PSYCHOLOGY

Fourth Edition

PSYCHOLOGY

Peter Gray
Boston College

WORTH PUBLISHERS

Psychology, *Fourth Edition*

Copyright © 1991, 1994, 1999, 2002 by Worth Publishers

All rights reserved

Manufactured in the United States of America

ISBN: 0-7167-5162-3

First Printing: 5 4 3 2 1

Senior Sponsoring Editor: Jessica Bayne

Development Editor: Cecilia Gardner

Senior Marketing Manager: Renee Altier

Art Director: Barbara Reingold

Designer: Paul Lacy

Photo Research Manager: Patricia Marx

Photo Editors: Patricia Marx, Julie Tesser

Photo Researchers: Deborah Goodsite, Vikii Wong, and Ariana Green

Illustration Coordinator: Bill Page

Illustrations: J/B Woolsey Associates and TSI Graphics, Inc.

Production Editor: Margaret Comaskey

Production Manager: Barbara Anne Seixas

Page Layout: Paul Lacy

Composition: TSI Graphics, Inc.

Printing and Binding: R. R. Donnelley & Sons Company

Cover art: *Jeanne Hebuterne*, Amedo Modigliani (1884–1920), oil on canvas.
    Christie's Images/The Bridgman Library. Researched by Vikii Wong.

Illustration credits begin on page IC-1 and constitute an extension of the copyright page.

Library of Congress Cataloging-in-Publication Data

Gray, Peter (Peter O.)

   Psychology / Peter Gray.—4th ed.

      p. cm.

   Includes bibliographical references and indexes.

   1. Psychology. I. Title.

   BF121.G667 2001

   150—dc21

                                                          2001026103

Worth Publishers

41 Madison Avenue

New York, NY 10010

http://www.worthpublishers.com

In loving memory of Anita, Mary Jane,
Charlie, Rebecca, and Albion

About the Author

Peter Gray is professor of psychology at Boston College, where he has served his department as Department Chair, Undergraduate Program Director, and Graduate Program Director. He has published research in physiological, developmental, and educational psychology; published articles on innovative teaching methods; taught more than twenty different undergraduate courses, including, most regularly, introductory psychology; helped develop a university-wide program to improve students' study and learning skills; and developed a program of research practicum courses. Before joining Boston College, he studied psychology as an undergraduate at Columbia University and earned a Ph.D. in biological sciences at Rockefeller University. He earned his way through college by coaching basketball and working with youth groups in New York City. As a graduate student, he directed a summer biology program for talented high school students from impoverished neighborhoods. His avocations today include long-distance bicycling, kayaking, and backwoods cross-country skiing.

Contents in Brief

Contents

PART 4
Sensation and Perception   231

PART 5
The Human Intellect   323

PART 4

Sensation and Perception   231

PART 5

The Human Intellect   323

PART 6
Growth of the Mind and Person 407

CHAPTER **11**
The Development of Thought and Language 409

CHAPTER **12**
Social Development 451

PART 7

The Person in a World of People   495

CHAPTER **13**

Social Perception and Attitudes   497

CHAPTER **14**

Social Influences on Behavior   533

PART 8

Personality and Disorders   571

CHAPTER **15**

Personality   573

Preface

My immodest goal has been to write an introduction to psychology that describes the main ideas of the field, and the evidence behind them, in as logically coherent and intellectually stimulating a manner as possible—one that excites students' interest by appealing to their intelligence. As cognitive psychologists have shown repeatedly, the human mind is not particularly good at absorbing and remembering miscellaneous pieces of information. It is designed for thinking, figuring out, understanding; and it remembers what it understands. I want students to join you and me in *thinking about* behavior—its functions, causes, and mechanisms.

Toward achieving this goal, I have entered each domain of psychology with the aim of identifying its main questions, its main approaches to answering questions, and its most durable and interesting theories and findings. I have striven to describe these as clearly as possible and have provided concrete, real-life examples to help readers see their relevance. The book is organized around ways of thinking about behavior, in a manner that permits the development of extended arguments while still covering the traditional ground of the introductory course. Focus questions in the margins continuously call attention to the main ideas and lines of evidence. My aim throughout has been to depict the science of psychology as a human endeavor in which progress comes through the work of thoughtful, if fallible, people who make observations, conduct experiments, reason, and argue about behavior.

One of my dearest aims has been to achieve some small measure of the personal touch that William James accomplished so masterfully in *The Principles of Psychology*—the book that still stands, in my mind, as far and away the best introduction to psychology ever written. I hope that students will read my text—as anyone must read James's—not as Truth with a capital T, nor as an unbiased distillate of all of psychology, but rather as one person's honest attempt to understand the field and to convey that understanding as best he could. Toward that end, in writing the book I constantly imagined myself carrying on a dialogue with an inquiring, thinking, appropriately skeptical student.

I must also confess to sharing two of James's biases: rationalism and functionalism. As a rationalist, I am uncomfortable presenting findings and facts without trying to make sense of them. Sometimes in our teaching of psychology we overplay the methods for gathering and analyzing data and underplay the value of logical thought. I want students always to think about findings in relation to larger ideas and not to get the impression that the discipline is simply a piling of fact upon fact. As a functionalist, I want to know why, in terms of survival or other benefit, people (or animals) behave as they do. The functionalist theme runs through the book and is part of the reason why the first major unit (following the brief *Background to the Study of Psychology* unit) is entitled *The Adaptiveness of Behavior* and deals with behavioral evolution and learning in back-to-back chapters. Natural selection and learning are the two reasons why behavior is functional, and I want students to know something about those processes, and their interaction, right from the start.

The functionalist orientation also leads me, in the second half of the book, to pay more than the usual amount of attention to cross-cultural research and to behavioral processes as they operate in the contexts of people's everyday lives.

An issue faced by any textbook author is how much attention to pay to current as opposed to classic work. Clearly, the primary task of any introductory psychology text published today is to represent the field as it is today, but, in my view, that cannot be accomplished without a historical perspective. One cannot adequately depict psychology for the future by providing a snapshot of the present. Ideas and approaches in psychology (or any other scholarly field) emerge and evolve over time, and a reasoned presentation must portray something of that evolution. This book contains plenty of current research, but it sets that research in the context of ideas that have been around for a long time and are associated with such names as Helmholtz, Darwin, Pavlov, Piaget, Vygotsky, Lewin, and Freud.

THE FOURTH EDITION

The positive responses of instructors and students to the previous editions convinced me not to modify the book's original goal and style of writing or to change radically the overall organization. Yet, within the original framework, I have made substantial changes. These changes, like those I made in the previous revisions, serve four main purposes:

1. **To extend the evolutionary theme more fully throughout the book.** When the book first appeared, its pathbreaking functionalist, evolutionary orientation was received enthusiastically. Since then, evolutionary thinking has become increasingly part of mainstream psychology and has generated a solid body of research findings in nearly every subfield of the discipline. Consistent with this trend and with the urgings of many of the book's users, I have extended the evolutionary theme further with each new edition. I have found that this theme does not negate or reduce the value of traditional research findings in psychology, but rather helps us and our students to integrate those findings and make sense of them. In the third edition, I increased considerably the use of the evolutionary theme in the chapters on human development, social psychology, and personality. In this edition, I have reorganized the material in Chapters 7, 8, and 9 in ways that have allowed me to integrate the evolutionary, functional theme more fully and logically with the discussion of mechanisms of sensation, perception, attention, and memory than had been true in the earlier editions.

2. **To enhance and extend the emphasis on cultural influences.** Equally important and complementary to the evolutionary theme is the cultural theme. Evolution underlies human nature, but we are, by our evolved nature, cultural animals. The human mind is biologically predisposed to develop within a cultural context and to operate with symbols acquired from that context. Many psychological principles that were once presented as if they were true of people everywhere are now known to apply primarily to people in Western cultures. These points were prominent in the earlier editions and are developed even more fully in this edition. Among these changes are an expanded and updated discussion of the historical and cultural influences on IQ, an expanded discussion of ecological perspectives on intelligence, updated discussions of cross-cultural differences in self-construal and attitudes, updated and expanded discussions of the role of culture (as well as evolution) in shaping gender differences in behavior and personality, and new discussions of cultural influences on the frequency of particular mental disorders.

3. **To make the book even more accessible and intellectually engaging to the typical student**. A book becomes more accessible not by being "dumbed down" but by being "smartened up." The clearer the logic and the more precisely it is expressed, the easier a book is to understand and the more engaging it is. With each revision, and with feedback from adopters and students, I find new ways to make difficult ideas clearer without ignoring their inherent subtlety or complexity. Sometimes this involves a simple change in wording or a minor alteration in the sequence of an argument's elements or a new example or visual illustration that captures the essence of the argument. At other times the change is more fundamental and reflects a true rethinking of the argument and an altered conclusion. In this edition, for example, by moving the discussion of attention into the chapter on memory and integrating it with the discussion of sensory memory and working memory, I was able to combine classic models of attention with classic models of memory in a way that abolishes what had previously been an arbitrary and potentially confusing distinction. A pedagogical innovation of this edition is the "Section Summary" that follows each major section of a chapter. The summary reminds students of the issues they have just read about and prompts them to review before moving on to the next section. The primary study aid in the book, however, continues to be the focus questions that appear in the margins and are meant to guide students' initial reading as well as review.

4. **To keep the book current and accurate.** Most of the work and fun of each revision lies in my own continued learning about and rethinking of each field of psychology. In producing this revision, I skimmed thousands of new research articles and chapters and read hundreds carefully to determine which new developments warrant inclusion in the introductory course. The result was not so much the discovery of new ideas as the determination of how long-standing ideas are playing themselves out in current research and debate. This edition contains approximately 470 new references, mainly to work published within the past few years, in a total reference list of approximately 2,100. Of course, that statistic means little by itself; the significance lies in whether the new references pertain to true advances in psychological theory and knowledge and whether those advances are presented in an intellectually engaging manner, and that is for you to judge. In order to add new material without increasing the overall length of the book, I have dropped or shortened some arguments that seem relatively less important to psychology today than they seemed a few years ago.

The most extensive changes in this edition occur in Chapters 7–9. In previous editions, Chapter 7, on sensation, was concerned mostly with physiological mechanisms and Chapter 8, on perception, was concerned mostly with information-processing models. In the new edition—reflecting psychology's increased understanding of brain mechanisms of perception—the physiological and cognitive approaches are integrated in a manner that ties them to each other and permits more extensive functional analyses of sensory/perceptual processes. Now, Chapter 7 is on smell, taste, pain, hearing, and psychophysics and Chapter 8 is on vision. This organization helps students understand more clearly the relationships between information-processing models (such as Treisman's feature-integration theory) and neurophysiological findings (such as those concerning visual feature detectors and the "what" and "where" pathways of vision). The discussions of smell, taste, and pain in the first parts of Chapter 7 connect logically with the discussions of motivation and emotion in Chapter 6 and add a strong functionalist flavor to the chapter. The discussions of visual perception in the last half of Chapter 8 connect logically to the topics of Chapter 9.

Chapter 9, which in previous editions was entitled *Memory*, is now entitled *Memory and Consciousness*. By moving the discussion of attention into this chapter, by enlarging the discussion of working memory, and by placing more emphasis on the interactions between implicit and explicit memory processes, the chapter now provides students with an understanding of cognitive psychology's manner of dealing with questions of consciousness as well as questions of memory.

All the other chapters have retained the same organization that they had in the third edition, but have been updated with new research and ideas. Among these additions are an expanded discussion of observational learning in nonhuman animals (Chapter 4); recent findings concerning neuroplasticity, neural neogenesis, and Hebbian synapses (Chapter 5); recent research involving functional neuroimaging (Chapters 5, 8, and 9); recent findings relevant to the false-memory controversy (Chapter 9); an expanded discussion of ways by which parents influence children's development (Chapter 12); a new section on the functions of adolescents' peer groups (Chapter 12); a new discussion of the controversy concerning the possible iatrogenesis of dissociative identity disorder (Chapter 16); and a new section on placebo effects in drug treatments of depression and anxiety (Chapter 17). A more detailed description of the changes made in each chapter can be found in the *Instructor's Resource Manual*.

GENERAL ORGANIZATION

Over the decades, a nearly uniform way of dividing up and arranging topics has emerged and taken hold in introductory psychology. For the most part, I have followed that standard organization: It is comfortable; it fits reasonably well with the ways that research psychologists divide up the discipline; and it makes considerable logical sense. My slight departures reflect three developments in contemporary psychology: (1) Knowledge of heredity and evolution is increasingly recognized to be essential for understanding the origins and functions of basic psychological processes. (2) Developments in the study of basic learning processes (which has always been conducted largely with nonhuman animals) link that field more closely than ever to an evolutionary perspective. (3) Developments in cognitive psychology have strengthened the link between its componential model of the mind and the traditional psychometric model of the mind.

The book is divided into eight units, or parts, each of which consists of two or (in one case) three chapters.

Part 1, *Background to the Study of Psychology*, has two relatively brief chapters. Chapter 1, on the history and scope of psychology, shows how some of psychology's most basic ideas and ways of conducting research have developed over time. Chapter 2, on methods, lays out some general elements of psychological research that will be useful to students in later chapters. (If you prefer a more thorough discussion of statistics than Chapter 2 contains, you might supplement it with the first three sections of the *Statistical Appendix*.)

Part 2, *The Adaptiveness of Behavior*, is devoted explicitly to the functionalist theme that reappears frequently in the book. Behavior can be understood as adaptation to the environment, which occurs at two levels—the phylogenetic level (through natural selection) and the individual level (through learning). These themes are developed in two chapters that emphasize the interaction of nature and nurture in behavioral adaptation. Chapter 3, on heredity and the evolution of behavior, includes the idea that even behaviors that are most highly prepared by evolution must develop, in the individual, through interaction with the environment. Chapter 4, on basic processes of learning, includes the idea that learning mechanisms themselves are products of evolution.

Part 3, *Physiological Mechanisms of Behavior*, is concerned with psychologists' attempts to explain behavior in terms of the neural and hormonal mechanisms that produce it. Chapter 5 is a functional introduction to the nervous system and to the actions of hormones and drugs. In addition to providing a background that is useful for the rest of the book, this chapter continues the theme of adaptiveness with an up-to-date discussion of neuroplasticity and brain mechanisms of learning. Chapter 6 is about basic mechanisms of motivation and arousal; here the ideas about the nervous system and hormones developed in the preceding chapter are applied to the topics of hunger, sex, reward mechanisms, sleep, and emotionality. Although this chapter centers on physiological mechanisms, it is not exclusively physiological. The discussions of motives and emotions pay ample attention to environmental influences.

Part 4, *Sensation and Perception*, is about the processes through which the brain or mind gathers information about the outside world. Chapter 7 is about smell, taste, pain, and hearing, and Chapter 8 is about vision. The main question for both chapters is this: How does our nervous system respond to and make sense of the patterns of energy in the physical world? In both chapters the discussion of sensory and perceptual mechanisms is placed in a functionalist context. The senses are understood as survival mechanisms, which evolved not to provide full, objective accounts of the world's physical properties but, rather, to provide the specific kinds of information that are needed to survive and reproduce.

Part 5, *The Human Intellect*, is about the ability of the brain or mind to store information and use it to solve problems. Chapter 9, on memory and consciousness, focuses on the distinctions between—and interactions of—unconscious and conscious mechanisms in the processes of attention, memory encoding, and memory retrieval. The chapter includes an analysis of the multiple memory systems that have evolved to serve different adaptive functions. Chapter 10, on intelligence and reasoning, deals with the structure and measurement of human intelligence, the cognitive components of problem solving, and the relation of language to thought. Throughout these chapters, the information-processing perspective is highlighted but is tempered by ecological discussions that draw attention to the functions of each mental process and the environmental contexts within which it operates.

In sum, Parts 2, 3, 4, and 5 are all concerned with basic psychological processes—processes of learning, motivation, emotion, sensation, perception, attention, memory, and problem solving—and each process is discussed in a manner that integrates ideas about its mechanisms with ideas about its adaptive functions. The remaining three parts are concerned with understanding the whole person and the person's relationships to the social environment.

Part 6, *Growth of the Mind and Person*, is about developmental psychology. In both its chapters the book's functionalist perspective is continued by emphasizing the interactions between evolved human tendencies and environmental experiences in shaping the individual person. Chapter 11, on cognitive development, deals with the development of thought and language. A major goal here is to show how the adult mind can be understood by identifying and describing the steps through which it is built in the developing child. Chapter 12, on social development, is concerned with the changes in social relationships and life tasks that occur throughout the life span and with ways in which these relationships and tasks vary across cultures. Chapter 12 also sets the stage for the next pair of chapters.

Part 7, *The Person in a World of People*, is about social psychology. Chapter 13, on social cognition, is concerned with the mental processes involved in forming judgments of other people, perceiving and presenting the self in the social environment, and forming and modifying attitudes. Chapter 14, on social influence, deals with compliance, obedience, conformity, cooperation, competition, group decision making, conflict, and the social regulatory roles of emotions. A theme of this chapter is the contrast between normative and informational influences. This unit on social psychology is placed before the one on personality and mental disorders because the insights of social psychology—especially those pertaining to social cognition—are increasingly becoming incorporated into personality theories and approaches to understanding and treating mental disorders.

Part 8, *Personality and Disorders*, consists of three chapters on topics that students most strongly identify as "psychology" before they enter the course. Chapter 15, on personality, has sections on the nature and origins of traits, the adaptive value of individual differences, and the classic theories of personality. Chapter 16, on mental disorders, begins by discussing the problems involved in categorizing and diagnosing disorders and then, through the discussion of specific disorders, emphasizes the notion of multiple causation and the theme that the symptoms characterizing disorders are different in degree, not in kind, from normal psychological experiences and processes. Chapter 17, on treatment, offers an opportunity to recapitulate many of the main ideas of earlier chapters—now in the context of their application to therapy. Ideas from Parts 2, 3, 5, and 7 reappear in the discussions of biological, behavioral, and cognitive therapies, and ideas from the personality chapter reappear in the discussions of psychodymanic and humanistic therapies.

Although this ordering of topics makes the most sense to me, I recognize that other sensible arrangements exist and that time limits may prevent you from using the entire book. Therefore, each chapter is written so that it can be read as a separate entity, independent of others. Links are often made to material presented in another chapter, but most of these cross-references are spelled out in enough detail to be understood by students who have not read the other chapter. The only major exception falls in the physiological unit: Chapter 6, on motivation, sleep, and emotion, assumes that the student has learned some of the basic information presented in Chapter 5, on the nervous system. Specific suggestions for making deletions within each chapter can be found in the *Instructor's Resource Manual*.

FEATURES

The main pedagogical feature of this or any other textbook is, of course, the narrative itself, which should be clear, logical, and interesting. Everything else is secondary. I have avoided the boxes and inserts that are often found in introductory psychology texts, because such digressions add to the impression that psychology is a jumble of topics that don't fit together very well. I have aimed, to the degree that the field allows it, to produce a logical flow of ideas.

One nondisruptive feature I have included is *focus questions*, located in the margins, which direct students' attention to the main idea, argument, or evidence addressed in the adjacent paragraphs of text. In a separate preface *To the Student* I offer advice for using the focus questions to guide both the initial reading and the review of each chapter. The focus questions also offer instructors a means to make selective assignments within any chapter. The questions are numbered so instructors can easily let students know, with a list of numbers, which issues will be fair game for exams. Many of the multiple-choice questions in the *Test Bank* are keyed by number to the focus questions. In my own course I tell students that tests will consist of multiple-choice and essay questions that are derived from the book's focus questions. This makes clear what students must do to prepare.

A new feature in this edition is the inclusion of a *Section Summary* at the end of each major section of each chapter. The summary briefly restates the main ideas discussed in the section and serves as a prompt for students to review that section—ideally by testing themselves on their ability to answer the section's focus questions—before moving on to the next section.

Because the focus questions and section summaries make a traditional end-of-chapter review unnecessary, I end each chapter with a section called *Concluding Thoughts* that expands on the broad themes of the chapter, points out relationships to ideas discussed in other chapters, and sometimes even offers a new idea or two for students to consider as they reflect on the chapter. My hope is that students will read this as the final section of the chapter's narrative and not view it as optional endmatter. *Concluding Thoughts* is followed by a brief section called *Further Reading*, which contains thumbnail reviews of several relevant and interesting books that are sufficiently nontechnical to be read by first-year students. At the very end of each chapter, a short section called *Looking Ahead* is designed to entice the reader into the next chapter and to show its relationship to the chapter just read.

SUPPLEMENTS

An excellent student study guide called *Focus on Psychology* has been prepared to accompany this textbook. Its author, Mary Trahan, is a cognitive psychologist who has a special interest in applying the insights of her field to the teaching of psychology. Trahan's guide is designed to be used in tandem with the reading of each textbook chapter, and its contents are linked to the textbook's focus questions. Students who used the previous editions of the study guide have praised it highly.

A *Test Bank* of multiple-choice questions has been prepared by Lori Bica of the University of Wisconsin, Eau Claire, Mary Trahan, and a team of psychologists. Each question has also been reviewed by Mary Trahan to make sure that it aligns with the content of the study guide. All the items in the *Test Bank* have been keyed to the focus questions in the text so that instructors can easily identify for students the material they should concentrate on when studying for exams. The *Test Bank* is also available on a CD-ROM with the Diploma computerized testing program for Windows and Macintosh computers. Instructors wishing to test over the Internet may use these test materials and the Diploma software.

With this edition of *Psychology*, Worth Publishers offers a new CD-ROM, called *Focus on Research*, developed by Thomas Ludwig of Hope College and Connie Varnhagen of the University of Alberta. It includes dozens of interactive activities, interactive three-dimensional models of the human eye and brain, and student quizzes. A sample version of the CD with the materials for Chapter 8 accompanies the examination copies of this book. The full version is available to be packaged with the book for a small fee. In addition, students and faculty may use the resources on the fourth edition's Web site at www.worthpublishers.com/gray. This site includes detailed chapter overviews, simulations and animations, an online version of Thomas Ludwig's *PsychSim* and *PsychQuest*, student quizzes, and PowerPoint® slides.

For instructors wishing to add articles to their course, a selection of 8 classic articles from *Scientific American* is available to be packaged with the text upon request. The articles are by Solomon Asch, Michael Gazzaniga, Eleanor Gibson and Richard Walk, Harry Harlow, Elizabeth Loftus, James Olds, B. F. Skinner, and Nikolaas Tinbergen.

An extremely useful manual of *Instructor's Resources* has been prepared for use with this textbook by Steven Heinrichs of Boston College and a team of psychologists. For each chapter of the textbook, this manual offers interesting class demonstrations, suggestions for incorporating the Internet and other media into classroom work, ideas for lecture elaborations and class discussions, and writing and research exercises. I have contributed to this manual some general thoughts about teaching introductory psychology and some specific teaching suggestions for each chapter, including possible ways of cutting the chapter down for shorter courses.

Worth Publishers offers a variety of materials for classroom presentations. A set of approximately 135 acetate *Transparencies* derived from charts, graphs, and other illustrations in the textbook is available on request. All the illustrations from the text are available at the Worth instructor's Image and Lecture Gallery, accessible on the

Web at www.worthpublishers.com/ilg. Also available are a customizable set of PowerPoint slides that includes text and illustrations from the textbook and a second set that includes additional graphs, figures, and tables, developed by Harvey Shulman of Ohio State University. Both sets of slides can be accessed on the book's Web site or on the *Presentation Manager Pro Instructor's Resource CD-ROM*. The *Presentation Manager Pro CD-ROM* also includes a unique "presentation maker" that allows instructors to customize classroom presentations. For instructors who wish to use the book with a classroom management system, materials from the Web site are available in WebCT and Blackboard E-Packs. Further online learning materials are also available, from Thomas Ludwig's *PsychOnline*, for Web-enhanced courses and distance learning.

An enormous number of video segments is available for use with this book. The *Scientific American Frontiers Video Collection* for introductory psychology includes 26 segments, each 8 to 25 minutes long, that feature the work of such notable researchers as Renée Baillargeon, Michael Gazzaniga, and Steven Pinker. The second edition of *The Mind* teaching modules is a collection of 35 video clips edited by Frank J. Vattano, Colorado State University, and produced by Worth Publishers and WNET. The second edition of *The Brain* teaching modules, edited by Frank J. Vattano, Thomas L. Bennet, and Michelle Butler, all of Colorado State University, includes 32 modules. The newest addition to the Worth Publishers collection of videos for introductory psychology is 3 hours of clips from *Psychology: The Human Experience*, a video telecourse produced by Coast Learning Systems. Finally, a collection of more than 20 short clips from classic experiments is also available on CD-ROM for instructors' use as part of the Worth Psychology Digital Archive.

ACKNOWLEDGMENTS

Nobody writes a textbook alone. Hundreds of people contributed directly or indirectly to the development and revision of this one, of whom I can list only a few here.

Herbert Terrace's inspiring introductory psychology course at Columbia University enticed me, at age 18, to turn away from a planned career in physics toward one in psychology. In graduate school at Rockefeller University, I was inspired and taught by Neal Miller, Jay Weiss, Bruce McEwen, William Estes, Peter Marler, and many others. My outlook has also been strongly influenced by my colleagues at Boston College, some of whom have contributed in very direct ways to the development of this book. They include (in alphabetical order) Ali Banuazizi, Norm Berkowitz, Hiram Brownell, Donnah Canavan, Randy Easton, Lisa Feldman, Steven Heinrichs, Murray Horwitz, Marianne LaFrance, Ramsay Liem, Michael Moore, Gilda Morelli, Michael Numan, Karen Rosen, Bill Ryan, Diane Scott-Jones, Jeanne Sholl, Kavitha Srivinas, Joe Tecce, and Ellen Winner.

Mary Trahan, who wrote the wonderful study guide for each edition of this book, has also improved the textbook through her perceptive eye and valuable suggestions. I also owe special thanks to my friend Michael Moore, who worked closely with me on early drafts of the first edition and taught me much about cognitive and developmental psychology. I thank, too, my friends Daniel and Hanna Greenberg, educational innovators and philosophers who have contributed greatly to my own thinking in both psychology and education. My greatest debt of gratitude is to my wonderful son, Scott, and my late, dear wife, Anita, who together contributed enormously to all aspects of my growth and to many of the ideas in this book.

Before writing this fourth edition, I sent notes to a number of prominent researchers inviting them to critique and make suggestions concerning my treatment of their own work and work closely related to theirs. Among those who responded with particularly helpful comments and suggestions are (in alphabetical order): Alan Baddeley, Robert Bell, Stephen Ceci, Anders Ericsson, Philip Johnson-Laird, Annette Karmiloff-Smith, Mark Leary, Joseph LeDoux, Dan McAdams, William Miller, Susan Mineka, Irene Miura, Randolph Nesse, Holly Prigerson, Robert Rescorla, Emilie Rissman, Shalom Schwartz, Shepard Siegel, Robert Siegler, Anne Treisman, Harry Triandis, and Leslie Zebrowitz.

Every draft of this manuscript was reviewed by experts in each area of psychology and by notably successful teachers of the introductory course. I was greatly impressed by the seriousness with which the reviewers approached this task; they taught me a great deal, and each one influenced the final outcome. For their thoughtful, sometimes challenging, and always helpful reviews, I thank:

Thomas R. Alley, *Clemson University*
Trevor Archer, *University of Goteborg*
Lori A. Bica, *University of Wisconsin, Eau Claire*
Hart Blanton, *SUNY at Albany*
Jim Calhoun, *University of Georgia*
Dennis Cogan, *Texas Tech University*
Thor Eysteinsson, *University of Iceland*
Jayne Florence, *University of Alberta*
Sandra P. Frankmann, *University of Southern Colorado*
Nellie Georgiou-Karistianis, *Monash University, Clayton*
Norma Graham, *Columbia University*
Yvette R. Harris, *Miami University*
Carol A. Hayes, *Delta State University*
Gail D. Heyman, *University of California, San Diego*
Tiffany Ito, *University of Colorado*
Ulla Karilampi, *University of Goteborg*
Wendy Kliewer, *Virginia Commonwealth University*
Neil Lutsky, *Carleton College*
Jennifer MacLean, *University of Alberta*
Stephen G. Misovich, *Providence College*
Cynthia O'Dell, *Indiana University Northwest*
Robert Pasnak, *George Mason University*
Erika Peterson, *George Washington University*
Donald J. Polzella, *University of Dayton*
Gary Poole, *University of British Columbia*
Gabriel Radvansky, *University of Notre Dame*
Thomas Rieg, *Union College*
Hillary Rodman, *Emory University*
Bryan E. Shepp, *Brown University*
Robert Turnbull, *Concordia University*
Connie K. Varnhagen, *University of Alberta*
Anne C. Watson, *West Virginia University*
Fiona White, *West Sydney University*
Peter Wright, *University of Edinburgh*
Karen Yu, *University of the South*

This edition of the text owes much to the reviewers who helped shape the first three editions. Once again, I thank:

Valerie Ahl, *University of Wisconsin, Madison*
George W. Albee, *University of Vermont*
Janet Andrews, *Vassar College*
Michael L. Atkinson, *University of Western Ontario*
Gregory Ball, *Johns Hopkins University*
Ali Banuazizi, *Boston College*
Lewis M. Barker, *Baylor University*
Byron Barrington, *University of Wisconsin, Marathon County*
F. Samuel Bauer, *Christopher Newport University*
Steve R. Baumgardner, *University of Wisconsin, Eau Claire*
John B. Best, *Eastern Illinois University*
Fredda Blanchard-Fields, *Georgia Institute of Technology*
Anthony Blum, *Stetson University*
Toni L. Blum, *Stetson University*
Galen Bodenhausen, *Michigan State University*
Susan Boon, *University of Calgary*
Brian Bornstein, *Louisiana State University*
Sharon Brehm, *State University of New York, Binghamton*
Nathan Brody, *Wesleyan University*
Michael F. Brown, *Villanova University*
Gary Byrd, *Texas A & M University*
William H. Calhoun, *University of Tennessee*
John L. Caruso, *University of Massachusetts, Dartmouth*
Robert B. Cialdini, *Arizona State University*
Stanley Coren, *University of British Columbia*
Katherine Covell, *University of Toronto*
Catherine Crosbie-Currie, *St. Lawrence University*
Martin Daly, *McMaster University*
Richard B. Day, *McMaster University*
V. J. DeGhett, *State University of New York, Potsdam*
Patricia G. Devine, *University of Wisconsin, Madison*
Timothy J. DeVoogd, *Cornell University*
R. Dale Dick, *University of Wisconsin, Eau Claire*
Francine Dolins, *Centre College*
Donald D. Dorfman, *University of Iowa*
Michael J. Dougher, *University of New Mexico*
John Dovidio, *Colgate University*
Bruce Earhard, *Dalhousie University*
David C. Edwards, *Iowa State University*
Gilles O. Einstein, *Furman University*
Nancy Eisenberg, *Arizona State University*
Fernanda Ferreira, *Michigan State University*
Peter R. Finn, *Indiana University*
Owen R. Floody, *Bucknell University*
Christina Frederick, *Southern Utah University*
Janet J. Fritz, *Colorado State University*
Bennett G. Galef, Jr., *McMaster University*
Preston E. Garraghty, *Indiana University*
Mary Gauvain, *Scripps College*
Don J. Gawley, *AT&T Bell Laboratories*
Daniel Gilbert, *University of Texas, Austin*
G. P. Ginsburg, *University of Nevada, Reno*
Norma Graham, *Columbia University*

Gary Greenberg, *Wichita State University*
W. Larry Gregory, *New Mexico State University, Las Cruces*
Alan Gross, *University of Mississippi*
Ed Haas
Andrea Halpern, *Bucknell University*
Benjamin Harris, *University of Wisconsin, Parkside*
Marie Hayes, *University of Maine*
John Henderson, *Michigan State University*
Bryan Hendricks, *University of Wisconsin, Marathon Center*
Stephen P. Hinshaw, *University of California, Berkeley*
Jill M. Hooley, *Harvard University*
David Hothersall, *Ohio State University*
Valerye A. Hunt, *Fraser Valley College*
Linda Hynan, *Baylor University*
John C. Jahnke, *Miami University of Ohio*
Sybillyn Jennings, *Russell Sage College*
Justin M. Joffe, *University of Vermont*
Ronald W. Johnson, *St. Francis Xavier University*
Douglas E. Jorenby, *University of Wisconsin*
Saul M. Kassin, *Williams College*
Lloyd Kaufman, *New York University*
Carolyn F. Keating, *Colgate University*
Ernest Keen, *Bucknell University*
Emily Kleyman, *Brooklyn College*
Terry J. Knapp, *University of Nevada, Las Vegas*
Daniel Langmeyer, *University of Cincinnati*
Kevin Lanning, *Oregon State University*
Theresa M. Lee, *University of Michigan*
Mary F. Lombard, *Regis College*
Thomas W. Lombardo, *University of Mississippi*
Stephen Madigan, *University of Southern California*
Leonard S. Mark, *Miami University (Ohio)*
Alan Marks, *Berry College*
Merrill J. May, *Weber State University*
Donald H. McBurney, *University of Pittsburgh*
Sallyanne McColgan, *clinical psychologist*
Matt McGue, *University of Minnesota*
Patricia A. McMullen, *Dalhousie University*
Steven Meier, *University of Idaho*
Daniel Miller, *Carthage College*
David B. Miller, *University of Connecticut, Storrs*
Douglas Mook, *University of Virginia*
Cathleen Moore, *Pennsylvania State University*
Greg Moran, *University of Western Ontario*
Gilda A. Morelli, *Boston College*
Daniel D. Moriarty, Jr. *University of San Diego*
James L. Mosley, *University of Calgary*
Darwin Muir, *Queen's University*
Margaret Munger, *Davidson College*
Harry G. Murray, *University of Western Ontario*
Lynn M. Musser, *Purdue University*
Andy Neher, *Cabrillo College*
Randy J. Nelson, *The Johns Hopkins University*

John B. Nezlek, *College of William and Mary*
James Nickels, *University of Manitoba*
Julie K. Norem, *Northeastern University*
Michael Numan, *Boston College*
David L. Oden, *LaSalle University*
Elizabeth Weiss Ozorak, *Allegheny College*
Chris Pagano, *Clemson University*
Tibor Palfai, *Syracuse University*
Hal Pashler, *University of California, San Diego*
David G. Payne, *SUNY-Binghamton*
Sergio M. Pellis, *University of Lethbridge*
Ed L. Pencer, *St. Francis Xavier University*
Peter Platenius, *Queen's University*
Steve Anderson Platt, *Northern Michigan University*
Gary Poole, *Simon Fraser University*
Dennis R. Proffitt, *University of Virginia*
Jesse E. Purdy, *Southwestern University*
Leon Rappoport, *Kansas State University*
Marc Riess, *Middlebury College*
David C. Rowe, *University of Arizona*
Joseph F. Rychlak, *Loyola University of Chicago*
Neil J. Salkind, *University of Kansas*
Eugene Schmidt, *Scottsdale Community College*
Matthew Sharps, *California State University*
Bonnie Sherman, *Saint Olaf College*

Irwin Silverman, *York University (Ontario)*
Stephen Siviy, *Gettysburg College*
John J. Skowronski, *Ohio State University at Newark*
Steven M. Smith, *Texas A & M University*
Kathryn T. Spoehr, *Brown University*
Kavitha Srinivas, *Boston College*
James R. Stellar, *Northeastern University*
Michelle K. Surbey, *Mount Allison University*
Ross Thompson, *University of Nebraska, Lincoln*
James Todd, *Eastern Michigan University*
Mary Trahan, *Randolph-Macon College*
Eric Turkheimer, *University of Virginia*
Robert Turnbull, *Concordia University*
Jonathan Vaughan, *Hamilton College*
Victor Villa, *University of Texas, San Antonio*
T. Joel Wade, *Bucknell University*
William P. Wallace, *University of Nevada, Reno*
Gillian Watson, *University of British Columbia*
Douglas Weldon, *Hamilton College*
Lawrence Wichlinski, *Carleton College*
Mark Winter, *Southern Utah University*
W. Scott Wood, *Drake University*
Murray S. Work, *California State University, Sacramento*
Otto Zinser, *East Tennessee State University*

I have been blessed by the opportunity to work, on earlier editions of this book, with two truly outstanding developmental editors—Phyllis Fisher and Susan Seuling. Because I stubbornly insisted that they not change any of my writing, but only make suggestions, these two remarkably talented people had to become my teachers. They had to convince me of their views, to the point where their views became mine, in order to improve the book. In the process they helped me become a better thinker, psychologist, and writer than I was before. Phyllis, who has an extensive background in psychology, worked closely with me in developing the ideas, organization, and writing style of the first and third editions. Susan showed me how to sharpen my writing, in the second and third editions, in ways that made the book's logic clearer and more accessible. Phyllis's and Susan's influence continues in this fourth edition through the lasting effects that they had on me as a writer. This edition and I as a writer have also benefited greatly from the superb line editing skills of Cele Gardner, a master of precision in language.

Many others at Worth Publishers also deserve my heartfelt thanks. First among them are Jessica Bayne, who coordinated all of the work pertaining to this edition, and Margaret Comaskey, who managed the book's production. Both of these women worked with great skill, tact, and energy, for which I am deeply grateful. Barbara Seixas ably managed the book's production, and Stacey Alexander, Graig Donini, and Eve Moeller worked diligently to produce the many supplementary materials that accompany the book.

Natick, Massachusetts
August 2001

Peter Gray

To the Student

Welcome to your psychology textbook. I hope you will enjoy it. It is about a question that, to me, is one of the most fascinating anyone can ask: What makes people feel, think, and behave the way they do? That, really, is what psychology is about. In this book you will read, in different units, about different approaches to answering that big question; and you will discover dozens of specific findings and ideas that help to answer it.

I hope that, as you read this book, you will allow yourself to become intrigued by psychology; that you will not focus too narrowly on getting a good grade; that you will think about, challenge, and discuss with others the book's ideas; and that you will keep constantly in mind that ideas in psychology come from people who are basically no different from you—so your own insights, questions, and thoughts are legitimate. Psychology is a science, and the essence of science is this: We do not accept anything on authority. It doesn't matter *who* says that something is or isn't true; what matters is the *evidence*—the facts and logic upon which the ideas are based, which are open for evaluation by any thinking person. In this book I have tried to present both the main ideas in psychology and some of the evidence. Each page is offered for your consideration, not for your unquestioned acceptance.

USING THE FOCUS QUESTIONS FOR STUDY AND REVIEW

To help you study and review the text, I have supplied for each chapter a set of *focus questions*, which can be found in the book's margins. Each question directs your attention to the main idea or line of evidence discussed in the paragraph or paragraphs that follow it. On page 3, for example, you will find that the first focus question of Chapter 1 is *How can psychology be defined, and what are three ways of expanding on that definition?* That question tells you exactly what the adjacent paragraphs are about. If you read it first, before reading the paragraphs, it will help you to focus your attention and to read actively—you will read to answer the question. The questions become even more effective in guiding your study if you rephrase them in your own words and spend a little time thinking about them before reading to answer them. For example, after reading the first question, you might say to yourself, "OK, how does this author define *psychology*? Will his definition match my own view of what psychology is about? And what are his three ways of expanding on the definition?"

Many of the focus questions break down into several questions when you think about them. For instance, the second question of Chapter 1 is *What was Descartes' version of dualism, and how did it help pave the way for a science of behavior?* When you think about that question, you might wonder, "What exactly is *dualism*? And what is Descartes' specific version of it? And how did his version help provide the basis for the scientific study of behavior?" After posing those questions in your own words, you are ready to read and think about the answer presented in the adjacent paragraphs. Your thoughts about the answer presented there will help prepare you for the next focus question, which introduces a criticism of Descartes' theory.

After reading the paragraphs that answer a particular focus question, stop for a moment and think about the answer, and maybe jot down in the margin your own note concerning the answer. In later chapters you will discover that many focus questions ask about the evidence for or against some idea. Be sure to think especially carefully about the answers you read to those questions and ask yourself whether or not you find the evidence convincing. At first, the focus-question approach to reading your textbook may seem awkward and annoying. Your natural tendency may be to read straight through the text and ignore the focus questions, or to glance at them without thinking about them as you read. But experience has shown that, with practice, the recommended way of using the questions becomes natural and pays big dividends in comprehension, enjoyment, and test performance. You may also apply this skill to your reading of textbooks in other courses. In those books you will probably not find focus questions already written for you, but you can use such cues as section headings and opening sentences to generate your own focus questions as you read. For more information about this study method you might turn to pages 342 and 343, where textbook reading is discussed in the context of a more general discussion of ways to improve memory.

Although using the focus questions in the recommended way will probably increase the time you need to read each chapter the first time through, it will probably decrease the total time you need to learn and remember the chapter's ideas and lines of evidence. Your first reading will be more purposeful and thoughtful, so the time required for rereading or review will be reduced. The focus questions are also a very useful aid in reviewing. To review each chapter, read each focus question again and try to answer it. If you cannot answer a question fully, read that portion of text again, and if the question still gives you trouble, mark it and ask your instructor or study companions to help you clarify it.

An excellent study guide called *Focus on Psychology* has been written by Mary Trahan and published as a separate volume to be used with this textbook. The contents of the guide are tied closely to the textbook's focus questions, so you can use the guide to supplement the method of study just described. The guide asks questions and provides exercises that help you to elaborate on the focus questions as you read, and it also contains review questions and practice tests that you can use at various points to assess your understanding. Students who have used the study guide in preceding editions praise it highly and credit it with improving their grade.

USING THE BOOK'S OTHER FEATURES

In addition to the focus questions, you should pay close attention to the *numbered figures* in each chapter. In some cases a figure will help you understand a point that would be difficult to grasp from words alone, and in other cases it will provide you with information that supplements or complements what is in the text. Whenever the text says, "see Figure ___," take a few moments to study that figure and read the caption. Many of the figures are graphs of data that back up an idea described in the text. If you have not had much experience reading graphs, please do not feel embarrassed about mentioning that to your instructor. He or she might then present some sample graphs in class and explain how to read them.

Another feature is the use of ***bold italics*** to highlight important terms. I suggest that you *not* devote much effort, on your first reading, to learning term definitions. Rather, read with the aim of understanding and thinking about the main *ideas* and the lines of evidence supporting or refuting them. In that process you will learn many of the terms, in the context of the ideas, without explicitly trying to learn them. The bold italics will be more useful in your later review. As you are reviewing the margin notes, look also for each of the terms in bold italics and check your knowledge of its meaning. These terms are also defined in the *Glossary* at the back of the book. If an important term has been defined in an earlier chapter, it is sometimes, but not always, defined again when it reappears. If it is not defined, you can use the glossary to find both the term's definition and the number of the page on which it was first used.

Each major section of each chapter ends with a brief *Section Summary*. Reading this will remind you of the section's main ideas and should prompt you to think about those ideas and review the section before proceeding to the next section. The most useful way to review, in my opinion, would be to answer each of the section's focus questions in your own words. Each chapter concludes with a section called *Concluding Thoughts*. This is not a summary, but rather provides some ideas and integrating themes designed to help you organize your own thoughts about and review of the chapter as a whole. My intention is that this section should be read as the final section of the chapter, not as optional, tacked-on "endmatter." Many instructors include, in their tests, questions that are based on this section.

A feature that this book shares with other books and articles in psychology is the use of *reference citations*, which can be found in the narrative on nearly every page. Each citation consists of the name of one or more researchers followed by a year. Sometimes both the name (or names) and the year are in parentheses, such as (*Jones & Smith, 1999*) and other times, when the name or names are part of the sentence, only the year is in parentheses, such as *According to Alice Jones (2001)*. . . . In either case, the year refers to the year of publication of an article or book, by the person or persons named, which describes more fully the idea or the research study being mentioned or discussed. The full reference to that article or book can be found in the *References* section at the back of the textbook. At first you may find these citations disruptive to the flow of your reading, but you will soon learn to read right through them. Their purpose is to give credit to the people whose work or ideas are being described and to give you the opprtunity to look up, and read more about, any ideas or research findings that intrigue you. In addition, at the end of each chapter, in a section called *Further Reading*, you will find brief reviews of several interesting books that you might use to supplement your study of specific areas of psychology.

And now—let's discuss psychology.

Natick, Massachusetts
August 2001

Peter Gray

PSYCHOLOGY

Anxiety of Waiting, Giorgio De Chirico

Background to the Study of Psychology

part 1

*You and I stand at a moment in time preceded by Aristotle,
Descartes, Darwin, and millions less known. Psychology today is
the accumulated and sifted ideas of all people before us and with us
who have attempted to fathom the mysteries of the human mind.
It is also, by its own definition, a science, using methods as objective
as the subject matter will allow. In this background unit, we
examine the history and methods of psychology.*

Chapter 1

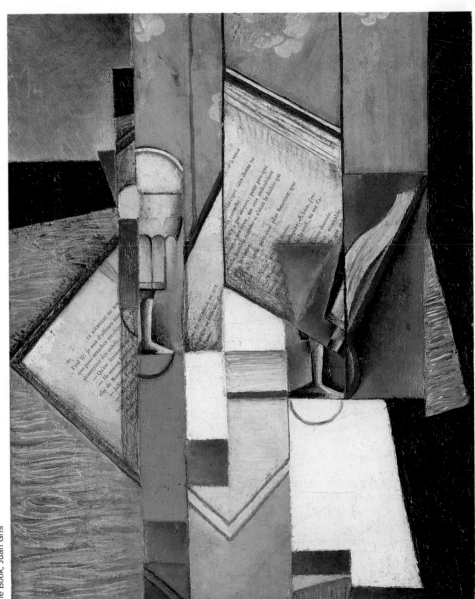

The Book, Juan Gris

The History and Scope of Psychology

The human being, as far as any human being can tell, is the only creature that contemplates itself. We not only think, feel, dream, and act but also wonder why and how we do these things. Such contemplation has taken many forms, ranging from just plain wondering, to folk tales and popular songs, to poetry and literature, to formal theologies and philosophies. A little more than a century ago, human self-contemplation took a scientific turn, and we call that science psychology.

Psychology is the *science* of *behavior* and the *mind*. In this definition *behavior* refers to the observable actions of a person or an animal. *Mind* refers to an individual's sensations, perceptions, memories, thoughts, dreams, motives, emotional feelings, and other subjective experiences. As a *science,* psychology endeavors to answer questions through the systematic collection and logical analysis of objectively observable data. The data in psychology are always based on observations of behavior, because behavior is directly observable and mind is not; but psychologists often use these data to make inferences about the mind.

Beyond the simple definition just presented, we can characterize psychology in many ways. Three have been particularly useful to me in developing this book:

1. *Psychology is a set of questions.* Psychology is the set of all questions about behavior and mind that are potentially answerable through scientific means. Some of the questions are very broad, with answers that are necessarily complex, qualified, or tentative: How are memories stored and retrieved? In what ways are people influenced by their perceptions of what other people think of them? How do genes and environment contribute to the psychological differences among people? Other questions are narrower, with answers that are more specific or definite: Why does a mixture of blue light and yellow light look white to people? What parts of the brain are most directly involved in the ability to understand and produce language? At what age do children begin to fear strangers? Each chapter of this book, beyond the second, probes a different set of broad and narrow questions.

2. *Psychology is a set of theories and procedures for asking and answering questions.* Psychology, like any other science, can be understood as a set of theoretical perspectives, which help researchers decide what questions to ask, and as a set of research methods and tools, which researchers use to answer questions. Throughout this book, we will be at least as concerned with the logic and evidence behind conclusions as with the conclusions themselves, because the latter can make sense or be convincing only in the light of the former.

3. *Psychology is a product of history.* Like any other organized human endeavor, psychology is what it is today because of a historical evolution. Viewed this way, psychology is a set of questions, theories, methods, and tentative answers that have been passed on and modified through successive generations. To understand psychology today, it is necessary to know something of that history.

1.

How can psychology be defined, and what are three ways of expanding on that definition?

Note to students: This is the first focus question of the book. A good way to study this book is to read each focus question before you read the adjacent paragraphs of text. After completing the paragraphs, you might then look back at the question to see if you can answer it. For more study ideas, read the section labeled "To the Student" following the Preface.

3

As you read this chapter on the history of psychology, think of history not simply as a record of the past but also as an explanation of the present.

BEFORE PSYCHOLOGY: PREPARING THE INTELLECTUAL GROUND

Before a science of psychology could come to pass, people had to conceive of and accept the idea that questions about human behavior and the mind can be answered scientifically. By the mid-nineteenth century, developments in philosophy, physiology, and evolutionary biology had paved the way for such a science.

Philosophical Developments: From Spirit to Machine

For the philosophical roots of psychology we could easily turn to the ancient Greeks, some of whom speculated about the senses, the human intellect, and the physical basis of the mind in ways that seem remarkably modern. But such ideas became dormant in the Middle Ages and did not begin to sprout again until the fifteenth century (the Renaissance) or to take firm hold until the eighteenth century (the Enlightenment).

Philosophy was tightly bound to religion through the seventeenth century. The church maintained that each human being consists of two distinct but intimately conjoined entities—a material body and an immaterial soul—a view referred to today as *dualism*. The body is part of the natural world and can be studied scientifically, just as inanimate matter can be studied. The soul, in contrast, is a supernatural entity that operates according to its own free will, not natural law, and therefore cannot be studied scientifically. This was the accepted religious doctrine, which—at least in most of Europe—could not be challenged publicly without risk of a charge of heresy and consequent death. Yet the doctrine left some room for play, and one who played dangerously near the limits was the great French mathematician, physiologist, and philosopher René Descartes (1596–1650).

Descartes' Version of Dualism: Focus on the Body

Prior to Descartes, most dualists assigned all the interesting qualities of the human being to the soul. The soul was deemed responsible for the body's heat, for its ability to move, for life itself. In *Treatise of Man* (1637/1972), and even more explicitly in *The Passions of the Soul* (1649/1985), Descartes challenged this view. He had performed dissections of animals and of human cadavers, was familiar with research on the flow of blood, and began to regard the body as an intricate, complex machine that generates its own heat and is capable of moving even without the influence of the soul. Although little was known about the nervous system in his time, Descartes' conception of the mechanical control of movement resembles our modern understanding of *reflexes*, which are involuntary responses to stimuli (see Figure 1.1).

Descartes believed that even quite complex behaviors can occur through purely mechanical means, without involvement of the soul. Consistent with church doctrine, he contended that nonhuman animals do not have souls, and he pointed out a logical implication of this belief: Any activity performed by humans that is qualitatively no different from what a nonhuman animal

René Descartes

Descartes' speculations, in the seventeenth century, about reflexes and the interaction of the body and soul in controlling voluntary actions were an important step toward a scientific analysis of human behavior.

Corbis-Bettmann

2.

What was Descartes' version of dualism, and how did it help pave the way for a science of behavior?

FIGURE 1.1 *Descartes' depiction of a reflex*

Descartes believed that reflexes occur through purely mechanical means. In describing this figure, Descartes (1637/1972) suggested that the fire causes movement in the nearby particles of skin, pulling on a "thread" (marked "CC") going to the brain, which, in turn, causes a pore to open in the brain, allowing fluid to flow through a "small conduit" to the muscles that withdraw the foot. What Descartes called a "thread" and a "small conduit" are today called nerves, and we now know that nerves operate through electrical means, not through physical pulling or the shunting of fluids.

Corbis-Bettmann

does can, in theory, occur without the soul. If my dog (who can do some wondrous things) is just a machine, then a good deal of what I do might occur purely mechanically as well.

In Descartes' view, the one essential ability that I have but my dog does not is *thought*, defined by Descartes as conscious deliberation and judgment. Whereas previous philosophers ascribed many functions to the soul, Descartes ascribed just one—thought. But even in his discussion of thought, Descartes tended to focus on the body's machinery. To be useful, thought must be responsive to the sensory input channeled into the body through the eyes, ears, and other sense organs, and it must be capable of directing the body's movements by acting on the muscles.

How can the thinking soul interact with the physical machine—the sense organs, muscles, and other parts of the body? Descartes suggested that the soul, though not physical, acts on the body at a particular physical location. Its place of action is a small organ (now known as the pineal body) buried between the two hemispheres (halves) of the brain (see Figure 1.2). Threadlike structures, which we now call nerves, bring sensory information by physical means into the brain, where the soul receives the information and, by nonphysical means, thinks about it. On the basis of those thoughts, the soul then wills movements to occur and executes its will by triggering physical actions in nerves that, in turn, act on muscles.

Descartes' dualism, with its heavy emphasis on the body, certainly helped open the door for a science of psychology. It is a popular theory among nonscientists even today, because it acknowledges the roles of sense organs, nerves, and muscles in behavior without violating people's religious beliefs or their intuitive feelings that conscious thought occurs on a nonphysical plane. But the theory has serious limitations, both as a philosophy and as a foundation for a science of psychology. As a philosophy, it stumbles on the question of how a nonmaterial entity (the soul) can have a material effect (move the body), or how the body can follow natural law and yet be moved by a soul that does not (Campbell, 1970). As a foundation for psychology, the theory sets strict limits, which few psychologists would accept today, on what can and cannot be understood scientifically. The whole realm of thought and all behaviors that are guided by thought are out of bounds for scientific analysis if they are the products of a willful soul.

3.

Why was Descartes' theory, despite its intuitive appeal, unsuitable as a foundation for a complete psychology?

FIGURE 1.2 *Descartes' depiction of how the soul receives information through the eyes*

Descartes believed that the human soul is housed in the pineal gland, depicted here as the tear-shaped structure in the center of the head. In describing this figure, Descartes (1637/1972) suggested that light from the arrow enters the eyes and opens pores in structures that we now know as the optic nerves. Fluid flows from the eyes through the opened pores, causing movement in the pineal gland, which, in Descartes' words, "renders the idea" of the arrow to the soul.

Materialism and Empiricism

At about the same time that Descartes was developing his machine-oriented version of dualism, an English philosopher named Thomas Hobbes (1588–1679) was going much further. It should be no surprise that an Englishman, not a Frenchman, was first to break from dualism entirely. The church and state were constantly feuding in seventeenth-century England, and inklings of democracy were emerging. Hobbes had been employed as a tutor to the future King Charles II and, when

4.

How did Hobbes's materialism and the subsequent development of empiricist philosophy help lay the groundwork for a science of psychology?

the latter came to power, enjoyed considerable protection. When a committee of bishops petitioned that Hobbes be burned to death for his blasphemous book *Leviathan*, Hobbes received instead a stern warning (Hunt, 1993). The church burned copies of his book, but Hobbes, promising not to repeat his heresy, lived to the ripe age of 91.

In the first chapter of *Leviathan*, Hobbes (1651/1962) argued that spirit, or soul, is a meaningless concept and that nothing exists but matter and energy, a philosophy now known as *materialism*. In Hobbes's view, all human behavior, including the seemingly voluntary choices we make, can in theory be understood in terms of physical processes in the body, especially the brain. Conscious thought itself, he maintained, is purely a product of the brain's machinery and therefore subject to natural law. Most of Hobbes's work was directed toward the implications of materialism for politics and government, but his ideas helped initiate a school of thought about the mind known as *British empiricism*, which was carried on by such English philosophers as John Locke (1632–1704), David Hume (1711–1776), James Mill (1773–1836), and John Stuart Mill (1806–1873).

Empiricism, in this context, refers to the belief that all human knowledge and thought ultimately derive from sensory experience (vision, hearing, touch, and so forth). The British empiricists' central belief was that the human mind consists of basic units, or elementary ideas (such as the idea of a chair), that originate from sensory experiences. These elementary ideas become associated (linked together) in certain ways, based on the pattern of one's sensory experiences, and the links, in turn, provide the foundation for the chaining together of ideas into the flow that we call thought. You will read more about empiricist philosophy in later chapters and see it contrasted with *nativism*, the view that elementary ideas are innate to the human mind and do not have to be gained through experience. The important point for now is simply that the empiricist philosophers believed that thought is not a product of free will but is a reflection of one's experience in the physical world. From this point of view, thought obeys natural law and can be studied scientifically.

Nineteenth-Century Physiology: Learning About the Machine

5.

How did the nineteenth-century conception of the nervous system inspire a theory of behavior called reflexology?

The nineteenth century was a time of great advances in physiology, the science of the body's machinery. One especially important development for the later emergence of psychology was an increased understanding of reflexes. The basic arrangement of the nervous system—consisting of a central nervous system (brain and spinal cord) and peripheral nerves that connect the central nervous system to sense organs and muscles—was well understood by the beginning of the century. In 1822 in England, François Magendie demonstrated that nerves entering the spinal cord contain two separate pathways, one for carrying messages into the central nervous system from the skin's sensory receptors and one for carrying messages out to operate muscles. In experiments with animals, scientists began to learn about the neural connections that underlie simple reflexes, such as the automatic withdrawal response to a pin prick, and found brain areas that, when active, could either enhance or inhibit such reflexes.

Some of these physiologists began to suggest that all human behavior occurs through reflexes, that even so-called voluntary actions are actually complex reflexes involving higher parts of the brain. One of the most eloquent proponents of this view, known as *reflexology*, was the Russian physiologist I. M. Sechenov. In his monograph *Reflexes of the Brain*, Sechenov (1863/1935) argued that every human action, "[b]e it a child laughing at the sight of toys, or . . . Newton enunciating universal laws and writing them on paper," can in theory be understood as a reflex. All human actions, he claimed, are initiated by stimuli in the environment. The stimuli act on a person's sensory receptors, setting in motion a chain of events in the nervous system that culminates in the muscle movements that constitute the action. Sechenov's work inspired another Russian physiologist, Ivan Pavlov (1849–1936), whose work on reflexes played a critical role in the development, in North America, of a school of thought in psychology called *behaviorism* (discussed later in this chapter).

Another important advance in nineteenth-century physiology was the concept of ***localization of function*** in the brain—the idea that specific parts of the brain serve specific functions in the control of mental experience and behavior. In Germany, Johannes Müller (1838) proposed the idea that the different qualities of sensory experience come about because the nerves from different sense organs excite different parts of the brain. Thus we experience vision when one part of the brain is active and hearing when another part is active. In France, Pierre Flourens (1824) performed experiments with animals showing that damage to different parts of the brain results in different kinds of deficits in animals' ability to move. And Paul Broca (1861), also in France, published clinical evidence that people who suffer injury to a very specific area of the brain's left hemisphere lose the ability to speak but not other mental abilities. All such evidence about the relationships between mind and brain helped lay the groundwork for a scientific psychology because it gave substance to the idea of a material basis for mental processes. The discovery of localization of function also led to the idea that natural divisions may exist among various mental processes and that the mind can be understood by identifying those basic processes and discovering how they interact. As you will see, this idea is central today in the psychological approach called *cognitive psychology*.

6.

How did discoveries of localization of function in the brain help establish the idea that the mind can be studied scientifically?

Paris Museum

Early evidence for localization of function

Shown here is the preserved brain of Paul Broca's patient known as Tan, who lost his ability to speak after suffering brain damage. The damage is in the left frontal lobe, in an area now called Broca's area (discussed in Chapter 5).

Darwin and Evolution: A New Unity of Person and Nature

In 1859, the English naturalist Charles Darwin (1809–1882) published *The Origin of Species*, a book that was destined to revolutionize biology, mark a new age in philosophy, and provide, along with the developments in physiology, a scientific grounding for psychology. Darwin's fundamental idea (discussed in Chapter 3) was that living things have arrived at their present forms through a long evolutionary process involving natural selection, in which those individuals whose inherited characteristics were best adapted to their environment survived and reproduced, while others died. Because of evolution, each part of any given plant or animal can be examined for the function it serves in allowing the individual to survive and reproduce in its natural environment. To understand, for example, why one species of bird has a stout beak and another has a slender beak, one must know what foods the birds eat and how they use their beaks to obtain those foods. The same principle

7.

How did Darwin's theory of natural selection offer a scientific basis for functional explanations of behavior?

Granger Collection

Charles Darwin

Darwin's principle of evolution by natural selection helped provide a scientific footing for psychology. The principle links humans to the rest of the biological world and explains the origin of brain mechanisms that promote the individual's survival and reproduction.

Note to students: Each major section in each chapter of this book is followed by a brief summary. Reading the summary should remind you of the ideas and information in the section and thereby help you to think about them. This would also be a good time to review the section by testing your ability to answer each of the focus questions in the margin and to define each of the section's boldfaced terms.

that applies to anatomy applies to behavior. Through natural selection, living things have acquired innate predispositions to behave in ways that promote their survival and reproduction in their natural environment. A key word here is *function*. While the physiologists were concerned with the neural mechanisms of behavior, Darwin was concerned with the functions of behavior, that is, with the ways in which an organism's behavior helps it to survive and reproduce.

In *The Origin of Species*, Darwin discussed only plants and nonhuman animals, but in later writings he made it clear that he viewed humans as no exception. Humans also evolved through natural selection, and their anatomy and behavior can be analyzed in the same ways as can those of other living things. In a book entitled *The Expression of the Emotions in Man and Animals*, Darwin (1872/1965) illustrated how evolutionary thinking can contribute to a scientific understanding of human behavior. He argued that the basic forms of human emotional expressions (such as laughing and crying) are inherited, as are those of other animals, and may have evolved because survival advantages accompanied the ability to communicate one's emotions or intentions to others of one's kind. In addition to providing the foundation for functionalism, Darwin's work provided a scientific foundation for nativist philosophy. The inborn knowledge and mechanisms of the human mind are not mystically created but are products of evolution by natural selection.

Darwin, perhaps more than anyone else, helped convince the intellectual world that human beings, despite their pretensions, are as much a part of nature as all other creatures and can be understood through the methods of science. The world was ripe for psychology.

SECTION SUMMARY

Philosophical and scientific developments in the seventeenth, eighteenth, and nineteenth centuries laid the groundwork for the emergence of a science of psychology. Among these developments were (a) Descartes' idea that much of human behavior occurs through purely physical means; (b) Hobbes's idea that all of human behavior occurs through such means; (c) the British empiricists' idea that all of human knowledge and thought depends on sensory experiences in the physical world; (d) physiologists' findings, in the nineteenth century, about reflexes and the localization of mental functions in specific areas of the brain; and (e) Darwin's idea that human beings, like all other forms of life, are part of the natural world and evolved through natural selection.

THE EVOLUTION OF PSYCHOLOGY: A HISTORY OF ALTERNATIVE PERSPECTIVES

Psychology became a recognized scientific discipline in the latter half of the nineteenth century. Then came a rather contentious period of rapid development in which various competing schools of thought arose, each offering a new view on the subject matter and methods appropriate to this new science. As in most intellectual disputes, a degree of truth lay on every side. Psychology today can be understood as a synthesis of ideas that had seemed contradictory to one another in the field's earlier history. Let us look at some of the schools of thought, or approaches in psychology, for what they can tell us about present-day psychology.

Origins of Experimental Psychology: How Can the Mind Be Studied?

The first research psychologists were Germans who were impressed by the success of laboratory methods in physiology and wished to apply similar techniques to the study of the mind. Their view was that the proper way to begin this study was to examine the simplest kinds of mental processes—simple sensations, memories, and judgments. If these could be understood, then the science could progress to more complex processes. Among these first psychologists, the one most often credited as the founder of our science was Wilhelm Wundt.

Wundt and the Laboratory Dissection of the Mind

Although others had conducted psychological research before him, Wundt (1832–1920) is considered the founder of scientific psychology for two reasons. First, he wrote the first textbook of psychology that defined the discipline as a science and reviewed psychological research that had been done up to that time (published in two parts, in 1873 and 1874). Then, in 1879, at the University of Leipzig, he opened the first university-based laboratory of psychology. This event—the official acceptance of psychology as a science by a respected university—is usually taken to mark psychology's birth (Blumenthal, 1985). The first official graduate students in psychology were Wundt's.

Before starting his psychological research, Wundt had worked as an assistant to the eminent physiologist Hermann von Helmholtz on projects such as measuring the speed of neural impulses. From this work, Wundt acquired the insight that mental processes, as products of the nervous system, do not occur instantaneously but take time. One of his aims in psychology was to measure the speed of simple mental processes. The fastest-occurring processes would be the most elementary, the "atoms of the mind." After identifying them, he could begin to test hypotheses about how these elements combine to form more complex mental processes.

One of Wundt's methods was to test people in two reaction-time tasks, one slightly more complex than the other, and to subtract the shorter time from the longer to determine the time required for the mental step or steps that differentiated the two tasks. Thus in one experiment (Kendler, 1987), the simple task was to release a telegraph key, connected to an electrical timer, as quickly as possible when a light came on. This took an average of 0.20 second. In the more complex task, the person was to release one key, held down by the left hand, if the light was red, and a different key, held down by the right hand, if the light was green. The average reaction time for this was 0.29 second. Subtracting the former from the latter, Wundt determined that the time needed to categorize the color and decide which key to release was 0.09 second. The most elementary mental processes, according to Wundt, are those that can be completed most quickly. Wundt's ideas that complex mental processes can be understood as sequences of more elementary processes and that the latter can be measured as reaction times are foundations for the field of research that today is called *cognitive psychology*.

8.

Why is Wundt considered the founder of scientific psychology? How are two of his key ideas illustrated by his reaction-time experiments?

Archives of the History of American Psychology

Wilhelm Wundt

Wundt, the long-bearded man in the center of this photograph, was a pioneer in the application of scientific methodology to psychology. His opening of a laboratory at the University of Leipzig in 1879 is often taken to mark the birth of psychology as a science. Here he and his colleagues are probably setting up a lecture demonstration of one of his famous reaction-time experiments, as indicated by the large timer and poster in the background.

9.

What was the goal of Titchener's structuralism? Why did his introspective approach to the structure of the mind fail as a scientific method?

Titchener's Structuralism and the Problem of Introspection

The school of psychological thought that descended most directly from Wundt's approach is called ***structuralism***, a term used not by Wundt but by one of his students, Edward Titchener (1867–1927). Titchener, an Englishman educated at Oxford, went to Leipzig to earn a Ph.D. in psychology under Wundt and then moved to the United States to head the newly established Department of Psychology at Cornell University. Like Wundt, Titchener believed that the proper goal of psychology was to identify the elements of the mind and determine how they combine with one another. His aim was to learn about the *structure* of the mind through analyzing elementary conscious experiences, which he considered to be the mind's building blocks.

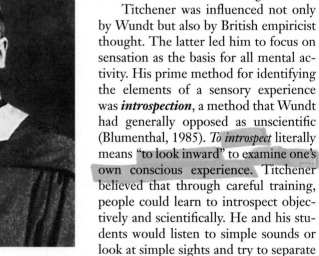

Archives of the History of American Psychology

Titchener was influenced not only by Wundt but also by British empiricist thought. The latter led him to focus on sensation as the basis for all mental activity. His prime method for identifying the elements of a sensory experience was ***introspection***, a method that Wundt had generally opposed as unscientific (Blumenthal, 1985). *To introspect* literally means "to look inward" to examine one's own conscious experience. Titchener believed that through careful training, people could learn to introspect objectively and scientifically. He and his students would listen to simple sounds or look at simple sights and try to separate their experience of the sound or sight into its elements. Through such work, Titchener concluded that every sensation has four basic dimensions: quality, intensity, duration, and clarity (Kendler, 1987). Thus he might describe the sensation produced by a particular flash of light as blue, strong, brief, and clear.

Edward Titchener

A student of Wundt, Titchener was one of the first psychologists in North America. His goal was to learn about the structure of the mind through the introspective analysis of its elements.

Today, nearly all psychologists agree that Titchener's method failed. Wundt had been right in warning about the limitations of introspection. Suppose that you, a student of Titchener's, look into your mind while gazing at a flash of light and decide that the sensation it produces has four elemental qualities and that I, trained in introspection by another master, look into my mind while gazing at the same flash and decide that it has only three. To you, the clarity and intensity of the flash are two separate elements, but I claim that they are one. How can we resolve our disagreement? Whose introspection is more accurate? Are we just using words differently, or do our two minds really differ in some fundamental way? I can't look into your mind to see what you see when you look at the flash, and you can't look into mine. The problem is that introspection is a private technique, and science requires public techniques. A public technique is one that produces data that can be observed by outsiders, not just by the individual user of the procedure.

James's Functionalism: Examining the Purposes of Behavior

10.

How was James's functionalism different from Titchener's structuralism? How did James's use of introspection differ from Titchener's?

A contemporary of Titchener, William James (1842–1910) held professorships at Harvard in both philosophy and psychology (the latter beginning in 1889). James is famous today as a great thinker, writer, and teacher who helped make psychology known to the intellectual world and who established some of its philosophical foundations. He had a small laboratory at Harvard, primarily for teaching purposes, but he was not by nature a laboratory scientist. In describing the work of the German experimentalists, James (1890/1950) wrote, only half in jest, "This method taxes patience to the utmost, and could hardly have arisen in a country whose natives could be bored." More important, he opposed Wundt and Titchener's view that one can understand the structure of the mind by analyzing its elementary parts. In one article, James (1884) compared their approach to that of a person attempting to understand a house by analyzing the content of each of its bricks. He argued that to understand a house or a mind, one must first ask what it is for and then look at the whole thing and its larger parts to see how it fulfills its purposes. Because of his emphasis on the purposes and functions of the mind, James's psychological perspective is called *functionalism.*

While the structuralists were most influenced by physiology, which attempted to understand behavior in terms of the machinery that produces it, James and other functionalists were most influenced by Darwin, who had shown that behavior can be understood in terms of its purposes without analyzing its mechanisms. To illustrate this perspective, in the first chapter of his classic textbook *The Principles of Psychology*, James (1890/1950) contrasted Romeo and Juliet's attraction to each other with that between iron filings and a magnet:

> Romeo wants Juliet as the filings want the magnet; and if no obstacles intervene he moves toward her by as straight a line as they. But Romeo and Juliet, if a wall be built between them, do not remain idiotically pressing their faces against the opposite sides like the magnet and the filings with the card. Romeo soon finds a circuitous way, by scaling the wall or otherwise, of touching Juliet's lips directly. With the filings the path is fixed; whether it reaches the end depends on accidents. With the lover it is the end which is fixed, the path may be modified indefinitely.

James was eclectic in his views about methods. He respected the experimental method, but his own contributions were more philosophical. He relied heavily on introspection but used it more loosely and broadly than did Titchener, as a source of ideas rather than as proof, and made no claim that he was being rigorously scientific. To develop a theory about emotions, he looked into his own mind while in various emotional states and described what he was feeling; to get ideas about the concept of the self (what people mean when they say "I" or "me"), he thought about the various meanings that this concept had to him and the functions that it served in his daily life. You will read more about James's view of emotions in Chapter 6 and his view of the self-concept in Chapter 13.

James's functionalism did not lead directly to a lasting, unified school of thought in psychology, partly because it was based so heavily on introspection, but it did provide a rich set of ideas that have since been pursued by others through more rigorous means. As you will discover in many places in this book, functionalism is thriving today

Courtesy of the Harvard University Archive

William James

A contemporary of Titchener, James is considered to be the founder of the school of philosophical and psychological thought called functionalism. He believed that the main objective of psychology should be to understand the mind's functions, not its structures.

Wellesley College Archives

FIGURE 1.3 *A pioneering woman in psychology: Mary Calkins*

In the nineteenth century women were barred from Ph.D. programs in psychology. In 1890, against the stern admonitions of Harvard's president, William James admitted Mary Calkins (1863–1930) into his graduate seminar. When she joined the seminar, all the other students dropped it, apparently in protest, and James tutored her alone. Calkins later completed the requirements for the Ph.D., outperforming all the male students on the qualifying exams, yet Harvard refused to grant her the degree. Despite this obstacle, she went on to a distinguished career as a researcher and professor at Wellesley College and became the first woman president of the American Psychological Association (Scarborough & Furumoto, 1987).

among psychologists who have adopted an evolutionary perspective in their research. These psychologists make explicit use of Darwin's evolutionary theory to frame their questions and theories about the ways that human mental processes promote the individual's survival and reproduction.

One of the many students inspired by James was Edward Thorndike (1874–1949), who studied under James for a while at Harvard and then went to Columbia University for a Ph.D. and a long career as a professor of educational psychology. Thorndike was one of the first psychologists to perform systematic experiments on the learning process, with both animals and humans. His main contribution was the development of an explicitly functionalist theory of learning that describes the learning process in terms of its value to the learner (discussed in Chapter 4). Another of James's students, Mary Calkins, who was a pioneer in another sense, is shown in Figure 1.3.

Gestalt Psychology: The Whole Is Different from the Sum of Its Parts

11.

How did a perceptual effect, the phi phenomenon, help promote Gestalt psychology as an alternative to structuralism?

In 1912, two years after James's death, a German psychologist named Max Wertheimer (1880–1943) published an article on a perceptual effect that he labeled the *phi phenomenon*. The phenomenon can be described as follows: Blink a single light at a rapid rate (about 20 times per second) against a dark background. What you see (no surprise) is one blinking light. Now add a second light, near the first, and blink it at the same rate but in alternation with the first; thus when the first is on, the second is off, and vice versa. The sensory result is not what you would expect if you consider the two lights separately. You see not two blinking, stationary lights but one unblinking light moving rapidly back and forth. In his paper on this phenomenon, Wertheimer (1912/1965) pointed out that it violates the atomistic view of perception favored by Wundt and Titchener. The two blinking lights together produce in the observer a sensory experience of movement that does not exist in the physical lights themselves or in the sensory experience that either light produces alone. The movement can be understood only as a sensory product of the whole complex stimulus—both blinking lights together.

On the basis of this study and others that followed, Wertheimer and a group of other German psychologists—including Kurt Koffka, Wolfgang Köhler, and Kurt Lewin—founded a school called ***Gestalt psychology***. *Gestalt* is a German word that can be translated roughly as "organized shape" or "whole form." The premise of this new school was that the mind must be understood in terms of organized wholes, not elementary parts. A melody is not the sum of individual notes, a painting is not the sum of the individual dots of paint, an idea is not the sum of its elementary concepts. The meaningful units of consciousness are whole, organized constructs—whole melodies, whole scenes, whole ideas—that cannot be understood by analyzing elementary judgments and sensations of the sort that Wundt and Titchener studied.

12.

How was the Gestalt school of thought applied to descriptions of perception and problem solving?

Most early research in Gestalt psychology was in the area of visual perception (discussed in Chapter 8). In many laboratory demonstrations, Gestalt psychologists showed that in conscious experience whole objects and scenes take precedence over parts. For example, when looking at a chair, people perceive and recognize the chair as a whole before noticing its arms, legs, and other components. Moving away from the area of perception, Köhler (1917/1973) performed experiments on problem solving with chimpanzees. He argued that these animals hit upon solutions through sudden flashes of insight, in which the whole solution (such as moving a box to a position underneath a banana dangling on a string in order to reach it) comes at once rather than in bits and pieces. Other Gestalt psychologists, including Lewin, took their principles into the realm of social psychology in ways that are discussed in Chapters 13 and 14.

Gestalt psychology started in Germany, but by the mid-1930s, with the increased threats against Jews and their supporters that accompanied Nazification, all

Nostell Priory, Yorks / Bridgeman Art Library London / Superstock

Seeing the whole or the parts

Long before Gestalt psychologists considered the question of part–whole relationships scientifically, artists were exploring and playing with such relationships. Viewed as a whole, this whimsical painting by Giuseppe Arcimboldo (1527–1593) is a face. Viewed as parts, it is fruits and vegetables.

its founders—including Wertheimer, Koffka, Köhler, and Lewin—had moved to North America and established research laboratories in colleges and universities there (Ash, 1985). Gestalt psychology eventually lost its position as a discrete school of thought, but it became integrated into many different lines of psychological work.

Psychological Perspectives Based on Research with Animals

All the perspectives in psychology that we have considered so far defined the field as the science of the human mind—the normal, adult human mind at that (and some might add *male* and *European* to the set of adjectives). But other psychologists, at the same time, were developing broader conceptions of psychology. Some of them studied nonhuman animals and defined psychology as the science of all animal behavior, human and nonhuman. They were interested in other animal species both for their own sake and as substitutes for humans in research that could not readily be done on people. Their approach was influenced by Darwin, who had argued convincingly for the continuity of life. If humans are biologically related to other species, then some principles of behavior that apply to other species may likewise apply to humans. Three psychological perspectives that make especially heavy use of animals are *behaviorism, ethology,* and *physiological psychology.*

Watson and the Emergence of Behaviorism

John B. Watson (1878–1958), one of the most influential of the early psychologists to study animals, began this work as a graduate student at the University of Chicago in 1901, and he continued it as a professor at Johns Hopkins University. Over the years, he performed experiments with monkeys, chickens, dogs, cats, frogs, and fish (Hothersall, 1995), but his usual research animal was the rat, which he studied in mazes and other such testing apparatuses.

Watson was impressed with the amount he could learn about an animal's behavior with no consideration of the animal's mind. Laws could be described that related changes in behavior directly to events in the environment, with no mention of thought or other mental processes. For example, a rat's route and rate of movement through a maze toward food could be predicted on the basis of where food had been placed during previous trials, without concern for the rat's "knowledge," "perceptions," "decisions," or other mental events. In fact, Watson became convinced that reference to the mind only obscured the explanation, because there was no direct way to observe the animal's mind. All one could observe were the external environmental conditions (such as the shape of the maze and the type of reward in its goal box) and the animal's actions. As he reflected on this, Watson became convinced that mental constructs were of no value in explaining human behavior either. When we observe humans, just as when we observe other species, all we can observe directly and objectively are behavior and environment, and psychology should limit itself to those two constructs.

On the basis of such considerations, Watson began to advocate a new perspective in psychology, which he called **_behaviorism_**. In 1913, he published a manifesto entitled "Psychology as the Behaviorist Views It," the main ideas of which can be summarized as follows:

1. The proper subject of study in psychology is not the mind but behavior, defined as the observable actions of people and other animals.

2. The appropriate goal of psychology is to identify the environmental conditions that cause individuals to behave in particular ways.

3. The achievement of this goal does not require reference to the mind or to any unobservable events occurring within the individual. In fact, such reference should be avoided. It is enough simply to describe the reliable environment–behavior relationships.

4. No fundamental difference exists between the behavior of humans and that of other animals or between the methods that should be used to study humans and other animals.

Many North American psychologists responded enthusiastically to Watson's ideas. They wanted to throw out the introspective techniques and convoluted mental terminology that they regarded as carryovers from stuffy European traditions. Within a decade after Watson's 1913 article, behaviorism had replaced Titchener's structuralism as the most influential school in North American psychology, and it remained in that position into the 1960s. Watson himself, however, was forced to leave the academic world before the school that he had founded achieved its greatest influence. In 1920, an extramarital affair with his research assistant Rosalie Rayner became public, and the scandal was cause for Johns Hopkins University to fire him and for no other university to hire him. He continued publishing books and articles on behaviorism, and he and Rayner (whom he later married) conducted some highly publicized research with nursery school children. But his main employment after 1920 was in the advertising world. In an autobiographical sketch, Watson (1936) wrote, perhaps wistfully, "I began to learn that it can be just as thrilling to watch the growth of a sales curve of a new product as to watch the learning curve of animals and men."

Watson (1924) argued that all behavior is essentially reflexive; that is, all behavior can be understood as reactions (responses) to events in the environment (stimuli). For this reason, his brand of behaviorism is often called *S-R psychology*, where *S* stands for stimulus and *R* for response. But not all of Watson's successors in behaviorism agreed with this reflex formulation of all behavior.

Skinner and a New Version of Behaviorism

Of the many behaviorists who succeeded Watson, by far the most influential was B. F. Skinner (1904–1990). As a graduate student at Harvard, Skinner developed a new kind of apparatus for studying learning in animals and a new way of describing

13.

What are four principles of behaviorism set forth by its founder, John B. Watson?

John B. Watson

On the grounds that the proper study of psychology is observable, verifiable behavior and not hidden mental processes, Watson founded behaviorism. The goal of this approach is to describe the environmental causes of behavioral effects.

the learning process. In 1938, he published *The Behavior of Organisms*, which summarized his research and the ideas behind it. The book helped bring him fame, and from soon after its publication until his death, more than 50 years later, he was the recognized leader of behaviorism.

Skinner agreed with the four just-summarized tenets of Watson's behaviorism, but he explicitly disagreed with Watson's idea that all, or even most, behaviors can be understood as reflexes. Skinner's emphasis was not on stimuli that precede responses but on stimuli that are *consequences* of responses. He coined the term *operant response* to refer to any behavioral action that operates on the environment to produce a consequence (such as food, water, or electric shock). The foundation of his theory lay in the simple observation that operant responses increase or decrease in frequency depending on their consequences. If a hungry rat receives a pellet of food each time it presses a lever, the rat will press the lever with increasing frequency (see Figure 1.4). Elaborating on this observation, Skinner and his followers discovered numerous reliable relationships between the rate at which an animal will produce an operant response and the nature, timing, and probability of the response (discussed in Chapter 4).

In emphasizing the role of consequences in controlling behavior, Skinner was following in the footsteps of Thorndike, who, as noted earlier, was influenced by William James's functionalism. Skinner's behaviorism is grounded in functionalism. Its focus is not on the mechanics of behavior but on the relationship between behavior and its beneficial or harmful effects upon the behaving animal. Skinner is frequently referred to as an S-R psychologist, like Watson, but he objected to that label (Epstein, 1991; Skinner, 1974). Skinner's brand of behaviorism is more appropriately called *operant psychology*, because its focus is on the consequences of behavioral actions, not on stimuli that precede and evoke such actions.

Like Watson, Skinner had a knack for stating his case strongly, clearly, and sometimes in terms that seemed deliberately designed to provoke controversy. The mere title of one of his books, *Beyond Freedom and Dignity* (1971), elicited a storm of protest. His basic argument in that book was that concepts such as freedom and dignity, like all other concepts referring to the mind, have no explanatory value. Skinner's message was that human behavior is a product of the conditions in which a person grows and lives and that words like *freedom, dignity, willpower,* and *decisions* only obscure our understanding of the lawful relationships between behavior and its consequences. The hero is merely the person who has been rewarded often for actions we call "good," and the villain is the person who has been rewarded often for actions we call "bad."

Ethology: The Study of Behavior in the Natural Environment

In the 1930s, while behaviorism was flourishing in North America, a quite different approach to the study of behavior was taking hold in Europe. The leaders of this movement—most notably Konrad Lorenz (1903–1989) in Austria and Nikolaas Tinbergen (1907–1988) in Holland—were genuine animal enthusiasts who studied animals for their own sake, not as substitutes for humans. Rather than focusing on domesticated breeds in laboratory settings, they preferred to study wild animals in their natural habitats—woods, fields, and ponds. Lorenz named this science *ethology*, a term that today can be defined simply as the study of animal behavior in the natural environment (Gould, 1982). Ethology originated as a branch of zoology, not psychology. But neither nature nor good scientists respect the arbitrary disciplinary boundaries that universities establish for administrative purposes. Ethologists and psychology's behaviorists were studying the same thing, animal behavior, and it was inevitable that the two would begin to interact.

At first, the interactions between ethologists and behaviorists took the form of arguments. Both groups were studying animal behavior, but from different points of view and with different methods. The behaviorists were interested almost solely

14.

How was Skinner's version of behaviorism similar to Watson's, and how was it different?

Nina Leen / *LIFE Magazine*, © Time Warner, Inc.

FIGURE 1.4 *B. F. Skinner and the Skinner box*
Skinner, who devoted a long career to the study of animal learning and to wide-ranging speculation about human behavior, was the acknowledged leader of behaviorism for about five decades. To study operant responses in rats and other animals, he invented an apparatus widely known as the Skinner box. The rat here receives a food pellet for pressing the lever.

15.

How did ethology and behaviorism differ? Why did they later begin to merge?

in learning. They brought to their work a philosophical bias, dating back to British empiricism, that behavior is a reflection of previous experience and the way to understand it is to understand learning. They were impressed by the degree to which they could train animals in the laboratory to behave in very unnatural ways by controlling the animals' experiences. Skinner even trained pigeons to play a version of Ping-Pong.

In contrast, ethologists were influenced most strongly by Darwin. They were impressed by the highly complex and adaptive behavior patterns that animals display without any apparent learning, at least not learning as defined by behaviorists. Lorenz studied courtship patterns in ducks and geese, and Tinbergen studied mating rituals in stickleback fish and various species of gulls. Their experiments showed that these behaviors occur in essentially normal form even in animals that have never observed the behaviors or been rewarded for practicing them. Lorenz and Tinbergen developed the idea that many survival-related behavior patterns are "wired into" an animal's nervous system and are triggered at the appropriate time by the co-occurrence of specific stimuli in the environment (such as the sight of an appropriate mate) and events inside the body (such as the heightened production of sex hormones in the spring).

By the 1960s, however, developments in both ethology and behaviorism began to bring the two schools together in cooperative ways. Behavioral researchers were increasingly reporting biologically based constraints on animals' learning abilities and describing differences in the kinds of responses that different species could learn (Shettleworth, 1972). For example, they found that migratory birds are biologically predisposed to learn landmarks that guide their migratory flight and that seed-eaters are predisposed to learn the locations of seeds. Behaviorists had always recognized that the underlying mechanisms of learning are themselves a product of evolution, and, increasingly, they began to acknowledge that quite different learning mechanisms may have evolved to serve different survival needs. At the same time, some ethologists began to turn their attention to mammals, and they found the behavior of mammals to be far more flexible and dependent on prior experiences than that of insects, fish, and birds, which had been the focus of earlier ethological studies. As you will see in Chapter 3, some ethologists even went on to study humans, and they developed new insights about the interactions between innate predispositions and environmental experiences in human behavior.

Konrad Lorenz and followers

Ethologists described a form of learning known as imprinting, in which newly hatched ducks or geese follow and become attached to the first moving object they see or hear. These geese, which were hatched by Lorenz in an incubator, responded to him as if he were their mother.

Nina Leen / *LIFE Magazine*, © Time Warner, Inc.

Physiological Psychology: The Search for Biological Mechanisms of Behavior

The progress made during the nineteenth century in understanding the nervous system helped make possible a science of psychology, but once psychology emerged as a formal discipline, most psychologists preferred to ignore the nervous system because of its extraordinary complexity. To explain behavior, they referred either to reliable relationships between behavior and events in the environment or to hypothetical mental processes, without worrying about how they are executed by the brain.

But not all early psychologists ignored the nervous system. One who did not was Karl Lashley (1890–1958), who had been one of Watson's graduate students at Johns Hopkins. Lashley learned a lot from Watson about observing animal behavior and constructing well-designed experiments, but he was not satisfied with Watson's S-R mode of explanation (Bruce, 1991). After receiving his degree in 1915, he went on to conduct numerous experiments with rats, monkeys, and other animals that were aimed at identifying the neural bases of learning. His work led him to conclude that complex behavior does not consist of chains of reflexes, as Watson had believed, but is the output of elaborate neural programs in the brain that are preformed by heredity and modified by experience (Lashley, 1930, 1951). His research showed that these programs can generate well-organized behaviors, such as running, jumping, and climbing, even without any sensory input. Lashley's work suggested that learning operates not by piecing together new chains of reflexes but by modifying inherited neural programs. Thus Lashley's work helped unite the North American behaviorists' interest in learning with the European ethologists' interest in instincts.

Lashley was one of the pioneers in *physiological psychology*, or what is often today called *behavioral neuroscience*—the attempt to understand the physiological mechanisms, in the brain and elsewhere, that organize and control behavior. In laboratory studies with animals, physiological psychologists can assess, under controlled conditions, the behavioral effects of damage to or artificial stimulation of specific parts of the brain. As you will discover in Chapter 6, physiological psychology has been especially successful in learning about basic motivational and emotional mechanisms that we share with other animals, such as those involved in hunger, sex, fear, and aggression.

16.

How did Lashley's early work in physiological psychology challenge Watson's behaviorism? How did it help bring behaviorism and ethology closer together?

Views from the Clinic: Understanding Individual Minds

Simultaneously with early developments in experimental and animal psychology, which were centered at universities, another important strand in the twine of psychology was being spun in a very different setting—the offices of health professionals who were attempting to help people overcome psychological problems. The most influential of these clinical pioneers was Sigmund Freud.

Freud and Psychoanalysis: Probing the Unconscious Mind

Sigmund Freud (1856–1939) was a creative thinker whose work and ideas were outside the mainstream of academic research and thought. Unlike the other pioneers we have been discussing, Freud was not a university professor. He was a physician who specialized in neurology and, from 1886 on, worked with patients at his private office in Vienna. He found that many people who came to him had no detectable medical problems but seemed to suffer from their memories, especially those of disturbing events in their early childhood. In many cases, they could not recall such memories consciously, but clues in their behavior led Freud to believe that disturbing memories were present nevertheless, buried in what he referred to as the *unconscious mind*. From this insight, Freud developed a method of treatment

17.

How did Freud arrive at his concept of an unconscious mind that influences conscious thought and behavior? How was Freud's work different from that occurring in academic circles, and how did it broaden the range of psychological inquiry?

Edmund Engelman

Sigmund Freud

As a Viennese physician specializing in neural disorders, Freud came to believe that many of his patients' physical and mental problems originated as a way of keeping certain disturbing memories out of consciousness. He went on to develop a theory of the mind and an approach to psychotherapy called psychoanalysis. Here he is shown in his office in Vienna in 1938.

18.

In what sense does humanistic psychology present an optimistic view of human nature? What is the goal of humanistic therapy?

in which his patients would talk freely about themselves and he would analyze what they said in order to uncover the buried memories. The goal was to bring the memories to a patient's conscious attention so that his or her conscious mind could work out ways of dealing with them.

Freud coined the term *psychoanalysis* to refer both to his method of treatment and to his theory of the mind (discussed in Chapters 15 and 17). Freud's most fundamental concept was that of a dynamic (forceful) unconscious mind. While Wundt, Titchener, James, Wertheimer, and others had defined the mind entirely in terms of conscious experience, Freud argued that the conscious mind is only the tip of the iceberg and that the bulk of mental activity is unconscious. Not only does the unconscious mind contain buried memories, but it is also the source of instinctive drives, particularly sexual and aggressive drives. Although the conscious mind has no direct access to the content of the unconscious mind, it is strongly affected by that content. Conscious thoughts and wishes can be understood as products of the unconscious mind that have been modified to become acceptable to the conscious mind. For example, a child's wish to kill a parent might be so terrifying that it would be converted unconsciously into an obsessive conscious fear that the parent might die. The child would never be aware of the original wish unless it arose later in the course of psychotherapy.

Freud considered his methods to be scientific, but relatively few psychologists in academic circles have ever agreed with him on that. The most common criticism is that psychoanalysis leaves too much room for the analyst's subjective interpretation. So many alternative ways of putting the clues together exist that any given analysis is at least as much the analyst's creation as a true account of the mind of the person being analyzed. Still, many research psychologists today do accept Freud's general theory that unconscious mental processes influence conscious thought and action. Freud's work also helped bring psychology's attention to a wide range of issues that the field had previously ignored. The role of childhood experiences in later development, the sexual drive and its various manifestations, and the whole realm of irrational, emotional behavior and thought became appropriate subjects for psychological research.

Humanistic Psychology: Focus on the Conscious, Striving Person

In reaction to both behaviorism and psychoanalysis, which seemed to devalue the conscious, human mind, some psychologists developed theories and clinical practices that centered on people's conscious understanding of themselves and capacity for self-control. This movement—led by such therapists and scholars as Carl Rogers (1902–1987) and Abraham Maslow (1908–1970)—came to be called *humanistic psychology.*

A central concept of humanistic psychology is that each person has an *actualizing tendency*, an inborn set of drives that go beyond basic animal needs and lead the individual to engage in creative activities, which contribute to the well-being of both the person and society at large (Maslow, 1970; Rogers, 1963). This actualizing tendency can be stunted, however, by parents, teachers, and others who criticize children's self-initiatives, thereby convincing them that they are unable or unworthy. Rogers (1951) and other early humanistic therapists reported that people who came to them for therapy usually had negative views of themselves, which prevented them from taking control of their lives. A central goal of humanistic therapy is to help people acquire positive self-concepts.

Like psychoanalysis, humanistic psychology has had a major impact on the practice of psychotherapy and on the ways in which people in our culture think and talk about themselves and others. Research psychologists often criticize humanistic psychology as unscientific. Yet, as discussed in Chapter 15, this approach has generated some interesting research and, with its emphasis on people's conscious thoughts, has influenced the course of modern cognitive and social psychology.

Cultural and Social Psychology: The Social Nature of the Mind

Those of us who are products of Western cultures tend to regard the human mind as the property of the individual. You have your mind; I have mine. But think about that for a moment. Consider how much overlap exists between your mind and mine and how dependent both of our minds are on the culture in which we live. Were it not for that overlap, I could not be writing to you and you could not make sense of what I am writing. We share knowledge and ways of thinking, feeling, and behaving that are aspects of the broad culture to which we both belong. In that sense, your mind and my mind are one.

Leonard Doob (1990) has used the example of sneezing to illustrate the pervasiveness of social and cultural influences. At one level, sneezing is a simple, reflexive reaction to irritation in the nose, common to people everywhere. But Doob asked questions that carry us beyond the reflex level: "Will [the person who senses the urge to sneeze] try to inhibit this reflex action? What will he say, what will bystanders say, when he does sneeze? What will they think of him if he fails to turn away and sneezes in their faces? Do they and he consider sneezing an omen and, if so, is it a good or bad omen?" Clearly, to answer such questions, we would have to know about the social context in which the urge to sneeze occurred and about the beliefs and customs of the culture in which the sneezer was raised.

As a different illustration, imagine that you grew up on an island and never had contact with another human being. What kind of person would you be? You would lack the knowledge, ideas, values, and customs that characterize and unify people who live intertwined lives in other parts of the world. You would lack language and, therefore, the ability for verbal thought, the kind of thought that uses words as mental symbols to represent objects, events, and ideas. You would lack social ties and the opportunity to express all the emotions associated with such ties. Biologically you would be a recognizable human being, but psychologically you would not be. Aristotle was right when, 23 centuries ago, he declared that human beings are by nature social animals. Normal human development occurs in a context of continual interaction with other humans.

Cultural Psychology: The Mind as a Product of History

The psychological perspective that emphasizes most strongly the dependence of the human mind on the culture in which it develops is ***cultural psychology*** (Miller, 1999). It can be defined as the study of the psychological differences among people who live in different cultural groups and of the ways by which people's thoughts, feelings, and behavior are influenced by their culture. Only recently has this approach taken shape as a recognized field within psychology. Yet its basic premises go back to the very beginnings of the discipline.

One of the first to advocate a cultural psychology was none other than Wilhelm Wundt, the same man who is credited with founding experimental psychology. Wundt argued that the experimental method he practiced in the laboratory was useful for understanding the elementary machinery of the mind but could not, by itself, constitute a complete psychology (Blumenthal, 1985). He claimed that the higher workings of the mind depend on culture—the language, knowledge, beliefs, and other forms of information that accumulate in a population over time and are passed from one generation to the next. These cultural variables influence all aspects of

What is human nature?

Humans are by nature social and cultural beings. Our abilities to speak, understand language, and think in words, for example, depend on our developing in a social environment, with other people. Occasionally a child is discovered who managed to survive outside of human contact, presumably raised by wolves. Such children are reported to act in many ways more wolflike than humanlike—to run on all fours, howl, and prefer raw meat over cooked. One such child, Victor, was discovered near Aveyron, France, in 1798, and was studied and tutored by Jean-Marc Itard. Under Itard's tutelage, Victor gradually became more humanlike (and Frenchlike), but he never became fully acculturated. Shown here is a still from François Truffaut's film *The Wild Child*, based on Itard's writings about Victor.

19.

What are the basic premises of cultural psychology as advocated by Wundt and Vygotsky?

motivation, emotion, thought, and action. To understand these effects, Wundt argued, psychologists would have to move out of the lab and observe people in different cultures as they engage in their normal, daily activities. Within any given culture, psychologists would also have to study history in order to understand how the culture evolved and affected the psychology of its people. Wundt himself read extensively about the languages, religions, and customs of people in different parts of the world, and between 1900 and 1920 he published a 10-volume work, *Völkerpsychologie*, on cultural psychology.

Another groundbreaker in cultural psychology was Lev Vygotsky (1896–1934). A leader of psychology in what was then called the Soviet Union, during the years immediately following the revolution that formed that country in 1917, Vygotsky was strongly influenced by the ideas of Karl Marx. Like Marx, he considered the human mind to be a product of history. From this perspective, each culture, which has its own distinct history, has produced a somewhat different version of the human mind. As you will discover in Chapters 11 and 12, Vygotsky's research focused on the ways in which children, through their social interactions with one another and with adults, acquire the mind of their culture.

Social Psychology: How People Are Influenced by One Another

In contrast with cultural psychology, **social psychology** is a well-established, long-accepted, large subfield of contemporary psychology (discussed in Chapters 13 and 14). Gordon Allport (1968) aptly defined this subfield as "an attempt to understand and explain how the thought, feeling, and behavior of individuals are influenced by the actual, imagined, or implied presence of others."

Compared with cultural psychology, which focuses on cross-cultural differences, history, and the long-term processes of human development, social psychology focuses more on the here and now. Its primary goal is to identify and understand general psychological processes through which people are influenced by other people at any given moment. Social psychology is concerned with such issues as conformity, obedience, the effects of others' expectations, and the ways by which people form impressions of other people and attitudes about social issues. Also unlike cultural psychology, social psychology relies heavily on experimental procedures, often conducted in university laboratories with college students as subjects. Of course, social psychologists recognize that results with college students may not apply to everyone, and many do conduct cross-cultural research to assess the generality of their concepts.

One of the pioneers of social psychology as a laboratory science was Kurt Lewin (1890–1947). Originally a Gestalt psychologist working in Germany, Lewin emigrated to the United States in the early 1930s. As an observer of the early stages of Nazism and as an immigrant to a new country, he was profoundly aware of the powerful influence of the social environment, for good or ill, on the thinking and behavior of individuals. Lewin's Gestalt background led him to reject the S-R behaviorism that dominated much of American psychology at the time, but he embraced the experimental method. He developed a perspective in social psychology called *field theory* (discussed in Chapter 14), which centers on the idea that each human being, at any given moment, exists in a psychological "field" composed of forces that tend to push or pull the person in various directions (Lewin, 1951). These forces include the individual's own goals and values as well as the person's beliefs about what others expect him or her to do.

The Rise of Modern Cognitive Psychology

Psychologists often speak of a "cognitive revolution" occurring in the 1960s and 1970s, during which **cognitive psychology** replaced behaviorism as the dominant school of thought in North American psychology (see Figure 1.5). The term *cogni-*

20.

How does social psychology differ from cultural psychology? What role did Lewin play in the development of modern social psychology?

A laboratory experiment in social psychology
This social psychological experiment, on how people judge others' personality, lacks the rich social context in which people normally interact. The starkness of the situation permits the researcher to isolate and vary systematically the factors that might affect the judgments being studied. Many social psychologists are concerned about the degree to which the results of such experiments can be generalized to settings outside the laboratory and to people other than college students, the usual subjects in such research.

tion refers to knowledge, and cognitive psychology can be defined as the study of people's ability to acquire, organize, remember, and use knowledge to guide their behavior. Although cognitive psychologists study the mind, they do so not through introspection but through inferences drawn from observable behavior. Cognitive psychologists develop models or theories about mental processes that mediate behavior, and they test them in controlled situations where people would be expected to behave in one way if the model is correct and in a different way if it is incorrect.

Although cognitive psychology began to come into its own in the 1960s, it was not suddenly born then. For many years before, some research psychologists who called themselves behaviorists—such as Clark Hull (1882–1952) and Edward Tolman (1886–1959)—were in fact practicing what would now be called cognitive psychology. Their brand of behaviorism was sometimes referred to as S-O-R behaviorism to distinguish it from Watson's S-R behaviorism. The *O* in this formulation stands for hypothetical processes inside the organism that mediate the relationship between stimuli and responses. Tolman (1948), for example, studied maze learning in rats and developed the view that rats acquire a cognitive map, a mental representation of the spatial layout of the maze, and use it to guide their

21.

What were some historical precursors to modern cognitive psychology?

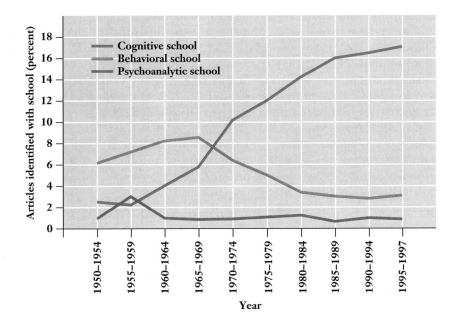

FIGURE 1.5 *The rise of cognitive psychology*
During the second half of the twentieth century, cognitive psychology rose sharply in prominence in academic psychology, while behaviorism declined and psychoanalysis remained at a relatively low level. The measure here is based on articles appearing in four "flagship" periodicals in psychology—*American Psychologist*, *Annual Review of Psychology*, *Psychological Bulletin*, and *Psychological Review*—all of which aim to publish articles representing the entire field of psychology. A keyword computer search was used to find articles in each periodical that were identified with each school of thought. Because some articles identified with a school would not have contained the keywords, the graph probably underestimates the true percentages for each school, but the trends shown are accurate and are confirmed by other measures. (Adapted from Robins & others, 1999.)

movements (discussed in Chapter 4). Going back still further, Wundt's laboratory methods and ideas, over 100 years ago, were remarkably similar to those of present-day cognitive psychologists (Blumenthal, 1985).

The Influence of Piaget and Chomsky

22.

How did Piaget's and Chomsky's ideas contribute to the rise of cognitive psychology?

The ascendance of cognitive psychology in the 1960s was spurred in part by theories about the human mind that were developed outside the mainstream of North American psychology. Especially influential was the work of the Swiss psychologist Jean Piaget (1896–1980). Piaget studied reasoning in children by observing the kinds of mistakes that they made when solving problems and by asking them to explain the reasons behind their solutions. From these studies, Piaget developed the idea that children undergo a series of mental metamorphoses from infancy through adolescence, at each of which they become able to reason in a qualitatively different and more advanced way. He attempted to describe the manner of thinking that characterizes each stage of this development in terms of hypothetical mental constructs called *schemes*. Roughly, a scheme can be thought of as a blueprint for acting upon the world and for using information about the world to control the actions. By 1960, American psychologists were aware of Piaget's work, and many began to perform experiments to test some of his ideas. Although Piaget's specific, mathematical manner of describing schemes did not catch on, his general approach of trying to explain behavior in terms of internal mental constructs was widely adopted and contributed greatly to the cognitive movement.

A second name for special mention is that of Noam Chomsky (b. 1928), who is not a psychologist but a linguist. In 1957, Chomsky published *Syntactic Structures*, which spurred a revolution in linguistics and had an enormous impact on psychology. In this book, and even more explicitly in later writings, Chomsky argued that language must be understood as a system of mental rules, not as stimulus–response chains as some behaviorists had proposed. He also held that these rules are constrained and partially predetermined by the innate capacities of the human mind. Many psychologists eagerly began to test Chomsky's ideas experimentally. The results they published contributed to the rapid growth of *psycholinguistics* (the study of the psychological bases for human language), which is today a major subfield of cognitive psychology. More generally, Chomsky's ideas prompted psychologists to think of other behaviors, not just linguistic statements, as products of mental rules.

The Impact of the Computer

23.

How did the computer analogy contribute to the rise of cognitive psychology?

Perhaps the strongest stimulant for the blossoming of cognitive psychology in the past three decades has been the emergence and growing popularity of computer technology. In every age, the concepts that people have of the brain and mind are influenced by the kinds of machines that are available as analogies (Rose, 1973). Descartes explicitly compared mechanical aspects of human behavior to the hydraulic mechanisms used to move the robotlike statues that decorated public gardens in seventeenth-century France. Nineteenth-century reflexologists compared the brain to the telephone switchboard, an analogy that was also implicit in the theories of some early-twentieth-century behaviorists. Today the machine that most influences people's conception of the brain is the computer. A computer receives coded information (the input), reorganizes the information, compares it with other information stored in its memory, performs calculations on it, and uses the results to determine what signals to send to the computer's output system. All this is analogous to what the brain does: Input is analogous to the receipt of information by sensory systems, output is analogous to behavioral action, and everything in between is analogous to thought.

The workings of a computer can be studied in two quite different ways. One is to learn about its hardware—that is, the electrical system through which the computer operates. This is analogous to studying the physiology of the brain. The other is to learn about the computer's software—that is, its set of programs. A computer program can be understood as a set of clearly specified steps for operating on specific kinds of information. The steps have to be written in such a way that the machine can follow them, but they can also be translated into English. We can write them out in the form, "First do _____, then _____, then _____." When cognitive psychologists talk about understanding the mind, they are usually referring to a process similar to specifying the steps of a computer program. They are asking: Through what steps is information transformed as a person perceives, remembers, thinks, and makes decisions? From this perspective, if you can program a computer to respond in the same way as a human does to a set of input stimuli, then you have provided a plausible explanation of the human's behavior (Simon, 1992).

The Diversity of Cognitive Psychology

Cognitive psychology cannot be described today as a single approach or school of thought. Rather, it is a constellation of approaches unified only in their attempt to explain observable behavior by reference to hypothetical mental structures or processes. Some cognitive psychologists, who call themselves *information-processing theorists*, use the computer analogy directly and try to spell out their theories of the mind in terms that a computer can follow (Massaro & Cowan, 1993). Others warn that the computer analogy can be misleading. The human being is not just an "information-processing device" but also a biological survival machine with motives and emotions that are foreign to computers but color all aspects of human thought and behavior. Those researchers often bring a functionalist perspective to bear on their theories about the mind, based on evolutionary theory (Barkow & others, 1992). Others combine the information-processing approach of cognitive psychology with the study of the brain—an endeavor called *cognitive neuroscience* (Gazzaniga, 2000). They attempt to identify the brain areas responsible for specific mental tasks, with the goal of understanding how the brain carries out those tasks. Cognitive psychology has also merged with social psychology to form *social cognition*, which develops cognitive models to explain how people influence each other.

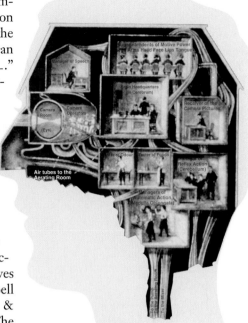

An early analogy

The analogies used to understand the brain are not limited to machines. In the 1930s, a children's encyclopedia used the notion of a factory to represent the complex information-organizing activities of the brain.

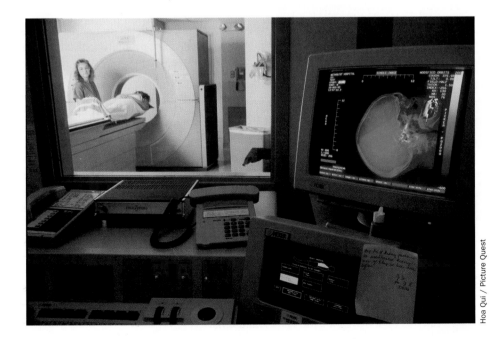

Hoa Qui / Picture Quest

Viewing the active brain

In recent years the field of cognitive neuroscience has advanced greatly, due in part to new techniques for assessing the amount of activity that occurs in specific brain locations as a person performs mental tasks. These neuroimaging techniques are discussed in Chapter 5.

SECTION SUMMARY

Psychology today is an amalgam of ideas and approaches derived from various schools of thought and lines of research that have emerged in the field's history. Wundt's early cognitivism, Titchener's structuralism, James's functionalism, and Gestalt psychology were prominent among the early laboratory approaches to the human mind. Watson's and Skinner's behaviorism, European ethology, and physiological psychology came about as three quite different ways of studying animals to learn about basic processes and mechanisms of behavior. Freud's psychoanalysis and the humanistic psychology of Rogers and Maslow were among the approaches that were developed to help people with psychological problems and to understand the differences between healthy and unhealthy human functioning. Social psychology and cultural psychology came about as ways of understanding how human behavior is influenced by other people and by the culture in which one develops. Modern cognitive psychology, which is very much in the tradition begun by Wundt, emerged as a multifaceted attempt to understand the elements of human thought and the relationship between thought and action.

PSYCHOLOGY AS A DISCIPLINE AND A PROFESSION

Psychology is an extraordinarily vast and diverse field. The historical account that you have just read describes not just an evolution but a mushrooming. Each school of thought brought with it new questions about the mind and behavior, and new techniques for trying to answer them. Psychology today is an amalgam of all those questions and techniques.

The Connections of Psychology to Other Scholarly Fields

24.

How does psychology link the three main divisions of academic studies?

In concluding this chapter, you might think for a few minutes about the place of psychology among the spectrum of disciplines that form the departments of a typical college of arts and sciences. Figure 1.6 illustrates a scheme that I call (with tongue only partly in cheek) the *psychocentric theory of the university*. The disciplines are divided roughly into three broad areas. One division is the *natural sciences*, the sciences of nature—including physics, chemistry, and biology—shown on the left-hand side of the figure. The second division is the *social sciences*, the sciences of

FIGURE 1.6 *Connections between psychology and other scholarly areas* Psychology bridges the natural and social sciences, and it has strong connections to the humanities. In this sense, it lies in the center of the academic pursuits of the university.

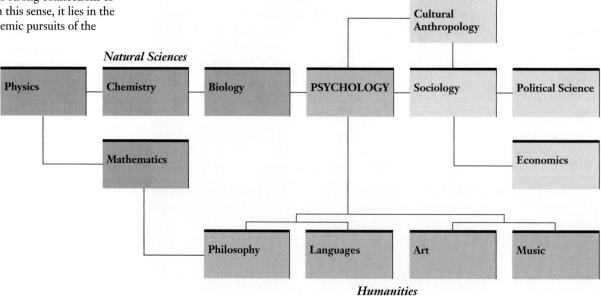

society and the individual's relationships to society—including sociology, anthropology, political science, and economics—shown on the right-hand side of the figure. The third division is the *humanities*—including languages, philosophy, art, and music—shown in the lower part of the figure. The humanities represent things that *humans* do. Humans, unlike other animals, talk to one another, develop philosophies, and produce art and music.

Where does psychology fit into this scheme? Directly in the center, tied to all three of the broad divisions. On the natural science end, it is tied most directly to biology by way of physiological psychology and ethology. On the social science end, it is tied most directly to sociology and anthropology by way of social and cultural psychology. In addition to bridging the natural and social sciences, psychology ties the whole spectrum of sciences to the humanities, through its interest in how people produce and understand languages, philosophies, art, and music.

If you were to look at the research activities of psychologists, you would find that some behave like natural scientists. They have labs, wear white coats, perform experiments, and spend a good deal of time over in Biology, Chemistry, and Physics exchanging ideas and equipment. Others, you would find, behave more like social scientists. They use surveys, historical documents, and interviews as sources of data, and they find intellectual companionship in the various social science departments. The distinction between these two groups, however, is often fuzzy. Social psychologists often have labs and fancy data-collecting equipment, and biologically oriented psychologists can be found whose data come mainly through their own two eyes, out in the field.

The link between psychology and the humanities is provided by individuals who ask questions about how and why people do such things as talk, reason, and create art or music. For example, consider the link between psychology and the study of languages. If you are interested in describing the structure of one or another of the world's languages, you are a linguist. But if you are interested in how people are able to learn and use that structure, and how this may affect other aspects of their behavior, you are a psycholinguist (a psychologist of language). Similarly, some psychologists are interested in how and why people respond to and create art, music, literature, and philosophies.

25.

How can psychology be understood historically in terms of alternative ways of characterizing the human mind? What is the value of a historical perspective in psychology?

Psychology as a Profession

Psychology is not only an academic discipline but also a profession. As a profession, it includes both academic psychologists, who are engaged in research and teaching, and practicing psychologists, who apply psychological knowledge and ideas in clinics, businesses, and other areas. The majority of professional psychologists in the United States hold doctoral degrees in psychology, and most of the rest hold master's degrees (Landrum & others, 2000). The main settings in which they work and the kinds of services they perform in each are:

+ *Academic departments in universities and colleges* Academic psychologists are employed to conduct basic research and to teach psychology courses.

+ *Clinical settings* Clinical and counseling psychologists work with clients who have psychological problems or disorders, in independent practice or in hospitals, mental health centers, clinics, and counseling or guidance centers.

+ *Elementary and secondary schools* School psychologists administer psychological tests, supervise programs for children who have special needs, and may help teachers develop more effective classroom techniques.

+ *Business and government* Psychologists are hired by businesses and government agencies for such varied purposes as conducting research, screening candidates for employment, helping design more pleasant and efficient work environments, and counseling personnel who have work-related problems.

ARLO & JANIS® by Jimmy Johnson

The decision to major in psychology in college does not necessarily imply a choice of psychology as a career. Most students who major in psychology do so primarily because they find the subject fun to learn and think about. Most go on to careers in other fields—such as social work, law, education, and business—where they are quite likely to find their psychology background helpful (Carroll & others, 1992; Landrum & others, 2000).

CONCLUDING THOUGHTS

At the end of each chapter I offer several "concluding thoughts," which in some cases might help you organize your review of the chapter and in other cases might add an insight or two to those that you generate yourself as you think about the chapter's contents. (Another useful way to review each chapter is to try to answer each of the focus questions that appear in the margins throughout the chapter.) Here are two concluding thoughts for the chapter you have just read:

1. Ways to characterize the mind The history of psychology can be viewed in part as a history of alternative ways of characterizing the human mind. Most of the early psychologists were interested primarily in conscious, rational thought. Following the lead of philosophers before them, their broad question was, How do people think? Wundt and Titchener (structuralists), in their different ways, tried to understand thought in terms of its elementary parts. That tradition persists in cognitive psychology's studies of the elementary processes involved in perception, memory, judgment, and so on. James (a functionalist), in contrast, contended that thought loses its very essence if it is broken down. He characterized thought as a continuous flow, which must be understood in terms of its broad goals or purposes rather than its parts. The Gestaltists also argued that thought must be understood in wholes rather than parts. Freud (a psychoanalyst) added a new twist to the problem, arguing that the study of conscious thought is insufficient; unconscious, irrational thoughts affect the conscious ones and also influence behavior in ways that bypass consciousness. Finally, Watson and Skinner (behaviorists) rejected the issue of thought entirely, changing the question from How do people think? to How is behavior controlled by stimuli and consequences in the environment?

2. The value of a historical perspective A temptation exists, today, to think of everything old as obsolete. In psychology, that temptation is manifest in the tendency to avoid reading the works of the early psychologists and other thinkers who set forth the questions and pioneered the methods that constitute the field of psychology as we know it today. But those who do read such works are often rewarded by the breadth of mind, clarity of vision, and sheer intelligence they find therein. Sometimes psychology seems to be a hodgepodge of specific facts, findings, theories, and techniques. Reading about the broader issues, in the original words of psychology's pioneers, can elevate one's vision and help put the details in perspective. One work to which I will refer occasionally throughout this book is William James's two-volume *Principles of Psychology*, first published in 1890. Take a look at that work in your library, or maybe even buy a copy (it's available in paperback). If you do buy it, you might very well enjoy reading it along with this textbook. As you go from topic to topic in this book, look up what James had to say on the topic and see if progress has occurred. On some topics you will be quite impressed with how far psychology has moved in a hundred years, and on others you might decide that the field has barely budged.

Further Reading

David Hothersall (1995). *History of psychology* (3rd ed.). New York: McGraw-Hill.

This lively historical account begins with the psychological theories of the ancient Greeks and ends with the behaviorism and neobehaviorism of the mid-twentieth century.

Robert Bolles (1993). *The story of psychology: A thematic history.* Pacific Grove, CA: Brooks/Cole.

In an informal, storytelling style, Bolles relates developments in psychology to developments in the culture at large. Kings as well as philosophers, and political movements as well as ideas, figure into the story. The subtitle, "a thematic history," refers to the focus on certain recurring themes: atomism, mechanism, empiricism, and associationism. The book leads us from Descartes to modern cognitive psychology.

Raymond Fancher (1996). *Pioneers of psychology* (3rd ed.). New York: Norton.

This is a beautifully written, fun-to-read history of the ideas that led to modern psychology. The pioneers whose ideas and lives are sketched here include Descartes, Locke, Helmholtz, Wundt, Darwin, Galton, James, Pavlov, Skinner, Freud, Binet, and Piaget. The book's last chapter deals with ideas underlying the modern field of artificial intelligence.

Elizabeth Scarborough & Laurel Furumoto (1987). *Untold lives: The first generation of American women psychologists.* New York: Columbia University Press.

This book tells the story of courageous women who managed to break into the previously all-male ranks of academic psychology and to open the doors for other women to enter. Included are separate chapters on Mary Calkins, Milicent Shinn, Ethel Puffer, Margaret Washburn, and Christine Ladd-Franklin.

Eric Landrum, Stephen Davis, & Teresa Landrum (2000). *The psychology major: Career options and strategies for success.* Upper Saddle River, NJ: Prentice-Hall.

If you are considering psychology as a major, this 160-page paperback can help you decide. If you have already chosen to major in psychology, it can help guide you through your years of study. It is packed with practical information and suggestions—about jobs and careers, how to conduct library research and write papers, how to find research and internship opportunities, and how to prepare for and apply for graduate study.

Julie DeGalan & Stephen Lampert (2000). *Great jobs for psychology majors* (2nd ed.). Lincolnwood, IL: NTC Contemporary Publishing.

This book contains useful information about jobs available for psychology majors (including jobs that do not require a postgraduate degree), how to find such jobs, and how to apply for them.

Looking Ahead

As you have seen, psychology has always been defined as a science. It became a formally recognized area of study when people accepted the idea that behavior and the mind are subject to natural law and can be studied by scientific methods. But what are scientific methods, and what special problems occur in applying such methods in psychology? These are the main questions of the next chapter.

Chapter 2

4 x 5 = 20, Wassily Kandinsky

Methods of Psychology

In Chapter 1, *psychology* was defined as the *science* of behavior and the mind. But what does it mean to say that psychology is a science? Science is the attempt to answer questions through the systematic collection and analysis of objective, publicly observable data (data that all observers can agree on). In psychology, the data are usually measures or descriptions of some form of behavior produced by human or animal subjects. Special problems exist in choosing what data to collect, collecting the data, and drawing conclusions from them.

This chapter is about scientific methods as applied to psychology. You will read sections on the research strategies psychologists use to answer questions, the statistical procedures they use to analyze data, the safeguards they employ to avoid biased results, and the protections they provide to human and animal research subjects. But first, to ease ourselves into the topic, here is a story about a horse . . . and a psychologist.

LESSONS FROM CLEVER HANS

This story, a true one, took place in Germany near the beginning of the twentieth century. The horse was Clever Hans, famous throughout Europe for his ability to answer questions, and the psychologist was Oskar Pfungst. In a preface to the original account (Pfungst, 1911/1965), James Angell wrote, "Were it offered as fiction, it would take high rank as a work of imagination. Being in reality a sober fact, it verges on the miraculous." I tell the story here because of its lessons about scientific attitude and methods.

The Mystery

Hans's owner, a Mr. von Osten, was an eccentric retired schoolteacher and devoted horseman who had long believed that horses would prove to be as intelligent as people if only they were given a proper education. To test his theory, von Osten spent 4 years tutoring Hans in the manner employed in the most reputable German schools for children. Using flash cards, counting frames, and the like, he set about teaching his horse reading, arithmetic, history, and other scholarly disciplines. He always began with simple problems and worked toward more complex ones, and he rewarded Hans frequently with praise as well as carrots. Recognizing that horses lack the vocal apparatus needed for speech, von Osten taught Hans to spell out words using a code in which the letters of the alphabet were translated into hoof taps and to answer yes–no questions by tossing his head up and down for yes and back and forth for no. After 4 years of this training, Hans was able to answer practically any question that was put to him in either spoken or written German, whether about geography, history, science, literature, mathematics, or

Clever Hans at a mathematics lesson

Mr. von Osten believed that his horse was intellectually gifted, and so did many other people until the psychologist Oskar Pfungst performed some simple experiments.

current events. Remarkably, he could also answer questions put to him in other languages, even though he had never been trained in them.

Now you might think that von Osten was a charlatan, but he wasn't. He genuinely believed that his horse could read and understand a variety of languages, could perform mathematical calculations, and had acquired a vast store of knowledge. He never charged admission or sought other personal gain for displaying Hans, and he actively sought out scientists to study the animal's accomplishments. Indeed, many scientists, including some eminent zoologists and psychologists, came to the conclusion that von Osten's claims were true. The evidence that most convinced them was Hans's ability to answer questions even when von Osten was not present, a finding that seemed to rule out the possibility that the horse depended on secret signals from his master. Moreover, several circus trainers, who specialized in training animals to give the appearance of answering questions, studied Hans and could find no evidence of trickery.

1.

How did Clever Hans give the appearance of answering questions, and how did Pfungst unveil Hans's methods?

The Solution

Hans's downfall finally came when the psychologist Oskar Pfungst performed a few simple experiments. Pfungst (1911/1965) theorized that Hans answered questions not through understanding them and knowing the answers but through responding to visual signals inadvertently produced by the questioner or other observers. Consistent with this theory, Pfungst found that the animal failed to answer questions when he was fitted with blinders so that he could not see anyone, and that even without blinders he could not answer questions unless at least one person in his sight knew the answer. With further study, Pfungst discovered just what the signals were.

Immediately after asking a question that demanded a hoof-tap answer, the questioner and other observers would naturally move their heads down just a bit to observe the horse's hoof. This, it turned out, was the signal for Hans to start tapping. To determine whether Hans would be correct or not, the questioner and other observers would then count the taps and, unintentionally, make another response as soon as the correct number had been reached. This response varied from person to person, but a common component was a slight upward movement of either the whole head or some facial feature, such as the eyebrows. This, it turned out, was the signal for Hans to stop tapping. Hans's yes–no head-shake responses were also controlled by visual signals. Questioners and observers would

Cues from the audience

When members of the audience knew the answer to a question asked of Clever Hans, they inadvertently signaled the horse as to when to start and stop tapping, or which way to shake his head, through their own head movements.

unconsciously produce slight up-and-down head movements when they expected the horse to answer yes and slight back-and-forth head movements when they expected him to answer no, and Hans would shake his head accordingly.

All the signals that controlled Hans's responses were so subtle that even the most astute observers had failed to notice them until Pfungst pointed them out. And Pfungst himself reported that the signals occurred so naturally that, even after he had learned what they were, he had to make a conscious effort to prevent himself from sending them after asking a question. For 4 years, von Osten had believed that he was communicating scholarly information to Hans, when all he had really done was teach the horse to make a few simple responses to a few simple, though minute, gestures.

Facts, Theories, and Hypotheses

The story of Clever Hans illustrates the roles of facts, theories, and hypotheses in scientific research. A *fact* (also called a *phenomenon* or an *observation*) is an objective statement, usually based on direct observation, that reasonable observers agree is true. In psychology, facts are usually particular behaviors, or reliable patterns of behaviors, of persons or animals. When Hans was tested in the manner typically employed by von Osten, the horse's hoof taps or head shakes were such as to give the appearance that he was answering questions correctly. That is the fact, which no one involved in the adventure disputed.

A *theory* is an idea, or a mental model, that is designed to explain existing facts and make predictions about new facts that might be discovered. Any prediction about new facts that is made from a theory is called a *hypothesis.* I have no idea what facts (or perhaps delusions) led von Osten to develop his theory that horses have humanlike intelligence. However, once he conceived his theory, he used it to hypothesize that his horse, Hans, could learn to give correct answers to verbally stated problems and questions. The psychologist, Pfungst, had a quite different theory of equine intelligence: Horses don't think like humans and can't understand human language. In keeping with this theory, and to explain the fact that Hans seemed to answer questions correctly, Pfungst developed the more specific theory that the horse responded to visual cues produced by people who were present and knew the answers. This theory led Pfungst to hypothesize that Hans would not answer questions correctly if fitted with blinders or if asked questions to which nobody present knew the answer.

Facts lead to theories, which lead to hypotheses, which are tested with experiments or other research studies, which lead to new facts, which sometimes lead to new theories, which . . . . That is the cycle of science.

The Lessons

In addition to illustrating the roles of fact, theory, and hypothesis, the story contains three more specific lessons about scientific research. One lesson concerns human gullibility and the value of skepticism. People are fascinated by extraordinary claims and often act as though they want to believe them. This is as true today as it was in the time of Clever Hans. We have no trouble at all finding otherwise rational people who believe in astrology, psychokinesis, water divining, telepathy, or other occult phenomena, despite the fact that all these have consistently failed when subjected to controlled tests. Von Osten clearly wanted to believe that his horse could do amazing things, and so to a lesser degree may have the scholars who had studied the horse before Pfungst. Pfungst learned the truth partly because he was highly skeptical of such claims. Instead of setting out to prove them correct, he set out to prove them wrong. His skepticism led him to look more carefully, to notice what others had missed, to think of an alternative, more mundane explanation, and to pit the mundane explanation against the paranormal one in controlled tests.

2.

How are facts, theories, and hypotheses related to one another in scientific research?

3.

How does the Clever Hans story illustrate the value of skepticism, the value of controlled experimentation, and the need to rule out observer-expectancy effects?

Skepticism should be applied not only to extraordinary theories that come from outside of science but also to the usually more sober theories produced by scientists themselves. The ideal scientist always tries to disprove theories, even those that are his or her own. The theories that scientists accept as correct, or most likely to be correct, are those that could potentially be disproved but have survived all attempts so far to do so.

The second lesson has to do with the value of careful observations under controlled conditions. Pfungst solved the mystery of Clever Hans by isolating the conditions under which the horse could and could not respond correctly to questions. He tested Hans repeatedly, with and without blinders, and recorded the percentage of correct answers in each condition. The results were consistent with the theory that the animal relied on visual signals. He then pursued the theory further by carefully observing Hans's examiners to see what cues they might be sending. And when he had an idea what they might be, he performed further experiments, in which he deliberately produced or withheld the signals and recorded their effects on Hans's hoof-tapping and head-shaking responses. Careful observation under controlled conditions is a hallmark of the scientific method.

The third lesson concerns *observer-expectancy effects*, which plague a great deal of psychological research (Rosenthal, 1976). A general problem in studies of humans and other sentient animals is that researchers may quite unintentionally communicate to subjects their expectations about how the subjects "should" behave, and the subjects, intentionally or not, may respond by doing just what the researchers expect. The same is true in any situation in which one person administers a test to another. Have you ever taken an oral quiz and found that you could tell whether you were on the right track by noting the facial expression of your examiner? By tentatively testing various tracks, you may have finally hit on just the answer that your examiner wanted. Clever Hans's entire ability depended on his picking up such cues. We will discuss the general problem of expectancy effects later (in the section on avoiding biases).

SECTION SUMMARY

Hans, the horse, appeared to be able to answer questions correctly by tapping his hoof an appropriate number of times. In a series of experiments, Oskar Pfungst, a psychologist, showed that Hans's hoof tapping was controlled by cues that observers unconsciously sent as to when they expected him to start and stop tapping. The story illustrates (a) the concepts of fact, theory, and hypothesis; (b) the value of skepticism and controlled experimentation; and (c) the need to rule out observer-expectancy effects.

TYPES OF RESEARCH STRATEGIES

Throughout this book you will read about research evidence for or against the theories under discussion. You will find such evidence easier to evaluate if you have some general knowledge of the various kinds of research strategies you will encounter. One approach to categorizing research strategies in psychology is to think of them as varying along three dimensions (Hendricks & others, 1990). One dimension is the *research design*, of which there are three basic types—descriptive studies, correlational studies, and experiments. The second dimension is the *setting* in which the study is conducted, of which there are two basic types—field and laboratory. And the third dimension is the *data-collection method*, of which there are again two basic types—self-report and observation. Each of these dimensions can vary independently from the others, resulting in 12 different kinds of studies, each defined by its combination of design, setting, and data-collection method (see

TABLE **2.1**   *Three dimensions of research strategy exemplified by studies of children's violence after viewing a violent film*

		Research Setting and Data-Collection Method			
		Field		**Laboratory**	
		Self-report	**Observation**	**Self-report**	**Observation**
Research Design	**Descriptive study**	Interview children leaving local theaters after watching violent films. Ask how they feel. Analyze for amount and types of violent feelings reported.	Observe children leaving local theaters after violent films. Make notes about their behavior. Analyze the notes for amount and types of violent actions.	Have children watch a violent film in the lab. Then interview them about their feelings. Analyze for amount and types of violent feelings reported.	Have children watch a violent film in the lab. Then videotape them as they play in a laboratory playroom. Analyze the tapes for amount and types of violent actions.
	Correlational study	Interview children leaving local theaters after watching violent and nonviolent films. Analyze for amount of violent feelings reported. Compare this amount for those who saw a violent film with the amount for those who saw a nonviolent film.	Observe children leaving local theaters after watching violent and nonviolent films. Make notes about their behavior. Analyze the notes for amount of violence. Compare this amount for those who saw a violent film with the amount for those who saw a nonviolent film.	In the laboratory, allow children to watch a violent or a nonviolent film—their choice. Then interview them. Analyze for amount of violent feelings reported. Compare this amount for those who saw the violent film with the amount for those who saw the nonviolent film.	In the laboratory, allow children to watch a violent or a nonviolent film—their choice. Then videotape them as they play in a laboratory playroom. Analyze the tapes for amount of violence. Compare this amount for those who saw the violent film with the amount for those who saw the nonviolent film.
	Experiment	Randomly sort neighborhood children into two groups. Give one group tickets to a violent film and the other tickets to a nonviolent film at a local theater. Interview them as they leave the theater. Analyze for amount of violent feelings reported. Compare this amount for the two groups.	Randomly sort neighborhood children into two groups. Give one group tickets to a violent film and the other tickets to a nonviolent film at a local theater. Observe and make notes about their behavior as they leave the theater. Analyze for amount of violence. Compare this amount for the two groups.	Divide children randomly into two groups and have one group watch a violent film and the other a nonviolent film in the laboratory. Interview them afterward. Analyze for amount of violent feelings reported. Compare this amount for the two groups.	Divide children randomly into two groups and have one group watch a violent film and the other a nonviolent film in the laboratory. Then videotape them as they play in a laboratory playroom. Analyze the tapes for amount of violence. Compare this amount for the two groups.

Each of the 12 studies outlined in this table is defined by a unique combination of *research design* (descriptive, correlational, or experimental), *research setting* (laboratory or field), and *data-collection method* (self-report or observational). After you have read the textbook section on research strategies, return to this table and read all 12 sketches carefully. For each study, think about the particular problems a researcher would have to solve to carry it out and the types of conclusions that the researcher could and could not reasonably draw from it.

Table 2.1). We will first discuss the three types of designs and then turn briefly to the other two dimensions.

Research Designs

Experiments

An experiment is the most direct and conclusive approach to testing a hypothesis about a cause–effect relationship between two variables (a variable is simply anything that can vary). In describing an experiment, the variable that is hypothesized to cause some effect on another variable is called the ***independent variable,*** and the

4.

How does an experiment test causal hypotheses?

5.

What are the independent and dependent variables in (a) Pfungst's experiment with Hans and (b) DiMascio's experiment on treatments for depression?

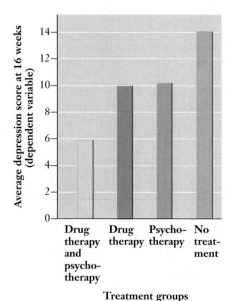

FIGURE **2.1** *Effect of treatment condition on depression*
Subjects who received both drugs and psychotherapy were the least depressed at the end of the 16-week treatment period (according to the results of a standard interview procedure scored on a 17-point scale). In contrast, subjects who received no treatment were the most depressed. (From DiMascio & others, 1979.)

variable that is hypothesized to be affected is called the ***dependent variable.*** The aim of any experiment is to learn how the dependent variable is affected by (*depends* on) the independent variable. In psychology, dependent variables are usually measures of behavior, and independent variables are factors that are hypothesized to influence those measures.

More specifically, an ***experiment*** can be defined as a procedure in which a researcher systematically manipulates (varies) one or more independent variables and looks for changes in one or more dependent variables, while keeping all other variables constant. The reason for keeping other variables constant is to ensure that any change observed in a dependent variable is really caused by the change in an independent variable, not by some other factor that happened to vary.

Consider, for example, the variables in one of Pfungst's experiments with Clever Hans. To determine whether or not visual cues were critical to Hans's ability to respond correctly to questions, Pfungst tested the horse sometimes with blinders and sometimes without. In that experiment the independent variable was the presence or absence of blinders, and the dependent variable was the percentage of questions the horse answered correctly. The experiment could be described as a study of the effect of blinders (independent variable) on Hans's percentage of correct responses to questions (dependent variable). Pfungst took care to keep other variables, such as the difficulty of the questions, constant across the two test conditions. This experiment is an example of a *within-subject experiment*, because the different conditions of the independent variable were applied to the same subject—in this case, Hans.

As a second example, consider an experiment in clinical psychology conducted by Alberto DiMascio and his colleagues (1979). These researchers identified a group of patients suffering from major depression (defined in Chapter 16) and randomly assigned them to different treatments. One group received both drug therapy and psychotherapy, a second received drug therapy alone, a third received psychotherapy alone, and a fourth received no scheduled treatment (but the patients were assigned to a psychiatrist whom they could call when needed). The drug therapy consisted of daily doses of an antidepressant drug, and the psychotherapy consisted of weekly sessions with a psychiatrist that focused on the person's social relationships. After 16 weeks of treatment, the researchers rated each patient's degree of depression using a standard set of questions about mood and behavior. In this experiment, the independent variable was the kind of treatment given, and the dependent variable was the degree of depression after 16 weeks of treatment.

This is an example of a *between-groups experiment*, because the manipulations of the independent variable (that is, the different treatments used) were applied to different groups of subjects. Notice that the researchers randomly assigned the subjects to the treatment groups. Because of the law of averages, random assignment tends to produce groups that are approximately equivalent on variables such as motivation that can affect the results. If the researchers had allowed the subjects to choose their own treatment group, those who were most likely to improve even without treatment might have disproportionately chosen one treatment over the others. Then we could not know whether the greater improvement of one group compared with the others was due to the treatment or to preexisting differences in the subjects.

The results of this experiment are shown in Figure 2.1. Following a common convention in graphing experimental results, which is used throughout this book, the figure depicts variation in the independent variable along the horizontal axis and variation in the dependent variable along the vertical axis. As you can see in the figure, those in the drug-plus-psychotherapy group were the least depressed after the 16-week period, and those in the no-treatment group were the most depressed. The results support the hypothesis that both drug therapy and psychotherapy help relieve depression and that the two treatments together have a greater effect than either alone.

Correlational Studies

In an experiment, as you have just seen, the researcher deliberately manipulates one variable (the independent variable) to determine its effect on another variable (the dependent variable). But many of the questions that psychologists ask are about relationships between variables over which the researcher has no reasonable means of control. In such cases, an experiment is not possible, but a correlational study is. A *correlational study* can be defined as a study in which the researcher does not manipulate any variable but observes or measures two or more variables to find relationships between them. Correlational studies can identify lawful relationships, and thereby help us make predictions, but they do not tell us in any direct way whether change in one variable is the cause of change in another.

Suppose, for example, that you are interested in the relation between the disciplinary styles of parents and the psychological development of their children. Perhaps you entertain the theory that strict punishment is harmful, that it promotes aggressiveness or other unwanted characteristics. To test that theory with an experiment, you would have to manipulate the discipline variable and then measure some aspect of the children's behavior. You might consider randomly assigning some families to a strict punishment condition and others to other conditions. The parents would then have to raise their children in the manners you prescribe. But you know that you cannot control families that way; it's not practical, not legal, and not ethical. So, instead, you conduct a correlational study.

Diana Baumrind (1971) used a correlational method in her now-classic study of the relationship between parents' disciplinary styles and children's development. Instead of manipulating disciplinary style, she measured it. Through questionnaires and home observations, Baumrind classified disciplinary styles into three categories: *authoritarian* (high exertion of parental power), *authoritative* (a more democratic style, but with the parents still clearly in charge), and *permissive* (parental laxity in the face of their children's disruptive behaviors). She also rated the children on various aspects of behavior, such as cooperation and friendliness, through observations in their nursery schools. The main finding (discussed more fully in Chapter 12) was that children of authoritative parents scored better on the measures of behavior than did children of authoritarian or permissive parents.

It is tempting to treat Baumrind's study as though it were an experiment and interpret the results in cause–effect terms. More specifically, it is tempting to think of the parents' discipline style as the independent variable and the children's behavior as the dependent variable, and to conclude that differences in the former caused the differences in the latter. But because the study was not an experiment, we cannot justifiably come to that conclusion. Because neither variable was manipulated by the researchers, we cannot be sure what was cause and what was effect. Maybe the differences in the parents' style caused the differences in the children's behavior, but you can probably think of some other possible ways to explain the correlation.

Maybe the differences in the children's behavior caused the differences in discipline style, rather than the other way around. Perhaps some children are better behaved than others for reasons quite separate from parental style, and perhaps parents with well-behaved children simply glide into an authoritative mode of parenting, while those with more difficult children fall into either of the other two approaches as a way of coping. Or perhaps the causal relationship goes in both directions—parents affect children and children affect parents. Still another possibility is that a third variable influences both parental style and children's behavior. For example, anything that makes families feel good about themselves (such as having good neighbors, good health, and an adequate income) might promote an authoritative style in parents and, quite independently, also lead children to behave

6.

How do correlational studies differ from experiments, and why must caution be exerted in inferring causal relationships from them?

Peter Byron / Monkmeyer Press

What causes what?

Although many correlational studies have found a relationship between the viewing of televised violence and the displaying of aggressive behavior, such studies cannot tell us whether television inspires the aggressive behavior or whether aggressive individuals are more likely than others to watch violent television programs.

well. Or maybe the correlation stems from the genes shared by parents and children: The same genes that predispose parents to behave in an authoritative manner may lead children to behave well. In many correlational studies one causal hypothesis may seem more plausible than others, but that is a judgment based on reasoning about possible causal mechanisms or on evidence from other sources, not from the correlation itself.

In Baumrind's study, one variable (parents' style) was used to place subjects into discrete groups, and the other (children's behavior) was compared across those groups. Many correlational studies are analyzed in that way, but in many others both variables are measured numerically and neither is used to assign subjects to groups. In the latter case, the data are assessed by a statistic called the correlation coefficient, which will be discussed later (in the section on statistical methods).

Descriptive Studies

7.

How do descriptive studies differ from experiments and from correlational studies?

Sometimes the aim of research is to describe the behavior of an individual or set of individuals without systematically investigating relationships between specific variables. A study of this sort is called a ***descriptive study.*** Descriptive studies may or may not make use of numbers. As an example of one involving numbers, researchers might survey the members of a given community to determine the percentage who suffer from various mental disorders. This is a descriptive study if its aim is simply to describe the prevalence of each disorder without correlating the disorders to other characteristics of the community's members. As an example of a descriptive study not involving numbers, an ethologist might observe the courtship behaviors of mallard ducks to describe in detail the sequence of movements that are involved. Some descriptive studies are narrow in focus, concentrating on one specific aspect of behavior, and others are very broad, aiming to learn as much as possible about the habits of a particular group of people or species of animal. One of the most extensive and heroic descriptive studies ever conducted is Jane Goodall's study of wild chimpanzees in Africa. She observed their behavior over a period of 30 years and provided a wealth of information about every aspect of these animals' lives.

Research Settings

8.

What are some advantages and disadvantages of laboratory studies compared with field studies?

The second dimension of research strategy shown in Table 2.1 is the research setting, which can be either the laboratory or the field. A ***laboratory study*** is any research study in which the subjects are brought to a specially designated area that has been set up to facilitate the researcher's ability to collect data or to control the environmental conditions. A ***field study*** is any research study conducted in a setting other than the laboratory. Laboratory and field settings offer opposite sets of advantages and disadvantages. The laboratory allows the researcher to collect data under more uniform, controlled conditions than are possible in the field. However, the strangeness or artificiality of the laboratory may induce behaviors in subjects that obscure those which are of interest to the researcher. A laboratory study of parent–child interactions, for example, may produce results that reflect not so much the subjects' normal ways of interacting as their reactions to a strange environment in which they know that they are being observed. To counteract such problems, some researchers combine laboratory and field studies. When the same conclusions emerge from tightly controlled laboratory studies and less controlled but more natural field studies, as often happens, researchers can be relatively confident that the conclusions are meaningful (Anderson & others, 1999).

As you might expect, experiments are most often conducted in the laboratory because of the greater control of variables that is possible in that setting, and correlational and descriptive studies are more often conducted in the field. But these relationships between research design and setting are by no means inevitable. Experiments are sometimes performed in the field, and correlational and descrip-

A field study

Social psychologist Harold Takooshian and his colleagues found that passersby rarely intervene when they observe a man apparently attempting to break into a car. Staged incidents like this are often part of field studies in social psychology.

Michael Abramson / Gamma Liaison

tive studies are sometimes carried out in the laboratory (as shown in Table 2.1).

A *field experiment* can be conducted by manipulating some aspect of the natural environment in a controlled way. In one field experiment (discussed more fully in Chapter 14), for example, schoolteachers were instructed to praise some of their students, selected at random, about their ability at math and not to praise others, and the effect of this manipulation on the students' scores on subsequent math tests was observed (Miller & others, 1975). This is a field study because it was conducted in the children's regular classrooms. However, it is also an experiment, with an independent variable manipulated by the researchers (praise or no praise) and a dependent variable that the researchers hypothesized would be affected by the independent variable (grades on subsequent math tests).

Data-Collection Methods

The third dimension of research shown in Table 2.1 is the data-collection method, of which there are two broad categories: self-report and observational.

Self-report methods are procedures in which people are asked to rate or describe their own behavior or mental state in some way. This might be done through a *questionnaire,* in which people produce self-descriptions either by checking off items on a printed list or by writing answers to essay questions. Or it might be done through an *interview,* in which people describe themselves orally in a dialogue with the interviewer. An interview may be tightly structured, with the interviewer asking questions according to a completely planned sequence, or it may be more loosely structured, with the interviewer following up on some of the subject's responses with additional questions. Researchers have developed numerical methods for scoring some structured interviews. For an example, look back at the method used to rate depression in the experiment depicted in Figure 2.1.

Observational methods include all procedures by which researchers themselves observe and record the behavior of interest rather than rely on subjects' self-descriptions. In one subcategory, *naturalistic observation,* the researcher avoids interfering with the subject's behavior. For example, an ethologist might unobtrusively watch a duck's courtship behavior, or a developmental psychologist might observe children through a one-way window in a laboratory playroom. In the other subcategory, *tests,* the researcher deliberately presents stimuli or problems for the subject to respond to. Examples include reaction-time tests, in which a person is asked to respond in a particular way as quickly as possible when a specific stimulus is presented, and problem-solving tests, such as maze problems for animals or paper-and-pencil logic problems for people.

None of these data-collection methods is in any absolute sense superior to another. Each has its purposes, advantages, and limitations. Questionnaires and

9.

How do self-report methods, naturalistic observations, and tests differ from one another? What are some advantages and disadvantages of each?

Courtesy of David S. Wilke

Observing without interfering

An obstacle to naturalistic observation is that the researchers may inadvertently, by their mere presence, influence the behavior they are observing. To minimize the degree to which her presence would affect the behavior of the Efe people she was studying, Gilda Morelli (at left) spent many months living among the Efe in Africa. People go about their daily activities more naturally in the presence of someone who is familiar and has proved trustworthy than they do in the presence of a stranger.

interviews can provide information that researchers would not be able to obtain by watching subjects directly, but the validity of such data is limited by the subjects' ability to observe and remember accurately their own behaviors or moods and by their willingness to report those observations frankly, without distorting them to look good or please the researcher. Naturalistic observations allow researchers to learn firsthand about their subjects' natural behaviors, but the practicality of such methods is limited by the great amount of time they take, the difficulty of observing ongoing behavior without disrupting it, and the difficulty of coding results in a form that can be used for statistical analyses. Tests are convenient and easily scored but are by nature artificial, and the relationship between test results and everyday behaviors is not always clear. What is the relationship between a rat's ability to run a maze and the kinds of behaviors that rats engage in normally? What is the relationship between a person's score on an IQ test and his or her ability to solve the problems of daily living? These are the kinds of questions that psychologists must try to answer whenever they generalize from test results to behaviors beyond the test environment.

SECTION SUMMARY

Research strategies vary along three dimensions: design, setting, and data-collection method. The three basic types of design—experiments, correlational studies, and descriptive studies—differ in the kinds of questions they can potentially answer. The two basic types of research setting—laboratory and field—and the two basic types of data-collection method—self-report and observational—each have distinct advantages and disadvantages. You might look again at Table 2.1 and think about the advantages, disadvantages, and special problems associated with each of the 12 studies outlined there, which represent all possible combinations of the basic types of design, setting, and data-collection method.

STATISTICAL METHODS IN PSYCHOLOGY

When the data in any research study have been collected, they must be summarized and interpreted to detect reliable patterns or relationships in them. Statistical procedures are mathematical aids for summarizing and interpreting data. The procedures can be divided into two categories: (1) ***descriptive statistics,*** which are used to summarize sets of data, and (2) ***inferential statistics,*** which help researchers decide how confident they can be in drawing specific conclusions (inferences) from the data. We will look briefly here at some commonly used descriptive statistics and then at the rationale behind inferential statistics. A more detailed discussion, with examples, can be found in the Statistical Appendix at the back of this book.

TABLE **2.2** *Two sets of data, with the same mean but different amounts of variability*

Set A	Set B
7	2
7	4
8	8
11	9
12	14
12	16
13	17
Median = 11	Median = 9
Total = 70	Total = 70
Mean = 70/7 = 10	Mean = 70/7 = 10
Standard deviation = 2.39	Standard deviation = 5.42

Descriptive Statistics

Describing the Central Tendency and Variability of a Set of Scores

Descriptive statistics include all numerical methods for summarizing a set of data. If we classified a group of individuals according to whether or not they showed a particular behavior, we might summarize the data by calculating the percentage who showed it. If our original data were a set of numerical measurements (such as depression ratings), we might summarize them by calculating either the mean or the median. The ***mean*** is simply the arithmetic average, determined by adding the scores and dividing the sum by the number of scores. The ***median*** is the center score, determined by ranking the scores from largest to smallest and finding the score that has the same number of scores above it as below it. (The Statistical Appendix explains when the mean or the median is the more appropriate statistic.)

For certain kinds of comparisons, researchers need to describe not only the central tendency but also the variability of a set of numbers. *Variability* refers to the degree to which the numbers in the set differ from one another or from their mean. In Table 2.2 you can see two sets of numbers that have identical means but different variabilities. In set A the scores cluster close to the mean (low variability), and in set B they differ widely from it (high variability). A common measure of variability is the ***standard deviation,*** which is calculated by a formula (described in the Statistical Appendix) that takes into account the difference between each score and the mean. As indicated in Table 2.2, the greater the average difference between each score and the mean, the greater the standard deviation.

10.

How do the mean, median, and standard deviation help describe a set of numbers?

Describing a Correlation

Correlational studies, you recall, assess two or more variables to determine whether or not a relationship exists between them. When both variables are measured numerically, the strength and direction of the relationship can be assessed by a statistic called the ***correlation coefficient.*** Correlation coefficients are calculated by a formula (described in the Statistical Appendix) that produces a result ranging from +1.00 to −1.00. The sign (+ or −) indicates the direction of the correlation (positive or negative). A positive correlation is one in which an increase in one variable coincides with a tendency for the other variable to increase, and a negative correlation is one in which an increase in one variable coincides with a tendency for the other variable to decrease. The absolute value of the correlation coefficient (the value

11.

How does a correlation coefficient describe the direction and strength of a correlation?

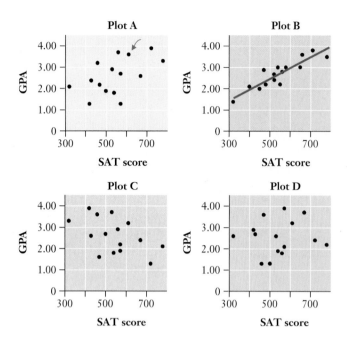

FIGURE **2.2**   *Scatter plots relating grade-point average (GPA) to verbal SAT score*

In these scatter plots, each dot denotes the GPA and SAT scores for one person. By comparing the plots, you can see the difference between weaker and stronger correlations and between positive and negative correlations. (The actual correlation coefficients calculated for the data shown here are +0.52 for A, +0.89 for B, −0.52 for C, and +0.08 for D. The data are hypothetical.)

with sign removed) indicates the strength of the correlation. To the degree that a correlation is strong (close to +1.00 or −1.00), you can predict the value of one variable by knowing the other.

As an example, consider a hypothetical study correlating students' scores on the verbal portion of the College Board scholastic assessment test (SAT) with their college grade-point averages (GPAs), in which the raw data consist of an SAT score and a GPA for each of 15 students. To visualize the results, the researchers might produce what is called a *scatter plot*, in which each student's pair of scores is designated by a single point on a graph. The scatter plots for four different hypothetical sets of results are shown in Figure 2.2. Plot A illustrates a *moderate positive correlation*. Notice that each point represents both the SAT score (marked on the horizontal axis) and the GPA (marked on the vertical axis) for a single student. Thus the point indicated by the red arrow denotes a student whose SAT score is 620 and GPA is 3.60. By looking at the whole constellation of points, you can see that, in general, higher GPAs correspond with higher SAT scores. This is what makes the correlation positive. Plot B illustrates a *strong positive correlation*. Notice that in this plot the points fall very close to an upwardly slanted line. The closer the points are to forming a straight line, the stronger is the correlation between the two variables. The stronger the correlation, the more accurately you can predict someone's GPA from his or her SAT score, or vice versa. Plot C illustrates a *moderate negative correlation*. In this case, GPAs tend to decrease as SAT scores increase. A negative correlation between GPA and SAT is unlikely, but it is easy to think of variables that probably are negatively correlated—such as GPA and number of days absent from class. Finally, plot D represents uncorrelated data—a coefficient close to or equal to 0. Here the two variables are unrelated: Knowing a person's SAT score does not help you predict that person's GPA, or vice versa.

Inferential Statistics

Any set of data collected in any research study contains some degree of variability attributable to chance. In the experiment comparing treatments for depression summarized in Figure 2.1, the average depression scores obtained for the four groups reflect not just the effects of treatment but also random effects caused by uncontrollable variables. For example, more patients who were predisposed to improve could by chance have been assigned to one treatment group rather than to another. Or measurement error due to imperfections in the rating procedure could have contributed to differences in the depression scores. If the experiment were repeated several times, the results would be somewhat different each time because of these uncontrollable random variables. Given that results can vary due to chance, how confident can a researcher be in inferring a general conclusion from the study's data? Inferential statistics are means to answer that question using the laws of probability.

Statistical Significance

The inference to be assessed in any given study is the *research hypothesis*. In an experiment, the research hypothesis is usually that the independent variable influences the dependent variable. In a correlational study, the research hypothesis is usually that two measured variables are correlated either positively or negatively. Inferential statistical methods, applied to either an experiment or a correlational study, are procedures for calculating the probability that the research hypothesis is

12.

What might you infer about your hypothesis if your experimental results were statistically significant at the 5 percent level?

wrong (the independent variable does *not* affect the dependent variable, or two variables are *not* correlated), given the observed data. The lower that probability is, the more confident the researcher can be that the research hypothesis is correct. A long-standing convention in psychology is to label results as **statistically significant** if the probability is less than 5 percent that the research hypothesis is wrong.

DiMascio and his colleagues (1979) reported that the effect of drug therapy in reducing depression (again, refer to Figure 2.1) was statistically significant at the 5 percent level. This means that their inferential statistics revealed less than a 5 percent chance that the drug had no effect and the difference observed between the drug and nondrug groups resulted just from random variability. Similarly, they reported that the effect of psychotherapy was also significant at the 5 percent level.

"He's charged with expressing contempt for data-processing."

The Components of a Test of Statistical Significance

One element of a test of statistical significance, clearly, is the *size of the observed effect*, as calculated by the descriptive statistics. Other things being equal, the larger the observed difference in the dependent variable between groups in an experiment, or the larger the correlation coefficient in a correlational study, the more significant the results.

A second element is the *number of individual subjects or observations* in the study. Other things being equal, the greater that number, the more likely the results are to be significant. If the number of subjects or observations is huge, even very small effects will be statistically significant.

A third element, applicable when the data are numerical and are summarized as means, is the *variability* (commonly measured as the standard deviation) of the data within each group. Variability within the group can be thought of as a direct assessment of the degree of randomness operating on the dependent variable, or the degree to which the dependent variable is affected by uncontrolled variables. For example, in the experiment assessing treatments for depression, greater variability in depression scores within each treatment group would reflect greater randomness.

In sum, the likelihood of finding statistical significance in the difference between the mean scores for two different groups increases as (1) the size of the difference between the means increases, (2) the number of subjects in each group increases, and (3) the variability of the data within each group decreases. (We need not concern ourselves here with the exact formula by which these factors are mathematically combined in an inferential test, but if you are curious, you can look up the formula for a *t*-test in any textbook on psychological statistics.)

Statistical significance tells us that a result probably did not come about by chance, but it does not by itself tell us that the result has practical value. Don't confuse statistical significance with practical significance. If I were to test a new weight-loss drug in an experiment that compared 1000 people taking the drug with a similar number not taking it, I might find a high degree of statistical significance even if the drug produced an average weight loss of only a few ounces. In that case, most people would agree that, despite the high statistical significance, the drug has no practical significance in a weight-loss program.

13.

How is statistical significance affected by the size of the effect, the number of subjects or observations in each group, and the variability of the scores within each group?

SECTION SUMMARY

Descriptive statistics are mathematical aids for summarizing sets of numerical data. Examples are the mean and median (indices of the central tendency), the standard deviation (an index of variability), and the correlation coefficient (an index of the degree to which the scores on one measure predict the scores on a different measure). Inferential statistics are mathematical means of determining how confident one can be in drawing specific conclusions from sets of data. The difference between the means of two sets of scores is statistically significant to the degree that it is unlikely to be due to chance.

14.

What is the difference between error and bias, and why is bias the more serious problem?

MINIMIZING BIAS IN PSYCHOLOGICAL RESEARCH

Good scientists strive to minimize both error and bias, especially the latter, in their research. ***Error,*** as a technical term, refers to random variability in results. Some degree of error is inevitable in psychological research, as a researcher can never precisely control all the extraneous variables that can influence a measure of behavior. The occurrence of error does not imply that the researcher has made a mistake. Individual differences among the research subjects and imperfections in the measure of behavior, for example, contribute inevitably to error. Because error is random, its consequences tend to disappear when averages are calculated, especially when the data set is large. Moreover, researchers can measure error precisely, by calculating the standard deviation, and can take it into account in their inferential statistics. Therefore, error is not a devastating problem in research. But bias is a devastating problem. ***Bias,*** as a technical term, refers to nonrandom (directed) effects caused by some factor or factors extraneous to the research hypothesis.

The difference between error and bias can be visualized by thinking of the difference between the sets of bullet holes produced by two men engaged in target practice. One is a novice. He hasn't learned to hold the gun steady, so it wavers randomly as he shoots. The bullets rarely hit the bull's-eye but scatter randomly around it (target A of Figure 2.3). His average shot, calculated as the average geometric location of his entire set of shots, is on or near the bull's-eye, even if few or none of his individual shots are on or near it. Those bullet holes exemplify error. The other man is an experienced marksman, but the sights on his rifle are out of alignment. Because of that defect, all his bullets strike the target about a foot to the right of the bull's-eye (target B). Those misses exemplify bias, and they are not correctable by averaging. No matter how many times the man shoots or how carefully he aims at the bull's-eye, the average location of the whole set of bullet holes will be about a foot away from the bull's-eye. Of course, error and bias can occur together, as happens when a novice shooter is given a defective rifle (target C). In that case the holes are widely scattered around a center that is a foot to the right of the bull's-eye.

Bias is a very serious problem in research because statistical techniques cannot identify it or correct for it. Whereas error only reduces the chance that researchers will find statistically significant results, bias can lead researchers to the false conclu-

FIGURE **2.3** *Error, bias, and both*
The difference between error and bias in research is like the difference between the sets of bullet holes produced by a novice shooter (target A) and by a skilled marksman whose rifle sights are misaligned (target B).

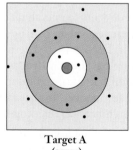

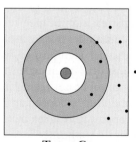

Target A
(error)   **Target B**
(bias)   **Target C**
(error and bias)

sion that their hypothesis has been supported when, in fact, the results came out as they did for a different reason.

Avoiding a Biased Sample

One source of bias in research has to do with the way in which the individuals to be studied are selected or assigned to groups. If the members of a particular group differ in some systematic way, to begin with, from the members of another group in an experiment, or from the larger population that the researcher is interested in, then that group is a **biased sample.** Conducting research with a biased sample is like shooting a rifle whose sights are misaligned. No matter how large the sample, the results will be off target.

Suppose that in the experiment on depression (Figure 2.1 again), the researchers had not randomly assigned the subjects to the different treatments but had allowed them to choose their own. In that case, biased samples could have resulted, because people's choices might have been based on preexisting differences among them. For example, those who felt most motivated to overcome their depression might have chosen the psychotherapy condition more often than those who felt less motivated. Thus any greater improvement by those in psychotherapy compared with the others might have resulted not from the psychotherapy but from the preexisting difference in motivation. When subjects are assigned randomly to groups, their individual differences are merely a source of error (and can be taken into account by the statistics); but when subjects are not assigned randomly, their differences can be a source of bias as well as error.

In descriptive research, a sample is biased when the people in it are not representative of the larger population that the researchers are trying to describe. A classic example of what can happen in such a case is the *Literary Digest*'s poll of U.S. voters in 1936, which led the *Digest* to announce that Alf Landon would beat Franklin D. Roosevelt in the presidential election that year by a margin of 2 to 1 (Huff, 1954). It turned out that the publication's conclusion could not have been more mistaken—Roosevelt won by a landslide. The *Digest* had conducted its poll by telephoning magazine subscribers. In 1936, in the midst of the Great Depression, people who could afford magazine subscriptions and telephones may indeed have favored Landon, but the great majority of voters, as the election showed, did not.

Avoiding Measurement Bias

Psychological researchers must give careful thought to their measures of behavior. A good measure is reliable and valid. Reliability has to do with measurement error, not bias. A measure is **reliable** to the degree that it yields similar results each time it is used with a particular subject under a particular set of conditions. Measuring height with an elastic ruler would not be as reliable as measuring it with a stiff ruler because the elasticity would cause the results to vary from one time to the next. A psychological test is not reliable if the scores vary widely due to uncontrolled variables in how it is administered or how it is interpreted by subjects. Because it is a source of error, low reliability decreases the chance of finding statistical significance in a research study.

Validity is an even more critical issue than reliability, because lack of validity can be a source of bias. A measurement procedure is **valid** if it measures or predicts what it is intended to measure or predict. A procedure may be reliable and yet not be valid. For example, assessing intelligence in adults by measuring thumb length is highly reliable (you would get nearly the same score for a given person each time) but almost certainly not valid (thumb length is almost assuredly unrelated to adult intelligence). This invalid measure exemplifies bias because it would produce false conclusions—for example, that tall people are more intelligent than short people,

15.

How can a nonrepresentative selection of research participants introduce bias into (a) an experiment and (b) a descriptive study?

16.

What is the difference between reliability and validity of a measurement procedure?

since thumb length correlates with height. If common sense tells us that a measurement procedure assesses the intended characteristic, we say the procedure has *face validity*. A test of ability to solve logical problems has face validity as a measure of intelligence, but thumb length does not.

A more certain way to gauge the validity of a measurement procedure is to correlate its scores with another, more direct index of the characteristic that we wish to measure or predict. In that case, the more direct index is called the *criterion*, and the validity is called *criterion validity*. Suppose, for example, that I defined intelligence as the quality of mind that allows a person to achieve greatness in any of various realms, including business, diplomacy, science, literature, and art. With this definition, I might use the actual achievement of such greatness as my criterion for intelligence. I might identify a group of people who have achieved such greatness and a group who, despite similar environmental opportunities, have not, and assess the degree to which they differ on various potential measures of intelligence. The more the two groups differ on any of the measures, the greater the correlation between that measure and my criterion for intelligence, and the more valid the test. If thumb length turned out to distinguish the two groups better than did a test of logical thinking, I would have to conclude that thumb length has the greater criterion validity despite its lower face validity. As you can see from this example, the assessment of validity requires a clear definition of the characteristic to be measured or predicted. If your definition of intelligence differs from mine, you will choose a different criterion than mine for assessing the validity of possible intelligence tests.

As another illustration of how an invalid measure can bias a research study, think once more about the study of depression (Figure 2.1). Suppose that the interview procedure used in the study was not a valid measure of depression but actually measured subjects' desire to appear depressed or not. In that case, the results would still be statistically significant, but the researchers' conclusion (that treatment affects depression) would be mistaken. A more accurate conclusion would be that some treatments lead to a stronger desire to appear not depressed than do others.

Avoiding Biases from Observers' and Subjects' Expectancies

Being human, researchers inevitably have wishes and expectations that can affect how they behave and what they observe when recording data. The resulting biases are called ***observer-expectancy effects.*** A researcher who desires or expects a subject to respond in a particular way may unintentionally communicate that expectation and thereby influence the subject's behavior. As you recall, Pfungst discovered that this sort of effect provided the entire basis for Clever Hans's apparent ability to answer questions. That episode occurred nearly a century ago, but the power of observer expectancies to delude us is as strong today as ever. A dramatic recent example concerns a technique designed to enable people with autism to communicate.

The Facilitated-Communication Debacle

Autism is a congenital (present at birth) disorder of development, characterized principally by a deficit in the ability to form emotional bonds and to communicate with other people. Some people with autism fail almost completely to develop either spoken or written language. In 1990, in the prestigious *Harvard Educational Review*, Douglas Biklen described an apparently remarkable discovery, made originally by Rosemary Crossley in Australia. The discovery was that people with severe autism, who had previously shown almost no language ability, could type meaningful statements with one finger on a keyboard. They could answer questions intelligently, describe their feelings, display humor, and write emotionally moving poetry by typing. To do this, however, a "facilitator" had to help by holding the typing hand and finger of the autistic person. According to Crossley and Biklen, the hand-

17.

How can the validity of a measurement procedure be assessed, and how can the lack of validity contribute to bias?

18.

How can the supposed phenomenon of facilitated communication by persons with autism be explained as an observer-expectancy effect?

holding was needed to calm the person, to keep the typing hand steady, and to prevent repeated typing of the same letter (people with autism tend to repeat their actions).

The community concerned with autism—including special educators and parents of autistic children—responded with great excitement to this apparent discovery. It is hard, emotionally, to care for and work with people who don't communicate their thoughts and feelings; it takes enormous dedication. You can imagine the thrill that parents and teachers felt when their autistic child typed on the keyboard, for the first time, something like "I love you." The motivation to believe in this new method was enormous. Workshops were held to teach people to be facilitators, and thousands of teachers and parents learned the technique. By 1993, over $100 million a year was being spent by the educational system on equipment and personnel for facilitated communication (Levine & others, 1994).

Yet, from the beginning, there were skeptics. The credulity of some observers was strained by the sudden appearance of literary skills and erudition in people who had never previously shown evidence that they could read. As an alternative theory, the skeptics proposed that the messages were not communications from the autistic persons but unconscious creations of the facilitators (Dillon, 1993; Levine & others, 1994). The skeptics suggested that subtle hand movements, made unconsciously by the facilitator, guided the autistic person's finger to the keys, just as unconsciously produced hand movements can cause a Ouija board to spell out messages (Spitz, 1997). Consistent with this view, some skeptics noticed that the autistic persons often did not even look at the keyboard as they ostensibly did their typing but that the facilitators always looked. The issue became important for legal reasons, as well as educational and scientific ones. Facilitated communication had barely become popular when some autistic children, working with facilitators, typed out messages that accused a parent or another caregiver of sexually abusing them (Bligh & Kupperman, 1993; Heckler, 1994). Could facilitated communication be used by child-welfare authorities as a basis for taking a child from a parent?

Within the past few years, well over a hundred different autistic person–facilitator pairs have been tested under controlled conditions, in many experiments, and the results have been consistently negative concerning the validity of facilitated communication. In the typical experiment, the pairs are chosen on the basis of their extensive experience and putative skill at using the technique together, and the autistic person is asked questions under conditions in which the facilitator either knows or does not know the answer. The inevitable result has been that many questions are answered correctly in the first condition, but in the second condition no more are answered correctly than would be expected by random guessing (Jacobson & others, 1995; Spitz, 1997). Other research has shown that people newly trained in facilitated communication immediately and unconsciously begin to control the other person's hand movements. It does not feel to them that they are creating the messages, even though they are (Burgess & others, 1998).

Avoiding Observer-Expectancy Effects in Typical Experiments

In the experiments on facilitated communication, the influence of observer expectancy was the focus of study and was assessed by varying the observers' (in this case, the facilitators') knowledge. In a more typical psychological experiment, the objective is not to study observer-expectancy effects but to eliminate them in order to observe other effects without bias. A researcher who expects subjects in one condition to behave differently from those in another condition may send different unintentional signals in the two conditions, and thereby elicit the expected difference

Facilitated water finding

In many communities, people hire a "water diviner" or "dowser," who uses a forked stick to locate a place to dig a well. The front of the stick is believed to be drawn down by a magnetic-like force stemming from the underground water. Skeptics (such as the author of your textbook) contend that dowsing is similar to facilitated communication. The actual force affecting the stick derives from subtle hand movements, of which the dowser may be unaware. The dowser's success at finding water may derive not from the pull of water but from the dowser's own good sense about where water is likely to be, which influences his hand movements.

19.

What are two ways by which an observer's expectations can bias results in a typical experiment? How does blind observation prevent such bias?

in behavior. In addition to influencing subjects' behavior, expectancy may affect the observer's perception or judgment of that behavior. For example, an observer who expects to find that people smile more in one condition than in another may interpret an ambiguous facial expression as a smile in the one condition and as something else in the other.

The best way to prevent observer-expectancy effects is to keep the observer *blind*—that is, uninformed—about those aspects of the study's design that could lead to differential expectations. Thus in a between-groups experiment, a blind observer would be kept ignorant as to which treatment any given subject had received. Not knowing who is in which group, the blind observer has no basis for expecting a particular behavior from a particular subject. In the study of treatments for depression (illustrated in Figure 2.1), the clinicians who evaluated the patients' depression at the end of the treatment period were blind to treatment condition. To keep them blind, patients were instructed not to say anything about their treatment during the evaluation interview.

Avoiding Subject-Expectancy Effects

Subjects also have expectations. If different treatments in an experiment induce different expectations in subjects, then the expectations, rather than anything else about the treatments, may account for observed differences in how the subjects respond. Effects of this sort are called *subject-expectancy effects.* For example, people who take a drug may subsequently behave or feel a certain way simply because they believe that the drug causes such behavior or feeling. Similarly, subjects who receive psychotherapy may improve simply because they believe that psychotherapy will help them.

Ideally, to prevent bias due to subject expectancy, subjects should be kept blind about the treatment they are receiving. Any experiment in which both the observer and the subjects are kept blind in this way is called a *double-blind experiment.* In double-blind drug studies, for example, some subjects receive the drug while other subjects receive a *placebo,* an inactive substance that looks like the drug, and neither subjects nor observers are told who took the drug and who did not. Consequently, any observed difference between those who got the drug and those who did not must be due to the drug's chemical qualities, not to the subjects' or observers' expectancies.

Subjects cannot always be kept blind concerning their treatment. For instance, you can't administer psychotherapy to people without their knowing it. As a partial control in some psychotherapy experiments, subjects in the nonpsychotherapy group are given a fake form of therapy designed to induce subject expectancies equivalent to those induced by psychotherapy. In the depression experiment described earlier, subjects were not blind about their treatment. Those in the nondrug groups did not receive a placebo, and those in the nonpsychotherapy groups did not receive fake psychotherapy. The results depicted in Figure 2.1 could therefore be placebo effects. Other experiments (discussed in Chapter 17) have shown that placebos can indeed reduce depression (Kirsch & Sapirstein, 1998).

20.

How can subjects' expectancies bias the results of an experiment? How does a double-blind procedure control both subjects' and observers' expectancies?

SECTION SUMMARY

Error refers to random effects that contribute to variability in a measure, and bias refers to directed effects that may lead to false support for a research hypothesis. Bias may derive from the manner in which research participants are chosen or assigned to groups, from an invalid measure, from an observer-expectancy effect, or from a subject-expectancy effect. The problem of observers' expectations is illustrated by the early, false evidence for facilitated communication by people suffering from autism. Observer- and subject-expectancy effects can be eliminated by keeping both the observer and the subject ignorant (blind) concerning key facts pertaining to the study (such as which subjects are receiving which treatment).

ETHICAL ISSUES IN PSYCHOLOGICAL RESEARCH

Psychologists must consider ethical as well as scientific issues in designing their studies. DiMascio and his colleagues (1979) could, from a scientific vantage point, have improved their study of treatments for depression by using a placebo in the nondrug conditions and a fake form of psychotherapy in the nonpsychotherapy conditions to reduce differences among the groups in subject expectancies. But the researchers felt that their subjects should know the form of treatment they were getting so that they could make an informed decision about whether or not to participate and could understand the side effects that might arise as treatment progressed.

In research with humans, ethical considerations revolve around three interrelated issues: (1) the person's right to privacy, (2) the possible discomfort or harm that a research procedure can produce, and (3) the use of deception that characterizes some research designs. Concerning the first two issues, the usual ethical safeguards include obtaining informed consent from subjects before they take part in a study, advising subjects that they can quit at any time (and respecting their right to do so), and keeping records and reports in a way that ensures subjects' anonymity. In addition, whenever the possibility of discomfort or harm exists, researchers are obliged to determine whether the same question can be answered in a study that involves less risk and, if the answer is no, to demonstrate that the human benefits of the study outweigh any possible costs. In reality, the great majority of psychological studies involve completely harmless procedures, such as reading rapidly flashed letters, memorizing lists of terms, or carrying on a discussion with other subjects.

The most controversial ethical issue in human psychological research concerns deception. In a small minority of experiments, the independent variable involves a lie. Subjects may be falsely told or led to believe that something is happening, or is going to happen, so that the researcher can study the effects of that belief. Some psychologists are opposed to all use of deception on the grounds that deception (a) is intrinsically unethical and (b) undermines the possibility of obtaining truly informed consent (Carroll & others, 1985). Others, however, justify deception on the grounds that some psychological processes cannot be studied effectively without it. These psychologists further contend that (a) research deception usually takes the form of benign "white lies," which are cleared up when the researcher informs the subject of the true nature of the study after the session has ended, and (b) informed consent can still be obtained by telling subjects that some details of the study must be withheld until the data have been collected and by advising them of any realistic dangers that could be involved.

The use of nonhuman animals in research presents another area of ethical controversy. Most people agree that some procedures that would be unethical to use with humans can be used ethically with other animal species. One can breed animals in controlled ways, raise them in controlled environments, and surgically intervene in their physiology for research purposes. Basic biological mechanisms underlying animal behavior are similar to those underlying human behavior, so such research contributes to our understanding of humans as well as the species studied. Still, research on nonhuman animals can sometimes cause them to suffer, and any researcher who employs animals has an ethical obligation to balance the animals' suffering against the potential benefits of the research. Animals must be well cared for and not subjected to unnecessary deprivation or pain. Some people question whether subjecting animals to pain or deprivation for research purposes is ever justifiable. But others, pointing to the enormous gains in knowledge and the reduction in human (and animal) suffering that have come from such research, have turned the ethical question around. In the words of one (N. E. Miller, 1986): "Is it morally justifiable to prolong human (and animal) suffering in order to reduce suffering by experimental animals?"

21.

What are the ethical concerns pertaining to privacy, discomfort, deception, and animal welfare? How do researchers strive to meet these concerns?

A rat with an electrode in its brain

Experiments in physiological psychology frequently involve operations on animal brains. For scientific as well as ethical reasons, conscientious researchers are scrupulous about minimizing discomfort to the animals. Discomfort can produce behaviors that interfere with those that the researcher wishes to study.

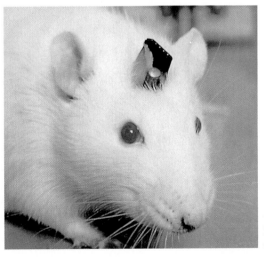

Joel Gordon

The American Psychological Association (1992) has established a set of ethical principles for psychological research, which researchers must follow if they are to publish their results in the research journals of that association. Moreover, in the United States, Canada, and many other countries, publicly funded research institutions are required by law to have ethics review panels, whose task is to evaluate all proposed studies that have any potential for ethical controversy. Such panels often turn down research proposals that once were regarded as quite acceptable. A few studies that are now considered classics and are cited in most general psychology textbooks, including this one, would not be approved today. As you read about some of the studies in the chapters that follow, questions of ethics may well occur to you from time to time. Such questions are always legitimate, as are those about the scientific merit of a study's design and the interpretation of its results. Psychology needs and usually welcomes people who raise those questions.

CONCLUDING THOUGHTS

1. How does science compare with everyday observation and thought? No sharp dividing line exists between science and the kinds of observation and thought that all of us use every day to learn about the world around us. In our everyday learning, we begin with the data of our senses and use those data to draw tentative conclusions (make inferences) about specific aspects of our world. For example, we might one day observe someone from town X acting politely and someone from town Y acting rudely and infer from those observations that people from X are more polite than people from Y. Most of us make such inferences all the time, often on scarcely more evidence than that. Science is simply the attempt to improve on our natural ways of learning by systematizing the data-collection procedures, controlling conditions to be more certain about which variables are having which effects, striving to eliminate sources of bias, deliberately thinking of alternative explanations, and using statistical procedures to assess the degree of confidence we should have in our tentative conclusions. As you review each of the main concepts discussed in the sections on research strategies, statistical methods, and sources of bias in this chapter, you might think about how that concept applies—somewhat less formally—to the distinctions between good and poor observation and thought in everyday life. We are observing and thinking poorly when we draw firm conclusions from too little evidence, or neglect to think about alternative explanations, or fail to see what is really there because of our biased expectations.

2. What is a science of psychology for? I remember, as a college freshman on a visit home, flaunting my pride about an A that I had received in calculus. My mother, hearing me brag and having a knack for deflating undue pride and putting things into perspective, asked a simple question: What is calculus for? I was floored. I could rattle off terms and equations about calculus, and I could solve the problems as they were given to me in the class, but I had no understanding at all of what calculus was for. Perhaps that is why, by a few months after the class had ended, I had completely forgotten the terms, the equations, and the way to solve them. So what is a science of psychology for?

Some people think of psychology purely in applied terms, as a means of solving human problems. These people are likely to appreciate the study on treatments for depression (illustrated in Figure 2.1) but are less likely to understand Wilhelm Wundt's desire to measure the speed of human judgments or Konrad Lorenz's desire to describe the courtship behaviors of ducks (both noted in Chapter 1). The issue of pragmatism occurs in other sciences as well. What good does it do us to know what the other side of the moon looks like?

For the most part, people go into psychological research, or any other research field, because they are curious or because they are thrilled by the prospect of being the first to uncover some mystery of nature, large or small. So psychology, like any other science, has two purposes: to solve practical problems and to satisfy the human quest for knowledge. It is hard to separate the two, however, because research done solely to satisfy curiosity very often reveals solutions to practical problems that at first seemed unrelated to the research. As you read the remaining chapters of this book, I hope you will allow yourself to become engaged by the questions for their own sake, regardless of whether you think they have practical applications. Each chapter contains mysteries—some solved, some not.

Further Reading

Randolph A. Smith & Stephen F. Davis (2000). *The psychologist as detective: An introduction to conducting research in psychology* (2nd ed.). Upper Saddle River, NJ: Prentice-Hall.

By presenting the research psychologist as a detective, and by giving many examples of the solving of psychological mysteries, this book enlivens the often dry stuff of research methodology. It deals with all aspects of the research process: forming hypotheses or questions, using the library, designing research studies, considering ethical issues, analyzing and graphing data, and writing reports.

Keith E. Stanovich (2001). *How to think straight about psychology* (6th ed.). New York: HarperCollins.

This fun-to-read book deals with popular misconceptions about psychological phenomena, the faulty uses of evidence and logic that lead to such misconceptions, and the processes through which enduring psychological knowledge has been developed. The author's goal, well achieved, is to help readers acquire the tools needed for critical thinking in psychology.

Darrell Huff (1954). *How to lie with statistics.* New York: Norton.

This witty paperback, filled with anecdotes and cartoons, has a serious message. It tells you how not to lie with statistics and how to spot lies when they occur. It is guaranteed to make you a more critical consumer of statistical information. Don't be put off by its date; it is reprinted regularly and is widely available.

Robert J. Sternberg (1993). *The psychologist's companion: A guide to scientific writing for students and researchers* (3rd ed.). Cambridge, England: Cambridge University Press.

Psychologists, like scholars in every field, must communicate their ideas and findings in writing. This book, by one of psychology's most prolific writers, is a practical guide to the writing of psychological papers of all types, ranging from library papers and lab reports by first-year college students to papers for publication by full-fledged researchers.

Looking Ahead

This is not the only chapter of this book that deals with methods. In effect, all the chapters that follow are about methods, because our knowledge in every area of psychology is inseparable from our ways of knowing. Each chapter offers at least some discussion of the methods used to test the ideas being discussed. The specific concepts described in this chapter that will be especially useful in later chapters are (a) the difference between an experiment and a correlational study and (b) the meanings of the terms correlation coefficient, statistical significance, measurement validity, and double-blind experiment. More generally, I hope that this chapter has encouraged you to ask about, and think critically about, the evidence underlying any claim that you read or hear. Now, we move from the background to the substance of psychology. The two chapters in Part 2 are about the ways by which behavior adapts to the environment and helps us survive. Chapter 3 is on evolution, and Chapter 4 is on learning.

The Adaptiveness of Behavior

*We are the products of our genes and our environments. Our genes have
been shaped by millions of years of evolution, adapting us to the general
conditions of human life on earth. Through this process, we have acquired,
among other things, an immense capacity to learn. This unit consists of
two chapters. Chapter 3 examines the role of genes and evolution in the
production of the underlying mechanisms of behavior. Chapter 4 deals
with basic processes of learning, which constantly modify behavior to meet
the unique conditions of each individual's life.*

Chapter 3

Monkey Frieze, Franz Marc

Genetic and Evolutionary Foundations of Behavior

In 1859, a book was published in England that helped change the way people think about themselves and the organic world in which they live. In that book, *The Origin of Species*, Charles Darwin set forth a theory of evolution that restructured biological thought, revolutionized philosophy, and helped make possible the emergence of a scientific psychology (see Chapter 1). The basic idea of evolution—that modern forms of life came about through gradual changes from earlier forms— had been around for centuries, but only after *The Origin of Species* was published did the idea begin to gain wide acceptance in the intellectual world. The book had its strong effect for two reasons. First, it presented massive amounts of evidence— based partly on patterns of variation that exist in present-day forms of life and partly on the fossil record—for the existence of an evolutionary process. Second, and more important, it described a mechanism by which evolution could occur: natural selection.

In essence, the theory of evolution by natural selection is this: *All living species, including humans, arrived at their present biological structures and mechanisms through a historical process involving random inheritable changes. Those changes that enhanced an individual's ability to survive and reproduce in the environmental conditions in which it lived were passed along in increasing number from generation to generation, and those that hindered survival and reproduction were lost.*

Darwin's theory has clear implications for all psychology. As was mentioned in Chapter 1, it provides the basic rationale for *functionalism* in psychology—that is, for thinking about psychological processes in terms of their value to the individual. From the perspective of Darwin's theory, all the complex biological mechanisms that underlie human behavior and experience—the mechanisms of motivation, emotion, perception, learning, memory, and thought—came about because they promoted the survival and reproduction of our ancestors. In later chapters of this book, I will often invite you to think about specific psychological theories and findings in the light of this functionalist idea. Darwin's theory also provides the rationale for comparing humans with other animal species, and, as you will see later in this chapter, it helps us decide what comparisons will be useful for what purposes.

This chapter is the first of a two-chapter sequence on the *adaptiveness of behavior*. Adaptation refers to modification to meet changed life circumstances. Evolution is the long-term adaptive process, spanning generations, that equips each species for life in its natural habitat. The next chapter is on learning, which refers to a set of shorter-term adaptive processes that occur within the life span of the individual. The mechanisms that permit learning to occur are themselves products of evolution.

Darwin developed his theory of evolution without any knowledge of genes, but the theory is best understood today in the light of such knowledge. This chapter begins with a discussion of basic genetic mechanisms and their implications for the inheritance of behavioral characteristics. Then, with that as background, the rest of the chapter is concerned with the evolution of behavior in humans and other animal species. In successive sections, we will examine the basic process of evolution and its implications for psychology; the evolution of instinctive behavioral responses; and the evolution of general patterns of mating, aggression, and helping.

GENES AND THE INHERITANCE OF BEHAVIORAL CHARACTERISTICS

Genes are the biological units of heredity. They are replicated and passed along from parent to offspring, and they are crucial to the development of each new individual. To the degree that any characteristic is inherited biologically, it is inherited through genes.

How Genes Affect Behavior

1.

How can genes affect behavioral traits through their role in protein synthesis?

Sometimes, as a sort of shorthand (which I will use occasionally in this book), researchers speak of genes "for" particular behavioral traits. For example, they might speak of genes for singing ability, for aggression, or for cooperation. But, of course, genes never produce or control behavior directly. All the effects that genes have on behavior occur through their role in building and modifying the physical structures of the body, and those structures, interacting with the environment, produce behavior. Thus, a gene might influence musical ability by promoting the development of a brain system that analyzes sounds or by promoting certain physical aspects of the vocal cords. Similarly, a gene might affect aggressiveness by fostering the growth of brain systems that respond to irritating external stimuli and organize aggressive behavior. In a sense, all genes that contribute to the body's development are "for" behavior, since all parts of the body are involved in behavior. Especially relevant for behavior, however, are genes that contribute to the development of sensory systems, motor systems (muscles and other organs involved in movement), and, most especially, the nervous system (which includes the brain).

Genes Provide the Codes for Proteins

Genes affect the body's development through, and only through, their influence on the production of *protein molecules*. The human body is made up of roughly 70,000 different kinds of protein molecules (Wahlsten, 1999). We are what we are, biologically speaking, because of our proteins. A class of proteins called *structural proteins* forms the structure of every cell of the body, and another, much larger class called *enzymes* controls the rate of every chemical reaction in every cell.

How do genes organize the production of proteins? Physically, genes are components of extremely long molecules of a substance called DNA (deoxyribonucleic acid). These molecules exist in the egg and sperm cells that join to form a new individual, and they replicate themselves during each cell division in the course of the body's growth and development. A replica of your whole, unique set of DNA molecules exists in the nucleus of each of your body's cells, where it serves as a template (that is, a mold or pattern) for producing another molecular substance called RNA (ribonucleic acid), which in turn serves as a template for producing protein molecules. Each protein molecule consists of a long chain of smaller molecules called amino acids. The 20 distinct amino acids can be arranged in countless sequences to form different protein molecules. The job of each gene is to provide the code that dictates the particular sequence of amino acids for a single type of protein. From a molecular vantage point, a *gene* can be defined as the segment of a DNA molecule that contains the code for manufacturing one specific type of protein molecule.

Genes Work Only Through Interaction with the Environment

At every level, from biochemical to behavioral, the effects of genes are entwined with the effects of the environment. The term *environment*, as used in this context, refers to every aspect of an individual and his or her surroundings except the genes themselves. It includes the nourishing womb and maternal bloodstream before birth; the internal chemical environment of the developing individual; and all the events, objects, and other individuals encountered after birth. Foods—a part of the environment—supply genes with amino acids, which are needed to manufacture proteins. Environmental effects also turn genes "on" and "off," resulting in bodily changes that alter the individual's behavioral capacity. Such changes can occur in adulthood as well as earlier in development. For example, physical exercise modifies the chemical environment of muscle cells in a way that activates genes that promote further growth of the muscle. One's body and behavioral capacities result from a continuous, complex interplay between genes and environment (see Figure 3.1). In no sense is one more basic than the other.

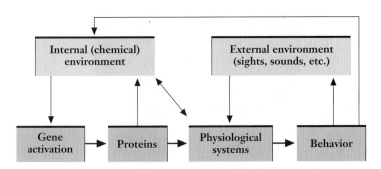

Researchers are only now beginning to learn about the specific mechanisms through which experiences can alter characteristics of the brain and thereby alter behavior (Wahlsten, 1999). They have found, for example, that adult mice and rats of either sex can become nurturant toward newborns through environmentally induced gene activation (Brown & others, 1996; Numan & Numan, 1995). The sight, sound, or smell of newborns acts on the adult's brain in such a way as to activate genes that produce a particular protein molecule. The gene activation occurs specifically in a cluster of brain cells that are known to be crucial for the motivation and organization of nurturant behavior, and the protein that is produced apparently alters the function of those critical cells. The result is that a mouse or rat that did not take care of young is transformed into a mouse or rat that does. There is good reason to believe that all sorts of prolonged behavioral effects that derive from experience, including those that we call "learning," involve the activation of genes. The experience activates genes, which produce proteins, which in turn alter the function of some of the neural circuits in the brain and thereby change the manner in which the individual behaves. More about this is discussed in Chapter 5.

Geneticists use the term *genotype* to refer to the set of genes that the individual inherits and the term *phenotype* to refer to the observable properties of the body and behavioral traits. The same genes can have different effects, depending on the environment and the mix of other genes. Two people with the same genotype can be quite different in phenotype. Identical human twins (who have the same genes) will differ phenotypically in muscle strength if one exercises a lot and the other does not. Genetically identical mice will differ phenotypically in their behavior toward infant mice if one has been exposed to infant mice and the other has not. You will see other examples as the chapter progresses.

2.

What does it mean to say that genes can influence behavioral traits only through interaction with the environment? How, in general, do genes figure into long-term behavioral changes that derive from experience?

FIGURE **3.1** *Route through which genes affect behavior*
Genes build proteins, which form or alter the body's physiological systems (including brain systems), which, in turn, produce behavior. Each step in this process involves interaction with the environment. Aspects of the internal environment control gene activation, and aspects of both the internal and the external environments act on physiological systems to control behavior. Behavior, in turn, can affect gene activation through direct and indirect effects on the internal environment.

Identical twins

These 13-year-old girls have the same genotype, but they obviously differ in at least one aspect of their phenotype.

How Genes Are Passed Along in Sexual Reproduction

To understand how genes are passed along in sexual reproduction, it is useful to know something about their arrangement within cells. The genetic material (strands of DNA) exists in each cell in structures called **chromosomes**, which are usually dispersed throughout the cell nucleus and are not visible. Just prior to cell division, however, the chromosomes condense into compact forms that can be stained, viewed through a microscope, and photographed. The normal human cell has 23 pairs of chromosomes, 22 of which are identical in both sexes. The remaining pair are the sex chromosomes. In the normal human male cell, they consist of a large chromosome labeled X and a small chromosome labeled Y (see Figure 3.2). The chromosomes in the normal human female cell are identical to those in the male, except that the female cell has a second X chromosome rather than a Y.

FIGURE 3.2 *Chromosomes of a normal human male cell*
The 22 numbered pairs of chromosomes are the same in a normal female cell and a normal male cell. The remaining two, labeled X and Y, are the sex chromosomes. The normal human female cell (not shown) has a second X chromosome instead of a Y.

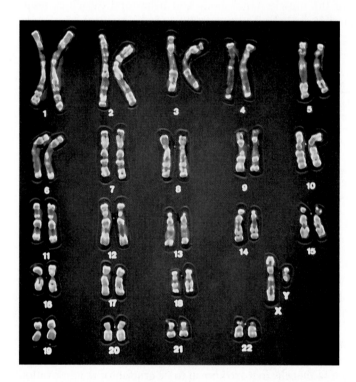

The Production of Genetically Diverse Egg and Sperm Cells

3.

How does meiosis produce egg or sperm cells that are all genetically different from one another, and what consequence does this have for the offspring of sexually reproducing creatures?

When cells divide to produce new cells *other than* egg or sperm cells, they do so by a process called **mitosis**. Each chromosome precisely replicates itself and then the cell divides, with one copy of each chromosome moving into each of the two cell nuclei thus formed. Because of the faithful copying of genetic material in mitosis, all your body's cells, except your egg or sperm cells, are genetically identical to one another. The differences among different cells in your body—such as liver cells and skin cells—arise from the differential activation of their genes, not from different gene content.

When cells divide to produce sperm or egg cells, they do so by a process called **meiosis**, which involves two divisions rather than just one and results in cells that are not genetically alike. Meiosis operates on precursor cells in the male's testes to produce sperm cells and in the female's ovaries to produce egg cells. At the beginning of meiosis, the two members of each pair of chromosomes in the precursor cell line up next to each other, and the DNA in each chromosome reproduces itself, resulting in sets of four identical-looking incomplete chromosomes called chromatids (see Figure 3.3). Then the cell divides, with two chromatids from each set of

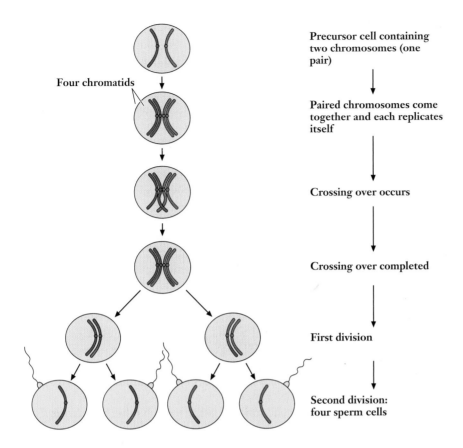

Four chromatids

Precursor cell containing two chromosomes (one pair)

Paired chromosomes come together and each replicates itself

Crossing over occurs

Crossing over completed

First division

Second division: four sperm cells

FIGURE **3.3**

Schematic representation of meiosis in sperm production

This illustration is for a creature that has only one pair of chromosomes rather than the 23 pairs that exist in humans. Although the drawing shows crossing over as occurring only at one place, it actually occurs at multiple places for each of the four chromatids. After the chromosomes have reproduced themseves and crossing over has occured, the cell divides twice, resulting in four sperm cells, each of which has one reshuffled member of the original pair of chromosomes. Meiosis in egg production is similar to that in sperm production, but only one of the two cells produced at each division survives.

four going to each of the two cells thus formed. In the male, both of these new cells then divide again, after the chromatids have developed into full chromosomes, and one chromosome from each set goes to each of the new cells. The result is four sperm cells, each of which has half the normal number of chromosomes, one member of each original pair. Egg production is similar to sperm production, except that only one of the four potential eggs derived from the two divisions survives the process.

A given person's egg or sperm cells look alike in terms of the number and shape of their chromosomes (except that half of the male's sperm cells have an X chromosome and the other half have a Y), but they are all different from one another in the genes they contain. To understand this, you must first realize that paired chromosomes, despite looking identical, do not have identical genes. During meiosis, after the chromosomes have reproduced but before the first cell division, sections of DNA are interchanged between chromosomes within each set of four in a random manner, a process called *crossing over* (illustrated in Figure 3.3). Then during each meiotic cell division, the chromosomes within each set are randomly divided between the new cells thus formed. Because of both crossing over and the random assortment of chromosomes, the DNA content of a precursor cell can be divided among the resulting egg or sperm cells in a virtually infinite number of ways. Thus the chance that a person will produce two genetically identical eggs or sperm is, for all practical purposes, nil.

The Genetic Diversity of Offspring

It may seem ironic that the very cells you use for "reproduction" are the only cells in your body that cannot, in theory, reproduce you. They are the only cells in your body that do not have all your genes. In sexual reproduction you are, of course, not really reproducing yourself. Rather, you are creating a genetically unique individual who has half of your genes and half of your partner's genes. When a sperm and an egg unite, the result is a single new cell, the **zygote**, which contains the full complement of 23 paired chromosomes, one member of each pair coming from each parent. The zygote then grows, through mitosis, eventually to become a new adult. Because each sperm or egg is different from any other sperm or egg (even from the same parent), each zygote is different from any other.

Biologists even today are uncertain as to why so many species of animals and plants have evolved to reproduce sexually instead of by simple cloning (the asexual production of offspring that are genetically identical to the parent). Most theories center on the evolutionary value of producing genetically diverse offspring. In a world where the environment keeps changing, genes have a better chance of surviving if they are rearranged at each generation in many different ways, to produce different kinds of bodies, than if they are all put into the same kind of basket, so to speak. The most prominent specific version of this theory focuses on the value of genetic diversity in resisting viruses, bacteria, and other parasites that cause disease (Hamilton & others, 1990; Ridley, 1994). Such parasites evolve to be able to attach themselves to the specific proteins of their hosts. By continually producing offspring with new mixtures of proteins, the hosts (including humans) at least partly foil the parasites.

The only people who are genetically identical to each other are **identical twins**. They are formed when two bundles of cells separate from each other during the early mitotic divisions following the formation of a zygote. Because they originate from one zygote, identical twins are also known as *monozygotic twins*. **Fraternal twins**, or *dizygotic twins*, originate from two zygotes, formed when each of two eggs is joined by a sperm. Fraternal twins are no more or less similar to each other genetically than are any two nontwin siblings. In later chapters of this book (especially Chapter 10), you will see how psychologists make use of twins in research aimed at understanding how much of the variability among people, in certain psychological traits, is due to differences in their genes and how much is due to differences in their environments.

Consequences of the Fact That Genes Come in Pairs

You have seen that genes exist on long DNA strands in chromosomes, rather like beads on a string, and that chromosomes come in pairs. The two genes that occupy the same **locus** (location) on a pair of chromosomes are sometimes identical to each other and sometimes not. When they are identical, the individual is said to be **homozygous** at that locus, and when they are not identical, the individual is said to be **heterozygous** at that locus (see Figure 3.4). Different genes that can occupy the same locus, and thus can potentially pair with each other, are referred to as **alleles**.

4.

What is the difference between a dominant and a recessive gene (or allele)?

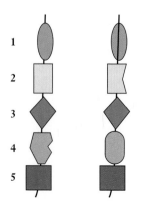

FIGURE **3.4**   *Schematic illustration of gene loci on a pair of chromosomes*

Successive genes are depicted here as beads on a string. This pair of chromosomes is homozygous at loci 1, 3, and 5 (the paired genes there are identical to each other) and heterozygous at loci 2 and 4 (the paired genes there are not identical to each other). Nonidentical genes that can occupy the same locus on a pair of chromosomes are referred to as alleles of each other. Thus the two genes at locus 2 are alleles, as are the two at locus 4.

For example, a gene for brown eyes and a gene for blue eyes in humans are alleles because they can occupy the same locus. If you are homozygous for brown eyes, you have two copies of a gene that manufactures an enzyme that makes your eyes brown. What if you were heterozygous for eye color, with one copy of the allele for brown eyes and one copy for blue eyes? In this case, you would have brown eyes, phenotypically indistinguishable from the eye color you would have if you were homozygous for brown eyes. This effect is described by saying that the allele for brown eyes is *dominant* and the one for blue eyes is *recessive*. A ***dominant*** gene (or allele) is one that will produce its observable effects in either the homozygous or the heterozygous condition, and a ***recessive*** gene (or allele) is one that will produce its effects in the homozygous condition only. But not all pairs of alleles manifest dominance or recessiveness. Some pairs blend their effects. For example, if you cross red four-o'clocks (a kind of flower) with white four-o'clocks, the offspring will be pink, because neither the red nor the white allele is dominant over the other.

The fact that genes come in pairs provides the basis for calculating what geneticists call *percent relatedness*. Because you received one member of each of your paired genes from your mother and the other from your father, you are said to be 50 percent related to each of your two parents. You are also considered to be 50 percent related to any full sibling you have, because any given gene that you received from your mother or father had a 50 percent chance of also being received by your sibling. An extension of this reasoning can be used to calculate the percent relatedness of other classes of relatives (see Table 3.1). Percent relatedness is a useful index of the likelihood that any given rare gene that exists in one individual will also exist in a relative. Most genes are very common in the population, so any two people chosen at random share much more than 50 percent of their total genes. But no matter how rare a particular gene is, if one of your parents has it, the chance that you will have it is at least 50 percent.

5.

What does it mean to say that you and a specific relative are x percent related?

TABLE **3.1** *Genetic relatedness*

Relationship	Degree of relationship	Percent relatedness
Identical twins		100.00%
Parent/child Full brothers, full sisters Fraternal twins	First degree	50.00
Grandparent/grandchild Uncle or aunt/nephew or niece Half-brothers, half-sisters	Second degree	25.00
First cousins	Third degree	12.50
Second cousins	Fourth degree	6.25

Mendelian Patterns of Heredity

The idea that the units of heredity come in pairs and that one member of a pair can be dominant over the other was developed in the mid-nineteenth century by Gregor Mendel, on the basis of his experiments breeding peas. In a typical experiment, Mendel would start with two purebred strains of peas, differing in one or more easily observed traits, and cross them to observe the traits of the offspring, called the F_1 (first filial) generation. Then he would breed the F_1 peas among themselves to produce the F_2 (second filial) generation. In one experiment, for example, Mendel crossed a strain of peas that regularly produced round seeds with a strain that regularly produced wrinkled seeds. His famous findings were that (a) all of the

F_1 generation had round seeds and (b) three-fourths of the F_2 generation had round seeds and one-fourth had wrinkled seeds.

Mendel's findings make perfect sense if we assume that seed texture is controlled by a single pair of genes, with the allele for round dominant over that for wrinkled. To illustrate this, let us use the capital letter R to stand for the dominant, round-producing allele and the small letter r for the recessive, wrinkle-producing allele. The purebred round strain is homozygous for the "round" allele (RR), and the purebred wrinkled strain is homozygous for the "wrinkled" allele (rr). (Purebred strains are homozygous for all observed traits.) Since one allele must come from each parent, the only possible result for the F_1 generation, produced by crossing the two purebred strains, is the heterozygous condition (Rr). This explains why all the F_1 peas in Mendel's experiment were round. At the next step, when Rr peas are bred with each other to produce the F_2 generation, four equally likely combinations can occur: (1) an R from each parent (RR), (2) an R from the female parent and an r from the male (Rr), (3) an r from the female parent and an R from the male (rR), and (4) an r from each parent (rr). (See Figure 3.5.) Since only one of these possible outcomes (rr) is wrinkled, the expectation is that one-fourth of the F_2 generation will be wrinkled and the other three-fourths, round. This, of course, is just what Mendel found.

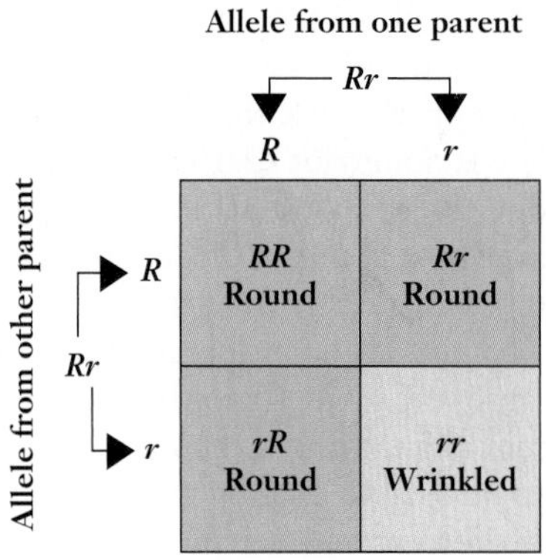

Note that although the Rr peas look the same as the RR peas, they are not genetically the same. In other words, even though they have the same phenotype, they have different genotypes. An Rr pea plant, if crossed with either an Rr or an rr variety, is capable of producing offspring with wrinkled seeds (rr). An RR plant, though, can produce only round-seeded offspring (Rr or RR) regardless of the variety of pea plant with which it is crossed.

One way to study the role of genes in behavior is to look for behavioral traits that are inherited in accordance with Mendel's ratios, indicative of control by a single pair of genes. Let us look at three examples of the many such traits that have been found.

A Breed Difference in Fearfulness in Dogs

In pioneering research on the role of genes in behavior, John Paul Scott and John Fuller (1965) studied the behavior of basenji hounds, cocker spaniels, and their mixed-breed offspring. Basenjis are timid dogs, showing fear of people until they have been much handled and gentled. Cockers, in contrast, show little fear under normal rearing conditions. In a standard test with 5-week-old puppies, Scott and Fuller found that all the basenji puppies yelped and/or ran away when approached by a strange person, whereas only a few of the cocker puppies showed these reactions. When cockers and basenjis were crossbred (see Figure 3.6), the offspring (F_1 hybrids) were like basenjis in this test: All showed signs of fear when approached. Since this was as true of hybrids raised by cocker mothers as of those raised by basenji mothers, Scott and Fuller concluded that the effect stemmed from the hybrid dogs' genes and not from the way they were treated by their mothers.

The fact that the F_1 hybrids were as fearful as the purebred basenjis suggested to Scott and Fuller that the difference in fearfulness between the two purebred strains might be controlled by a single gene locus, with the allele promoting fear dominant over that promoting confidence. If this were so, then mating F_1 hybrids with each other should produce a group of offspring (F_2 generation) in which

FIGURE **3.5**
Explanation of Mendel's 3:1 ratio
When two pea plants that are heterozygous for round versus wrinkled seeds are cross-bred, four possible gene combinations occur. Here R stands for the dominant, round-producing allele, and r for the recessive, wrinkle-producing allele. The phenotype of three of the offspring will be round and that of one, wrinkled. This 3:1 ratio was Mendel's famous finding.

6.

Why do three-fourths of the offspring of two heterozygous parents show the dominant trait and one-fourth show the recessive trait?

7.

How did Scott and Fuller show that the difference between cocker spaniels and basenji hounds in fearfulness is controlled by a single gene locus with the "fear" allele dominant over the "nonfear" allele?

FIGURE **3.6** *Dogs used in Scott and Fuller's research*
At left are a male basenji and a female cocker spaniel; at right are two F_1 (first-generation) hybrids resulting from a basenji-cocker cross.

three-fourths would show basenjilike fear and one-fourth would show cockerlike confidence—the same ratios that Mendel had found with seed texture in peas. Scott and Fuller did this experiment and, indeed, found ratios very close to those predicted. As additional evidence, they also mated F_1 hybrids with purebred cockers. About half the offspring of those *backcrosses* were basenjilike in fear, and the other half were cockerlike in confidence—just as expected if the "fear" allele is dominant over the "nonfear" allele (see Figure 3.7).

Be careful not to misinterpret this finding. It concerns a difference between two breeds of dogs in certain behavioral tests. It would not be reasonable to conclude that fear in all its various forms is controlled by a single gene. Many different genes must contribute to building the complex neural structure needed to experience fear and express it in behavior. Scott and Fuller's work demonstrates only that the difference between cocker spaniels and basenji hounds in a particular test of fear is controlled by a single gene. Recognize also that their studies do not diminish the role of environmental influences. Scott and Fuller could detect the effect of a specific gene pair because they raised all the dogs in similar environments. In other research, Scott (1963) showed that any puppy isolated from people for the first 4 months of life will be fearful of humans. Had Scott and Fuller isolated the cockers from all human contact and given the basenjis lots of kind handling before the behavioral test, they might well have found the cockers to be more fearful than the basenjis, despite the genetic predispositions toward the opposite.

8.

Why would it be a mistake to conclude from Scott and Fuller's work either that fear in dogs is due to a single gene or that it is due to genes and not environment?

FIGURE **3.7** *Explanation of Scott and Fuller's results of mating basenji-cocker hybrids with purebred cockers*
The finding that half the offspring were fearful and half were not makes sense if fearfulness results from a dominant allele (F) and lack of fearfulness results from a recessive allele (f). Because half the offspring receive F from their hybrid parent and all receive f from the purebred parent, half the offspring will be Ff (phenotypically fearful) and the other half, ff (not fearful).

Allele from cocker-basenji hybrid

— Ff —

	F	f
f	fF Fearful	ff Not fearful
f	fF Fearful	ff Not fearful

Allele from purebred cocker

ff

PKU: A Recessive Developmental Disorder in Humans

Most of the behaviorally relevant traits identified so far in humans as being controlled by a single gene locus are disorders—failures of normal development due to a relatively rare, mutant, malfunctioning gene that is passed along from generation to generation. One of the most well-understood examples is phenylketonuria, usually called **PKU**, which is inherited through a recessive gene (see Figure 3.8). The

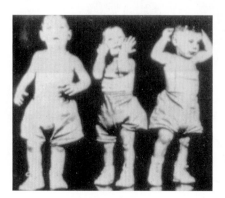

disorder occurs in about 1 of every 10,000 newborns. If untreated, it usually results in reduced brain size, poor motor coordination, and severe mental retardation, including, in many cases, an inability to speak or understand language (Hay, 1985). The gene responsible for this disorder can be any of several different defective alleles of a gene that normally directs the synthesis of an enzyme that controls the body's use of phenylalanine (an amino acid present in milk and other protein-containing foods). The defective allele creates a defective enzyme, which is anywhere from 0 to 50 percent as effective as the normal enzyme in breaking down phenylalanine (Okano & others, 1991). In the absence of the normal enzyme, phenylalanine accumulates in the body and is converted to an acidic substance that, in high quantities, is poisonous to the brain and other tissues.

FIGURE **3.8** *Triplets, two with PKU and one without*
The two children at the right are genetically identical and have PKU (the child at the left is their fraternal triplet). Their arm posturing is typical of severely affected PKU individuals. Today the most severe effects of PKU are prevented by starting affected infants on a diet low in phenylalanine immediately after birth.

Although inherited genetically, PKU can be treated by environmental means. Most hospitals today routinely test newborns for PKU and immediately place affected infants on a diet low in phenylalanine. With low phenylalanine intake, little of the poisonous acid is created, and the baby can grow up quite normally. The diet must be started soon after birth, because the most severe and irreversible effects of the acid on brain development occur in infancy. Later in life, PKU sufferers can be somewhat less diligent about their diet, although a mild reduction in mental abilities can still occur if the phenylalanine level gets too high (Welsh & others, 1990). Also, pregnant women with PKU must go back onto the diet to prevent brain damage to the fetus during prenatal development.

9.

How has knowledge of the genetic basis of PKU led to an environmental treatment?

To say that a PKU-producing allele is recessive is to say that its effects will not occur if it is paired with a normal, non-PKU-producing allele. Thus a child can be born with the disease only if both parents carry the abnormal allele. Let's use the capital letter *P* for the dominant normal allele and the small letter *p* for any of the various PKU-producing alleles. If two parents who don't have PKU have a PKU baby, both must be heterozygous (*Pp*) carriers of the disease, which, in turn, means that there is 1 chance in 4 that any future child they have will be born with PKU (as was shown in Figure 3.5 for wrinkled peas). Most single-gene disorders are like PKU in that they are caused by recessive alleles. In other words, most such disorders occur only if a faulty gene exists on both chromosomes at the same gene locus. It is fortunate that genes come in pairs. If one is defective, then its mate on the homologous chromosome can usually make up for the deficit. It's like carrying a spare tire. Only if both members of a gene pair are defective will the person be harmed.

10.

How does the paired nature of genes reduce the incidence of genetic disorders?

A Specific Language Disorder due to a Dominant Gene

A more subtle example of a deficit controlled by a single gene locus has to do with language learning. As will be discussed in Chapter 11, most human beings are remarkably adept at learning, at an early age, the grammatical constructions of the language to which they are exposed. But a few, who are otherwise quite normal, have a terrible time learning grammar and never really master it (Gopnik, 1999).

11.

What is the evidence that a particular deficit in language acquisition may depend on a single dominant gene?

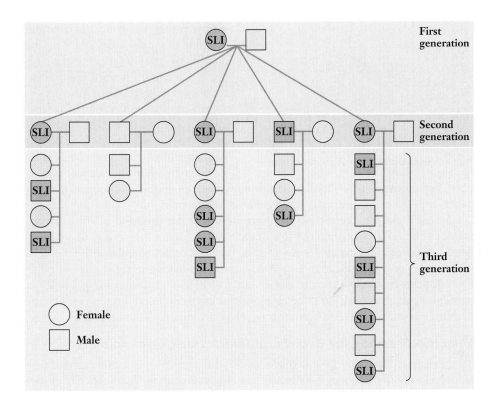

FIGURE **3.9**
Inheritance of a specific language impairment
This diagram shows the members of three generations of a family in which a specific language impairment (SLI) recurred. Circles depict females; squares, males; horizontal lines, marriage bonds; and slanted or vertical lines, lines of descent. "SLI" indicates presence of the disorder. Notice that approximately half (10 of 21) of the third-generation children who had one parent with SLI also had SLI. This pattern is consistent with the theory that the disorder is inherited through a single dominant gene. (Based on Gopnik & Crago, 1991.)

They can learn intellectually, for example, to add *-s* onto nouns to make them plural, or *-ed* onto verbs to make them past tense, but to follow such rules they must exert conscious effort, and they often make mistakes. They don't automatically distinguish the different grammatical categories (verbs, nouns, and so on) as even most 3-year-olds do. Their lack is referred to as a *specific language impairment (SLI)*, and at least one version of this impairment is inherited in a manner suggesting that it is due to a single dominant gene.

Myrna Gopnik and Martha Crago (1991) studied three generations of a single family in which SLI was common and found the pattern of heredity shown in Figure 3.9. As you can see by examining the results for the third generation, when neither parent had SLI, no child had it, and when one parent had SLI and one did not, about half the offspring had it—just what you would expect if the impairment results from a single dominant gene. The logic behind this expectation is identical to that shown in Figure 3.7 for fearfulness in dogs. If one parent is heterozygous for the SLI gene and the other parent completely lacks the gene, each offspring has a 50 percent chance of inheriting a copy of the gene. Because the gene is dominant, each person inheriting it manifests the trait.

Polygenic Characteristics and Selective Breeding

Thus far our focus has been on traits that derive from alleles at a single gene locus. Those variations are typically of type, not degree. Peas are either wrinkled or round; mixed-breed basenji-cockers differ so sharply in fearfulness that they can be categorized into two clear groups; and people either have or don't have PKU or SLI. But most measurable anatomical and behavioral differences among individuals of any species are of degree, not type. That is, the measures taken from individuals do not fall into two or more distinct groups but can lie anywhere within the observed range of scores. Most often the set of scores obtained on such measures

12.

How does the distribution of scores for a polygenic trait differ from that usually obtained for a single-gene trait?

FIGURE **3.10**   *Normal distribution*
When many individuals are tested for a polygenic characteristic, the majority usually fall in the middle of the range of scores and the frequency tapers off toward zero at the extremes. Mathematically, this defines a normal curve. (For a more complete description, see the Statistical Appendix at the end of the book.)

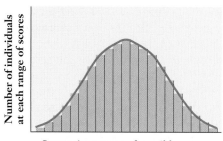

Successive ranges of possible scores

approximates a ***normal distribution***, meaning that most scores fall near the middle of the range and the frequency tapers off toward the two extremes (see Figure 3.10). Measures of aggressiveness in mice, of maze learning in rats, and of conscientiousness in people are just a few of the behavioral measures that are consistently found to fit a normal distribution.

Characteristics that vary in a continuous way are generally affected by many genes and are therefore called ***polygenic characteristics*** (the prefix *poly-* means "many"). Of course, these traits are also influenced by variation in the environment, so the variability observed in a graph such as Figure 3.10 is due to a combination of genetic differences at many gene loci and environmental differences. In Chapter 10, you will discover how behavioral geneticists—using studies of twins and adoptive families—estimate the extent to which variations among people in particular polygenic traits are due to genetic or environmental differences. For the present, our concern is with a procedure used only with nonhuman animals.

Selective Breeding for Behavioral Characteristics in Animals

To the degree that individuals within a species differ in any measurable characteristic because of differences in their genes, that characteristic can be modified over successive generations through ***selective breeding***. This procedure involves the mating of individuals that lie toward the desired extreme on the measure in question. For single-gene characteristics the effects of selective breeding are immediate, but for polygenic characteristics the effects are gradual and cumulative over generations.

The basic procedure of selective breeding is by no means new. For thousands of years before a formal science of genetics existed, plant and animal breeders used selective breeding to produce new and better strains of every sort of domesticated species. Grains were bred for fatter seeds; cows, for docility and greater milk production; horses, along separate lines for working and racing; canaries, for their song; and dogs, along dozens of different lines for such varied purposes as following a trail, herding sheep (running around them instead of at them), and being gentle playmates for children. The procedure in every case was essentially the same: The members of each generation that best approximated the desired type were mated to produce the next generation, resulting in a continuous genetic molding toward the varieties we see today.

Under controlled laboratory conditions, researchers have used selective breeding to produce many behaviorally specialized strains of animals. Fruit flies have been bred to move instinctively either toward or away from a source of light; mice, to be either more or less inclined to fight; and rats, to either prefer or not prefer alcohol over water (Crabbe & others, 1999; Wimer & Wimer, 1985). That selective breeding can influence essentially any behavior should come as no surprise. It follows logically from the fact that all behaviors depend on particular sensory, motor, and neural structures, all of which are built from proteins whose production depends on genes.

A fox bred for tameness
Since 1959, researchers in Russia have been selectively breeding silver foxes for tameness. At each generation, only those foxes that show the least fear and aggression and the most affection to humans have been bred. The result, after 30 to 35 generations, is a breed of foxes that are as friendly to humans as are dogs (Trut, 1999).

Tryon's Classic Study of Maze-Learning Ability

The first long-term, systematic study of selective breeding in psychology was begun in the 1920s by Robert Tryon (1942), partly in reaction to the belief then held by some psychologists that individual differences in behavior are due entirely to environmental, not at all to genetic, differences. Tryon wanted to demonstrate that a type of behavior frequently studied by psychologists could be strongly influenced by variation in genes.

Tryon began by testing a genetically diverse group of rats for their ability to learn a particular maze. Then he mated the males and females that had made the fewest errors in the maze to begin what he called the "maze bright" strain and those that had made the most errors to begin the "maze dull" strain. When the offspring of succeeding generations reached adulthood, he tested them in the same maze and mated the best-performing members of the bright strain, and the worst-performing members of the dull strain, to continue the two lines. Some of his results are shown in Figure 3.11. As you can see, with each generation the two strains became increasingly distinct, until by the seventh there was almost no overlap between them. Almost all seventh-generation bright rats made fewer errors in the maze than even the best dull rats. To control for the possibility that the offspring were somehow learning to be bright or dull from their mothers, Tryon cross-fostered the rats so that some of the offspring from each strain were raised by mothers in the other strain. He found that rats in the bright strain were equally good in the maze, and those in the dull strain equally poor, regardless of which mothers raised them.

Once a strain has been bred to show some behavioral characteristic, the question arises as to what other behavioral or physiological changes accompany it. Tryon referred to his two strains as "bright" and "dull," but all he had measured was their performance in a particular type of maze. Performance in the maze no

13.

How did Tryon produce "maze bright" and "maze dull" strains of rats? How did he show that the difference was due to genes, not rearing?

14.

Why is the strain difference produced by Tryon not appropriately characterized in terms of "brightness" or "dullness"?

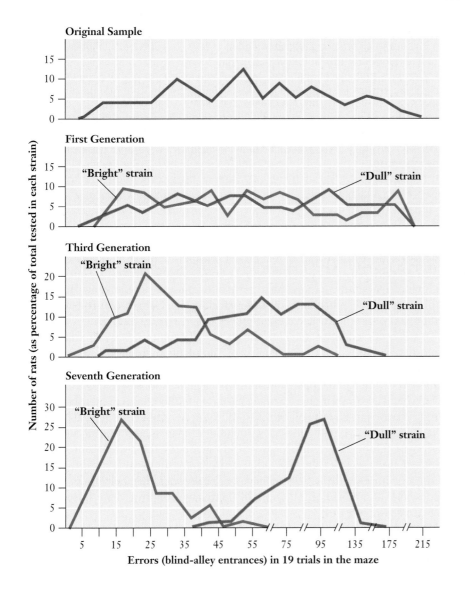

FIGURE 3.11 *Selective breeding for "maze brightness" and "maze dullness" in rats*

The top graph shows, for the original parent stock, the distribution of rats according to the number of errors they made in the maze. Subsequent graphs show this distribution for the "bright" and "dull" rats. With successive generations, an increasing percentage in the "bright" strain made few errors and an increasing percentage in the "dull" strain made many errors. (From Tryon, 1942.)

doubt depended on many sensory, motor, motivational, and learning processes, and specific changes in any of them could in theory have mediated the effects that Tryon observed. In theory, Tryon's "dull" rats could simply have been those that had less acute vision, or were less interested in the variety of food used as a reward, or were more interested in exploring the maze's blind alleys. In later studies, another researcher found that Tryon's "dull" rats were as good as the "bright" ones, and sometimes even better, at other learning tasks (Searle, 1949). We do not know what underlying abilities or dispositions changed in Tryon's two strains of rats to produce their difference in maze performance, but the change was apparently not one of general learning ability. This problem still occurs in modern behavioral genetics research, in which new strains of animals (usually mice) are created by adding, deleting, or modifying known genes using sophisticated genetic-engineering methods. The behavioral differences between two strains found in one laboratory often fail to occur in another laboratory, apparently due to subtle differences in environment or testing conditions (Cabib & others, 2000; Crabbe & others, 1999b).

SECTION SUMMARY

Genes, interacting with the internal and external environments, control the synthesis of proteins, which influence the structure and functioning of physiological systems, thereby influencing behavior. Genes exist in pairs, on paired chromosomes, and the process of meiosis results in egg and sperm cells that contain just one randomly selected member of each gene pair. The result is that every egg and sperm cell is genetically unique, so all offspring (except identical twins) are genetically unique.

Some behavioral characteristics—such as the difference in fearfulness between basenji hounds and cocker spaniels—are due to differences in a single pair of genes. Such characteristics are inherited in a Mendelian manner—that is, in the ratios that Mendel found in his classic experiments with peas. Many genetic disorders in humans, such as PKU, are inherited in this way. Most behavioral traits, however, are polygenic (influenced by many genes) and are alterable only gradually through selective breeding, as exemplified by Tryon's classic study in which rats were bred to perform well or poorly in a maze.

NATURAL SELECTION AND ITS IMPLICATIONS FOR PSYCHOLOGY

15.

How is natural selection similar to and different from artificial selection?

Long before Darwin developed his theory of evolution, people knew that animals and plants could be modified over generations by human-controlled selective breeding, a process that Darwin (1859/1963) called *artificial selection*. In *The Origin of Species*, Darwin led his readers into his theory of evolution by reminding them of the enormously diverse varieties of animals and plants that have been produced by artificial selection. Then he pointed out that breeding in nature is also selective and can also produce changes in living things over generations. Selective breeding in nature, which Darwin labeled **natural selection**, is dictated not by the needs and whims of humans but by the obstacles to reproduction that are imposed by the natural environment. Those obstacles include predators, limited food supplies, extremes of temperature, difficulty in finding mates for sexual reproduction—anything that can cut life short or otherwise prevent an organism from producing offspring. Animals and plants that have characteristics that help them overcome such obstacles are, by definition, more likely to have offspring than those that don't have these characteristics.

Darwin's essential point was this: Individuals of a species vary in the number of offspring they produce. Some produce none, because they die early or fail to mate, and others produce many. Any inherited trait that increases the number of offspring that an individual produces is automatically "selected for," as the trait is passed on to those offspring. Conversely, any inherited trait that decreases one's number of offspring is automatically "selected against," appearing in fewer members of the next generation. Thus, as long as inheritable differences exist among individuals in an interbreeding population, and as long as some of those differences affect survival and reproduction, evolution will occur.

Non Sequitur by Wiley
© 1997 Washington Post Writers Group

Modern Understanding of Evolution

Darwin knew nothing of genes. He realized that something must change and be passed along through eggs and sperm for evolution to occur, but he did not know what. Mendel's work, which was the first step toward a knowledge of genes, was unknown to most scientists until about 1900. Today we know that genes are the units of heredity and that evolution entails changes, from generation to generation, in the frequency of particular genes in an interbreeding population. Genes that improve an individual's ability to survive and reproduce in the existing environment increase from generation to generation, and genes that impede this ability decrease from generation to generation.

16.

How do mutations and natural selection combine to produce evolution?

The genetic variability that provides the fodder for evolution comes from two main sources: (1) the reshuffling of genes that occurs in sexual reproduction (which we have already discussed) and (2) mutations. **Mutations** are errors that occasionally and unpredictably occur during DNA replication, causing the "replica" to be not quite like the original. In the long run of evolution, mutation is the ultimate source of all genetic variation. As would be expected of any random change in a complex, organized structure, new mutations are more often harmful than helpful, and natural selection usually weeds them out. But occasionally a mutation is useful, producing a protein that affects the organism's development in a way that increases its ability to survive or reproduce, and the gene arising from that mutation increases in frequency from generation to generation. At the level of the gene, that is evolution.

Prior to the modern understanding of genes, many people believed that changes in an individual that stem from practice or experience could be inherited and therefore provide a basis for evolution. For example, some argued that early giraffes, by frequently stretching their necks to reach leaves in trees, slightly elongated their necks in the course of their lives and that this change was passed on to their offspring, resulting, over many generations, in the long-necked giraffes we see today. That idea, referred to as the *inheritance of acquired characteristics*, is most often attributed to Jean-Baptiste de Lamarck (1744–1829), although many other evolutionists, both before and after Lamarck, held the same view (Futuyma, 1997). Even Darwin did not reject that idea but added to it the concepts of random variation and natural selection. Now, however, we know that evolution is based entirely on genetic changes and that no amount of practice or experience can change one's genes in such a way as to affect the next generation. Random change followed by natural selection, not directed change stemming from individual experience, provides the basis for evolution.

Evolution Observed: The Role of Environmental Change

Evolution is spurred by changes in the environment. If the environment were completely stable, organisms would adapt as fully as possible and change little or not at all thereafter. But the environment keeps changing. Climates change, sources of food change, predators change, and so on. When the conditions of life change, what was previously a useful characteristic may become harmful, and vice versa.

Darwin believed that evolution is a slow and steady process. But today we know that it can occur rapidly, slowly, or almost not at all, depending on the rate and nature of environmental change and on the degree to which genetic variability already exists in a population (Gould & Eldredge, 1993). Environmental change spurs evolution *not* by causing the appropriate mutations to occur but by promoting natural selection. Some mutations that previously would not have been advantageous, and would have been weeded out by natural selection, are advantageous in the new environment, so they are passed along from generation to generation in increasing numbers. Evolution sometimes occurs so quickly that people can see it happen. In fact, scientists since Darwin's time have reported more than a hundred cases of observed evolution (Endler, 1986; Weiner, 1994).

One of the most well-documented examples comes from the work of Peter and Rosemary Grant, who for more than 20 years studied a species of finch that inhabits one of the Galápagos Islands, about 600 miles off the coast of Ecuador (Grant, 1991; Weiner, 1994). The Grants found that the members of this species differ somewhat in body size, that the variation is inheritable, and that environmental changes result sometimes in selection for large size and other times for small size. During years of drought, when most of the finches died because the plants that produce the seeds they eat failed to grow, the birds that survived and produced offspring tended to be the larger ones, apparently because their beaks were thick and powerful enough to crack open the large, hard-shelled seeds that were last to be consumed (see Figure 3.12). During rainy years, when an abundance of seeds caused a population explosion among the finches, the smaller birds did better. Apparently, in those conditions, their young could grow to full size and reproduce more quickly than the young of the larger finches.

The evolution of simple or small changes, such as in skin pigmentation or in body size, can occur in a few generations when selection conditions are strong, but more complex changes require much more time. The difference, say, between a chimpanzee brain and a human brain could not have come about in a few generations, as it must have involved many mutations, each of which would have promoted a slight selective advantage to the chimpanzee (in its environment) or the human (in our environment). When evolutionists talk about "rapid" evolution of complex changes, they are usually talking about periods measured in hundreds of thousands of years (Gould & Eldredge, 1993).

Evolution Has No Foresight

People sometimes mistakenly think of evolution as a mystical force working toward a predetermined end. One manifestation of this belief is the idea that evolution could produce changes for some future purpose, even though they are useless or harmful in the present environment. But evolution has no foresight. The finches studied by the Grants could not have evolved thicker beaks in anticipation of drought. Only genetic changes that increase survival and reproduction in the immediate environment can proliferate through natural selection.

Another manifestation of the belief in foresight is the idea that present-day organisms can be ranked according to the distance they have moved along a set evolutionary route, toward some planned end. For example, some may think of humans as the "most evolved" creatures, with chimpanzees next and amoebas way down on the list. But evolution has no set route or planned end. Humans, chimps, and amoebas have taken their different forms and behavioral characteristics because of chance events that led them to occupy different niches in the environment, where the selection criteria differed. The present-day amoeba is not an early step toward humans but a creature that is at least as adapted to its environment as we are to ours. The amoeba has no more chance of evolving to become like us than we have of evolving to become like it.

17.

How did a study of finches illustrate an effect of environmental change on evolution?

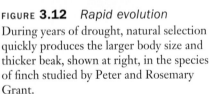

Natural History Magazine

FIGURE **3.12**   *Rapid evolution*
During years of drought, natural selection quickly produces the larger body size and thicker beak, shown at right, in the species of finch studied by Peter and Rosemary Grant.

18.

What are three mistaken beliefs about evolution, all related to the misconception that foresight is involved?

A third manifestation of the belief in foresight is the idea that natural selection is a moral force, that its operation and its products are in some sense right or good. In everyday talk, people sometimes imply that whatever is natural (including natural selection) is good and that evil stems from society or human contrivances that go beyond nature. But nature is neither good nor bad, moral nor immoral. To say that natural selection led to such and such a characteristic does not lend any moral virtue to that characteristic. As you will see, fighting is as much a product of evolution as is cooperation, but that is no reason to consider them morally equivalent.

Thinking About Behavior in Terms of Its Functions

The mechanisms underlying behavior are products of natural selection, and, like all products of natural selection, they came about because they promoted survival and reproduction. Just as Tryon, through artificial selection, bred rats to be better at learning a particular maze, natural selection breeds animals to be better at doing what they must to survive and reproduce in their natural environments. This idea provides a foundation for the psychological approach (introduced in Chapter 1) known as *functionalism*—the attempt to explain behavior in terms of what it accomplishes for the behaving individual.

When applied to understanding the most general behavioral traits of a species, the functionalist approach in psychology is essentially the same as the functionalist approach in anatomy: Why do giraffes have long necks? Why do humans lack fur? Why do male songbirds sing in the spring? Why do humans have such an irrepressible ability to learn language? The anatomist trying to answer the first two questions, and the behavioral researcher or psychologist trying to answer the latter two, would look for ways by which each trait helped ancestral members of the species survive and reproduce.

Ultimate and Proximate Explanations of Behavior

Biologists and psychologists who think in evolutionary terms find it useful to distinguish between two kinds of explanations of behavior: ultimate and proximate. *Ultimate explanations* are functional explanations at the evolutionary level; that is, they are statements of the role that the behavior plays in the animal's survival and reproduction. *Proximate explanations* are explanations that deal not with function but with mechanism; they are statements of the immediate conditions, both inside and outside the animal, that bring on the behavior.

Consider, for example, why male songbirds (of many species) sing in the spring. An ultimate explanation goes something like this (Koodsma & Byers, 1991): Over the course of evolution, songbirds have adapted to a mating system that takes place in the spring. The male's song serves to attract a female with which to mate and to warn other males to stay away from the singer's territory in order to avoid a fight. In the evolution of these birds, males whose genes promoted such singing produced more offspring (more copies of their genes) than those whose genes did not promote such singing. A proximate explanation, in contrast, might go as follows (Ball & Hulse, 1998): The increased period of daylight in the spring triggers, through the birds' visual system, a physiological mechanism that leads to the increased production of the sex hormone testosterone, which in turn acts on certain areas of the brain (which we might call the "song areas"), promoting the drive to sing. Notice the complementarity of these explanations. The ultimate

19.

How does an understanding of evolution provide a basis for functionalism in psychology?

20.

What is the difference between ultimate and proximate explanations of behavior?

A yellow-throated western blackbird at home
This male's singing warns other males of the species to stay away.

Robert Ballou / Animals, Animals

explanation states the survival or reproductive value of the behavior, and the proximate explanation states the stimuli and physiological mechanisms through which the behavior occurs.

Nonfunctional Evolutionary Changes

It is much easier to make up ultimate explanations (or proximate ones) than it is to prove them. Richard Lewontin and Stephen J. Gould (1978) have referred to some of the ultimate explanations proposed by biologists and psychologists as "Panglossian myths," named after the optimistic Dr. Pangloss of Voltaire's novel *Candide*, who believed that every detail of everything on earth was placed here to serve a useful function. For example, according to Pangloss, the human nose was given its peculiar shape to enable us to wear glasses. To avoid creating Panglossian myths, we must base ultimate explanations on appropriate evidence and realize that not every characteristic of humans or other animals is the direct result of natural selection.

Some inheritable characteristics are inconsequential for survival and reproduction. Different races of people have somewhat differently shaped noses. *Maybe* that variation is due to natural selection. Perhaps one shape worked best in one climate and another worked best in another climate, so natural selection molded the noses differently. But we can't automatically assume that. The different shapes might be due to mutations that didn't matter and therefore were never weeded out by natural selection. Maybe the small group of people who migrated to a specific part of the world, and who were the ancestors of a particular racial group, just happened to carry along genes for a nose shape that was different from the average for the group they left. Such variation, due to chance alone without selection, is referred to as *genetic drift*.

Other inheritable characteristics may be *side effects* of natural selection rather than directly selected effects. A useless or even harmful change might be an unavoidable consequence of selection for a useful change. An example discussed by Gould (1983) is the female spotted hyena's extraordinarily large clitoris, which is almost indistinguishable in size and shape from the male's penis. *Perhaps* the large clitoris plays some useful function and is a direct effect of natural selection, but it seems more likely that it came about as a side effect of natural selection for another fascinating characteristic of this species. The spotted hyena is one of the few mammals in which the female is larger than the male and aggressively dominant over the male (Glickman & others, 1992). In all mammals, large size and aggressiveness are promoted by a class of hormones called androgens (including testosterone), and biologically the spotted hyena achieves its large size and aggressiveness through the production of large quantities of androgens. A result is that all spotted-hyena fetuses—female as well as male—are exposed to high levels of androgens coming from their mother's bloodstream (Yalcinkaya & others, 1993). In other mammals, only the male is exposed to high levels of androgens before birth (coming from his own developing testes), and high androgen levels in any fetal mammal cause the precursor of the clitoris or penis to develop as the latter rather than the former.

Thus we have the following plausible scenario: Natural selection led to the production of large amounts of androgens by female spotted hyenas as a means of promoting strength and aggressiveness, with the enlarged clitoris emerging as a side effect of the androgens. If this scenario is right, then the appropriate question to ask about evolutionary function pertains not to the female's large clitoris but to her large body size and aggressiveness: What is it about the habitat and lifestyle of the spotted hyena that makes it valuable for the female to be larger, stronger, and more aggressive than the male?

The point here is that a degree of caution is wise in asking functionalist questions. Some characteristics may not themselves be functional but may result from genetic drift or be side effects. These alternative explanations are far more likely to apply to relatively simple modifications of existing structures (such as changes in size or color) than to the basic organization of the structures themselves. A struc-

21.

What are two means by which characteristics that do not contribute to survival or reproduction might emerge in evolution?

E.R. Degginger / Animals, Animals

A female spotted hyena

She produces high levels of androgen hormones and is larger and more aggressive than a typical male of her species.

ture as complex as an eye, or a brain, or the set of vocal and neural mechanisms that enable and motivate a bird to sing or a person to talk could not plausibly have evolved without the directive effect provided by natural selection. Such structures would not have come about if they did not in some way promote the individual's survival and reproduction.

SECTION SUMMARY

Natural selection is selective breeding imposed by the conditions of nature. All species of animals and plants are products of evolution by natural selection. Mutations and meiotic recombinations result in new variations in traits, and natural selection leads to the proliferation of those variations that promote survival and reproduction. In some cases, such as that involving body size and beak thickness among Galápagos finches, natural selection alters successive generations of animals at a pace that is rapid enough to be observed by scientists. Natural selection cannot anticipate the future; evolution results merely from the fact that some individuals in each generation have characteristics that lead them to produce more offspring than do others.

Natural selection has bred into animals traits that are adaptive, or functional, meaning that they promote survival and reproduction. It would be a mistake, however, to assume that every characteristic of an animal is adaptive. Useless traits can result from genetic drift or emerge as side effects of traits that do serve a function.

ETHOLOGY: THE STUDY OF SPECIES-TYPICAL BEHAVIOR PATTERNS

Suppose you saw an animal that looked exactly like a dog, but it went "meow," climbed trees, and ignored the mail carrier. Would you call it a dog or a cat? Clearly, we identify animals as much by their behavior as by their anatomy. Behavior patterns that are so characteristic of a given species of animal that they can be used to help identify that species are called **species-typical behaviors**. Meowing, tree climbing, and acting aloof are species-typical behaviors of cats. Dam building is species-typical of beavers. Talking and two-legged walking are species-typical of humans.

The field of behavioral study that has concentrated most explicitly on species-typical behaviors is **ethology**, which originated in Europe in the 1930s as a branch of zoology concerned with animal behavior in the natural environment (see Chapter 1). In contrast to psychologists, who studied animals in mazes and other artificial contrivances and who were looking for general principles of learning that cut across species, ethologists were more interested in the behavioral differences among species, which they attributed to the species' disparate evolutionary histories. Ethologists were (and still are) interested in (a) identifying and describing species-typical behaviors, (b) understanding the environmental requirements for the development of such behaviors in the young animal, and (c) tracing the evolutionary pathway through which the genetic basis for the behavior came about.

Describing Species-Typical Behaviors

Fixed Action Patterns and Sign Stimuli

The early ethologists, including Konrad Lorenz and Nikolaas Tinbergen (the field's main founders), studied various species of insects, fish, reptiles, and birds and found that many aspects of their behavior are quite predictable. Different members of the same species produce identical responses to specific environmental stimuli. The ethologists referred to such responses as **fixed action patterns**, emphasizing the idea that the controlling mechanisms are "fixed" in the animals' nervous system by heredity and are relatively unmodifiable by learning. The ethologists also coined

22.

How did Tinbergen identify the sign stimulus for the attack response in the male stickleback?

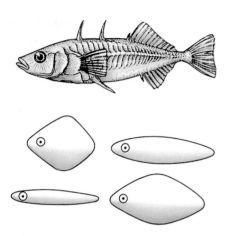

FIGURE 3.13 *Stickleback models used in the test of sign stimuli*
Models that had a red belly provoked aggression in male sticklebacks no matter how crude they were, whereas even a perfect replica of a male stickleback with no red belly did not. (From Tinbergen, 1951.)

23.

What evidence supports the idea that humans are biologically predisposed to express particular emotions in particular species-typical ways?

the term **sign stimulus** to refer to any stimulus that elicits a fixed action pattern. The relationship between a sign stimulus and a fixed action pattern is essentially that of a reflex, except the response is generally more complex than that of a typical reflex and more sensitive to the context. In many cases, a sign stimulus triggers a fixed action pattern only when the animal is in a physiological condition and an environmental context that make the response appropriate.

Tinbergen (1951, 1952) studied fixed action patterns and sign stimuli in a little European fish, the stickleback. During the breeding season, the male stickleback's belly turns from dull gray to bright red, and he builds a nest and defends the area around it by attacking other male sticklebacks that come too close. To determine what triggers the attack on other males, Tinbergen made stickleback models of varying accuracy and trailed them on thin wires through a male's territory. He found that any model with a red belly, no matter how little it resembled a real stickleback in other respects, would elicit a vigorous attack from the defending male (see Figure 3.13). A model without a red belly, no matter how much it resembled a real stickleback in other respects, failed to elicit an attack. Thus Tinbergen showed that the red belly is the sign stimulus for the attack response in the male stickleback. More recently, other researchers have shown that the red coloration on a stickleback image elicits an attack only when the male is in his home territory (Bolyard & Rowland, 1996). The action thus serves to protect the nesting area and does not occur, uselessly, in other contexts.

Human Emotional Expressions as Species-Typical Behaviors

Darwin noted that we humans, like other animals, automatically communicate moods and behavioral intentions to one another through body postures, movements, and facial expressions. In his book *The Expression of the Emotions in Man and Animals*, Darwin (1872/1965) argued that specific facial expressions accompany specific emotional states in humans and that these expressions are universal, occurring in people throughout the world and even in people who were born blind and thus could not have learned them through observation.

In an extension of Darwin's pioneering work, Paul Ekman and Wallace Friesen (1975, 1982) developed an atlas that describes and depicts the exact facial-muscle movements that make up each of six basic emotional expressions in people: surprise, fear, disgust, anger, happiness, and sadness (see Figure 3.14). They then showed photographs of each expression to individuals in many different cultures—including members of a preliterate tribe in the highlands of New Guinea who had little previous contact with other cultures—and found that people in every culture

FIGURE 3.14 *Six basic human emotional expressions*
These expressions were produced by a model who was asked to move specific facial muscles in specific ways. As you study each figure, try to describe the positions of the facial features for each expression. For example, surprise can be described as follows: (1) The brows are pulled upward, producing horizontal wrinkles across the forehead; (2) the eyes are opened wide, revealing white above the iris; (3) the lower jaw is dropped; and (4) no tension exists around the mouth.

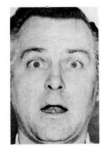

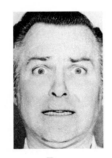
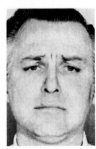

Surprise   **Fear**   **Disgust**   **Anger**   **Happiness**   **Sadness**

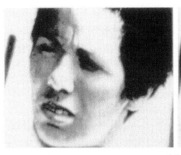

(a)   (b)

FIGURE 3.15 *The eyebrow flash*
This universal signal of greeting is shown in adjacent frames from films of (a) a French woman and (b) a Yanomami man (of the Brazil-Venezuela border).

described each depicted emotion in a way that was consistent with descriptions in the United States (Ekman, 1973; Ekman & others, 1987). In a reversal of this procedure, they also photographed members of the New Guinea tribe who had been asked to act out various emotions and showed the photographs to college students in the United States. The college students were highly accurate in labeling the emotions portrayed by the New Guineans.

In a further extension of Darwin's work, Irenäus Eibl-Eibesfeldt documented the cross-cultural universality of many nonverbal signals, including one that he labeled the ***eyebrow flash***, a momentary raising of the eyebrows lasting about one-sixth of a second, usually accompanied by a smile and an upward nod of the head (see Figure 3.15). He observed this expression in every culture he studied—including those in New Guinea, Samoa, and various parts of Africa, Asia, South America, and Europe—and concluded that it is a universal sign of greeting among friends (Eibl-Eibesfeldt, 1989). Raised eyebrows are also a component of the emotional expression of surprise (look at Figure 3.14 again), so the eyebrow flash with its accompanying smile might be interpreted as a nonverbal way of saying, "What a happy surprise to see you."

Eibl-Eibesfeldt (1975) also filmed children who were born blind, or both blind and deaf, and found that they manifest emotions in the same basic ways as sighted children do (see Figure 3.16). Such observations provide the most direct evidence that at least some human expressions do not have to be learned through observing them in others or hearing descriptions of them.

Taking all the evidence together, there can be little doubt that we are biologically predisposed to express certain emotions in certain species-typical ways. It is also clear, however, that we can control and modify our emotional expressions and

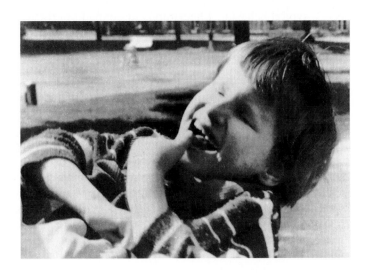

FIGURE 3.16 *Some emotional expressions need not be learned through observation*
This young girl, manifesting joy, has been blind and deaf since birth.

learn new ones. Even researchers who focus on universal expressions are quick to point out cross-cultural differences. For example, Eibl-Eibesfeldt (1975) found that despite its cross-cultural similarity in form and general meaning, large cultural differences exist in the use of the eyebrow flash. The Japanese, who are reserved in social expressions among adults, use it mainly when greeting young children, whereas Samoans, at the other extreme, greet nearly everyone in this way.

Biological Preparedness as the Basis for Species-Typical Behaviors

Fixed action pattern and *sign stimulus* seem to be appropriate terms for describing the species-typical behaviors that ethologists first studied in fish and insects. In mammals, however, species-typical behaviors are more flexible in form and less tightly controlled by particular stimuli than is implied by those terms. That is true of the human emotional expressions we just examined, and it is even more true of other species-typical human behaviors. A scientist from outer space making a study of earthly life would almost certainly point to two-legged walking and use of a grammar-based language as being among the species-typical behaviors of humans, but these are neither rigid in form nor tightly controlled by stimuli, and they obviously involve a great deal of learning. At the same time, it is clear that humans are biologically predisposed to engage in these behaviors.

Evolution has provided humans with anatomical features—such as strong hindlimbs with feet, weaker forelimbs without feet, an upwardly tilted pelvis, and a short, stiff neck—that combine to make it more convenient for us to walk upright than on all fours. Moreover, we are born with neural systems in the brain and spinal cord that enable us to move our legs and other body parts correctly for coordinated two-legged walking and with neural structures that help motivate this behavior at the appropriate stage of our development. Consider the difference between two-legged walking in humans and in dogs. Dogs are capable of learning to walk on two legs, and much is made of that fact by circus trainers, but they are never very good at it. They do not have the appropriate muscular and skeletal systems to coordinate the behavior properly, and they have no natural impulse to walk in this manner. A dog, unlike a human child, will practice two-legged walking only if it receives immediate rewards, such as food, for doing so. Thus two-legged walking is not a species-typical behavior in dogs.

The same is true for talking. Humans are born with anatomical structures, including a tongue and larynx, that can produce a wide range of sounds and with a brain that has special neural centers for understanding and producing language (discussed in Chapter 5). Infants begin talking at a certain stage even if they receive little outside inducement (discussed in Chapter 11). Of course, to acquire a language, a child must hear others use it and have others around with whom to speak it. But the fact that learning is involved does not negate the point that talking is a species-typical behavior. The natural environment of the human being, the one in which we have been evolving for millions of years, is one in which children are surrounded by adults who communicate through spoken language. Chimpanzees can be taught to simulate some aspects of human language, just as dogs can be taught to walk on their hind legs, but they are never very good at it.

Having characterized the concept of species-typical behavior in terms of biological preparedness, I must now add that the concept is relative rather than absolute. No behavior stems just from biological preparation; some sort of experience with the environment is always involved. Conversely, any behavior that an animal can produce—no matter how artificial it may seem or how much training is required—must make use of the animal's inherited biological capacities. The concept of species-typical behavior is useful as long as we accept it as relative and do not argue about whether one or another behavior really should or should not be called species-typical. *Big* and *little* are useful words in our vocabulary, but there is no

24.

Why are species-typical behaviors in mammals better characterized in terms of biological preparedness than as fixed action patterns, and how is such preparedness evident for two-legged walking and language in humans?

25.

Why is the concept of species-typical behavior relative rather than absolute?

point in arguing about whether a bread box is properly called one or the other. Two-legged walking is more species-typical for humans than for dogs, as a bread box is bigger than a matchbook.

The question to ask when we study a particular behavior is not, Is this a species-typical behavior? Rather, the meaningful questions are these: What are the environmental conditions needed for the full development of this behavior? What internal mechanisms are involved in producing it? What is its function in the individual's daily life? In the course of evolution, why would the genes that make this behavior possible have been favored by natural selection? These questions can in principle be asked of any behavior, whether it is thought of as species-typical or not.

Development of Species-Typical Behaviors: The Role of the Environment

After identifying species-typical behaviors, ethologists were curious to learn about their development in the individual animal. What aspects of the animal's natural environment are needed for a behavior to develop in its normal, species-typical form? To answer this kind of question, they devised ***deprivation experiments***, in which young animals were not exposed to selected aspects of their normal environment.

For some behaviors, such as fighting in rats, such experiments have shown that the species-typical movement patterns can develop quite normally even in animals that had no opportunity to observe them in others (see Figure 3.17). In other cases, deprivation experiments have helped pinpoint experiences that are necessary for a species-typical behavior to develop. For example, Peter Marler (1970) found that white-crowned sparrows develop the ability to sing their species-typical song only if they are permitted to hear it during their first summer after hatching. Indeed, populations of the species living in different areas have somewhat different dialects, and a white-crowned sparrow learns to sing the dialect of the adult that it hears. Yet the range of possible songs that the birds can learn is limited. No matter what environmental experiences it has, a white-crowned sparrow cannot learn to sing like a canary or like any species other than a white-crowned sparrow. In Chapter 4, you will encounter other examples of species-typical behaviors that require specific learning experiences to develop normally.

26.

What is the purpose of deprivation experiments, and how is that purpose illustrated in studies of fighting in rats and singing in white-crowned sparrows?

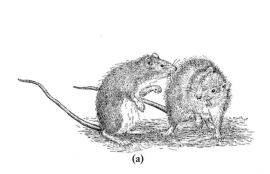  

(a)   (b)   (c)

FIGURE **3.17** *Species-typical fighting postures in rats*
When aggressive rats meet, they first (a) circle each other with arched backs and then (b) rise into a boxinglike position and (c) push each other with their paws. Deprivation experiments show that rats fight in this way even if raised in isolation from other rats, with no opportunity to observe the behavior.
(From Eibl-Eibesfeldt, 1961.)

Tracing the Evolution of Species-Typical Behaviors

Scientists interested in the evolution of anatomical traits, especially bones, can compare fossils of different ages. But behavior does not fossilize (except occasionally in remnants such as footprints or, for humans, in products of behavior such as tools). How can ethologists make reasonable inferences about the evolutionary pathway of species-typical behaviors? The answer, as pointed out by Darwin and pursued by ethologists, is through the systematic comparison of behaviors in present-day species.

Two Forms of Cross-Species Comparisons: Homologies and Analogies

27.

How can researchers determine whether a behavioral similarity between two species is a homology or an analogy?

To understand the logic of comparing present-day species to infer an evolutionary pathway, we must distinguish between two conceptually different classes of similarities among species: homologies and analogies. A **homology** is any similarity that exists because of different species' common ancestry. All animals originated from a common ancestor, so it is not surprising that some homologies—such as those in the basic structure of DNA molecules and of certain enzymes—can be found between any two species. But the more closely related two species are, the more homologies they will show. An **analogy**, in contrast, is any similarity that stems not from common ancestry but from *convergent evolution*. Convergent evolution occurs when different species, because of some similarity in their habitats or lifestyles, independently evolve a common characteristic.

As an illustration, consider some comparisons among species that can fly. Flying has arisen separately in three taxonomic groups: birds, some insects (such as butterflies), and some mammals (bats). Similarities across these three groups in their flying motions, and in the anatomical structures that permit flight, are examples of analogies because they do not result from common ancestry (see Figure 3.18). However, similarities in flight and wings among species within any of these groups, such as between crows and sparrows, are likely to be homologies.

Aside from evidence based on knowledge about the relatedness of the species being compared, analogies and homologies can often be distinguished by the nature of the observed similarity (Lorenz, 1974). Analogies entail similarity in function and gross form, but not in detail and underlying mechanism. Thus the wings of birds, bats, and butterflies are similar at the functional and gross anatomical level in that they provide broad, flappable surfaces that enable flight; but they are very different from one another in the details of their construction and in the neural and muscular mechanisms that control them. In contrast, because homologies arise from shared genes, they entail similarities in their underlying construction and physiological mechanisms, even when, because of divergent evolution, large differences have emerged in gross form or function (for example, see Figure 3.19).

FIGURE **3.18**
Analogous wings
Similarities in the wings and flying behavior of birds, bats, and butterflies are considered to be analogies, not homologies, because they arose independently in evolution.

Joe McDonald / Earth Scenes / Animals, Animals

M. Tuttle / Photo Researchers

James Carmich / Bruce Coleman

Whale flipper   Human arm   Bear leg

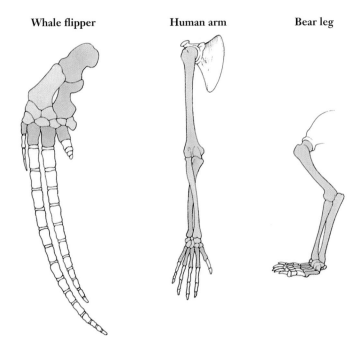

FIGURE **3.19** *Homologous forelimbs* Similarities in the forelimbs of different species of mammals are considered to be homologies because they arose from common ancestry. Although the limbs of the whale, human, and bear differ in function and gross structure, they are similar in certain structural details, as is characteristic of homologies. Behaviors, too, can be homologous, and a key to their homology is similarity in mechanism and detail, even when function differs. (Adapted from Lorenz, 1974.)

Analogies are useful as clues in understanding the evolutionary function of species-typical behaviors (as you will see later), but only homologies are useful in inferring the actual pathways along which they evolved. The pioneer in the use of this method was Darwin himself, so it seems most fitting to illustrate it by describing one of Darwin's studies, taken from his chapter on instinct in *The Origin of Species*.

Darwin's Study of Hive Building in Bees

Have you ever examined the hive that honeybees make? It is a marvelous piece of work, which the bees build with wax secreted from special glands in their bodies. Each comb in the hive consists of a double layer of thin-walled, hexagonally shaped cells, with their bases beveled to enable the two layers of cells to fit perfectly together (see Figure 3.20a). Mathematicians in Darwin's time had shown that this design is the most efficient possible, allowing for the storage of the greatest amount of honey and larvae with the least use of wax. The cells' exquisite design and apparent difficulty of fabrication had been used as evidence that a divine and unfathomable intelligence lay behind their construction. Darwin knew that for his theory of evolution to be accepted, he would have to show how such a marvelous behavior as building combs of hexagonal cells, accomplished by such a simple animal as the bee, could have come about through natural selection.

FIGURE **3.20**
Cells built by honeybees and bumblebees
The hexagonal cells of the honeybee's hive (a) are the optimal shape for storing large amounts of honey and larvae using the least amount of wax. Darwin suggested that ancestors of modern honeybees built their hives in a way similar to that of modern bumblebees (b) but, through evolution, began placing their cells closer together and patching up the points of intersection, resulting eventually in the kind of hive honeybees build today.

M. A. Chappell / Animals, Animals

(a)

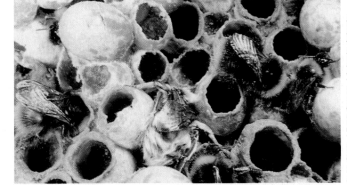

D. M. Shale / Earth Scenes / Animals, Animals

(b)

28.

How did Darwin use comparison by homology to infer the evolutionary steps through which honeybees acquired their hive-making ability?

Darwin (1859/1963) began his study of the honeybee's hive building by surveying the storage structures built by other living bee species. He discovered that the structures could be arranged in a series from very simple to complex. The simplest, produced by bumblebees, consisted of small clusters of spherical cells (see Figure 3.20b). Darwin noted that spherical cells are easy to construct and that insects commonly build them by sweeping their bodies compasslike around a fixed point. Another species of bee, *Melipona domestica*, which is anatomically more similar to the honeybee than is the bumblebee, builds much larger clusters of spherical cells that are more closely compacted than those of the bumblebee. Darwin found that this species constructs its cells in essentially the same way as the bumblebee, but closer together, patching up intersecting cells with flat walls. This insight provided the key to explaining the honeybee's hive-building ability.

Darwin reasoned that if a group of honeybees began building spherical cells a certain distance apart (which they could do by using their own bodies as a measure) and then patched up the points of intersection between adjacent cells with flat walls, doing this in two layers, they would produce precisely the structures found in the honeybee hive. They would not have to calculate the sizes of the planes and angles of hexagonal prisms in order to build them but would simply have to add another, not terribly complex step (that of building the cells equal distances apart) to the behaviors already present in the *Melipona* bees. Subsequently, Darwin developed a method for observing honeybees directly as they built their combs, and he confirmed that this indeed was how they worked.

On the basis of his comparisons of different bee species, Darwin proposed that the early ancestors of honeybees built spherical cells, as do present-day bumblebees, but that some aspect of their environmental niche made efficient storage vessels more valuable to them than to bumblebees. Through natural selection, they gradually came to position their cells closer together, sharing more walls, until they arrived at the "perfect" form of the present-day comb. Each small step in this process would represent a selective advantage to the bees, allowing for the construction of more cells (to store more honey and house more larvae) with less expenditure of precious wax.

Evolution of Two Kinds of Human Smiles

Darwin also used homologies to understand species-typical behaviors in humans. At the London Zoo, he watched monkeys and apes and noted that a number of their expressions seem to be homologous to human expressions, including the smile (Darwin, 1872/1965). Research following up on Darwin's work has suggested that people may produce two kinds of smiles, which may have separate evolutionary origins.

People smile in two quite different contexts: (1) when genuinely happy and (2) when wishing to show another person that they are favorably disposed toward that person. The latter situation need not entail happiness at all; in fact, people are especially likely to smile at others in potentially tense circumstances, apparently as a means of reducing the tension (Goldenthal & others, 1981). Darwin (1872/1965) himself pointed out that these two smiles are anatomically distinct. The *happy smile* involves not just the turning up of the corners of the lips but also the pulling in of the skin near the outside corners of the eyes. This creates the creases called crow's feet, which radiate from the eyes and seem to make them sparkle. The other smile, in contrast, typically involves the lips alone, without the eyes. This distinction has been confirmed in many studies with both adults and young children (Ekman, 1992). In one study, for example, 10-month-old infants smiled with eyes and mouth when approached by their mother (presumably a happy situation) but smiled with mouth alone when approached by a stranger (a possibly tense situation) (Fox & Davidson, 1988).

Ekman (1992) considers the mouth-alone smile to be a derivative of the happy smile. He emphasizes its use in masking one's true feelings and calls it a "false smile." An alternative possibility, supported by research with monkeys and apes, is that the mouth-alone smile is a unique expression—let's call it the *greeting smile*—that arrived through a different evolutionary route from the happy smile (Redican, 1982; van Hooff, 1976).

Nonhuman primates manifest two distinct smilelike displays. The one that seems most clearly to be homologous to the human greeting smile is the *silent bared-teeth display* (see Figure 3.21a). If you have ever watched a cage of macaque monkeys at a zoo, you have almost certainly observed this display, a grimace usually shown by the more submissive of two monkeys as it glances nervously toward the more dominant. A direct stare in macaques (and other primates) is an aggressive signal, which precedes attack and can precipitate an attack by the other, and the silent bared-teeth display seems to have evolved as a means for a more submissive monkey to look at a more dominant one without provoking a fight. If it could be translated into words, it might be rendered as, "I'm looking at you but I'm not going to attack, so please don't attack me." In some monkey species, it is also used to promote affiliation after an aggressive encounter (Preuschoft & van Hooff, 1997).

J. A. van Hooff (1972, 1976) found that among chimpanzees this display takes on a new function, more similar to that of the human smile of greeting. *Both* the more submissive and the more dominant of two chimpanzees show the display upon meeting, and it usually precedes friendly interaction between them. From such observations, van Hooff proposed that the silent bared-teeth display originated in monkeys as a submissive gesture, but in the evolutionary line leading to chimpanzees and humans it evolved further into a general form of greeting. As used by the more submissive individual, it may retain its original meaning, "Please don't attack me," but as used by the more dominant, it may mean, "Rest assured, I won't attack," and as used by both it may mean, "Let's be friends."

The other primate smilelike expression is the *relaxed open-mouth display* (see Figure 3.21b), which occurs mostly in young primates during playful fighting and chasing and may be homologous to both laughter and the happy smile in humans. In chimpanzees, it is often accompanied by a vocalized *ahh ahh ahh*, which sounds like a throaty human laugh. Van Hooff believes that this display originated as a means for young primates to signal to each other that their aggressivelike behavior is not to be taken seriously; nobody will really get hurt. Interestingly, in human children, laughter occurs during playful fighting and chasing more reliably than during any other form of play (Blurton-Jones, 1967), and even among us "sophisticated" adults, pie throwing, chase scenes, mock insults, and other forms of fake aggression are among the most reliable ways to elicit laughter. Thus our laughter not only is similar in form to the relaxed open-mouth display of other primates but, at least in some cases, seems to serve a similar function. The laughing smile is similar in form to the nonlaughing

29.

How do studies of monkeys and apes support the view that the human greeting smile and happy smile have separate evolutionary origins?

(a)

(b)

FIGURE **3.21** *Possible homologues to the human smile of greeting and the human laugh and smile of happiness*
The silent bared-teeth display (a) is believed to be homologous to the human greeting smile, and the relaxed open-mouth display (b) is believed to be homologous to the human laugh and happy smile. The animals in both photos are chimpanzees.

Tim Davis / Animals, Animals

Norman Tomalin / Bruce Coleman

happy smile, so the latter, too, may have its roots in the relaxed open-mouth display (Redican, 1982). There is, it seems to me, some poetry in the thought that the smile of happiness may have originated from a signal indicating that, although the world can be frightening and full of conflict, the aggression going on now is just in fun and we are safe.

Vestigial Characteristics

Some species-typical behaviors do not make sense as adaptations to the current environment but do make sense as adaptations to conditions present at an earlier time. These behavioral remnants of the past are called ***vestigial characteristics***, and they can often be understood through homologies. An example is the *grasp reflex*, by which newborn human infants close their fingers tightly around objects placed in their hands. This reflex may well be useful in the development of the infant's ability to hold and manipulate objects, but that does not explain why prematurely born infants grasp so strongly that they can support their own weight, why they grasp with their toes as well as their hands (see Figure 3.22), and why the best stimulus for eliciting the response is a clump of hair (Eibl-Eibesfeldt, 1975). These aspects of the reflex make more sense when we observe the homologous behavior in other primates. To survive, infant monkeys and apes cling tightly with hands and feet to their mother's fur while she swings in trees or goes about her other daily business. In the course of our evolution from apelike ancestors, we lost our fur, so our infants can no longer cling to us in this way, but the grasp reflex remains.

30.

How can comparison by homology be used to infer the original functions of behaviors that are now vestigial?

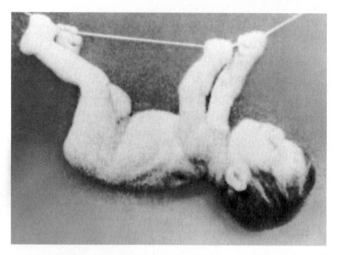

FIGURE 3.22 *Premature infant clinging with hands and toes*
This ability may be a vestigial carryover from an earlier evolutionary time, when the infants of our ancestors clung to their parents' fur.

The concept of vestigial traits becomes especially relevant to psychologists when applied to our inherited drives, or motives. Because of culture, our habitat and lifestyle have changed dramatically in just a few centuries, a speck on the evolutionary time scale. The great bulk of our evolution occurred in conditions that were quite different from those present today, and some of our inherited tendencies may be harmful in the habitat that some of us occupy. An example is our great appetite for sugar. In the world of our ancestors, sugar was a rare and valuable commodity. It existed primarily in fruits and provided energy needed for life in the wild, as we can see by looking at the diets of present-day monkeys and apes. But today, at least in our culture, sugar is readily available, and life (for many of us) is less physically strenuous. Yet our preference for sugar persists as strong as ever, despite such negative consequences as tooth decay and obesity.

SECTION SUMMARY

The early ethologists, who focused mostly on nonmammals, described species-typical behaviors in terms of fixed action patterns and sign stimuli, as exemplified by Tinbergen's work on aggression in stickleback fish. Facial expressions of emotion are a well-studied category of human species-typical behaviors. The same basic expressions occur across cultures and even in people born blind and deaf. In humans and mammals generally, species-typical behaviors are better described in terms of the degree to which they are biologically prepared than as fixed action patterns. Through deprivation experiments, researchers have identified the environmental conditions required for particular species-typical behaviors to develop normally.

Similarities in the species-typical behaviors of different species may be homologies (derived from common ancestry) or analogies (derived from convergent evolution). In his study of hive building in bees, Darwin showed how homologies among living species can be used to reconstruct the stages through which a complex behavior may have evolved. Similarly, studies of homologous smilelike displays in primates have shed light on the evolution of the human greeting smile and happy smile. Homologies can also inform us of the original functions of vestigial characteristics.

SOCIOBIOLOGY: THE COMPARATIVE STUDY OF ANIMALS' SOCIAL SYSTEMS

An animal alone is in some ways not a complete animal. That is certainly true of the highly social species, from honeybees to humans. A bee without other bees cannot build a hive or tend a queen. A human without other humans cannot build a village or exchange ideas. Recognizing the close interdependence of animals with others of their kind, many ethologists and other animal behaviorists have concentrated on the study of social systems in animals, a study called *sociobiology*.

As a school of thought, sociobiology arose partly from ethology, but it took a somewhat different direction. While ethologists typically focus on the specific movement patterns involved in species-typical behaviors, sociobiologists focus more often on the ultimate functions of such behaviors. Not surprisingly, sociobiologists have paid most attention to patterns of mating, aggression, and cooperation—patterns that are central to the functioning of social groups and are quite clearly related to the individual's goal of survival and reproduction. Why do some animal species bond as male–female pairs for extended periods, while others don't? Why do some spread themselves out over the available territory, while others live in concentrated groups? Why do animals sometimes compete with, and at other times help, one another in their struggle for survival? These are the kinds of questions that sociobiologists address.

A standard method in sociobiology is comparison by analogy. If different species have independently evolved a particular social pattern, then comparing the species may reveal commonalities of habitat and lifestyle that are clues to the ultimate function of that pattern. Here we will examine some sociobiological theories about the conditions of life that promote particular patterns of mating, aggression, and cooperation.

Patterns of Mating in Relation to Parental Investment

From an evolutionary perspective, sex is the prime reason for society. Were it not necessary for female and male to come together to reproduce, members of a species could, in theory, go through life completely oblivious to one another.

Countless varieties of male–female arrangements for sexual reproduction have evolved in different species of animals. One way to classify them is according to the number of partners a male or female mates with over a given period of time, such as a breeding season. Four broad classes are generally recognized: *polygyny*, in which one male mates with more than one female; *polyandry*, in which one female mates with more than one male; *monogamy*, in which one male mates with one female; and *polygynandry*, in which members of a group consisting of more than one male and more than one female mate with one another (Rees & Harvey, 1991). (These terms are easy to remember if you know that *poly-* means "many"; *mono-*, "one"; *-gyn*, "female"; and *-andr*, "male." Thus, for example, *polygynandry* literally means "many females and males.") As illustrated in Figure 3.23, a feature of both polygyny and polyandry is that some individuals are necessarily deprived of a mating opportunity—a state of affairs associated with considerable conflict. Why have different species evolved these different mating systems, and how do the mating systems affect other aspects of the animals' lives?

FIGURE **3.23** *Four mating systems*
In a polygynous system (common in mammals), the unmated males are a threat to the mated male, and in a polyandrous system (present in some birds and fishes), the unmated females are a threat to the mated female. Threat is reduced by monogamy and polygynandry, because with those systems, most individuals find mates.

31.

What sorts of questions do sociobiologists ask, and how do they use comparison by analogy to help answer them?

Polygyny

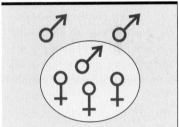

Polyandry

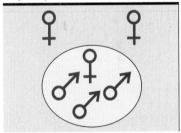

Monogamy

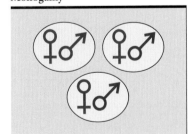

Polygynandry

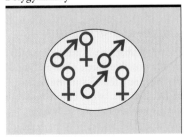

In one of the most frequently quoted papers in sociobiology, Robert Trivers (1972) outlined a theory relating courtship and mating patterns to sex differences in **parental investment**. Parental investment can be defined roughly as the time, energy, and risk to survival that are involved in producing, feeding, and otherwise caring for each offspring. More precisely, Trivers defined it as the loss, to the adult, of future reproductive capacity that results from the production and nurturance of any given offspring. Every offspring in a sexually reproducing species has two parents, one of each sex, but the amount of parental investment from the two is usually not equal. The essence of Trivers's theory is this: *In general, for species in which parental investment is unequal, the more parentally invested sex will be (a) more vigorously competed for than the other and (b) more discriminating than the other when choosing mates.* To illustrate and elaborate on this theory, let us apply it, as many sociobiologists have (for example, Davies, 1991), to evolutionary thinking about the four classes of mating systems.

Polygyny Is Related to High Female and Low Male Parental Investment

Most species of mammals are polygynous, and Trivers's theory helps explain why. Mammalian reproductive physiology is such that the female necessarily invests a great deal in the offspring she bears. The young must first develop within her body and then must obtain nourishment from her in the form of milk. Because of the female's high investment, the number of offspring she can produce in a breeding season or a lifetime is limited. A female whose gestation and lactation periods are such that she can bear at most four young a year can produce no more than that regardless of the number of different males with which she mates.

Things are different for the male. His involvement with offspring is, at minimum, simply the production of sperm cells and the act of copulation. These require little time and energy, so his maximum reproductive potential is limited not by parental investment but by the number of fertile females with which he mates. A male that mates with 20 females, each of which can bear 4 young, can in theory produce 80 offspring a year. When a greater evolutionary advantage accrues to the male for multiple matings than to the female, a pattern evolves in which males compete with one another to mate with as many females as they can.

Among mammals, competition among males for females often involves one-on-one battles, which the larger and stronger combatant most often wins. This

32.

Based on Trivers's theory of parental investment, why does high investment by the female lead to (a) polygyny, (b) large size of males, and (c) high selectivity in the female's choice of mate?

Who's bigger and stronger?
These male elephant seals are sizing each other up for possible battle over mating rights to the many females in the background. Because the larger combatant usually wins, male elephant seals have through natural selection become huge compared with females.

Ben Osborne / Earth Scenes / Animals, Animals

leads to a selective advantage for increased size and strength in males, up to some maximum beyond which the size advantage in obtaining mates is outweighed by disadvantages, such as difficulty in finding sufficient food to support the large size. In general, the more polygynous a species, the greater is the average size difference between males and females. An extreme example is the elephant seal. Males of this species fight one another, sometimes to the death, for mating rights to groups averaging about 50 females, and the males outweigh females severalfold (Hoelzel & others, 1999). In the evolution of elephant seals, those males whose genes made them large, strong, and ferocious enough to defeat other males sent many copies of their genes on to the next generation, while their weaker opponents sent few or none.

For the same reason that the female mammal usually has less evolutionary incentive than the male to mate with many individuals, she has more incentive to be discriminating in her choice of mate (Trivers, 1972). Because she invests so much, risking her life and decreasing her future reproductive potential whenever she becomes pregnant, her interests lie in producing offspring that will have the highest possible chance themselves to survive and reproduce. To the degree that the male affects the young, either through his genes or through other resources he provides, females would be expected to select males whose contribution will be most beneficial. In elephant seals, it is presumably to the female's evolutionary advantage to mate with the winner of battles. The male victor's genes increase the chance that the female's sons will win battles in the future and produce many young themselves.

Polyandry Is Related to High Male and Low Female Parental Investment

Polyandry is not the primary mating pattern for any species of mammal, but it is for some species of fishes and birds (Clutton-Brock & Vincent, 1991; Erckmann, 1983). Polyandry is more likely to evolve in egg-laying species than in mammals, because a smaller proportion of an egg layer's reproductive cycle is tied to the female's body. Once the eggs are laid, they can be cared for by either parent, and, depending on other conditions, evolution can lead to greater male than female parental investment.

Consistent with Trivers's theory, females of polyandrous species are the more active and aggressive courters, and they have evolved to be larger, stronger, and in some cases more brightly colored than the males. An example is the spotted sandpiper, a common freshwater shorebird. A female spotted sandpiper can lay up to three clutches of eggs in rapid succession, each cared for by a different male that has mated with her (Oring, 1995). At the beginning of the breeding season, the females—which outweigh the males by about 20 percent and have somewhat more conspicuous spots—stake out territories where they actively court males and drive out other females.

Monogamy Is Related to Equivalent Male and Female Parental Investment

According to Trivers's theory, when the two sexes invest approximately equally in their young, their degree of competition for mates will also be approximately equal and monogamy will prevail. Equal parental investment is most likely to come about when conditions make it impossible for a single adult to raise the young but quite possible for two to raise them (Dewsbury, 1988). Under these circumstances, if either parent leaves, the young fail to survive, so natural selection favors genes that lead parents to stay together and care for the young together. Because neither sex is much more likely than the other to fight over mates, there is little or no natural selection for sex differences in size and strength, and, in general, males and females of monogamous species are nearly identical in these characteristics.

An aggressive female

The spotted sandpiper is a polyandrous species. The female mates with several males and defends her territory from invading females. This female is stretching her wings in a threat display.

33.

What conditions promote the evolution of polyandry, and how do sex differences within polyandrous species support Trivers's theory?

34.

What conditions promote the evolution of monogamy, and why are sex differences in size and aggressiveness generally lacking in monogamous species?

Consistent with the view that monogamy arises from the need for more than one adult to care for offspring, over 90 percent of bird species are predominantly monogamous (Lack, 1968) compared with only about 3 percent of mammals (Kleiman, 1977). Among most species of birds, unlike most mammals, a single parent would usually not be able to raise the young. Birds must incubate and protect their eggs until they hatch and then must guard the hatchlings and fetch food for them until they can fly. One parent alone cannot simultaneously guard the nest and leave it to get food, but two together can. Among mammals, monogamy has arisen in some species that are like birds in the sense that their young must be given food other than milk, of a type that the male is capable of providing. The best-known examples are certain carnivores, including foxes and coyotes (Malcolm, 1985). Young carnivores must be fed meat until they have acquired the necessary strength, agility, and skills to hunt on their own, and two parents are much better than one at accomplishing this task. Monogamy also occurs in several species of rodents, where the male may play a crucial role in protecting the young from predators while the mother forages (Sommer, 2000).

With modern DNA techniques to determine paternity, researchers have learned that *social monogamy* (the faithful pairing of female and male for raising young) does not necessarily imply *sexual monogamy* (fidelity in copulation between that female and male). Researchers commonly find that between 5 and 35 percent of offspring in socially monogamous birds are sired by a neighboring male rather than by the male at the nest (Birkhead & Moller, 1992), and for one species, the superb fairy wren, that average is 75 percent (Mulder, 1994). Why does such extra-mate copulation occur? From the female's evolutionary perspective, copulation

35.

For what evolutionary reasons might monogamously mated females and males sometimes copulate with partners other than their mate?

A not-so-faithful couple

The superb fairy wren is socially but not sexually monogamous. The male (at the left) and the female stay together at the nest and raise the young together, but DNA testing has shown that about 75 percent of the offspring, on average, are sired by a neighboring male.

with a male that is genetically superior to her own mate (as manifested in song and feathers) results in genetically superior young, and extra-mate copulation with any male increases the chance that all her eggs will be fertilized (Ketterson & Van Nolan, 1994). For the male, evolutionary advantage rests in driving neighboring males away from his own mate whenever possible and in copulating with neighboring females whenever possible. Genes that build brain mechanisms that promote such behaviors are passed along to more offspring than genes that do not.

Polygynandry Is Related to Investment in the Group

36.

What appear to be the evolutionary advantages of polygynandry for chimpanzees and bonobos, and in what ways is it more fully developed for the latter than the former?

Among the clearest examples of polygynandrous species are chimpanzees and bonobos, which happen to be our two closest animal relatives (see Figure 3.24). *Bonobos* are similar in appearance to chimpanzees but are rarer and have only recently been studied in the wild. The basic social structure of both species is the

Frans Lanting / Minden Pictures

Bonobo sex

Bonobos seem to live by the motto, "Make love, not war." Research suggests that they are the most sexually active and the most peaceful of all primates. Here a male has mounted a female in a face-to-face position—a position long thought to be unique to humans. But bonobo sex occurs in all possible partner combinations (homosexual as well as heterosexual) and essentially all imaginable positions.

colony, which consists usually of two or three dozen adult males and females and their offspring. When the female is ovulating, she develops on her rump a prominent pink swelling, which she actively displays to advertise her condition. During the time of this swelling, which lasts about a week in chimps and 3 weeks in bonobos, she is likely to mate with most of the adult males of the colony (Goodall, 1986; Kano, 1992).

Polygynandry has apparently evolved in these ape species because it permits the adult males and females to live together in relative harmony, without too much fighting over who mates with whom. A specific related advantage, especially from the female's evolutionary perspective, is *paternity confusion* (Hrdy, 1981, 1997; Wrangham, 1993). Among many species of primates, males kill young that are not their own, and such behavior has been observed in chimpanzees when a female migrates into a colony bringing with her an infant that was sired elsewhere (Wrangham, 1993). Because almost any chimp or bonobo male in the colony could be the father of any infant born within the colony, each male's evolutionary interest lies not in attacking the young but in helping to protect and care for the group as a whole.

Polygynandry seems to be more fully developed in bonobos than in chimps. Male chimps do fight with one another over females that are at peak fertility, and sometimes a single male manages to monopolize the sexual activity of a female throughout her ovulatory cycle (Goodall, 1986; Wrangham, 1993). In contrast, bonobo males rarely compete physically to copulate (Wrangham, 1993). In fact, for bonobos sex appears to be more a reducer of aggression than the cause of it. Unlike any other apes, female bonobos copulate at all times of their reproductive cycle, not just near the time of ovulation (Wrangham, 1993). In addition to their frequent heterosexual activity, bonobos of the same sex often rub their genitals together, and genital stimulation of all types occurs most often following conflict and in situations that could potentially elicit conflict, such as when a favorite food is discovered (Hohmann & Fruth, 2000; Parish, 1996). Field studies suggest that bonobos are the most peaceful of primates and that their frequent, polygynandrous sexual activity helps keep them that way (Kano, 1992).

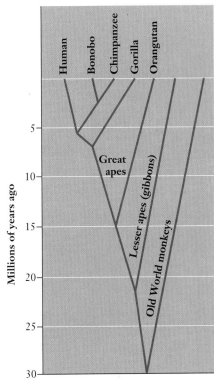

FIGURE **3.24**
Relationship of humans to apes and Old World monkeys
The ancestral line leading to humans split off from that leading to Old World monkeys 30 million years ago, and it split off from that leading to bonobos and chimpanzees 5.6 million years ago. (Data from Corballis, 1999.)

Patterns of Aggression

Aggression, as the term is used by ethologists and sociobiologists, refers to fighting and threats of fighting among members of the same species. Physiological mechanisms that motivate and organize such behavior have presumably evolved because they help animals acquire and retain resources needed to survive and reproduce. As already discussed, much animal aggression centers on mating. Polygynous males and polyandrous females fight for mates; monogamous males fight to prevent other males from copulating with their mate; and monogamous females fight to keep other females from leading their mate away (Slagsvold & others, 1999; Tobias & Seddon, 2000). Aggression can also serve to protect a feeding ground for oneself and one's offspring, to drive away individuals that may be a threat to one's young, and to elevate one's status within a colony. Here we will look briefly at two broad classes of aggressive behavior: territorial aggression and within-group aggression related to dominance.

Territorial Aggression

Animals of many species establish home territories, either permanently or for the duration of a breeding season, that they defend from others of their kind. Monogamous birds and mammals guard the territory around their nest or den partly to keep away potential sexual competitors but also to preserve a feeding ground for themselves and their young. Animals that live in large groups—including wolves, macaque monkeys, and chimpanzees—often defend large feeding ranges, sometimes many square miles in size, from invasion by other groups of their species. At times of food shortage or overpopulation, territorial battles can be bloody. But at other times, life-threatening battles are avoided by a combination of territorial signaling, through which residents warn others not to enter, and a tendency to respect one another's signals and stay out of occupied territories.

Methods of territorial signaling vary from species to species. Such diverse groups as birds, crickets, and alligators loudly announce by song that they are home and defending their area. Territorial troops of monkeys warn off other approaching troops by running up into trees and noisily shaking the branches. Certain other mammals mark their territories with odor trails deposited either in their urine (as in the case of bears and wolves) or from special scent glands (as in the case of badgers and rabbits). When you walk your male dog and observe him urinating on every lamppost and fire hydrant in the neighborhood, you are observing a vestige of the territorial-marking behavior of his wolf ancestors.

In some species, prolonged fights are also avoided through a tendency for individuals that find themselves in another's territory to become less aggressive and more inclined to flee than they would be in their own territory. When fights do occur, the territory owner fights more viciously than the intruder and usually succeeds in driving the intruder out, even if the intruder is the larger of the two. As an example, Lorenz (1966) described the behavior of two cichlid fish in a tank. When first placed in the tank, fish A, the bigger of the two, drove fish B into a tiny corner near the surface (the most dangerous place for fish to live in nature, where predatory birds can attack them) and forced it to stay there for several days. Gradually, however, B expanded its territory until it occupied approximately half the tank. After that, the two fish coexisted peacefully, fighting only when one by chance swam over the boundary into the territory of the other. When A swam into B's territory, B would drive A out; when B swam into A's territory, A would drive B out. This example is typical of much (although not all) animal territorial aggression: The defender wins, the invader retreats, and no blood is spilled in the process.

Within-Group Aggression and Dominance

Animals that live in large groups may appear to get along peacefully, but closer examination usually reveals much within-group bickering. They squabble over such

37.

How do territorial signaling and the home-court advantage help reduce bloodshed in territorial animals?

resources as food, mates, and the best location in the group (the center is usually preferred because it offers the most protection from predators). When group members fight, they must have a means of terminating the fight other than one in which the loser flees to another territory. The loser's interest lies in remaining in the group, and the winner's interest lies in allowing the loser to remain (otherwise, there would be no group, with its attendant advantages to each individual). To permit fights to terminate without the loser's running far away, a variety of submissive signals have evolved that allow one animal to signal to another that it has lost and will no longer challenge the victor. The silent bared-teeth display, which you already read about, is used by some primates for this function as well as to avoid future fights (Preuschoft & van Hooff, 1997). In some mammals, the exaggerated exposure of a vulnerable body part signals submission (see Figure 3.25).

Another great aid in reducing fighting within a colony is memory. Animals recognize other colony members and remember the results of their previous aggressive encounters. If A has beaten B in a fight, then B will be less inclined to challenge A the next time, and A will have established *dominance* over B. In some species, including barnyard chickens, rather strict *dominance hierarchies* are established, in which the individuals in the group can be ranked from highest to lowest, with each being dominant over those lower in rank and submissive to those higher. In other species, how-

Zig Leszcynski / Earth Scenes / Animals, Animals

ever, dominance hierarchies are not so rigid and are not always based on individual fighting ability. In chimpanzees, cleverness can play a role. Jane Goodall (1988) observed a relatively small male chimp achieve dominance over the entire colony by charging at the other chimps while banging together empty kerosene cans, which he had stolen from Goodall's camp. In other cases, she saw chimps raise their rank by forming coalitions and challenging a more dominant chimp together.

In chimpanzee and bonobo colonies, females have separate dominance hierarchies from those of males, and the female hierarchy helps establish the male hierarchy of the next generation (Goodall, 1986; Kano, 1992). Mother chimps and bonobos commonly aid their sons in aggressive encounters. The more dominant the mother, the more successful she is at providing such support, and through this means she teaches other young males not to attack her sons. The lessons apparently last into adulthood and help the sons of dominant females assume high rank in the male hierarchy. Chimp and bonobo mothers also aid their daughters in aggressive encounters, but this assistance does not have the same lasting effect as help to sons has, because female chimps and bonobos, on reaching adulthood, leave their mother's colony and join a new colony, where they must start from scratch to build their reputation.

Patterns of Helping

Animals of the same species bicker, fight, and sometimes kill one another in their competition for resources, but they also help one another. From an evolutionary perspective, *helping* can be defined as any behavior that increases the survival chance or reproductive capacity of another individual. Given this definition, it is useful to distinguish between two categories of helping: cooperation and altruism.

38.

How do submissive signals and dominance hierarchies help reduce aggression among animals that live in a group?

FIGURE **3.25**
Submissive response in a wolf
Animals that live in groups have evolved signals to terminate or prevent fights so that the loser need not flee and can remain in the group. Here a wolf shows its submissive status by rolling over onto its back in a defenseless posture. Dogs also show submission in this manner.

39.

How can male chimpanzees and bonobos achieve dominance through means other than their own fighting ability?

Cooperation occurs when an individual helps another while helping itself. This sort of helping happens all the time in the animal world. It occurs when a mated pair of foxes work together to raise their young, a pack of wolves work together to kill an antelope, or a troop of macaque monkeys work together to repel a troop invading their territory. Most of the advantages of social living lie in cooperation. By working with others for common ends, each individual has a better chance of survival and reproduction than it would have alone. Whatever costs accrue are more than repaid by the benefits.

Altruism, in contrast, occurs when an individual helps another while *decreasing* its own survival chance or reproductive capacity. Animals do sometimes behave in ways that at least appear to be altruistic. For example, some animals, including female ground squirrels, emit a loud, distinctive call when they spot an approaching predator. The cry warns others of the predator's approach and, at the same time, tends to attract the predator's attention to the caller (Sherman, 1977). (See Figure 3.26.) The selfish response would be to remain quiet and hidden, or sneak off quietly, rather than risk being detected by warning others. How can such behavior be explained from an evolutionary perspective? As Trivers (1971) pointed out, any evolutionary account of apparent altruism must operate by showing that from a broader perspective the behavior is not truly altruistic. Sociobiologists have developed two broad theories to account for ostensible altruism in animals: the kin selection theory and the reciprocity theory.

The **kin selection theory** holds that behavior that seems to be altruistic came about evolutionarily because it is most likely to help close relatives—that is, those that have the same genes (Hamilton, 1964). What actually survives over evolutionary time, of course, is not the individual but the individual's genes. Any gene that promotes the production and preservation of copies of itself can be a fit gene, from the vantage point of natural selection, even if it reduces the survival chances of a particular carrier of the gene.

Imagine a ground squirrel with a rare gene that promotes the behavior of calling out when a predator is near. The mathematics of inheritance are such that, on average, one-half of the offspring or siblings of the individual with this gene would be expected to have the same gene, as would one-fourth of the nieces or nephews and one-eighth of the cousins (look back at Table 3.1). Thus if the altruist incurred a small risk (Δ) to its own life while increasing an offspring's or a sibling's chances of survival by more than 2Δ, a niece's or nephew's by more than 4Δ, or a cousin's by more than 8Δ, the gene would increase in the population from one generation to the next.

Many research studies have shown that animals do help kin more than nonkin. Paul Sherman (1977) found that ground squirrels living with kin are more likely to emit alarm calls than are ground squirrels living with nonkin. Goodall (1986) and Nishida (1990) found that chimpanzees are far more likely to help close kin than nonkin in all sorts of ways. For these and many other examples, helpers can apparently distinguish kin from nonkin and selectively direct help toward the former (Pfennig & Sherman, 1995). In theory, however, altruistic behavior can evolve through kin selection even without such discrimination. A tendency to help any member of one's species, indiscriminately, can evolve if the animal's usual living arrangements are such that, by chance alone, a sufficiently high percentage of help is directed toward kin.

The **reciprocity theory** provides an account of how acts of apparent altruism can arise even when nonkin are helped as often as kin. According to this theory, behaviors that seem to be altruistic are actually forms of long-term cooperation (Trivers, 1971). Computer simulations of evolution have shown that a genetically induced tendency to help nonkin can evolve if it is tempered by (a) an ability to remember which individuals have reciprocated such help in the past and (b) a tendency to refrain from helping again those that failed to reciprocate previous help

40.

How do the kin selection and reciprocity theories take the altruism out of "altruism"?

FIGURE **3.26** *An alarm-calling ground squirrel*
When they spot a predator, female ground squirrels often emit an alarm call, especially if they are living in a group of close kin. Males are less likely to live near close kin and do not show this response.

L. D. Klein / Photo Researchers

(Axelrod, 1984; Nowack & Sigmund, 1992). Under these conditions, helping another is selfish because it increases the chance of receiving help from that other in the future. Behavior fitting this pattern is quite common in the animal world. As one example, vampire bats frequently share food with unrelated members of their species that have shared food with them in the past (Wilkinson, 1988). As another example, bonobo females that establish friendship coalitions—and are known to be unrelated to one another, having immigrated from different natal colonies—reciprocate in such activities as grooming and sharing food (Kano, 1992; Parish, 1996).

Some Sociobiological Thoughts About Humans

Does a sociobiological analysis—of the kind just applied to systems of mating, aggression, and helping in nonhuman animals—shed light on human social interactions? Certainly most sociobiologists think it does, and so do a growing number of other psychologists, some of whom call themselves *evolutionary psychologists*. We are animals; we have an evolutionary history; we have drives, behavioral tendencies, and learning mechanisms that were shaped by natural selection. Still, perhaps mainly because of past political misuses of evolutionary theory, some psychologists are reluctant to think about human behavior in such terms. Let's examine briefly those misuses, before considering some sociobiological ideas about ourselves.

Fallacies to Avoid

Two general errors of logic prevail in the misuses of evolutionary theory. One, called the **naturalistic fallacy**, is the equation of "natural" with "moral" or "right." If male mammals in nature dominate females through force, then aggressive dominance of women by men is right. If natural selection involves self-interested struggle among individuals, then selfishness is right. Such equations are logically indefensible, because nature itself is neither moral nor immoral except as judged so by us. Morality is a product of the human mind. We have acquired, in our evolution, the capacity to think in moral terms, and we can use that ability to develop moral philosophies that go in many possible directions, including those that favor real altruism and constrain individual self-interest for the good of the larger community.

The term *naturalistic fallacy* was coined by the British philosopher G. E. Moore (1903) as part of an argument against the views of another British philosopher, Herbert Spencer. A contemporary of Darwin, Spencer considered himself a strong believer in Darwin's theory, and his goal was to apply it to the sphere of social philosophy and ethics (Spencer, 1879). Unlike Darwin, however, Spencer implicitly thought of natural selection as guided by a moral force. He believed that one could find "more evolved" and "less evolved" behaviors in nature and that "more evolved" meant more moral. Although Spencer discussed cooperation as highly evolved and virtuous, his philosophy leaned more toward the virtues of individualism and competition. Spencer's writings were especially popular in the United States, where they were championed by such industrialists as John D. Rockefeller and Andrew Carnegie (Rachels, 1990). It was Spencer, not Darwin, who popularized the phrase "survival of the fittest," and some of the so-called *social Darwinists*, who were inspired by Spencer, used that phrase to justify even the most ruthless extremes of capitalism. In their view, the fittest were those who rose to the top in unchecked capitalism, and the unfit were those who fell into poverty or starvation.

Darwin himself was not seduced by the naturalistic fallacy. He was repulsed by much of what he saw in nature and marveled at the human ability to rise, sometimes, above it. He conscientiously avoided phrases such as "more evolved" that would imply that evolution is a moral force, and he felt frustrated by his inability to stop others from assuming that it is. In a letter to a friend, shortly after publication of *The Origin of Species*, he wrote wryly, "I have noted in a Manchester newspaper a

41.

Why is the equation of "natural" with "right" considered a fallacy?

42.

Why is it a mistake to believe that characteristics that are influenced by genes cannot be changed except by modifying genes?

rather good squib, showing that I have proved 'might is right' and therefore Napoleon is right and every cheating tradesman is also right" (Rachels, 1990).

The second general error, called the ***deterministic fallacy***, is the assumption or implication that genetic influences on our behavior take the form of genetic control of our behavior, which we can do nothing about (short of modifying our genes). The mistake here is assuming or implying that genes influence behavior directly, rather than through the indirect means of working with the environment to build or modify biological structures that then, in interplay with the environment, produce behavior. Some popular books on human evolution have exhibited the deterministic fallacy by implying that one or another behavior—such as fighting for territories—is unavoidable because it is controlled by our genes. That implication is unreasonable even when applied to nonhuman animals. Territorial birds, for example, defend territories only when the environmental conditions are ripe for them to do so. We humans can control our environment and thereby control ourselves. We can either enhance or reduce the environmental ingredients needed for a particular behavioral tendency to develop and manifest itself.

We also can and regularly do, through conscious self-control and well-learned social habits, behave in ways that are contrary to biases built into our biology. One might even argue that our capacity for self-control is the essence of our humanity. In our evolution, we acquired that capability in a greater dose than seems apparent in any other species, perhaps because of its role in permitting us to live in complex social groups. Our ability for self-control, itself, is part of our biological heritage, and it liberates us to some degree (but by no means completely) from that heritage.

Our great capacity for knowledge, including knowledge of our own biological nature, can also be a liberating force. Many sociobiologists and evolutionary psychologists contend that an understanding of human nature, far from implying fatalism, can be a step toward human betterment. For example, in a sociobiological analysis of male violence against women, Barbara Smuts (1992) wrote:

> Although an evolutionary analysis assumes that male aggression against women reflects selection pressures operating during our species' evolutionary history, it in no way implies that male domination of women is genetically determined, or that frequent male aggression toward women is an immutable feature of human nature. In some societies male aggressive coercion of women is very rare, and even in societies with frequent male aggression toward women, some men do not show these behaviors. Thus, the challenge is to identify the situational factors that predispose members of a particular society toward or away from the use of sexual aggression. I argue that an evolutionary framework can be very useful in this regard.

Let's proceed, now, unblinded by the moralistic and deterministic fallacies, to examine several ideas about human nature that are much discussed by sociobiologists. Some of these ideas appear again, with greater elaboration, later in the book.

Human Communities

43.

What evidence suggests that we are predisposed to live in communities, and how do our communities compare with those of other primates?

In no part of the world do people regularly live like orangutans (for which the only social group is the mother and her children), or gibbons (which live as isolated monogamous families), or gorillas (which live as isolated polygynous families). Human communities everywhere are more like the gregarious chimpanzee and bonobo model. That is, most people live, and apparently prefer to live, in at least moderately large communities that include many adults of both sexes, who interact with one another regularly in smaller groups of various types within the larger community (Rodseth & others, 1991). In non-Western, nonindustrialized cultures, most people live in tribes or villages consisting of a few dozen to a few hundred individuals.

People everywhere feel lonely when alone too long, and loneliness drives them to seek other people, much as hunger drives them to seek food. No population of humans anywhere is unconcerned about making friends. Hermits exist, but they are

Human gregariousness

Humans everywhere live and interact regularly with others of their kind. In this, we are like chimpanzees, not orangutans.

everywhere regarded as peculiar. It is uncertain what factors in our evolution led to our tendency to live in groups, but observations of present-day villages suggest that they include cooperation in hunting and gathering food, in caring for children, in building dwellings, in defending against predators and human invaders, and, most human of all, in exchanging, through language, information that bears on all aspects of the struggle for survival.

Nepotism

In accord with the kin selection theory, nonhuman animals help close relatives more than they help nonrelatives. Among humans, the selective aiding of kin is called *nepotism*, and cross-cultural research shows that such behavior is common everywhere (Essock-Vitale & McGuire, 1980). If a mother dies or for other reasons is unable to care for a child, the child's grandmother, aunt, or other close relative is by far the most likely adopter (Kurland, 1979). Close kin are also most likely to share dwellings or land, hunt together, or form other collaborative arrangements. On the other side of the same coin, studies in Western culture indicate that genetic kin living in the same household are less often violent toward one another than are nonkin living in the same household (Daly & Wilson, 1988), and studies in other cultures have shown that villages in which most people are closely related have less internal friction than those in which people are less closely related (Chagnon, 1979).

When leaders call for patriotic sacrifice or universal cooperation, they commonly employ kinship terms (Johnson, 1987). At times of war, political leaders ask citizens to fight for the "motherland" or "fatherland"; at other times, religious leaders and humanists strive to promote world peace by speaking of our "brothers and sisters" everywhere. The terms appeal to our instincts to be kind to relatives. Our imagination and intelligence allow us, at least sometimes, to extend our concept of kin to all humanity.

44.

What evidence suggests that the kin selection theory of altruism applies to humans, as it does to other species?

45.

What evidence suggests that humans evolved as a moderately polygynous species?

Human Mating Patterns

Although we live in groups a bit like chimpanzees and bonobos, we do not appear anywhere to be quite as sexually promiscuous as they. In every culture, people tend to form mating bonds that are legitimized through some sort of culturally recognized marriage contract, and males in most cultures play at least some role in caring for their children (Dewsbury, 1988; Eibl-Eibesfeldt, 1989). Anthropologists have found that the great majority of non-Western cultures, where Western influence has not made polygyny illegal, practice a mixture of polygyny and monogamy (Low, 2000; Murdock, 1981). In such cultures, men with sufficient wealth or status have more than one wife, while the majority of men have either one wife or none.

The moderate size difference between men and women is another bit of evidence that humans evolved as a moderately polygynous species (Dewsbury, 1988). As noted earlier, the degree to which males are larger than females correlates positively, across mammalian species, with the degree to which the species is polygynous. Cross-cultural observations of parental investment by men and women also fit the theory (Geary, 2000). In some societies, especially where monogamy is enforced, fathers are almost as invested in their children as are mothers, and in other societies they are much less invested; but nowhere are fathers routinely *more* invested than mothers (the condition that would promote polyandry).

Recently, psychologists have renewed the debate over some old questions about the possible evolutionary basis of differences between men and women in mating strategies and sexual appetite (for example, Buss, 1994a, 1998). Are men, for biological reasons, most attracted to women whose bodies have clues that they can bear healthy children; and are women, for biological reasons, most attracted to men who manifest a capacity and willingness to provide material resources for raising children? Are men, for biological reasons, more motivated than women to have sex with many different partners; and are women, for biological reasons, less interested than men in one-night stands? On the basis of what you have read in this chapter, I am sure you can develop for yourself the evolutionary arguments that have been used by some psychologists to answer each of these questions in the affirmative. Other psychologists, however, argue that these sex differences could arise purely from what people learn in cultures where men control most of the financial resources and political power (Eagly & Wood, 1999). Such ideas are examined more fully in Chapter 12.

Male Violence

Among the great majority of mammals, males not only are larger and stronger than females but also are more inclined to fight. Human beings are no exception to this general pattern. Cross-cultural studies show that everywhere men are more violent, more likely to maim or kill, than women. In fact, in a survey of cross-cultural data on this issue, Martin Daly and Margo Wilson (1988) were unable to find any society in which the number of women who killed other women was even one-tenth as great as the number of men who killed other men. On average, in the data they examined, male–male killings outnumbered female–female killings by more than 30 to 1. One might construe a scenario through which such a difference in violence would be purely a product of learning, in every culture, but the hypothesis that the difference resides at least partly in inherited sex differences seems more plausible.

According to Daly and Wilson's analyses, the apparent motives underlying male violence and homicide are very much in accord with sociobiological theory. Among the leading motives for murder among men in every culture is sexual jealousy. In some cultures, men are *expected* to kill other men who have sex with their wives (Symons, 1979), and in others, such murders are common even though they are illegal (Daly & Wilson, 1988). Why are men more prone to violent sexual jealousy than are women? According to Daly and Wilson, the ultimate explanation lies at least partly in the asymmetry of reproduction. Men tend to act violently toward sexual competitors because in the long run of evolution those who behaved that way fathered more children than those who did not. Through most of history (and for most people today), the only way a man could be certain that his wife's children were also *his* children was to prevent her from having sex with anyone else. Women never had that problem; they always knew that their children were theirs, regardless of who the father might be. Their reproductive interest lay more strongly in staying alive than in fighting with sexual competitors.

Sociobiological analyses such as this are often objected to more strongly than are other, less plausible accounts that completely neglect the role of evolution. The reason for the objection, I think, lies in concern about the naturalistic and deterministic fallacies. People fear that an evolutionary explanation of male violence, for example, will be used to justify such violence or will be taken as evidence that nothing can be done about it. If we can resist these fallacies, however, we have nothing to fear in looking at ourselves as products of natural selection and much to gain in terms of insight.

46.

How do sociobiologists explain the link between sexual jealousy and violence in men?

SECTION SUMMARY

Sociobiologists learn about the ultimate (evolutionary) functions of particular behavioral characteristics by comparing species that show analogous behaviors. Such work, applied to patterns of mating, led Trivers to develop his theory of parental investment. According to this theory, in any species the sex that invests the most in bearing and caring for offspring will be the more discriminating sex in choosing when and with whom to mate, and the sex that invests the least will be the more eager sex to mate and will expend the most effort in courtship and competition for mating opportunities. The theory helps explain why among most mammals males are larger and more aggressive than females, females are less quick than males to mate, and polygyny is common. It also helps explain why monogamy is common among birds and how polyandry has evolved in some species of birds and fish.

Cross-species comparisons have also shed light on patterns of aggression and helping. Animals of some species fight with others of their kind not only for mating opportunities, but also to preserve feeding territories. Territorial marking reduces fighting for territories. Within colonies, animals squabble over resources, and dominance hierarchies reduce such squabbling. Animals within a colony cooperate in such activities as finding food and warding off predators. Animal behaviors that appear to be altruistic are best explained by kin selection and reciprocity.

Sociobiological thinking has been applied usefully to human behavior, in ways that avoid the naturalistic and deterministic fallacies. Human beings across cultures show many behavioral similarities, which collectively constitute human nature. For instance, people everywhere are gregarious, tend to favor genetic relatives over nonrelatives, form long-lasting monogamous or polygynous mating bonds (marriages), and exhibit more violence by men than by women.

CONCLUDING THOUGHTS

As you review and think about the ideas in this chapter, you might find it useful to reflect on the following four general lessons, which have come to psychology from evolutionary thinking or from research inspired by such thinking.

1. The indirect nature of genetic influences on behavior Genes are simply DNA molecules, which provide the code for building the body's proteins. Variation in that code across species is the basis for species-typical behaviors, and variation in

47.

What four lessons are proposed as coming to psychology from evolutionary thought and research? Through what examples was each lesson supported in this chapter?

that code among members of a species is one basis for individual differences in behavior within a species. But genes in no case produce behaviors directly. Genes always work in conjunction with the environment, and so their effects depend on environmental conditions. Neither genes nor environment "determines" our behavior. Our behavior results from an interplay between the environment in which we live and our bodies' biological mechanisms, which themselves were built through an interplay between genes and environment.

2.   **Evolution as a basis for functionalism in psychology** Our genes were selected, over countless generations, to build into our bodies mechanisms that help us survive and reproduce under the varying conditions in which our species evolved. That insight is worth keeping in mind throughout this book, for it bears on every general theory in psychology. All our complex biological machinery, including the brain processes that underlie our psychological nature, came about because they helped our ancestors survive and reproduce. We can expect, therefore, that all our basic motivational and emotional mechanisms are biased toward generating behaviors that promote survival and reproduction; and we can expect that our sensory, perceptual, memory, and reasoning mechanisms are biased toward picking up and using information essential to those purposes. We are not general learning or thinking machines that indiscriminately analyze all information available; we are biological survival machines designed to use information selectively to achieve our ends.

3.   **The value of studying behavior in the natural environment** Behavioral mechanisms evolve over generations and develop in the individual to deal with the problems that animals routinely face in their natural environments. When animals (including people) are tested in unnatural settings, their behaviors may make little sense. The early ethologists often made this point in their arguments with psychologists who limited themselves to laboratory studies. If Tinbergen had begun his research on sticklebacks by testing them in isolated laboratory aquariums, his discovery that males attack objects that have red undersides would have simply been a source of puzzlement. But because he began the other way around, first learning all he could about their mating habits and other aspects of their natural lives, he was able to make sense of this behavior. People, too, have acquired their species-typical behaviors and their learned habits in the contexts of their everyday lives, and often those behaviors don't make sense in the stark or strange conditions of the laboratory. Today psychologists, like ethologists, are increasingly concerned with the natural contexts and real-life meanings of the behaviors they study. The laboratory is a fine place for controlled experiments aimed at understanding causal mechanisms but not such a great place to learn about the real-life functions of behavior.

4.   **Evolutionary rationales for cross-species comparisons** Psychologists have long studied the behavior of other animals as one route to understanding the behavior of humans. Evolutionary thinking not only provides a general rationale for that enterprise, by pointing out our relatedness to other animals, but also helps us decide which animals to compare ourselves with. If we want to understand the underlying mechanism of some form of human behavior by studying it in an animal, we should choose a species for which the behavior is homologous (not just analogous) to that in humans. As you will see in Chapters 6 through 8, researchers have learned much about basic motivational and sensory mechanisms in humans by studying their homologous forms in other mammals. Analogies are useful for developing hypotheses about the evolutionary functions of behaviors, and for that reason are widely employed by sociobiologists. But analogies are not so useful for learning about mechanisms, because convergent evolution can produce superficially similar behaviors that involve very different mechanisms.

Further Reading

Charles Darwin (1859; reprinted 1963). *The origin of species.* New York: Washington Square Press.

Darwin was an engaging writer as well as a brilliant thinker. Why not read at least part of this book, which revolutionized the intellectual world? The most relevant chapter for the psychologist is Chapter 8, entitled "Instinct," which includes Darwin's research on hive building in bees and many other other insights about the behavior of wild and domesticated animals.

Steven Pinker (1997). *How the mind works.* New York: Norton.

This is a witty, fast-paced introduction to many of psychology's basic issues from an evolutionary perspective. Pinker's theme—which he develops in chapters on seeing, thinking, emotions, and family relationships—is that the human mind is a set of relatively separate organs that came about through natural selection to solve the problems faced by our foraging ancestors. The final chapter offers some interesting speculation about art, music, humor, and religion from an evolutionary perspective.

Bobbi S. Low (2000). *Why sex matters: A Darwinian look at human behavior.* Princeton, NJ: Princeton University Press.

Low is an anthropologist who has conducted wide-ranging research into sex differences in animals and people, the latter across cultures and historical time. This scholarly but highly readable book is about sex, the differences between the sexes, and all that relate to these—beauty, bonding, reproduction, parenting, division of labor, cooperation, competition, wealth, power, and politics. It's an excellent introduction to evolutionary psychology from an anthropological perspectives.

Jane Goodall (1988). *In the shadow of man* (rev. ed.). Boston: Houghton Mifflin.

Goodall's study of wild chimpanzees, which began in 1960, ranks as one of the most courageous and scientifically valuable studies of animal behavior ever undertaken. This book, first published in 1971, is an exciting account of her early struggle to locate and study the animals and of her early findings about their behavior. For a more complete and scientific account of her research, I recommend Goodall's 1986 book, The Chimpanzees of Gombe.

Frans de Waal, with photographs by **Frans Lanting** (1997). *Bonobo: The forgotten ape.* Berkeley: University of California Press.

Bonobos—the apes that are tied with chimpanzees as our closest animal relatives—were rediscovered in the 1980s, after decades of scientific neglect. Among the scientists who have studied them intensively is Frans de Waal, and here he describes their ecology and habits in a narrative that is accompanied by dozens of full-color, full-page photographs of these endangered apes, famous for their make-love-not-war style of life. Chapter 4 is X-rated.

Looking Ahead

Among the products of evolution are the basic mechanisms of learning, which allow people and other animals to benefit from experience and adapt to their environments within their lifetimes. The study of learning has long been one of the most central activities of psychology. We turn to it in the next chapter.

Chapter 4

Le duc de Bordeaux, Francois-Edouard Picot

Basic Processes of Learning

To survive, animals must adapt to their environments. Evolution by natural selection, discussed in Chapter 3, is the long-term adaptive process that equips each species for life within a certain range of environmental conditions. But the environment is never constant; it changes from place to place and from time to time, even within short periods in an individual's life. In response to such continual change, natural selection has built into animals many adaptive mechanisms that operate within the individual's life span. For instance, human skin has adaptive mechanisms for dealing with exposure to hot sun (the skin develops a suntan, which helps protect it from the damaging effects of further exposure to the sun) or repeated friction (the skin develops a callus, which helps protect it from the damaging effects of further friction). Some mechanisms of adaptation involve the central nervous system, and among them are those that promote what psychologists call learning.

The term *learning* is used in various ways by different psychologists to refer to a wide variety of phenomena. For our purposes, however, we can define it broadly as *any process through which experience at one time can alter an individual's behavior at a future time*. *Experience* in this definition refers to any effects of the environment that are mediated by the individual's sensory systems (vision, hearing, touch, and so on). *Behavior at a future time* refers to any subsequent behavior that is not part of the individual's immediate response to the sensory stimulation during the learning experience. If I make a clicking sound just before flashing a bright light into your eyes, your immediate response to the click or to the light (such as blinking) does not exemplify learning, but your increased tendency to blink to the click alone, the next time I present that sound, does exemplify learning.

Most of psychology is in one way or another concerned with learning—that is, with effects of experience on subsequent behavior. Social psychologists try to explain people's beliefs and social behaviors in terms of their past experiences. Clinical psychologists try to explain people's emotional problems in terms of their past experiences. Cognitive psychologists try to understand the basic perceptual, memory, and thought processes that are involved in people's ability to learn. Thus most of the chapters in this book, or in any other introductory psychology text, are in one way or another about learning.

In this chapter, our concern is with the most basic attempts to characterize or describe learning processes. We will examine learning from three perspectives: (1) the *behavioral perspective*, which characterizes learning in terms of observable stimuli and responses; (2) the *cognitive perspective*, which characterizes learning in terms of information stored in the mind; and (3) the *ecological perspective*, which identifies separate, specialized learning mechanisms that have been built through evolution to meet specific survival needs. As you will see, much of the research within each perspective has been conducted with nonhuman animals. That is partly because greater control can be exerted over their environments and partly because basic learning mechanisms are assumed to be more easily uncovered in animals whose nervous systems and behavioral repertoires are less complex than ours.

The Behavioral Perspective on Learning: Acquiring New Reponses to and for Stimuli

Classical Conditioning

Phenomena Associated with Classical Conditioning

Operant Conditioning

Phenomena Associated with Operant Conditioning

The Cognitive Perspective on Learning: Acquiring Information About the World

The Cognitive Nature of Stimuli

The Cognitive View of Classical Conditioning

The Cognitive View of Operant Conditioning

Place Learning

Observational Learning

The Ecological Perspective on Learning: Filling the Blanks in Species-Typical Behavior Patterns

Learning What to Eat

Other Examples of Selective Learning Abilities

THE BEHAVIORAL PERSPECTIVE ON LEARNING: ACQUIRING NEW RESPONSES TO AND FOR STIMULI

1.

What is behaviorism, and what two classes of learning are identified by this perspective?

Behaviorism, as described in Chapter 1, is the attempt to understand behavior in terms of relationships between observable *stimuli* (events in the environment) and observable *responses* (behavioral actions). The early behaviorists were in the forefront of the effort to make psychology an objective science, and, in support of objectivity, they proposed dropping from psychology terms that refer to unseen, inner, mental entities such as thoughts or feelings. As John B. Watson (1913), the acknowledged founder of behaviorism, put it, "In a system of psychology completely worked out, given the response the stimuli can be predicted, and given the stimuli the response can be predicted." Neither Watson nor subsequent behaviorists denied the existence of mental processes, but they believed that these are too obscure to be studied scientifically.

In addition to developing objective, stimulus-response descriptions of behavior, the early behaviorists established learning as their main explanatory concept. They maintained that a person's behavior at any given time is the product of that person's past experiences. In a famous boast illustrating this view, Watson (1924) wrote, "Give me a dozen healthy infants, well-formed, and my own specified world to bring them up in and I'll guarantee to take any one at random and train him to become any type of specialist I might select—doctor, lawyer, artist, merchantchief, and yes, even beggar-man and thief, regardless of his talents, penchants, tendencies, abilities, vocations, and the race of his ancestors." Of course, Watson did not mean his boast to be taken literally. He meant simply to dramatize his view that behavioral differences among people stem mainly from their varying experiences, mediated by learning.

As behaviorism developed, its main goal became to identify basic learning processes that could be described in terms of stimuli and responses. By the late 1930s, B. F. Skinner, Watson's successor as behaviorism's most recognized leader, was able to describe, in such terms, what he took to be two separate learning processes (Skinner, 1938). One, now most often called *classical conditioning*, is a process by which a stimulus that previously did not elicit a response comes to elicit a response, in reflexlike fashion, after it is paired for one or more trials with a stimulus that already elicits a response. Your blinking to a clicking sound that was previously paired with a bright flash of light is an example of classical conditioning. The other, which Skinner emphasized more strongly and labeled *operant conditioning*, is a process by which the consequences of a response increase or decrease the likelihood that the response will occur again. Your increased rate of smiling at people if that behavior brings you favorable consequences is an example of operant conditioning. The main task of behaviorism throughout its history has been to discover and apply the principles associated with classical and operant conditioning. Let us look now at those principles.

Classical Conditioning

2.

What is a reflex, and how can it change through habituation?

Classical conditioning has to do with the formation of new reflexes. A *reflex* is a simple, relatively automatic, stimulus-response sequence mediated by the nervous system. If your knee is tapped with a rubber mallet, your leg will jerk. If a bright light is flashed in your eyes, you will blink. If lemon juice is squirted into your mouth, you will salivate. If a loud alarm suddenly clangs, your muscles will tighten. In each of these examples, a particular, well-defined event in the environment, a *stimulus*, results in a particular, well-defined bit of behavior, a *response*. The tap on the knee, the flash of light, the squirt of lemon juice, and the sudden alarm are stimuli. The leg jerk, the eye blink, the salivation, and the muscle tightening are responses. It is not surprising that behaviorists, early on, were interested in reflexes. With reflexes, the rather vague and wishy-washy statement "Behavior is influenced by the environment" can be replaced by the more definite and stronger statement "A response is caused by a stimulus." Some early behaviorists hoped to be able to characterize all behavior in terms of reflexes.

To be considered a reflex, the response to a stimulus must be mediated by the nervous system. Messages carried by nerves from the eyes, ears, or other sensory organs enter the spinal cord or brain and act there to produce messages in nerves running outward to muscles and glands. If something hits you and you fall down as a result of the direct force of the impact, that is not a reflex. But if something hits you and your muscles respond in a way that tends to keep you from falling down, that is a reflex. Because reflexes are mediated by the nervous system, they can be modified by experience.

One simple effect of experience is **habituation**, defined as a decline in the magnitude of a reflexive response when the stimulus is repeated several times in succession. Not all reflexes undergo habituation. One that does is the startle response to a loud sound. You might jump the first time the sound occurs, but each time the sound is repeated, you respond less and soon show no visible response at all. In some cases, habituation persists over long periods and thus can be considered a simple form of learning. Habituation does not produce a new stimulus-response sequence but only weakens an already existing one. Classical conditioning, in contrast, is a form of reflex learning that does produce a new stimulus-response sequence. Classical conditioning was first described and most extensively studied by a Russian physiologist, Ivan Pavlov.

Pavlov's Discovery

Ivan Petrovich Pavlov (1849–1936) was the personification of the dedicated scientist. By the time of his most famous research on classical conditioning, he was in his fifties and had already earned a Nobel Prize for studies of the reflexes involved in digestion. His research so engulfed his life that he is said to have hardly noticed such events as the Bolshevik Revolution of 1917, which transformed his country. One former co-worker (Gantt, 1975, as quoted by Hothersall, 1990) recalled, many years later, Pavlov's angry scolding of an assistant who arrived 10 minutes late to start an experiment: "But Professor," exclaimed the assistant, "there's a revolution going on, with shooting in the streets." To which Pavlov replied, "What the ____ difference does that make when you've work to do in the laboratory? Next time there's a revolution, get up earlier!"

Pavlov's initial discovery of what we now call classical conditioning emerged from his earlier studies of digestive reflexes in dogs. Using permanently implanted tubes to collect salivary and stomach juices from dogs, he and his team of researchers found, for example, that a dog salivates differently when different kinds of food are placed in its mouth. Juicy meat triggers a very thick saliva; dry bread, a wetter saliva; and acidic fluids, a wetter one yet. In a fine-grained analysis, then, these represent three different reflexes, with three different stimuli eliciting three measurably different salivary secretions (see Figure 4.1).

In the course of these studies, Pavlov encountered a problem. Dogs that had been given food on previous occasions in Pavlov's experiments would salivate before receiving food. Apparently, signals that regularly preceded food, such as the sight of the food or the sound associated with its delivery, alerted the dogs to the upcoming stimulation and caused them to salivate. At first Pavlov was content to treat this simply as a source of experimental error. He called it "psychic secretion," implying that it was outside the physiologist's realm of study, and he attempted to eliminate it by developing ways to introduce the food into the dog's mouth without any warning. But then it occurred to Pavlov that this might well be a phenomenon that could be studied physiologically. Rather than call it psychic secretion, perhaps he could consider it a reflex and analyze it objectively, just as he had analyzed the reflexive salivary response to food in the mouth. This insight led Pavlov (1927/1960) to his first experiments on conditioned reflexes.

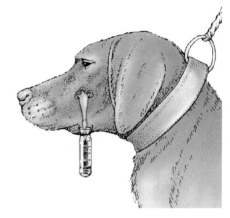

FIGURE 4.1 *Pavlov's method for measuring salivation*
One of the dog's salivary ducts is surgically connected to a glass tube. In his early experiments, Pavlov learned that dogs produce different salivary secretions in response to different kinds of food. Later he found that the dogs could be conditioned to produce these secretions in response to stimuli that reliably precede the presentation of food. (Adapted from Yerkes & Morgulis, 1909.)

3.

How did Pavlov discover the conditioned reflex? How did he then systematize the process of conditioning, and what names did he give to the relevant stimuli and responses?

The Procedure and Generality of Classical Conditioning

To study such reflexes, Pavlov deliberately controlled the signals that preceded food. In one experiment he sounded a bell just before placing food in the dog's mouth. After several such pairings of a bell with food, the dog would salivate in response to the bell sound alone; no food was necessary. Pavlov referred to this new reflex as a *conditioned reflex*, because it depended on the unique conditions present in the dog's previous experience—the pairing of the bell sound with the food-in-mouth stimulus. He referred to the stimulus in a conditioned reflex (the bell sound, in this case) as a *conditioned stimulus* and to the learned response to it (salivation) as a *conditioned response*. Likewise, he referred to the original, unlearned reflex as an *unconditioned reflex* and to its stimulus (food placed in the mouth) and response (salivation) as an *unconditioned stimulus* and *unconditioned response*. For a diagram of Pavlov's basic procedure, called *classical conditioning*, see Figure 4.2.

Pavlov (1927/1960) was impressed in these studies by the similarity between the dog's salivary response to a conditioned stimulus and its response to the unconditioned stimulus. A sound that had been paired with meat elicited a thick saliva, similar to that elicited by meat; and a sound that had been paired with bread elicited a thinner, wetter saliva, similar to that elicited by bread. In other experiments, Pavlov and his colleagues varied the stimulus used as the conditioned stimulus. They concluded that essentially any environmental event that the animal could detect could become a conditioned stimulus for salivation. Sounds produced by bells, buzzers, or tuning forks were highly effective and used most often because they were the easiest to control. But Pavlov's group also produced conditioned responses to visual stimuli, such as a black square; to olfactory stimuli, such as the odor of camphor; and to tactile (touch) stimuli, such as pressure applied to a spot on the animal's skin. In each case, the stimulus initially did not elicit the salivary response, but it did after having been paired with food a number of times.

Of course, classical conditioning is not limited to salivary responses. Researchers have shown this in hundreds of laboratory experiments, and you have

FIGURE **4.2**
Classical-conditioning procedure
A neutral stimulus initially does not elicit a response. After it is paired for several trials with an unconditioned stimulus, however, it becomes a conditioned stimulus and does elicit a response.

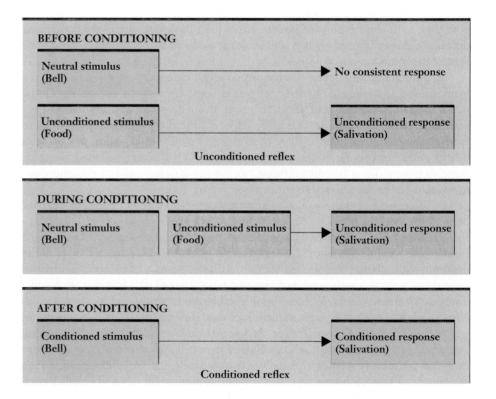

Pavlov conducting an experiment

To conduct his pioneering research on conditioning, Pavlov developed means to control the presentation of stimuli, such as the sight of food, and to measure the dog's reflexive salivary response.

experienced countless examples of such conditioning in your everyday life. The sound of a dentist's drill may elicit a conditioned cringing response because of its previous pairing with pain. The mere smell of coffee may help wake you up because of its previous pairing with coffee's effects. The sight of the toilet when you enter a bathroom to comb your hair may elicit a previously unfelt urge to urinate due to previous pairings of that sight with that urge. If you once had an automobile accident at a curve in the road on a wet day, each new encounter with such a curve on such a day may elicit a conditioned tensing of muscles. If you go through a day recording instances of conditioned responses, you will find that the list quickly becomes quite long.

The Value of Pavlov's Discovery for the Emergence of a Science of Learning

To understand the importance of Pavlov's work on conditioning, it is useful to view it in the context of earlier, philosophical thought about learning. For centuries before Pavlov, one of the most influential ideas about learning was the ***law of association by contiguity***, originally proposed by Aristotle (Hothersall, 1995). *Contiguity* means closeness in space or time, and the law of association by contiguity can be stated as follows: If a person experiences two environmental events (stimuli) at the same time or one right after the other (contiguously), those events will become associated in the person's mind, such that the thought of one will, in the future, tend to elicit the thought of the other. If your thought "ice cream" is followed more often by the thought "spoon" than by the thought "pencil," that is because in your past experience ice cream has been accompanied more often by a spoon than by a pencil. If the sound of the word *ball* evokes in a child's mind an image of a spherical object, that is because in the child's past experience that sound has often been paired with the sight of a spherical object. Thus, according to Aristotle and subsequent philosophers, association by contiguity plays a major role in determining the flow of a person's thoughts and is involved in all sorts of learning, including the learning of language.

4.

How can classical conditioning be understood as an objective reformulation of the philosophers' law of association by contiguity?

Association by Contiguity

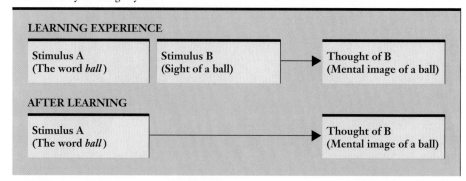

Classical Conditioning

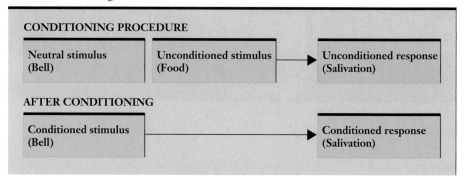

FIGURE **4.3** *Comparison of the law of association by contiguity with the principle of classical conditioning* Philosophers, from Aristotle on, argued that if two stimuli are paired in a person's experience, the recurrence of one will tend to elicit the thought of the other. Pavlov's principle of conditioning parallels the philosophers' law, with one important difference. Because Pavlov began with a stimulus (unconditioned stimulus) that reflexively elicited an observable response, he could measure learning objectively as the increased likelihood that the response would occur to the new stimulus (conditioned stimulus).

Now consider the similarity between the philosophers' law of association by contiguity and Pavlov's principle of conditioning (outlined in Figure 4.3). Both propose that learning occurs when two stimuli are paired in a person's experience. The essential difference is that in the philosophers' formulation one stimulus comes to elicit a *thought* that was previously elicited just by the other, while in Pavlov's formulation one stimulus comes to elicit a *behavioral response* that was previously elicited just by the other. The great advantage of Pavlov's formulation is that a response is publicly observable, whereas a thought is not. A researcher using Pavlov's method can look at a person or nonhuman animal and see the change in response and use it to chart the course of learning. Philosophers could only speculate about the association of thoughts, but Pavlov could do experiments. He could vary the conditions and objectively measure the effects on an individual's behavior. This idea, of course, was not lost on Watson and other American behaviorists. To them it was a step that helped make possible a science of learning.

Phenomena Associated with Classical Conditioning

Pavlov and scientists after him performed hundreds of experiments on classical conditioning and identified many phenomena related to conditioning, including those discussed below.

Extinction and Recovery from Extinction

One question that interested Pavlov had to do with the permanence, or lack of permanence, of a conditioned reflex. Once a dog has learned to salivate to a bell, does this reflex continue to occur if the bell is sounded for many trials without the unconditioned food-in-mouth stimulus? Pavlov's group found that without food, the bell elicits less and less salivation on each trial and eventually none at all, a phenomenon that they labeled ***extinction***. But they also found that extinction does not return the animal fully to the unconditioned state. The mere passage of time fol-

5.

How can a conditioned reflex be extinguished? What evidence indicates that extinction does not return the animal to the untrained state?

lowing extinction can partially renew the conditioned reflex, a phenomenon now known as ***spontaneous recovery*** (see Figure 4.4). And a single pairing of the conditioned stimulus with the unconditioned stimulus can renew the conditioned reflex, which can be abolished again only by another series of extinction trials. On the basis of such findings, Pavlov (1927/1960) concluded that the conditioned reflex is not truly lost during extinction, but is somehow inhibited, and that it can be disinhibited by such means as the passage of time or the recurrence of the unconditioned stimulus. This conclusion has been validated in many experiments since Pavlov's time (Bouton, 1994).

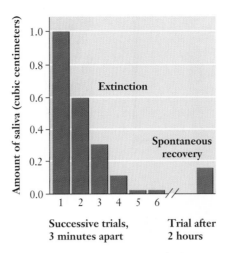

FIGURE **4.4** *Extinction and spontaneous recovery of conditioned salivation*
The conditioned stimulus in this case was the sight of meat powder, presented repeatedly out of the animal's reach at 3-minute intervals. Extinction was complete by the fifth and sixth presentations, but when 2 hours were allowed to elapse before the seventh presentation, the reflex was partially renewed. (Data from Pavlov, 1927/1960.)

Generalization and Discrimination

After conditioning, stimuli that resemble the conditioned stimulus will elicit the conditioned response even though they themselves were never paired with the unconditioned stimulus. This phenomenon is called ***generalization***. The magnitude or likelihood of a response to the new stimulus is correlated with its degree of similarity to the original conditioned stimulus. Thus a dog conditioned to salivate to a 1000-hertz (cycles-per-second) tone also salivated to tones of other frequencies. But the farther the tone was in frequency from the original conditioned stimulus, the less the dog would salivate to it (Pavlov, 1927/1960).

Generalization between two stimuli can be abolished if the response to one is reinforced while the response to the other is extinguished, a procedure called ***discrimination training***. As an example of this procedure, Pavlov's group used a dog whose conditioning to the sight of a black square had generalized to a gray square. After a series of trials in which presentations of the gray square were never followed by food and presentations of the black square were always followed by food, the dog stopped salivating to the gray square and continued to salivate to the black one. The researchers continued this procedure with ever-darker shades of gray, until they eventually conditioned the dog to discriminate a black square from a gray one that was so nearly black that a human observer had difficulty telling them apart (Pavlov, 1927/1960).

Classical conditioning coupled with discrimination training provides an excellent tool for studying an animal's sensory capacities. A dog cannot tell you what it can or cannot hear, but you can find out by doing a conditioning experiment. If an animal can be conditioned to respond to a stimulus, we know that it can sense the stimulus; and if an animal can be trained to respond to one stimulus and not to another, we know that it can sense the difference between the two. Pavlov's team conditioned dogs to salivate to tones so high-pitched as to be inaudible to humans and to discriminate between pitches less than one-eighth of a note apart (Pavlov, 1927/1960).

Conditioned Emotional Responses

We move temporarily from Pavlov's laboratory to that of John B. Watson. Watson was one of the first psychologists to describe human learning explicitly in Pavlovian terms and to demonstrate directly how an emotional response—fear—can be conditioned in human infants. Consistent with his behavioral perspective, Watson (1924) defined fear not as a feeling but as a set of observable responses: "a catching of the breath, a stiffening of the whole body, a turning away of the body from the

6.

How can generalization in classical conditioning be abolished through discrimination training, and how can discrimination training be used to assess an animal's sensory capacities?

7.

How did Watson demonstrate that an emotional reaction can be conditioned?

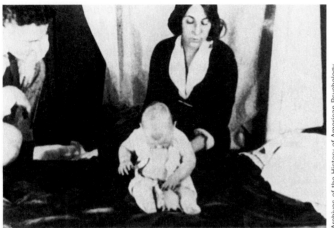

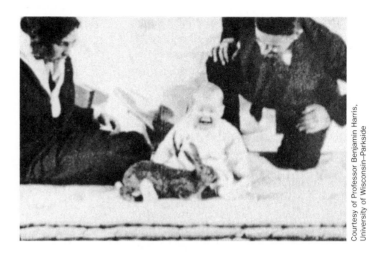

Little Albert with Watson, Rayner, and furry animals

Prior to the conditioning experience, 11-month-old Albert played happily with a live laboratory rat *(left)*. After he was conditioned to respond fearfully to the rat, he also cried at the sight of other furry objects, including a rabbit, thereby exhibiting generalization *(right)*.

source of stimulation, a running or crawling from it." On the basis of this definition, Watson found two unconditioned stimuli for fear in young infants—sudden loud sound and sudden loss of support (as when a baby slips out of a person's hands). Other stimuli, he argued, come to elicit fear only as a result of conditioning.

In a classic demonstration of such conditioning, Watson and Rosalie Rayner (1920) conditioned an 11-month-old baby named Albert to fear laboratory rats. At first, Albert played happily and fearlessly with a rat that was placed in front of him. To condition the fear, the experimenters struck a steel bar with a hammer to produce a loud sound on two occasions when Albert was paying close attention to the rat. Each occurrence of the loud sound elicited the fear response, and after the second occurrence Albert showed the fear response each time he saw the rat, even though the loud sound was not repeated. Thus, in the terminology of classical conditioning, the rat had become a conditioned stimulus for fear through being paired with a loud sound, which was an unconditioned stimulus for fear.

You might wonder about the ethics of this experiment. In fairness to Watson, I should note that he was far more interested in how to eliminate unwanted fears than in how to produce them. In Chapter 17, you will see how Watson's research and ideas helped lead to clinical methods for extinguishing irrational fears through exposing the person to the fear-producing stimuli at gradually increasing magnitudes in a safe, relaxing context.

Fear, of course, is not the only emotional response that can be conditioned through Pavlovian procedures. When beer and car advertisers pair their products with scenes of beautiful people having wonderful times, they are trying to get you to drool with pleasure, like Pavlov's dogs, whenever you see their products.

Conditioning young humans to love beer

The unconditioned stimulus is the happy, sexually suggestive scene. The conditioned stimulus is the Budweiser label.

Conditioned Drug Reactions

In one of their most intriguing experiments, Pavlov's group conditioned a dog to show a drug reaction to a nondrug stimulus. After repeated pairing of a tone with injection of a drug that elicited restlessness and vomiting, the dog began to exhibit those responses to the tone alone (Pavlov, 1927/1960). This discovery suggests that stimuli normally present when a drug is taken may, through conditioning, come to induce the symptoms of the drug. Because of conditioning, the sight of a coffee cup or the smell of coffee might give you a lift, and a visit to a hospital where you were previously given a sedative might make you feel sleepy.

Research conducted more recently has shown that conditioned effects of stimuli paired with some drugs are the *opposite* of the most prominent unconditioned effects of the drugs. Morphine, for example, reduces sensitivity to pain. When rats are repeatedly injected with morphine in a distinctive environment and then are placed in that environment without morphine, they become temporarily more sensitive to pain, not less (Hinson & others, 1986). What happens in such cases might be understood as follows (Siegel, 1999): The drug produces, through nonreflexive means, a direct effect (which in this case includes reduced sensitivity to pain). The direct effect, in turn, activates a reflexive physiological response that tends to counteract the direct effect (tends to increase pain sensitivity). Only the counteractive response is a reflex, so only it becomes conditioned to the cues present in the environment in which the drug was taken. Thus when the animal is later placed in that environment without receiving the drug, the cues stimulate an increase in pain sensitivity, not a decrease.

You might think of such conditioning as analogous to what would happen if a bell sound (conditioned stimulus) reliably preceded a shove from the front (unconditioned stimulus). The shove would tend to push you backward, but you would counteract that with a reflexive movement forward. Only the reflexive movement forward would be conditioned, so if the bell were sounded without the shove, you might fall on your face—a reaction opposite to the most direct effect of the shove. The body protects itself with counteractive reflexes to interventions (such as shoves and drugs) that disrupt its normal functioning. The conditioning of those reflexes is normally useful because it allows the counteraction to begin even before the potentially harmful stimulus strikes (Dworkin, 1993; Ramsay & Woods, 1997).

The discovery of conditioned counteractive effects of drugs may help explain an important observation associated with human drug abuse. A study of heroin overdose cases revealed that quite often the "overdose" was not larger than the addict's usual drug dose but was taken in an unusual environment (Siegel, 1984). Apparently, when an addict takes a drug in the usual drug-taking environment, cues in that environment, because of past conditioning, produce a physiological counteraction that allows the addict's body to tolerate a large dose of the drug. If the addict takes the same amount of the drug in a novel environment, where the conditioned cues aren't present, the full impact of the drug kicks in before a counteractive reaction begins—resulting in extreme illness or death. Consistent with this interpretation, rats that had received many morphine injections in a specific, highly distinctive cage were much more likely to survive a high dose of the drug if it was given to them in the same cage than if given in a different setting (Siegel, 1976, 1984). Similar effects have been shown in animal experiments using alcohol (Melchior, 1990) and various other drugs (Goudie, 1990).

8.

Why is the conditioned response to a drug-related stimulus often the opposite of the most direct effect of the drug?

9.

How does the conditioning of counteractive drug effects help explain why an addict's usual dose can sometimes be an "overdose"?

Operant Conditioning

We are pulled as well as pushed by events in our environment. That is, we do not just react to stimuli; we also behave in ways that seem designed to *produce* or *obtain* certain environmental changes or stimuli. My dog rubs against the door to be let out. I flip a switch to illuminate a room, press keys on my computer to set up words on a screen, and say "Please pass the potatoes" to get potatoes. Most of my day seems to consist of behaviors of this sort, and I expect that most of my dog's day would too if there were more things that she could control. Surely if Pavlov's dogs had had some way to control the delivery of food into their mouths, they would have done more than salivate—they would have pushed a lever, bitten open a bag, or done whatever was required to get the food.

Actions such as those just listed are called **operant responses** because they *operate* on the world to produce some effect. They are also called *instrumental responses* because they function like *instruments*, or tools, to work some change on the environment. The learning process by which the consequence of such a response affects the likelihood that the response will recur in the future is called **operant conditioning** or *instrumental conditioning*. Although the labels "operant" and "instrumental" were not coined until the 1930s, this learning process was studied extensively before that time, most notably by E. L. Thorndike.

Thorndike's Puzzle-Box Procedure

At about the same time that Pavlov began his research on conditioning, a young American student of psychology, Edward Lee Thorndike (1898), published a re-

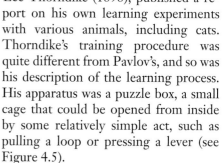

port on his own learning experiments with various animals, including cats. Thorndike's training procedure was quite different from Pavlov's, and so was his description of the learning process. His apparatus was a puzzle box, a small cage that could be opened from inside by some relatively simple act, such as pulling a loop or pressing a lever (see Figure 4.5).

In one experiment, Thorndike deprived cats of food long enough to make them hungry, and then he placed them inside the cage, one at a time, with food just outside it. When first placed inside, the cat would engage in many actions—such as clawing at the bars or pushing at the ceiling—in an apparent attempt to

Edward Lee Thorndike

After earning his Ph.D. in psychology with his puzzle-box experiments, Thorndike became a professor of educational psychology at Columbia University. Perhaps partly because of his early animal research, he maintained throughout his career that intelligence is a collection of separate learned skills, not a unitary characteristic of the person.

Courtesy of Columbia University

FIGURE 4.5 *One of Thorndike's puzzle boxes*

Thorndike was a great psychologist, not a great carpenter! Shown here is a photograph of one of his actual puzzle boxes. A cat placed inside could open this box by pulling down on the loop hanging from the ceiling, which would pull up the bolt and allow the door to fall forward.

Yale University Library

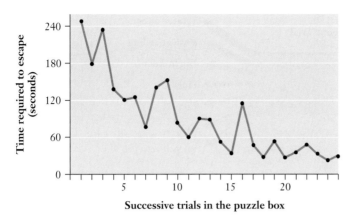

escape from the cage and get at the food outside. Finally, apparently by accident, the cat would pull the loop or push the lever that opened the door to freedom and food. Thorndike repeated this procedure many times with each cat. He found that on early trials they made many useless movements before happening on the one that released the latch, but, on average, they escaped somewhat more quickly with each successive trial. After about 20 to 30 trials, most cats would trip the latch to freedom and food almost as soon as they were shut in (see Figure 4.6). An observer who joined Thorndike on trial 31 might have been quite impressed by the animal's intelligence; but, as Thorndike himself suggested, an observer who had sat through the earlier trials might have been more impressed by the creature's stupidity than its intelligence. In any event, Thorndike came to view learning as a trial-and-error process, through which an individual gradually becomes more likely to make those responses that produce beneficial effects.

Thorndike's Law of Effect

Thorndike's basic training procedure differed fundamentally from Pavlov's. Pavlov could directly *elicit* the response he wished to condition in his animal. For example, he could elicit salivation by putting food in the dog's mouth. His conditioning method was to pair a new stimulus with a stimulus that already elicited the response. Thus Pavlov was concerned only with environmental events that *preceded* the response that he wished to condition, not with the effect or consequence of the response. With Pavlov's procedure, the animal can be thought of as a passive, responsive machine: Push button X and get response Y. Thorndike, in contrast, could not directly elicit the response that he wished to condition. There was no known unconditioned stimulus, no button Thorndike could push, that would make the animal open the latch. With Thorndike's procedure, the animal has to be thought of as an active creature, one that produces or *emits* various responses, seemingly of its own accord. Most of the cat's initial movements in the box were ineffective, and Thorndike had to wait patiently until the animal emitted the correct one. To gain some control over the cat's behavior, Thorndike had arranged the environment in such a way that only one type of response would open the box. Thus, with Thorndike's method, the important environmental event (the opening of the box) was a *consequence* of the response, not a precursor to it.

Partly on the basis of his puzzle-box experiments, Thorndike (1898) formulated the ***law of effect***, which can be stated, in somewhat abbreviated form, as follows: *Responses that produce a satisfying effect in a particular situation become more likely to occur again in that situation, and responses that produce a discomforting effect become less likely to occur again in that situation.* In Thorndike's puzzle-box experiments, the situation presumably consisted of all the sights, sounds, smells, internal feelings, and

10.

How did Thorndike's training procedure differ from Pavlov's, and how did it help lead Thorndike to formulate the law of effect?

FIGURE **4.7**
Thorndike's law of effect
According to Thorndike, the stimulus situation (being inside the puzzle box) initially elicits many responses, some more strongly than others, but the satisfying consequence of the successful response (pressing the lever) causes that response to be more strongly elicited on successive trials.

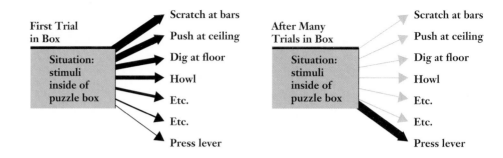

so on that were experienced by the hungry animal in the box. None of them initially elicited the latch-release response in reflexlike fashion; rather, taken as a whole, they set the occasion for many possible responses to occur, only one of which would release the latch. Once the latch was released, the *satisfying effect*, including freedom from the box and access to food, caused that response to become more firmly bonded to the situation than it was before, so the next time the cat was in the same situation, the probability of that response's recurrence was increased (see Figure 4.7).

Skinner's Method of Studying and Describing Operant Conditioning

11.

How did Skinner's method for studying learning differ from Thorndike's, and why did he prefer the term reinforcer *to Thorndike's* satisfaction?

The psychologist who did the most to extend and popularize the law of effect for more than half a century was Burrhus Fredric Skinner. As a graduate student at Harvard around 1930, Skinner developed an apparatus for studying learning in animals that was considerably more convenient than Thorndike's puzzle boxes. His device, commonly called a "Skinner box," is a cage with a lever or another mechanism in it that the animal can operate to produce some effect, such as delivery of a pellet of food or a drop of water (see Figure 4.8). The advantage of Skinner's apparatus is that the animal, after completing a response and experiencing its effect, is still in the box and free to respond again. With Thorndike's puzzle boxes and similar apparatuses such as mazes, the animal has to be put back into the starting place at the end of each trial. With Skinner's apparatus, the animal is simply placed in the cage and left there until the end of the session. Throughout the session, there are no constraints on when the animal may or may not respond. Responses (such as lever presses) can easily be counted automatically, and the learning process can be depicted as change in the rate of responses (see Figure 4.9).

FIGURE **4.8**   *Skinner box, or operant-conditioning chamber*
When the rat presses the lever, it activates an electrical relay system that causes the delivery of a food pellet or drop of water into the cup next to the lever. Each lever press can be automatically recorded to produce a cumulative record, such as that shown in Figure 4.9.

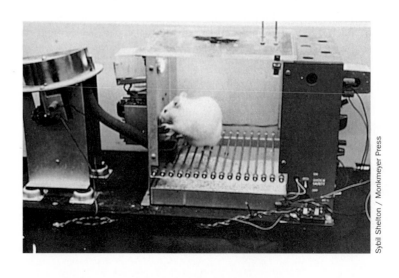

Sybil Shelton / Monkmeyer Press

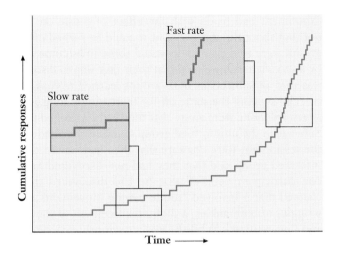

FIGURE **4.9** *Typical cumulative response curve for a rat learning to press a lever in a Skinner box* This graph is called a cumulative response curve because the height of the curve at any point indicates the total (cumulative) number of responses that the rat has made up to that time. The graph is automatically produced, while the rat is responding, by a recording machine outside the Skinner box. A pen moves horizontally across a roll of paper at a constant rate, and each lever press made by the rat produces a slight vertical movement of the pen. Thus, the degree to which the curve slopes upward is a measure of the animal's response rate. Note that early in learning the response rate was very low and then it gradually increased to a fast, steady rate.

Skinner developed not only a more efficient apparatus for studying such learning but also a new vocabulary for talking about it. As a confirmed behaviorist, he wanted to describe learning in terms that refer to observable stimuli and responses and to avoid words that refer to mental events. It was he who coined the terms *operant response* to refer to any behavioral act that has some effect on the environment and *operant conditioning* to refer to the process by which the effect of an operant response changes the likelihood of the response's recurrence. Thus, in a typical experiment with a Skinner box, pressing the lever is an operant response, and the increased rate of lever pressing that occurs when the response is followed by a pellet of food exemplifies operant conditioning. Applying the same terms to Thorndike's experiments, the movement that opens the latch is an operant response, and the increased speed of making that movement from trial to trial exemplifies operant conditioning.

Skinner (1938) proposed the term **reinforcer**, as a replacement for such words as *satisfaction* and *reward*, to refer to a stimulus change that occurs after a response and increases the subsequent frequency of that response. Thus, in a typical Skinner-box experiment, the delivery of a pellet of food or drop of water following a lever-press response is a reinforcer. In Thorndike's experiment, the opening of the cage, which allowed the cat to escape its confines and obtain the food outside, was the reinforcer.

The Scope of Operant Conditioning

To Skinner and his followers, operant conditioning is not simply one kind of learning to be studied but represents an entire approach to psychology. In his many books and articles, Skinner argued that essentially all the things we do, from the moment we arise in the morning to the moment we fall asleep at night, can be understood as operant responses that occur because of their past reinforcement. In some cases we are clearly aware of the relationship between our responses and reinforcers, as when we place coins in a vending machine for a candy bar or study to obtain a good grade on a test. In other cases we may not be aware of the relationship, yet it exists and, according to Skinner (1953, 1966), is the real reason for our behavior. To Skinner, awareness—which refers to a mental phenomenon—is not a useful construct for explaining behavior. We can never be sure what a person is aware of, but we can see directly the relationship between responses and reinforcers and use that to predict what a person will learn to do.

An illustration of conditioning without awareness comes from an experiment conducted many years ago, in which adults listened to music over which static was occasionally superimposed (Hefferline & others, 1959). Unbeknownst to the subjects, they could turn off the static by making an imperceptibly small twitch of the left thumb. Some subjects (the completely uninformed group) were told that the

12.

How were people conditioned without awareness to make a tiny thumb twitch, and how is this relevant for understanding the acquisition of motor skills?

experiment had to do with the effect of music on body tension; they were told nothing about the static or how it could be turned off. Others (the partly informed group) were told that static would sometimes come on, that they could turn it off by a specific response, and that their task was to discover that response. The result was that all subjects in both groups learned to make the thumb-twitch response, thereby keeping the static off for increasingly long periods. But, when questioned afterward, none were aware that they had controlled the static with thumb twitches. Subjects in the uninformed group said that they had noticed the static decline over the session but were unaware that they had caused the decline. Most in the partly informed group said that they had not discovered how to control the static. Only one participant believed that he had discovered the effective response, and he claimed that it involved "subtle rowing movements with both hands, infinitesimal wriggles of both ankles, a slight displacement of the jaw to the left, breathing out, and then waiting"! While he was consciously making this superstitious response, he was unconsciously learning to make the thumb twitch.

If you think about it, the results of this experiment should not come as a great surprise. We constantly learn finely tuned muscle movements as we develop skill at playing the violin, riding a bicycle, hammering nails, or whatever. The reinforcers, presumably, are the improved sound from the violin, the steadier movement on the bicycle, or the straight downward movement of the nail we are pounding; but often we do not know just what we are doing differently to produce these good effects. Our knowledge is often similar to that of the neophyte carpenter who said, after an hour's practice at hammering, "The nails you're giving me now don't bend as easily as the ones you were giving me before."

Therapeutic Applications of Operant Conditioning

13.

How can biofeedback training be described as operant conditioning?

Aside from its importance as a concept for understanding everyday behavior, operant conditioning is used by some clinical psychologists, called *behavior therapists*, to help clients change their behavior in desired ways. From an operant perspective, many of the problems that lead people to seek therapy are best thought of as bad habits, learned and maintained because they are reinforced in the short run even though they are harmful in the long run. Such behaviors as overeating, overdrinking, and smoking are obvious examples. Ultimately, these are unhealthy, but the immediate effect of each bite of food, each sip of alcohol, or each drag on the cigarette is pleasure, relief from discomfort, or both, and that is why the behaviors continue. To help a client give up such habits, a behavior therapist suggests ways to change the reinforcement contingencies, so as to increase the immediate reinforcement that comes from healthful pursuits and decrease that which comes from harmful pursuits. (More about behavior therapy can be found in Chapter 17.)

Even physiologically based problems, such as high blood pressure and migraine headaches, can sometimes be controlled through an interesting variation of operant conditioning called **biofeedback training**. In this procedure, a signal, such as a tone or light, is made to come on whenever a certain desirable physiological change occurs, and the person is instructed to try to keep the signal on for increasing periods of time. For example, a man being trained to lower his blood pressure might hear a tone every time his pressure falls below a certain level. The tone al-

Biofeedback training

In this procedure, sensors record scalp-muscle movements and finger temperature. (Muscle contractions are a source of tension headaches, and cold fingers often indicate tension.) Learning to control these physiological reactions has proved to be an effective means of warding off tension headaches.

lows him to detect a favorable consequence (reduced blood pressure) that he otherwise would not be able to sense. In operant terminology, the tone is a reinforcer (assuming that the subject is motivated to succeed at the task) for the response of decreasing blood pressure. As was the case for the subjects in the thumb-twitch experiment, the client need not discover or be aware of just how he is reducing his blood pressure for successful learning to occur. Using a similar method, biofeedback trainers have also reported success in teaching people with irregular heart rates to produce more regular heartbeats and people who suffer from headaches to reduce muscle tension in the scalp and thereby decrease the incidence of headaches (Andrasik, 2000; Mercer, 1986).

Phenomena Associated with Operant Conditioning

Skinner and his followers identified and studied many behavioral phenomena associated with operant conditioning, including the ones described below.

Shaping

Suppose you put a rat in a Skinner box, and it never presses the lever; or you place a cat in a puzzle box, and it never pulls the loop. In operant conditioning, the reinforcer comes only after the subject emits the desired response. But what happens if that response never occurs? The solution to this problem is a technique called *shaping*, in which successively closer approximations to the desired response are reinforced until the response finally occurs.

> **14.**
>
> *How can operant conditioning be used to get an animal to do something that it currently doesn't do?*

Imagine that you want to shape a lever-press response in a rat whose initial rate of lever pressing is zero or so low that you don't have the patience to wait for the response to occur. To begin, you might present the reinforcer (such as a pellet of food) whenever the rat goes anywhere near the lever. As a result, the rat will soon be spending most of its time near the lever and occasionally will touch it. When that happens, you might provide the reinforcer only when the rat touches the lever, which will increase the rate of touching. Some touches will be more vigorous than others and produce the desired lever movement; when that has happened a few times, you can stop reinforcing any other response—your animal's lever pressing has now been shaped. Animal trainers regularly use this technique in teaching domestic or circus animals to perform new tricks or tasks (for example, Prior, 1985), and we all tend to use it, more or less deliberately and not always skillfully, when we teach new skills to people. For example, when teaching a novice to play tennis, we tend at first to offer praise for any swing of the racket that propels the ball in the right general direction, and as improvement occurs, we gradually reserve praise for closer and closer approximations to an ideal swing.

Extinction and Schedules of Partial Reinforcement

An operantly conditioned response declines in rate and eventually disappears if it no longer results in a reinforcer. Rats stop pressing levers if no food pellets appear, cats stop scratching at doors if nobody responds, and people stop smiling at those who don't smile back. The absence of reinforcement of the response and the consequent decline in response rate are both referred to as *extinction*. Extinction in operant conditioning is analogous to extinction in classical conditioning. Just as in classical conditioning, extinction in operant conditioning is not true "unlearning" of the response. Passage of time following extinction can lead to spontaneous recovery of responding, and a single reinforced response following extinction can lead the individual to respond again at a rapid rate.

> **15.**
>
> *How do the four types of partial-reinforcement schedules differ from one another, and why is it generally adaptive to respond faster to ratio schedules than to interval schedules?*

In many cases, both in the real world and in laboratory setups, a particular response only sometimes produces a reinforcer. This is referred to as *partial reinforcement*, to distinguish it on the one hand from continuous reinforcement, where the response is always reinforced, and on the other hand from extinction, where the

Basis for reinforcement (number of responses or elapsed time)

	Ratio schedules	Interval schedules
Fixed schedules	In a fixed-ratio (FR) schedule a reinforcer occurs after every *n*th response, where *n* is some whole number greater than 1. For example, in an FR 5 schedule every fifth response is reinforced.	In a fixed-interval (FI) schedule a fixed period of time must elapse between one reinforced response and the next. Any response occurring before that time elapses is not reinforced. For example, in an FI 30-second schedule, the first response that occurs at least 30 seconds after the last reinforcer is reinforced.
Variable schedules	A variable-ratio (VR) schedule is like an FR schedule except that the number of responses required before reinforcement varies unpredictably around some average. For example, in a VR 5 schedule every fifth response on average is reinforced.	A variable-interval (VI) schedule is like an FI schedule except that the period that must elapse before a response will be reinforced varies unpredictably around some average. For example, in a VR 30-second schedule the average period required before the next response will be reinforced is 30 seconds.

(Left axis label: Predictability or lack of predictability of reinforcement on any given trial)

FIGURE **4.10** *Four types of partial-reinforcement schedules*

Ratio schedules (fixed or variable) generally produce higher response rates than do interval schedules, and variable schedules (ratio or interval) generally produce greater resistance to extinction than do fixed schedules.

16.

Why do partial-reinforcement schedules produce behavior that is very resistant to extinction?

response is never reinforced. In initial training, continuous reinforcement is most efficient, but once trained, an animal will continue to perform for partial reinforcement. Skinner and other operant researchers have described four basic types of partial-reinforcement schedules—*fixed ratio, variable ratio, fixed interval,* and *variable interval*—which are explained in Figure 4.10. The different schedules produce different response rates, which make sense if one assumes that the person or non-human animal is striving to maximize the number of reinforcers obtained and minimize the number of unreinforced responses. *Ratio* schedules (whether fixed or variable) produce reinforcers at a rate that is directly proportional to the rate of responding, so, not surprisingly, such schedules typically induce rapid responding. With *interval* schedules, in contrast, the maximum number of reinforcers available is set by the clock, and such schedules result, not surprisingly, in relatively low response rates that depend on the length of the interval, whether fixed or random.

Compared with continuous reinforcement, partial-reinforcement schedules, especially variable ratio and variable interval, cause behavior to be more resistant to extinction. This phenomenon is known as the *partial-reinforcement effect*. If a rat is trained to press a lever only on continuous reinforcement and then is shifted to extinction conditions, the rat will typically make a few bursts of lever-press responses and then quit. But if the rat has been shifted gradually from continuous reinforcement to an ever-stingier variable schedule and then finally to extinction, it will often make hundreds of unreinforced responses before quitting. Rats and humans who have been reinforced on stingy variable schedules have experienced reinforcement after long unpredictable periods of no reinforcement, so they have learned (for better or worse) to be persistent. Skinner (1953) and others (Rachlin, 1990) have used this phenomenon as a basis for explaining why gamblers often persist at the slot machine or dice game even after long periods of losing; they are hooked by the variable-ratio schedule of payoff that characterizes nearly every gambling device or game.

Stimuli That Set the Occasion for Operant Behavior

Responses that are reinforced in one setting or set of conditions are not necessarily reinforced in other settings or conditions. A rat trained in a Skinner box has learned to make a lever-press response in a particular context, which includes being inside the Skinner box. The rat does not go foolishly about making the lever-pressing movement in its home cage or in other places where the response has never been reinforced.

Partial reinforcement in daily life
Winning at slot machines occurs on a variable-ratio schedule, which produces a rapid and steady style of play. Success at reaching a previously busy telephone number occurs on a variable-interval schedule, which results in a slow and steady rate of redialing.

In his original formulation of the law of effect, Thorndike (1898) emphasized the importance of the *situation* in which the animal is trained, saying, "Of several responses made to the same situation, those which are accompanied or closely followed by satisfaction to the animal will, other things being equal, be more firmly connected with the situation, so that when it recurs, they will be more likely to recur." The set of stimuli inside a puzzle box or a Skinner box is an example of a Thorndikian situation (look back at Figure 4.7). Only in the presence of those stimuli is the response reinforced; therefore, the response becomes likely to occur when those stimuli are present.

Through *discrimination training*, an operant response can be brought under the control of a more specific stimulus than the entire inside of a Skinner box. Discrimination training in operant conditioning is analogous to discrimination training in classical conditioning. The essence of the procedure is to reinforce the animal's response when a specific stimulus is present and to extinguish the response when the stimulus is absent. Thus to train a rat to respond to a tone by pressing a lever, a trainer would alternate between reinforcement periods with the tone on (during which the animal gets food pellets for responding) and extinction periods with the tone off. After considerable training of this sort, the rat will begin pressing the lever as soon as the tone comes on and stop as soon as it goes off. The tone in this example is called a ***discriminative stimulus***. A discriminative stimulus can be thought of as a cue; it is present when a particular response will be reinforced and absent when the response will not be reinforced. A discriminative stimulus in operant conditioning is similar to a conditioned stimulus in classical conditioning in that it promotes a particular response as a result of the subject's previous experience, but it does so in a less reflexive way. It *sets the occasion* for responding, rather than reflexively eliciting the response.

Operant discrimination training, like the analogous procedure in classical conditioning, can be a powerful tool for learning about the sensory abilities of animals and human infants, who cannot describe their sensations in words. In one experiment, for example, researchers trained 1-day-old human babies to turn their heads in one direction—using a sip of sugar water as the reinforcer—whenever a tone was sounded and in the other direction whenever a buzzer was sounded (Siqueland & Lipsitt, 1966). Thus the babies learned to make two different responses to two different discriminative stimuli. This demonstrated, among other things, that the newborns could hear the difference between the two sounds. (More is said about such experiments in Chapter 11.)

17.

How can a neutral stimulus be turned into a discriminative stimulus to control an operant response?

18.

How can a discriminative stimulus for one response serve as a reinforcer for a new response and thereby link two responses together in a chain?

The Amazing Barnabus

Through the systematic process of chaining, Barnard College students trained an ordinary rat named Barnabus to climb a spiral ramp, push down a drawbridge, cross a moat, climb a staircase, crawl through a tunnel, enter an elevator, operate the elevator, raise a miniature Columbia University flag, and finally press a lever, all in the proper sequence for the ultimate reward of a pellet of food (Pierrel & Sherman, 1963).

Chaining, Secondary Reinforcement, and Tokens

Let's return to the rat that has been conditioned to press a lever whenever a tone comes on. Because the tone sets the occasion for receiving a reinforcer, the tone itself acquires reinforcing value. If the trainer arranges the environment so that the tone comes on whenever the rat pulls a string, the rat will learn to pull the string. After such training, the animal's behavior in the Skinner box consists of a chain of two operant responses linked by the tone. The tone serves as a reinforcer for one response (the string pull) and a discriminative stimulus for the next (the lever press):

string-pull response → tone → lever-press response → food

With further training, this chain could be extended by establishing a discriminative stimulus for the string-pull response (say, a green light) and then using that as the reinforcer for yet a new response (say, turning a wheel). By this stepwise procedure, rats have been trained to complete chains of as many as a dozen separate responses in order to obtain in the end a pellet of food or a drop of water (Pierrel & Sherman, 1963). Similar techniques have been used to train severely retarded people to complete such response sequences as those involved in dressing themselves. First the person learns the last step in the sequence, for a reinforcer, and then new steps are added, each of which is reinforced by the opportunity it provides to perform the next step.

NYT Pictures

Through the procedure just described, almost any kind of stimulus can become a reinforcer. A ***primary reinforcer*** is a stimulus, such as food or water, that is reinforcing even without previous training, and a ***secondary reinforcer*** is a stimulus, such as the tone in the above example, that has acquired its reinforcing value through previous training. In the example just discussed, the tone could serve as a secondary reinforcer for the string-pull response because it had set the occasion for obtaining food. From this perspective, a secondary reinforcer is reinforcing because it permits an individual to obtain a primary reinforcer. Operant theorists point out that much human behavior is reinforced by secondary reinforcers—such as money, certificates, and grades—which have acquired their reinforcing status because of their previous use in obtaining primary reinforcers. With money in my hand I can buy food; therefore, I will work for money:

work → money → buy food → food

In this chain, unlike the one described for the rat, a considerable delay may occur between one response (working for money) and the next (using the money to buy food). A secondary reinforcer, such as money, which can be saved and exchanged later for another reinforcer, is called a ***token***.

In a classic experiment with chimpanzees, J. B. Wolfe (1936) demonstrated that humans are not the only animals that can learn to work for tokens. Wolfe first

Joel Gordon

Joel Gordon

In a token economy

These volunteers at the Brooklyn Developmental Center (New York) wait on "customers" at the Center's "store." Staff members give tokens to their severely retarded clients to reward and motivate them for learning, maintaining, or improving a skill. Clients can then use the tokens to purchase different items at the store.

trained chimpanzees to place poker chips into a machine that dispensed grapes, and then he trained them to make new responses to obtain poker chips. Because the poker chips could be used to obtain grapes, they served readily as secondary reinforcers. Interestingly, the chimpanzees would work for poker chips even when the grape machine was temporarily removed and the chips could not be used immediately to get grapes, indicating that the chips now functioned as true tokens. The chimpanzees would save them and cash them in for grapes when the machine again became available.

Negative Reinforcement

In Skinner's terminology, *reinforcement* refers to any process that increases the likelihood that a particular response will occur. Reinforcement can be positive or negative. *Positive reinforcement*, the type that you have been reading about so far, occurs when the *arrival* of some stimulus following a response makes the response more likely to recur. The stimulus in this case is called a *positive reinforcer*. Food pellets, grapes, money, words of praise, and everything else that organisms will work to obtain are positive reinforcers. *Negative reinforcement*, in contrast, occurs when the *removal* of some stimulus following a response makes the response more likely to recur. The stimulus in this case is called a *negative reinforcer*. Electric shocks, loud noises, unpleasant company, scoldings, and everything else that organisms will work to get away from are negative reinforcers. The one example of negative reinforcement discussed so far was the experiment in which a thumb-twitch response was reinforced by the temporary removal of unpleasant static. Notice that *positive* and *negative* here do *not* refer to the direction of change in the response rate—that increases in either case. Rather, they indicate whether the response causes a particular stimulus to arrive (positive) or be removed (negative).

Punishment

In Skinner's terminology, *punishment* is the opposite of reinforcement. It is the process through which the consequence of a response *decreases* the likelihood that the response will recur. As with reinforcement, punishment can be positive or negative. In *positive punishment*, the arrival of a stimulus, such as electric shock for a rat or scolding for a person, decreases the likelihood that the response will occur again. In *negative punishment*, the removal of a stimulus, such as taking food away from a hungry rat or money away from a person, decreases the likelihood that the

19.

How does negative reinforcement differ from positive reinforcement?

20.

How does punishment differ from reinforcement, and how do the two kinds of punishment parallel the two kinds of reinforcement?

FIGURE **4.11**
Two types of reinforcement and two types of punishment
Reinforcement (whether positive or negative) increases the response rate, and punishment (whether positive or negative) decreases the response rate. The terms *positive* and *negative* refer to whether the reinforcing stimulus arrives or is removed when the response is made.

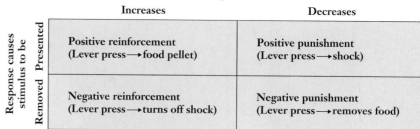

		Response rate	
		Increases	Decreases
Response causes stimulus to be	Presented	Positive reinforcement (Lever press → food pellet)	Positive punishment (Lever press → shock)
	Removed	Negative reinforcement (Lever press → turns off shock)	Negative punishment (Lever press → removes food)

response will occur again. Both types of punishment can be distinguished from extinction, which, you recall, is the decline in a previously reinforced response when it no longer produces any effect.

To picture the distinction between positive and negative punishment, and to see their relation to positive and negative reinforcement, look at Figure 4.11. The terms are easy to remember if you recall that *positive* and *negative* always refer to the arrival or removal of a stimulus and that *reinforcement* and *punishment* always refer to an increase or decrease in the likelihood that the response will recur.

The figure also makes it clear that the same stimuli that can serve as positive reinforcers when presented can serve as negative punishers when removed, and the same stimuli that can serve as positive punishers when presented can serve as negative reinforcers when removed. It is easy to think of the former as "desired" stimuli and the latter as "undesired," but Skinner urged us to avoid such mentalistic terms. He argued that the only way we can tell whether a stimulus is desired or undesired is by observing the manner in which it serves as a reinforcer or punisher to the individual in question, so the mentalistic terms add nothing to our understanding.

Effective and Ineffective Punishment

21.

What are some problems with the use of punishment to improve a child's behavior?

Punishment is interesting to many people because of its common use to control children's behavior. Skinner (1953) and many other psychologists (Martin & Pear, 1996; Newsom & others, 1983) have pointed out that punishment—especially painful positive punishment such as spanking—often has undesired consequences. Punishment can elicit negative emotions, such as fear and anger, which may result in further misbehavior. Through classical conditioning, any stimuli present during punishment—including the caregiver who administers it—may become conditioned stimuli for the negative emotions, so the child may learn to feel fear or anger toward the caregiver. Through observational learning (to be described later), the caregiver's use of punishment may inadvertently teach the child to use punishment to control others' behavior; the child may learn to hit or verbally berate. In addition, while punishment may lead to the suppression of the specific punished behavior, it is unlikely to promote desired substitutes for that behavior. A child punished for bad table manners, for example, may learn to refrain from certain undesired actions but not learn new desired actions. For these and other reasons, psychologists typically advise that caregivers use positive reinforcement rather than punishment to modify children's behavior. A child who is complimented and treated well for showing good table manners may exhibit increasingly good manners until the bad manners are pushed out by the good, and that procedure is better for everyone's digestion than is spanking.

Sometimes, however, immediate intervention is required to stop a young child's seriously disruptive or dangerous actions. A technique often recommended by child-care experts is *time-out*, in which the child is removed temporarily from the scene of the misbehavior and required to sit quietly and alone for a brief period—typically a minute or two—before regaining freedom (Turner & Watson, 1999).

This technique is categorized as negative punishment, because it involves the temporary removal of the opportunity to engage in enjoyable activities. Research in which parents have been trained to use the technique in a calm, firm, nonemotional manner, without threats or scolding, suggests that it can reduce disruptive behavior without producing the negative consequences that positive punishment does (Rortvedt & Miltenberger, 1994).

SECTION SUMMARY

In their attempt to develop an objective psychology, behaviorists focused on the influences of observable environmental conditions on behavior. They used the term conditioning as a synonym for learning and identified two types: classical and operant. In classical conditioning a new stimulus is paired with a stimulus (the unconditioned stimulus) that reflexively elicits some response, and, as a consequence, the new stimulus (now called the conditioned stimulus) acquires the capacity to elicit that response or one related to it (now called the conditioned response). This process can be understood as an objective manifestation of the law of association by contiguity, long central to empiricist philosophy. In experiments with dogs Pavlov uncovered many phenomena associated with classical conditioning, including extinction, spontaneous recovery, generalization, and discrimination. Watson used classical conditioning as a foundation for behaviorism, and he performed experiments showing that fears could be acquired through this process. Classical conditioning of counteractive responses to drugs explains why an addict can tolerate a larger drug dose in the usual environment than in a novel environment.

Operant conditioning was first studied by Thorndike and later named by Skinner. Thorndike formulated the law of effect to account for animals' tendencies to repeat, ever more quickly, responses that had previously led to a satisfying end, such as escape from a puzzle box. Skinner proposed the term reinforcer to refer to the stimulus or event that Thorndike considered to be the satisfying end, and he reformulated the law of effect as the principle of operant conditioning: A response followed by a reinforcer increases in frequency. Operant behavior is often considered to be voluntary rather than reflexive, but, as demonstrated in Hefferline's thumb-twitch conditioning experiment, it can occur in people without their conscious awareness. In experiments in which animals pressed levers for pellets of food or drops of water, Skinner and his followers identified many phenomena associated with operant conditioning, including shaping, extinction, effects of various schedules of partial reinforcement, discrimination training, chaining, secondary reinforcement, and distinctions between positive and negative reinforcement and positive and negative punishment.

THE COGNITIVE PERSPECTIVE ON LEARNING: ACQUIRING INFORMATION ABOUT THE WORLD

22.

In the most general terms, how does the cognitive perspective differ from the behavioral perspective?

The behavioral perspective, in the pure forms advocated by Watson and Skinner, avoids explanations in terms of unseen events in the mind or brain; it seeks instead to describe learning and other behavioral processes in terms of observable stimuli and responses. But many of Watson's and Skinner's contemporaries argued that unseen mental constructs that are inferred from observed behavior can be very useful in predicting and explaining what organisms will learn or do. They pointed out that many constructs in science—such as gravity and the idea of force—are not directly observable but are inferred from the way things behave and are useful in predicting future behavior. Some of these contemporaries called themselves *liberalized behaviorists* or *S-O-R theorists*. The *O* in *S-O-R* stands for "organism" or, more precisely, for some sort of interpretation of the stimulus that occurs inside the organism and determines the response:

$$\text{stimulus} \rightarrow \text{interpretation} \rightarrow \text{response}$$

Today the approach advocated by those liberalized behaviorists is called **cognitive psychology** (see Chapter 1). Cognitive psychology is the attempt to explain the behavior of humans and other animals in terms of mental entities, such as knowledge and beliefs, that are inferred from observable behavior. You will read much more about cognitive psychology in later chapters (especially Chapters 8 through 13). Here we will focus on the perspective's contributions to the understanding of basic learning processes.

The Cognitive Nature of Stimuli

As you have seen, a fundamental concept in the behaviorist's view of learning is that of the *stimulus*. But what precisely is a stimulus? Cognitive theorists argue that to understand the role of stimuli in conditioning, one must consider not just their physical aspects but also their meaning to the individual being conditioned. To predict how a given individual will respond to a given stimulus, we must know how that individual will interpret that stimulus, and to know that is to know something about the structure of the subject's mind.

23.

What is some evidence, from people and pigeons, that conditioned and discriminative stimuli are interpreted before they are responded to?

Meaning as a Basis for Generalization

Consider, for example, an experiment in classical conditioning conducted long ago by Gregory Razran (1939), who used college students as subjects, a squirt of lemon juice into the mouth as the unconditioned stimulus, and printed words as conditioned stimuli. By pairing each word with a squirt of lemon juice, Razran conditioned students to salivate to the words *style*, *urn*, *freeze*, and *surf*. He then tested the students to see if the conditioned response would generalize to other words that had never been paired with lemon juice. Of most interest, he found that the students salivated more to the words *fashion*, *vase*, *chill*, and *wave* than to the words *stile*, *earn*, *frieze*, and *serf*. That is, the conditioned response generalized more to words that resembled the original conditioned stimuli in meaning than to words that resembled the originals in physical appearance or sound. Thus the true conditioned stimuli were not the physical sights or sounds of the words but the subjects' interpretation of them.

An even more dramatic demonstration of stimulus generalization based on word meaning was conducted by a Soviet psychologist (Volkova, 1953). A Russian schoolboy was conditioned to salivate to the Russian word for *good* and, by discrimination training, not to salivate to the word for *bad*. When the discrimination was well established, the boy was found to salivate copiously to such statements as *The Soviet army was victorious* and not at all to statements such as *The pupil was fresh to the teacher*. In other words, those statements that the boy interpreted as good elicited

FIGURE 4.12
Tree pictures similar to those used to study concepts in pigeons
Pigeons that had been trained to peck whenever a slide contained a tree, or part of a tree, pecked when they saw slides such as these and refrained from pecking when they saw similar slides that did not include a tree.

salivation, and those that he interpreted as bad did not. A child who had a different set of conceptions of what is good or bad might have shown the opposite pattern of salivation.

Concepts in Pigeons

We need not look to humans or language to make the point that stimuli are interpreted before they are responded to. Consider an experiment conducted by Richard Herrnstein (1979), who operantly conditioned pigeons to peck a key for grain, using slides depicting natural scenes as discriminative stimuli. Herrnstein divided the slides into two categories—those that had at least one tree or portion of a tree somewhere in the scene and those that didn't (see Figure 4.12). The pigeons received grain for pecking the key whenever a "tree" slide was shown and nothing when a "nontree" slide was shown. In the first phase, 80 slides were presented each day, 40 of which contained trees and 40 of which didn't. By the end of 5 days of such training—that is, after five presentations of all 80 slides—all the birds were successfully discriminating between the two categories of slides, pecking when the slide contained a tree and not pecking otherwise.

Now, the question is: What did the pigeons learn in Herrnstein's experiment? Did they learn each slide as a separate stimulus, unrelated to the other slides, or did they learn a rule for categorizing the slides? Such a rule might be stated by a person in the following terms: "Respond whenever a slide includes a tree or part of a tree, and don't respond otherwise." To determine whether the pigeons had acquired such a rule, Herrnstein tested them with new slides, which they had never seen before, and found that they immediately pecked at a much higher rate when a new slide contained a tree than when it did not. In fact, the pigeons were as accurate with new slides as they were with slides that had been used during training. The birds apparently based their responses on a *concept* of trees (Herrnstein, 1990). A concept, as the term is used here, can be defined as a rule for categorizing stimuli into groups. The pigeons' tree concept, in this case, must have guided their decision to peck or not to peck.

How might one describe the pigeons' tree concept? That question is not easily answered. It is *not* the case, for example, that the pigeons simply learned to peck at slides that included a patch of green. Many of the nontree slides had green grass, and some of the tree slides were of fall or winter scenes in New England, where the trees had red and yellow leaves or none at all. In some slides, only a small portion of a tree was apparent or the tree was in the distant background. So the method by which the pigeons distinguished tree slides from nontree

It's a flower

Researchers have developed various means to test animals' abilities to categorize complex objects. In the experiment illustrated here, Edward Wasserman (1995) trained pigeons to peck a different one of four keys depending on whether the slide shown was of a car, cat, chair, or flower. The birds proved to be quite accurate at classifying objects that they had never seen before.

slides cannot be easily stated in stimulus terms, although ultimately it must have been based on the birds' analysis of the stimulus material. Other experiments have shown that pigeons can acquire concepts pertaining to such objects as cars, chairs, and even abstract symbols that do not have counterparts in the natural environment of pigeons (Wasserman, 1995; Zentall, 2000). The point is that, even for pigeons and certainly for humans, sophisticated analysis of the stimulus information occurs before the stimulus is used to guide behavior.

The Cognitive View of Classical Conditioning

What does an animal learn in classical conditioning? Watson (1924) and other early behaviorists believed that the animal learns a new reflex, that is, a new stimulus-response connection. From their perspective, Pavlov's conditioned dog salivated to the bell because of a direct, learned connection between the bell and salivation. This *stimulus-response (S-R)* theory of classical conditioning is diagrammed in the top part of Figure 4.13. Pavlov (1927/1960) himself, however, had a different theory.

Classical Conditioning Interpreted as Stimulus-Stimulus Association

Consistent with the earlier associationist philosophers, Pavlov believed that the animal does not learn a direct stimulus-response connection but, rather, learns a connection between two stimuli, the conditioned stimulus and the unconditioned stimulus. Because the bell and food have been paired in past experience, a physiological bond is formed between their representations in the brain, such that the sound of the bell now activates the part of the brain that was formerly activated by food, and that, in turn, elicits salivation. Using mental rather than physiological terms, we could say that the dog salivates to the bell because the bell sound elicits in the dog a mental representation of food (bell → mental representation of food → salivation). This *stimulus-stimulus (S-S)* theory of classical conditioning is illustrated in the bottom part of Figure 4.13.

Many experiments have been conducted to test the S-R and S-S theories of classical conditioning, and the weight of evidence favors the latter for most examples of conditioning in mammals and birds (Anderson, 2000). As an illustration, consider an experiment conducted by Robert Rescorla (1973) using rats as subjects, a loud sound as the unconditioned stimulus, and a signal light as the conditioned stimulus. The loud sound elicited freezing (a fear response in which the rats stand

24.

How does an experiment involving habituation support the S-S theory of classical conditioning over the S-R theory?

FIGURE **4.13** *Comparison of S-R and S-S theories of classical conditioning*
According to the S-R theory, conditioning produces a direct bond between the conditioned stimulus and the response. According to the S-S theory, conditioning produces a bond between the conditioned stimulus and the unconditioned stimulus. Support for the S-S theory comes from experiments showing that weakening the unconditioned reflex (through habituation), after conditioning, also weakens the conditioned reflex.

S-R Theory of Classical Conditioning

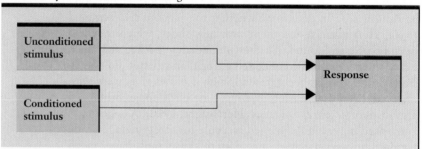

S-S Theory of Classical Conditioning

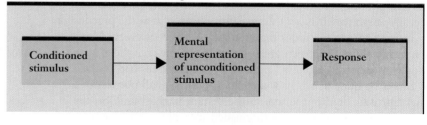

motionless) as an unconditioned response. By pairing the signal light with the loud sound, Rescorla conditioned the rats to freeze when the signal light came on. Now, the question was: Did the rats freeze in response to the signal light because of a direct, learned connection between the light and freezing, in accordance with the S-R theory (light → freezing)? Or did they freeze because of a learned connection between the light and the loud sound, in accordance with the S-S theory (light → mental representation of loud sound → freezing)?

To answer the question, Rescorla habituated the response to the loud sound in half of the conditioned rats. That is, he presented the loud sound many times without the signal light until the rats no longer froze in response to it. Then he again tested the rats with the signal light. Would the rats that no longer froze in response to the loud sound continue to freeze in response to the light? The S-R and S-S theories make different predictions. According to the S-R theory, the habituated rats should continue to freeze in response to the light because conditioning would have produced a direct connection between the light and freezing. But according to the S-S theory, the habituated rats should not freeze in response to the light because conditioning would have produced a connection between the light and a representation of the loud sound, which itself no longer elicits freezing. Rescorla's results supported the S-S theory. Habituation to the sound greatly reduced the degree to which the rats froze in response to the light.

Classical Conditioning Interpreted as Learned Expectancy

The S-S theory of classical conditioning, by its nature, is more cognitive than the S-R theory. The S-S theory holds that the observed stimulus-response relation is mediated by an inner, mental representation of the original unconditioned stimulus. Cognitive theorists argue that the inner representation may be best understood as an *expectation* of the unconditioned stimulus. In this view, Pavlov's dog learned to expect food when it heard the bell.

The *expectancy theory* helps make sense of the observation that a conditioned response is often quite different from the unconditioned response. Consider again a dog being conditioned to a bell that precedes food. In response to food, the dog not only salivates but also chews (if it is solid food) and swallows. Salivation becomes conditioned to the bell, but chewing and swallowing usually do not. Moreover, the bell comes to elicit not only salivation but also responses that do not usually occur in response to the food-in-mouth stimulus—such as tail wagging, food begging, and looking in the direction of the usual source of food (Jenkins & others, 1978). According to the expectancy theory, all these responses, including salivation, occur *not* because they were previously elicited by the unconditioned stimulus but because they are the dog's responses to the *expectation* of food:

bell → expectation of food → tail wagging, food begging, salivation, etc.

Rescorla (1988) has summed up his cognitive view of classical conditioning as follows: "[Classical] conditioning is not a stupid process by which the organism willy-nilly forms associations between any two stimuli that happen to co-occur. Rather, the organism is best seen as an information seeker using logical and perceptual relations among events, along with its own preconceptions, to form a sophisticated representation of its world."

25.

How does the construct of expectancy help explain the ways in which a conditioned response is different from an unconditioned response?

Expectancy

There is nothing inscrutable about this young tiger cat. The sound of the can being attached to the opener permits her to predict the arrival of food. Her response is not identical to her response to food itself, but one of rapt attention.

Mark Sherman / Bruce Coleman

26.

What are three conditions in which the pairing of a new stimulus with an unconditioned stimulus does not result in classical conditioning? How do these observations support a cognitive view of conditioning?

Conditioning Depends on the Predictive Value of the Conditioned Stimulus

Support for Rescorla's view comes from research showing that classical conditioning occurs only, or at least mainly, when the new stimulus provides information that the animal can use to predict the arrival of the unconditioned stimulus, and thereby prepare itself for that event. Here are three classes of such findings:

1. ***The conditioned stimulus must precede the unconditioned stimulus.*** Classical conditioning is most effective if the onset of the conditioned stimulus slightly precedes the unconditioned stimulus; it commonly doesn't occur at all if the conditioned stimulus comes either simultaneously with or just after the unconditioned stimulus (Lieberman, 2000). This observation makes sense if the animal is actively seeking predictive information; a stimulus that does not precede the unconditioned stimulus is useless as a predictor, and thus is ignored by the animal.

2. ***The conditioned stimulus must signal heightened probability of occurrence of the unconditioned stimulus.*** Not all stimuli that are present just prior to an unconditioned stimulus become conditioned stimuli. Conditioning depends not just on the number of pairings of the potential conditioned stimulus with the unconditioned stimulus but also—negatively—on the number of times the unconditioned stimulus occurs in the absence of the potential conditioned stimulus (Rescorla, 1988; Rescorla & Wagner, 1972). In fact, if the unconditioned stimulus is as likely to occur when the potential conditioned stimulus is absent as when it is present, conditioning usually does not occur at all (see Figure 4.14). The animal's behavior suggests that in some way its nervous system computes two probabilities—the probability that the unconditioned stimulus occurs in the presence of (or just after) the potential conditioned stimulus and the probability that it occurs in the absence of that stimulus—and accepts the potential conditioned stimulus as a predictor only if the first probability is greater than the second.

3. ***Conditioning is ineffective when the animal already has a good predictor.*** A number of experiments have shown that if one conditioned stimulus reliably precedes an unconditioned stimulus, the animal will not become conditioned to a new conditioned stimulus that is presented simultaneously with the first one. This failure of conditioning is called the *blocking effect*; the already-conditioned stimulus *blocks* conditioning to the new stimulus. For example, Leon Kamin (1969) showed that if a sound reliably precedes the onset of a shock and on later trials a light is added so that both the light and the sound come on simultaneously just before the shock, a rat does *not* develop a conditioned response to the light. A cognitive interpretation of this is that the rat has already solved the problem of predicting shock (by listening for the

FIGURE **4.14** *Stimulus relationships that will result in good, moderate, or no conditioning*

Rescorla and other researchers have found that a perfect correlation (top line) between a potential conditioned stimulus and an unconditioned stimulus results in rapid, strong classical conditioning; a moderate correlation (middle line) between the two results in a slower, weaker conditioning; and a zero correlation (bottom line) usually results in no conditioning.

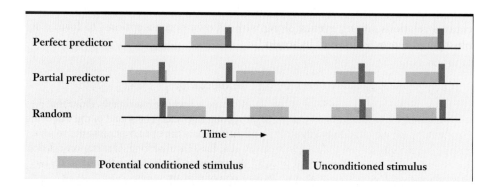

sound) and has no reason to learn a new way of predicting it. Only if the sound becomes an unreliable predictor does the animal look for another predictor, and in that case the animal does learn to respond to the light.

Cognitive psychologists often emphasize that their use of terms such as *expectation* and *prediction* does not imply anything mystical. The terms describe the kind of information that underlies the behavior but do not say anything about the physical form of that information, which presumably involves neural connections in the brain. To illustrate that such processes can occur through purely physical means, cognitive psychologists have programmed computers to behave in ways that simulate the processes of expectation and prediction (Commons & others, 1991). In fact, it is not difficult to design a machine that manifests all three of the conditioning phenomena listed above and in that sense is capable of learned prediction.

The Cognitive View of Operant Conditioning

What is learned in operant conditioning? Historically, theories about this have paralleled those about what is learned in classical conditioning. According to the S-R theory, held by many early behaviorists (Guthrie, 1952), operant conditioning entails the strengthening of a bond between the reinforced response and stimuli that are present just before the response is made (the discriminative stimuli). Thus, for a rat learning to press a lever in a Skinner box, the learned connection could be described as: stimuli inside Skinner box → lever press. Or if a more specific discriminative stimulus such as a tone is used, it could be described as: tone → lever press. According to this view, the reinforcer (such as a pellet of food), which follows the response, is involved in learning only insofar as it helps stamp in the connection between the antecedent stimuli and the response.

Other theorists, however, taking a more cognitive perspective, have argued—with evidence—that during operant conditioning the animal learns much more than the S-R relationship. The animal also learns the S-S relationship between the discriminative stimuli and the reinforcing stimulus (Mowrer, 1960) and the R-S relationship between the response and the reinforcing stimulus (Mackintosh & Dickinson, 1979). In other words, a rat in a Skinner box learns that the discriminative stimuli within the box signal that food is available there (S-S relationship) and that pressing the lever will make the food appear (R-S relationship). In an early cognitive theory, Edward Tolman (1959) described operant conditioning as the learning of means-end relationships.

Operant Conditioning Interpreted as Means-End Relationships

A *means-end relationship* is the animal's knowledge or belief that a particular response, in a particular situation, will have a particular effect. Thus, according to Tolman, if a rat is reinforced with a specific kind of food for pressing a lever when a tone is on, the rat acquires the knowledge that pressing the lever when the tone is on will produce that food. In the future, the occurrence of the tone does not automatically produce a lever-press response, as the S-R theory would hold, but, rather, activates the animal's knowledge that a lever press will bring a certain food—will be the means to an end. The animal can then press the lever or not, depending on its current interest in the food. Thus, in Tolman's view, the rat's behavior is best understood as:

tone → knowledge that lever press will now bring a certain kind of food
 → decision to press lever or not, depending on whether the food is desired

In support of this cognitive view, animals that have learned an operant response have been shown to vary their response rate in ways that are predictable on the premise that the animals have learned a means-end relationship (Dickinson, 1989; Dickinson & Balleine, 2000). For example, in one experiment, some hungry

27.

How can the view that operant conditioning involves means-end knowledge be experimentally tested? What are the results of one such test?

FIGURE **4.15** *Evidence that rats learn what reinforcer a response produces*

All the rats were trained to press the lever when hungry. Some had received drops of sugar water as their training reinforcer, and others had received dry food pellets. When tested under extinction conditions (no reinforcer given), the animals that had been trained with sugar water made about the same number of responses whether they were thirsty or hungry. In contrast, those that had been trained with food pellets made fewer responses when thirsty than when hungry. These results suggest that the rats had a conception of the reinforcer that the response would produce and knew whether it would satisfy both thirst and hunger or only hunger. (Adapted from Dickinson & Dawson, 1987.)

28.

How are reward contrast effects explained from a cognitive perspective, and what is the evidence that they depend on brain structures not present in fish and reptiles?

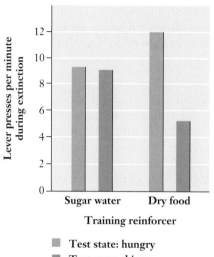

rats were trained to press a lever for sugar water and others were trained to press a lever for dry food pellets as a reinforcer (Dickinson & Dawson, 1987). Later all the rats were tested under extinction conditions (no reinforcer given), after having been deprived of either food or water. The interesting result was that when tested in the new drive state (thirst), those that had been reinforced with sugar water (which would satisfy thirst as well as hunger) pressed at a high rate, and those that had been reinforced with dry pellets (which would not satisfy thirst) pressed at a low rate (see Figure 4.15). The most direct way to explain this difference is to assume that the rats had acquired knowledge of the kind of reinforcer they would receive for pressing the lever and were able to use that knowledge to decide whether or not the reinforcer would satisfy their current drive state.

Reward Contrast Effects in Operant Conditioning

Further evidence that animals learn to expect a certain reinforcer for making a certain response is found in the existence of *reward contrast effects*, which involve shifts in the response rate when the size of the reward changes. Suppose that one group of rats is trained to press a lever for relatively large pellets of food as reinforcers and another group is trained to press for smaller pellets. As you might predict, rats in the first group would typically respond at a somewhat faster rate than those in the second. So far, this is consistent with S-R theory. Presumably, the S-R connection built by the larger reinforcer is stronger than that built by the smaller reinforcer, resulting in faster response rates in the first group. But now suppose that the rats receiving the large reinforcer are suddenly shifted to the small reinforcer. According to the S-R model, they should continue, at least for a while, to respond at a higher rate than the other rats, because of the stronger S-R connection built during the first phase of the experiment. But what actually happens is the opposite. Rats shifted from a large to a small reinforcer show a sharp drop in their response rate, to a slower rate than that of rats that had been in the small-reinforcer condition all along. This illustrates the **negative contrast effect**. Conversely, rats shifted from a small to a large reinforcer show an increase in their response rate, to a higher rate than that of rats that had been in the large-reinforcer condition all along. This illustrates the **positive contrast effect**.

Not surprisingly, reward contrast effects also occur for people. If you have been getting $1 per page for typing term papers, you will probably be delighted to discover that your pay is now $2 per page, and you may type with renewed vigor; but if you have been getting $4 per page, that same discovery (that you are now getting only $2) may lead you to quit. Clearly, our experience of reward size is relative to what we are used to receiving. From a cognitive perspective, these contrast effects—in rats as in humans—are explained by assuming that the animal (a) has learned to expect a certain reward and (b) is able to compare the actual reward with the expected one. If the comparison is favorable, the animal increases its response rate; if unfavorable, the animal decreases its rate. The animal is constantly out to do better, and if a particular response leads to less reinforcement than it did before, the animal might do better by spending less time at it and more time looking for reinforcers elsewhere. In fact, animals that have experienced a downshift in reward size do engage in increased exploration, as if looking for the larger reward (Pecoraro & others, 1999).

Reward contrast effects have been observed in many species of mammals and in pigeons (Flaherty, 1996). However, such effects apparently do not occur in fish and reptiles (Bitterman, 2000). For example, in one experiment fish trained to push a key for a large reinforcer (40 worms per response) and then switched to a small reinforcer (4 worms per response) continued, after the switch, to respond at a faster rate than fish that were initially trained with the small reinforcer (Bitterman, 1975). In certain other ways, too, researchers have found that the behavior of fish and reptiles conforms more closely to S-R predictions than does the behavior of mammals and birds (Bitterman, 2000). Perhaps, in the evolution of mammals and birds from their reptilelike ancestors, changes occurred in the brain that permitted more complex cognitive processes, including the ability to compare present rewards with past ones, and these were added on to a basic S-R learning mechanism. This view is supported by an experiment showing that rats treated with amobarbital, a drug that reduces neural activity in some of the higher parts of the brain, failed, like fish and reptiles, to show the negative contrast effect, while undrugged rats clearly showed it (Rosen & others, 1967). The same is true of immature rats, whose higher brain structures are not fully developed (Amsel, 1986).

The Overjustification Effect

In humans, rewards can affect the likelihood of engaging in a particular form of behavior by changing the person's understanding of the meaning of that behavior. Consider an experiment conducted with nursery school children (Lepper & Greene, 1978). Children in one group were rewarded with attractive "Good Player" certificates for drawing with felt-tipped pens. This had the immediate effect of leading them to spend more time at this activity than did children in the other group (who were not rewarded). Later, however, when certificates were no longer given, the previously rewarded children showed a sharp drop in their use of the pens—to a level well below that of children in the unrewarded group.

Many subsequent experiments, with people of various ages, have produced similar results. The drop in performance following a period of reward is particularly likely to occur when the task is something that is initially viewed as fun and the reward is given in such a manner that it seems to be designed to coerce the participants into engaging in the rewarded task (Deci & others, 1999; Newman & Layton, 1984). This decline is called the *overjustification effect* because the reward presumably provides an unneeded justification for engaging in the behavior. The result, according to the usual cognitive interpretation, is that the person comes to regard the task as work (the kind of thing one does for external rewards such as money, certificates, or an improved résumé) rather than play (the kind of thing that one does for its own sake). When the participants come to regard the task as work, they stop doing it when they no longer receive a reward for it, even though they would have continued to do it for fun if they had never been rewarded for it. The overjustification effect suggests that some rewards used in schools might have negative long-term effects. For example, rewarding children for reading might cause them to think of reading as work rather than fun, which would lead them to read less on their own. The broader point is that one must take into account the cognitive consequences of rewards in predicting their long-term effects.

29.

How does the overjustification effect illustrate a limitation in the use of reward to promote certain behaviors in people?

When does play become work?

Many people play tennis purely for pleasure, but some become so good at it that they are paid. In some cases, but certainly not all, payments for a previously enjoyed activity can change the way the activity is viewed, from play to work.

Tommy Hindly / Pro Sport / Topham / The Image Works

Place Learning

Much of the early impetus for a more cognitive view of learning came from research by Tolman and his students, using rats in mazes. Behaviorists in Tolman's time (the 1920s to 1940s) often interpreted maze learning in stimulus-response terms. They believed that an animal learns a sequence of responses—such as turn right, go forward, turn left—each signaled by stimuli that are present at the critical-choice points in the maze. Tolman's research led him to reject that view. He proposed instead that animals allowed to explore either a maze or a more natural terrain do not learn a specific sequence of responses but, rather, acquire a *cognitive map*—a mental representation of the spatial layout of the maze or terrain. He also proposed that animals acquire that representation just from exploring, whether or not they find any rewards.

Tolman's Evidence That Animals Learn Cognitive Maps

Tolman (1948) and his students showed that when faced with a change in their starting place, or with blockades placed in their usual routes, rats behave as if they are able to consult a map and work out the best available route to the goal. In one experiment, for example, Tolman and Honzik (1930a) used the maze depicted in Figure 4.16, which contains three possible routes from the start box to the goal box (and food). After sufficient experience, rats showed a strong preference for route 1 (the shortest), less preference for route 2 (the next shortest), and the least for route 3 (the longest).

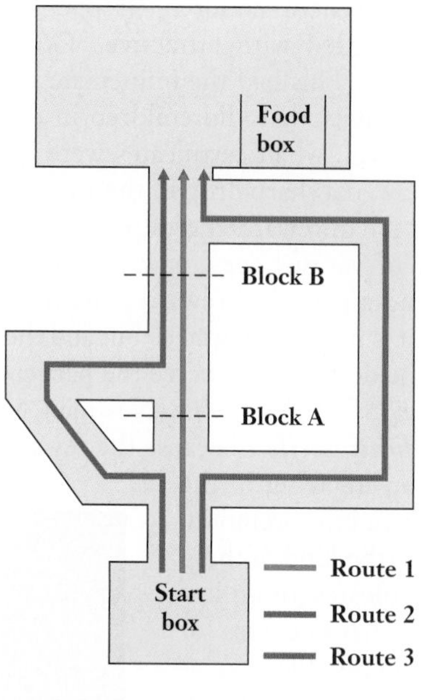

In the critical phase of the experiment, route 1 was blocked at one of two points, as shown in Figure 4.16. When the block was at point A, most rats ran down route 1, reached the block, and then went back and took route 2. But when the block was at point B, most rats ran down route 1, reached the block, and then went back and took route 3, previously their least preferred route. By inspecting Figure 4.16 (which literally is a map), you can see that this is exactly what an intelligent individual with maplike knowledge of the maze would be expected to do in this situation. The block at point B blocks routes 1 and 2, so now only route 3 leads to the goal. According to Tolman, such behavior—occurring as it did the first time the rats were faced with the blockade—cannot be interpreted in terms of learned stimulus-response habits but must be understood as insight based on maplike knowledge of the maze.

30.

How did Tolman show that rats use cognitive maps and that they learn such maps whether or not they are rewarded?

FIGURE **4.16**
Maze used to demonstrate insightful use of cognitive maps
Rats well trained in this maze normally took route 1, the most direct route to the food. When a block was placed at point A, they ran back and took route 2, the shortest unblocked route. When a block was placed at point B, rather than A, they ran back and took route 3, the only unblocked route. Most rats made these adaptive responses during the first trial in which the obstacle appeared, which led Tolman and Honzik to conclude that the rats had spatial knowledge (a cognitive map) of the maze that they could use intelligently. (Adapted from Tolman & Honzik, 1930a.)

Tolman's Evidence That Place Learning Does Not Require Reward

Do animals learn the spatial layout of their environment only when they receive some reward, such as food, for finding a particular location, or do they learn it even without such rewards? To answer that question, Tolman and Honzik (1930b) tested three groups of rats in a complex maze under different reward conditions. Group 1 received one trial per day in the maze with no food or other reward in the goal box. As expected, the rats in this group showed little improvement from day to day in the time it took them to reach the goal box (the goal box contained no "goal" for them). Group 2 received one trial per day with food in the goal box. As expected, this group improved considerably from day to day. The most interesting group was group 3. Rats in this group received one trial per day with no reward for 10 days,

Samuel Gross © 1994. *The New Yorker Magazine.*

"Well, you don't look like an experimental psychologist to me."

like group 1, but, beginning on the eleventh day, they received one trial per day with a food reward, like group 2. These rats improved dramatically between days 11 and 12. On day 11, they were no better than the other unrewarded group (group 1), but on day 12, after just one experience with the reward, they were as fast at reaching the goal box as the rats that had been rewarded all along (see Figure 4.17).

On the basis of this and other experiments, Tolman (1948) argued that rewards affect what animals *do* more than what they *learn*. Animals learn the location of distinctive places in their environment whether or not they have ever found rewards there, but they do not run directly to those places unless they have found rewards there. Tolman used the term **latent learning** to refer to learning that is not immediately demonstrated in the animal's behavior. In the experiment just described, the rats in group 3 learned the maze in the first 10 trials, but that learning remained *latent*, not manifested in their behavior, until the addition of a reward in the goal box gave the rats a reason to use their cognitive maps to run to that location.

Tolman's conclusion that animals acquire maplike representations of the terrains they explore has been confirmed in hundreds of subsequent experiments with many animal species, including humans (Gallistel, 1990). We will consider some of this research near the end of this chapter.

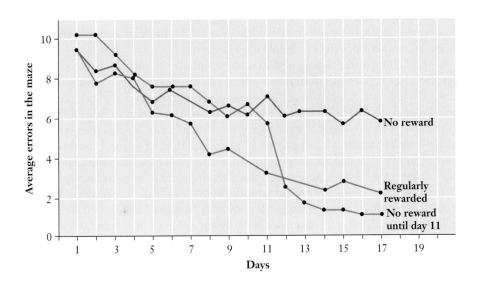

FIGURE 4.17
Latent learning of a maze
Each rat received one trial per day in the maze, with or without a food reward in the goal box. The group that received its first reward on day 11 performed as well on day 12 (and thereafter) as the group that had received a reward every day. From this, Tolman and Honzik concluded that the rats had learned the spatial layout of the maze even without a reward, but the rats did not use that knowledge until the changed conditions made it worthwhile for them to do so. (From Tolman & Honzik, 1930b.)

Observational Learning

If you examine learning in everyday human life, you cannot help noticing that people learn to a great extent by watching other people. Imagine what life would be like if such skills as driving a car or performing surgery were learned purely by trial and error! Fortunately, people learn such skills partly by observing closely and mimicking the behavior of those who have already mastered them. On a grander scale, learning by watching others seems to be a prerequisite for human culture. The skills and rituals acquired by each generation are passed on to the next not so much because the older generation deliberately trains the younger (though that is part of it) but more because members of the younger generation intently observe their elders to learn to behave as they do. Learning by watching others is called ***observational learning***.

31.

How does observation of skilled performers facilitate the learning of new operant tasks by nonprimate animals? How does imitation differ from stimulus enhancement and goal enhancement, and what evidence suggests that chimpanzees can learn through imitation?

Observational Learning by Nonhuman Animals

Observational learning is especially apparent in humans, but it can be seen to varying degrees in other creatures as well. For example, kittens can learn more quickly to press a lever for food if they have seen their mother do so than if they have not (Chesler, 1969), and goslings can learn to open a box to get food more quickly if they have seen a person perform the task than if they have not (Fritz & others, 2000). How do such observations help the observer learn the task? A common view today is that the help occurs largely through stimulus enhancement and goal enhancement (Byrne & Russon, 1998).

Stimulus enhancement refers to an increase in the salience or attractiveness of the object that the observed individual is acting upon, and *goal enhancement* refers to an increased drive to obtain rewards similar to what the observed individual is receiving. Thus a kitten that sees its mother pressing a lever for food pellets may become attracted to the lever (stimulus enhancement) and motivated to eat food pellets (goal enhancement). In this case, stimulus enhancement increases the likelihood that the kitten will press the lever, goal enhancement increases the reward value of the pellets, and the two combined increase the rate at which the kitten learns through operant conditioning to press the lever for pellets.

Stimulus enhancement and goal enhancement are cognitively simpler than imitation. *Imitation* refers to instances in which the observer reproduces the specific actions of the observed individual (Byrne & Russon, 1998). If two individuals perform the same actions because they are instinctive to both of them, or because they have separately learned them through trial and error, that is not imitation. Imitation is cognitively complex because it requires that the learner remember the novel actions that were observed and then map them onto its own movement control system. Debate exists as to whether or not any animals other than primates can imitate, but at least some primates clearly can. The most thoroughly studied primate imitators (other than humans) are chimpanzees.

Wild chimpanzees living in different groups, geographically isolated from one another, have different cultural traditions, which pass from generation to generation. For example, chimpanzees in some colonies crack hard-shelled nuts by placing the nut on a carefully selected rock and hitting it with another carefully selected rock. The young in these colonies learn this difficult skill by observing their elders closely and practicing elements of it over a period of several months (Inoue-Nakamura & Matsuzawa, 1997). In other colonies, however, chimpanzees have never been observed to crack nuts, even though plenty of nuts and stones are available (Whiten & others, 1999). Apparently, in those colonies the discovery that nuts can be cracked was never made, so it could not be passed along. In a recent count, researchers studying wild chimpanzees at seven different field stations listed 39 behaviors, ranging from tool design to mating displays, that are distinct to specific groups and that seem to arise from cultural tradition rather than from ecological

A not completely attentive observer
Chimpanzees learn through observation to crack nuts with rocks. This infant is too young to work seriously at nut cracking but may be learning something about it through watching the older master.

constraints (Whiten & others, 1999). In laboratory studies, captive chimpanzees have been shown to observe both human and chimpanzee "tutors" closely to learn new, sometimes complex sequences of actions to obtain rewards (Hirata & Morimura, 2000; Whiten, 1998).

Bandura's Research on Observational Learning by People

Albert Bandura (1977)—the psychologist who, over the years, has most vigorously studied observational learning in humans—has emphasized that people observe others to learn not just specific motor skills (such as driving a car and performing surgery) but also more general modes or styles of behaving. When you enter a new situation, you probably look around to see what others are doing before doing much yourself. When you do begin to act, you may mimic rather precisely some of the actions you have observed—such as the maneuvers required to coax coffee from the newfangled coffeemaker in the room. But beyond that (unless you are a clown), you probably don't imitate many of the exact actions of others. Rather, you adopt a general style of behavior that fits with what seems to be acceptable in the setting.

Bandura demonstrated both of these functions of observational learning—acquiring specific actions and learning general styles of behavior—in experiments with kindergarten children. In one experiment, one group of children observed an adult behaving very aggressively toward a large inflated Bobo doll (Bandura, 1969). The aggression included specific verbal insults and such physical acts as banging the doll with a mallet, hurling it down, kicking it, and bombarding it with balls. A second group watched the adult model behave in a gentle manner toward the doll, and a third group was not shown any model. Later, when each child was allowed to play in the room with a variety of toys, including the Bobo doll, those in the first group behaved more aggressively, and those in the second group behaved more gently, than those in the third group. The children in the first group not only mimicked many of the aggressive actions that they had observed in the adult model but also improvised many new aggressive actions of their own and directed them toward other toys as well as toward the Bobo doll. The children had learned not only specific ways of being aggressive but also the more general message that an appropriate way to play in this particular playroom was to act aggressively.

Bandura's theory of observational learning is an explicitly cognitive one. Just as Tolman posited that rats actively explore mazes to develop cognitive maps, Bandura (1977, 1986) proposes that people actively observe the behavior of other people to gain knowledge about the kinds of things that people do, and use that knowledge in situations where it is useful. He also developed methods of therapy in which people overcome fears by watching others engage in the feared activity, such as handling snakes (Bandura & others, 1982).

32.

How did Bandura demonstrate two functions of observational learning in experiments with children?

SECTION SUMMARY

Cognitive theorists explain the behavior of animals and people in terms of mental entities—such as knowledge, concepts, expectancies, and mental maps—that are inferred from observable behavior. They point out, for example, that stimulus generalization by people, and by pigeons, is based not just on the physical features of the stimulus but also on the meaning, or concept, that the person or pigeon attaches to the stimulus.

Cognitive theorists interpret classical conditioning as the learning of mental associations between conditioned and unconditioned stimuli. Cognitivists point out that classical conditioning occurs only when the conditioned stimulus is a useful predictor of the unconditioned stimulus and that conditioned responses help prepare the animal for the unconditioned stimulus. Similarly, cognitivists interpret operant conditioning as learned means-end relationships. In experiments that involve shifts in the animal's motivational state, and in experiments that demonstrate reward contrast effects, animals behave as though they expect certain consequences for their operant responses.

> Cognitive theorists contend further that some forms of learning cannot be described simply in terms of classical operant conditioning. For example, Tolman found evidence that rats that explore a maze acquire maplike knowledge of its spatial layout, whether or not they receive rewards in the maze. Chimpanzees and people can learn new skills through imitation, a process that requires the learner to remember the actions of the model and to repeat them effectively. Children who observed an adult behave aggressively in a particular setting learned not only to produce the specific behaviors demonstrated by the adult but also that aggressive behavior in general was appropriate in that setting.

33.

How does the ecological perspective differ from the behavioral and cognitive perspectives?

THE ECOLOGICAL PERSPECTIVE ON LEARNING: FILLING THE BLANKS IN SPECIES-TYPICAL BEHAVIOR PATTERNS

The behavioral and cognitive approaches to learning emphasize processes that are assumed to operate across a wide range of learning situations, and for that reason they are both considered to be part of a *general-process perspective*. Behaviorists have looked for general laws related to classical and operant conditioning, expressible in terms of stimuli and responses, that apply to all sorts of learning situations. And cognitivists have tried to describe general mental constructs, such as expectancies, that likewise apply to all sorts of learning situations. The alternative to the general-process perspective is called either the *specific-process perspective*, or, more often, the **ecological perspective** (Hollis, 1997; Johnston & Pietrewicz, 1985).

According to the ecological perspective, learning must be understood in relation to the natural environment, or ecology, in which a species evolved. Through natural selection, animals acquire instinctive, species-typical behavior patterns (discussed in Chapter 3) that help them survive and reproduce in their natural environments. The mechanisms that underlie many of these behaviors have evolved in such a way that they are not rigid but can be modified by specific aspects of the animals' experience. Thus the abilities of animals to find food, avoid predators, find mates, raise their young, and do whatever else they must to survive and reproduce depend on inherited behavioral tendencies coupled with inherited means to modify or refine those tendencies. The latter, taken together, make up the collection of mechanisms called *learning*. Many learning mechanisms have evolved to meet specific survival-related purposes, and to understand how these mechanisms work, we must think about them in relation to those purposes.

In Chapter 3, the white-crowned sparrow's ability to learn its parents' song was cited as an example of a specific learning mechanism designed to supplement a specific instinctual tendency. In Chapter 11, the idea that human language is acquired through a unique, specialized learning ability will be discussed. Now we will look at the learning of food aversions and preferences and then, more briefly, at a few examples of other specialized learning mechanisms.

Learning What to Eat

For some animals, learning what to eat is a relatively minor problem. Koalas, for instance, eat only the leaves of eucalyptus trees. Through natural selection, koalas evolved a food-identifying mechanism that tells them that eucalyptus leaves are food and everything else is not. That simplifies their food choice, but if eucalyptuses were to vanish, so would koalas. Other animals are more flexible in their diets. Most flexible of all are omnivorous creatures, such as rats and humans, which treat almost all organic matter as potential food and must *learn* what is safe to eat. Such animals have, through natural selection, acquired special mechanisms for learning to identify healthful foods and to avoid potential poisons.

Food-Aversion Learning

If rats become ill after eating a novel-tasting food, they subsequently avoid that food (Garcia & others, 1972). In experiments demonstrating this, researchers induce illness by adding a toxic substance to the food or by administering a drug or a high dose of x-rays to the animals after they have eaten. Similarly, people who by chance get sick after eating an unusual food often develop a long-term aversion to the food (Bernstein, 1991; Logue, 1988). For years as a child, I hated the taste and smell of a particular breakfast cereal, because once, a few hours after I ate it, I happened to develop a bad case of stomach flu. I knew, intellectually, that the cereal wasn't the cause of my illness, but that didn't help. The learning mechanism kicked in automatically and made me detest that cereal.

Many psychologists choose to describe such cases of food-aversion learning in terms of classical conditioning. Thus the feeling of illness or nausea induced by the x-ray treatment or drug is the unconditioned stimulus for a reaction of aversion or revulsion, and the taste and smell of food become conditioned stimuli for that reaction. But John Garcia, the researcher who pioneered the study of food-aversion learning, argues that such learning is quite different from standard cases of classical conditioning (Garcia & others, 1989).

Courtesy of UCLA Media

One special characteristic of food-aversion learning has to do with the optimal delay between the conditioned and unconditioned stimuli. In typical cases of classical conditioning, such as the salivary reflex studied by Pavlov, conditioning occurs only when the unconditioned stimulus follows immediately (within a few seconds at most) after the conditioned stimulus. But food-aversion learning has been demonstrated even when the x-rays were administered as much as 24 hours after the animals had eaten the food (Etscorn & Stephens, 1973). In fact, food-aversion learning fails to occur if the gap between tasting the food and the induction of illness (by means of a drug injected directly into the bloodstream) is less than a few minutes (Schafe & others, 1995).

Another special characteristic has to do with the sorts of stimuli that can serve as conditioned stimuli for such learning. In typical cases of classical conditioning, almost any kind of detectable stimulus can serve, but in food-aversion learning the stimulus must be a distinctive taste or smell (and taste works better than smell). Rats that become ill after eating a particular food subsequently avoid food that tastes or smells like what they have eaten, even if it looks different, but they do not avoid

34.

What are two ways in which food-aversion learning differs from typical examples of classical conditioning, and how do these differences make sense in terms of the function of such learning?

John Garcia

In the 1960s, Garcia discovered that food-avoidance learning violates certain principles of conditioning that had been accepted by many psychologists as general laws of learning. He pursued this work despite the "better judgment" of his thesis advisers and even though the editor of a leading psychological journal refused to publish his early findings on the grounds that they could not be true. One historian of psychology (Bolles, 1993) describes Garcia as a charismatic Spanish American fond of saying *Viva yo*, which translates literally into "Long live me" but actually means something like "To hell with you guys."

Learning to hate mutton

Coyotes are omnivorous, like rats and humans, and will learn to avoid foods that make them sick. In an experimental attempt to control coyote predation of sheep, sheep carcasses were treated with a drug that induces nausea. Captive coyotes that ate such carcasses subsequently stayed away from sheep (Gustavson & others, 1976).

food that looks like what they have eaten if it tastes and smells different (Garcia & others, 1968, 1989).

The distinguishing characteristics of food-aversion learning make excellent sense when considered in the light of the function that such learning serves in the natural environment. In general, poisons and spoiled foods do not make an individual ill immediately, but only after many minutes or several hours. Moreover, it is the chemical quality of a food, detectable in its taste and smell, not the visual quality, that affects health. For example, a food that has begun to rot and makes an animal sick may look just like one that has not begun to rot, but its taste and smell are quite different. Thus, to be effective, a learning mechanism for food aversion must tolerate long delays and be tuned especially to those sensory qualities that correspond with the food's chemistry.

Food-Preference Learning

35.

How might rats learn which food contains a needed vitamin?

The other side of the coin from learning to avoid harmful foods is that of learning to choose foods that satisfy a specific nutritional requirement. In a series of experiments on food-preference learning, researchers deprived rats of thiamine (one of the B vitamins, essential for health) for a period of time and then offered them a choice of foods, only one of which contained thiamine (Overmann, 1976; Rozin & Kalat, 1971). Each food had a distinct flavor, and thiamine—which itself has no flavor—was added to a different food for different rats. The result was that, within a few days of experience with the foods, most rats strongly preferred the thiamine-containing food.

How did the rats "figure out" which food contained the thiamine? Close inspection of their eating patterns suggests a possible answer (Rozin & Kalat, 1971). When first presented with the choices, a rat usually ate just one or two of them. Then, typically after several hours, the rat would switch to a different food or two. Such behavior—eating just one or two foods at a time—seems ideally suited for isolating particular foods that lead to an increase or a decrease in health. If the rat had sampled all the foods at once, it would have had no basis for knowing which food had affected its health. Thus, just as rats can learn to associate the taste of a food with subsequent illness and therefore avoid that food, they may also (to a lesser extent) be able to associate a taste with a subsequent improvement in health and thereafter prefer that food (Rozin & Schull, 1988).

A Food-Selection Experiment with Human Infants

36.

How are Davis's observations with human babies similar to results of food-selection experiments with rats? Why should we be cautious in interpreting Davis's study?

In the 1920s, before food-selection experiments with rats had been performed, a pediatrician named Clara Davis performed a bold experiment on food selection with human infants—so bold, in fact, that it would probably not pass the ethics review board of a modern research institution (which helps explain why the experiment has never been repeated). The subjects were newly weaned baby boys whose mothers consented to their participation, and the object was to determine whether the babies would feed themselves a nutritionally balanced diet if they could choose their own foods (Davis, 1928). For 6 months or longer, beginning at the age of 35 weeks, the babies lived in the children's ward of a hospital. At each meal, a tray containing about a dozen different foods was placed before each infant. The choices were all natural, wholesome foods—including cereals, fruits, ground meats, fish, eggs, and vegetables—but no single food contained all the required nutrients. To remain healthy, the infants would have to select a variety. At first a nurse had to help the babies eat, but she was allowed to feed a baby only what he had chosen through reaching or pointing. Within a few weeks, all the babies had learned to feed themselves, usually with their fingers, and the nurse's assistance was no longer needed.

The results of the experiment can be summarized as follows: All the babies developed clear food preferences, but the preferences varied from time to time such that over the long run each infant ate a nutritionally balanced diet. An infant would usually eat just two or three foods in quantity at any given meal and might stick to those for as long as a week but then would switch to other foods and stick with them for a similar period. One baby, who had rickets (due to lack of vitamin D) at the beginning of the experiment, self-selected cod-liver oil (which is rich in vitamin D) until his rickets was cured, and he stopped selecting it after that. All in all, the babies' behavior was rather similar to that of rats in food-selection experiments. It was as if they were following a logic that goes like this: Eat only a few foods at a time; if you feel well later, stick with those foods, but if you begin to feel less well, switch. Of course, if the infants could talk, they would probably express a different logic: "Last week I loved the applesauce, but this week it tastes awful and the mashed eggs are great."

We should be cautious, however, in interpreting these results. The observation that the boy with rickets self-selected cod-liver oil is made less surprising by evidence that (contrary to popular opinion) some young children like the taste of cod-liver oil, whether or not they have a vitamin D deficiency (Richter, 1942–1943). It is also possible that the changes in the infants' food preferences arose not from their associating tastes with changes in their health but simply from their becoming bored with a food they had eaten for several days (Galef, 1991). Moreover, the experiment probably would not have worked had unnaturally sweet foods, like fudge bars or sweetened cereals, been included among the choices. Even rats have great difficulty learning which food is good for them if one or more of the deficient foods is laced with sugar (Beck & Galef, 1989). From an ecological perspective, that is not surprising. The food-learning systems in rats and humans evolved long before refined sugar and fudge bars were invented.

The Role of Social Learning in Food Selection

In addition to learning from the individual trial-and-error mechanisms described above, rats learn what to eat from one another. Newly weaned wild rats generally limit their diets to foods that older rats in the colony regularly eat (Galef, 1985). Through this means, they can avoid even tasting a food that older animals have learned is poisonous (Galef & Clark, 1971) and can choose, from the beginning, a nutritious food that older animals have learned to prefer (Beck & Galef, 1989). Similar results have been found with kittens (Wyrwicka, 1996). Even in adulthood, rats are strongly influenced by one another's food choices. Bennett Galef (1990) has found that rats in a colony sniff near the mouth of a rat that has recently eaten and then show a strong preference for the food they had smelled on the demonstrator rat's breath. Through this and other means, adult rats introduced into a new colony acquire the colony's food preferences (Galef & Whiskin, 1997).

We humans, presumably, don't learn food preferences by smelling one another's breath, but we are certainly influenced by our observations of what those around us eat. In one experiment, children between 1 and 4 years old were more willing to taste a new food if they saw an adult eat it first than if they had never seen anyone eat it (Harper & Sanders, 1975). Other research suggests that children are most open to new foods from about 1 to 2 years of age, which is when they are most likely to be closely watched and fed by adults, and most unwilling to try new foods between about 4 and 8 years of age, a time when they are often on their own and thus more vulnerable to eating something harmful (Cashdan, 1994).

37.

What evidence, with rats and people, points to the importance of social learning in food selection?

Observational learning has its limits

Children acquire the food preferences of their culture by observing their elders, but sometimes it takes a while.

Mitch York / Tony Stone

38.

In sum, what has natural selection imparted to young omnivores about food selection?

Summary of Rules for Learning What to Eat

Suppose that you were a wise teacher of young omnivorous animals and wanted to equip your charges with a few rules for food selection that could be applied no matter what food was available. Two that you would probably come up with are these: (1) When possible, eat what your elders eat. Such food is probably safe, as evidenced by the fact that your elders have most likely been eating it for some time and are still alive. (2) When you eat a new food, remember its taste and smell. If you don't feel sick within a few hours, continue choosing foods of that taste and smell, but if you do feel sick, avoid such foods.

Notice that these rules don't specify exactly what to eat but, instead, specify *how to learn* what to eat. The first rule describes a variety of observational learning, and the second denotes a particular kind of associative learning in which the stimuli that one should pay attention to are spelled out in a way that makes the learning most efficient. As you have just seen, rats do in fact behave in accordance with these rules, and young humans may also. Of course, we assume that these rules have been imparted not by a wise teacher of young omnivores but by natural selection, which has shaped the brain to operate in accordance with the rules. Again, during evolution, animals have acquired instincts to learn about food in particular ways.

Other Examples of Selective Learning Abilities

Food selection is by no means the only functional area in which special learning abilities have apparently come about through evolution. Here are some other well-studied examples.

39.

What is some evidence that people and monkeys are biologically predisposed to learn to fear some things more easily than other things?

Innate Biases in Fear-Related Learning

Do you remember the demonstration by Watson and Rayner (1920), in which Little Albert was conditioned to fear a white rat through pairing the rat with a loud noise? Several years later, Elsie Bregman (1934), a graduate student working with Thorndike, tried to repeat that demonstration with one important modification. Instead of using a rat as the conditioned stimulus, she used various inanimate objects, including wooden blocks and pieces of cloth. Despite numerous attempts, with 15 different infants as subjects, she found no evidence of conditioning. What are we to make of this apparent discrepancy? One possibility, suggested by Martin Seligman (1971), is that people are biologically predisposed to acquire fears of situations and objects, such as rats, that posed a threat to our evolutionary ancestors and are less disposed to acquire fears of other situations and objects.

More recently, Susan Mineka and her colleagues have shown that rhesus monkeys are not afraid of snakes when first exposed to them but very easily learn to fear them. In one experiment, monkeys raised in the laboratory did not react fearfully to snakes until they saw another monkey (one raised in the wild) do so. After that, they showed strong fear reactions themselves (Mineka & others, 1984). In subsequent experiments, Michael Cook and Mineka (1989, 1990) used splicing to produce videotapes in which a monkey was shown reacting fearfully in the presence of various different objects, including toy snakes, flowers, and a toy rabbit. Through observing the tapes, monkeys that previously feared none of these objects developed a fear of toy snakes (and real snakes) but not of flowers or toy rabbits.

From an ecological perspective, this learning bias makes a good deal of sense. In some regions (depending on the kinds of snakes that are present), snakes are dangerous, and in other areas they are not. In places where snakes are harmless, an inflexible instinctive fear of them would be maladaptive. Thus, the learning mechanism may have evolved because it allows monkeys living in areas where snakes are dangerous to learn quickly to fear and avoid them, while it allows monkeys living elsewhere to go about their business relatively oblivious to snakes. We humans also vary greatly in the degree to which we fear snakes, and research suggests that we

Susan Minaka

Yikes!
Monkeys that have never been harmed by snakes nevertheless learn quickly to fear them through watching the fearful reactions of other monkeys.

learn to fear them—and other objects, such as spiders and angry faces, that posed threats to our evolutionary ancestors—more readily than we learn to fear equally dangerous objects that were not present in our early evolutionary history, such as electrical outlets, sharp knives, and automobiles (Öhman, 1986; Seligman, 1971).

Imprinting in Precocial Birds

Some of the earliest evidence for specialized learning abilities came from studies of young precocial birds. Precocial birds are those species—such as chickens, geese, and ducks—in which the young can walk almost as soon as they hatch. Because they can walk, they can get separated from their mother, and because of that they have acquired, through evolution, an efficient means to recognize their mother and remain near her. In the nineteenth century, Douglas Spalding (1873/1954) observed that when newly hatched chicks saw him, rather than their mother, move past their nest shortly after they hatched, they followed him as if he were their mother. They continued to follow him for weeks thereafter, and once attached in this way, they would not switch to following the mother hen. Some 60 years later, Konrad Lorenz (1935) made essentially the same discovery with newly hatched goslings. He labeled the phenomenon *imprinting*, a term that emphasizes the very sudden and apparently irreversible nature of the learning process involved.

One interesting feature of imprinting is the rather restricted ***critical period*** during which it can occur. Spalding (1873/1954) found that if chicks were prevented from seeing any moving object during the first 5 days after hatching and then he walked past them, they did not follow him but, rather, showed "great terror" and ran away. In more detailed studies, Eckhard Hess (1958, 1972) found that the optimal time for imprinting mallard ducklings is within the first 18 hours after hatching.

Although early studies suggested that young birds could be imprinted on humans or other moving objects as easily as on their mothers, later studies proved otherwise. Given a choice between a female of their species and some other object, newly hatched birds invariably choose to follow the female of their species. Experiments with chicks indicate that this initial preference centers on visual features of the head. Newly hatched chicks will follow a box with a chicken head attached to it as readily as they will a complete stuffed chicken and more readily than any object without a chicken head (Johnson & Horn, 1988). The experience of following the object brings the imprinting mechanism into play, and this mechanism causes the chicks to be attracted thereafter to all the features of the moving object

40.

What aspect of a young fowl's ability to follow its mother depends on learning, and how is that learning guided by inborn biases?

"The Far Side" cartoons by Gary Larson are reprinted by permission of Chronicle Features, San Francisco.

When imprinting studies go awry . . .

(Bateson, 2000). Under normal conditions, of course, the moving object is their mother, and imprinting leads them to distinguish their mother from any other hen. In sum, we have here a learning process for which the timing (the critical period), the stimulus features (characteristics typical of a mother bird of the species), and the motor response (following) are all genetically predisposed in ways that are optimal for its specific adaptive function.

Place Learning Revisited

Earlier we examined Tolman's classic research on place learning as support for a cognitive view of learning. Subsequent studies of place learning have provided many examples of special learning abilities that can be understood in relation to an animal's natural ecology. Consider the behavior of a rat in a simple T-shaped maze. If the rat has, on one trial, found food in the right arm of the maze, what should the rat do on the next trial—turn right or turn left? A straightforward application of operant-conditioning theory would have the rat turn right, because it was rewarded for that response on the previous trial. But if you think of this behavior in relation to normal foraging, turning right does *not* make the most sense. The rat has just cleaned out all the food hidden in the right compartment, and in the wild food does not magically replenish itself in a given place within seconds or minutes after it has been taken. After removing food from one place, it makes sense for the rat to look anywhere other than that place to find more food. How do rats actually behave in such situations? In general, early in training, they behave in accordance with the ecological prediction, not the operant prediction. They tend to avoid the arm in which they have already been, whether or not they found food there, and to choose the other arm (Gaffan & others, 1983). Only after many trials in the maze do they learn to go always to the same arm if the reward is always in that arm.

Some research on maze learning employs conditions more in keeping with natural foraging. David Olton (1979) used a radial maze in which each arm led away from a center platform like the spokes on a wheel and food was hidden at the end of each arm. When the food was found and eaten in a particular arm, it was not replaced, so efficient behavior in this case involved avoiding the arms in which food had already been found. Rats quickly learned to behave very efficiently in this task, rarely returning to an arm from which they had already taken food until all the other arms had been explored, even when there were as many as 17 arms to remember. Olton and his colleagues showed that the rats achieved this efficient be-

41.

How might the ecological perspective help us predict which place-learning tasks an animal will find easy or difficult to master? What special place-learning abilities have been observed in (a) rats, (b) birds that hide food, and (c) Pacific salmon?

A seed-hiding species

Perhaps you have seen black-capped chickadees, like this one, make visit after visit to the bird feeder, each time flying off with a single seed. Chickadees, like many bird species, hide seeds in many different sites for the winter. Their ability to remember each hiding place is an example of a specialized learning ability.

Lee Foster / Bruce Coleman, Inc.

havior by remembering the location of each place that they had been and using visual cues to avoid that location.

In other species, even more dramatic evidence of specialized place learning has been discovered. As one example, Clark's nutcrackers (a species of bird inhabiting the southwestern United States) bury food in literally thousands of different sites, to which they return during the winter when the food is needed (Gould-Beierle & Kamil, 1999). Experiments have shown that the birds' ability to find each location depends on their memory of visual landmarks, such as stones, near the site (Kamil & Balda, 1985; Shettleworth, 1983). In other experiments (for example, Olson & others, 1995), various bird species that hide seeds have been found to remember spatial locations better than do species that don't hide seeds. A quite different example of specialized place learning is the ability of Pacific salmon to return to their hatching grounds. Salmon that hatch in small streams in the northwestern United States migrate into the Pacific Ocean, where they swim around for 5 years or more, carrying with them a memory of the exact smell of the water in which they hatched. Then, when they are ready to spawn, they use their sense of smell to find their way back to the same stream from which they had come (Hasler & Larsen, 1955; Navitt & others, 1994).

While the cognitive perspective often emphasizes the general intelligence of an animal (its ability to bring sophisticated cognitive processes to bear on a learning problem), the ecological perspective reminds us that animals appear much more intelligent when faced with problems similar to those posed by their natural environment than when faced with other problems. The intelligence comes not from a general ability to reason but from specialized learning abilities that have evolved over thousands of generations in the wild. This will be an interesting point to keep in mind when reading about human intelligence in Chapters 10 and 11. Might it be that we humans, too, have not one general intelligence but various specialized intelligences that evolved to solve different kinds of problems faced by our evolutionary ancestors?

SECTION SUMMARY

The basic premise of the ecological perspective on learning is that natural selection has endowed animals with many specialized learning mechanisms for acquiring particular kinds of information related to survival and reproduction. The perspective is illustrated by the problem of learning what is safe to eat. Omnivorous mammals are able to associate feelings of illness with the flavor (but not with the sight) of any new food that they have eaten, even though many hours may have elapsed between the time the food was eaten and the onset of illness. This is a specialized mechanism for learning to avoid poisonous foods; it has characteristics quite different from typical examples of either classical or operant conditioning. Special learning mechanisms also apparently underlie the abilities of rats and young humans to select foods that contain needed vitamins and the ability of rats to identify and eat what other rats have eaten. Other special learning mechanisms underlie the learning of fears by people and monkeys, the imprinting of ducklings and chicks upon their mothers, and the ability of some bird species to recall the locations of the thousands of sites at which they have hidden food.

CONCLUDING THOUGHTS

You have read about learning from three different perspectives. What is a *perspective?* It is a point of view, a framework, a set of ground rules and assumptions that scientists bring to the topic studied. The perspective helps determine the kinds of questions asked, the kinds of evidence regarded as important, the kinds of studies conducted, and the vocabulary used to describe observations. As you review the

42.

What features of each perspective on learning are noted here as an aid in beginning your review of and reflection on the ideas in this chapter?

chapter, think about how each idea is related to the larger perspective within which it falls. Here are some further thoughts about each perspective on learning:

1. The behavioral perspective   Behaviorists such as Watson and Skinner began with the assumption that learning is best described in terms of observable stimuli and responses. Although they acknowledged that inner processes are involved in learning, they assumed that these are too obscure to study scientifically and that lawful relations between stimuli and responses can be identified without worrying about the inner events that mediate them. Borrowing from Pavlov's terms for describing classical conditioning, and adding a parallel set of terms for operant conditioning, the behaviorists brought to psychology a rich, objective vocabulary for talking about learning and many learning-related phenomena. That vocabulary is still very much a part of psychology. As you review the terms and concepts in the behavioral section, try to avoid the temptation to translate them into mental terms. Try instead to define each in terms of relationships between responses and stimuli, including reinforcers.

2. The cognitive perspective   This perspective emerged from the behavioral perspective by way of psychologists, like Tolman, who called themselves S-O-R behaviorists and conducted experiments to understand the O. These psychologists argued that you can go just so far without talking about inner processes. You can establish very general principles, but you can't predict how they will apply in a given situation. For example, you can establish the principle of stimulus generalization in classical conditioning, but you can't predict the degree to which an individual will generalize from one stimulus to the next unless you understand something about the individual's mental concepts, which can lead to the perception of two stimuli as similar even if they aren't physically similar. Other cognitive constructs—such as expectancies, predictions, means-end relationships, and cognitive maps—can also be inferred from subjects' behavior and used to help predict their future behavior. As you think about these constructs, try to imagine them not as conscious thoughts but as the kinds of rules for guiding behavior that one might program into a computer. That is how cognitive psychologists generally think of them.

3. The ecological perspective   This is the perspective that most closely unites the two chapters on adaptation—the preceding one on evolution and the present one on learning. While behaviorism and cognitivism have roots in empiricist philosophy, which attempts to understand human behavior and the human mind in terms of general principles (such as the law of association by contiguity), the ecological perspective grew out of biology, which recognizes the diversity of life processes. The view that learning mechanisms are a product of natural selection implies that they should be specially designed to solve biologically important problems related to survival and reproduction. Different animal species, whose ecological niches pose different problems, may have evolved different species-typical learning mechanisms to solve those problems. This idea has been developed most fully for nonhuman animals, but psychologists are increasingly applying it also to humans. We appear to have relatively distinct learning mechanisms for such domains as language, spatial relations, motor skills, and emotionality, just as we do for food selection. Closer ties between the cognitive and ecological perspectives have emerged in all realms of psychology.

Further Reading

B. F. Skinner (1978). *Reflections on behaviorism and society.* Englewood Cliffs, NJ: Prentice-Hall.

Skinner—who wanted to be a novelist before he went into psychology—is always fun to read, and there is no better way to begin than with this collection of some of his essays. The titles include "Human Behavior and Democracy," "Why I Am Not a Cognitive Psychologist," "The Free and Happy Student," "The Force of Coincidence," and "Freedom and Dignity Revisited." You will find here Skinner's basic philosophy about psychology and his suggestions for using behavioral learning principles to improve society.

John D. Baldwin & Janice I. Baldwin (2001). *Behavior principles in everyday life* (3rd ed.). Upper Saddle River, NJ: Prentice-Hall.

This is an easy-to-read introduction to the principles of classical conditioning, operant conditioning, and observational learning, with examples taken from everyday human existence. Readers will discover many ways by which their own behavior is influenced by conditioned stimuli and reinforcers and may learn how to use learning principles to modify their own behavior in desired ways.

David A. Lieberman (2000). *Learning: Behavior and cognition* (3rd ed.). Belmont, CA: Wadsworth.

This is one of several excellent midlevel undergraduate textbooks on learning. It deals with learning primarily from the behavioral and cognitive perspectives but also has a chapter on the evolutionary perspective. Most of the ideas you have read about in the chapter just completed can be found in greater elaboration in this book.

Robert C. Bolles & Michael Beecher (Eds.) (1988). *Evolution and learning.* Hillsdale, NJ: Erlbaum.

This collection of essays, each by one or more specialists in the subject, shows how the traditions of behaviorism and ethology have merged and begun to provide rich detail about species-typical learning processes. The book begins with historical chapters about the relationship of learning theory to evolutionary theory and then turns to contemporary research on learning in such biologically important domains as feeding, defending against predators, and sexual behavior.

Looking Ahead

In the two-chapter unit just completed, you have read about how evolution and learning adapt behavior to the environment. All such adaptations involve changes in the body, particularly in the nervous system. The nervous system contains the mechanisms for organizing all behaviors, and modifications in the nervous system underlie all instances of learning. The next chapter is about the nervous system.

Visage, Jean Dubuffet

Physiological Mechanisms of Behavior

Behavior is a product of the body's machinery, especially the nervous system. The nervous system receives information about the internal and external environments, integrates that information, and controls the body's movements. This unit consists of two chapters. Chapter 5 examines the overall structure of the nervous system and its principles of operation. Chapter 6 is concerned with the neural and hormonal mechanisms underlying motivation, sleep, and emotion.

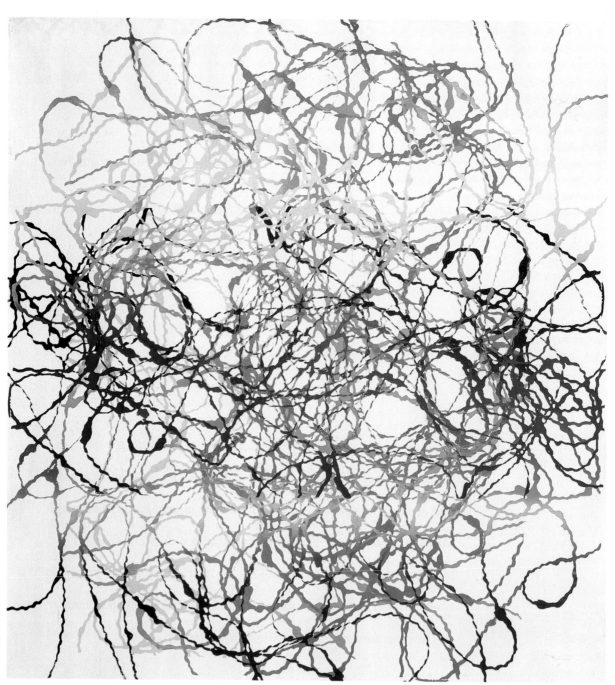

Yarn, Andy Warhol

The Nervous System

A human brain is, I must admit, somewhat disappointing in appearance. It is about the size and shape of a cantaloupe, but more gnarled. To the eye it seems quite dormant, even when viewed in a living person. Aristotle and many other ancient Greeks—who were among the first to try to figure out what the various parts of the body are for—were not much impressed by the brain. Noticing that the blood vessels leading into it are larger than those entering other organs, they suggested that the brain's main function was to cool the blood. They were much more impressed by the heart, an obviously dynamic organ, and proposed that the heart and blood are the source of feelings, thoughts, and all else that today we call "psychological."

Not all the ancients agreed with the heart theory of psychology. One who didn't was the Greek physician Hippocrates, whose observations on the effects of head injuries on people's thoughts and actions led him to postulate that the brain is the organ of psychology. In the fourth century B.C.E., Hippocrates (1923) wrote that "from the brain, and from the brain only, arise our pleasures, joys, laughter and jests, as well as our sorrows, pains, griefs and tears. Through it, in particular, we think, see, hear. . . . Eyes, ears, tongue, hands and feet act in accordance with the discernment of the brain." Hippocrates was right, of course, and that is why nearly every introductory psychology text ever written, from William James's (1890) classic on, contains a chapter about the nervous system, especially the brain. As psychologists and neuroscientists learn more about the brain, the nervous-system chapter becomes ever more closely connected to the rest of the book, and material on the brain spills ever more freely out of that chapter and into the rest of the book. Psychology is the study of what the nervous system does; it is especially the study of the most complex aspects of what the nervous system does.

Every chapter of this book is at least indirectly about the nervous system, and this chapter is directly about it. The first and longest section of the chapter describes the overall structure of the nervous system and the main functions of each of its parts; the second section concerns the workings of individual neurons and how they are modified by experience; and the final section has to do with the ways by which drugs and hormones act on the nervous system to modify behavior.

FUNCTIONAL ORGANIZATION OF THE NERVOUS SYSTEM

The nervous system is fundamentally a communication network for coordinating and directing the body's actions effectively within the environment. To do that, it must (1) receive sensory messages that provide information about the environment; (2) organize that information and integrate it with other, already-stored information in useful ways; and (3) use that integrated information to send out messages to the muscles and glands, thereby producing organized movements and adaptive

1.

What are three basic tasks of the nervous system?

secretions. As part of these processes, the nervous system also somehow provides the basis for what we call *conscious experience*—the stream of perceptions, thoughts, and feelings that make up a person's mental life.

The system that does all this is sketched in Figure 5.1. The brain and spinal cord (which extends from the brain down through the bones of the spinal column) together make up the **central nervous system**. Extensions from the central nervous system, called *nerves*, make up the **peripheral nervous system**. The elementary units of the nervous system are **neurons**, or nerve cells, and we begin our tour by looking briefly at them.

The Basic Functions and Structures of Neurons

Neurons are cells that have become specialized to carry information rapidly from one place to another and to integrate information from various sources. They can be classified by function into three types that relate, respectively, to the three tasks of the nervous system listed above (see Figure 5.2): (1) **Sensory neurons** carry information from sensory organs, through nerves, into the central nervous system. (2) **Interneurons** exist entirely within the central nervous system and carry messages from one set of neurons to another. They bring together messages from various sources and thereby organize and integrate information. (3) **Motor neurons** carry messages out from the central nervous system, through nerves, to activate muscles and glands. The task of the interneurons is by far the most complex, and interneurons greatly outnumber the other two types. The human nervous system contains a few million sensory neurons and motor neurons and roughly 100 *billion* interneurons.

Figure 5.3 shows the main components of a typical motor neuron. The **cell body** is the widest part and contains the cell nucleus and other basic machinery common to all cells. The **dendrites** are thin, tubelike extensions that typically branch repeatedly near the cell body, forming a bushlike structure. Their function is to increase the surface area of the cell to allow for receipt of signals from many other neurons. The **axon** is another thin, tubelike extension. Its function is to carry electrical impulses, called *action potentials*, away from the cell body to other cells. Although microscopically thin, the axon is in some cases extraordinarily long. You have axons extending all the way from your spine down to the muscles of your big toe—a distance of over a meter. The axons of some neurons are surrounded by a casing called the **myelin sheath**, made up of the cell membranes of special nonneural cells that are wrapped tightly around the axon. The axon usually branches some distance away from the cell body, and each branch ends with a small swelling called the **axon terminal**.

The action potentials travel along the axon to the axon terminals. As each action potential reaches a terminal, it causes the terminal to release a chemical substance called a **neurotransmitter**, or *transmitter*, onto a receiving cell. Interneurons and sensory neurons release transmitter molecules onto the dendrites and cell bodies of other neurons. Motor neurons release transmitter molecules onto muscle cells and gland cells. The place at which an axon terminal passes transmitter molecules to a receiving cell is called a **synapse**. At the synapse, the transmitter molecules diffuse across a small cleft, or gap, and act on the membrane of the receiving cell.

2.

What are the three types of neurons and the function of each?

3.

What are the main parts of a motor neuron, and what is the function of each?

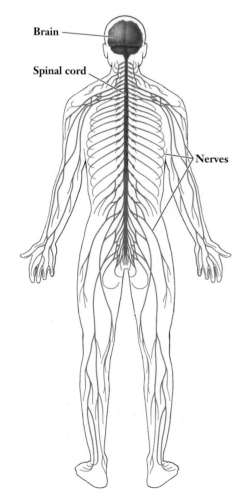

Brain

Spinal cord

Nerves

FIGURE **5.1**

The human nervous system

The central nervous system consists of the brain and the spinal cord, which runs through the bones of the spinal column down the center of the back. The peripheral nervous system consists of the entire set of nerves, which connect the brain and spinal cord to the sensory organs, muscles, and glands.

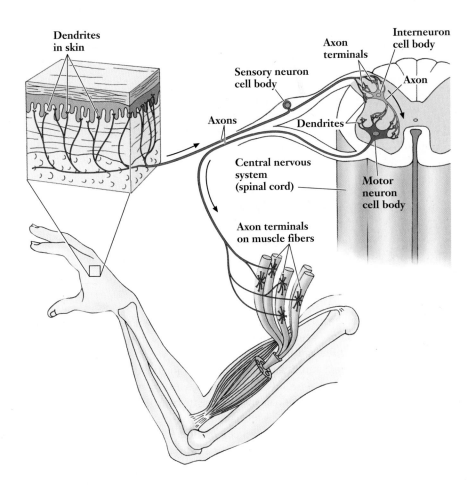

FIGURE **5.2**
The three classes of neurons
This illustration shows the positions in the nervous system of the three types of neurons. On the right is the central nervous system (more specifically, a cross section of the spinal cord), and on the left are muscles and skin. Motor neurons send electrochemical messages from the central nervous system to muscles and glands. Sensory neurons send messages into the central nervous system from sensory organs, such as the skin. And interneurons, located entirely within the central nervous system, carry messages between neurons.

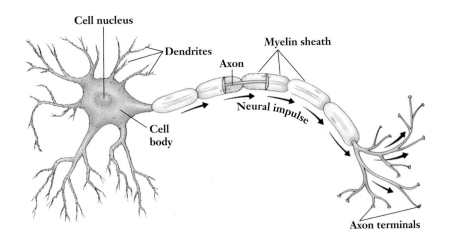

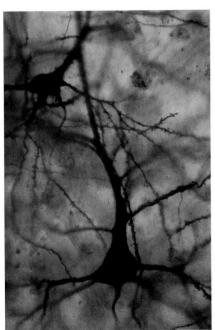

FIGURE **5.3**   *A motor neuron*
The parts common to many neurons can be seen in this diagram of a motor neuron. The neuron receives input from other neurons on its dendrites and cell body and sends its own output down the axon to the axon terminals. The myelin sheath is not part of the neuron; it is formed of separate glial cells that are wrapped around the axon.

Motor neurons in the spinal cord
In this photograph taken through a microscope, you can see the cell bodies and some of the branching dendrites of several motor neurons.

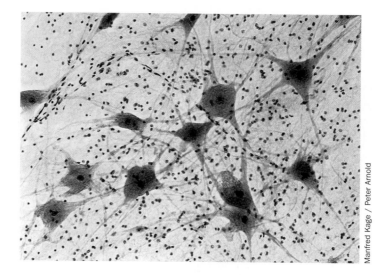

Manfred Kage / Peter Arnold

The molecular mechanisms of action potentials and synapses will be described later in this chapter, in the section on how neurons work. For now it is enough to know that a neuron's message lies in the number of action potentials that move down the axon per second and cause the release of transmitter molecules from each axon terminal. In the case of an interneuron or a sensory neuron, the transmitter acts on another neuron to either *excite* it (increase its rate of action potentials) or *inhibit* it (decrease its rate of action potentials). In the case of a motor neuron, the transmitter acts on a muscle cell or gland cell to alter its activity.

To compare the parts of a typical interneuron and sensory neuron with those of a motor neuron, look again at Figure 5.2 and read the labels. Interneurons come in an enormous variety of shapes and sizes, but the largest and most well studied are similar in structure to motor neurons. The main difference is that the interneuron's axon does not leave the central nervous system, and its terminals form synapses on other neurons rather than on muscle cells. Sensory neurons, in contrast, have a quite different structure from the other two types. The sensory neuron shown in Figure 5.2 carries information about touch or pressure on the skin (you will read about other kinds of sensory neurons in Chapters 7 and 8). Its cell body (unlike that of the motor neuron or interneuron) lies outside the central nervous system; its axon extends in both directions from the cell body; and its dendrites protrude from one end of the axon (the end in the skin) rather than directly from the cell body. In this cell, the tips of the dendrites are specialized to respond to physical stimulation of the skin, and the axon is designed to carry the action potentials initiated by that stimulation past the cell body and into the central nervous system.

The amazing abilities of the nervous system reside not so much in the individual neuron as in the organization of the billions of neurons that make up the whole system. The following paragraphs and accompanying figures paint a picture of that organization. We begin with the peripheral nervous system (cranial and spinal nerves) and then turn to the central nervous system (spinal cord and brain), working upward from the more primitive lower parts to the more recently evolved higher parts. As you read about each component, pay particular attention to its main behavioral functions and its relationship to other structures already described.

4.

How do interneurons and sensory neurons differ anatomically from motor neurons?

The Peripheral Nervous System

As noted earlier, the peripheral nervous system consists of the entire set of nerves. A **nerve** is a bundle of axons of sensory neurons, motor neurons, or both, existing anywhere outside of the central nervous system.

Cranial and Spinal Nerves

Nerves are divided into two classes based on the portion of the central nervous system from which they protrude. *Cranial nerves* project directly from the brain, and *spinal nerves* project from the spinal cord. Like most other structures in the body, nerves exist in pairs; there is a right and a left member in each pair. Humans have 12 pairs of cranial nerves and 31 pairs of spinal nerves. With their various branches, these nerves form an enormous network extending to all portions of the body.

Some pairs of cranial nerves are highly specialized. Three pairs are purely sensory: One of them conveys input just from the nose; another, from the eyes; and a third, from the ears. Five other pairs are purely motor: Three of them control eye movements; another pair, tongue movements; and another pair, the neck muscles that move the head. The remaining cranial nerves and all the spinal nerves contain axons of both sensory and motor neurons. The spinal nerves carry motor output to muscles and glands below the neck and convey sensory input into the spinal cord from the bodily senses collectively referred to as *somatosensation*. *Soma* means "body," and somatosensation is the set of senses that derive from the whole body—such as from the skin, muscles, and tendons—as opposed to those that come from the special sensory organs of the head.

The Autonomic Compared with the Skeletal Motor System

Motor neurons act on two broad classes of structures. One class consists of the *skeletal muscles*, the muscles that are attached to bones and that produce externally observable movements of the body when contracted. The other class consists of the visceral muscles and glands. *Visceral muscles* are internal muscular structures that do not move the skeleton, such as the heart, arteries, and gastrointestinal tract. *Glands* are structures that produce secretions, such as the salivary glands and sweat glands. Neurons that act on skeletal muscles make up the *skeletal* portion of the peripheral motor system, and those that act on visceral muscles and glands make up the *autonomic* portion.

Whereas skeletal motor neurons initiate activity in the skeletal muscles, autonomic motor neurons typically *modulate* (modify) rather than initiate activity in the visceral muscles. Skeletal muscles are completely inactive in the absence of neural input, but visceral muscles have built-in, nonneural mechanisms for generating activity. The heart continues to beat and the muscular walls of such structures as the intestines and arteries continue to contract in response to local influences, even if all the nerves to these organs are destroyed. Most visceral muscles and glands receive two sets of neurons, which produce opposite effects and come from two anatomically distinct divisions of the autonomic system: the sympathetic and parasympathetic (see Figures 5.4 and 5.5).

The *sympathetic division* responds especially to stressful stimulation and helps prepare the body for possible "fight or flight." Among its effects are (a) increased heart rate and blood pressure, (b) the release of energy molecules (sugars and fats)

5.

How do the autonomic and skeletal motor systems differ from each other?

6.

How do the sympathetic and parasympathetic portions of the autonomic system differ from each other?

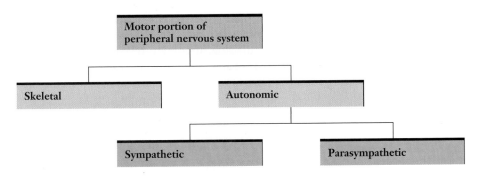

FIGURE **5.4** *Divisions of the motor portion of the peripheral nervous system*
The motor portion of the peripheral nervous system consists of the skeletal and autonomic systems, and the autonomic system consists of the sympathetic and parasympathetic systems.

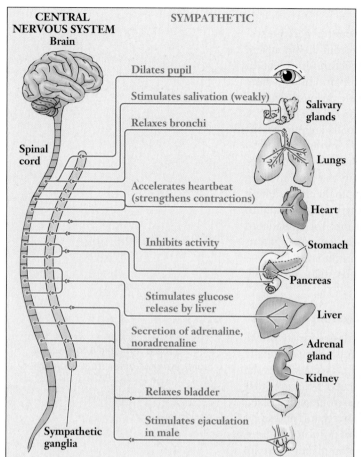

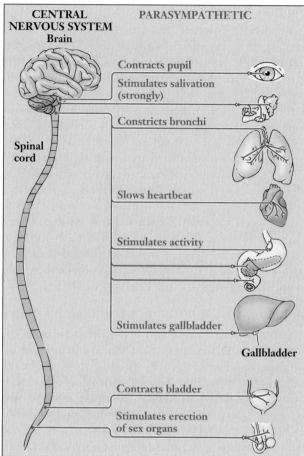

FIGURE **5.5**   *The autonomic nervous system*

The sympathetic portion of the autonomic nervous system derives from spinal nerves, and the parasympathetic portion derives from three pairs of cranial nerves and several of the bottommost pairs of spinal nerves. The two portions act on many of the same structures, but have opposite effects on them. Unlike skeletal motor neurons, individual autonomic motor neurons do not extend the full distance from the central nervous system to the organ they affect. Autonomic motor neurons with cell bodies in the central nervous system terminate instead in a ganglion (a group of neural cell bodies that is outside the central nervous system), where they form synapses with a second set of neurons that do send axons to the muscle or gland. In this diagram, ganglia are indicated by small circles.

from storage deposits to permit high energy expenditure, (c) increased blood flow to the skeletal muscles, and (d) inhibition of digestive processes (which helps explain why a heated argument at the dinner table can lead to a stomachache). Conversely, the ***parasympathetic division*** serves regenerative, growth-promoting, and energy-conserving functions through effects that include the opposites of those just listed for the sympathetic division. If you are relaxed while reading this book, your parasympathetic activity probably predominates over your sympathetic, so your heart is beating at a slow, normal rate and your digestion is working fine.

The Spinal Cord

The spinal cord is, among other things, a conduit between the spinal nerves and the brain. Any bundle of axons coursing together within the central nervous system is called a **tract**, which is analogous to a nerve in the peripheral nervous system. The spinal cord contains *ascending tracts*, which carry somatosensory information brought in by spinal nerves up to the brain, and *descending tracts*, which carry motor-control information down from the brain to be transmitted out by spinal nerves to muscles. A person who has an accident that completely severs the spinal cord will be completely paralyzed and lacking in sensation in those parts of the body that are innervated by spinal nerves that come from below the place of injury. As you can see by looking back at Figure 5.1, the closer the place of injury to the neck or head, the greater the number of spinal nerves cut off from the brain and the greater, therefore, the extent of paralysis and insensitivity. Thus if the spinal cord is cut through just below the brain, the paralysis and insensitivity will include the arms, trunk, and legs; but if the cut is farther down, it may include only the legs.

But the spinal cord is more than just a pathway between the spinal nerves and the brain. It can also organize some behaviors on its own, as you know if you have ever witnessed the wing-flapping and running movements of a newly decapitated chicken. The spinal cord contains networks of neurons that stimulate one another in a cyclic manner and thereby produce bursts of action potentials that wax and wane in a regular, repeating rhythm. These networks, called *pattern generators*, activate motor neurons in the spinal cord in such a way as to produce the rhythmic sequence of muscle movements that results in flying, walking, running, or swimming (Grillner, 1996; Pearson & Gordon, 2000). In some animals, the pattern generators become active when released from the brain's inhibitory control over them, which accounts for the flying and running motions of the headless chicken. Normally, in animals that still have their heads, pattern generators are controlled by neurons descending from the brain; they can be either inhibited, producing a motionless animal, or activated to varying degrees, producing varying rates of locomotion (Pearson & Gordon, 2000). Thus one function of the spinal cord is to provide the rhythmic organization of locomotor movements.

In addition, the spinal cord organizes many reflexes, as can be demonstrated in animals whose spinal cords have been surgically separated from the brain. (Such experiments might seem cruel, but the knowledge gained from them has been extremely valuable in helping people who have spinal cord injuries.) Such animals, referred to as *spinal animals*, still have both a brain and a spinal cord, but these structures can no longer communicate with each other. If the paw of a spinal cat is pricked with a pin, the animal does not hiss or show facial signs of pain, as a normal cat would, because the stimulus input cannot reach the pain and vocalization centers of the brain. The cat cannot feel sensations from below the neck because feeling is mediated by the brain. Nevertheless, the animal's paw quickly withdraws from the pin. This reflex is called the *flexion reflex* because it involves contraction of the flexor muscles—the muscles that bend the limb at each joint, causing it to be pulled inward (flexed) toward the body. The adaptive advantage of the flexion reflex is obvious: It quickly and automatically moves the limb away from potentially damaging stimuli.

The mechanism of the flexion reflex (in simplified form) can be traced in Figure 5.2. A stimulus such as a pinprick triggers action potentials in a set of pain-sensitive sensory neurons in the skin, which, in turn, excite a set of interneurons in the spinal cord, which, in their turn, excite a set of motor neurons going to the flexor muscles of the same limb from which the sensory stimulus arose. In a normal cat, other interneurons would at the same time transmit a sensory message to the brain, and the animal would experience pain.

In sum, the spinal cord serves three important functions: (1) It carries messages upward and downward between the spinal nerves and the brain; (2) it generates the rhythmic component of locomotion (walking, flying, and swimming); and (3) it organizes certain reflexes, such as the flexion reflex.

7.

How does the spinal cord serve as (a) a conduit between spinal nerves and the brain, (b) an organizer of rhythmic locomotor movements, and (c) an organizer of certain reflexes?

Subcortical Structures of the Brain

Atop the spinal cord sits the brain, the most complex biological organ that ever evolved on this planet, with its many billions of neurons and trillions of synaptic connections. It would be hopeless, with present technology, to try to work out all the details of the brain's wiring, as one might do with a human-made machine such as a radio or a computer. Fortunately, though, for those of us who wish to understand what we can of it, patterns exist in the trillions of connections. Axons do not run willy-nilly but course together in tracts from one cluster of neural cell bodies to another. Any cluster of cell bodies of neurons in the central nervous system is called a ***nucleus*** (not to be confused with the cell nucleus within each cell). In general, neurons whose cell bodies occupy the same nucleus and whose axons run along the same tract have similar functions. Moreover, groups of nuclei that exist in the same area of the brain often have functions that are closely related to one another. Because of this, we can talk about the functions of various relatively large anatomical structures within the brain.

Here we will examine the most general functions of the largest subdivisions of the brain, beginning with the *subcortical* structures, so called because of their position beneath the *cerebral cortex*, the topmost part of the brain. Working our way upward from the bottom, we begin our tour of the brain with the brainstem.

The Brainstem and Thalamus

As it enters the head, the spinal cord enlarges and becomes the ***brainstem***. The parts of the brainstem, beginning closest to the spinal cord and going upward toward the top of the head, are the ***medulla***, ***pons***, and ***midbrain*** (see Figure 5.6). The brainstem is functionally and anatomically quite similar to the spinal cord, but more elaborate. The spinal cord is the site of entry of spinal nerves, and the brainstem is the site of entry of most (10 of the 12 pairs) of the cranial nerves. The spinal cord contains ascending (sensory) and descending (motor) tracts connecting nerves to higher parts of the central nervous system, as does the brainstem. Also like the spinal cord, the brainstem has some neural centers that organize reflexes and other neural centers that help organize more complex behaviors that are governed by higher parts of the brain.

The medulla and pons organize reflexes that are more complex and sustained than those produced by the spinal cord. They include *postural reflexes*, which help an animal maintain balance while standing or moving, and certain so-called *vital reflexes*, such as those that regulate breathing rate and heart rate in response to input signaling the body's metabolic needs. The midbrain contains neural centers that

8.

How is the brainstem similar to and different from the spinal cord? What role does the brainstem play in the control of behavior?

FIGURE **5.6**

The brainstem and thalamus

This figure makes clear why the medulla, pons, and midbrain are collectively called the *brainstem*. They form a stemlike continuation from the spinal cord, to which other brain structures are connected. The thalamus is attached to the top of the brainstem.

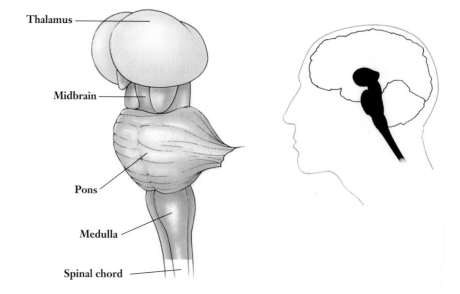

Thalamus

Midbrain

Pons

Medulla

Spinal chord

help govern most of an animal's basic movement patterns, such as those involved in eating, drinking, attacking, or grooming (Klemm, 1990). Also in the midbrain are neurons that act on pattern generators in the spinal cord to increase or decrease the speed of locomotion (Pearson & Gordon, 2000). And together the midbrain and pons contain neural systems that help control sleep and level of arousal (to be discussed in Chapter 6).

An animal (such as a cat) whose central nervous system is cut completely through just above the midbrain can produce almost the entire set of behaviors that a normal animal can produce (Klemm, 1990; Schmidt, 1986). It can walk, run, jump, climb, groom, attack, produce copulatory movements, chew, swallow, and so on. Unlike a normal animal, however, it makes these responses only when provoked by immediate stimuli; it does not behave in either a spontaneous or a goal-directed manner. If placed on a pole, for example, the animal climbs, but it does not itself *choose* to climb a pole that has food at the top or avoid one that does not. Such behavior indicates that the midbrain and the structures below it contain neural systems that organize movements but do not contain neural systems that permit deliberate decisions to move or refrain from moving in accordance with the animal's long-term interests.

Directly atop the brainstem is the ***thalamus*** (see Figure 5.6). This structure, seated squarely in the middle of the brain, is most conveniently thought of as a relay station that connects various parts of the brain with one another. Most of the sensory tracts that ascend through the brainstem terminate in special nuclei in the thalamus, which in turn send their output to specific areas in the cerebral cortex (discussed in Chapter 7). The thalamus also has nuclei that relay messages from higher parts of the brain to movement-control centers in the brainstem.

The Cerebellum and Basal Ganglia

Cerebellum means "little brain" in Latin, and the ***cerebellum*** indeed looks something like a smaller version of the rest of the brain, riding piggyback on the rear of the brainstem (see Figure 5.7). Its best-known function is to help control rapid movements of the limbs. People with damage in the cerebellum are often incapable of rapid, coordinated movements, such as kicking and throwing, but can still use their legs and arms for slower movements, such as walking and reaching (Kornhuber, 1974). It is noteworthy that birds and monkeys have particularly large, well-developed cerebellums. Birds must continuously make rapid, well-timed movements when flying, and monkeys must do the same when leaping about in trees.

9.

In what sense is the thalamus a relay station?

10.

What are the main functions of the cerebellum and basal ganglia? Why are these structures classed together even though they are anatomically distinct?

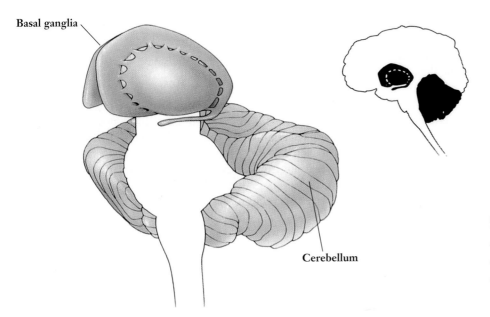

Basal ganglia

Cerebellum

FIGURE **5.7**
The cerebellum and basal ganglia
These two structures are critically involved in the initiation and coordination of movements.

The cerebellum has been likened to a highly sophisticated computer (Houk & others, 1996). It receives and integrates information from all the senses, including visual information about relevant objects in the external world and somatosensory information about the current positions of the limbs, and it makes rapid-fire calculations as to just which muscle groups must be activated, by how much, and when, in order to perform a certain movement—to leap over a hurdle, hit a baseball, or swing from branch to branch in the treetops. It is most active during the learning of new movements or the performance of chains of movements in which each motion cannot be predicted in advance of the previous one (Ghez & Thach, 2000; Houk & others, 1996).

The **basal ganglia** are large structures lying on each side of the thalamus (see Figure 5.7). They have movement-control functions that complement those of the cerebellum. While the cerebellum is more involved in rapid movements, the basal ganglia are more involved in slower, deliberate movements, such as reaching for an object and walking (Kornhuber, 1974). Parkinson's disease, which is characterized by difficulty in starting and stopping deliberate movements and by involuntary muscle tremors, results from the deterioration of a neural tract that runs from the brainstem into the basal ganglia (Sourkes, 1989). Destruction of portions of the basal ganglia results in loss of the ability to produce both instinctual and learned movement sequences in laboratory animals. In one study, for example, rats with parts of their basal ganglia destroyed could still perform each of the individual tongue and paw movements involved in grooming their bodies but could not put those movements together into the systematic, species-typical sequence by which rats normally groom themselves (Aldridge & others, 1993).

Research with humans suggests that the cerebellum and basal ganglia are involved in the sequencing and timing not just of muscle movements but also of mental events that do not manifest themselves as movements—such as shifting attention from one stimulus to another or even from one memory to another in a chain of thought (Allen & others, 1997; Middleton & Strick, 1994). In the course of human evolution, the abilities of the cerebellum and basal ganglia to sequence muscle movements was apparently exploited in the development of new capacities for planning and other forms of thought that involve the chaining of mental events. Consistent with this view, large tracts connect the human cerebellum and basal ganglia to areas of the cerebral cortex that are known to be involved in such thought (Middleton & Strick, 1994).

The Limbic System and Hypothalamus

11.

Why is the limbic system so named, and what functions does it perform?

The term *limbic* comes from the Latin word *limbus*, meaning "border" or "edge." The **limbic system** can be thought of as the border dividing the evolutionarily older parts of the brain, below it, from the newest part (the cerebral cortex), above it. The limbic system consists of several distinct structures—including the **amygdala** and **hippocampus**—that interconnect with one another in a circuit wrapped around the thalamus and basal ganglia (see Figure 5.8). These structures are involved in the regulation of basic drives and emotions (discussed in Chapter 6). The limbic system is believed to have evolved originally as a system for the sophisticated analysis of olfactory input (Thompson, 1985), and its connections with the nose remain strong. This may help explain the special influence that smells—such as the aroma of good food or perfume, or the stench of vomit—can have on drives and emotions. But the limbic system also receives input from all the other sensory organs. In addition, it is intimately connected to the basal ganglia, and that connection is believed to help translate emotions and drives into actions.

At least one part of the limbic system, the hippocampus, is also critical to the formation of memories. People who have suffered extensive damage to the hippocampus on both sides of the brain can remember events that occurred before the damage but cannot form new, long-term memories of events that occur after the

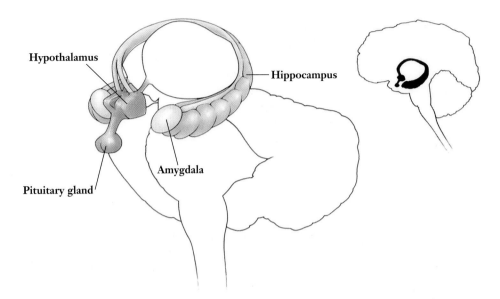

FIGURE **5.8** *The limbic system and hypothalamus*
The most conspicuous structures of the limbic system are the hippocampus and the amygdala, which have strong connections to the hypothalamus. The pituitary gland is not technically part of the brain but is strongly tied to the hypothalamus and is controlled by it.

damage. You will read in Chapter 9 of a man who sustained such damage and could read the same story day after day without realizing that he had read it before.

The *hypothalamus* is a small but extraordinarily important structure. Its name derives from its position directly underneath the thalamus (*hypo* in this case means "underneath"). The hypothalamus is not technically part of the limbic system but is intimately connected to all the structures of that system. Its primary task is to help regulate the internal environment of the body. This it accomplishes by (a) influencing the activity of the autonomic nervous system, (b) controlling the release of certain hormones (to be described later), and (c) affecting certain drive states, such as hunger and thirst. In addition, through its connections with the limbic system, the hypothalamus helps regulate emotional states, such as fear and anger. You will read in Chapter 6 about the role of the hypothalamus in drives and emotions. If I had to give up a cubic millimeter (a tiny speck) of tissue from some part of my brain, the last place I would want it taken from is the hypothalamus. Depending on just which part was taken, I could be left without one or more of my basic drives, without a normal cycle of sleep and wakefulness, or without the ability to regulate my body metabolism.

12.

What are the three ways by which the hypothalamus controls the body's internal environment?

The Cerebral Cortex

We move now up to the anatomically topmost and evolutionarily newest part of the brain, the *cerebral cortex*. *Cerebrum* is the Latin word for "brain" (the term is now sometimes used to refer to all parts of the brain other than the brainstem and cerebellum). *Cortex* is the Latin word for "bark," and in anatomical usage it refers to the outside layer of any structure. The cerebral cortex, therefore, is the outermost layer—the bark—of the brain. It is by far the largest part of the human brain, accounting for approximately 80 percent of its total volume (Kolb & Whishaw, 1996). Its surface area is much greater than it appears because it folds inward in many places. Only about one-third of the surface of the human cortex is visible in a view of the undissected human brain; the remaining two-thirds lies buried within the folds. The entire cerebral cortex is divided into left and right *hemispheres*, and each hemisphere is further divided into four lobes, or

A human brain

Only one-third of the surface area of the brain's cortex is visible from the outside. The remaining two-thirds is hidden in the folds and fissures.

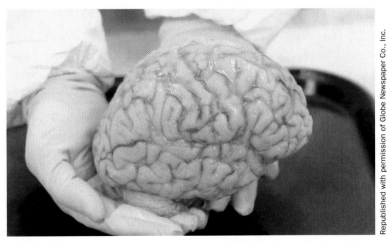

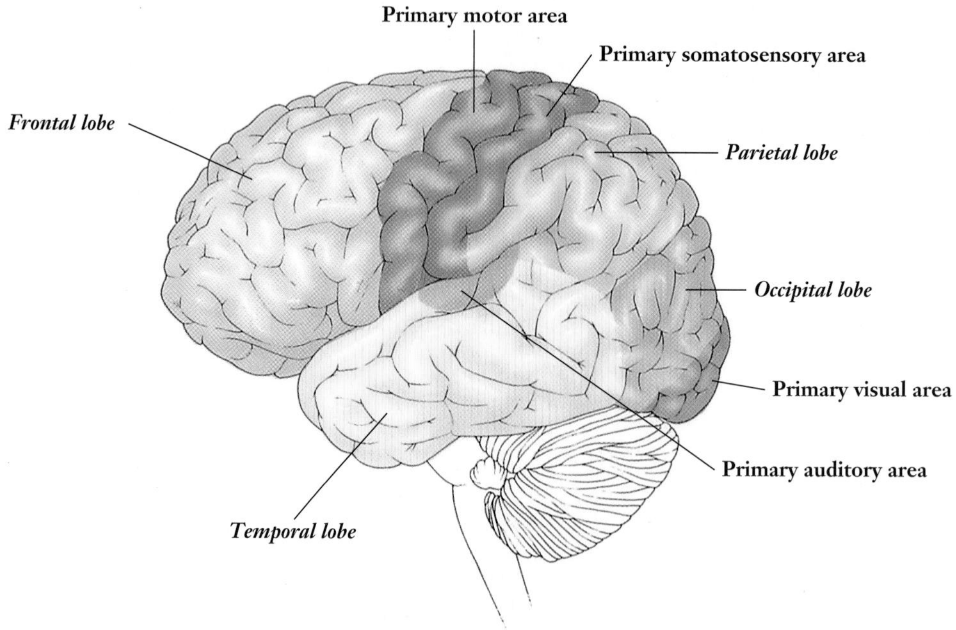

FIGURE **5.9**   *The cerebral cortex*
This figure shows the four lobes of the cortex, as well as the locations of the primary motor area and the primary sensory areas for vision, hearing, and somatosensation.

Primary motor area

Primary somatosensory area

Frontal lobe

Parietal lobe

Occipital lobe

Primary visual area

Primary auditory area

Temporal lobe

13.

What are the four lobes of the cortex, and what are the three functional categories of areas that exist within these lobes?

FIGURE **5.10**   *Comparison of the brains of four mammals*
All the brains contain the same structures, but in the chimpanzee and human proportionately much more cortical space is devoted to association areas than in the rat and cat.

segments, demarcated at least partly by rather prominent folds. The lobes, whose positions you can see in Figure 5.9, are, from back to front, the *occipital, temporal, parietal,* and *frontal lobes*.

Researchers who study the functions of the cortex divide it into three functional categories of regions, or areas. One category consists of the *primary sensory areas*, which receive signals from sensory nerves and tracts by way of relay nuclei in the thalamus. As shown in Figure 5.9, primary sensory areas include the visual area in the occipital lobe, the auditory area in the temporal lobe, and the somatosensory area in the parietal lobe. A second category is the *primary motor area*, which sends axons down to motor neurons in the brainstem and spinal cord. As shown in Figure 5.9, this area occupies the rear portion of the frontal lobe, directly in front of the somatosensory area. The third category consists of the remaining parts of the cortex, which are called *association areas*. These areas receive input from the sensory areas and lower parts of the brain and are involved in the complex processes that we call perception, thought, and decision making. As shown in Figure 5.10, the amount of association cortex, relative to the other two categories, increases dramatically as one goes from simpler mammals, such as the rat and the cat, to more complex ones, such as the chimpanzee and the human.

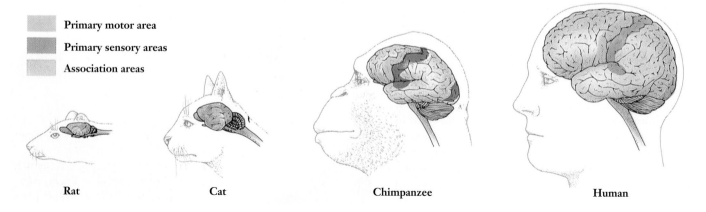

Primary motor area

Primary sensory areas

Association areas

Rat   Cat   Chimpanzee   Human

Topographic Organization of the Primary Sensory and Motor Areas

The primary sensory and motor areas of the cortex are organized such that adjacent neurons receive signals from or send signals to adjacent portions of the sensory or muscular tissue to which they are ultimately connected. This fact is referred to as the *principle of topographic organization*. For example, neurons that are near one another in the visual cortex receive signals from receptor cells that are near one another in the retina of the eye. Similarly, neurons that are near one another in the somatosensory cortex receive signals from adjacent areas of the skin, and neurons that are near one another in the primary motor cortex send signals to adjacent sets of muscle fibers. It is possible to map onto the somatosensory cortex the part from which each portion of the cortex receives its signals or onto the motor cortex the part to which each portion sends its signals.

The resulting maps, depicted in Figure 5.11, show a distorted view of the human body. This is because the amount of cortex devoted to each part of the body corresponds not to the size of the body part but to the degree of sensitivity of that part (in the case of a sensory map) or the fineness of its movements (in the case of a motor map). As you can see, huge areas of the human primary motor cortex are devoted to control of the fingers and vocal apparatus, where fine control is needed. In other animals, other body parts have greater representation, depending on the range and delicacy of their movements. In a cat, for example, large portions of the somatosensory and primary motor areas of the cortex are devoted to the whiskers, and in a spider monkey—a creature that uses its tail as a fifth arm and hand—large areas are devoted to the tail (Walker, 1973).

14.

What does it mean to say that cortical sensory and motor areas are organized topographically?

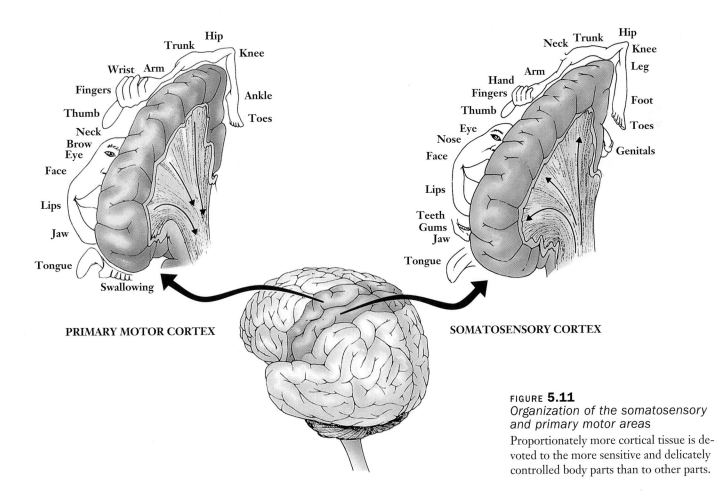

PRIMARY MOTOR CORTEX

SOMATOSENSORY CORTEX

FIGURE 5.11
Organization of the somatosensory and primary motor areas
Proportionately more cortical tissue is devoted to the more sensitive and delicately controlled body parts than to other parts.

15.

What is some evidence that the primary motor cortex comes relatively late in the chain of command preceding an action and that its function is to refine the more delicate parts of the action?

16.

What is some evidence that the premotor and supplementary motor areas of the cortex help establish programs for skilled actions?

Cortical Control of Movement

The primary motor area of the cortex is part of the chain of command in controlling movements but is not at the top of that chain and is not essential for all types of movements. The primary motor area receives input from the basal ganglia and cerebellum and is specialized to fine-tune the signals going to the smaller muscles that must operate in a finely graded way. Experiments in which monkeys must make well-controlled hand movements to obtain a food reward have shown that each movement is preceded first by a burst of activity in the basal ganglia and then by a burst in the motor cortex (Evarts, 1979; Kornhuber, 1974). This is part of the evidence that the primary motor cortex comes later than the basal ganglia and the cerebellum in the chain of command. In other experiments, monkeys whose primary motor cortex had been entirely destroyed behaved normally in most respects but were unable to make delicate hand movements, such as those needed to lift a small piece of food out of a narrow hole (Passingham & others, 1983). Modern means of measuring activity in the intact human brain (to be discussed later) have revealed that large portions of the primary motor area become active during movements of the fingers and wrist and during the movements of the vocal apparatus that occur when speaking (Petersen & others, 1989; Sanes & others, 1995).

Directly in front of the primary motor area lie two other cortical areas devoted to motor control: the *premotor area* and the *supplementary motor area* (see Figure 5.12). Both are involved in the planning and initiation of goal-directed movements, and they exert their control partly by acting on neurons in the primary motor area. The premotor area is particularly involved in an animal's or person's choosing of the appropriate movement to make when more than one movement is possible, and the supplementary motor area is particularly involved in the performance from memory of skilled, complex, learned motor sequences (Krakauer & Ghez, 2000). In one experiment, human subjects learned a complex sequence of finger movements. When they were subsequently asked to perform the sequence, strong neural activity occurred in the supplementary motor area and the primary motor area; but when they were asked only to rehearse the task mentally, without actually performing it, strong activity occurred in the supplementary motor area but not the primary motor area (Roland & others, 1980). Perhaps when divers, gymnasts, or pianists "visualize" their performance before they act, what they are doing, partly, is warming up specific neurons in the supplementary motor area and elsewhere (such

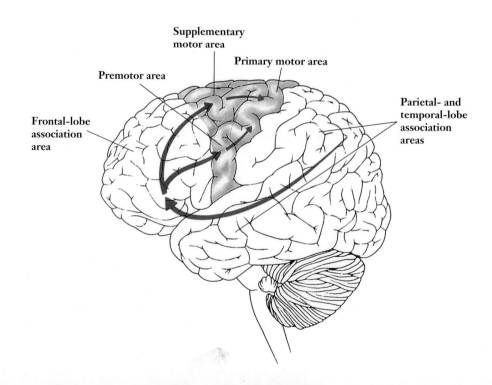

FIGURE **5.12** *Control of movement by the cerebral cortex*
The frontal-lobe association areas integrate information received from other brain areas and make a general plan for action. The premotor and supplementary motor areas convert this plan into neural programs for movement, which are then executed through connections to the primary motor cortex or through downward connections to the cerebellum and basal ganglia.

as in the basal ganglia and cerebellum) and in that way setting up the neural programs that will eventuate in the perfect performance.

Other areas of the cortex also contribute to the development of plans for action, in ways that are more complicated and less well understood than those just described. To get an idea of the general flow of information in the cortex in the control of movement, notice the arrows in Figure 5.12. Association areas in the rear parts of the cortex, especially the parietal and temporal lobes, are involved in the analysis of information that comes to them from sensory areas. These areas, in turn, send output to the association areas of the frontal lobe, which also receive information about the internal environment through strong connections with the limbic system. Combining all this information, the frontal association areas set up general plans for action that can be put into effect through connections to the premotor and supplementary motor cortex and through downward links to the basal ganglia.

Consistent with this interpretation, damage to the frontal-lobe association areas does not, as a rule, harm one's ability to extract information from the environment, but it does harm one's ability to use that information effectively to control behavior. Depending on the location and extent of the injury, it can destroy either short-range planning, such as working out the series of movements needed to solve a particular puzzle, or long-range planning, such as organizing one's day, week, or life (Kolb & Whishaw, 1996).

Hierarchical Organization in the Control of Movement: A Summary

The preceding discussion emphasized the role that each part of the nervous system plays in the control of movement. From an evolutionary perspective, movement control is the overarching purpose of the nervous system. The nervous system integrates information to provide a basis for effective, life-preserving movement. The simplest nervous systems—in the simplest invertebrate animals—control movement largely through means that are best described as reflexes. A stimulus produces a response, with relatively little intervening processing of the stimulus information. The evolution of more complex movement-control systems occurred not so much by replacing earlier systems as by building onto them. Thus the human nervous system can be viewed as a *hierarchy* of systems, ranging from the most primitive, reflexive levels in the spinal cord up to the most complex, analytical levels involving association areas in the cerebral cortex. To a large degree, the higher and evolutionarily newer levels exert their effects by controlling the activity of the lower and older levels.

To review the functions of the various parts of the nervous system and to visualize how the parts interact, look at Figure 5.13. Structures are organized in this figure according to their general roles in controlling movement, not according to their anatomical position. At the top are structures involved in motivation and planning, and proceeding down are those involved in refining and executing the plans, turning them into action. Notice that subcortical structures (shown on the left side of the diagram) and cortical structures (shown on the right side) are involved at each of the top three levels in the hierarchy.

To illustrate the hierarchy further, imagine events occurring in the nervous system of a person who hasn't eaten in a while and sees some peanuts. At the top of the hierarchy, the limbic system (which most directly monitors the internal state of the body) senses that food is needed and sends a message of "hunger" to the cortical association areas with which it is connected. These areas, which share the top of the hierarchy with the limbic system, analyze information coming to them from the visual cortex and determine that some peanuts lie in a bowl across the room. Other information is also considered by the association areas, including memories about

17.

How do association areas in (a) the frontal lobe and (b) the parietal and temporal lobes contribute to control of movement?

18.

From an evolutionary perspective, why does it make sense to regard the nervous system as a hierarchy of movement-control mechanisms?

19.

How is the hierarchy of motor control illustrated by an imaginative tour through the nervous system of a person who decides to eat some peanuts?

FIGURE **5.13**
A hierarchy of motor control
This figure summarizes the broad functions of various structures of the nervous system in the control of movement. The structures shown higher up are involved in the more global aspects of an action, and those shown farther down are involved in the finer details of carrying it out. Notice that both subcortical and cortical structures exist at each of the top three levels of the hierarchy. Although this portrayal does not show all the known pathways, it provides a useful way to think about the neural flow of information from the planning of an action to its execution. (Based partly on information in Ghez & Krakauer, 2000, and Schmidt, 1986.)

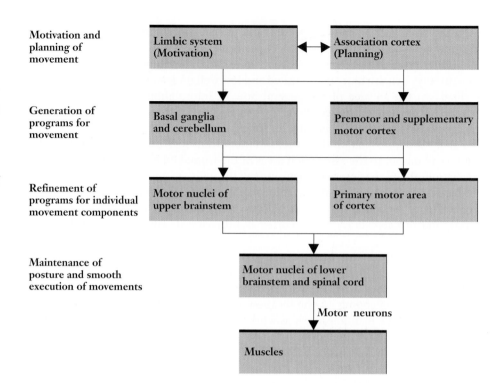

the taste of peanuts, about how to eat them, and about the propriety of eating them in this room at this time. Such information, integrated by association areas in the frontal lobes, leads to a decision to cross the room, take a few peanuts, and eat them.

At the second level, the basal ganglia and cerebellum, as well as the premotor and supplementary motor areas of the cortex, receive the broad program from the limbic system and association cortex. They also receive direct somatosensory input about the exact position of parts of the body and visual input about the exact location of the peanuts. They use this information to refine the motor program, working out the specific timing and patterning of the movements to be made.

At the third level, the motor program is conveyed through two pathways for further refinement. The program for larger movements, such as walking toward the peanuts, is sent directly down to a set of nuclei in the upper part of the brainstem. The program for delicate movements, such as those needed for removing the peanuts from their shells, is conveyed to the motor cortex, which, in turn, sends its output down to the brainstem and spinal cord. The motor cortex also receives sensory feedback from the fingers by way of the somatosensory cortex, which helps it make fine adjustments in the finger movements needed to shell the peanuts.

Finally, at the fourth level of the hierarchy are the motor neurons of the lower brainstem and spinal cord. In the words of the pioneering neurophysiologist Charles Sherrington, these neurons, which send their axons to muscles and glands, are the "final common path" of the nervous system. From an evolutionary perspective, the whole function of all the billions of other neurons is to operate these few million motor neurons in a reasonable, life-promoting way.

A Word of Caution

The hierarchy just described is useful as a first approach to understanding the nervous system, and it accurately reflects the kinds of behavioral deficits that occur when different parts of the nervous system are damaged. However, there is a possible danger in this portrayal: It can seduce us into believing that we know more than we actually do know. Specifically, the knowledge that certain parts of the brain are

20.

What is the difference between knowing where a brain function occurs and knowing how it occurs?

essential for certain aspects of behavioral control can be mistaken for knowledge about *how* those processes are accomplished. But the discovery of "where" does not answer "how." In illustrating the hierarchy, I spoke of a "decision" made in association areas of the cortex and of programs for action developed and refined by other brain areas. What do such statements mean? They mean only that individuals who suffer damage in one part of the brain lose the ability to make reasonable choices for action and that those who suffer damage in another part retain the ability to make reasonable choices but lose the ability to carry them out in a coordinated manner. Such statements don't address the far more difficult question of how the association cortex makes decisions or how various other structures develop and refine programs for action.

Asymmetry of Higher Functions of the Cerebral Cortex

Nearly every part of the brain exists in duplicate. We have a right and a left member of each anatomical portion of the brainstem, thalamus, cerebellum, and so on. The part of the brain in which the right-left division is most evident, however, is the cerebral cortex. Each half of the cortex folds inward where it would abut the other half, forming a deep, fore-to-aft *midline fissure* that divides the cortex into distinct right and left *hemispheres*. The two hemispheres are connected, however, by a massive bundle of axons called the ***corpus callosum*** (see Figure 5.14).

Each hemisphere has the same four lobes, and the same primary sensory and motor areas, that are shown in Figure 5.9. Most of the neural paths between the primary sensory and motor areas and the parts of the body to which they connect are crossed, or *contralateral*. Thus sensory neurons that arise from the skin on the right side of the body send their signals to the somatosensory area of the left hemisphere, and vice versa. Similarly, neurons in the primary motor area of the left hemisphere send their signals to muscles in the right side of the body, and vice versa. The two hemispheres are quite symmetrical in their primary sensory and motor functions. Each does the same job, but for a different half of the body. But the symmetry breaks down in the association areas.

In humans, the most obvious distinction between the two cortical hemispheres is that certain association areas in the left are specialized for language and comparable areas in the right are specialized for nonverbal, visuospatial analysis of information. The earliest evidence for this differentiation came from observations of people who had suffered strokes or other injuries that affected one hemisphere of the cortex and not the other. In general, damage to the left hemisphere results in

21.

In what ways are the two hemispheres of the cortex functionally symmetrical and in what ways asymmetrical?

FIGURE **5.14**   *The corpus callosum*
The corpus callosum is a huge bundle of axons that connects the right and left hemispheres of the cerebral cortex. You can see it here in an inside view of the right hemisphere of a human brain that has been cut in half. This photograph and matched diagram also give you an inside view of other brain structures.

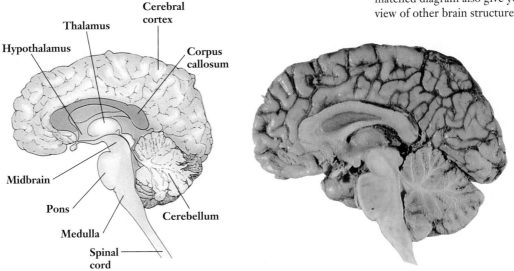

Thalamus
Cerebral cortex
Hypothalamus
Corpus callosum
Midbrain
Pons
Medulla
Cerebellum
Spinal cord

Martin Rotker

deficits in using and comprehending language, and damage to the right hemisphere results in deficits in such tasks as recognizing faces, reading maps, and drawing geometric shapes, all of which depend on perceiving spatial relationships. The most dramatic evidence for the separate abilities of the two hemispheres, however, appeared when Roger Sperry and Michael Gazzaniga began in the 1960s to study people who, as a last-resort treatment for epilepsy, had undergone an operation in which the corpus callosum had been severed so that the two hemispheres were separated.

The Split-Brain Syndrome

22.

How is it possible to test each hemisphere separately in split-brain patients, and how do such tests confirm the view that the left hemisphere controls speech and the right hemisphere has superior spatial ability?

Earlier, more casual observations had revealed no remarkable deficits in people whose corpus callosums had been severed. The operation was generally successful in reducing or eliminating epileptic seizures, and, after a period of recovery, there was usually no drop in measured IQ, in conversational facility, or even in ability to coordinate the two sides of the body in skilled tasks. But Sperry and Gazzaniga showed that under special test conditions, in which information was provided to just one hemisphere or the other, these people behaved in some ways as though they had two separate minds with different abilities (Gazzaniga, 1967, 1998).

The split-brain studies take advantage of the crossed sensory and motor connections of the brain. Recall that each hemisphere most directly controls movement in, and receives somatosensory information from, the opposite half of the body. As illustrated in Figure 5.15, connections from the eyes to the brain are such that input from the right visual field (the right-hand half of a person's field of view) goes first to the left hemisphere and input from the left visual field goes first to the right hemisphere. In the normal brain, all information that goes first to one hemisphere subsequently travels to the other through the corpus callosum. But the split-brain operation destroys those connections. Therefore, with the testing apparatus shown in Figure 5.16 and with split-brain patients as subjects, it is possible to (a) send visual information to just one hemisphere by presenting the stimulus in only the opposite half of the visual field, (b) send tactile information to just one hemisphere by having the subject feel an object with the opposite hand, and (c) obtain a response from just one hemisphere by having the subject point to an object with the opposite hand.

In a typical experiment, pictures of common objects were flashed in either the right or the left visual field. When a picture was flashed in the right field (projecting to the left hemisphere), the split-brain patient described it as well as someone with an intact brain would; but when a picture was flashed in the left field (projecting to the right hemisphere), the patient either claimed that nothing had been flashed or made a random guess. Then the researchers asked the same person to reach under a barrier with one hand or the other and identify, by touch, the object that had been flashed. The fascinating result was that the person could reliably identify with the left hand (but not with the right) the same object that he or she had just vocally denied having seen (Gazzaniga, 1967). Thus if the object flashed to the right hemisphere was a pencil, the subject's left hand picked out the pencil from a set of objects even while the subject's voice was continuing to say that nothing had been flashed. In other tests, Sperry and Gazzaniga found that split-brain patients were much better at solving spatial puzzles or drawing geometric diagrams with

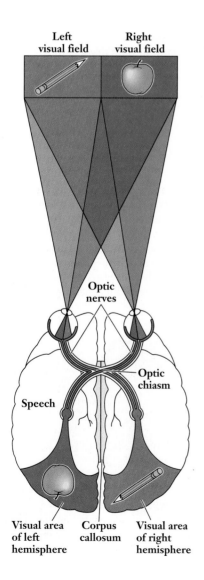

FIGURE 5.15
Neural pathways from the eyes to the right and left hemispheres of the cortex
Neurons of the optic nerves either cross or don't cross at the optic chiasm in such a way that those that receive input from the left visual field go to the right hemisphere of the brain, and vice versa.

FIGURE **5.16** *Testing apparatus for split-brain subjects*

With this apparatus, it is possible to flash a stimulus to either visual field (or both at once) and to ask the person to identify objects by touch with either hand. With the image of a pencil flashed in his left visual field, this split-brain subject will be able to identify the pencil by touch with his left hand. Vocally, however, he will report having seen nothing on the screen. (Adapted from Gazzaniga, 1967.)

their left hand than with their right, indicating right-hemisphere superiority in spatial tasks (see Figure 5.17).

Researchers have found large individual differences among split-brain patients in the degree to which the right hemisphere can comprehend speech. Some show essentially no right-hemisphere comprehension. They cannot participate in experiments such as that just described, because their right hemispheres don't understand such instructions as "Pick up the object that you saw on the screen." Some have right-hemisphere comprehension that is nearly as good as their left, although their right hemisphere is still unable to facilitate speech production; and a few show a reversal, with the right hemisphere superior to the left in language comprehension and production. Other tests, on people without the corpus callosum cut, indicate that about 4 percent of right-handed individuals and 15 percent of left-handed individuals have their speech centers located in the right hemisphere rather than the left (Rasmussen & Milner, 1977).

Perhaps you are wondering how people who have had the split-brain operation get along in the world as well as they do. What keeps their two hemispheres from going off in opposite directions and creating conflict between the two halves of the body? In some instances, especially shortly after the surgery, conflict does occur. One man described a situation in which, while dressing in the morning, his right hand was trying to pull his pants on while his left hand was trying to pull them back off (Gazzaniga, 1970); apparently, his right hemisphere wanted to go back to bed. But such conflicts are rare, and when they do occur the left hemisphere (right hand) usually wins.

The patient's ability to coordinate the two hemispheres probably involves several mechanisms. First, only the cerebral cortex and some parts of the limbic system are divided when the corpus callosum is cut. Motor centers that control such whole-body movements as walking lie in the lower, undivided parts, and some sensory information also passes from one hemisphere to the other by way of those lower routes (Reuter-Lorenz & Miller, 1998). The intact connections also apparently allow each hemisphere to inhibit the motor output of the other, so the more competent hemisphere can take control of any given task (Reuter-Lorenz & Miller, 1998). In addition, under normal conditions, when the eyes can move around and things can be felt with both hands, the two hemispheres can receive the same or similar information through their separate channels. Finally, each hemisphere apparently learns to communicate indirectly with the other by observing and responding to the behavior that the other produces, a process that Gazzaniga (1967) labeled *cross-cuing*. For example, the right hemisphere may perceive something unpleasant and precipitate a frown, and the left may feel the frown and say, "I'm displeased."

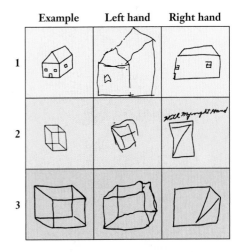

	Example	Left hand	Right hand
1			
2			
3			

FIGURE **5.17** *Evidence for right-hemisphere superiority in spatial representation*

Although the split-brain patient who produced these drawings was right-handed, he could copy geometric figures much better with his left hand (controlled by his right hemisphere) than with his right hand. (From Gassaniga, 1967.)

Specialized Language Areas: Evidence from Brain Damage

Within each hemisphere, specific areas of association cortex appear to be designed to carry out specific kinds of mental tasks. The most long-standing evidence for this comes from the effects of relatively localized areas of brain damage, and the most fully studied such deficits have to do with language comprehension and production. Any loss in language ability resulting from brain damage is called *aphasia*. Aphasias can be classified into a number of types, depending on the specific nature and degree of language loss (Dronkers & others, 2000), but the most well known are Broca's aphasia and Wernicke's aphasia, named after the nineteenth-century neurologists Paul Broca (1861/1965) and Carl Wernicke (1874/1977), who were among the first to describe them.

In **Broca's aphasia**, also called *nonfluent aphasia*, speech is labored and telegraphic—that is, the minimum number of words are used to convey the message. The speech consists mostly of nouns and verbs, and a sentence is rarely more than three or four words long. If you ask a person with this disorder what he or she did today, the answer might be, "Buy bread store." Broca's aphasics show relatively good language comprehension but often have difficulty understanding grammatically complex sentences. They become confused, for example, by sentence constructions in which the agent and object of an action are reversed from the usual word order and the meaning cannot be inferred from the individual word meanings alone (Grodzinsky, 2000; Zurif, 1990). Thus they easily understand *The boy pushed the girl* (a simple, active sentence) or *The apple was eaten by the boy* (which can be understood from the content words, because apples don't eat boys), but *The girl was pushed by the boy* leaves them unsure as to who pushed whom. The brain damage coinciding with Broca's aphasia usually encompasses a specific portion of the left frontal lobe, referred to as *Broca's area* (see Figure 5.18).

An early theory to explain Broca's aphasia focused on the deficit in language production coupled with the relative preservation of language comprehension. This theory proposed that Broca's area generates the motor programs needed to articulate sentences and transmits those programs to the nearby portion of the motor cortex that controls the lip, tongue, and laryngeal movements involved in speaking (Geschwind, 1972). A more recent theory suggests that Broca's area is crucial for holding in mind the overall grammatical structure of complex sentences (Dunbar & others, 2000). This theory accounts for the deficit in the comprehension of complex sentences, as well as the difficulty in producing sentences that are more than a few words long, that occurs when Broca's area is destroyed.

In contrast, **Wernicke's aphasia**, also called *fluent aphasia*, is characterized by a marked deficiency in language comprehension as well as production. The most obvious characteristic is a loss in the ability to understand word meanings and to produce the appropriate words to express meanings. The speech of Wernicke's aphasics is almost the opposite of that of Broca's aphasics. It is rich in the little words that serve primarily to form the grammatical structure of a sentence—the articles (*a*, *the*), prepositions (such as *of*, *on*), and conjunctions (*and*, *but*)—but is markedly deficient in nouns, verbs, and adjectives, which give most of the meaning to a sentence. One such patient, trying to describe a simple picture, said: "Nothing the keesereez the, these are davereez and these and this one and these are living. This one's right in and these are . . . uh . . . and that's nothing, that's nothing" (Schwartz, 1987). The inability to come up with the correct names of objects and actions leads to a heavy use of pronouns and nonsense words as substitutes. The speech retains its grammatical structure but loses its meaning. The brain damage coinciding with Wernicke's aphasia usually encompasses a specific portion of the left temporal lobe, referred to as *Wernicke's area*, which lies adjacent to the primary auditory area (see Figure 5.18). Theories concerning the role of Wernicke's area generally propose that it is involved in translating the sounds of words into their meanings and in locating, through connections to other cortical association areas,

---

23.

What is the difference between Broca's and Wernicke's aphasias in (a) language production, (b) language comprehension, and (c) area of the brain damaged?

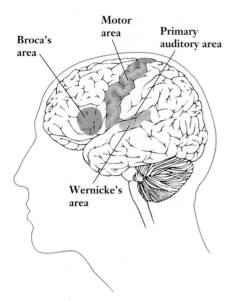

FIGURE **5.18** *Left-hemisphere language areas*

Damage to Broca's area leads to a loss of the ability to generate fluid, grammatically complete sentences but not to a loss of the ability to supply the words needed to convey the main content of the sentence. Damage to Wernicke's area has the opposite effect on speech production; it also greatly impairs speech comprehension.

the content words needed to express intended meanings (Dronkers & others, 2000; Geschwind, 1972).

Neuroimaging: Observing the Brain's Activity

Until relatively recently, knowledge about the functions of specific brain areas in humans depended almost entirely on studies of people who had suffered brain damage. Now, however, sophisticated computer and scanning technology makes it possible to create images of the brain that reflect the relative amount of neural activity occurring in each of its parts.

Two Methods of Neuroimaging: PET and fMRI

Like other tissues in the body, the brain is permeated by tiny blood vessels. When a portion of the brain becomes more active, blood vessels there enlarge, allowing more blood, which is carrying oxygen and glucose to the tissues, to flow into that portion. The two most common methods of assessing the activity of the human brain both make use of the fact that the amount of blood flowing into a given area of the brain at a given time correlates positively with the amount of neural activity occurring in that area at that time.

In the technique referred to as *positron emission tomography*, or **PET**, a radioactive form of glucose or of water (both of which are safe at low levels) is injected into a vein so that it flows into all the body's blood vessels, including those in the brain. The radioactive molecules emit subatomic particles called *positrons*, which quickly degrade and give off gamma rays, which are detected by sensors that surround the subject's head. A computer analyzes the information from the sensors and uses it to reconstruct an image (called a *tomograph*) of the brain in which variations in the density of gamma rays coming from each area are indicated by variations in color. The radiation from any given brain area reflects the amount of blood that has entered that area, which, in turn, reflects the amount of neural activity occurring in that area.

The technique referred to as *functional magnetic resonance imaging*, or *fMRI*, makes use of the fact that the protons in certain molecules can be made to resonate and give off radio waves when subjected to a strong magnetic field. The protons in hemoglobin molecules are particularly susceptible to this effect. Hemoglobin is the substance that holds on to oxygen in the blood until the oxygen is delivered into the surrounding tissues. Oxygenated hemoglobin responds differently to the magnetic field than does deoxygenated hemoglobin, and a certain radio wave frequency coming from the tissues reflects the ratio of oxygenated to deoxygenated hemoglobin. When an area of the brain is active, the increased blood flow to that area results in a local increase in this ratio (oxygenated hemoglobin moves into the active area faster than the oxygen is used). As in the case of PET, sensors around the head pick up the signal (radio waves in this case) and a computer analyzes the information and uses it to construct an image of the brain in which variations in the signal are indicated by variations in color. Once again, the color variations that are produced by the computer reflect the relative amount of neural activity occurring in each portion of the brain.

At any given time, the brain is doing many things, and most portions of it are almost always active to some degree. In order to determine, with either PET or fMRI, which brain areas are involved in a particular task, researchers need to employ an appropriate control condition. By subtracting the activity measured in each brain area in the control condition (when the person is not performing the specific task) from the activity measured in the same areas in the experimental condition (when the person is performing the task), the researcher can determine which areas show the greatest increase in activity during the task.

24.

How have the PET and fMRI techniques allowed researchers to see the relative amounts of activity in various parts of a person's brain as the person engages in a cognitive task?

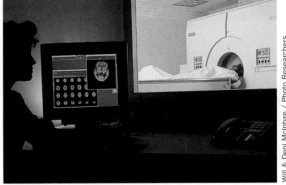

Will & Deni McIntyre / Photo Researchers

PET scanning

Sensors around the subject's head detect gamma rays, which will be used to construct an image depicting the relative amounts of activity in each part of her brain.

25.

How was PET used to identify brain areas involved in word perception and production?

An Example of Neuroimaging for Tasks Relevant to Language

The use of PET in language research is nicely illustrated by an experiment in which the procedure was applied to people as they carried out four types of tasks that varied stepwise in level of complexity (Petersen & others, 1989; Posner & Raichle, 1997). At the first level (simplest task), the subjects simply gazed at a spot marked by crosshairs in the center of a television screen. At the second level, they continued to gaze at the crosshairs while they either saw (superimposed on the crosshairs) or heard (through earphones) a series of common English nouns. The third level was just like the second, except that now they were asked to speak aloud each word that they saw or heard. The fourth level was like the third, except that instead of simply repeating each noun, they were asked to generate and say aloud a verb that represented an action appropriate to the noun (for example, in response to *hammer*, they might say "pound").

In order to identify the brain areas brought into play by each type of task, the researchers had the computer calculate, for each small area of the brain, the difference between the average gamma activity during that task and the average gamma activity during the task one level below that task. The results are depicted in Figure 5.19 and can be summarized as follows: (a) Viewing words produced high activity in visual sensory areas of the occipital lobe, at the rear of the brain. (b) Listening to words produced high activity in auditory sensory areas of the temporal lobe and in nearby association areas, including Wernicke's area. (c) Speaking words produced high activity in large portions of the primary mortor cortex. And (d) Generating appropriate verbs produced high activity in a portion of the frontal lobe that encompassed Broca's area and in a portion of the temporal lobe somewhat behind Wernicke's area.

These findings, as well as the results of other neuroimaging studies, are not completely consistent with expectations derived from traditional theories about the roles of Broca's and Wernicke's areas. The theories that you have just read about would predict that Broca's area should be involved in speaking words that have just been seen or heard, not just in generating words, and that Wernicke's area—rather than the spot behind it—should be involved in generating words with the appropriate meaning. At present, the neuroimaging findings are contributing to new theories about brain involvement in language that place relatively less emphasis on Broca's and Wernicke's areas and more on other regions of the left hemisphere (Dronkers & others, 2000).

FIGURE **5.19** *Brain activity during word-processing tasks, as revealed by PET*
Each figure shows the amount of activity in each part of the left hemisphere during the performance of the indicated task relative to the amount of activity in that part during the performance of the task one level below it in the hierarchy. The colors violet, blue, green, yellow, and red, in that order, represent increasing amounts of activity.

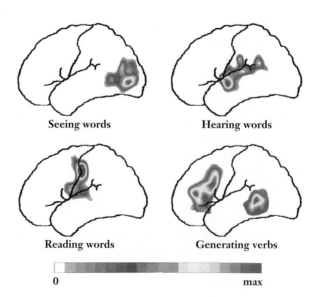

Seeing words   Hearing words

Reading words   Generating verbs

0   max

SECTION SUMMARY

The nervous system functions as an integrated whole but is thought of as consisting of interacting subsystems. The spinal cord and brain constitute the central nervous system, and the spinal and cranial nerves constitute the peripheral nervous system. Sensory neurons carry impulses from sensory organs into the central nervous system, interneurons interconnect neurons within the central nervous system, and motor neurons carry impulses from the central nervous system to muscles and glands. Motor neurons that activate skeletal muscles compose the skeletal motor system, and those that activate visceral muscles and glands compose the autonomic motor system. The autonomic system is further divided into the sympathetic portion, which prepares the body for emergencies, and the parasympathetic portion, which promotes digestion, energy conservation, and growth.

The central nervous system is divisible into several distinct structures. The spinal cord contains tracts connecting spinal nerves to the brain; it also contains interneurons that organize rhythmic locomotor movements and spinal reflexes. Tracts from the spinal cord continue into the brainstem (the medulla, pons, and midbrain), which organizes postural and vital reflexes and many species-typical movements. The thalamus is a relay center, which sends sensory input to the cerebral cortex and output from the cortex down to movement-control centers in the brainstem. The cerebellum and basal ganglia are involved in the sequencing and timing of muscle movements and the learning of motor skills. The limbic system and hypothalamus contain centers for motivation, emotion, and regulation of the internal environment.

The largest, outermost portion of the brain, the cerebral cortex, is divided into right and left hemispheres, each of which has four lobes: the occipital, temporal, parietal, and frontal. Each hemisphere contains several primary sensory areas devoted to specific senses, association areas that integrate information from more than one sense and formulate plans for action, and a motor area that participates directly in the control of muscle movements. The entire brain can be thought of as a system for movement control, organized hierarchically in the manner summarized in Figure 5.13.

The association areas of the two hemispheres of the human cortex are functionally asymmetrical. In most people, the left hemisphere has superior linguistic ability and the right has superior spatial ability. These differences are dramatically demonstrated in patients whose hemispheres were surgically separated to control epilepsy. Studies of people with localized areas of brain damage indicate that Broca's and Wernicke's areas, both in the left hemisphere, play special roles in language. Recently researchers have used neuroimaging methods—PET and fMRI—to assess the neural activity that occurs in each portion of the brain as a person engages in specific mental tasks.

HOW NEURONS WORK AND INFLUENCE ONE ANOTHER

Thus far our concern has been with the broad functions of large areas of the nervous system, each of which involves many millions of neurons. Now we move down to the microscopic level and ask questions about the workings of individual neurons and their connections with one another. How do neurons transmit their messages? How do neurons influence the activity of other neurons at their synaptic connections? How do connections among neurons change as a result of experience?

Molecular Basis of the Action Potential

The message that a neuron sends lies in the frequency of all-or-none ***action potentials***—electrical impulses that move down a neuron's axon and influence the activity of other cells. Action potentials are described as "all or none" for two reasons: (a) Each action potential produced by a given neuron is the same strength as any other action potential produced by that neuron, and (b) the action potential retains its full strength all the way down the axon.

FIGURE 5.20 *The resting potential*
Illustrated here is a portion of a neuron's cell membrane with ions dissolved on each side. Negatively charged protein molecules (A⁻) exist only inside the cell. Potassium ions (K⁺) exist mostly inside the cell. Sodium ions (Na⁺) and chloride ions (Cl⁻) exist mostly outside the cell. Because channels in the membrane that are permeable to potassium remain open, some potassium ions diffuse out, resulting in a surplus of positive charges outside the cell and a deficit of positive charges inside. For this reason, the resting membrane has an electrical charge across it of about 70 mV, with the inside negative compared to the outside. (Adapted from Koester, 1991.)

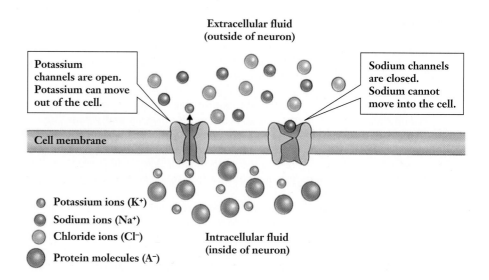

Extracellular fluid (outside of neuron)

Potassium channels are open. Potassium can move out of the cell.

Sodium channels are closed. Sodium cannot move into the cell.

Cell membrane

● Potassium ions (K⁺)
● Sodium ions (Na⁺)
○ Chloride ions (Cl⁻)
● Protein molecules (A⁻)

Intracellular fluid (inside of neuron)

26.

How does the resting potential arise from the distribution of ions across the cell membrane?

27.

How do the two phases of the action potential (depolarization and repolarization) result from the successive opening and closing of two kinds of channels through the cell membrane?

The Electrical Charge Across the Membrane of a Resting Neuron

To understand how action potentials are propagated, you have to know something about the functioning of the **cell membrane** that encloses each neuron. The membrane is a porous "skin" that permits certain chemicals to flow into and out of the cell and blocks the passage of others. You can think of the neuron as a membrane-encased tube filled with a solution of water and dissolved chemicals called *intracellular fluid* and bathed on the outside by another solution of water and dissolved chemicals called *extracellular fluid*.

Among the various chemicals dissolved in the intracellular and extracellular fluids are some that have electrical charges. These chemicals include *soluble protein molecules* (A⁻), which have negative charges and exist only in the intracellular fluid; *potassium ions* (K⁺), which are more concentrated in the intracellular than the extracellular fluid; and *sodium ions* (Na⁺) and *chloride ions* (Cl⁻), which are more concentrated in the extracellular than the intracellular fluid. For the reason described in Figure 5.20, more negatively charged particles exist inside the cell than outside. This imbalance results in an electrical charge across the membrane, with the inside typically about −70 millivolts (a millivolt [mV] is one-thousandth of a volt) relative to the outside. This charge across the membrane of an inactive neuron is called its **resting potential**. Just as the charge between the negative and positive poles of a battery is the source of electrical energy in a flashlight, so the resting potential is the source of electrical energy that makes an action potential possible.

The Action Potential Is Mediated by a Change in Membrane Permeability

An action potential is initiated at one end of the axon and moves along the axon through a chain reaction that is sometimes likened to the way a row of dominoes falls after the first one is tipped. As the action potential occurs at any given place on the axon (akin to the falling of one domino), thousands of tiny channels in the axon's membrane that are permeable to sodium open up, allowing some of the positively charged sodium ions in the extracellular fluid to pass into the intracellular fluid (see Figure 5.21). Two forces tend to drive sodium into the cell when the channels are open: (1) a concentration force, which occurs simply because more sodium ions exist outside the cell than inside; and (2) an electrical force, which occurs because like charges repel each other, so the positive electrical environment outside the cell pushes the positive sodium ions inward. As a result of these two forces, enough sodium moves inward to cause the electrical charge across the membrane to reverse itself and become momentarily positive inside relative to outside. This sudden shift constitutes the *depolarization phase* of the action potential.

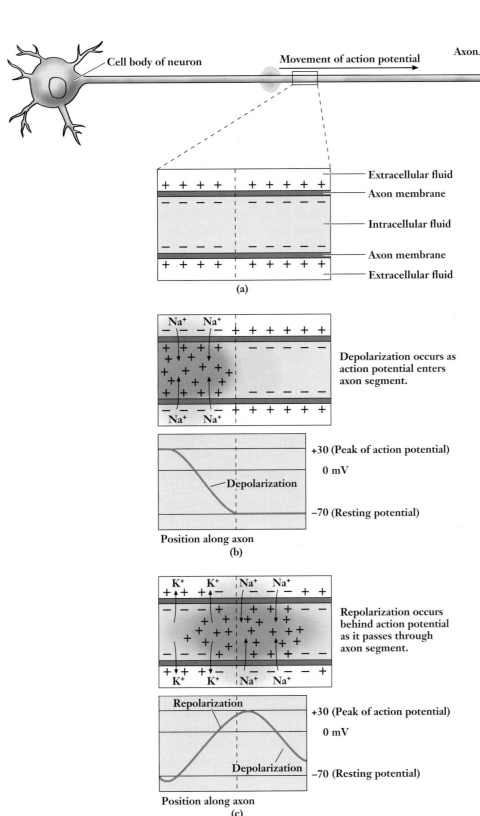

(a)

Extracellular fluid
Axon membrane
Intracellular fluid
Axon membrane
Extracellular fluid

Depolarization occurs as action potential enters axon segment.

+30 (Peak of action potential)
0 mV
Depolarization
−70 (Resting potential)

Position along axon
(b)

Repolarization occurs behind action potential as it passes through axon segment.

Repolarization
+30 (Peak of action potential)
0 mV
Depolarization
−70 (Resting potential)

Position along axon
(c)

FIGURE **5.21** *The action potential*
Shown here are the changes that occur at a given portion of the axon (indicated as a blue rectangle) as an action potential (indicated as an orange spot) passes through on its way from the neuron's cell body to its axon terminals. (a) During the resting state, this portion of the axon is electrically polarized such that it has a charge of about −70 mV inside compared with outside, as described in Figure 5.20. (b) The approaching action potential triggers sodium channels to open, which allows Na⁺ to pass into the axon, causing a depolarization, which itself is the first phase (depolarization phase) of the action potential. The influx of sodium ions causes the axon to lose its electrical polarity and, at the peak, to slightly reverse its polarity such that the inside becomes slightly positive compared with the outside (by about +30 mV). (c) The action potential continues to move through this portion of the axon by triggering sodium channels to open ahead of it. In the wake of the action potential, potassium channels open, which allows K⁺ to move out of the axon, restoring the membrane potential to its original value; this is the repolarization phase of the action potential.

As soon as depolarization occurs, the channels that permitted sodium to pass through close, and channels that permit only potassium to pass through open (Brown, 1997). Because potassium ions are more concentrated inside the cell than outside, and because they are repelled by the temporarily positive environment inside the cell, they are pushed outward. In this process, enough positively charged potassium ions move out to reestablish the original resting potential. This constitutes the *repolarization phase* of the action potential. The entire action potential, from depolarization to repolarization, takes less than a millisecond (one-thousandth of a second) to occur at any given point on the axon.

With each action potential, a small amount of sodium enters the cell and a small amount of potassium leaves it. To maintain the original balance of these ions across the membrane (and thereby retain the resting potential), each portion of the membrane contains a chemical mechanism, referred to as the *sodium-potassium pump*, that continuously moves sodium out of the cell and potassium into it. One can think of it as the neuron's battery recharger. Any recharger requires energy; to keep the pump going, the neuron constantly needs food and oxygen, which come from the blood. (Remember the ancient Greeks' observation, mentioned earlier, that the brain has particularly large blood vessels entering it? You now know a reason why.)

The Movement of Action Potentials Along the Axon

Action potentials are triggered at one end of the axon by influences that tend to reduce the electrical charge across the membrane at that point. In sensory neurons these influences derive from sensory stimuli acting on the dendritic ends of the axon; in motor neurons and interneurons they derive from effects of other neurons acting eventually on the axon at its junction with the cell body. The axon's membrane is constructed in such a way that depolarization, or reduction in charge, to some critical value causes the sodium channels to open, thereby triggering an action potential. This critical value (for example, to −60 millivolts inside, compared with a resting potential of −70 millivolts inside) is referred to as the cell's *threshold*. Once an action potential occurs at one end of the axon, it depolarizes the area of the axon just ahead of where it is occurring, thus triggering the sodium channels to open there. In this way the action potential keeps renewing itself and moves continuously along the axon. When an axon branches, the action potential follows each branch and thus reaches each of the possibly thousands of axon terminals.

The speed at which an action potential moves down an axon is affected by the axon's diameter. Large-diameter axons present less resistance to the spread of electric currents and therefore conduct action potentials faster than thin ones. Another feature that helps speed up the rate of conduction in many axons is the presence of a myelin sheath. The cells that form the sheath insulate the axon's membrane, so ions can move through it only at spaces (nodes) between adjacent cells. Each action potential skips down the axon, from one node to the next, faster than it could move as a continuous wave. The thickest and most thoroughly myelinated axons in the nervous system can conduct action potentials at a velocity of about 100 meters per second. Thus it takes about one-hundredth of a second for an action potential to run along that kind of axon from the central nervous system to a muscle about 1 meter away (a toe or finger muscle, for example). Very thin axons without a myelin sheath, in contrast, may conduct at rates as slow as 1 or 2 meters per second. When you poke your finger with a pin, you feel the pressure of the pin before you feel the pain. That is partly because the sensory neurons for pressure are large and myelinated and those for pain are thin and mostly unmyelinated.

Molecular Basis of Neural Communication at Synapses

As you learned earlier, neurons exert their influences on one another by releasing chemical neurotransmitter molecules at special junctions called synapses. Such synapses can be categorized into two basic types: *fast synapses* and *slow synapses*. The classic, most fully studied synapses are of the fast type.

Fast Synaptic Transmission: Quickly Exciting or Inhibiting Postsynaptic Neurons

The best-understood fast synapses are those between an axon terminal and either a muscle cell or the dendrite or cell body of another neuron. The axon terminal is separated from the membrane of the cell that it influences by a very narrow gap, the *synaptic cleft*. The membrane of the axon terminal that abuts the cleft is the

28.

How is an axon's conduction speed related to its diameter and to the presence or absence of a myelin sheath?

presynaptic membrane, and that of the cell on the other side of the cleft is the *postsynaptic membrane*. Within the axon terminal are hundreds of tiny globelike vesicles, each of which contains several thousand molecules of a chemical neurotransmitter. All these structures are depicted in Figure 5.22.

When an action potential reaches the axon terminal, it causes some of the vesicles to spill their neurotransmitter molecules into the cleft. The molecules then diffuse through the fluid in the cleft, and some become attached to special binding sites on the postsynaptic membrane. Each molecule of transmitter can be thought of as a key, and the binding sites can be thought of as locks. A molecule key entering a binding-site lock opens a gate in the channel, allowing ions to pass through. If the postsynaptic cell is a muscle cell, this flow of ions triggers a biochemical process that causes the cell to contract. If the postsynaptic cell is a neuron, one of two opposite effects occurs, depending on the type of synapse (Rockhold, 1997). At an *excitatory synapse* (as shown in Figure 5.22), the transmitter opens sodium (Na^+) channels. The movement of the positively charged sodium ions into the cell causes a slight depolarization of the receiving neuron (the neuron becomes less negative inside), which tends to increase the rate of action potentials triggered by that neuron. At an *inhibitory synapse*, the transmitter opens either chloride (Cl^-) channels or potassium (K^+) channels. The movement of negatively charged chloride ions into the cell or of positively charged potassium ions out of the cell causes a slight hyperpolarization of the receiving neuron (the neuron becomes even more negative inside than it was before), which tends to decrease the rate of action potentials triggered by that neuron.

All the chemical substances that have been identified as fast synaptic transmitters are small molecules (containing fewer than 10 carbon atoms) that can diffuse

29.

How do neurotransmitters at excitatory and inhibitory fast synapses affect the rate at which action potentials are produced in the postsynaptic neuron?

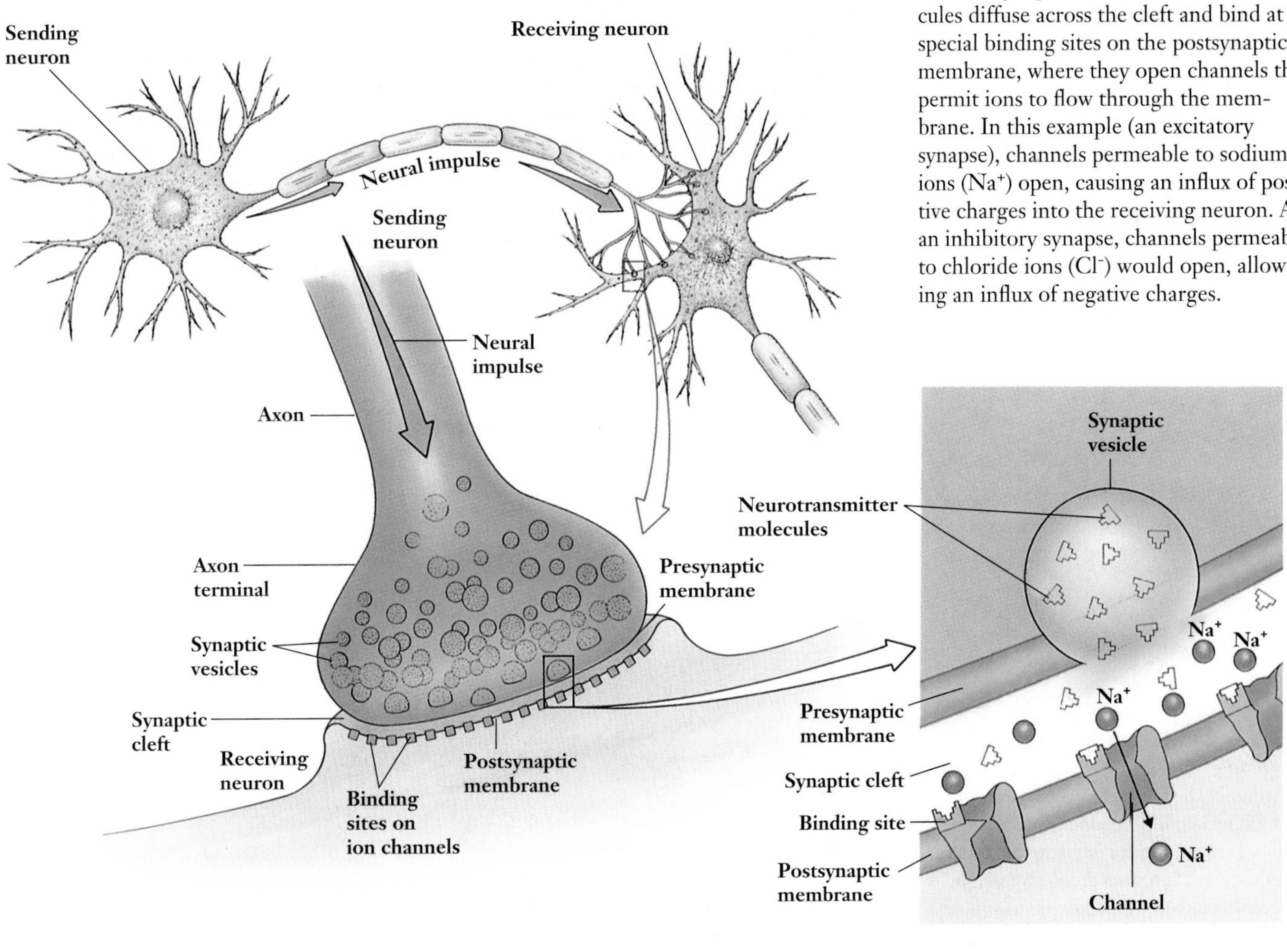

FIGURE **5.22**
Transmission across the synapse
When an action potential reaches an axon terminal, it causes some of the synaptic vesicles to spill their transmitter molecules into the synaptic cleft. Some of the molecules diffuse across the cleft and bind at special binding sites on the postsynaptic membrane, where they open channels that permit ions to flow through the membrane. In this example (an excitatory synapse), channels permeable to sodium ions (Na^+) open, causing an influx of positive charges into the receiving neuron. At an inhibitory synapse, channels permeable to chloride ions (Cl^-) would open, allowing an influx of negative charges.

quickly across a synaptic gap. Many of them fall into the chemical class called *amino acids*, which are also the basic building blocks of protein molecules. The most prevalent excitatory neurotransmitter in the brain is the amino acid *glutamate*, and the most prevalent inhibitory neurotransmitter is the amino acid *GABA* (*gamma-aminobutyric acid*) (Rockhold, 1997). Most of the other known fast transmitters fall into the chemical class called *biogenic amines*, which includes *acetylcholine*, *dopamine*, *norepinephrine*, and *serotonin*. They can be either excitatory or inhibitory, depending on the properties of the postsynaptic membrane on which they act.

Integration of Excitatory and Inhibitory Inputs from Fast Synapses

Any given neuron receives input via many synapses. In fact, the cell body and dendrites of some neurons are completely blanketed with axon terminals from thousands of other neurons (see Figure 5.23). Some of these synapses are excitatory and some inhibitory, and at any given moment transmission is occurring at some, but not all, of them (see Figure 5.24). At each excitatory synapse the transmitter causes a slight depolarization, and at each inhibitory synapse the transmitter causes a slight hyperpolarization. These effects spread passively through the cell body and affect the electrical charge across the membrane of the axon at its junction with the cell body. Recall that whenever the axon membrane is depolarized below the critical value, action potentials are triggered. The greater the degree of depolarization below that value, the greater the number of action potentials per second. Thus the rate of action potentials generated in the postsynaptic neuron's axon depends on the relative amount of activity at the excitatory as opposed to the inhibitory synapses on that neuron. In this way, the neuron integrates the total number of excitatory and inhibitory signals to it and sends a message (in its rate of action potentials) reflective of that integration.

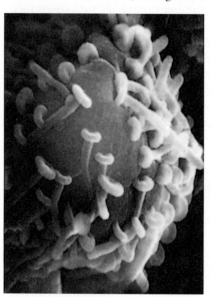

FIGURE 5.23 *Axon terminals*
This electron micrograph shows the terminals of many axons forming synapses on the cell body of a single neuron. Synaptic vesicles, filled with neurotransmitter molecules, reside within the buttonlike swelling of each axon terminal. In the central nervous system, the cell bodies and dendrites of motor neurons and some interneurons are blanketed with thousands of such terminals.

E. R. Lewis

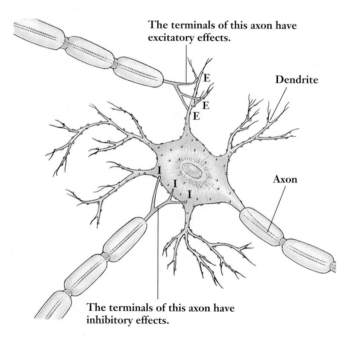

The terminals of this axon have **excitatory effects.**

Dendrite

E
E
E

I
I I

Axon

The terminals of this axon have **inhibitory effects.**

FIGURE 5.24 *Excitatory and inhibitory synapses*
Neurons in the central nervous system receive many synaptic connections from other neurons, some excitatory and some inhibitory. All synapses from any single neuron are either excitatory or inhibitory.

Slow Synaptic Transmission: Prolonged Alteration of Postsynaptic Neurons

At slow synapses, neurotransmitter molecules are released from the presynaptic neuron much as they are at fast synapses, but the effect on the postsynaptic neuron is different. Instead of directly opening ion channels for brief periods (a few milliseconds), slow neurotransmitters trigger a series of biochemical events in the postsynaptic neuron that take time to develop and can alter the functioning of that neuron for periods ranging from several hundred milliseconds up to hours or longer (Rockhold, 1997). In some cases, the neuron becomes excited or inhibited (produces more or fewer action potentials) for a prolonged period. In addition, or in other cases, growth processes are triggered, which result in the strengthening of old synapses or the production of new ones that can permanently alter the neuron's structure and functioning. Through such means, transmission at slow synapses can produce sustained effects on a person's behavior, such as altering mood or sensitivity to pain for a period of time or restructuring neural connections involved in learning.

Most of the chemical substances that serve as slow transmitters fall into the chemical class referred to as *neuropeptides*. These are relatively large molecules consisting of chains of amino acids. One class of neuropeptides about which you will read in Chapter 7 is the *endorphins*, which can reduce the experience of pain through their actions in pain pathways in the spinal cord and brain.

30.

How does slow synaptic transmission differ from fast transmission, and, in general, what sorts of functions are served by slow transmission?

Modification of Neural Connections as a Basis for Learning

As you have seen, the nervous system consists of an enormous network of neurons connected with each other at synapses. Researchers sometimes refer to these connections as "wiring," but that metaphor has limits. The nervous system is not hard-wired like a computer or other human-made electrical device. Neurons are soft, pliable, living cells. They can change their sizes, shapes, excitabilities, and patterns of connections in ways that help adapt their possessor to life's circumstances. Every day you grow millions of new synapses and lose millions of others, and at least part of that change apparently depends on the unique experiences you have that day.

Brain Growth Resulting from Experience

Evidence that the brain can change its structure in response to experience arose, beginning in the 1960s, from experiments conducted with rats housed in *enriched* and *deprived* environments (Greenough & Black, 1992; Rosenzweig, 1984). The enriched environments were large cages in which rats lived with others and had many objects to explore; the deprived environments were small cages in which each rat lived alone and had no objects except food and a water bottle. After weeks in these environments, the brains of the two groups of rats showed many differences. The brains of the enriched group had thicker cerebral cortexes, larger cortical neurons, more acetylcholine (a prominent neurotransmitter in the cortex), and thicker, more fully developed synapses than did those of the deprived group. These changes occurred even when rats were not placed in the differing environments until well into adulthood.

31.

What brain changes have been observed in rats and mice caged in enriched environments?

A playground for mice

In mice, as well as in rats, experience in an enriched environment enhances growth in the brain.

The researchers who performed these early experiments assumed that the brain growth they observed must derive solely from modifications of existing neurons and possibly the addition of new glial cells (the nonneural cells in the brain that provide structural and nutritional support to neurons). It was believed at that time that the mammalian brain was incapable of producing new neurons after birth. In the late 1990s, however, that belief crumbled as researchers using new techniques found ample evidence that new neurons are constantly being generated in the brain, including the adult human brain (Kempermann & Gage, 1999). The parts of the brain in which such growth has been most clearly observed are the hippocampus and the association areas of the cortex (Gould & others, 1999)—areas that have long been known to be important for learning and memory. In a study with adult mice, Gerd Kempermann and his colleagues (1997) found that new neurons were generated in the hippocampus at a rate 60 percent faster in an enriched environment than in a deprived environment.

Restructuring of the Brain Resulting from Experience

32.

What evidence shows that practice at specific sensory tasks alters neural connections so that more neurons become devoted to the task?

Other research has revealed that practice at sensory discrimination tasks can restructure brain pathways that are involved in performing those tasks. In one study, monkeys were trained to discriminate between subtly different rates of vibration applied to a particular patch of skin on one finger. (They received banana pellets for making a certain response each time the vibration rate increased above 20 cycles per second.) Subsequently, the researchers mapped the somatosensory area of the cortex of these and other monkeys by stimulating points on the skin with a thin probe while recording the activity of cortical neurons. They found that the area of cortex that received input from the "trained" spot of skin was, on average, two to three times larger than the comparable area in untrained monkeys, which had received the same vibrations but had not been required to discriminate among them for food reward (Recanzone & others, 1992). Apparently, the brain reorganization resulted not from the stimulation per se but from the monkeys' use of the stimulus input to guide their behavior. Similar studies have revealed comparable brain changes in visual and auditory sensory areas when animals are trained to discriminate among subtly different sights or sounds (Bakin & others, 1996; Zohary & others, 1994).

Through the use of PET neuroimaging, comparable results have been found in humans. In one such study, stringed-instrument players (six violinists, two cellists, and a guitarist) manifested unusually large areas of somatosensory cortical activation in response to stimulation of the fingers of the left hand—the same fingers that they had used for years in fingering the strings of their instruments (Elbert & others, 1995). In other studies, blind people who read Braille showed unusually large areas of cortical activation in response to stimulation of the index finger that they used in reading Braille (Pascual-Leone & Torres, 1993; Sadato & others, 1996). Apparently, we learn new skills at least partly through a process that modifies connections in the brain so that more neurons can be devoted to analyzing the pertinent sensory information.

Long-Term Potentiation as a Basis for Learning

Over 50 years ago, the Canadian psychologist Donald Hebb (1949) suggested that learning involves the selective strengthening of synapses in the brain. More specifically, he theorized that some synapses have the property of growing stronger (and more effective) whenever the presynaptic and postsynaptic neurons are active simultaneously (see Figure 5.25). Through this means, Hebb suggested, neurons could acquire the property of responding to stimuli that they previously didn't respond to, which could provide a basis for classical conditioning and other forms of learning. More than 20 years later, Timothy Bliss and Terje Lømo (1973) discovered a phenomenon called ***long-term potentiation***, or ***LTP***, which strongly supports Hebb's theory.

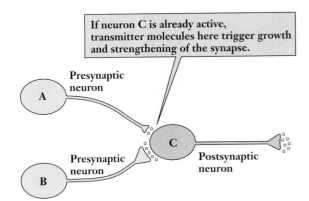

If neuron C is already active, transmitter molecules here trigger growth and strengthening of the synapse.

Presynaptic neuron

A

Presynaptic neuron

B

C

Postsynaptic neuron

FIGURE 5.25 *A Hebbian synapse*

The synapse between neuron A and neuron C is initially weak, so neuron A is ineffective in stimulating neuron C. However, if neuron C is already active (due in this case to the firing of neuron B), then transmitter molecules released at the synapse between A and C stimulate growth of that synapse. If this happens a sufficient number of times, the synapse will become sufficiently strong that neuron A will be able to trigger action in neuron C even when neuron B is inactive. This type of synapse is called *Hebbian* because its existence was first postulated by Donald Hebb. Recent research into the phenomenon of long-term potentiation confirms the existence of such synapses.

In the laboratory, LTP is produced by artificially stimulating, with a burst of electrical pulses, a bundle of neurons entering a particular region of an animal's brain. The result is that the synapses that those neurons form with postsynaptic neurons become stronger, so subsequent weak stimulation of the same bundle elicits a stronger response in the postsynaptic neurons than it would have done before. This *potentiation* is *long-term*: It lasts for hours or even weeks, depending on the conditions. Subsequent research has shown that, at least in some brain areas, LTP works in the manner depicted in Figure 5.25. The strengthening of a synapse from neuron A to neuron C (in the figure) occurs only if the latter neuron is already active when the former neuron releases its transmitter on it. Special receptors on the postsynaptic membrane, which are different from the receptors involved in normal, fast synaptic transmission, become primed to receive the transmitter when the postsynaptic neuron is active. When the primed receptors receive molecules of the transmitter, the receptors trigger a set of biochemical processes that strengthen the existing synapses between the presynaptic and postsynaptic neuron and in some cases generate the growth of new synapses between them (Toni & others, 1999).

Evidence that LTP is actually involved in learning comes from experiments showing that interference with the brain's normal capacity for such potentiation interferes with the animal's ability to learn. In one study with mice, genetic engineering was used to abolish the capacity for LTP to occur in a portion of the hippocampus known to be crucial for spatial learning. The mice treated in this way failed to form new spatial memories when tested in a maze (Tsien & others, 1996). In another study with mice, a drug that prevents LTP was injected into a portion of the amygdala that is known to be crucial for fear learning. After this treatment, the researchers tried, through classical conditioning, to train the mice to fear a tone that was paired with an electric shock. (As you may recall from Chapter 4, classical conditioning occurs when a *conditioned stimulus*, which does not initially elicit the response, is paired a sufficient number of times with an *unconditioned stimulus*, which does elicit the response, with the effect that after such pairing the conditioned stimulus will elicit the response even in the absence of the unconditioned stimulus.) The LTP-inhibited mice failed to learn such fear. They responded to the shock as did normal mice, but, unlike normal mice, they did not subsequently show fear responses to the tone (Maren, 1999).

Given such evidence that LTP is essential for learning, what would happen if the capacity for LTP were increased above the normal level? Joe Tsien (2000) and his colleagues found a way to answer that question. The postsynaptic receptors that are involved in initiating LTP come in two forms, a strong form (which is highly effective in triggering LTP) and a weak form (which is less effective). Through genetic engineering, Tsien and his colleagues produced a strain of mice—which they named "Doogie", after the boy genius of the television show *Doogie Howser, M.D.*—that had many more of the strong receptors and fewer of the weak ones than do

33.

How has the discovery of LTP tended to confirm Hebb's theory about synaptic strengthening, and what evidence shows that LTP is involved in learning?

Peter Murphy

FIGURE **5.26**   *A genetically altered "smart" mouse being tested for object recognition*
Mice, like other mammals, explore new objects more than familiar ones. In this test, each mouse was exposed to two objects: one that it had explored in a previous 5-minute session and one that was new. Genetically altered Doogie mice explored the new object (in this case, the one on the right) more than the old one even when several days had elapsed since the initial session. In contrast, unaltered mice explored the new object more than the old one only when a shorter period of time had elapsed. Tsien and his colleagues took this as evidence that the altered mice remembered the original object for a longer period of time than did the unaltered mice. (Photogaph from Tsien, 2000.)

normal mice. As predicted, brain neurons in the Doogie mice showed more LTP in response to electrical stimulation than did those in the normal, unaltered mice. Remarkably, but just as predicted, the Doogie mice also showed better memory than the unaltered mice in a series of three widely different tests: maze learning, classical conditioning of a fear response, and object recognition (see Figure 5.26). In each case, the altered mice behaved similarly to the unaltered mice during the learning experience but showed significantly better memory when tested 1 or more days later (Tang & others, 1999; Tsien, 2000).

The results of this study raise many questions that have not yet been answered. Will similar results be found with other animals and other forms of learning? Could memory in people be improved through methods that increase LTP? If a simple genetic change can improve memory by increasing LTP, then why hasn't evolution already produced that change through natural selection? That last question is an important one. Perhaps increased LTP, or even increased memory, is maladaptive for one reason or another.

How a Mollusk Learns

34.

How can the gill-withdrawal reflex be classically conditioned in Aplysia, and what is the neural mechanism of such conditioning?

Although the research just described has generated some provocative ideas about how learning occurs in the mammalian brain, researchers still don't know exactly which changes in which neurons underlie any specific instance of learning in any mammal. They do know that for some much simpler invertebrate animals, however.

The most detailed analyses of neural mechanisms of learning have been conducted by Eric Kandel (2000a) and his colleagues on a shell-less sea-dwelling mollusk commonly called a sea slug, or sea hare, and known to scientists by its genus name, *Aplysia*. While even the simplest of vertebrate animals has millions of neurons, *Aplysia* has a mere 20,000, some of which are quite large and easy to identify.

Several of *Aplysia*'s natural behaviors can be modified by classical conditioning, and some of them involve as few as 100 neurons (Bailey & Chen, 1991). One such behavior is the gill-withdrawal reflex.

When a strong stimulus, such as an electric shock, is applied anywhere on its skin, *Aplysia* reflexively pulls its gill into its body as protection against attack. A weaker stimulus, such as a light touch to the skin, normally does not elicit this response, but it can be made to do so through classical conditioning. Shock (or any other strong stimulus) applied anywhere on the skin can serve as the unconditioned stimulus to elicit *Aplysia*'s gill-withdrawal reflex, and a light touch anywhere else on the animal's skin can serve as the conditioned stimulus.

In the example diagrammed in Figure 5.27, the shock is applied to the tail, and the light touch is applied to an organ called the siphon. At first the light touch alone does not elicit gill withdrawal, but after several pairings with the shock it does. The effect is long-lasting. Even after several weeks, a light touch applied to the siphon elicits gill withdrawal. The effect is also specific. Light touch applied elsewhere, such as to the mantle skin, will not elicit the reflex, although it would if that had been where the stimulus was applied during initial conditioning. Through a long series of experiments, Kandel and his colleagues worked out the precise mechanism by which such conditioning occurs. As you read the following description, you will find it useful to refer repeatedly to Figure 5.27.

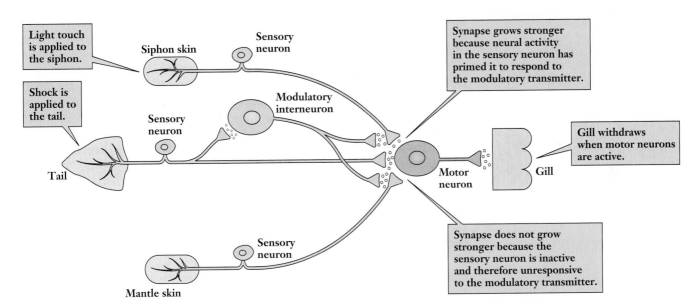

FIGURE 5.27 *Neuronal basis for gill-withdrawal learning in* Aplysia
Each neuron depicted in this diagram stands for a set of neurons that operate in parallel. Sensory neurons from various parts of the *Aplysia*'s body (the tail, siphon, and mantle) all have synapses on motor neurons that act to withdraw the gill. Stimulation at any of these areas produces the gill-withdrawal reflex. Strong stimulation also activates modulatory interneurons, releasing a neuromodulator substance on synaptic terminals of sensory neurons, which causes a long-term strengthening of those synaptic terminals and growth of new ones if the sensory neuron has just been active. This long-term strengthening of synapses from sensory neurons to motor neurons underlies classical conditioning of the reflex. In the example shown here, strong stimulation applied to the tail is the unconditioned stimulus for gill withdrawal, and weak stimulation to the siphon is the conditioned stimulus. After several pairings of the two stimuli, the weak stimulus, which previously did not elicit gill withdrawal, does elicit it.

Aplysia

Because of its relatively simple nervous system, this marine mollusk has become a favorite subject for studies of the neuronal basis of learning.

The gill-withdrawal reflex is mediated by sensory neurons that come from various places on the animal's skin and terminate at synapses on motor neurons, which, when active, cause contraction in muscles that pull the gill inward. These sensory neurons also terminate on special interneurons called *modulatory neurons*. The modulatory neurons are activated only when the sensory neurons are unusually active, as in response to an electric shock or (in natural conditions) a bite from a predator. When activated, the modulatory neurons release their transmitter substance, called a *neuromodulator*, at special *slow* synapses directly onto the axon terminals of sensory neurons. The neuromodulator molecules can initiate a series of biochemical processes in the sensory neurons on which they act, which cause the existing synapses between those neurons and motor neurons to strengthen and new synapses to grow. However—and this is the key point—these long-term growth processes are much more strongly triggered in neurons that have just fired action potentials than in inactive neurons.

So classical conditioning of the gill-withdrawal reflex works as follows: The light touch, applied just before the shock, elicits action potentials in sensory neurons coming from the siphon. These action potentials are insufficient in number to release enough neurotransmitter onto the motor neurons to cause gill withdrawal. However, they are sufficient to prime the sensory neurons in which they occur to respond to the neuromodulator. The shock to the tail causes strong activation of sensory neurons from the tail, which triggers motor neurons to cause gill withdrawal and, simultaneously, activates modulatory interneurons. The modulatory interneurons, in turn, release their neuromodulator onto the terminals of sensory neurons coming from various areas of the skin, including the siphon. Because the sensory neurons coming from the siphon have been primed by the light touch, they are especially sensitive to the effects of the neuromodulator, with the result that new and stronger synaptic connections are made between those sensory neurons and motor neurons to the gill. Because of that change, subsequent light touches to the siphon, but not to other areas of the skin, activate the gill-withdrawal reflex.

Thus a stimulus that formerly would not have elicited *Aplysia*'s gill-withdrawal reflex comes to elicit it, through a process of synaptic strengthening that is quite in line with Hebb's prediction. Most human learning is far more complex than that of *Aplysia*, but future research may well show that at its base are cellular processes similar to those in *Aplysia*.

SECTION SUMMARY

The semiporous nature of the neuron's cell membrane and the actions of the sodium-potassium pump maintain an electrical charge—the resting potential—across the membrane. When an action potential is triggered, an influx of sodium ions causes a momentary reversal of the charge across the membrane—the action potential—followed quickly by an outflux of potassium ions that restores the resting potential. Action potentials move wavelike down the axon, from its junction with the cell body to its axon terminals, at rates between 1 and 100 meters per second, depending on the axon's thickness and myelination.

Neurons influence the activity of other neurons at synapses. At a fast synapse, transmitter molecules released from axon terminals diffuse across the synaptic cleft and bind to the postsynaptic membrane on the cell body or on a dendrite of the postsynaptic neuron. Excitatory transmitters cause a slight depolarization of the postsynaptic membrane, and inhibitory transmitters have the opposite effect. The balance of excitatory and inhibitory synapses that are active at any given time on an interneuron or motor neuron determines the frequency at which that neuron produces action potentials. At slow synapses, transmitters trigger long-lasting changes in the activity and structure of the postsynaptic neuron.

The brain changes constantly as a function of experiences. New neurons grow, and new or strengthened connections develop between existing neurons. When animals or people develop skill at a specific task, neural connections change so that larger portions of the brain become devoted to that task. In line with Hebb's theory about the neural basis of learning, research on long-term potentiation (LTP) shows that simultaneous neural activity in two neurons strengthens the synaptic connections between them. In research on classical conditioning in the mollusk Aplysia, Kandel uncovered the details of one mechanism by which such synaptic strengthening can occur.

HOW HORMONES AND DRUGS INTERACT WITH THE NERVOUS SYSTEM

When the ancient Greeks argued that the heart is the seat of thought, feeling, and behavioral control, they were not entirely without reason. Like the brain, the heart is an organ that has long protrusions from it (blood vessels, in this case), connecting it with other parts of the body. Blood vessels are easier to see than nerves, and because they can be found in all the sense organs and muscles, as well as in other tissues, early theorists believed that blood vessels were the conduits of sensory and motor messages. Today we know that the circulatory system does indeed play a vital communicative role in the body. A slower messenger system than the nervous system, it carries chemicals that affect both physical growth and behavior. Among these chemicals are hormones, which are secreted naturally into the bloodstream, and drugs, which may enter the blood artificially through various routes.

Hormones

Hormones are chemical messengers that are secreted into the blood. They are carried by the blood to all parts of the body, where they act on specific *target tissues*. Dozens of hormones have been identified. The classic hormones—the first to be identified and the best understood—are secreted by special *endocrine glands* (see Figure 5.28). But many other hormones are secreted by organs not usually classed as endocrine glands, such as the stomach, intestines, kidneys, and brain.

Comparison of Hormones and Neurotransmitters

Hormones and neurotransmitters appear to have a common origin in evolution (Snyder, 1985). The earliest multicellular animals evolved a system of chemical messengers that allowed the cells to communicate and coordinate their actions, enabling the animal to behave as a unit. As organisms grew more complex, the chemical communication system differentiated along two distinct routes. One route involved the nervous system and was designed for rapid, specific, point-to-point communication. Here the primitive chemical messengers evolved into neurotransmitters. The other route involved the circulatory system and was designed for relatively slow, diffuse, widespread communication. Here the primitive chemical messengers evolved into hormones.

The main difference between a hormone and a neurotransmitter is the distance that each must travel through fluid between its site of release and its site of action. Neurotransmitter molecules released from an axon terminal must diffuse across the synaptic cleft—a distance of about 20 nanometers (20-billionths of a meter)—in order to affect the postsynaptic cell. In contrast, hormone molecules often must travel through the entire circulatory system before they bind to their target cells and exert their effects.

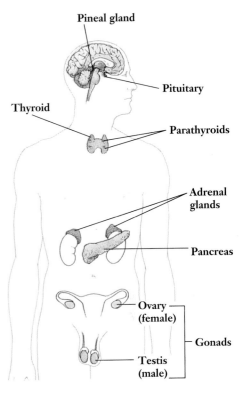

FIGURE **5.28** *Endocrine glands*
These are some of the glands that secrete hormones into the bloodstream. The pituitary, which is controlled by the brain, secretes hormones that, in turn, control the production of hormones by the thyroid, adrenals, and ovaries or testes.

35.

How are hormones similar to and different from neurotransmitters?

36.

What two lines of evidence support the idea that hormones and neurotransmitters have a common evolutionary origin?

One line of evidence for a common origin of hormones and neurotransmitters lies in their chemical similarity. In fact, some hormones are chemically identical to some neurotransmitters. The chemical *norepinephrine*, for example, is a hormone when secreted into the blood by the adrenal gland (shown in Figure 5.28) but is a neurotransmitter when released by sympathetic motor neurons of the autonomic nervous system on visceral muscles and glands. It is also a neurotransmitter in certain pathways in the brain. In each of these roles, norepinephrine helps arouse and alert the body. As a hormone and a sympathetic transmitter, it has effects such as increasing the heart rate; as a brain transmitter, it helps produce a state that we experience psychologically as high arousal or alertness.

Other evidence for a common origin of hormones and neurotransmitters lies in the existence of **neurohormones**. Like neurotransmitters, these chemicals are produced by neurons and released from axon terminals in response to action potentials. But they are classed as hormones because they are released not into a synaptic cleft but into a bed of capillaries (tiny blood vessels), where they are absorbed into the bloodstream. As you will see, some neurohormones promote the secretion of other hormones, and in that way they provide a means by which the nervous system controls the activity of the endocrine system. To compare the four modes of chemical communication just discussed, see Figure 5.29.

How Hormones Affect Behavior

Hormones influence behavior in many ways. They affect the growth of peripheral body structures, including muscles and bones, and in that way influence behavioral capacity. Hormones also affect metabolic processes throughout the body and thereby influence the amount of energy that is available for action. Of greatest interest to psychologists, hormones also act in the brain in ways that influence drives and moods.

Some effects of hormones are long term or irreversible, and some of these occur before birth. For example, essentially all the anatomical differences between newborn boys and girls are caused by the hormone testosterone, which is produced

FIGURE **5.29**
Four modes of chemical communication between cells
The primitive mode of intracellular chemical communication (a) evolved to form three more complex modes of chemical communication: (b) a neural mode, in which chemicals from a neuron diffuse across a small synaptic gap to their target cell (another neuron or muscle cell); (c) a neurohormonal mode, in which chemicals from neurons enter the bloodstream and are carried to target cells; and (d) a hormonal mode, in which chemicals from an endocrine gland enter the bloodstream and are carried to target cells. (Based on figure in Snyder, 1985.)

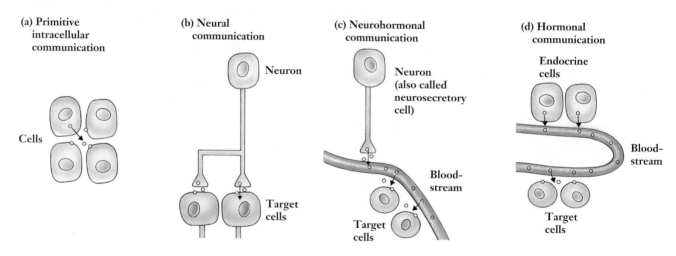

by the male fetus but not the female. These anatomical differences are evident in the brain as well as in the genitals. The brain differences provide a basis for sex differences in the adult sexual behavior of nonhuman animals and may do so in humans as well (discussed in Chapter 6). At puberty, the increased production of sex hormones—especially testosterone in the male and estrogen in the female—stimulates a new set of growth processes that further differentiate males and females anatomically and thereby influence their behavior.

The shorter-term effects of hormones range in duration from a few minutes to many days. In response to stressful stimulation, for example, the adrenal cortex (the external layer of the adrenal gland) secretes various hormones, including cortisol, that act on tissues throughout the body to help prepare it to expend energy and withstand wounds. These hormones promote the release of sugar and fat molecules into the blood to supply energy and help suppress inflammation at wound sites. Experiments with rats and other animals show that these hormones are also taken up by neurons in the limbic system, especially in the hippocampus (McEwen & others, 1986). Just what role they play there is uncertain, but some evidence suggests that they help the animal calm down after a period of stress and promote the formation of long-term memories related to the stressful experience (McEwen, 1989).

At the molecular level, hormones can work on cells in various ways. Most hormones fall into one of two chemical classes: *peptides*, which are short-chain protein molecules, and *steroids*, which are chemically related to cholesterol. Neurohormones and all hormones produced by the pituitary gland are peptides; hormones produced by the adrenal cortex and the gonads (ovaries in the female and testes in the male) are steroids. Peptides do not easily pass through cell membranes, so they usually exert their effects at receptor sites on the outside of the cell membrane. There they may act like neurotransmitters to alter the balance of ions across the membrane and may stimulate more sustained changes by activating messenger systems that work inside the neuron. Steroids, in contrast, pass through cell membranes easily, and commonly exert their effects within the cell nucleus. There they may activate or inhibit specific genes and thereby increase or decrease the production of specific protein molecules, which, in turn, can alter the neuron's activity in either a short-term or a long-term manner (McEwen, 1989).

How Hormones Are Controlled by the Brain

The pituitary, which sits at the base of the brain, is sometimes called the master endocrine gland because it produces hormones that, in turn, stimulate the production of other hormones in other glands, including the adrenal cortex and the gonads. But we might more accurately say that the brain is the master endocrine gland, because through neurohormones it controls the pituitary.

To visualize the intimate relationship between the brain and the pituitary, look at Figure 5.30. The rear part of the pituitary, the *posterior lobe*, is in fact a part of the brain. The posterior lobe consists mainly of modified neurons, referred to as *neurosecretory cells*, that extend down from the hypothalamus and secrete neurohormones into a bed of capillaries. Once these hormones enter the capillaries, they are transported into the rest of the circulatory system to affect various parts of the body. The remainder of the pituitary, the *anterior lobe*, is not part of the brain (no neurons descend into it) but is intimately connected to the brain by a specialized set of capillaries, as shown in Figure 5.30. Neurosecretory cells in the brain's hypothalamus produce *releasing factors*, neurohormones that are secreted into the capillary system and are carried to the anterior pituitary, where they cause the synthesis and release of pituitary hormones. Different releasing factors, produced by different sets of neurosecretory cells in the hypothalamus, act selectively to stimulate the production of different anterior pituitary hormones.

37.

What are examples of long-term and short-term effects of hormones?

38.

At the molecular level, how do hormones exert their effects?

39.

How does the brain control the release of hormones from the two lobes of the pituitary and thereby control the release of other hormones as well?

FIGURE **5.30** *How the hypothalamus controls pituitary hormones*
Specialized neurons in the hypothalamus, called neurosecretory cells, control the activity of the pituitary gland. Some neurosecretory cells secrete hormones directly into capillaries in the posterior pituitary, where they enter the general bloodstream. Others secrete hormones called *releasing factors* into a special capillary system that carries them to the anterior pituitary, where they stimulate the release of hormones manufactured there.

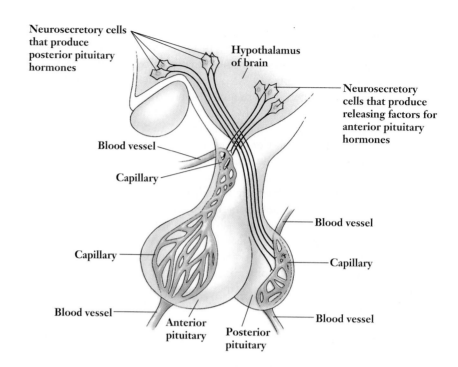

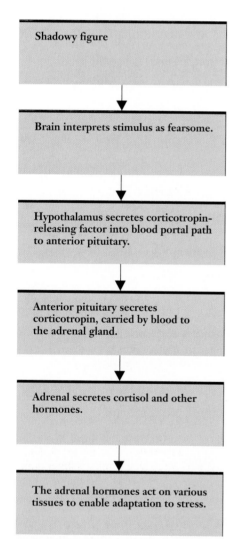

FIGURE **5.31** *Brain-pituitary-adrenal response to a fearful stimulus*
This is one example of a brain-mediated hormonal response to sensory stimulation.

Consider the sequence of hormonal events, triggered by the brain, that is diagrammed in Figure 5.31: (1) A shadowy figure is seen at night, and the brain interprets it as fearsome. (2) The association cortex sends a neural message to the viewer's hypothalamus that causes it to secrete *corticotropin-releasing factor*. (3) The specialized capillary system transports this releasing factor to the anterior pituitary, where it stimulates the release of another hormone, *corticotropin*, into the bloodstream. (4) From the bloodstream, corticotropin enters the adrenal cortex, where it causes the release of adrenal cortical hormones, including cortisol. (5) These adrenal hormones are carried throughout the body to help prepare it for a possible emergency. At the same time, many other brain-controlled effects are also occurring to deal with the possible emergency suggested by the sight of the shadowy figure. They range from the activation of the sympathetic portion of the autonomic nervous system to the development of a plan to escape.

Drugs

The main difference between a hormone and a drug is that the former is produced in the body and the latter is introduced from the outside. Like hormones, drugs are carried by the blood and taken up in target tissues in various parts of the body.

How Drugs Get to Neurons in the Brain

To be carried to potential sites of action, a drug first must get into an individual's bloodstream. Sometimes drugs are introduced directly into the blood by intravenous injection, but more commonly they are administered by routes that bring them into contact with capillaries, where they are gradually absorbed into the blood. Drugs are absorbed by capillaries in the intestines if taken orally, by capillaries in the lungs if taken by inhalation, by capillaries in the rectum if taken by rectal suppository, and by capillaries under the skin or in the muscles if taken by subcutaneous or intramuscular injection. The preferred route of administration depends largely on the properties of the drug and the desired time course of action. A drug that is destroyed by digestive juices in the stomach, for example, cannot be taken orally. A drug that is injected intravenously will act more quickly than one that is administered by any other route.

If a drug is going to act in the brain, it must pass from the blood into the extracellular fluid that surrounds neurons in the brain. The capillaries in the brain are much less porous than those in other tissues. In addition, they are tightly surrounded by the fatty membranes of a certain variety of glial cells. The tight capillary walls and the surrounding glial cells form the ***blood-brain barrier***, which helps protect the brain from poisons. To act in the brain, a drug (or hormone) must be able to pass through this barrier. In general, fat-soluble substances pass through easily, and non-fat-soluble substances may or may not pass through, depending on other characteristics of their chemistry.

How Drugs Can Alter Synaptic Transmission

Many different drugs are used in psychiatry and neurology to alter a person's mood or behavioral capacities. Nearly all such drugs work by enhancing or blocking synaptic transmission somewhere in the nervous system (Stone, 1995). In normal synaptic transmission, neurotransmitter molecules are released from the presynaptic neuron, diffuse across the narrow synaptic cleft, and then bind to the membrane of the postsynaptic cell and alter its activity (to review this process, look back at Figure 5.22).

Drugs can influence activity at a synapse in three ways: (1) They can act on the presynaptic neuron to either facilitate or inhibit the release of the transmitter, thereby affecting the amount of it that enters the cleft. (2) They can act in the cleft to either facilitate or inhibit the processes that normally terminate the action of the transmitter once it has been released, either prolonging or shortening the amount of time that the transmitter remains in the cleft and exerts its effects. (3) They can act directly on postsynaptic binding sites, either producing the same effect as the transmitter or blocking the transmitter from producing its normal effect.

Of the three, the postsynaptic effect is best understood. To visualize how the postsynaptic effect occurs, recall the comparison of neurotransmitter molecules to keys and binding sites on postsynaptic membrane channels to locks (and look at Figure 5.32). A drug molecule that diffuses into a synapse may act as a substitute key, producing the same effect as the transmitter would, or it may act as a misshapen key, filling the keyhole without turning the lock, thereby preventing the transmitter from having its normal effect. Many different neurotransmitters exist in the nervous system, and a particular drug may alter the activity of just one or several different transmitters. Thus drugs can be more or less specific, affecting either a small or a large class of synapses, and hence can be more or less specific in the effects they produce on behavior.

40.

What are three ways in which drugs can alter activity at a synapse?

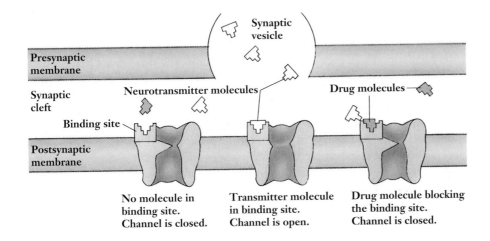

FIGURE 5.32 *Lock-and-key view of drug effects in a synapse*
Each binding site on the membrane of the postsynaptic cell can be thought of as a keyhole, and each neurotransmitter molecule as a key that fits into it and opens the lock, causing the ion channel in the cell membrane to open. A drug molecule can serve as a substitute key and produce the same effect as the neurotransmitter, or it can serve as a misshapen key (as shown here) that occupies the keyhole without activating the lock and thus prevents the neurotransmitter from acting.

Synaptic vesicle

Presynaptic membrane

Synaptic cleft

Neurotransmitter molecules

Drug molecules

Binding site

Postsynaptic membrane

No molecule in binding site. Channel is closed.

Transmitter molecule in binding site. Channel is open.

Drug molecule blocking the binding site. Channel is closed.

How Drugs Act at Different Levels of the Behavior-Control Hierarchy

One way to imagine the many kinds of effects that drugs can have on behavior is to think of them in relation to the hierarchy of behavioral control depicted in Figure 5.13 (on page 158). Drugs that act at a particular level of the hierarchy have behavioral effects that are consistent with the functions of that level, as described in the figure.

Curare is a drug that acts at the lowest level, at synapses between motor neurons and skeletal muscle cells. This poison, long used by certain South American Indians on the tips of their arrows for hunting, paralyzes the animal that is hit. Curare produces paralysis by blocking the postsynaptic binding sites for acetylcholine, which is the transmitter released by skeletal motor neurons onto muscle cells. Because the muscle cells can no longer respond to acetylcholine, they can no longer contract, so the animal is unable to move. Acetylcholine is also a transmitter at many places within the central nervous system, but curare does not act in those places because it cannot pass the blood-brain barrier.

A drug that acts somewhat higher up in the movement-control hierarchy is *L-dopa*, which is used to treat Parkinson's disease. As you may recall, Parkinson's disease is caused by the degeneration of certain neurons whose axons originate in the brainstem and terminate in the basal ganglia. The disease is characterized by muscle tremors and severe difficulty in initiating movements. These symptoms are manifested when the degenerating neurons fail to release a sufficient quantity of the neurotransmitter *dopamine*. It might seem logical to treat these symptoms by introducing additional dopamine into the body, but dopamine cannot cross the blood-brain barrier. However, L-dopa, a precursor in the synthesis of dopamine, can cross the barrier. Once in the brain, L-dopa is converted to dopamine.

Drugs that work still farther up in the behavior-control hierarchy may alter mood or general arousal or may affect one's thoughts and perceptions. These drugs are called *psychoactive drugs* because they influence processes that we think of as psychological. Chapter 17 describes some of the clinical uses of psychoactive drugs in the treatment of severe anxiety, depression, and other disorders. Meanwhile, Table 5.1 shows one way of categorizing psychoactive drugs and what is known about the action mechanism of some of them, including such everyday examples as caffeine and nicotine.

Tolerance, Withdrawal Symptoms, and Addiction

Some drugs produce progressively smaller physiological and behavioral effects if taken repeatedly, a phenomenon known as **drug tolerance**. Because of tolerance, people who regularly take a drug may have to increase their dose over time to continue to achieve the original effect. In addition, some drugs can produce disturbing or even life-threatening *withdrawal symptoms* when their habitual use is abruptly stopped. Withdrawal symptoms are commonly the opposite of the initial direct effects of the drug. Thus drugs taken repeatedly to treat some symptom—such as constipation, headaches, sleeplessness, or anxiety—can have counterproductive effects in the long run. Upon withdrawal, the symptom may return at a higher level of severity than ever. In general (although not always), the same drugs that produce tolerance when taken repeatedly also produce withdrawal symptoms when stopped (Fishbein & Pease, 1996).

A general theory to explain both tolerance and withdrawal symptoms relates them to long-term adjustments that the body makes to adapt itself to a drugged condition (Poulos & Cappell, 1991). During prolonged drug use, physiological changes occur that serve essentially to *counteract* the effects of the drug, permitting the individual to function more normally while in the drugged state. These changes may involve a reduction in the activity of physiological systems that are excited by the drug or an increase in the activity of systems that are depressed by the drug. Because of these long-term compensatory changes, an ever-increasing dose of the drug is needed to achieve the original effect, and absence of the drug results in an

41.

How can the effects of curare, L-dopa, and psychoactive drugs be interpreted in terms of the hierarchical model of movement control?

42.

How can drug tolerance and withdrawal symptoms be explained in terms of physiological adaptation to a drugged state? For amphetamines, how might this adaptation occur at the molecular level?

TABLE **5.1** *Some categories of psychoactive drugs*

1. Behavioral stimulants and antidepressants

Drugs that increase alertness and activity level and elevate mood, including:

◆ *Amphetamines and cocaine* Often abused because of the psychological "high" they produce, these drugs increase the release of norepinephrine and dopamine into synapses and prolong their action there.

◆ *Clinical antidepressants* These counteract depression but do not produce the sleeplessness or euphoria that amphetamines and cocaine produce. One class, the *monoamine oxidase inhibitors*, increases the synaptic activity of monoamine neurotransmitters (serotonin, norepinephrine, and dopamine) by inhibiting the enzyme that breaks them down (discussed in Chapters 16 and 17).

◆ *Caffeine* Found in coffee, tea, and cocoa beans, this drug promotes arousal partly by activating the peripheral sympathetic nervous system. In the brain, it increases neural activity by inhibiting the postsynaptic action of adenosine, which functions as an inhibitory neuromodulator.

◆ *Nicotine* Found in tobacco, this drug increases activity in many neurons in the brain by acting on some of the same postsynaptic receptor sites as does the neurotransmitter acetylcholine (through the substitute-key mechanism). In this way, it also activates portions of the peripheral sympathetic nervous system, causing, as one effect, increased heart rate.

2. Tranquilizers and central-nervous-system depressants

Drugs that counteract anxiety and/or decrease alertness and activity level, including:

◆ *Benzodiazepines* Prescribed to counteract anxiety, these drugs (including diazepam, sold as Valium) act on postsynaptic receptors to make them more responsive to GABA, which is an inhibitory transmitter. Increased responsiveness to GABA causes a decrease in neural activity in those parts of the brain where it is present.

◆ *Alcohol and barbiturates* These often-abused drugs depress neural activity throughout the brain by a variety of means that are not well understood. Low doses may produce relief from anxiety, and higher doses produce sedation, sleep, unconsciousness, coma, and death, in that order. Their antianxiety effects are believed to work in the same way as those of benzodiazepines.

3. Opiates

These include *opium*, a crude extract from the opium plant; *morphine*, the most active ingredient in opium; *codeine*, an extract from opium that is chemically similar to morphine but less active; and *heroin*, which is synthesized by chemical modification of morphine. All are potent pain reducers and can cause feelings of euphoria. They produce at least some of their effects by activating neurons that normally respond to *endorphins*, a class of slow-acting transmitters that are part of the body's natural system for relieving pain (discussed in Chapter 7).

4. Antipsychotic drugs

Prescribed mostly to treat schizophrenia, most of these drugs (including chlorpromazine and haloperidol) are believed to work by decreasing activity at synapses where *dopamine* is the transmitter (discussed in Chapters 16 and 17).

5. Hallucinogenic drugs

These induce hallucinations and other sensory distortions. Some, such as *mescaline* and *psilocybin*, exist naturally in plants and have a long history of use among various peoples, including Native Americans, in religious rites. Others, such as *LSD* (lysergic acid diethylamide), are synthetic compounds. Most are structurally similar to neurotransmitters, and they are believed to act either by mimicking or blocking transmitters that they resemble. Both LSD and psilocybin resemble the transmitter *serotonin*.

Source: Compiled largely from W. A. McKim, *Drugs and behavior: An introduction to behavioral pharmacology* (4th ed.) (2000) Upper Saddle River, NJ: Prentice-Hall.

unbalanced state in which the long-term compensatory changes are not counteracted by the drug.

To illustrate how tolerance and withdrawal symptoms may develop, consider *amphetamines*, a class of drugs that are often used (and abused) to sustain wakefulness or to produce a psychological feeling of elation (a drug "high"). Amphetamines promote the release of the neurotransmitter norepinephrine into synapses in the brain, and this provides at least part of the physiological basis for the arousal and mood elevation. Prolonged use of an amphetamine results in tolerance, and subsequent abstinence results in withdrawal symptoms, including extreme fatigue and psychological depression, which are the opposite of the direct effects of the drug (McKim, 1997). Research suggests that both the tolerance and the withdrawal symptoms come about at least partly because the brain, reacting to the repeated, drug-induced oversupply of norepinephrine, begins to produce a specific chemical that blocks the postsynaptic binding sites for norepinephrine by the misshapen-key method illustrated in Figure 5.32 (Caldwell & others, 1980).

Because many of the binding sites are blocked, more norepinephrine is needed in the synapse to activate the postsynaptic neurons. Thus a higher dose of amphetamine is needed to achieve the effect that was once achieved by a low dose, and when no amphetamine is taken, the postsynaptic neurons are unusually inactive, resulting in feelings of fatigue and depression. After a sufficient period of drug abstinence, however, the brain stops making the blocking chemical, and the person returns to a normal mood and alertness without the amphetamine.

Thus far I have avoided the term *addiction*. People are said to be addicted to a drug if, despite contrary intentions, they cannot refrain from continuing to take it. Physiological withdrawal symptoms can certainly provide part of the basis for addiction, since some people continue to take a drug almost entirely to alleviate the effects of withdrawal. But addiction may be present even without physiological withdrawal symptoms.

You can read more about addiction in Chapter 16, including evidence that it is a product not just of the direct biological effects of a drug but also of the learned expectancies and values concerning the drug, which people acquire from their social experience. In Chapter 4, evidence was presented that classical conditioning can also affect the way a person reacts to a drug, so the same drug dose can have different effects, depending on the environment in which it is taken. Whether we are talking about drugs or any other class of influences on human behavior, the effect can be fully understood only by considering it in the context of a great deal of other information about the person and the setting.

SECTION SUMMARY

Hormones are chemical messengers that act over much longer distances within the body than do neurotransmitters. They are secreted by endocrine glands into the bloodstream and act on various target tissues, including the brain. Hormones can stimulate growth in specific areas of the brain and elsewhere in the body, thereby producing long-term behavioral effects. They can also temporarily activate particular areas of the brain, producing short-term behavioral effects. Through its neural and vascular connections to the pituitary gland, the brain regulates the secretion of many hormones.

Drugs are substances introduced into the body from the outside, which make their way into the bloodstream and act on various target tissues. Many drugs alter behavior by interfering with synaptic transmission or by acting like transmitters in specific areas of the brain. Such drugs may be classified in terms of where in the hierarchy of movement control they exert their influence. Psychoactive drugs act at the highest level, altering mood, perception, and thought. Drug tolerance and withdrawal symptoms occur because of bodily processes that tend to counteract the direct effects of the drug.

CONCLUDING THOUGHTS

Hippocrates was right: The brain is the organ of the mind. The mind is a set of processes (feeling, thinking, initiating action, and so on) carried out by physical activities in the brain and interfered with by lesions in the brain. The brain, of course, does not work in isolation from the rest of the body or the environment. It needs input from sensory nerves, it is affected by chemicals carried in the blood, and it acts through motor nerves and (to a smaller degree) hormones. Yet the brain is the center of all that we call the mind: It contains the mechanisms needed to analyze all inputs and organize all outputs.

In reviewing this chapter, so full of terms and details, you may find it useful to keep the following broad points in mind:

43.

What three broad ideas are suggested as a framework for reviewing the chapter?

1.   The value of a functional perspective   As you list the structures described in this chapter—ranging from the little ones, such as *synaptic vesicles* and *neurohormones*, to the big ones, such as the *limbic system* and *autonomic nervous system*—ask yourself, for each: What is it for? That is, what role does it play in the larger machine that is the human being? How is it related to other parts of the machine, and how can variations in it affect human behavior? The structures are a lot easier to remember, and certainly more interesting, if you think of them in terms of their roles in a larger system rather than as isolated entities.

2. **Uses of the hierarchical model** The hierarchical model described in this chapter (summarized in Figure 5.13) provides a way to organize thinking about the nervous system. It is a useful memory scheme because it allows us to see each part in relation to the whole. It summarizes, in a very general way, the effects of damage to different parts of the nervous system. It also summarizes, again in a general way, the effects of drugs that act in different parts of the nervous system. As you review the discussion of the central nervous system, and the later discussion of drugs, tie the bits and pieces together into the hierarchical model.

3. **Brain science in relation to the rest of psychology** As more is learned about the brain, knowledge about it becomes relevant to broader areas of psychology. In later chapters, you will read about the brain in relation to psychology's attempt to understand basic processes of motivation, sensation, memory, and thought. Still later, you will read of brain-based theories of mental disorders and of drugs that are believed to alleviate specific mental disorders through their interactions with neurotransmitters. Your review of this chapter may be more effective if you try to anticipate the ways that each topic discussed here might be relevant later. Ask yourself: Why might a *psychologist* want to know about this structure or process? You may surprise yourself with the frequency with which you come up with a good answer.

Further Reading

Floyd Bloom, Charles Nelson, & Arlyne Lazerson (2001). *Brain, mind, and behavior* (3rd ed.). New York: Worth.

This is a beautifully illustrated, lucidly written introduction to the brain and its functions of creating the mind and controlling behavior. It begins with chapters on the basic workings and development of the brain and then proceeds through chapters on the brain's role in sensation, movement control, circadian rhythms, emotions, memory, thinking, and mental disorders.

John Dowling (1998). *How the brain works.* New York: Norton.

This 200-page paperback provides a briefer, simpler tour of the brain than that provided by Bloom and colleagues. It is clearly written, and, throughout, it ties information about the brain to practical problems and issues such as diseases, mental illness, aging, and brain injury. The first half presents the basics of the brain; the second half deals with the brain's role in vision, perception, language, memory, emotion, and consciousness.

Sally Springer & Georg Deutsch (1997). *Left brain, right brain* (5th ed.). New York: Freeman.

Research on right- and left-hemisphere differences, including the split-brain studies, is always interesting. This book provides a well-documented account of such research in a form that can be understood by the beginning student.

William McKim (2000). *Drugs and behavior: An introduction to behavioral pharmacology* (4th ed.). Upper Saddle River, NJ: Prentice-Hall.

Each major class of drugs that alters mood or behavior is discussed here in a separate chapter. McKim describes clearly not just the behavioral effects and physiological mechanisms of each drug but also the drug's role in human history and culture.

Looking Ahead

You now have—stored somehow in that gnarled, cantaloupe-sized knot of protoplasm under your skull—a little knowledge about the extraordinary organization that exists within that knot, how it can change with experience, and how hormones and drugs can act on it. Hold on to that knowledge. At least some of it will be useful in the next chapter, as we examine the physiological underpinnings of some psychological states: hunger, sexual drive, sleep, arousal, and emotionality.

Chapter 6

Boy with grapes, Joaquin Sorolla y Bastida

Mechanisms of Motivation, Sleep, and Emotion

The kaleidoscope that makes a day or a year of mental life has both fast-moving and slow-moving components. Sensations, perceptions, thoughts, and muscle movements flit through our consciousness and behavior at speeds measured in milliseconds. But slower changes, measurable in minutes or hours, modulate and help direct these rapid changes. The slower changes are referred to as *mental* or *behavioral states*; they include variations in motivation, sleep and arousal, and emotion.

Are you hungry right now, or sleepy, or angry? Even as you attempt to study this chapter, your mental state affects your capacity to attend, and it may direct your attention to some things over others. If you are hungry, your thoughts of food may be capturing most of your attention. If you are sleepy, your reaction even to the most interesting ideas in the chapter may be "oh hmmmm . . . *zzzzzzzz*." Clearly, your mental state affects your momentary thoughts and actions. But what affects your mental state? What exactly makes you hungry, or sleepy, or angry? This is a fundamental question, one that links psychology tightly to the study of the brain and its interactions with the body's internal environment as well as the external environment. This chapter is about the physiological underpinnings of motivation and emotion. You will read first about the general concept of motivation, from a physiological perspective, and then about hunger, sexual drive, reward, sleep, dreams, and emotionality—in that order. Social and cultural influences on motivation and emotion, which are only touched on here, are discussed more fully in later chapters.

MECHANISMS OF MOTIVATION

To *motivate*, in the most general sense of the term, is to set in motion. In psychology, the term **motivation** is often used to refer to the entire constellation of factors, some inside the organism and some outside, that cause an individual to behave in a particular way at a particular time. Motivation defined this way is a very broad concept, almost as broad as all of psychology. Every chapter in this book deals with one or another facet of motivation. Genes, learning, physiological variables, perceptual and thought processes, developmental variables, social experiences, and personality characteristics are all constructs that psychologists describe as contributors to motivation.

A more precise label for the specific topic of our present discussion is **motivational state** or **drive**. These terms are used interchangeably to denote an internal condition, which can change over time in a reversible way, that orients an individual toward a specific category of goals. Different drives have different goals. *Hunger* orients one toward food, *sex* toward sexual gratification, *curiosity* toward novel stimuli, and so on. For the most part, drives are thought of in psychology as hypothetical constructs. The psychologist does not observe a state of hunger, thirst, or

Cvele Zamur / Gamma

Hunger
Many of us have no idea what real hunger feels like, but the faces of these Serbian refugees give us a hint.

1.

How do drives and incentives (a) complement one another and (b) influence one another in their contributions to motivation?

curiosity inside the animal but infers the existence of that state from the animal's behavior. An animal is said to be hungry if it behaves in ways that bring it closer to food, to have a sex drive if it behaves in ways that bring it into contact with a sexual partner, to be curious if it seeks out and explores new environments. To say that the drive varies over time is to say that the animal will work harder, or accept more discomfort, to attain the goal at some times than at others. The assumption is that something inside the animal changes, causing the animal to behave differently in the same environment.

But the inside interacts constantly with the outside. Motivated behavior is directed toward ***incentives***, the sought-after objects or ends that exist in the external environment. Incentives are also called *reinforcers* (the term used in Chapter 4), *rewards*, or *goals*. The motivational state that leads you to stand in line at the cafeteria is presumably hunger, but the incentive for doing so is the hamburger you intend to purchase. Drives and incentives complement one another in the control of behavior; if one is weak, the other must be strong to motivate the goal-directed action. Thus, if you know that the cafeteria's hamburger tastes like cardboard (weak incentive), you are likely to wait in line for it only if your hunger drive is strong; but if the cafeteria serves a really great hamburger (strong incentive), you are likely to wait even if your hunger drive is weak.

Drives and incentives not only complement each other but also influence each other's strength. A strong drive can enhance the attractiveness (incentive value) of a particular object: If you are very hungry, even a hamburger that tastes like cardboard might seem quite attractive. Conversely, a strong incentive can strengthen a drive: The savory aroma of a broiling hamburger wafting your way as you wait in line might increase your hunger drive, which might in turn induce you to eat something that previously wouldn't have interested you if, by the time you get to the grill, all the hamburgers are gone.

The Physiological Approach to the Study of Drives

The very notion of drives, as defined above, almost begs us to look inside the organism to see what has happened there to cause a change in behavior. The goal of the physiological approach to the study of drives is to give substance to the hypothetical inner state, to make it no longer hypothetical. What really happens inside to make a person hungry or driven in some other way? Historically, to answer such questions, some researchers have focused on the needs of the body's tissues, and others have focused on states of the brain.

Drives as Tissue Needs: The Concept of Homeostasis

In an influential book entitled *The Wisdom of the Body* (1932), the physiologist Walter B. Cannon described simply and elegantly the requirements of the tissues of the human body. For life to be sustained, certain substances and characteristics within the body must be kept within a restricted range, going neither too high nor too low. These include body temperature, oxygen, minerals, water, and energy-producing food molecules. Physiological processes, such as digestion and respiration, must continually work toward achieving what Cannon termed **homeostasis**, the constancy of internal conditions that the body must actively maintain. Most important, Cannon pointed out that maintenance of homeostasis involves the organism's outward behavior as well as its internal processes. To stay alive, individuals must find and consume foods, salts, and water and must maintain their body temperature through such means as finding shelter. Cannon theorized that the basic physiological underpinning for some drives is a loss of homeostasis, which induces behavior designed to correct the imbalance.

Following Cannon, psychologists and physiologists performed experiments showing that animals indeed do behave in accordance with their tissue needs. For example, if the caloric (energy) content of its food is increased or decreased, an animal will compensate by eating less or more of it, keeping the daily intake of calories relatively constant. As another example, removal of the adrenal glands causes an animal to lose too much salt in its urine (because one of the adrenal hormones is essential for conserving salt). This loss of salt dramatically increases the animal's drive to seek out and eat extra salt, which keeps the animal alive as long as salt is available (Richter & Eckert, 1938; Stricker, 1973).

The force of homeostasis in human behavior was dramatically and poignantly illustrated by the clinical case of a boy, referred to as D. W., who when 1 year old developed a great craving for salt (Wilkins & Richter, 1940). His favorite foods were salted crackers, pretzels, potato chips, olives, and pickles; he would also take salt directly from the shaker. When salt was denied him, he would cry until his parents gave in, and when he learned to speak, *salt* was one of his first and favorite words. D. W. survived until the age of 3½, when he was hospitalized for other symptoms and placed on a standard hospital diet. The hospital staff would not yield to his demands for salt, and he died within a few days. An autopsy revealed that his adrenal glands were deficient; only then did D. W.'s doctors realize that his salt craving came from physiological need. His strong drive for salt and his ability to manipulate his parents into supplying it, even though they were unaware that he needed it, had kept D. W. alive for 2½ years—powerful evidence for "the wisdom of the body."

Limitations of Homeostasis: Regulatory and Nonregulatory Drives

Homeostasis is a useful concept for understanding thirst, hunger, and the drives for salt, oxygen, and temperature control but not for understanding certain other drives. Consider sex, for example. People are highly motivated to engage in sex, but there is no tissue need for it. No vital bodily substance is affected by engaging in sexual behavior; nobody can die from lack of sex (despite what an overly amorous someone may have told you). In their desire to develop a unitary theory of drives, some psychologists proposed hypothetical needs for sex and other drives for which no tissue need can be found. But by doing so, they were destroying the original advantage of the homeostatic theory. If needs cannot be identified in the

2.

How is the concept of homeostasis related to that of drive, and how is this relationship demonstrated by the case of a little boy who craved salt?

Photo Edit

Ahh, homeostasis
When the body's water level is reduced from prolonged athletic exertion, nothing is more satisfying than replenishing it. Thirst is a typical example of a regulatory drive.

3.

What is the difference between regulatory and nonregulatory drives, and why is "need" not useful in explaining the latter?

body, independently of the behaviors they are believed to motivate, then the concept of need is not an objective explanation. In fact, it is no explanation at all, as the term *need* in that case is simply a substitute for the term *drive*. Psychologists today find it useful to distinguish between regulatory drives and nonregulatory drives. A ***regulatory drive*** is one, like hunger, that helps preserve homeostasis, and a ***nonregulatory drive*** is one, like sex, that serves some other purpose.

Drives as States of the Brain

If drives are inner states, how can they best be described physiologically? Early theories, based on the concept of homeostasis, attempted to define drives as tissue needs. But such definitions were never fully satisfactory, even when applied to regulatory drives. For example, under certain conditions hunger can be high when the tissue need for more food is low, or low when the need for food is high. Most physiological psychologists today think of drives not as states of peripheral tissue but, rather, as states of the brain. According to most versions of this ***central-state theory of drives***, different drives correspond to neural activity in different sets of neurons in the brain (Stellar & Stellar, 1985). The set of neurons in which activity constitutes a drive is called a ***central drive system***. Although the central drive systems for different drives must be at least partly different from one another, they may have overlapping components. For example, because hunger and sex are different drives, the neural circuits for them cannot be identical; yet they may share components that keep the animal alert and increase its general level of motor activity, which are behavioral aspects of both drives.

What characteristics must a set of neurons have to serve as a central drive system? First, concerning input, it must receive and integrate the various signals that can raise or lower the drive state. For hunger, these signals include chemicals in the blood, the presence or absence of food in the stomach, and the sight and smell of food in the environment. Second, concerning output, a central drive system must act on all the neural processes that would be involved in carrying out the motivated behavior. It must direct perceptual mechanisms toward stimuli related to the goal, cognitive mechanisms toward working out strategies to achieve the goal, and motor mechanisms toward producing the appropriate movements. Look back at Figure 5.13 (p. 158), which depicts a hierarchical model of the control of action, with mechanisms involved in motivation and planning at the top. The central drive systems are part of that top level of the hierarchy. To affect behavior (for example, to cause a hungry person to cross a room for some peanuts), they must influence the activity of motor systems at lower levels of the hierarchy.

Researchers have sound reasons to believe that a hub of many central drive systems lies in the hypothalamus. Anatomically, this brain structure is ideally located to play such a role (see Figure 6.1). It is centered at the base of the brain, just above the brainstem, and is strongly interconnected with higher areas of the brain. It also has direct connections to nerves that carry input from, and autonomic motor output to, the body's internal organs. It has many capillaries and is more sensitive to hormones and other substances carried by the blood than are other brain areas. Finally, through its connections to the pituitary gland, it controls the release of many hormones (as described in Chapter 5). Thus, the hypothalamus has all the inputs and outputs that central drive systems would be expected to have. And, as you will soon see, small disruptions in particular parts of the hypothalamus can have dramatic effects on an animal's drives.

Some Techniques for Studying Central Drive Systems

As explained in Chapter 5, neurons within specific *nuclei* (clusters of neural cell bodies) and *tracts* (bundles of axons running together) in the brain tend to have similar functions. To identify those functions, researchers may either damage or stimulate nuclei or tracts and assess the effect on the animal's behavior.

4.

In theory, what characteristics must a set of neurons have to function as a central drive system? What characteristics of the hypothalamus seem to suit it to be a hub of such systems?

5.

Why and how are localized areas of the brain damaged or stimulated in research on drives?

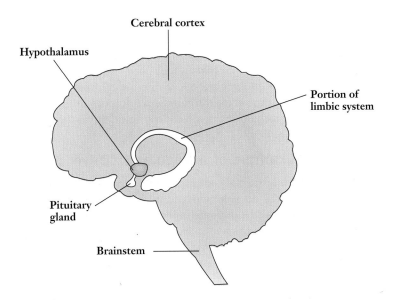

FIGURE 6.1 *Location of the hypothalamus*
The hypothalamus is ideally situated to serve as a hub for central drive systems. It has strong connections to the brainstem below, the limbic system and cerebral cortex above, and the endocrine system (by way of its tie to the pituitary gland).

Small (typically a fraction of a millimeter in diameter), localized areas of damage, called *lesions*, can be produced in the brain through either electrical or chemical means. To produce a lesion electrically, a thin wire *electrode* is inserted into the brain with the help of a *stereotaxic instrument* (see Figure 6.2), and enough current is sent through the electrode to destroy the neurons adjacent to its tip (the rest of the electrode is electrically insulated). To produce a lesion chemically, a tiny tube called a *cannula* is inserted into the brain, again using a stereotaxic instrument, and a small amount of a chemical is injected through the cannula, destroying neurons whose cell bodies are located near the cannula's tip. Lesions usually are made *bilaterally*, in the same area in both the right and left halves of the brain. Because the right and left halves of such structures as the hypothalamus and limbic system generally serve identical functions, the same part of the structure must be destroyed on both sides to eliminate a function. If, after a bilateral lesion, an animal no longer shows a particular drive (for example, no longer responds to food but does respond to other incentives), a researcher would infer that the destroyed area is a critical part of the central system for that drive.

Stimulation of specific brain areas can also be accomplished either electrically or chemically. To stimulate neurons electrically, an electrode is permanently implanted in the brain, as shown in Figure 6.2. The electrode can be activated at any time after surgery, through either a wire connection or radio waves. The electrical current used for stimulation is much weaker than that for producing a lesion—it is strong enough to activate, but not destroy, neurons near the electrode's tip. To stimulate neurons chemically, a cannula is permanently implanted in the brain, and shortly before behavioral testing a tiny amount of a transmitter or other chemical known to activate neurons is injected through it.

If electrical or chemical stimulation of a specific brain area elicits a drive (for example, if a previously nonhungry animal responds to the stimulus by seeking food and eating), a researcher would infer that the stimulated area is part of the central system for the drive elicited.

Recent advances in genetics have resulted in methods of interfering with specific biochemical processes in the nervous system, and these methods have been applied to the study of motivational mechanisms. Researchers can produce

FIGURE 6.2
Method for making lesions in or stimulating a rat's brain
A stereotaxic instrument (*left*) is used to insert an electrode into a precise location in the anesthetized (unconscious) animal's brain. To produce a lesion, an electric current that is strong enough to destroy neurons near the electrode tip is sent through the electrode, and then the electrode is removed. To prepare the animal for electrical brain stimulation, the electrode is cemented in place (*right*) so that it can be stimulated through wire leads during behavioral tests after the animal has recovered from surgery.

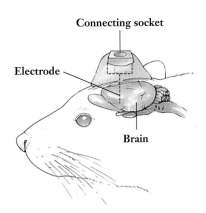

mutations in specific genes and in that way produce breeds of mice, rats, or other animals that are lacking in a specific type of protein—such as a particular neurotransmitter or hormone or a receptor site for a neurotransmitter or hormone. Such animals are referred to as *knockout* animals, because one gene (and its resultant protein molecule) has been knocked out by the genetic manipulation. This technique has contributed to some remarkable recent advances in understanding the neurochemical control mechanisms involved in specific drives, particularly hunger.

Hunger: An Example of a Regulatory Drive

No drive has been more fully studied physiologically than hunger. In fact, a major impetus for the initial development of the central-state theory of drives, beginning over 50 years ago, was the demonstration that lesions and electrical stimulation applied to specific areas of the hypothalamus can drastically alter an animal's tendency to seek food and eat (Morgan, 1943; Stellar, 1954). More specifically, the early work suggested that neural activity in the *lateral area* of the hypothalamus promotes hunger and food seeking and that neural activity in the *ventromedial area* of the hypothalamus promotes satiety. (To see the relative locations of the lateral and ventromedial areas of the hypothalamus, look at Figure 6.3.) Research since then has led to an increasingly sophisticated understanding of the roles of these and other brain areas in the regulation of hunger and body weight.

A General Motivational System
Runs Through the Lateral Hypothalamus

6.

What early evidence suggested that the lateral hypothalamus is a "hunger center," and how was this view confounded by further studies involving incentives other than food?

Animals with bilateral lesions in the lateral area of the hypothalamus ignore food and will starve to death if not fed artificially through a stomach tube. Conversely, animals receiving electrical stimulation to the lateral hypothalamus eat food in direct response to the stimulation, even if they have just previously eaten their fill. These dramatic, oft-repeated findings led in the early 1950s to the idea that the lateral hypothalamus is a "hunger center" (Stellar, 1954). Neural activity there promotes hunger, and lack of neural activity there abolishes hunger. Today we know the story is more complex than that.

Complications to the hunger-center view arose when researchers began to test animals in the presence of other incentives, not just food (Stricker, 1982). Animals with lesions in the lateral hypothalamus failed not only to eat but also to drink, copulate, build nests, care for young, hoard objects, or attack enemies. They would still move around in non-goal-oriented ways and would effectively move away from painful stimuli. But they lacked the whole set of behaviors that involve goal-directed movement toward objects in the environment. Moreover, electrical stimulation in the lateral hypothalamus could produce any of those behaviors, depending on what incentives were available. Thus, if only food was avail-

FIGURE **6.3** *The lateral and ventromedial areas of the hypothalamus*

This schematic diagram shows the relative location of some of the parts of the hypothalamus where lesions or electrical stimulation produce dramatic effects on behavior. To interpret the diagram, imagine that you are looking straight down through the top of the animal's head and can see an x-ray view of the lower part of the hypothalamus, at the very bottom of the brain. The paired central structures lie along the midline of the brain, and the paired lateral areas lie to their right and left. For a bilateral lesion, both the right and the left structures must be damaged.

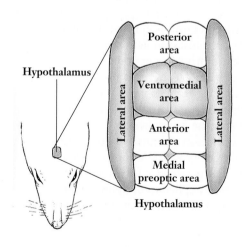

able, the animal would eat in response to the stimulus, but if water and a sexual partner were also available, the animal might drink or copulate instead.

Other experiments revealed that the most critical neurons for producing these effects of lesions and stimulation are not those with cell bodies in the lateral hypothalamus, as had previously been believed, but are those whose cell bodies exist elsewhere and whose axons form a tract through the hypothalamus, connecting parts of the brainstem (below the hypothalamus) with the basal ganglia (above the hypothalamus). Lesions or electrical stimulation anywhere along this tract, including in the brainstem or at its entrance to the basal ganglia, were as effective as those in the lateral hypothalamus in abolishing or stimulating drives (Grossman, 1979). Researchers now believe that this tract through the lateral hypothalamus is part of a general motor-activation system, which prepares the basal ganglia to initiate deliberate movements regardless of the specific drive (Mogenson & Yim, 1991). Electrical stimulation here seems to give the message, "Do something," leaving the animal to respond to whatever incentives are present in the environment.

Some Lateral Hypothalamic Neurons Are Part of a Special Hunger System

But all is not lost for the theory that some lateral hypothalamic neurons are specifically involved in hunger. Using chemical rather than electrical means, researchers can destroy neurons whose cell bodies are located in the lateral hypothalamus without destroying neurons whose axons pass through the area (the chemical must adhere to the cell body in order to destroy the neuron). Such lesions reduce the animals' eating but do not abolish it. The animals eat enough to survive, but at a lower-than-normal weight, and most of their other drives appear to be relatively normal (Stellar & Stellar, 1985; Winn, 1995).

Neurons in the lateral hypothalamus receive input from neurons whose cell bodies are in another part of the hypothalamus, the *paraventricular area* (Winn, 1995). Electrical stimulation of the paraventricular area promotes eating, and neurons coming from this area release a slow-acting neurotransmitter called *neuropeptide Y* onto neurons in various other brain regions, including the lateral hypothalamus. Neuropeptide Y is the most potent appetite stimulator yet discovered. This substance, injected into any of various regions in the hypothalamus, causes a previously sated animal to eat voraciously (Stanley & Gillard, 1994). Unlike fast transmitters, slow transmitters (discussed in Chapter 5) have the capacity to alter neural activity for long periods of time—in this case for periods ranging from minutes to several hours. It is not surprising that slow transmitters would be involved in the prolonged brain changes that underlie motivational and other mental states.

Further evidence for involvement of lateral hypothalamic neurons in hunger comes from yet another way of exploring the brain, that of recording activity in single neurons through permanently implanted microelectrodes (very tiny electrodes). Using this method with monkeys, Edmond Rolls (1982) found neurons in the lateral hypothalamus that produced bursts of action potentials only when the monkey was hungry (from having been deprived of food) and was exposed to food-related stimuli. The cells would become active when the hungry monkey saw or smelled food, or saw a conditioned stimulus that had previously been used to signal the delivery of food, but not when the monkey was exposed to stimuli that had never been associated with food. Moreover, if the monkey was fed its fill of one food (for example, bananas), the cells would stop responding when that food was present but would continue to respond to other foods (peanuts and oranges) with which the animal was not yet satiated (Rolls & others, 1986).

Rolls's discovery provides insight into the physiological basis of the interaction of drives and incentives. The motivational state of hunger apparently includes, as one of its components, the sensitization of certain neurons in the lateral

7.

What is the evidence that hunger is maintained by a certain slow neurotransmitter in the hypothalamus?

8.

How have recordings from neurons in the hypothalamus shed light on the interaction between drive and incentive in the control of eating?

hypothalamus, such that they respond to an incentive (food signals) to which they would not respond otherwise. Researchers have found that these same neurons both receive axons from and send axons to the association areas in the frontal lobes of the cerebral cortex, which are known to be important for planning and organizing goal-directed movements (Karadi & others, 1990; Rolls, 1982). Such findings help validate the theory (outlined in Chapter 5) that motivational mechanisms in the hypothalamus and limbic system work closely with planning mechanisms in the cerebral cortex, enabling drives to be turned into useful actions.

Role of the Ventromedial Hypothalamus

Bilateral lesions in the ventromedial area of the hypothalamus have an effect on eating opposite to that of bilateral lesions in the lateral area: Ventromedial lesions cause an animal to eat much more than normal and to gain weight. This was the leading evidence supporting the early view that the ventromedial area is a "satiety center." The animal without this brain region appears to eat insatiably.

Researchers have since learned that most of the effect of such lesions on weight and hunger results not from directly abolishing or reducing the capacity for satiation but, rather, from altering digestive and metabolic processes. The ventromedial hypothalamus contains neurons that regulate activity in peripheral autonomic nerves. Bilateral lesions of the ventromedial hypothalamus cause parasympathetic neurons involved in digestion and metabolism to become overactive. This causes food to be digested more rapidly than normal (Duggan & Booth, 1986) and food molecules in the blood to be converted very quickly to fat, leaving less for use as fuel for other tissues in the body (King & others, 1984). The result is that messages are sent from the body's tissues to the brain signaling that more food is needed. In other words, the lesioned animals are hungry and overeat because they are converting most of their food to fat rather than to the energy molecules needed to fuel the body. Occasionally a tumor at the base of the brain causes damage to the ventromedial hypothalamus in humans, and in such cases the person becomes obese, apparently for the same reasons that experimental animals do (Bray & Gallagher, 1975).

Courtesy of Neal E. Miller, Yale University

9.

Why do animals with lesions in the ventromedial hypothalamus overeat and become obese?

Effect of a lesion in the ventromedial area of the hypothalamus

After receiving a bilateral lesion, this rat overate and gained weight to the point where it tipped the scale at 1080 grams (80 grams more than the 1000-gram capacity of this scale)—about three times what a normal rat weighs.

Stimuli That Act on the Brain to Increase or Decrease Hunger

To be effective in promoting survival, hunger systems in the brain must be responsive to the body's signals indicating need or lack of need for more food. In the early days of hunger research, many researchers hoped to find *the* signal to the brain that turns hunger on or off. Some thought it might be glucose (a sugar molecule that is the main source of energy for the brain) or some other type of food molecule carried by the blood. Others thought it might be signals from the stomach. Today, researchers know that the brain's hunger system is responsive to many signals, none of which has full control. Among these are the following (schematized in Figure 6.4):

+ **Satiety signals from the stomach and intestines** Signals indicating when to *stop* eating come from the stomach and intestines. Food in these organs stimulates them to secrete a chemical called *cholecystekinin* (*CCK*), which, in turn, activates sensory neurons that run—by way of the vagus nerve (one of the

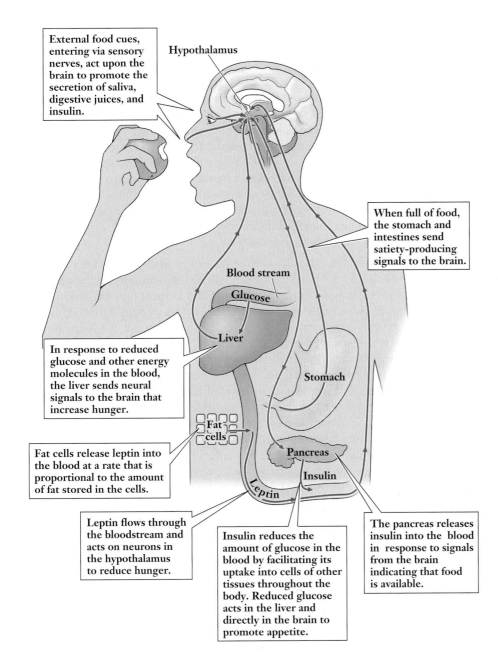

External food cues, entering via sensory nerves, act upon the brain to promote the secretion of saliva, digestive juices, and insulin.

Hypothalamus

When full of food, the stomach and intestines send satiety-producing signals to the brain.

Blood stream

Glucose

Liver

In response to reduced glucose and other energy molecules in the blood, the liver sends neural signals to the brain that increase hunger.

Stomach

Fat cells

Fat cells release leptin into the blood at a rate that is proportional to the amount of fat stored in the cells.

Pancreas

Insulin

Leptin

Leptin flows through the bloodstream and acts on neurons in the hypothalamus to reduce hunger.

Insulin reduces the amount of glucose in the blood by facilitating its uptake into cells of other tissues throughout the body. Reduced glucose acts in the liver and directly in the brain to promote appetite.

The pancreas releases insulin into the blood in response to signals from the brain indicating that food is available.

FIGURE **6.4**
Some hunger-control mechanisms
Sensory input from the environment, glucose receptors in the liver and brain, sensory receptors in the stomach, leptin secreted by fat cells, and insulin secreted by the pancreas all contribute to the control of hunger through the effects they have on the brain, especially the hypothalamus.

cranial nerves)—from the stomach and intestines to the brain (Woods & others, 2000). In addition, receptors in the walls of the stomach respond directly to pressure exerted on them when the stomach is full, and these receptors also trigger activity in neurons of the vagus nerve (Deutsch, 1990). Input from the vagus nerve activates neural mechanisms in the brain that produce the sense of satiety that leads one to stop eating. Cutting the branch of the vagus nerve that goes from the stomach and intestines to the brain causes animals to eat larger-than-normal meals (Gonzalez & Deutsch, 1981); and artificially stimulating those same neurons, either with injections of CCK or with a water-filled balloon that distends the stomach, causes animals to eat smaller-than-normal meals (Geliebter & others, 1987; Woods & others, 1998).

◆ **Signals indicating the amount of food molecules in the blood**   Foods are broken down to their molecular components (digested) in the stomach and

10.

How is appetite regulated by (a) signals from the stomach and intestines, (b) the concentration of food molecules in the blood, (c) the amount of fat stored in fat cells, and (d) signals in the external environment indicating the availability of food?

intestines, and then the molecules enter the bloodstream and are carried to all the body's tissues. Two organs that are especially sensitive to the level of food molecules in the blood are the liver and the brain. Receptors in the liver respond to a variety of food molecules and send messages to the brain that activate hunger when blood-borne food supplies are low (Novin & others, 1983). Receptors in the brain respond specifically to glucose that reaches the brain in the blood. In fact, many of the same neurons in the lateral hypothalamus that respond to food-related cues in the environment are also sensitive to glucose (Karadi & others, 1990; Winn, 1995). When glucose is high, the neurons become less active (thereby, presumably, decreasing hunger), and when glucose is low, they become more active. Normally, food molecules in the blood remain relatively constant in amount; the mechanisms just described probably evolved more for emergencies than for the normal, daily control of the onset and cessation of eating (Woods & others, 2000).

◆ **A hormone indicating the amount of fat in the body**   The concentration of food molecules in the blood remains relatively constant between meals, even when meals are delayed, because such molecules are sent into the blood from storage supplies when needed. Food is stored primarily in the form of fat, in special fat cells. A major purpose of hunger, over the long run, is to regulate the amount of fat that is stored in such cells. Fat cells (in mice, humans, and other mammals) secrete a hormone, called ***leptin***, at a rate that is directly proportional to the amount of fat that is in the cells (Woods & others, 2000). Leptin is taken up into the brain and acts in various parts of the hypothalamus to inhibit the activity of neurons that produce neuropeptide Y as their neurotransmitter. Neuropeptide Y, as mentioned earlier, is itself the major neurotransmitter involved in stimulating hunger in the hypothalamus. Thus, we have the following chain of events: high fat → much leptin enters the brain → reduced release of neuropeptide Y in the hypothalamus → reduced activity in the brain's hunger system → reduced eating (Woods & others, 2000). Animals lacking the specific gene needed to produce leptin lack this signal and become extraordinarily obese (see Figure 6.5), as do animals lacking the specific gene needed to produce the receptor sites for leptin in the hypothalamus (Friedman, 1997). Very rarely a person is found who lacks the genes needed to produce leptin. Such people are extremely obese but reduce their eating and lose weight rapidly when given injections of leptin (Farooqi & others, 1999).

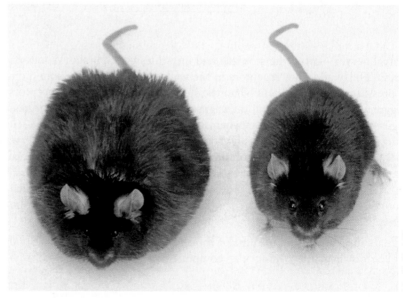

FIGURE 6.5 *Lacking leptin*
The mouse on the left, which lacks the gene needed to synthesize the weight-regulating hormone leptin, outweighs two genetically normal mice. Without leptin, the animal overeats and becomes obese.

John Sholtis / AP

✦ **Signals indicating the availability of food in the environment**   In normal conditions, initiation of eating probably has more to do with timing and environmental circumstances than with true need for food. As one group of researchers (Woods & others, 2000) put it, "Animals do not [typically] initiate meals because one or another tissue's supply of available energy is about to be compromised, but rather an animal eats when it is accustomed to eating, or when its predators have left, or when it has a break between classes." We learn to respond to cues indicating that it is time to eat and that good food is available. The cues might include such stimuli as a clock indicating dinnertime, a gathering of people that one usually eats with, and the aroma of good food. Through classical conditioning, stimuli that are regularly paired with eating come to elicit internal responses that help prepare the body for food intake, and these responses contribute to the feeling of hunger. The responses include the secretion of saliva and digestive juices, which we associate with hunger. They also include the secretion of insulin, which causes a small but sudden drop in blood glucose (because insulin promotes the uptake of glucose from the blood into the cells of other tissues), which may stimulate hunger through the mechanism already described (Campfield & Smith, 1990). Such responses can also become entrained to the time of day, even without specific external cues. Animals that are regularly fed at specific times of day begin to secrete appetite-regulating hormones and transmitters—such as insulin and neuropeptide Y—just before their mealtimes (Woods & others, 2000; Yoshihara & others, 1996).

Genes, Environment, and Body Weight

Human evolution occurred almost entirely in environments where the food choices were far fewer, and far lower in fat and sugar content, than the foods available to people in modern Western cultures. Natural selection built into us excellent mechanisms to defend against weight loss in times of scarcity but rather poor mechanisms to defend against obesity in times of plenty. Obesity is a cultural disease of our time and place. According to criteria developed by the World Health Organization, 54 percent of adults in the United States are overweight and 22 percent are obese (Hill & Peters, 1998). (These criteria are based on a measure called the *body mass index*, or *BMI*, defined as body weight in kilograms divided by the square of the person's height in meters. A BMI of 25 or more is considered overweight, and one of 30 or more is considered obese. Thus a person who is 1.7 meters [5 feet 7 inches] tall and weighs 73 kilograms [161 pounds] is deemed overweight [BMI = $75/1.7^2$ = 25.3].)

Within modern Western cultures, the determination of who does or does not become obese depends very much on genes and relatively little on the specific home environment (Barsh & others, 2000). The weights of adopted children correlate much more strongly with the weights of their biological parents than with those of their adoptive parents; identical twins usually have very similar weights even if raised in different homes; and pairs of biological siblings raised in different homes are, on average, nearly as similar to each other in weight as are pairs raised in the same home (Grilo & Pogue-Geile, 1991; Stunkard & others, 1986). This does not mean that the environment is an unimportant influence on body weight. It simply means that the environmental conditions that promote obesity are fairly constant within Western cultures, so differences in weight have mostly to do with genetic differences in how individuals respond to those conditions.

Across cultures, environmental differences can have a large effect on body weight. As one example, obesity is very common among Pima Indians living in

11.

What is the evidence that differences in body weight within a culture are due mostly to genes but that across cultures environment plays a large role?

Felicia Martinez / Photo Edit

I'll have just one muffin

In an environment in which "just one muffin" could be that one on the right, regulating one's weight can be a challenge.

FIGURE **6.6** *Effect of culture on body weight*

If the only Pima Indians you ever saw were those living in Mexico and following traditional Pima practices (like these photographed at a holy festival), you might conclude that they are genetically predisposed to be slender. Obesity is almost nonexistent among the Mexican Pima. However, their close relatives living across the border in the United States are often obese. The difference lies not in genes but in the choices of foods available.

John Annerino

Arizona but is essentially absent among their genetic relatives living in Mexico (see Figure 6.6). The Mexican Pimas subsist mainly on grains and vegetables; their culture does not include the high-calorie sugary and fatty foods available to the American Pimas (Gibbs, 1996). The genes that promote obesity in our culture apparently do so both by increasing the person's attraction to high-calorie foods and by decreasing the body's ability to burn up such foods quickly (Barsh & others, 2000). Where high-calorie foods are unavailable, the same genes don't lead to obesity.

Problems of Dieting

12.

How is the difficulty of losing weight explained in terms of fat cells and basal metabolism? What can people do who would like to maintain a lower weight?

Weight gained is often very difficult to lose. One reason for this may have to do with an increase in the number of fat-storage cells in the body. In experiments with rats, animals that were placed on a high-fat diet gained weight, and examination of their fat tissues showed that the gain was due partly to an increase in the size of each fat cell and partly to an increase in the number of fat cells (Bray & Popkin, 1998; Faust, 1984). When the rats were subsequently returned to a normal diet, they lost some of the weight they had gained but not all of it. The amount lost was accounted for by the return of their fat cells to normal size, and the amount *not* lost was accounted for by the increased number of fat cells (see Figure 6.7).

In addition, research with people shows that dieting to lose weight can cause a decline in *basal metabolism* (the rate at which calories are burned up while the individual is at rest), so food is converted more efficiently to fat (Keesey & Corbett, 1984; Leibel & others, 1995). In one extreme case, a woman managed to reduce her weight from 312 pounds to a still-obese but much healthier 192 pounds through diet. For at least 18 months after that she maintained her new weight, without losing any more, by eating a total of 1000 to 1200 calories a day—less than half of what most women would have to eat to maintain that weight (Rodin & others, 1989).

Despite the odds, some people do lose significant amounts of weight and avoid regaining it. A recent study of 2500 people who had lost at least 30 pounds and kept the weight off for a year or longer revealed that they succeeded primarily by avoiding high-fat foods and by greatly increasing their exercise (Fritsch, 1999). Regular, vigorous exercise not only burns up calories immediately but also builds muscle, and muscle cells burn up calories, even in the resting state, at a higher rate than does other body tissue (VanItallie & Kissileff, 1990).

Researchers who study metabolism and diet often have a few sensible words of advice for people who want to lose weight: Don't try to lose rapidly. Don't go on a diet that you can't stay on for the rest of your life; it may be better in the long run

Fat cells

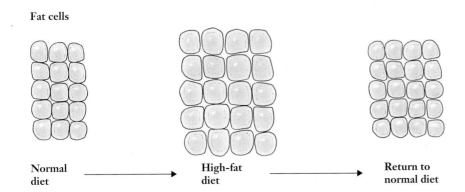

Normal   High-fat   Return to
diet   diet   normal diet

FIGURE **6.7** *Effect of a high-fat diet on fat cells*
As illustrated by this diagram, when rats were placed on a high-fat diet, their fat cells increased in both number and size. When they were subsequently returned to a normal diet, their fat cells returned to normal size but did not decrease in number. Consequently, the rats remained heavier than they would have been had they never been on the high-fat diet.

to keep your present weight than to lose weight rapidly and gain it back (Brownell & others, 1986). Instead of reducing food intake to a level that leaves you hungry, shift the kind of food you eat, away from fatty and sugary foods and toward complex carbohydrates (breads, cereals, and vegetables), which are less readily converted into body fat and are less likely to overwhelm the body's natural satiety mechanisms (which, after all, evolved in an environment where sugary and fatty foods were rare). If you have a sedentary job or are a student, try to develop some pleasurable hobbies that involve muscle-building exercise for at least a few hours a week. (I, for one, can't stand jogging or weight lifting, but I love bicycling, kayaking, and cross-country skiing.) And when you need to get from one place to another, use your muscles rather than an automobile or elevator to convey you whenever you can. Through such changes in habits, many people can lose a fair amount of weight and keep it off, without feeling deprived at all.

Sex: An Example of a Nonregulatory Drive

Just as hunger is the most thoroughly studied regulatory drive, sex is the most thoroughly studied nonregulatory drive. As with hunger, most research on the physiological basis of the sex drive has been conducted with laboratory animals.

There are limits, of course, in the degree to which we can understand hunger, sex, or any drive in humans by studying them in other animals. Human culture, intellect, sensibility, and capacity for conscious self-control affect all human behavior in ways that cannot be studied in laboratory animals. People don't just eat; they *dine*, which connotes all sorts of social, cognitive, and aesthetic influences. And people don't just copulate; they fall in love, compose romantic sonnets, gaze into each other's eyes over candlelit dinners, swear by the moon to be faithful, have affairs, suffer guilt, and engage in long, intimate discussions with their beloved. Keep in mind, as you read on, that our concern here is the basic physiological mechanisms that we humans share, more or less, with other mammals, not the whole range of issues concerning human sexuality. (Sex is discussed more from a social and cultural perspective in Chapter 12.)

Even when dealing with the copulatory act itself, humans differ quite sharply from rats and other laboratory animals on which most research is conducted. Among nonhuman mammals, including most other primates, copulation occurs in a stereotyped way, with one set of postures and movements for the female and a different set for the male (see Figure 6.8). Among humans, by contrast, the variety of ways to copulate is limited only by imagination. As you will discover as you read further, differences between humans and other species exist also in the hormonal regulation of the sexual drive, especially in females.

13.

Why is caution advised in extrapolating from laboratory animals to humans in the study of drives, especially the sex drive?

FIGURE **6.8** *Copulation in rats*
Rats, like most other nonhuman mammals, have a stereotyped (unvarying) pattern of copulation, with clearly different postures for the female and the male.

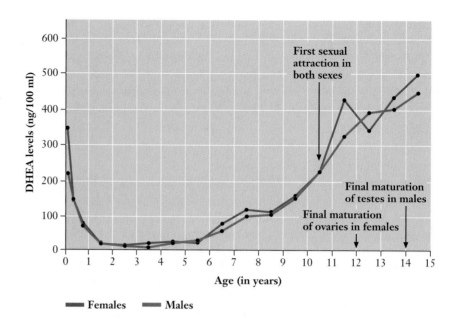

FIGURE **6.9**
A sex hormone that increases at the same rate in girls and boys
Shown here are the average blood levels of the adrenal androgen DHEA (dehydroepiandrosterone) in boys and girls as a function of age. This hormone is believed to activate the brain in a way that enables the young person, whether male or female and regardless of sexual orientation, to feel sexually attracted toward others, beginning at about age 10. (Adapted from McClintock & Herdt, 1996, p. 181.)

14.

What roles are played by testosterone, estrogen, and adrenal DHEA in the developmental changes of puberty?

Hormones and the Onset of Puberty

In both humans and other mammals, the production of sex hormones greatly increases at the onset of the developmental stage called *puberty*. In men, increased *testosterone*, produced by the *testes*, stimulates such changes as beard growth and the male pattern of muscle development; in women, increased *estrogen*, produced by the *ovaries*, stimulates such changes as breast growth. Less well known is the fact that, in humans as well as other animals, and in both sexes, the *adrenal glands* also produce sex hormones. In humans the primary adrenal sex hormone is *dehydroepiandrosterone*, mercifully abbreviated *DHEA*. This substance is commonly classed as a "male hormone"—that is, as an *androgen*—because it has effects in men similar to those of testosterone; but it is produced as much in women as in men, and there is reason to believe that it is the primary hormone responsible for the onset of sexual feelings and attractions in young humans of both sexes (McClintock & Herdt, 1996).

Boys' and girls' adrenals begin to secrete DHEA at about 6 years of age, and the amount secreted rises continuously until the mid-teenage years, when it stabilizes at adult levels (see Figure 6.9). Several interview studies have shown that most people, of both sexes, recall their earliest clear feelings of sexual attraction to another person as occurring at about 10 years of age, well before the prominent physical changes brought on by testosterone or estrogen (Herdt & Boxer, 1993; Pattatucci & Hamer, 1995). If testosterone and estrogen brought on this developmental effect, then we would expect girls to experience sexual attraction at an earlier age than boys, since the rise in estrogen precedes the rise in testosterone by about 2 years, on average. But repeated studies find no difference between the sexes in the age of earliest sexual attraction, which is consistent with the idea that this feeling is brought on by DHEA, which increases at the same rate in the two sexes. DHEA, like other sex hormones, passes into the brain and alters activity in certain neural centers there, especially in the hypothalamus.

Activating Effects of Hormones on the Sex Drive in Male Mammals

15.

What is some evidence that testosterone is needed to maintain the male's sex drive and that, at least in some species, it does so by direct action in the hypothalamus?

In male mammals, including humans, the most crucial hormone for the maintenance of the sexual drive during adulthood is not DHEA but testosterone. Castration (removal of the testes and hence the main supply of testosterone) causes a marked decline in the sex drive—not all at once, but gradually over time (it takes days to occur in rats, weeks in dogs, sometimes months in monkeys) (Feder, 1984).

But the injection of testosterone into the bloodstream of castrated animals fully restores their drive.

The sex drive can also be restored in castrated male animals by implanting a tiny crystal of testosterone into an area of the hypothalamus called the *medial preoptic area* (see Figure 6.10 for its location) (Davidson, 1980). The same amount of testosterone placed elsewhere in the brain does not produce this effect. Neurons in the medial preoptic area contain many receptor sites for testosterone, and small lesions there abolish sexual behavior in male rats (Meisel & Sachs, 1994). Apparently, the medial preoptic area of the hypothalamus is a crucial part of the central drive system for sex in male rats (and various other male animals that have been studied), and testosterone acts there in a rather prolonged way to augment neural activity and sustain the drive (Pfaff & Modianos, 1985).

Testosterone is also crucial for maintaining the sex drive in human males. Men castrated in an accident or for medical reasons almost always experience a decline (though often not a complete loss) in sex drive and behavior, and testosterone injections restore their drive, usually fully (Money & Ehrhardt, 1972). In other studies, testosterone injections administered to noncastrated men whose testes were producing abnormally low amounts of the hormone sharply increased their sexual behavior (Davidson & Myers, 1988; Davidson & others, 1979). This effect was more on drive than on sexual capability. Men with abnormally low levels of testosterone were fully capable of the mechanics of sexual behavior—including erection and ejaculation—but had little desire for it until injected with testosterone. The subjects in this research did not know when they were receiving testosterone and when they were not, so the results must have been due to the effects of the hormone and not to their expectations.

Activating Effects of Hormones on the Sex Drive in Female Mammals

After puberty, a female's ovaries begin to secrete estrogen and progesterone in a cyclic pattern over time, producing the cycle of physiological changes referred to as the *menstrual cycle* in humans and the *estrous cycle* in other mammals. In both humans and nonhumans, this cycle controls ovulation (the release of one or more eggs so that pregnancy can occur). In most mammals, it also tightly controls the sex drive—which ranges from very strong at the time of ovulation to nonexistent at other times. Removal of the ovaries completely abolishes sexual behavior in most nonhuman female mammals, and injection of hormones can fully restore it. For some species an injection of estrogen alone is most effective, and for others (including the rat) a sequence of estrogen followed 2 or 3 days later by progesterone (another female hormone) is most effective.

At least in rats, the *ventromedial area* of the hypothalamus (for location, see Figure 6.10) plays a role in sexual behavior in the female analogous to that of the preoptic area in the male. Neurons in this area contain receptors for estrogen and progesterone; insertion of small amounts of one or both of these hormones directly into this area brings on sexual behavior in rats whose ovaries have been removed, and lesions in this area abolish sexual behavior in otherwise intact female rats (Mani & others, 1994; Pleim & Barfield, 1988; Schwartz-Giblin & others, 1989). Apparently the cyclic variation in ovarian hormones acts on the ventromedial area to cause the cyclic waxing and waning of sexual drive.

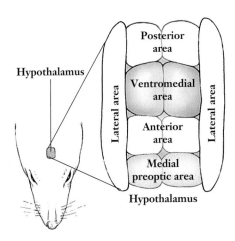

FIGURE **6.10** *Hypothalamic areas where hormones activate sexual behavior*
In rats, testosterone promotes male sexual behavior by activating neurons in the medial preoptic area of the hypothalamus, and estrogen promotes female sexual behavior by activating neurons in the ventromedial area of the hypothalamus.

16.

What evidence suggests that ovarian hormones act directly on the brain to activate the sexual drive in female rats? How do nonhuman primates and humans differ from each other, and from rats, regarding the role of hormones in regulating the sexual drive?

Female monkeys and apes depend less on ovarian hormones for sexual behavior than do most other female mammals. Most primate females can, and sometimes will, copulate with a sexually active male at any time in their hormone cycle, though they are more likely to seek out and initiate sexual contact with a male at the time in their cycle when they are ovulating and the level of ovarian hormones is high (Wallen, 1990). In at least some species of primates, including rhesus monkeys, adrenal androgens apparently help maintain sexual drive and behavior during times in the estrous cycle when ovarian hormones are low (Wallen, 1990).

Human females show still greater liberation of sexual behavior from cyclic hormonal control than do other primates. Women can experience a high or low sex drive at any time in their hormone cycle. In fact, debate exists as to whether women's sex drive is affected in a consistent way at all by the hormone cycle. Some studies in which women kept records of their daily sexual activities or thoughts showed an enhanced sexual drive around the time of ovulation (Adams & others, 1978), but other studies have shown negative or mixed results (Davidson & Myers, 1988; Hill, 1988). In women, ovarian hormones apparently play a rather small role, if any, in regulation of the sex drive, and adrenal hormones play a larger role. The adrenals of adult women produce both DHEA and testosterone. In clinical studies, women whose adrenal glands have been removed often report a decline in sex drive whereas women whose ovaries have been removed generally do not, and treatment with testosterone reliably increases the sex drive reported by low-sex-drive women (Bancroft, 1978; Sherwin & Gelfand, 1987; Sherwin & others, 1985).

Another animal for which androgens are more crucial than estrogen for sexual drive is the *musk shrew*. Females of this rodentlike species do not have estrous cycles and will mate at any time. In these females testosterone is the primary sex-drive hormone, and it stimulates the drive by direct action in the medial preoptic area of the hypothalamus, the same area where testosterone acts to promote sexual motivation in the males of all other mammals studied so far, including musk shrews (Rissman, 1995). Musk shrews are believed to be similar to the earliest-evolved mammals, which leads to an interesting hypothesis about evolution. Perhaps in the earliest mammals the central sex-drive system in females was essentially the same as that in males. In the course of evolution the advantage of synchronizing sexual behavior with the period of maximal fertility led to a new control system, involving ovarian hormones and the ventromedial hypothalamus, in the females of most mammals. In human evolution, however, there was apparently an advantage to women in engaging in sexual behavior at any time of the hormone cycle, so the more primitive system was regained. At present this idea is speculative. We do know that androgens promote sexual drive in women as well as men, but we do not know if the brain areas on which androgens act to stimulate the drive are the same in the two sexes.

What in evolution might have made it advantageous to women to experience sexual drive at any time in the ovarian cycle? Nobody knows the answer, but there has been no lack of speculation (Schröder, 1993). One theory is that this capacity helps promote long-term pair bonding; a male may be more likely to remain with a partner who is potentially interested in sex at any time than with one who isn't. Another theory, not necessarily incompatible with the first, is that lack of cyclicity in sexual drive, coupled with lack of external evidence as to when she is ovulating, allowed females greater choice in sexual partners. A male consort might be able to guard a female for a few days each month, to prevent her from becoming pregnant by anyone but him, but would not be able to guard her continuously. In the absence of clues as to her hormonal state, the male does not know when to guard, which increases the female's opportunity to engage in clandestine sex with another male, who may have better genes to offer (see also the discussion of mating strategies in Chapter 3).

17.

How has research on female musk shrews contributed to a theory about the evolution of sexual-drive systems in female mammals in general and particularly in humans?

Joe B. Blossom

A musk shrew

Sexual drive in the female of this small mammal is controlled by the same mechanism that controls sexual drive in the male, that is, by testosterone acting in the medial preoptic area of the hypothalamus.

Brain-Differentiating Effects of the Early Presence or Absence of Testosterone

In addition to their role in activating sexual-drive systems in the adult brain, sex hormones are also involved in the growth of those drive systems prior to birth (or in some species shortly after birth).

As noted in Chapter 3, the only *genetic* difference between the two sexes is that females have two X chromosomes whereas males have a small Y chromosome in place of the second X. A specific gene on the Y chromosome causes the growth of testes (the male gonads) from structures that would otherwise develop into ovaries (the female gonads) (Page & others, 1987). Before birth the testes begin to produce testosterone, which acts on the brain and other bodily structures to tip development in the male direction. The rudimentary genitals of the fetus develop into male structures (including the penis and scrotum) if testosterone is present, and they develop into female structures (including the clitoris and vagina) if testosterone is absent. This early testosterone also acts in the brain to promote the development of neural systems involved in the male sex drive and to inhibit the development of neural systems involved in the female sex drive (Gorski, 1996). For an example of one such effect, see Figure 6.11.

In order to produce these brain-differentiating effects, testosterone must act within a critical period in the animal's development. In rats, this period runs from a few days before birth to a day or so after birth. In many other species, the critical period ends before birth. The critical period for testosterone's effect on the brain is later than that for its effect on the genitals. Thus, manipulation of hormones at the appropriate time can produce animals that have the genitals of one sex but the brain structures and behavior of the other sex (Feder, 1984; Ward, 1992).

In a fascinating series of experiments, Ingeborg Ward and her colleagues (Ward, 1992; Ward & others, 1999) showed that stressful events experienced by pregnant rats can influence the future sexual behavior of their male offspring, apparently by reducing the level of prenatal testosterone. When the researchers subjected pregnant rats, late in pregnancy, to bright lights and physical restraint, the rats' male offspring manifested less male sexual behavior and more female sexual behavior (in response to injected estrogen and progesterone) in adulthood than did the male offspring of unstressed mothers. These researchers also found that males born to stressed mothers had unusually low levels of testosterone in their blood at the time of birth. Other researchers found that prenatal stress inhibits malelike development of a nucleus in the medial preoptic area that normally distinguishes the male hypothalamus from the female hypothalamus (the nucleus depicted in Figure 6.11) (Anderson & others, 1986). Apparently, in response to stress, the mother secretes hormones that inhibit the production of testosterone in male fetuses, and this in turn causes their brains to be less masculinized and more feminized than they would be otherwise.

18.

What are some effects of the presence or absence of testosterone before birth on development of the genitals, the brain, and behavior?

19.

How can prenatal stress affect the sexual development of male rats?

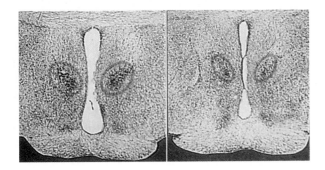

FIGURE **6.11** *A sex difference in the rat's hypothalamus* Shown here is a cross section of the medial preoptic area of the hypothalamus of a male rat (*left*) and a female rat (*right*). The dark spots represent cell bodies of neurons, and the dense cluster of them represents the *sexual dimorphic nucleus* (marked by red circles). The nucleus receives its name from the fact that it is clearly different in the two sexes; it is about five times larger, on average, in the male than in the female (Gorski & others, 1980). The difference is due entirely to the presence or absence of testosterone early in the rat's development. Early treatment with testosterone in females and early deprivation of testosterone in males can reverse this sex difference. The nucleus is believed to be part of the neural circuitry controlling male sexual drive and behavior (DeJonge & others, 1989).

Perhaps you are wondering why a male hormone, not a female hormone, plays the key role in early sexual differentiation in mammals. The answer is that the female hormones (progesterone and estrogen) are produced by pregnant females at high levels and get into the tissues of all fetuses, of both sexes. If female hormones promoted growth of female structures during fetal development, all mammalian infants would be born looking like females. In birds and reptiles—which develop in eggs outside the mother's body—early sexual differentiation is determined by the presence or absence of estrogen, not testosterone (Adkins-Regan, 1981).

Brain Development and Sexual Orientation in Humans

It is quite possible that the brain mechanisms for male and female sexual motivation are less different from one another in humans than in most other mammalian species. As already noted, in people, unlike most other mammals, androgens may be the primary sex-drive hormones in both sexes. Moreover, men and women show similar patterns of physiological changes during sexual arousal and orgasm (Masters & others, 1992) and describe the subjective feelings they have during sex in similar ways (Vance & Wagner, 1976). But one way in which most men and women do clearly differ in sex drive is in the object of the drive: Most men are attracted to women, and most women are attracted to men. Might this difference result from a structural difference in the brain? If so, what creates the brain difference? Nobody knows the answers to those questions, but some interesting ideas about them have emerged from studies of people who are sexually attracted to members of their own sex rather than the opposite sex.

In the past many psychologists argued that sexual orientation derives primarily from social learning, and some still argue that today. But the existence of a significant homosexual population in every culture—including cultures where homosexuality is frowned upon, punished, or outlawed—presents a challenge to that hypothesis (LeVay & Hamer, 1994). Using various criteria and survey methods, researchers estimate that between 1 and 5 percent of men and women are almost exclusively homosexual and a larger percentage, even harder to estimate, are bisexual (attracted to members of both sexes) (Bell & others, 1981; Kinsey & others, 1948, 1953; LeVay & Hamer, 1994). If sexual orientation is learned through social experiences, then why would anyone developing in a society that glorifies heterosexuality and strongly discourages homosexuality grow up as a homosexual? Over the years psychologists have suggested many possible answers to that question aimed at preserving the learning hypothesis, but none has so far withstood the test of research.

Interviews and surveys of thousands of homosexuals and heterosexuals have found no consistent relationship between sexual orientation and the kinds of experiences in childhood or adolescence that have at times been theorized to cause homosexuality. In the largest such study to date, no evidence was found that style of parenting, absence of the father or mother, early seduction or rape by someone of the same or opposite sex, or degree of opportunity for one or another type of sexual experience in adolescence contributes significantly to the development of sexual orientation (Bell & others, 1981). That study and others (Herdt & Boxer, 1993; Pattatucci & Hamer, 1995) did show, however, that whatever its cause or causes, sexual orientation is usually a deeply ingrained and early-emerging aspect of one's being. Homosexuals and heterosexuals alike generally reported that their sexual orientation was present, though not necessarily understood or accepted, in their childhood thoughts and fantasies, typically by the age of about 10 or 11. The feeling of strong attraction to one sex or the other often existed for years before it was expressed. Most psychologists are now convinced that sexual orientation is not something that most people can choose or change through willpower or psychotherapy but, rather, is something that one discovers about oneself.

20.

What evidence suggests that in humans sexual orientation (a) is not correlated with environmental variables that in the past were hypothesized as causal, (b) appears early in development, (c) is at least partly influenced by differences in genes, and (d) is correlated with a measurable difference in a portion of the hypothalamus?

Gay rights

Advocates for gay rights often express the hope that a better understanding of the biological underpinnings of homosexuality will foster acceptance of it as a normal human variation that, like left-handedness, is better to accept than to try to change. The people depicted here believe they deserve the same freedoms and rights as are accorded to heterosexuals.

Genetic differences among individuals apparently play some role in determining sexual orientation but are not solely responsible. Several studies indicate that roughly 50 percent of the identical twin brothers of homosexual men are also homosexual, compared with about 15 percent of the nonidentical twins or nontwin brothers of homosexual men (Bailey & Pillard, 1991; Gladue, 1994), and one study revealed comparable figures for women (Bailey & others, 1993). Other studies, which are still quite controversial, suggest that sexual orientation might be affected by any of various factors—ranging from prenatal stress to certain medications taken during pregnancy—that alter the amount of androgens available to the fetus's brain during a critical period in development (Ellis & Ames, 1987; Ellis & others, 1988; Meyer-Bahlburg & others, 1995). Such work suggests that a high level of androgens during the critical period might promote the development of brain systems that predispose sexual attraction toward women and not toward men and that a relative lack of androgens during the same period might promote the opposite.

Simon LeVay (1991) compared the brains of a group of homosexual men who had died of AIDS with the brains of two other groups: heterosexual men, some dead of AIDS and some of other causes; and heterosexual women, all dead of causes other than AIDS. He focused on a particular nucleus in the hypothalamus, which other researchers had already shown to be much smaller in heterosexual women than in heterosexual men. LeVay not only confirmed that previous finding but also discovered that the nucleus was much smaller in the homosexual than in the heterosexual males' brains he studied. The difference was apparently not due to AIDS. The nucleus was not smaller in the heterosexual men who had died of AIDS than in the other heterosexual men, and the difference between the brains of the homosexual and heterosexual men remained statistically significant even when the comparison was restricted to victims of AIDS.

It is tempting to conclude from LeVay's study that the observed brain difference is the underlying cause of the motivational and behavioral differences between homosexual and heterosexual men, or at least part of the cause. But such a conclusion would be premature. Keep in mind that LeVay's study is correlational, not an experiment, and correlations by themselves do not tell us what is cause and what is effect. As LeVay himself points out, it is possible that the brain difference and behavioral difference do not bear a causal relation to each other at all but are both caused by some as yet unidentified third variable (LeVay & Hamer, 1994). It is even conceivable that the brain difference emerged in adulthood as a result of, rather than a cause of, some difference in the behaviors or experiences of homosexuals and heterosexuals (Byne, 1994).

21.

How are reward pathways within the brain identified by the self-stimulation technique?

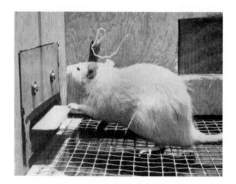

FIGURE **6.12** *Lever pressing for electrical stimulation to the brain* Each time this rat presses the lever, it receives a brief pulse of electrical current through an electrode implanted in its brain. Some rats continued to press the lever for 24 hours without rest, as often as 5000 times per hour. (From Olds, 1956.)

22.

What is some evidence that a particular neural tract that releases the neurotransmitter dopamine is critical for the rewarding effects of electrical brain stimulation and certain abused drugs?

Reward Mechanisms and Their Relationship to Drives

We are endowed with a wonderful capacity to experience pleasure, which must have come about in evolution because it promoted survival and reproduction. The pleasure brought by good food when hungry, water when thirsty, or drifting off to sleep when tired; the pleasure of sex; the pleasure of the company of good friends, or praise, or our own assessment of a job well done—it is easy to see how pleasures such as these can promote survival and reproduction. Of course, some activities that people find pleasurable, such as taking cocaine, threaten rather than promote survival and reproduction. But cocaine and other such drugs, as you will see, act directly on brain mechanisms that are normally stimulated by less direct means—such as by eating when hungry or by copulating when sexually motivated.

Rewards from Electrical Stimulation of the Brain

In the early 1950s, James Olds and Peter Milner made a remarkable discovery. They observed, by accident at first, that rats that received electrical stimulation in certain brain areas behaved as if they were trying to get more of it. For example, if a rat happened to receive the stimulation while exploring a particular corner of the cage, the animal would return repeatedly to that corner. To determine systematically if the brain stimulation would serve as a reward, Olds and Milner tested rats to see if they would stimulate their own brains by pressing a lever (see Figure 6.12). With certain electrode placements, rats learned very quickly to press the lever and would continue to press at high rates, sometimes for many hours without stopping (Olds & Milner, 1954).

Although Olds and Milner's rats behaved as if they liked the electrical stimulation, we can't know for sure what they were actually feeling. Very shortly after the initial discovery with animals, some researchers tried electrical stimulation in the brains of human patients as a possible treatment for various disorders, including epilepsy and severe schizophrenia (reviewed by Valenstein, 1973). With some electrode placements (mostly in the limbic system), patients reported intense pleasure, sometimes equating it with the feeling experienced during sexual orgasm (Heath, 1972). Other patients spoke vaguely of warm, glowing feelings. Patients who had electrodes in more than one brain area described the feeling differently depending on which electrode was stimulated. In no case did this procedure produce compulsive self-stimulation. Patients would stimulate their own brains when given the chance, and they liked it, but they had no difficulty stopping when they wished or were asked to stop. However, none of the electrodes were in the brain areas known to be most effective in rats for self-stimulation. Today such research with humans has been discontinued, apparently because the procedure is not sufficiently useful therapeutically to justify the risks involved.

Subsequent research has shown that rats will work hardest and longest to stimulate a specific tract in the brain called the *medial forebrain bundle*, which runs from the midbrain up through the lateral area of the hypothalamus into a particular nucleus in the basal ganglia called the *nucleus accumbens*. The neurons of this tract secrete the neurotransmitter dopamine into the nucleus accumbens. Chemicals that selectively block the release of dopamine reduce or abolish animals' self-stimulation of this tract, and various manipulations that enhance the release of dopamine increase the rate of self-stimulation (Milner, 1991; Wise, 1996).

Actions of Abused Drugs on Reward Areas of the Brain

This same neural system also underlies the pleasurable effects of certain drugs. Drugs that people use and abuse for the feeling of euphoria they produce act either directly or indirectly to increase the level of dopamine in the just-described neural pathway (Spanagel & Weiss, 1999).

Rats fitted with tubes and mechanisms for pumping drugs into their bloodstream will self-administer cocaine, amphetamine, and opiates (such as morphine or heroin) but will stop self-administering any of these drugs if the nucleus accumbens is destroyed or chemically blocked (Wise, 1996). Rats will work as hard to administer tiny amounts of amphetamine or cocaine through a cannula directly into the nucleus accumbens as they will work to administer much larger amounts into the bloodstream (Hoebel & others, 1983; Wood & Emmett-Oglesby, 1989). Mice will also self-administer these drugs, but not if they have been genetically altered so that their dopamine transmitter system can no longer respond to the drugs (Maldonado & others, 1997).

Brain-Stimulation Reward and Natural Drives

The neural circuitry underlying the reward effects just described surely did not come about in evolution to respond to drugs or to stimulation through wire electrodes. It must have evolved as part of the brain's mechanism for motivating behaviors that promote survival and reproduction, such as eating and copulating. Consistent with this view, rats will stimulate their brains faster, with some electrode placements, if a particular natural drive is strong than if it is weak. For instance, rats will self-stimulate much faster at certain sites in the lateral hypothalamus if they have been made hungry by food deprivation than if they have not (Fulton & others, 2000; Olds & Fobes, 1981). Leptin—the hormone that reduces hunger when body fat is elevated—apparently acts to reduce the rewarding effect of stimulation in these sites. When food-deprived rats are treated with leptin, their rate of self-stimulating at these sites declines (Fulton & others, 2000). In another, much earlier experiment, male rats self-stimulated their brains at certain sites more slowly when their sex drive was reduced through castration and faster again when they were injected with testoterone (Caggiula & Hoebel, 1966). Food tastes better when one is hungry than when one is sated; sex is more pleasurable when the sex drive is strong than when it is weak. Perhaps the mechanism for such effects involves sensitization of the same neural pathways that provide the rewarding effect of electrical brain stimulation.

Other research has shown that dopamine is released naturally from axon terminals in the nucleus accumbens when hungry rats eat or when sexually motivated rats copulate (Damsma & others, 1992; Phillips & others, 1991). Moreover, blockage of dopamine receptors may block the rewarding effect of food or sexual contact (Wise & Rompre, 1989). In one experiment, Roy Wise and his colleagues (1978) trained rats to press a lever for food pellets. Then, at a time when the rats were hungry, the researchers injected some with a dopamine-blocking drug and tested their rate of lever pressing. The drugged rats started off by pressing the lever and consuming pellets at the same high rate as did the undrugged rats, indicating that they were motivated for food. But within a few minutes their rate of pressing and eating slowed down and eventually fell nearly to zero. Apparently, the drug deprived the rats not of hunger but of the rewarding experience that normally comes from eating when hungry. Hence, their lever pressing underwent extinction, similar to that of undrugged, hungry rats whose lever presses brought no food.

Much remains to be learned about the roles of the brain's pleasure systems in motivation and learning. These brain systems may provide a basis for all forms of positive reinforcement in operant conditioning (the learning process discussed in Chapter 5), but little is known about the mechanisms by which such effects occur. For instance, researchers do not yet know to what degree different drives have their own associated sets of reward neurons or to what degree they share a common set (Nader & others, 1997). That issue bears on the larger issue, discussed in Chapter 4, of the degree to which the brain contains separate learning mechanisms or common mechanisms that underlie learning motivated by different drives. Future research on the brain's reward systems will no doubt continue to bring theories of motivation and of learning closer together.

23.

What is some evidence that the neural systems involved in reward from electrical stimulation are also involved in reward related to natural drives such as hunger and sex?

SECTION SUMMARY

Drives are states of the brain that orient a person or animal toward particular goals or incentives. In general, a drive is activated by internal and external conditions that occur when the behaviors motivated by that drive are likely to promote the individual's survival or reproduction. Conversely, drives are generally inhibited by conditions that occur when those behaviors would be useless or harmful.

Hunger is an example of a regulatory drive. Its function is to regulate body weight and the level of specific nutrients in the body. Neurons in the lateral hypothalamus are part of a hunger system that is activated by external cues indicating that food may be available and is inhibited by the presence of food in the stomach and intestines, by high levels of glucose and other energy-providing molecules in the blood, and by high levels of the hormone leptin (reflective of ample stores of body fat). Obesity results from an interaction of genes and culture. Among genetically susceptible people, the food regulation system is thrown off by the easy availability of high-calorie foods and the many external cues promoting appetite.

The sex drive is an example of a nonregulatory drive—that is, a drive whose purpose is something other than that of promoting homeostasis. This drive depends on a combination of appropriate external stimulation (such as signals from an available sexual partner) and a brain state primed by hormones. In all male mammals, apparently, the crucial hormone for this drive is testosterone, which acts on the medial preoptic area of the hypothalamus. In most female mammals (but not in women), the sex drive is primed by action, on the ventromedial nucleus of the hypothalamus, of the same hormones that promote ovulation (usually estrogen followed by progesterone), so the drive coincides with the period of fertility. In human females, in contrast, the sex drive is primed by the relatively constant production of androgens (DHEA and testosterone) by the adrenal glands. The basic differences in the responsiveness of male and female brains to hormones and external stimuli depend on the presence or absence of testosterone during prenatal development.

Drive satisfaction entails a pleasurable or rewarding effect that contributes to motivation and learning. Apparently, different sets of neurons underlie the pleasure associated with different drives, but they are anatomically near one another as they course through the lateral hypothalamus into the nucleus accumbens. The greater the drive, the more rapidly an animal will self-stimulate, electrically, the neurons associated with satisfaction of that drive. These same reward systems are also the sites of action of drugs that are used and abused for the sense of euphoria that they produce.

SLEEPING AND DREAMING

Sleepiness can be thought of as a drive. A sleepy person is motivated to go to sleep and will expend some effort to reach a safe, comfortable place to do so. Achieving this goal and drifting off to sleep provide a sense of pleasure analogous to that which comes from eating when hungry. But sleep is more than the end state of a drive: It is an altered state of consciousness, in which the brain for a time gives up some of its functions, leaving the person in a condition of reduced activity and responsiveness to the environment. Most of us spend about a third of our lives in this behavioral state. How, more precisely, can sleep be described? What is its function? What causes it physiologically? During sleep we dream. What are the function and cause of dreams? These are the questions we turn to now.

The Electroencephalographic Description of Sleep

Because sleep is a state in which people show little overt behavior and cannot answer questions, scientists who study it must focus on subtle behavioral and physiological changes. The most valuable index of sleep is based on a recording of brain activity called the *electroencephalogram* (abbreviated *EEG*).

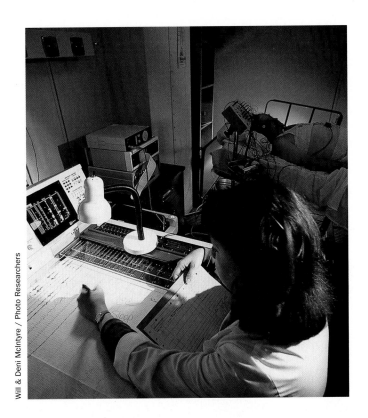

Will & Deni McIntyre / Photo Researchers

FIGURE 6.13 *Recording an EEG in a sleep laboratory*
Electrodes pasted to this man's scalp pick up weak electrical signals from his brain, which are then amplified and used to produce an EEG (recorded as ink tracings on the continuously moving roll of graph paper in the foreground). Other physiological changes, such as eye movements, can also be electrically recorded in this way.

As you know (from Chapter 5), neural activity is electrochemical activity and can be measured as electrical change. The brain, with its billions of neurons, produces constant electrical "chatter," which to some degree penetrates the overlying skull and scalp. By placing electrodes on a subject's scalp, researchers can detect and amplify these signals. The signals can be stored and analyzed by computer and can also be used to move pens up and down on a roll of paper that moves continuously under the pens, resulting in a permanent record of the signals (see Figure 6.13). The resulting EEG recording is a gross index of the electrical activity of the brain, representing a sort of average of activity of billions of neurons, with the greatest weight given to those lying closest to the recording site. By correlating the pattern of waves observed in the EEG with subjects' overt behavior or reported moods, researchers have developed a basis for using the EEG as a rough indicator of psychological states.

24.

What does the EEG actually measure?

EEG Waves Accompanying Wakefulness and Stages of Sleep

When a person is relaxed but awake, with eyes closed, and not thinking of anything in particular, the EEG typically consists of large, regular waves called *alpha waves*, which occur at a frequency of about 8 to 13 cycles per second (see Figure 6.14b). These relatively slow waves stem from a synchronized pulsing of neurons in the thalamus and cerebral cortex that occurs in the absence of focused mental activity or emotional excitement. When a person concentrates on an external stimulus or tries to solve a problem or becomes excited, the EEG pattern changes to low-amplitude, fast, irregular waves called *beta waves* (see Figure 6.14a). The low amplitude of these waves indicates that neurons are firing in an unsynchronized manner, such that their contributions to the EEG tend to cancel one another out. Whereas alpha waves are analogous to the large, regular waves that occur on a pond undisturbed by anything but the wind, beta waves are more akin to the effect of a million pebbles tossed suddenly onto the surface of the pond. The crests of the ripples created by some pebbles would cancel out the troughs created by others, resulting in a chaotic, high-frequency, low-amplitude pattern of ripples.

25.

How does a person's EEG change as the person goes from alert to relaxed to various stages of sleep?

FIGURE **6.14** *EEG waves of waking and sleep stages*

In general, as one goes from an alert to a relaxed state, and then to ever-deeper stages of sleep, the EEG waves become slower in frequency and higher in amplitude. The brief bursts of rapid waves called *sleep spindles* that appear in stage 2 are the most distinctive markers of the onset of sleep. Sleep stage 3 is not shown here; it is arbitrarily defined as the period when 10 to 50 percent of the EEG consists of delta waves. REM sleep, also not shown, is characterized by beta waves that look like those of the awake, attentive state. (From Snyder & Scott, 1972.)

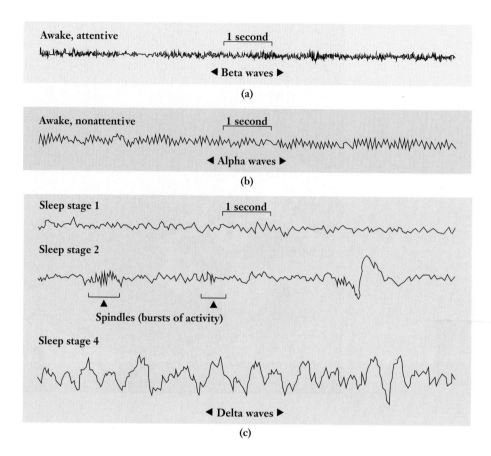

26.

How do REM and slow-wave sleep differ, and how do they cycle through the night?

When a person falls asleep, the EEG goes through a fairly regular sequence of changes, which are used by researchers to divide sleep into four stages, illustrated in Figure 6.14c. *Stage 1* is a brief transition stage, when the person is first falling asleep, and *stages 2* through *4* are successively deeper stages of true sleep. As sleep deepens, an increased percentage of the EEG is devoted to slow, irregular, high-amplitude waves called *delta waves*. These waves, like others, are controlled by neurons in the thalamus that respond in an oscillating manner and synchronize the activity of billions of neurons in the cerebral cortex (Steriade & others, 1993). Corresponding to this EEG change, muscle tension, heart rate, and breathing rate decline, and the person becomes increasingly hard to awaken.

Sleep Cycles

Having reached stage 4, a person does not remain there for the rest of the night. Instead, after about 80 to 100 minutes of total sleep time, sleep rapidly lightens, returning through stages 3 and 2, and then a new, quite fascinating stage of sleep appears for a period of about 10 minutes or more. During this new stage the EEG is unsynchronized, looking much like the beta waves of alert wakefulness. On the basis of the EEG alone, one might think that the person had awakened, but direct observation shows that the person is sound asleep, and the record of muscle tension shows that the muscles are more relaxed than at any other sleep stage. Yet, consistent with the unsynchronized EEG, other indices of high arousal are apparent: Breathing and the heart rate become more rapid and less regular; penile erection occurs in males (even in infants and young boys); twitching movements occur in the small muscles of the fingers and face; and, most indicative of all, the eyes move rapidly back and forth and up and down under the closed eyelids. These eye movements, which can be recorded electrically along with the EEG, give this stage of sleep its name, **REM sleep** (rapid-eye-movement sleep). As you may have guessed, it is during REM sleep that most dreams occur—a topic to which we will return.

REM sleep is also sometimes called *emergent stage 1*, because, even though it is different from the original stage 1, it marks the onset of a new sleep cycle. Stages 2, 3, and 4 are referred to collectively as **slow-wave sleep**, because of the slow EEG waves that characterize those stages.

In a typical night's sleep, a person goes through four or five sleep cycles, each involving gradual descent into deeper stages of slow-wave sleep, followed by a rapid lightening of slow-wave sleep, followed by REM sleep (Hobson, 1995). Each complete cycle takes about 90 minutes. As you can see in Figure 6.15, the deepest slow-wave sleep occurs in the first cycle or two. With each successive cycle, less time is spent in the deeper stages of slow-wave sleep (stages 3 and 4), and more is spent in light slow-wave sleep (stage 2) and REM sleep.

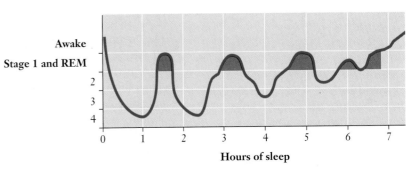

FIGURE 6.15 *The cycle of sleep stages through a night*
People usually go through four or five sleep cycles per night, each ending with a period of REM sleep. With successive cycles the depth of slow-wave sleep becomes less, and the amount of time spent in REM sleep increases. (Adapted from Snyder & Scott, 1972.)

Functions of Slow-Wave Sleep

Why must we sleep? Countless children have asked that question to protest being put to bed, and many scientists have asked it, too. Researchers have proposed two different theories to explain why a tendency to sleep came about in evolution. The two theories are not incompatible with each other, and there is reason to believe that both contain more than a grain of truth.

The Restoration Theory

The *restoration theory* is the one that most people intuitively believe. It is the theory that your parents probably repeated to you as their reason for requiring that you go to bed at a certain hour. According to this view, the body wears out during the day and sleep is necessary to put it back in shape. Scientific support for this theory includes the observation that sleep *is* a time of rest. The muscles are relaxed, the metabolic rate is down, and the rate of neural activity in the brain is reduced—although only by about 10 percent, according to recordings from individual neurons in various brain structures (Hobson, 1987).

The restoration theory predicts that the sleep drive should be greater after a day of strenuous exercise than after a day of rest. Research testing this prediction has produced mixed results but generally tends to validate it. In one study, regular aerobic exercise led to faster sleep onset and somewhat greater sleep time in a group of elderly people who initially suffered from mild insomnia, though it is not clear if the increased sleep resulted from the energy expenditure itself or from other physical and psychological benefits that a regular exercise program might provide (King & others, 1997). The increased sleep began to occur only after 2 or more weeks of the exercise program. In another study, extreme physical exercise—running a 92-kilometer (57-mile) marathon—significantly increased the amount and depth of sleep for 2 nights afterward (Shapiro & others, 1981; see Figure 6.16). Also consistent with the restoration theory, prolonged complete sleep deprivation in rats results in breakdown of various bodily tissues (for example, skin sores fail to heal) and death within about 3 weeks (Everson, 1993; Everson & others, 1989).

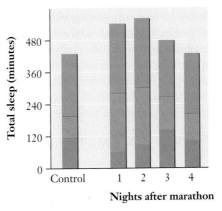

Light sleep (stages 1 and 2)
Deep sleep (stages 3 and 4)
REM sleep

FIGURE 6.16 *Effect on sleep of running a marathon*
Shown here is the average time spent in each sleep stage by athletes on each of 4 nights following a 92-kilometer (57-mile) marathon, compared with control nights (2 weeks before and 2 weeks after the marathon). Notice that the main effects were an increase in the time spent in deep slow-wave sleep (stages 3 and 4) and a decrease in REM sleep on the first 2 nights after the marathon. (From Shapiro & others, 1981.)

27.

What are two theories about the functions of sleep, and what is some evidence supporting each theory?

The Preservation and Protection Theory

The *preservation and protection theory* is less intuitive than the restoration theory and is based primarily on comparisons of sleep patterns in different species of animals. It posits that sleep came about in evolution to preserve energy and protect the individual during that portion of each 24-hour day when there is relatively little value and considerable danger in moving about. An animal needs only a certain number of hours per day to do the things that are necessary or useful for survival, and the rest of the time, according to this theory, it is better off asleep—quiet, hidden, and protected from predators and other possible dangers.

Support for this theory comes from evidence that variations in sleep time among different species do not correspond with differences in physical exertion while awake but do correspond with feeding habits and ways of achieving safety (Allison & Cicchetti, 1976; Webb, 1982). At one extreme, large grazing animals such as bison and horses average only 2 or 3 hours of sleep per 24-hour day. Because of their large size and because they eat grass and other vegetation, which are extremely low in calories, they must spend most of their time eating, and therefore they have little time to sleep. Moreover, because of their size and the fact that they cannot burrow or climb trees, such animals are not adept at finding safe nooks in which to sleep. Thus, they are safer awake. (The fact that such animals sleep at all might be taken as evidence that some minimal amount of sleep is necessary for restorative functions.) At the other extreme, opossums and bats sleep an average of about 20 hours each 24-hour day. These two species need relatively little time to obtain food (such as high-calorie insects), and they are adapted to hide in out-of-the-way places. Presumably, they sleep so much because they have no need to be awake for long and are protected from predators while asleep.

In addition to explaining species differences in total amount of sleep, the preservation and protection theory also helps explain differences in the time of day at which different species sleep. Animals that rely heavily on vision generally forage during the day and sleep at night. Conversely, animals such as mice and rats that rely more on other senses, and are preyed upon by animals that use vision, generally sleep during the day and forage at night. The theory also offers an explanation for the fact that infants in most species of mammals sleep much more than adults. Infants who are being cared for by adults do not need to spend time foraging, and sleep protects them from wandering away into danger. Their sleep also gives their caregivers an opportunity to rest or attend to other needs.

It is interesting to speculate, in this vein, about the evolutionary conditions behind the 8-hour nighttime sleep pattern that characterizes adult humans throughout the world. Humans are highly visual creatures who need light to find food and do other things necessary for survival. At night it may have been best for us, during most of our evolution, to be tucked away asleep in a cave or other hiding place, so as not to be tempted to walk about and risk falling over a cliff or being attacked by a nocturnal predator. Only during the past few centuries—an insignificant speck of evolutionary time—have lights and other contrivances of civilization made the night relatively safe for us. According to this line of thinking, our pattern of sleep might be in part a vestigial trait, a carryover from a period when the night was a time of great danger. To the degree that nighttime is still more dangerous than daytime, our pattern of sleep may continue to serve an adaptive function.

Sleep as a Biological Rhythm

One approach to understanding sleep is to view it in relation to other biologically based changes that accompany the 24-hour cycle of day and night. The day-night cycle has been a stable feature of our planet since its beginning, and all plants and animals have mechanisms that accommodate it. Among the physiological changes in humans that follow a daily rhythm are body temperature, which falls at night and rises during the day, and secretion of the adrenal hormone cortisol, which follows an opposite pattern.

Experiments with animals have shown that cyclic changes in temperature, hormone levels, and behavioral activity (indicative of sleep or wakefulness) continue even when the animals are maintained in a time-free environment—an environment in which there is no regular change in lighting or other cues that could indicate the time of day. In such an environment the cycle is typically somewhat longer or shorter than 24 hours, and it varies from individual to individual but is remarkably constant within a given individual (Takahashi & Zatz, 1982). Experiments with human volunteers—who agreed to live for days or weeks in rooms with no windows, clocks, or other time cues—have produced results quite similar to those found with other species. Temperature, cortisol production, and sleepiness continue to oscillate at close to a 24-hour period (see Figure 6.17).

The technical term for any rhythmic change that continues at close to a 24-hour cycle in the absence of external 24-hour cues is ***circadian rhythm*** (from the Latin words *circa*, meaning "about," and *dies*, meaning "day"). Such rhythms are governed by cyclic changes in activity in the nervous system that can occur independently of external cues. Under normal conditions, however, the circadian clock is reset each day by the onset of daylight, so rhythms occur in periods of exactly rather than approximately 24 hours. Experiments with animals show that the cycle can be shortened or stretched somewhat—say, to a 22-hour or 26-hour period—by artificially changing the period of light and dark. And experiments with humans as well as other animals show that the cycle can be reset through carefully timed exposure to bright fluorescent lights.

Charles Czeisler and his colleagues (1989) found that just a few hours of bright fluorescent lighting at night, coupled with avoidance of daylight, over 3 successive days is enough to reverse a person's circadian clock so that he or she becomes sleepy

28.

What is some evidence that sleepiness is affected by an internal clock that can operate even without external time cues but is continuously reset by daily changes in light?

FIGURE **6.17** *Human circadian rhythm in a time-free environment*
These data are from a single male subject. Each horizontal bar represents one circadian period of wakefulness followed by sleep, with successive periods drawn below each other. The triangles indicate the time of lowest body temperature in each period. Notice that during the period of isolation from time cues, the cycle period became somewhat longer than 24 hours, so the man fell asleep and woke up later each day. (Adapted from Aschoff, 1969.)

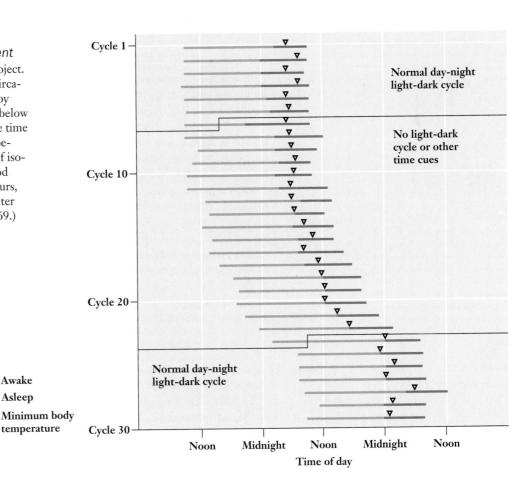

FIGURE **6.18**
Resetting the circadian clock
Charles Czeisler treats a woman for a sleep problem. Before treatment, she would routinely drop off to sleep at about 9 P.M. and awaken at about 4 A.M. After treatment—3 evenings of bright lights—she would fall asleep at about 11 P.M. and awaken at about 7 A.M., her preferred schedule. If her circadian clock were to drift back, it could be reset with another evening or two of lights. Other research by Czeisler and his colleagues suggests that even normal room lights can influence the circadian clock, but the very bright lights shown here are more effective.

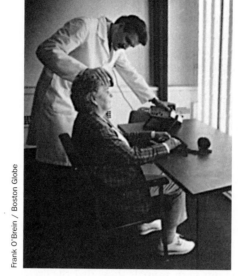

Frank O'Brein / Boston Globe

29.

What are some effects of staying awake through several days and nights?

during the day and alert at night. Very bright light is most effective, but even levels comparable to those already occurring in well-lit offices or factories can significantly affect the cycle (Boivin & others, 1996). Such knowledge can be applied to help night workers adapt their bodily rhythms to their work hours. In one experiment, people simulating night work for a week were more alert at work, slept better during the day, and showed a more complete shift in their body temperature cycle if their work environment was very brightly illuminated and their daytime sleep room was completely darkened than they did under more typical lighting conditions (Czeisler & others, 1990). Czeisler has also used lighting to help people with unusual sleep cycles achieve a more normal pattern (see Figure 6.18).

Behavioral Effects of Sleep Deprivation in People

The long periods of sleep deprivation that cause bodily damage to rats have, for obvious reasons, not been attempted in people. Thus far the longest recorded period of sleep deprivation is that of Randy Gardner, who, as a college student, stayed awake for 11 consecutive days and nights as a publicity stunt for a radio station. During the final hours of his vigil, he played a penny-arcade baseball game 100 times with sleep researcher William Dement and won every one. Just before going to bed, after 264 consecutive hours without sleep, Gardner held a news conference at which, according to Dement (1972), he was "very coherent and conducted himself in impeccable fashion."

Other, more systematically controlled research indicates that there are large individual differences in response to sleep deprivation. After 3 or 4 days without sleep some people begin to experience such symptoms as distorted perceptions and extreme irritability (Borbély, 1986). Yet, all in all, such sleep deprivation has remarkably little effect on participants' performance of tasks requiring physical skill or intellectual judgment. As a rule, sleep deprivation hurts performance on simple, boring tasks more than on challenging ones (Dement, 1979; Horne, 1979, 1988). Impaired performance, when it occurs, seems to derive primarily from dozing off for brief periods. The most reliable effect of sleep deprivation is sleepiness itself. (This is also the most dangerous effect, because it can cause one to fall asleep at the wrong time, such as when driving.) Yet even this effect is not simply related to the amount of time that one has gone without sleep. During sleep deprivation the circadian rhythm maintains its 24-hour cycle, so participants who manage to remain awake all night usually find it much easier to remain awake after daybreak than before (see Figure 6.19).

FIGURE **6.19**   *Rhythm of fatigue during 72 hours of sleep deprivation*
In this experiment, 15 women went for 72 hours without sleep. Every 3 hours they rated their subjective feeling of tiredness on a scale on which 100 meant "normal fatigue" and 200 meant "twice as fatigued as normal." Notice that in each successive 24-hour period, the highest fatigue ratings occurred around 2 to 6 A.M. and the lowest ratings occurred around 2 to 8 P.M. (From Akerstedt & Fröberg, 1977.)

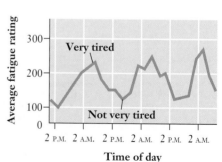

Individual Variation in the Sleep Drive

Some people seem to need more sleep than the typical 8 hours a night to function well, and others seem to need less. At the extreme are rare people, referred to as *nonsomniacs*, who sleep far less than most of us and yet do not feel tired during the day. Such people are particularly interesting with respect to theories about the functions of sleep. If 8 hours of sleep were essential for physical restoration, we would expect nonsomniacs to be extremely inactive during the day or to suffer in some way from their lack of sleep. But a study conducted by Ray Meddis (1977) suggests that nonsomniacs are generally vigorous and healthy. One of Meddis's subjects was a nurse who reported that for most of her life she had slept about 50 minutes per night. She was very active during the day and usually spent the night in quiet activities, such as reading or painting. To verify her nonsomnia, Meddis tested her in the sleep lab. She slept not at all the first three nights in the lab, remaining cheerful and talkative throughout. Finally, on the fourth night, she slept a total of 99 minutes and awoke feeling fully rested.

I hasten to add that for most people 8 or so hours of sleep per night *is* necessary. It is important to distinguish nonsomnia, which is rare, from *insomnia*, which is relatively common. An insomniac is someone who has a normal desire for sleep but who, for some reason (such as worry), is unable to sleep at night. Unlike a nonsomniac, an insomniac feels tired all day as a result of not sleeping. And so do most people who voluntarily reduce their sleep. Again, the desire to sleep can be thought of as a drive, similar in some but not all ways to hunger. To oversimplify somewhat, we sleep because we have a mechanism in the brain that makes us want to sleep at certain periodic intervals. If we yield to this want, we experience pleasure as we drift off; if we resist it, we experience discomfort and an increased craving to sleep until we finally give in. The sleep drive varies from person to person. Most of us have a drive that can be satisfied by about 8 hours of sleep per night; but some have a drive that requires more, and others have a drive that requires less.

Dreams and REM Sleep

Dreams have always been a mystery to people. In sleep one travels to distant places, speaks with friends long dead, and performs impossible feats as if they were commonplace. People at various times and places have believed that dreams foretell the future or are instructions from the spiritual world. Others (most notably Sigmund Freud), less mystically inclined, have held that dreams express hidden wishes and can be used to unlock the secrets of the unconscious mind. Today our knowledge of dreams has been advanced by studies in sleep laboratories, where sleep stages are monitored physiologically and people are periodically awakened and asked to report what was on their mind just before awakening.

True Dreams Contrasted with Sleep Thought

When people are awakened during REM sleep, they usually (in about 90 percent of the cases) report a mental experience that researchers call a *true dream* (Foulkes, 1985). A true dream is experienced as if it were a real event rather than something merely imagined or thought about. The dreamer has the feeling of actually seeing or in other ways sensing various objects and people and of actually moving and behaving in the dream environment. Moreover, the true dream usually involves a progression of such experiences, woven into a somewhat coherent though often bizarre story. The more time the sleeper spends in REM sleep before awakening, the longer and more elaborate is the reported dream. Studies show that essentially everyone dreams several times a night. People who believe that they rarely dream, or who can recall only fragments of dreams upon normal awakening in the morning, describe vivid, detailed dreams if awakened during REM periods. Dreams are fleeting experiences, quickly lost from memory unless we catch them and think about them immediately upon awakening.

30.

What is the difference between a nonsomniac and an insomniac?

31.

How do researchers know that true dreams generally accompany REM sleep and that other forms of sleep thought generally occur in other sleep stages?

People who are awakened during slow-wave sleep report some sort of mental activity just before awakening roughly half the time (Foulkes, 1985; Hobson, 1995). Such reports are usually not of true dreams but of *sleep thought*, which lacks the vivid sensory and motor hallucinations of true dreams and is more akin to day-time thinking. Often the subject of sleep thought is some problem that had been of concern during the day. For example, a student who had been cramming for a math exam might report working on a calculus problem while sleeping. A major difference between sleep thought and daytime thought is that the former is usually ineffective. Although the sleeper may feel that he or she is solving a calculus problem, questions upon awakening indicate that no real progress was made (Hobson, 1987).

Dreams Viewed as Side Effects of Neural Exercise

Research has not answered the question: What are true dreams for? One view prevalent among researchers today is that dreams don't serve any special purpose at all but are side effects of physiological changes in REM sleep that do serve a purpose (Antrobus, 2000; Hobson, 1988). According to one version of this view, the purpose of REM sleep is to provide regular exercise to groups of neurons in the brain. Synapses can degenerate if they go too long without being active (Edelman, 1987), so neural activity during REM sleep may help preserve important circuits. Some of the neurons are in perceptual and motor circuits, and perceptual and movement hallucinations may be inevitable consequences of their activity. In research done many years ago, electrical stimulation in portions of the cerebral cortex produced dreamlike hallucinations in people who were awake (Penfield & Perot, 1963). A similar phenomenon may well occur in REM sleep. In addition to producing hallucinations, the brain continues in REM sleep to engage in some degree of thought, just as it does in slow-wave sleep. But now the thought becomes wrapped up in trying to make sense of the hallucinations. The result is the weaving of a story connecting one hallucination to the next—hence, the dream. Because of reduced mental capacity during sleep, the story is less logical than one the awake brain would develop, but it still contains some degree of logic.

Consistent with the view that the purpose of REM sleep is to exercise brain pathways, with dreams as a side effect, is the observation that REM sleep occurs in mammals besides humans and occurs to a much greater degree in fetuses and infants of all species than in adults (see Figure 6.20). In fact, the peak of REM sleep in the human occurs in the 30-day-old fetus, who spends almost 24 hours a day in this state (Parmelee & others, 1967). Why should fetuses spend so much time in REM sleep? Perhaps as their brains are developing in the relative isolation of the womb they need to exercise sensory and motor pathways, and REM sleep is their means for doing that (Hobson, 1988). In the fetus, REM sleep is accompanied by body movements such as kicking and twisting, which are apparently triggered by the bursts of activity in motor areas of the brain. By the time of birth a neural inhibitory system matures, which inhibits most motor neurons during REM sleep and thus prevents most movements that would otherwise occur. The motor neurons to the eyes, however, remain uninhibited, so eye movements remain as a visible effect of the brain's activity.

Sometimes the side-effect theory just described is interpreted as an argument against the psychoanalytic view that dream analysis can be useful for understanding the mind. But that interpretation seems unjustified. Even if dreams are triggered by random events in the brain, the actual images, emotions, and story lines that constitute the dream are not random. They certainly contain elements based on the dreamer's experience, and because they occur at a time of reduced mental capacity, ideas or feelings that are normally suppressed by higher mental processes could emerge and perhaps be useful in psychoanalysis (Reiser, 1991). Evidence for or against this view would have to come from studies in which dream experiences are correlated with other aspects of a person's life.

32.

According to one theory, what is the function of REM sleep, and how might dreams be a side effect? How is this theory supported by the high rate of REM sleep in fetuses and infants?

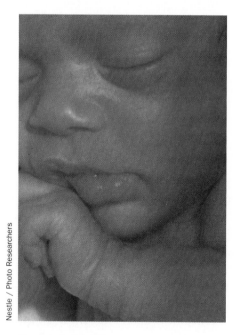

Nestle / Photo Researchers

Sweet dreams?
We have no idea whether human fetuses, such as this one of 7 months, experience dream sensations or not, but we do know that they spend most of their time in REM sleep.

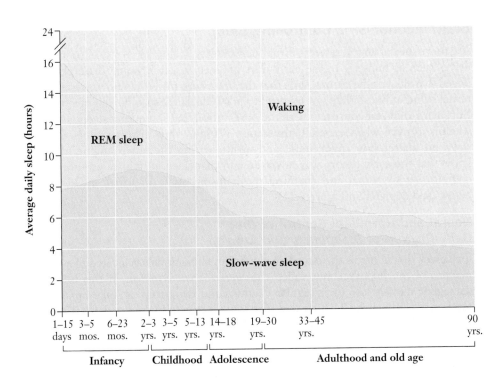

FIGURE **6.20** *Changes in sleep over the course of life*
As shown here, both the total daily sleep time and the percentage of sleep time spent in REM sleep decrease as a person gets older. If the curves were extended to the left, they would show that prior to birth, REM sleep occupies most of each 24-hour day. (Adapted from Snyder & Scott, 1972.)

Possible Role of REM Sleep in Memory Consolidation

In addition to keeping existing neural connections intact through exercise, neural activity in REM sleep may help strengthen newly formed connections and thereby help consolidate new memories. In many experiments, laboratory animals newly trained in a task performed the task better after several hours if they were permitted REM sleep during that period than if they were not permitted such sleep (Smith, 1995). Similar experiments with people have produced mixed results, depending perhaps on the kind of task. There is little evidence that REM sleep improves subsequent recall for verbally learned factual information, but there is considerable evidence that it improves performance on perceptual-motor tasks in people—tasks that are more similar to those used with laboratory animals.

In one experiment, college students were trained at a task in which they had to locate, as quickly as possible, specific visual targets hidden in textured backgrounds (Karni & others, 1994). After the training the students slept in the laboratory for about 8 hours and were deprived either of REM sleep (by being awakened regularly during that sleep stage) or of slow-wave sleep (through regular awakening during slow-wave sleep) or were allowed to sleep soundly through the night. The results were quite dramatic. Those who were deprived of slow-wave sleep or were not sleep-deprived at all performed the perceptual task better right after the sleep period than they had just before the sleep period, but those deprived of REM sleep showed no such improvement. This effect occurred only for the newly learned task; none of the just-described sleep conditions influenced performance of a similar task that had been learned several days earlier.

More recently, using PET neuroimaging (described in Chapter 5), researchers have shown that patterns of brain activity during REM sleep can be influenced in predictable ways by daytime experiences. In one experiment, students who had practiced a particular skill involving eye-hand coordination exhibited, during subsequent REM sleep, extra neural activity in some of the same visual and motor areas of the brain that had been most active during the skill training session (Maquet & others, 2000). Such findings are consistent with the view that neural pathways related to the day's learning are activated and strengthened during REM sleep.

33.

What evidence suggests that REM sleep may help consolidate the effects of recent training or practice?

Brain Mechanisms Controlling Sleep

Are there special neural systems for inducing sleep, analogous to those for inducing drives such as hunger? In the early days of sleep research, some researchers believed that sleep is the natural state that the brain slips into when not aroused by external stimulation, so they saw no need to posit special sleep-inducing mechanisms. But such a view is inconsistent with the observation that sometimes sleepiness overwhelms us even when external stimulation is high, while at other times we can't sleep no matter how quiet, dark, and unstimulating the environment. We now know that the early theory was mistaken and that sleep is actively promoted by a complex set of neural and chemical mechanisms, some of which are described below (and depicted in Figure 6.21).

Neural and Hormonal Control of the Daily Rhythm of Sleepiness and Arousal

The clock that controls the circadian rhythm in all mammals is located in a specific nucleus of the hypothalamus called the *suprachiasmatic nucleus*. If this nucleus is damaged, animals lose their regular rhythms and fall asleep or wake up at rather random times over the 24-hour day. The same is true of human patients (Cohen & Albers, 1991). This nucleus contains rhythm-generating neurons, which gradually increase and decrease their rate of action potentials over a cycle of approximately 24 hours, even when surgically isolated from other parts of the brain (Shearman & others, 2000; Silver & others, 1996). This neural rhythm accounts for the circadian rhythm of sleep and wakefulness that occurs in an environment free of time cues. The same nucleus also receives direct input from the eyes by way of a special set of neurons in the optic nerve, through which the daily changes in sunlight synchronize the circadian clock to the 24-hour pattern of the earth's rotation (Freedman & others, 1999; Takahashi & Zatz, 1982).

Another structure that contributes to the daily rhythm of sleep and arousal is the *pineal gland*. This structure resides in the middle of the brain, right above the brainstem, but is not part of the brain; rather, it is an endocrine gland, which se-

34.

What is known about the roles of (a) the suprachiasmatic nucleus in controlling daily rhythms, (b) the pineal gland and melatonin in inducing sleep, (c) the anterior hypothalamus in controlling slow-wave sleep, and (d) two brainstem centers in controlling REM sleep?

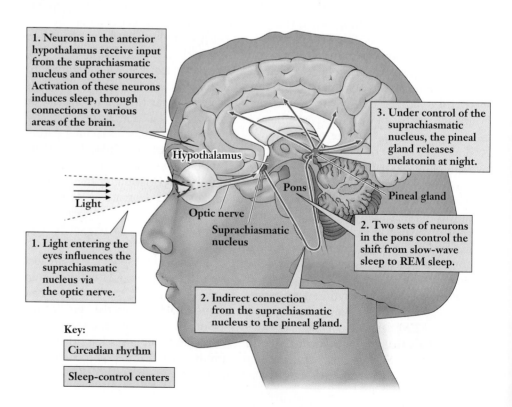

1. Neurons in the anterior hypothalamus receive input from the suprachiasmatic nucleus and other sources. Activation of these neurons induces sleep, through connections to various areas of the brain.

3. Under control of the suprachiasmatic nucleus, the pineal gland releases melatonin at night.

Hypothalamus

Pons

Pineal gland

Light

Optic nerve

Suprachiasmatic nucleus

2. Two sets of neurons in the pons control the shift from slow-wave sleep to REM sleep.

1. Light entering the eyes influences the suprachiasmatic nucleus via the optic nerve.

2. Indirect connection from the suprachiasmatic nucleus to the pineal gland.

Key:

Circadian rhythm

Sleep-control centers

FIGURE 6.21 *Some sleep-control mechanisms*
Connections from the optic nerve to the suprachiasmatic nucleus of the hypothalamus help synchronize the body's circadian rhythms to the 24-hour change in lighting, and connections from that nucleus to the pineal gland help promote sleepiness at night by stimulating the secretion of melatonin. Sleepiness is also promoted by activity in a set of neurons in the anterior (front) portion of the hypothalamus, and the shift from slow-wave sleep to REM sleep is promoted by activity in two sets of neurons in the pons.

cretes the hormone *melatonin*. In mammals the pineal gland's secretion of mela-tonin is controlled by the suprachiasmatic nucleus, through connections to sympa-thetic control centers in the hypothalamus that act on a peripheral sympathetic nerve that runs to the pineal gland. The pineal gland produces large quantities of melatonin at night and little or none during the day. Melatonin circulates in the blood and acts on various tissues, including the brain.

Research shows that melatonin helps bring on sleepiness in humans, though it is not essential for sleepiness. In one study, people who were treated at various times of day with melatonin manifested significantly more sleep 2 hours after the treatment than people who received a placebo (Haimov & Lavie, 1996). Melatonin treatment has proved useful in helping blind people regulate their sleep. Without sensitivity to light, blind people often manifest a circadian rhythm that is out of sync with the 24-hour light-dark cycle and have erratic sleep patterns; but daily treatment with melatonin, taken 2 hours before the desired bedtime each evening, can regulate their circadian rhythms and lead to more regular sleep patterns (Haimov & Lavie, 1996).

Neural Centers for Slow-Wave and REM Sleep

Researchers have located several areas of the brain where neural activity seems to promote sleep. One such area is the anterior portion of the hypothalamus (Jones, 2000). Electrical stimulation in this area can cause a previously alert animal to fall asleep, and lesions there can result in permanent sleeplessness, eventuating in death. The anterior hypothalamus receives neural connections from the suprachi-asmatic nucleus, and these connections may be part of the means by which that nu-cleus regulates the 24-hour sleep-wake rhythm. At present it is unknown where in the brain melatonin acts to help bring on sleepiness, but the anterior hypothalamus is one likely candidate.

The shift from slow-wave to REM sleep involves two interconnected sets of neurons in the pons. One set generates the increased brain activity that occurs in REM sleep, through connections to the cortex by way of the thalamus (Steriade, 1996), and the other set inhibits motor neurons and thereby produces the extreme loss of muscle tension that occurs in REM sleep. Cats with lesions in these in-hibitory neurons begin to move about every time they fall into REM sleep and wake themselves by their own movements (Jouvet, 1972). People who have brain damage to this area produce, in fact, the movements that they dream they are pro-ducing—sometimes with quite harmful consequences—unless such movements are prevented by drug treatment (Culebras & Moore, 1989).

So the sleeping brain is an active brain. The brain actively brings on sleep, con-trols each shift from one sleep stage to another, exercises its own neural pathways, and inhibits motor output—all in a night's work.

SECTION SUMMARY

The quality of sleep varies cyclically through the night. Each cycle (lasting roughly 90 minutes) begins with a period of progressive deepening of slow-wave sleep, character-ized by delta waves in the EEG, and ends with rapid lightening of slow-wave sleep fol-lowed by a period of REM sleep, characterized by beta waves like those of alert wakefulness. Some amount of sleep is apparently needed for body restoration, but the restoration theory does not account for the large differences among animal species in the quantity and timing of sleep. Such differences are best explained by the preserva-tion and protection theory, which holds that sleep protects the individual and pre-serves energy during that portion of each 24-hour day when the cost—in risk and energy expenditure—of moving about outweighs its value.

The mind does not stop functioning during sleep but does become less logical. Sleep thought occurs during all sleep stages, and true dreams occur mostly during REM sleep. REM sleep may function to exercise neural pathways in the brain, and dreams may stem from the sleeping mind's attempt to make sense of the sensations and feelings that result from such exercise. There is also evidence that newly learned sensory-motor skills are consolidated by the strengthening of neural pathways during REM sleep.

The 24-hour sleep-wake rhythm is regulated by a circadian clock in the suprachiasmatic nucleus of the hypothalamus, which is kept synchronous with the day-night cycle by its responsiveness to variations in sunlight. This nucleus affects sleepiness at least partly through its effect on the secretion of melatonin by the pineal gland. It may also act directly on neurons in the anterior hypothalamus that bring on sleep. The switch from slow-wave sleep to REM sleep is controlled by neurons in the pons.

AROUSAL AND EMOTION

Enough sleep; wake up and face the challenges of the day. Midterm exams are just around the corner, your family is after you to get your life in order, your lover has just left you for another, the surgeon says your nose and left ear will have to go, and a hungry tiger is crouched behind you. Are you awake? All these events have something in common: All are likely to be psychologically disturbing, and all have the potential to stimulate a pattern of physiological reactions referred to as *high arousal*. In this section we will look first at the arousal response and its effects and then at the psychological experience called *emotion*, which is often (but not always) accompanied by high arousal. (By the way, I was only kidding about your left ear.)

High Arousal

35.

How does the arousal response help prepare the body for fight, flight, and possible wounds?

The *arousal response* is a pattern of measurable physiological changes that helps prepare the body for "fight or flight" (to use Walter Cannon's famous phrase). The pattern varies from person to person and situation to situation, but it commonly includes the following elements: (1) Skeletal muscles become tense, and blood is diverted from other parts of the body to muscles, preparing them to spring into action. (2) The heart rate, blood pressure, and breathing rate increase, and sugar and fat molecules are released into the blood from storage deposits—all of which help prepare the body metabolically for a possibly prolonged expenditure of energy. (3) Changes occur in the blood that enable it to clot more easily, and pain-relieving hormones called endorphins (discussed in Chapter 7) are released—both of which help prepare the body for possible injury. (4) Alerting mechanisms of the brain are strongly activated, and cognitive processes are narrowly focused on the arousing stimulus or thought. This pattern seems nicely designed to cope with the proverbial tiger about to attack or with a bully at the neighborhood playground. But it can also occur in response to such challenges as taking midterm exams or asking someone out on a date, where neither fight nor flight is called for, and in these cases it may do more harm than good.

36.

What is the relationship between degree of arousal and task performance? In what way does that relationship depend on the kind of task?

In the short run, as shown by many experiments with both humans and other animals, the arousal response can be either helpful or harmful, depending on the task at hand. In general, high arousal is beneficial for tasks that require a good deal of physical energy, or when the task is very well practiced or instinctive, but is harmful for tasks that call for novel (unpracticed) movements, creativity, or careful judgment. In other words, for any given task some level of arousal is optimal, and the optimal level is lower for intellectually difficult tasks than for those defined more by endurance, persistence, or ability to stay alert (see Figure 6.22).

This relationship between optimal arousal and type of task is called the **Yerkes–Dodson law**, because a version of it was first proposed by Robert Yerkes and John Dodson (1908). These researchers conducted experiments in which mice could avoid electric shocks by entering the brighter of two compartments. They varied the arousal level in the mice by varying the intensity of the shocks, and they varied the task difficulty by varying the contrast in brightness between the two

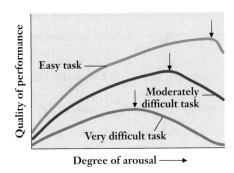

FIGURE **6.22** *The relationship between degree of arousal and quality of performance for three different tasks*
For any given task, quality of performance increases as arousal increases, up to some peak, and then declines as arousal increases still further. In this illustration, peak performance for each task is indicated by the arrow. As shown, peak performance occurs at a lower arousal level for cognitively difficult tasks than for cognitively easy tasks. This relationship is referred to as the Yerkes–Dodson law.

compartments. When the task was easy (a big difference between the two compartments), the mice did best with high arousal (from strong shocks). But when the task was difficult (little difference between the compartments), the mice performed best with lower arousal (from weak shocks). Chapter 14 discusses experiments showing a comparable effect in people—where arousal level was manipulated by the presence or absence of an audience. An audience, as the Yerkes–Dodson law would predict, typically improves performance on routine tasks and worsens it on tasks requiring calm judgment or creativity.

If the arousal response is too strong and prolonged, and occurs too often, it can have harmful effects on the body. It can contribute to the development of stomach ulcers, promote chronic high blood pressure, contribute to vascular and heart damage, and promote infectious disease by suppressing the immune system. People vary in the degree and type of arousal response they show in similar situations, and these differences correlate with their likelihood of developing particular physical ailments—an idea discussed more fully in Chapter 16.

The Concept of Emotion

Stimuli that produce high physiological arousal also, in general, produce strong feelings, such as *terror*, *rage*, or *passion*, which in everyday life we refer to as emotions. Consistent with everyday usage of the term, many psychologists define **emotion** as a particular class of subjective feeling. It is a feeling elicited by objects or events, real or imagined, that have high significance to the individual. The significance may have to do with perceived threat or benefit. Thus, I might be terrified by a real or imagined tiger behind me or elated by my real or imagined winning of a sought-after prize. Emotions tend to come on rapidly and automatically and may be based on an unreasoned evaluation of the event or object that can contradict rational thought. A garter snake might elicit fear in a person who is afraid of snakes, despite the person's rational knowledge that the snake is harmless.

Our capacity for emotions must have come about, through natural selection, because of their value for survival and reproduction. This line of thinking draws attention to the motivating qualities of emotions. When fearful, we run away, or freeze, or try to look inconspicuous, or in other ways manifest caution. When angry, we puff ourselves up, make threats, and sometimes even fight. When passionately in love, we behave in all sorts of ways—some of which would otherwise seem foolish—to gain the attention of our beloved. The social emotions of guilt, shame, embarrassment, and pride motivate us to behave in ways that help us get along with other people (as discussed in Chapter 14). So emotions are not just feelings; they are feelings associated with tendencies to behave in particular ways, toward particular ends.

How many different emotions are there? The answer to that is quite arbitrary; it depends on how finely graded a taxonomy we wish to create. You may recall from Chapter 3 that Paul Ekman and Wallace Friesen identified what they consider to be six basic emotions—surprise, fear, disgust, anger, happiness, and

37.

How are emotions characterized in terms of subjective feelings, relative independence of rationality, and action tendencies?

FIGURE **6.23** *Spectrum of positive and negative emotions*
Shown here is an attempt to arrange emotions along two dimensions: the degree to which the emotion is experienced as positive or negative and the level of bodily arousal involved. Because emotional feelings are subjective, no such classification will be completely agreed upon by all observers. (From Kissin, 1986.)

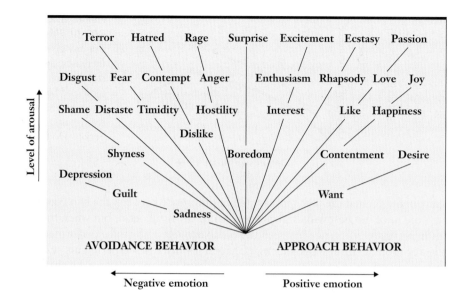

sadness—each expressed by a unique set of muscle contractions in the face, and suggested that most other emotions are blends or variations of those six. Another way to classify emotions is illustrated in Figure 6.23, which portrays various emotions in a two-dimensional array. One dimension is the degree to which the emotion is associated with approach or avoidance, and the other is the degree of bodily arousal associated with it. The way we label emotions and think about them is also very much affected by the culture we live in (discussed in Chapter 14). For the present, however, our focus is on the physiological underpinnings of emotions, in the brain and elsewhere in the body.

Theories of Emotion That Emphasize Peripheral Feedback

Because emotions are associated with peripheral changes in the body, psychologists have long wondered if those changes contribute to or are essential for emotional feelings. By peripheral changes, I mean all bodily changes that occur outside the central nervous system, including changes in heart rate, breathing rate, muscle tension, body posture, and facial expressions.

James's Peripheral Feedback Theory

38.

What was James's theory of emotion, what evidence did he supply for it, and how does it depend on his specific definition of emotion?

In his famous textbook, *The Principles of Psychology*, William James (1890) argued that bodily arousal causes emotion. More specifically, he argued that arousal occurs immediately in response to the perception of certain kinds of environmental events and that emotions are one's sense of arousal. In James's words,

> Our natural way of thinking . . . is that the mental perception of some fact excites the mental affection called the emotion, and that this latter state of mind gives rise to the bodily expression. My theory, on the contrary, is that *the bodily changes follow directly the perception of the exciting fact, and that our feeling of the same changes as they occur IS the emotion.* Common sense says, we lose our fortune, are sorry, and weep; we meet a bear, are frightened, and run; we are insulted by a rival, are angry, and strike. The hypothesis here to be defended says that this order of sequence is incorrect . . . and that the more rational statement is that we feel sorry because we cry, angry because we strike, afraid because we tremble, and not that we cry, strike, or tremble because we are sorry, angry, or fearful. . . . Without the bodily states following on the perception, the latter would be purely cognitive in form, pale, colorless, destitute of emotional warmth. We might then see the bear, and judge it best to run, receive the insult, and deem it right to strike, but we should not actually feel afraid or angry.

James's evidence for his theory came not from experiments but from introspection—looking inward at his own emotions. From his attempt to analyze his own emotional feelings, James concluded that the feelings were really sensations stemming from bodily changes. Thus, his feeling of fear was really his feeling of a quickened heart, shallow breathing, goose-bumpy flesh, and trembling limbs. Similarly, his feeling of anger was his feeling of a tightened chest, flushed face, dilated nostrils, and clenched teeth. James believed that he could identify a different constellation of bodily changes for each emotion and that if he could not feel these changes, he would not feel the emotion. In line with James's view, researchers have found that people throughout the world describe their emotions in terms of bodily changes and are quite consistent in the kinds of changes they associate with each emotion (Cacioppo & others, 1992; Rime & others, 1990).

Much of the controversy over James's theory pertains to people's differing definitions of the term *emotion*. In the excerpt above, James was clearly using the term to refer to one's conscious experience of a particular internal state. He was not using it to refer to one's immediate assessment of the stimulus (for example, the assessment that a bear is dangerous). If he had defined that initial assessment as the emotion, then clearly the emotion would have to precede the body's arousal reaction, since the reaction depends on the assessment of the stimulus. The essence of James's theory is that the initial assessment and the subsequent arousal response occur quickly, automatically, without consciousness of how one is feeling. The emotion, which is the conscious feeling, comes later and is based on sensations coming from the aroused body. The contrast between James's theory and what he called the common-sense theory is illustrated in the top two portions of Figure 6.24.

Common-Sense Theory

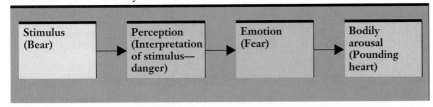

James's Theory

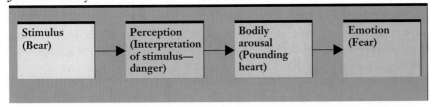

Schachter's Theory

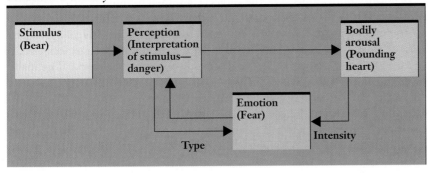

FIGURE **6.24**
Three theories of emotion
Each theory proposes a different set of causal relationships among perception of the stimulus, bodily arousal, and emotional feeling. According to the common-sense theory (so labeled by James), the emotional feeling precedes and causes the bodily arousal. James's theory reverses that relationship, and Schachter's theory holds that the intensity of the emotional feeling depends on the bodily response but the type of emotion experienced (such as fear, anger, or love) depends on the person's cognitive assessment of the external stimulus or situation.

39.

How does Schachter's theory differ from James's?

40.

How did Schachter support his theory in laboratory experiments?

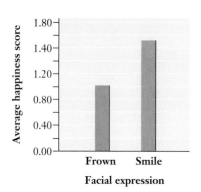

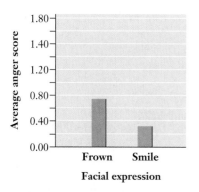

FIGURE **6.25** *Effect of facial molding on self-reported happiness and anger*

Adult subjects were asked to contract certain facial muscles, which effectively molded their faces into either a smile or a frown, while viewing a picture. The smile increased self-reported happiness, and the frown increased self-reported anger. (Data from Laird, 1974.)

Schachter's Cognition-Plus-Feedback Theory

In the 1960s, Stanley Schachter developed a theory of emotion that can be understood as a variation of James's theory. According to Schachter, the feeling of an emotion depends not just on sensory feedback pertaining to the body's response but also on one's perceptions and thoughts concerning the environmental event that presumably evoked the body's response. More specifically, he proposed that perception and thought about the environment influence the type of emotion felt and that sensory feedback about the degree of bodily arousal influences the intensity of the emotion felt (see the bottom portion of Figure 6.24). Thus, if you see a bear, your perception that it is dangerous determines that the emotion you feel will be fear, and your perception of your own pounding heart, sweating, and so on determines how much fear you will feel. Schachter also proposed that the intensity of the emotional feeling influences the interpretation of the stimulus. Thus, if your bodily arousal were already high, perhaps from drinking too much coffee, that arousal would contribute to your emotional intensity and might lead you to perceive the bear as more dangerous than you would otherwise.

In experiments testing his theory, Schachter (1971) injected people with either epinephrine (a substance also known as adrenaline, which raises heart rate and produces other effects associated with high arousal) or a placebo (an inactive substance) and then exposed them to various emotion-eliciting conditions. He found that epinephrine by itself did not produce any particular emotion (the subjects just said they felt jumpy) but that when it was combined with an emotion-inducing situation, such as a horror film, it increased the intensity of the subject's emotion. As predicted by his theory, the kind of emotion subjects felt depended on the external situation, but the intensity was heightened by epinephrine. The epinephrine-injected subjects manifested and reported more anger when insulted, more fear when watching a frightening film, and more hilarity when watching a slapstick comedy than did placebo-injected subjects. This emotion-enhancing effect occurred only if the subjects had *not* previously been informed of the physiological effects of epinephrine. Thus, according to Schachter, high physiological arousal increases emotion only when people believe that the arousal is caused by the external situation.

A Facial Feedback Theory

Paul Ekman (1984) has proposed a theory of emotions that is similar to James's peripheral feedback theory but focuses particularly on the role of the face. As discussed in Chapter 3, Ekman and others have found that each basic emotion is associated with a unique facial expression. Ekman believes that those expressions are produced rapidly and automatically (though they can be inhibited) and that sensory feedback from the expression contributes to the emotional feeling. If Ekman is right, then people should be able to augment their own feeling of an emotion by mimicking the facial expression of that emotion.

If you form your face into a smile, will you feel happier? A Polyannaish suggestion, perhaps, but research suggests that there may be some truth to it. In one experiment (Laird, 1974), each subject was asked to contract certain facial muscles in ways that were (unbeknownst to the subject) designed to mold the face into a smile or a frown. While they were maintaining these facial postures, the subjects were asked to examine pictures that were designed to instill emotional feelings, such as a picture of children playing. Then, as if it were incidental to the experiment, they were asked to fill out a questionnaire designed to assess their mood. The main result was that the subjects' self-reported moods were affected not just by the specific pictures they saw but also by the induced facial expression. Those whose faces had formed a smile reported themselves to be more happy and less angry than did those whose faces had formed a frown (see Figure 6.25). In another experiment, people reported themselves to be happier after repeating the vowel sound of a long *e*,

(a)   **(b)**   **(c)**

Paul Ekman

FIGURE **6.26** *Inducing an expression of fear*
Shown here are frames from a videotape of a man following the instructions used by Ekman and his colleagues (1983) to induce an expression of fear: (a) "Raise your brows and pull them together," (b) "now raise your upper eyelids," and (c) "now stretch your lips horizontally, back toward your ears." Other instructions were used to induce other emotional expressions, producing the results shown in Figure 6.27.

which forces the face into a smile, than after repeating other vowel sounds (Zajonc & others, 1989).

Induced facial expressions not only can alter self-reports of emotion but also can produce physiological responses throughout the body that are consistent with the induced expression. In one experiment, Ekman and his colleagues (1983) asked subjects to move specific facial muscles in ways designed to mimic each of the six basic emotional expressions (see Figure 6.26). For comparison, they asked other subjects to feel each emotion by mentally reliving an event in which that emotion had been strong. As the subjects held the facial expressions or imagined the emotional event, various indices of their physiological arousal were recorded. The main finding was that different patterns of arousal accompanied different emotions, but the pattern for a given emotion was the same whether the person had been asked to relive that emotion or simply to move certain facial muscles (see Figure 6.27). For instance, anger, whether it was relived or mimicked by facial molding, was accompanied by an increase in skin temperature that did not occur for the other emotions (consistent with evidence that blood tends to flow into the skin during anger). As another example, both anger and fear—in both the mimicking and the reliving conditions—increased the subjects' heart rate more than did any of the other emotions. Researchers subsequently replicated these findings with a wide variety of people and various experiment conditions (Levenson, 1992; Levenson & others, 1990). The results are consistent with Ekman's view that sensory feedback from the face influences both the feeling and the bodily state associated with the emotion.

41.

What is some evidence that molding the face into an emotional expression can affect mood and that it may do so partly by producing changes elsewhere in the body?

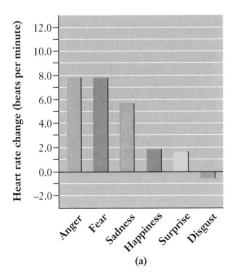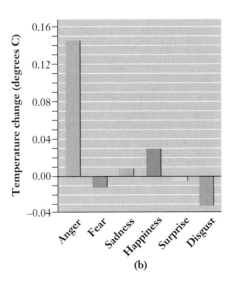

(a)   **(b)**

FIGURE **6.27** *Effect of induced emotional expressions on heart rate and skin temperature*
Ekman and his colleagues (1983) found that (a) heart rate increased most when the induced facial expression was of anger, fear, or sadness, and (b) skin temperature increased most when the induced expression was of anger. Although not shown here, the same pattern of effects also occurred when subjects were asked to relive specific emotional experiences through imagination. (From Ekman & others, 1983.)

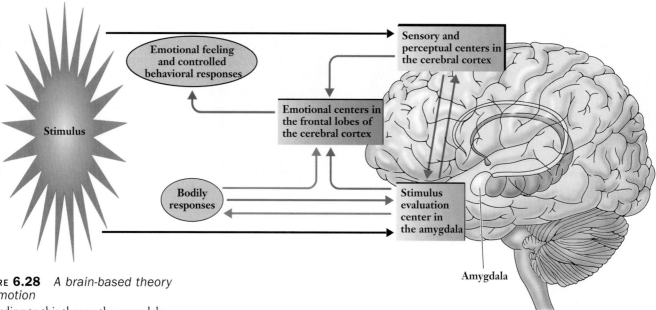

FIGURE **6.28**   *A brain-based theory of emotion*

According to this theory, the amygdala and the frontal lobes are essential to the generation and experience of emotion, especially fear. As the flowchart shows, the amygdala receives sensory information about the external environment through both a subcortical route and a route that involves the sensory and perceptual areas of the cerebral cortex. The amygdala is crucial for evaluating the emotional significance of that sensory input and generating immediate bodily reactions. It also sends output to the frontal lobes of the cortex, which are crucial for experiencing the emotion consciously and controlling deliberate behavioral responses. The model also shows that feedback from the bodily responses might act both in the amygdala and in the frontal lobes of the cortex to modify the emotion, in line with James's, Schachter's, and Ekman's feedback theories.

42.

What is some evidence that the amygdala is critical in evaluating the significance of stimuli and generating emotional reactions?

A Brain-Based Theory of Emotion

Thus far I have focused on the role of the peripheral bodily changes in emotion and have said nothing about the brain. But of course the brain is the center both for producing the bodily changes and for experiencing emotions. Research on the brain's emotional systems has focused especially on two structures: (1) the ***amygdala***, a portion of the limbic system, and (2) the ***frontal lobes*** of the cerebral cortex. Such research has led to the brain-based theory of emotion diagrammed in Figure 6.28 (LeDoux, 1992, 1996). According to this theory, the amygdala plays a central role in assessing the emotional significance of stimuli and generating some of the body's immediate responses, and the frontal lobes are crucial for the conscious experience of emotion and the initiation of the more deliberate, controlled aspects of emotional behavior.

Role of the Amygdala in Computing the Emotional Significance of Stimuli

Many years ago, Walter Cannon (1927) proposed that some neural system in the brain must quickly and automatically assess stimulus input to determine if some survival-promoting response is needed. He argued that this system, not the peripheral feedback mechanism postulated by James, is the key to understanding emotion. Cannon suggested that the center for this neural system lies in the hypothalamus, but subsequent research led others to focus on the amygdala.

In experiments with monkeys, removal of the amygdala along with nearby portions of the temporal lobe of the cerebral cortex on both sides of the brain produced a dramatic set of changes in behavior described as *psychic blindness* (Klüver & Bucy, 1937; Weiskrantz, 1956). The monkeys could still see objects and could move in a coordinated fashion, but they seemed indifferent to the psychological significance of objects. They no longer responded fearfully to objects that had previously frightened them or aggressively to objects that had previously angered them. They attempted to eat just about anything, showing little discrimination between what they previously would have considered good food or not food, and some also attempted to copulate with just about anything, animate or inanimate. Remarkably similar observations were subsequently made of human beings whose amygdalas, along with surrounding portions of the cortex, had been destroyed by disease (Marlowe & others, 1975).

Recently, more subtle disruptions in ability to assess the emotional significance of stimuli have been observed in people whose brain damage was confined to portions of the amygdala (Allman & Brothers, 1994). For instance, one woman, after bilateral destruction of portions of the amygdala as treatment for epilepsy, was no longer able to recognize expressions of fear or anger in people's faces or in the sounds of their voices, even though she could still recognize individuals by face and had no difficulty understanding the words that people spoke (Scott & others, 1997). Another woman with damage to the amygdala failed to react fearfully, or even to show much concern, when she and her husband were mugged (described by Bruce & Young, 1998). Neuroimaging studies show that the human amygdala becomes especially active in response to fearful stimuli (such as frightening film clips or signals predicting possible electric shock) and in response to facial or vocal expressions of fear by others (Whalen, 1998). Somewhat less consistently, such research also shows involvement of the amygdala during experiences of anger and disgust but not, apparently, during experiences of various other emotions.

Further evidence for the involvement of the amygdala in fear comes from extensive research with laboratory animals. Such research shows that neural activity in the amygdala indeed can, through connections to the hypothalamus, generate the hormonal secretions and autonomic responses (such as change in heart rate) that typically accompany strong emotions (Davis, 1992). Moreover, rats with lesions in a particular part of the amygdala fail to react fearfully to sights or sounds that had previously been paired with painful shock, whereas rats with lesions destroying the entire visual or auditory cortex without damage to the amygdala still do show such reactions (LeDoux, 1992, 1996; LeDoux & others, 1989). The latter finding is particularly interesting because it suggests that the amygdala can evaluate the emotional significance of stimuli through a route that, in humans, does not involve conscious perception. At least since Freud's time, many psychologists have contended that emotional reactions to a stimulus can occur without conscious perception of the stimulus. The subcortical connections from sensory systems to the amygdala may well provide neural routes through which such unconscious evaluation occurs.

Role of the Frontal Lobes in Emotional Experience

The amygdala also has strong connections to the frontal lobes of the cerebral cortex, and through these it apparently influences people's conscious emotional feelings and their ability to act in deliberate, planned ways based on those feelings. One line of evidence for this comes from observations many years ago of people who were subjected to *prefrontal lobotomy*—an operation that cut off the frontmost portion of the frontal lobes from the rest of the brain and was, before the development of drug treatments, a relatively common treatment for severe mental disorders (discussed further in Chapter 17). The operation usually relieved people of their crippling emotions, but it also left them unable to plan and organize their lives effectively (Valenstein, 1986).

More recently, evidence has mounted that the left frontal lobe may be most involved in positive emotions and the right may be most involved in negative emotions (Haller & others, 1998; Sutton & Davidson, 1997). Some of the evidence comes from experiments in which people were presented with emotion-eliciting stimuli while the overall rate of neural activity in each frontal lobe was recorded by means of an electroencephalograph. In one such experiment, the left frontal lobes of adult subjects became most active in response to happy films of a puppy playing with flowers or a gorilla taking a bath, and the right frontal lobes became most active in response to medical films showing third-degree burns or a leg amputation (Davidson & others, 1990). In a similar experiment, 10-month-old babies showed more activity in the left frontal lobe when their mothers approached them and more activity in the right when a stranger approached them (Fox & Davidson, 1988). Other evidence comes from studies of people who suffered damage in one or the other frontal lobe due to a stroke. Damage in the left frontal lobe commonly

43.

What is some evidence that the frontal lobes are involved in the conscious feelings of emotions and that the right and left frontal lobes are involved with different classes of emotions?

produced a decline in positive emotions, and damage in the right more often produced a decline in negative emotions (Robinson & others, 1984).

Such research on the brain and emotions illustrates nicely the increasing conjoining of psychological theories with knowledge of physiological mechanisms. Conscious and unconscious emotional assessments, and positive and negative emotions, differ not just in the realm of subjective experience but also, apparently, in the brain pathways that underlie them.

SECTION SUMMARY

High arousal, which prepares the body for "fight or flight," typically facilitates performance of tasks that are physically strenuous, instinctive, or highly practiced, but it interferes with performance of novel or intellectually challenging tasks. In people, high arousal is typically accompanied by strong feelings of emotion.

Classical theories of emotion differ in their view of the relationship between emotion and arousal: Does emotion cause arousal (the common-sense theory), or does arousal cause emotion (James's theory), or is emotion caused by a combination of arousal and cognitive assessment of the situation (Schachter's theory)? The facial responses that accompany emotional feelings apparently contribute to those feelings and play some role in controlling the pattern of bodily arousal.

Ultimately, emotions are products of the brain. The amygdala is particularly crucial for the automatic evaluation of a stimulus as fearful. It influences the body's arousal response through connections to the hypothalamus, and it promotes the conscious experience of fear through its connections to the frontal lobes of the cerebral cortex.

CONCLUDING THOUGHTS

44.

What is the general goal of the physiological approach to the study of behavioral states, and what different types of contributions are made toward this goal by the methods of intervention and correlation?

As you review the mechanisms of hunger, sexual drive, reward, sleep, and emotions described in this chapter, you might find the following two points useful in organizing some of your thoughts:

1.   The attempt to relate behavioral states to physiological states   Hunger, sexual drive, sleep, and emotions are examples of *behavioral states*. They all involve somewhat sustained but reversible changes in the way a person or other animal behaves in a given environment. In this chapter you read many examples of research aimed at finding relationships between behavioral states and *physiological states*. The goal of such work is to identify the somewhat sustained but reversible changes in the brain that provide the foundation for behavioral states and to identify the various neural and chemical inputs to the brain that bring on or terminate a given behavioral state. This goal is both fascinating and difficult to achieve because the machine being studied is so extraordinarily complicated. As you think about each type of behavioral state discussed in this chapter, ask yourself: What changes in the brain correspond to this state, and how are these changes regulated through means that promote the individual's survival?

2.   Two categories of methods in the physiological study of states   Like all the other chapters in the book, this chapter is about methods and evidence, not just about findings. As you review the specific methods described in the chapter, you will find that they fall into two broad categories. One category involves *intervention* in ongoing physiological processes to see what happens to the behaviorally measured state. What happens to hunger, or the sex drive, or sleep, or an emotion if a particular part of the brain is destroyed or stimulated or if the receptors for a particular hormone or transmitter in the brain are depleted or increased in number? As you review the chapter, notice how often such methods were mentioned. Intervention is a powerful way to identify causal relationships between physiology and behavior. But most intervention procedures are harmful or at least risky to the subject, so they are used primarily in studies of animals other than humans. The intervention approach is approximated, however, in studies of people whose natural physiology has been disrupted through accident or disease. Several studies of that sort were described in the chapter.

The other category involves the *measurement* of physiological processes and the *correlation* of the measures with changes in behavioral state. What natural changes in brain activity (measured by EEG or by neuroimaging) or in hormonal secretions, heart rate, or other physiological variables accompany specific changes in behavioral state? Most measurement procedures are safe and can be used with humans. Notice, as you review the chapter, how often this correlational method was used in the human studies described. This method helps identify reliable relationships but does not, by itself, tell us about cause and effect. The observation that brain waves slow down during sleep, or that skin temperature goes up during anger, or that the amygdala is active during fear tells us about correlations but not necessarily about cause and effect. To test cause-effect hypotheses, researchers seek to manipulate the physiological system and measure the effect on behavior.

Further Reading

Elizabeth Capaldi (1996). *Why we eat what we eat: The psychology of eating.* Washington, DC: American Psychological Association.

Eating is much more than a matter of ingesting an appropriate number of calories each day. To remain healthy, we must consume foods that contain needed vitamins, minerals, and other nutrients and do not contain poisons. This book—with each chapter written by one or more experts in the field—describes the basic learning, sensory, neural, hormonal, social, and cultural mechanisms that influence our food choices.

Simon LeVay (1993). *The sexual brain.* Cambridge, MA: MIT Press.

This brief (161-page) book by a prominent neuroscientist and gay rights activist is essentially a series of essays about the biology of sex and sex differences. In the course of telling about sex, LeVay gently teaches his readers a good deal of biology—about chromosomes, hormones, brain circuits, and evolution as well as behavior.

Donald Pfaff (1999). *Drive: Neurobiological and molecular mechanisms of sexual motivation.* Cambridge, MA: MIT Press.

In elegant prose directed to the intelligent nonspecialist, Pfaff takes sex as a prototypical drive for understanding the general ways by which genes, proteins, neurotransmitters, receptor sites, hormones, neurons, neural systems, and environmental stimuli interact to regulate motivation and behavior in a functionally adaptive manner.

J. Allen Hobson (1995). *Sleep* (paperback edition). New York: Scientific American Library.

Fun to read and beautifully illustrated, this nontechnical book on sleep and dreaming was written by one of the world's foremost experts on these topics.

Joseph LeDoux (1996). *The emotional brain.* New York: Simon and Schuster.

This well-documented book of ideas and evidence about the brain's control of emotionality is written in a lucid, nontechnical style that appeals to the first-year student as well as the more seasoned scholar. The focus is primarily on the control of fear, as that emotion is better understood physiologically than any other, thanks in part to LeDoux's own research.

Looking Ahead

Many issues concerning drives and emotions that are hinted at in this chapter are discussed more fully in chapters to come. The role of social factors in human sexuality is discussed in Chapter 12. The social functions of emotions are discussed in Chapter 14. Human motives and emotions having to do with affiliation, achievement, and self-esteem are themes running through the chapters on social development, social psychology, and personality (Chapters 12 to 15). Emotional problems and treatments for them are the subjects of Chapters 16 and 17.

Now we turn from the slower-moving components of the kaleidoscope of mental life to the fast-moving components. The next chapter is on sensation and perception.

Sensation and Perception

All that we learn we learn through our senses. All that attracts, repels, interests, or bores us does so through our senses. All of the images that we bring to mind when we remember or think are derived from our sensory experiences. Our senses are the conduits that connect our brains and minds to the rest of the world. Nothing is more fundamental to psychology than an understanding of the senses. Chapter 7 is about smell, taste, pain, and hearing; Chapter 8 is about vision. In both chapters the main question is this: How does our nervous system respond to and make sense of the patterns of energy in the physical world?

Chapter 7

Concert in the Egg, Hieronymus Bosch

Smell, Taste, Pain, Hearing, and Psychophysics

What would your mental life be like if you had no senses? What if, from birth, you could not see, hear, touch, taste, smell, or in any other way sense the world around you? You would not be able to react to anything, because reaction requires sensory input. You would not be able to learn anything, because learning begins with sensory input. Would you be able to think? What could you think about with no knowledge gained from the senses? Philosophers, from Aristotle on, have pondered these questions and have usually concluded that without sensation there would be no mental life. It is no wonder that the study of the senses has always been a fundamental part of the science of psychology.

Sensory systems have evolved in all animals for the purpose of guiding their behavior. To survive and reproduce, animals must respond to objects and events in the world in which they live. They must move toward food and mates, for example, and away from predators and other dangers. Sensory systems evolved not to provide full, objective accounts of the world's physical properties but, rather, to provide the specific kinds of information that the animal needs to survive and reproduce. To understand an animal's sensory systems is to understand its ways of life. For instance, frogs' eyes contain "bug detectors," neurons that respond only to small, moving dark spots and that trigger tongue movements in the spot's direction; they also contain color detectors that are ideally tuned to distinguish the hue of the pond from that of the grass and lily pads (Muntz, 1964). Many species of migrating birds have a magnetic sense, sensitive to the earth's magnetic field, that allows the birds to fly north or south even on a cloudy night, when visual cues to direction are not available (Hughes, 1999). Bats, which fly at night, have tiny, almost useless eyes but huge ears. They emit ultrasonic beeps and hear the echoes, which they use to detect objects (such as edible insects) and barriers as they navigate in complete darkness (Griffin, 1986).

This chapter and the next are about sensation and perception. Roughly speaking, *sensation* refers to the basic processes by which sensory organs and the nervous system respond to stimuli in the environment and to the elementary psychological experiences that result from those processes (such as our experience of the bitterness of a taste, loudness of a sound, or redness of a sight). *Perception*, in contrast, refers to the more complex organizing of sensory information within the brain and to the meaningful interpretations extracted from it (such as "This is strong coffee," "My alarm clock is ringing," or "That object is a fire engine"). Thus, the study of perception is more closely tied to the study of thought and memory than is the study of sensation. The distinction is fuzzy, however, because the organizing of stimulus information in ways useful for extracting meaning actually begins during the earliest steps of taking that information in. *Sensation* and *perception* are often used as synonyms.

This chapter begins with a brief overview of basic processes involved in sensation. It continues with sections on smell, taste, pain, and hearing, and it concludes with a discussion of psychophysics, which is a nonphysiological approach to describing the relationships between physical stimuli and sensory experiences. The next chapter deals exclusively with vision, which is by far the most studied of the senses. Whereas the research on smell, taste, and pain provides us with an opportunity to link the senses to basic drives and emotions (discussed in the preceding chapter), the research on vision links more strongly to cognition—to issues of memory and thought that are discussed in the chapters that follow the next one.

OVERVIEW OF SENSORY PROCESSES

Most broadly, the process of sensation can be diagrammed as follows:

physical stimulus ⟶ physiological response ⟶ sensory experience

We have here three classes of events, each of which is entirely different from the others: (1) The *physical stimulus* is the matter or energy of the physical world that impinges on sense organs; (2) the *physiological response* is the pattern of chemical and electrical activity that occurs in sense organs, nerves, and the brain as a result of the stimulus; and (3) the *sensory experience* is the subjective, psychological sensation or perception—the taste, sound, sight, or whatever—experienced by the individual whose sense organs have been stimulated. The sensory experience generally tells us something about the physical stimulus, but it is a very different thing from the physical stimulus. We receive molecules of caffeine on our tongue and we experience a bitter taste. The bitterness is not a chemical property of the caffeine molecules; it lies only in our sensory experience triggered by the molecules. We receive electromagnetic energy of a certain wavelength and we experience the color red. The redness is not a property of the electromagnetic energy that impinges on our eye but is only in our sensory/perceptual experience.

To be studied scientifically, events must be measurable. The first two classes of events in the chain above can be measured by direct physical means, using such tools as light meters, recording electrodes, and neuroimaging machines. The third class cannot be measured directly—there are no meters that can be plugged into the head to read out sensory experiences—but it can be measured indirectly through observations of behavior.

The most useful indices of human sensory experience are verbal answers to carefully worded questions about stimuli presented under controlled conditions. If we present two different sounds to a person, and the person repeatedly says that sound A is louder than sound B, we can conclude that the person experiences the difference between the two on a dimension that he or she has learned to call loudness. If other people make the same judgment, we can conclude that loudness is a sensory experience that is regularly affected, in people, by whatever the physical difference is between sounds A and B. In studies of nonhuman animals or human infants, we can obtain information about sensory experiences through nonverbal means. For example, we might train a pigeon to peck one key when one stimulus is present and a different key when another stimulus is present. Whether we are working with humans or other animals, it is not raw sensory experience that is assessed but the individual's ability to use that experience to guide a behavioral choice.

Another way to represent the three classes of events in the process of sensation is shown in Figure 7.1. Each arrow in the figure represents a different set of questions about sensation and, to some degree, a different domain of research, all of which are considered in this chapter.

1.

How can the process of sensation be depicted as a chain of three different kinds of events, and how can each class of event be measured?

FIGURE **7.1** *Three domains in the study of sensation*

Sensory physiology, sensory physiological psychology, and psychophysics are each concerned with a different pair from among the three classes of events involved in sensation. *Sensory physiology* is concerned with the relationship between the physical stimulus and the physiological response. What effect does the stimulus have on the nervous system, and how does it produce that effect? *Sensory physiological psychology* is concerned with the relationship between the physiological response and the sensory experience. What neurons are active when I experience, for example, a bitter taste or a high-pitched tone? Finally, *psychophysics* is concerned with the relationship between the physical stimulus and the sensory experience, ignoring the physiological response that mediates that relationship. If the physical stimulus is changed in such-and-such a way, how will the sensory experience change? (Adapted from Uttal, 1973.)

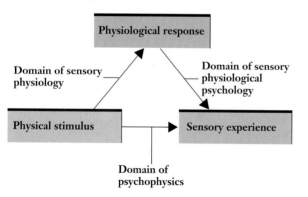

The Basic Anatomy of the Human Senses

Ever since Aristotle, people have spoken of the *five senses*, identifying them as smell, taste, touch, hearing, and vision. Actually, humans have more than five senses, and any attempt to tally them up to an exact number is arbitrary, because what one person thinks of as one sense may be thought of as two or more by another. For example, our skin is sensitive not just to touch but also to temperature and pain, neither of which is included in Aristotle's five senses. Other senses omitted by Aristotle have to do with body position and the body's internal environment. We have a sense of balance mediated by a mechanism in the inner ear, a sense of limb position and movement mediated by receptors in muscles and joints, and senses pertaining to homeostatic needs (such as sensitivity to the inner supply of food molecules, discussed in Chapter 6).

Each sense has its own set of **receptors**, specialized structures that respond to the physical stimulus by producing electrical changes that can initiate neural impulses, and its own set of **sensory neurons**, which carry neural impulses from the receptors to the central nervous system (the structure of sensory neurons was described in Chapter 5). For some senses the receptors are simply the sensitive ends of sensory neurons, and for others they are separate cells that form synapses upon sensory neurons. For some senses the receptors all exist in a specific, localized sensory organ, such as the ear, eye, or nose, and for others they exist in a wide variety of locations. Pain receptors, for example, exist not just in the skin but also in muscles, tendons, joints, and many other places. The stimuli, receptors, and peripheral nerves involved in the most thoroughly studied senses are identified in Table 7.1 (page 236). Regardless of whether they come from one location or many, the neurons for any given sense lead to sensory-specific pathways in the central nervous system. These pathways in turn lead to specific **sensory areas** in the cerebral cortex (see Figure 7.2), which receive and analyze the neural input.

Every sensation that you experience is a product, ultimately, of some pattern of activity within the brain. You see light because your eyes (with their light receptors) are connected to visual areas of your brain, and you hear sound because your ears (with their sound receptors) are connected to auditory areas of your brain. If we could somehow rewire those connections, sending your optic nerves to your auditory brain areas and your auditory nerves to your visual brain areas, you would hear light and see sound. When you bump your head and "see stars," you are activating visual areas of your brain artificially.

2.

What are the common anatomical elements of all our senses?

FIGURE **7.2** *Primary sensory projection areas of the cerebral cortex*

The conscious perception of sensory stimulation requires activation of sensory areas in the cerebral cortex. Shown here are the locations of the primary cortical areas for vision, hearing, somatosensation (which includes touch, temperature sensitivity, and pain), taste, and smell. The primary taste area overlaps with the primary somatosensory area for the tongue and mouth, and it lies buried in the fold between the parietal and temporal lobes. The primary olfactory area lies in a portion of the frontal lobe (the orbitofrontal cortex) that wraps underneath the brain. Secondary sensory processing areas generally surround the primary areas. The secondary areas for vision (discussed in Chapter 8) occupy all of the occipital lobe and much of the parietal and temporal lobes.

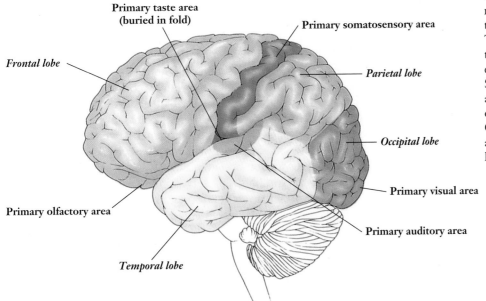

Primary taste area (buried in fold)
Primary somatosensory area
Frontal lobe
Parietal lobe
Occipital lobe
Primary visual area
Primary olfactory area
Primary auditory area
Temporal lobe

TABLE **7.1**   *Stimuli, receptors, and the pathways to the brain for various senses*

Sense	Stimulus	Receptors	Pathway to the brain
Smell	Molecules dissolved in fluid on mucous membranes in the nose	Sensitive ends of olfactory neurons in the olfactory epithelium in the nose	Olfactory nerve (1st cranial nerve)
Taste	Molecules disolved in fluid on the tongue	Taste cells in taste buds on the tongue	Portions of facial, glossopharyngeal, and vagus nerves (7th, 9th, and 10th cranial nerves)
Touch	Pressure on the skin	Sensitive ends of touch neurons in skin	Trigeminal nerve (5th cranial nerve) for touch above the neck; spinal nerves for touch elsewhere
Pain	Wide variety of potentially harmful stimuli	Sensitive ends of pain neurons in skin and other tissues	Trigeminal nerve (5th cranial nerve) for pain above the neck; spinal nerves for pain elsewhere
Hearing	Sound waves	Pressure-sensitive hair cells in cochlea of inner ear	Auditory nerve (8th cranial nerve)
Vision	Light waves	Light-sensitive rods and cones in retina of eye	Optic nerve (2nd cranial nerve)

3.

How do receptors respond to stimulus energy and code information about the amount and kind of energy?

Transduction and Coding: Preserving Information About the Stimulus

The process by which a receptor cell produces an electrical change in response to a physical stimulus is called *transduction*. It is the process by which receptors in the eye respond to light, receptors in the ear respond to sound, receptors on the tongue respond to chemicals dissolved there, and so on. Although the details of transduction are different for different senses, basic similarities exist across the senses. In every case, the membrane of the receptor cell becomes more permeable to certain electrically charged particles, such as sodium or potassium ions, when the appropriate type of stimulus energy acts on the receptor cell. These charged particles then flow through the membrane, either from outside the cell to inside or vice versa, and change the electrical charge across the membrane. This electrical change is called the *receptor potential*, and it is analogous to the postsynaptic potential produced on neurons by the action of synaptic transmitters (described in Chapter 5). Receptor potentials in turn trigger events that lead to the production of action potentials (also described in Chapter 5) in the axons of sensory neurons.

For senses to be useful, they not only must respond to a particular class of stimulus energy (such as sound or light) but must also respond differently to variations in the energy. Every form of energy varies along at least two dimensions, a quantitative and a qualitative dimension. The *quantitative variation* has to do with the amount or intensity of energy present. A sound or light can be weak or strong; molecules stimulating taste or smell can be diluted or highly concentrated. The *qualitative variation* has to do with the precise kind of energy present. Lights of different wavelengths (which we perceive as different colors) are considered to be qualitatively different, as are sounds of different frequencies (which we perceive as different pitches), as are different chemicals (which we perceive as different smells or tastes). In every sense, transduction occurs in such a way that information about the quantity and quality of the stimulus is preserved in the pattern of action potentials sent to the brain. That preservation of information is referred to as *coding*.

Coding of stimulus *quantity* results from the fact that stronger stimuli produce larger receptor potentials, which in turn produce faster rates of action potentials in sensory neurons. The brain interprets a fast rate of action potentials as a strong stimulus and a slow rate as a weak stimulus. Coding of stimulus *quality* occurs because different receptors within any given sensory tissue are tuned to respond best

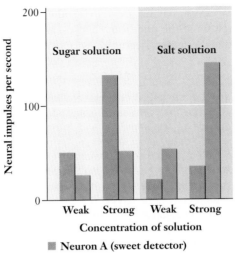

FIGURE **7.3** *Quantitative and qualitative coding of taste*
Shown here are the rates of action potentials in two different taste neurons when a weak or strong solution of sugar or salt is placed on the tongue. Each neuron responds at a faster rate to a strong solution of a given substance than to a weak one (quantitative coding); but neuron A always responds at a faster rate than neuron B when the stimulus is sugar, and the reverse is true when the stimulus is salt (qualitative coding). (Data are hypothetical but are based on findings, such as those of Nowlis & Frank, 1977, with laboratory animals.)

to somewhat different forms of energy. In the eye, for example, three different kinds of receptor cells, each most sensitive to a different range of wavelengths of light, provide the basis for color vision. In the ear, different receptors are most sensitive to different sound frequencies. And in the nose and mouth, different receptors are most sensitive to different molecules. Thus, in general, qualitative variations are coded as different *ratios* of activity in sensory neurons coming from different sets of receptors. For an illustration of qualitative and quantitative coding for the sense of taste, see Figure 7.3.

Sensory Adaptation: Responding to Change More Than to Steady States

Our senses are designed to alert us to *changes* in our sensory environment and to be relatively oblivious to steady states. When you first put on your wristwatch, you feel the pressure on your skin, but later you don't. When you first enter a well-lit room from the dark, the room seems very bright, but later not so bright. When you first wade into a lake, the water may seem terribly cold, but later only slightly cool. When you first enter a chemistry lab, the odor may seem overwhelming, but later you hardly notice it. The change in sensitivity that occurs when a sensory system is either stimulated or not stimulated for a length of time is called ***sensory adaptation***. In general, in the absence of stimulation a sensory system becomes temporarily more sensitive (it will respond to weaker stimuli), and in the presence of stimulation it becomes temporarily less sensitive (it requires stronger stimuli to produce a response).

In many cases, sensory adaptation is mediated by the receptor cells themselves. If a stimulus remains for a period of time, the receptor potential and rate of action potentials are at first great, but over time they are much reduced, resulting in reduced sensation. In other cases, however, adaptation is mediated at least partly by changes farther inward, in the central nervous system. You can prove this yourself for the sense of smell (Matlin & Foley, 1997). If you place an odorous substance (such as an open bottle of nail polish remover or cologne) on a desk in front of you, with one nostril plugged, you will adapt to it within about 5 minutes (it won't smell as strong). Then, if you unplug that nostril and quickly plug the other, you will find that you are still partly (but not completely) adapted to the odor, even though it is now acting on receptors in the other nostril, different from those that it was acting on before. Thus, adaptation for smell must be due in part to changes in neurons in the brain that receive input from both nostrils.

4.

What is the value of sensory adaptation? How can you demonstrate that adaptation can occur in neurons in the brain, not just in receptors?

Sabine Weiss / Photo Researchers

It's a nice place to work, but I wouldn't want to visit

Can you imagine the pungent smell you would experience if you walked into this cave full of Roquefort cheese? Yet, as suggested by this worker's equable expression, one adapts after a while. In general, our senses are designed to register changes in the environment, not steady states.

Now, having previewed some of the general characteristics of the sensory systems and the questions that researchers try to answer, let us look in more detail at specific senses, beginning with smell and taste.

SECTION SUMMARY

To study sensation fully, researchers must distinguish among, and be able to measure, three distinct classes of events: the physical stimulus, the physiological (neural) response to the stimulus, and the resultant psychological sensory/perceptual experience. Anatomically, a unique set of receptors, sensory neurons, and brain areas is devoted to each sensory modality (such as vision, hearing, or taste). The receptor cells transduce the energy of the physical stimulus into patterns of neural responses that preserve (in coded form) information that was in the stimulus. In general, variations in the quantity (intensity or amount) of a stimulus are coded as variations in the rate of action potentials in a given set of neurons, and variations in the quality (type) of stimulus are coded as variations in the ratios of activity across sets of neurons activated by different sets of receptors. Most sensory systems become less sensitive during prolonged stimulation by the same type of stimulus and more sensitive after a period in which stimulation is absent. These processes of adaptation leave the individual highly responsive to changes in stimuli and relatively oblivious to steady states.

THE CHEMICAL SENSES

Smell and taste are called chemical senses because the environmental stimuli for them are chemical molecules. The stimuli for smell are molecules that evaporate into the air and are taken with air into the nose. The stimuli for taste are molecules that become dissolved in the fluid on the tongue and other parts of the mouth when taken in as food. The chemical senses are first and foremost systems for warning and attraction. They play on our drives and emotions more than on our intellects. Think of the effects produced by a valentine gift of chocolates, perfume, or fresh roses; by the aroma and taste of your favorite meal; or by the stench of feces or rotting meat.

Smell

The human sense of smell is underappreciated. People often think of it as highly developed in dogs and other animals, but as an almost useless evolutionary vestige in people. In fact, although our sense of smell is much less sensitive than that of many other animals, it is still remarkably sensitive and useful. We can smell smoke at concentrations well below that needed to trigger even the most sensitive of household smoke detectors. We can distinguish among roughly 10,000 different chemicals by their smell (Axel, 1995). Blind people regularly identify other individuals by each person's unique odor, and sighted people can do that too when they try. Much, if not most, of what we call the flavor of foods is actually smell, not taste.

Anatomy and Physiology of Smell

The basic layout of the olfactory (smell) system is illustrated in Figure 7.4. The *olfactory epithelium*, in the nasal cavity, contains the sensitive ends of roughly 10 million olfactory sensory neurons. Each sensitive end contains 5 to 20 hairlike *cilia*, and each cilium contains many *receptor sites*, which are large protein molecules woven into the cell membrane that are capable of binding molecules of specific odorants (odorous substances). The binding of a molecule to a receptor site changes the structure of the cell membrane, which results in an electrical charge across the membrane that triggers action potentials in the neuron's axon. The

5.

How do transduction, qualitative coding, and quantitative coding occur for the sense of smell?

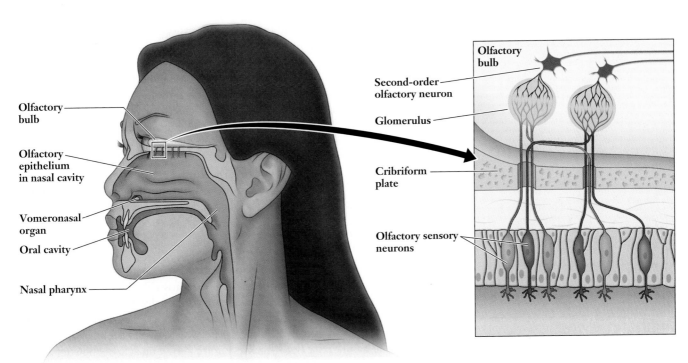

FIGURE 7.4 *The anatomy of smell*
Odorants enter the nose through the nostrils and through the nasal pharynx that links the nose to the mouth. Molecules of odorants become dissolved in the fluid coating the olfactory epithelium, where they bind to specific binding sites on the cilia of olfactory sensory neurons. The axons of the sensory neurons pass through the cribriform plate that separates the nose from the brain, and they terminate in a glomerulus in the olfactory bulb. Different types of olfactory sensory neurons differ in the nature of their binding sites, and sensory neurons of a given type send their axons to the same glomerulus. There is at least one glomerulus (and possibly two or three) for each different type of olfactory sensory neuron (Axel, 1995; Buck, 2000a). The human olfactory epithelium contains roughly 10 million receptor cells, of roughly 1000 different types. From each glomerulus, second-order olfactory neurons carry messages to the hypothalamus, limbic system, and orbitofrontal cortex. The drawing also shows the location of the vomeronasal organ, which may or may not be functional in humans but which in other mammals is specialized for sensing pheromones.

greater the number of binding sites activated by odorous molecules, the greater is the rate of action potentials triggered in the axon. The whole process is similar to that of synaptic transmission, described in Chapter 5, but here the effective molecules are odorants brought by air into the nose rather than transmitters released by other neurons.

Recent research has shown that approximately 1000 different types of receptor sites, each characterized by a different protein molecule, exist within the human nose and that all the receptor sites on any given olfactory sensory neuron are of the same type (Buck, 2000b). Stated differently, the olfactory nerve contains roughly 1000 different types of sensory neurons, each of which has a distinct type of binding site within the olfactory epithelium. Any given type of binding site can bind more than one odorant, but any given odorant binds more readily to some types than to others. Thus, each type of olfactory neurons differs from the other types in its degree of sensitivity to particular odorants.

The axons of the olfactory sensory neurons pass through a thin, porous bone (called the cribriform plate) into the *olfactory bulb* of the brain, where they form synapses upon other neurons in structures called *glomeruli* (see Figure 7.4). The pattern of these connections is remarkably orderly (Buck, 2000b). Each glomerulus in the olfactory bulb receives input from several thousand olfactory sensory neurons, but all these neurons are of the same type. For each of the 1000 different types of olfactory sensory neurons, there is a different receiving glomerulus in the olfactory bulb.

From this work, researchers have inferred the process by which qualitative and quantitative coding occurs in the sense of smell. Each odorant that we can distinguish is apparently characterized by its ability to produce a unique pattern of activity in the glomeruli of the olfactory bulb. Thus, odorant A might trigger a lot of activity in one specific glomerulus, a moderate amount in several other glomeruli, and a little in another set of glomeruli. The greater the amount of odorant A, the greater would be the total amount of activity triggered in each of the glomeruli that it affects, but the ratio of activity across glomeruli would be the same. Thus, the ratio indicates type of odorant (quality), and the total amount of activity indicates amount of odorant (quantity).

The glomeruli in turn send output to various other parts of the brain. Most of this output goes to structures in the limbic system and the hypothalamus, which (as discussed in Chapters 5 and 6) are involved in basic drives and emotions. These connections, presumably, help account for the strong and often unconscious effects that smell can have on our motivational and emotional states. The connections from the olfactory bulb to the limbic system are so strong, in fact, that the limbic system was at one time often referred to as the *rhinencephalon*, which literally means "nose brain." Some of the output from the olfactory bulbs, however, goes eventually to a portion of the neocortex located on the underside of the frontal lobe (where the frontal lobe wraps down underneath the rest of the brain), called the *orbitofrontal cortex*. The orbitofrontal cortex is crucial for the ability to make fine distinctions among odors and to use those distinctions consciously to control behavior (Buck, 2000b; Tanabe & others, 1975).

Smell as a Component of Flavor

6.

How do we smell foods that are already in our mouths, and what evidence indicates that smell contributes greatly to flavor?

Odorants can reach the olfactory epithelium through two different routes. The route that everyone knows about is through the nostrils. That's the route that allows you to smell smoke, roses, skunks, and other odor sources that are outside your mouth. The other route allows you to smell foods that have already entered your mouth. An opening called the *nasal pharynx* connects the back of the mouth cavity with the nasal cavity (look back at Figure 7.4). The acts of chewing and swallowing push air from the mouth up into the nose—air that carries volatile molecules of whatever you are eating. What most people call taste—and what is properly called *flavor*—consists not just of true taste (from taste receptors in the mouth) but also of smell that has been triggered through this mouth-to-nose, backdoor route. Remarkably, you *experience* this sensation as coming from the mouth, where the food exists, and as indistinguishable from taste, even though it actually comes from the olfactory epithelium (Bartoshuk & Beauchamp, 1994).

If you pinch your nostrils shut, you cut off both routes to the olfactory epithelium. If air can't flow out through the nostrils, it can't stream into the nasal cavity from the mouth. Experiments have shown that people's ability to identify foods and drinks by flavor declines markedly when the nostrils are shut. In one such experiment, 21 different beverages and liquefied foods were dripped onto the tongues of people whose nostrils were either open or closed (Mozel & others, 1969). All the substances were identified by more subjects with nostrils open than with nostrils closed, and for most substances the difference was dramatic. Cherry, apricot, cranberry, grape, pineapple, root beer, coffee, chocolate, and garlic were among the flavors that were identified by most of the subjects with nostrils open and by none or almost none with nostrils closed. You can easily demonstrate the role of smell in your own ability to identify flavors, using jelly beans as stimuli (suggested by Schiffman, 1996). With eyes closed, chew one jelly bean at a time and try to identify its flavor. You will probably find this task to be relatively easy as long as you keep your nostrils open (though you may need a little practice at first, with eyes open, relating the flavor to the color). Then try the same task with your nostrils pinched shut. You will most likely find that now all the jelly beans taste the same; all you can taste is the sugar.

As we get older, our sense of smell declines. By age 65 about 25 percent of people have serious olfactory impairment, and by age 80 the number is 75 percent (Doty & others, 1984). Many elderly people complain of loss in ability to taste foods, but tests typically show that their real loss is not taste but smell (Bartoshuk & Beauchamp, 1994). What people miss most when they lose their sense of smell is the flavors of foods, but what may be more serious is the increased danger they are in when they cannot smell smoke or gas in the air they are breathing. A high proportion of people who die from asphyxiation are elderly people who have lost much or all of their olfactory ability.

Smell as a Mode of Communication: Pheromones

A *pheromone* is a chemical that is released by an animal and that acts on other members of the species to promote some specific behavioral or physiological response. Some of the most dramatic examples occur in insects. For instance, sexually receptive female cabbage moths secrete a pheromone that attracts male cabbage moths from as far as several miles away (Lerner & others, 1990). Most species of mammals also produce pheromones, which serve such functions as sexual attraction, territorial marking (discussed in Chapter 3), and regulation of hormone production (Hughes, 1999). Most species of mammals have in their nasal cavity a structure called the *vomeronasal organ*, which contains receptor cells specialized for responding to pheromones. Whereas the main olfactory epithelium is designed to distinguish somewhat imprecisely among many thousands of different odorants, the vomeronasal organ appears to be designed for very precise recognition of, and exquisite sensitivity to, a small number of specific substances, the species' pheromones (Buck, 2000a).

Do humans communicate by pheromones? We do have the structures that would make such communication possible. Like other mammals, we have specialized glands in the skin that secrete odorous substances. Such glands are especially concentrated in areas of the body where our species has retained hair—such as in the axillary region (armpits) and genital region (see Figure 7.5). One theory is that the function of hair in these locations is to hold on to the secretions and to provide a large surface area from which they can evaporate, so as to increase their effectiveness as odorants (Stoddart, 1990). Some of the substances secreted by these glands are steroid molecules that resemble substances known to serve as pheromones in other mammals. We also have a vomeronasal organ (as shown in Figure 7.4, page 239), but the evidence to date is inconclusive as to whether it functions in our species or is vestigial (McClintock, 2000).

Motivated partly by the perfume and cologne industry, most human pheromone research has centered on whether or not we produce sex-attractant pheromones. In many experiments, men and women have been exposed to various secretions taken from the other sex and have rated the attractiveness of the odor or changes in their own mood. To date, such experiments have failed to yield convincing evidence that we do produce such pheromones (Hughes, 1999; McClintock, 2000). Certainly some people find some of the odorous substances secreted by other people to be pleasant, but individual differences are great and no specific

7.

What anatomical characteristics of our species are consistent with the possibility that we produce and respond to pheromones? What evidence and logic suggest that we do not produce sex-attractant pheromones?

Scala / Art Resource

FIGURE **7.5** *Locations of maximal scent production by humans*
In humans, specialized scent-producing glands (apocrine glands) are concentrated most highly in the axillary region (underarms) and also exist in high concentrations in the genital area, the alveolar area (around the nipples), the navel area, on the top of the head, and on the forehead and cheeks (Stoddart, 1990), as shown by the added circles. (The statue here is Michelangelo's *Aurora*, from the tomb of Lorenzo de Medici, in Florence.)

human secretion has been found to be consistently attractive to members of the opposite sex. Perhaps that should not be surprising. Sex-attractant pheromones are valuable for animals that mate only at certain times of the year or only when the female is ovulating, as a means of synchronizing the sex drives of males and females to maximize the chance of conception. As discussed in Chapter 6, humans have taken a different evolutionary route, such that sexual drive and behavior are not tied to a season, cycle, or variable physiological state. For that reason, perhaps, there is little or no need for us to advertise by scent our readiness to mate.

The most solid evidence to date for pheromones in our species concerns an effect not on sex drive but on women's menstrual cycles. In a now-classic study, conducted when she was still an undergraduate at Wellesley College, Martha McClintock (1971) found that college women who lived together and spent much time together tended to have synchronized menstrual cycles. Within 3 months after the start of the school year, women who spent a great deal of time together typically began to ovulate and menstruate at nearly the same time as one another. McClintock suggested that this effect might be mediated by chemical communication, and research since then has confirmed that hypothesis.

In several experiments, secretions were collected daily from "donor women," who agreed to wear cotton pads in their underarms, and the secretions were then wiped onto the upper lips, under the noses, of "recipient women," who did not know the donor women. Over time, the recipients' menstrual cycles tended to shift to be synchronous with those of the donors whose scents they were exposed to (Preti & others, 1986; Russell & others, 1980). Using a variation of this procedure, Kathleen Stern and McClintock (1998) have found evidence that at least two different chemicals, secreted at different times of the cycle, are involved in producing this effect. One substance tends to lengthen another woman's cycle, and the other tends to shorten it. At present it is not known what the active chemicals are or whether they act on receptors in the main olfactory epithelium or in the vomeronasal organ. Interestingly, tests revealed that the recipients could not consciously smell the difference between cotton pads that contained chemicals from a donor and those that contained only the alcohol solvent that was present in all the pads. This result is consistent with other evidence that pheromones can influence physiology and behavior through means that do not involve conscious detection (McClintock, 2000). Pathways from receptor cells in the nose to brain areas in the hypothalamus that control hormone cycles need not involve brain areas in the cerebral cortex that are crucial for consciousness.

Discriminating Among Individuals by Smell

As dog owners well know, dogs greet and recognize others of their kind (and sometimes of our kind too) by smell. We humans living in a somewhat odor-phobic culture may not often admit it, but we too can identify individuals of our species by smell. In a typical experiment, one set of subjects wear initially clean T-shirts for a day without washing or using deodorants or perfumes, and then other subjects are asked to identify by smell alone which shirt had been worn by whom. Such experiments have revealed that parents can tell which of their children wore the shirt, children can tell which of their siblings wore it, and people generally can distinguish between the odors of two strangers (Porter, 1991; Wallace, 1977).

Among some mammals, notably goats and sheep, odor recognition is a crucial part of the bond between mother and young (Kendrick & others, 1992). Might smell play a role in human mother-infant bonding? In one study conducted in a hospital maternity ward, 90 percent of mothers who had been exposed to their newborn baby for just 10 to 60 minutes after birth were able to identify by smell alone which of several undershirts had been worn by their own baby (Kaitz & others, 1987). In another study, breast-fed babies as young as 6 days old turned their heads reliably toward a cotton pad that their own mother had worn against her

8.

What evidence suggests that women influence other women's menstrual cycles through the production of pheromones?

9.

What is the evidence that people can identify other individuals by odor, that mothers can identify the smell of their newborns very soon after birth, and that nursing babies can identify and prefer their mothers' smell?

breast, when given a choice between that and an identical-looking pad that had been worn against the breast of another lactating woman (Macfarlane, 1975). Such evidence suggests that odor may very well figure into the complex of stimuli that are involved in the attachment between infants and their caregivers, but so far no evidence suggests that odor is in any way critical to such attachment.

In mice, odor has been shown to play a role in mating choices. Mice, like dogs and humans, can identify other individuals of their species by odor, and, remarkably, they prefer to mate with opposite-sex mice whose smell is *most different* from their own (Potts & others, 1991; Yamazaki & others, 1988). Why this preference? Researchers have found that the individual differences in smell that determine these mating preferences result from a set of about 50 highly variable genes (genes with many different alleles) referred to collectively as the *major histocompatibility complex (MHC)* (Yamazaki & others, 1994). The same genes also determine the precise nature of the cells used by the immune system to reject foreign substances and kill disease-producing bacteria and viruses. Thus, by choosing mates who smell most different from themselves, mice choose mates who (a) are not likely to be close relatives of themselves and (b) will add much new genetic variation to the mix of disease-fighting cells that develop in the offspring. As explained in Chapter 3, such genetic variety increases the chance that the offspring will survive.

The MHC also exists in human beings, and in us too this set of genes apparently contributes greatly to individual differences in odor (Bartoshuk & Beauchamp, 1994). The advantages of mating with someone who has a very different MHC presumably exist in humans as much as in mice. So do humans, to any degree at all, prefer sexual mates who smell most different from themselves and differ most in MHC? At present, the answer to that question is not known, but research by Claus Wedekind and his colleagues suggests that it might be yes (Wedekind & Füri, 1997; Wedekind & others, 1995). These researchers asked young men and women to rate the "pleasantness" (and in one study the "sexiness") of the odors of T-shirts that had been worn by a set of other young men and women. All the subjects were assessed biochemically for differences in their MHCs. The result was that any given donor's odor was, on average, rated as more pleasant by raters who differed from that person in MHC than by raters who were similar to that person in MHC. It remains to be seen whether this odor preference affects people's actual mating choices, either in our culture (where we tend to hide our odors) or any other.

Taste

Some insects have taste receptors on their feet, which allow them to taste what they are walking on. Fish have taste receptors not just in their mouths but all over their bodies (Hara, 1994). They can taste their prey before they see it, and they use taste to help them track it down. For us and other mammals, taste has a more limited but still important function. Our taste receptors exist only in our mouth, and their function is to help us decide whether a particular substance is good or bad to eat.

Anatomy and Physiology of Taste

Taste receptor cells exist in spherical structures called *taste buds*. Each bud contains between 50 and 150 taste receptor cells, arranged something like segments in an orange (see Figure 7.6 on page 244). Most people have between 2000 and 10,000 taste buds, about two-thirds of which are on the tongue and the rest of which are on the roof of the mouth and in the opening of the throat (Herness & Gilbertson, 1999).

For many years Western scientists believed that human taste receptors (and those of other mammals) were of just four types—*sweet, salt, sour,* and *bitter*—each named after the taste sensation that results when that type is activated. Every taste, it was believed, could be understood as a combination of those four primary tastes.

10.

From an evolutionary perspective, why might mice prefer to mate with others that smell most different from themselves, and what evidence suggests that the same might be true of humans?

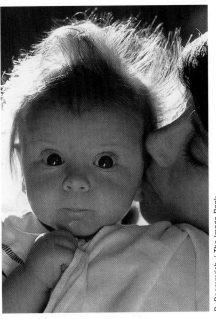

B. Daemmrich / The Image Bank

A sweet aroma
Every human being has a unique, identifiable odor.

11.

What are the five primary tastes, and what is known about the transduction mechanism for each?

FIGURE **7.6** *A taste bud*

Taste buds are found in the surface tissue of the tongue and elsewhere in the mouth. Each one contains 50 to 150 taste receptor cells. From the tip of each cell, hairlike extensions make contact with the fluid lining the tongue or other epithelial tissue. These extensions contain the binding sites and channels where substances to be tasted exert their effects on the taste cells. The receptor cells produce action potentials in response to such input and, in turn, induce action potentials in taste sensory neurons through synaptic transmission (Herness & Gilbertson, 1999).

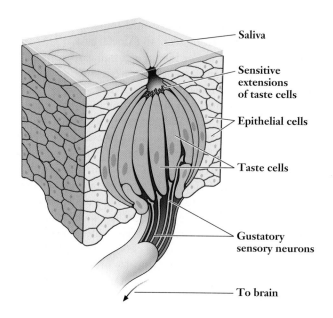

Saliva

Sensitive extensions of taste cells

Epithelial cells

Taste cells

Gustatory sensory neurons

To brain

Surface of the tongue

The red disklike structures are fungiform papillae. Most taste buds are located within the walls of these papillae with their sensitive ends oriented toward the surrounding saliva-filled trough. The magnification is about 100X.

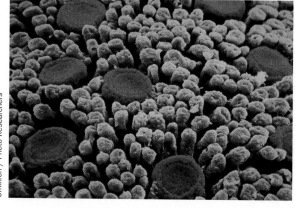

Omikron / Photo Researchers

Japanese scientists, in contrast, generally spoke of *five* primary tastes—the four just mentioned plus *umami*, which, loosely translated, means "savory" or "delicious" (Kurihara & Kashiwayanagi, 1998). Umami, they held, is not experienced subjectively as similar to any combination of the other primaries and is a major contributor to the taste of many natural foods, especially those that are high in protein, such as meats, fish, and cheese. Umami is also the taste produced by monosodium glutamate (MSG), a substance frequently used as a flavor enhancer in Asian cuisine. Taste researchers have recently found strong evidence of separate receptor cells and brain areas responsive to MSG, and now even Western taste specialists write of five rather than four primary tastes and types of taste receptors (Chaudhari & others, 2000; Rolls & others, 1998).

To be tasted, a chemical substance must first dissolve in saliva and come into contact with the sensitive ends of appropriate taste receptor cells, where it triggers electrical changes that result in action potentials first in the taste receptor cell and then, by synaptic transmission, in sensory neurons that run to the brain (see Figure 7.6). The specifics of the transduction mechanism vary from one type of taste receptor cell to another (Bartoshuk & Beauchamp, 1994; Herness & Gilbertson, 1999). *Salt receptor cells* respond most strongly to sodium chloride (NaCl) and lithium chloride (LiCl). These substances break up into ions in solution, and the positively charged ions (Na$^+$ or Li$^+$) flow through channels into the salt receptor cell, altering the electrical charge across the membrane in a manner that triggers action potentials. *Sour receptor cells* respond most strongly to acids, which release hydrogen ions (H$^+$) in solution. Hydrogen ions flow through special channels in the sour receptor cell, altering the charge and triggering action potentials.

Unlike salt and sour tastes, bitter taste is stimulated by a large set of chemically diverse substances. *Bitter receptor cells* have on their surfaces a large number of binding sites, which consist of specialized protein molecules that bind certain molecules that come into contact with them. In all, there are between 50 and 80 different types of such sites, each specialized for binding one or more substances. Each bitter receptor cell apparently contains all these binding sites and is therefore capable of responding to the whole set of substances that we taste as bitter (Adler & others, 2000; Dulac, 2000). The binding of any substance to these sites triggers a chemical change in the cell that eventuates in action potentials. *Sweet receptor cells* appear to operate in a manner similar to that for bitter receptors, though the details are less well understood. A number of chemically diverse substances (not just sugars) taste sweet, and sweet receptors are believed to have different binding sites for these different substances (Herness & Gilbertson, 1999). Little is known about *umami receptor cells*, except that they appear to respond maximally to *glutamate*, an amino acid present in monosodium glutamate and in many natural foods (Chaudhari & others, 2000).

It was once believed (primarily by textbook writers and their readers) that the different types of taste receptors are concentrated in different parts of the tongue, with sweet tasted in one place, bitter in another, and so on. In fact, taste researchers have long known that the different types of receptors are quite evenly distributed over the whole tongue (Bartoshuk & Beauchamp, 1994). Spatial separation of different tastes does occur in the brain, however. The neural connection from the receptors to the brain is such that the different types of receptors ultimately stimulate different portions of the primary taste area of the cerebral cortex. This cortical area, which lies in a fold between the temporal and parietal lobes, is apparently essential for the conscious perception of tastes. People with extensive damage here lose their experience of taste (Pritchard, 1991), and artificial stimulation here produces experiences of taste in the absence of any taste stimuli on the tongue (Penfield & Faulk, 1955).

Jeff Greenberg / The Image Works

Umami

The savory umami taste of Chinese food is often enhanced by monosodium glutamate. Umami is believed to be one of the five primary tastes.

An Evolutionary Account of Taste Quality: The Bitter Rejection Response

The purpose of taste is to motivate us to eat some substances and avoid eating others. Generally speaking, salty, sweet, and umami are pleasant tastes, which, in the course of evolution, became attached to substances that are good for us (or at least were good for our evolutionary ancestors). A certain amount of salt intake is needed to maintain a proper salt balance in bodily fluids. Sugars, in fruits and other natural foodstuffs, were a valuable source of energy to our evolutionary ancestors. Protein (a source of umami flavor) is essential for building and restoring tissues.

Still speaking generally, sour and bitter are unpleasant experiences, which evolution has attached to certain substances that are bad for us. Bacterial decay produces acidic compounds. Since decaying substances can cause disease when eaten, natural selection produced a taste system that experiences most acids as unpleasant (sour). Many plants and some insects and animals, as part of their own evolution, have concentrated toxic substances into their tissues—substances that can harm or kill animals that eat them. As a consequence, our ancestors evolved a taste system that experiences most of those toxic substances as unpleasant (bitter).

To pursue this line of thinking further, let's take the example of the relationship between bitter taste and poisons. In nature, a wide variety of chemical substances that might be taken in by mouth are poisonous. Many of these are very different from one another; they have entirely different molecular structures and potential chemical actions. The only thing they have in common is that they are all capable, in one way or another, of damaging an animal that eats them. Imagine some early animal species that eats plants, some of which contain substance X, a poison that kills by interfering with the animal's respiratory system. Any mutations affecting

12.

From an evolutionary perspective, (a) why do so many chemically diverse substances taste bitter; (b) why are carnivores more sensitive to bitter taste than are herbivores; and (c) why does bitter sensitivity increase in women at pregnancy?

the taste system of this animal in such a way as to lead it to dislike the taste of X would promote the animal's survival, and those new genes would multiply from generation to generation.

Now imagine a species that does experience substance X as having a negative, bitter taste. Members of this species are successfully avoiding X but are still eating plants that contain another poison, Y, which kills animals by paralyzing the muscular system. Because Y is an entirely different compound from X, it does not attach to the X receptors on the taste cells that trigger bitterness, so the animals have no sensory grounds for avoiding it. Now imagine a single mutation, which results in a new variety of receptor protein on the surface of bitter taste cells, a protein that can bind molecules of Y. The animal with this mutation would experience the same bitter sensation upon eating leaves containing Y as it experiences when eating leaves containing X, and it would avoid both of them. It would be more likely to survive and send progeny into the next generation than would other members of the species, and many of those progeny would inherit the new gene. Extending this scenario, you can imagine how natural selection might have produced modern mammals that have bitter taste cells containing 50 to 80 different types of receptor proteins, able collectively to bind molecules of most of the toxic substances found in plants and other potential foods. We can't go back and prove with certainty that this is how the present state of affairs relating to bitter taste came about, but this account helps make sense of the facts of bitter taste. Various toxic substances all taste bitter not because of any physical similarity among them but because different receptor sites on bitter receptor cells are able to bind them.

This evolutionary account also helps us make sense of some differences among species in their sensitivity to bitter taste. Carnivores (exclusive meat eaters) are most sensitive to bitter taste, omnivores (meat and plant eaters) are next most sensitive, and herbivores (exclusive plant eaters) are least sensitive (see Figure 7.7). At first thought, this order may seem the opposite of what an evolutionary perspective would lead us to expect. Plant tissues much more often contain poisons than do animal tissues, so why wouldn't evolution have made herbivores most sensitive to bitter and carnivores least sensitive? John Glendinning (1994) has suggested a quite plausible answer. Plants protect themselves from being eaten not just by concentrating truly poisonous substances but also by concentrating non-poisonous substances that are chemically similar to poisons and that therefore bind to receptors on bitter taste cells and trigger the animal's bitter rejection response. Plants have been so successful in doing this that a herbivorous animal that avoided all bitter tastes would find little or nothing to eat. In response, herbivores have evolved chemical and physiological defenses against the most common toxins in plants, so they can tolerate a greater amount of them in their diets without ill effect (Glendinning, 1994), and, coupled with that, have evolved a taste system that is less sensitive than that of other mammals to bitter tastes.

Extending the argument, carnivores are most sensitive to bitter because they can afford to be. So few of their potential foods taste bitter that they can afford to reject all bitter substances, even though most of them might not be truly poisonous. Omnivores, such as rats and humans, lie in between. In life little is certain; evolution merely leads to better ways of hedging one's bets, and when it comes to a decision to eat or avoid possibly poisonous foods, the odds are stacked somewhat differently for carnivores, omnivores, and herbivores.

Among humans, women are generally more sensitive to bitter taste than are men, and women become still more so during the first 3 months of pregnancy (Duffy & Bartoshuk, 1996). A possible reason is found in evidence that the human fetus is highly subject to damage by poisons, especially during the first 3 months of its development (Profet, 1992). With the stakes being survival of genes, the value of avoiding even mild toxins increases during pregnancy, and so does sensitivity to bitter taste.

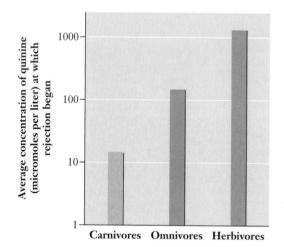

FIGURE **7.7** *Acceptance of a bitter-tasting substance by carnivores, omnivores, and herbivores*
The graph is based on many experiments in which mammals, representing 30 different species, were tested to determine the highest concentration of quinine in water that they would tolerate (as demonstrated by their willingness to drink it at a certain minimal rate in a test in which they could drink either that or plain water). Quinine is a standard stimulus used to study bitter taste. Shown here are the averages for the carnivorous (meat-eating), omnivorous (meat- and plant-eating), and herbivorous (plant-eating) species that were tested. (Based on data in Glendinning, 1994.)

We and other animals also refine our dietary bets through learning (as discussed in Chapter 4). The bitter rejection response is not absolute; it is moldable in ways that make evolutionary sense. If a young animal detects that others of its species regularly eat a certain food and don't get sick or die, then that young animal would probably do well to eat it too, even if it tastes bitter. Young children everywhere appear to dislike greens such as Brussels sprouts and spinach because of their bitter taste, but in societies where adults regularly eat these highly nutritious foods, most children eventually learn to like them.

SECTION SUMMARY

The human olfactory epithelium contains the sensitive endings of roughly 1000 types of olfactory neurons. Each type differs from the others in its relative sensitivity to different odorous chemicals, and each type sends its output to a different location in the brain's olfactory bulb. Odorants can reach the olfactory epithelium either through the nostrils or through an opening at the back of the mouth. The latter route permits smell to contribute to the flavors of foods.

Many animals communicate by way of odorous secretions called pheromones. The best evidence for human pheromones comes from studies showing that the sense of smell is involved in the synchronization of menstrual cycles among women who spend much time together.

People, like other animals, can identify each other by smell. Mice prefer to mate with others who smell most different from themselves, and this preference may provide a basis for ensuring genetic diversity in offspring. There is some evidence that people too may be attracted to body smells that are most different from their own.

In contrast to the 1000 types of olfactory receptors, there appear to be only five types of taste receptors, responsible, respectively, for the sensations of sweet, salt, sour, bitter, and umami. Taste (along with smell) motivates us to eat some substances and avoid eating others. An evolutionary account explains why many chemically diverse poisons all taste bitter, why herbivores are less sensitive to bitter taste than are carnivores, and why women's sensitivity to bitter taste is heightened during the first 3 months of pregnancy.

PAIN

Pain is one of the somatosenses (introduced in Chapter 5). That is, like touch, temperature sensitivity, and proprioception (the sense of body position), pain is a sense that can originate from multiple places throughout the body rather than just from specialized sensory organs in the head. (Recall that *soma* means "body.") Pain receptors exist over the whole surface of the skin and in many other bodily tissues.

Pain is a "body" sense in another way, too. When you see, hear, smell, taste, or touch something, you experience the sensation as coming from outside yourself (from the thing you are seeing, hearing, smelling, tasting, or touching); but when you feel pain, you experience it as coming from your own body. If you cut yourself with a knife, your feeling of pain is a sense not of the knife (that comes from your vision and touch) but of your own injured bodily state. Pain is not only a sense but also a drive. A person in pain is motivated both to reduce the pain and to avoid future behaviors like the one that produced it (such as careless handling of knives). In psychology, pain is by far the most studied of the somatosenses (Craig & Rollman, 1999). That, no doubt, is largely due to the dramatic ways by which pain can both affect and be affected by one's other psychological experiences.

The value of pain—the reason, presumably, that it came about in evolution—is dramatically illustrated by those rare, unlucky people who are born with a genetic disorder that makes them insensitive to it (Brand & Yancey, 1993). They can experience all other sensations, including touch and temperature, and they can report increasing intensities of those feelings, but pain, with its warning and motivating

13.

In what ways is pain a "body" sense, and what is its value?

qualities, is missing. Children with this disorder are not motivated to remove their hands from a hot stove, or to refrain from chewing on their tongues as they eat, or to change their body positions (as most of us do from minute to minute) to relieve the strain on muscles and joints. Even if they are constantly watched throughout childhood, and even if they learn intellectually to avoid certain activities, people with this disorder usually die young from the tissue deterioration and infections that result from their wounds.

Neural Pathways for Pain

Anatomically, pain is closely related to the other somatosenses, such as touch and temperature sensitivity. For all these senses, the receptors are the sensory neurons themselves, which have receptive endings in the skin and long axons that enter the central nervous system by way of a spinal nerve or (in the case of neurons coming from the head) a cranial nerve. Pain neurons are thinner than other neurons from the skin, and their sensitive terminals, called **free nerve endings**, are not encased in special capsules, or end organs, as are the endings of touch and temperature receptors (see Figure 7.8). Free nerve endings can be found in all body tissues from which pain is sensed (Lynn & Perl, 1996)—not just the skin but also the pulp of the teeth (from which comes the dreaded toothache), muscles (giving us the pain of cramps and muscle aches), membranes around bones and joints (from which we experience arthritis), and various visceral organs (giving us stomachaches and other inner pains).

FIGURE **7.8**
Pain receptors in the skin
The pain receptors are the sensitive endings of sensory neurons, called *free nerve endings*. The slower, second wave of pain is carried by the very thin C fibers, and the faster, first wave is carried by the thicker A-delta fibers. The sense of touch is carried by still thicker (and faster) A fibers, whose endings are not "free" but, rather, are surrounded by a capsule, or end organ, that modifies the pressure stimulus.

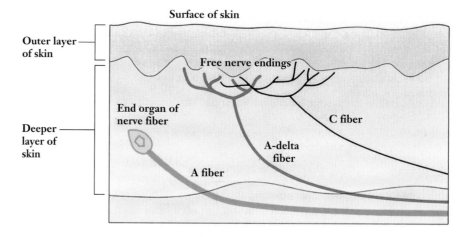

14.

What is the anatomical basis for a distinction between first and second pain?

Sensory Neurons for Two Waves of Pain

Pain sensory neurons are of two general types—very thin, unmyelinated, slow-conducting neurons called *C fibers* and slightly thicker, myelinated, faster-conducting neurons called *A-delta fibers* (again see Figure 7.8). Some A-delta fibers are specialized to respond to strong pressure (such as from a pinprick), other A-delta fibers are specialized to respond to extremes of temperature (hot or cold), and C fibers respond to all sorts of stimuli that produce pain, including strong pressure, heat and cold, and chemicals that produce pain when applied to the skin (Basbaum & Jessell, 2000). When your skin is pricked or burned, you feel two separate waves of pain: a *first pain*, which is sharp and highly localized, followed by a *second pain*, which is more diffuse and longer-lasting. The first is mediated by A-delta fibers, and the second by the slower C fibers (Basbaum & Jessell, 2000). The C fibers also respond in a more prolonged way to a variety of chemicals that are released by damaged or infected cells, accounting for the persistent pain that accompanies burns, wounds, and infections.

Pain neurons enter the spinal cord (via a spinal nerve) or the brainstem (via the fifth cranial nerve) and terminate there on neurons that send their axons upward to higher parts of the brain. Some of these neurons send their output to structures that promote reflexive responses—such as increased physiological arousal—independent of conscious pain experience. Others send their axons to the thalamus, which, in turn, sends output to portions of the brain that are involved in the conscious experience of pain.

Brain Areas for Three Aspects of Pain Experience

A simplified model that relates different aspects of conscious pain experience to different areas of the brain is shown in Figure 7.9. The basic ability to perceive pain as a sensation, to describe its intensity and qualities (as dull or sharp, for example), and to locate it in a particular portion of the body depends on the *somatosensory cortex*, the area of the parietal lobe of neocortex that receives input for touch and temperature as well as pain (for its location, look back at Figure 7.2, page 235).

The immediate motivational qualities of pain, however, depend on certain areas of the limbic system and on the *insular cortex*, which lies buried in one of the folds of the brain's frontal lobe. People with damage to the insular cortex experience a condition called *asymbolia for pain*. They can perceive a painful stimulus and describe it as such, identify the location of the pain, describe its qualities, and rate its intensity; but they do not feel a normal desire to escape the pain. The pain doesn't bother them.

A third aspect of normal pain experience in humans is the more cognitively based suffering that derives from the person's worrying about the future or about the meaning of the pain. The brain area that is crucial for this troubled state is the prefrontal lobe, the frontmost portion of the neocortex. People with damage here feel pain and experience its immediate threat and unpleasantness, but they do not worry about it, just as they do not worry about or make plans based on other experiences. The prefrontal lobes are involved in all aspects of long-term planning (as noted in Chapter 5).

The experience of pain, even of well-localized pain, does not always originate from stimulation of pain receptors. This fact is all too well known by many people who have had a limb amputated. Such people often feel as if the missing limb were still present and feel pain in that limb. Such *phantom-limb pain* can persist even if all the nerves from the limb's stump have been destroyed and even if the pain pathways entering the brain from the spinal cord have been destroyed (Melzack, 1992). Apparently, in such cases the brain's mechanism for experiencing pain and assigning that experience to a particular body location can be activated without sensory input from that part of the body. In fact, the *lack* of sensory input might trigger phantom-limb pain by removing a source of inhibition to the pain mechanism.

15.

What are three different aspects of pain experience in people, and what evidence links these to three different portions of the brain?

16.

What is one line of evidence that the brain's pain mechanisms can become active without sensory input?

FIGURE **7.9** *Brain areas involved in three aspects of pain experience* Pain input from tracts through the spinal cord and midbrain is relayed by one portion of the thalamus to the somatosensory cortex and by another portion of the thalamus to certain areas of the limbic system (specifically to the cingulate gyrus and insula). These areas in turn send output to the prefrontal cortex. The somatosensory cortex is essential for judging the sensory aspects of pain, such as its quality (hot, cold, sharp, dull), location, and intensity. The limbic areas are essential for the immediate emotional response to pain and desire to escape. The prefrontal cortex is involved in planning for the future and is essential for the worry initiated by pain. (Based on information reviewed by Price, 2000.)

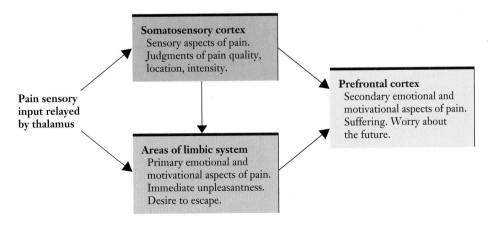

The Modulation of Pain

The experience of pain depends not just on the physical stimulus or its damaging effects but also on other conditions that exist at the time the stimulus or damage occurs. The same degree of wound may at one time feel excruciatingly painful and at another time be barely detected. Over 35 years ago, Ronald Melzack and Patrick Wall (1965, 1996) proposed a ***gate-control theory*** of pain, aimed at explaining such variability. In essence, the theory holds that the experience of pain depends on the degree to which input from pain sensory neurons can pass through a neural "gate" and reach higher pain centers in the brain. Conditions can increase or decrease pain by opening or closing the gate. Much research has confirmed this general theory and has added many details to it.

The major gate, where pain input is most strongly enhanced or inhibited, is at the first way station in the central nervous system. Pain sensory neurons enter the spinal cord and brainstem and terminate there on second-order pain neurons that send their axons upward. These second-order neurons are highly variable in their responsiveness. This variability is controlled in part by pain-enhancing and pain-inhibiting neurons coming down from the brain, as illustrated in Figure 7.10.

Mechanisms of Pain Enhancement

As you probably know only too well, a general enhancement of pain sensitivity all over the body accompanies illness, especially if high fever is involved. This effect may have evolved to motivate ill individuals to rest rather than move around, since a great deal of energy is required to fight disease (Kluger, 1991). Although the details are not known, this illness-induced effect is believed to occur through an action of the immune system on a set of neurons in the brain that send their axons downward to terminate on and increase the excitability of pain-carrying neurons in the brainstem and spinal cord, as illustrated in Figure 7.10 (Watkins & Maier, 2000).

Pain sensitivity can also be increased in specific locations of the body as a result of injury at those locations. Even light touch to a recently burned or wounded area

17.

How does illness produce a general increase in pain sensitivity, and how does injury produce a localized increase in pain sensitivity? Why do surgeons today use local anesthetics more often than they did in the past?

FIGURE **7.10**   *Gate control of pain*
Pain transmission neurons in the spinal cord, which receive input from pain sensory neurons coming from the body, can be made more or less excitable by descending connections from the brain. In the figure, + indicates excitatory connections and – indicates inhibitory connections. Although not shown in the drawing, the pain inhibitory and excitatory systems can also produce their effects by inhibiting or facilitating the release of neurotransmitter from the sensory neurons. (Modified from Watkins & Maier, 2000, p. 31.)

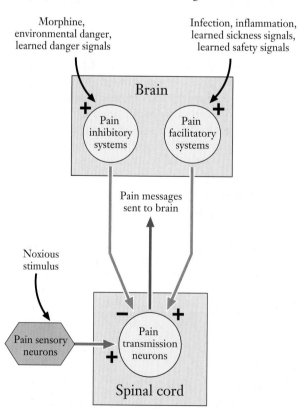

of skin can be intensely painful. This heightened sensitivity occurs partly because of changes in the free nerve endings of C fibers and A-delta fibers that are induced by chemicals released from damaged cells (Basbaum & Jessell, 2000). The sensitized sensory neurons respond to much weaker stimuli than they would have before the injury. In addition, second-order pain neurons in the spinal cord and brainstem become sensitized by intense activation, such that they become more responsive to subsequent input for periods ranging from minutes to many days or even weeks (Keefe & France, 1999; Woolf & Salter, 2000). Such pain-enhancing systems presumably evolved as a means of motivating individuals to be gentle with damaged areas of their body, but in some cases the effects appear to outlive their usefulness and cause needless suffering.

The discovery of central pain sensitization stemming from strong pain input has begun to influence surgical practice (Basbaum & Jessell, 2000). General anesthetics, which produce overall unconsciousness, prevent patients from experiencing pain during surgery, but they do not prevent the strong activation of pain neurons in the spinal cord and brain during surgery and do not prevent the consequent long-term sensitization of those neurons. Increasingly, surgeons now are using local anesthetics, at the site of incision or in the spinal cord, in addition to or instead of general anesthetics. The local anesthetics prevent the activation and sensitization of central pain neurons and thereby reduce the pain that patients experience during the postoperative period.

Neural and Chemical Mechanisms of Pain Reduction

A major neural center for pain inhibition exists in a portion of the midbrain called the *periaqueductal gray* (abbreviated *PAG*). Neurons in this area send their axons down into the lower brainstem and spinal cord to inhibit pain input there, as illustrated in Figure 7.10. Electrical stimulation of the PAG has a powerful analgesic (pain-reducing) effect—so powerful, in fact, that abdominal surgery can be performed without drugs in animals that are receiving such stimulation (Reynolds, 1969). Electrical stimulation of this area has also, in humans, successfully reduced or abolished chronic pain that could not be relieved by other means (Hosobuchi & others, 1979).

Morphine and other *opiate drugs* (derivatives of opium) exert their well-known analgesic effects partly through direct action in the PAG. Morphine that passes into the brain is taken up at special binding sites on neurons in the PAG, where it increases neural activity and thereby reduces pain (Basbaum & Fields, 1984). Morphine binding sites are also found on neurons in the spinal cord, and injections of a tiny amount of morphine directly into the spinal cord can greatly reduce or eliminate pain in the part of the body that sends its sensory neurons into that spinal cord area (Basbaum & Jessell, 2000).

Of course, the pain-inhibiting system did not evolve to respond specifically to morphine or other foreign substances. Its basic function is to mediate the body's own capacity to reduce pain. The body produces a variety of chemicals that act like morphine. These are collectively called **endorphins**, a term that is short for *endogenous morphinelike substances* (*endogenous* means "created within the body"). Some endorphins are produced in the brain or spinal cord and serve as neurotransmitters or neuromodulators to alter the activity or excitability of neurons that they bind to. Others are secreted from the pituitary and adrenal glands, as hormones, into the blood and have a variety of effects both peripherally and in the central nervous system (Henry, 1986). Endorphins are believed to inhibit pain by acting both in the PAG and at the point where pain-carrying neurons enter the spinal cord and lower brainstem.

Stress-Induced Analgesia

During his search for the source of the Nile River, the famous explorer David Livingston was attacked by a lion. He survived the incident and later wrote that

18.

How can pain input be inhibited at its entry into the central nervous system, and how might endorphins be involved in this process?

Excitement-induced analgesia
Situations that call for vigorous action tend to promote the secretion of endorphins and to reduce the experience of pain.

Doug Pensinger / All Sport

although the lion shook him "as a terrier does a rat" and crushed his shoulder, he had felt "no sense of pain nor feeling of terror, though quite conscious of all that was happening" (Livingston, 1857). Other people have had similar experiences. For example, soldiers severely wounded in battle often do not notice their wounds until the battle is over. We are apparently endowed with a mechanism that prevents us from feeling pain at times when, for survival purposes, it is best to ignore our wounds. A person or nonhuman animal faced with a predator or similar threat cannot afford to nurse a wound or favor it by limping; all the body's resources must be used to fight or flee. There is now good evidence that ***stress-induced analgesia***, as this phenomenon is called, occurs in response to many forms of stressful stimulation and is at least partly dependent on endorphins. Endorphins are secreted along with various other hormones by the pituitary and adrenal glands as part of the body's general response to stressful events (Terman & others, 1984).

19.

What is some evidence that stress-induced analgesia is at least partly mediated by endorphins?

In one study of stress-induced analgesia, rats that were subjected to a series of electric shocks to their feet (the source of stress) became relatively insensitive to pain for several minutes afterward, as indicated by their lack of response to normally painful heat that was applied to their tails (Lewis & others, 1980). Rats treated with a drug that blocks the action of endorphins did not show this stress-induced analgesia, indicating that the effect must have been mediated by endorphins. In similar experiments, the mere presence of a cat (Lichtman & Fanselow, 1990) produced analgesia in rats; the presence of biting flies produced analgesia in mice (Kavaliers & others, 1999); a stressful math test produced analgesia in students (Bandura & others, 1988); and films depicting combat produced analgesia in veterans who had experienced the trauma of war (Pitman & others, 1990). In all these cases the analgesic effect was shown to depend on endorphins, since the effect was prevented by a drug that blocks the action of endorphins.

Endorphins are also produced during periods of prolonged, strenuous physical exertion, such as long-distance running, and may account for the pain reduction and euphoric "high" that many people enjoy during and after such exertion. In one experiment both the reduced pain and the sense of euphoria failed to occur in runners who had been treated with an endorphin-blocking drug (Janal & others, 1984).

Belief-Induced Analgesia

20.

What is some evidence that pain can be reduced by belief?

In humans, dramatic reduction in pain can also, at times, be produced by the power of *belief* or faith. Some religious groups engage in practices that most of us would regard as torture, yet the participants appear to feel no pain. One group in India, for example, practices a hook-hanging ritual. A man who has been chosen to represent the power of the gods is secured to a rope by two steel hooks that pierce the skin and muscles on his back. He hangs from this rope, swinging back and forth, while he blesses the children and the crops of the village. He is honored to have been chosen and apparently feels little or no pain (Melzack & Wall, 1996). A less dramatic example in our culture, where faith is more often placed in science and medicine, is the *placebo effect* on pain. In many cases a pill or injection that contains no active substance (the placebo) can reduce pain in a person who believes that the drug is a painkiller.

Endorphins are apparently not involved in all cases of placebo-induced pain reduction (Montgomery & Kirsch, 1996) but are involved in some. In one experiment demonstrating such involvement, people who had undergone a tooth extraction reported less pain if given a placebo than if not, and this reduction in pain was abolished in subjects who were treated with an endorphin-blocking drug (Levine & others, 1979). Other experiments have shown that various cognitive techniques for relieving pain, such as meditating on the idea that the pain is disconnected from the rest of the body, also work at least partly through endorphins (Bandura & others, 1987). Might the man hanging from hooks in India also be secreting large quantities of endorphins? Much remains to be learned about the brain's ability to control pain, but the discovery of the endorphin system is a great stride in that endeavor.

SECTION SUMMARY

The sense of pain motivates individuals to avoid injuring themselves. Fast-conducting A-delta fibers and slow-conducting C fibers provide the bases for two waves of pain with different psychological properties. Within the brain, the somatosensory cortex is crucial for perceiving pain and identifying its bodily location, the insular cortex is crucial for the immediate aversive qualities of pain, and the prefrontal cortex is crucial for the worry and planning initiated by pain. The gate-control theory of pain, which posits that pain pathways in the spinal cord can be sensitized and inhibited, helps explain various phenomena involving temporarily enhanced or reduced pain sensitivity. These phenomena include the general increase in pain sensitivity that accompanies illness, the heightened sensitivity that occurs in recently injured areas of the body, the analgesic effects of opiate drugs and endorphins, and stress-induced and belief-induced analgesias.

HEARING

Among mammals, the greatest listeners are the bats. In complete darkness, and even if blinded, bats can flit around obstacles such as tree branches and capture insects that themselves are flying in erratic patterns to escape. Bats navigate and hunt by sonar. They send out high-pitched chirps, above the frequency range that we can hear, and analyze the echoes in a way that allows them to *hear* the scene in front of them. From echoes, they can hear such characteristics as the size, shape, position, direction of movement, texture, and pattern of wingbeats of a target insect (Feng & Ratnam, 2000).

Hearing may not be as well developed or as essential for us as it is for bats, but it is still enormously effective and useful. It allows us to detect and respond to potentially life-threatening or life-enhancing events that occur in the dark, or behind our backs, or behind occluding objects. We use it to identify animals and events such as upcoming storms. And, perhaps most important, it is the primary sensory modality of human language. We learn from each other through our ears.

Sound and Its Transduction by the Ear

If a tree falls in the forest where no one hears it, does it make a sound? This old riddle plays on the fact that the term *sound* refers both to a type of physical stimulus and to the sensation produced by that stimulus. As a physical stimulus, sound is the vibration of air or some other medium produced by an object such as a tuning fork, one's vocal cords, or a falling tree. The vibration moves outward from the sound source in a manner that can be described as a wave (see Figure 7.11, page 254). The height of the wave indicates the total pressure exerted by the molecules of air (or

John Mitchell / Photo Researchers

An auditory animal

Bats, which navigate and hunt by sonar, have large, mobile outer ears. This is especially true of some species, such as *Plecotis auritus*, pictured here.

FIGURE **7.11**
Characteristics of sound
The oscillating tuning fork (a) causes air molecules to vibrate in a manner that can be represented as a wave of pressure. Each wave contains an area in which the air molecules are more compressed (the dark regions in the upper diagram) and an area in which they are less compressed (the light regions) than normal. The peak pressure (the highest compression) of each wave defines the amplitude of the sound, and the number of waves that pass a given point per second defines the frequency. The higher the amplitude, the louder the sound; and the higher the frequency, the higher the pitch (b). All the wave drawings in this figure are sine waves, indicative of pure tones. (Adapted from Klinke, 1986.)

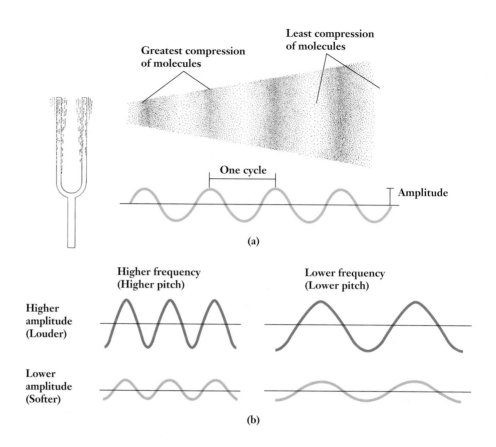

another medium) as they move back and forth, which is referred to as the sound's **amplitude** or intensity and corresponds to what we hear as the sound's **loudness**. Sound amplitude is usually measured in logarithmic units of pressure called *decibels* (abbreviated *dB*). (See Table 7.2, which further defines decibels and contains the decibel ratings for a number of common sounds.)

In addition to varying in amplitude, sound waves vary in **frequency**, which we hear as the sound's **pitch**. The frequency of a sound is the rate at which the molecules of air or another medium move back and forth. Frequency is measured in *hertz* (abbreviated *Hz*), which is the number of complete waves (or cycles) that occur at any given point per second. Sounds that are audible to humans have frequencies ranging from about 20 to 20,000 Hz. To give you an idea of the relationship between frequency and pitch, the dominant (most audible) frequency of the lowest note on a piano is about 27 Hz, that of middle C is about 262 Hz, and that of the highest piano note is about 4186 Hz (Matlin & Foley, 1997). The simplest kind of sound is a pure tone, which is a constant-frequency wave of vibration that can be described as a sine wave (depicted in Figure 7.11). Pure tones, which are useful in auditory experiments, can be produced in the laboratory, but they rarely occur in other contexts. Natural sources of sound, including even musical instruments and tuning forks, vibrate at several frequencies at once and thus produce more complex waves than that shown in Figure 7.11. Natural sounds can be thought of as consisting of many different tones at once.

How the Ear Works

21.

What are the functions of the outer ear, middle ear, and inner ear?

Evolutionarily, hearing is a variation of touch. Touch is sensitivity to pressure on the skin, and hearing is sensitivity to pressure on a special sensory tissue in the ear. In some animals, such as moths, sound is sensed through modified touch receptors located on flexible patches of skin that vibrate in response to sound waves. In humans and other mammals the special patches of skin for hearing have migrated to a

TABLE 7.2   *Sound-pressure amplitudes of various sounds, and conversion to decibels**

Example	P (in sound-pressure units)	Log P	Decibels
Softest detectable sound	1	0	0
Soft whisper	10	1	20
Quiet neighborhood	100	2	40
Average conversation	1,000	3	60
Loud music from a radio	10,000	4	80
Heavy automobile traffic	100,000	5	100
Very loud thunder	1,000,000	6	120
Jet airplane taking off	10,000,000	7	140
Loudest rock band on record	100,000,000	8	160
Spacecraft launch (from 150 ft.)	1,000,000,000	9	180

*One sound-pressure unit (P) is defined as 2×10^{-5} newtons/square meter (Klinke, 1986). When measured in sound-pressure units, the amplitude range of human hearing is enormous. A reason for converting to logarithmic units is to produce a smaller range of numbers. The logarithm (log) of a number is the power to which 10 must be raised to produce that number. For example, the log of 10,000 is 4, because $10^4 = 10,000$. A decibel (dB) is defined as $20 \log P$. Thus, 4 log units = 80 dB.

Sources: Human information processing, 2nd ed. (p.161) by P. H. Lindsay & D. A. Norman, 1977, New York: Academic Press. *Sensation and perception,* 4th ed. (p. 281) by M. W. Matlin & H. J. Foley, 1997, Boston: Allyn and Bacon.

location inside the head, and special organs, the ears, have developed to magnify the pressure exerted by sound waves as they are transported inward. A diagram of the human ear is shown in Figure 7.12. To review its structures and their functions, we will begin from the outside and work inward.

The **outer ear** consists of the *pinna*, which is the flap of skin and cartilage forming the visible portion of the ear, and the *auditory canal*, which is the opening into the head that ends at the *eardrum* (or tympanic membrane). It can be thought of as an air-filled funnel for receiving sound waves and transporting them inward. The vibration of air outside the head (the physical sound) causes air in the auditory canal to vibrate, which in turn causes the tympanic membrane to vibrate.

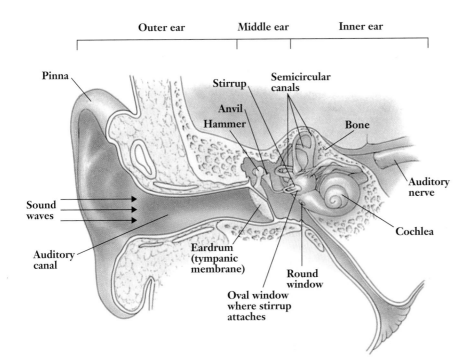

FIGURE 7.12
Parts of the human ear
Sound waves (vibrations of air) that enter the auditory canal cause the eardrum to vibrate, which causes the ossicles (the hammer, anvil, and stirrup bones) to vibrate, which causes the oval window to vibrate, setting up waves of motion in the fluid inside the cochlea. The semicircular canals are involved in the sense of balance, not hearing.

The **middle ear** is an air-filled cavity, separated from the outer ear by the eardrum. Its main structures are three tiny bones collectively called *ossicles* (and individually called the *hammer*, *anvil*, and *stirrup*, because of their respective shapes), which are linked to the eardrum at one end and to the *oval window*, a membrane of the cochlea, at the other end. When sound causes the eardrum to vibrate, the ossicles vibrate and push against the oval window. Because the oval window has only about one-thirtieth the area of the tympanic membrane, the pressure (force per unit area) that is funneled to it by the ossicles is about 30 times greater than the pressure on the eardrum. Thus, the main function of the middle ear is to increase the amount of pressure that sound waves exert upon the inner ear so that transduction can occur.

The coiled **cochlea**, in the **inner ear**, is where transduction finally takes place. As depicted in the uncoiled view in Figure 7.13, the cochlea contains a fluid-filled *outer duct* that begins at the oval window, runs to the tip of the cochlea, and then runs back again to another membrane, the *round window*, located near the oval window. Sandwiched between the outgoing and incoming portions of the outer duct is another fluid-filled tube, the *inner duct*. Forming the floor of the inner duct is the **basilar membrane**, on which are located the receptor cells for hearing, called **hair cells**. There are four rows of hair cells (three outer rows and one inner row), each row running the length of the basilar membrane. Tiny hairs (called *cilia*) protrude from each hair cell into the inner duct and abut against another membrane, called the *tectorial membrane*. At the other end from its hairs, each hair cell forms synapses with several *auditory neurons*, whose axons form the *auditory nerve* (eighth cranial nerve), which runs to the brain.

The process of transduction in the cochlea can be summarized as follows: The sound-induced vibration of the ossicles against the oval window initiates vibration in the fluid in the outer duct of the cochlea, which produces an up-and-down waving motion of the very flexible basilar membrane. The tectorial membrane above the basilar membrane is less flexible and does not move when the basilar membrane moves, so the hairs protruding from the hair cells in the basilar membrane bend against the tectorial membrane each time the basilar membrane moves upward. This bending causes a physical change in the hair cell's membrane, which leads to

22.

How does transduction occur in the inner ear?

FIGURE **7.13** *Transduction mechanism in the inner ear*
This diagram depicts a longitudinal section of the cochlea (partially uncoiled), showing the outer and inner ducts. Sound waves in the fluid of the outer duct cause the basilar membrane to wave up and down. When the basilar membrane moves upward, its hairs bend against the tectorial membrane, initiating receptor potentials in the hair cells.

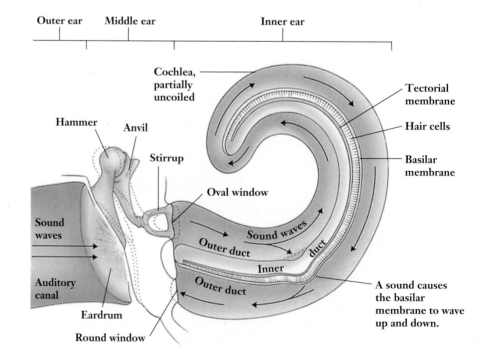

an electrical change across the membrane (the receptor potential). This in turn causes each hair cell to release neurotransmitter molecules at its synapses upon auditory neurons, thereby increasing the rate of action potentials in those neurons (Hudspeth, 2000b).

Deafness and Hearing Aids

With this knowledge of the ear it is possible to understand the physiological bases for two varieties of deafness. ***Conduction deafness*** occurs when the ossicles of the middle ear become rigid and cannot carry sounds inward from the tympanic membrane to the cochlea. People with conduction deafness can hear vibrations that reach the cochlea by routes other than the middle ear. A conventional hearing aid is helpful for such people, because it magnifies the sound pressure sufficiently for vibrations to be conducted by other bones of the face into the cochlea.

   Sensorineural deafness occurs from damage to the cochlea, the hair cells, or (less often) the auditory neurons. People with complete sensorineural deafness are not helped by a conventional hearing aid but can in many cases be helped by a newer form of hearing aid called a ***cochlear implant***. This device performs the transduction task normally done by the ear's hair cells (though it does not do it nearly as well). It transforms sounds into electrical impulses and sends the impulses through thin wires permanently implanted into the cochlea, where they stimulate the terminals of auditory neurons directly. It can be used when deafness is due to the destruction of hair cells, but not when the auditory nerve has been destroyed. The best cochlear implants today permit sufficient sound resolution to enable at least some deaf children to acquire vocal language at a nearly normal rate and to allow adults who became deaf after learning language to regain their ability to understand speech (Rauschecker, 1999; Svirsky & others, 2000).

Pitch Perception

How do receptors on the basilar membrane code the differences in sound frequency that permit pitch detection? Historically, that is one of the first questions that scientists asked about the workings of the ear. In the mid-nineteenth century, the great German physiologist Hermann von Helmholtz suggested a possible analogy between the ear's basilar membrane and the strings of a harp. A harp's strings vibrate not only when plucked but also when sound waves strike them, and different strings vibrate more readily to different frequencies. Helmholtz proposed that the basilar membrane may contain separate fibers that, like a harp's strings, resonate to different tonal frequencies and activate different neurons in the auditory nerve (Zwislocki, 1981). We now know that Helmholtz was correct in theorizing that different portions of the basilar membrane are most sensitive to different sound frequencies, but he was wrong about the details.

The Traveling Wave as a Basis for Frequency Coding

Considerably after Helmholtz, in work begun in the 1920s that eventuated in a Nobel Prize, Georg von Békésy developed a way to observe directly the action of the basilar membrane, and he discovered that it behaves not like a harp with separate strings but, rather, like a bedsheet when someone shakes it at one end. Sound waves entering the cochlea set up traveling waves on the basilar membrane, which move from the proximal end (closest to the oval window) toward the distal end (farthest away from the oval window). As each wave moves, it gradually increases in amplitude up to a certain maximum and then rapidly dissipates. Of most importance, Békésy found that the position on the membrane at which the waves reach

23.

How do two kinds of deafness differ from each other in their physiological bases and in possible treatment?

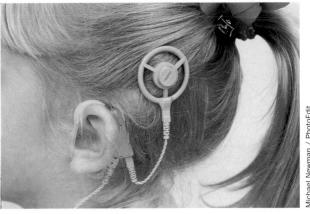

Michael Newman / PhotoEdit

*External portions
of a cochlear implant*

A microphone hooked around the girl's ear picks up sound waves and sends signals down, through a cable connection, to an auditory processor attached to a belt around her waist. The auditory processor converts the signals into electrical pulses, suitable for stimulating the cochlea, and sends those pulses up the cable to a transmitter fastened to the girl's head behind her ear. The transmitter sends the pulses through the skin to a receiver implanted in her skull, and from there the pulses are sent by thin wire electrodes to stimulate appropriate sets of auditory neurons in the cochlea of the inner ear.

24.

How does the basilar membrane of the inner ear operate to ensure that different neurons are maximally stimulated by sounds of different frequencies?

their peak depends on the frequency of the tone. High frequencies produce waves that travel only a short distance, peaking near the proximal end, and low frequencies produce waves that travel farther, peaking near the distal end. From this observation, Békésy hypothesized that (a) rapid firing in neurons that come from the proximal end of the membrane, accompanied by little or no firing in neurons coming from more distal parts, is interpreted by the brain as a high-pitched sound and (b) rapid firing in neurons coming from a more distal portion is interpreted as a lower-pitched sound.

Subsequent research has confirmed the general validity of Békésy's hypothesis and has shown that the waves on the intact, living basilar membrane are in fact much more sharply defined than those that Békésy had observed. There is now strong evidence that the primary receptor cells for hearing are the inner row of hair cells and that the outer three rows serve mostly a different function. They have the capacity to stiffen when activated, and they do so in a manner that amplifies and sharpens the traveling wave (Zhao & Santos-Sacchi, 1999). For an illustration of the effects that different tones and complex sounds have upon the basilar membrane, see Figure 7.14.

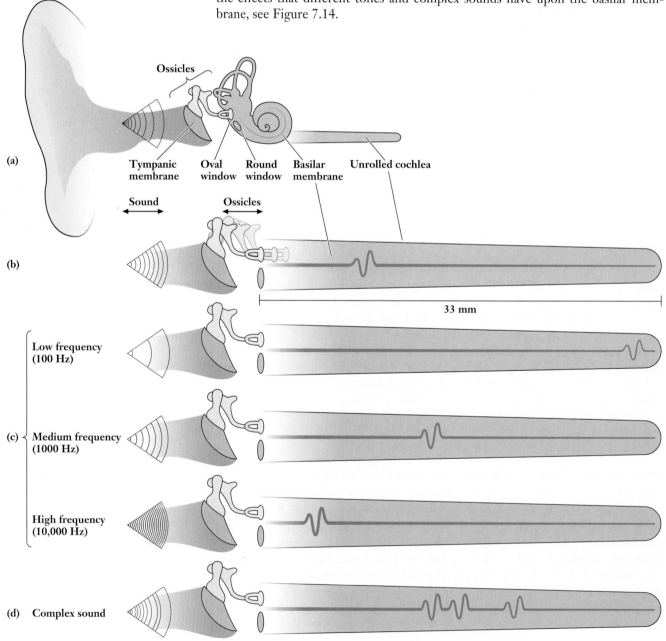

Two Sensory Consequences of the Traveling-Wave Mechanism

The manner by which the basilar membrane responds to differing frequencies helps us make sense of a number of auditory phenomena. One such phenomenon is *asymmetry* in *auditory masking*, which is especially noticeable in music production. *Auditory masking* refers to the ability of one sound to mask (prevent the hearing of) another sound. Auditory masking is asymmetrical in that low-frequency sounds mask high-frequency sounds much more effectively than the reverse (Scharf, 1964). A bassoon can easily drown out a piccolo, but a piccolo cannot easily drown out a bassoon. To see how this can be explained in terms of the waves the two instruments produce on the basilar membrane, look at Figure 7.15. The wave produced by a low-frequency bassoon note encompasses the entire portion of the basilar membrane that is encompassed by the piccolo note (and more). Thus, if the bassoon note is of sufficient amplitude, it can interfere with the effect of the piccolo note; but the piccolo note, even at great amplitude, cannot interfere with the effect that the bassoon note has on the more distal part of the membrane, because the wave produced by the piccolo note never travels that far down the membrane.

Another effect of the traveling-wave mechanism concerns the pattern of hearing loss that occurs as we get older. We lose our sensitivity to high frequencies to a much greater degree than to low frequencies. Thus, young children can hear frequencies as high as 30,000 Hz, and young adults can hear frequencies as high as 20,000 Hz, but a typical 60-year-old cannot hear frequencies above about 15,000 Hz (to see a graph of this, look ahead to Figure 7.18, page 264). This decline is greatest for people who live or work in noisy environments (see Figure 7.16, page 260) and is caused by the wearing out of hair cells with repeated use (Kryter, 1985). But why should cells responsible for coding high frequencies wear out faster than those for coding low frequencies? The answer may lie in the fact that the former are acted upon by all sounds (as shown in Figure 7.15), while the latter respond only to low-frequency sounds.

25.

How does the traveling-wave theory explain (a) an asymmetry in auditory masking and (b) the pattern of hearing loss that occurs as we get older?

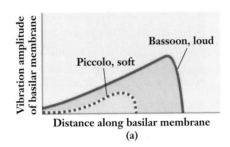

Effect of bassoon on basilar membrane

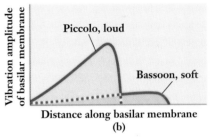

Effect of piccolo on basilar membrane

FIGURE **7.15** *Why a low-frequency tone masks a high-frequency tone better than the reverse*
(a) When a low-frequency tone (such as that from a bassoon) and a high-frequency tone (such as that from a piccolo) are played simultaneously, the bassoon can mask the piccolo because the bassoon's action on the basilar membrane encompasses the entire portion on which the piccolo acts. (b) But the piccolo cannot mask the bassoon because, even when played at high amplitude, the piccolo does not affect the distal part of the membrane to which the bassoon's waves extend. (Adapted from Scharf, 1964.)

FIGURE **7.14** *Waves on the basilar membrane*
In this highly schematic diagram, the cochlea is uncoiled and stretched out and the basilar membrane is depicted as a straight line running down the center of the cochlea. Part (b) illustrates the back-and-forth movement of the ossicles in response to sound and the traveling wave that that motion sets up on the basilar membrane. Part (c) illustrates the relationship between the frequency of a tone and the place on the basilar membrane where the traveling wave reaches its peak amplitude. Part (d) shows that a complex sound, comprising more than one frequency, produces wave peaks simultaneously at more than one location on the basilar membrane. The sizes of the wave peaks are grossly exaggerated in the diagram. If they were drawn to actual scale, the peaks would be less than 1/100 of the width of the lines representing the basilar membrane in these drawings. The waves are shown only at the places where they peak. In fact, each wave must travel the length of the basilar membrane to the place where it reaches its peak, and then it dies out shortly after that. (Based on Figure 30-3 in Hudspeth, 2000a, p. 595.)

FIGURE **7.16**
Warning: Noise can be dangerous
These electron micrographs show hair cells on the basilar membrane of a guinea pig (a) before and (b) after exposure to 24 hours of sound at an intensity comparable to a rock concert. The tiny hairs are disarranged on some cells and completely destroyed on others.

(a)

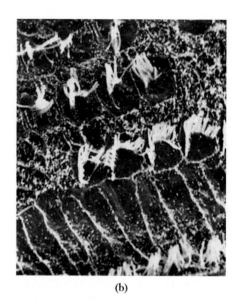

(b)

26.

How does the timing of action potentials code sound frequency, and how do the best cochlear implants produce perception of pitch?

Another Code for Frequency

Although the traveling-wave theory of frequency coding has been well validated, it is not the whole story. For frequencies below about 4000 Hz (which includes most of the frequencies in human speech), perceived pitch depends not just on which part of the basilar membrane is maximally active but also on the timing of that activity (Moore, 1997). The electrical activity triggered in sets of auditory neurons tends to be locked in phase with sound waves, such that a separate burst of action potentials occurs each time a sound wave peaks. The frequency at which such bursts occur contributes to the perception of pitch.

Interestingly, the most sophisticated cochlear implants use both place and timing to produce pitch perception (Moore, 1997). These devices break a sound signal into separate frequency ranges and send electrical pulses from each frequency range through a thin wire to a different portion of the basilar membrane. Pitch perception is best (but still not nearly as good as that accomplished by the normal ear) when the electrical signal sent to a given locus of the membrane is pulsed at a frequency similar to that of the sound wave that would normally act at that location.

Making Sense of Sounds

Think of the subtlety and complexity of our auditory perception. With no cues but sound, we can locate the direction of a sound source within about 5 to 10 degrees of its true direction (Hudspeth, 2000a). At a party we can distinguish and listen to one person's voice in a noisy environment that includes many other voices and a band in the background. To comprehend speech, we hear the tiny difference between *plot* and *blot*, while ignoring the much larger differences between two different voices that speak either of those words. All sounds set up patterns of waves on our basilar membranes, and from those seemingly chaotic patterns our nervous system extracts all the information needed for auditory perception.

The auditory sensory neurons send their output to nuclei in the brainstem, which in turn send axons upward, ultimately to the auditory area of the cerebral cortex, located in each temporal lobe (see Figure 7.2, page 235). Neurons in the primary auditory cortex are *tonotopically* organized. That is, each neuron is maximally responsive to sounds of a particular frequency, and the neurons are systematically arranged such that high-frequency tones activate neurons at one end of this cortical area and low-frequency tones activate neurons at the other end. Ultimately, the pitch or set of pitches we hear depends largely on which neurons in the auditory cortex are most active. The experience of a sound includes not only its loudness and pitch but also its location in space, its *timbre* (the quality, based on the exact form of the sound wave, that allows us to discriminate one natural sound from another even if they have the same dominant pitch), its time of onset and offset, and its inflection (the rise and fall of the dominant pitch). Most sounds, such as spoken words, consist of simultaneous waves of many frequencies, which change continuously in both frequency and amplitude from the beginning of the sound to the end. All the information that allows you to distinguish one such sound from another must be extracted by the brain from the pattern of action potentials in the auditory nerves.

The response characteristics of neurons in the auditory cortex are modifiable by experience. When guinea pigs were trained by either classical or operant conditioning to use a particular tone frequency as a cue guiding their behavior, the number of auditory cortical neurons that responded strongly to that frequency greatly increased (Bakin & others, 1996; Edeline & others, 1993). In auditory cortical areas near the primary auditory area, some neurons respond only to certain combinations of frequencies, others only to rising or falling pitch, others only to brief clicks or bursts of sound, and still others only to sound sources that are moving in a particular direction (Baumgart & others, 1999; Phillips, 1989). In macaque monkeys, some neurons in the auditory cortex respond selectively to particular macaque calls (Rauschecker & others, 1995). In the end, activity in some combination of neurons in your cerebral cortex must provide the basis for the specific auditory experience that occurs when you hear a canary singing or your professor enunciating the sweet word *psychology*.

Locating Sounds

The ability to tell the direction of a sound source contributes greatly to the usefulness of hearing. When startled by an unexpected rustling, we reflexively turn toward it to see what might be causing the disturbance. Even newborn infants do this (Muir & Field, 1979), indicating that the ability to localize a sound does not require learning. Such localization is also a key component of our ability to keep one sound distinct from others in a noisy environment. People can attend to one voice and ignore another much more easily if the two voices come from different locations in the room than if they come from the same location (Feng & Ratnam, 2000).

Sound localization depends partly on the timing at which each sound wave reaches one ear compared to the other. A wave of sound coming from straight ahead reaches the two ears simultaneously, but a wave from the right or the left reaches one ear slightly before it reaches the other (see Figure 7.17). A sound wave that is just slightly to the left of straight ahead reaches the left ear a few microseconds (millionths of a second) before it reaches the right ear, and a sound wave that is 90 degrees to the left reaches the left ear about 700 microseconds before it reaches the right ear. Neurons in at least one way station in the auditory system receive input from both ears, with some of these neurons most responsive to waves that reach both ears at once and others most responsive to waves that reach one ear some microseconds—ranging from just a few on up to about 700—before or after reaching the other ear. These neurons, presumably, are part of the mechanism by which the nervous system identifies the direction from which a sound is coming (Hudspeth, 2000a).

27.

How do differences between the two ears in the timing and amplitude of sound waves contribute to our ability to tell the direction from which a sound is coming?

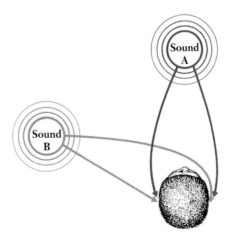

FIGURE **7.17** *Locating a sound*
Sound waves coming from the left (sound B) reach the left ear sooner than the right ear. The converse would be true of sound waves coming from the right. Neurons receiving input from the two ears are sensitive to this difference, which provides a code for sound localization. Without moving the head, it is difficult to distinguish a sound directly in front (sound A) from one directly behind the head, because in both cases the sound waves reach both ears simultaneously.

Differences between our two ears in the amplitude of the sound wave also contribute to localization, especially for high-frequency sounds. High-frequency (short-wavelength) sounds do not easily travel around the head but do travel through the head, and in doing so their amplitude is reduced. The result is that the ear farthest from the sound source receives a weaker sound wave than the ear closest to the sound source. Some neurons in the auditory system are excited by input from one ear and inhibited by input from the other (Hudspeth, 2000a), and the amount of activity in these neurons may indicate the degree to which a sound is coming from the right or the left. For example, a neuron that is excited by input from the right ear and inhibited by that from the left will be most active when the sound is 90 degrees to the right and least active when the sound is directly in front of (or directly behind) the listener.

Differences in the timing and intensity of input to the two ears cannot, by themselves, indicate whether a sound is coming from in front of or behind the head. In humans, that ability probably depends mostly on head movements. Rotating the head even slightly in either direction has opposite effects depending on whether the sound is from the front or the rear. For instance, rotating the head to the right will cause the sound to reach the left ear more quickly and with greater amplitude, relative to the right ear, if the sound comes from the front, and will have the opposite effect if the sound comes from behind. In the absence of head movement, any ability to distinguish between front and back may depend on the shape of the pinna of the outer ear, which alters the sound waves somewhat differently for sounds coming from behind than for sounds coming from the front. The shape of the pinna probably also contributes to the ability to judge the vertical (up or down) location of a sound source (Brown, 1994). The pinnas of some animals (such as bats, rabbits, and deer) are large and mobile and contribute much more to sound localization than do our pinnas.

Phonemic Restoration: An Auditory Illusion

In certain situations our auditory system provides us with the perception of sounds that are not really present as physical stimuli. A well-documented example is the sensory illusion of *phonemic restoration*. **Phonemes** are the individual vowel and consonant sounds that make up words (discussed further in Chapter 11), and phonemic restoration is an illusion in which people hear phonemes that have been deleted from words or sentences as if they were still there. The perceptual experience is that of really *hearing* the missing sound, not that of inferring what sound must be there.

28.

Under what conditions does our auditory system fill in a missing sound, and what might be the value of such an illusion?

Richard Warren (1970) first demonstrated this illusion in an experiment in which he removed an *s* sound and spliced in a coughing sound of equal duration in the following tape-recorded sentence at the place marked by an asterisk: *The state governors met with their respective legi*latures convening in the capital city.* People listening to the doctored tape could hear the cough, but it did not seem to coincide with any specific portion of the sentence or block out any sound in the sentence. Even when they listened repeatedly, with instructions to determine what sound was missing, people were unable to detect that any sound was missing. After they were told which sound was missing, they still claimed to hear that sound each time they listened to the tape. In other experiments, thousands of practice trials failed to improve people's ability to judge which phoneme was missing (Samuel, 1991).

Which sound is heard in phonemic restoration depends on the arrangement of the surrounding phonemes and the meaningful words and phrases they produce. The restored sound is always one that turns a partial word into a whole word that is consistent in meaning with the rest of the sentence. Most remarkably, even words that occur *after* the missing phoneme can influence which phoneme is heard. For example, people heard the stimulus sound **eel* (again, the asterisk represents a coughlike sound) as *peel*, *heel*, or *wheel*, depending on whether it occurred in the phrase *The *eel was on the orange, The *eel was on the shoe,* or *The *eel was on the axle* (Warren, 1984). The illusory phoneme was heard as occurring at its proper place, in the second word of the sentence, even though words coming after it were critical in determining which phoneme was heard.

One way to make sense of this phenomenon is to assume that much of our perceptual experience of hearing actually depends on a brief auditory sensory memory, which lasts for a matter of seconds and is modifiable. The later words generate a momentary false memory of hearing, earlier, a phoneme that wasn't actually present, and that memory is indistinguishable from a true auditory memory. Such brief, compelling memories and their role in perceptual experiences are discussed more fully in Chapter 9. Illusory restoration has also been demonstrated in music perception. People hear a missing note, in a familiar tune, as if it were present (DeWitt & Samuel, 1990).

A limiting factor in these illusions is that the gap in the sentence or tune must be filled with noise; it can't be a silent gap. In everyday life the sounds we listen to are often masked by bits of noise, never by bits of silence, so perhaps illusory sound restorations are an evolutionary adaptation by which our auditory system allows us to hear meaningful sound sequences in a relatively uninterrupted stream. When a burst of noise masks a phoneme or a note, our auditory system automatically, after the fact, in auditory memory, replaces that burst with the auditory experience that, according to our previous experience, belongs there.

SECTION SUMMARY

Sound waves entering the outer ear initiate vibration of the ossicles of the middle ear, which sets up waves of motion in the fluid of the inner ear's cochlear duct. This motion generates traveling waves in the cochlea's basilar membrane. These waves activate auditory receptor cells (hair cells) located on that membrane and trigger action potentials in auditory sensory neurons. The distance that the traveling waves move along the basilar membrane, and the place at which they peak, depends on the frequency of the tone; the lower the frequency, the farther the wave moves. This, along with the timing of the waves (for low tones), provides the basis for pitch perception. The mechanics of the basilar membrane's response to tones of different frequencies also helps explain why low tones can mask high tones more readily than the reverse and why the ability to hear high tones declines more rapidly with age than does the ability to hear low tones. The ability to locate the direction of a sound source depends on the brain's ability to compare the timing and intensity of sound waves as they reach one ear compared to the other. The phonemic-restoration illusion illustrates that what we hear is determined not just by the physical stimulus but also by the meaning that we attribute to the stimulus.

PSYCHOPHYSICS

Psychophysics is the study of the relationship between the physical characteristics of a stimulus and the sensory experience that it produces (look back at Figure 7.1, page 234). (You can remember *psychophysics* by recalling that it relates the *psychological* sensory experience to *physical* characteristics of the stimulus.) The sensory experience is typically assessed by asking subjects to make some judgment about the stimulus, such as whether it is present or absent or whether it is the same as or different from another stimulus. Many experiments already alluded to in this chapter were psychophysical, including those assessing people's abilities to detect or identify particular substances by taste or smell and those relating the frequency of a tone to its perceived pitch.

This section describes some psychophysical methods and findings related to (a) the detection of weak stimuli, (b) the detection of small changes in stimuli, and (c) the attempt to develop a general law relating the physical intensity of a stimulus to the intensity of the sensory experience it produces. As you will see, psychophysics is more mathematical than most other areas of psychology. That is one of the reasons why some psychologists find it exciting. Psychophysics is just the right cup of tea for those psychologists who like a degree of precision in their science, are drawn by the elegance of mathematics, and are fascinated by the idea that certain psychological phenomena can be described meaningfully with algebraic equations. Historically, research in psychophysics by such scientists as Ernst Weber and Gustav Fechner, in the nineteenth century, played a vital role in the founding of psychology as a science, and many of the specific questions they raised are still topics of research and debate today.

Detecting Weak Stimuli and Small Differences

The Absolute Threshold, and Why It Is Not Absolute

How sensitive are our senses? What is the faintest sound that we can hear or the dimmest light that we can see? Psychophysicists refer to the faintest detectable stimulus, of any given type, as the **absolute threshold** for that type of stimulus. The absolute threshold within any sensory system—let's take hearing as our example—depends on a number of variables. It depends on who is tested (some people have more sensitive hearing than others), the precise kind of stimulus used as the signal (we are more sensitive to sounds at some frequencies than at others), and the precise conditions in which the test is conducted (such as the amount of background noise).

You can see the influence of the first two of these variables by looking at Figure 7.18, which shows an audiogram for a typical 60-year-old and a typical 20-year-old. An *audiogram* is a graph depicting a person's absolute thresholds for tones of various frequencies. Notice that the 60-year-old has a higher absolute threshold than the 20-year-old at every frequency. That is, the tone must be more intense to be heard by the older person. The figure also shows how the absolute threshold varies with frequency. Both individuals are most sensitive (have the lowest thresholds) to tones in the range of 1,000 to 3,000 Hz. As the frequency becomes lower or higher than this, sensitivity decreases (the absolute threshold increases).

To determine a person's absolute threshold for a particular kind of stimulus (such as a 5,000-Hz tone), a psychophysicist might present the stimulus many times, at various low intensities, each time asking the person if he or she detects it. The procedure sometimes also includes control trials in which the stimulus is not presented. When the stimulus is near the threshold level, it is sometimes detected and sometimes not, and sometimes the person believes the stimulus is present when it really isn't. Presumably, various random events—including outside noises and

29.

What are some variables that influence the absolute threshold, and why must it be arrived at by averaging?

FIGURE **7.18** *Audiogram for a typical 60-year-old and 20-year-old*
The audiogram is a graph of the minimum intensity that the person can hear (the absolute threshold) for each tone frequency. Notice that the younger person has a lower threshold than the older person for each frequency and that the difference increases as the frequency rises. For example, the graph shows that for a 5,000-Hz tone the 60-year-old's absolute threshold is nearly 30 dB and the 20-year-old's is about 10 dB.

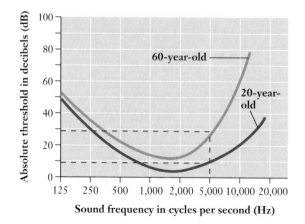

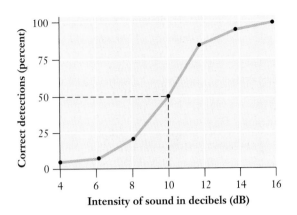

FIGURE 7.19 *The absolute threshold is statistically derived*

If a stimulus—say, a 5,000-Hz tone—is presented many times at each of several weak intensities, the proportion of times that the person correctly detects it increases as the intensity increases. Arbitrarily, the intensity at which correct detection occurs in 50 percent of the trials—in this case, 10 dB—is taken as the absolute threshold. (Data are hypothetical.)

occurrences within the person's nervous system—may either mask the signal or mimic it. Thus, the absolute threshold is not truly "absolute" but, rather, is arrived at by statistical averaging. For a given study, it may be defined as that intensity of the stimulus that is detected on some specified percentage of the trials in which it is present (see Figure 7.19).

Signal Detection as a Decision-Making Task

A problem arising from the arbitrary nature of absolute thresholds is that reported stimulus detection depends not just on sensory ability but also on *response bias*, the tendency to favor a particular response when uncertain about whether the stimulus is present or not. Some subjects might adopt a conservative response bias and say yes (present) only when they are certain that the stimulus is present. Others might adopt a liberal response bias and say yes when they think it is present but are less than certain. Subjects who expect the stimulus to be present on most trials or who are highly motivated to detect its presence are more inclined to say yes on a given trial than are those who expect that it will rarely be present or who are highly motivated to avoid falsely saying it is present when it isn't.

Differences in subjective expectation and motivation take on great significance in signal-detection tasks in real-life settings. Consider, for example, a radiologist scanning x-ray images for faint signs of cancer. The likelihood of putting a particular set of x-rays in the possible-cancer pile versus the clean-bill-of-health pile may depend on (a) the radiologist's prior beliefs about the likelihood that the patient would have cancer and (b) the balance between the radiologist's motivation, on the one hand, to detect cancer whenever it is present and, on the other hand, to avoid unduly frightening or inconveniencing patients when it is not present. Some radiologists are more liberal in their willingness to say "cancer may be present here," and others are more conservative.

In order to compare people's actual sensory abilities, psychophysicists have developed ways to specify the degree to which a person responds according to a liberal or conservative bias and to correct for that bias. To do this, they include trials in which the stimulus is not present as well as trials in which it is, and then they separate the subject's responses into four categories: (1) *hits* (the stimulus is present and the subject reports sensing it); (2) *misses* (the stimulus is present and the subject reports not sensing it); (3) *false alarms* (the stimulus is absent and the subject reports sensing it); and (4) *correct rejections* (the stimulus is absent and the subject reports not sensing it). A liberal bias would increase the number of hits and false alarms and decrease the number of misses and correct rejections, and a conservative bias would have the opposite effect (see Figure 7.20, page 266). By comparing the proportion of hits to false alarms, psychophysicists can derive a measure of sensitivity that is independent of response bias; it is called *d prime* (written *d′*) (Green, 1964). The greater the ratio of hits to false alarms, the greater the person's sensitivity to the stimulus. In real-life signal-detection tasks—such as those of radiologists looking at

30.

How is the measure of absolute threshold affected by a liberal or conservative response bias, and how can the bias be assessed by a signal-detection experiment?

Actual stimulus condition

	Present	Absent
"Present"	Hit	False alarm
"Absent"	Miss	Correct rejection

Subject's response

(a)
Possible outcomes
on each trial

Actual stimulus condition

	Present	Absent
"Present"	Hit 90%	False alarm 30%
"Absent"	Miss 10%	Correct rejection 70%

Subject's response

(b)
Sample results with
liberal response bias

Actual stimulus condition

	Present	Absent
"Present"	Hit 60%	False alarm 10%
"Absent"	Miss 40%	Correct rejection 90%

Subject's response

(c)
Sample results with
conservative response bias

FIGURE **7.20**
Signal-detection outcomes
Part (a) shows the definition of hits, misses, false alarms, and correct rejections. Parts (b) and (c) show hypothetical results for a person adopting a liberal or conservative response bias, with a signal near the absolute threshold. Notice that the liberal bias increases hits but also increases false alarms.

31.

How did Weber derive a law from data on just-noticeable differences (jnd's)? How can Weber's law be used to predict the degree to which two stimuli must differ for a person to tell them apart?

x-ray images or of airport guards scanning luggage with metal detectors—the hit and false-alarm rate, and hence the person's response bias and actual sensitivity to the signal, can be assessed by periodic tests with planted stimuli, which are known to contain or not contain the signal.

The Difference Threshold and Weber's Law

Whereas the absolute threshold is the minimum intensity of a stimulus that a person can detect, the ***difference threshold*** is the minimum difference that must exist between two stimuli for the person to detect them as different. To determine a difference threshold for sound intensity, a person is presented on each trial with a standard tone, always of the same intensity, and a comparison tone, which is sometimes the same intensity as the standard tone and sometimes not, and is asked to report whether the two tones are the same or different. Like the absolute threshold, the difference threshold is a statistical concept. It is commonly defined as the amount of difference between the standard and comparison stimuli required for correct detection of the difference in 50 percent of the trials (although in some situations, where guessing would produce 50 percent correct, 75 percent is used as the criterion). Another name for the difference threshold is the ***just-noticeable difference***, abbreviated *jnd*.

The first scientist to study the jnd systematically was the nineteenth-century German physiologist Ernst Weber (1834). Weber asked: What is the relationship between the jnd and the intensity (or magnitude) of the standard stimulus? That is, if the standard stimulus is increased in intensity, does the jnd stay the same, or does it change in some systematic way? In one series of experiments Weber applied this question to people's ability to judge differences between weights. On each trial he asked the subjects to pick up each of two weights (the standard weight and a comparison weight), one at a time, and judge which was heavier. Weber found that the jnd varied in direct proportion to the weight of the standard. Specifically, he found that for any standard weight that he used (within a certain range), the jnd was approximately 1/30 of the standard weight (Gescheider, 1976). Thus, a typical subject could just barely discriminate between a 15-gram and a 15.5-gram weight or between a 90-gram and a 93-gram weight. In the first case the jnd was 0.5 gram, and in the second it was 3 grams, but in both cases it was 1/30 of the standard weight. In other experiments, Weber studied people's ability to discriminate between the lengths of two lines, one presented after the other, and again he found a constant proportionality between the standard stimulus and the difference threshold. For this task, however, the constant fraction was 1/100 rather than 1/30. Thus, a typical subject could just barely detect the difference between a 100- and a 101-millimeter line or between a 1000- and a 1010-millimeter line.

On the basis of these and similar experiments, Weber formulated a general law, now called **Weber's law**, stating that *the jnd for stimulus magnitude is a constant proportion of the magnitude of the standard stimulus.* The law can be abbreviated as

$$\text{jnd} = kM$$

in which M is the intensity or magnitude of the stimulus used as the standard and k is a proportionality constant referred to as the *Weber fraction*, which is different for different sensory tasks (1/30 for weight judgment and 1/100 for length judgment in the examples cited previously). Since Weber's time, psychophysical experiments have confirmed Weber's law for many different types of stimuli. The law holds rather well over a wide portion of the possible range of intensities or magnitudes for most types of stimuli, but not at the very low (near the absolute threshold) and very high ends of the range.

Relating the Psychological Amount of a Stimulus to the Physical Amount

When a physical stimulus increases, our sensory experience of it also increases. When a sucrose solution becomes more concentrated, we taste its sweetness as stronger; when a sound increases in amplitude, we hear it as louder; when a light becomes more intense, we see it as brighter; and so on. Is it possible to specify in a mathematical equation the relationship between the magnitude of a stimulus and the magnitude of the sensory experience produced by it? Such an equation was proposed in the nineteenth century and tested experimentally and modified in the twentieth.

Fechner's Logarithmic Law

Gustav Fechner (1860/1966), like Weber a nineteenth-century German, used Weber's law to derive a mathematical relationship between stimulus magnitude and sensory magnitude. The jnd is measured in physical units (such as grams or sound-pressure units), yet it reflects a sensory phenomenon, the just-noticeable difference between two sensations. Therefore, Fechner reasoned, the jnd could serve as a unit for relating physical and sensory magnitudes. His crucial assumptions were (a) that every jnd along a sensory dimension is equivalent to every other jnd along that dimension in the amount it adds to the sensory magnitude and (b) that jnd's can be added together. In other words, he assumed that a sound that is 100 jnd's above threshold would sound twice as loud as one that is 50 jnd's above threshold, or one-tenth as loud as one that is 1000 jnd's above threshold.

Fechner assumed that jnd's are subjectively equal, but he knew from Weber's work that they are not physically equal. As you just saw, the jnd is directly proportional to the magnitude of the original stimulus. Thus, Fechner assumed that the amount of physical change needed to create a constant sensory change is directly proportional to the magnitude of the stimulus, and he showed mathematically that this can be expressed as a logarithmic relationship (if you wish to see how he could prove this, turn to page A-9 of the Statistical Appendix at the back of the book). Thus, Fechner derived what he believed to be a general psychophysical law, now called **Fechner's law**, stating that *the magnitude of the sensory experience of a stimulus is directly proportional to the logarithm of the physical magnitude of the stimulus.* This law can be abbreviated as

$$S = c \log M$$

where S is the magnitude of the sensory experience, c is a proportionality constant, and M is the magnitude of the physical stimulus.

32.

How did Fechner use Weber's law to formulate a law relating sensory magnitude to the logarithm of stimulus magnitude?

TABLE **7.3**   *Illustration of the relation between physical magnitude (M) and sensory magnitude (S) according to Fechner's law*

Number of light bulbs	M	S* (1 log M)	
1	100	2.00	
2	200	2.30	+.30
3	300	2.48	
4	400	2.60	+.30
5	500	2.70	
6	600	2.78	
7	700	2.84	+.30
8	800	2.90	

*In this hypothetical example, c in the formula $S = c \log M$ is 1. A change in c would change the values of S but would not change the fact that each doubling of M adds a constant increment to S, which is the point that the table is designed to illustrate.

To gain a sense of the meaning of Fechner's law (if you are a bit foggy on logarithms), look at Table 7.3, which shows hypothetical data that are consistent with the law. Imagine a person judging the brightness of a room's illumination with one light bulb on, then two bulbs, then three bulbs, and so on. Although each successive bulb adds a constant amount (100 units) to the physical intensity (M) of the room's illumination, each bulb adds a progressively smaller amount to the perceived brightness (S). Thus, in the example, the second bulb adds 0.30 unit to the brightness, the third adds another 0.18 unit, the fourth adds 0.12, and so on. Notice too that every time the physical intensity (M) doubles, the sensed brightness (S) increases by a constant amount (0.30 unit in the example). Stated differently, as the physical scale increases geometrically, the sensory scale increases arithmetically. That is the essence of a logarithmic relationship. Consequently, a huge intensity range on the physical scale is condensed to a much smaller range on the psychological scale.

Stevens's Power Law

Although Fechner believed his law was valid on theoretical grounds, he did not believe it could be tested experimentally. He wrote (in 1860), "A real measure of sensation would demand that we be able to call a given sensation twice, thrice, or so-and-so as many times as intense as another—but who would say such a thing?" (quoted in Stevens, 1975). The belief that people could not report the magnitudes of their sensations in a consistent way went relatively unchallenged until the early 1950s, when S. S. Stevens, a Harvard psychologist, began a series of experiments in which he asked people to do exactly that.

33.

How did Stevens test Fechner's law, and what did he find? How does Stevens's law differ from Fechner's?

Stevens's technique, called the ***method of magnitude estimation***, was to ask subjects to assign numbers to the magnitudes of their sensations. For example, he would present a standard stimulus and call that a "10," and then he would present a comparison stimulus and ask the subject to give it a number that best approximated its sensory magnitude compared with that of the standard. Thus, a sensation that appeared to the subject to be twice that of the standard would be called "20," one that seemed half that of the standard would be called "5," and so on. Stevens found that people had little difficulty carrying out these instructions and that their responses were remarkably consistent for any given set of stimuli.

If Fechner's law were correct, Stevens should have found that his subjects' magnitude estimates were directly proportional to the logarithms of the stimulus intensities he used. He found, however, that the logarithmic relationship was only roughly accurate for most senses and very inaccurate for some senses and that for every sense the results could be described better by a different mathematical relationship—a power relationship. On this basis, Stevens proposed a **power law** as an alternative to Fechner's logarithmic law. According to Stevens's power law, *the intensity of a sensation is directly proportional to the intensity of the physical stimulus raised by a constant power*. The law can be abbreviated as

$$S = cMp$$

where S is the reported magnitude of the sensory experience, M is the physical magnitude of the stimulus, p is the power (or exponent) to which M must be raised (which differs from one sensory dimension to another), and c is a constant that depends on the size of the measurement units used.

How does Stevens's law compare with Fechner's? If you transform each side of the above equation logarithmically, the equation becomes

$$\log S = \log(cMp)$$

which can be rewritten as

$$\log S = \log c + p \log M$$

Because $\log c$ is simply a constant, the equation now shows that the logarithm of S is directly (linearly) related to the logarithm of M. In other words, whereas Fechner's law holds that the sensory magnitude is directly proportional to the logarithm of the physical magnitude, Stevens's law maintains that the *logarithm* of the sensory magnitude is directly proportional to the logarithm of the physical magnitude.

Stevens and his colleagues performed dozens of experiments, involving magnitude estimates for many different kinds of stimuli, and they almost always found that the results could be quite well represented by a power equation. For each kind of stimulus, they could determine a unique exponent (p) to which the physical magnitude had to be raised to approximate the experienced magnitude. Table 7.4 shows the exponents that they compiled for several different kinds of stimuli. Notice that for most tasks shown in the table the exponent is less than 1, but for one task (estimating the length of a line) it is exactly 1, and for another (estimating the pain of an electric shock) it is greater than 1. In cases where p is less than 1, equal physical changes produce smaller sensory changes at the high end of the scale than at the low end, as was also true with Fechner's logarithmic law. When p is greater than 1, however, the opposite relationship holds. Thus, adding a certain amount of electric shock to a relatively strong shock produces a greater increase in pain than does adding the same amount to a relatively weak shock. Finally, when p is equal to 1,

TABLE **7.4**   *Power-law exponents for various stimuli*

Type of stimulus	Measured exponent (p)*
Brightness of a spot of light in the dark	0.33
Loudness of a 3000-cps tone	0.67
Smell of heptane	0.60
Taste of saccharine	0.80
Length of a line	1.00
Pain of an electric shock on the fingers	3.50

*The exponent (p) is the power to which the stimulus magnitude must be raised to approximate the sensory magnitude.

Source: From *Psychophysics: Introduction to its perceptual, neural, and social prospects* (p.13) by S. S. Stevens, 1975, New York: Wiley.

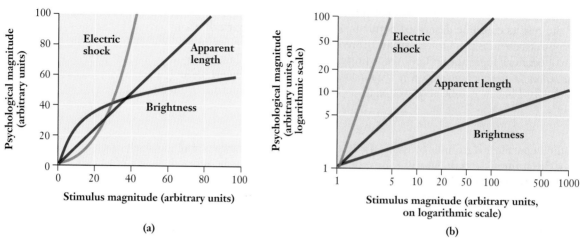

FIGURE 7.21   *Stevens's power law illustrated for three sensory dimensions*
Graph (a) shows how subjects' estimates of the sensory magnitude that they experienced in-creased as the stimulus magnitude increased, with separate data for the pain of an electric shock, the length of a line, and the brightness of a spot of light. Notice that the curvature is upward or downward depending on whether the exponent, *p*, is greater or less than 1. Graph (b) depicts the same data (with different arbitrary units) after both scales have been converted to logarithms. Now all the lines are straight. By definition, a power law specifies a relationship in which the logarithm of one variable is linearly related to the logarithm of the other. (Adapted from Stevens, 1962.)

equal physical changes produce the same amount of sensory change whether one is starting with a strong or a weak stimulus. All these relationships are graphically portrayed in Figure 7.21a. In Figure 7.21b, you can see that the results for each magnitude-estimation task fit a straight line when graphed on log–log coordinates; that is the proof of a power law. If Fechner's law had been correct, a straight line would have resulted from converting just the physical scale (the horizontal axis) to logarithms, without converting the sensory scale (the vertical axis) to logarithms.

Why a Power Law?

Why do our senses obey a power law for so many different kinds of stimuli? Is it just coincidence, or is there some advantage that would lead each sense, in the course of evolution, to operate in accordance with a power law? Stevens (1975) thought a good deal about that question, and the answer he suggested was essentially the following:

Our world of stimuli is constantly changing. As we move closer to or farther from the sources of stimulation, or as day turns to dusk, the overall intensity of the energy reaching us from specific objects in the environment changes greatly. If we are to recognize the same scenes, sounds, and smells under such varying conditions, then we must extract those features of each stimulus constellation that remain con-stant. One such constancy is the ratio of the magnitudes of the stimulus elements with respect to each other.

As you move toward or away from a sound source, the ratio of the amplitudes of the various tones in the sound remains relatively constant, even though the over-all amplitude increases or decreases greatly. Similarly, the ratio of light reflected from a darker compared with a lighter portion of a visual scene remains nearly con-stant as the overall intensity fades at dusk. A power law, and only a power law, pre-serves constant sensory ratios as the overall intensity waxes or wanes. (You can find a proof of this statement on page A-10 of the Statistical Appendix at the back of the book.) For example, in the case of the power function for brightness, with an expo-nent of 0.33, every eightfold change in light intensity results in a twofold change in

34.

Why is it advantageous that our senses operate according to a power law rather than a logarithmic law?

apparent brightness, no matter where on the intensity continuum we start. Thus, if the light illuminating a visual scene decreases in physical intensity to one-eighth of what it was before, each part of the scene will appear half as bright as before, and the ratios of brightnesses among the parts will remain what they were before. The elegant feature of the power law, with p less than 1, is that it compresses large physical changes down to smaller sensory changes, as does the logarithmic law; but, unlike the logarithmic law, it does this while preserving the constancy of stimulus ratios.

SECTION SUMMARY

Psychophysics deals with relationships between physical measures of stimuli and psychological, or behavioral, measures of sensory experiences. In assessing the minimal intensity of a stimulus that a person can reliably detect (the absolute threshold), psychophysicists take into account the person's response bias by comparing the number of hits to the number of false alarms. In the nineteenth century, Weber found that the minimal difference in physical magnitude between two stimuli (a standard and a comparison stimulus) that is required for a person to detect them as different (the jnd) is a constant proportion of the magnitude of the standard stimulus. On this basis, plus questionable assumptions about the equivalence and additivity of jnd's, Fechner formulated a psychophysical law claiming that for any type of stimulus the sensory magnitude is directly proportional to the logarithm of the physical magnitude of the stimulus. Much later, with experiments using the method of magnitude estimation, S. S. Stevens disproved Fechner's logarithmic law and replaced it with a power law: The sensory magnitude is directly proportional to the physical magnitude of the stimulus raised by a constant power. Natural selection apparently favored a power law because a power law, unlike a logarithmic law, can compress large physical changes into smaller sensory changes while preserving constant ratios of magnitudes in the sensory environment.

CONCLUDING THOUGHTS

Broad themes can get lost in a chapter as full of details as this one. Yet if you focus on the themes as you review, even the details will be easier to understand and remember. Here are three themes that might help you think about and review the chapter:

1. **The mechanisms of transduction and coding**   All sensory systems respond to physical stimuli by producing action potentials (the process of transduction), and all sensory systems do this in such a way as to preserve useful information about the stimulus (coding). For each sense discussed in this chapter—smell, taste, pain, and hearing—you might think about each of the following questions pertaining to transduction and coding: (a) To what type of physical stimulus does this sense respond, and what is the range of stimuli to which it responds? (b) How is the sensory organ designed for receiving (and possibly concentrating or amplifying) the stimulus? (c) What are the receptors for the stimulus, and how do they respond in such a way as to generate action potentials in sensory neurons? (d) How does the transduction process code the different qualities of stimuli to which the sensory system responds? (e) How do neural mechanisms in the central nervous system alter or reorganize the input and for what purposes? The chapter does not answer all these questions (especially not the last) completely for each sense, but the questions will provide a good framework for organizing and thinking about the information that is provided.

2. **The survival functions of sensory processes**   Our sensory systems, like all the basic mechanisms underlying our behavior, evolved through natural selection because they promoted our ancestors' survival and reproduction. They are not unbiased

35.

What are some findings that illustrate the theme that sensory systems promote survival through means other than faithful recording of the physical properties of stimuli?

recorders of physical energies but biological tools designed to pick out from the sea of energy around us the information that is potentially most useful. We are sensitive to some kinds of energies and not others, and, within the kinds to which we are sensitive, our senses extract and enhance some relationships and not others.

Here are some examples, described in the chapter, of how specific sensory processes can be understood in terms of their survival advantages: (a) Sensory adaptation (the decline in sensitivity to prolonged, constant stimuli) helps us to ignore stimuli that remain unchanged and to notice changes. (b) Smell and taste work together to produce flavors that are experienced as pleasant or unpleasant, in ways that as a rule are consistent with what is good for us or bad for us (or for our evolutionary ancestors) to eat. The bitter rejection response is an example, and variations of this reaction across species occur in a manner that makes evolutionary sense. (c) Pain is a sensory system for warning us when our actions are damaging our tissues and for motivating us to avoid such actions. Evolved mechanisms increase pain sensitivity at times of illness, when it is best to rest, and decrease pain sensitivity at times of threat, when strenuous action without favoring one's wounds may be necessary. (d) The phonemic-restoration illusion helps us to hear speech in a continuous flow and ignore extraneous noises, which may increase comprehension. (e) The fact that our senses obey a power law in converting stimulus magnitude to sensory magnitude may have come about because the power law preserves the constancy of ratios, helping us recognize a pattern in sound or light as the same pattern even when its overall intensity increases or decreases.

3. The problem of objective assessment of subjective experience   A problem running through all of psychology is that of assessing what is in people's minds through objective, behavioral means. In the study of sensation that problem can be confronted in a more straightforward way than in other areas of psychology because sensations are the aspects of mental life that are most reliably related to measurable aspects of the physical world. Psychophysics is the subfield that assesses these relationships most directly. Psychophysicists have developed means to assess the absolute threshold, the difference threshold, and the relative magnitude of one sensory experience compared with another, and they have tied these to measures of the physical stimulus. Psychologists in other fields sometimes borrow the methods of psychophysics to study subjective judgments that are far removed from raw sensations. The signal-detection procedure for assessing response bias has been applied in such tasks as the judgment of guilt or innocence on the basis of the evidence that a juror might hear; and Stevens's method of magnitude estimation has been used for such tasks as estimating the relative amount of pleasure that would be gained from winning various amounts of money.

Further Reading

Constance Classen (1993). *Worlds of sense: Exploring the senses in history and across cultures.* London: Routledge.

This book treats sensation from a cultural rather than physiological perspective. People learn in different cultures to respond very differently to particular sights, sounds, tastes, and smells. Moreover, as this book makes clear, words having to do with the senses become culture-specific metaphors for more abstract concepts—such as, in English, blue, bland, bitter, sweet, foul, hot, cold, see, and sensitive.

Howard C. Hughes (1999). *Sensory exotica: A world beyond human experience.* Cambridge, MA: MIT Press.

The fit between an animal's senses and its habitat and behavior becomes most apparent when we look at animals whose sensory world is very different from our own. This fascinating, well-researched book is about sonar in bats and dolphins, magnetic-field sensitivity in migrating birds, sun compasses in bees and ants, electroreception in fishes, and pheromone communication in insects and mammals.

Gary K. Beauchamp & Linda Bartoshuk (Eds.) (1997). *Tasting and smelling.* San Diego: Academic Press.

This brief, scholarly book is clearly written and quite readable by the serious beginning student. It consists of six chapters, each by a different expert or pair of experts, which deal with the transduction mechanisms of taste, coding in taste, psychophysics of taste, psychophysics of smell, clinical disorders of taste and smell, and the development of flavor perception in infants.

Brian C. J. Moore (1997). *An introduction to the psychology of hearing* (4th ed.). San Diego: Academic Press.

Clear and up to date, this paperback textbook discusses all aspects of the physiology and psychology of hearing. Separate chapters are devoted to the auditory perception of loudness, pitch, space, and temporal qualities (such as rhythm). The final two chapters deal with speech perception and with practical applications in such realms as development of sound reproduction systems (such as compact disc players) and aids for the hard of hearing.

Paul Brand & Philip Yancey (1993). *Pain: The gift nobody wants.* New York: HarperCollins.

For over 50 years and in three cultures (England, India, and the United States), Paul Brand worked as a surgeon among people who suffered from pain and others who suffered from lack of ability to feel pain (due in most cases to leprosy). Through numerous case examples this book tells us how people experience and manage their pain. We learn of pain as both a cultural phenomenon and an intensely personal phenomenon. We gain respect for our most despised sense.

S. S. Stevens (1975). *Psychophysics: Introduction to its perceptual, neural, and social prospects.* New York: Wiley.

A brilliant description of the research leading to the power law and the implications of that law, this slender classic is quite readable by the beginning student who is not intimidated by exponents or algebraic equations. Stevens also shows how the power law applies to magnitude judgments other than those about sensations, such as judgments about the seriousness of crimes.

Looking Ahead

Most psychological research on sensation and perception has centered on vision, so that sense receives a chapter of its own—the next in our sequence. Whereas the research on smell, taste, and pain provided us with an opportunity to link the senses to basic drives and emotions, the research on vision links more strongly to cognition—to issues of memory and thought that are discussed in the chapters that follow the next one. With vision, then, we shift our primary focus from the "sensation" end of the sensation-perception spectrum toward the "perception" end. What cues do we use to perceive the sizes, shapes, and distances of objects in our three-dimensional world? How do we translate the images on our retinas into recognizable, meaningful objects?

Vision

At the start of the last chapter I pointed out the close tie between an animal's sensory systems and its natural habits of life. We humans are highly visual animals. Our sleep system (as discussed in Chapter 6) evolved to keep us quiet and hidden at night and active during the day, largely because we depend on vision to find food, avoid dangers, and do what else we must to survive. We are also cognitive animals. We are specialists in thinking. Our senses don't just guide our immediate actions; they also provide us with *information* about the world in which we live—information that we remember, think about, and use in planning future actions. Our visual system is a major route of such information. Vision may or may not be the most important human sense (I could argue the question either way), but it is by far the most thoroughly studied sense, especially by psychologists. It is also true that a greater portion of our cerebral cortex is devoted to vision than to any other sense.

At the start of the last chapter I described the rough distinction between sensation and perception. *Sensation* refers generally to the basic processes by which sensory organs and the nervous system respond to sensory stimuli and encode information about those stimuli. It refers also to the elementary experiences (such as the pitch of a sound or the color of a patch of light) that result from such encoding. *Perception* refers generally to the processes by which sensory information is selected, organized, and in other ways manipulated by the nervous system to extract or construct meaningful representations of objects and events that exist in the external environment. From a cognitive perspective, perception is the ultimate purpose of sensation. Our senses evolved their present capacities not primarily because these capacities allowed our ancestors to distinguish yellow from green or middle C from C sharp but because they allowed our ancestors to identify bananas, tigers, and the calls and words of their friends.

This chapter, on visual sensation and perception, is divided into three main sections. The first section deals with physiological bases for vision and is largely concerned with the more "sensory" aspects of vision: How does the eye work? How is information in light coded so as to allow us to see variations in color and brightness? What is known about brain areas involved in organizing and analyzing visual input? The other two sections deal with issues that are most commonly classed as "perceptual": How do we see patterns and recognize objects in the visual array that strikes our eyes? What information in the visual input allows us to perceive the distances, sizes, and movements of objects in three-dimensional space?

PHYSIOLOGICAL FOUNDATIONS FOR SEEING

Life on earth evolved in a world illuminated by the sun during the day and by starlight and the moon's reflected sunlight at night. Most forms of earthly life are sensitive in one way or another to that light (Land & Furnald, 1992). Even single-celled organisms contain chemicals that respond to light and alter the organism's

275

activity in survival-promoting ways. In many species of multicellular animals, specialized light-detecting cells called **photoreceptors** evolved and became connected to the animal's nervous system. Earthworms, for example, have photoreceptors distributed throughout their skin. Stimulation of these cells by light causes the worm to wriggle back down into the earth, where it finds food and safety.

A standard, partly speculative account of the evolution toward eyes like ours goes as follows (after Gregory, 1996): In some organisms photoreceptors became concentrated into groups, forming primitive light-detecting organs, or *eye spots*, on the animal's skin. With further evolution these eye spots became recessed into depressions, or pits, a step that reduced glare and increased the animal's chance of detecting moving boundaries of light and dark that could signal an approaching predator. Subsequent evolution led to the development of a transparent membrane covering such pits, protecting them from becoming filled by sand particles or other debris that could block incoming light. Mutations that thickened the center of this membrane converted it into a crude lens, which at first may have served merely to magnify the light reaching the photoreceptors but which with further refinement became capable of projecting an image onto the lining of photoreceptors. Through these and further steps, coupled with appropriate changes in the nervous system, the primitive ability to detect light and shadows evolved into the more advanced ability to see the shapes of things and eventually into the marvelously complex and precise visual ability that this chapter is about.

Functional Organization of the Eye and the Process of Transduction

The main parts of the human eye are shown in Figure 8.1. The photoreceptors lie in the **retina,** a membrane lining the rear interior of the fluid-filled eyeball. The rest of the eye is a device for focusing light reflected from objects in such a way as to form an image on the retina. The front of the eyeball is covered by the **cornea,** a transparent tissue that, because of its convex (outward) curvature, helps focus the light that passes through it. Immediately behind the cornea is the pigmented, doughnut-shaped **iris,** which provides the color (usually brown or blue) of the eye. The iris is opaque, so the only light that can enter the interior of the eye is that which passes through the **pupil,** which is simply the hole in the center of the iris. Muscle fibers in the iris enable it to increase or decrease the diameter of the pupil to allow more or less light to enter. Behind the iris is the **lens,** which adds to the focusing process begun by the cornea. Unlike the cornea, the lens is adjustable—it becomes more spherical when focusing on objects close to the eye and flatter when focusing on those farther away. Light rays diverge as they move toward the eye from any given point on a visual object. The focusing properties of the cornea and lens bring the light rays back together at a particular point on the retina, thereby forming an image of the object on the retina.

1.

Through what steps might sophisticated eyes like ours have evolved from primitive beginnings?

2.

How do the cornea, iris, and lens help form images on the retina?

FIGURE 8.1 *Cross section of the eye, depicting the retinal image* The light rays that diverge from any given point on the surface of an object are brought back together (focused) at a distinct point on the retina to create an image of the object on the retina. This drawing shows light rays diverging and being brought together for just two points on the leaf, but the same process is occurring for light rays coming from every point.

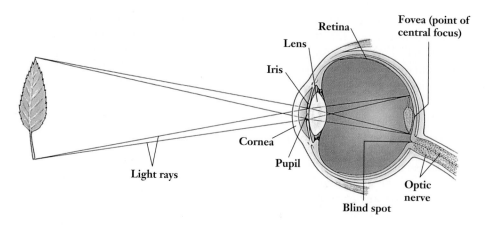

FIGURE 8.2 *Rods and cones*
This electron micrograph shows that the photoreceptors are aptly named. Rods are responsible for vision in dim light, and cones for vision in bright light.

As discussed in Chapter 7, the process by which a stimulus from the environment generates electrical changes in neurons is referred to as *transduction*. In vision, transduction is the function of the photoreceptors. In each eye millions of photoreceptor cells are arranged, mosaiclike, in one thin layer of the multilayered retina. These cells are of two types: ***cones,*** which permit sharply focused color vision in bright light, and ***rods,*** which permit vision in dim light. They are so named because of their general shapes (see Figure 8.2). Cones are most concentrated in the ***fovea,*** the pinhead-size area of the retina that is in the most direct line of sight (look again at Figure 8.1), which is specialized for high visual *acuity* (the ability to distinguish minute details). The concentration of cones decreases sharply with increasing distance from the fovea. Rods, in contrast, exist everywhere in the retina except in the fovea and are most concentrated in a ring about 20 degrees away from the fovea (see Figure 8.3). Each human retina contains about 6 million cones and 120 million rods (Wade & Swanston, 1991).

3.

How are cones and rods distributed in different parts of the retina, and how do they respond to light?

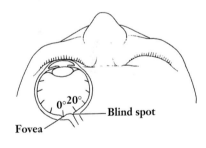

FIGURE 8.3 *Distribution of cones and rods in the retina*
Cones are most concentrated in the fovea. Rods are absent from the fovea and most concentrated in a ring 20 degrees away from it. No receptors at all exist in the blind spot.

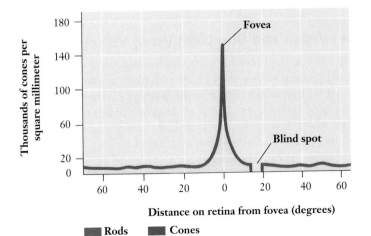

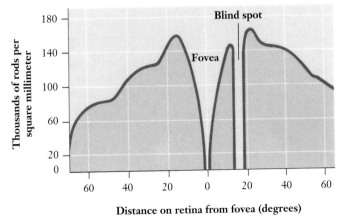

The outer segment of each photoreceptor contains a *photochemical*—a chemical that reacts to light. The rods' photochemical is called **rhodopsin**. When hit by light, rhodopsin molecules undergo a structural change that triggers a series of chemical reactions in the rod's membrane, which in turn causes an electrical change across the membrane (Schnapf & Baylor, 1987). The transduction process for cones is similar to that for rods, but (for reasons discussed in the section on color vision) three varieties of cones exist and each contains a different photochemical. The electrical changes in rods and cones cause electrical responses in other cells in the retina, which lead to the production of action potentials (neural impulses) in neurons that form the **optic nerve,** which runs from the back of the eye to the brain. At the place on the retina where the axons of these neurons converge to form the optic nerve there is a **blind spot,** due to the absence of receptor cells (shown in Figure 8.3). We normally do not notice the blind spot, but you can demonstrate its existence by following the instructions in Figure 8.4.

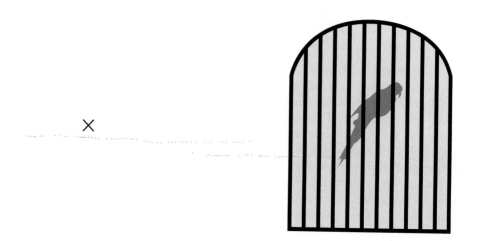

FIGURE 8.4
Demonstration of the blind spot
Close your left eye and focus on the X with your right eye. Start with the page a little more than a foot from your eye and move it gradually closer, still focusing on the X. At about 10 inches, the bird will disappear. At that location, the image of the bird falls on the blind spot of the retina, shown in Figure 8.3. Yet you will probably still see the bars of the cage running across the area where the bird was located, and the background color may fill the space previously occupied by the bird. The bars and color are perceptually filled in by a process called surface interpolation, which is discussed later in the chapter.

One of the many problems that our visual system has to solve is that of adjusting to the enormous range of light intensities that occur over a 24-hour day. A white object in sunlight at noon reflects roughly 100 million times as much light as the same object reflects on a starlit but moonless night (Riggs, 1965), yet we can see the object in either condition. The iris, which dilates (widens) the pupil in darkness and constricts (narrows) it in bright light, provides part of the solution to the problem of adjusting to variations in brightness: A fully dilated pupil allows in about 16 times as much light as a fully constricted pupil (Matlin & Foley, 1997). The major part of the solution, however, lies in the fact that our two different types of photoreceptors, cones and rods, are differentially sensitive to bright and dim light.

Bright-Light (Cone) Vision and Dim-Light (Rod) Vision

4.

How do cone vision and rod vision differ?

Cones and rods provide the starting point for what can be thought of as two separate but interacting visual systems within the human eye. **Cone vision** (also called *photopic vision* or *bright-light vision*) is specialized for high acuity and for the perception of color. **Rod vision** (also called *scotopic vision* or *dim-light vision*) is specialized for sensitivity (the ability to see in very dim light). It lacks acuity (the edges of objects appear fuzzy) and the ability to distinguish colors. Rod vision is so sensitive that, according to calculations from laboratory studies, it should be possible on a clear night to see a single candle flame on a hill 30 miles away if no other lights are present (Galanter, 1962).

In very dim light, too dim to activate cones, you see only with rod vision; you can make out the general shapes of objects but not their details and colors. In such light you can see dim objects best when you don't look directly at them—because, as noted before, the fovea (the part of the retina in the direct line of sight) contains no rods. If you find yourself in the country on a starry but moonless night, away from all artificial lights, try to stare at the dimmest star that you can see. It will disappear when you look straight at it, but reappear when you look just a little away. You can see it best when looking 20 degrees away, because this angle allows the light from the star to strike the part of the retina where rods are most concentrated.

The Separate Adaptation Curves of Cones and Rods

As you know from experience, it takes time for your vision to adapt to a sudden large change in illumination. The gradual increase in sensitivity to light that occurs after you enter a darkened room or turn off the lights is called *dark adaptation,* and the more rapid decrease in sensitivity that occurs after you turn on a bright lamp or step out into sunlight is called *light adaptation.* These processes are mediated in part by changes in the sensitivities of cones and rods and by a shift from predominantly cone vision to predominantly rod vision, or vice versa. In bright light, the photochemical molecules tend to break down quite rapidly to two inactive substances, and in dim light or darkness they gradually re-form. The cone photochemicals do not break down as fully as the rod photochemical (rhodopsin), and this is part of the reason why cones are more responsive than rods in normal to bright light. For the same reason, when you first move from bright illumination into a dark room, whatever you can see immediately you are seeing more with cones than with rods.

For the first 7 or 8 minutes in the dark, after being in bright light, you are seeing mostly with cones, and the improvement in vision that occurs during that time is due mostly to the regeneration of the cone photochemicals. Further improvement after that, however, is due to rods, as rhodopsin continues to regenerate for another 15 to 20 minutes after the cones have become as sensitive as they can. This two-part dark-adaptation process is graphed in Figure 8.5. The blue, lowest curve depicts the shift in sensitivity for people with normal vision, who have both cones and rods. People who are completely color-blind show the rods-only (green) curve because they have no cone photochemicals (Grüsser & Grüsser-Cornehls, 1986), and people who have no rhodopsin (as a result of severe vitamin A deficiency) show the cones-only (red) curve (Hecht & Mandelbaum, 1938). Complicating this otherwise tidy story, recent research has shown that light and dark adaptation are mediated not just by the breakdown and regeneration of the photochemicals but also by poorly understood changes in the sensitivity of cells in the retina that receive input from the photoreceptors (Hood, 1998).

5.

What is the chemical basis for light and dark adaptation, and why do we see mostly with cones in bright light and with rods in dim light?

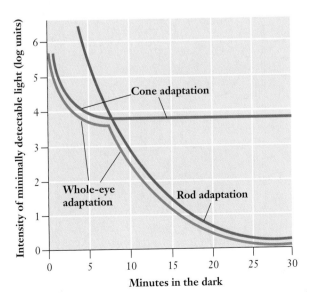

FIGURE **8.5** *Dark-adaptation curves* The blue curve depicts the minimal intensity of a spot of light that a person with normal vision can see after varying periods in the dark. The lower the curve, the greater the sensitivity to light. For the first 7 minutes or so, the cones are more sensitive than the rods, but after that the rods are more sensitive. The two-part nature of the curve can be understood by comparing it to the dark-adaptation curve obtained for a person who has only rods (the green curve) and to that obtained if the light is presented in such a way that it strikes only the fovea, where only cones exist (the red curve). (From Grüsser & Grüsser-Cornehls, 1986.)

In today's world of artificial lights and rapid changes in degree of lighting, the slowness of dark adaptation seems maladaptive. In the world of our ancestors, however, it probably had little effect. As day became dusk and dusk became night, the dimming of light was gradual, so a gradual process of dark adaptation would generally have served perfectly well.

Neural Convergence as a Basis for Differences Between Cone Vision and Rod Vision

6.

How does the pattern of neural connections within the retina help account for the greater sensitivity and reduced acuity of rod vision compared with cone vision?

The superiority of rods over cones in detecting dim light stems not just from the greater sensitivity of rhodopsin but also from a difference in the way rods and cones are connected to neurons of the optic nerve. As shown in Figure 8.6, both rods and cones form synapses on short neurons called *bipolar cells,* which in turn form synapses on larger neurons called *ganglion cells.* The ganglion cells have their cell bodies in the retina, and they have long axons that leave the eye at the blind spot to form the optic nerve. Other neurons (horizontal cells and amacrine cells) within the retina interconnect adjacent bipolar and ganglion cells, creating a good deal of complexity in the connections within the retina.

The net effect of these connections is that each ganglion cell receives input from a set of rods and/or cones, which are located adjacent to one another and define the *receptive field* of that cell. To understand the concept of a receptive field, imagine an experiment in which a dot of light is shined into an animal's eye and moved so that it strikes various parts of the retina while a recording is made of the electrical activity of a particular ganglion cell or other neuron in the animal's visual system. The localized portion of the retina within which the dot of light can alter the electrical activity of the cell is the receptive field for that cell. The receptive field is larger for ganglion cells that receive input primarily or wholly from rods than for those that receive input primarily or wholly from cones.

To visualize this difference and how it bears on acuity and sensitivity, look at Figure 8.7. As depicted in the left-hand portion of the figure, each ganglion cell in the fovea receives input from a small number of cones—often just one (Masland, 1996)—which means that its receptive field is very small. Consequently, two dots of light very close to each other will act on separate ganglion cells, resulting in two

FIGURE 8.6 *Diagram of cells in a cross section of the retina*
Light that reaches the retina must pass through its relatively transparent inner layers of cells before reaching the sensitive ends of the rods and cones in the outermost layer, at the back of the eye.

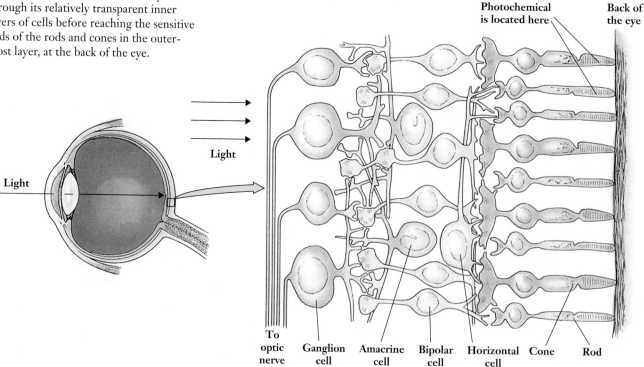

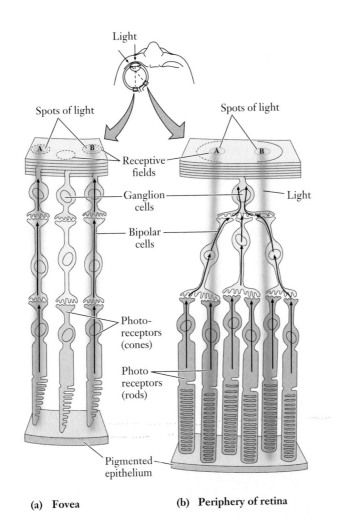

FIGURE **8.7** *Relationship of receptive-field size to visual acuity and sensitivity*

Ganglion cells in the fovea have smaller receptive fields than do those in the periphery; in other words, they receive input from fewer receptor cells. This difference accounts for high acuity in the fovea and high sensitivity (but low acuity) in the periphery. Spots A and B of light on the fovea (diagram a) will activate two different ganglion cells, and hence maintain their distinctiveness (high acuity). The same two spots in the periphery (diagram b) will activate the same ganglion cell and lose their distinctiveness (low acuity), but each spot will add to the total activity of that cell (high sensitivity). (*Note*: For the sake of simplicity, this figure omits the horizontal and amacrine cells and underestimates the actual amount of convergence that occurs in both the fovea and the periphery.)

distinct messages to the brain—a condition that permits them to be seen as separate dots (high acuity) rather than as a single blurred-together dot (low acuity). The right-hand portion of the figure illustrates peripheral portions of the retina, where rods predominate. Here each ganglion cell receives input from a large number of receptor cells (thousands, in some cases) spread out over a relatively large area, which means that its receptive field is large. Two dots of light very close to each other will therefore act on the same ganglion cell, and thus lose their distinctiveness, causing them to blur into one dot in the person's perception (low acuity). For the same reason that acuity is decreased, however, sensitivity is increased. A small amount of electrical activity coming from each receptor cell, when stimulated by dim light, can add up to produce a relatively large amount of electrical activity in the ganglion cell. The funneling of the activity of many receptor cells to fewer sensory neurons is called ***neural convergence.*** In general, in other sensory systems as well as vision, high neural convergence increases sensitivity at the expense of acuity.

Seeing Colors

Many animals—including humans, other primates, birds, and bees—that depend greatly on vision to identify objects have evolved color vision, which helps to make objects stand out vividly from their backgrounds. The colors that we see in objects depend on the *wavelengths* of the light that is reflected from those objects.

Light is a form of electromagnetic energy, and like all such energy it can be described as both particles and waves. The particles, or individual packets of light, are called *photons*, and as they travel through space they pulsate in a wavelike way. Light travels at a constant speed (186,000 miles per second), and the distance that photons travel between the beginning of one pulse and the beginning of the next

7.

How can light be described physically, and what is the relationship of its wavelength to its perceived color?

defines the wavelength of the light. The wavelengths of light visible to humans range from about 400 to 700 nm (1 nm, or nanometer, is a billionth of a meter). Shorter waves of electromagnetic energy, below the visible range, include ultraviolet rays, x-rays, and gamma rays; longer waves, above the visible range, include infrared rays, radar rays, and radio waves. White light, such as that from the sun, contains all visible wavelengths combined (plus some of the nonvisible wavelengths). When the wavelengths in white light are separated (by shining the light through a prism, for example), the visual effect is an array of colors like that of a rainbow, because different wavelengths of visible light are seen as different colors. Progressing from the shortest to the longest wavelengths of visible light, we see the familiar rainbow spectrum, from violet through shades of blue, blue-green, green, green-yellow, yellow, orange, and red, in that order (see Figure 8.8).

FIGURE **8.8**
The electromagnetic spectrum
Light is the visible portion of the electromagnetic spectrum. White light, separated according to wavelength with a prism, produces the spectrum of visible colors, extending from violet and blue at the short-wavelength end to red at the long-wavelength end.

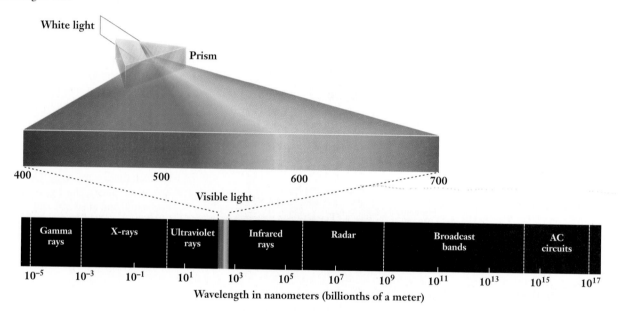

8.

How do pigments affect the perceived color of an object in white light? How does the mixing of pigments affect color by subtracting from the light that is reflected to the eye?

Objects vary in the wavelengths of light they reflect because they have on their surfaces different *pigments*, chemicals that absorb some wavelengths of light and thereby prevent them from being reflected. A pigment that absorbs short and medium waves, for example, appears red, because only long (red-appearing) waves are reflected. Similarly, a pigment that allows only short waves to be reflected appears violet or blue, and one that allows only medium waves to be reflected appears yellow or green. A surface that reflects all wavelengths about equally appears white, gray, or black, depending on whether the relative amount of each wavelength reflected is, respectively, high (none absorbed), moderate (some absorbed), or low (all absorbed).

Subtractive Color Mixing

Because pigments create the perception of color by *subtracting* (absorbing) some of the light waves that would otherwise be reflected to the eye, the mixing of pigments is called **subtractive color mixing**. As illustrated in Figure 8.9, if a blue pigment, which absorbs long waves, is mixed with a yellow pigment, which absorbs short waves, only medium-length waves will be reflected, and the mixture will be seen as green. When you were a child playing with watercolors, you probably proved the basic facts of subtractive color mixing many times. You may remember being disappointed when you mixed all the paints together and produced something pretty close to black rather than the brilliant reddish-yellowish-greenish-blue that you had hoped for. In that experiment you subtracted all the wavelengths by combining all the pigments.

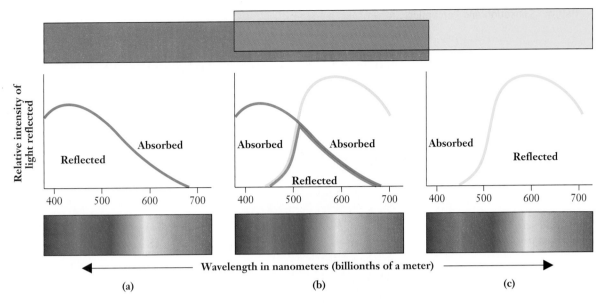

Reflected — Absorbed

Absorbed — Reflected — Absorbed

Absorbed — Reflected

400   500   600   700

400   500   600   700

400   500   600   700

◄——— Wavelength in nanometers (billionths of a meter) ———►

(a)   (b)   (c)

FIGURE **8.9** *Subtractive color mixing*
In this example, the blue pigment (a) absorbs most of the light that has wavelengths above 550 nm, and the yellow pigment (c) absorbs most of the light that has wavelengths below 500 nm. When the two pigments are mixed (b), the only light that is not strongly absorbed is that with wavelengths lying between 500 and 550 nm. This is the light that will be reflected, causing the mixture to appear green.

Two Laws of Additive Color Mixing

The opposite of subtractive color mixing is *additive color mixing,* which occurs when colored lights rather than pigments are mixed. Additive color mixing can be demonstrated by shining two or more beams of light of different wavelengths at the same spot on a white screen; the screen then reflects them back mixed together (see Figure 8.10). By the early eighteenth century, experiments had led to two general laws of additive color mixing. According to the *three-primaries law,* three different wavelengths of light (called *primaries*) can be used to match any color that the eye can see if they are mixed in the appropriate proportions. The primaries can be any three wavelengths as long as one is taken from the long-wave end of the spectrum (red), one from the short-wave end (blue or violet), and one from the middle (green or green-yellow). According to the *law of complementarity,* pairs of wavelengths can be found that, when added together, produce the visual sensation of white. The wavelengths of light in such a pair are referred to as *complements* of each other.

9.

How does additive color mixing differ from subtractive color mixing? What are the two laws of additive color mixing, and how is each illustrated in the standard chromaticity diagram?

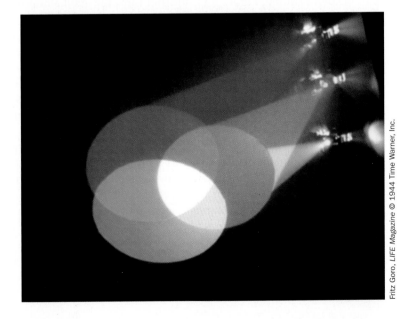

Fritz Goro, *LIFE Magazine* © 1944 Time Warner, Inc.

FIGURE **8.10** *Additive color mixing*
Additive color mixing occurs when lights of different wavelengths are mixed by shining them together on a surface that reflects all wavelengths. By varying the intensity of the three lights shown here, it would be possible to produce all the colors that the eye can see.

FIGURE 8.11 *The standard chromaticity diagram*

All the facts of additive color mixing—related to both the three-primaries law and the law of complementarity—are summarized in this diagram. The three primaries here are lights of 460 nm (blue), 530 nm (green), and 650 nm (red). The proportions of red and green primaries that must be added to the blue primary to match any given color on the diagram are shown, respectively, on the horizontal and vertical axes. The proportion of blue can be calculated by subtracting the other two proportions from 100 percent. For example, if you wish to match the blue-green produced by a 490-nm light, the figure indicates that your mixture must contain about 5 percent red primary, 30 percent green primary, and 65 percent blue primary (100% − 5% − 30% = 65%). As another example, the figure shows that the best white is produced by approximately equal (33.3 percent) proportions of the three primaries.

The chromaticity diagram can also be used to find all possible pairs of complementary colors. Two colors are complementary if their additive mixture produces white. In the diagram, the possible colors produced by mixing any two wavelengths lie along the straight line connecting the points representing the two wavelengths on the diagram. Thus, the two ends of any straight line passing through the white center of the diagram represent complementary colors. Two such lines are drawn on the figure for purposes of illustration. Notice that wavelengths in the red to orange part of the spectrum have their complements in the green to blue-green part and that wavelengths in the yellow part of the spectrum have their complements in the blue part.

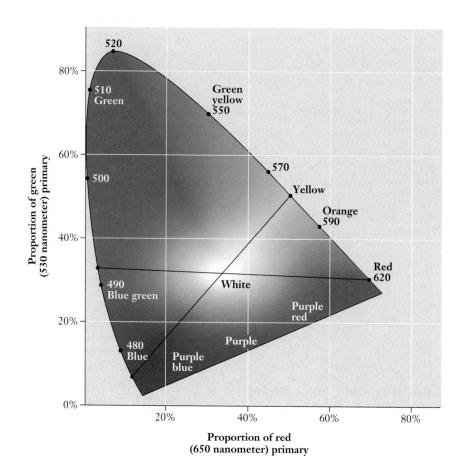

All the facts associated with the two laws of additive color mixing are taken into account in the *standard chromaticity diagram* (Figure 8.11). The colors in the periphery of the diagram are produced by single wavelengths and are called saturated colors. As you move from any point on the periphery toward the white center, the color comes more and more to resemble white; that is, it becomes increasingly unsaturated (white is regarded as fully unsaturated). For example, as you go along the line from the 620-nm point on the periphery to the center, you go from red to progressively whiter shades of pink (unsaturated red) to white. (Because of the limitations of color printing, Figure 8.11 does not show the gradualness of this change in saturation, but you can imagine it.) The figure's caption describes how the diagram can be used to determine (a) the color that will result from mixing the three standard primaries in any given proportion and (b) which pairs of wavelengths are complements of each other.

It is important and rather exciting to realize that the facts of color mixing portrayed by the chromaticity diagram are facts of *psychology*, not physics. The wavelengths of the three primaries do *not* become physically blended into one wavelength when added together to match the color produced by a fourth wavelength. A machine that detects wavelengths has no difficulty distinguishing, say, a 550-nm light from the mixture of three primaries that would exactly match its greenish-yellow color. Similarly, when two complementary wavelengths are mixed to produce the sensation of white, they do not physically produce white light (which contains all the wavelengths). Such color matches, in which physically distinct stimuli look identical, occur because of processes in the eye and the brain. Indeed, the matches just described provided the insight that led, in the nineteenth century, to the development of two physiological theories of color vision: the trichromatic and the opponent-process theories.

The Trichromatic Theory of Color Vision

According to the ***trichromatic theory***, color vision is mediated by three different types of receptors, each most sensitive to a different range of wavelengths. This idea was proposed first (in 1802) by Thomas Young and later by Hermann von Helmholtz (1852) as an attempt to explain the three-primaries law of color vision. Young and Helmholtz reasoned that if every color we see is the result of a unique proportion, or ratio, of activity among three types of receptors, then it would be possible to match any visible color by varying the relative intensities of three primary lights, each of which acts maximally on a different type of receptor. Young and Helmholtz developed their theory purely from behavioral data on perceptual effects of color mixing, at a time when nothing was known about photoreceptors in the retina. We now know from physiological studies that their theory was correct. Three types of cones indeed exist in the human retina, each with a different photochemical that makes it most sensitive to the light within a particular band of wavelengths.

In Figure 8.12 you can see an approximation of the actual sensitivity curves for each type of cone. The cones are labeled blue, green, and red, after the color that is experienced when that type of cone is much more active than the other types. Notice that any given wavelength of light produces a unique ratio of activity in the three types of cones. For example, a 550-nm light, which is seen as a greenish-yellow, produces a slightly larger response in red cones than in green cones and a very low response in blue cones. That same ratio of response in the three cone types could be produced by shining into the eye a mixture of red, green, and blue primaries, with the first two much more intense than the last. The result would be a perceptual experience of greenish-yellow indistinguishable from that produced by the 550-nm light.

Some people, referred to as *dichromats*, have only two types of cone photochemicals. These people, as you might expect, obey a two-primaries law of color mixing rather than the three-primaries law. For them, any color that they can see can be matched by varying the proportion of just two different wavelengths of light. The most common forms of dichromia involve the absence of the normal photochemical for either the red or the green cones (usually the green) due to a defect in the gene that produces that photochemical (Neitz & others, 1996). Because the defective gene is recessive and the genes for both the red and the green photochemicals are located on the X chromosome, this trait appears much more often in

10.

How does the trichromatic theory explain the three-primaries law? How was the theory validated by the discovery of three cone types?

11.

Why does vision in some people obey a two-primaries law rather than the three-primaries law, and why are these people not good at picking cherries?

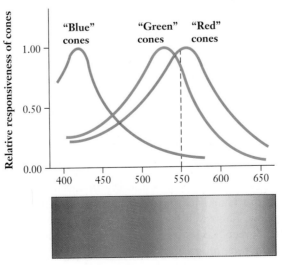

Wavelength in nanometers
(billionths of a meter)

FIGURE **8.12** *How the three types of cones respond to different wavelengths of light*

Any given wavelength produces a unique ratio of activity in the three cone types, and that ratio provides the initial code that permits us to see different wavelengths as different colors. For example, a 550-nm light, which is seen as greenish-yellow, produces a slightly larger response in red cones than in green cones and a very low response in blue cones. Any combination of lights that would produce that same ratio of responses would be seen as greenish-yellow. (For precise data, see Bowmaker & Dartnall, 1980, or Merbs & Nathans, 1992.)

The value of color vision
Our sensitivity to the wavelength of reflected light helps us to distinguish objects of interest from their background.

David Frazier / The Image Works

men than in women. Men (as discussed in Chapter 3) have only one X chromosome, inherited from the mother, so a single defective gene on that X chromosome can produce color blindness. Women have two X chromosomes, one inherited from each parent, and are color-blind only if the defective gene exists on both of them.

People who lack either the red or the green cone photochemical are red-green color-blind, meaning that they have difficulty distinguishing colors ranging from green to the red end of the spectrum. If you look again at Figure 8.12, you will see why this is so. The normal ability to distinguish colors in this range (from about 500 to 700 nm) is mediated almost entirely by differential activity in the red and green cones, because blue cones are quite inactive in this range. If either the red or the green cone photochemical is missing, then the person has no or little physiological basis for distinguishing one wavelength from another in this range. Many people who have red-green color blindness don't know it and may wonder why certain perceptual tasks that are hard for them are easy for others. One man's red-green color blindness was not discovered until he told his family how much he admired the perceptual skill of cherry pickers: "After all," he said, "the only thing that tells 'em it's a cherry is . . . that it's round and the leaves aren't. I just don't see how they find 'em in those trees!" (Coren & Ward, 1989).

Very rarely, a person is dichromatic in one eye and has normal, trichromatic vision in the other. Such people's normal eye dominates their everyday perceptual experience, so they see colors and learn color names just as the rest of us do, and this allows them to tell us what colors they see or don't see when looking just with their dichromatic eye. Many years ago a woman was studied who lacked the green cone photochemical in one eye and had full color vision in the other (Graham & others, 1961). She reported that everything seen with just her dichromatic eye appeared to be a shade of blue, yellow, or gray. When tested with the full range of single-wavelength lights, she reported seeing all wavelengths below about 500 nm as blue (similar to what a trichromatic person reports) and all wavelengths longer than that as yellow. This result makes sense if we assume that, lacking the green photochemical, her "green" cones became partly coated instead with the red cone photochemical. If the red and green cones have the same photochemical but the red cones have somewhat more of it, then any wavelength above 500 nm will produce a relatively strong response in the red cones, a slightly weaker response in the green cones, and a very weak response in the blue cones, which is the response combination that normally results in the sensation of yellow (look once more at Figure 8.12).

The Opponent-Process Theory of Color Vision

The trichromatic theory explains the three-primaries law and certain types of color blindness well, but it does not explain the law of complementarity—how certain pairs of wavelengths produce the experience of white. To explain that, Ewald Hering, another nineteenth-century scientist, developed the **opponent-process theory.** Hering was most impressed by the observation that complementary colors (blue and yellow, or green and red) seem to swallow each other up, erasing each other's color, when added together. For example, if you begin with blue light and gradually add more of its complement (yellow), the result is not "bluish-yellow" but an ever-paler (more unsaturated) blue, which finally becomes white. To explain such observations, Hering (1878/1964) proposed that color perception is mediated by physiological units (which we now call cells) that can be either excited or inhibited, depending on the wavelength of light, and that complementary wavelengths have opposite effects (activate "opposing processes") on these opponent-process cells.

More specifically, Hering proposed that the ability to see blues and yellows is mediated by blue-yellow opponent cells, which are excited by wavelengths in the blue part of the spectrum and inhibited by those in the yellow part, or vice versa. Similarly, he proposed that the ability to see greens and reds is mediated by green-red opponent cells, which are excited by wavelengths in the green part of the spectrum and inhibited by those in the red part, or vice versa. In addition, he proposed that the ability to distinguish bright from dim light, independent of wavelength, is mediated by a third set of cells (brightness detectors), which are excited by lights of any wavelength. This theory nicely accounts for the facts of complementary colors. A mixture of wavelengths from the blue and yellow parts of the spectrum, or from the green and red parts, appears white (colorless but bright) because the two sets of wavelengths have opposite effects on the opponent cells that promote color detection. Thus, they cancel each other out in their effect on color detectors but act in concert to excite brightness detectors.

The opponent-process theory also accounts wonderfully for another psychological phenomenon, that of *complementarity of afterimages.* For a demonstration of this phenomenon, follow the instructions in the first paragraph of the caption of Figure 8.13. You will see that the colors in the afterimage are the complements of those in the original: What was green becomes red; what was yellow becomes blue; and what was black becomes white. How does the opponent-process theory explain this phenomenon? Consider the example of green becoming red in the afterimage. The units in the retina that receive the green-appearing (middle-wavelength) light as you stare at the picture become fatigued. Therefore, when you shift your eyes to the white paper (which reflects all wavelengths), those units don't respond as strongly as they normally would, but other units, including those that respond to red-appearing (long-wavelength) light do respond strongly. Thus, opponent-process cells that are normally excited by red-appearing light and inhibited by green-appearing light in that part of the retina become excited, resulting in the perception of red. To convince yourself that this adaptive process occurs early in the visual pathway, before the input from the two eyes converges, follow the instructions in the second paragraph of the caption of Figure 8.13.

12.

How does the opponent-process theory explain (a) the law of complementarity in color mixing and (b) the complementarity of afterimages?

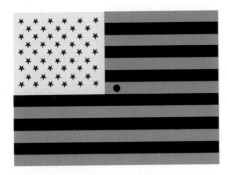

FIGURE **8.13**
Complementarity of afterimages
Stare at the dot in the middle of the flag for at least half a minute. Then look at the dot on the white space beside the flag. What do you see?

To demonstrate that this effect involves a change within the retina, or at least somewhere early in the visual system before the input from the two eyes converges, repeat the demonstration but this time keep one eye closed as you stare at the middle of the flag. Then look at the dot in the white space first with one eye and then with the other. What happens?

FIGURE **8.14** *Reconciliation of the trichromatic and opponent-process theories*

Shown here is a simplified wiring diagram illustrating how connections from the three types of cones can result in opponent-process cells—cells that are excited by blue and inhibited by yellow (B+Y−) and cells that are excited by red and inhibited by green (R+G−). Excitatory neural connections are shown as arrowheads, and inhibitory connections are shown as straight lines perpendicular to the axon. The cells marked "I" are inhibitory intermediary neurons. Notice that the B+Y− cell is excited by input from blue cones and inhibited by input from an intermediary neuron that, itself, is excited by input from both green and red cones. Since yellow light stimulates both red and green cones strongly, yellow light would be the most effective inhibitor of the B+Y− cell. As an exercise, try constructing wiring diagrams that result in B−Y+ and R−G+ opponent neurons.

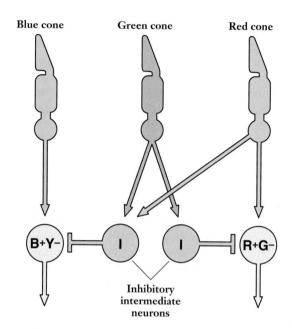

13.

How has the opponent-process theory been validated in studies of the activity of neurons that receive input from cones?

A Physiological Reconciliation of the Two Theories

For many years the trichromatic and opponent-process theories were thought to be contradictory, but in the 1950s and 1960s research showed that both theories are fundamentally correct (De Valois & others, 1966; Hurvich & Jameson, 1957). The retina indeed contains three types of cones, consistent with Young and Helmholtz's trichromatic theory. But the cones feed into ganglion cells (the neurons of the optic nerve) in a pattern that translates the trichromatic code into an opponent-process code, conforming to Hering's theory. Some ganglion cells behave in a red-green opponent manner: They receive excitatory input from "red" cones and inhibitory input from "green" cones, or vice versa. Others behave in a blue-yellow opponent manner: They receive excitatory input from "blue" cones and inhibitory input from both "green" and "red" cones, or vice versa (see Figure 8.14). Neurons in the cerebral cortex that are most directly involved in color perception maintain these opponent-process characteristics (Engel, 1999; Schiller, 1994).

The research and theories on color vision just presented are a wonderful, early illustration of the value of combining behavioral and physiological research. The trichromatic and opponent-process theories were developed, in the nineteenth century, from behavioral evidence having to do with the perceptual effects of additive color mixing, before anything was known about the physiology of receptors and neurons. Later, both theories were confirmed physiologically, and today both physiologists and psychologists are working out the finer details of the theories.

The Coding of Light-Intensity Patterns

The ultimate perceptual purpose of our vision is not to detect the simple presence or absence of light or differing wavelengths but, rather, to identify objects. Color vision helps toward this end to the degree that different objects reflect different wavelengths of light, but we also make use of differences in the amount, or *intensity*, of light reflected by different objects, which we perceive as differences in *brightness*. The pencil on my desk not only reflects different wavelengths of light compared with its background (the desk) but also reflects a different intensity of light, which allows me to see it as lighter or darker than the desk even in a black-and-white photograph or even in dim light when only my color-blind rod vision is working. How does the visual system organize information about light intensity in a way that helps us identify objects?

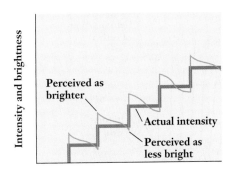

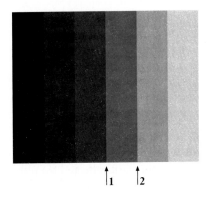

FIGURE **8.15** *Enhancement of contrast*
Each solid gray stripe appears lighter near its boundary with a darker stripe and darker near its boundary with a lighter stripe. Compare the perceived brightness just above arrow 1 with that just above arrow 2, for example. The graph above the stripes shows how the actual brightness (purple line) and the perceived brightness (thin orange line) change from stripe to stripe in the figure. (Adapted from Matlin & Foley, 1997.)

Enhancement of Contrast

Objects are defined principally by their *contours* (that is, their edges or borders). Visually (ignoring the role of color), contours are lines of contrast created when one amount of brightness appears next to another. The visual system exaggerates that contrast, thereby increasing the clarity of our visual perceptions.

A greater difference in brightness between adjacent visual stimuli is registered by the visual system than would be registered by a machine that faithfully recorded the actual physical difference in the light. If you look at a television screen with the set turned off, it appears a relatively light shade of gray. Yet when the TV is turned on, the same screen can create the impression of black objects, even though no part of the screen can send less light to the eye when the screen is on than when it is off. The same intensity of light that formerly looked gray looks black when surrounded by higher-intensity light. This is an example of heightened contrast created by the visual system. Another example, which shows that contrast enhancement is strongest at borders, can be seen in Figure 8.15.

A clue to the mechanism by which the nervous system enhances contrast was uncovered by Stephen Kuffler (1953), who recorded the activity of individual ganglion cells (the cells whose axons form the optic nerve) in anesthetized cats while stimulating various parts of the retina with small spots of light. He found that any given ganglion cell produces a relatively steady baseline rate of action potentials when not stimulated and that the cell's activity could be either increased or decreased by stimulating different parts of its retinal receptive field. That is, he found that the receptive fields for most ganglion cells contain two portions: an *"on"* portion, where light increases activity in the cell, and an *"off"* portion, where light decreases activity. These fields are circular, with the *"on"* and *"off"* regions arranged concentrically, such that a given receptive field has either an *"on"* or an *"off"* center and an opposite surround. Figure 8.16 on page 290 shows the pattern of connections from receptors to the ganglion cell that could create such receptive fields. An important consequence of this arrangement is that ganglion cells are more sensitive to contrast than to uniform areas of illumination.

14.

What is the value of the visual system's ability to exaggerate contrast, and how can that ability be demonstrated?

15.

How do connections from receptor cells to ganglion cells produce "on" and "off" receptive field areas and provide a basis for the coding of contrast?

This simplified diagram traces the neural
connections between light receptors (rods
and cones) and a ganglion cell into which
their impulses feed. Receptors in the "on"
area of the receptive field directly excite
the bipolar cell. Receptors in the "off"
area excite horizontal cells, which then inhibit the bipolar cell. The resulting activity in the bipolar cell is then transmitted
to the ganglion cell. (Adapted from De
Valois & De Valois, 1988.)

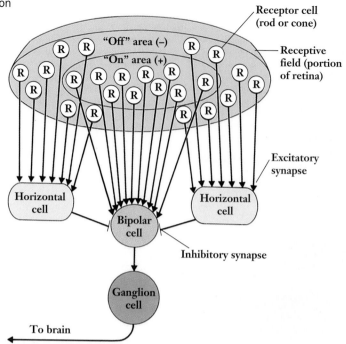

FIGURE **8.17**   *Neural explanation of*
contrast heightening
Depicted here are the receptive fields of
four ganglion cells that fall within adjacent rectangles of light striking the retina.
For simplicity, only receptive fields with
"on" centers (+) and "off" surrounds (–)
are shown. Because of the unequal distribution of light on their "on" and "off"
areas, the cells whose receptive fields
partly overlap the boundary between the
two rectangles will be either more or less
active than the other cells. In this case, A
is most active and C is least active.

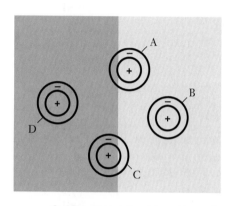

16.

How do the unique receptive fields of
neurons in the primary visual cortex
provide a foundation for detecting
edges, bars, and the orientations of
edges and bars?

Figure 8.17 can help you understand how Kuffler's discovery explains contrast
heightening at edges. When you look at the figure, the light reflected from the two
adjacent rectangular gray patches strikes adjacent areas on your retina and acts
there on rods and cones, which act on bipolar cells, which act on ganglion cells.
Ganglion cells whose receptive fields lie entirely within one patch or the other (B
and D in the figure) respond only moderately because the light acts uniformly on
their "on" (+) and "off" (–) receptive-field areas, which tend to cancel each other
out. In contrast, ganglion cells whose receptive fields cross the boundary between
the two patches respond more strongly or more weakly than the other cells. The
ganglion cell whose receptive field is marked A in the figure produces a relatively
high rate of action potentials because its "on" area receives more total light than its
"off" area (its entire "on" area is on the lighter-gray patch, but part of its "off" area
is in the darker-gray patch). Conversely, the ganglion cell whose receptive field is
marked C produces a relatively low rate of action potentials because its "off" area
receives more total light than its "on" area. Thus, the ganglion cells whose receptive-field centers are aligned along the two sides of the edge differ from one another in rate of activity more than do other ganglion cells, and this provides a
neural basis for the edge to stand out sharply in your visual experience.

Coding the Orientation of Contrasting Elements

To identify objects, we must detect not only contrast but also the orientation, or
slant, of contrasting areas. The contours that define the sharp point of my pencil
have a different slant than do the long, parallel contours that define most of the
pencil's boundary. A few years after Kuffler's pioneering work, David Hubel and
Torsten Wiesel (1962, 1979) performed similar studies with cats and monkeys.
Rather than recording from ganglion cells, however, they recorded the electrical
activity of individual neurons in the primary visual area of the cortex (see Figure
8.18).

Hubel and Wiesel found that the receptive fields for neurons in the primary visual cortex are not small circles, as Kuffler had found for ganglion cells, but are
larger, oblong areas, with "on" and "off" regions that run parallel to each other
along the long axis of the oblong. For some cells, one whole side of the field is an
"on" area and the other side is an "off" area [example (a) in Figure 8.19]. These
cells respond best when the edge between areas of dark and light is aligned precisely along the line separating the "on" and "off" portions of the receptive field.

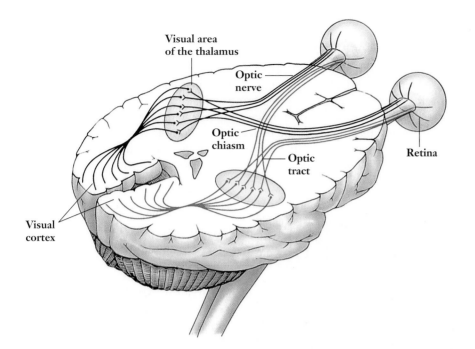

FIGURE **8.18** *Pathway from the eyes to the visual cortex*
Neurons in the optic nerves come together at the optic chiasm at the base of the brain and form the optic tracts, which run to nuclei in the thalamus, where they synapse on neurons that run to the visual cortex.

For other cells, either an "on" or an "off" area runs lengthwise down the middle of the oblong, with its opposite on either side [examples (b), (c), and (d) in Figure 8.19]. These cells respond best to narrow bars of light or dark appropriately placed in the receptive field. Hubel and Wiesel hypothesized that each of these cortical cells receives neural input from a set of ganglion cells whose receptive fields lie adjacent to one another in a straight line; research done since their work tends to corroborate that hypothesis (Ferster & others, 1996; Hubel, 1996).

Because of their elongated receptive fields, with parallel "on" and "off" areas, neurons in the primary visual cortex are sensitive to the orientation of the edges or bars that stimulate them. The cells respond maximally when the edge or bar of light is slanted at the same orientation as the long axis of the oblong visual field. Hubel and Wiesel found a systematic change across columns of cells in the visual cortex in the orientation to which the cells were most responsive. For example, all cells in one column might respond best to a vertical bar, all cells in the next column might respond best to a bar rotated 5 degrees clockwise, and so on. Thus, these neurons, taken as a whole, have the potential to keep track of the relative orientation of each contrasting area in a visual scene. They apparently provide a neural basis for detecting borders and patterns in objects, thereby providing part of the basis for identifying objects.

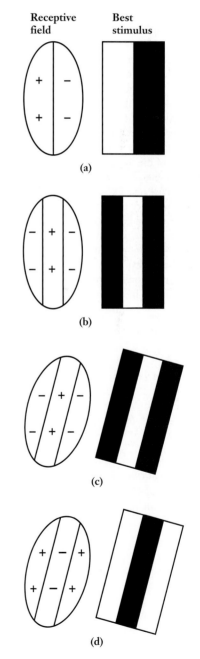

FIGURE **8.19** *Retinal receptive fields for four cells of the visual cortex*
In each of these four examples, the whole oval represents a receptive field, the area on the retina where a change in lighting can affect the rate of action potentials in the cortical cell. Areas with plus signs ("on" areas) are places where a spot of light increases activity in the cell, and areas with minus signs ("off" areas) are places where a spot of light decreases activity in the cell. The best stimulus for eliciting a high rate of response in the cell is shown to the right of each receptive field. To serve as a best stimulus, each rectangle would have to be centered over the receptive field in such a way that its dark bars fell on the "off" areas and its light bars fell on the "on" areas.

17.

How can cortical neurons code the spatial frequency of repeated elements of a pattern, and why might such coding be valuable in identifying objects?

Spatial-Frequency Coding

The neurons studied by Hubel and Wiesel are sensitive not only to the orientation of bars and edges but also to a characteristic called ***spatial frequency*** (De Valois & De Valois, 1988). In a pattern of repeating elements, such as that created by blades of grass on a lawn or bricks on a walkway, spatial frequency is the number of repetitions per unit of distance in the pattern's image on the retina. Figure 8.20 shows two stimuli with different spatial frequencies; it also shows how the width of "on" and "off" receptive-field regions can provide the basis for distinguishing one spatial frequency from another.

FIGURE 8.20   *Spatial frequency*
A stimulus of higher spatial frequency (a) produces an image on the retina that contains more repeating elements per unit of distance than a stimulus of lower spatial frequency (b). Some visual neurons respond more strongly to higher spatial frequencies, others to lower spatial frequencies, depending on the nature of the neuron's receptive field. Depicted in (c) are the receptive fields of three cortical neurons superimposed on the retinal image of a gridlike stimulus. This stimulus evokes the strongest response from the neuron with receptive field A because its "on" and "off" areas are the same width as the bars of the image. The neuron with receptive field B does not respond strongly because its "on" and "off" areas are too wide for the grid; this neuron would respond better to a lower spatial frequency. The neuron with receptive field C does not respond strongly because its "on" and "off" areas are too narrow; this neuron would respond better to a higher spatial frequency.

(a) High-spatial-frequency stimulus

(b) Low-spatial-frequency stimulus

(c) Receptive fields of three neurons

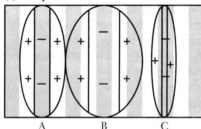

Vision researchers today are interested in spatial frequency primarily because of its relation to a procedure called *Fourier analysis*, by which any possible pattern of changes in intensity in a visual scene can be described in terms of multiple, overlapping, regular, wavelike patterns. Fourier analysis is the most efficient means that mathematicians have been able to devise for describing all possible visual patterns, and some researchers suggest that the nervous system may use this same efficient code. For our purposes, however, an easier-to-understand rationale for interest in spatial frequency lies in the observation that the visual world in fact contains many repeating elements. Ripples on a pond, blades of grass in a field, leaves along a stem, bark on a tree trunk, scales on a fish—these are just a few examples of repeating visual patterns found in nature. Such repeating elements are sometimes referred to as the ***visual texture*** of an object. Different objects in our visual world differ in their texture, and neurons sensitive to spatial frequency are ideally designed to encode those differences.

In sum, along with our sensitivity to the wavelengths and overall intensity of the light reflected from objects, our sensitivity to regular patterns of change in the intensity of that light may contribute to our ability to distinguish one object from another. Abrupt changes in what we see as color, brightness, and texture can signal the boundaries between objects in our visual world. In fact, there is evidence that the visual system devotes most of its resources to detecting such changes and devotes few resources to the homogeneous surfaces in between.

Surface Interpolation

Our visual system seems to abide by the following rule: *In the absence of information to the contrary, assume that any given area in a visual scene has the same color, brightness, and texture as the immediately surrounding areas.* When researchers produce a gap in a visual scene by preventing their subjects' eyes from receiving any information at all from a specific area, the subjects do not detect a gap; the gap is filled in perceptually with a surface identical to the one that surrounds it (Pessoa & others, 1998; Ramachandran, 1992). This filling-in process is called *surface interpolation*. If the blind-spot demonstration described in Figure 8.4 (page 278) worked for you, then you experienced an effect of surface interpolation. The bird disappeared, but the area previously occupied by the bird did not—it probably looked yellow and had black bars running through it, just like the surrounding area.

Surface interpolation may make normal vision more efficient than it otherwise would be. Because of surface interpolation, visual neurons do not have to keep con-

18.

How can surface interpolation be demonstrated, and what might be the value of this process in normal vision?

stant track of every single spot in the visual field. By devoting fewer resources to the analysis of information within uniform surfaces, the visual system may devote more resources to areas where surfaces change—areas that typically define objects' boundaries. The neural mechanism of surface interpolation is not yet fully known, but it seems to involve a network of neurons that interconnect visual cortical neurons whose receptive fields lie adjacent to one another (Fiorani & others, 1992; Gilbert & Wiesel, 1992).

Beyond the Primary Visual Cortex: Two Streams of Visual Processing

The cortical visual neurons that you have just been reading about lie in the *primary visual cortex*, which occupies the rearmost part of the occipital lobe. But this is only the first way station for visual information processing in the cerebral cortex. The primary visual cortex sends its output to many other visual-processing areas, which taken as a whole occupy the rest of the occipital lobe and extend forward into much of the temporal and parietal lobes. Researchers studying macaque monkeys have found over two dozen distinct cortical areas devoted to vision, and all evidence to date indicates that our own cortical areas for vision are laid out in much the same way as those of macaques (Ungerleider & Haxby, 1994; Van Essen & others, 1992). Between 25 and 40 percent of our entire cerebral cortex is devoted to analyzing visual information, and the percentage is even higher in macaques and other monkeys (Gross, 1998; Sereno & others, 1995).

Different visual areas of the cortex are specialized for processing different kinds of visual information (Lennie, 1998). The primary visual cortex contains neurons that are sensitive to all the important features of visual stimuli—intensity, wavelength, line orientation, spatial frequency, movement, and so on. But somehow, through the pattern of neural connections, these different features are separated from one another at subsequent stations. Thus, visual neurons in one area of the cortex are sensitive primarily to wavelength, those in another are sensitive primarily to spatial frequency, those in another primarily to movement, and so on. In humans, the evidence for this comes partly from studies of people who have specific visual deficits due to strokes that damaged particular portions of the cortex on both sides of the brain. Through such damage, people have lost the ability to see colors while retaining the ability to see contours, or lost the ability to see movements while retaining the ability to see colors and contours, or lost the ability to locate objects in three-dimensional space while retaining the ability to identify the objects they see (McCloskey & Palmer, 1996; Ungerleider & Haxby, 1994). Other evidence comes from positron emission tomography (PET) and functional magnetic resonance imaging (fMRI) applied to people with normal, intact vision. Such studies have shown that the peak of neural activity shifts from one brain area to another as the subjects are asked to make judgments about different features of the same stimulus, such as its color, shape, or direction of movement (Corbetta & others, 1991; Sereno & others, 1995).

Some years ago, Leslie Ungerleider and Mortimer Mishkin (1982) proposed that the visual areas beyond the primary area exist in two relatively distinct pathways, or "streams" (see Figure 8.21). One stream runs into the lower portion of the temporal lobe and is specialized for processing all the information needed to identify objects. The other runs into the parietal lobe and is specialized for maintaining a map of three-dimensional space, for locating objects in that space, and for using visual input to guide movements. Ungerleider and Mishkin's theory has been

19.

What evidence suggests that visual areas beyond the primary visual cortex are specialized for processing particular features of a visual stimulus?

FIGURE **8.21** *The "what" and "where" visual pathways*
Neurons in the primary visual area send output into two relatively distinct streams for further visual processing. The "what" pathway, into the lower temporal lobe, is specialized for perceiving shapes and identifying objects. The "where" pathway, into the parietal lobe, is specialized for perceiving spatial relationships and for guiding actions.

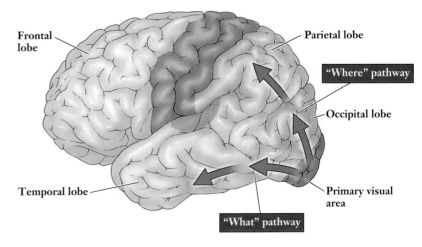

widely accepted and has guided much of the recent research on higher brain processes in vision. On the basis of their functions, the two streams are often referred to as the *"what"* and *"where"* pathways, respectively. "What?" and "Where?" are the two big questions that our visual system is designed to answer about any object that we see.

A Brain System for Identifying Objects: The "What" Pathway

The functional value of distinguishing and recognizing objects is obvious. How our brain accomplishes this is perhaps the most central and difficult question of visual science. Neurons in the *"what" pathway*—in the lower portions of the occipital and temporal lobes of the cortex—respond selectively to those features of visual stimuli, such as color and shape, that are most crucial for identifying objects (Janssen & others, 2000; Ungerleider & Haxby, 1994). Such evidence comes from single-cell recording (in monkeys) and from PET and fMRI neuroimaging (in humans) done while the subject is attending to visual stimuli that vary systematically in shape, color, or other such dimensions. Further evidence is found in the perceptual deficits of people who have brain damage restricted to these areas of the cortex.

People who have suffered damage in specific portions of the "what" pathway on both sides of the brain typically can see but cannot make sense of what they see, a condition called *visual agnosia*. Visual agnosias have been classified into a number of general types (Farah, 1990; Milner & Goodale, 1995). People with *visual form agnosia* can see that something is present and can identify some elements of what is present, such as its color and brightness, but cannot perceive the object's shape (Milner & Goodale, 1995). They are unable to describe or draw the outlines of objects or patterns that they are shown (see Figure 8.22). In contrast, people with *visual object agnosia* can identify and draw the shapes of objects they are shown but cannot identify the objects. For instance, shown an apple, such a person might draw a recognizable apple but would still be unable to say what he or she had just drawn. The problem is not one of language, since the person can name objects identified through other means, such as touch.

The existence of these two types of agnosia is evidence that the visual perception of an object involves a sequence of separable processes. First the individual sensory elements are picked up and analyzed, then these are grouped by the brain into basic shapes, and finally the shapes are organized into a whole and recognized as a particular object. Destruction of the brain mechanisms needed for the second of these steps results in visual form agnosia, and destruction of the brain mechanisms needed for the final step results in visual object agnosia.

In a famous essay entitled "The Man Who Mistook His Wife for a Hat," the neurologist Oliver Sacks (1970) described the plight of one of his patients, who,

20.

What perceptual disorders are observed in people who have damage to the "what" pathway on both sides of the brain? How do these observations support the idea that object perception occurs in a sequence of steps?

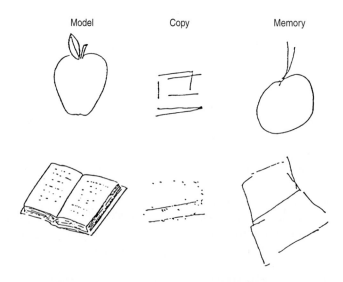

FIGURE **8.22** *Drawings made by a person with visual form agnosia*
The patient D. F. was unable to recognize the drawings on the left. When she was asked to try to copy these models, she produced drawings (middle column) that bore no or very little resemblance to the originals. When asked to draw an apple and a book from memory, however, she succeeded (right-hand column). Later, when she was shown the drawings she had produced from memory, she had no idea what they represented. (From Milner & Goodale, 1995, p. 127.)

after a stroke, suffered from visual object agnosia. When Sacks offered the man a rose and asked him to identify it, the man's response was, "About six inches in length. A convoluted red form with a linear green attachment. It lacks the simple symmetry of the Platonic solids, although it may have a higher symmetry of its own. . . . " After a period of such reasoning about the object's parts, the man finally guessed, uncertainly, that it might be some kind of flower. Then Sacks asked him to smell it. "Beautiful!" he exclaimed. "An early rose. What a heavenly smell!" He could tell a rose by smell but not by sight, even though he could see and describe each of its parts in terms of geometry and color.

One category of object that is particularly important for human beings to recognize is that of individual human faces. Most of us can recognize hundreds of different people by face, even though the facial differences are often very subtle. The ability to recognize people quickly by face provides an important foundation for our social relationships, which are critical for survival and reproduction, so it would not be surprising if natural selection had provided us with a special brain mechanism for recognizing faces. Evidence that we may in fact have such a mechanism comes from the existence of **prosopagnosia**—a deficit in the ability to recognize individual faces—which generally results from damage to a particular part of the lower temporal cortex (Bruce & Young, 1998; Farah & others, 1998). People with this disorder can tell that they are looking at a human face, but they are unable to say whose face it is, even if it is their own or that of a close friend. In some cases people with this disorder show a relatively normal ability to recognize individual members of other object categories. For example, one sheep rancher who could not recognize people by face after he had suffered a stroke could still recognize individual sheep by sight (McNeil & Warrington, 1993).

A Brain System for Locating Objects and Guiding Actions: The "Where" Pathway

Second only to knowing what an object is, we want to know where it is. Damage on both sides of the brain in the **"where" pathway**—in the upper parts of the occipital and parietal lobes of the cortex—interferes with the ability to locate objects and to guide one's own actions appropriately. People with such damage can identify objects, but they lose much of their ability to perceive spatial relationships among objects, to judge the distances of objects, to follow moving objects with their eyes or hands, to move around obstacles, or to learn and remember routes (Gross, 1998). Single-cell recording in monkeys shows that neurons in the "where" pathway are most responsive to spatial aspects of a visual stimulus, such as its distance from the eyes or its direction of movement. This pathway is crucial for our conscious perception of objects' locations (Ungerleider & Haxby, 1994), and it provides continuous unconscious visual information that guides our moment-to-moment movements.

A. David Milner and Melvyn Goodale (1995) have argued convincingly that the "where" stream is first and foremost a visual system for guiding action. As we look at and reach for objects, our eye and hand movements are constantly guided by visual input. As we walk through a world of objects, our ability to stay on the path and avoid bumping into things depends on visual input. We are generally not aware of this visual guidance, but its existence can be demonstrated with a simple exercise. If you focus your eyes at a specific point and someone places an object in your peripheral vision, far enough away from your direct line of sight that you can just barely see that something is there but can't make out its size and shape, you can, without moving your eyes, reach out and grab that object, accurately and without fumbling (Goodale & Murphy, 1997). As you do this, you make hand movements that are precisely attuned to the object's size and shape, even though you can't consciously see that size and shape. Apparently, the visual system that guides your hand has detailed information about the size and shape of the object, as well as about its location, that is unavailable to your conscious perception.

21.

What evidence suggests that we (and other primates) have a specialized neural mechanism for recognizing faces?

22.

What evidence suggests that the "where" pathway (a) contributes to conscious perception of objects' locations and (b) provides unconscious information that is used in guiding actions?

According to Milner and Goodale, the "where" pathway is sensitive to the shapes of objects as well as to their spatial positions, even though it does not contribute to the conscious perception of shapes. The most dramatic evidence for this comes from research on people who suffer from visual form agnosia resulting from damage to the "what" stream. Milner and Goodale (1995) have extensively studied one such person, a woman known by the initials D. F., the same person whose drawings are reproduced in Figure 8.22. Despite her complete inability to perceive consciously the shapes of objects, D. F. responds to objects in ways that take into account shape as well as size, position, and movement. When she walks, she moves around obstacles with ease. She is good at catching objects that are thrown to her, even though she can't consciously see the object. In experiments, she fails at tasks that require her to report in words the shape or orientation of an object but regularly succeeds on tasks that require her to act on the object in a way that takes into account shape or orientation. In one experiment, for example, she was shown an upright disk with a slot cut through it. She claimed to be unable to see the orientation of the slot and, indeed, when she was asked to hold a card at the same angle as the slot, her accuracy (over several trials with the slot at varying orientations) was no better than chance. But when she was asked to slip the card into the slot as if mailing a letter, she did so quickly and accurately on every trial, holding the card at just the right orientation before it reached the slot! She could not use conscious perception to guide her hand, but her hand moved correctly when she wasn't trying to use conscious perception to guide it.

In later chapters you will read of much more evidence that our brains can use information that we are not consciously aware of to guide our actions. In the next section, however, we turn back to the realm of conscious perception. It is one thing to know that certain brain areas are involved in the perception of objects. It is quite another thing to know *how* such perception is achieved. Researchers are a long way from understanding, at the level of neural activity, how we identify objects. However, many useful ideas about object identification have been generated through experiments showing how people's perceptions are affected by variations in the stimulus input. We turn now to those ideas and experiments.

SECTION SUMMARY

Light that is reflected from an object is focused by the eye's cornea and lens to form an image on the retina, where rods and cones are activated. Because of the great sensitivity of rhodopsin and amount of neural convergence from rods to ganglion cells, rod vision allows us to see in very dim light. Cones, whose photopigments are less sensitive than rhodopsin, and which show relatively little convergence, are specialized for high-acuity vision in bright light. Cone vision is also color vision.

Objects with different pigments on their surfaces reflect different wavelengths of light, and this property leads us to see them as having different colors. The three-primaries law of additive color mixing—the fact that any perceived color can be matched by a mixture of three primary wavelengths—led to the trichromatic theory of color vision. According to this theory, each color corresponds to a unique ratio of activity in three types of receptors that differ from one another in their relative sensitivity over the wavelength spectrum. The three types of cones in the human eye indeed do behave as the trichromatic theory would predict. The theory's logic is also supported by the fact that people who have just two types of cone pigments obey a two-primaries law of color mixing. The law of complementarity in additive color mixing—the fact that pairs of lights of certain wavelengths cancel out each other's color and produce the sensation of white—led to the opponent-process theory of color vision. Consistent with this theory, blue-yellow and red-green opponent cells have been found. Both theories have been proved correct: The three types of cones send their outputs to ganglion cells in a manner that translates the trichromatic code into an opponent-process code.

The receptive fields of ganglion cells are divided into concentric "on" and "off" portions, and this property provides a foundation for the exaggeration of brightness contrast that helps us see the borders of objects. Farther inward, neurons in the primary visual cortex have receptive fields that are well designed for detecting the orientations of visual edges and bars and the spatial frequencies of texture elements in a visual scene. The primary visual cortex appears to devote most of its resources to identifying the colors, brightnesses, and visual textures that exist at and near areas of contrast and to fill in other areas by surface interpolation. Output from the primary visual cortex enters two parallel pathways for further processing. The "what" pathway is specialized for identifying objects, and the "where" pathway is specialized for locating objects and for controlling body movements in ways that take objects into account.

SEEING PATTERNS AND RECOGNIZING OBJECTS

As I look at the top of my desk, what strikes my retinas is a continuous field of light, varying from point to point in amplitude and wavelength. But I see the scene neither as a continuous field nor as a collection of points, and I certainly do not see it as existing on my retinas. Instead, I see objects: a computer, a pencil, a stapler, and a pile of books. The objects look solid, and they appear to occupy definite positions in the three-dimensional space atop my desk.

My experience is no illusion. The objects I see on my desk really exist and are located precisely where I see them. I can prove that: With vision as my only guide, I can reach out directly to the pencil and pick it up, without fumbling, and then use it to write a note. If you were here now, you could do the same, even though you never experienced my desk before. Now, that is truly amazing!

The study of our capacity to identify objects through vision is roughly at the same stage today as was the study of color vision in the nineteenth century, when the trichromatic and opponent-process theories were developed. Those theories, as you recall, were based on purely behavioral data concerning people's responses to mixtures of wavelengths of light, but they made certain predictions about what happens in the nervous system. Only much later were the models verified by physiological studies of the nervous system. In what follows you will read about similar theories, or models, of more complex perceptual processes, which have not yet been verified physiologically. We are now moving into the heart of what has long been called *perceptual psychology*.

Most perceptual psychologists conceive of object perception as a form of unconscious problem solving, in which sensory information from the object provides clues that are analyzed using concepts already in the person's head. From this perspective, the mental processes involved in perception are classed into two categories: **Bottom-up processes,** or *data-driven processes*, are those that register and integrate the sensory information; and **top-down processes,** or *concept-driven processes*, are those that use preexisting knowledge to interpret the sensory information.

The pencil on my desk is characterized by a point, a yellow color, two parallel lines that form most of its contour, and several other features. Bottom-up processes must somehow bring those features together, enabling me to see the pencil as a whole. But how does my perceptual system know which features to bring together? How does it know to combine the parallel lines with the yellow color and the point rather than, say, with the blue color and flat plane of the blotter on which the pencil rests? Scientists who have tried to build computers that can recognize objects have found that bottom-up processes cannot work alone (Watt, 1988). The computer must be provided with information that helps it decide which features to combine. For example, to recognize a pencil, the computer must be programmed with some facts about what pencils look like and with general rules for distinguishing objects from their backgrounds. The top-down perceptual processes are those that use such knowledge.

My perception of the pencil (or anything else) requires an interplay of bottom-up and top-down processes. A simplified model might go something like this (see

23.

What is the difference between bottom-up and top-down perceptual processes, and how are they assumed to interact in perceiving an object?

FIGURE **8.23** *Model of bottom-up and top-down perceptual processes*
Bottom-up (data-driven) processes detect and organize the features of the sensory stimulus. Top-down (concept-driven) processes use preexisting knowledge and expectancies to direct attention to relevant features and to recognize an object.

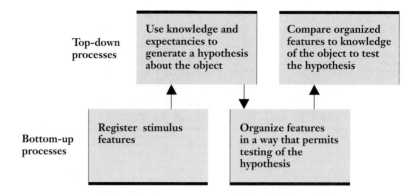

also Figure 8.23): (1) Bottom-up processes register a set of elementary features in the scene before me—lines, angles, colors, and so forth. (2) Top-down processes, using my knowledge of objects and my expectations about which objects are likely to be present, perform a preliminary analysis of the features and form the hypothesis that a pencil lies before me. (3) In response to the pencil hypothesis, bottom-up processes integrate the sensory features in such a way that the hypothesis can be tested. For example, bottom-up processes combine the parallel lines, yellow color, and sharp point into a coherent whole. (4) Top-down processes compare that whole with information in my memory about the appearance of pencils and confirm the pencil hypothesis. All this occurs almost instantly, with little or no conscious effort on my part.

Integrating Sensory Information into Coherent Patterns

Logically, in order to see an object, the perceptual system must somehow group the sensed elements (such as the color and contour) of that object together into a coherent whole. Here we will examine some ideas about how that grouping is accomplished.

Treisman's Feature-Integration Theory

24.

What is the difference between parallel processing and serial processing, and what roles do they play in Treisman's feature-integration theory?

To explain the bottommost of bottom-up perceptual processes, Anne Treisman (1986, 1998) developed what she called a *feature-integration theory*. Any perceived stimulus, even a simple one such as the X shown in Figure 8.24, consists of a number of distinct *primitive sensory features*, such as its color and the slant of its individual lines. To perceive the stimulus as a unified entity, the perceptual system must detect these individual features and integrate them into a whole. The essence of Treisman's theory is that the detection and integration occur sequentially in two fundamentally different steps or stages.

The first stage, *detection of features*, occurs automatically (it is not controllable by top-down mental processes) and involves **parallel processing.** Parallel processing means that this step operates simultaneously on all parts of the stimulus array. That is, according to Treisman, our visual system picks up at once all the primitive features of all the objects whose light rays strike our retinas. Even if we are paying attention just to the X in Figure 8.24, our visual system picks up at the same time the primitive features of the V in that figure and of all other stimuli in our field of view.

The second stage is the *integration of features*, which is less automatic (more controllable by top-down processes) and leads eventually to our conscious perception of whole, spatially organized patterns and objects. This step involves **serial processing,** which occurs sequentially for the features at one spatial location at a time, rather than simultaneously over the entire array. When looking at Figure 8.24, we can integrate the features of the X and then, an instant later, the features of the V, but we cannot integrate the two sets of features simultaneously.

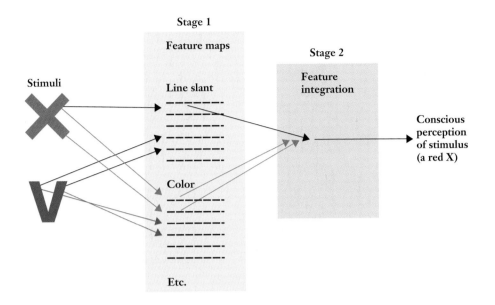

Stage 1

Feature maps

Stage 2

Stimuli

Line slant

Feature
integration

Conscious
perception
of stimulus
(a red X)

Color

Etc.

FIGURE **8.24** *Treisman's theory of feature detection and integration*
According to Treisman, stimulus features are detected and integrated in two separate stages of information processing. During stage 1, the primitive features of all stimuli that reach the eyes are registered automatically and simultaneously. The parallel processing is illustrated here by showing that all the features of both the X and the V are detected at once (registered in the appropriate feature-mapping areas of the brain). Integration of features occurs at stage 2, during which information is processed serially from one localized area of the visual field at a time. Serial processing is illustrated here by showing that only the information from one stimulus, the X, is being processed. An instant later, stage 2 could operate on the V, but it does not operate on the X and V at the same time.

Research Support for Treisman's Theory

To understand some of the evidence on which Treisman based her theory, look at the array of stimuli in Figure 8.25a on page 300. Notice that no effort is needed to find the single slanted line. You don't have to scan the whole array in serial fashion to find it; it just "pops out" at you. According to Treisman, this is because line slant is one of the primitive features that is processed automatically through parallel processing. Now look at Figure 8.25b and find the single slanted green line among the vertical green lines and slanted red lines. In this case the target does not pop out; you have to scan through the array in serial fashion to find it (though you can still find it quite quickly).

In controlled experiments, Treisman and Stephen Gormican (1988) measured the time it took for people to locate specific target stimuli in arrays like those of Figure 8.25 but with varying numbers of *distractors* (defined as the nontarget stimuli). As long as the target differed from all the distractors in one or more of Treisman's list of primitive features—such as slant, curvature, color, brightness, or movement—subjects detected it equally quickly no matter how many distractors were present. This lack of effect on detection time is indicative of parallel processing. But when the target combined two or more primitive features present in the distractors, as in Figure 8.25b, the amount of time required to locate the target increased in direct proportion to the number of distractors. This increase in detection time is indicative of serial processing, the necessity to attend to each item (or to small groups of items) separately until the target is found. Identification of a single unique feature can be accomplished in stage 1, but identification of a unique conjoining of two or more features requires stage 2.

Treisman also found that subjects who saw simple stimuli flashed briefly on a screen easily identified which primitive features were present but sometimes misperceived which features went together, a phenomenon called *illusory conjunctions*. For example, when shown a straight red line and a green curved one, all subjects knew that they had seen a straight line and a curved line, and a red color and a green color, but some were mistaken about which color belonged to which line. Such findings led Treisman to conclude that stage 1 (parallel processing) registers features independently of their spatial location and that different features that coincide in space (such as the color and curvature of a given line) are joined perceptually only at stage 2 (serial processing), which requires separate attention to each spatial location.

25.

How do pop-out phenomena and mistakes in joining features provide evidence for Treisman's theory?

FIGURE **8.25** *Stimuli that pop out or do not pop out*

These stimulus arrays are similar to those used by Treisman and Gormican (1988). In (a) the target stimulus (slanted green line) differs from the distractor stimuli in a primitive feature; it is the only slanted line in the array. Here the target pops out at you; you notice it immediately even if you aren't looking for it. In (b) the target stimulus (slanted green line) does not differ from the distractors in a primitive feature; its greenness is matched by some distractors and its slant is matched by other distractors. Rather, this target is distinct in the way its features are conjoined. It is the only line that is both green and slanted. This target does not pop out at you; you have to look for it to notice it. [*Note:* Through practice, with arrays like the one shown in (b), people can make the target pop out (Treisman, 1998). Subjects learn to inhibit the red input and attend only to the green, and then the single slanted green line pops out. Or they learn to inhibit the vertical lines and attend only to the slanted lines, and then the single green slanted line pops out. This shows that conscious perceptual strategies can be used to affect even very early stages of visual processing.]

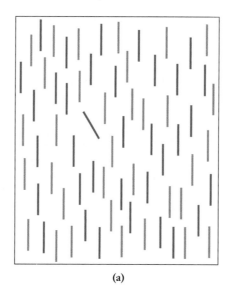

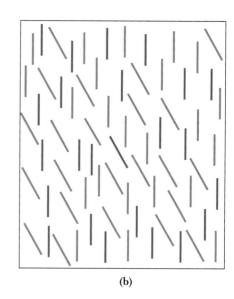

(a)   (b)

More recently, Treisman and her colleagues reported on a man who had suffered damage in both hemispheres to the portion of the parietal cortex that is most critical for identifying the spatial location of visual stimuli (Friedman-Hill & others, 1995; Treisman, 1998). The man could see objects but often made mistakes when asked to point to them or to say where they were. As would be predicted by Treisman's theory, he was especially prone to illusory conjunctions. He had no difficulty registering the primitive features of briefly flashed stimuli but had great difficulty integrating those features, apparently because of the loss in his visual ability to represent spatial locations. He found that he could see objects better if he looked at them one at a time through a narrow viewing tube. By cutting off his view of other objects, he prevented the melding of their features into those of the object that he was inspecting.

Gestalt Principles of Perceptual Grouping

Long before Treisman developed her model of feature integration, **Gestalt** psychologists argued that we automatically perceive whole, organized patterns and objects without needing to register their individual components separately. The Gestalt school arose in Germany during the early twentieth century in response to the then-dominant *structuralist* school (discussed in Chapter 1). The structuralists were interested in the basic elements of sensory experience and believed that all perceptions are best understood as combinations of such elements. For example, Edward Titchener and his students attempted to count the number of brightnesses and hues that people could see in visual stimuli. The Gestaltists, in contrast, argued that perception is a matter not of combining separate elements in consciousness but of responding immediately to large, whole patterns. One of the leaders of the Gestalt movement, Max Wertheimer (1923/1938), argued against the structuralists as follows: "I stand at the window and see a house, trees, sky. Now on theoretical grounds I could try to count and say: 'here they are . . . 327 brightnesses and hues.' Do I have '327'? No, I see sky, house, trees." Treisman and other modern perceptual psychologists would not necessarily disagree with Wertheimer. In our conscious experience we do typically perceive wholes before we perceive parts; the building up of the wholes from the parts occurs automatically, without conscious awareness.

The Gestalt point of view is characterized by the statement, "The whole is different from the sum of its parts." The

Principle of similarity

Groups of individuals in this crowd stand out as perceptual units because of similarity in the color of their clothing.

Paul Chesley / Stone

whole is different because it not only contains the parts but contains them organized in a certain way. The meaningful information that is perceived lies in the organization. The German word *Gestalt* translates roughly to "organized whole," and the Gestaltists believed that the gestalt, not the individual sensory elements, is the proper unit of study. To them, the structuralist approach was like trying to account for the beauty of the *Mona Lisa* by carefully weighing the amount of paint used to produce each part of the masterpiece.

The Gestaltists proposed that the nervous system is innately predisposed to respond to patterns in the stimulus world according to certain rules or *principles of grouping.* These principles include the following (Koffka, 1935; Wertheimer, 1923/1938):

1. *Proximity*   We tend to see stimulus elements that are near each other as parts of the same object and those that are separated as parts of different objects. This helps us segregate a large set of elements into a smaller set of objects (see Figure 8.26a).

2. *Similarity*   We tend to see stimulus elements that physically resemble each other as parts of the same object and those that do not resemble each other as parts of different objects. This helps us distinguish between two adjacent or overlapping objects on the basis of a change in their texture elements. (Texture elements are repeated visual features or patterns that cover the surface of a given object, as illustrated in Figure 8.26b.)

3. *Closure*   We tend to see forms as completely enclosed by a border and to ignore gaps in the border. This helps us perceive complete forms even when they are partly occluded by other objects (see Figure 8.26c).

4. *Good continuation*   When lines intersect, we tend to group the line segments in such a way as to form continuous lines with minimal change in direction. This helps us decide which lines belong to which object when two or more objects overlap (see Figure 8.26d).

5. *Common movement*   When stimulus elements move in the same direction and at the same rate, we tend to see them as part of a single object. This helps us distinguish a moving object (such as a camouflaged animal) from the background. If the dots marked by arrows in Figure 8.26e were all moving as a group, you would see them as a single object.

6. *Good form*   The perceptual system strives to produce percepts that are elegant—simple, uncluttered, symmetrical, regular, and predictable (Chater, 1996; Koffka, 1935). This rather unspecific principle encompasses the other principles listed above but also includes other ways by which the perceptual system organizes stimuli into their simplest (most easily explained) arrangement (as illustrated in Figures 8.26f and 8.29).

26.

What are some principles of grouping proposed by Gestalt psychologists, and how does each help explain our ability to see whole objects?

FIGURE **8.26**   *Gestalt principles of grouping*
(a) *Proximity*: We see 3 sets of dots rather than 13 individual dots. (b) *Similarity*: Because we group similarly textured elements together, we see two separate forms here. (c) *Closure*: We assume that the boundary of the circle is complete, continuing behind the square. (d) *Good continuation*: We see two smooth lines here, ab and cd, rather than four shorter lines or two sharply bent lines such as ac or bd. (e) *Common movement*: If the dots and arrows were moving as a group, we would see the dots as a single object. (f) *Good form*: Because of its symmetry, the left-hand figure is more likely than the middle figure to be seen as a single object. The middle figure is likely to be seen as two separate objects, like those depicted more clearly in the right-hand figure.

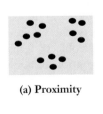

(a) Proximity

(b) Similarity

(c) Closure

(d) Good continuation

(e) Common movement

(f) Good form

27.

How do reversible figures illustrate the mind's strong tendency to separate figure and ground, even in the absence of sufficient cues for deciding which is which?

Figure and Ground

In addition to proposing the six principles of grouping just listed, the Gestaltists (particularly Rubin, 1915/1958) called attention to our automatic tendency to divide any visual scene into *figure* (the object that attracts attention) and *ground* (the background). As an example, look at Figure 8.27. The illustration could be described as two unfamiliar figures, one white and one black, whose borders coincide, but you probably do not see it that way. Most people automatically see it as just one white figure against a black background. According to the Gestaltists, the division into figure and ground is not arbitrary but is directed by certain stimulus characteristics. In Figure 8.27, the most important characteristic is probably *circumscription:* Other things being equal, we tend to see the circumscribing form (the one that surrounds the other) as the ground and the circumscribed form as the figure.

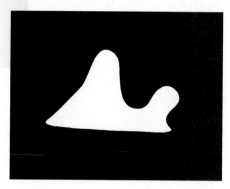

FIGURE 8.27 *Figure and ground*
Because the white form is completely surrounded by the black form, we tend to see the white form as the figure and the black form as the ground.

The figure-ground relationship is not always completely determined by characteristics of the stimulus. You can reverse your perception of figure and ground in Figure 8.27 by imagining that the illustration is a black square with an oddly shaped hole cut out of it, sitting on a white background. When cues in the scene are sparse or ambiguous, the mind may vacillate in its choice of which shape to see as figure and which as ground. This is illustrated by the *reversible figure* in Figure 8.28, where at any given moment you may see either a white vase against a dark ground or two dark profiles against a white ground. In line with the Gestalt figure-ground principle, the same part of the figure cannot simultaneously be both figure and ground, and thus at any instant you may see either the vase or the faces, but not both.

FIGURE 8.28 *Reversible figure*
Because it lacks strong cues as to which is figure and which is ground, this image—developed by the Danish Gestalt psychologist Edgar Rubin—may be seen either as a white vase against a dark ground or as two dark profiles against a white ground. If you stare at it, your perception may alternate between the two.

Illusions That Promote the Perception of Wholes

The tendency to perceive whole, organized patterns and objects is so compelling that in some cases the perceptual system fills in missing elements, thereby creating illusions. An example is the *illusory-contour* illustration in Figure 8.29. You probably see a solid white triangle sitting atop some other objects. The contour of the white triangle appears to continue across the white space between the other objects. This is not simply a misperception caused by a fleeting glance. The longer you look at the whole stimulus, the more convinced you may become that the contour (border) between the white triangle and the white background is really there; the triangle seems *whiter* than the background. But if you try to look at the contour isolated from the rest of the stimulus, by covering the black portions with your fingers

FIGURE 8.29 *Illusory contour*
In response to this stimulus, the perceptual system creates a white triangle, the borders of which appear to continue across the white page, such that the triangle seems whiter than the white page. (Adapted from Kanizsa, 1976.)

or pieces of paper, you will see that the contour isn't really there. The white triangle and its border are illusions.

Some researchers have suggested that the illusion in Figure 8.29 may derive entirely from bottom-up processes. Lateral connections in the visual cortex can under some conditions cause edge detectors (neurons responsive to edges) to respond to appropriately lined-up edges that are outside their own visual field (Rubin & others, 1996; Winklegren, 1992). Thus, at an early stage in visual processing, without influence from higher up, the brain may respond as if a discontinuous edge is actually a continuous edge.

Other researchers, however, explain the illusion in terms of top-down processes that attempt to make sense of initial sensory input (Hoffman, 1998; Parks & Rock, 1990). The most elegant means of interpreting the figure—consistent with the Gestalt principle of good form—is to assume that it contains a white triangle lying atop a black triangular frame and three black disks. That is certainly simpler and more likely than the alternative possibility—three disks with wedges removed from them and three unconnected black angles, all oriented with their openings aimed at a common center. According to this explanation, the perceptual system decides on the basis of the initial input that a white triangle must be present (because that makes the most sense), and then it *creates* the white triangle, top-down, by influencing contour-detection processes in such a way as to produce a border where one does not physically exist in the stimulus. For a demonstration that tends to support this top-down explanation, look at Figure 8.30. Regardless of which type of explanation is correct, illusory contours appear to be a consequence of a perceptual system designed to allow us to see whole, organized objects even when some of the stimulus input is missing.

28.

How do illusory contours illustrate the idea that perception of the whole influences perception of the parts? How are these illusions explained in terms of bottom-up and top-down processes?

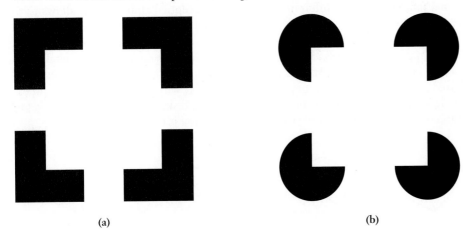

(a)   (b)

FIGURE **8.30** *Which pattern shows the clearer illusory contour?* Most people see an illusory contour (outlining a white square) in pattern (b) more clearly than in (a). Why? The actual black-white borders at the corners of the imagined white square are just as long in (a) as in (b), so it is difficult to see how bottom-up border-extension processes, by themselves, would create a stronger illusion in one case than in the other. A top-down explanation begins with the observation that the arrangement of four black angular objects in pattern (a) is more likely to occur in our everyday experience than is the arrangement of four disks with wedges cut out in pattern (b). Thus, pattern (a) presents less need for our visual system to superimpose a white square to make sense of it than does pattern (b). (Based on Hoffman, 1998, p 58.)

Recognizing Objects

To recognize an object is to categorize it. It's a bird, or an airplane, or Superman. To recognize an object visually, you must combine your perception of its visual pattern with your previously learned knowledge about that class of object. One problem is that any given class of object can produce a countless number of possible visual patterns.

Recognizing Objects on the Basis of Components

Think of all the different visual patterns that you would recognize as, say, an airplane. An airplane produces a very different array of stimuli depending on whether it is viewed from the bottom, or the side, or the front, and different airplanes differ in many of their visual aspects, yet you can recognize all of them as airplanes. How do you accomplish those perceptual feats? There are an infinite number of different specific arrangements of visual elements that you will call an airplane. It seems logical that you must somehow reduce that infinite set to something finite as part of the process of deciding what you are looking at. In what he calls a *recognition-by-components theory*, Irving Biederman (1987, 1989) has proposed that in recognizing any three-dimensional object, the visual system first organizes the stimulus information in such a way as to recognize a set of basic three-dimensional shapes (components) and then uses the arrangement of those shapes to recognize the object.

The theory may be best understood by relating it to the process of recognizing (reading) a printed word. The components of words are letters, which themselves are made up of a number of straight or curved lines (features) arranged in a certain way. As a skilled reader, when you read the word *airplane* quickly in a sentence, you probably do not consciously notice its individual letters, and you certainly do not consciously notice the individual lines that make up the letters. Yet, logically, your visual system must have picked up at least some of those lines, in order to pick up at least some of the letters, in order to recognize the word. Thus, the bottom-up processes in reading a word can be diagrammed as *features → letters → word*. For a skilled reader these processes are automatic and unconscious, but they still must occur.

According to Biederman's theory, recognizing any common three-dimensional object is like reading a word. You must pick up enough of the elementary features of the object to identify its basic components, and then, on the basis of the arrangement of those components, you recognize the object. The components of three-dimensional objects are not letters but are geometric forms that Biederman refers to as *geons*. Thus, in Biederman's theory, the bottom-up processes in recognizing any three-dimensional object can be diagrammed as *features → geons → object*. Just as there are a finite number of different letters in the English alphabet, there are also a finite number of different geons in the perceptual alphabet that allows us to recognize objects. On the basis of fundamental properties of three-dimensional geometry, Biederman has proposed that there are 36 different geons, some of which appear in Figure 8.31. By smoothing the edges and ignoring the details, any object, according to Biederman, can be seen as a small subset of such geons organized in a certain way. You may already be familiar with this general idea from experience with learn-to-draw books that recommend sketching any object as a set of three-dimensional geometric shapes before fleshing it out with details.

29.

According to Biederman's theory, how might a finite set of geometric forms (geons) provide the basis for perception of an infinite set of objects?

FIGURE **8.31**   *Some geons*
From principles of geometry, Biederman developed a list of 36 simple, three-dimensional forms, which he labeled "geons," six of which are shown here. He suggests that geons provide the basic perceptual components of more complex forms. (Adapted from Biederman, 1987.)

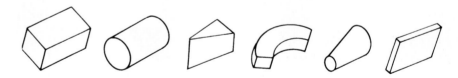

30.

How is the recognition-by-components theory supported by experiments on object recognition and by evidence from certain brain-damaged individuals?

Some Evidence for the Recognition-by-Components Theory

If Biederman's recognition-by-components theory is correct, then object recognition depends on the ability to detect at least some of the object's geons and their arrangement relative to one another. Evidence supporting the theory comes from experiments in which Biederman (1987) asked people to identify objects in pictures that were flashed briefly on a screen. He found that the speed and accuracy of recognizing the objects depended very much on the intactness and arrangement of an object's geons and very little upon other aspects of the stimulus, such as the amount of detail occurring within the geons or the exterior outline of the object as a whole. Figure 8.32 shows some of the stimuli that Biederman used. The airplane in Figure 8.32a was recognized as an airplane even when most of its geons were removed (changing its overall outline), as long as the geons still present were intact and properly arranged. The various objects in Figure 8.32b were recognized when the lines were degraded in a way that preserved the recognizability of individual geons

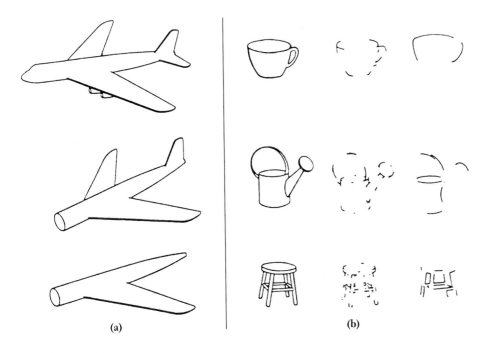

FIGURE **8.32**
Support for Biederman's recognition-by-components theory
Part (a) shows an airplane consisting of nine, four, or two components (geons). Even with just a few components present, it is recognizable. Part (b) shows a set of line drawings of objects degraded in two different ways. The degradation in the middle column preserves the connections between adjacent components, and that in the right-hand column does not. When subjects saw the degraded figures alone, they recognized those in the middle column but not those in the right-hand column. (Adapted from Biederman, 1987.)

and their connections to one another (middle column) but not when the same amount of line degradation occurred in a way that obscured the geons and their connections (right-hand column).

Biederman's theory is also supported by studies of people with visual object agnosia, who can identify geometric shapes (such as Biederman's geons) by sight yet cannot identify whole, meaningful objects by sight. You read earlier in this chapter about one such person, who, when shown a rose, could describe its parts but could not identify it as a rose until he smelled it. Another patient with this disorder described a bicycle that he was shown as a pole and two wheels but could not identify it as a bicycle or guess its function (Hécaen & Albert, 1978). Apparently, the combining of components into recognizable whole objects is a separate step from the perception of components, and it is carried out by a unique set of neurons in the cortex.

Learning Which Parts to Attend To

We may be able to recognize that an object is an airplane on the basis of the arrangement of its component geons, but how do we distinguish between a Boeing 727 and a Boeing 747? These finer distinctions must be learned through experience in which, for one reason or another, the distinction is important (Archambault & others, 1999). Many years ago, Eleanor Gibson (1969) developed a *distinctive-feature theory* of that learning process. In essence, her theory is that we learn to notice the *distinctive features* of objects—those features that most clearly distinguish an object from others with which it might be confused—and to disregard other features.

According to Gibson, the kinds of features that we learn to notice for any particular object depend on the kind of distinction that we need to make. Consider the problem (suggested by Gibson) of identifying goats. One level of identification involves distinguishing goats, as a category, from other barnyard animals, such as pigs or sheep. That is the level with which most of us are concerned when we identify goats, and so we learn to pay attention to the properties that are common to all goats but not to other animals. We notice, for example, the beardlike tuft of hair on the chin and use that as one of the distinctive features—a feature that is exaggerated in cartoon drawings of goats to make for easy recognition. But a specialist in goats, someone who tends them or sells them, not only must distinguish

31.

According to Eleanor Gibson, what do expert identifiers know that the rest of us do not know? What is some evidence that this knowledge can be unconscious?

goats from other animals, or one breed of goat from another, but must also distinguish individual goats within a breed. This is a difficult task for someone who is unfamiliar with goats, but it is easy for the goat expert because he or she has learned to notice the features that vary from goat to goat, such as the specific placement of spots of color or the amount of separation between the eyes.

People often are not conscious of the features they use in making such distinctions, which explains why someone can be an expert identifier without necessarily being able to teach that skill to others. I remember, years ago, working on a maple sugar farm in Vermont and having to identify sugar maples without their leaves in late winter. The old hands teased me about tapping the wrong kinds of maple (they said I also tapped pine trees and utility poles, but they exaggerated). Yet none of them—and I think they really tried—were able to tell me how to distinguish sugar maples from other leafless deciduous trees. After several frustrated attempts, one expert concluded, "Well, you know, it just looks more *sugary* than other trees." Obviously he knew at some level of his mind what to look for, because he never made a mistake, but not at a level that was connected to his speaking ability.

In a formal study, Irving Biederman and Margaret Shiffrar (1987) found that expert chicken sexers—people who could classify a newly hatched chick as male or female by glancing at the cloaca (the bird's genital opening)—typically could not explain just how the cloacae of males and females differed. Many claimed that this skill must be learned gradually through months or even years of experience. Yet Biederman and Shiffrar discovered that the difference, though subtle, could be described easily and that a person who could describe it could, in just 15 seconds, train people who had no previous chicken-sexing experience to make the discrimination as accurately as the experts (Biederman, 1988). (It is nice to know that in one realm, at least, 15 seconds with a good teacher is worth months of real-world experience.)

Recognizing Objects on the Basis of Context

Our recognition of objects depends not just on stimuli from those objects but also on other stimuli, which provide a context that may lead us to expect or not expect a particular object to be present. For example, when you look at a tree, you can perceive leaves and twigs that, because of their angle or distance from you, would be unrecognizable if seen away from the tree. Likewise, you probably recognize your psychology professor more easily in the classroom than you would at a shopping mall and more easily at a shopping mall than at a rock concert. Numerous experiments have shown that people recognize objects more quickly and accurately in accustomed contexts than in unaccustomed contexts (Henderson & Hollingworth, 1999). Try to identify the four objects depicted in Figure 8.33, and then turn to Figure 8.47 on page 319 and identify the same four objects there. Expectations based on context provide part of the top-down contribution to object identification.

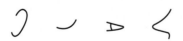

Recognizing Objects on the Basis of Motion

Perceptual psychologists most often study the perception of static images, typically using still pictures as the to-be-identified stimuli. But in the real world many of the things we observe (including people, animals, and vehicles) move, and their movement helps us identify them. To study the role of movement cues independent of other indices of shape, Gunnar Johansson and his colleagues in Sweden attached a small light to each major joint of a person's body and then filmed the person in such a way that only the lights could be seen as the person engaged in various activities (see Figure 8.34). When observers saw a single still frame of the film, they had no

Sondra Dawes / The Image Works

Learning to look

For these birdwatchers, field guides may be as useful as field glasses. By highlighting the features that distinguish each species from the most similar other species, the guides help hobbyists identify species quickly and accurately. Field guides can also facilitate the identification of trees, even sugar maples in winter.

32.

How does context affect the top-down processes involved in object recognition?

FIGURE **8.33**   *Objects out of context* Can you identify these objects? After making your guesses, turn to Figure 8.47 at the end of the chapter.

33.

How has research shown that patterns of movement provide a basis for object identification?

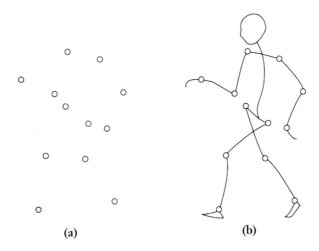

FIGURE **8.34** *Lights that are perceived as a person when the person moves*
Lights attached to a person's major joints (a) are not perceived as a recognizable object in the dark when the person stands still. However, when the person begins to move (b), the lights are perceived immediately as a human form. (From Michaels & Carello, 1981.)

idea what they were looking at; but as soon as the lights began to move, they recognized the object as a person performing a particular action. Just $\frac{1}{10}$ second of viewing time, enough to go through two frames of the film, was sufficient for most viewers to see the lights as a human being walking (Johansson, 1976/1994). Other experiments have shown that viewers can identify the moving lights as a person regardless of the direction in which the person is walking (Bradshaw & others, 1999) and can even judge the sex of the person according to how the tiny lights move as the person walks or jumps (Cutting & others, 1978; Runeson & Frykholm, 1986). Our ability to perceive subtle differences in movement patterns may play a larger role than we normally realize in identifying people and other animate objects.

SECTION SUMMARY

Visual object perception can be understood as an interaction between bottom-up (data-driven) and top-down (concept-driven) mental processes. Treisman's feature-integration theory, dealing with early bottom-up processes, proposes that primitive visual features of objects are registered simultaneously—that is, in parallel—and then are integrated spatially by slower, serial processing within the visual system. Long before Treisman developed her theory, Gestalt psychologists had proposed a number of principles—proximity, similarity, closure, good continuation, common movement, good form, and figure-ground division—that the visual system seems to follow automatically in grouping stimulus elements. Gestalt principles help us understand such phenomena as illusory contours.

Biederman's recognition-by-components theory, dealing with later stages of object perception, proposes that the visual system first organizes the stimulus information from an object into a set of geons (basic three-dimensional shapes) and then identifies the object on the basis of the arrangement of geons. Other theories and research on visual object perception have been concerned with the perceptual system's use of distinct features, context, and patterns of movement to facilitate object recognition.

SEEING IN THREE DIMENSIONS AND SEEING CONSTANCIES

In the preceding discussion we took for granted the capacity to see three-dimensional shapes (such as geons) in three dimensions. Objects occupy and move in space that includes not only a vertical (up-down) and a horizontal (right-left) dimension but also a dimension of depth, or distance from our eyes. The images focused on our flat, two-dimensional retinas clearly contain the information we need to perceive in three dimensions. What information is that? How does that information contribute to our

34.

How did Helmholtz describe perception as a problem-solving process?

Hermann von Helmholtz

Considered by many to be the greatest of all nineteenth-century physiologists, Helmholtz was also a pioneer of what we now call cognitive psychology. His unconscious-inference theory of perception posits that the mind constructs, through unconscious calculations, meaningful percepts from cues picked up by the senses.

35.

How can binocular disparity serve as a cue for depth?

perception of the depth, size, and three-dimensional shapes of objects? These questions have long interested philosophers, psychologists, and other scholars.

A critical step toward answering these questions was the publication of a treatise on vision, in the mid-nineteenth century, by Hermann von Helmholtz (1867/1962), the same German physiologist who developed the trichromatic theory of color vision. Helmholtz argued that visual perception is not a passive response of the visual system to the light entering the eyes but is an active mental process. The light focused onto our retinas is not the scene we see but is simply a source of cues about the scene. Mechanisms in our brain identify the critical cues and use them to construct a mental representation of what must be out there in the world before us.

Thus, according to Helmholtz, visual perception is always a matter of inference. We infer the characteristics and positions of objects from cues in the reflected light, and those inferences are our perceptions. Helmholtz also pointed out that some of the steps in this inferential process can be expressed mathematically, in equations relating information in the reflected light to conclusions about the positions, sizes, and shapes of objects in the visual scene. Helmholtz realized that people are not conscious of performing calculations as they look and perceive, so he coined the term ***unconscious inference*** to refer to the active processes that underlie perception. The top-down and bottom-up processes discussed earlier in the chapter are extensions of Helmholtz's concept of unconscious inference. Now, in the more direct tradition of Helmholtz, let us examine how unconscious inferences may provide the basis for our ability to perceive the depth and size of objects.

Cues for Depth Perception

What cues in the light focused on our retinas allow us to perceive three-dimensional space? It is relatively easy to understand how we can perceive the vertical and horizontal dimensions of space; those are represented directly on the two-dimensional surface of each retina (as shown in Figure 8.1). But what cues enable us to perceive the third dimension, depth (distance from our eyes)? Drawing on the work of earlier researchers, Helmholtz (1867/1962) was able to describe an impressive number of such cues, including all those discussed below.

Binocular Cues for Depth

Depth perception works best when you use both eyes. You can prove that with a simple demonstration. Pick up two pencils and hold them in front of you, one in each hand, with their points toward each other. Close one eye and move the pencils toward each other to make the points touch at their tips. Chances are, you will miss by a little bit on your first attempt, and your subsequent adjustments will have something of a trial-and-error quality. Now repeat the task with both eyes open. Is it easier? Do you find that now you can see which adjustments to make to bring the points together and that you no longer need trial and error?

Two types of cues contribute to the binocular (two-eye) advantage. The less important is *eye convergence*, the inward turning of the eyes that occurs when you look at an object that is close to you. The closer an object is, the more the two eyes must converge in order to focus on it. To experience eye convergence consciously, try focusing both eyes on your finger as you hold it a few inches in front of your nose. In theory, the perceptual system could judge the distance of an object from the degree to which the eyes converge when looking at it. In practice, however, researchers have found that eye convergence is a poor distance cue even for objects close to the eyes and a useless one for objects more than a few feet away (Arditi, 1986; Hochberg, 1971).

The other, far more important cue requiring two eyes is ***binocular disparity,*** which refers to the slightly different (disparate) view that the two eyes have of the same object or scene. Because the eyes are a few centimeters apart, they view any

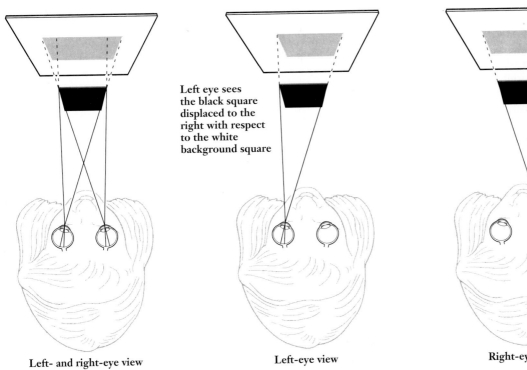

Left eye sees
the black square
displaced to the
right with respect
to the white
background square

Left- and right-eye view   **Left-eye view**

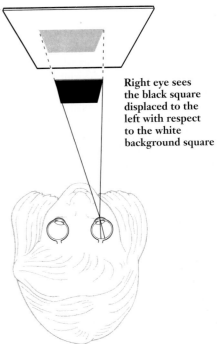

Right eye sees
the black square
displaced to the
left with respect
to the white
background square

Right-eye view

FIGURE **8.35** *Demonstration of binocular disparity*
The two eyes see somewhat different views of the relationship between the closer figure and the more distant figure. The disparity (degree of difference) between the two views is proportional to the distance between the two objects, and that information is used by the perceptual system to perceive the depth between them.

given object from slightly different angles. To see how the degree of binocular disparity varies depending on an object's distance from your eyes, hold your index finger about a foot in front of your eyes and then look at it with just your right eye open, then with just your left eye open, alternately back and forth. As you alternate between the two eyes, your finger appears to jump back and forth with respect to the background wall. That is because each eye views the finger from a different angle. Now move your finger farther away (out to full arm's length), and notice that your view of it jumps a smaller distance with respect to the wall as you again alternate between right-eye and left-eye views. The farther your finger is from your eyes, the smaller is the difference in the angle between each eye and the finger; the two lines of sight become increasingly parallel. Thus, the degree of disparity between the two eyes' views can serve as a cue to judge an object's distance from the eyes: The less the disparity, the greater the distance. In normal, binocular vision your brain fuses the two eyes' views to give a perception of depth. Helmholtz (1867/1962) showed mathematically how the difference in two objects' distance from the eyes can be calculated from differences in the degree of binocular disparity. For another demonstration of binocular disparity, see Figure 8.35.

Illusions of Depth Created by Binocular Disparity

The ability to see depth from binocular disparity—an ability called *stereopsis*—was first demonstrated in the early nineteenth century by Charles Wheatstone (described by Helmholtz, 1867/1962). Wheatstone wondered what would happen if he drew two slightly different pictures of the same object or scene, one as seen by the left eye and one as seen by the right, and then viewed them simultaneously, each with the appropriate eye. To permit such viewing, he invented a device called a *stereoscope*. The effect was dramatic. When viewed through the stereoscope, the two pictures were fused perceptually into a single image containing depth. Stereoscopes became a great fad in the late nineteenth century. People could see scenes such as Buckingham Palace or the Grand Canyon in full depth by placing cards that contained two photographs of the same scene, shot simultaneously from slightly different angles, into their stereoscope. (The Viewmaster, a child's toy, is a

36.

How do stereoscopes and autostereograms provide illusions of depth?

(a)   (b)

FIGURE **8.36**   *A depth illusion created by binocular disparity*

The two patterns are constructed to appear as they would to the left and right eye, respectively, if the dark square actually sat a certain distance in front of the white square (like that shown in Figure 8.35). In order to experience the three-dimensional effect, hold the book about a foot in front of your eyes and let your eyes drift in an unfocused way until you see double images of everything. You will see four renditions of the white frame with a darker square center—two renditions of (a) and two of (b). When all four of these images are clear, converge or diverge your eyes a little in order to get the right-hand image of (a) to sit right atop the left-hand image of (b). You have fused your left eye's view of (a) and your right eye's view of (b) into a single image, which now appears to be three-dimensional: The dark square seems to float in space in front of the white square.

type of stereoscope in common use today.) Three-dimensional motion pictures and comic books employ the same general principle. In the simplest versions, each frame of the film or comic strip contains an overlapping pair of similar images, each in a different color, and the viewer wears colored glasses that allow only one image to enter each eye. You can demonstrate stereopsis without any special viewer by looking at the two patterns in Figure 8.36 in the manner described in the caption.

In the 1960s Bela Julesz discovered that stereopsis could be achieved even with patterns of random dots that have no clear objects or borders within them (see Julesz, 1995). To achieve this effect, he created two versions of the same random pattern but displaced one segment of the dots slightly to the right or left in one pattern compared with the other. When people viewed one version with the left eye and the other with the right, the two merged into a single pattern and the region of displaced dots appeared to lie either in front of or behind the rest of the figure, depending on the direction of displacement. By varying the amount of displacement, he could vary the amount of perceived depth.

Subsequently, Christopher Tyler and Maureen Clarke (1990) found that a similar illusion of depth could be created by superimposing two repeating patterns of dots in a single filled space, somewhat offset from each other, in such a way that some segments of repeated dots in one pattern were displaced farther from their counterparts in the other pattern than were others. When people viewed these patterns with eyes converged or diverged so that different sets of repeating elements merged with each other in the two eyes' views, they saw clear illusions of depth. Tyler and Clarke referred to these depth-producing printed images as *autostereograms*, and during the 1990s they became a popular form of art and amusement. To experience the effect and to learn a little more about how autostereograms work, see Figure 8.37.

FIGURE **8.37**   *An autostereogram*

To view this image in three dimensions, place the book a foot or so in front of your eyes and look through it rather than at it. The two fixation spots at the top will appear as four spots. Slightly converge or diverge your eyes, or move the book, until the center two spots overlap, so that you see a row of three spots. Focus on the middle spot until you see the rest of the display as a three-dimensional checkerboard. It may take a little time for this image to develop—keep looking until you see it clearly. Once you have experienced the three-dimensional effect, refocus your eyes directly on the display to study it. Notice that each row consists of a random pattern of black and white dots that repeats itself almost exactly at cycles that are 20 dots long and equivalent to the distance between the two fixation spots. However, in every alternate repetition, the first of the repeated 20 dots is missing. When you saw the three-dimensional effect, your brain was matching up your right-eye view of one cycle in the repeating pattern with your left-eye view of the adjacent cycle. Because alternate squares of spots in the figure have slightly different degrees of displacement, the amount of binocular disparity is different for alternate squares of perceived dots, and this is what causes the two sets of squares to appear in different planes. (From Tyler & Clarke, 1990.)

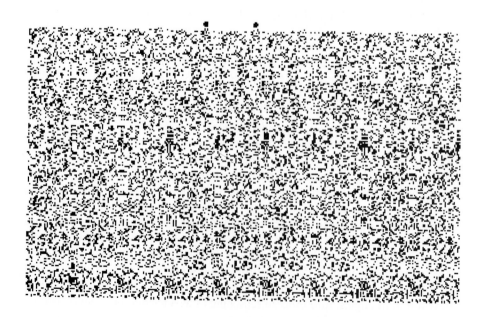

J. R. Eyerman, *LIFE Magazine,* ©Time Warner, Inc.

Entertainment in depth

The three-dimensionality of some movies is achieved by projecting an overlapping dual image on the screen and viewing it through special lenses that filter a different image to each eye, producing binocular disparity.

Monocular Cues for Depth

Although depth perception is most vivid with two eyes, it is by no means absent with one. An important monocular (one-eye) cue is ***motion parallax,*** which refers to the changed view one has of a scene or object when one's head moves sideways to the scene or object. To demonstrate motion parallax, hold your finger up in front of your face and view it with one eye as you rock your head back and forth. As your head moves, you gain different views of the finger, and you see it being displaced back and forth with respect to the wall in the background. If you now move your finger farther away from your eye, the same head movement produces a less changed view. Thus, the degree of change in either eye's view at one moment compared with the next, as the head moves in space, can serve as a cue for assessing the object's distance from the eyes: The smaller the change, the greater the distance.

As you can see from this demonstration, motion parallax is very similar to binocular disparity. In fact, binocular disparity is sometimes called *binocular parallax.* The word *parallax* refers to the apparent change in an object or scene that occurs when it is viewed from a new vantage point. In motion parallax the changed vantage point comes from the movement of the head, and in binocular parallax (or disparity) it comes from the separation of the two eyes. Motion parallax also accounts for a phenomenon that you have probably noticed many times while staring out the side window of a moving train or car: Objects that are farther away cross your field of view more slowly than do those that are nearby. Thus signs or utility poles next to the road race past you, while trees off in the distance pass leisurely by. At the farthest extreme, the sun (which, for perceptual purposes, is infinitely distant) doesn't move past you at all but seems to float through the sky at the same speed and direction as you and the train or car. Again, the closer the scene or object, the more sharply your view of it changes as your head moves sideways to it.

Motion parallax depends on the geometry of true three-dimensionality and cannot be used to depict depth in two-dimensional pictures. All the remaining monocular depth cues, however, can provide a sense of depth in pictures as well as in the real three-dimensional world, and thus they are called ***pictorial cues for depth.*** You can identify some of these by examining Figure 8.38 on page 312 and thinking of all the reasons why you see some objects in the scene as standing in the foreground and others as more distant. The pictorial cues include the following:

1. ***Occlusion***   The man partially occludes (cuts off) the view of the house, which indicates that the man is closer to us than is the house. Near objects occlude more distant ones.

2. ***Relative image size for familiar objects***   The image of the man (both in the picture and on the viewer's retina) is taller than that of the house. Because we know that people are not taller than houses, we take the man's larger image as a sign that he must be closer to us than is the house.

37.

How can motion parallax serve as a cue for depth, and how is it similar to binocular disparity?

38.

What are some cues for depth that exist in pictures as well as in the actual, three-dimensional world?

FIGURE 8.38
Pictorial cues for depth
Depth cues in this picture include occlusion, relative image size for familiar objects, linear perspective, texture gradient, position relative to the horizon, and differential lighting of surfaces.

3. **Linear perspective**   The lines marking the sides of the driveway converge as they go from the man to the house, indicating that the house is farther away. Parallel lines appear to converge as they become more distant.

4. **Texture gradient**   Texture elements in the picture, such as the stones on the driveway and the grass blades on the lawn, are smaller and more densely packed near the base of the house than near the man's feet. In general, a gradual decrease in the size and spacing of texture elements in a picture indicates depth.

5. **Position relative to the horizon**   The house is closer to the horizon than is the man. In outdoor scenes, objects nearer the horizon are usually seen as farther away than those that are displaced from the horizon either up or down. Similarly, the bird that is closer to the horizon appears farther away than the one that is higher up.

6. **Differential lighting of surfaces**   In real three-dimensional scenes the amount of light reflected from different surfaces varies as a function of the orientation of each surface with respect to the sun or other source of light and also as a function of shading from other objects. The fact that one side of each of the house's chimneys is darker than the other sides makes them appear three-dimensional rather than flat, thus showing the viewer which surface is farther away. For a more dramatic demonstration of an effect of lighting, see Figure 8.39.

FIGURE 8.39 *Depth perception created by light and shade*
Because we automatically assume that the light is coming from above, we see the smaller disruptions on the surface here as bumps and the larger ones as pits. Turn the picture upside down and see what happens. (The bumps and pits reverse.)

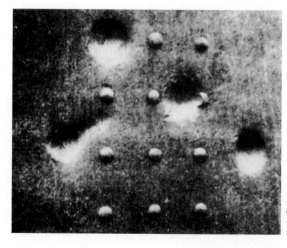

Kevin Berbaum

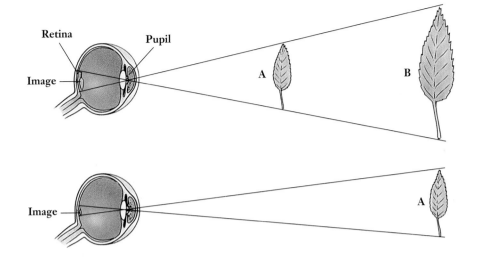

FIGURE **8.40**
*Relationship of retinal-image size
to object size and distance*
If, as in the upper sketch, object B is twice
as tall and wide as object A and also twice
as far away from the eye, the retinal images that the two objects produce will be
the same size. If, as in the lower sketch,
object A is moved twice its former distance from the eye, the retinal image produced will be half its former height and
width.

The Role of Depth Cues in Size Perception

The ability to judge the size of an object is intimately tied to the ability to judge its distance. As Figure 8.40 illustrates, the size of the retinal image of an object is inversely proportional to the object's distance from the retina. Thus, if an object is moved twice as far away, it produces a retinal image half the height and width of the one it produced before. But you don't see the object as smaller, just farther away. The ability to see an object as unchanged in size, despite change in the image size as it moves farther away or closer, is called *size constancy.* For familiar objects, such as a pencil or a car, previous knowledge of the object's size may contribute to size constancy. But size constancy also occurs for unfamiliar objects if cues for distance are available, and even familiar objects can appear to be drastically altered in size if misleading distance cues are present (for an example, see Figure 8.41).

39.

*In theory, why does size perception
depend on distance perception?*

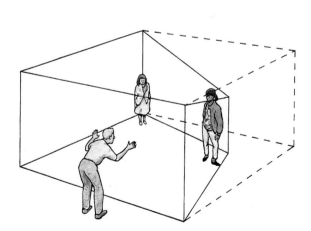

FIGURE **8.41**   *A size-distance illusion*
We know that these young women must be approximately the same size, so what explains this illusion? It's the room they're standing in that's distorted. The back wall and both windows are actually trapezoidal in shape, and the wall is slanted so that its left-hand edge is actually twice as tall and twice as far away from the viewer as its right-hand edge (see drawing at right). When we view this scene through a peephole (or the camera's eye), we automatically assume that the walls and window are normal, that the occupants are the same distance away, and therefore that their size is different. This distorted room is called an *Ames room,* after Adelbert Ames, who built the first one.

40.

How might the unconscious assessment of depth provide a basis for the Müller-Lyer, Ponzo, and moon illusions?

Unconscious Depth Processing as a Basis for Size Illusions

It is not difficult to produce drawings in which two identical lines or objects appear to be different in size. Two classic examples are the ***Müller-Lyer illusion*** (first described by F. C. Müller-Lyer in the mid-nineteenth century) and the ***Ponzo illusion*** (first described by Mario Ponzo in 1913), both of which are illustrated in Figure 8.42. In each illusion two horizontal bars appear to be different in length; but if you measure them, you will discover that they are in fact identical. Some years ago, Richard Gregory (1968) offered a *depth-processing theory* to account for these and various other size illusions. This theory—consistent with everything said so far about the relation between size and distance—maintains that one object in each illusion appears larger than the other because of distance cues that, at some early stage of perceptual processing, lead it to be judged as farther away. If one object is judged to be farther away than the other but the two produce the same-size retinal image, then the object judged as farther away will be judged as larger. This theory applies most readily to the Ponzo illusion, in which the two converging lines provide the depth cue of linear perspective, causing (according to the theory) the upper bar to be judged as farther away and hence larger than the lower one. The photograph in Figure 8.43 makes this point clear.

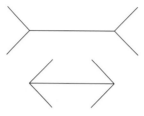

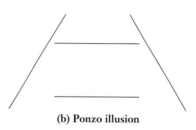

(a) Müller-Lyer illusion

FIGURE 8.42 *The Müller-Lyer and Ponzo illusions*

In both (a) and (b), the top horizontal bar looks longer than the bottom one, although they are actually the same length.

(b) Ponzo illusion

The application of the depth-processing theory to the Müller-Lyer illusion is a bit more subtle. The assumption in this application is that people see the figures as three-dimensional objects, something like sawhorses viewed from above. The object with wings extending outward (top drawing in Figure 8.42a) may be seen as an upside-down sawhorse, with legs toward the viewer, and the one with inward wings (bottom drawing) may be seen as a right-side-up sawhorse, with its horizontal bar closer to the observer. If real sawhorses were viewed this way, the horizontal bar of the upside-down one would be farther from the observer than that of the right-side-up one, and if it produced the same-size retinal image, it would in fact be longer (see Figure 8.44).

FIGURE 8.43 *Depth-processing explanation of the Ponzo illusion*

If this were a real, three-dimensional scene, not a photograph, and the red bars really existed as shown, the one in the background would not only look larger but be larger than the one in the foreground. (Adapted from Gregory, 1968.)

The depth-processing theory seems to offer an elegant explanation of the Ponzo and Müller-Lyer illusions, but perhaps you have already thought of an objection to it. Most people see the Müller-Lyer figures not as three-dimensional objects but as flat, arrowlike objects, yet they see the illusion. Even with the Ponzo illusion, many people do not notice depth in the picture; they do not see the top bar as being farther away than the bottom one, yet they see the illusion. Researchers who support the depth-processing theory of these illusions are well aware of this objection, but it does not lead them to abandon the theory. They remind the dissenters, as did Helmholtz, that the mental processes leading to perceptions are unconscious. The cues to depth in the Müller-Lyer and Ponzo figures may be too weak, or too ambiguous, to lead to a conscious perception of depth, yet they may still lead to an *unconscious* assessment of depth. That unconscious assessment may enter into the mental calculation that leads to a conscious perception of size differences.

Joel Gordon

The Moon Illusion

The *moon illusion* has provoked debate since ancient Greek and Roman times. You have probably noticed that the moon looks huge when it is near the earth's horizon, just above the trees or buildings in the distance, but looks much smaller when it is closer to the zenith (straight up). This difference is truly an illusion. Objectively, the moon is the same size, and the same distance from us, whether it is at the horizon or the zenith. If you view the horizon moon through a peephole, so that you see it in isolation from other objects such as trees and buildings, the illusion disappears and the moon looks no larger than it does at the zenith.

A depth-processing account of this illusion was first proposed by the Greek astronomer Ptolemy in the second century, was revived by Helmholtz (1867/1962) in the nineteenth century, and has been supported by modern research conducted by Lloyd Kaufman and his colleagues (Kaufman & Kaufman, 2000; Kaufman & Rock, 1962). The account can be summarized as follows: Our visual system did not evolve to judge such huge distances as that from the earth to the moon, so we automatically assess its distance in relation to more familiar earthly objects. Most objects that we see near the earth's horizon are farther away than objects that we see near the zenith. For example, birds or clouds seen near the horizon are usually farther away than those seen straight up (look back at Figure 8.38, page 312). Thus, our perceptual system assumes that the moon is farther away at the horizon than at the zenith, even though in reality it is the same distance away from us in either position. As in the case of the Ponzo and Müller-Lyer illusions, when two objects produce the same-size retinal image and are judged to be different distances away, the one that is judged to be farther away is seen as larger than the other.

Even today, the main objection to this explanation of the moon illusion is that people do not consciously see the horizon moon as farther away than the zenith moon (Hershenson, 1989). When people see the large-appearing horizon moon and are asked whether it seems farther away or closer than usual, they usually say closer. Again, however, as with the Ponzo and Müller-Lyer illusions, Kaufman and Irving Rock (1989) contend that we must distinguish between unconscious and conscious assessments. From their perspective, the sequence of perceptual assessments about the horizon moon might be described as follows: (1) Unconscious processes judge that the moon is farther away than usual (because objects near the horizon are usually farthest away). (2) Unconscious processes judge that the moon is larger than usual (because if it is farther away but produces the same-size retinal image, it must be larger). (3) The judgment that the moon looks larger than usual enters consciousness and leads to the conscious judgment that it must be closer than usual (because we know that the moon doesn't really change size, so its large apparent size must be due to closeness).

Not all perceptual psychologists agree with the depth-processing account of the moon illusion, or of the Müller-Lyer or Ponzo illusions, but the depth-processing account seems to be supported by at least as much evidence and logic as any other explanations that have been offered (Hershenson, 1989; Kaufman & Kaufman, 2000; Rock, 1995).

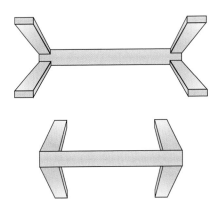

FIGURE 8.44
Depth-processing explanation of the Müller-Lyer illusion
Compare these sawhorses with the Müller-Lyer drawings in Figure 8.42. If these were real sawhorses, viewed from above in the three-dimensional world, the upside-down one would be longer than the right-side-up one.

The moon illusion
The moon at the horizon looks very large. Seen in isolation, with no cues indicating that it is at the horizon, the moon would appear to be the same size at the horizon as at the zenith.

Two Perspectives on the Perception of Constancies

We have seen that the perceptual system uses information about *relationships* among different parts of a scene to perceive the distance, size, and movement of any given part. Thus, perception of the distance of an object depends on such relationships as whether the object occludes or is occluded by other objects, and perception of size depends on the relationship between distance cues and the object's retinal-image size. For many years, psychologists have debated the merits of two general ways of thinking about the ability of the perceptual system to use such relationships. One is the unconscious-inference theory, and the other is the direct-perception theory.

To compare the two theories concretely, the following discussion focuses on how each theory explains three types of **visual constancies.** Visual constancies are those characteristics of objects that appear to remain the same despite retinal-image changes that occur when viewing conditions change. The three types discussed are (1) *size constancy* (on page 313), by which an object appears to remain the same size, even though its retinal image changes size when the object moves farther away or closer; (2) **shape constancy,** by which an object appears to maintain the same shape, even though its retinal image changes shape when the object is rotated in space; and (3) **lightness constancy** (also called *whiteness constancy*), by which a white, gray, or black object appears constant in the degree to which it looks light or dark (white or black), even though the amount of light reflected from the object changes when the amount of light shining on it changes.

Helmholtz's Unconscious-Inference Perspective

You have already read of Helmholtz's theory that unconscious inference underlies perception, and you have seen applications of that idea in discussions of depth perception, size perception, and size illusions such as the Müller-Lyer illusion and moon illusion. The unconscious-inference perspective posits that perception involves problem solving, though at an unconscious level. The sensory input provides cues that the brain uses to figure out, or infer, the distance, size, movement, and other characteristics of an object.

To apply Helmholtz's theory to the problem of size constancy, look at Figure 8.45, which depicts a cylinder as it would appear at position A, close to the viewer, and at position B, farther away. The cylinder appears to be the same size at each position, despite the difference in size of the retinal image that it produces. (If this were a real, three-dimensional scene, this constancy would be even more apparent than it is in the picture.) Helmholtz would explain this constancy as follows: The brain first uses depth cues, such as the linear perspective and texture gradient provided by the brick wall, to judge how far away the cylinder is. Then it uses that distance information to calculate the object's size and concludes that the object is the same size at each distance.

To see how the theory applies to shape constancy, look at Figure 8.46. A square sheet produces a trapezoidal retinal image when viewed at a slant, yet we see it as a square, not a trapezoid. (Again, this constancy is more apparent in a real, three-dimensional scene than in a picture.) According to the unconscious-inference theory, depth cues are used to assess shape in much the same way they are used to assess size. The brain calculates the distance of various parts of the object from the eyes and then uses those calculations, along with the shape of the retinal image, to calculate the shape that the image would take if the object were viewed from any other angle (Rock, 1995). In this way, all retinal images that can be produced by the same object result in equivalent perceptions of the object's shape.

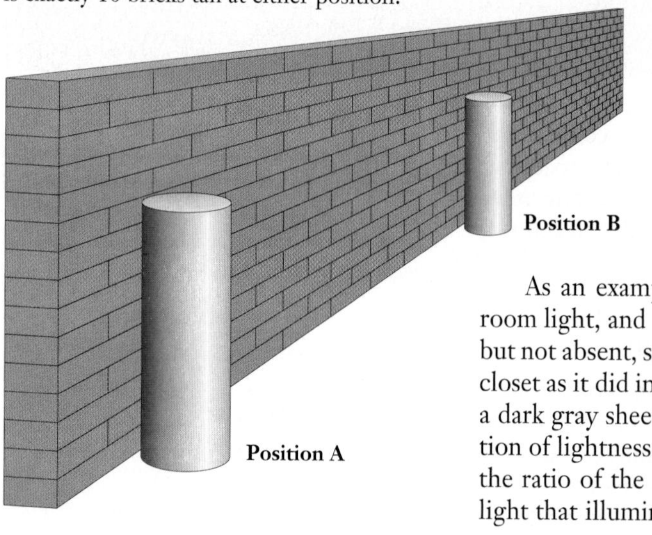

As an example of lightness constancy, look at a page of this book in normal room light, and then move it to a place where illumination is considerably dimmer but not absent, such as a closet with the door ajar. The page will look as white in the closet as it did in the brighter room, even though it now reflects no more light than a dark gray sheet of paper would have reflected in the brighter room. Our perception of lightness is directly related to the degree of *reflectance* of an object, which is the ratio of the amount of light reflected by the object divided by the amount of light that illuminates (falls upon) the object. Reflectance remains constant regard-

41.

How can constancies of size, shape, and lightness be explained by the unconscious-inference theory?

FIGURE **8.45** *Size constancy explained by two theories*

This illustration shows the same cylinder as it would appear close to the viewer and farther away. According to the unconscious-inference theory, we use linear perspective to assess the distance of the object at both positions, and we use that assessment, along with the size of the retinal image, to judge the stimulus as the same size in either position. According to Gibson's direct-perception theory, however, no such calculations are necessary. The size is seen directly in the higher-order stimulus, which includes the texture elements (bricks) of the adjacent wall. The cylinder is exactly 10 bricks tall at either position.

Position B

Position A

less of level of illumination, and so does perceived lightness (at least over a wide range of illumination levels). Helmholtz was aware of this (Gilchrist & others, 1999), and by now you may be able to guess how he would explain this constancy. He would say that your perceptual system must (a) assess the overall level of illumination in the room, (b) use that assessment in order to estimate the amount of light striking the page, (c) assess the amount of light reflected from the page, (d) divide the amount of light reflected from the page by the amount of light striking the page to determine reflectance, and (e) use reflectance as the foundation for perceiving the page's whiteness.

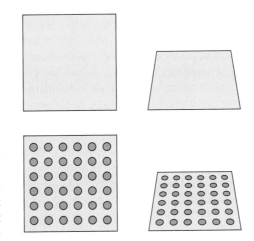

FIGURE **8.46** *Shape constancy explained by two theories*
You cannot tell whether the upper right-hand object is a trapezoid or a tilted square because it contains no texture elements or other depth cues. You can tell that the bottom right-hand object is a tilted square because of the texture elements (shown here as dots). According to the unconscious-inference theory, we use the change in size and placement of texture elements as depth cues to judge the degree of tilt and then use that to judge the true shape of the object. According to the direct-perception theory, however, we can see that this is a square without calculating depth, because each side spans the same number of texture elements.

Gibson's Direct-Perception Perspective

An alternative approach to understanding how the perceptual apparatus perceives constancies stems from a broad theoretical perspective called ***direct-perception theory***. This theory was developed by James Gibson in work that began in the 1940s. Gibson was influenced in his thinking by a modern understanding of biological evolution. We evolved through natural selection in the real, three-dimensional world, and that process eventuated in a perceptual system that is extremely efficient at picking up the kinds of information needed for survival in that world. An exquisite ability to perceive the distance, size, and motion of objects is essential for capturing prey, avoiding predators, and engaging in other survival-promoting actions. Such perceptions are too important to be left to an inferential process, which would take time and effort and could result in errors. Evolution created a more efficient system attuned to the kinds of information that directly signal depth, size, and motion. Gibson (1966, 1979) referred to his theory as an *ecological theory* to emphasize the intrinsic, inseparable relationship between the perceptual system and the physical and biological environments in which it evolved.

Unlike the unconscious-inference theory, which assumes that the stimulus information is insufficient and must be supplemented with calculations and inferences, the direct-perception theory assumes that the stimulus information is sufficient. According to Gibson, psychologists and philosophers had focused too much on mental processes and not enough on the stimulus array itself and the kinds of information it provides. Thus, Gibson shifted the emphasis from the study of the perceiver to the study of the external stimulus information that must be perceived.

Like the unconscious-inference theory, the direct-perception theory emphasizes the use of information about relationships; but while the former theory assumes that the relationships emerge from mental calculation, the latter assumes that they exist directly in the sensory stimuli. Gibson referred to the relational aspects of sensory stimuli as ***higher-order stimuli*** and argued that the perceptual system evolved to respond to these directly. Just as different wavelengths of light are picked up and experienced as different colors (without calculations), somewhat more complex stimulus information is picked up and experienced directly as depth, size, shape, and movement. In Gibson's view there is no difference between sensation and perception.

Concerning the size-constancy example in Figure 8.45, Gibson would contend that the cylinder and the bricks are not separate stimuli to be analyzed separately and then compared. Rather, they are parts of the same higher-order stimulus. Nearly all natural scenes include texture elements, and we know innately that

42.

In what sense is the direct-perception theory an ecological theory, and how can it explain the constancies of size, shape, and lightness?

James J. Gibson (1904–1979)
A leading perceptual psychologist, Gibson argued that perception must be understood in relation to the higher-order stimuli that exist in the physical and biological world in which human beings and other animals evolved.

texture elements on a continuous surface are generally constant in size. The visual system automatically registers the object in relation to the texture elements surrounding it. Thus, we perceive the cylinder at position B as being the same size as it is at position A because, in terms of the number of texture elements spanned, it is the same size (in both positions the cylinder is exactly 10 bricks tall). Notice that in this account, size constancy is explained in terms of a constancy that actually exists in the stimulus. According to Gibson, the visual system evolved so as to ignore the size of the retinal image and automatically perceive an object's size in relation to other parts of the scene, especially texture elements.

Concerning shape constancy, Gibson argued that the visual system is attuned not just to the borders of objects but also to surfaces, and surfaces normally have texture. Thus, the surface in Figure 8.46 is seen as a square because, regardless of its slant, it remains a surface whose sides each have an equal number of texture units (represented by the dots in the figure). By defining a square in terms of a scale of texture units, the perceptual system makes its job much easier; it need not calculate the relative depth of each side in order to see an object as a square. Of course, the texture elements would be misleading if they varied in real size in a gradual way over the surface of the object, but this rarely happens in the real world. Most changes that do occur in texture are abrupt, and the perceptual system perceives them as borders between differently textured surfaces.

By now you can probably guess how the direct-perception theory would explain the example of lightness constancy. From this perspective, separate assessments of the room illumination and the light reflecting from the page are not necessary and not performed. Rather, the page and its surrounding environment are all part of the same scene, and the visual system responds directly to the *ratios* of illumination in different parts of the scene (Wallach, 1948). Whether we view the page in bright light or dim light, it always reflects a high ratio of light compared with other objects near it, and that ratio is the higher-order stimulus from which we see the page as white. As was discussed earlier in this chapter, neurons in the optic nerve and visual cortex are relatively insensitive to changes in overall level of illumination but are highly sensitive to the amount of contrast between lighter and darker regions within their receptive fields. That evidence is very much in line with the direct-perception theory.

The Complementarity of the Two Perspectives

Gibson offered his theory of direct perception nearly a century after Helmholtz had developed the unconscious-inference theory. In the interim, however, Helmholtz's theory did not go unchallenged (Meyering, 1989). A contemporary of Helmholtz, Ewald Hering (the same person who developed the opponent-process theory of color vision), developed an *intuition theory* of spatial perception that can be viewed as a precursor to Gibson's direct-perception theory. According to Hering's theory, we perceive depth and other spatial characteristics of objects automatically, with no need for complex mental operations. Hering maintained that Helmholtz's theory was implausible because perception occurs too quickly to be mediated by cumbersome calculations and inferences. In reply, Helmholtz (1867/1962) contended that Hering's theory simply avoided the real problems of spatial perception by failing to specify a mechanism, in the brain or mind, through which it can occur.

43.

How can the direct-perception and unconscious-inference theories be understood as complements rather than mutually exclusive opposites?

Perceptual psychologists still debate occasionally along the same lines as Hering and Helmholtz. But the great majority now see the two theories as complementary to one another rather than mutually exclusive. The theories emphasize opposite sides of the same coin. Consistent with Gibson's direct-perception theory and Hering's intuition theory, the information needed to see lightness, depth, size, shape, motion, and so on does lie in relationships that exist in the stimulus input, and those relationships are registered quickly, efficiently, and effortlessly. Nevertheless, perception is also clearly a function of the brain. The brain somehow extracts the relevant relationships from the stimulus information, and the unconscious-inference theory calls our attention to that process.

Much of the attraction of the direct-perception theory lies in its assumption that the brain does not have to perform complex calculations to perceive the relevant stimulus relationships. But what does it mean to say that the brain directly "picks up" or "is attuned to" the correct relationships? How does the tuner work? Surely a complex neural system is involved. Any attempt to specify how neurons can pick up the relational information in higher-order stimuli might lead to a model that is as complex as—and perhaps not much different from—a model that specifies how neurons pick up elementary stimuli, integrate them, and perform the relevant calculations. By any account, the brain is an extraordinarily complex machine, vastly more sophisticated than our best computers. It is not unreasonable, therefore, to assume that the brain can perform with split-second timing the complex calculations that are required of it by the unconscious-inference theory.

Comstock

A textured world
Texture elements—provided here by the plants in the field—allow us automatically to perceive the shaptes and slants of surfaces and to perceive the junctions between surfaces, according to Gibson.

SECTION SUMMARY

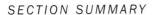

Helmholtz's unconscious-inference theory of perception led him and subsequent researchers to seek out the cues that the mind uses to infer the depths and sizes of objects in three-dimensional space. The major depth cue requiring both eyes is binocular disparity, the potency of which is illustrated by the depth illusions one sees in stereograms and autostereograms. Monocular cues for depth include motion parallax and a set of pictorial cues (occlusion, relative image size for familiar objects, linear perspective, texture gradient, position relative to the horizon, and differential lighting of surfaces). According to the unconscious-inference perspective, cues for depth also contribute to our perception of the sizes of objects. In theory, at least, an object's size (in height and width) is proportional to the size of the retinal image of the object times the object's distance from the eyes. Unconscious inferences of depth are believed to underlie visual size illusions, including the Ponzo, Müller-Lyer, and moon illusions.

Gibson developed his direct-perception theory as an alternative to the unconscious-inference theory. Gibson's theory explains such phenomena as size, shape, and lightness constancies in terms of higher-order stimuli rather than in terms of mental processes that combine elementary stimulus cues. Many perceptual psychologists today view the two perspectives as complementary rather than competing; Gibson's theory focuses on the richness of the information that is available in natural stimuli, and Helmholtz's focuses on how that information is extracted and used by the nervous system to produce meaningful percepts.

CONCLUDING THOUGHTS

As you review this chapter, you may find it useful to think about the following three themes:

1. The survival functions of vision Our visual system, like all the basic mechanisms underlying behavior, evolved through natural selection on the basis of its usefulness in promoting our ancestors' survival and reproduction. Our visual system is not an unbiased recorder of physical patterns of light. Rather, it is a biological tool designed to pick out the information in patterns of light that is potentially

FIGURE 8.47 *Objects in context*
The schematic ear, mouth, eye, and nose are easy to recognize in the context of the face, but they may not have been recognizable in Figure 8.33 (on page 306), where they were shown out of context.

most useful. As you review, think about the survival advantage of each of the following processes or mechanisms: (a) the processes of light and dark adaptation, (b) the distinctions between cone vision and rod vision, (c) color vision, (d) the enhancement of contrast at borders, (e) sensitivity to spatial frequency, (f) surface interpolation, (g) the distinction between "what" and "where" systems, (h) the evidence of a special neural system for face recognition, (i) Treisman's two-stage theory of perception and the complementary roles of parallel and serial processing, (j) the Gestalt laws of perceptual grouping and of figure and ground, (k) illusory contours, (l) Biederman's idea of geons serving as a basic alphabet of perception, (m) the distinctive-feature theory of perceptual learning, (n) the roles of context and motion in object identification, (o) the multiple cues that allow us to assess depth, (p) the role of depth cues in perception of size, and (q) the constancies of size, shape, and lightness.

2. The distinction between top-down and bottom-up processes   This distinction between two directions of mental processes is based on the idea that any perceptual act requires some kind of matching of stimulus input with knowledge already in the mind. The processes that bring in the stimulus information are bottom-up, or data-driven, and those that bring preexisting knowledge to the interpretation of the incoming information are top-down, or concept-driven. As you review the various perceptual processes discussed in the chapter, you might think about whether they are bottom-up, top-down, or both.

If you think critically about the distinction between top-down and bottom-up, you will find that it is often fuzzy. For example, Gestalt principles of grouping are considered by some perceptual psychologists to be top-down and by others to be bottom-up. If you think of them as items of general knowledge applied to the analysis of stimuli, they are top-down. But if you think of them as automatic consequences of the way the brain registers and integrates stimulus input, they are bottom-up. The selective use of distinctive stimulus features in skilled, learned acts of recognition can likewise be thought of as either bottom-up or top-down. If you think of such skills as involving modification of the stimulus-input channels, so certain features automatically are accented at the expense of others, then they are bottom-up. But if you think of such skills as learned knowledge applied to the stimulus input in order to recognize it, then they are top-down. Thus, depending on your perspective, you can often think of the same phenomenon as a demonstration of either bottom-up or top-down processing. Gibson's direct-perception perspective leads one to think of most or all perceptual processes as bottom-up, whereas Helmholtz's unconscious-inference perspective emphasizes top-down processes.

3. Studying perception under restricted versus rich stimulus conditions   Helmholtz's perspective—which regards perception as a matter of drawing inferences from stimulus cues—encourages the use of restricted stimulus conditions in perceptual research. To isolate and describe both the cues and the mental steps involved in acts of perception, researchers in the Helmholtzian tradition perform experiments in which stimulus input is restricted in ways designed to produce illusions or ambiguous perceptions. This approach coincides with a general approach in other realms of psychology—and in other sciences—of trying to understand how normal processes work by testing them in artificial conditions, where individual variables contributing to the processes can be separated and controlled. For example, if you want to describe mathematically the force of gravity, you will conduct your tests in a place with no air to interfere with falling objects, even though you know that in the real world falling objects are affected by air as well as by gravity. The same logic applies in trying to identify the roles that specific stimulus cues play in visual perception by testing those cues in isolation from others.

Gibson criticized the Helmholtzian approach partly on the grounds that it focuses too narrowly on isolated cues and ignores the rich set of stimulus relationships—the higher-order stimuli—that are available in real-world scenes. He argued that the isolation of stimuli results in artificial conditions to which the visual system is not adapted to respond normally. Gibson referred to his direct-perception theory as an *ecological* theory because of its premise that researchers must begin by considering the full range of stimuli available in the world in which people and animals evolved and live. In nearly every realm of psychology there is or has been tension between the desire to isolate variables in the laboratory and the desire to observe behavior in the far more complex real world. For instance (as described in earlier chapters), the early ethologists, who studied animals in the natural environment, contended that the early behaviorists underestimated the instinctive capacities of animals because of the restrictive laboratory conditions in which they studied them.

Further Reading

Richard Gregory (1997). *Eye and brain: The psychology of seeing* (5th ed.). Princeton, NJ: Princeton University Press.

This relatively brief book is an oft-referred-to classic. With clear prose and illustrations, Gregory introduces the reader to the entire range of issues concerning visual psychology, beginning with a chapter on the nature of light and then progressing through chapters on the eye, the visual brain, brightness perception, movement perception, color perception, the role of learning in vision, art, and illusions.

A. David Milner & Melvyn Goodale (1995). *The visual brain in action.* Oxford: Oxford University Press.

Milner and Goodale develop here their thesis that the brain contains two rather distinct visual-processing systems, one for conscious visual perception and one for immediate, unconscious guidance of action. The book is clearly written, assumes little prior knowledge about the visual brain, and summarizes many fascinating experiments on visual processes in monkeys and humans. Included is a full account of the visual abilities and deficits of D. F., the patient who suffers from visual form agnosia but can nevertheless act on objects in ways that take form into account.

Vicki Bruce & Andy Young (1998). *In the eye of the beholder: The science of face perception.* Oxford: Oxford University Press.

You can enjoy this book, and learn a lot, just by looking at the pictures and captions. The illustrations are packed with information, ideas, humor, and beauty, and they will probably tempt you to read the book's narrative. One chapter deals with the basics of light, color, and shape perception as they have to do with perceiving faces. Other chapters discuss such issues as the facial features that people use in recognizing faces, the recognition of emotions in facial expressions, the attractiveness of faces, and brain mechanisms involved in face perception.

Roger Shepard (1990). *Mind sights.* New York: Freeman.

This is a book of playful drawings by a distinguished cognitive psychologist who is also a talented artist and humorist. The drawings use size illusions, figure-ground ambiguities, and other visual tricks to present jokes and puns. The author's commentary on his drawings explains what the various tricks tell us about perception.

Looking Ahead

Perception is the first step in cognition. The way we initially see or hear something influences the way we subsequently remember and think about it. Memory and thought are the topics of the next two chapters, and many of the ideas that have just been discussed will be enlarged upon there. In particular, the distinction between bottom-up and top-down processes, the distinction between conscious and unconscious information, and the strategy of describing the mind in terms of compartments that serve differing information-processing functions will be applied to an analysis of memory.

The Human Intellect

The effectiveness of our behavior depends on knowledge we have stored as memory. It also depends on our ability to call up and combine the portions of that knowledge that are useful for the task at hand. How do we store and organize our experiences as memories for future use? How do we recall memories when they are needed? How do we manipulate knowledge in our minds in order to reason and solve problems? What differences among individuals account for differences in problem-solving ability? These are big questions that concern us in Chapter 9, on memory and consciousness, and Chapter 10, on intelligence and reasoning.

Chapter 9

The Happy Donor, René Magritte

Memory and Consciousness

Repeatedly, while working on this book, I have lamented my seeming lack of memory. I can't remember who did that experiment. I forgot to bring home the articles I need for this section. I've looked up that word a thousand times but still don't remember how to spell it; now where did I put my dictionary? Like digestion, memory is one of those abilities that we tend to take for granted except when it fails us. Usually we are more aware of forgetting than of remembering. But if we stop to think about it, we realize that our memory is far more impressive than our forgetting. Every waking moment is full of memories. Every thought, every learned response, every act of recognition is based on memory. It can reasonably be argued that memory is the mind.

Memory, clearly, is intimately tied to learning. Memory is often thought of as the change within an individual, brought on by learning, that can influence the individual's future behavior: Learning → memory → effect on future behavior. Chapter 4 of this book examines basic learning processes (especially classical and operant conditioning) that occur in other animals as well as humans. Consistent with its behavioral theme, the focus in that chapter is on the relationship between observable aspects of the learning experience (the training conditions) and subsequent behavior, with little concern for memory. Only the section called "The Cognitive Perspective" deals with the inner change (memory) that mediates that relationship. The present chapter, in contrast, is primarily about that inner change, and it deals with types of learning and memory that may be more or less unique to human beings. Our focus here is on the conscious, human mind.

Consciousness is one of those words that different philosophers and psychologists use in different ways and about which they often debate. For our discussion here, and with the hope of avoiding currently unresolvable controversy, I define *consciousness* simply as the experiencing of one's own mental events in such a manner that one can report on them to others. Defined this way, *consciousness* and *awareness* are synonyms. If you tell me, correctly, that a picture I show you has a bluebird in it, then I assume that you consciously see the the bluebird. If, sometime later, you respond "a bluebird" to my question as to what was in the picture, then I assume you have consciously recalled the bluebird. One of our concerns in this chapter will be with influences that *unconscious* information can have on the stream of one's conscious thought and behavior.

The chapter begins with a general model of memory that cognitive psychologists use as a framework for talking and thinking about the human mind. It then discusses issues pertaining to attention, mental imagery, the formation and recall of long-term memories, and the idea that the human mind is composed of several different but interacting memory systems that have distinct neural bases. Because memory is the core topic of cognitive psychology, this chapter, more than any other, presents a strong flavor of how cognitive psychologists think and conduct research.

OVERVIEW: AN INFORMATION-PROCESSING MODEL OF THE MIND

Cognitive psychologists commonly look at the mind (or brain) as a processor of information, analogous to a computer. Information is brought into the mind by way of the sensory system, and then it can be manipulated in various ways, placed into long-term storage, and retrieved when needed to solve a problem. *Memory*, broadly defined from this perspective, refers to all of the information in a person's mind and to the mind's capacity to store and retrieve that information. Memory is too large and multifaceted a topic to be studied or talked about all in one piece. Progress has been made in understanding memory by breaking it into components that can be described and studied separately. But any such breakdown implies a theory about memory—a theory that memory consists of the proposed components, that these can be studied relatively independently, and that an understanding of the components contributes to an understanding of the whole.

Theories in cognitive psychology are commonly called *models* and are often presented visually in diagrams that use boxes to represent the mind's components and arrows to represent interactions among components. Such models do not attempt to explain how mental tasks are accomplished at the level of neural activity. Rather, they attempt to describe the function and general characteristics of each task in a way that is useful in predicting how people will behave under particular conditions. The model that guides much of the discussion in this chapter (shown in Figure 9.1) has been so influential that it has come to be called the ***modal model of the mind***, where *modal* means "standard." Versions of this model were first proposed in the 1960s (by Waugh & Norman, 1965, and Atkinson & Shiffrin, 1968), and ever since it has served as a general framework for thinking and talking about the mind. As you use this model throughout this chapter, keep in mind that it is only a model. Like any general model in psychology, it is simply one way of trying to make sense of the data from many behavioral studies. And like any model, it can place blinders on thought and research if taken literally rather than as a metaphor.

The model portrays the mind as containing three types of ***memory stores***—sensory memory, working (or short-term) memory, and long-term memory—conceived of as places where information is held. Each store type is characterized by its *function* (the role it plays in the overall workings of the mind), its *capacity* (the amount of information it can hold at any given instant), and its *duration* (the length of time it can hold an item of information). In addition to the stores, the model specifies a set of ***control processes***, including *attention*, *rehearsal*, *encoding*, and *retrieval*, which govern the processing of information within stores and the movement of information from one store to another. As a prelude to the more detailed later discussion, here is a brief description of the three stores and the control processes.

1.

What are the main components of the so-called modal model of the mind? What is the purpose of such a model?

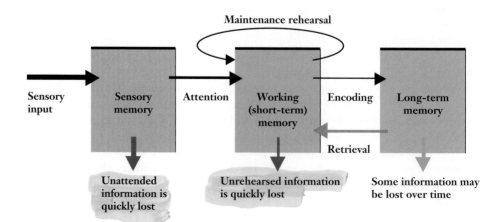

FIGURE 9.1
The modal model of the mind
This model has long served as a framework for thinking about the human mind, and we will use it for that purpose throughout the chapter.

Sensory Memory

When lightning flashes on a dark night, you can still see the flash and the objects it illuminated for a split second beyond its actual duration. Somewhat similarly, when a companion says, "You're not listening to me," you can still hear those words, and a few words of the previous sentence, for a brief time after they are spoken. Thus, you can answer (falsely), "I was too listening. You said . . ."—and then you can repeat your annoyed companion's last few words even though, in truth, you weren't listening when the words were uttered. These observations demonstrate that some trace of sensory input stays in your information-processing system for a brief period—less than 1 second for sights and longer (up to several seconds) for sounds—even when you are not paying attention to the input. This trace and the ability to hold it are called *sensory memory.*

A separate sensory-memory store is believed to exist for each sensory system (vision, hearing, touch, smell, and taste), but only those for vision and hearing have been studied extensively. Each sensory store is presumed to hold, very briefly, all the sensory input that enters that sensory system, whether or not the person is paying attention to that input. The function of the store, presumably, is to hold onto sensory information long enough for it to be analyzed by unconscious mental processes and for a decision to be made as to whether or not to bring that information into the next store, that of working memory. We are unconscious of most of the information held in our sensory store. We are conscious only of those items that are brought by the selective process of *attention* into working memory.

2.

What is the function of sensory memory?

Why don't we see this way?
If you're wondering why multiple representations of the icon don't distort your view of the visual world, the answer is that each new image from instant to instant blocks out the previous image.

Working Memory

According to the modal model, some of the information processed in the sensory store moves into the next compartment, that called *working memory* (look again at Figure 9.1). This is conceived of as the major workplace of the mind. It is, among other things, the seat of conscious thought—the place where all conscious perceiving, feeling, comparing, computing, and reasoning take place. An older and still often-used alternative name for this memory compartment is *short-term memory,* a term that calls attention to the relatively fleeting nature of information in this store; each item fades quickly (within seconds) when it is no longer actively attended to or thought about. Although some cognitive psychologists ascribe somewhat different meanings to the terms *working memory* and *short-term memory,* there is no consistency in such differential usage, and others use them as synonyms, as I do here (Miyake & Shah, 1999). Both terms refer to the content of conscious perception and thought and to the mental processes that operate on that content.

As depicted by the arrows in Figure 9.1, information can enter working memory from both the sensory-memory store (representing the present environment) and the long-term-memory store (representing knowledge gained from previous experiences). In this sense, working memory is analogous to the central processing unit of a computer. Information can be transmitted into the computer's central processing unit from a keyboard (analogous to input from the mind's sensory store), or

3.

What are the basic functions of working memory, and how is this memory store equated with consciousness? In what way is working memory like the central processing unit of a computer?

The passing moment
The flow of thought through working memory is not unlike the flow of scenery past the window of a moving train.

it can be entered from a floppy disk or other long-term storage device (analogous to input from the mind's long-term store). The real work of the computer—the computations and manipulations of the information—occurs within its central processing unit.

The sensory store and long-term-memory store both contribute to the continuous flow of conscious thought that constitutes the content of working memory. *Flow* is an apt metaphor here. The momentary capacity of working memory is very small—only a few items of information can be perceived or thought about at once. Yet the total amount of information that moves through working memory over a period of minutes or hours can be enormous, just as the amount of water flowing through a narrow channel over time can be enormous.

Long-Term Memory

4.

In the modal model, what is the function of long-term memory, and how is this memory store different from working memory?

Once an item has passed from sensory memory into working memory, it may or may not then be encoded into **long-term memory** (again, see Figure 9.1). Long-term memory corresponds most closely to most people's everyday notion of memory. It is the stored representation of all that a person knows. As such, its capacity must be enormous. Long-term memory contains the information that enables us to recognize or recall the taste of an almond, the sound of a banjo, the face of a grade-school friend, the names of the foods eaten at supper last night, the words of a favorite sonnet, and the spelling of the word *sonnet*. Usually we are not aware of the millions of items of information in our long-term store. According to the model, the items lie dormant (or relatively so) like books on a library shelf or signals on a computer disk until they are called into working memory and put to use.

In the modal model, long-term memory and working memory are sharply differentiated. Long-term memory is passive (a repository of information), and working memory is active (a place where information is thought about). Long-term memory is of long duration (some of its items last a lifetime), and working memory is of short duration (items disappear within seconds when no longer thought about). Long-term memory has essentially unlimited capacity (all your long-lasting knowledge is in it), and short-term memory has limited capacity (only your present thoughts are in it).

Control Processes

5.

In the modal model, what are the functions of attention, encoding, and retrieval?

According to the modal model, the movement of information from one memory store to another is regulated by the control processes of attention, encoding, and retrieval, all indicated in Figure 9.1 by arrows between the boxes. **Attention** is the process that controls the flow of information from the sensory store into working memory. Since the capacity of sensory memory is large and that of working memory is small, attention must restrict the flow of information from the first into the second. **Encoding** is the process that controls movement from working memory into the long-term store. When you deliberately memorize a poem or a list of names, you are consciously encoding it into long-term memory. Most encoding, however, is not deliberate; rather, it occurs incidentally as a side effect of the special interest that you devote to certain items of information. **Retrieval** is the process that controls the flow of informa-

Control processes at play

The man who best controls his control processes of attention, encoding, and retrieval is likely to win this game, unless, of course, he was dealt a lousy hand.

tion from the long-term store into working memory. Retrieval is what we commonly call *remembering*. Like both attention and encoding, retrieval can be either deliberate or automatic. Sometimes we actively search our long-term store for a particular piece of information. More often, however, information seems to flow automatically into the working store from the long-term store. One image or thought in working memory seems to call forth the next in a stream that is sometimes logical, sometimes fanciful.

Now, having overviewed the memory stores and processes represented in the model, let's examine them in more detail, beginning with sensory memory and attention.

SECTION SUMMARY

The framework that psychologists most often use for thinking about the mind is the modal model; it divides the mind into three memory stores. The first store is sensory memory, which holds sensory information briefly before it is either lost or transferred into the next store, working memory (also called short-term memory). The sensory store has a very large capacity, but working memory has a limited capacity. It can hold only a few items at any given instant, items that are actively being thought about. Sensory information that has entered working memory may or may not then pass into the large-capacity, long-duration store called long-term memory. Long-term memory is the repository of all one's knowledge. In addition to the three stores, the model identifies the control processes of attention, encoding, and retrieval, which, respectively, regulate the flow of information from sensory memory into working memory, working memory into long-term memory, and long-term memory back into working memory.

SENSORY MEMORY AND ATTENTION: THE PORTAL TO CONSCIOUSNESS

As I sit on my porch composing this paragraph, my senses are bombarded by countless stimuli, but I can choose from among them those to which I will attend. I can stop writing and attend to the chirping of a single bird. As I listen to the bird, I am vaguely aware of my neighbors arguing through the open window next door, of traffic on the street, and even of other birds chirping nearby, but these do not enter my consciousness in a clear and detailed way, as does the song to which I am attending. Everything else is part of the background. If I wish, however, I can shift my attention from the birdsong to any of the other sounds. I can choose to listen to the neighbors' argument, and when I do that, the birdsong becomes part of the background. I can do the same with sight as I do with hearing—shift my focus, say, from the bird, to the twig that it is standing on, to anything else in my field of view. From the viewpoint of the modal model, all the sounds, sights, and other stimuli impinging on my senses enter my sensory-memory store briefly, but only a few of them make their way into my working-memory store, where they become part of my flow of conscious thought. My process of attention determines which ones will pass through that gate.

Sensory Memory as a Store to Which Attention Can Be Directed

Before we examine the process of attention itself, it would be useful to look more closely at the nature of sensory memory for vision and hearing.

Visual Sensory Memory: The Icon

Visual sensory memory is also called **iconic memory,** and the brief memory trace for a specific visual stimulus is called the *icon*. The first psychologist to suggest the existence of iconic memory (or any form of sensory memory) was George Sperling

(1960). In experiments on visual perception, Sperling found that when slides containing arrays of letters were flashed for only one-twentieth of a second, people could read the letters, as if they were still physically present, for up to one-third of a second after the slide was turned off. This led him to propose that a memory store must hold representations of the letters, in essentially their original sensory form, for about a third of a second.

More direct evidence that iconic memory holds information in its original sensory form was provided by Charles Eriksen and James Collins (1967), who found that superimposing two icons produces an effect comparable to that of superimposing two pictures. The researchers devised pairs of dot patterns that appeared random when shown separately but formed a three-letter syllable when superimposed (see Figure 9.2). When the two patterns of such a pair were flashed successively, with a very brief delay between them, most subjects saw the syllable, just as they did when the two patterns were flashed simultaneously. As the delay was increased (up to 0.3 second), the frequency with which the subjects saw the syllable dropped sharply.

6.

How did Eriksen and Collins demonstrate that seeing the icon is like seeing the original stimulus?

FIGURE 9.2
Sample stimuli used to show the picturelike nature of iconic memory
When (a) and (b) are superimposed, the dot patterns form a visible syllable (c). The same effect occurs when (a) and (b) are flashed in rapid succession (less than 0.3 second apart), so that their icons are fused in sensory memory. (From Eriksen & Collins, 1967.)

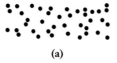 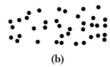 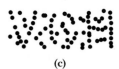

(a)   (b)   (c)

Normally, we are not conscious of iconic memory. As our eyes move (in jumps called *saccades*) while scanning a visual scene, the image from each new fixation point blocks out our conscious perception of the icon from the previous fixation point, so we do not see two images superimposed. Researchers are at present uncertain about just what role iconic memory plays in normal visual perception. One hypothesis is that it preserves sensory information during the brief time that it takes for the eyes to move from one fixation point to another, allowing us to integrate the information over time and to see both the consistencies and the changes in the scene before us (Irwin, 1992).

Auditory Sensory Memory: The Echo

Auditory sensory memory is called **echoic memory,** and the brief trace for a specific sound is called the *echo.* Early studies of echoic memory suggested that it lasts 2 or 3 seconds (Darwin & others, 1972), but research since then indicates that under some conditions it may last as long as 8 to 10 seconds (Cowan & others, 2000; Gomes & others, 1999).

In a typical experiment on echoic memory, subjects are asked to focus their attention on a particular task, such as reading a prose passage that they will be tested on, and to ignore spoken words (typically digit names, such as "seven, two, nine, four") that are presented as they work. Occasionally, however, their work on the task is interrupted by a signal, and when that occurs they are to repeat the spoken words that were most recently presented. The results, typically, are that subjects can repeat accurately the last few words from the spoken list if the signal follows immediately after the last word, but performance drops off as the delay between the last word and the signal is increased up to about 10 seconds (e. g., Cowan & others, 2000). The subjective experience of people in such an experiment is that they are only vaguely aware of the spoken words as they attend to their assigned task, but when the signal occurs, they can still "hear" the last few words and they can shift their attention to those words and repeat them. The relatively long duration of echoic memory may be important for speech perception, which, by its nature, is a process that requires the integration of information over time. To understand a spoken sentence, for example, we must accumulate over time a series of separate sounds; and a prolonged sensory memory for speech sounds may help us do that.

7.

How has echoic memory been demonstrated and measured, and what evidence suggests that sounds can be modified within echoic memory before they are consciously heard?

Perhaps you recall the experiment on phonemic restoration (by Warren, 1984) described in Chapter 8, showing that the way people hear a word can depend on words that follow it. Subjects who were presented with the sound *eel (where the asterisk was a cough) heard it as *peel* when the subsequent words were *was on the orange* and as *heel* when the subsequent words were *was on the shoe*. Their experience was not of inferring the first consonant but of actually hearing it. For that to have happened, the sound *eel must have remained in sensory memory while the rest of the phrase was spoken and must have been modified there before entering full consciousness. This suggests that echoic memory is not an entirely passive store; some modification of sensory information apparently can occur within echoic memory in order to produce meaningful patterns.

The Selective Nature of Attention

Attention is selective. Of all of the sensory input that is registered briefly in sensory stores, only some is selected to pass into working memory, where it is consciously perceived and thought about. How is that selection accomplished? That is the fundamental question of attention, and researchers are far from an answer.

Figure 9.3 depicts a very general model, in which attention is portrayed as a gate that lies between sensory memory and working memory. For the gate to be effective, it must somehow discriminate between items of information that are useful—that contribute meaningfully to the task at hand or that signal possible danger—and items that are not so useful. But how does the attention gate make that discrimination? Logically, to determine which stimuli might be worth passing into working memory, the mind must perform some sort of preliminary analysis of them. That analysis occurs at an unconscious level, and in the model it is referred to as *preattentive processing*. Logically, such processing must involve some comparison of the sensory input to information already stored in working memory and long-term memory. Without such comparison, there would be no basis for distinguishing what is relevant from what is not. Activity in the working-memory compartment must somehow operate on the selective gate to help determine what kind of information will be allowed to pass through at any given moment. In the model, that top-down control is indicated by the arrow running from the working-memory compartment to the selective gate.

All theories of attention posit that the mind monitors a great deal of stimulus input, through some sort of preattentive processing, and uses the results of such monitoring to select some of that information for further, potentially conscious analysis. Different theories of attention differ in their descriptions of the kind of preattentive processing that occurs and in their descriptions of the postattentive (working-memory) compartment (LaBerge, 1995; Pashler, 1998). According to some theories (Broadbent, 1958; Kahneman & Treisman, 1984), preattentive processing is concerned only with physical features of the stimuli, not with meaning, and the gate allows all stimuli that have the appropriate physical features to pass through. In those theories, however, the post-attentive, or working-memory, compartment is not equated with consciousness. According to those theories, processing for meaning occurs at an unconscious or semiconscious level after it has passed through the gate, and only some of that information then becomes fully conscious. According to other theories, however, stimuli are processed for meaning preattentively, at least to some degree, and all the information that passes through becomes conscious (Shiffrin & Schneider, 1977). To a considerable degree the differences among theories depend

8.

What are the main components of any model or theory of attention, and how do different theories of attention differ from each other?

FIGURE **9.3** *A generalized model of attention*
All sensory input enters the sensory memory store, where it is processed preattentively. Then some of it is selected into conscious, working memory. The arrow going from working memory to the selector indicates top-down control of the selection criteria.

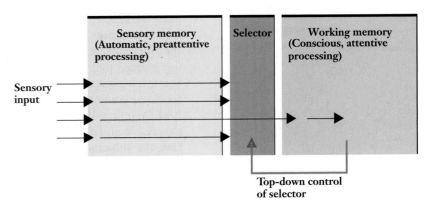

on the theorist's conception of the working-memory compartment. If working memory is equated with full consciousness, then everyone would agree that some processing for meaning must occur before the selection is made as to which stimuli will enter that compartment.

With this background in mind, let's now consider some classic experiments concerned with the selectivity of attention.

Selective Listening

The pioneering research on attention, beginning in the 1940s and 1950s, centered on the so-called *cocktail-party phenomenon*, the ability to listen to and understand one person's voice while disregarding other voices nearby. In the laboratory this ability is usually studied by playing two spoken, tape-recorded messages at once and asking the subject to *shadow* one message—that is, to repeat immediately each of its words as they are heard—while ignoring the other message.

The early experiments (reviewed by Hawkins & Presson, 1986) showed that successful shadowing depends primarily on physical differences between the two voices and differences in their spatial location. Shadowing is very poor if the two messages are read by the same voice and played through speakers that are near each other. It improves greatly if the messages are read by different voices (especially if one is a woman's and the other is a man's) or if the voices are altered electronically to make them different in pitch. It also improves greatly if the messages come through speakers located in different parts of the room or if they are played through separate earphones, one into each ear—a procedure called *dichotic listening*. Differences in the meaning of words in the two messages have much less impact. When the two messages are read by the same voice, shadowing a passage of English prose is only slightly easier if the distracting message consists of nonsense words or is in a foreign language than if it is another passage of English prose. Other dichotic-listening studies showed that subjects usually noticed and could report upon physical characteristics of the unattended message, such as the gender of the speaker or variation in pitch, but usually were unaware of any of the message's meaning or even whether the speaker switched to a foreign language (Cherry, 1953; Cherry & Taylor, 1954).

Such research led Donald Broadbent (1958) to develop the earliest specific version of the generalized model of attention shown in Figure 9.3—a version he called the *filter theory of attention*. Broadbent likened the selector to a filter (or sieve), which completely blocks passage of most particles but allows through those that have a particular physical definition. He proposed that the preattentive stage analyzes the physical features of all the sounds striking the ears and sights striking the eyes and allows through only those that have the physical features to which the selector has been tuned. Another metaphor, which may capture the essence of Broadbent's theory even better than that of a filter, is that of a tuner on a radio. Changing attention is like adjusting the tuner to pick up a different band of frequencies from the spectrum of radio waves that strike the antenna.

Subsequent research, however, showed that some meaning can be picked up from the unattended message and can promote a shift in attention from one message to another. In one experiment, subjects who failed to identify most words in the unattended message, including one that had been repeated 35 times, nevertheless noticed their own names in that message on about one-third of all occasions that it was presented (Moray, 1959). In another experiment, subjects shadowed sentences containing words with two possible meanings, such as *They threw stones at the bank* (MacKay, 1973). At the same time, the other ear was presented with a word that resolved the ambiguity (*river* or *money* in this example). After the shadowing task, the subjects were asked to choose from a pair of sentences the one that was most like the shadowed sentence. In the example just cited, the choice was between *They threw stones at the savings and loan association* and *They threw stones toward the side of the river*. Although the subjects could not report the nonshadowed word, they

9.

What evidence indicates that selective listening depends on physical qualities of the stimulus, and how did that support a filter theory of attention?

Jonathan Kirn / Tony Stone Worldwide

Selective listening
Cocktail parties are not the only setting in which the ability to attend to one voice and ignore others is valuable.

10.

What evidence indicates that unattended words are to some degree processed for meaning?

usually chose the sentence that was consistent with the meaning of that word. Thus, the unattended word apparently influenced their interpretation of the shadowed message, even though they were unaware of having heard that word. Results such as these convinced researchers that meaning can be processed at an unconscious level, and this led them to revise Broadbent's theory.

Selective Viewing

On the face of it, selective viewing seems to be a simpler task than selective listening; we can control what we see just by moving our eyes, whereas we have no easy control over what we hear. But we can also attend selectively to different, nearby parts of a visual scene without moving our eyes.

An experiment by Irvin Rock and Daniel Gutman (1981) offers evidence for selective viewing without eye movement. The researchers presented, in rapid succession, a series of slides to viewers whose eyes were fixed on a spot at the center of the screen. Each slide contained two overlapping forms, one green and one red, and subjects were given a task that required them to attend to just one color (see Figure 9.4). Most of the forms were nonsense shapes, but some were shaped like a familiar object, such as a house or a tree. After viewing the sequence, subjects were tested for their ability to recognize which forms had been shown. The result was that they recognized most of the forms that had been presented in the attended color but performed only at chance level on those that had been presented in the unattended color, regardless of whether the form was nonsensical or familiar. Still, they did notice and remember unusual physical characteristics of the unattended forms, as occurred when a form was unusually large or small or was composed of a dotted line rather than a solid line. As was typical in selective-listening studies, subjects frequently picked up the basic physical features but not the meaning of unattended visual stimuli.

An even more dramatic example of selective viewing comes from the work of Robert Becklen and Daniel Cervone (1983), which is illustrated and described in Figure 9.5. Apparently, people who focus intently on a visual task quite effectively screen out irrelevant information.

Unconscious, Automatic Processing of Stimulus Input

The modal model, as depicted in Figure 9.1 (its usual depiction), is a useful beginning point for thinking about the mind, but it is far from complete. Perhaps its most glaring deficiency is its failure to account for unconscious effects of sensory

11.

What is some evidence that people effectively screen out irrelevant visual stimuli that overlap relevant visual stimuli?

FIGURE 9.4 *Overlapping forms used in an experiment on attention*
To assess the degree to which vision can be selective, Rock and Guttman (1981) directed subjects to attend to either just the red or just the green shape in slides such as this and then tested their recognition of both shapes in each slide.

FIGURE 9.5 *Attending to one of two overlapping videos*
Becklen and Cervone (1983) made two separate videos of the same three men moving around a room, throwing a basketball to one another. In one video the men wore black shirts, and in the other they wore white shirts. Then the researchers showed the two videos fully overlapping on the same screen, creating the effect of a television set showing two channels at once. A casual viewer would see six men moving around, throwing basketballs, with one man or a ball sometimes passing ghostlike through another. In the experiment, subjects were asked to attend just to the black-shirted players and to press a button each time one of them passed the ball, a task that they performed quite accurately. Midway through the 1-minute film, an event occurred that, to a casual observer, was very noticeable. A woman carrying a large white umbrella sauntered across the playing area, spending a total of 5.5 seconds on screen, walking right through some of the players and the ball they were throwing. Remarkably, when questioned immediately afterward, only 18 of the 85 subjects had any memory of seeing a woman carrying an umbrella.

input. In the model, sensory information can influence behavior and consciousness only if it is attended to and enters the conscious working-memory compartment; otherwise, it is simply lost from the system with no consequence. In fact, however, there is much evidence that sensory input can alter behavior and conscious thought without itself becoming conscious to the person. One means by which it can do this is called priming.

Unconscious Priming of Mental Concepts

Priming can be defined as the activation, by sensory input, of information that is already stored in long-term memory. The activated information then becomes more available to the person, altering the person's perception or chain of thought. The activation is not experienced consciously, yet it influences consciousness. Most relevant for our present discussion, there is good evidence that such activation can occur even when the priming stimulus is not consciously perceived.

MacKay's (1973) experiment on dichotic listening, already discussed, provides a good illustration of unconscious priming. Words that were not attended to and were not consciously heard influenced subjects' interpretation of ambiguous sentences that were attended to. For example, the word *river*, even though not consciously heard, activated a set of concepts related to river in the person's long-term memory store, which led the person immediately to interpret the word *bank*, in the sentence *They threw stones at the bank*, as the bank of a river, not a place where money is deposited. In everyday life, priming provides a means by which contextual information that we are not attending to can help us make sense of information that we are attending to. I might not consciously notice a slight frown on the face of a person I am listening to, yet that frown might prime my concept of sadness and allow me to experience more clearly the sadness in what he is saying.

Another example of priming without awareness of the priming stimulus is found in an experiment (by Eagle & others, 1966) in which researchers briefly showed students either of the two visual stimuli shown in Figure 9.6. The left-hand stimulus contains the outline of a duck, formed by the tree trunk and its branches. The researchers found that subjects who were shown the duck-containing stimulus did not consciously notice the duck. Yet when all subjects were subsequently asked to draw a nature scene, those who had been shown the duck-containing stimulus were more likely to draw a scene containing a duck or a duck-related object (such as a pond) than were the other subjects.

Other experiments have shown that pictures or words that are flashed too quickly to be consciously recognized or read can nevertheless alter the person's subsequent thought and perception in ways that are consistent with the meaning of the picture or word (Greenwald & others, 1996). Some experiments of this type, in which people's judgments of other people were altered by this means, are described in Chapter 13.

12.

What is some evidence that concepts stored in long-term memory can be primed by stimuli that are not consciously perceived?

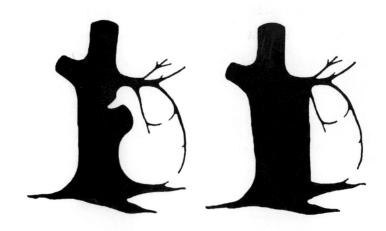

FIGURE **9.6**
Tree with and without a duck
When subjects were shown the stimulus on the left (in three 1-second presentations on a screen), they were aware of seeing a tree but not a duck. Yet when subsequently asked to draw a nature scene, they more frequently drew a scene having to do with ducks than did those who had been presented with the stimulus on the right. (From Eagle & others, 1966.)

Automatic and Obligatory Processing of Stimuli

A wonderful adaptive characteristic of the mind is its capacity to perform routine tasks automatically, which frees its limited, effortful, conscious working memory for more creative purposes or for dealing with emergencies. When you were learning to drive a car, you probably had to devote most of your attention to that task; you couldn't drive and carry on a meaningful conversation at the same time. With practice, however, an increasing amount of the skill of driving probably became automatic. Your visual system began to pick up and interpret automatically much of the information from the road that you needed to drive safely, allowing you to devote ever more of your conscious attention to other tasks.

Many experiments have demonstrated that extensive practice can lead people to perform a previously difficult task with little conscious attention, a situation that allows them to use their attention for other purposes. For example, Ulrich Neisser and his colleagues have shown that, with many hours of practice, people could learn to write down dictated words or sentences at the same time that they read a story or encyclopedia article, with no reduction in their rate of reading or comprehension (Hirst & others, 1980; Spelke & others, 1976). A reasonable interpretation of this result is that the subjects learned to take dictation automatically and thus were able to devote all their attention to the story or article they were reading.

Some highly practiced perceptual skills become not only automatic and unconscious but obligatory—we can't prevent ourselves from carrying them out. An often-cited example of this is the **Stroop interference effect,** named after J. Ridley Stroop (1935), who was the first to describe it. Stroop presented words or shapes printed in colored ink to subjects and asked them to name the ink color of each as rapidly as possible. In some cases each word was the name of the color in which it was printed (for example, the word *red* printed in red ink); in others it was the name of a different color (for example, the word *blue* printed in red ink); and in still others it was not a color name. Stroop found that subjects were slowest at naming the ink colors for words that named a color different from the ink color. To experience this effect yourself, follow the instructions in the caption of Figure 9.7.

A variety of specific explanations of the Stroop effect have been offered (for example, Luo, 1999), but all agree that the effect depends on people's inability to prevent themselves from reading the color words. Apparently, when primed to report color names, we find it impossible *not* to read a color name that we are looking at, and that interferes with our ability to think of and say quickly the ink color name when the two are different. As you would expect, children who have not yet learned to read are not susceptible to the Stroop effect, and children who are just learning

13.

How is the concept of automatic, unconscious processing of stimuli used to help explain (a) people's ability to do two tasks at once and (b) the Stroop interference effect?

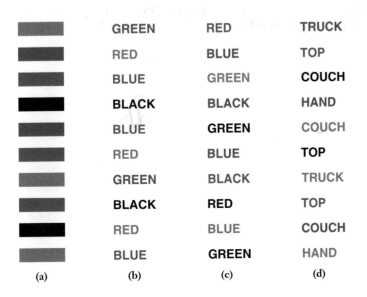

	(a)	(b)	(c)	(d)

FIGURE **9.7**
The Stroop interference effect
Time yourself (or a friend) on each of the following tasks: (1) Name the colors in each box in column (a). (2) Name the ink colors used to print the words in columns (b), (c), and (d), timing each column separately. Column (c) will take the longest, because the color words interfere with naming the ink colors—that is the Stroop interference effect. Column (d) may also take somewhat longer than either (a) or (b), because the noncolor words interfere somewhat with naming the ink colors. Column (b) should be quickest, because there the words facilitate naming the ink colors.

to read are only slightly susceptible to it (Gibson, 1971). In fact, the Stroop effect is sometimes used as an index of the extent to which reading has become automatic for a child.

SECTION SUMMARY

Visual sensory (iconic) memory lasts about one-third of a second; auditory sensory (echoic) memory may last as long as 8 to 10 seconds. Information that is still in sensory memory can be attended to and experienced as if the physical stimulus were still present. The phenomenon of phonemic restoration suggests that information can be modified in echoic memory before it is heard.

To be experienced consciously, sensory information must be attended to and thereby moved from sensory memory into working memory. Models of attention posit that unconscious, preattentive processing must occur in order to determine what information is to be selected for transfer into working memory. Experiments on selective listening and viewing suggest that nonattended items are processed most fully for their physical characteristics but also to some degree for their meaning. Information that is not brought into conscious, working memory can nevertheless alter the flow of conscious thought, as demonstrated in experiments on unconscious priming of mental concepts. In highly practiced tasks, a great deal of sensory information may be processed and responded to automatically. As illustrated by the Stroop interference effect, such processing can in some cases be obligatory; one can't ignore certain stimuli even if one tries.

WORKING MEMORY: THE ACTIVE, CONSCIOUS MIND

As defined earlier in the chapter, working memory, or short-term memory, is the center of conscious perception and thought. This is the part of the mind that thinks, makes decisions, and controls such processes as attention and retrieval of information from long-term memory. Most cognitive psychologists today conceive of working memory as consisting of a number of separate but interacting components. According to one influential theory, proposed by Alan Baddeley (1986, 2000), these include a ***phonological loop***, responsible for holding verbal information; a ***visuospatial sketch pad***, responsible for holding visual and spatial information; and a ***central executive***, responsible for coordinating the mind's activities and for bringing new information into working memory from the sensory and long-term stores. We have already discussed one process of the central executive (attention) and will discuss other processes of it later in this chapter and in Chapter 10. Here we'll focus on the phonological loop and visuospatial sketch pad.

The phonological loop

Keeping a telephone number in mind long enough to dial it may occupy this man's phonological loop, but other components of his mind are free to play nonverbally with his child.

© Esbin-Anderson / The Image Works

Verbal Working Memory: The Phonological Loop

As a test of one aspect of your own short-term memory, read the digits at the end of this sentence and then close your eyes and try to keep them in mind for a minute or so: 2 3 8 0 4 9 7. What did you do to keep them in mind? If you are like most people, you repeated the digit names over and over to yourself in the order you read them: *two three eight zero four nine seven*. Some IQ tests (discussed in Chapter 10) include a measure of the number of digits that the person can keep in mind for a brief period and report back accurately, a measure called the *digit span*. Most people have a digit span of about seven digits. More generally, the number of pronounceable items—such as digits, other words, or nonsense syllables—that a person can keep in mind and report back accurately after a brief delay is called the *span of short-term memory*. According to Baddeley's model, it might better be called the *span of the phonological loop of working memory*. The phonological loop is that part of working memory that holds on to verbal information by subvocally repeating it.

Research has shown that the span of short-term memory, measured this way, depends on how rapidly the person can pronounce the to-be-remembered items (Baddeley, 1986, 2000). As a general rule, people can keep in working memory about as much verbal material as they can state aloud in 2 seconds (Baddeley & others, 1975). Unrehearsed items fade quickly; some of them disappear within 2 seconds or slightly longer. People who can speak rapidly have larger spans than people who cannot speak so rapidly. The span for single-syllable words is greater than that for multiple-syllable words. Try repeating from memory the following seven-word list, with eyes closed, immediately after reading it: *disentangle appropriation gossamer anti-intellectual preventative foreclosure documentation*. Was that list harder than the list of digits? Any intervention that interferes with a person's ability to articulate the words to be remembered interferes with verbal short-term memory (Baddeley, 2000). Try to hold seven digits in mind while repeating over and over, out loud, the word *the*. You probably can't do it; the act of saying *the* interferes with your ability to articulate to yourself the digit names.

Keeping a list of memory items in the phonological loop is a bit like a circus performer's keeping a set of plates spinning on the ends of sticks. As the number of plates increases, the performer must work more frantically to get back to each and renew its spinning before it falls. Performers who can move quickly can spin more plates than performers who move slowly. Larger plates take longer to set in motion than smaller ones, so the performer can't spin as many large plates as small ones. If the performer attempts to do at the same time another task that involves his or her arms and hands—such as building a tower of cups and saucers—the number of plates he or she can spin decreases. Of course, in everyday life we don't normally use our phonological loop to keep nonsensical lists in mind, any more than we use our hands to keep plates spinning. Rather, we use it for useful work. We say words silently to ourselves, and we bring ideas together in the form of words, as we reminisce about our experiences, solve problems, make plans, or in other ways engage in *verbal thought* (discussed in Chapter 10).

Baddeley and his colleagues (1998) have recently suggested that a large short-term-memory span may be most useful for vocabulary learning. In a series of studies, they found that people with unusually small short-term-memory spans performed quite normally on most intellectual tasks but were very poor at learning new words (Baddeley & others, 1998). In another study, a group of students who were unusually adept at learning foreign languages were found to have digit spans that averaged 1.6 digits more than otherwise comparable students who had no special flare for languages (Papagno & Valler, 1995). A large short-term-memory span may help a person to hold new words in mind while thinking about their meaning.

Visual Working Memory: The Visuospatial Sketch Pad

We think not only with words but also with mental pictures. We are especially likely to think in pictures when concerned with the spatial layout of things. I can never remember which way is west when I am facing south unless I picture myself standing on a map of North America looking toward South America. Then I can "see" immediately that the West Coast is on my right. Similarly (but at a slightly higher level of thought), Albert Einstein claimed that the concept of relativity came to him through visualizing what would happen if he chased a beam of light and caught up to it (Kosslyn & Koenig, 1992).

14.

What is some evidence that people keep information in the phonological loop through subvocal repetition?

15.

What evidence suggests that the phonological loop may be especially useful for vocabulary learning?

16.

How do we use the visuospatial sketch pad to make judgments about spatial relationships?

FIGURE **9.8**   *Sample stimulus used
in a mental-imagery experiment*
Subjects saw line drawings such as this,
and later, when answering questions based
on their memory of a drawing, showed reaction times suggesting that they were
scanning a mental image. (From Kosslyn,
1980.)

17.

*What is the evidence that the visuospa-
tial sketch pad and the phonological
loop are distinct from each other? How
did Kosslyn demonstrate a similarity
between examining a visual image and
actual looking?*

If you rotate a *p* 180 degrees clockwise, do you get a *b* or a *d*? Who had a longer nose, your fifth-grade teacher or your sixth-grade teacher? Examine the boat in Figure 9.8 for a few seconds; then turn to page 340 and answer the question posed there in the margin near the top. If you are like most people, you probably answered each of these questions by creating and examining a visual image. According to Baddeley's model, you held that image on the visuospatial sketch pad of your working memory, where you examined and possibly manipulated the image to answer the question.

Just as working in the phonological loop has some of the properties of listening to sounds, working in the visuospatial sketch pad has some of the properties of looking at sights (Baddeley, 2000; Kosslyn & Koenig, 1992). People are slowed down in answering questions of the type just posed if, at the same time, they must also attend to visual signals on a screen. They are not slowed down, however, or at least not as much, if they are asked to attend to auditory signals or to say the word *the* repeatedly as they perform the imagery task. People are much better at doing two mental tasks at once if one task involves the phonological loop and the other involves the visuospatial sketch pad than if both involve the same component of working memory (Baddeley, 1986). You can easily rotate a *p* in your mind to see what it looks like upside down while repeating from memory a set of digit names, but you cannot so easily do so while trying to visualize those same digits as mental pictures. Such findings led Baddeley to conclude that the phonological loop and the visuospatial sketch pad are two separate components of working memory rather than two aspects of the same component.

No cognitive psychologist would say that a visual image really is, physically, a picture in the mind; but examining such an image is in some ways like examining a picture. In one study demonstrating that, Stephen Kosslyn (1973) showed people drawings, including the one in Figure 9.8, and later asked them to visualize each drawing from memory. He asked them to focus, in their memory, on either the left or the right end of the drawing and then, as quickly as possible, to indicate (by pushing one of two buttons) whether or not a particular named component was present in the drawing. For example, referring to the boat drawing, he would say "motor" or "porthole" or "anchor" while the person was focusing at either the left or the right end of the boat in memory. He found that the farther away the named object was from the place of focus, the longer it took subjects to push the correct button. These time lags suggested that the subjects had to scan across the mental image to find the named component before they could respond, just as they would if they were looking at an actual picture. Kosslyn took the lags as evidence that mental images indeed are organized spatially, like pictures.

Brain Areas Involved in Working Memory

18.

*How do neuroimaging studies support
the idea that mentally rehearsing words
is like repeating words aloud and that
mentally humming a tune is like
humming aloud?*

Using PET and fMRI neuroimaging methods (discussed in Chapter 5), it is possible to determine which areas of the brain show the most increase in activity as a person engages in various mental tasks (see Figure 9.9). When people are asked to hold a list of words in mind (that is, to exercise the phonological loop), extra activity occurs in a portion of the left frontal lobe that is known to be involved in the articulation of words and in a portion of the left temporal lobe that is known to be involved in listening to words (Awh & others, 1996; Paulesu & others, 1993). When people are asked to imagine a particular familiar melody, without words, a

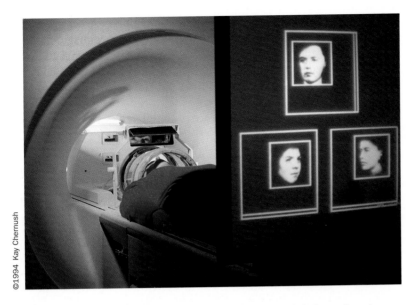

©1994 Kay Chernush

FIGURE **9.9** *Imaging a brain at work*
The magnetic resonance imaging (MRI) machine in which this volunteer lies assesses (by means described in Chapter 5) the amount of neural activity that occurs in each part of her brain as she engages in various mental tasks. In the mirror she can see words or pictures to respond to mentally in accordance with the researcher's instructions.

comparable pattern of activity occurs in the *right* rather than left frontal and temporal lobes (Halpern & Zatorre, 1999). These results are consistent with other evidence (discussed in Chapter 5) that in humans the left hemisphere is specialized for language and the right is specialized for various nonverbal tasks, including music. Apparently, the mental rehearsal of words involves the same brain areas as are involved in the actual speaking and hearing of words, and the mental rehearsal of a melody involves the same brain areas as are involved in the actual humming and hearing of a melody.

When people engage in mental tasks that entail visual imagery, extra activity occurs in visual areas of the brain, in patterns that depend on the specific nature of the task in the same way as occurs when actual visual objects or scenes are inspected. As was discussed in Chapter 8, visual areas of the cerebral cortex are divisible into two pathways. The "what" pathway is involved in recognizing patterns and objects, and the "where" pathway is involved in perceiving spatial locations of objects and controlling a person's movements in relation to those objects. When people hold visual images in their working memory for the purpose of recognition—for example, to compare a just-seen face with a previously seen face to see whether they are the same—the brain areas of the "what" pathway become most active. In contrast, when people hold visual images for the purpose of solving a spatial task—such as saying where in a previously viewed scene a particular face was located—the "where" pathway becomes most active (Smith, 2000).

People who have deficits in visual perception resulting from brain damage have deficits in visual working memory that are directly comparable to their perceptual deficits (Farah, 1989). For example, after suffering damage in the "what" pathway of his cortex, one man lost much of his ability to see the shapes of objects even though he could still see the relative locations of objects in a scene. In memory tests for information that he would have learned before the accident, he performed poorly on such shape-dependent questions as "Does a bear have a long tail or a short tail?" and "What does a cocker spaniel's ear look like?" Just as he was unable to see shapes in objects before his eyes, he was unable to "see" them in images recalled from memory. Yet he had no difficulty answering questions about the relative locations of objects. He could describe accurately, from memory, the layout of the furniture in his living room or the arrangement of buildings along a familiar street. Another man, with damage in the "where" pathway, showed just the opposite pattern of deficits: He could see and describe from memory the shapes of objects but not their locations.

In addition to the brain areas just described, working-memory tasks also generally involve the prefrontal cortex (the frontmost portion of each frontal lobe).

19.

What are two lines of evidence that the "what" and "where" pathways of visual perception are also involved in inspecting visual images drawn from memory?

The prefrontal cortex appears to be the neural hub of the central executive portion of working memory (Smith & Jonides, 1999). In neuroimaging studies, increased activity in the prefrontal cortex occurs whenever a person engages in a task that requires organized, conscious mental activity. People who have damage in the prefrontal lobes suffer from an inability to organize their behavior in meaningful, goal-directed ways, apparently because they cannot maintain focus on a plan or call forth information in the right sequence to complete a task (Kimberg & others, 1997).

SECTION SUMMARY

Working memory is divisible into several relatively independent components. The phonological loop is involved in the mental repetition of words. Anything that interferes with one's ability to "say" words subvocally and "hear" them interferes with the phonological loop. The visuospatial sketch pad is involved in visual imagery, and its activity is disrupted by visual tasks but not by verbal tasks. Neuroimaging studies have shown that verbal working memory involves activity in the same brain areas as are involved in speaking and hearing words and that visual working memory involves activity in the "what" or "where" visual pathway, depending on the nature of the task.

Answer this question from your memory of the boat in Figure 9.8: Is the anchor closer to the front of the boat or to the center of the boat?

20.

What is some evidence for and against the idea that repetition in working memory promotes encoding into long-term memory?

ENCODING INFORMATION INTO LONG-TERM MEMORY

As you read a book, or attend to a conversation, or admire the scenery you pass on a walk, some of the sensory information that reaches your conscious mind enters your long-term-memory store, allowing you to recall it later. Why does some but not all of the information that reaches working memory get encoded into long-term memory?

In the early days of memory research, most studies had to do with the memorization of lists of nonsense syllables or meaningless strings of unrelated words. Such items can be kept in the phonological loop of working memory by simple repetition—either aloud or silently—and it seemed reasonable to suppose that the longer an item is kept in working memory or the more frequently it is repeated, the greater is its likelihood of being encoded into long-term memory. The pioneer of such research was Hermann Ebbinghaus, a nineteenth-century German who conducted countless memory experiments with himself as the only subject. In a typical experiment, Ebbinghaus (1885/1913) would read a list of randomly selected three-letter nonsense syllables (*rup, gox, pim,* and the like), one or more times and then, either immediately or after a delay, would try to repeat the list from memory. One of his many unsurprising findings was that the more times he read a list, the more likely he was to remember it when he tested himself sometime later. Many subsequent studies likewise showed a positive relationship between number of repetitions and probability of later recall (Atkinson & Shiffrin, 1971).

It is not clear exactly what Ebbinghaus and research subjects after him were doing when they rehearsed items in lists in order to memorize them, but they were probably not simply passively reciting the items. Everyday observation, as well as research evidence, suggests that recitation, by itself, does not encode information into long-term memory. Many years ago a psychologist named Edmund Sanford (1917/1982) illustrated this point by describing his own poor memory of four short prayers that he had read aloud thousands of times over a 25-year period as part of his daily religious practice. He found, when he tested himself, that he could recite, on average, no more than three or four successive words of each prayer from memory before having to look at the printed text for prompting. I myself have looked up a certain telephone number dozens of times and held it in working memory long enough to dial it, without ever encoding it into long-term memory. Yet I remember some other numbers that I have looked up only once or twice. Experiments in which subjects held specific words in working memory for varying periods of time have shown little or no relationship between the duration of those periods and the likelihood that subjects would recall the words later in a surprise test of long-term memory (e.g., Craik & Watkins, 1973).

A weakness of the original version of the modal model was its failure to distinguish the rehearsal processes that maintain information in working memory from those that encode information into long-term memory. The model assumed that the longer an item is held in working memory, or the more frequently it is repeated, the more likely it will be to enter long-term memory (Atkinson & Shiffrin, 1968; Waugh & Norman, 1965). Today, however, psychologists distinguish between two kinds of rehearsal. *Maintenance rehearsal* is the process by which a person holds information in working memory for a period of time, and *encoding rehearsal* is the process by which a person encodes information into the long-term store. The activities that are effective for maintenance are not necessarily effective for encoding. What is effective for encoding? Research suggests that some of the most effective strategies involve elaboration, organization, and visualization.

Elaboration

Most of what we learn and remember in our everyday lives does not come from consciously trying to memorize. Rather, we remember things that capture our interest and stimulate our thought. The more deeply we think about something, the more likely we are to remember it later. To think deeply about an item is to do more than simply repeat it; it is to tie that item to a structure of information that already exists in long-term memory. This process is called *elaboration,* or *elaborative rehearsal,* by psychologists who study its effect on memory. The immediate goal of elaboration is not to memorize but to understand, yet the attempt to understand is perhaps the most effective of all ways to encode information into long-term memory.

Memory techniques centering on elaborative rehearsal capitalize on the human tendency to remember things that conform to some sort of logic, even if the logic is fictional. There is no intrinsic logic to the fact that stone formations hanging down in a cave are called *stalactites* while those pointing up are called *stalagmites*. But you can invent a logic: A stalactite has a *c* in it, so it grows from the *ceiling*; a stalagmite has a *g*, so it grows from the *ground*. Memory of a person's name can be improved by thinking of a logical relation between the name and some characteristic of the person. Thus, you might remember Mr. Longfellow's name by noting that he is tall and thin or, if he is actually short and stout, by recalling that he is definitely not a long fellow. I suspect that my students easily remember my name by relating it to the color of my hair.

Evidence for the Value of Elaboration

A number of laboratory experiments have demonstrated that people can remember factual information better if it is presented in a relevant context, which presumably stimulates thought about it (elaboration), than if it is presented alone or in an irrelevant context (Bradshaw & Anderson, 1982). Other experiments have shown that instructions to elaborate can improve memory even for sets of unrelated words.

In one such experiment, Fergus Craik and Endel Tulving (1975) showed subjects a long series of printed words, one at a time, and for each word asked a question that required a different form of thought about the word. In some cases, the question was simply about the printing of the word ("Is it in capital letters?"). In other cases, the question asked about the word's sound ("Does it rhyme with *train*?"). In still others, the question referred to the word's meaning ("Would it fit in the sentence, *The girl placed the _____ on the table*?"). As you can see by looking at Figure 9.10 on page 342, subjects remembered many more words when they had been asked questions that focused on meaning than they did when asked the other types of questions. Other experiments have shown that memory is even better when people are asked to relate each word's meaning to their own experiences or characteristics ("Does the word describe you?") (Rogers & others, 1977).

Robert McElroy / Woodfin Camp & Associates

Thinking through the lines

It is not exactly clear how performers commit long passages to memory, but, as suggested by the thoughtful expression on opera star Marilyn Horne's face, they apparently do much more than repeat the passages over and over.

21.

What is some evidence, from both the laboratory and the classroom, that the more deeply a person thinks about an item of information, the more likely it is that the item will be encoded into long-term memory?

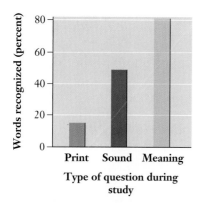

FIGURE 9.10
The method of elaboration used influences the likelihood of encoding into long-term memory
Subjects were shown a long sequence of words and were asked questions that required them to focus on the way the word was printed, how it sounded, or what it meant. The type of question dramatically affected the subjects' later ability to recognize the word as one that had appeared in the sequence. (Adapted from Craik & Tulving, 1975.)

A difference in elaboration

Flash cards and counting frames are both traditional ways to learn number facts. Their difference in effectiveness may depend on the amount of elaboration that they induce in the learner.

In a study of fifth-graders, John Bransford and his colleagues (1982) found that students who received high marks in school were far more likely to use elaborative rehearsal than were those who received lower marks. The researchers gave the children written passages to study for a later test and asked them to explain what they did as they studied each passage. For example, one passage described two different kinds of boomerangs, a returning kind and a nonreturning kind, each used for different purposes. Academically successful students often reported that they rehearsed the material by asking themselves questions about it. They might wonder what a nonreturning boomerang looked like or why it would be called a boomerang if it didn't return, and this caused them to think deeply about what a boomerang really was and about the information in the passage. Less successful students, in contrast, usually studied the passages simply by rereading them.

Bransford's study was correlational in nature, so it does not prove that elaborative study caused improved test performance; it shows only that the two tended to go together. But research with college students suggests that elaborative study can improve students' grades. In one college learning program, developed by Marcia Heiman (1987), students are taught to write down questions about every textbook section that they read as they read it and about the lecture notes they take as they take them. The process of generating these questions and thinking about the answers presumably produces deeper thinking about the information than would otherwise be achieved and thereby improves both understanding and memory. In a series of field experiments, Heiman found that students who were taught these techniques subsequently achieved higher grades in their college courses than did otherwise comparable students who received either subject-matter tutoring or no special help.

Such findings are compatible with the following advice for studying this or any other textbook:

◆ Don't highlight or copy out passages as you read; rather, question the text. Focus on the ideas, not the author's exact words.

◆ Constantly ask yourself questions such as these: Do I understand the idea that the author is trying to convey here? Do I agree with it? Is it relevant to my own life experiences? Has the author given evidence supporting it? Does the evidence seem reasonable? How is this idea relevant to the larger issues of the chapter? (In this textbook, the numbered focus questions that appear in the margins give you a start on this task.)

◆ As you ask such questions, jot down notes in the margins that bear on your answers, such as "This idea seems similar to . . . ," or "I don't understand what he means by . . . ."

Through this active process, you will encode the material in a far richer and more lasting way than you could accomplish by simple rereading. You will also, in the process, generate questions that you might ask other students or your instructor.

Organization

As a memory strategy, organization is closely tied to elaboration. Organizing items to be remembered is itself a means of elaboration; you must think about the items, not just repeat them, in order to organize them. Moreover, organization can improve memory by revealing or creating links among items that would otherwise be perceived as separate.

Chunking

One way to increase memory efficiency is to group adjacent items that are at first perceived as separate, thus making them a single item. This procedure, known as **chunking,** decreases the number of items to be remembered and increases the amount of information in each item (Miller, 1956). As a simple illustration, if you had to memorize the series *M D P H D U S A T W A*, your task would be made easier if you saw it not as a set of 11 independent letters but as a set of four common abbreviations—M.D., Ph.D., U.S.A., and TWA. You could make your task still easier if you then chunked these four abbreviations into one sentence: "The M.D. and Ph.D. left the U.S.A. on TWA." In developing such a story, you would not only be chunking but also elaborating—making the information more meaningful by adding some new information of your own to it.

Beginning music students find it easier to remember the notes on the lines of the treble clef as one sentence, *"Every Good Boy Does Fine,"* than as the senseless string of letters *E G B D F*. Similarly, physiology students can recall the seven physiological systems (skeletal, circulatory, respiratory, digestive, muscular, nervous, and reproductive) by matching their first letters to the consonants in SACRED MANOR. Both devices involve chunking. In the first example, the five notes are chunked into one meaningful sentence, and in the second the seven systems are chunked into two meaningful words. By reducing the number of separate items, and by attaching more meaning to each item, chunking provides an advantage both for maintaining information in working memory and for encoding it into long-term memory.

The Role of Chunking in Expert Memory

We are all much better at forming long-term working memories for information that is within rather than outside our realm of expertise. For example, master chess players can look for just a few seconds at a chess game in progress and form a long-term memory of the locations of all the pieces on the board (de Groot, 1965). Similarly, football coaches have excellent memories for diagrams of football plays (Garland & Barry, 1991), architects have excellent memories for floor plans (Atkin, 1980), and physicians have excellent memories for information gained in diagnostic interviews of patients (Coughlin & Patel, 1987).

As a step toward explaining the expertise advantage in memory, K. Ander Ericsson and his colleagues have posited the existence of a special kind of long-term memory, called *long-term working memory* (Ericsson & Delaney, 1999; Ericsson & Kintsch, 1995). They conceive of this as memory for the interrelated set of items (such as a patient's case history or the pieces on a chess board) that is crucial for solving the problem or completing the task at hand. Such memories are encoded into long-term storage in a manner that makes the entire structure of information easily accessible to working memory, at least until the problem is solved or the task is finished. Such memories allow a physician to puzzle over a particular patient's symptoms as she drives home from work and back again the next morning or a chess master to mull over the possibilities inherent in a particular set of chess positions while away from the game.

22.

How can chunking be used to increase the amount of information that can be maintained in short-term memory or encoded into long-term memory?

23.

How does chunking figure into experts' excellent memories for information that is within their realm of expertise?

Chunking plays a major role in the formation of long-term working memories. In order to form such a memory for, say, a particular arrangement of pieces on a chess board, the person must already have in long-term storage a great deal of well-established information about possible and likely ways that such items might be arranged. This knowledge provides a foundation for the efficient chunking of new items of information. Chess games normally progress in certain logical ways, so logical relationships exist among the pieces, which experts can chunk together and remember as familiar formations rather than as separate pieces. If the chess pieces are arranged randomly rather than in ways that could occur in a real game, masters are no better than novices at remembering their locations (Chase & Simon, 1973).

The Value of Hierarchical Organization

Perhaps the most useful format for organizing information is the hierarchy. In a hierarchy, related items are clustered together to form categories, related categories are clustered to form larger (higher-order) categories, and so on.

In an experiment demonstrating the advantage of hierarchical organization for long-term memory, Andrea Halpern (1986) gave subjects a chart listing 54 well-known song titles to be memorized. In some cases the chart was organized in a hierarchical manner, with songs arranged according to meaningful categories and subcategories. In other cases a similar chart was used but organized randomly, with no systematic relation among categories, subcategories, and song titles. When tested later for their memory of the song titles, subjects who had studied the organized chart recalled accurately many more titles than did those who had studied the disorganized chart. During the test the former group of subjects would first recall a category name and then the songs that had been listed under that name.

The information in this textbook (like that in nearly all textbooks) is hierarchically arranged: Each main heading refers to a large set of ideas, and each subheading refers to a smaller subset of ideas within the larger set. An efficient way to summarize the information in almost any textbook chapter is to sketch it out in a manner that preserves the author's hierarchical organization. As an illustration, a hierarchical sketch of the section you are now reading appears in Figure 9.11. Notice that the top node indicates in key words the theme of the section, the nodes subordinate to it indicate the main ideas pertaining to that theme, and the comments under them indicate the examples or evidence provided for each idea. You

24.

What is a hierarchical organization, and how can such an organization improve long-term memory?

FIGURE **9.11** *Hierarchical summary of a textbook section*
Summarized here are the ideas and evidence presented in this section (pp. 340–346) of the textbook. Such a chart is an aid to thought and memory because it reveals the logical connections among the items of information. Notice that most of the boxed items correspond to headings within the section.

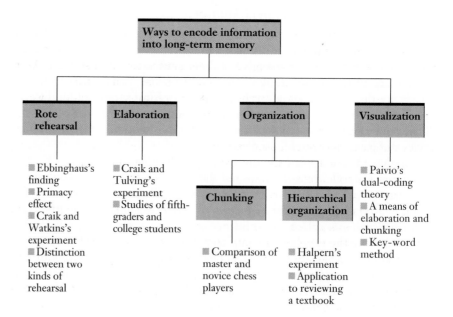

could summarize the whole chapter with six such sketches, one for each of the chapter's main sections. Such a summary would be a far more efficient aid in helping you commit the information to memory for a test than would a string of terms and names that does not preserve the connections of ideas to each other or of ideas to evidence.

Visualization

Our discussion of encoding so far has centered mostly on memory for verbal information. But we can also encode pictures or visual scenes into long-term memory, apparently in a nonverbal form, which can be recalled later into the visuospatial sketch pad of working memory. Visual and verbal memories interact and supplement one another in our everyday experience. If you asked me to describe my living room, I would summon a pictorial memory of that room and then find the words to describe it. Researchers have found that memory for information in news stories improves if the information is also presented in pictures accompanying the stories, even though the pictures are completely redundant with information in the stories (Prabu, 1998). The pictures in this textbook may serve more than just an aesthetic function. Even those that add nothing to your ability to understand what you are reading may, by supplementing your verbal memory with a visual memory, contribute to your ability to recall what you have read.

Some years ago, Allan Paivio (1971, 1986) developed a *dual-coding theory* of mental representation and memory. According to this view, we have two separate but interacting forms of long-term memory: a linguistic form specialized for storing verbal information and a visual form specialized for encoding the patterns and spatial arrangements of objects and scenes that we see. Paivio's research suggests that in many cases we can improve our memory by encoding information into both of these systems at once. Thus, in memorizing a list of objects, picturing each object while thinking of its name may produce better memory than picturing or naming alone. The theory helps explain why, in list-learning experiments, people find concrete words, such as *accordion* or *dress*, easier to remember than abstract words, such as *satire* or *effort* (Paivio & others, 1968). The referents for concrete words are easier to visualize than are those for abstract words.

In addition to providing a second memory trace, the visualization of verbally presented information may improve memory by providing a means of elaboration and chunking. You have to think about (elaborate on) a word's meaning before you can form an image of it, and an image can chunk otherwise separate items of information together in a single scene. Consistent with the chunking interpretation, visualization is especially effective in *paired-associate learning*, in which people study pairs of words and then recite the second member of each pair after seeing or hearing the first member (Marschark & Hunt, 1989). To use visual imagery in such learning, a person forms for each pair of words a single image that ties the two together. To remember the association *accordion–dress*, for example, a person might form a mental image of an accordion wearing a dress.

One practical application of such research is the *key-word method* for learning foreign-language vocabulary (Atkinson 1975). With this method, the student thinks of some easily visualized English word (the key word) that sounds like some portion of the target foreign word; then the student forms a visual image of that word interacting with the translated meaning of the foreign word. For example, see Figure 9.12 on page 346. In one experiment, students who studied a Spanish vocabulary list by the key-word method got 88 percent correct on a subsequent test, contrasted to 28 percent correct for those who studied for the same length of time by the more common method of rote rehearsal (Raugh & Atkinson, 1975). The method has also proved useful for learning other types of vocabulary, such as medical terminology (Troutt-Ervin, 1990).

25.

How does Paivio's dual-coding theory explain the value of visualization in memory encoding? How does the key-word method involve both visualization and chunking?

FIGURE **9.12** *How mental images can be used to learn foreign vocabulary*

A student using the key-word method to remember that *pato* (pronounced "pot-o") is the Spanish word for "duck," might choose the English word *pot* as the key word and then imagine a duck with a pot over its head. Later, in a vocabulary test on translating from Spanish to English, the student would associate *pato* with *pot* (because of the similarity in sound) and *pot* with *duck* (because of the mental image). In a test on translating from English to Spanish, this would be reversed: *Duck* would remind the student of *pot*, which would remind the student of *pato*. Similarly, the Spanish word *caballo* (pronounced "cob-eye-o"), meaning "horse," might be remembered by associating it with the English word *eye* and then creating a mental picture associating *eye* with *horse*. (Adapted from Atkinson, 1975.)

Pato—pot—duck

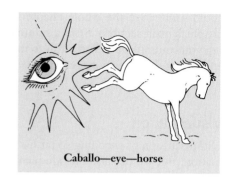

Caballo—eye—horse

SECTION SUMMARY

Rote rehearsal is effective for holding information in working memory but not for encoding it into long-term memory. Laboratory and classroom studies have shown that elaborative thought about an item of information greatly increases the chance that it will be encoded into long-term memory. Mentally chunking items together into a smaller number of meaningful units also increases the efficiency of encoding. Experts easily chunk items that are within their realm of expertise, and this contributes to their ability to hold relevant information in a form called long-term working memory that is useful for problem solving. Information that is organized hierarchically, into meaningful catergories and subcategories, is easier to remember than information that is disorganized. Converting verbal information into a visual image improves memory both by providing an alternative memory trace (a visual one as well as a verbal one) and by chunking otherwise separate items into a single image.

RETRIEVING INFORMATION FROM LONG-TERM MEMORY

Once an item is encoded into long-term memory, it may or may not be available for use when we need it. Why are we sometimes unable to remember a name or fact that we once knew well? Why do we at other times remember a name or fact that we thought we had long since forgotten? Why, in some cases, do we remember an event differently each time we retell it, or remember an event that didn't really happen as if it did? These are some of the questions that cognitive psychologists have addressed in theories concerning the retrieval of information from long-term memory.

The Role of Time

Clearly, time plays a role in remembering and forgetting. In general, our ability to retrieve an item from long-term memory declines over time unless we retrieve the item frequently. But the rate of decline varies tremendously, depending on the depth at which the information was originally encoded and the circumstances under which we attempt to retrieve it. In Figure 9.13 you can see two very different forgetting curves. The first is from Ebbinghaus's classic research with lists of nonsense syllables. As you can see, most forgetting occurred within the first hour; then the rate of loss became increasingly gradual, with little difference between tests conducted 1 day or 1 month thereafter. The second is from a study by H. P. Bahrick and his colleagues (1975) of people's memories for names and faces of their former high school classmates—information that would have been learned more solidly than Ebbinghaus's nonsense syllables. As you can see, in this study people who had graduated 34 years earlier were as good as recent graduates at matching names to faces in a recognition (multiple-choice) test. But a different test (recalling class-

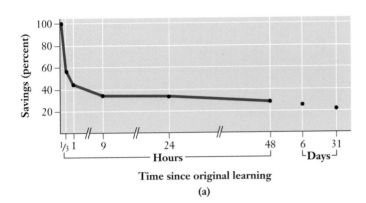

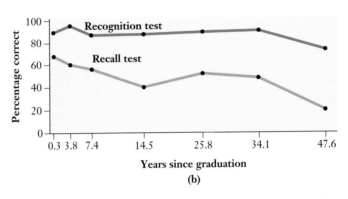

FIGURE **9.13**

Forgetting curves for (a) nonsense syllables and (b) high school classmates
Graph (a) depicts the results of a classic experiment in which Hermann Ebbinghaus tested his own memory for 13-item lists of nonsense syllables at various intervals after original learning. The measure of memory (percent saved) was the number of repetitions required to relearn a list expressed as a percentage of the number of repetitions required for original learning. (Based on Ebbinghaus, 1885/1913.)

Graph (b) depicts the results of an experiment in which memories for names and faces of high school classmates were tested in people who had graduated 3 months to nearly 50 years before testing. In the *recognition test*, subjects had to match each name to one out of a set of yearbook portraits. In the *recall test*, they were shown yearbook portraits and had to recall the names without any other cues. (Adapted from Bahrick & others, 1975.)

mates' names from pictures with no other cues) revealed a considerable loss in memory since graduation.

What happens over time to cause forgetting? Is information lost *from* the long-term-memory store, like a book that has disintegrated or been stolen from the library? Or is it lost *in* the long-term store, like a book that has been miscataloged or misshelved? One early theory held that memories simply fade away or decay gradually with disuse (Thorndike, 1913). Consistent with that theory, research with invertebrate animals indicates that the neural synaptic connections that are strengthened by learning experiences gradually weaken over time if the learning experiences are not renewed (Bailey & Chen, 1989). At present, however, we have no way to determine whether such synaptic weakening accounts for memory losses in humans. Whatever role time may play in forgetting, that role clearly depends greatly on the type of memory and the manner in which the memory is tested, as indicated by data such as that in Figure 9.13. A problem with the decay theory is that there is currently no way to test it. We cannot be sure that a memory is gone forever just because it can't be retrieved at a given time. You have probably often had the experience of recalling suddenly an item of information—such as the name of a childhood friend—that you thought you had long since forgotten.

Alternatives to the decay theory are *interference theories*, which maintain that other memories may interfere with the ability to retrieve any given memory, and *retrieval-cue theories*, which maintain that the ability to retrieve information depends on the availability of appropriate cues (reminders).

26.

What is the decay theory of forgetting, and why is it presently untestable?

Interference as a Cause of Forgetting

Learning one set of items can, in some cases, interfere with one's memory for another set of items. Experiments have demonstrated two types of such interference: **retroactive interference**, which stems from material learned *after* the test material is learned, and **proactive interference**, which stems from material learned *before* the

TABLE 9.1 *Experimental designs used to access retroactive and proactive interference*

	Task 1	Task 2	Task 3
Retroactive interference			
Interference group	Learn A	Learn B	Test on A
Control group	Learn A	—	Test on A
Proactive interference			
Interference group	Learn A	Learn B	Test on B
Control group	—	Learn B	Test on B

test material is learned. Both types are commonly studied in the laboratory by giving subjects lists of words or nonsense syllables to memorize. If two lists are learned, the inhibiting effect of the second on a person's memory of the first is retroactive interference and the inhibiting effect of the first on a person's memory of the second is proactive interference (see Table 9.1).

A particularly striking example of proactive interference is shown in Figure 9.14. Subjects who learned 36 successive word lists, each separated by a 2-day interval, showed progressively poorer memory of the most recently learned list as the experiment continued. In the last 18 tests they remembered on average less than 15 percent of the words, compared with 70 percent in the first test. Proactive interference does not affect either the rate at which a new list is learned or the immediate memory for the list, but it leads to more rapid forgetting. The steep rate of forgetting shown by Ebbinghaus (look again at Figure 9.13a) is probably due to proactive interference, although he was apparently unaware of that phenomenon. Ebbinghaus learned hundreds of lists of nonsense syllables over the course of his experiments, so each new list would have been interfered with by the previous ones.

What causes retroactive and proactive interference? Nobody knows for sure, and the answer may be different for different situations. According to one theory, both forms of inhibition occur in list-learning experiments because the separately learned lists lose their distinctiveness with time and tend to merge in memory, forming one large pool of information rather than two or more smaller ones (Ceraso, 1967). It is harder to search through a large pool of information and find an appropriate item than to search through a smaller pool. Consistent with that theory, many experiments have shown that interference is greatest when the different learning tasks involve similar items, which are presumably more likely than dissimilar items to merge into one pool (Wickens, 1972). Lists of nonsense syllables interfere with other lists of nonsense syllables but not with lists of words; and lists of words drawn from the same category (say, animals) interfere with each other but not with those drawn from a different category (say, household furniture). I once heard a story about an absentminded ichthyology professor (fish specialist) who refused to learn the names of his students. Asked why, he responded, "Every time I learn a student's name, I forget the name of a fish." Had he studied cognitive psychology, he would have known that learning the names of a group of students might interfere with his memory for names of another group of students but not with his memory for names of fish (that is, unless students and fish were similar entities in his mind).

27.

How can the concept of interference explain Ebbinghaus's rapid forgetting in his list-learning experiments?

28.

In list-learning experiments, what conditions increase or decrease the amount of retroactive and proactive interference?

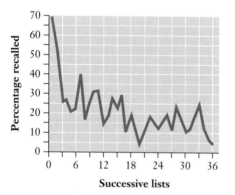

FIGURE 9.14 *Proactive interference*
Subjects learned a new list every 2 days and were tested before each new session on only the most recently learned list. As the experiment progressed, performance deteriorated, indicating proactive interference. (Adapted from Keppel & others, 1968.)

Mental Associations and Memory Retrieval Cues

To be retrievable, information must be organized. In a dictionary, information is retrievable because the entries are organized alphabetically. There it is easy to find every word that starts with *A* but hard to find every word that is the name of a fruit. In a supermarket, items are organized in a different way. There it is easy to find the fruits but hard to find all the items that start with *A*. We can draw an analogy here to our ability to find items in long-term memory. If I ask you to name things that start with *A*, you can easily reel off a long string of such items from your memory. If I ask you to name fruits, you can do that just as easily. Similarly, if I ask you to name things that are red, or that rhyme with *cat*, or that happened yesterday, or that taste sweet, you can use any of those categories to probe your memory and come up quickly with a number of items. In such cases, the categories I give you serve as mental prods, or **retrieval cues,** which help you probe your memory to find appropriate items. The most remarkable aspect of human long-term memory is not the enormous number of items it contains but the sophistication of its organization.

Mental Associations as Bases for Retrieval

The question of how knowledge is organized in the mind has been a subject of philosophical speculation at least since the time of Aristotle. Aristotle himself described that organization in terms of the *association* of elementary ideas or concepts. He considered two concepts to be associated if the thought of one tends to evoke (call forth from long-term memory) the thought of the other, and he proposed several principles of association, the most central of which are the principles of contiguity and similarity.

According to the principle of **association by contiguity** (also discussed in Chapter 4), some concepts are associated because their referents have occurred together (contiguously) in a person's previous sensory experience. Thus, *napkin* and *plate* might be associated in your mind because you have frequently seen napkins and plates together. This principle also accounts for our ability to bring quickly to mind the various properties of an object when we hear its name. If I hear *apple*, I can immediately think *red, round, sweet, tart, grows on trees, good in pies* because I have experienced all those properties of apples contiguously with apples themselves and with the word *apple*.

Association by contiguity cannot, however, by itself account for our ability to generate quickly, from memory, a list of items that are red or whose names start with *A*. To account for this ability, Aristotle proposed the principle of **association by similarity**. According to that principle, similar items—items that share some property in common—are linked in memory whether they were ever experienced contiguously or not. Your thought *apple* might evoke the thought *fire engine* because both are red, even if you have never seen an apple and a fire engine together.

As William James (1890/1950) pointed out, association by similarity can be thought of as a derivative of the more primitive and fundamental principle of association by contiguity. Contiguity allows us to think of the properties of any given object or idea and then allows us to think of other objects that have those same properties, leading to associations by similarity. Thus, my thought *apple* leads to my thought *red* (because of contiguity), and my thought *red* leads to my thought *fire engine* (again because of contiguity), with the result that my thought *apple* leads to *fire engine* (similarity). James suggested that the ability to separate mentally the various properties of objects and events from their concrete referents and to use those properties to link objects and events that were never experienced contiguously represents the basic difference between the human mind and that of other animals. He expressed this idea when he wrote: "Thoughts [in dogs] will not be found to call up their similars, but only their habitual successors. Sunsets will not suggest heroes' deaths, but supper-time. This is why man is the only metaphysical animal."

Network Models of Memory Organization

Continuing the tradition begun by Aristotle, many cognitive psychologists today depict the mind's storehouse of knowledge as a vast network of mental concepts linked by ties that could be called associations (but are commonly given other names, such as *pointers*). Figure 9.15 on page 350 illustrates one such model. Allan Collins and Elizabeth Loftus (1975) developed this model to explain the results of experiments concerned with people's ability to recognize or recall specific words very quickly after exposure to other words. For example, a person can recognize the

29.

What do the principles of association by contiguity and association by similarity say about retrieval from long-term memory? According to James, how does the second principle depend on the first?

30.

What sorts of experimental results was Collins and Loftus's spreading-activation model designed to explain? How does the model expand on the idea that mental associations provide a basis for memory and thought?

FIGURE **9.15**   *A network model of memory organization*
This diagram depicts schematically some of the links, or associations, among a tiny fraction of the thousands of different concepts that are stored in a typical person's long-term memory. The shorter the path between two concepts, the more strongly they are associated in memory. To say that two items are associated is to say that the thought of one will tend to activate the other, making it more easily retrievable. (From Collins & Loftus, 1975.)

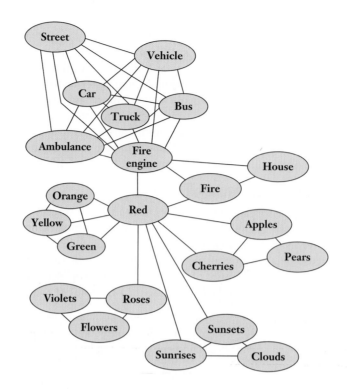

word *apple* more quickly if the previous word was *pear* or *red* than if it was *bus*. Collins and Loftus assumed that the degree to which one word speeds up the ability to recognize or recall another reflects the strength of the mental association between the two words or concepts.

In Figure 9.15, the shorter the path between two concepts, the more strongly they are associated. Notice how the model incorporates the idea that common properties of objects often provide the basis for their link in memory. *Roses, cherries, apples,* and *fire engines* are all linked to the concept *red,* and through that common tie they are all linked to each other. The model is called a *spreading-activation model* because it proposes that the activation of any one concept initiates a spread of activity to nearby concepts in the network, which primes those concepts, so they become temporarily more retrievable than they were before. The spreading activity declines with distance, so concepts that are closely linked with the active concept receive more priming than those that are more distantly linked. Such models are convenient ways to depict the results of many memory experiments, and they help us visualize the patterns of associations that make up the mind.

Concepts Present at Encoding Become Excellent Retrieval Cues

How you place new information into your network of associations has a big effect on your subsequent ability to retrieve it. This brings us back to the role of elaborative rehearsal in memorization, discussed earlier. The more links you create in learning a new item of information, the more ways will be available for you to retrieve it later.

31.

How does the encoding-specificity principle help explain the value of elaborative encoding and the remarkable performance of experimental subjects on a recall test for 500 nouns?

Suppose you are learning for the first time that the capital of Vermont is Montpelier. You might notice, as you encode this new fact, that the syllable *mont* appears in both the capital name and the state name, and you might then think about the fact that *mont* is French for *mountain,* that Vermont is known as the Green Mountain state, and that many of the early settlers were French. Through such observations and thoughts you are setting up many possible retrieval cues for remembering, later, that the capital of Vermont is Montpelier. According to the **encoding-specificity principle,** the stimuli or ideas that are prominent in a person's mind during the original encoding of an item of information into long-term memory often become the most effective cues for retrieval (Tulving, 1974).

Consistent with the encoding-specificity principle, people have extraordinary recall ability if they make up their own retrieval cues at the time of encoding and are given the same cues at the time of testing. In one experiment demonstrating this, Timo Mäntylä (1986) presented 500 nouns to people, one by one, all in one very long session. He did not ask the subjects to memorize the nouns but asked them to write down either one or three words that they regarded as properties of the object named by each noun. For example, for the word *barn* they might write *large, wooden, red*. He then surprised the subjects with a test of their ability to recall all 500 nouns. As cues, he gave them either their own self-generated properties or those generated by a different subject in the same experiment. Subjects who received three self-generated properties for each word were able to recall correctly more than 90 percent of the 500 nouns. When only one property was available or when the properties had been generated by someone else, recall was much poorer (see Figure 9.16).

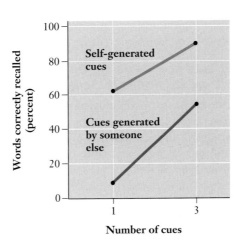

FIGURE 9.16 *Value of self-generated retrieval cues*
Subjects generated either one or three single-word properties related to each of 500 nouns. Later they were tested for their ability to recall each noun, using either their own self-generated properties or another subject's self-generated properties as retrieval cues. (Data from Mäntylä, 1986.)

Context-Dependent Memory

According to the encoding-specificity principle, memory retrieval is facilitated not just by cues that are properties of the learned material but also by cues that are incidental to the learned material but happened to be present at the time of encoding. Have you ever returned to a former school or to a neighborhood where you once lived and found that the sights and sounds, even the odors, evoked memories of people you knew or things you did—memories you thought were forgotten? Recall that depends on similarity between the test environment and the encoding environment is called *context-dependent memory*. In one series of experiments demonstrating context-dependent memory, Frank Schab (1990) found that people who studied a list of words in a room that smelled of chocolate or cinnamon/apple or mothballs performed better on a recall test if the same smell was again present than they did if a different smell, or no smell, was present. In other experiments, students showed slightly better recall for information learned in a classroom when learning and testing occurred in the same room than when they occurred in different rooms (Metzger & others, 1979).

Memory Construction as a Source of Distortion

Remembering is not just a process of retrieving traces that were laid down during the original encoding. The brain is not a tape recorder or video camera, which records information at high fidelity, and remembering is not a matter of finding the right cassette and playing it back. Instead, remembering is an active, inferential process guided by a person's general knowledge and intuitions about the world and by cues in the present environment. When you hear a story or experience an event, your mind encodes into long-term memory only some parts of the available information. Later, when you try to recount the story or event, you retrieve the encoded fragments and fill in the gaps through your logic and knowledge, which tell you what must have happened even if you can't quite remember it. With repeated retelling, it becomes harder to distinguish what was present in the original encoding from what was added later. Thus, memory of the story or experience is not a simple readout of the original information but a *construction* built and rebuilt from various sources. Our ability to construct the past is adaptive because it allows us to

32.

How can context-dependent memory be demonstrated, and how is it consistent with the encoding-specificity principle?

33.

What does it mean to say that memories are constructed?

make logical and useful sense of our incompletely encoded experiences. But the process can also lead to distortions.

Effects of Preexisting Beliefs: Fitting Memories to Schemas and Scripts

One of the first psychologists to call attention to the role of people's general knowledge or beliefs in their more specific memories was the British psychologist Frederick Bartlett. Bartlett (1932) used the term *schema* to refer to one's generalized mental representation, or concept, of any given class of objects, scenes, or events. He used the term especially in relation to concepts that may vary from culture to culture and that involve spatial or temporal relationships among the individual units of the object, scene, or event. For example, in our culture today people might share a relatively common schema of a living room, perhaps including a couch, an easy chair, and a rocking chair, all oriented around a television set, with a coffee table in front of the couch. When we enter a new living room, we recognize it as a living room and assess its unique features by comparing it with our already existing schema. Schemas that involve the organization of events in time, rather than of objects in space, are commonly called *scripts* by today's cognitive psychologists (Schank & Abelson, 1977). The typical birthday party is a good example: There are games, followed by the presentation of the cake, the singing of "Happy Birthday," the blowing out of the candles, the eating of the cake, the opening of the presents, and then more games.

According to Bartlett and the results of many studies since his time, schemas do not just help us recognize and label the objects, scenes, and events that we encounter in daily life; they also affect the way we remember them later. We tend to remember any particular living room or birthday party as being more like the standard living room or birthday party than it really was. That is because we fill gaps in our memory of the particular with information from our schemas and scripts for the general.

In a classic demonstration of the effect of general knowledge on memory for the specific, Bartlett (1932) asked British university students to listen to a Native American story entitled "The War of the Ghosts" and later asked them to retell the story from memory. He found that the story often changed in the retelling, and he noticed certain consistencies in those changes. Details not essential to the plot tended to drop out, and those that were essential were often exaggerated. Also, points in the story that were consistent with Native American beliefs but not with the students' own beliefs were often changed to be more consistent with the latter.

34.

How did Bartlett demonstrate that culture-specific schemas affect the way that people remember a story?

A typical birthday party

Years from now, this boy may construct a memory of his seventh-birthday party largely from his knowledge of the typical birthday-party script.

Esbin-Anderson / The Image Works

For example, the protagonist's obligation to specific spirits—a key component of the original story—tended to be transposed into an obligation to his parents. The changes were not deliberate; the students were trying to retell the story accurately, but they inevitably used their own ways of understanding things—their own schemas—to fill the gaps in their memory.

Effects of Suggestion and Imagination on Memory Construction

Memory construction is affected not just by preexisting schemas but also by events that occur after the to-be-remembered event was encoded. Such effects assume more than academic importance in such settings as courtrooms and psychotherapy offices. When eyewitnesses are questioned repeatedly about a crime, does the manner of questioning affect the memories that are generated? If an adult begins to recall instances of having been abused in childhood, do the memories reflect the truth, or might they have been constructed from ideas implanted by a well-intentioned therapist or friend? Do instructions to "imagine" a past event increase or decrease the accuracy of one's subsequent memory for that event? A number of high-profile court cases have revolved around such issues. People have sued their parents for past abuse based on memories that they claimed had been discovered, or released from repression, during psychotherapy. Parents have sued therapists for implanting false memories of childhood abuse in their adult children. Day-care providers have been charged with heinous crimes on the basis of testimony elicited from very young children through repeated questioning and hints about what might have happened. In response to all this, research psychologists have conducted many dozens of experiments aimed at understanding the variables that can lead people to construct false memories.

In a classic experiment concerned with eyewitness testimony, Elizabeth Loftus and J. C. Palmer (1974) had adults view a film depicting a traffic accident. Later, the researchers asked some of the subjects how fast the cars were going when they *hit* each other, and they asked others how fast the cars were going when they *smashed into* each other. The question with the word *smashed* elicited estimates of faster speed than did the question with the word *hit*. Moreover, when the subjects returned a week later and were asked to remember the film and say whether there was any broken glass in the accident, those who had heard the word *smashed* were more likely to say they saw broken glass (though actually there was none in the film) than were those who had heard the word *hit*. In subsequent studies, Loftus and others showed that such memory distortion is especially likely if the misinformation is introduced in just the manner that a clever but biased detective or cross-examiner is likely to introduce it—repeatedly but subtly, in the context of recounting aspects of the event that really did occur (Loftus, 1992; Zaragoza & Mitchell, 1996).

Other studies have shown that strong suggestion can lead people to "remember" entire episodes in their own lives that in fact never happened. In one such study, Loftus and Jacqueline Pickrell (1995) led adults to believe that at age 5 they had been lost in a specific shopping mall or department store and had been helped and comforted there by an elderly woman—an experience that in fact had never happened, according to the subjects' parents and other close relatives who served as informants. Yet 25 percent of the subjects maintained—both at initial questioning and in follow-up interviews 1 and 2 weeks later—that they could remember the event. Some even elaborated upon it with further details.

In a subsequent study, using a more unlikely false event, Ira Hyman and Joel Pentland (1996) showed that the construction of a false memory can be abetted by imagination. These researchers tested college students for their memory of three true childhood events (reported by subjects' parents to have happened) and one false childhood event (reported by the parents not to have happened). In this case the false event was an incident in which the subject, at age 5, had been running around with other children at a wedding reception and had knocked over the punch

35.

How did Loftus demonstrate that information added after an event can affect people's apparent memory for the event?

Courtesy of Elizabeth F. Loftus, Ph. D.

Elizabeth Loftus

Loftus is one of psychology's leading memory researchers. She often testifies in court cases that rest on a witness's or victim's memory. Her research on constructed memories has led her to be especially skeptical of memories that were recovered in psychotherapy or under the pressure of a prosecutor's persistent goal-directed questioning.

36.

How have false memories for childhood events been implanted in experiments, and what evidence indicates that imagination can increase false-memory construction?

FIGURE **9.17**   *Effect of imagery on development of a false memory*
Adult subjects were told about three events from their early childhood that did happen and one that did not happen and were asked to try to remember each event. Subjects who failed to remember an event were asked either to think about the event (control condition) or to develop a vivid mental image of what might have happened (imagery condition). This procedure was repeated in a second session the next day, and the subjects' memories were again assessed in a third session, 2 days after the first. In the false event, the subject was said to have spilled the punch at a wedding at age 5. The graph shows the percentage of subjects in each condition, at each interview, who claimed to remember the punch-spilling episode. (Based on data in Hyman & Pentland, 1996.)

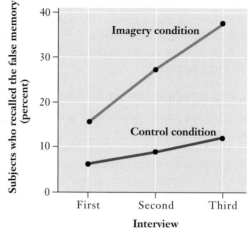

37.

How can false memory be explained as source confusion, and how might social pressure contribute to false-memory construction?

bowl, spilling punch on the bride's parents. Half of the subjects—those in the *imagery condition*—were told that their memory for each event would improve if they vividly imagined it, as it might have happened. They were asked to spend some time imagining each event that they could not immediately recall and to describe in detail the contents of their imagination to the researcher. The other half—those in the *control condition*—were told that sitting quietly and thinking about an event would help them remember it, and they were asked to do that for each event that they could not immediately recall. In a second interview, a day later, the subjects were again asked to report on their memories for the events and to again imagine or think about (depending on condition) any event they didn't remember. In a third interview, another day later, their memories were probed once more. The main result was that imagery sharply increased memory for the false event. By the third interview, 38 percent of the subjects in the imagery condition, compared to only 12 percent in the control condition, claimed they could remember the incident of spilling punch at the wedding (see Figure 9.17). In contrast, imagery had little effect on memory for the true events; over 80 percent of those were remembered by subjects in either condition.

Possible Causes of False-Memory Construction

According to some theorists, a basic cause of most if not all cases of false-memory constructions is *source confusion* (Mitchell & Johnson, 2000). We acquire information from various sources—including firsthand experiences, stories we have heard, and scenes we have imagined—and our minds reorganize the information in ways that may be meaningful but that obscure the ties between each item and its original source. Events that are conceptually linked but came from different sources may become confounded in memory. The memory for the actual traffic accident witnessed becomes confounded with the memory for what the cross-examiner implied about the accident. The memory of an actual event in childhood becomes confounded with a story heard from others or with an imagined scene constructed by free association in a psychotherapy session.

Social pressure also, no doubt, figures into many cases of false memory (Loftus, 1997). In all the experiments just described, subjects were in one way or another led to believe that they should remember the suggested events. Similar pressure occurs in courtrooms, where the cross-examiner acts as if any normal person should remember the incident's details. And, too often apparently, it also occurs in psychotherapists' offices, where the therapist conveys the message that certain kinds of incidents, such as childhood abuse, must have happened and that the patient's task is to remember those incidents. A person who feels pressured to come up with a memory is more likely than an unpressured person to identify a vague, possible memory as an actual memory. The situation here is like that of a subject in a signal-detection study (discussed in Chapter 7). Pressure to detect the signals (in this case, to remember specific incidents) increases the chance of both hits (remembering incidents that actually happened) and false alarms (remembering incidents that didn't happen).

SECTION SUMMARY

Because we store so much information in long-term memory, a major challenge in retrieval is to locate the particular item or items we are looking for. When people memorize multiple lists, retroactive and proactive interference occur, perhaps because the lists become merged so that each item becomes more difficult to find. Aristotle noted that concepts are organized mentally in accordance with the principles of association by contiguity and association by similarity. James suggested that the second principle is a derivative of the first: Similar objects are associated because each is associated with their common property, and those associations resulted from contiguity. Network models of memory expand on the concept of association by proposing that all concepts are associated with all others in a vast network. When any one concept is active in the mind, other concepts become primed (temporarily easier to retrieve) to the degree that they lie close, in the network, to the active concept. According to the encoding specificity principle, cues that are present when a new item of information is encoded become associated with that item and can serve later as retrieval cues.

Episodes in our life and stories we hear are not stored in full detail in our memories. When we recall an episode or story, we construct it by adding to the bits and pieces that are stored inferences that we make from our general knowledge and beliefs. As Bartlett showed, this process can lead to systematic memory distortions. Subsequent research has shown that eyewitness testimony can be altered by suggestive comments and that false memories of childhood events can be implanted by researchers who claim that the events occurred. Source confusion, including the confusion of imagined events with real ones, and social pressure underlie most cases of false-memory construction.

MULTIPLE MEMORY SYSTEMS: BEYOND THE MODAL MODEL

Most of the research and ideas about memory described thus far have fit at least moderately well into the framework of the modal model. The model has helped differentiate active (working) from passive (long-term) memory and has provided a basis for defining the processes of attention, encoding, and retrieval. But does the model work well for describing the entire range of phenomena that can reasonably be classified as memory?

Look again at the diagram of the modal model in Figure 9.1 (page 326). Its central feature is the box labeled "Working memory," which is equated with conscious perception and thought. According to the model, new information can be encoded into long-term memory only if it is first perceived consciously in working memory. To influence behavior at a future time, that information must be retrieved from long-term memory back into working memory, where it again becomes part of the flow of conscious thought. In its broadest sense, *memory* refers to all effects of prior experience on subsequent behavior. Do all such effects involve the conscious mind, as indicated by the model? To that, nearly all cognitive psychologists today would answer no. The memories that best fit the model are called *explicit memories*, and those that do not are called *implicit memories*.

38.

What types of memories are not accounted for by the modal model?

Distinctions Among Explicit and Implicit Memory Systems

Explicit memory is the type of memory that can be brought into a person's consciousness. It provides the content of conscious thought, and it is highly flexible.

39.

What are the differences between explicit memory and implicit memory, and how is each memory type assessed? In what sense are implicit memories more context-dependent than explicit memories?

Explicit memories can be called to mind even in settings quite different from those in which they were acquired and can be combined with other explicit memories for purposes of reflection, problem solving, and planning. Such memory is called *explicit* because it is assessed through explicit tests—tests in which the person is asked to report directly (explicitly) what he or she remembers about a particular entity or event. It is also called *declarative memory* because the remembered information can be declared (stated in words).

Implicit memory, in contrast, is the type of memory that does not enter into the contents of consciousness. It consists of all the unconscious means through which previous experiences can influence a person's actions and thoughts. Such memory is called *implicit* because it is assessed through implicit tests—tests in which the memory is not reported directly but is inferred from behavioral responses. I would test your memory for balancing on a bicycle not by asking you *how* to do it but, rather, by asking you *to* do it. Your good performance on the bicycle would *imply* to me that you know how to balance on it. Because people are unable to report in words the relevant information, implicit memory is also called *nondeclarative memory.* Implicit memories are much more closely tied to the contexts in which they were acquired than are explicit memories. Whereas explicit memories can be called forth voluntarily outside their original context, implicit memories exert their effects automatically in the context of the specific stimuli, tasks, or problems to which they pertain.

Over time, with routine tasks, explicit memories are in some cases replaced by implicit ones. When I began commuting between my home and job, I developed a set of explicit memories of street names and landmarks to guide me along the way. I could call up those memories, any time, to think about the route or to tell another person how to make that trip. Now that I have made the trip hundreds of times, however, my commute is guided by implicit memories, which lead me automatically to turn at the correct places, and I have forgotten many of the explicit memories. The description of my route that I could give you today is much less clear than the description I could have given you on my second day of commuting. (If you want a clear explanation of how to do something, ask a novice; if you want to *see* how to do it, watch an expert!)

In addition to distinguishing between explicit and implicit memories, cognitive psychologists also distinguish among subclasses of each type, along the lines depicted in Figure 9.18 (Squire & others, 1993; Tulving, 1985).

Varieties of Explicit Memory

As shown in Figure 9.18, explicit memory is divisible into two subclasses. *Episodic memory* is the explicit memory of one's own past experiences. Your memory of

40.

How do the two subclasses of explicit memory differ from each other?

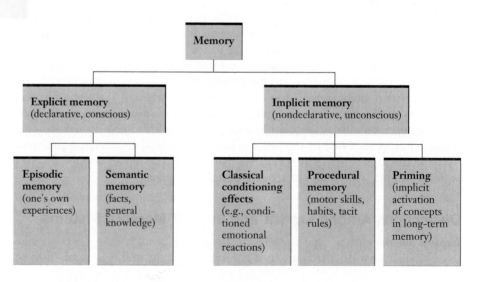

FIGURE **9.18**
Types of long-term memory
Explicit- and implicit-memory systems follow different rules and involve different neural systems in the brain. The implicit- and explicit-memory categories can be further subdivided into narrower categories that may also involve different neural systems. (Based on Tulving, 1985, and Squire, 1992.)

what you did and how you felt on your sixteenth birthday or of what you ate for dinner last night or of any other specific episode in your life is episodic memory. Episodic memories always have a personal quality. As an integral part of your episodic memory for an event, you remember yourself experiencing that event—as participant, witness, or learner.

Semantic memory, by contrast, is explicit memory that is not tied mentally to a particular past experience. It includes knowledge of word meanings (which is one definition of *semantics*) plus the myriad facts, ideas, and schemas that constitute one's general understanding of the world. It also includes knowledge of oneself that is not mentally tied to the reexperiencing of a particular episode in one's life. Your memories that apples are red, that penguins are birds, that you were born in March (or whatever month), and that psychology is the most fascinating of all academic subjects are examples of semantic memory. Of course, all such information had to have been acquired through past events in your life, but your memory of that information does not depend on remembering those events. To remember that penguins are birds or that you were born in March, you do not have to remember anything about the circumstances in which you learned that fact. Recalling an item from semantic memory is a bit like looking for information in an encyclopedia. To find an item that doesn't come easily to mind, you probe your mind with terms or concepts that have meaningful associations to that item. The network model of knowledge organization that you saw in Figure 9.15 has to do with the organization of semantic memory.

Here is a test question: What is classical conditioning? After answering that question, think about *how* you answered it. Did you think back to your experience of reading about classical conditioning earlier in this book, or to your experience of hearing your professor define classical conditioning, and try to reconstruct the definition from your memory of that experience? Or did you just *know* the answer, without having to reflect on any particular past experience? If the first is the case, then your memory of the definition of classical conditioning is an episodic memory (or at least partly so); if the second is the case, it is a semantic memory. In general, episodic memories are more fleeting, less stable, than semantic memories. Over time, we forget most of our memories for our specific past experiences, but the general knowledge that we extract from those experiences often stays with us.

In a research study, Martin Conway and his colleagues (1997) assessed the degree to which students' memories for information learned in an introductory psychology course were episodic or semantic. They did this by asking students to indicate, for each test question, whether their subjective experience in answering the question was one of "remembering" (recalling a past experience) or "knowing" (accessing present knowledge). In an initial test, given shortly after the information was learned, students more often reported that their experience was that of remembering rather than knowing; but in a retest for the same information, given several months later, the opposite pattern held, especially for those items that they got correct. Moreover, this shift from remembering to knowing was sharpest for those students who received the highest grades.

Varieties of Implicit Memory

Implicit memory is also often divided into subclasses, and one way of doing so is depicted in the right-hand portion of Figure 9.18. One subclass consists of the memories produced by classical conditioning—the internal changes produced by conditioning experiences that lead a person or animal to respond to conditioned stimuli (discussed in Chapter 4). A second subclass is a broad one referred to as ***procedural memory,*** which includes motor skills, habits, and unconsciously learned (tacit) rules. With practice you improve at a skill such as riding a bicycle, hammering nails, or weaving a rug. The improvement is retained (remembered) from one practice session to the next, even though you are unaware of the changes in muscle movements that make the difference. (For an operant-conditioning account of such

Thompson McClellan / The Picture Cube

Procedural memory
The learned skill of balancing on a bicycle is retained as implicit procedural memory. You can't say just how you do it, but you don't forget it.

41.

What evidence indicates that memory for newly learned concepts shifts with time from episodic to semantic memory?

42.

What are some examples of procedural memory, and why are such memories classed as implicit?

improvement, see Chapter 4.) You can even learn to make decisions based on complex rules without ever becoming aware of the rules (Greenwald, 1992), and that phenomenon, too, exemplifies procedural memory.

Some experiments demonstrating rule-based procedural memories use what are called *artificial grammars* (Reber, 1989). The grammars consist of sets of rules specifying which letters may or may not follow certain other letters in strings that are several letters long. For example, one rule might be that an *X* at the beginning of a string must be followed either by another *X* or a *V*, and another rule might be that a *J* anywhere in the middle of a string must be followed by a *B*, *X*, or *T*. Subjects are not told the rules. Instead, they are shown examples of grammatical and nongrammatical strings, labeled as such, and then are asked to categorize new examples as grammatical or not, on the basis of their "gut feelings." The subjects typically do not learn any of the rules explicitly—they cannot state the rules—yet they learn to make correct categorizations at a rate significantly better than chance. The memories that guide their correct choices are implicit.

A third variety of implicit memory, much studied in recent years, is priming (Tulving, 2000). *Priming* was defined earlier in this chapter as the activation, by sensory input, of information that is already stored in long-term memory. This activation is not experienced consciously, yet it influences subsequent conscious perception and thought and thus provides a link between implicit and explicit memory. Priming helps keep our stream of thought running along consistent, logical lines. When we see or think about an object, event, or idea, those elements of our semantic memory that are relevant to that perception or thought become activated (primed) for a period of time, so they are more easily retrievable into conscious, working memory. The network model of semantic memory organization shown in Figure 9.15 was derived from experiments on priming, and, indeed, the whole discussion of mental associations and retrieval cues (on pages 348–351) could be rephrased as a discussion of priming.

Priming is classed as implicit memory because it occurs independently of the person's conscious memory for the priming stimulus. Thus, the term *fire engine* in a list of priming stimuli will increase the person's ability to recognize objects related to fire engines whether or not the person remembers, in an explicit test, that that word was in the list (Tulving & Schacter, 1990). As noted in the discussion of attention, priming can even occur when the priming stimulus is presented in such a way that it enters sensory memory but is not consciously perceived.

Neuropsychological Evidence for Separate Memory Systems

You have read in this chapter of distinctions between working memory and long-term memory, and between explicit and implicit varieties of long-term memory, as they appear in people's normal experience. Further evidence for multiple, distinct memory systems comes from studies of people who have impaired memory (amnesia) due to brain damage and from neuroimaging studies that relate patterns of brain activation to types of memory tasks.

Role of Temporal-Lobe Structures in Encoding Explicit Long-Term Memories

No human being has contributed more to our modern understanding of brain mechanisms of memory than a man known in the psychological literature as H. M. In 1953, at age 27, H. M. underwent surgery in which a portion of the temporal lobe of the cortex and underlying parts of the limbic system on each side of his brain were removed as treatment for severe epilepsy. The surgery was effective against the epilepsy, but it left him with a drastic impairment in memory, which was studied extensively first by Brenda Milner (1965, 1970) and then by many other researchers. In presenting their original version of the modal model, Richard

43.

Why is priming considered to be implicit memory? How was priming used to develop the network model of semantic memory organization, and what function does priming play in a person's everyday thought and speech?

Eve-Lucie Bourque

Brenda Milner

The Canadian neuropsychologist is best known for her long-term studies of memory loss in a surgical patient (H. M.). The work of Milner and her colleagues has left little doubt that structures in the temporal lobe are directly associated with memory in humans.

Atkinson and Richard Shiffrin (1968) referred to the case of H. M. and other (less fully studied) cases like his as "perhaps the single most convincing demonstration for a dichotomy in the memory system." They were referring to the dichotomy between explicit-long-term and working memory.

H. M.'s most obvious deficit is an almost complete inability to encode new explicit-long-term memories. He can still remember events that occurred before the operation. He can converse, read, solve problems, and keep new information in mind as long as his attention remains focused on it. But the minute his attention is distracted, he loses the information he had just been thinking about, and he cannot recall it later. To hold information in mind for a period of time, H. M. sometimes uses elaborate memory schemes. In one test, for example, he successfully kept the number 584 in mind for 15 minutes, and when asked how he did this, he replied: "It's easy. You just remember 8. You see, 5, 8, 4 add to 17. You remember 8; subtract from 17 and it leaves 9. Divide 9 by half and you get 5 and 4, and there you are—584. Easy." Yet a few minutes later, after his attention had shifted to something else, he could not remember the number or the memory scheme he had used, or even that he had been given a number to remember (Milner, 1970).

Of course, H. M.'s memory impairment has had an enormous impact on his life. For many years now he has lived in a nursing home (Hilts, 1995). He must be accompanied wherever he goes and needs constant reminders of what he is doing. He is aware of his memory deficit and once described it in the following way (Milner, 1970): "Right now, I'm wondering, have I done or said anything amiss? You see, at this moment everything looks clear to me, but what happened just before? That's what worries me. It's like waking from a dream. I just don't remember."

Many other people have been studied who have a similar loss of memory (though usually not as complete) after strokes or other sources of brain damage. The disorder is called ***temporal-lobe amnesia,*** and the areas of destruction most strongly correlated with it are the hippocampus (the limbic-system structure buried within the temporal lobe, depicted in Figure 9.19) and cortical and subcortical structures closely connected to the hippocampus in both halves of the brain (Squire, 1992). Complementing the evidence from brain damage is that from neuroimaging studies. When people with intact brains are presented with new information to learn, they manifest increased activity in the hippocampus and adjacent parts of the temporal lobe, and the degree of that increase correlates positively with the likelihood that they will recall the information successfully in a later test (Fernandez & others, 1998; Nyberg & Cabeza, 2000).

44.

How does the case of H. M. support the idea of a sharp distinction between working memory and explicit-long-term memory?

45.

What evidence indicates that the hippocampus and temporal-lobe structures near it are involved in encoding explicit-long-term memories?

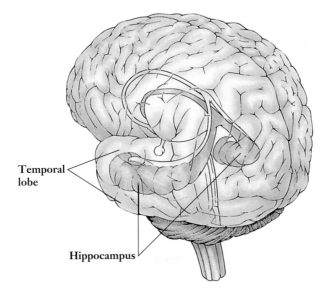

Temporal lobe

Hippocampus

FIGURE **9.19** *Brain area involved in temporal-lobe amnesia*
The hippocampus is buried within the temporal lobe of the brain. Destruction of this structure in both sides of the brain produces a severe deficit in ability to encode new episodic memories. Destruction of this structure plus some of the surrounding areas of the temporal lobe produces a severe deficit in ability to encode new explicit memories of both types—semantic and episodic.

46.

What is the evidence that the hippocampus and nearby temporal-lobe structures are not essential for forming or using implicit memories?

Implicit Memory in Amnesic Patients

Despite their severe deficit in explicit memory, H. M. and other temporal-lobe patients typically exhibit normal memory in all sorts of implicit-memory tests. If classically conditioned to blink their eyes in response to a conditioned stimulus, they show the conditioned response as strongly in subsequent tests as do nonamnesic subjects (Daum & others, 1989). If given practice with a new motor skill, such as tracing a pattern that can be seen only in its mirror image, they show normal improvement from session to session and retain the effects of previous learning even if months elapse between one session and the next (see Figure 9.20; Gabrieli & others, 1993; Milner, 1965). Similarly, they can learn and retain artificial grammars and tacit rules for grouping objects into categories (Knowlton & Squire, 1993; Knowlton & others, 1992), and in experiments on priming they show as much activation of long-term semantic memories in response to priming stimuli as do normal subjects (Gabrieli, 1998; Vaidya & others, 1995). In all these examples the implicit memory is manifested even when the amnesic subjects cannot consciously

FIGURE **9.20** *Implicit memory without explicit memory*

As shown in the graphs, the patient H. M. improved from session to session in a mirror-tracing task and retained the skill over an interval of nearly a year (from day 25 to day 358), even though at each session he could not remember having performed the task before. In general, people with temporal-lobe amnesia show normal ability to form new implicit memories despite their inability to form new explicit memories. The task in this case was to trace the outline of the star under conditions in which the star and hand could be seen only in a mirror, so that movements had to be made in the opposite direction from the way in which they appeared. An error was counted whenever the stylus moved off the star's outline. The data points on the graph represent the average number of errors per trial for the seven trials that occurred at each session. (Graphs adapted from Gabrieli & others, 1993.)

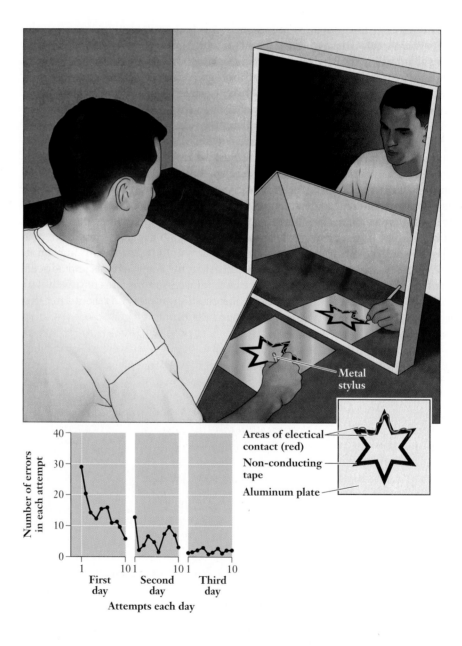

remember anything at all about the learning experience. In one experiment, a severely amnesic patient learned to program a computer over a series of sessions. At each session his programming ability was better than that in the previous session, even though he had no explicit memory of ever having programmed a computer before (Glisky & others, 1986).

In sum, research on people with full temporal-lobe amnesia indicates that the hippocampus and associated structures are essential for one very specific but extraordinarily important memory task. Such people are quite normal in their ability to (a) attend to sensory information and form new working memories from such information, (b) retrieve long-term explicit memories that were acquired well before the brain damage, and (c) acquire and use new implicit memories. Their one clear deficit is their inability to encode new long-term explicit memories. For that reason they live a moment-to-moment existence, constantly feeling that they have just become conscious. They are able to think about the immediate present but are unable to connect that present to the recent past or to recall it in the future.

Separation of Episodic and Semantic Memories in Amnesic Patients

The most severe cases of temporal-lobe amnesia entail loss of both episodic- and semantic-memory encoding. H. M. not only fails to remember anything about his own experiences that occurred after his surgery (in 1953) but also fails to remember factual information that he has experienced since then. He cannot name new world leaders or entertainers, and if asked to draw a car or a radio from memory, he persists in drawing the 1950s versions (Milner, 1984). But patients with less severe forms of amnesia typically manifest a greater deficit in episodic memory than in semantic (Wheeler, 2000).

People who suffer from a rare disorder called *developmental amnesia* show severe deficits in episodic memory coupled with normal or near-normal semantic memory. These people have bilateral damage to the hippocampus, but not to structures surrounding it, caused by temporary loss of blood flow to the brain at the time of birth or in early childhood. Apparently, the hippocampus is more susceptible to permanent damage due to lack of oxygen than is the rest of the brain. Recently, Faraneh Vargha-Khadem and her colleagues identified and studied eight young people who suffer from this disorder (Gadian & others, 2000; Vargha-Khadem & others, 1997). All these individuals have severe deficits of episodic memory. If asked what happened a few hours ago or yesterday or at their last birthday party, they can recount little or nothing. Yet, despite this, they developed speech, reading, vocabulary, and other verbal capacities within the normal range. They all attended mainstream schools and learned and remembered facts well enough to perform passably on school tests. Their abilities are consistent with other evidence that the hippocampus may be essential for episodic memory but not for semantic memory (Eichenbaum, 1997b). Amnesics such as H. M., who lose semantic as well as episodic memory, have damage not just to the hippocampus but also to other portions of the temporal lobes.

Another group who manifest greater loss of episodic than of semantic memory are patients who have suffered damage to the prefrontal areas of the cortex, usually due to strokes (Wheeler, 2000). In one study a group of people with such damage were compared with age-matched control subjects in tests of both semantic and episodic memory (Janowsky & others, 1989). In one session the subjects were given a series of facts to learn, such as: "The last name of the actor who portrayed Dr. Watson in the *Sherlock Holmes* series was Bruce." Then, a week later, they were tested for their memory for those facts and for other facts, which had not been presented to them in the laboratory session but which they would likely have learned from previous life experiences outside the laboratory. After each correct response in this memory test, they were asked to say whether they had learned that fact in the previous laboratory session or in life outside the laboratory. The result was that

47.

What is some evidence that the hippocampus and prefrontal cortex are more essential for episodic memory than for semantic memory?

the brain-damaged subjects remembered as many of the facts—both old and new—as did the brain-intact subjects, but performed much more poorly on the test for the source of their memory. Their memory for the facts (semantic memory) was normal, but their memory for the experience of learning the facts (episodic memory) was deficient. Apparently, an intact prefrontal cortex, as well as hippocampus, is essential for normal encoding of episodic memories.

It may at first seem surprising that people can remember new information without remembering the experience of learning that information. Yet, with a little poking around in your own semantic store, you can probably find many facts that you yourself know but can't relate to any episodes in your life (though it probably took you longer to forget the episodes than amnesic patients would take). I know that kumquats are a kind of fruit, but I can't recall any instance in my life of ever seeing, reading about, or hearing of kumquats. Older people are especially familiar with the phenomenon of knowing without knowing how they know. In old age, the capacity to form new episodic memories generally declines more rapidly than does the capacity to form new semantic memories (Johnson & others, 1993). Another group who show excellent semantic memory and poor episodic memory are young children. During their first 4 years of life, children acquire an enormous amount of semantic information—including word meanings and facts about their world—that will stay with them throughout their lives. But children under 4 are relatively poor at recalling specific episodes in their lives, and none of us in adulthood can recall much about our own childhood prior to about age 4—a phenomenon known as *childhood amnesia* (Eacott, 1999). Apparently the human ability for episodic-memory encoding develops more slowly than that for semantic-memory encoding.

The relatively poor episodic memory at both ends of the life span may be related to prefrontal cortical functioning (Wheeler & others, 1997). The prefrontal cortex develops more slowly in childhood and tends to suffer more damage in old age than does the rest of the brain. This brain area, which is much larger in humans than in other species (see Figure 9.21) and which is so important for planning and complex thought (as discussed in Chapter 5), may be essential for our sense of ourselves, including our sense of our own past experiences. We are not only a conscious species but a *self*-conscious species. We—probably much more than any other animal—reminisce about our past, think about our position in the present, and project ourselves into the future as we make plans and contemplate their consequences. Such abilities are intimately tied to our capacity to form episodic memories. This evolutionarily recent addition to the mammalian cognitive machinery is apparently more fragile—more destructible by aging and injuries—than is the more ancient semantic-memory system or the still more ancient implicit-memory system (Tulving, 1985; Wheeler & others, 1997).

48.

How might frontal-lobe functioning be related to childhood amnesia and to a fundamental distinction between humans and other animal species?

FIGURE **9.21**   *Prefrontal cortex in cat, chimpanzee, and human*
The evolution of primates, and especially of humans, entailed a mushrooming of the prefrontal cortex. In humans, this part of the brain is responsible for many of what we consider to be our unique traits, including our capacity for episodic memory and self-reflection.

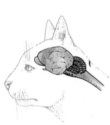

■ Motor area of frontal lobe

■ Prefrontal cortex

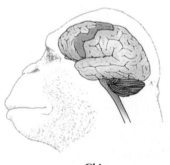

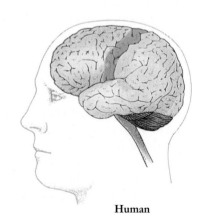

Cat   Chimpanzee   Human

SECTION SUMMARY

*A broad distinction is made between explicit memories, which can be consciously re-
called, and implicit memories, which do not enter into the contents of consciousness
but which nevertheless influence the flow of conscious thought and behavior. Explicit
memories are classified into two subtypes: episodic memories, which are memories of
one's own past experiences, and semantic memories, which are memories for facts
that are not experienced as a reliving of the past. Implicit memories are classified into
a number of subtypes, including effects of classical conditioning, procedural memories, and priming. People such as H. M., who suffer from full temporal-lobe amnesia,
can form new long-term implicit memories but not new long-term explicit memories. In
contrast, people with damage confined to the hippocampus or to the prefrontal cortex
manifest poor ability to form episodic memories but normal or near-normal ability to
form semantic memories as well as implicit memories.*

CONCLUDING THOUGHTS

Memory indeed is the central topic of cognitive psychology. It is relevant to all aspects of both conscious and unconscious mental activity. To help yourself organize,
elaborate upon, and thereby encode into long-term memory the ideas in this chapter, you may find useful the following general thoughts:

1. The modal model as a functional representation of the mind   Throughout
this chapter, the modal model served as the organizing structure for thinking about
memory and the mind. You have read of three memory stores, of control processes
related to the stores, and of research aimed at characterizing the stores and
processes. Your review and thoughts about all this will be most effective, I think, if
you adopt a functionalist perspective. From that perspective, each store and process
represents not a different part (or structure) of the mind but a different job that the
mind performs in its overall task of acquiring and using information. As you review
each mental component and process, think first of its main function—how it contributes to normal, everyday thought and behavior—and then think about how its
special characteristics help it serve that function. You might apply such elaborative
reasoning to each of the following: (a) sensory memory and differences between
iconic and echoic memory; (b) the process of attention, including roles played by
the unconscious, automatic processing of unattended stimuli; (c) working memory
and differences between the phonological loop and the visuospatial sketch pad;
(d) the process of encoding information into long-term memory, including elaboration, organization, and visualization as encoding strategies; (e) the process of retrieving information from long-term memory, including interference effects,
retrieval cues, and means by which memory constructions can be influenced by
one's general knowledge; (f) distinctions between semantic and episodic forms of
long-term explicit memories; and, going beyond the modal model, (g) the roles of
implicit-memory systems, particularly procedural memories and priming.

2. The modal model as an example of a schema   To the degree that you and I
have incorporated the modal model into our own minds, it has become our schema
for understanding memory. As noted by Bartlett, schemas allow us to recognize,
label, and make sense of phenomena in the world around us, but in doing so they
can also distort our perceptions and thoughts. The model is a valuable schema for
organizing research and thought about an extraordinarily complicated topic; but by
encouraging us to fit all observations about memory into that model, it can con-
strict and bias the observations we make and the conclusions we draw. To some degree, I may have distorted the field of memory research in this chapter because I
have written it with the model strongly in mind. To some degree, you may have distorted the research and findings even further to fit the model as you understand it.

To some degree, cognitive psychology as a whole may have distorted the knowledge of memory by directing research toward aspects of memory that are most consistent with the model while ignoring other aspects that are equally important. The creative thinkers in this science, as in any other, are those who are not bound by current models or schemas but find new ways to look at the topic and in that way open up new lines of research. Current research on implicit memory and its interaction with explicit memory may produce a new, improved schema of the human mind.

3. Unconscious supports for conscious thought and behavior   Long ago, Sigmund Freud (1933/1964) drew an analogy between the human mind and an iceberg. Consciousness, he suggested, is the small visible tip of the mind, which is supported by massive unconscious portions of the mind that are invisible, submerged under the ocean's surface. Although Freud's concept of the functions of the unconscious mind (discussed in Chapter 15) is different from that presented here, the analogy remains apt. All we are conscious of are the perceptions and thoughts that course through our limited-capacity working memory. We are unconscious of all the preattentive analysis of information and of the top-down control of selective attention that help determine which stimuli make it into working memory. We are also unconscious at any given time of the vast store of information we have in long-term memory and of the priming processes that determine which portions of that store will, at that moment, be most available for retrieval into consciousness. And we are unconscious of the vast set of procedural memories and effects of conditioning that allow us to carry out routine tasks and respond adaptively to stimuli without conscious attention. As you review the chapter, think about all the ways in which unconscious information and processes support that small part of our mental activity that enters our consciousness.

4. The mind as a product of the brain   In cognitive psychology the term *mind* refers to the entire set of processes—unconscious as well as conscious—by which information is acquired and used within a person to organize and direct the person's behavior. The mind is entirely a product of the brain. In recent times, cognitive psychology has merged increasingly with neuropsychology into what is now often called *cognitive neuropsychology*. The development of fMRI and PET neuroimaging methods has allowed psychologists to identify which parts of the human brain become most active as people engage in specific mental tasks, and to relate those findings to findings that come from the more traditional neuropsychological studies of mental deficits in people who have suffered damage to specific portions of the brain. Of course, there is a big difference between knowing *where* in the brain a particular task is accomplished and knowing *how* it is accomplished. At this point we are far from knowing how neural activity in the brain provides the basis for memories, thoughts, and decisions (but see Chapter 5 for work on how new and strengthened synaptic connections may provide a basis for implicit memories). The brain may be a computer, but it is vastly more complex than any nonbiological computer yet built. At this point the mapping of mental tasks upon brain areas is useful primarily as an adjunct to behavioral evidence in helping us to categorize mental tasks. The idea that two mental tasks are fundamentally similar to or different from each other is supported by evidence that they do or do not involve the same areas of the brain.

As you review the results of neuroimaging and brain-damage studies presented in this chapter, think about how each helps to validate the distinctions among the different memory systems and processes described in the chapter. Which findings regarding brain locations support each of the following ideas? (a) Verbal working memory and visuospatial working memory are distinct from each other; (b) verbal working memory is like talking and listening; (c) using remembered visual images to answer questions about what and where is like looking at an actual object or scene to answer those questions; (d) long-term memory is distinct from working memory; (e) explicit memory is distinct from implicit memory; and (f) episodic memory is at least partly distinct from semantic memory.

Further Reading

Larry R. Squire & Eric R. Kandel (1999). *Memory: From mind to molecules.* New York: Scientific American Library.

Larry Squire is a leader in the cognitive neuroscience of memory, and Eric Kandel is a Nobel laureate known especially for his research on the neural and molecular bases of learning and memory in invertebrates (discussed in Chapter 5 of the book you have in hand). In Memory, a beautifully illustrated 230-page book, they combine their two realms of expertise to present the general reader with a story about the nature and neuronal bases of implicit- and explicit-memory systems that is as coherent as the data reasonably allow.

Endel Tulving & Fergus I. M. Craik (Eds.) (2000). *The Oxford handbook of memory.* Oxford: Oxford University Press.

With this 700-page compendium, you can look up and read about, and find further references concerning, almost any memory topic that you wish to pursue. Each of the book's 39 chapters is written by one or more specialists on a particular aspect of memory, in language that requires no more knowledge of technical jargon than you would have picked up from the textbook chapter you have just read. Among the chapters that relate directly to what you have read are Baddeley's on working memory; Brown and Craik's on encoding and retrieval of explicit-long-term memories; Toth's on nonconscious forms of memory; Neisser and Libby's on remembering life experiences; Zola and Squire's on the roles of the temporal lobe and hippocampus; Wheeler's on episodic memory; and Schacter, Wagner, and Buckner's on multiple memory systems.

Steven Jay Lynn & Kevin M. McConkey (Eds.) (1998). *Truth in memory.* New York: Guilford.

The unifying assumption of this book, in the editors' words, is that "memory is a dynamic medium of experience shaped by expectancies, needs, and beliefs, imbued with emotion, and enriched by the inherently human capacity for narrative creation." How, then, does one find truth in memory? In 19 chapters, each by a different expert or set of experts, this book presents a variety of views and lines of evidence concerning this problem as it relates to such issues as memories of childhood experiences, children's suggestibility, psychotherapy procedures, eyewitness testimony in courtrooms, and the truthfulness of reports in the media.

Philip J. Hilts (1995). *Memory's ghost: The strange tale of Mr. M. and the nature of memory.* New York: Simon & Schuster.

This is a literary essay on the role of memory in human existence, and it is also the biography of a man who has no autobiography of adult life. It is the story of H. M., who at age 27 (42 years before Hilts's book) lost his ability to form new explicit-long-term memories. We learn here something of what it is like to live in a disconnected series of eyeblinks, where the past is but a few seconds long.

Charles P. Thompson, Thaddeus M. Cowan, & Jerome Frieman (1993). *Memory search by a memorist.* Hillsdale, NJ: Erlbaum.

Many stories have been told about people with amazing memories. Do such people have brains that are fundamentally different from yours and mine? Is it all a matter of practice? This slim book is by three psychological researchers who performed a series of experiments on the memory abilities of Rajan Srinivasan Mahavedan, who was once listed in the Guiness Book of World Records *for reciting 31,811 decimal digits of pi without error. (His record has since been topped by Hideaki Tomoyori, who recited 40,000 digits of pi.) The experiments described here help demystify Mahavedan's memory. The book also contains a brief discussion of the memory abilities of 13 other memorists whose abilities were studied by psychologists.*

Looking Ahead

In studying the topic of memory, we have entered the gate to the human intellect. Memories provide the basis for ideas, reasons, decisions, plans, and verbal utterances. Thinking and speaking are the abilities that appear to distinguish humans most from the other animals, and these are the central topics of the next two chapters, which deal with human intellect and its development.

Chapter 10

The Gifted Boy, Paul Klee

Intelligence and Reasoning

Compared with other species, we are not the most graceful, nor the strongest, nor the swiftest, nor the fiercest, nor the gentlest, nor the most long-lived, nor the most resistant to the poisons accumulating in our atmosphere. We do, however, fancy ourselves to be the most intelligent of animals; and, at least by our own definitions of intelligence, our fancy is apparently correct. We are the animals that know and reason; that classify and name the other animals; that try to understand all things, including ourselves. We are also the animals that tell each other what we know, with the effect that each generation starts off with more knowledge, if not more wisdom, than the previous one.

Research on human intelligence has taken two different but overlapping tracks. The first track, historically, is that of intelligence testing, which focuses on measuring and explaining differences among individuals in intellectual ability. The second track is that of cognitive psychology, which focuses on the question of how people reason and solve problems and is concerned more with universals than with individual differences. Cognitive psychologists examine the errors that people make on problems, including intelligence-test problems, not to rank people but to find clues as to how the human mind works.

In this chapter we begin with intelligence testing and move toward the questions of cognitive psychology. The first section describes intelligence testing and some of the controversies it has generated. The second section is concerned with genetic and environmental sources of individual differences in measured intelligence. The third section examines the idea that the human mind is better characterized as a set of separate abilities than as a single global intelligence. The fourth section focuses on the mental processes involved in logic and insight, and the fifth considers the role that language plays in reasoning.

PROBLEMS OF IDENTIFYING AND MEASURING INTELLIGENCE

Intelligence, of course, is just a word. Like many words, it is used by different people to refer to different concepts. To find out how psychologists and educators who specialize in intelligence define it, Mark Snyderman and Stanley Rothman (1987) asked more than 1000 of them to examine a list of human abilities and check off those that they considered to be aspects of intelligence. Nearly all checked off abstract reasoning, problem solving, and the capacity to acquire knowledge; more than half checked off memory, adaptability to one's environment, mental speed, linguistic competence, mathematical competence, general knowledge, and creativity; and about one-fourth checked off sensory acuity, goal-directedness, and achievement motivation. Thus, some experts conceived of intelligence as specific to higher-order reasoning and knowing, while others conceived of it as a broad set of characteristics that help people deal with their environment. Given this lack of consensus about how to define *intelligence*, it is not surprising that experts have long disagreed over how intelligence can best be measured. In this section we examine the origin of modern intelligence testing and some of the controversies such testing has engendered.

IQ Tests as Measures of a Collection of Mental Abilities

Intelligence testing has always served primarily practical concerns. The first applied psychologists—practitioners who try to solve real-world problems using insights from psychology—were intelligence testers. School systems wanted intelligence tests to determine who could profit most from education; employers wanted them to help decide whom to hire; armies wanted them to help decide how to assign recruits to ranks and tasks.

Binet's Development of a Test of School-Related Abilities

1.

What was the purpose and form of Binet's intelligence test, and how did he develop it?

The first widely used intelligence test, the *Binet-Simon Intelligence Scale*, was developed in France in 1905 by Alfred Binet (1857–1911) and his assistant Théodore Simon. Binet had been hired by the French Ministry of Education to develop a test that would be used to help determine the grade level in which children should be placed at school. Binet conceived of intelligence not as a single entity, and not as something fixed by heredity, but as a collection of higher-order mental abilities that are only loosely related to one another and are nurtured through interaction with the environment (Binet & Henri, 1896; Binet & Simon, 1916/1973). In fact, he believed that a proper goal of schooling is to increase intelligence, and he proposed that his test be used to identify children who were not profiting as much as they should from schooling so that they might be given special attention.

Binet and Simon's test was oriented explicitly toward the skills required for schoolwork. It included questions and problems designed to test memory, vocabulary, common knowledge, use of numbers, understanding of time, and ability to combine ideas. The problems were selected by pretesting them with schoolchildren of various ages and comparing the results with teachers' ratings of each child's

Alfred Binet and subject

Before he was asked by the French Ministry of Education to develop a measure of intelligence, Binet experimented with various tests of motor and sensory capacities in children, using methods similar to those pioneered by Galton. The apprehensive expression on this boy's face reminds us that part of doing well on any ability test is overcoming the fear that stems from the novelty of the test situation.

Archives of the History of American Psychology, University of Akron

classroom performance (Binet & Simon, 1916/1973). Items were kept in the test only if more of the high-rated than low-rated children answered them correctly; otherwise, they were dropped. Binet was aware of the circularity of this process: His test was intended to measure intelligence better than existing measures did, but to develop it, he had to compare results with an existing measure (teachers' ratings). Yet once developed, the test would presumably have advantages over teachers' ratings. Among other things, it would allow for comparison of children who had had different teachers or no formal schooling at all.

In 1908, Binet and Simon revised their test and incorporated the concept of *mental level*, referred to by others as *mental age*, into the scoring system. With this new scoring system, a child was assigned a mental level corresponding to the age group whose average score the child's test result best matched. Thus, a child of any age who performed as well as an average 10-year-old would be assigned a mental level of 10. For better or worse, this system probably did much to popularize the test. Mental level indicated directly whether a child was advanced or behind and thus played on the pride and anxiety of parents and teachers. Within a few years, English translations of the Binet-Simon test were available, and testing caught on in England and North America even more readily than it had in France.

Modern IQ Tests Patterned After Binet's

The first intelligence test commonly used in North America was the Stanford-Binet Scale, a modification of Binet and Simon's test that was developed in 1916 at Stanford University under the direction of Lewis Terman. By this time Binet's original mental-age scoring system had been modified to produce the *intelligence quotient*, or *IQ*, which was determined by dividing a child's mental age (MA) by his or her actual chronological age (CA) and multiplying by 100. Thus, IQ = (MA/CA) × 100. If a child's mental age as measured by the test was 11.5 and chronological age was 10, then the child's IQ would be (11.5/10) × 100 = 115. An IQ of 100 would mean that a child was average for his or her age, and scores above or below 100 would mean that the child was above or below average.

The Stanford-Binet Scale has been revised over the years and is still used quite widely, but the most common individually administered intelligence tests today are variations of a test that was developed by David Wechsler in the 1930s and was modeled after Binet's. Wechsler's original purpose was to construct an intelligence test for adults, because the Stanford-Binet Scale was appropriate only for children, but later he modified his own adult test to produce a children's version. The descendants of Wechsler's tests that are most widely used today are the *Wechsler Adult Intelligence Scale, Third Edition (WAIS-III)*, and the *Wechsler Intelligence Scale for Children, Third Edition (WISC-III)*. Table 10.1 on page 370 summarizes the various subtests of the WAIS-III. The WISC-III is similar to the WAIS-III but contains simpler problems.

By the time Wechsler was developing his intelligence test for adults, the term *IQ* was so ingrained in public consciousness that he retained it in the scoring system even though its original meaning had to be abandoned. (It

How many objects can you name?

As part of the original Binet intelligence test, children were asked to name common household objects in this picture. Obviously, a child whose home contained such objects would do better than a child whose home did not.

2.

How was IQ calculated in the original Stanford-Binet procedure, and how was the procedure changed when tests for adults were developed?

Stanford-Binet test materials

These materials are from the current version of the test. In addition to an overall IQ score, separate scores are obtained for verbal reasoning, abstract/visual reasoning, quantitative reasoning, and short-term memory.

TABLE 10.1 *Subtests of the WAIS-III*

Verbal subtests

Vocabulary   A set of words are to be defined.

Similarities   On each trial the examinee must say how two objects or concepts are alike.

Information   Questions are asked about generally well-known people, places, events, and objects.

Comprehension   Questions that require rather detailed answers tap practical knowledge, social judgment, and ability to organize information.

Digit Span   Strings of orally presented digits must be recited verbatim (and, in a second phase, in reverse order) to test short-term memory span.

Letter-Number Sequencing   After hearing each list of letters and numbers in random order, the examinee repeats the numbers in ascending order, followed by the letters in alphabetical order.

Arithmetic   Arithmetic problems are to be solved mentally.

Performance subtests

Block Design   Blocks are to be arranged in such a way as to match specific designs.

Picture Completion   The examinee identifies the missing elements in each picture.

Picture Arrangement   Sets of pictures are to be arranged in a way that tells a story (similar to a comic strip).

Object Assembly   Puzzle pieces are put together to form a picture.

Matrix Reasoning   Geometric shapes that change according to some rule are presented in an incomplete grid, and the examinee chooses from a set of options the shape that completes the grid.

Digit-Symbol Coding   The examinee translates a series of single-digit numbers into symbols as quickly as possible, on the basis of a code that is provided.

Symbol Search   On each trial a target set and search set of symbols are presented. The examinee says as quickly as possible whether a target symbol appears in the search set.

Subtests used to calculate various IQ indexes

Verbal Comprehesion Index   Vocabulary, Similarities, Information.

Working-Memory Index   Digit Span, Letter-Numbering Sequencing, Arithmetic.

Perceptual Organization Index   Block Design, Picture Completion, Matrix Reasoning.

Processing-Speed Index   Digit-Symbol Coding, Symbol Search.

Crystallized Intelligence   Vocabulary, Similarities, Information, Comprehension, Picture Arrangement.

Fluid Intelligence   Similarities, Arithmetic, Block Design, Picture Arrangement, Object Assembly, Matrix Reasoning.

Source: Compiled from information in A. S. Kaufman & E. O. Lichtenberger (1999), *Essentials of WAIS-III Assessment*. New York: Wiley.

---

would be senseless to say that a 20-year-old who scores as well as an average 60-year-old has an IQ of 300.) The scoring system for the WAIS-III (and also for the WISC-III) is based on the results obtained from large samples of individuals in various age groups. Those whose performance is average for their age group are assigned an IQ of 100, and those whose performance is above or below average are assigned an IQ above or below 100, in such a way that the overall distribution of scores takes the bell-shaped form known as a normal distribution, depicted in Figure 10.1. For more on normal distribution and the method for standardizing test scores, see the Statistical Appendix at the end of the book.

The Validity of IQ Tests as Predictors of Achievement

A test is *valid* if it measures what it is intended to measure (as discussed in Chapter 2). If intelligence tests measure intellectual ability, then IQ scores should correlate with other indices of a person's intellectual ability. For the most part, researchers have considered the question of IQ validity to be directly tied to the practical question of whether or not such tests predict success in school and careers. Not surprisingly—given that most modern intelligence tests are direct or indirect descendants

3.

How have psychologists attempted to assess the validity of IQ tests, and what have been the results of those assessments?

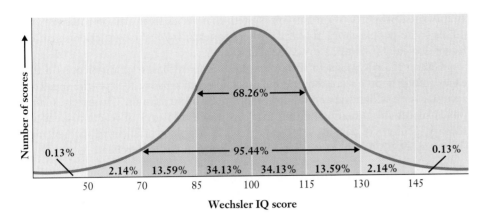

FIGURE 10.1 *Standardized scoring of Wechsler IQ tests*
The scoring system for Wechsler IQ tests is based on the assumption that intelligence is distributed in the population according to a normal distribution (represented by the bell-shaped curve). Thus raw scores on the test are converted into IQ scores in such a way as to produce a normal distribution. Notice that with this system about 68 percent of IQ scores are between 85 and 115 and about 95 percent are between 70 and 130.

of Binet's and that Binet's test was explicitly designed to measure school abilities—IQ scores do correlate moderately well with grades in school; the correlation coefficients in various studies range from 0.30 to 0.70 (Brody, 1992; Jensen, 1980).

How well do IQ scores predict achievement outside of school? That is a more difficult question to answer, partly because there is no convenient measure of out-of-school achievement comparable to school grades and partly because access to intellectually demanding employment is constrained by social and economic factors that themselves may or may not be related to IQ. Large-scale correlational studies in North America have shown that the likelihood of achieving employment in a prestigious occupation—such as doctor, lawyer, or business executive—is predicted better by the socioeconomic status of one's parents than by IQ or by any other single measure (Jencks, 1979; McClelland, 1993). Higher socioeconomic status leads to increased access to education, more personal connections to the employment community, and higher job status regardless of measured intelligence.

To get around such confounds, a number of researchers have correlated IQ and on-the-job performance, as measured by supervisors' ratings or direct observation, for people already involved in a particular career. In general, such studies reveal that, other things being equal, the higher a person's IQ, the better his or her performance, especially in jobs acknowledged to require high intellectual ability (Ree & Earles, 1992; Schmidt & others, 1992). The correlations usually fall in the range of about 0.20 to 0.40. Such research also indicates that IQ predicts performance better for people who are in the training or novice phase of employment than for those who have been at the job a long time (Hunt, 1995; Wigdor & Green, 1991). Apparently, the abilities measured by IQ tests are more closely related to the ability to learn new job skills rapidly than to performance after the skills have been acquired. Job performance has also been found to correlate positively with years of experience, measures of achievement motivation, and a personality trait labeled conscientiousness (Schmidt & Hunter, 1992). No surprise—if you ever find yourself in the position of employer, look for people who are smart, motivated, experienced, and conscientious!

The research just referred to has convinced many people in the fields of educational and industrial-organizational psychology that IQ tests are sufficiently valid predictors of scholastic and employment performance to justify their use. Some argue that failure to use such tests would cause socioeconomic status to become an even greater determinant of access to higher education and employment than it currently is and would reduce the role of ability.

The Concept of General Intelligence and Attempts to Explain It

Historically, concern with practical purposes of intelligence tests has always been paralleled by debates and research aimed at characterizing intelligence as a basic human attribute. Well before Binet developed the first widely used intelligence test, the English scientist Sir Francis Galton (1822–1911) had described intelligence as

Francis Galton

Galton's genius was wide ranging. In addition to his studies of individual differences and his development of the statistical concept of correlation, Galton invented a variety of mathematical devices, including a data-storage system and a periscope that enabled him to see over the heads of taller people.

an inherited property of the nervous system that varies from person to person and makes some people more able than others to learn from their experiences and to reason logically (Galton, 1869/1962, 1885).

Galton (1885) hoped to show that the biological bases for intellectual differences among people were their neural quickness and sensory acuity—the speed and accuracy with which they could detect and respond to stimuli. Ultimately, Galton was unsuccessful in demonstrating that his simple measures of reaction speed and sensory acuity correlated significantly with people's intellectual achievement (Fancher, 1985), but his work helped inspire subsequent researchers.

Spearman and the Statistical Derivation of g

Charles Spearman (1863–1945), a British psychologist and mathematician, praised Galton's seemingly elegant idea that intelligence is a single entity reflecting an inherited property of the nervous system, but he objected that Galton's tests of motor and sensory abilities were too simple to measure it (Spearman, 1904, 1927). He considered Binet's tests of memory, understanding, and reasoning to be more appropriate measures of intelligence, but he objected to Binet's theoretical writing on intelligence, calling it self-contradictory and scientifically displeasing. Why, asked Spearman (1927), would Binet score intelligence with just one number—the mental-level score—if he believed that intelligence is a mixture of separate abilities?

Combining Galton's perspective on intelligence with Binet's testing strategy, Spearman developed a new battery of mental tests and a new statistical procedure called *factor analysis* to make sense of the results. Factor analysis, essentially, is a procedure for finding patterns of correlations among scores or measures in order to identify underlying "factors" (in this case mental abilities) that account for the correlations. In a long series of studies using a wide variety of mental tests similar to those used by Binet—including tests of memory, pattern perception, logic, and verbal fluency—Spearman found that the score on virtually every test correlated positively with that on essentially every other test. In other words, people who scored higher than average on memory tests also tended to score higher than average on perceptual tests, logic tests, and so on. Most of the correlations were of moderate strength, typically in the range of 0.30 to 0.60. Spearman's application of factor analysis to the pattern of correlations indicated to him that the pattern is best explained by assuming that each test is influenced by two separate factors. One factor, which he called *g*, for *general intelligence,* was meant to explain why all tests correlated positively with one another, and the other factor, which he called *s*, for *specific ability*, was meant to explain why the correlations were not perfect. Thus, according to Spearman, a person's score on any given test depends on a combination of *g* (the person's general intelligence) and *s* (the person's presumably learned ability to perform the specific tasks of the particular test). That is, *g* accounts for the similarity of the person's scores from one test to another, and *s* accounts for the differences (see Figure 10.2).

Notice that Spearman's *g*, unlike Galton's notion of intelligence, is a statistical abstraction. Spearman (1927) defined *g*, essentially, as the hypothetical mental

4.

How did Spearman's view of intelligence draw from both Galton's and Binet's views, and what evidence led him to posit a general intelligence (g)?

FIGURE **10.2**   *Spearman's theory of intelligence*
To explain why people who score high on one kind of mental test also tend to score high on other kinds, Spearman hypothesized that people differ in general intelligence (*g*). To explain why the correlation among tests is not perfect, he hypothesized that each test score is also affected by a person's specific ability (*s*) related to that particular test. Thus, according to Spearman, a person's score on each test is affected by his or her amount of general intelligence plus his or her specific ability for that test.

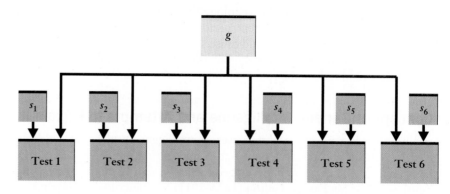

factor that accounts for the positive correlations among scores on different mental tests. He did not identify it directly with a concrete aspect of the nervous system, as Galton had tried to do. Yet Spearman assumed that *g* does represent a biologically endowed ability, and he suggested that it may be best understood as the capacity to detect relationships among different stimuli (for example, to detect the similarities between two different words or to see one pattern as the inverse of another). He noted that this ability is involved to some degree in all the mental tests that correlate with one another. Because any given test is influenced by a specific ability as well as by *g*, Spearman (1927) believed that the best measure of *g* is the total or average score on a wide variety of tests.

Cattell and the Distinction Between Fluid Intelligence and Crystallized Intelligence

Raymond Cattell (1905–1998) was a student and research associate of Spearman in England in the 1930s, until he moved to the United States in 1937. He devoted most of his subsequent long career to developing a personality theory (described in Chapter 15), but he also developed a new theory of intelligence, which he considered to be a modification of Spearman's theory. Cattell (1943, 1971) agreed with Spearman that scores on mental tests reflect a combination of general intelligence and a specific factor that varies from test to test, but he contended that general intelligence itself is not one factor but two. More specifically, he proposed that Spearman's *g* must be divided into two separate *g*'s. He called one of them *fluid intelligence*, abbreviated g_f, and the other *crystallized intelligence*, abbreviated g_c.

Fluid intelligence, as defined by Cattell (1971), is the ability to perceive relationships independent of previous specific practice or instruction concerning those relationships. It is best measured by tests in which people identify similarities or lawful differences between stimulus items that they have never previously experienced or between items so common that everyone in the tested population would have experienced them. An example of the first type is the *Raven Progressive Matrices Test*, illustrated and described in Figure 10.3 An example of the second type is the following verbal analogy problem (Horn, 1985):

> SOON is to NEVER as NEAR is to (a) NOT FAR, (b) SELDOM, (c) NOWHERE, or (d) WIDELY?

Essentially all adults who speak English know the meanings of all the words in this problem, so performance depends on the ability to perceive relationships among the meanings, not on knowledge of the meanings themselves. A verbal analogy problem that would *not* be a good measure of fluid intelligence is the following (modified from Herrnstein & Murray, 1994):

> RUNNER is to MARATHON as OARSMAN is to (a) BOAT, (b) REGATTA, (c) FLEET, or (d) TOURNAMENT?

Solving this problem is limited not just by ability to perceive relationships but also by knowledge of uncommon words (*marathon* and *regatta*), which reflects crystallized intelligence.

Crystallized intelligence, according to Cattell (1971), is mental ability derived directly from previous experience. It is best assessed in tests of knowledge, such as knowledge of word meanings, of cultural practices, and of how to use particular tools. Although people may differ in the domains of their knowledge (one person may know a lot of words but little about tools, for example), Cattell considered crystallized intelligence to be a general intelligence, not a set of test-specific abilities like the *s*'s in Spearman's theory. One's accumulated knowledge can be applied broadly to solve a wide variety of problems.

Like Spearman, Cattell based his theory largely on the factor analysis of scores on many different mental tests. Cattell's use of factor analysis showed him that mental tests tend to fall into two clusters—those that seem to depend mostly on

5.

How did Cattell modify the theory of his former mentor, Spearman? What evidence led him to distinguish between fluid intelligence and crystallized intelligence?

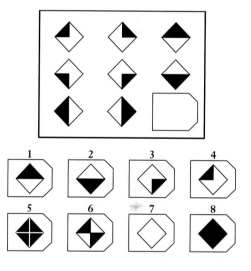

FIGURE 10.3
Sample Raven problem
All problems in the Raven Progressive Matrices Test are structured this way. The task is to figure out the rules by which the pattern changes from column to column, and from row to row, and then to choose, from the set of eight choices, the pattern that belongs in the blank space. In this example, within each row the pattern in the first column is superimposed on that in the second column to produce the pattern in the third column. The same rule also applies within each column, going from the top row to the bottom. The correct answer is 8. (Example is from Carpenter & others, 1990, p. 409. It is similar to problems in the Raven test but is not taken from the actual test.)

FIGURE **10.4** *Hypothetical correlations among test scores, suggestive of two underlying intelligences*

Each coefficient in the matrix is the correlation between the two tests indicated by its row and column. Thus, 0.35 is the correlation between test 1 and test 2. All the correlations are positive. Notice, however, that the correlations among tests 1, 3, and 5 (in gold) and among tests 2, 4, and 6 (in purple) are higher than any of the other correlations. A factor analysis of this pattern would suggest that the tests measure two different abilities. Tests 1, 3, and 5 are the best measures of one ability, and tests 2, 4, and 6 are the best measures of the other. This result could be taken as support for Cattell's theory if the items in one cluster of tests seem to measure raw reasoning ability and those in the other seem to measure learned information.

Tests	2	3	4	5	6
1	0.35	0.62	0.40	0.59	0.45
2	–	0.41	0.55	0.39	0.64
3	–	–	0.28	0.63	0.30
4	–	–	–	0.34	0.60
5	–	–	–	–	0.38

raw reasoning ability and those that seem to depend mostly on previously learned information. Test scores within each cluster correlate more strongly with each other than with scores in the other cluster (see Figures 10.4 and 10.5). In addition, Cattell found that measures of fluid and crystallized intelligence behave differently as a function of age. Fluid ability typically peaks at about age 20 to 25 and declines gradually after that, while crystallized ability typically continues to increase until about age 50 (Cattell, 1971; Horn, 1985). Cattell suggested that the decline in fluid intelligence stems from gradual biological deterioration and that the increase in crystallized intelligence stems from the continued accretion of knowledge.

The evidence from factor analysis, and the differing effects of age, led Cattell to argue that fluid and crystallized intelligences are distinct from one another. He did not, however, think they are entirely independent. He noted that within any given age group crystallized- and fluid-intelligence scores correlate positively with one another. This, he suggested, is because people with higher fluid intelligence learn and remember more from their experiences than people with lower fluid intelligence. In that sense, he claimed, crystallized intelligence depends on fluid intelligence.

Mental Speed and Working Memory as Possible Bases for g

As noted earlier, Galton had hoped to characterize intelligence in terms of basic properties of the nervous system, measurable in simple behavioral tests such as speed of reacting to stimuli. In recent times, researchers have revived this quest, using more sophisticated measures and measuring devices, and have found positive correlations between a number of simple reaction-time measures and scores on conventional IQ tests (Vernon & others, 2000).

One such measure is *inspection time*—the minimal time that subjects need to look at or listen to a pair of stimuli to detect the difference between them. In one common test of inspection time two parallel lines, one of which is 1.4 times as long as the other, are flashed on a screen and subjects must say which line is longer. The duration of the stimulus varies from trial to trial, and inspection time is the shortest duration at which a subject can respond correctly most of the time. Studies correlating fast inspection time with IQ scores have typically revealed correlation coeffi-

6.

What findings have revived Galton's idea of mental quickness as a basis for general intelligence?

FIGURE **10.5**
Cattell's theory of intelligence
To explain why the correlations among some mental tests are greater than those among others (as in Figure 10.4), Cattell hypothesized that the human mind consists of two separate intelligences. Tests that correlate most strongly with one another are the best measures of one intelligence (as indicated by the heavy arrows). To explain why tests in different clusters also correlate (to a smaller degree) with one another, Cattell hypothesized that no test is a pure measure of one intelligence but that each test to some degree measures the other intelligence as well. Cattell's analysis of the items in the two clusters led him to characterize the two intelligences as *fluid* and *crystallized*.

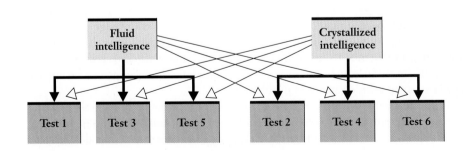

cients of 0.4 to 0.5 for measures of fluid intelligence and coefficients of about 0.2 for measures of crystallized intelligence (Deary, 2000). The correlations are about as strong when untimed IQ tests are used as when timed tests are used (Vernon & Kantor, 1986), so they are not simply the result of the fact that the subtests of some standard IQ tests require quick reaction.

How might mental quickness help people perform well on IQ tests? One possibility is that it does so by improving the capacity of working memory. According to the standard information-processing model of the mind, described at length in Chapter 9, working memory is the center of conscious thought (look back at Figure 9.1, page 326). Information enters working memory from the environment (through the senses) and from one's long-term-memory store (through the act of retrieval). To solve a problem on an intelligence test, according to this model, you must bring the appropriate information from the senses and from long-term memory into the working store and combine the information in an appropriate way to come up with a solution. But working memory can hold only a limited amount of information at any given time. While it is the center of conscious thought, it is also a bottleneck that limits the amount of information you can bring together to solve a problem. Information fades quickly from working memory when it is not being acted upon, so the faster you can process information, the more items you can bring together to make a mental calculation or arrive at a reasoned decision.

Working-memory capacity is often measured as *digit span*, the number of single-digit numbers that a person can hold in mind and report back accurately after hearing the list just once (discussed in Chapter 9). Consistent with the idea that mental speed improves reasoning ability by increasing the capacity of working memory, researchers have found that mental speed correlates positively with digit span and that digit span correlates even more strongly with problem-solving ability and overall IQ than does mental speed (Kyllonen & Christal, 1990; Miller & Vernon, 1992).

Not surprisingly, both mental speed and working-memory capacity correlate more strongly with measures of fluid intelligence than with measures of crystallized intelligence (Carpenter & others, 1990; Deary, 2000). Presumably, it is the combining of information to perceive relationships, not the acquisition of factual knowledge, that is most limited by mental quickness and working memory. Mental speed and working-memory capacity tend to decline as we grow older in adulthood, which helps explain the effect of age on fluid intelligence, noted earlier (Salthouse, 1994; Schretlen & others, 2000).

Mental Self-Government

While some psychologists have looked to simple measures of mental speed and working memory to understand variation in intelligence, others have looked to more complex decision-making abilities. Robert Sternberg (1986b) has described intelligence as "mental self-government." By this he means that people who perform well on intelligence tests are people who can control their mental resources in a way that allows for efficiency in problem solving.

In what he calls a "componential" model of intelligence, Sternberg (1985) posits that the mind consists of various components, each of which is responsible for a different type of task in solving problems. For example, there are components for encoding information, for comparing items of information to infer relationships, and for applying the inferred relationships to solve the problem. The components that Sternberg associates most directly with intelligence are those that he labels *metacomponents*. The prefix *meta-* in this context means "beyond" or "transcending,"

7.

Logically, how might working-memory capacity provide a basis for individual differences in intelligence, and how might mental quickness affect that capacity? What evidence supports this logical possibility?

Rob Van Petten / Image Bank

High-speed information processing

Regardless of whether mental quickness is the basis for general intelligence, it is certainly important in many human endeavors. These stock exchange traders must routinely make crucial decisions under extreme time pressure.

8.

In Sternberg's theory, what are the functions of metacomponents in solving problems? How was such functioning illustrated in a comparison of people who did well with those who did poorly on tests of logic?

and in Sternberg's theory the metacomponents transcend the other components. The metacomponents can be thought of as executive officers of the mind, dealing with overall goals and strategies and exerting their effects by controlling the lower components. Indeed, other theorists use the term *central executive* to refer to these components of the mind. Metacomponents define the problem, decide whether or not it is worth solving, select the lower components needed to solve it, control the order in which those components are activated, and decide when the problem is solved.

Consistent with Sternberg's theory, differences in problem-solving performance have been found to correlate with differences in the general strategies adopted by the people who are tested. Sternberg (1985), for example, found that people who performed well on logical-reasoning problems spent relatively more time encoding the problem (thinking about the meaning of each statement in it), and relatively less time on subsequent steps, than did people who performed poorly. If you think about it, this is not a terribly surprising result. Understanding the problem fully is a key to solving almost any problem. How many times have you lost points on a test because you didn't read the question carefully or take the time to figure out exactly what was being asked before you started to work out the answer? In Sternberg's theory of intelligence, deciding how much time to devote to each step in solving a problem is a task of the metacomponents.

The ability to control one's mental resources efficiently might, at least in theory, even help explain the correlation between IQ and mental speed or working-memory scores (an idea suggested by Marr & Sternberg, 1987). People who can think of good strategies for solving IQ problems might also be able to think of good strategies for focusing their attention, preventing boredom, and responding quickly in simple tests of speed and memory.

The aspects of mind that Sternberg refers to as "metacomponents" and others refer to as "the central executive" appear to be functions largely of the frontal lobes of the cerebral cortex. In PET neuroimaging studies, problems that are deemed to be the best measure of fluid intelligence all trigger strong activity in the frontal lobes of subjects trying to solve them (Duncan & others, 2000). Other studies have revealed that the size of the frontal lobes correlates more strongly with IQ than does the size of any other area of the cerebral cortex and that the decline in IQ with age appears to correspond with a shrinkage with age in the frontal lobes that is greater than shrinkage elsewhere (Schretlen & others, 2000).

SECTION SUMMARY

The history of intelligence testing is one of controversy. Galton defined intelligence as innate mental quickness and sensory acuity, but his measures of these did not correlate strongly with academic achievement. Binet defined intelligence essentially as the constellation of abilities that allows one to perform well in school, and he developed a test that tapped such abilities. Spearman demonstrated that performance on any mental test correlates positively with that on any other mental test, and from that he posited the existence of a general intelligence (g) that varies from person to person and gives some people an advantage over others in every mental realm. Cattell showed that mental tests can be divided into two types based on the degree to which scores on the tests correlate with one another, and from that he distinguished between two types of intelligence—fluid and crystallized.

Modern Wechsler intelligence tests are patterned after Binet's test. They can be used to produce an overall IQ score as well as separate scores for fluid intelligence, crystallized intelligence, and various more specific abilities. Scores on such tests correlate reasonably well with school performance and less well (but still positively) with performance in jobs and careers. In the search to understand the mental basis for g, some researchers have focused on measures of mental quickness and working memory, and other researchers have focused on people's varying abilities to coordinate their own mental activities in goal-directed ways—abilities that are ascribed to the mind's "metacomponents" or central executive.

THE NATURE-NURTURE DEBATE CONCERNING IQ

Galton's research on intelligence, over a century ago, marked the beginning of what is often called the **nature-nurture debate,** which in various guises has continued throughout psychology's history. *Nature* here refers to a person's biological inheritance, and *nurture* refers to the entire set of environmental conditions to which the person is exposed. In essence, the question of the debate is this: *Are psychological differences among people primarily the result of differences in their genes (nature) or in their environments (nurture)?* The psychological differences that have been most often subjected to this debate are differences in personality (discussed in Chapter 15), in susceptibility to mental disorders (discussed in Chapter 16), and, especially, in intelligence as measured by IQ.

You might think that the nature-nurture question concerning IQ is the same as the question we have just been discussing, that of the extent to which IQ tests measure basic capacities of the nervous system (such as mental speed) or measure skills and knowledge that have been learned. But the two questions are not the same. To the degree that differences in genes affect learning ability, IQ differences might reflect genetic differences even if the tests measured only what one has learned. Conversely, to the degree that environmental differences (including differences in nutrition and training) alter one's mental speed, IQ differences might reflect environmental differences even if the tests measured only mental speed. As you will see, the research strategies that one can use to address the nature-nurture question depend on whether one is concerned with IQ differences among individuals who are part of the same cultural group or with IQ differences between cultural groups.

Like parents, like child

Eminent people often pass on more than genes to their offspring. Anthropologist Richard Leakey, shown here discussing a fossil with his father, has benefited from the genes and the wisdom of both his eminent parents—anthropologists Louis and Mary Leakey.

IQ Differences Among Individuals Within a Cultural Group

A common misunderstanding is that the nature-nurture question, as applied to individuals, concerns the degree to which a particular trait stems from genes or environment. Some might ask, for example, "Is a person's intelligence due more to genes or to environment?" But if you think about that question, you will realize it is absurd. With no genes there would be no person and hence no intelligence, and with no environment there would also be no person and no intelligence. Given that genes and environment are both absolutely essential for any trait to develop, it would be absurd to think that one contributes more than the other to the trait. But it is not absurd to ask whether *differences* in a trait among individuals are due more to *differences* in their genes or in their environments.

A useful analogy (suggested by Hebb, 1958) concerns the contribution of length and width to the areas of rectangles. It is absurd to ask whether the area of any given rectangle is due more to length or width, because both dimensions are absolutely essential to the area. If you shrink either to zero, there is no rectangle and no area. But it is not absurd to ask whether the differences in area among a given set of rectangles are due more to differences in their length or in their width. As illustrated in Figure 10.6, the answer could be length or it could be width, depending on the specific set of rectangles asked about. Similarly, when we ask

9.

What is the difference between the absurd form of the nature-nurture question and the reasonable form? Why is one absurd and the other reasonable?

FIGURE 10.6 *A geometric analogy to heritability*

It makes no sense to ask whether a given rectangle's area is due more to its width or to its length. Shrink either to zero and the area goes to zero. But one can sensibly ask whether variation in area in a specific group of rectangles is due more to differences in their length than in their width. In group A, variation in area is due to differing lengths, and in group B it is due to differing widths. Similarly, for variation in a characteristic such as IQ, one can imagine one group of people in which variation is due mostly to their differing genes and another group in which it is due mostly to their differing environments.

GROUP A

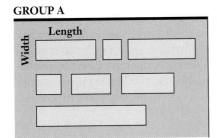

GROUP B

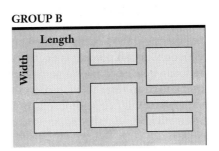

whether differences in intelligence are due primarily to differences in genes or in environment, the answer might be genes for one set of people and environment for another. Logic tells us, for example, that IQ differences are likely to be due more to environmental differences if the people we are studying live in very diverse environments than if they live in similar environments. If you were raised in a typical middle-class environment and I were raised in a closet, the difference between us in IQ would certainly be due mostly to differences in our environments; but if we were both raised in typical middle-class environments, then whatever difference exists between us in IQ might well be due more to differences in our genes than to those in our environments.

10.

How is heritability defined? Why would the logic of the concept, and the formula, lead you to expect to find higher heritability in a population whose members all share similar environments than in an environmentally diverse population?

The Concept of Heritability and Environmentality

The central concept in any modern scientific discussion of the nature-nurture question is **heritability**. Heritability is the degree to which variation in a particular trait, within a particular set or population of individuals, stems from genetic differences among those individuals as opposed to environmental differences. Heritability is often quantified by a statistic called the **heritability coefficient**, abbreviated h^2. This coefficient is technically defined as the proportion of the variance of a trait, in a population, that is due to genetic variation. As a formula, it can be written

$$h^2 = \frac{\text{variance due to genes}}{\text{total variance}} = \frac{\text{variance due to genes}}{\text{variance due to genes} + \text{variance due to environment}}$$

The denominator (total variance) is simply a measure of the degree to which the individuals being studied differ from one another in the characteristic that was measured. It can be calculated directly from the set of scores obtained from the individuals in the group (the formula for variance can be found in the Statistical Appendix). The numerator (variance due to genes), in contrast, cannot be calculated directly but must be estimated by comparing sets of individuals who differ in their degree of genetic relationship to one another (by methods to be explained soon). Examination of the formula shows that the heritability coefficient can, in theory, vary from 0.00 to 1.00. A coefficient of 0.00 means that none of the observed variance in the characteristic is due to genetic differences (and all of it is due to environmental differences); a coefficient of 1.00 means that all the variance is due to genetic differences (and none of it is due to environmental differences); and a coefficient of 0.40 means that 40 percent of the variance is due to genetic differences (and the remaining 60 percent is due to environmental differences).

Notice how the heritability formula reflects the logic of the nature-nurture question. Total variance (the denominator of the ratio) is equal to variance due to genes (the numerator of the ratio) plus variance due to environment. Therefore, if variance due to environment is small, the denominator will be only slightly higher than the numerator and the heritability coefficient will be high (close to 1). Conversely, if variance due to environment is large relative to variance due to genes, the denominator will be large compared with the numerator and heritability will be small (approaching zero).

Some researchers prefer not to use the term *heritability* because it focuses too much attention on genes and not enough on the environment. But, logically, the heritability coefficient is as much a measure of the environmental contribution to variability as it is a measure of the genetic contribution. For example, a heritability coefficient of 0.40 means that 40 percent of the measured variance is due to genetic variation and 60 percent is due to environmental variation. To create greater equity in focus, some behavioral geneticists have proposed that the term ***environmentality*** be used to refer to the proportion of the variance that is due to environmental variation (Fuller & Thompson, 1978). A heritability coefficient of 0.40 corresponds to an environmentality coefficient of 0.60.

The Value of Twins in Separating Effects of Environment from Effects of Genes

To the degree that a trait is heritable, people who are closely related to one another genetically should be more similar in the trait than are people who are less closely related genetically. A difficulty with using this logic to estimate heritability, however, is that related people also typically share similar environments. Thus, the observation that siblings are, on average, more similar to each other in IQ than are unrelated people does not, by itself, tell us the degree to which their similarity is due to similarity in genes or in environment.

In an attempt to separate the contributions of genes and environment to IQ differences, behavior geneticists often compare pairs of individuals who differ from other pairs in their degree of genetic relatedness and were either raised in the same home or adopted at an early age into different homes. Twins are especially valuable subjects in such studies, because some pairs of twins are genetically identical and other pairs (fraternal twins) are, like nontwin siblings, only 50 percent related to each other (as explained in Chapter 3).

Galton (1876) himself pioneered the study of twins as a basis for understanding the contributions of heredity to psychological characteristics. On the basis of self-report questionnaires and other biographical materials, he concluded that twins who were "alike at birth" remained similar psychologically throughout their lives, even after they left home and entered different environments. By contrast, those who were "different at birth" remained dissimilar throughout their lives. From this, Galton argued that the degree of similarity of twins must be due more to nature than to nurture; otherwise, all twins should grow more different when they leave home and enter different environments. Galton was unaware of the full significance of his work, because the genetic basis for the distinction between the two classes of twins was not yet known (Rende & others, 1990).

Since Galton's time, many researchers have addressed the question of heritability of IQ systematically by comparing the correlation in IQ scores of identical twins with that of fraternal twins. As explained in Chapter 2, correlation coefficients can run from 0.00 to either plus or minus 1.00. A correlation of 0.00 in this case would mean that the IQs of twins are no more alike on average than are those of any two people chosen at random from the population being studied; at the other extreme, a correlation of +1.00 would mean that the twins in each pair have identical IQs. In Figure 10.7, the IQ correlations between twins raised in the same home are shown, separately, for identical and fraternal twins in various age groups (McGue & others, 1993). As you can see, in each age group the correlation coefficient is considerably greater for identical twins than for fraternal twins, indicating that genes play a relatively large role. The difference between the two classes of twins is especially great for adults, because of a drop in the correlation that occurs during adulthood for fraternal twins but not for identical twins. Consistent with Galton's observation long ago, when fraternal twins leave home and go their separate ways, they become more different from each other in IQ than they were before, but when identical twins leave home, their IQs remain as similar as ever.

> **11.**
>
> *What logic lies behind the focus on twins in studies aimed at assessing the relative contributions that genetic variability and environmental variability make to variability in a trait? What did Galton find in his study of twins? How has that finding been corroborated in more recent studies involving IQ?*

> **12.**
>
> *How can IQ heritability be estimated by studying identical and fraternal twins raised together? What is the evidence from such studies that IQ heritability is greater for adults than for children? How can IQ heritability be estimated by studying identical twins who were adopted into different homes?*

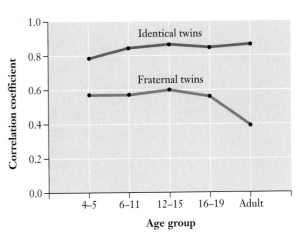

FIGURE **10.7** *IQ correlations between twins who were raised together*

The correlations in IQ between identical twins remains high throughout their lives. That between fraternal twins declines as they enter adulthood and go their separate ways. The data are averages for studies published prior to 1993. (McGue & others, 1993, p. 63.)

IQ Heritability Assessed from Studies of Twins

Correlation coefficients are not the same as heritability coefficients, but they can be used to estimate heritability coefficients. One common method is simply to subtract the correlation for fraternal twins from that for identical twins and multiply the difference by 2 (Plomin & others, 1990). The precise logic behind this method, which relates the method to the general formula for heritability presented earlier, involves more mathematical detail than most readers would desire, but you can get a sense of that logic without the mathematics. The assumption is that the environment is equally similar for the two categories of twins, so the difference between the two in IQ correlation must be due to the difference in their degree of genetic relatedness; that is, the difference must reflect heritability. Because fraternal twins are themselves 50 percent related, the difference between the two correlation coefficients is assumed to reflect only half the total amount of difference in correlation coefficient that would be present if the comparison were between identical twins and completely unrelated individuals. Therefore, the difference is doubled to arrive at an estimate of the heritability coefficient.

If we apply this formula to the data in the figure, we arrive at a heritability coefficient of 0.46 for the 12-to-16 age group ([0.83 − 0.60] × 2 = 0.46) and 0.86 for the adults ([0.83 − 0.40] × 2 = 0.86). In other words, according to these calculations, about half of the IQ variance in the teenagers and younger children is due to genetic variance, but over 80 percent of the IQ variance in the adults is due to genetic variance. Apparently, the environment plays a greater role in IQ variation among younger people than it does among adults—an idea that we will return to later.

Another way to assess heritability of IQ is to locate pairs of identical twins who were adopted at an early age into separate homes and determine their IQ correlation. Based on the assumption that the environments of raised-apart identical twins are no more similar to each other than are the environments of any two members of the study population chosen at random, the correlation coefficient for raised-apart identical twins is itself an estimate of the heritability coefficient (Loehlin & others, 1988). The average coefficient determined from essentially all such studies published prior to 1993 is 0.73 (McGue & others, 1993). Most of the twin pairs in those studies were adults, but a few were adolescents, and no attempt was made to determine the coefficient separately for different age groups.

Every procedure for assessing heritability involves assumptions that may not be entirely true, so any heritability coefficient should be taken as only a rough estimate. But the studies suggest, overall, that genetic differences account for about half of the IQ variance among children and adolescents and for considerably more than half of the IQ variance among adults in the populations that were studied. Contrary to what might be expected, those studies that have assessed fluid and crystallized intelligence separately indicate that the two are about equally heritable (Horn, 1985). Apparently, within the populations that have been studied, genetic differences influence the amount of factual knowledge that people have learned just as much as they influence people's ability to think quickly or see relationships in novel stimuli. It is not hard to think of many ways by which genetic differences could have such an effect. Genes can influence curiosity, reading ability, long-term memory, or any of countless other traits that influence the acquisition and recall of facts.

The Transient Influence of the Family in Which One Is Raised

It seems reasonable to expect that the IQs of children raised in the same family would be more similar than average not just because of shared genes but also because of shared environments. Children in the same family are exposed to the same parents, the same neighborhoods, the same schools, and the same learning opportunities at home.

The most direct way to assess the degree to which shared family leads to similarity in IQ is to study pairs of adoptive siblings who are genetically unrelated but are raised together. Assuming that such pairs are genetically no more similar to one another than any two random people from the study population, any correlation greater than 0 in their IQs must be due to their shared environment. Several such studies have been done, and the results tell a remarkably consistent story. As long as the unrelated siblings are still children, their IQs do correlate positively with one another; but the correlation is lost completely when they reach adulthood. Taking all such studies together, the average IQ correlation for genetically unrelated children living in the same family is 0.25, and the average for genetically unrelated adults who had been raised in the same family is –0.01, or essentially 0 (McGue & others, 1993). Other studies have shown that the IQ correlations for other categories of children raised in the same family also decline as the children enter adulthood, but the greater the degree of genetic relationship, the smaller the decline (Plomin & Daniels, 1987). You saw that effect in Figure 10.7, where the IQ correlations for fraternal twins declined at adulthood while that for identical twins did not. Apparently, families have a rather strong early influence on children's IQ, but the effect fades as the children become adults.

The transient nature of the effect of the family on IQ is perhaps the most surprising result that has emerged from studies of IQ correlations. Not long ago many psychologists believed that even subtle differences in the early environments of children would give some an advantage in intellectual development that would last a lifetime. But the results of the studies just summarized indicate that the advantage or disadvantage that comes from being raised in a particular home, within the range of homes the studies sampled, disappears by early adulthood. One way to explain this finding is to assume that as children grow into adulthood, they increasingly choose their own environments, and their genetic differences influence the kinds of environments they choose (Dunn & Plomin, 1990; Scarr & McCartney, 1983). Those who are genetically similar, and therefore more similar in interests and temperament, may choose more similar environments than those who are genetically different, and so they remain more similar in intelligence. If you think of intelligence as analogous to muscle strength, which can wax and wane depending on exercise, then you can understand why an adult's IQ may be more influenced by his or her current environment than by his or her past, childhood environment.

IQ Differences Between Cultural Groups

All the conclusions about the heritability of IQ drawn in the discussion so far were properly qualified by the phrase "for the populations that were studied." In almost all cases that population was white, North American or European, and in the upper two-thirds of the socioeconomic scale (Stoolmiller, 1999). Heritability coefficients are always limited to the population that was studied. The more uniform that population, the smaller is the proportion of IQ variance that is due to environmental variation and the greater is the heritability coefficient. If heritability studies included people occupying the entire range of human environments rather than just a slice of that range, the resultant heritability coefficients would be much smaller than those presented above.

Comparisons of racial or cultural groups in IQ routinely reveal average differences. The difference that has attracted the most attention, and on which we will focus here, is that between blacks and whites in the United States: Blacks, on average, score about 15 points lower than whites on standard IQ tests (Herrnstein & Murray, 1994). The question is why. Some people who have heard of the heritability studies that you have just read about assume that those studies can be applied to understand the black-white difference. They assume that if IQ is x percent heritable within a group, then any IQ difference between two groups must also be x percent due to genetic differences. But that assumption is false.

13.

What is the evidence that the effect of a shared family environment on IQ correlations is lost in adulthood? How might this loss be explained?

FIGURE **10.8** *Why high within-group heritability tells us nothing about group differences*
The same genetically diverse mix of wheat seeds was planted in two fields. If each field is quite uniform in the environmental conditions it provides, then the differences in plant size within each must be due mostly to genetic differences (high heritability). However, the difference between the two fields in average plant size in this case cannot be due to genes, because genetic differences would cancel out in the averages. The difference between the two fields must be due to differences in environment; one field may have more fertilizer than the other.

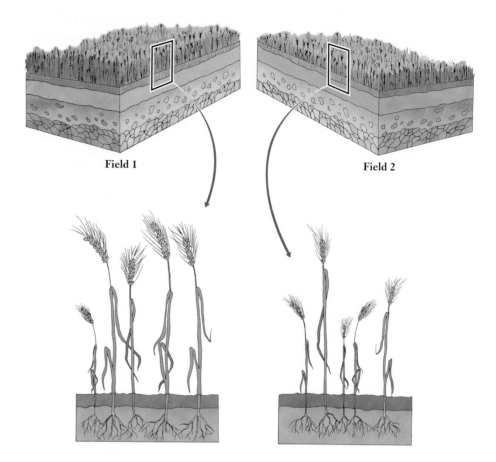

Field 1   Field 2

14.

Why can't heritability coefficients found within groups be used to infer the source of differences between groups?

The heritability coefficient for variance in a trait within a group, in fact, tells us nothing about differences between groups. To understand why, consider the example illustrated in Figure 10.8. Imagine two wheat fields, each planted from the same package of genetically diverse wheat seeds. Imagine further that the soil fertility is relatively constant within each field but quite different between the two—one has lots of manure and the other has little. Within either field, differences in the sizes of individual plants would be the result primarily of genetic differences in the seeds, yet the average difference between the two fields would almost certainly be due entirely to the difference in the environment (the amount of manure). To take another example, height in people is more than 90 percent heritable when measured for a given cultural group, yet group differences in height can be found that are clearly the result of the environment (Ceci, 1996). In the 1950s, for example, researchers found that men of full Japanese ancestry born in California were nearly 3 inches taller, on average, than Japanese men born in Japan (Greulich, 1957). That difference was almost certainly due to the difference between the diets of the two groups.

Evidence That Black-White IQ Differences Are Cultural in Origin

In the examples just given, we could be quite certain that the group differences were environmental in origin because there was reason to believe that the members of the two groups (of wheat plants and of Japanese men) did not differ genetically, on average. In contrast, many people automatically think of differences between the so-called black and white "races" as racial differences, and they automatically assume that *racial* means "genetic." In the United States and many other countries, however, blacks and whites are not truly distinct races in a biological sense but, rather, are different cultural groups. We classify people as "black" who have any detectable black African ancestry, no matter how small a proportion it is. Thus, a person who is half English, one-fourth French, and one-fourth African is called black, whereas that person's cousin, who is half English, one-fourth French, and one-fourth Polish, is called white. While some average genetic differences exist between the two groups—which show up in skin pigmentation, for example—the amount of genetic variation *within* each group is far greater than the average difference *between* them.

Researchers who have attempted to separate the effect of black African ancestry from the effect of the social designation "black" have consistently failed to find evidence that genetic ancestry plays a role in the black-white IQ difference. In the first such study, Paul Witty and Martin Jenkins (1935) attempted to determine if high-IQ black children have more European and less African ancestry than blacks who have lower IQs. They identified a sample of black children in Chicago who had IQs in the superior range (125 or better) and then interviewed their parents to see if they had more European ancestry than the average black person. The results were negative. The proportion of European ancestry in the high-IQ black children was neither more nor less than that in the black population at large. (The highest IQ of all in that study, incidentally, was a whopping 200 scored by a girl with 100 percent black African ancestry.) More recently, other researchers have performed similar studies, using modern biochemical methods to determine the degree of black African and European ancestry (Loehlin & others, 1973; Scarr & Carter-Saltzman, 1983). Like Witty and Jenkins, they found no relationship between ancestry and IQ, and they concluded that the *social* designation of black, not biological ancestry, is most likely the critical variable in determining the black-white IQ difference.

How might the social designation of black affect IQ? Nobody knows for sure, but John Ogbu (1986, 1994) has suggested an interesting line of thought about it. On the basis of cross-cultural research, Ogbu distinguishes among three classes of minority groups. *Autonomous minorities* are groups, such as the Amish in the United States, who have deliberately separated themselves from the mainstream and are proud of their heritage. *Immigrant minorities* are groups, such as Japanese or Chinese Americans, who emigrated in hopes of bettering themselves, who see themselves as well-off compared with those they left behind, and who see themselves as on their way up, regardless of how the dominant majority may see them. The third class, *involuntary minorities* or *castelike minorities*, are groups, such as the Harijans (formerly, Untouchables) in India, who did not choose their minority status, who are routinely judged as inferior by the dominant majority, and who see little hope of improvement through the traditional routes open to the majority. Ogbu argues that blacks in North America even today occupy a castelike status. According to research summarized by Ogbu, castelike minorities everywhere perform more poorly in school, and score an average of 10 to 15 points lower on IQ tests, than the dominant majority.

Particularly informative, in Ogbu's work, is the comparison of the Buraku outcasts of Japan with blacks of the United States. The Buraku, who are a purely cultural class, not racially distinct from other Japanese, were emancipated from official pariah status by a royal edict in 1871, just 8 years after blacks in the United States were emancipated from slavery; yet both groups, to this day, typically occupy menial positions and are implicitly, if not explicitly, perceived as inferior by the dominant majority. The gap in school achievement and IQ between the Buraku and the majority group in Japan is about the same as that between blacks and whites in the United States; but the gap disappears when Buraku move to the United States. Most people in the United States do not know the difference between Buraku and other Japanese, and the two groups of immigrants are treated the same and perform equally well in school and on IQ tests. According to Ogbu, it is the sense that one is a pariah, and that standard routes to achievement are cut off, that oppresses castelike minorities and depresses their scholastic achievement and IQs.

15.

What evidence suggests that the IQ difference between black and white Americans originates in culture, not genes?

16.

What evidence suggests that the status of castelike minorities may be particularly detrimental to IQ development?

A Buraku protest

The Buraku people of Japan are descendants of people who worked as tanners and butchers, jobs that were traditionally believed to be unclean and worthy only of lowly people in Japan. Although they are no longer legally categorized as outcasts, they continue to be discriminated against. Like outcast groups elsewhere, they perform more poorly in school and have lower average IQ scores than other citizens of their nation. Here a group of Buraku activists protest the continuing discrimination.

Tom Wagner / SABA

17.

How does history provide further evidence that IQ is highly susceptible to cultural influences? On which measures has IQ increased the most?

Historical Increase in IQ

Perhaps the most dramatic evidence of cultural influence on IQ is found in the improved performance on intelligence tests, worldwide, over the years since they were first invented. As you know, IQ tests are literally graded on a curve, with the average score for the population at any given time in history assigned a value of 100. But the average score keeps rising, indicating that the tests become easier for each successive generation, so researchers periodically modify the scoring system and increase the difficulty of the questions. James Flynn (1987, 1999) has compiled data on norm adjustments for many different countries, from the dawn of IQ testing to present times, and has concluded that the increase in IQ has occurred worldwide at a rather steady rate of about 9 to 15 points every 30 years, depending on the type of test (for examples, see Figure 10.9). The greatest increases, interestingly, are in the tests geared toward fluid intelligence, such as Raven's Progressive Matrices—the very tests that were originally conceived of as least affected by cultural experience and most indicative of raw reasoning ability.

FIGURE **10.9** *Examples of the rise in intelligence-test scores*
The red line shows the mean full-scale IQ scores that Americans would have obtained on Stanford-Binet and Wechsler IQ tests each year if the standard that was used in 1932 had remained unchanged. The blue line shows the mean IQ that 18-year-old Dutch males would have obtained each year on Raven's Progressive Matrices—a test of fluid intelligence—if the standard that was used in 1952 had remained unchanged. (Adapted from Neisser, 1998, p. 14, Figure 2.)

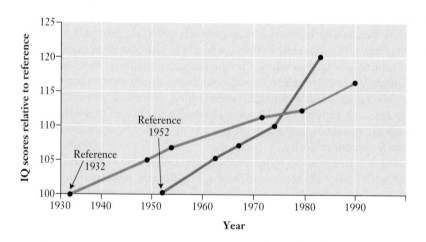

What accounts for these massive gains in IQ from one generation to the next? Flynn (1999) argues against the idea that increased or improved schooling has much to do with it. He points out that the tests that are most reflective of school learning—such as the Arithmetic and Vocabulary subtests of Wechsler's IQ tests—have shown the *least* improvement. It seems likely that the improvement comes instead from a variety of broad cultural changes. Increased travel, increased access to information and ideas (through television and other media), and increased use of technologically complex tools (such as computers) have led people to live in increasingly rich and varied environments that require and promote abstract thinking

(Greenfield, 1998). In addition, improved prenatal care and nutrition have almost certainly fostered healthier brain development (Sigman & Whaley, 1998).

SECTION SUMMARY

The nature-nurture debate has to do with whether differences among individuals in a trait are due primarily to genetic or environmental differences. To address that question, researchers devise ways to estimate heritability, defined as the proportion of variance in a trait that is due to genetic variation. Logically, heritability depends not just on the trait but also on the amount of genetic and environmental variation that exists in the population that is studied. The greater the genetic variation and the smaller the environmental variation, the greater is heritability. Studies of twins and adopted children within the same general (middle-to-upper-class) culture have led to high estimates of heritability for IQ. Within the range of families sampled in such studies, adult IQ depends very little on the specific family in which one was raised.

IQ differences between cultural groups, such as between black and white Americans, however, appear to result primarily or wholly from environmental differences. Researchers have generally failed to find average IQ differences between people who differ in racial ancestry but are identified as members of the same cultural group. Conversely, they have found substantial IQ differences between people who are indistinguishable in racial ancestry but are identified as members of different groups. The most dramatic evidence that IQ is affected by culture is the continuous increase in intelligence-test scores from one generation to the next.

VARIETIES OF INTELLIGENCE

Measuring intelligence with a single IQ score is a methodological convenience, but is intellectual ability properly described as a single dimension, measurable with a single number, or is it better described as a constellation of separate abilities? Historically, the most compelling argument for the unidimensional theory of intelligence was Spearman's research showing that all mental tests tend to correlate positively with one another. As you recall, the statistical procedure of factor analysis that Spearman developed led him to postulate *g*, general intelligence, as the factor that accounts for the positive correlations.

But not all tests correlate equally with one another. Some sets of tests correlate more strongly with each other, within the set, than with tests from other sets. Factor analysis applied to such correlational patterns sometimes reveals distinguishable factors, each potentially representing a different intelligence. Cattell's distinction between fluid and crystallized intelligence, as you recall, was based on evidence from factor analysis. In other research, Philip Vernon (1961) found evidence that verbal ability and visuospatial (or mechanical) ability are distinguishable factors—a distinction that provides part of the basis for the two categories of subtests in Wechsler IQ tests (look back at Table 10.1, page 370). Now let us consider some other lines of evidence concerning the multiplicity of intelligence.

Evidence from Brain Damage and Cases of Unusual Development

In contrast to the factor-analytic approach, which involves examining correlations among test scores in the population at large to identify separate intelligences, the neuropsychological approach involves examining the abilities of people who are clearly exceptions to the norm, either because of brain damage or because of other unusual, often unidentified, influences on their mental development. If some people are capable of superb or normal performance in one intellectual realm but only of poor performance in another realm, that is evidence that the human intellect can be partitioned into relatively separate abilities.

Left- Versus Right-Hemisphere Brain Damage

People who study the effects of brain damage on the intellect often express bewilderment at the uniqueness of each case and the remarkable specificity of some of the deficits observed. Contrary to what would be expected from the theory of general intelligence, people after brain damage are often as intelligent as they were before in some intellectual realms and very deficient in others. Some of the cases do not make sense in terms of any universal theory of separate intelligences but probably reflect individual differences in how information is stored in the brain. An example is the case of a 54-year-old woman who, after a stroke, recovered nearly all her intellectual abilities except the capacity to deal with numbers higher than 4. She could not add, subtract, multiply, divide, or even count if any of the numbers involved were 5 or higher (Sutherland, 1991). Despite such idiosyncrasies, certain general patterns can be discerned in the relation between place of brain damage and effects on the intellect. The clearest and most studied pattern pertains to the distinction between left-hemisphere and right-hemisphere damage.

Chapter 5 presented evidence that the left hemisphere of the brain is specialized for language and the right is specialized for various nonverbal functions, including the analysis of the spatial arrangement of objects. That evidence has led some psychologists to posit that verbal intelligence and nonverbal, pictorial, or spatial intelligence are separate abilities with separate neural mechanisms. A left-hemisphere lesion in the language areas can completely abolish a person's ability to speak or to think in words without affecting the ability to read maps or solve spatial puzzles, and a right-hemisphere lesion in a specific location can have just the opposite effect. Other research has shown that lesions anywhere in the left hemisphere tend to depress people's scores on Wechsler IQ subtests that are designed to measure verbal knowledge and verbal reasoning (particularly the Vocabulary, Comprehension, Similarities, and Information subtests) more than on other subtests; and, conversely, lesions anywhere in the right hemisphere tend to depress scores on the subtests designed to measure visuospatial reasoning (particularly the Block Design, Object Assembly, and Picture Completion subtests) more than on others (Kaufman, 1990).

Retarded Savants: Extreme Intellectual Specialists

The most striking examples of people with specialized intellectual abilities are so-called *retarded savants*. These are people who are born with a condition that severely retards their development in most intellectual realms but who nevertheless develop superior ability in one intellectual realm, such as music, art, language, or mental arithmetic. Although savants' abilities have often been dismissed as imitation or rote memorization, careful studies have revealed that savants master the rule systems of their specialty and can use the rules flexibly and creatively (Miller, 1999).

In an analysis of the case histories of 13 musical savants, Leon Miller (1989) found that at least 12 of them had absolute pitch; that all 13 had severe deficits in ability to understand and use language; that 5 were blind or partially so; and that all 13 showed an extraordinarily intense interest in performing music beginning at a very young age, usually before age 4. One of these individuals, 5-year-old Eddie, was so motivated to play the piano that the opportunity to play it was used to reward him for eating his meals. Perhaps a preserved or enhanced neural capacity for music, coupled with a low level of language comprehension and vision, led in these cases to the extraordinary focus on music. In a series of experiments conducted with five musical savants, Miller found that although they had a remarkable ability to play from memory a piece that they had heard, they also could transpose pieces to new keys, add chords and flourishes that were appropriate to the style of the piece, and compose new pieces that followed the rules of Western music.

Savants with other special abilities have likewise been shown to use rules, not just rote memory. Calendar calculators—who can tell you the day of the week that

18.

How do studies of brain-damaged individuals support the idea of a distinction between verbal intelligence and visuospatial intelligence?

19.

What evidence has been found that retarded savants behave intelligently, not just by rote, in their specialty?

corresponds with any given day of any given month and year, past or future—apparently extract and learn, through their own studies of calendars, a set of rules for making those calculations, which a normal graduate student can learn to use with about a month's deliberate training (Ericsson & Faivre, 1988). A well-publicized artistic savant named Nadia mastered the rules for drawing in perspective at a much younger age than most artists do (see Figure 10.10). Like many other artists, Nadia used photographs and other pictures as models for her work, but she did not just copy; she created her own versions, which were sometimes oriented in space quite differently from the originals (Selfe, 1977). Retarded savants often score rather high on one or more Wechsler IQ subtests—typically Digit Span, Block Design, and/or Object Assembly—while scoring very low on other subtests (Miller, 1999).

An Ecological Perspective on Intelligence

Quite different from either the traditional testing approach or the neuropsychological approach to intelligence is that of examining intelligence as it is manifested in people's daily activities. Some psychologists involved in such studies have adopted an *ecological perspective* on intelligence, which holds that intelligence is a property not of the person alone but, rather, of the person in combination with an environmental context (Ceci, 1996; Lave, 1988; Scribner, 1986). From this perspective, we would speak not of person A's intelligence but, rather, of person A's intelligence in context X. Person A might behave more intelligently than person B in context X, but the reverse might be true in context Y. A *context* here is an environmental setting that poses particular types of problems to be solved. From this view, it does not make sense to speak of any finite number of intelligences at all; there are as many intelligences as there are person-context combinations. Each human mind adapts to the context within which it operates, so its operation must be understood in terms of that context. This is the approach that takes literally the idea that intelligence is mental adaptation to one's environment.

Intelligence at Work

The ecological perspective has generated a good deal of research showing that people are far more successful at solving problems in the context of their everyday employment than at solving formally equivalent problems taken from other contexts. Much of this research has focused on mathematical problems, partly because they have clear-cut right and wrong answers, so it is possible to measure success objectively, and partly because it is easy to generate various math problems that are identical in their formal, abstract properties but differ in the concrete terms in which they are stated.

Children aged 10 to 12 who worked as candy vendors on the streets of a Brazilian city and had no more than 2 years of schooling quickly figured out in their heads how much change to give customers who purchased sets of candies at various prices, yet the same children could not solve the equivalent addition and subtraction problems when they were presented in the more abstract manner usually employed in school (Saxe, 1988). Construction foremen with less than a third-grade education could figure out how much sand was needed when they were told the area and depth of the concrete floor to be laid and the proportion of sand and cement to use in the concrete, but they were lost when given formally identical problems in an unfamiliar work context (making a juice drink) or in the abstract manner of noncontextual school problems (Ceci, 1993). Frequent grocery shoppers in California who had been out of school for many years were far better at judging which of two packages of oatmeal differing in price and amount was the better bargain than they were at solving formally identical school problems (Lave, 1988).

When the subjects in such studies were questioned about their procedure, or were asked to think aloud, they often revealed clever ways of simplifying problems,

20.

How does the ecological perspective on intelligence differ from the traditional view of intelligence? How has the ecological perspective been supported by research on the use of math in various work settings?

FIGURE **10.10** *Drawing produced by a child who is deficient in other intellectual areas*
This remarkable drawing was produced by a 5-year-old girl, Nadia, afflicted with autism, a condition that includes severe retardation in development of speech and social interaction. Her artistic skill emerged from her own efforts, without any training. (From Selfe, 1977.)

which they would not have learned in school. For instance, when a grocery shopper was asked to judge which of two rolls of paper towels was the better deal—one containing 119 sheets and costing 82 cents or one containing 104 sheets and costing 79 cents—she did not solve it by the laborious means of dividing each price by the number of sheets to determine the price per sheet. Instead, she took a route that is much easier to pursue in one's head. She subtracted the smaller number of sheets from the larger one, and the smaller price from the larger one, and concluded immediately that 15 extra sheets for 3 extra cents is a good deal, much lower than the usual cost per sheet (Lave, 1988).

Stephen Ceci (1993) has pointed out that school itself is a specific work environment, and he has provided some evidence that abilities learned in school do not generalize any better to other contexts than do abilities learned in occupations outside school. In one study in Brazil, for example, Ceci and his colleagues found that adults with 9 years of schooling could solve proportion problems that were presented in the typical school format but could not solve the same problems when they were presented in the practical context of construction work. They were no better at solving construction problems than unschooled construction foremen were at solving school problems.

The Intelligence of Experts

Most people become good at the things that they do regularly, but a few become *really* good. They become virtuoso violinists, chess grand masters, or Nobel laureate scientists. What distinguishes outstanding performers from those who are merely good? It seems reasonable to suppose that genetic differences play at least some role; but a fact that is easier to prove is that practice plays a huge role.

On the basis of many studies of experts, in many realms of expertise, Anders Ericsson (1998) has concluded that top performers practice longer and more intensely than merely good performers. In a study of elite violinists, for example, Ericsson and his colleagues (1993) found that those who were at the highest level had practiced an average of more than 10,000 hours by the age of 20 (that amounts to nearly 3 hours per day, 7 days a week, for 10 years). They had practiced 33 percent more than had those in the next most accomplished group and 50 percent more than those in the third tier down. With other studies, Ericsson and his colleagues established what they call "the 10-year rule." In such diverse realms as mathematics, chess, science, music, and sports, the people at the top have spent at least 10 years immersed in the activity (Ericsson & Lehmann, 1996). Moreover, according to Ericsson, the kind of practice that leads to superior performance is not just time spent doing the activity but is highly focused, effortful, and intense, aimed always at improvement.

Consistent with a basic tenet of the ecological perspective, the mental skills that experts develop are generally highly specific to their domain of expertise

21.

How is the ecological perspective on intelligence supported by studies of experts?

(Ericsson, 1998). For example, experts typically manifest excellent memory for information that is relevant to their domain but not for conceptually similar information outside their domain (discussed in Chapter 9). A common component of many IQ tests is a test of digit span—the maximum number of randomly presented single-digit numbers that a person can recite after hearing them just once. In a laboratory demonstration of the effect of practice on mental performance, a young man increased his digit span from the usual 6 or 7 digits to approximately 80 by practicing for more than 200 one-hour sessions (Ericsson & Chase, 1982). Yet when he was given letters instead of digits to recite, his memory was no better than average. The strategies he had invented and honed through practice were specific for numbers; they couldn't be applied to letters. According to Ericsson, similar limitations apply to most of the skills that experts develop.

Cross-Cultural Differences in Reasoning

Another strategy of the ecological approach is to compare standard test results of people from different cultures to see how culture affects mental development. One general conclusion from such research is that the way people approach intelligence tests—their understanding of what is expected of them—is culturally dependent. People of non-Western cultures often find it absurd or presumptuous to respond to questions outside their realm of concrete experiences (Cole & Means, 1981; Scribner, 1977). Thus, the logic question, "If John is taller than Carl, and Carl is taller than Henry, is John taller than Henry?" is likely to elicit the polite response, "I'm sorry, but I have never met these men." Yet the same person has no difficulty solving similar logic problems that present themselves in the course of everyday experience.

Researchers have also found that non-Westerners who have not received Western-style schooling are more likely than Westerners to answer intelligence-test questions in practical, functional terms and less likely to answer in terms of abstract properties (Hamill, 1990). To solve classification problems, for example, Westerners generally consider it smarter to sort things by taxonomic category than by function, but people in other cultures do not. For instance, consider this problem: Which of the following objects does not belong with the others: ax, log, shovel, saw? The correct answer, in the eyes of Western psychologists, is *log*, because it is the only object that is not a tool. But when the Russian psychologist Alexander Luria (1971) presented this problem to unschooled Uzbekh peasants, they consistently chose *shovel* and explained their choice in functional terms: "Look, the saw and the ax, what could you do with them if you didn't have a log? And the shovel? You just don't need that here."

22.

How do unschooled members of non-Western cultures typically perform on classification problems, and what evidence suggests that this may be more a matter of preference than of ability?

Rick Smolan / Stock, Boston

Another cultural context

The ecological approach emphasizes the importance of the context in which intelligent behavior occurs. Micronesians' skill at navigating long distances using information from the stars and from ocean currents reflects intelligence that is well adapted to their environment.

This difference in reasoning may be more one of preference than of ability. Michael Cole and his colleagues (1971) described an attempt to test a group of Kpelle people in Nigeria for their ability to sort pictures of common objects into taxonomic groups. No matter what instructions they were given, the Kpelle persisted in sorting the pictures by function until, in frustration, the researchers asked them to sort the way stupid people do. Then they sorted by taxonomy!

Other cross-cultural studies have demonstrated that the specific abilities tested by the subtests of standard IQ tests may be affected by cultural variation. People who survive by hunting and fishing, for example, commonly perform better on visuospatial tests (such as Block Design and Object Assembly, described in Table 10.1) than do people who survive by other means, such as farming (Berry, 1971). The likely explanation is that the long distances traveled in hunting and fishing require that people keep track of landmarks and make mental maps of their routes, activities that strengthen visuospatial intelligence. The Eskimos living north of the Arctic Circle seem to have particularly well-developed abilities in this area (McShane & Berry, 1988). The Arctic environment provides very few clues telling hunting parties which way is home, so to find their way back from an excursion, they must constantly construct mental maps based on the turns they make and the estimated distances between turns.

23.

What is one line of evidence that a culture's means of existence affect the mental abilities its people develop?

SECTION SUMMARY

While some psychologists strive to understand general intelligence, others conceive of the intellect as a set of several or many qualitatively distinct intelligences. Evidence for distinct intelligences is found in the simultaneous existence of high and low abilities in the same individual, resulting from brain damage or genetic causes. In general, left-hemisphere damage impairs verbal reasoning more than visuospatial reasoning, and right-hemisphere damage does the reverse. Retarded savants exhibit high ability in such domains as music, drawing, or mental arithmetic, coupled with very low ability in other domains.

The ecological perspective views intelligence as context-specific adaptation to the mental challenges encountered regularly in life. Consistent with this perspective, researchers have found that (a) workers readily solve problems at their jobs that they cannot solve when phrased in terms other than those relating to their jobs; (b) experts' skills are generally specific to their much-practiced domains of expertise; and (c) cross-cultural differences in mental abilities relate logically to cross-cultural differences in people's daily experiences and livelihoods.

HOW PEOPLE REASON AND SOLVE PROBLEMS

Thus far we have been more concerned with *what* people can do than with *how* they do it. We now shift our focus to questions about how people reason and solve problems: Why do we find some problems much more difficult than others? Why do we often make what seem later to be "dumb" mistakes? Are there any general strategies that we can employ to become better reasoners?

Psychologists tend to look at reasoning differently from the way logicians (philosophers interested in reason or logic) do. Logicians are most interested in the ideal case, that is, in the laws that describe reasoning as it is most efficiently and effectively performed. Cognitive psychologists, in contrast, are more interested in reasoning as it is *typically* performed; hence, their theories are messier than those of the logicians. A theme running through this section is that human beings are not abstract-thinking machines. Our thought is grounded in the concrete experiences and routines that make up our daily lives. Natural selection endowed us with a brain designed to help us survive, not necessarily to analyze information objectively and establish logical truths. Yet, amazingly, we can, to some degree, think logically.

Inductive Reasoning and Biases in It

Philosophers and psychologists alike distinguish between two general classes of logical reasoning—deductive (to be discussed later) and inductive. ***Inductive reasoning***, or *induction*, is the attempt to infer some new principle, or proposition, from a set of observations or facts that serve as clues. Inductive reasoning is also called *hypothesis construction* because the inferred proposition is at best an educated guess, not a logical necessity. Scientists engage in inductive reasoning all the time as they try to infer rules of nature from their observations of specific events in the world. Cognitive psychologists use inductive reasoning when they make guesses about the workings of the human mind on the basis of observations of many instances of human behavior under varied conditions.

As an example of an inductive-reasoning task, consider the following series-completion problem:

$$1 \quad 2 \quad 4 \quad \underline{\quad} \quad \underline{\quad}$$

What numbers did you place in the two blanks? You might have constructed the hypothesis that each number in this series is double the previous number, which would have led you to complete the series with 8 and 16. But suppose I now inform you that the first blank should be filled with a 7. With that, you would know that your original hypothesis was incorrect, and you might generate a new hypothesis—that each number is the sum of the previous two numbers plus 1. With this hypothesis, you would place a 12 in the final blank. Notice that the more numbers you are given, the more certain you can be that your hypothesis is correct, as long as all the numbers are consistent with it. But you can never be absolutely certain. No matter how many numbers you have seen, the next one might prove your hypothesis wrong.

As another, quite different inductive-reasoning task, consider the following (modified from Tversky & Kahneman, 1974):

> Steve is meek and tidy, has a passion for detail, is helpful to people, but has little real interest in people or real-world issues. Is Steve more likely to be a librarian or a salesperson?

Notice that this question asks you to combine some new information, about Steve, with ideas and information that you have already acquired from life, in order to make a reasonable guess about Steve's profession. Psychologists who study inductive reasoning are interested in the kinds of information that people typically use, or ignore, in answering inductive questions. On the basis of such studies, psychologists have proposed that certain systematic biases exist in people's inductive-reasoning strategies, which sometimes lead to less-than-optimal guesses. Let's examine some of these biases.

The Overuse of Representativeness and Underuse of Base Rates

What answer did you give to the question about Steve? More important, what information did you consider in making your choice? Did you compare the description of Steve's personality with your beliefs about the personalities of typical librarians and typical salespeople? If so, you used the kind of information that Amos Tversky and Daniel Kahneman (1974) call *representativeness*, which refers to the extent to which the item to be classified (Steve, in this case) has characteristics that are typical or representative of the possible classes into which the item might be placed (librarian or salesperson, in this case). Another kind of information that you might have used is *base rate*, which in this case refers to the likelihood that any randomly chosen man would be a librarian or a salesperson. If you know that salespeople vastly outnumber librarians and if you thought to consider this information, you might reasonably conclude that, even though Steve's personality is typical of a librarian's, he is more likely to be a salesperson.

24.

What is inductive reasoning, and why is it also called hypothesis construction?

" HOLMES OPENED IT AND SMELLED THE SINGLE CIGAR WHICH IT CONTAINED."

The Granger Collection

Gathering the evidence

Arthur Conan Doyle conveyed the thrill of inductive reasoning in his stories of Sherlock Holmes, who could form a plausible hypothesis as to who committed the murder and how from the subtlest of clues.

25.

How did Tversky and Kahneman demonstrate that people ignore base rates and overuse representativeness in making inferences?

Tversky and Kahneman (1974) found that people often ignore base rates in answering such questions, even if those rates are made explicit in the statement of the problem. In one experiment, they asked people to estimate the likelihood that a particular individual was either an engineer or a lawyer. One group of subjects was told that the individual had been randomly selected from a set of 70 engineers and 30 lawyers, and another group was told that the set consisted of 30 engineers and 70 lawyers. When subjects were asked to make the judgment with no other information, they used the 70:30 ratios effectively: Most in the first group said there was a 70 percent likelihood that the person was an engineer, and most in the second group said this likelihood was 30 percent. But when a personality description was added, most people ignored the stated proportions (base rates), even when the personality description provided no useful information. For example, a man described as "30 years old, married with no children, and high in ability and motivation" was judged as 50 percent likely to be an engineer regardless of whether the stated proportion of engineers in the set was 70 percent or 30 percent.

The Availability Bias

26.

What kinds of false inferences is the availability bias likely to produce?

One of the least surprising biases identified by Tversky and Kahneman (1973, 1974) is *availability*: In making inferences, people are more likely to use information prominent in their senses or memory at the time of the test than information that is more difficult to summon. For example, when asked whether the letter *d* is more likely to occur in the first position or third position of a word, most people said the first. In reality, *d* is more likely to be in the third position; but, of course, people find it much harder to think of words with *d* in the third position than to think of words that begin with *d*. As another example, when asked to estimate the percentage of people who die from various causes, most people overestimate causes that have recently been emphasized in the media (such as traffic accidents, fires, or murders) and underestimate less publicized but still well-known causes (such as heart disease).

The Confirmation Bias

27.

How has a confirmation bias been demonstrated in research in which subjects were asked to discover a sequence rule or test a hypothesis about someone's personality?

Textbooks on scientific method (and this book, in Chapter 2) explain that scientists should design studies aimed at *disconfirming* their currently held hypotheses. In principle, one can never prove absolutely that a hypothesis is correct, but one can prove absolutely that it is incorrect. The most creditable hypotheses are those that survive the strongest attempts to disprove them. Nevertheless, research indicates that people's natural tendency is to try to confirm rather than disconfirm their current hypotheses (Lewicka, 1998).

In an early demonstration of this *confirmation bias*, Peter Wason (1960) engaged subjects in a game in which the aim was to discover the experimenter's rule for sequencing numbers. On the first trial the experimenter presented a sequence of three numbers, such as 6 8 10, and asked the subject to guess the rule. Then, on each subsequent trial, the subject's task was to test the rule by proposing a new sequence of three numbers to which the experimenter would respond yes or no, depending on whether or not the sequence fit the rule. Wason found that subjects overwhelmingly chose to generate sequences consistent with, rather than inconsistent with, their current hypothesis and quickly became confident that their incorrect rule was correct. For example, after hypothesizing that the rule was *even numbers increasing by twos*, a person would, on several trials, propose sequences consistent with that rule—such as 2 4 6 or 14 16 18—and, after getting a yes on each trial, announce confidently that his or her initial hypothesis was correct. Such persons never discovered that the experimenter's actual rule was *any increasing sequence of numbers*.

In contrast, the few people who discovered the experimenter's rule proposed, on at least some of their trials, sequences that contradicted their current hypothesis. A successful subject who initially guessed that the rule was *even numbers increasing by twos* might, for example, offer the counterexample 5 7 9. The experimenter's *yes* to that would prove the initial hypothesis wrong. Then the subject might hypothesize that the rule was *any sequence of numbers increasing by twos* and test that with a counterexample, such as 4 7 32. Eventually, the subject might hypothesize that the rule was *any increasing sequence of numbers* and, after testing that with counterexamples, such as 5 6 4, and consistently eliciting *no* as the response, announce confidence in that hypothesis.

In other experiments demonstrating a confirmation bias, subjects were asked to interview another person to discover something about that individual's personality (Skov & Sherman, 1986; Snyder, 1981). In a typical experiment, some subjects were asked to assess the hypothesis that the person is an *extrovert* (socially outgoing), and others were asked to assess the hypothesis that the person is an *introvert* (socially withdrawn). The main finding was that subjects usually asked questions for which a *yes* answer would be consistent with the hypothesis they were testing. Given the extrovert hypothesis, they tended to ask such questions as "Do you like to meet new people?" And given the introvert hypothesis, they tended to ask such questions as "Are you shy about meeting new people?" This bias, coupled with the natural tendency of interviewees to respond to all such questions in the affirmative, gave most subjects confidence in the initial hypothesis, regardless of which hypothesis that was or whom they had interviewed.

Why do people show the confirmation bias? One possibility, which pertains to the examples just noted, is that *yes* is much more pleasant to hear than *no* in social exchanges, and so we may have learned to bias our statements in ways designed to elicit agreement. A deeper possibility, which would apply to a larger set of examples, is that in everyday life the goal of gathering information for the long term often conflicts with the goal of being rewarded, or avoiding disaster, at any given moment (Lewicka, 1998). Through evolution or learning or both, we might have developed an adaptive tendency to stick with hypotheses that seem to be working rather than to test their limits by behaving in ways that violate them. I don't honestly know that wearing my orange vest while bicycling helps keep motorists from hitting me; but I wear it each time I ride, and so far I haven't been hit. If my primary goal were knowledge rather than survival, I might perform an experiment: Wear the vest some days and not others and tally the number of times I get hit in either condition.

28.

How might a confirmation bias be adaptive (useful) in everyday life?

The Concrete Nature of Deductive Reasoning

Deductive reasoning, or *deduction*, is the attempt to derive logically the consequences that *must* be true if certain premises are accepted as true. Whereas inductive reasoning is logical guesswork, deductive reasoning (when done correctly) is logical proof, assuming the premises really are true. If you studied plane geometry, you exercised deductive reasoning when you tried to prove or disprove various correlates based on axioms that you were told were true. Table 10.2 on page 394 illustrates two examples of deductive problems. The first is a *series problem*, which requires you to organize items into a series based on a set of comparison statements and then arrive at a conclusion that was not contained in any single statement. The second is a *syllogism*, which presents a major premise and a minor premise that you must combine mentally to see if a particular conclusion is true, false, or indeterminate (cannot be determined from the premises).

The traditional theories of deductive reasoning, long held by most philosophers and some psychologists (for example, Inhelder & Piaget, 1958), are *formal-logic theories*. According to these, deductive reasoning is based on an underlying abstract mental calculus, which makes use of the formal structure of the problem, not the concrete content. Most psychologists who study reasoning today reject formal-logic

29.

What is the difference between deductive and inductive reasoning, and how is deductive reasoning illustrated by series problems and syllogisms?

TABLE **10.2**   *Deductive-reasoning problems*

Series problem	Syllogism	
John is taller than Henry.	All chefs are violinists (major premise).	*Answers:*
John is shorter than Mary.	Mary is a chef (minor premise). Is Mary a violinist?	(˙ou 'ǝʇɐuᴉɯɹǝʇǝpuᴉ 'ǝʇɐuᴉɯɹǝʇǝpuᴉ
Mary is shorter than Billy.	*Alternative forms, based on different minor premises:*	:sɯɹoɟ ǝʌᴉʇɐuɹǝʇן∀) ˙sǝʎ :ɯsᴉƃoןןʎS
Is Billy shorter than Henry?	Mary is a violinist. Is she a chef?	˙ou :ɯǝןqoɹd sǝᴉɹǝS
	Mary is not a chef. Is she a violinist?	
	Mary is not a violinist. Is she a chef?	

theories because they do not explain why some problems are much more difficult to solve than others that have identical formal structures. If people used formal logic to solve syllogisms, for example, then it should not matter whether the major premise fits with common experience (*All chefs are humans*), violates common experience (*All chefs are violinists*), or is a bit of nonsense (*All quilogogs are boomjams*). All that should matter is the abstract form of the problem and the relationship expressed by the words, "All _____ are _____." But numerous experiments have shown that the specific content does matter. The specific content of a problem may facilitate the solution by providing images for development of a *mental model* with which to solve the problem.

Phillip Johnson-Laird (1985) contends that deduction is primarily a problem of understanding the information in the premises, forming mental models (mental representations) of that information, and then examining the models to find the answer to the question. Although Johnson-Laird does not claim that the models must take the form of visual images, the easiest such models to understand are those that do.

When you solved the series problem in Table 10.2, you probably—either on paper or in your head—made little stick figures to represent the relative heights of each of the four individuals—a longer stick for John than for Henry, a longer one yet for Mary, and a still longer one for Billy. Then all you had to do was examine the drawing or mental model and see that the stick for Billy is longer than that for Henry. Similarly, you might have solved all four versions of the syllogism in the table with a model—either on paper or in your head—that represented all the conditions of the major premise, as illustrated in Figure 10.11.

30.

How do mental-model theories of deductive reasoning differ from formal-logic theories, and what evidence suggests that the models we use often take the form of visual images?

FIGURE **10.11**

An image that can be used to solve a specific set of syllogisms

To represent the major premise *All chefs are violinists*, you might draw or imagine a set of people, some of whom (the violinists) are holding violins and some of whom (the chefs) are wearing chefs' hats. To be consistent with the major premise, all the chefs must be holding violins. The premise does not say that all violinists are chefs, so you must provide for the possibility that some are not chefs by including some violinists without chefs' hats. In addition, of course, there may be some people who are neither chefs nor violinists. The result might resemble the diagram shown here but would probably be more schematized. By looking at the diagram, you can now easily answer all four versions of the syllogism presented in Table 10.2. From a logical standpoint, this is a cumbersome way to solve syllogisms; but according to research by Johnson-Laird and others, this is how people typically do solve them or attempt to solve them.

As evidence that people construct models to solve deductive problems, Johnson-Laird and his colleagues (1994, 2000) have shown that the difficulty people have with such problems correlates positively with the number and complexity of the models required to represent the information in the premises. Consistent with the idea that the models often take the form of visual images, some researchers have found that performance on syllogisms correlates more strongly with visuospatial ability than with verbal ability, as measured by standard intelligence tests (Frandsen & Holder, 1969; Guyote & Sternberg, 1981), and others have found that deduction problems are easier to solve if the premises are easy to visualize than if they aren't.

In one such experiment, Catherine Clement and Rachel Falmagne (1986) presented college students with conditional-reasoning problems such as these:

> If the man wants plain doughnuts, then he walks to the bakery across the intersection. The man walked to the bakery across the intersection. Did he want plain doughnuts?

> If the woman reorganizes the company structure, then she makes a profit for the year. The woman made a profit for the year. Did she reorganize the company structure?

Notice that these problems are identical in form and similar in linguistic complexity and the degree to which the premises seem sensible. But most people can more easily form a mental picture of someone crossing an intersection than of someone reorganizing the company structure. Clement and Falmagne found that problems whose premises had been rated as easy to visualize were solved correctly by a higher percentage of students than those whose premises had been rated as hard to visualize. (Incidentally, the correct answer to both of these problems is indeterminate.)

Some Strategies for Solving Problems: Elements of Insight

The function of reasoning is to help us achieve desired goals, that is, to help us solve problems. A *problem* exists whenever we are trying to reach some goal and are not sure how to get there. Any problem—whether it is a puzzle, a mathematical equation to be solved, or a real-life question such as how to improve your relationship with your family—has an *initial state* (the disarranged puzzle pieces, the unsolved equation, or the present state of your family relationship); a *goal state* to be achieved; and a set of possible moves or *operations* for achieving the goal. To solve a problem, one normally must (a) understand the problem, (b) identify the operations that could lead to a solution, (c) carry out the operations, (d) check the results, and (e) return to some earlier point in this chain if the results do not achieve the goal. The first two steps (understanding the problem and identifying a possible route to a solution) are the most critical for solving many problems. They are the steps in which processes collectively called *insight* or *creative ingenuity* are often required.

How do people find a possible solution to a problem that at first seems unsolvable? Research on this question has focused on the value of breaking out of an unproductive mental set, finding a useful analogy to the problem, representing the problem information efficiently, and establishing subgoals based on an explicit statement of the overall problem (Chi & Glaser, 1985; Robertson, 1999). Let's look a bit at each of these paths to insight.

Breaking Out of a Mental Set

Some problems are difficult because their solutions depend on breaking a well-established habit of perception or thought referred to as a **mental set**. Two problems often used to illustrate mental sets are the nine-dot problem and the candle problem, depicted in Figures 10.12 and 10.13, respectively. Before reading further,

31.

How is the concept of a mental set illustrated by the nine-dot problem and the candle problem?

FIGURE **10.12** *The nine-dot problem*
Without ever lifting your pencil from the page or retracing any line, draw four straight lines, no more and no less, that connect all nine dots shown above.

FIGURE 10.13 *The candle problem*
Using only the objects shown here—a candle, a book of matches, and a box of tacks—attach the candle to the bulletin board in such a way that the candle can be lit and will burn properly.

32.

What is some evidence that a light-hearted mood can help a person transcend a mental set?

try to solve these "brain teasers" and then check Figure 10.15 at the end of the chapter for solutions.

If you solved one or both problems, congratulations; if you didn't, join the crowd. Most people fail to solve the nine-dot problem because they approach it from the mental set that each straight line must begin and end on a dot. Perhaps this mental set comes partly from connect-the-dots drawings done in childhood. Most people fail to solve the candle problem because they see the box as nothing but a container for the tacks; it never occurs to them that it could also serve as a shelf and candle holder. Karl Duncker (1945), who invented the candle problem and performed the first experiments with it, referred to this type of mental set as *functional fixedness*, the inability to see an object as having a function other than its usual one. The candle problem is easier for most people if the box and tacks are presented separately rather than with the tacks inside the box (Adamson, 1952). Apparently, alternative functions for an object are easier to see if the object is not currently being used for its more common function.

What allows people to overcome a mental set at some times but not others? Earlier in this century, Gestalt psychologists argued that problems such as those just described are a bit like reversible figures (such as the one shown in Figure 8.28 on page 302) and that finding a solution is a matter of perceptual reorganization. You look at the problem from different angles, turn away from it for a while, look back again, try a few different manipulations of the objects, and then suddenly you see it differently from the way you did before, and the solution becomes obvious. Any conditions, therefore, that would allow your thought and perceptual processes to run more freely might help. Consistent with this view, experimental conditions that increase subjects' anxiety, such as the presence of a judge, tend to inhibit the solution of insight problems, and conditions that promote lightheartedness tend to facilitate their solution (Ashby & others, 1999). Alice Isen and her colleagues (1987), for example, found that college students who had just watched a comedy film were far more successful in solving the candle problem than college students who had seen either a serious film or no film.

Finding a Useful Analogy

Insight is more than just a matter of overcoming a prior mental set. To solve an insight problem, you must not only set aside an approach that doesn't work but also find an approach that does work. As William James (1890) pointed out long ago, problem solving is often a matter of finding a useful analogy (similarity) between the present problem or situation and some other problem or situation with which you are more familiar. A creative genius, according to James, is a person who finds useful analogies where others would not think to look for them. For example, Charles Darwin came up with the concept of natural selection as the mechanism of evolution in part because he could see the similarity between selective breeding by horticulturists and conditions that limit breeding in nature.

A useful analogy in solving the candle problem likens the tack box to a shelf; both can be attached to a wall and can provide a horizontal surface on which to mount a candle. Your reasoning in solving that problem might go something like this: *I know that I could set the candle upright on the wall if I had a shelf. Is anything in the picture like a shelf? Aha, the box—it has a flat surface and can be attached to the wall with tacks so the surface sticks out horizontally!* Thus, you may have solved the problem in a less mysterious way than that implied by the Gestalt psychologists' notion of perceptual reorganization. You may have solved it through a deliberate search for a useful analogy.

Representing the Information Efficiently and Finding Shortcuts

Many problems are difficult because of the sheer quantity of information that must be considered. Efficient representation of the information is often the key to the solution, an idea you encountered already in the discussion of mental models in deductive reasoning. One reason why experts in any given domain outperform novices is that they have learned to distinguish relevant from irrelevant items of information and to group the former into meaningful chunks that can be manipulated mentally to solve the problem (discussed in Chapter 9).

Sometimes, restating a problem in different terms can lead to a more efficient way to organize the information. Look at the stick-configuration problem in Figure 10.14 and see if you can solve it before reading on. The original problem statement (in the figure caption) leads many people to focus on the sticks and to remove different sets of five sticks, in trial-and-error fashion, in the hope of finding the solution. The difficulty with this approach is that more than 6000 combinations of five sticks exist in the seventeen sticks available, so most people give up or lose track of which combinations they have already tried long before solving the problem (Fischler & Firschein, 1987). Success is more likely if you think in terms of squares rather than sticks. Thus, you might restate the problem, "Find three squares, out of the six available, which, if preserved, would allow for the removal of exactly five sticks." There are only 20 combinations of three squares out of six, so trying all possible combinations of the squares would not be too taxing. Focusing on squares reduces the number of trials needed for a trial-and-error solution by a factor of 1/300. But focusing on squares can also lead to a more elegant solution, involving deductive logic rather than trial and error. A square has four sides, so the only way that twelve sticks (the number remaining after five are removed) can form three squares with no sticks left is if they share no sides in common. Inspection of the figure reveals immediately that only two three-square sets have that characteristic: (1) upper left, middle right, lower left; and (2) upper right, middle left, lower right.

33.

How can the deliberate search for an analogy help a person solve a problem that at first seems unsolvable?

34.

How can a problem sometimes be simplified by stating it differently?

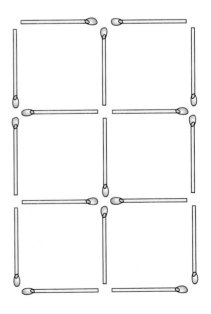

FIGURE **10.14** *Stick-configuration problem*
Find all possible ways to remove exactly five sticks from the pattern so that only three squares are left, with no sticks left over.

35.

What is the difference between an algorithm and a heuristic, and why are heuristics needed more by humans than by computers?

The stick-configuration problem provides a nice example for distinguishing between two general classes of rules for solving problems: algorithms and heuristics. An ***algorithm*** is any rule that, if followed correctly, will eventually solve the problem. For many problems, an algorithm may simply specify that the problem solver produce the entire set of available moves (as defined by the problem), one at a time, until the correct solution occurs. Algorithmic reasoning might in such cases be called the brute-force approach to problem solving; it succeeds not by cleverness but by tireless persistence. Computers use algorithms well because they can perform simple manipulations very rapidly, have perfect memories, and don't run out of patience. An algorithmic approach to the stick-configuration problem is to remove every possible combination of five sticks out of the seventeen available—about 6000 trials in all—and to note which trials leave just three squares. A computer could solve this problem almost instantly with such an algorithm, whereas a human might spend hours trying to solve it this way before flinging the sticks aside in frustration.

A ***heuristic*** is any rule that allows one to reduce the number of operations that are tried in solving a problem. In colloquial terms, a heuristic is a shortcut. In the stick-configuration problem, one heuristic would be to focus on squares rather than sticks and to search for three squares in the configuration whose boundaries are made up of twelve different sticks. In general, human problem solvers are successful to the extent that they can recognize or invent useful heuristics and are unsuccessful to the extent that they use heuristics that lead them off track. The biases discussed previously under the topic of inductive reasoning (such as the availability bias and the confirmation bias) are examples of heuristics that are often useful but can lead to wrong answers in logic problems. Computers can use heuristics, too, if they are programmed to do so, but they are not very good at developing their own, and they have less need for them.

Establishing Subgoals and Defining the Problem Explicitly

In games such as chess that involve a sequence of moves, and in most long-range problems of real life, it is not possible to map out a solution from beginning to end before making the first move. Each move in chess elicits a countermove, which must be taken into account in choosing the next move. Similarly, each step you take to reach your chosen career has some effect, not fully predictable, which you must take into account when you decide on the next step. In chess and in life, plans must usually center on shorter-term subgoals that bring one closer to the ultimate goal

36.

What is the value of subgoals and clear definitions in solving a problem? How can fixation on a subgoal sometimes interfere with successful problem solving?

of capturing the king or obtaining a desired life position. Experiments have shown that people who succeed in solving problems involving a series of choices typically establish explicit subgoals that lead ever closer to the final goal (Chi & Glaser, 1985).

A distinction between problems commonly studied in the laboratory and those confronted in real life lies in the extent to which they are well or ill defined. A *well-defined problem* is one in which the initial state, goal, and permissible operations for reaching the goal are all clearly stated; an *ill-defined problem* is one in which one or more of these is not clear (Voss & Post, 1988). Suppose you want to be happier. That is a problem worth tackling; everyone, I assume, wants to be happier. But it is an

Achieving a subgoal

Chess is won not by going directly for checkmate but by establishing and achieving subgoals that eventually get one's pieces into position for checkmate. A skilled player modifies the subgoals as the board changes while keeping the ultimate goal in mind.

ill-defined problem; where does one begin to solve it? Counselors and therapists hired to help people solve such problems emphasize the value of restating the problem in more explicit, well-defined terms. What would bring happiness—more friends? more money? a more fulfilling job? more time to relax? Once that can be established, the problem has become better defined; some subgoals can be established and steps laid out to achieve them.

A difficulty with subgoals, however, is that they can obscure the original purpose. Fixation on the subgoal itself can become a mental set that may blind a person to alternative routes to the larger goal. A chess player who focuses solely on trying to maneuver the bishop into a better position may overlook a shortcut to checkmate that was opened up by the opponent's last move. A person who focuses on more money as a path to happiness may lose sight of the original aim and devote his or her life to obtaining money for its own sake, overlooking other means to happiness that arise along the way. A successful problem solver establishes subgoals but keeps them subordinated to their original purpose.

SECTION SUMMARY

The psychological study of reasoning has focused on inductive reasoning, deductive reasoning, and creative problem solving. In inductive reasoning (the use of knowledge and clues to develop hypotheses) people often fail to take base rates into account and fall prey to the availability and confirmation biases. The confirmation bias may represent an evolved or learned tendency to stick with premises that seem to work rather than take risks. Deductive reasoning (proving the truth or falsity of specific conclusions from premises that are accepted as true) appears to be carried out through the construction and inspection of mental models. Difficult deductive problems are those whose premises are difficult to visualize or to represent mentally in other ways.

Problems that test insight or creative ingenuity are those for which the possible steps toward solution are not immediately obvious to most people. Strategies for solving such problems include breaking out of a mental set, finding a useful analogy, and restating the problem in new terms that make it simpler. Some real-life problems are ill defined; to solve them one must first define them in such a way as to establish explicit goals and steps for achieving those goals.

ROLES OF LANGUAGE IN THOUGHT

As you worked to solve the sample problems in the previous section, you undoubtedly called forth information from long-term memory that you had originally acquired through language. You may also have uttered words to yourself, subvocally, as part of your work on the problem.

We proudly conceive of ourselves as the thinking animal; but if beings from outer space were to contrast humans with other earthly creatures, they might well call us the linguistic animal. Other species can learn and use what they have learned to solve problems (discussed in Chapter 4), and they share with us a highly developed capacity for nonverbal communication (discussed in Chapter 3). But no other species has the well-developed, flexible, abstract, symbol-based mode of communication that we call *language*, which permits the conveyance of an infinite variety of facts and ideas.

Language allows us to tell each other not just about the here and now but also about the past, future, far away, and hypothetical. We are effective problem solvers largely because we know so much, and we know so much because we learn not only from our own experiences but also from others' reports. As the philosopher Daniel Dennett (1994) put it, "Comparing our brains with bird brains or dolphin brains is almost beside the point, because our brains are in effect joined together into a single cognitive system that dwarfs all others. They are joined by an innovation that has invaded our brain and no others: Language."

Language not only is a vehicle of communication that allows us to learn from each other but is also a vehicle of thought. To some extent, perhaps a great extent, we think with words. As the Russian psychologist Lev Vygotsky (1934/1962) pointed out, young children often speak words out loud as they think to themselves, but with time they learn to speak the words subvocally and then to use the words purely mentally in abbreviated forms that may no longer be recognized as words. Such thought, which uses symbols that were acquired originally in the form of words, is called *verbal thought*. Chapter 11 explains more about the nature of human language, its development in children, and its role in the development of thought. Right now our focus is on the possibility that one's particular language and linguistic habits can affect the way one thinks about particular classes of problems.

Thinking in Different Languages

If language is a basis for thought, then people who speak different languages might think differently because of their different languages. This idea, which is consistent with Vygotsky's, is most often attributed to the American linguists Edward Sapir (1941/1964) and Benjamin Whorf (1956). Sapir and Whorf both argued that language affects not only our higher thoughts but even our basic perceptions of the physical world. Whorf coined the term **linguistic relativity** to refer to all such effects. The idea that language influences perception of physical qualities of the environment, such as color and spatial relationships, is still much debated (Davidoff & others, 1999; Kay & Kempton, 1984; Levinson, 1996). Logically, however, we might expect that language would influence higher-order thinking much more than it influences basic perceptual processes. One realm of such thought is mathematics.

Number Words and Math Ability

In some instances the linguistic-relativity theory obviously holds true. English and other languages that contain a full set of number names organized in a base-10 system certainly give their speakers an advantage in all sorts of numerical reasoning compared with Australian Aborigines who speak Worora. The Worora language has only three number words, which translated to English are *one*, *two*, and *more than two* (Greenberg, 1978). If Worora speakers wanted to think mathematically, they would have to start by inventing or learning number names. The words, in this case, are essential tools.

A more subtle linguistic effect on numerical reasoning may lie in the comparison of people who speak English or certain other European languages with those who speak Asian languages such as Chinese, Japanese, and Korean. Asian children greatly outperform American and European children in mathematics at every stage of their schooling (Miller & others, 1995). Usually that effect is attributed to differences in how mathematics is taught, but some researchers have argued that the difference may stem at least partly from a difference in language.

In English and other European languages the number words do not precisely mirror the base-10 number system that is used in all of arithmetic, but in Chinese, Japanese, and Korean the number words do precisely mirror that system. While we count *one, two, . . . , nine, ten, eleven, twelve, thirteen, . . . , twenty, twenty-one, . . . ,* the speakers of the Asian languages count (if their words were translated literally into English) *one, two, . . . , nine, ten, ten one, ten two, ten three, . . . , two-tens, two-tens one, ...* The words *eleven* and *twelve* give the English-speaking child no clue at all that the number system is based on groups of 10, whereas *ten one* and *ten two* make that fact abundantly clear to the Asian child. Even many English-speaking adults do not know that *teen* means "ten" (Fuson & Kwon, 1992), and children do not automatically think of *twenty* as "two tens." Because the Asian count words make the base-10 system transparent, Asian children might develop an implicit grasp of that system and thereby gain an advantage in learning arithmetic.

37.

What differences are found between Asian children and American or European children in counting and mathematics, and how might the difference be attributed to a difference in language?

Consider children learning to add two-digit numbers, say, 34 plus 12. English-speaking children pronounce the problem (aloud or to themselves) as "*thirty-four* plus *twelve*," and the words give no hint as to how to solve it. Chinese-speaking children, however, pronounce the problem (in effect) as "*three-tens four* plus *ten two*," and the words themselves point to the solution. In the two numbers together, there are four tens (*three tens* plus *one ten*) and six ones (*four* plus *two*), so the total is *four-tens six* (46). From the perspective of Johnson-Laird's mental-model theory of reasoning (discussed earlier in the chapter), we might say that the words *three-tens four* and *ten two* lead directly to mental models that keep the tens and units separate, whereas the words *thirty-four* and *twelve* do not.

One line of evidence that the number words indeed do make a difference comes from a study showing that children in the United States learn to count to 10 at the same age, on average, as do Chinese children but fall behind Chinese children in learning to count beyond 10, which is where the languages begin to diverge (Miller & others, 1995). By age 4, most of the Chinese children studied could count to 40 or beyond, whereas most of the American children could not get past the low teens.

In an even more telling study, 6-year-olds in the United States and in France and Sweden (where number words contain irregularities comparable to those in English) were compared with 6-year-olds in China, Japan, and Korea on a task that directly assessed their use of the base-10 system (Miura & others, 1994). All the children had recently begun first grade and had received no formal training in place value. Each was presented with a set of white and purple blocks and was told that the white blocks represented units (ones) and the purple blocks represented tens. The experimenter explained, "Ten of these white blocks are the same as one purple block," and set out ten whites next to a purple to emphasize the equivalence. Each child was then asked to lay out sets of blocks to represent specific numbers—11, 13, 28, 30, and 42. The results were striking. The Asian children made their task easier by using the purple blocks correctly on over 80 percent of the trials, but the American and European children did so on only about 10 percent. While the typical Asian child set out four purples and two whites to represent 42, the typical American or European child laboriously counted out 42 whites. When they were subsequently asked to think of a different method to represent the numbers, most of the American and European children attempted to use the purple blocks, but made mistakes on about half the trials.

Linguistic Relativity in Bilingual People

A basic problem in the study of linguistic relativity is that any difference in thought observed between people who speak different languages might arise from other cultural differences between the two groups. For instance, in the studies just described, the Asian children might have had more experiences at home with numbers greater than 10, and some of them might even have had practice with the abacus, a mechanical calculating device often used in Asia, which has sliders in different tracks that represent different powers of 10 (although none of the children had yet been taught the abacus at school). To avoid the inevitable confound that occurs when linguistic effects are studied across culturally distinct groups, some researchers have studied language effects in bilingual people who are fluent in both languages. Such people often claim that they think differently in the two languages, and research tends to support their claim.

In one study, for example, Curt Hoffman and his colleagues (1986) found that bilingual speakers may develop different impressions of a person depending on which language they are using when forming an impression. In their experiment, Chinese students at the University of Alberta, in Canada, read descriptions of hypothetical individuals in either English or Chinese and then wrote essays about their impressions of each person described—using English when the original description was in English and Chinese when the original description was in Chinese.

38.

What problem in studying effects of language is avoided by studying people who speak two languages? How did one such study provide evidence of a linguistic effect on thought?

Two of the individuals described could easily be labeled by an English word but not by a Chinese word, and two were the reverse. For example, one description was designed to fit what in English is called an artistic character—a person with artistic ability, a temperamental disposition, a tendency toward fantasy, and an unconventional lifestyle. Another description was designed to fit what in Chinese is called a *shi gu* individual—a person with much worldly experience, a strong family orientation, and good interpersonal skills. The labels were not used in the descriptions, but the descriptions were written so as to be consistent with those labels.

As predicted by the linguistic-relativity hypothesis, the students formed a firmer, more consistent impression of the artistic character when reading and thinking in English and a firmer, more consistent impression of the *shi gu* character when reading and thinking in Chinese. On the basis of these results, Hoffman and his colleagues suggested that bilingual speakers have two different sets of schemas (mental representations of concepts), each tied to a different language. When the person thinks in one language, one set of schemas is evoked; in the other language, the other set is evoked.

Effects of Wording on Thinking Within a Language

Whether or not we store concepts in linguistic form and think in words, many problems are posed to us in words, and our understanding of those words is critical to solving the problem. Subtle differences in how a problem or question is worded, which from a formal-logic perspective should not matter, in fact do matter. Also, the labels we assign to objects in our environment can influence our ability to use those objects to solve problems.

How a Verbal Habit Can Affect Problem Solving

39.

How did practice with a new verbal habit improve performance on the candle problem?

In a clever set of experiments, E. Tory Higgins and William Chaires (1980) demonstrated an effect that wording can have on people's ability to solve the candle problem. As you recall, to solve the candle problem a person must think of the box full of tacks as something other than a container for tacks (to refresh your memory, look back at Figure 10.13 on page 396). Higgins and Chaires instilled in some of their college-student subjects a verbal habit designed to get them to separate containers and contents mentally. They showed a series of slides depicting containers with contents and described each to the students using an *and* construction: *a jar* and *cherries, a carton* and *eggs,* and so on. They showed other students the same slides but described the objects using the more familiar *of* construction: *a jar of cherries, a carton of eggs.* In one experiment, previous experience with the *and* constructions led students to label the box full of tacks as *a box and tacks* when they first saw it, and in another experiment students who had experience with the *and* construction were much faster at solving the candle problem than those who had experience with the *of* construction. Apparently their new verbal habit helped them see the box as something separable from the tacks and therefore suitable as a shelf.

Sexism and the Generic Man

The role of language in thought can have important real-life consequences. If language shapes thought, then one way to change long-established ways of thinking is to modify the language. This reasoning lay behind the movement, which began in the 1970s, to rid English of constructions that tend to characterize males as more human than females. One such construction is use of the word *man* to stand for both human beings in general (the generic *man*) and human males in particular. Many writers have argued that because these two concepts have the same label, they become fused into the same mental schema and lead English-speaking people to think of males as more typical examples of human beings than are females. This form of labeling is no accident. Historically, and still among many people today,

WHEN YOU GROW UP

What would you like to be when you are bigger? Would you like to be a good cook like your father? Would you like to be a doctor or a nurse?
What would you like to be?

policeman   fireman

WHEN YOU GROW UP

What would you like to be when you are bigger? Would you like to be a good cook like your father? Would you like to be a doctor or a nurse?
What would you like to be?

police officer   fire fighter

What a difference a decade makes

When Richard Scarry's *Best Word Book Ever* was first published, few people thought about the effect of books on children's developing sense of their gender. Studies of children's literature in the early 1970s changed all that, and publishers began to replace stereotyped images and language with material that provides equal treatment, as these pages from the 1963 (top) and 1980 (bottom) editions of the book show.

men have been considered quite explicitly to be the primary humans and women have been considered to be secondary.

To test the degree to which *man*, used in the generic sense, elicits a mental perception of humans in general versus males in particular, Joseph Schneider and Sally Hacker (1973) performed an experiment involving hypothetical titles for chapters of a sociology textbook. One set of titles used the generic *man* construction, which was still common in textbooks of that time: *Social Man, Urban Man, Economic Man*, and so on. Another set avoided that construction, with titles such as *Society, Urban Life*, and *Economic Behavior*. The researchers gave one set of titles to one group of students and the other set to a similar group and asked each student to find pictures from newspapers and magazines that would be suitable for illustrating each chapter. The result was that about 65 percent of the pictures brought back by students in the *man* group depicted males only (the rest contained either both genders or females only), compared with about 50 percent male-only pictures brought back by the other group. These percentages were about the same for female and male students. From this, the researchers argued that the two meanings of *man* are in fact not distinct in people's minds. The students in this experiment surely knew that *man* as used in those titles meant human beings in general, but their behavior suggested an unconscious mental compromise between that meaning and the male-only meaning.

Subsequent studies produced comparable results, not just for *man* but also for the use of *he* to refer to a person of unspecified gender (Harrison, 1975; Khorsroshahi, 1989; MacKay, 1980). Such research suggests that it has been worth the effort for me and others of my generation to consciously alter some of our ingrained ways of speaking and writing, ways that were considered proper when we attended school.

40.

What evidence suggests that the habit of using man *to refer to humans in general is worth changing?*

SECTION SUMMARY

Since much thought is verbal, it is not surprising that thought is influenced by the words of one's language. The explicit representation of the base-10 number system in various Asian languages appears to facilitate children's learning of mathematical concepts in those languages. People who are fluent in two languages find it easier to remember and think about a concept in the language that more clearly labels that concept than in the other language. Ease of solving the candle problem depends on the words that subjects have learned to use to label the box full of tacks. Experiments conducted in the 1970s and 1980s revealed that the use of man *and* he *to refer both to males and to humans in general led people unconsciously to think of males as more typical exemplars of human beings than are females.*

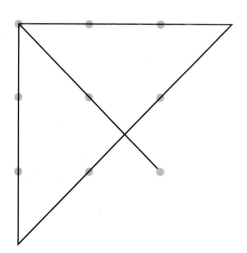

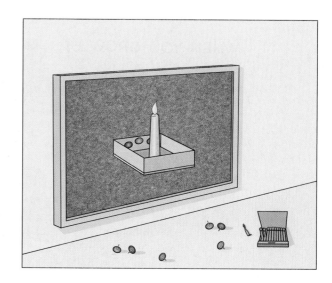

FIGURE **10.15**   *Solutions to the nine-dot and candle problems*
These are the solutions to the problems in Figures 10.12 and 10.13.

CONCLUDING THOUGHTS

In this chapter we considered some aspects of the mind that most clearly distinguish us from other animals. You might find it useful to organize your review around the following general themes:

1. Controversies about the measurement and heritability of intelligence   IQ tests have been around, and controversial, for most of the history of psychology, and the basic controversies have not changed much over the years. As you review the classic work and theories of Binet, Spearman, and Cattell, you might relate them to current research and ideas on (a) the validity of IQ tests; (b) the extent to which IQ scores reflect mental speed, working-memory capacity, mental self-government, and cultural influences; and (c) the heritability of intelligence. As you review the heritability discussion, be sure to keep in mind the definition of *heritability*; it will help you make sense of the research and understand how heritability can be high within groups and still be zero between them. Heritability is one of the most misunderstood concepts in psychology. It is worth making an effort to get the concept straight.

2. Theories about the structure of the human intellect   A major scientific goal of people involved in intelligence testing is to use individual differences as a basis for making inferences about the structure of the human intellect in general. How did Spearman and Cattell differ from each other in their interpretations of patterns of correlations among test scores to arrive at their differing theories of the structure of the mind? How do the neuropsychological and ecological approaches to intelligence each differ from the IQ-based approach in their claims and in the types of research they have inspired?

3. Ideas about how we reason   The theses of the last two major sections of the chapter are that people reason concretely and that reasoning is much affected by wording. As you review these sections, think about (a) the evidence for certain biases in inductive reasoning; (b) the evidence that we solve deductive-reasoning problems with mental models; (c) the evidence that certain deliberate strategies can improve one's ability to solve insight problems; and (d) the evidence that the words of a language, or the words chosen within a language, can markedly influence people's ability to reason in particular realms.

Further Reading

N. J. Mackintosh (1998). *IQ and human intelligence.* Oxford: Oxford University Press.

This is a thorough, balanced introduction to IQ testing and theories of intelligence. It discusses the development of IQ tests, issues of the reliability and validity of such tests, heritability of and environmental effects on IQ, group differences in IQ, factor analysis of IQ, the search for neural and elementary cognitive underpinnings for IQ differences, attempts to specify the cognitive processes underlying specific components of IQ, fluid intelligence and problem solving, and modern theories of intelligence.

Stephen J. Ceci (1996). *On intelligence: A bioecological treatise on intellectual development* (expanded ed.). Cambridge, MA: Harvard University Press.

This book's theses are that intelligence tests are not as valid as most IQ researchers believe them to be and that intelligence is best understood in relation to the social-environmental contexts of everyday life.

Neil Smith & Ianthi-Maria Tsimpli (1995). *The mind of a savant: Language learning and modularity.* Oxford: Blackwell.

This detailed study of Christopher—a retarded savant who by age 7 was reading technical works in foreign languages and by age 30 could translate, with varying degrees of success, from 20 different languages into English—illustrates the case-study approach at its scientific best. The research contributes to a theory of distinct intelligences by mapping out the boundaries of one person's abilities and inabilities.

S. Ian Robertson (1999). *Types of thinking.* London: Routledge.

In this brief, entertaining introduction to reasoning and problem solving, Robertson devotes separate chapters to everyday thinking, creative thinking, logical and scientific thinking, failures in thinking, and intelligent thinking.

Looking Ahead

In this chapter you have seen how psychologists attempt to understand the structure and functioning of the human intellect by studying individual differences in test performance and by comparing performance on systematically varied versions of the same problem. Still another route to understanding intellectual abilities is to watch them as they are built—that is, to observe how they grow in the developing child. The next chapter is about cognitive development; it deals with many of the same issues that were raised in this chapter but does so from a developmental perspective. What can we learn about thought and language by studying their development in children?

The House of Cards, Zinadia Serebriakova

Growth of the Mind and Person

part **6**

One way to understand any complex entity, be it a building under construction or a person growing, is to watch it develop over time. This is the approach taken by developmental psychologists, who study the changes through which human behavior becomes increasingly complex and sophisticated from infancy to adulthood. This unit consists of two chapters on developmental psychology. The first is about the development of thought and language. The second is about the development of social relationships and the roles they play in promoting other aspects of development.

Chapter 11

Yamauba and Kintoki, Kitagawa Utamaro

The Development of Thought and Language

When I first saw my newborn son, my words did not match my thought. I said something like, "Oh, he's beautiful," but my thought was, "My god, will this turn into a human being?" Of course, I knew intellectually that he already was a human being, but at the moment he looked more like a cross between that and a garden slug. Over the next weeks, months, and years the little slug's mother and I watched in amazement as he grew not only to look increasingly human but also to do the things that humans everywhere do. He began to smile in response to our smiles; he began eventually to walk upright on two legs and to talk, sometimes incessantly; and, true to his species' name (*Homo sapiens*, where *sapiens* means "wise"), he manifested from early on an insatiable curiosity and soon developed a remarkable store of knowledge and theories about his world.

This chapter is about the millions of new human beings who enter the world every year. More specifically, it is the first of two chapters concerned with ***developmental psychology,*** the study of changes that occur in people's abilities and dispositions as they grow older. Some developmental psychologists study changes that occur in adulthood (as you will discover in Chapter 12), but most study changes that occur in infancy and childhood. They do so not only because they find infants and children fascinating and worthy of understanding for their own sake but also because they see in infants and children the origins of adult abilities. Human thought and language in particular are extraordinarily complex abilities, and developmental psychologists have learned a great deal about them by watching them grow in infants and children.

This chapter begins by examining infants' explorations and knowledge of the physical world; then it turns to some theories and research concerning the development of reasoning, including reasoning about people's minds as well as about physical objects; and finally it discusses the acquisition of language. A theme throughout is that the exploratory and playful activities of young people can be understood as biological adaptations serving the purpose of development. Innate tendencies and drives, which are products of human evolution, motivate the child to learn about his or her physical and social worlds, to become an increasingly sophisticated reasoner, and to learn the specifics of his or her native language. These innate tendencies and drives, operating in a responsive social environment, enable the person to develop as one who can survive and thrive in the culture into which he or she is born. This theme is also pursued in the next chapter, focusing on the development of social relationships.

LEARNING, IN INFANCY, ABOUT THE PHYSICAL WORLD

Infancy, roughly the first 18 to 24 months after birth, is the time of most rapid developmental change—change that lays the foundation for further development. How do babies learn about the physical world around them? What do they know, early on, about that world?

The Infant as Explorer

Babies' sensory systems all function at birth (although one sense, vision, is still quite immature). On the day they are born, babies will turn toward sounds, turn toward anything that touches their face, turn away from unpleasant odors, suck a nipple more readily for a sweet liquid than for a sour one, and orient their eyes toward high-contrast or moving visual stimuli (Maurer & Maurer, 1988). Within a short time after birth, babies not only respond to stimuli, but respond selectively, in ways that seem well designed for learning.

Seeking Novelty and Control

Hundreds of experiments have shown that babies gaze longer at new stimuli than at familiar ones. When shown a pattern, they look at it intently at first and then, over the course of minutes, look at it less and less—a phenomenon referred to as *habituation*. This decline in attention is not due to general fatigue; if a new pattern is substituted for the old one, the infants immediately increase their looking time. Similarly, if shown the new and old patterns at the same time, infants look more at the new one than the old one. This preference is so reliable that developmental psychologists use it to assess infants' abilities to perceive and remember. Babies who look reliably longer at a new stimulus than at one they have already seen must perceive the difference between the two and must, at some level, remember having seen the old one before. In one such study, infants as young as 1 day old perceived the difference between two checkerboards differing in size of the squares and remembered that difference over the seconds that separated one trial from the next (Friedman, 1972).

Beginning within a few weeks after their birth, infants manifest a special interest in aspects of the environment that they themselves can control. In one experiment, 2-month-olds smiled and attended much more to a mobile that moved in response to their own bodily movement than to a motor-driven mobile that they could not control (Watson, 1972). In another experiment, 4-month-olds learned quickly to make a particular movement to turn on a small array of lights but lost interest and responded only occasionally once they became proficient. When the conditions were changed so that a different movement was needed to turn on the lights, the infants regained interest and made another burst of responses (Papousek, 1969). Their renewed attention must have been generated by the new relationship between a response and the lights, because the lights themselves were unchanged. Apparently, the babies were interested not so much in the lights per se as in their own ability to control them. In still another experiment, infants as young as 2 months old, who had learned to turn on a video and sound recording of the *Sesame Street*

1.

What is the evidence that infants prefer to look at novel stimuli?

2.

What is the evidence that infants are motivated to control their environment and are emotionally involved in gaining and retaining control?

Making the cow jump over the moon

Researchers have found that babies take more delight in objects they can control than in objects they can't control.

theme song by pulling a string tied to their wrist, showed facial expressions of anger when the device was disconnected so that they could no longer control it (Lewis & others, 1990). Apparently, even 2-month-olds experience joy in learning to control aspects of their environment and anger when they lose that control. That seems to be a facet of human nature that is true at every phase of development, and its function seems obvious. We, more than any other species, survive by controlling our environment.

Exploring Objects Using Eyes and Hands Together

Infants explore not only with their eyes but also with their mouth and hands, and their means of exploration changes in a regular way as they grow older. Babies as young as 5 days old will extend one or both hands toward objects they see, although at this age their reaching seems reflexive and they rarely succeed in touching or grasping the object (Streri, 1993). Within a few weeks, however, their reaches become better coordinated and apparently deliberate. Infants who are 2 or 3 months old often succeed in grasping an object that they reach toward, and then they typically bring it to their mouth and suck or chew on it in an apparently exploratory fashion. By 4 months of age, infants who grasp an object explore it with their fingers and eyes as well as their mouth; subsequently, their use of the mouth declines while their exploration with hands and eyes increases (Rochat, 1989).

By 5 or 6 months, infants regularly manipulate and explore objects in the sophisticated manner that researchers label *examining* (Ruff, 1986). They hold an object in front of their eyes, turn it from side to side, pass it from one hand to the other, squeeze it, mouth it, and in various other ways act as if they are deliberately testing its properties. Such actions decline dramatically as the infant becomes familiar with a given object but return in full force when a new object, differing in shape or texture, is substituted for the old one (Ruff, 1986, 1989). As evidence that examining involves active mental processing, researchers have found that babies are more difficult to distract, with bright visual stimuli, when they are examining an object than when they are involved in other activities (Oakes & Tellinghuisen, 1994).

Infants vary their examining in ways consistent with an object's properties. They preferentially look at colorfully patterned objects, feel objects that have varied textures, and shake objects that make a sound when shaken (Lockman & McHale, 1989). Other experiments have shown that infants indeed learn about objects' properties through such examination. In one experiment, 9-month-olds explored toys that produced interesting nonobvious effects when manipulated in certain ways, including a can that wailed when tilted and a doll that separated into two parts when pulled. The infants soon learned to produce each toy's unique effect, and when given a new toy that was similar (but not identical) to the one they had just explored, they immediately tried to produce the previously experienced effect. If the new toy differed in its basic structure from the original one, they did not try to produce the effect but explored the toy afresh as if intent on discovering its unique properties (Baldwin & others, 1993).

Infants do not have to be taught to examine objects. They do it in every culture, whenever objects are in their reach, regardless of whether or not such behavior is encouraged. Roger Bakeman and his colleagues (1990) studied the exploratory

3.

What is the evidence that infants' examining of objects (a) involves active mental processing, (b) helps them learn about the unique properties of specific objects, and (c) occurs regardless of whether or not adults encourage it?

Laura Dwight / PhotoEdit

A small scientist

By 5 to 6 months of age, infants learn about the properties of objects by manipulating them with their hands while watching intently to observe the effects.

behavior of infants among the !Kung San, a hunting-and-gathering group of people in Botswana, Africa, who have been relatively uninfluenced by Western cultures. (The *!K* in *!Kung* stands for a clicklike sound that is different from the pronunciation of our *K*.) !Kung adults do not make toys for infants or deliberately provide them with objects for play. Yet !Kung babies examine objects that happen to be within their reach—such as stones, twigs, food items, and cooking utensils—in the same manner as do babies in Western cultures; and, as in Western cultures, their examining increases markedly in frequency and intensity between about 4 and 6 months of age. The adults do not encourage such behavior because they see no reason to, yet they recognize its value and do not discourage it. Their view of child development seems to be well summarized by one of their folk expressions, which can be translated roughly as "Children teach themselves" (Bakeman & others, 1990).

The Use of Social Cues to Guide Exploration

4.

What are three ways by which infants, beginning at roughly 6 to 12 months, use their observations of adults' behavior to guide their own explorations?

Although infants act upon and explore their environment whether or not they are encouraged by others to do so, they regularly use social cues to guide such actions. By 6 months of age, infants often mimic adults' actions on objects. In one experiment, 6-month-olds frequently rolled a ball if they had recently seen their mother roll it, and they frequently pounded with a ball if they had seen their mother do that (Hofsten & Siddiqui, 1993).

Beginning sometime in the latter half of their first year of life, infants regularly engage in *joint visual attention* with adults (Moore & Corkum, 1994). A baby looks at an adult's eyes and then directs his or her own eyes toward whatever the adult is looking at. The baby may then gaze at the object for a while or may turn back to the adult, apparently to check again the adult's line of sight. Such behavior may help infants learn which objects and events are of greatest interest to their elders, which may be the objects and events most important to learn about for survival within that culture. Other experiments have shown that the reflexive tendency to follow another individual's gaze is present in infants as young as 3 months old (Hood & others, 1998) and occurs also in other primate species (Tomasello & others, 1998).

By the time they can crawl or walk freely on their own (toward the end of their first year), infants engage in what is called **social referencing**—they look to their caregivers' emotional expressions for clues about the safety or possible danger of

Inuit mother and baby
In many traditional cultures, infants are carried around by their mothers throughout the day, and they learn about the world by seeing it from their mother's vantage point.

their own actions (Walden, 1991). In one experiment with 12-month-olds, not one crawled over a slight visual cliff (an apparent 30-centimeter drop-off under a solid glass surface) if the mother showed a facial expression of fear, but most crawled over it if her expression was one of joy or interest (Sorce & others, 1985). In another experiment, 12-month-olds avoided a new toy if the mother showed a facial expression of disgust toward it, but they played readily with it otherwise (Hornik & others, 1987).

Infants' Knowledge of the Laws of Physics

You and I share certain assumptions about the nature of physical reality. We assume, for example, that objects continue to exist even when they disappear from view; that two solid objects cannot occupy the same space at the same time; and that if an object moves from one place to another, it must do so along a continuous path. Such assumptions constitute *core principles* of our knowledge of the physical world (Spelke & others, 1994). We expect these principles always to be true, and when they seem to be violated, we usually assume that our senses have been somehow deceived, not that the principles have really been contravened.

At what age do people begin to make these core assumptions about physical reality? This question has spurred much research in developmental psychology, partly because of its intrinsic interest and partly because of its relevance to a centuries-long philosophical debate. Empiricist philosophers, such as John Locke (1690/1975) and George Berkeley (1710/1820), argued that each person gradually acquires an understanding of core principles through use of the senses and general learning ability. In contrast, nativist philosophers, such as René Descartes (1649/1985) and Immanuel Kant (1781/1965), argued that knowledge of at least some core principles is inborn. According to the nativists, such principles are so central to human perception and thought that they must in some way be known from the beginning if useful learning is to occur. For instance, without the assumption that objects and parts of objects continue to exist when out of view, a baby who witnesses one object becoming partly occluded (hidden from view) by another would assume that the first object suddenly lost part of itself, which would lead to a false and ultimately maladaptive understanding of the world. Psychological research has not settled the question about the origin of knowledge of core principles, but it has shown that such knowledge is manifested in the patterns of infants' exploratory behavior beginning at a very young age.

5.

How have empiricist and nativist philosophers differed in their view of the origin of a person's knowledge of core physical principles?

Peek-a-boo

The results of selective-looking experiments suggest that babies even much younger than this one know that objects continue to exist when out of view. Nevertheless, they take delight in having that understanding confirmed, especially when the object is a familiar, friendly person.

Bob Daemmrich / Stock, Boston

6.

What is the rationale behind the habituation method of studying infants' knowledge of physical principles? With this method, what have researchers found about the knowledge of 2- to 4-month-olds?

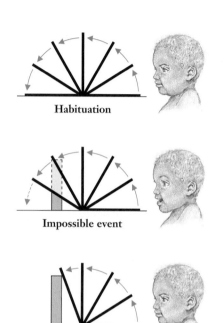

FIGURE 11.1 *Evidence for object permanence in very young infants*
Baillargeon (1987) first showed infants a hinged screen rotating back and forth over a 180° arc until they were bored with it (habituation). Then, using mirrors, she created the illusion that a brightly colored object had been put just behind the place where the screen was hinged. Finally, she manipulated the screen to produce either of two events: one possible and the other impossible. In the impossible event, the screen rotated over the entire arc, as though the object behind it magically disappeared and then reappeared on each rotation. In the possible event, the screen stopped in each rotation at the place where it would have bumped into the object had it been physically present. Infants as young as 3½ months old looked longer at the impossible than at the possible event, suggesting that they were more surprised by it. (Adapted from Baillargeon, 1987.)

Evidence from Selective-Looking Experiments

The most common method of assessing early knowledge of physical principles capitalizes on infants' preference for looking at novel rather than familiar events. Called the *habituation* or *selective-looking method*, it involves two phases. First, in the *habituation phase*, the infant is repeatedly shown a physical event until he or she is bored with it, as indexed by reduced time spent looking at it. Then, in the *test phase*, the infant is shown one of two variations of the original event. One variation, called the *impossible event*, appears (to adults) to violate a physical principle. The other variation, the *possible event*, does not appear to violate a physical principle. The two test events are designed so that, on purely sensory grounds, the possible event differs more from the original habituation event than does the impossible event. If their perception is based purely on sensory aspects of what they see, infants should see the possible event as most different from the original and should look longest at it. But if their perception is based partly on an understanding of the physical principle that is violated, infants should look longest at the impossible event, because that differs most from what they would expect to happen.

For an example of the method, look at Figure 11.1 and read the caption. In this case, the habituation event was a back-and-forth rotating screen, and each of the test events involved the same rotating screen with an apparently solid block behind it. The block was obscured from the baby's view by the screen each time the screen rotated up and back. In the impossible event, the screen continued to rotate all the way back and down to the tabletop, as though the block no longer existed once it was out of view. In the possible event, the screen stopped in each rotation, just at the point where you and I would expect it to hit the object behind it, and then it rotated forward again. In this experiment, Renée Baillargeon (1987) found that infants as young as 3½ months old—the youngest tested—looked longer at the impossible event than at the possible event. This result suggests that the infants believed the block was still present behind the screen, even though they couldn't see it, and believed that solid objects do not normally pass through and obliterate other solid objects. If the infants had not held those beliefs, then the impossible event should have been most boring and attracted their least attention, because it, unlike the possible event, involved the same movement of the screen as was used during habituation.

In such experiments, 3-month-olds have also manifested an understanding of other core principles. For instance, they expect a rolling ball to stop at a barrier rather than pass through it (Spelke & others, 1992) and a stationary ball to remain so unless hit or pushed by another object (Spelke & others, 1994). Of course, young infants do not manifest entirely the same expectations about the physical world that adults do. Core principles may be present early on, but nuances related to them are acquired with age and experience. Baillargeon (1994, 1998) and her colleagues found that 4-month-olds expected a box to fall to the ground when it was released in midair but did not expect it to fall when it was set on the edge of a shelf with most of its weight hanging off the shelf. Only by 6 to 7 months did infants show evidence that they expected the box on the edge to fall also.

Lag Between Selective Looking and Ability to Retrieve Hidden Objects

The findings supporting infants' early knowledge of core principles surprised many developmental psychologists, because previous research, using a different procedure, had suggested that infants only gradually develop an understanding of even the most basic principles of objects. The pioneer in the earlier research was the famous Swiss developmental psychologist, Jean Piaget (1936/1963). Piaget's observations of his own children's successes and failures in retrieving hidden objects led him to conclude that infants only gradually develop a comprehension of ***object permanence,*** the principle that objects continue to exist even when out of view.

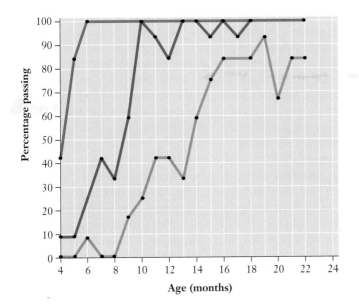

FIGURE **11.2** *Improvement in finding hidden objects*
This graph shows the percentage of infants at various ages who succeeded on each of the three kinds of search tasks developed by Piaget. The simple hiding and changed-hiding-place tasks were as described in the text, except that the objects were hidden under cups rather than under napkins. In the invisible displacement task, the infant watched as the researcher's hand closed around the toy, hiding it from view. The researcher's closed hand then moved under the cup and deposited the toy. When the hand was brought back into view, most infants under 14 months old looked in and under the hand for the toy, but not under the cup. According to Piaget, infants fail to find the toy because they do not understand that objects can be moved from one place to another when out of view. (Adapted from Wishart & Bower, 1984.)

———— Simple hiding task
———— Changed-hiding-place task
———— Invisible displacement task

To assess his children's understanding of object permanence, Piaget invented three kinds of search problems, which were later used with hundreds of infants by other researchers, who found results remarkably similar to Piaget's (see Figure 11.2). In the *simple hiding problem*, an attractive toy is shown to a baby and then is placed under a napkin as the baby watches. Babies younger than about 5 months typically follow the toy with their eyes as it disappears under the napkin but do not reach for it once it is there and almost immediately seem to lose interest in it. Piaget and his successors interpreted this result as evidence that babies this age completely lack the concept of object permanence.

Between about 6 and 9 months of age, most infants solve the simple hiding problem but fail the *changed-hiding-place problem*. In this test, first the toy is hidden under one napkin for a series of trials, and the baby retrieves it each time. Then it is hidden under another napkin, right next to the first. Despite having watched the object disappear under the new napkin, the baby reaches toward the original napkin. Piaget concluded that at this age the emerging understanding of object permanence is still very fragile; when pitted against a learned motor habit (reaching toward the original hiding place), the habit wins out. By about 10 to 12 months, most infants solve the changed-hiding-place problem but fail the *invisible displacement problem*, described in the caption to Figure 11.2. Not until about 18 months do infants regularly succeed at all three problems, by which time, according to Piaget, their understanding of object permanence is fairly complete.

Why do infants younger than 5 months fail all of Piaget's tests of object permanence yet appear to understand object permanence in the selective-looking studies of Spelke, Baillargeon, and others? Nobody knows for sure, but Baillargeon (1993) suggests that the developmental sequence observed by Piaget has less to do with the understanding of object permanence than with the ability to plan a sequence of movements needed to reach a hidden object. To succeed on Piaget's hiding problems, the baby must act on one object (the napkin) in order to get another object (the toy). Piaget (1952) himself pointed out, and others have confirmed (Willats, 1999), that babies typically fail to solve any problem in which they must act on one object to obtain another until they are about 7 or 8 months old. For instance, they do not pull on a cloth to bring into their reach a desired object that sits atop the cloth, even when the object is in full view.

7.

How did Piaget test infants' understanding of object permanence? How might the discrepancy between Piaget's results and the results of selective-looking experiments be explained?

8.

What evidence suggests that self-produced locomotion leads to improvement in retrieving hidden objects and to fear of heights? How might the latter effect be explained from an evolutionary perspective?

Another view, consistent with Piaget's own view, is that infants' knowledge is not separable from their actions. Infants act upon objects in various ways, triggered by a variety of sensory inputs. In the case of the changed-hiding-place problem, for example, a learned habit of reaching to one napkin is pitted against the baby's tendency to reach to the place where the toy was last seen. Depending on the strength of the learned habit and the relative salience of the new hiding place (the second napkin), the infant may reach to one place or the other (Smith & others, 1999).

Other studies have shown that dramatic improvement in the ability to retrieve hidden objects occurs shortly after infants can crawl or in other ways move about on their own (Campos & others, 2000). In one experiment, 8-month-olds were tested in a series of search tasks, including a version of Piaget's classic changed-hiding-place problem (Kermoian & Campos, 1988). One group had learned to crawl at least 9 weeks before the tests; a second group had not learned to crawl but had at least 9 weeks of experience moving around in walkers at home; and a third group had neither learned to crawl nor been provided with walkers. Approximately 75 percent of the babies in the first two groups succeeded on the changed-hiding-place problem, compared with only 13 percent of those in the third group. Self-produced locomotion requires that infants coordinate their vision with their muscular movements in new ways, to avoid bumping into objects, and affords them the opportunity to view stationary objects from varying perspectives. Such experience may well be crucial in developing the ability to use one's visual understanding of a hidden object's location to guide one's movements in retrieving that object manually.

Self-Produced Locomotion and Wariness of Heights

Self-produced motion also appears to be crucial to the development of wariness of heights. Eleanor Gibson and Richard Walk (1960) found that infants who are experienced crawlers will not crawl over a *visual cliff* (see Figure 11.3), even if their mother calls from that side of the table. Joseph Campos and Bennett Bertenthal found that 6- and 7-month-olds who had learned to crawl or who had been provided with about 40 hours of experience moving around in a walker showed an increased heart rate when lowered onto the glass over the deep side of the cliff, but those who could not crawl and had no walker experience showed either no change in heart rate or a slightly decreased heart rate when similarly placed (Bertenthal & others, 1984; Campos & others, 1992). On the basis of previous research, Bertenthal and Campos interpreted the increased heart rate as a sign of fear and the decreased heart rate as a sign of interest without fear.

Contrary to what most of us would guess, the fear of heights brought on by self-produced movement was not due to experience with falling. The infants who were provided with walkers were allowed to use them only in a setting where they did not (and could not) fall, so they had no more experience with falling than did the noncrawling infants without walkers. Campos and his colleagues (2000) propose that the new wariness of heights follows from a more general cognitive change induced by self-produced movement. To move successfully, either by crawling or using a walker, infants must learn to adjust their movements to the continuously changing view of their environment that occurs as they move, and this ability may lead them to a new level of understanding.

Although Campos and Bertenthal's account may explain infants' increased attention to heights, it does not in itself explain why infants who can move about on their own should begin to *fear* heights. The nonlocomotive infants placed face-down over the cliff surely saw the cliff (previous research has shown that depth perception is well developed even in infants much younger than 6 months), yet they did not show evidence of fear. My own interpretation of Bertenthal and Campos's finding is cast in evolutionary terms. Fear of heights is likely to be instinctive in humans, just as it is in other animals, resulting from countless generations in which those with the fear survived while those without it fell over cliffs. However, such a fear is of little value to infants who cannot yet move on their own, and it may even

Enrico Feorelli

FIGURE 11.3 *Visual cliff*
The apparatus consists of a drop-off underneath a solid glass tabletop. Although his mother is calling, this child will not venture over the deep side of the visual cliff.

be harmful to them because of the distress it might cause as they are carried about by adults, high above the ground. According to this reasoning, natural selection may have provided humans with (a) a tendency to fear heights and (b) an activating mechanism that causes this tendency to manifest itself after self-produced locomotion begins. The same or a similar activating mechanism may also bring on some other fears, such as fear of separation from caregivers and fear of strange places and people (to be discussed in the next chapter), which also emerge as infants become mobile. All these fears may motivate babies to constrain their explorations in ways that reduce the potential dangers and, as noted earlier, to look to their caregivers for guidance about what is safe or dangerous.

SECTION SUMMARY

Infants are active explorers. Within hours after they are born, they look longer at novel patterns than at patterns they have already seen. By 2 months of age, they show special interest in aspects of the environment that they can control. By 5 months, infants actively examine objects with their eyes and hands simultaneously. By 6 months, they mimic adults' actions. Before they are a year old, they look preferentially at objects that their caregiver is looking at and use their caregiver's emotional expressions as clues about the safety or danger of their own actions.

Infants as young as 2 to 4 months look preferentially at events that appear to violate certain core principles of physics, including the principle of object permanence, indicating that they are most surprised by those events. But their ability to retrieve hidden objects develops more slowly. Most infants fail to solve Piaget's simple hiding problem before they are 5 months old and cannot solve his changed-hiding-place problem until they are about 9 or 10 months old. Crawling and other means of self-produced locomotion promote a number of cognitive changes in infants, including improved performance on the changed-hiding-place problem and the emergence of fear of heights. The latter change does not require that the infant have any experience with falling.

DEVELOPMENT OF REASONING

As children grow from infancy to adulthood, their thinking becomes ever more logical, ever more effective in solving problems. How can these changes be characterized, and what are the processes through which they develop? The pioneer in the attempt to answer these questions was Jean Piaget, whose research and theory set much of the agenda that is still being pursued by developmental psychologists. We will begin, therefore, with Piaget's theory and then turn to two other perspectives—the information-processing and sociocultural perspectives—that were partly inspired by Piaget's theory.

Piaget's Theory

In his long career at the University of Geneva (from the 1920s until his death in 1980), Piaget wrote more than 50 books and hundreds of articles on children's reasoning. Piaget's goal was to understand how the adult mind, particularly its capacity for objective reasoning, develops from the child's more primitive abilities. His primary method was to ask children to solve specific problems and to question them about the reasons for the solutions they offered. From this work, Piaget developed an elaborate, comprehensive theory of cognitive development.

The Child's Own Actions Provide the Basis for Cognitive Development

Piaget's most fundamental idea was that mental development derives from the child's own actions on the environment. At first, according to Piaget (1936/1963),

Jean Piaget

Because of his interest in the influence of the environment on children's cognitive development, Piaget preferred to observe children in natural settings. Here he is shown during a visit to a nursery school.

9.

In Piaget's theory, (a) what is a scheme, (b) how do schemes develop through assimilation and accommodation, and (c) what is the special value of operations? How do all these concepts relate to Piaget's idea that mental growth occurs through the child's own, self-motivated actions?

Accommodation

This 11-month-old may be accommodating her "stacking scheme" in order to assimilate the experience of one block fitting inside another. From such experiences, a new "fits-inside" scheme may develop.

infants react toward events in their environment only through automatic, wired-in reflexes. Later, however, they gradually gain voluntary control of their actions as they develop internal, mental representations of the kinds of actions they can perform on particular categories of objects. Piaget called these internal representations **schemes**. Schemes serve as mental blueprints for actions. The earliest schemes are closely tied to specific objects and are called forth only by the object's immediate presence. Thus a young infant might have a sucking scheme most applicable to nipples, a grasping and shaking scheme most applicable to rattles, and a smiling scheme most applicable to human faces. As a child grows older, new, more sophisticated, more abstract schemes develop, which are less closely tied to the immediate environment or to actual actions. Piaget conceived of the growth of schemes as involving two complementary processes: assimilation and accommodation.

Assimilation is the process by which new experiences are incorporated into existing schemes. Piaget was a biologist by training, and he considered the assimilation of experiences to be analogous to the assimilation of food. Two people may eat the same type of food, but the food will be assimilated into the tissues differently, depending on the inner structures involved in digestion and building the body. Moreover, just as nondigestible foods will not result in body growth, new experiences that are too different from existing schemes to be mentally digested will not result in mental growth. A hand calculator given to an infant will not contribute to the child's arithmetic skills, because the infant has no calculating scheme into which to assimilate the calculator's functions. The infant will probably instead assimilate the calculator into his or her already well-developed sucking scheme or banging scheme.

Few new stimuli perfectly fit an existing scheme. Assimilation usually requires that existing schemes expand or change somewhat to accommodate the new object or event. Appropriately, Piaget referred to this process as *accommodation*. In Piaget's theory, the mind and its schemes are not like a brick wall, which only grows bigger as each new brick (unit of knowledge) is added; they are more like a spider's web, which changes its entire shape somewhat as each new thread is added. The web accommodates to the thread while the thread is assimilated into the web. The addition of new information to the mind changes somewhat the structure of schemes that are already present.

Consider an infant who in play discovers that an object placed above an open box will fall into the box. Perhaps the child already had a scheme for stacking objects, which included the notion that one object placed on top of another will remain on top. But now that scheme must be modified to accommodate this new experience, to include the notion that if one object is hollow and open-topped, another object placed on it may fall inside. At the same time, other schemes that include the notion that two objects cannot occupy the same place at the same time may also undergo accommodation. In Piaget's view, children are most fascinated by experiences that can be assimilated into existing schemes but not too easily, so that accommodation is required. This natural tendency leads children to direct their own activities in ways that maximize their mental growth.

As children grow beyond infancy, according to Piaget, the types of actions most conducive to their mental development are those called *operations,* defined as *reversible actions*—actions whose effects can be undone by other actions. Rolling a ball of clay into a sausage shape is an operation because it can be reversed by rolling the clay back into a ball. Turning a light on by pushing a switch up is an operation because it can be reversed by pushing the switch back down. Young children perform countless operations as they explore their environment, and in doing so, they gradually develop *operational schemes*—mental blueprints that allow them to think about the reversibility of their actions.

Understanding the reversibility of actions provides a foundation for understanding basic physical principles. The child who knows that a clay ball can be rolled into a sausage shape and then back into a ball of the same size as it was before has the basis for knowing that the amount of clay must remain the same as the clay changes shape—the principle of *conservation of substance*. The child who can imagine that pushing a light switch back down will restore the whole physical setup to its previous state has the basis for understanding the principle of cause and effect, at least as applied to the switch and the light.

Four Types of Schemes; Four Stages of Development

Piaget conceived of four types of schemes, which represent increasingly sophisticated ways of understanding the physical environment. His research convinced him that the four types develop successively, in stages roughly correlated with the child's age.

The most primitive schemes in Piaget's theory are **sensorimotor schemes,** which provide a foundation for acting on objects that are present but not for thinking about objects that are absent. During the *sensorimotor stage* (birth to roughly 2 years old), thought and overt physical action are one and the same. The major task in this stage is to develop classes of schemes specific for different categories of objects. Objects the child explores become assimilated into schemes for sucking, shaking, banging, squeezing, twisting, dropping, and so on, depending on the objects' properties. Eventually the schemes develop in such a way that the child can use them as mental symbols to represent particular objects and classes of objects in their absence, and then they are no longer sensorimotor schemes.

Preoperational schemes emerge from sensorimotor schemes and free the child's thought from strict control by the here and now. Children in the *preoperational stage* (roughly 2 to 7 years old) have a well-developed ability to symbolize objects and events that are absent, and in their play they delight in exercising that ability (Piaget, 1962). Put a saucepan into the hands of a preschooler and it is magically transformed into a ray gun or a guitar—the saucepan becomes a symbol in the child's play. The schemes at this stage are called preoperational because, although they can represent absent objects, they do not permit the child to think about the reversible consequences of actions. According to Piaget, understanding at this stage is based on appearances rather than principles. If you roll a ball of clay into a sausage shape and ask the child if the shape now contains more than, less than, or the same amount of clay as before, the child will respond in accordance with how it looks. Noting that the sausage is longer than the ball was, one preoperational child might say that the sausage has more clay than the ball had. Another child, noting that the sausage is thinner than the ball, might say that the sausage has less clay.

10.

In Piaget's stage theory, (a) what are the four stages and the ages roughly associated with each, (b) how are the child's capacities and limitations at each stage related to the kind of scheme that is most prominent, and (c) how does the child's behavior at each stage promote advancement toward the next stage?

The preoperational stage

Sarah, here age 5¾, does not pass Piaget's test of conservation. Even though she knows that the short glasses contain the same amount of milk and carefully watches the milk being poured into the tall glass, she still points to the tall glass when asked, "Which has more?"

Hazel Hankin

The concrete-operational stage
According to Piaget, thought becomes increasingly logical during middle childhood, but it still depends on the presence of real objects. Activities such as that shown here offer oportunities to learn about cause-effect relatioinships. From such activities, formal-operational thinking eventually emerges.

Although (or perhaps because) preoperational children have not yet internalized an understanding of operations, they continually produce operations as they explore their environment. As they push, pull, squeeze, mix, and so on, they gradually develop **concrete-operational schemes** and eventually enter the *concrete-operational stage* (roughly 7 to 12 years old). These schemes permit a child to think about the reversible consequences of actions and thereby provide the basis for understanding physical principles such as conservation of substance and cause and effect (Piaget, 1927). A concrete-operational child who has had experience with clay will correctly state that the sausage has the same amount of clay as the ball from which it was rolled because it can be rolled back into that ball (see Figure 11.4). A concrete-operational child who has had experience with bicycles will correctly say that the chain is crucial to the bicycle's movement but the fender is not, because the child can picture the reversible consequences of removing each and knows that the pedals can move the wheels only if there is a physical connection between the two.

The earliest schemes for operations are called concrete operational because they are still tied closely to the child's actual experiences in the world. The child might have schemes, for example, for the conservation of clay rolled into various shapes and of fluids poured from one container to another but still lack an understanding of conservation of substance as a general principle that applies regardless of the type of substance. Such schemes do, however, lead the child to think about the similarities of operations that can be performed on different entities, and such thought leads in time to the development of **formal-operational schemes,** which represent principles that apply regardless of the specific situation. When these schemes characterize a significant share of a person's thinking, the person is said to be in the *formal-operational stage* (which begins roughly at the onset of adolescence and continues throughout adulthood). Such schemes permit a person to think theoretically and apply principles even to actions that cannot actually be performed (Inhelder & Piaget, 1958).

FIGURE **11.4** *Tests of children's understanding of conservation*
The transition from the preoperational to the concrete-operational stage, in Piaget's theory, is marked by success on tests such as these. Children usually succeed on conservation-of-number and conservation-of-length tests before they succeed on conservation-of-substance tests.

In conservation-of-number tests, two equivalent rows of coins are placed side by side and the child says that there is the same number in each row. Then one row is spread apart, and the child is again asked if the two rows have the same number.

In conservation-of-length tests, two same-length sticks are placed side by side and the child says that they are the same length. Then one stick is moved, and the child is again asked if they are the same length.

In conservation-of-substance tests, two identical amounts of clay are rolled into similar-appearing balls and the child says that they have the same amount of clay. Then one ball is rolled out, and the child is again asked if they have the same amount.

You cannot really unbeat an egg, but with an appropriate formal-operational scheme you can understand the theoretical principle that an egg can be unbeaten and restored to its original form. Thus, you can answer correctly a conservation question about a beaten egg as well as about a rolled-out piece of clay: Is the amount of egg more, less, or the same after it is beaten compared with before? Formal-operational thinkers can extend principles into hypothetical realms that neither they nor anyone else has actually experienced. While the concrete-operational reasoner is limited to empirical (fact-based) science and arithmetic, the formal-operational reasoner is capable of theoretical (principle-based) science and formal mathematics.

Piaget believed that the transitions from stage to stage are gradual; each new type of scheme develops slowly, and a given child may use the more advanced type of scheme for one class of problems while still using the more primitive type for other problems. Piaget also believed that children vary in the age at which a type of scheme begins to predominate. The ages given earlier are only rough averages. The one constant in Piaget's stage theory is that each child, for any given category of problem, must progress through the stages sequentially: Children will not jump from the first to the third without going through the second, nor (barring brain damage) will they regress from one stage to an earlier one.

Limitations of Piaget's Theory

Piaget's theory is much admired by developmental psychologists, especially for its emphasis on the role of the child's own activity in cognitive development and its idea that children are self-motivated to behave in ways that stretch and improve their mental capacities. For many years, Piaget's theory—especially his theory of stages—provided the impetus for much of the research that psychologists performed on cognitive development. Research and thought since Piaget's time, however, have convinced many developmental psychologists of a number of serious limitations of the theory, including the following:

+ *Overestimation of age differences in ways of thinking*   Research conducted since Piaget's time suggests that people's basic ways of thinking do not change as much with age as Piaget believed. Piaget appears to have underestimated the abilities of young children and overestimated those of adolescents and adults. Earlier in this chapter you read about selective-looking experiments that showed that infants as young as 3 months expect objects to continue to exist when out of view and to obey certain universal physical principles. Children as young as 4 or 5 years regularly pass at least some tests indicative of operational reasoning (such as the number-conservation test illustrated in Figure 11.4) if the problems are presented clearly, without distracting information (McGarrigle & Donaldson, 1975). At the other end of the developmental scale, research with adults challenges the distinction between concrete and formal thought. Such research (discussed in Chapter 10) suggests that people who are good at solving abstract problems usually do so by thinking of analogies to more familiar problems or by turning the problem statement into a familiar visual image in order to convert a formal task into a concrete one.

  In light of such studies, it seems reasonable to suggest that all of us, throughout the great bulk of our childhood and throughout adulthood, are what Piaget would call concrete-operational thinkers. Our thinking may advance more because of our gradually increasing store of knowledge and ability to manipulate that knowledge efficiently than because of fundamental revolutions in our way of thinking.

+ *Vagueness about the process of change*   Some critics contend that Piaget's theory of the process by which the mind develops is too vague, too general, too distanced from the behavioral data. What precisely is a scheme? What information must a scheme have in order, say, to permit a child to succeed in the conservation-of-clay problem? What exactly changes when assimilation and

11.

What do developmental psychologists tend to admire most about Piaget's theory, and what criticisms have been raised concerning Piaget's (a) claims about age differences in reasoning, (b) theory of the process of change, and (c) emphasis on the physical rather than social environment?

Helping Grandma
Children learn even about physical concepts, such as quantity and mass, in interaction with other people. Piaget has been criticized by contemporary developmental psychologists for having underemphasized the role of social learning.

Lawrence Migdale / Stock, Boston

accommodation occur? Theorists in the information-processing tradition (to be described shortly) believe that theories of mental development should be more explicit than Piaget's in describing the links between the observed changes in behavior and the posited changes occurring in the mind.

✦ *Underestimation of the role of the social environment*   The children Piaget studied were growing up in a Western European culture where particular ways of thinking are valued and are taught in schools. Yet Piaget attributed the children's mental development primarily to their individual interactions with the physical world, not to their culture or schooling. He tended to conceive of each child as a lone scientist discovering anew the laws of nature. But cross-cultural research has shown that success on Piaget's tests of formal-operational reasoning, and even on some of his tests of concrete-operational reasoning, depends very much on experience with Western culture (Dasen & Heron, 1981; Segall & others, 1990). Theorists in the sociocultural tradition (to be described later) argue that mental development occurs more through interaction with other people than through solo interaction with nature.

The Information-Processing Perspective

Piaget treated the mind as a single entity that grows as a whole. In contrast, developmentalists who adopt the information-processing perspective treat the mind as a set of interacting components, any one of which might change as a child grows older. The goal, from this perspective, is to account for specific changes in children's mental abilities in terms of specific changes in one or another of the mind's components or in terms of specific knowledge the child has acquired.

The information-processing approach to cognition, as described in Chapter 9, begins with the assumption that the mind is a system, analogous to a computer, for analyzing information from the environment. According to the standard information-processing model (see Figure 9.1, page 326, the mind's basic machinery includes attention mechanisms for bringing information in, working memory for actively manipulating (or thinking about) information, and long-term memory for passively holding information so that it can be used in the future. Together these components are analogous to the all-purpose operating system that is built into a computer. In addition, the mind contains specific strategies and rules for analyzing particular types of information or solving particular types of problems. These strategies and rules are analogous to the specific programs, such as a word-processing program or a statistical package, that are loaded into a computer. From the information-processing perspective, cognitive development can stem from changes in the mind's general operating system or in its specific programs, or in both.

12.

What is the information-processing perspective on cognitive development, and how does it differ from Piaget's perspective?

Increased Capacity of Working Memory and Faster Speed of Processing

Developmentalists who have focused on the mind's general operating system have documented improvements, with age, in children's abilities to pay attention to relevant information, encode information into long-term memory, and retrieve specific items of information from long-term memory (Kail & Bisanz, 1992). The most fully studied general changes with age, however, are improvements in the capacity of working memory and in the speed at which simple information-processing steps of all kinds can be performed.

In the standard model of the mind, working (or short-term) memory is the center of conscious thought and the place where information is combined and manipulated to solve problems. As discussed in Chapters 9 and 10, working memory is limited in the amount of information it can hold and use at any given time, and this limit constrains a person's problem-solving ability. Some years ago, a mathematically oriented psychologist, Juan Pascual-Leone (1970), proposed that the most fundamental change underlying cognitive development is a gradual, maturational increase in the capacity of working memory, which he referred to as *M space* (mental space). Pascual-Leone and other researchers showed mathematically how the stages posited by Piaget could, in theory, be accounted for by a gradual change in M space (Case & others, 1982). Specific intellectual tasks require a certain minimal amount of M space, just as computer programs require a certain amount of computer memory; so as M space increases, a child can solve problems that he or she could not solve before. Consistent with Pascual-Leone's theory, many studies have shown that the number of items of information that can be held and manipulated in working memory increases with age throughout childhood (Swanson, 1999).

Closely correlated with increased working-memory capacity, and possibly a cause of it, is increased *speed of processing*—the speed at which elementary information-processing tasks of all sorts can be carried out. Speed of processing is usually assessed with reaction-time tests that require a very simple judgment, such as whether two letters or shapes flashed on a screen are the same or different or whether an arrowhead is pointing right or left. Such tests consistently reveal age-related improvement up to the age of about 15 years (Kail, 1993; see Figure 11.5). As was discussed in Chapter 10, faster processing speed permits faster mental movement from one item of information to another, which improves one's ability to keep track of (and thereby hold) a number of different items in working memory at once. Robbie Case (1992) and Robert Kail (1991) contend that faster speed of processing derives from biological maturation of the brain independent of specific experiences. Consistent with that view, 9- and 10-year-old boys who were judged as physically mature for their age—on the basis of the degree to which they had reached their predicted adult height—exhibited significantly faster processing speeds on reaction-time tests than did boys of the same age who were judged as physically immature for their age (Eaton & Ritchot, 1995).

13.

How might a continuous increase in the capacity of working memory produce stagelike development in problem-solving ability?

14.

What is the evidence that an increase in mental speed results from biological maturation, and how might that account for increased working-memory capacity?

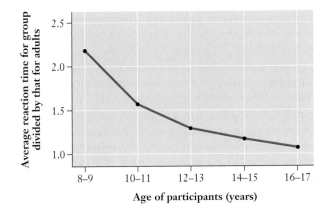

FIGURE 11.5
Reaction time for simple tasks decreases with age
Children and adolescents were tested for their speed in each of six different tests, including a test of elementary reaction time (releasing a button in response to a signal) and a test of picture matching (judging whether two pictures are identical or not). Each person's average time for each test was converted by dividing it by the average time achieved by adults on the same test, and the results were then averaged for each age group. Note that a decline in reaction time implies an increase in speed. (Data from Kail, 1993.)

The growth of cognitive strategies
Through video games and other forms of play, children learn to pay attention, remember relevant information, follow rules, and react quickly.

Reed Kaestner / Corbis

15.

How does Siegler's explanation of improvement in solving balance-beam problems differ from the kind of explanation that Piaget would offer?

Acquiring Rules to Solve Specific Classes of Problems

From the information-processing perspective, mental development occurs not just through improvement in the all-purpose mental machinery but also through the acquisition of particular rules and strategies for solving particular categories of problems (Siegler, 2000; Siegler & Jenkins, 1989). Consider, for example, the task of determining which side of a balance beam will tilt down when varying numbers of equally heavy weights are placed on each side at varying distances from the fulcrum (see Figure 11.6). This was one of the tasks that Piaget commonly used to test formal-operational thinking. Many years later, from an information-processing perspective, Robert Siegler (1983) described advancement in this problem in terms of the acquisition of four increasingly sophisticated rules, which are summarized in the caption to Figure 11.6. Siegler found that the rule a given person used to solve such problems could be discerned from that person's pattern of successes and errors on a set of balance-beam problems. In general, older children and adults used a more advanced rule than did younger children.

In some of his experiments, Siegler allowed children to gain feedback on each trial, after they had made their prediction, by releasing the balance so that they could see which end would go down. He found that the effect of feedback depended on the specific problem for which it was given. Children who behaved according to rule 1 profited from feedback on problems that disconfirmed rule 1 (the simplest rule) and confirmed rule 2 (such as problem A in Figure 11.6). These children did not, however, profit from feedback on problems that disconfirmed both rules 1 and 2 (such as problem B in the figure). From such data, Siegler suggested that children at one level of rule application are prepared to use information needed to acquire the next rule in the sequence but cannot fathom information that would require them to skip the next rule and go directly to a more advanced one.

Notice that Siegler's account differs from Piaget's not only in its explicitness regarding the mental change but also in its narrowness regarding the kinds of behaviors that change together. Moving to a higher level on conservation problems would not necessarily move a child to a higher-level on balance-beam problems. Whereas Piaget thought of the mind as developing more or less as a whole unit, information-processing theorists commonly study and write about *domain-specific* development. *Domain* refers to a class of problems that are linked by a set of principles they share. A domain might be as narrow as balance-beam problems or addition and subtraction problems (Siegler & Crowley, 1994) or as broad as all of physics or all of mathematics (Karmiloff-Smith, 1992). The principles that underlie and unite any given domain are likely to include some that are innate to the human mind and others that must be acquired through experience.

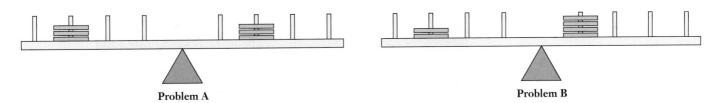

Problem A   Problem B

FIGURE **11.6** *Sample balance-beam problems used by Siegler*
Participants were informed that the weights of the rings were identical and the distances between pegs on each side of the fulcrum were identical. The participants' judgments as to which side would tip down on a series of such problems generally followed one of four rules, ranked from the most primitive to the most sophisticated: (1) Weight alone is considered; the end with more weight is predicted to go down. (2) Weight alone is considered unless the weights on the two sides of the fulcrum are the same (as in problem A), in which case the side with the weights farther from the fulcrum is predicted to go down. (3) Both weight and distance are considered, but when weight is greater on one side and distance is greater on the other (as in problem B), the person just guesses. (4) For each side the sum of the weights multiplied by their distances from the fulcrum is calculated; the side for which that sum is higher is predicted to go down. Siegler (1983) found that most 5-year-olds behaved according to rule 1, most 9-year-olds behaved according to either rule 2 or 3, and most adolescents and adults behaved according to rule 3.

Transforming Implicit Knowledge into Explicit Knowledge

One of Piaget's central ideas was that cognitive development involves not just the acquisition of new information from the environment but also the restructuring of information (schemes) already in the mind. Annette Karmiloff-Smith, a British psychologist who studied and collaborated with Piaget's group in Geneva toward the end of Piaget's career, has recently revived this Piagetian idea and combined it with modern concepts of domain-specific development and multiple forms of memory.

As described in Chapter 9, psychologists who study memory distinguish between *explicit memories*, which are available for conscious thought, and *implicit memories*, which can control behavior but are not available for conscious thought. When you answer questions verbally about what you know, you are calling on your explicit memories; but your everyday behavior is guided by your implicit as well as explicit memories. One large class of implicit memories is *procedural memories*, which include motor habits and tacit (unconscious) rules that guide behavior.

Karmiloff-Smith's (1992, 1994) theory centers on the idea that knowledge can be transformed, within the mind, from one memory type to the other, a process she calls *redescription*. One type of such transformation (discussed in Chapter 9) occurs when previously explicit knowledge becomes implicit through its repeated, routine, uncreative use, a process called *proceduralization*. Her main concern, however, is with the opposite process, called **explicitation**: the transformation of previously implicit memories into explicit ones or of explicit memories into more sophisticated types of explicit memories. Karmiloff-Smith (1994) defines explicitation as the process "by which information *in* the cognitive system becomes explicit knowledge *to* the system." While proceduralization allows us to perform routine actions without conscious thought, explicitation allows us to think about and deliberately modify actions that we previously performed automatically. Explicitation permits us to be inventors, creators, and theorists rather than mere practitioners.

To illustrate the process of explicitation, Karmiloff-Smith (1992) gives the example of a novice pianist who has learned to play a number of pieces by rote. The novice's knowledge is confined to the actual actions of playing. If she is interrupted midway through a piece, she cannot start again where she left off but must go back

16.

How does Karmiloff-Smith's theory of mental redescription build on the concepts of implicit and explicit knowledge to account for the emergence of creativity in a domain?

The advantage of explicit knowledge

According to Karmiloff-Smith, people who convert their implicit knowledge in a skilled domain into explicit knowledge can exhibit more deliberate control, flexibility, and creativity in that domain than they could before. Implicit ability to sing may suffice to be a member of the chorus, but explicitation may be required to become a soloist.

David Young-Wolff / Photo Edit

17.

How does the theory of explicitation account for the worsened block-balancing performance of 6-year-olds compared with 4-year-olds?

to the beginning. If she is asked to state verbally the sequence of notes, she cannot do so except by covertly or overtly playing them and noticing how her fingers move. She cannot produce variations on the piece but can play it only as she learned it. Her abilities are limited in all these ways because her knowledge is implicit, not available for conscious inspection and reorganization. To become a creative artist at the piano, her understanding of piano pieces would have to be redescribed in her memory in ways that permit explicit use of that information. The redescription of a given piece might occur through her repeated thought about the piece as she played it, or it might occur relatively automatically as a consequence of her acquiring, through training and experience, increasingly explicit ways of representing piano pieces in general.

According to Karmiloff-Smith, explicitation often entails some cost to performance early on. In one study she compared 4-, 6-, and 8-year-olds in their ability to balance blocks of various shapes on a narrow rail (Karmiloff-Smith, 1984). Unbeknownst to the children, some of the blocks had lead weights inside them on one side, which caused them to balance way off center. Karmiloff-Smith found that the 4-year-olds were much better than the 6-year-olds at balancing the weighted blocks. The 4-year-olds could not explain any principles of balancing, but their behavior followed the very effective implicit rule of sliding the block away from the direction of its tendency to tip until it balanced. The 6-year-olds, in contrast, had some explicit understanding that objects balance at their center of gravity. They would place a block down with its apparent center over the rail and then let it go. When the block fell, they would pick it up and set it down again at the same spot as before, but *more gently*—and, of course, it would fall again. In other words, the 6-year-olds behaved as blind theorists; they did not use the empirical data as did the 4-year-olds, and when their theory failed, they failed to balance the blocks. The 8-year-olds, however, were the best block balancers. According to Karmiloff-Smith, they had a more sophisticated explicit theory about balancing than did the 6-year-olds and could combine it with their sense of the direction in which the block was tipping.

Consistent with her domain-specific view of development, Karmiloff-Smith writes of *phases* in the development of any particular cognitive ability rather than of *stages* in overall development. She contends that explicitation occurs repeatedly, in many different domains, throughout a person's life depending on his or her experiences and interests. Applying her theory to Baillargeon's and Spelke's research on infants (pages 413–414), Karmiloff-Smith (1992) suggests that the knowledge of core physical principles exhibited by 3-month-olds in selective-looking experiments is implicit. With time, experience, and interest, at least some of that knowledge becomes explicit, and then the child can use those principles in new creative ways.

Vygotsky and the Sociocultural Perspective

The Piagetian and information-processing perspectives on cognitive development focus on the child's own activities and on processes that occur within the child's mind. But children do not develop in a social vacuum. They develop in a sociocultural milieu in which they interact constantly with other people and with products of their cultural history.

The person most often credited with originating the sociocultural perspective on cognitive development is Lev Vygotsky, a Russian scholar who died in 1934 at age 38, after devoting just 10 years to formal research and writing in psychology. Vygotsky agreed with Piaget that cognitive development can be described in terms of the child's internalization of experiences and that the main force for development is the child's active interaction with the environment. But he disagreed with Piaget's conception of the relevant environment. Whereas Piaget emphasized the child's interaction with the physical world, Vygotsky emphasized the child's interaction with the social world. In Vygotsky's view, cognitive development is largely a matter of internalizing the symbols, ideas, and modes of reasoning that have evolved over the course of history and constitute the culture into which the child is born.

The distinction between Vygotsky's and Piaget's perspectives can be illustrated by a story, related by Piaget (1970), about how a mathematician friend of his had, as a child, become fascinated by mathematics:

> When he was a small child, he was counting pebbles one day; he lined them up in a row, counted them from left to right, and got to ten. Then, just for fun, he counted them from right to left to see what number he would get, and was astonished that he got ten again. He put the pebbles in a circle and counted them, and once again there were ten. And no matter how he put the pebbles down, when he counted them, the number came to ten. He discovered there what is known in mathematics as commutativity, that is, the sum is independent of the order.

The story is prototypically Piagetian. The child, through acting on physical objects (pebbles), discovers and is exhilarated by a core principle of mathematics. As Piaget goes on to explain, "The knowledge that this future mathematician discovered that day was drawn, then, not from the physical properties of the pebbles, but from the actions that he carried out on the pebbles." How might Vygotsky have reacted to this story? It was told long after Vygotsky had died, but I imagine him saying: "Where did that young boy learn to count in the first place? Of all the things he might do with pebbles, why did he decide that counting them was worthwhile? The answer lies in the boy's social environment. He was growing up in a culture where number words are in the air and people value counting. He may have discovered with pebbles that day the principle of commutativity, but his social environment had prepared him to make that discovery."

The Role of Language in Cognitive Development

The distinction between Piaget and Vygotsky is typified by their different views on the role of language in the development of thought. Human beings (as I will argue later) are biologically predisposed toward acquiring language, but the specific language that a given child learns is a product of the cultural history of the society into which the child is born and must be acquired in interaction with other people. While Piaget (1970) considered language to be more or less a side effect of the child's development of thought and not essential to it, Vygotsky (1934/1962) argued that language is the foundation for the development of higher human thought. According to Vygotsky, children first learn words as means of communicating with others but then begin to use those words also as symbols for thinking. Their thought becomes *verbal thought*, which, according to Vygotsky, is more powerful than the child's earlier, nonverbal forms of thought. Words are symbols developed over countless generations of human language use. In internalizing language and using it for thought, children internalize a far richer set of symbols than they could possibly invent on their own.

18.

How does Vygotsky's perspective on cognitive development differ from Piaget's?

Ria-Novosti / Sovfoto

Lev Vygotsky

A leader of Russian psychology during the early days of the Soviet Union, Vygotsky developed a theory of human development that emphasized the roles of culture and social interaction.

19.

In Vygotsky's view, how does the acquisition of language lead to a higher form of thought?

The words of a language not only provide the building blocks for verbal thought but also direct it in ways that reflect the culture's activities and values. For example, cultures in which counting is important have developed an efficient set of number words. Children growing up in those cultures begin to recite number words sequentially even before they understand their meaning; and through that ritual act they eventually learn the meaning. As another example, consider the word *because*. Both Vygotsky (1934/1962) and Piaget (1927) noted that children begin to use this word (or rather its Russian or French equivalent) before they fully understand its meaning. Children younger than 6 or 7 years commonly reverse cause and effect, saying such things as "Billy fell off the porch because he broke his arm." To Piaget, the word is incidental to cognitive development; its correct or incorrect use only reflects the child's level of understanding. But to Vygotsky, the word is critical. Using the word in a communicative, social context induces the child to think about its meaning, which leads the child toward a more advanced understanding of cause-effect relationships. *Because* becomes not just a tool for communication but also a tool for private thought.

In support of his view of language as critical to thought, Vygotsky cited Piaget's observation that children of about 4 to 6 years old often talk aloud in a noncommunicative manner. Sometimes such speech occurs when the child is completely alone, and other times it takes the form of a pseudo-conversation. While working on separate projects at a kindergarten table, one child might say, "I'll make it green" (not indicating what he would make green), and another (attending to her own work) might respond, "Horses like sugar and oats."

As you might guess, Piaget and Vygotsky had very different interpretations of such noncommunicative speech. Piaget (1923) believed that it reflects the child's lack of a full understanding of the communicative purpose of language. He argued that children first learn to speak simply as a form of action upon the world and only gradually begin to use speech effectively for communication. Vygotsky (1934/1962), in contrast, contended that noncommunicative speech is a transition phase in the development of verbal thought. It declines at around age 7 because by then non-communicative speech has become silent *inner speech* (Vygotsky's term), or *verbal thought*. With experience, inner speech becomes increasingly abbreviated, and in older children and adults the words are usually not pronounced even to the self but are purely mental symbols.

Consistent with Vygotsky's view, researchers have since found that young children manifest more out-loud noncommunicative speech when working on difficult problems than when working on easy ones (Berk, 1994) and solve problems better when asked to think aloud than when asked to work silently (Kendler, 1972; Kohlberg & others, 1968). In another study, first- and second-graders who manifested the most muttering and lip movement while solving arithmetic problems showed the greatest improvement in their arithmetic ability over the course of a year (Bivens & Berk, 1990).

20.

According to Vygotsky, what is the function of noncommunicative speech in children? What evidence supports Vygotsky's view?

Elizabeth Crews

Thinking with lips and fingers

According to Vygotsky, young children talk to themselves as a means of solving problems. With time and experience, such talk becomes internalized in the form of verbal thought.

The Role of Dialogue and Collaboration in Mental Development

The most fundamental Vygotskian idea is that development occurs first at the social level and then at the individual level. People learn to converse with words (a social activity) before they learn to think with words (a private activity). People also learn how to solve problems in collaboration with more competent other people before they can solve the same kinds of problems alone. Vygotsky (1935/1978) coined the term *zone of proximal development* to refer to the difference between what a child can do alone and what the same child can do in collaboration with a more competent other.

As an example, imagine a 4-year-old girl who begins to play with crayons and paper while her mother is present. The mother, simply from curiosity and because she enjoys talking with her daughter, asks, "What are you going to draw?" The child had never thought of that question before, but to keep the conversation going, she answers, "A giraffe." Now she has a plan, and further conversation with her mother helps her keep it in mind as she draws. The mother makes such comments as "Giraffes have long necks," and the child responds with such comments as "I'll make a long neck." The result is a more purposeful and representational drawing than the child would or could have produced alone. With time, the girl will internalize such conversations and use them (probably out loud at first) to direct her own artistic endeavors. "What shall I draw?" she'll say to herself. "I'll draw a spaceship," she'll answer.

From a Vygotskian perspective, critical thinking—in adults as well as children—derives largely from the social, collaborative activity of dialogue. In actual dialogue, one person states an idea and another responds with a question or comment that challenges or extends the idea. In the back-and-forth exchange, the original statement is clarified, revised, used as the foundation for building a larger argument, or rejected as absurd. From many such experiences we internalize such dialogues, so that we (or what seem like voices within us that represent our friends and critics) question and extend our private thoughts and ideas and in that way improve them or throw them out. Consistent with Vygotsky's view, researchers have found that students who engage in covert dialogues with authors as they read, or who are asked to explain ideas they are studying to a real or imagined other person, acquire a more complete understanding of what they have studied than do those who don't engage in such activities (Chi & others, 1989, 1994; Heiman, 1987).

While Piaget's child can be characterized as a little scientist performing experiments on the world and discovering its nature, Vygotsky's child can be characterized as an apprentice (Rogoff, 1990). The child is born into a social world in which people routinely engage in such activities as drawing, setting the table, and discussing the nature of the universe. Children are attracted to these activities and seek to participate. At first the child's role is small, but it grows as the child gains skill and understanding. From this view, cognitive development is a progression not so much from simple tasks to more complex ones as from small roles to larger roles in the activities of the social world. Barbara Rogoff (1990, 1993) has documented many ways by which children in various cultures involve themselves in family and community activities.

Of course, one prediction of the apprenticeship analogy is that people who grow up in different cultures will acquire different cognitive abilities. A child surrounded by people who drive cars, use computers, and read books will not learn the same mental skills as a child surrounded by people who hunt game, weave blankets, and tell stories far into the night. The apprenticeship analogy also reminds us that logic itself is not the goal of mental development. The goal is to function effectively as an adult in one's society. Achieving that goal entails learning to get along with people and to perform economically valuable tasks. In our society, such ends may for some people entail the kind of mathematical and scientific thinking that Piaget labeled formal operational; but in another society, they may not.

Children's Understanding of Minds

Other people are not only the sources and vehicles of much of our learning but also the topics of much of our learning and thought. Most of us surely spend more time trying to understand other people than trying to understand inanimate objects, and we apply entirely different explanatory concepts to the two endeavors. In our explanatory frameworks, billiard balls move because they are hit by other balls or cue sticks, but people move because they want to get somewhere. We are all psychologists in our everyday lives, continually trying to account for people's behavior in

21.

According to Vygotsky, how are a child's abilities stretched and improved through collaboration with other people? How does Vygotsky's "apprentice" view of the child contrast with Piaget's "scientist" view?

Beryl Goldberg

Apprenticeship

Vygotsky pointed out that children are attracted to activities that involve them in family and community life. This Peruvian girl knitting alongside her mother is preparing for full adult participation in her culture.

22.

In what sense are we all psychologists in everyday life, and what evidence suggests that young children are, too?

terms of their minds. We attribute emotions, motives, feelings, desires, goals, perceptions, and beliefs to people, and we use those attributes to explain their actions.

By the time children have learned language sufficiently to offer verbal explanations—that is, by about 2½ to 3 years of age—they already explain people's behavior in terms of mental constructs (Bartsch & Wellman, 1995; Lillard & Flavell, 1990). They describe a crying person as sad; they say that a person filling a glass with water is thirsty and wants a drink. David Premack (1990) has suggested that, beginning at a very early age, humans automatically divide the world into two classes of entities, those that move on their own and those that don't, and attribute psychological properties to the former but not the latter. When 3- to 5-year-olds saw videos of balls moving like billiard balls, only in response to physical impacts, they described the movements in purely physical terms; but when they saw videos of balls moving and changing direction on their own, they immediately regarded the balls as representing people or animals and described the movements in mental terms (Premack, 1990). A child described one sequence of movements as one ball trying to help another ball get out of a hole. In another experiment, 18-month-old toddlers who observed an adult try but fail at certain tasks—such as inserting a stick into a hole—responded not by copying the adult's failed movements but by completing the tasks successfully (Meltzoff, 1995). Apparently the toddlers interpreted the adult's behavior in terms of an inferred goal, just as you or I would, not in terms of its actual physical movements.

23.

What evidence suggests that most 4-year-olds, but not most 3-year-olds, understand that people can hold false beliefs?

Delay in Understanding False Beliefs

You and I explain people's behavior in terms of their beliefs as well as their intentions, and we know that beliefs can be mistaken. For example, if we see a man carrying an umbrella on a sunny day, we might explain that he must have believed it was going to rain that day. Three-year-olds, however, rarely offer explanations in terms of beliefs (Bartsch & Wellman, 1995), and tests suggest that they do not clearly understand that beliefs can differ from reality (Flavell, 1999).

In one type of test—the *container test*—the child is shown a familiar kind of container, such as an M&Ms bag, which would normally contain a particular content well known to the child (M&M candies). In response to questioning, the child predicts that the familiar content will be found inside. Then the container is opened, and the child sees that it holds not what was predicted but something else, say, a pencil. The container is closed again, and the child is asked to guess what another person—who has not yet looked inside—will think is in it. Most 4-year-olds in the example just given say "M&Ms," just as you or I would; they understand that someone else will be fooled by the familiar bag. But most 3-year-olds say "pencil" (Flavell, 1999; Gopnik & Astington, 1988). Even more surprising, 3-year-olds typically also deny their own previous false belief. When asked, "What did you think would be inside before we opened it," they answer "pencil," in contradiction to what they had actually predicted (Gopnik, 1993).

The problem isn't simply poor memory, because the 3-year-olds in these experiments had no difficulty reporting accurately other things that they had said and done before the container was opened. Nor, apparently, are they lying. They seem not to understand that either they or anyone else can believe something that isn't true. Another type of false-belief test that 3-year-olds typically fail and 4-year-olds typically pass is the *displacement test*, described in Figure 11.7. False beliefs may be particularly difficult constructs to understand because, although they are false, they are by definition held by the believer to be true.

Make-Believe as a Precursor to the Belief-Reality Distinction

Three-year-olds may have difficulty understanding false beliefs, but they have no difficulty understanding pretense. Toddlers who are 2 and 3 years old, as well as older children, engage in an enormous amount of pretend play, and researchers have found that even 2-year-olds clearly differentiate between make-believe and re-

1. Maxi places ball in cupboard.

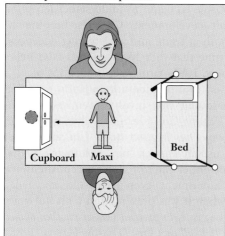

2. Maxi leaves and a second doll enters.

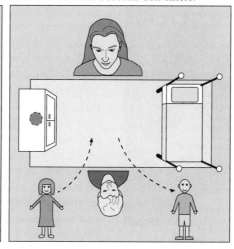

3. Second doll takes ball out of cupboard and puts it under bed.

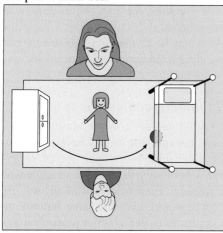

4. Maxi reenters.

Where will Maxi look for the ball?

FIGURE **11.7** *A test of children's understanding that one can have a false belief about an object's location*

In the displacement test of understanding false beliefs, the child watches a doll (Maxi, in this example) place an object (a ball) in a particular location (a cupboard). Then Maxi leaves, and another doll comes in and moves the ball to a new location (under the bed). Then Maxi returns, and the child is asked to predict where Maxi will look for the ball. Most 4-year-olds say that Maxi will look in the cupboard, but most 3-year-olds say that he will look under the bed (Perner, 1991; Wimmer & Perner, 1983). The 3-year-olds are able to report correctly where Maxi had originally put the ball and to report correctly that Maxi was out of the room when it was moved, yet they continue to maintain that Maxi will look for the ball in the new location.

ality. A 2-year-old who turns a cup filled with imaginary water over a doll and says, "Oh oh, dolly all wet," knows that the doll isn't really wet (Leslie, 1994). Alan Leslie (1987, 1994) has suggested that children's understanding of false beliefs emerges from their earlier understanding of pretense. Pretense is very similar to false belief. Both, by definition, are mental conceptions that depart from reality. The only difference between the two is that pretenders know that their conception doesn't match reality whereas believers think that theirs does. Three-year-olds, who fail false-belief tests, do not fail analogous tests in which they are asked to report what either they or another person had *imagined* or *pretended* was in a box before it was opened (Lillard & Flavell, 1992; Woolley, 1995).

Children everywhere engage in pretend play, whether or not they are encouraged to do so. Piaget (1962) regarded such play as an expression and exercise of the child's ability to symbolize objects in their absence, but many developmental psychologists today ascribe even further significance to it. Leslie (1991) suggests that the brain mechanisms that enable and motivate pretend play came about in evolution because such play provides a foundation for understanding nonliteral mental states, including false beliefs. A child who understands that pretense differs from reality has the foundation for understanding that people's beliefs (including the child's own beliefs) can differ from reality and that people can fool others by manipulating their beliefs. Certainly, in the history of human affairs, an understanding of deception has often marked the difference between survival and death, and

24.

What evidence suggests that pretend play may be an evolutionary adaptation whose function is to enable children to understand false beliefs and other nonliteral mental states?

Scott Barrows / International Stock

I'm flying (but not really)

A child of 2 or 3 years old who pretends that a box with its flaps out is an airplane knows that it is not really an airplane. The understanding that pretense and reality are different comes well before the understanding that people can hold sincere beliefs that are false.

25.

How does research on people with autism support the premise that the understanding of minds and the understanding of physical objects are fundamentally distinct abilities?

natural selection might well have produced brain mechanisms that allow people to begin to understand deception rather early in their development. Children become increasingly skilled both at using and at detecting deception at about the same time that they begin to pass false-belief tests (Sodian & others, 1991; Yirmiya & others, 1996).

Pretend play may also provide a foundation for other sorts of logical reasoning that involve premises not anchored in physical reality. Consider this syllogism: *All cats bark. Muffins is a cat. Does Muffins bark?* Children under about 10 years old usually answer "no," and their explanations show that they either can't or won't accept the initial premise. Yet in an experiment, even 4-year-olds succeeded on that syllogism when it was presented in a playful voice and in words that began *Let's pretend I'm on another planet. On that planet I see that all cats bark* (Dias & Harris, 1988). Children apparently have, early in their development, two separate modes of thinking: a fictional mode and a reality mode. Young children can apparently think quite well in either mode, but they do not at first combine the two. Advancement in thinking may entail, in part, the bringing together of these two modes for specific types of problems. Understanding false beliefs may be an early and quite universal result of such conjoining, and deductive reasoning from hypothetical premises may be a later, more culture-dependent result.

Autism: A Developmental Disorder in Understanding Minds

Suppose you were oblivious to the minds of other people. You would not feel self-conscious or embarrassed in others' presence, because you would have no understanding of, or concern for, their thoughts about you. You would not ask others about their thoughts or inform them of yours, because you would have no reason to. You would not look where others look, attend to their words, or in any way try to fathom their perceptions and beliefs. People would serve the same function to you as inanimate objects or machines. You might try to get a bigger person's attention to help you get a cookie from the top shelf in the kitchen, but that person's attention would have no value to you in and of itself.

If you had these characteristics, you would almost certainly be diagnosed as having **autism**, a congenital (present-at-birth) disorder that in some cases is genetic in origin and in others may stem from prenatal damage to the brain (Rodier, 2000). The major diagnostic features of autism are severe deficits in social interaction, severe deficits in acquiring language, a tendency toward repetitive actions, and a narrow focus of interest (American Psychiatric Association, 1994). Among the earliest signs of autism in infants are failure to engage in prolonged eye contact, failure to synchronize emotional expressions with those of another person, and failure to engage in shared visual attention (Baron-Cohen, 1995; Mundy & others, 1990). The deficit in language seems clearly to be secondary to the lack of interest in communication. Unlike children who fail to learn language because of deafness, autistic children rarely use gestures as an alternative form of communication, and when they do, it is almost always for instrumental purposes (for example, to get someone to help them reach a cookie). Those who learn language at all learn it late, almost invariably with the help of deliberate teaching, and their language always contains peculiarities that seem to reflect a lack of sensitivity to other people's minds and perspectives.

In a groundbreaking book about her own daughter's autism, Clara Park (1967) described how Elly at age 6 learned with ease such words as *curve*, *triangle*, and *heptagon*, which have objective definitions relating to the physical world, but had enormous difficulty with such typical 6-year-olds' words as *love*, *friend*, *good*, *bad*, *think*, and *see*, which pertain to the subjective, psychological world. She simply didn't have the mental concepts to which to tie the latter words. Like nearly all children with autism who learn language, Elly also had special difficulty with the pronouns *I* and *you*, whose definitions depend on the implicit understanding that two people in a conversation have different perspectives. As Park (1967) put it,

> It is perfectly logical, when one considers it. Elly [at age 8] thinks her name is *you* because everyone calls her that. No one ever calls her *I*. People call themselves *I*, and as a further refinement Elly began to call them *I* herself. . . . I have come to wonder how it is that ordinary two-year-olds can grasp anything so subtle [as the *I-you* distinction], yet they do. . . . The correct use of the first- and second-person pronouns cannot be grasped by logic. The social sense must take over and straighten things out. . . . Elly's usage is rigidly consistent, severely logical. What it lacks is that social instinct which guides even the dullest of normal children in the labyrinth of personal relations.

In view of what you have read so far, it should come as no surprise that people with autism perform poorly on false-belief tests and on tests of ability to deceive others or to detect deception (Baron-Cohen, 1995; Yirmiya & others, 1996). In one experiment (Leslie & Thaiss, 1992), relatively high-functioning autistic children and adolescents, whose ages averaged 12 years and whose verbal abilities were equivalent to those of normal 6-year-olds, were compared with normal 4-year-olds on two false-belief tests and two false-picture tests. The false-belief tests were versions of the container and changed-location tests described previously, and the false-picture tests were constructed to be analogous to those but to assess the understanding that a photograph, rather than a belief, might misrepresent reality. In one false-picture test, for example, the child saw a photograph being taken of an object at one location. Then the object was moved to a new location, and the child was asked where the object would be in the photograph when it was developed. The results of the experiment are shown in Figure 11.8. As you can see, the autistic children and adolescents performed much worse than the normal 4-year-olds on the false-belief tests but better on the false-picture tests. This experiment not only demonstrates the specificity of the intellectual impairment in autism but also suggests that the human capacity to understand mental representations (beliefs) is distinct from the capacity to understand physical representations (pictures).

In line with Leslie's theory that pretend play is a developmental precursor to understanding false beliefs and other nonliteral mental states, autistic children have consistently been found to lack such play (Wing & others, 1977; Wulff, 1985). Autistic children explore the real physical properties of objects, as do normal children, but they do not make one object stand for another or pretend that an object has properties different from those it actually has. In contrast, children with developmental disorders such as Down syndrome, including those who are more retarded than autistic children in their understanding of the physical world, do engage in pretend play (Hill & McCune-Nicolich, 1981) and eventually develop a much better understanding of false beliefs and deception than do autistic children (Baron-Cohen & others, 1985; Yirmiya & others, 1996).

A few people with autism can perform well in school and employment, but even they have difficulty understanding false beliefs and other nonliteral mental states. In describing one such person, who had earned a Ph.D. and developed a successful career in agricultural science, Oliver Sacks (1995) wrote: "In her ingenuousness and gullibility, Temple [Grandin] was at first a target for all sorts of tricks and exploitations; this sort of innocence or guilelessness arising not from moral virtue but from failure to understand dissembling and pretense." Grandin described herself as a literal thinker, concerned with facts more than theories and unable to appreciate most poetry and fiction. She explained that she could get along reasonably well in society not because she had any intuitive understanding of people's hidden thoughts and intentions but because she had carefully studied the surface forms of

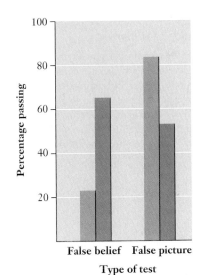

FIGURE **11.8** *Performance of autistic individuals and normal 4-year-olds on false-belief and false-picture tests*
Each person was tested in two false-belief tests and in two false-picture tests designed to be analogous to the false-belief tests. Shown here is the percentage of each group of subjects who passed both false-belief tests and the percentage who passed both false-picture tests. (Data from Leslie & Thaiss, 1992.)

26.

How does research on autism support the idea that an understanding of false beliefs and deception may derive, in part, from prior engagement in pretend play?

A voice of autism

Temple Grandin, despite having autism, has developed a successful career in agricultural science. She claims that her unique perspective on the world, in which she has had to learn about humans as though she were "an anthropologist on Mars," has given her a better understanding of nonhuman animals.

Michael Schwartz / Gamma Liaison

people's behavior, could mimic those forms, and could use them with moderate success to predict people's actions. She described herself in this endeavor as "an anthropologist on Mars" (Sacks, 1995).

SECTION SUMMARY

Piaget proposed that the mind consists of schemes, or mental blueprints for actions, and that mental growth occurs when children assimilate new experiences into their existing schemes and the schemes accommodate to those experiences. He proposed, further, that children progress through four stages of mental development, each characterized by a new type of scheme. During the sensorimotor stage, thought is inseparable from physical action. At the preoperational stage, children can symbolize objects and events that are absent. At the concrete-operational stage, children know that certain actions, called operations, are reversible, which allows them to understand principles of conservation. At the formal-operational stage, children have a more abstract understanding of the reversibility of operations, applicable to hypothetical as well as concrete situations. Piaget's theory is vague about the underlying causes of change during development and underestimates the role of the social environment.

From the information-processing perspective, the mind is in some ways like a computer. General reasoning ability improves throughout childhood as a result of increased mental speed and capacity of working memory. Reasoning in specific realms improves as knowledge in those realms increases and as implicit knowledge becomes increasingly explicit.

From the sociocultural perspective, initiated by Vygotsky, the major change underlying mental growth in young children is the acquisition and internalization of language. Language is a powerful tool for learning from other people, and it provides the foundation for verbal thought. Because words are symbols that are products of cultural history, verbal thought unites the child's mind with the culture as a whole. Vygotsky and researchers in his tradition have also pointed out many ways in which children learn, apprenticelike, through observing and interacting with people who are older and more skilled than themselves.

In recent times, much research has centered on young children's understanding of other people's minds. Children's early understanding of intentionality, imagination, and pretense may lay the groundwork for their later understanding—by about 4 years of age—that people's behavior is guided by their beliefs and that beliefs may be false. Autistic children are deficient in their ability to learn about minds. They do not engage in pretend play and do not learn that people may behave in accordance with false beliefs.

DEVELOPMENT OF LANGUAGE

Clara Park's observation of the difficulty that her autistic daughter had in learning many aspects of language led her to marvel at the ease with which nonautistic children learn language. Of all the things that people can do, none seems more complex than understanding and speaking a language. Thousands of words and countless subtle grammatical rules for modifying and combining words must be learned. Yet nearly all people master their native language in childhood; in fact, most are quite competent with language by the time they are 3 or 4 years old. How can children too young to tie their shoes or understand that 2 plus 2 equals 4 succeed at such a complex task? Most developmentalists agree that language learning requires innate mechanisms that predispose children to it, coupled with an environment that provides adequate models and opportunity to practice. In this section, we will first consider briefly the question of what language is, then chart the normal course of language development, and finally explore the innate and environmental requisites for that development.

The Nature of Language

Just what is it that children learn when they learn a language? Linguists estimate that approximately 3000 separate languages exist in the world today, all distinct enough that the speakers of one cannot understand those of another (Foss & Hakes, 1978). Yet these languages are all so fundamentally similar to one another that we can speak of *human language* in the singular (Pinker & Bloom, 1992).

Some Universal Characteristics of Human Language

Every language has a vocabulary consisting of a set of *symbols*, entities that represent other entities. The symbols in a language are called **morphemes,** defined as the smallest meaningful units of a language, that is, the smallest units that stand for objects, events, ideas, characteristics, or relationships. In all languages except the sign languages used by the deaf, morphemes take the form of pronounceable sounds. Most morphemes are words, but others are prefixes or suffixes used in consistent ways to modify words. Thus, in English, *dog* is both a word and a morpheme, *-s* is a morpheme but not a word, and *dogs* is a word consisting of two morphemes (*dog* and *-s*). The word *antidisestablishmentarianism* contains six morphemes (*anti-dis-establish-ment-arian-ism*), each of which has a separate entry in an English dictionary.

In any language, we can distinguish two general classes of morphemes. One class, **content morphemes,** includes nouns, verbs, adjectives, and adverbs—the morphemes that carry the main meaning of a sentence. The other class, *grammatical morphemes,* includes (in English) articles (*a, the*), conjunctions (such as *and, but*), prepositions (such as *in, of*), and some prefixes and suffixes (such as *re-, -ed*). These serve primarily to fill out the grammatical structure of the sentence, although they also contribute to meaning.

27.

What are the universal characteristics of morphemes, and how do morphemes differ from the signals used in nonverbal forms of communication?

Human language at the United Nations

Because all human languages contain certain underlying similarities, it is possible to translate any statement in one language into a corresponding statement in any other language. Language is a universal human trait, which, according to the spirit of the United Nations, can be used to help bring peace and unity to humankind.

Christopher Morris/Black Star

Morphemes in any language are both arbitrary and discrete. A morpheme is *arbitrary* in that no similarity need exist between its physical structure and that of the object or concept for which it stands. Nothing about the English morpheme *dog*, or the French morpheme *chien*, naturally links it to the four-legged, barking creature it represents. Because morphemes are arbitrary, new ones can be invented whenever needed to stand for newly discovered objects or ideas or to express newly important shades of meaning. This characteristic gives language great flexibility. A morpheme is *discrete* in that it cannot be changed in a graded way to express gradations in meaning. For example, you cannot say that one thing is bigger than another by changing the morpheme *big*. Rather, you must add a new morpheme to it (such as *-er*) or replace it with a different morpheme (such as *huge*).

In contrast, the types of signals used in nonverbal forms of communication found among other animals as well as humans (discussed in Chapter 3) are neither arbitrary nor discrete. Nonverbal signals typically develop from and bear physical resemblance to such actions as fighting or fleeing, the intentions of which they communicate. Moreover, nonverbal signals can be presented gradationally. One expresses *more* surprise, anger, or whatever nonverbally by presenting the signal more vigorously or with greater amplitude of movement. In everyday speech, you might communicate that one thing is bigger than another by saying, "This one is big but that one is *big*," but the vocal emphasis placed on the second *big* is a nonverbal addition. In speech, we commonly mix nonverbal with verbal communication to get our point across (which is one reason why speaking is easier than writing).

In addition to commonalities in their symbol systems, all languages share a particular hierarchical structure of units (see Figure 11.9). The top level (largest unit) is the sentence, which can be broken down into phrases, which can be broken down into words or morphemes, which can be broken down into elementary vowel and consonant sounds called **phonemes.** The power of this organization is that the relatively few phonemes (anywhere from 15 to 80 occur in any given language) can be arranged in different ways to produce an enormous number of possible words, which themselves can be arranged in different ways to produce a limitless number of possible phrases and sentences. Every language has rules—collectively referred to as the **grammar** of the language—that specify permissible ways to arrange units at one level to produce the next higher level in the hierarchy. Grammar includes rules of *phonology*, which specify how phonemes can be arranged to produce morphemes; rules of *morphology*, which specify how morphemes can be combined to form words; and rules of **syntax**, which specify how words can be arranged to produce phrases and sentences. These rules differ from language to language, but every language has them, and similarities exist across all languages in the fundamental nature of the rules (Pinker & Bloom, 1992).

28.

How can any sentence be described as a four-level hierarchy, and how can rules of grammar be described in relation to that hierarchy?

FIGURE **11.9** *The hierarchical structure of language*
These four levels of organization characterize every spoken language.

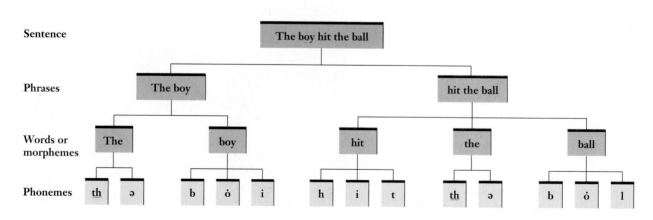

Sentence	The boy hit the ball
Phrases	The boy	hit the ball
Words or morphemes	The	boy	hit	the	ball
Phonemes	th ə	b ȯ i	h i t	th ə	b ȯ l

The Tacit Nature of Grammar

People often think of grammar as something they learned (or tried to learn) in elementary school (also called *grammar* school, perhaps for that very reason). But grammar is learned tacitly, without conscious effort, long before formal schooling. The fact that 4-year-olds can carry on meaningful conversations with adults, producing and understanding new and unique sentences, indicates that by age 4 children have already acquired the essential grammar of their native language. Four-year-olds can't name or describe the rules of grammar (nor can most adults), yet they use them every day. Indeed, even professional linguists have yet to describe the full grammar of any of the world's languages (Jackendoff, 1994). Grammatical rules in this sense are like the rules that underlie the sequence and timing of specific muscle movements in walking or running; both sets of rules are generally encoded in *implicit* rather than explicit memory. We generally can't state them, but we use them when we walk, run, or carry on a conversation.

People's tacit knowledge of grammar is demonstrated in their ability to distinguish acceptable from unacceptable sentences. Nearly every English speaker can identify *The mouse crawled under the barn* as a grammatical sentence and *The crawled barn mouse the under* as nongrammatical, although few can explain exactly why. The ability to distinguish grammatical from nongrammatical sentences is not based simply on meaning. As the linguist Noam Chomsky (1957) pointed out, English speakers recognize *Colorless green ideas sleep furiously* as grammatically correct but absurd.

The Course of Language Development

Early Perception of Speech Sounds

Infants seem to treat speech as something special as soon as they are born and maybe even before. When allowed to choose between tape-recorded sounds by sucking in different ways on a nipple, 3-day-olds chose to listen to human speech rather than to other sounds such as instrumental music (Butterfield & Siperstein, 1974). In other experiments, babies as young as 2 hours old, who had not heard their mother speak since their birth, chose their own mother's voice over that of another woman (DeCasper & Fifer, 1980; Querleu & others, 1984). The mother's voice is audible in the womb, and during the last few weeks before birth her voice has a quieting effect on the fetus, as indexed by reduced muscle movements (Hepper & others, 1993).

The ability of very young infants to hear the differences among speech phonemes has been demonstrated in many experiments. One technique is to allow an infant to suck on a pacifier that is wired to trigger the playing of a particular sound each time a sucking response occurs. When the baby becomes bored with a sound, as indicated by a reduced rate of sucking, the sound is changed (maybe from *pa* to *ba*). Typically, the rate of sucking increases immediately thereafter, which indicates that the infant hears the new sound as different from the previous one. Another method, which can be used with infants older than 5 months, is described in Figure 11.10 (page 438).

The results of such experiments suggest that babies younger than 6 months old hear the difference between any two sounds that are classed as different phonemes in any of the world's languages. After 6 months, however, they begin to lose the ability to distinguish between sounds that are classed as the same phoneme in their native language but as distinct phonemes in another language (Kuhl, 1987; Werker & Tees, 1999). For example, regardless of what culture they are growing up in, babies under 6 months old can distinguish among the subtly different /t/ sounds that constitute different phonemes in Hindi but not in English; but older children and adults in an English-speaking culture do not hear those differences (Werker & Tees, 1999; Werker & others, 1981). Similarly, children growing up in a Japanese

29.

What is meant by saying that rules of grammar are tacit?

30.

What is the evidence that humans pay special attention to speech even before birth and that during the first year after birth their perception and production of speech sounds are modified to conform with their native language?

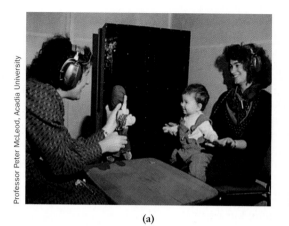
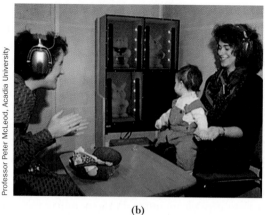

(a)   (b)

FIGURE **11.10**   *A procedure for testing infants' abilities to detect changes in a speech sound*

The infant sits on the mother's lap and attends to a toy held by the researcher while a speech sound is played repetitively through a loudspeaker (a). Occasionally the sound changes, and very shortly after each change an attractive toy to the infant's right is lit up and begins to move (b). Thus the infant is rewarded by the sight of the toy for turning to the right when the speech sound changes. After the infant is well trained in this procedure, the head-turn response can serve as an index that the infant distinguishes the new sound from the old one. The mother and researcher wear headphones that prevent them from hearing the critical sound and inadvertently cuing the infant as to when to turn. (From Werker & Tees, 1992.)

culture lose the distinction between the English /*l*/ and /*r*/, which belong to the same phoneme category in Japanese (Eimas, 1975). The sharpest loss occurs between 6 and 12 months of age, which is when babies are beginning to recognize and occasionally mimic words in their native language. The loss is not due to a decline in sensory acuity; with special training, adults can regain the ability to hear the sound differences (Lively & others, 1993; Werker & Tees, 1999). The loss is best understood as an adaptive change in how the sounds are automatically categorized and heard (Werker & Desjardins, 1995). Presumably, it is useful to hear different phonemes within one's native language as different, but it is confusing to hear different versions of the same phoneme as different.

Cooing and Babbling

Beginning at birth, infants can cry and produce various other vocal signs of distress, but at about 2 months they begin to produce a new, more speechlike category of sounds called *cooing*, which consists of repeated drawn-out vowels (*oooh-oooh, eeeh-eeeh*). Between about 4 and 6 months, cooing changes gradually to *babbling*, which consists of repeated consonant-and-vowel sounds such as *paa-paa-paa* or *tooda-tooda*. Cooing and babbling occur most often when the infant is happy. They seem to be forms of vocal play that have evolved to help the infant exercise and refine the complex muscle movements needed to produce coherent speech.

Coos and the earliest babbles do not depend on the infant's hearing spoken sounds. Deaf infants coo and begin to babble at about the same age and in the same manner as hearing infants (Lenneberg, 1969), and early babbles are as likely to contain foreign-language sounds as native-language sounds (Locke, 1983). By 8 months of age, however, hearing infants begin to babble in ways that mimic the rhythm and pitch patterns of the language they hear around them; the babbling of a French baby becomes recognizably French, and that of a British baby becomes recognizably British (de Boysson-Bardies, 1999). Beginning at about 10 months of age, hearing infants produce babbled sounds that increasingly resemble syllables and words of their native language (de Boysson-Bardies, 1999; Locke, 1983). Also, at this age, deaf infants who are exposed to a sign language begin to babble with their hands—repeating over and over some of the hand movements that are components of words in the language they see around them (Pettito & Marentette, 1991). Eventually, recognizable words appear in the hearing infant's vocal babbling and the deaf infant's manual babbling.

First Words

31.

When is a word really a word?

When my son Scott was about 10 months old, his mother and I noticed that some of his babblelike sounds were not random but occurred reliably in specific contexts. He would say *ticka-ticka-ticka* while tickling things, *gooda-gooda-gooda* while playfully eating baby food, and *hewo* into the receiver of our telephone when we let him play with it. We excitedly recorded these as our son's "first words." But now I have to ask: Were they really words? A word is a symbol. A symbol is an entity that refers to something outside itself—some object, action, event, characteristic, or abstract idea. Did Scott use *ticka*, *gooda*, or *hewo* to refer to anything, or were the sounds simply part of his action of tickling things, eating, and playing with the telephone, which he had learned by imitating his parents? There is no way to answer this question with certainty, but systematic observations have shown that babies very commonly produce wordlike sounds as components of other actions before they begin to produce them in a clearly referential way (Greenfield & Smith, 1976; Snow, 1999). Some developmental psychologists refer to these prewords as *performatives* to distinguish them from words that serve true symbolizing functions.

No sharp division exists between performatives and true words. The vocalization that we recorded as our son's sixth "word" was *ba*. At first he would say *ba* only after he had been given his bottle, so the sound may well have been a performative. He would say *ba-ba-ba-ba* as soon as he got the bottle, as part of the joyous act of taking it into his hands, and occasionally would repeat the sound between bouts of sucking. Eventually, however, he began to use the sound in different contexts. For example, one time he pointed to his bottle on the kitchen shelf and happily said *ba*. Now, at what may have been his first true use of a word, he seemed to be using the sound to label the object he saw. It is significant, too, that in this early use of *ba* as a label he was not hungry or asking for the bottle—he refused it when it was subsequently offered—but was simply pointing it out. A general rule, based on observations of many babies, is that early words are usually used first to name things that are present and only later to ask for things (Bloom & Lahey, 1978).

Mapping the World into Words

New words come slowly at first, but then, typically at about 15 to 20 months of age, the rate begins to accelerate. Between the ages of 2 and 5 years the typical child learns words at a phenomenal rate—an average of about 10 per day, or nearly 1 word every waking hour (Jackendoff, 1994). Relatively few of these are explicitly taught to the child; more often, the child must infer the meaning of a new word from the context in which others use it. How does the child draw these inferences?

Most of the earliest words learned, in any language culture, are nouns that refer to categories of objects in the child's environment (Golinkoff & others, 1994). Young children's tendency to look at whatever an older person is looking at (discussed earlier) no doubt helps them identify objects that the older person is referring to when speaking. Experiments have shown that infants are especially likely to follow an adult's gaze when the adult is labeling an object in the environment (Baldwin, 2000). In addition, young children seem to have a number of cognitive biases, or built-in assumptions, that help them narrow down the likely referent to a new word they hear (Golinkoff & others, 1994). One of these is a strong tendency to link new words with objects for which they do not already know a name.

Other things being equal, young children assume that a new word is not a synonym for a word they already know but a label for something whose name they don't know. In one experiment, 3- and 4-year-olds were presented with toy animals that they could name (a pig, a sheep, and a cow) plus one that they could not name (a tapir). When they heard the novel word *gombe* in the presence of these objects, all the children applied it to the novel animal (Clark, 1987). Other research indicates that toddlers begin to manifest this bias at about the same time, in their second year of life, that they begin their vocabulary spurt (Mervis & Bertrand, 1994). Although the bias leads to some mistakes, it is apparently much more helpful than harmful to their acquisition of words.

Laura Dwight / Peter Arnold

First words

Naming objects is an important step in the mastery of language. It is also a source of great delight to infants and their caregivers. Here 1-year-old Genevieve uses her favorite word, *light*.

32.

How do children make the link between new words that they hear and appropriate referents in their environment?

By the time they can understand multiword sentences, young children are able to use their tacit knowledge of grammar to help them infer the meaning of new words, including verbs and other parts of speech as well as nouns (Gleitman & Gillette, 1995; Naigles, 1990). Thus if they are shown a videotaped scene and told, "The duck and bunny are biffing," 2-year-olds—who understand *duck* and *bunny* and tacitly know that words ending in *-ing* refer to actions—infer that *biffing* means whatever the duck and bunny are both doing. If told, instead, "The duck is biffing the bunny," they infer that *biffing* means whatever the duck is doing to the bunny. As another example, 2-year-olds who heard "Mommy feeds the ferret" inferred that a ferret is an animal, not an inanimate object (Goodman & others, 1998).

Extending Words to Fit Appropriate Categories

33.

How might children's overextensions of new words be explained in terms of (a) their bias toward assuming that all nouns are common nouns, (b) learning based on features of the referent, and (c) their desire to communicate about entities for which they have no label?

In addition to linking a new word to its immediate referent, children must learn how to *extend* it to new referents. Common nouns such as *ball* refer to categories of objects, and a full understanding is demonstrated when a child applies the word to all members of the category and not to nonmembers. Researchers have found that young children, including even infants as young as 12 months, behave as though they assume that a newly heard label applies not just to the specific object that has been labeled but also to other objects that are perceptually like the original one (Golinkoff & others, 1995; Waxman & Markow, 1995). In other words, infants are biased toward assuming that labels are common nouns, not proper nouns. The bias leads to some mistakes, as when a child refers to all men as *Daddy*, but is useful overall because the vast majority of nouns to be learned are common nouns.

In addition to using proper nouns as though they were common nouns, children often *overextend* common nouns, using them more broadly than adult usage would allow. On the basis of an analysis of many examples, Eve Clark (1973) proposed that overextension results when a child implicitly defines a new word in terms of just one or a few of the prominent features of the original referent object. Thus a child who hears *ball* in association with a specific ball might take the object's most prominent feature—its roundness—as the defining characteristic and subsequently refer to all round objects, including oranges and full moons, as balls. In other cases, overextensions may not represent errors at all but simply derive from children's attempts to communicate about objects that they have not yet learned to name (Clark, 1995). A toddler who says, "Look doggie," while pointing to a cat, may in essence be saying, "Look at that thing that is something like a doggie." The same child, when asked which animals in a set are dogs, may pick the actual dogs and not the cats (Thomson & Chapman, 1977).

Children also *underextend* words, applying them to more narrowly defined categories than do adults (Anglin, 1977). In fact, some research suggests that underextension is more common than overextension (MacWhinney, 1998). But underextensions do not result in errors in children's spontaneous speech. They are difficult for researchers to detect and haven't been studied very much.

The remarkable fact, however, is not that children make errors in their extensions but that they so often extend new words appropriately. A child's ability to discern quickly the category that an adult is referring to with a new word is testament to the child's social sensitivity. Children with autism, who lack normal social sensitivity, have great difficulty learning the appropriate extensions of new words, even with deliberate training (Tomasello & others, 1993).

Using Grammatical Rules

34.

What evidence indicates that children use syntax to understand sentences even before they can speak in multi-word sentences?

All children go through a relatively prolonged period during which each of their utterances is only one word long. When they do begin to put words together, typically at about 18 to 24 months of age, they at first use content words almost exclusively, especially nouns and verbs, and usually arrange them in the grammatically correct sequence for simple, active sentences (Brown, 1973). For an English-speaking child, this means that subjects are placed before verbs, and verbs before objects. A child at the two-word stage will say "Billy kick" to mean that Billy is kicking something, and "Kick Billy" to mean that someone is kicking Billy. Apparently, children learn the rules of word order for simple sentences in the active voice before they begin to produce such sentences. Further evidence for that sequence comes from an experiment in which 16- to 18-month-olds, most of whom were still in the one-word stage of speaking, saw two simultaneous videos. One screen depicted Big Bird tickling Cookie Monster, and the other depicted the reverse. When the children heard the words "Look, Big Bird is tickling Cookie Monster!" they looked mostly at the first screen, and when they heard "Look, Cookie Monster is tickling Big Bird!" they looked mostly at the second screen (Hirsh-Pasek & Golinkoff, 1991).

When children acquire a new grammatical rule, such as adding *-ed* to the end of a verb to create the past tense, they almost invariably overgeneralize it at first (Kuczaj, 1977; Marcus & others, 1992). The 3-year-old who says "kicked," "played," and "laughed" also says "goed," "thinked," and "swimmed." Similarly, children who have just learned to add *-s* to pluralize nouns will talk about many *mouses*, *sheeps*, and *childs*. This overgeneralization confirms that children really know the rule. If they followed the rule only when adults did, their usage might be attributed to simple imitation. As further evidence suggesting that their grammar is based on rules, young children have been shown to use the rules with made-up words that they had never heard before (see Figure 11.11).

35.

What evidence suggests that young children's grammatical constructions are based on their knowledge of rules and do not result from simple mimicry?

This is a wug.

Children are not taught the rules of grammar explicitly; nobody sits a 2-year-old down and tries to explain how to create infinitives, possessives, or past-tense verbs. Some parents correct their children's grammar, but even this is rare (Brown & Hanlon, 1970), and long-term experiments in preschools have shown that deliberate programs of correcting grammar have little ef-

**Now there is another one.
There are two of them.
There are two _____.**

FIGURE 11.11
One wug and two _____?
With this test, Jean Berko found that children who had just begun to use the rule of forming plurals by adding *-s* would use the rule correctly even for words they had never heard before. (From Berko, 1958.)

fect on rule acquisition (de Villiers & de Villiers, 1979). Through their own devices, children actively (and mostly unconsciously) infer grammatical rules from examples of rule-based language spoken around them and to them.

Internal and External Supports for Language Development

How is it that children can learn language so early, with so little apparent conscious effort and without deliberate training? There is no doubt that humans enter the world in many ways equipped for language. We are born with (a) anatomical structures in the throat (the larynx and pharynx) that enable us to produce a broader range of sounds than any other mammal, (b) brain areas specialized for language (including Broca's and Wernicke's areas, discussed in Chapter 5), (c) a preference for listening to speech and an ability to distinguish among the basic speech sounds of any language, and (d) mechanisms that cause us to exercise our vocal capacities through a period of cooing and babbling regardless of experience. There is also no doubt that most of us are born into a social world that provides rich opportunities for learning language. We are surrounded by language from birth on, and when we begin to use it, we achieve many rewards through this extraordinarily effective form of communication.

36.

How did Chomsky link the study of grammar to psychology? What did he mean by a language-acquisition device?

Noam Chomsky and the Concept of an Innate Language-Learning Mechanism

The linguist Noam Chomsky, more than anyone else, was responsible for drawing psychologists' attention to the topic of language. In his enormously influential book *Syntactic Structures* (1957), Chomsky characterized grammatical rules as fundamental properties of the human mind. In contrast to an earlier view held by some psychologists that sentences are generated in chainlike fashion, with one word triggering the next in a sequence, Chomsky emphasized the hierarchical structure of sentences. He argued that a person must have some meaningful representation of the whole sentence in mind before uttering it and then must apply grammatical rules to that representation in order to fill out the lower levels of the hierarchy (phrases, morphemes, and phonemes) to produce the utterance. Similarly, he maintained that when listening to a sentence, a person must hear it as a whole (not as a chain of separate words) and apply grammatical rules to understand it.

To get an idea of the arguments that Chomsky employed, consider this sentence: *The boy who likes Mary hit the ball.* How do you know from the sentence that it was the boy and not Mary who hit the ball? Apparently, you are able to view the sentence as more than a sequence of individual words or word pairs and use its whole structure to understand its meaning. Some rule you know about English syntax tells you that in this case *Mary* does not belong with *hit* but, instead, is part of a set of words modifying *boy*. The rule tells you that the core sentence is *The boy hit the ball* and that *who likes Mary* has been inserted to clarify which boy. Even young children must know that rule, since they can understand the sentence.

Chomsky (1957, 1965, 1968) conceived of grammatical rules as aspects of the human mind that link spoken sentences ultimately (through one or more intermediary stages) to the mind's system for representing meanings.

Chris Felver / Archive Images

Noam Chomsky

In his book *Syntactic Structures*, Chomsky called attention to the idea that producing a verbal statement is a creative act guided by implicit mental rules. This work and the revolution in psycholinguistics that it inspired have enriched research and theory in cognitive psychology.

Although specific grammatical rules vary from one language to another, they are all, according to Chomsky, based on certain fundamental principles, referred to as *universal grammar*, that are innate properties of the human mind. These properties account for the universal characteristics of language discussed earlier and for other, more subtle language universals (Pinker, 1994). To refer to the entire set of innate mental mechanisms that enable a child to acquire language quickly and efficiently, Chomsky coined the term ***language-acquisition device,*** or ***LAD.*** The LAD includes the inborn foundations for universal grammar plus the entire set of inborn mechanisms that guide children's learning of the unique rules of their culture's language. Support for the concept of an innate LAD comes in part from observations of specific inabilities to learn particular aspects of language due to damage in particular brain areas (discussed in Chapter 5) or due to a genetic disorder (specific language impairment, discussed in Chapter 3).

Children's Invention of Grammar

Further support for the LAD concept comes from evidence showing that young children invent grammar when it is lacking in the speech around them. New languages occasionally arise when people from many different language cultures simultaneously colonize an area and begin to communicate with one another. These first-generation colonists communicate through a primitive, grammarless collection of words taken from their various native languages—a communication system referred to as a ***pidgin language.*** Subsequently, the pidgin develops into a true language, with a full range of grammatical rules, at which point it is called a ***creole language.*** Derek Bickerton (1984) studied creole languages from around the world and found that at least some of them became fully developed in one generation by the children of the original colonists. Apparently, the children imposed grammatical rules on the pidgin they heard and used those rules consistently in their own speech—powerful evidence, in Bickerton's view, that children's minds are innately predisposed to grammar. Bickerton also found that creole languages in various parts of the world, which emerged from different sets of parent languages, are more similar to one another in grammatical structure than are long-standing languages. Bickerton takes this, too, as evidence for innate grammar. Other languages have evolved away from the grammatical constructions that are most natural to the human mind, but creole languages have not existed long enough to undergo this transformation.

Bickerton's evidence of children's role in language invention is necessarily indirect, as he was studying languages that emerged many years ago. More recently, other researchers have documented the emergence of a new sign language among the deaf in Nicaragua (Kegl, 1994; Senghas, 1994). Prior to 1979, deaf Nicaraguans had little opportunity to meet other deaf people. There was no deaf community or common sign language, and the deaf were typically treated as though they were retarded. In 1980, the new Sandinista government created the first Nicaraguan schools for the deaf, so deaf people for the first time came into extended contact with one another. Based on outmoded ideas, the schools did not at first teach any sign language but, instead, attempted to teach the deaf to speak and lip-read the nation's vocal language (Spanish), a policy that almost always fails. Despite the official policy, the students began to communicate with one another using hand signs.

At first their signing system was a manual pidgin, an unstructured and variable amalgam of the signs and gestures that the individuals had been using at home. But over the course of a few years the signs became increasingly regularized and efficient, and a system of grammar emerged. All this occurred naturally, with no formal teaching, simply through the students' desire to communicate with one another. Of most significance for our discussion, the new grammar was produced not by the oldest, wisest members of the community but by the youngest. In fact, those who were more than about 10 years old when the deaf community was formed not only failed to contribute to the development of grammar but learned little of that which eventually did develop (Senghas, 1994). The sign language invented by the children has since become the official sign language in Nicaragua. It is a true language, comparable to American Sign Language, in which the morphemes are elementary hand movements and grammatical rules stipulate how the morphemes can be combined and sequenced into larger units.

Children's improvement of grammar may be viewed by us as a creative act, but it is almost certainly not experienced as that by the children themselves. Children tacitly assume that language has grammar, so they unconsciously read grammar

Stephen McBrady / PhotoEdit

The drive to communicate

When people lack the ability to hear, the drive to communicate manifests itself in sign languages. Whether they communicate by vocal language or a manual sign language, children infer or even invent the rules of grammar from the language that they have heard or seen around them.

into language even where it doesn't exist. Just as children learning English over-generalize grammatical rules when they say things like *goed* and *mouses*, and thereby temporarily make English grammar more consistent and elegant than it really is, children exposed to a pidgin language may accept the slightest, random hint of a grammatical rule as a true rule and begin to use it as such.

The Critical-Period Hypothesis

The research on sign language in Nicaragua is consistent with other evidence that the LAD functions much more effectively in childhood than later in life—an idea referred to as the *critical-period hypothesis* (Lenneberg, 1969). Occasionally a hearing person is discovered who has been deprived of language throughout childhood, and in each such case studied the person subsequently has been unable to learn language fully (Curtiss, 1989). The most thoroughly studied such person, known as Genie, was rescued in 1970, at age 13, from the inhuman conditions in which her deranged father and dominated, partly blind mother had raised her (Curtiss, 1977; Rymer, 1993). From shortly after birth until her rescue, Genie had been locked in a tiny bedroom and been exposed to almost no speech. At the time of her rescue she understood a few words but could not string words together and had learned no grammar. She was subsequently placed in a foster home where she was exposed to English much as infants normally are and received tutorial help. In this environment, she eventually acquired a large vocabulary and learned to produce meaningful, intelligent statements; but even after 7 years of language practice, when Genie was 20, her grammar lagged far behind other indices of her intelligence (Curtiss, 1977). A typical sentence she produced was "I hear music ice cream truck," and she often misunderstood sentences whose meaning depended on grammar.

The Language-Acquisition Support System

Children come into the world predisposed to acquire language, but they do not acquire it in a social vacuum. Neither Genie nor any other child has ever invented language alone. Normal language development requires not just the LAD but also the **LASS**—the **language-acquisition support system**—provided by the social world into which the baby is born (Bruner, 1983).

In our culture and many others, adults typically simplify their speech to infants and young children in ways that might help the children learn words and some aspects of grammar. They enunciate more clearly than when speaking to other adults (Kuhl & others, 1997), use short sentences that focus on the here and now, repeat salient words, and use gestures to help convey meaning (Snow, 1984). A 6-month-old playing with a ball might be told, "Oh, you have a *ball*. A nice *ball*. What a pretty *ball*." Such speech is often referred to as *parentese* (although it is not just par-

37.

What evidence supports the view that grammar is learned more readily in early childhood than later in life?

38.

What special aspects of the LASS in our culture may help infants acquire language? What light has been shed on the LASS by cross-cultural research?

Taking account of the listener
Most people automatically simplify their speech when talking to infants and young children. Even young children addressing younger children deliberately slow their rate of speech, choose simple words and grammatical structures, and gesture broadly.

Lew Merrim / Monkmeyer

ents who speak this way to babies), and some evidence suggests that it does help children learn language. In one study, 2- to 3-year-olds whose mothers had spoken the simplest forms of parentese to them during the previous year spoke more maturely than did those whose mothers had used more complex language (Furrow & others, 1979).

Research in other cultures, however, has revealed that parentese as we know it is by no means universal, yet children everywhere acquire language at roughly the same rate (Ochs & Schieffelin, 1995). Bambi Schieffelin and Elinor Ochs (1983) found, for example, that the Kalikuli people of the New Guinea rain forest believe that there is no reason to speak to babies who cannot yet speak themselves. These babies hear no parentese, but they go everywhere with their mothers and constantly hear the speech of adults and children. Once Kalikuli children do begin to speak, adults help them not so much by simplifying their own speech as by stating explicitly the proper way to say things. Apparently, large variations can occur in the LASS without impairing children's ability to learn language.

Language Learning by Nonhuman Apes

Our closest relatives, chimpanzees and bonobos (discussed in Chapter 3), have brains that are structurally quite similar to ours. Although neither species communicates in its natural environment with anything like the symbol-based, grammar-based system we call human language, both species are highly gregarious and have complex systems of nonverbal communication. What would happen if you took such a creature out of its natural community and raised it with humans, exposing it to language in the same rich way that human children normally are? Even dogs raised with us learn to make some use of our language. My golden retriever gets excited whenever she hears *outside* or *leash* in the conversation around her. What might a chimpanzee or bonobo learn in a similar living situation?

In an attempt to find out, Allen and Beatrix Gardner (1978, 1989) began in 1966 to raise a young female chimp named Washoe in the constant presence of people who directed language to her as well as to one another. Because the Gardners hoped that Washoe would learn to produce as well as understand language, they and others involved used a modified version of American Sign Language rather than a vocal language. Chimpanzees lack the vocal apparatus needed to produce the sounds of human speech, but they have flexible fingers capable of producing manual signs. Washoe's success in acquiring some of the elements of language inspired many subsequent ape-language projects. Researchers have since studied language learning in a number of other chimpanzees, several bonobos, a gorilla, and an orangutan (Miles, 1983; Patterson & Linden, 1981; Savage-Rumbaugh & Fields, 2000).

The Accomplishments of Kanzi

The most linguistically accomplished ape to date is a bonobo named Kanzi, whose learning has been nurtured and documented by Sue Savage-Rumbaugh and her associates. Before working with Kanzi, Savage-Rumbaugh had been using operant conditioning to teach chimpanzees to communicate through an invented language in which the words are geometric figures called *lexigrams* that are arranged on a keyboard (see Figure 11.12, page 446). In 1981, Savage-Rumbaugh was, with little success, training Kanzi's mother in the lexigram system when she noticed that young Kanzi, who had been allowed to run free in the laboratory, was learning to use some of the lexigrams correctly just by watching, even though he wasn't being rewarded. This inspired Savage-Rumbaugh to try a different method with Kanzi, that of immersion in a language culture rather than systematic training. Kanzi was continuously free, but not forced, to communicate, using a stationary keyboard in the lab and a portable one outdoors. Kanzi's caretakers used both spoken English

39.

What LASS was supplied for the bonobo Kanzi? What are Kanzi's (and other apes') linguistic accomplishments and limitations to date?

FIGURE **11.12** *Kanzi using the lexigram keyboard*
Kanzi is a bonobo, a species of ape very closely related to chimpanzees and humans. Each symbol on the keyboard is a word. When Kanzi depresses a key, it is illuminated both on the keyboard and on a larger screen that his caretakers can see. Kanzi also has a portable keyboard that he carries with him as he roams a forested area with his caretakers.

40.

What conclusions may be tentatively drawn from the ape-language studies?

and lexigrams with and around him, and they responded to Kanzi's lexigrams and gestures as parents might to the communicative attempts of their child. Their task was not to teach Kanzi language, but to communicate with him as best they could as they and he went about their daily activities. My inference from the reports and films on Kanzi is that he received more linguistic attention and heard more parentese than does a typical child.

Kanzi soon learned to use all the lexigrams appropriately, and his behavior indicates that he does not simply use them to get rewards (Savage-Rumbaugh & others, 1986, 1993). For example, he uses the lexigram for *apple* after he already has an apple. He also often announces his intentions before acting, even though he doesn't need permission to act. Before taking a trip to the tree house, he presses the lexigram for *tree house*. In addition, he regularly combines lexigrams with nonverbal gestures in order to get across more complex ideas than would be possible with the limited set of lexigrams on his board. For example, to get caretaker A to chase caretaker B, he presses the lexigram for *chase* and then pushes A's hand in the direction of B.

Even more impressive than Kanzi's use of lexigrams is his understanding of spoken English. His behavior suggests that he knows the meanings of at least 500 English words (Savage-Rumbaugh & Fields, 2000). When Kanzi was 8 years old, he was tested for his ability to carry out spoken requests that he had never heard before, such as "Put the egg in the noodles" and "Hammer the ball." The requests were made by a caretaker who stayed out of view so that nonverbal cues could not guide Kanzi's behavior. Kanzi carried out most of the requests successfully, performing at a rate comparable to that of a 2½-year-old human girl who was given the same requests (Savage-Rumbaugh & others, 1993). Kanzi also responded appropriately to requests whose meaning depended on word order, such as "Make the doggie bite the snake" and "Make the snake bite the doggie" (using a toy dog and toy snake as props). More recently, two other bonobos and a chimpanzee in Savage-Rumbaugh's care have been exposed to language in the same manner that Kanzi was, and their abilities approach that of Kanzi (Savage-Rumbaugh & Fields, 2000).

Tentative Conclusions from the Ape-Language Studies

Has Kanzi or any other ape learned human language? Some scholars argue about that as if it were a meaningful question, but it isn't. The answer depends entirely on how one chooses to define *human language*. A more sensible question is this: What aspects of human language have nonhuman apes been able to acquire, and what aspects, at least so far, seem beyond them? Taking all the studies together, apes appear to be relatively adept at acquiring a vocabulary, and systematic tests suggest that they can use signs and lexigrams as true symbols, standing for referents, and not merely as performatives or as operant responses to obtain rewards (Sevcik & Savage-Rumbaugh, 1994). Moreover, Kanzi can apparently use word order to decipher the meanings of some simple multiword sentences. However, no ape to date has acquired or invented a rule for distinguishing plural from singular nouns, for marking the tense of verbs, or for marking any words by grammatical class. Apparently, the brain mechanism that makes grammar so easy and natural for human children came about in our evolution sometime after we split off from the line leading to chimpanzees and bonobos.

To me, the most interesting general conclusion from the ape-language research has to do with the conditions that optimize learning. Attempts at deliberate, focused training, involving rewards for correct language usage, have generally failed (for example, Terrace, 1985). In those cases the animals learned to produce wordlike gestures as ways to get rewards rather than truly as symbols to label their experiences. Success has occurred when the focus was on communication rather than training. It has occurred when the researchers entered the ape's world for long periods and brought the ape into their world, using words and sentences along the way. This is similar to the conditions in which most human children learn language. The function of language is communication, and a major prerequisite for acquiring language is a desire to communicate.

SECTION SUMMARY

Human language is a hierarchically structured system of communication in which phonemes are combined into words, words into phrases, and phrases into sentences— all in accordance with rules of grammar. Infants come into the world with a strong tendency to attend to human speech and, apparently, with an ability to hear the differences among all the sounds that constitute distinct phonemes in any of the world's languages. They also go through stages of cooing and babbling that exercise their ability to articulate language sounds. During their second half-year, babies learn to hear as the same all sounds that are classed as a single phoneme within their native language, and, at the same time, their babbling begins to sound increasingly like the speech that surrounds them. Word learning begins in the second year and is facilitated by the child's tendency to look at what adults are looking at and by certain biases that help the child determine the most likely referent for a new word. Children tacitly learn most of the grammar of their language by the time they are 3 or 4 years old, and some of the mistakes they make—such as saying mouses or goed—indicate that they follow the rules even when the language makes exceptions.

The fact that humans learn grammar so quickly and well, with so little guidance, suggested to Chomsky that humans must be born with a "language-acquisition device" (LAD) that includes an implicit understanding of language universals and special neural mechanisms for picking up the specifics of one's native language. Consistent with Chomsky's view is research—including that on creole languages and on deaf children's communication—indicating that children growing up in social environments that lack a grammatical language impose grammar on the languagelike system to which they are exposed and thereby convert it into a full language. Language acquisition also depends on a "language-acquisition support system" (LASS) that includes other people who use the language. Nonhuman apes raised with people who attempt regularly to communicate with them linguistically acquire the ability to understand simple sentences and to communicate their experiences using wordlike symbols and gestures. Such research suggests that some aspects of the LAD had begun to evolve before the division between humans and the other apes, but that the full capacity for grammar came after that division.

CONCLUDING THOUGHTS

Thinking and talking are—to use a term introduced in Chapter 3—*species-typical* activities of humans. We are biologically predisposed for thought and language, just as we are predisposed to smile and walk on two legs. The human brain has been specialized for these activities in the course of evolution; people everywhere, in every culture, think and talk in ways that are recognizably human and distinguishable from the activities of any other species. Yet, despite their universality, these abilities must develop anew in each human being.

1. Why thought and language must develop Why aren't these species-typical abilities fully present at birth? An immediate answer is that birth occurs in humans at a relatively early stage in the body's growth. The brain, including the pathways required for thought and language, continues to mature after birth. A more profound answer, however, lies in the ultimate functions of thought and language. Thought serves to make sense of the environment so that we can navigate safely

41.

Why must thought and language develop, and how can this chapter be reviewed by considering the innate foundations and social supports for development?

through it and use parts of it to promote our survival and reproduction. We can survive in a wide range of conditions because we can think of ways to modify them to suit our needs. To do so, we must consider not just the universals of every environment, such as the fact that unsupported objects fall to the earth, but also the particulars of our specific environment, such as the foods that are available and tools that are needed. Similarly, to communicate effectively in our particular cultural group, we must acquire the specific linguistic devices (the words and grammar) that have emerged in our group's history and represent concepts that are crucial to survival in that group. In other words, to be effective, thought and language must be fine-tuned to the unique physical and social environment in which each individual must survive, and such adjustment can be accomplished only through development in that environment.

2.   Innate foundations for development   Evolution could not endow human beings with the specific knowledge and skills needed to survive in every human environment, but it could and did endow the species with a solid foundation for acquiring them. This theme, of innate foundations for development, can help you tie together many of the ideas and research findings that you have read about in this chapter. As you review, consider the following questions: What inborn assumptions may help each new person make sense of his or her physical, social, and linguistic worlds? What universal aspects of babies' and children's explorations and play may help them learn about the particulars of their native environment and language? How have studies of people raised in unusual conditions and of people with particular brain disorders contributed to psychologists' understanding of these innate foundations?

The findings and ideas to which you can relate these questions include (a) infants' preferences for novelty, their mode of examining objects, their drive to control their environment, and their knowledge of core physical principles; (b) Piaget's ideas about the roles of action, assimilation, and accommodation in development, and other researchers' theories about domain-specific development and the process of explicitation; (c) young children's understanding of false beliefs, the absence of such understanding in autistic children, and the possible role of make-believe in acquiring that understanding; (d) the roles of early attention to language, of vocal play, and of inborn biases and drives affecting vocabulary and grammar acquisition; and (e) Chomsky's concept of a language-acquisition device, and other researchers' studies of children who invented language.

3.   Social supports for development   The innate tendencies and drives that promote development are useless without a responsive environment. Babies need solid surfaces against which to exercise their muscles in order to learn to walk, objects to explore in order to learn about the physical world, and people to listen to and with whom to exercise their linguistic play in order to learn to talk. Young children may, as Piaget contended, choose what to assimilate from the smorgasbord of information around them, but adults help provide the smorgasbord. As you review the chapter, consider the specific ways in which the child uses and is influenced by the social environment. In particular, consider (a) infants' employment of mimicry, joint visual attention, and social referencing to guide their explorations; (b) Vygotsky's theory of the roles of language, dialogue, and cooperative action in the development of thought; and (c) the role, in language development, of the language-acquisition support system. In the next chapter, on the development of social relationships, you will read much more about ways in which variation in the social environment can influence development.

Further Reading

Kang Lee (Ed.) (2000). *Childhood cognitive development: The essential readings*. Malden, MA: Blackwell.

This is a collection of 19 articles published by contemporary developmental psychologists. They were selected because they are representative of current theory and research in the field of cognitive development and are quite readable by the nonspecialist. Included are articles on children's development of perception, motor control, attention, language, understanding of minds, mathematics, scientific reasoning, physical knowledge, and moral understanding.

Jean Piaget (1929). *The child's conception of the world*. London: Routledge & Kegan Paul.

Many of Piaget's books are difficult to read, but this one, written early in his career, is an exception. In the introduction, he spells out his method of learning about children's understanding through interviewing them. The book is about children's thoughts on such issues as where the names of things come from, where rain comes from, and what it means to think. The book provides a historical foundation not just for Piaget's subsequent work but for the whole subfield of psychology concerned with cognitive development.

Lev S. Vygotsky (1934; reprinted 1962). *Thought and language* (E. Haufmann & G. Vaker, Eds. and Trans.). Cambridge, MA: MIT Press.

This book was first published in the Soviet Union in 1934, shortly after Vygotsky's death from tuberculosis at age 38, but was not translated into English until 1962. It is a fascinating collection of papers in which Vygotsky sets forth his theory that the internalization of language is critical to the development of human thought.

Simon Baron-Cohen (1995). *Mindblindness: An essay on autism and theory of mind*. Cambridge, MA: Bradford Books/MIT Press.

This book, written for both specialists and nonspecialists, cogently summarizes research on young children's understanding of minds and explains how the study of people with autism has led to new insights about normal children's understanding.

Steven Pinker (1994). *The language instinct*. New York: Morrow.

Pinker is not only a leading expert on language but a gifted user of it. In delightfully clear and humorous prose, he elaborates on essentially all the ideas about language and its development that are touched on in this chapter, plus much more. Have you ever wondered why baseball announcers say the batter "flied out" the last time up, rather than "flew out"? Pinker answers this and dozens of other questions about language.

Looking Ahead

This chapter, on the development of thought and language, has already touched on the idea that development depends on children's social experiences. The next chapter, about the development of social relationships from birth through old age, elaborates much more fully on the theme that development is a social process.

Chapter 12

Fin del Corrido (detail), Diego Rivera

Social Development

Each of us is born into a social world to which we must adapt. Over the span of our lives we are involved continually in relationships with other people that sustain, enhance, and give meaning to our existence. As *infants* we depend physically and emotionally on adult caregivers. As *children* we learn to get along with others and to abide by the rules and norms of society. As *adolescents* we begin to explore romantic relationships and, in other ways, seek a niche in the adult world. As *adults* we assume responsibility for the care and support of others and contribute through work to the broader society.

Social development refers to the changing nature of our relationships with others over the course of life. What characterizes our ties to other people at each life phase? How do those relationships, at each phase, influence our subsequent development? How variable is social development from culture to culture and between males and females? These are the principal questions of this chapter, which begins with some general ways of thinking about social development and then proceeds, section by section, through the life span, from infancy through old age.

CONCEPTIONS OF SOCIAL DEVELOPMENT

Before we proceed to the sections on infancy, childhood, adolescence, and adulthood, it will be useful to consider some broad theoretical perspectives that have influenced research and theory on social development in each life stage. Such theories can be divided roughly into three classes, which are not mutually exclusive: (a) *biological theories*, which view development as maturation and the playing out of inborn social drives or instincts; (b) *cultural theories*, which regard development as adaptation to the particular norms and values of a person's culture; and (c) *cognitive theories*, which consider social development to be a product of an individual's more general growth in mental ability and ways of thinking.

The Playing Out of Inborn Drives or Instincts

Many of the earliest biologically based ideas about social development came from or were inspired by the work of Sigmund Freud (1856–1939). Freud's psychodynamic theory of personality (discussed in Chapter 15) centers on the role of universal human drives, particularly the sexual and aggressive drives, which often bring people into conflict with one another and with social norms. According to Freud, social development is fundamentally a matter of learning to channel one's sexual and aggressive drives in socially acceptable ways, a process that occurs most intensely during the first 5 to 6 years of life in the child's interactions with parents.

Following Freud, other psychodynamic theorists enlarged the number of drives that they deemed crucial to development and in some cases also expanded the age range over which significant development was posited to occur. The most influential such theory was developed by Erik Erikson.

Erikson's Psychosocial Theory of Life Stages

1.

What kinds of conflicts form the basis for Erikson's stages, and what are the consequences of positive or negative resolution of a given conflict?

Sarah Putnam / The Picture Cube

Erik H. Erikson

Erikson (shown here with his wife) was an intellectual nonconformist whose formal academic training ended with high school. His novel views have had a major impact on the study of children's development, and his clear and graceful literary style has made his books accessible to the general public.

2.

How do the writings of Bowlby and Konner reflect an application of Darwinian thinking to issues of social development?

Erik Erikson (1902–1994)—who was trained in psychoanalysis by Anna Freud, Sigmund Freud's daughter, and always considered himself to be a Freudian—developed a theory of the life course that divides it into a series of stages. Instead of focusing on sex and aggression, Erikson's theory centers on a set of *social drives*, which motivate people to develop social ties and to establish themselves as useful members of society. Erikson proposed that these drives are biologically based and operate to make the human being a fundamentally social animal.

More specifically, Erikson (1963) divided the life span into eight *psychosocial stages*, each associated with a particular problem or crisis to be resolved. Further, he posited that the manner in which a person resolves the crisis at each stage adds a new dimension to personality, which affects the person's life at all subsequent stages. As you study Erikson's stages, described in Table 12.1, notice that the outcome of each can vary along a continuum between two opposite poles, one positive (strengthening the person and fostering further healthy development) and the other negative. For example, an infant emerges from the first stage with a tendency toward either *basic trust* (the positive pole) or *basic mistrust* (the negative pole). Notice also how each stage builds on the one preceding it. According to Erikson, positive resolution at one stage is generally a prerequisite for positive resolution at the next, although all is not lost if a positive resolution eludes the person at a given stage. With an appropriate social environment and determination, a person can at least to some degree reverse the outcomes of previous stages.

Ethological and Evolutionary Perspectives

From an evolutionary perspective, the mechanisms underlying human behavior, including those that produce change in behavior with age, are products of natural selection; that is, they evolved because they helped our ancestors survive and reproduce (Bjorklund & Pellegrini, 2000). Freud, Erikson, and other early psychodynamic theorists claimed to be influenced by Darwin in their focus on biological underpinnings of human behavior, but they did not analyze their posited drives, instincts, and stages in terms of their specific functions in promoting survival and reproduction, as Darwin would have.

Ethologists in Europe began in the 1930s to examine animal behavior in explicitly Darwinian terms (as discussed in Chapter 3). They observed that many behavior patterns—including some that occur at specific stages of life—are universal among members of a species and can be understood in terms of their roles in helping individuals survive and reproduce. Attachment behaviors, for example, help bond infants with their parents during the time when much care is needed, and courtship behaviors help bond an adult male and female together to produce and care for young.

One of the first developmental psychologists to be influenced by ethology was John Bowlby (1907–1990), a British child psychiatrist. Bowlby (1982) contended, in particular, that the emotional bond between human infant and adult caregiver is promoted by a set of instinctive tendencies in both partners. They include the infant's crying to signal discomfort, the adult's distress and urge to help on hearing the crying, the infant's smiling and cooing when comforted, and the adult's pleasure at receiving those signals. Bowlby also discussed certain universal childhood fears, such as fear of the dark and of strangers, in terms of their roles in promoting survival.

Other proponents of the evolutionary perspective (e.g., Konner, 1981) have pointed out that some aspects of human development that seem puzzling when viewed in our culture become more understandable when viewed in the hunting-

TABLE 12.1 *Erikson's stages of psychosocial development*

A positive outcome at each stage increases the person's self-confidence and ability to relate constructively to others.

Stage 1: Basic trust versus mistrust (birth to 1 year)

Babies enter the world completely at the mercy of others. If the first caregiver (usually the mother) meets a baby's needs dependably, the baby learns to trust that person, and this generalizes into a trust of others and the self.

Stage 2: Autonomy versus shame and doubt (1 to 3 years)

As they gain voluntary control of their actions, children become increasingly willful. The resulting disputes with parents result in *autonomy* if the child gains a rewarding sense of self-control but in *shame and doubt* if the child acquires a punishing sense that whatever he or she does is inadequate or bad.

Stage 3: Initiative versus guilt (3 to 5 years)

Having gained control of their own actions, children begin to plan their actions in advance, which leads to a crisis about planning. A positive resolution entails a sense of *initiative* (confidence in ability to plan and initiate actions), and a negative resolution entails a sense of *guilt* about one's plans and a sense of inability to guide one's own future.

Stage 4: Industry versus inferiority (5 to 12 years)

As children become involved with such organized enterprises as chores, school assignments, and games and hobbies, they may experience the pleasure of work completion through perseverance, which will lead to a sense of competence, or *industry*, or they may experience the opposite, which will lead to a sense of *inferiority*.

Stage 5: Identity versus identity confusion (adolescence)

As their bodies become more adultlike, young people struggle for an *identity*—a sense of who they are and where they are going in life. Successful resolution leads to a *positive identity*, with an ability to function in ways beneficial to self and society. Unsuccessful resolution leads to either *identity confusion* (no stable identity) or a *negative identity* (one that is unhealthy or antisocial).

Stage 6: Intimacy versus isolation (young adulthood)

Young adulthood is a time for learning to share oneself with another person. Success leads to *intimacy*, the capacity to make and abide by concrete commitments to other people. Failure can lead to a lifelong sense of *isolation*, even if surrounded by other people.

Stage 7: Generativity versus stagnation (middle adulthood)

During this longest life stage, roughly from age 25 to 65, caring for others—in family, friendships, and work—leads to *generativity*, a sense of contributing to the next generation. Failure leads to *stagnation*, a sense of boredom and meaninglessness.

Stage 8: Integrity versus despair (late adulthood to death)

Successful resolution of the previous crises leads, finally, to a sense of *integrity*. The integrated person can look objectively at life, see broad truths, and counsel wisely those in earlier stages. Failure in the earlier crises may lead to *despair*, a helpless and bitter sense that life has been incomplete and will end so.

and-gathering cultures that characterized human existence through most of our evolutionary history. Later you will read about how knowledge of hunter-gatherer existence has shed light on such issues as infants' bedtime protests and children's patterns of play.

Adapting to Culture-Specific Norms and Values

Whereas biologically oriented theories emphasize the underlying similarities among humans in all cultures, which arose from our evolutionary history, cultural theories focus on cross-cultural differences that illustrate the flexibility of human nature. Human development is, at least in part, a matter of adapting to the social customs and economic conditions of the culture into which one is born. Therefore, a full account of development in any given culture requires an understanding of those customs and conditions.

Look back at Erikson's eight stages (Table 12.1) and consider them from a cultural perspective. Notice that the onset of Stage 4, *industry*, coincides with the age at which children in our society start primary school; Stage 5, *identity*, with the age at which people in our society are trying to decide on a career; Stage 6, *intimacy*, with the age at which people are expected to become engaged or married; Stage 7, *generativity*, with the age at which people are expected to be raising children and working hard at their careers; and Stage 8, *integrity*, with the age at which many people retire and hope to enjoy a more contemplative style of life. If Erikson had been raised in a non-Western, agrarian (agriculture-based) society, in which people

3.

How might the cultural perspective provide an alternative explanation of Erikson's stages?

Michael Krasowitz / FPG

4.

How does Bronfenbrenner's social ecology theory explain why any specific aspect of the immediate environment can produce different effects on children in different cultures?

Mother-Daughter interaction: A matter of culture

A phase of rebellion and psychological separation from parents may be a normal stage of development for young people in western cultures, but in Asian cultures—which place greater emphasis on family interdependence and less on individual independence—such a phase would be considered highly unusual. Increasingly, developmental psychologists have come to understand that human development varies significantly from culture to culture.

live in extended families and children work alongside their elders in the fields at a very early age, would he have come up with the same eight stages? To what degree do the stages represent human universals, and to what degree do they stem from traditions and practices that are specific to some cultures and not others? These are the kinds of questions that the cultural perspective begs us to ask.

One of the leaders in the attempt to account for cross-cultural differences in children's development is Urie Bronfenbrenner (1979, 1986), who proposed a *social ecology theory*. In biology, *ecology* refers to the entire network of interactions and interdependences among living things and their physical environment. In Bronfenbrenner's usage, **social ecology** refers to the entire network of interactions and interdependencies among people, institutions, and cultural constructs (such as tools, religions, and modes of communication) to which the developing person must adapt psychologically.

Bronfenbrenner depicts a child's social ecology as a set of concentric circles, illustrated in Figure 12.1. At the center is the individual child. The *immediate environment* surrounding the child consists of the people and things with which the child is in contact at any given moment. The next level, the *interrelation among immediate environments*, refers to the relationships among those parts of the world that serve as the child's immediate environment at different times. For example, home and school are two immediate environments of a child in our culture. According to Bronfenbrenner (1986), the relationship between home and school is as important to the child's development as are the separate qualities of the two. Thus a child's ability to learn at school depends not only on how he or she is taught there but also on the parents' attitudes about the school, which in turn affect the child's attitudes. The next circle in Bronfenbrenner's theory is the *social context*, which consists of aspects of society that affect the child even though the child does not come into direct contact with them. In our culture, the parents' places of work, the school board, the local government, the producers of television programming, and so on influence development through their effects on the child's environment. The outermost circle in Bronfenbrenner's theory is the *cultural context*, which is the entire set of beliefs, values, and accepted ways of behaving that characterize the historically connected group of people of which the child and his or her family are a part.

FIGURE 12.1
Bronfenbrenner's model of social ecology
Urie Bronfenbrenner conceives of the child as developing within a system of social influences, which can be visualized as a set of concentric circles arranged according to the degree to which they pertain specifically to the child or to the broader society and culture of which the child is a part. (Adapted from Bronfenbrenner, 1979, with descriptive labels replacing his original, technical designations.)

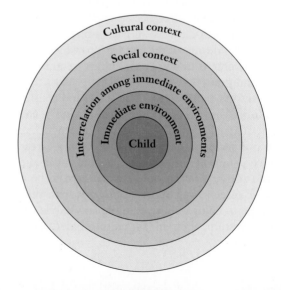

Growing Socially by Growing Mentally

Most developmental psychologists today consider the child to be a mentally active contributor to his or her own development, an idea most strongly emphasized by Jean Piaget (and discussed in Chapter 11). Piaget (1932/1965) argued further that changes in children's social behavior reflect changes in their more general understanding of the world. For example, as children become more cognizant of cause-effect relationships in the physical world, they also become more cognizant of cause-effect relationships in the social world; this understanding influences their views of right and wrong and their modes of interacting with others. You will read later of Lawrence Kohlberg's theory of moral development, which was inspired by Piaget's work.

Lev Vygotsky (1934/1962, 1935/1978), the Russian psychologist whose ideas about the social bases of human thought were introduced in Chapters 10 and 11, contended that children actively build mental models of appropriate behavior from examples in the social environment. Concepts such as right, wrong, female, male, friend, enemy, and responsibility exist in the social environment and are symbolized in the words that children learn. From these examples and symbols, children construct their own understanding and then use it to guide their behavior. Vygotsky's theory integrates the cultural and cognitive perspectives, and it is by no means incompatible with a biological perspective. Combining all three perspectives, we might posit that evolution has endowed children with social instincts that lead them to attend to and assimilate into their minds those facets of their environment that are most critical to survival and reproduction within their culture.

As we proceed through the life course in the rest of this chapter, you will encounter many examples that illustrate the value of a broad perspective that acknowledges the contributions of biology, culture, and cognition to social development. Indeed, I suspect that the more you think about what you read, the more convinced you will become that these three forces are inseparably intertwined in almost every developmental phenomenon of interest to psychologists.

5.

How have Piaget's and Vygotsky's theories of cognitive development influenced ideas about social development? How can the three perspectives—biological, cultural, and cognitive—be combined?

SECTION SUMMARY

Theories of social development fall into three rough categories. (1) Biological theories focus on universal drives, instincts, and stages that are understood as aspects of human nature. An example is Erikson's theory, which relates each life stage to a different psychosocial need and problem to be resolved. Also in this category are Bowlby's theory of infant-caregiver attachment and modern evolutionary theories that attempt to identify the survival value of behaviors that occur at various life stages. (2) Cultural theories—such as Bronfenbrenner's social ecology theory—view development as adaptation to the particular norms and values of the culture into which the child is born. (3) Cognitive theories, such as Kohlberg's theory of moral development, are concerned with the relationship between intellectual development and social development. As children aquire more understanding, they behave toward others in more advanced ways. Vygotsky's theory, which emphasizes the cultural locus of the knowledge that children aquire, combines the cultural and cognitive perspectives.

INFANCY: USING CAREGIVERS AS A BASE FOR GROWTH

Human infants are absolutely dependent on caregivers for survival, but they are not passively dependent. They enter the world biologically prepared to learn who their caregivers are and to elicit from them the help they need. By the time they are born, babies already prefer their own mother's voice to another woman's voice (discussed in Chapter 11), and within a short time they also prefer her smell and sight (Bushnell & others, 1989; Macfarlane, 1975). Newborns signal distress through fussing or crying, and by the time they are 3 months old they express clearly and effectively their interest, joy, sadness, and anger through their facial expressions and respond differentially to such expressions in others (Field, 1990; Izard & others, 1995). With such actions, infants help build an emotional bond between themselves and those on whom they most directly depend, and then they use those caregivers as a base from which to explore the world. In the 1950s, Bowlby began to use the term ***attachment*** to refer to such emotional bonds, and since then the study of infants' attachment to caregivers has become a major branch of developmental psychology.

Infants' Attachment to Caregivers

At about the same time that Bowlby was beginning to write about attachment, Harry Harlow initiated a systematic program of research on attachment with rhesus monkeys. With monkeys, Harlow could control conditions experimentally to learn about the developmental consequences that occurred when the infants were raised in isolation from their mothers and other monkeys. Most relevant to our present theme are experiments in which Harlow raised infant monkeys with inanimate surrogate (substitute) mothers.

Harlow's Monkeys Raised with Surrogate Mothers

In one experiment, Harlow (1959) raised infant monkeys individually in isolated cages containing two surrogate mothers—one made of bare wire and the other covered with soft terry cloth (see Figure 12.2). The infants could feed themselves by sucking milk from a nipple that for half of them was attached to the wire surrogate and for the other half was attached to the cloth surrogate. Harlow's purpose was to determine if the infants would become attached to either of these surrogate mothers, as they would to a real mother, and which characteristic—the milk-providing nipple or the soft cloth exterior—would be more effective in inducing attachment.

Harlow's main finding was that regardless of which surrogate contained the nutritive nipple, all infants treated the cloth-covered surrogate, not the wire one, as a mother. They clung to it for much of the day and ran to it when threatened by a strange object (see Figure 12.3). They also were braver in exploring an unfamiliar room when the cloth surrogate was present than when it was absent, and they pressed a lever repeatedly to look at it through a window in preference to other objects. This work not only demonstrated the role of *contact comfort* in the development of attachment bonds but also laid part of the foundation for understanding the specific functions of attachment in young primates (including humans).

6.

How did Harlow assess infant monkeys' attachment to surrogate mothers, and what did he find?

FIGURE **12.2**
Harlow's motherless monkeys
Harlow found that infant monkeys isolated from other monkeys and raised with two surrogate (substitute) mothers, one wire and one cloth, treated the cloth surrogate in many ways as they would their real mothers. The monkey shown here received its nourishment from a bottle attached to the wire surrogate but went to the cloth surrogate for comfort, affection, and reassurance.

Courtesy of University of Wisconsin Primate Lab, Madison, WI

Monkmeyer Press

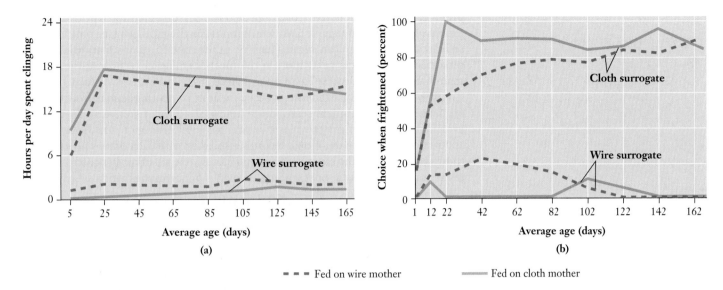

FIGURE **12.3** *Evidence of infant monkeys' preference for the cloth surrogate*
These graphs show (a) the average number of hours that Harlow's monkeys spent on each of the surrogate mothers and (b) the percentage of time that they ran to each when they were frightened by a strange object. Notice that the preference for the cloth surrogate was as strong for the monkeys that were fed on the wire surrogate as for those fed on the cloth surrogate. (Adapted from Harlow, 1959.)

The Form and Functions of Human Infants' Attachment

Bowlby (1958, 1982) began in the 1950s to develop a theory of human infant attachment. He observed that attachment is strongest in children between about 8 months and 3 years of age and is most clearly manifested in situations that are potentially frightening. He found that attached children (a) exhibit distress when the object of their attachment leaves them, especially if they are in an unfamiliar environment; (b) exhibit pleasure when reunited with that person; (c) exhibit distress when approached by a stranger unless reassured or comforted by the object of their attachment; and (d) are more likely to explore an unfamiliar environment if the object of their attachment is present than if that person is absent. Many research studies have since verified these general conclusions.

Consistent with his ethological perspective, Bowlby contended that attachment is a universal human phenomenon with a biological foundation that derives from natural selection. Infants are potentially in danger when out of sight of caregivers, especially in a novel environment. During our evolutionary history, infants who successfully scrambled after their mothers or protested their mothers' departure and thus secured their return, and who avoided unfamiliar objects when their mothers were absent, were more likely to survive to adulthood and pass on their genes than were those who blithely ignored their mothers' presence or absence. Evidence that similar behaviors occur in all human cultures (Kagan, 1976) and in other species of mammals (Kraemer, 1992) supports Bowlby's evolutionary interpretation.

Also consistent with the evolutionary explanation is the observation that attachment begins to strengthen at about the same age (6 to 8 months) that infants begin to move around on their own. A crawling or walking infant, who for good evolutionary reasons is intent on exploring the environment, can get into more danger than an immobile one. For survival, exploring and learning must be balanced by appropriate fears, and exploration is safer if the caregiver is present than if not. As was noted in Chapter 11, infants who can crawl or walk exhibit much *social referencing* as they explore; that is, they look to their caregivers for cues about danger or safety. To feel most secure in a novel situation, infants require not just the

7.

According to Bowlby, what infant behaviors indicate strong attachment, and why would they have come about through natural selection?

8.

From an evolutionary perspective, why does attachment strengthen at about 6 to 8 months of age, and why does perception of the mother's face become especially important at this time?

presence of their attachment object but also the person's emotional availability and expressions of reassurance. Infants who cannot see the mother's face typically move around her until they can see it (Carr & others, 1975), and infants who are approached by a stranger relax more if the mother smiles cheerfully at the stranger than if she doesn't (Broccia & Campos, 1989).

Bowlby emphasized the role of attachment in protecting infants from immediate dangers, but attachment serves other functions as well. Later you will encounter evidence that attachment provides a vehicle for the learning of rules, social norms, and values. The warm emotional feelings associated with each other's presence motivates the child and the caregiver to attend closely to each other in nonstressful contexts, not just in stressful ones, and this provides opportunities for social learning.

The Strange-Situation Measure of Attachment Quality

9.

How does the strange-situation test assess the security of attachment? What are some limitations of this measure?

In order to assess attachment systematically, Mary Ainsworth—who originally worked with Bowlby—developed the ***strange-situation test***. In this test the infant and mother (or another caregiver to whom the infant is attached) are brought into an unfamiliar room with toys. The infant remains in the room while the mother and an unfamiliar adult move out of and into it according to a prescribed sequence. The infant is sometimes with just the mother, sometimes with just the stranger, and sometimes alone. Infants are classed as *securely attached* if they explore the room and toys confidently when the mother is present, become upset and explore less when the mother is absent (whether or not the stranger is present), and show pleasure when the mother returns (see Figure 12.4). Other response patterns result in classifications of insecure attachment. Infants who avoid the mother and seem to act coldly toward her are said to have an *avoidant attachment*, and those who do not avoid the mother but continue to cry and fret despite her attempts to comfort are said to have an *anxious resistant attachment*. By these criteria, Ainsworth and other researchers have found that about 70 percent of middle-class North American infants in their second year of life are securely attached to their mothers, about 20 percent are avoidant, and about 10 percent are anxiously resistant (Ainsworth & others, 1978; Waters & others, 2000).

Like most measures of psychological attributes, the strange-situation test has limitations. The test assesses fear-induced aspects of attachment but fails to capture the harmonious caregiver-child interactions that can occur in less stressful situations (Field, 1996). Moreover, the test is designed to assess the infant's reactions to the caregiver in a *mildly* fearful situation, but for some infants, because of either innate temperament (Kagan & others, 1992) or past experience, the situation may be either too stressful or insufficiently stressful to induce the appropriate responses (Goldsmith & others, 1986). Some researchers in Japan have concluded that the strange situation is not a valid measure of attachment in their culture (Nakagawa & others, 1992; Rothbaum & others, 2000). Japanese infants are rarely separated

FIGURE 12.4

The strange-situation test

In this test of attachment, the mother (or other person to whom the infant is attached) moves into and out of an unfamiliar room, leaving the infant either with a stranger or alone. Here we see one infant, Brian, at different stages in the test: In (a) he plays confidently when his mother is present, in (b) he cries when she leaves, and in (c) he is comforted when she returns. Brian's behavior indicates that he is securely attached to his mother.

(a)   (b)   (c)

Courtesy of Mary Ainsworth

from their mothers, even briefly, and their abandonment in the strange situation leads many of them to become inconsolable when the mother returns—leading to the superficial appearance of a high rate of anxious resistant attachment.

Evidence That the Quality of Care Affects the Quality of Attachment

Ainsworth hypothesized that infants will become securely attached to a mother who provides regular contact comfort, responds promptly and sensitively to the infant's signals of distress, and interacts with the infant in an emotionally synchronous manner (see Figure 12.5). Consistent with that hypothesis, Ainsworth (1979) found that the mothers of infants who showed secure attachment in the strange-situation test were on average more attentive and comforting to their infants, in tests conducted in their homes, than were the mothers of infants who showed insecure attachment. Subsequent research has generally but not always produced similar correlations (Cox & others, 1992; Pederson & others, 1998; Seifer & others, 1996).

But as you by now well know, we must be cautious about inferring causal relationships from correlations. The assumption that the mothers' behavior causes the infants' attachment status may underestimate the power of infants to influence their mothers' behavior. Maybe some infants are, for genetic reasons, warmer and more sociable than others, and maybe that temperament leads those infants (a) to show the "secure" pattern in the strange situation and (b) to succeed in eliciting sensitive attention from their mothers at home. To test most directly Ainsworth's and Bowlby's causal hypothesis, one would have to conduct an experiment—get some mothers to behave in a more sensitive manner toward their infants than other mothers do, and then assess their infants for attachment security.

In the Netherlands, Dymphna van den Boom (1994) performed just such an experiment. She focused on mothers with temperamentally irritable babies—babies who by disposition are unusually fussy, easily angered, and difficult to comfort. Van den Boom (1991) had previously observed that mothers of such babies tended to withdraw emotionally from them, which seemed to set off a spiral of decline in the mother-infant relationship. For her experiment, she recruited 100 mother-infant pairs, in each of which the infant had been judged by a standard test of temperament to be highly irritable. Half the mothers, randomly chosen, participated in a 3-month training program, beginning when their infants were 6 months old, that was designed to help and encourage the mothers to perceive and respond appropriately to their babies' signals, especially to signals of distress. When the infants were 12 months old, all of them were tested with their mothers in the strange situation. The result was that 62 percent of the infants with trained mothers showed secure attachment and only 22 percent of the other infants did.

Other evidence of the relationship between sensitive care and attachment comes from studies involving caregivers other than the mother. Infants can become attached not only to mothers but also to fathers, grandparents, older siblings, and day-care providers. If the quality of the attachment simply reflected the infant's temperament and was unrelated to the quality of care, then an infant's attachment to one caregiver should predict well the type of attachment the same infant will show to all caregivers, but many studies indicate that it doesn't (Goossens & van Ijzendoorn, 1990; Howes & Hamilton, 1992b). In studies involving out-of-home caregivers, infants and toddlers became more securely attached to those who had been rated as responsive and warm than to those who had been rated as unresponsive or harsh (Howes & Hamilton, 1992a; Howes & Segal, 1993).

Possible Developmental Effects of Quality of Attachment

Many psychologists have theorized that the quality of an infant's early attachment to the mother or another caregiver strongly influences the child's later development. For instance, Erikson (1963) proposed that secure attachment in infancy results in "basic trust," which permits the infant to enter subsequent life stages in a confident, growth-promoting manner (see Table 12.1, page 453). Bowlby (1973) and Ainsworth (1989) postulated that infants develop an internal "working model,"

10.

What early caregiver behaviors are predictive of secure attachment? How do Bowlby and Ainsworth interpret the correlations, and how else might they be interpreted?

11.

What evidence supports Ainsworth's and Bowlby's theory that caregivers' responsiveness and warmth promote secure attachment?

Julie O'Neil / The Picture Cube

FIGURE **12.5** *Interactional synchrony* Researchers have found that interactions such as this during the first 3 months of life correlate with secure attachment measured several months later.

12.

What evidence supports the theory that infant attachment affects subsequent emotional and social development, and what are the limitations of that evidence?

Steven Rubin / The Image Works

Having a good day

Researchers may argue about the long-term effects of day care on children's social and emotional development, but high-quality settings like the one shown here seem to offer an excellent environment for development. Such centers provide toddlers a safe setting, with opportunities for exploration, and responsive, consistent, nurturing care.

or cognitive representation, of their first attachment relationship and that this model affects their subsequent relationships throughout life. Many research findings are consistent with such theories. Infants judged as securely attached in the strange-situation test have been found to be on average more confident, better problem solvers, emotionally healthier, and more sociable in later childhood than those who were judged as insecurely attached (Ainsworth, 1989; Frankel & Bates, 1990; Schneider & others, 2001).

Secure attachment in infancy clearly helps predict positive development in later life. Again, however, correlation does not tell us about the direction of causality. While it seems logical that the security of infant attachment would help produce the positive later effects, other explanations of the correlation are possible. Perhaps the correlation derives from the child's innate temperament. The same temperament that predisposes secure attachment in childhood might also predispose successful social interactions later in life. Or perhaps it derives from the continuity of parental behavior. Parents who are affectionate toward their children typically remain so throughout their children's development (Levitt, 1991), and the continuing emotional support may be more influential than the quality of infant attachment in promoting positive development. Consistent with this view is evidence that children who were emotionally deprived during infancy but were adopted later into affectionate homes usually developed warm relationships with their adoptive parents and adjusted positively to life's subsequent challenges (Tizard & Hodges, 1978).

Cross-Cultural Differences in Infant Care

Beliefs and practices regarding infant care vary considerably from culture to culture. Our Western, Euro-American culture is in many ways less indulgent of infants' desires than are other cultures. Are such differences in care associated with any differences in infant social behavior and subsequent development?

Sleeping Arrangements

13.

How do adults in different cultures justify their sleeping or not sleeping with their young children? What evidence suggests that co-sleeping may be beneficial?

Our culture is unusual in the expectation that infants and young children should sleep alone. A survey of 90 other cultures revealed that, in every one, infants and toddlers slept in the same room as the mother or another closely related adult, usually in the same bed (Barry & Paxson, 1971). Young chimpanzees, bonobos, and gorillas—our closest nonhuman relatives—sleep in direct contact with their mothers during their first few years of life (Mosko & others, 1993; de Waal, 1997).

Interviews with Mayan mothers in rural Guatemala and middle-class mothers in the United States revealed that differing beliefs and values support the differing sleeping practices (Morelli & others, 1992). The Mayan mothers, who all slept with their infants and toddlers, emphasized the comforting value of physical closeness. When told that young children in the United States often sleep alone, in their own rooms, they expressed dismay and pity at what seemed to them a heartless practice. In contrast, the U.S. mothers, none of whom slept regularly with their youngsters, expressed concern that to do so would establish a hard-to-break habit, would foster dependence, and might even be physically dangerous because the infant could be smothered. Moreover, the U.S. mothers saw bedtime as a time for intimate relations with their husbands, whereas the Mayan mothers saw it as a time for family togetherness. Not surprisingly, the task of putting young children to bed was much easier for the Mayan mothers than for the U.S. mothers, who commonly engaged in elaborate bedtime rituals.

Some researchers who began with the view that sleeping with parents is likely to be developmentally harmful—a view held by most pediatricians in the United States (Lozoff & others, 1984)—have concluded just the opposite. In one study, conducted in Spain, adult women who had slept with their parents up to the age of 4 or 5 years showed somewhat healthier, more mature personalities (higher "ego strength") on a standard paper-and-pencil test of personality than did otherwise-comparable women who had slept alone during infancy and early childhood (Crawford, 1994). In another study, conducted with U.S. military families in which the father was often away, children who had been diagnosed with behavioral or psychological problems were significantly *less* likely than other children to have slept regularly with their mothers (Forbes & Weiss, 1992). Again, of course, these are correlational studies, so we don't know for sure what is cause or effect.

One intriguing consequence of requiring infants and toddlers to sleep alone is their high rate of attachment to inanimate objects—the "security blanket" or the special doll or teddy bear. Several studies, some across cultures and some comparing different families within the same culture, have shown that infants who sleep alone are much more likely to develop such attachments than are those who sleep with or in the presence of an adult (Ahluvalia & Schaefer, 1994; Honig & Townes, 1976; Wolf & Lozoff, 1989). Perhaps, to relieve their fear at night, infants who sleep alone—much like Harlow's monkeys—attach themselves to the softest, most comforting mother substitute available. Unlike Harlow's monkeys, of course, the human infants are in contact with their mothers and other caregivers during the day, so the attachment to the inanimate object is in addition to other attachments.

Caregiving in Hunter-Gatherer Societies

During the great bulk of our species' history, our ancestors lived in small groups made up mostly of close relatives, who survived by gathering and hunting food cooperatively in the forest or savanna. The biological underpinnings of infants' and caregivers' behaviors evolved in the context of that way of life. Partly for that reason, an examination of infant care in the few hunter-gatherer cultures that remain is of special interest.

Melvin Konner (1976, 1982) studied the !Kung people, who live in Africa's Kalahari Desert (the *!K* stands for a clicklike sound that is different from the English *K*). He observed that !Kung infants spend most of their time during their first year in direct contact with their mothers' bodies. At night the mother sleeps with the infant, and during the day she carries the infant constantly in a sling at her side. The sling is arranged in such a way that the infant has constant access to the mother's breast and can nurse at will—which, according to Konner, occurs on average every 15 minutes. The infant's position also enables the infant to see what the mother sees and in that way to be involved in her activities. When not being held by the mother, the infant is passed around among others who cuddle, fondle, kiss, and enjoy the baby. According to Konner, the !Kung never leave an infant to cry alone, and usually they detect the distress and begin to comfort the infant before crying even begins.

M. Edrington / The Image Works

Security
In Western cultures, babies and young children are commonly required to sleep alone. As a consequence, they often develop a srong attachment to a blanket, teddy bear, or other soft inanimate object that they sleep with.

14.

How might our culture's typical sleeping arrangements explain infants' attachments to "security blankets"?

15.

What observations suggest that hunter-gatherers are highly indulgent toward infants? What parenting styles distinguish the !Kung, Efe, and Aka?

An Efe girl and her infant brother

In hunter-gatherer cultures, infants are in direct physical contact with a caregiver almost constantly. Among the Efe, the principal caregiver is the mother. The infant spends about half of each day with her and the rest of the day with other members of the group, most of whom are close relatives.

16.

What evidence suggests that responsiveness to infants' needs and desires does not spoil them? How might indulgence of infants be related to interdependence and to living in extended families?

Studies of other hunter-gatherer cultures have shown a similarly high degree of indulgence toward infants (Hewlett & others, 1998), but patterns of who provides the care can vary. Among the Efe—who gather and hunt in the Ituri forest of central Africa—infants are in physical contact with their mothers for only about half the day (Morelli & Tronick, 1991; Tronick & others, 1992). During the rest of the day they are in direct contact with other caregivers, including siblings, aunts, and unrelated women. Efe infants nurse at will, not just from their mothers but also from other lactating women in the group. However, at about 8 to 12 months of age—the age at which research in many cultures has shown that attachment strengthens—Efe infants begin to show an increased preference for their own mothers. They are less readily comforted by other people and will often reject the breast of another woman and seek the mother's.

In no culture yet studied is the average father nearly as involved as the average mother in direct care of infants and young children; but, in general, paternal involvement appears to be greater in hunter-gatherer cultures than in agricultural or industrial cultures (Hewlett, 1988; Konner, 1981). The record on this score seems to be held by the Aka of central Africa, a hunter-gatherer group closely related to the Efe (Hewlett, 1988). Aka fathers have been observed to hold their infants an average of 20 percent of the time during daylight hours and to get up with them frequently at night. Among the Aka, the whole family—mother, father, infant, and other young children—sleep together in the same bed.

Issues of Indulgence and Dependence

Books on infant care in our culture (for example, Spock & Rothenberg, 1985) commonly advise that indulgent parenting—including sleeping with infants and offering immediate comfort whenever they cry—can lead infants to become ever more demanding and prevent them from learning to cope with life's frustrations. Konner (1976, 1982), however, contends that such indulgence among the !Kung does not produce overly demanding and dependent children. In a cross-cultural test, !Kung children older than 4 years explored more and sought their mothers less in a novel environment than did their British counterparts (Blurton-Jones & Konner, 1973). By the time they are teenagers, !Kung children must do their share of providing food and other necessities in an environment that is full of dangers (such as wild animals) and hardships (such as prolonged droughts). If their indulgent child-rearing practices had produced uncooperative or incompetent adults, the !Kung would not have survived in their harsh environment.

Some researchers speculate that the high indulgence of infants' desires, coupled with the complete integration of infants and children into the community's social life, may foster long-lasting emotional bonds that are stronger than those developed by our Western practices (Rogoff, 1990; Tronick & others, 1992). The result is apparently not dependence, in the sense of fear when alone or inability to function autonomously, but *interdependence*, in the sense of strong loyalties or feelings of obligation to a particular set of people. In cultures such as the !Kung and the Efe, where people depend economically throughout their lives on the cooperative efforts of their relatives and other members of their tribe, such bonds may be more crucial to each person's well-being than they are in our mobile society, where the people with whom we interact change as we go from home to school to work or move from one part of the country to another.

In our culture, where nuclear families live in relative isolation from one another, most parents cannot indulge their infants to the degree seen in many other cultures. !Kung mothers are constantly in contact with their young infants, but they are also constantly surrounded by other adults who provide social stimulation and emotional and material support (Konner, 1976). A survey of infant care in 55 cultures in various parts of the world revealed a direct correlation between the degree of indulgence and the number of adults who live communally with the infant (Whiting, 1971). Indulgence is greatest for infants who live in large extended families or close-knit tribal groups and least for those who live just with one or both parents.

SECTION SUMMARY

Infants' first social ties are attachment bonds to their primary caregivers. Harlow showed that contact comfort is crucial to the development of attachment in monkeys and that infants explore much more when their attachment object is present than when it is absent. Bowlby observed that human infants, likewise, explore more when their attachment object (usually their mother) is present than when she is absent, are distressed when she leaves, and happily greet her and are comforted when she returns. In the strange-situation test, developed by Ainsworth, these behaviors are used as indices of secure attachment.

Secure attachment correlates positively with a sensitive and comforting style of caregiving. Evidence that such caregiving fosters secure attachment comes from an experiment in which infants whose mothers were trained to behave sensitively toward them became more securely attached than did infants whose otherwise-similar mothers were not given such training. Secure attachment generally correlates positively with healthy social and emotional development later in childhood, but it is uncertain to what degree the former causes the latter.

Parental practices vary across cultures. In non-Western cultures, infants and young children typically sleep with their mothers or other adult relatives. Although parents in Western cultures fear that sleeping with a child would produce harmful effects, the few existing studies of co-sleeping within Western cultures suggest the opposite. In hunter-gatherer cultures, adults are especially indulgent of infants' emotional needs. Infants are continually in close contact with their mother or another adult, are comforted at the first sign of distress, and are allowed to nurse at will. There is no evidence that such indulgence leads to "spoiling" within the context of the hunter-gatherer way of life.

CHILDHOOD: LEARNING TO PLAY BY AND WITH THE RULES

In addition to using their caregivers as sources of comfort and security, infants and children use them—and other people—as sources and vehicles for learning about and practicing their culture's values, morals, and manners. Such learning is referred to as **socialization**. In the past, philosophers who thought about socialization tended to view the young child as akin to either a wild animal that must be tamed or a lump of clay that must be shaped into a socially acceptable human. Most present-day developmental psychologists, in contrast, regard the child as the primary conductor of his or her own socialization, with caregivers, peers, and others in the child's environment serving as the substrate from which the child works. Of course, that substrate is important, because without good models of acceptable social behavior a child would be hard put to create an acceptable social self.

In this section, which focuses on the age range of late infancy to the start of adolescence (from 1 year to about 12), we will examine how a child's inborn socializing tendencies, coupled with a responsive social environment, produce a social person. We will look first at children's interactions with caregivers, then at their play with peers, and finally at the role that their gender plays in their social development.

Developing Through Interactions with Caregivers

Most of the child's earliest social interactions are with caregivers. These interactions involve sharing, caring, helping, complying with requests or prohibitions, and resolving conflicts when the interactants' needs or wishes differ.

17.

What evidence suggests that young children naturally enjoy giving, and how does the !Kung culture use that enjoyment for prosocial ends?

The Young Child's Giving, Helping, and Caring

Giving appears to be a human instinct, much like smiling and babbling. Near the end of their first year of life, infants routinely, without any special encouragement, begin to give objects to their caregivers and to delight in games of give-and-take, in which the child and caregiver pass an object back and forth to each other. In a series of experiments conducted in the United States, nearly every one of more than 100 infants, aged 12 to 18 months, spontaneously gave toys to an adult during brief sessions in a laboratory room (Hay & Murray, 1982; Rheingold & others, 1976). They gave not just to their mothers or fathers but also to an unfamiliar researcher, and they gave new toys as frequently as familiar ones. They gave when an adult requested a toy by holding a hand out with palm up (the universal begging posture), and they gave when no requests were made. Infants in a !Kung hunter-gatherer community were likewise observed to give objects regularly, beginning near the end of their first year of life (Bakeman & others, 1990).

In our culture, young children's enjoyment of giving is known to most parents but is not much commented on. Books on child care, for example, rarely mention it. In contrast, the !Kung treat a child's early acts of giving as a crucial developmental milestone, much as we treat a child's first words. The sharing of food and supplies often marks the difference between life and death for these hunting-and-gathering people, and the culture as a whole ascribes great value to its system of giving and receiving, referred to as *hxoro*. Grandmothers are especially charged with the task of initiating infants into *hxoro* by encouraging their giving and by guiding the infants' hands in the giving of beads to relatives (Bakeman & others, 1990; Wiessner, 1982). Whether or not such training increases the !Kung's tendency to give is unknown, but it surely must help alert young !Kung to the special significance of such behavior in their culture.

In addition to liking to give, young children enjoy helping with adult tasks. In one study, children between 18 and 30 months old were frequently observed joining their mothers, without being asked, in such household tasks as making the bed, setting the table, and folding laundry (Rheingold, 1982). Not surprisingly, the older children helped more often, and more effectively, than the younger children.

One might argue that young children's early giving and helping are largely self-centered rather than other-centered, motivated more by the child's own needs and wishes than by the child's perception of others' needs and wishes. But the very fact that such actions seem to stem from the child's own wishes is evidence that our species has evolved prosocial drives, which motivate us—with no feeling of sacrifice—to involve ourselves in positive ways with other people. Giving and helping

Giving is natural

Infants and young children all over the world delight in games of give and take with adults or older children. Sharing appears to be an aspect of human nature that begins to be exercised as soon as the child's capacity for motor coordination makes it possible.

Peter Southwick / Stock, Boston

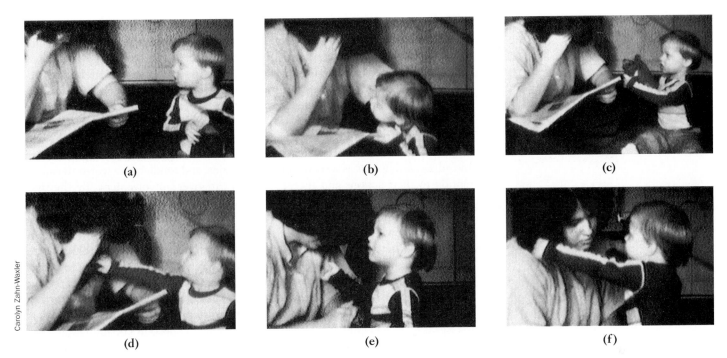

Carolyn Zahn-Waxler

FIGURE 12.6 *A toddler's empathic concern*
In this sequence, a 21-month-old (a) notices and (b) examines his mother's simulated expression of sadness; (c) tries to cheer her with a puppet; (d) expresses concern; (e) asks the researcher to come to help; and (f) gives his mother a hug while uttering consoling sounds and statements. (From Zahn-Waxler & Radke-Yarrow, 1990, pp. 116–117.)

become increasingly other-focused as they become linked to another apparently innate capacity in the child, that of *empathy*, the capacity to sense and feel the emotions that another person is feeling.

According to some researchers, the earliest elements of empathy are apparent in newborns' reflexive crying in response to other babies' crying (Hoffman, 1998) and in their mimicking of adults' facial expressions of emotion (Field & others, 1982). By the time they are 2 years old children clearly manifest concern for others and respond in ways designed to comfort or help (Young & others, 1999; Zahn-Waxler & others, 1992). For example, one 15-month-old boy was observed trying to comfort a crying peer. First he offered his own teddy bear to the peer, and when that didn't help, he brought, from an adjacent room, the distressed child's security blanket (Hoffman, 1975). For another example, see Figure 12.6.

In their relationships with caregivers, children are most often on the receiving end of acts of giving, helping, and comforting, and therefore have ample opportunity not only to witness such behaviors but also to feel their pleasurable and comforting consequences. Correlational studies indicate, in general, that children who are securely attached to their caregivers are themselves more giving and helpful to others than are those who are not securely attached (Bretherton & others, 1997; Liable & Thompson, 2000). Perhaps their increased giving and helping derive from the trusting relationship they have with their caregivers.

Learning Restraint, Compliance, and Negotiation

In their interactions with caregivers, children learn not only to channel their prosocial tendencies in useful ways but also to inhibit potentially harmful actions and to

18.

How might the capacity for empathy change the nature of the child's giving and helping, and what evidence suggests that this capacity develops during infancy?

19.

What roles might social referencing, temperament, and the capacity for guilt play in the emergence of restraint and compliance? How might guilt derive from empathy?

comply with requests that run counter to their urges. This learning, too, although it often involves temporary conflict, apparently occurs most effectively in child-caregiver relationships that are usually harmonious.

Robert Emde and his colleagues (1991) have proposed that much of such restraint learning derives initially from *social referencing*—the infant's tendency to look at a caregiver's face for cues as to whether an action is safe or dangerous (see Chapter 11). The 7- to 15-month-old baby will avoid approaching a novel object or person if the caregiver's expression is one of fear, disgust, or anger. During the second year of life, social referencing becomes increasingly verbal; caregivers warn and advise with words as well as facial expressions, and toddlers use words to call attention to their actions and thereby elicit a caregiver's involvement. By the time they are 2½ or 3 years old, toddlers can even reference an absent caregiver by recalling the caregiver's words. In one experiment, 36-month-olds resisted temptations to play with forbidden toys by saying things like, "Didn't you hear my mommy? We better not play with those toys" (Emde & Buchsbaum, 1990).

But compliance is almost never automatic. Even in their early social referencing, infants appear to negotiate with their caregivers (Emde & others, 1991). If the caregiver's expression is somewhat ambiguous and the object especially attractive, the infant may continue to approach despite a warning, while continuing to look at the caregiver's face. Only when the caregiver's warning becomes unambiguous does the baby back off. Between the second and third birthdays—the period known to many parents as the "terrible twos"—children become increasingly willful and ready to challenge authority. In laboratory studies, young, temperamentally bold children complied more frequently with their mothers' requests if they were securely attached to their mothers, as measured by the strange-situation test, than if they weren't (Kochanska, 1995). Apparently, secure attachment entails, among other things, a spirit of cooperation and mutual respect.

A developmental event that tempers the child's willfulness in the third year of life is the gradual emergence of the capacity for *guilt*. Many psychologists think of guilt primarily in negative terms, and it certainly is often harmful, as when children feel guilty about events that they cannot control (Donenberg, 1998) or about every attempt to assert their will (note, in Table 12.1 on page 453, that guilt is the potentially negative outcome of Erikson's Stage 3). But guilt about one's own hurtful actions, which one can control, may be crucial to human social interaction. Martin Hoffman (1982, 1998) distinguishes between *empathy-based guilt*, which is constructive, and *anxiety-based guilt*, which can be harmful. He suggests that empathy-based guilt emerges from the capacity for empathy coupled with the child's growing understanding of the relationship between his or her own actions and others' feelings. A child who can sense another's hurt, and who knows that the hurt came from his or her actions toward the other, can feel discomforting guilt. Guilt helps curb aggression and selfishness and promotes acts of kindness and helping. According to Hoffman, a constructive style of parenting can contribute to a child's development of empathy-based guilt.

Hoffman's Theory About the Role of Discipline in Moral Development

20.

What are Hoffman's three categories of discipline, and why does he favor the category called induction?

Discipline refers to the set of methods by which parents attempt to stop or correct their children's misbehavior. Hoffman (1983, 1998) has categorized disciplinary techniques into three classes. The first—which he most favors—is ***induction***, a form of verbal reasoning in which the parent induces the child to think about the harmful or helpful consequences of the child's actions. Induction draws on the child's capacity for empathy and empathy-based guilt. For example, a parent may say to a young child, "When you hit Billy, it hurts him and makes him cry," or to a somewhat older child, "When you tease Susan and call her names, it makes her feel that nobody likes her." Such statements demonstrate respect for the child's desire to act responsibly. The child who then stops hitting or teasing can attribute the change in behavior to his or her own moral standards ("I don't want to hurt anyone"). According to Hoffman, induction helps the child develop a set of personal moral standards that can promote good behavior even when no authority figure is watching.

The second category of disciplinary style in Hoffman's taxonomy is *power assertion*—the use of physical force, punishment, or (less often) rewards to control a child's behavior. The third is *love withdrawal*, which occurs when parents—often unwittingly—express disapproval of the child, rather than just of the child's specific action. Love withdrawal may take the form of verbal statements, such as "You are worthless," or nonverbal actions, such as coldly ignoring the child. Like many other psychologists, Hoffman points to the harmful effects of power assertion and love withdrawal. He argues that power assertion focuses attention on the punishments and rewards rather than on reasons why an action is wrong or right. A child so disciplined may continue the undesirable behavior when there is little chance of being caught and may behave well only when someone is sure to notice and provide a reward. Moreover, both punishment and love withdrawal elicit negative emotions in the child (anger in the case of punishment, anxiety in the case of love withdrawal) that interfere with the child's ability to experience empathy for the person that he or she has hurt and to grow morally from that experience. Anger and anxiety can also weaken the parent-child relationship and promote further misbehavior.

Hoffman acknowledges that sometimes a degree of power assertion may be necessary to stop a child from engaging in a seriously wrong or dangerous action; in that case, according to Hoffman, the additional use of induction can blunt the potentially harmful effects of the power assertion. The child who understands that he has been forcibly removed from the playground because he has been hurting another child, not because his parent hates him, has grounds for thinking morally.

"What do I think is an appropriate punishment? I think an appropriate punishment would be to make me live with my guilt."

The Cause-Effect Problem in Relating Children's Behavior to Parental Styles

Many research studies have shown correlations between parenting styles and children's behavior that are consistent with Hoffman's theory (Eisenberg, 2000). The best-known study was conducted many years ago by Diana Baumrind (1967, 1971). Baumrind assessed the behavior of young children by observing them at nursery school and in their homes, and she assessed parents' behaviors toward their children through interviews and home observations. On the basis of the latter assessments, she classed parents into three groups:

1. *Authoritarian* parents, who value obedience for its own sake and use a high degree of power assertion to control their children.

2. *Authoritative* parents, who are less concerned with obedience for its own sake and more concerned that their children learn and abide by basic principles of right and wrong. In Hoffman's terms, they prefer inductive discipline but couple it with power assertion when they feel it is needed.

3. *Permissive* parents, who are most tolerant of their children's disruptive actions and least likely to discipline at all. What responses they do show to their children's misbehavior seem to be manifestations of their own frustration more than reasoned attempts at correction.

Consistent with what one would expect from Hoffman's theory, Baumrind found that children of authoritative parents exhibited the most positive qualities. They

21.

How did Baumrind classify parents' disciplinary styles into three types, and how do her findings support Hoffman's theory?

22.

Why is caution needed in interpreting correlational results as evidence of parents' effects on children? What evidence exists that (a) children's behavior influences parents' disciplinary style and (b) parents' disciplinary style influences children's behavior?

were friendlier, more cooperative, and less likely to disrupt others' activities than were children of either authoritarian or permissive parents. In a follow-up study of the same children, the advantages for those with authoritative parents were still present at age 9 (Baumrind, 1986).

As always, however, we must be cautious in drawing causal inferences from correlational research. It is tempting to conclude from studies such as Baumrind's that the positive parenting style caused the good behavior of the offspring, but the opposite causal relationship may be just as plausible. Some children may be dispositionally less cooperative and more disruptive than others, and that behavior may elicit harsh, power-assertive discipline and reduced warmth from parents.

Evidence that this can happen is found in a recent study of adopted children and their mothers. Thomas O'Connor and his colleagues (1998) collected information about the antisocial behavior of the biological and adoptive mothers of infants who were adopted at birth. On the basis of the biological mothers' histories, they classified the infants as genetically "at risk" or "not at risk" of being disruptive and difficult to manage. Subsequently, when the children were between 7 and 12 years old, the behaviors of the children and of the adoptive mothers were studied. The main results were that (a) the children who had been classed as being at risk were in fact less cooperative and more antisocial than those who had been classed as being not at risk, and (b) the adoptive mothers of the at-risk children, on average, manifested more coercive, negative parenting than did the adoptive parents of the not-at-risk children. These results occurred despite the fact that the two groups of adoptive mothers were not different from each other in any initial measures of their behavior and despite the fact that the adoptive mothers did not know anything about the initial risk status of their adopted children. In this study, therefore, characteristics of the children must have played a role in causing the positive and negative parenting styles of the parents.

The best evidence to date that parenting styles do influence children comes from experiments that modify, by training, the styles of one group of parents and then compare the offspring of those parents with the offspring of an otherwise similar group of parents who did not receive such training (Collins & others, 2000). One such study focused on recently divorced mothers who had a biological son living with them. Divorce often leads to a serious deterioration in the relationship between mothers and their sons and to deterioration in the son's behavior, both at home and at school (Collins & others, 2000). To test a method of preventing such decline, Marion Forgatch and David DeGarmo (1999) recruited a sample of 238 divorcing mothers who had sons in grades 1 through 3. Half of the mothers, randomly selected, underwent a 16-week training program in which they were encouraged to interact with their sons in positive ways and to use firm and consistent yet kind methods of discipline when their sons misbehaved. Assessments 1 year later showed that the sons of mothers who had undergone the training had more positive relationships with their mothers, rated themselves as happier, and were rated by their teachers as more friendly and cooperative in school than was the case for the sons of the comparison mothers.

The Developmental Functions of Play

If developmental psychology were an endeavor pursued by children rather than by adults, I suspect that research and theory would focus more than it currently does on children's relationships with one another and less on their relationships with adults. Parents and other caregivers provide a base from which children grow, but peers are the target toward which children are oriented and about whom they often have the most conscious concerns. A mother and father want their daughter to wear a certain pair of shoes, but the neighborhood children think the shoes are "geeky" and a different style is "cool." Which shoes will the girl want to wear?

From an evolutionary perspective, the child's strong orientation toward peers—that is, toward people in his or her own generation—makes some sense. It is the peer group, after all, not the parental group, that will provide the child's most direct future collaborators in life-sustaining work and reproduction.

Across cultures and over the span of history, the child's social world is and has been largely a world of other children (Harris, 1995). In most cultures for which data are available, children beyond the age of about 4 or 5 years spend more of their daytime hours with other children than with adults (Konner, 1975; Whiting & Edwards, 1988). What are they doing together? Mostly they are playing. In every culture that has been studied, children play when they have the opportunity, and their play takes certain universal forms (Eibl-Eibesfeldt, 1989; Power, 2000; Schwartzman, 1978). The forms include *rough-and-tumble play* (play fighting and chasing), *constructive play* (building or making things for fun), *sociodramatic play* (acting out imaginary roles), and *formal games* (games and sports with prescribed rules, usually competitive in nature). Such play certainly provides a vehicle of social interaction that helps children learn to get along with one another, and it may also serve a set of more specific developmental functions.

Play as a Vehicle for Skill Development

Karl Groos (1898, 1901)—a German philosopher who was the first scholar to write extensively about play in terms of Darwin's theory of evolution—observed that play is common not just in young humans but in the young of essentially all mammals. He contended that the drive toward play came about through natural selection, because it motivates young mammals to practice skills that are required for survival and reproduction.

Consistent with Groos's view, mammals play in species-typical ways, and often in sex-typical ways, that seem well suited to their evolutionary needs. Lion cubs and the young of other predators play at stalking and chasing (Groos, 1898). Young horses and zebras, which in the wild are preyed on by lions and such, play at fleeing and dodging (Fagen & George, 1977). Young monkeys of various species play in ways that seem ideally designed to develop and maintain the muscular-skeletal flexibility needed to leap from branch to branch in trees (Fontaine, 1994). Among species in which adult males fight more than adult females (most species of mammals), juvenile males play at fighting more than juvenile females (Meaney & others, 1985). Among species of primates in which mothers are more involved in the care of infants than are fathers, juvenile females engage in more play with infants than do juvenile males (Goodall, 1986; Lancaster, 1971; Meaney & others, 1985).

The play of human children is often like that of other young primates and appears to serve many of the same functions. Children all over the world play chase games, which promote physical stamina, agility, and clever strategies to avoid getting caught. Play nurturing—often with dolls or other infant substitutes rather than with real infants—and play fighting are also universal, and everywhere the former is more prevalent among girls and the latter is more prevalent among boys (Eibl-Eibesfeldt, 1989). Yet, as Groos (1901) himself observed, human play is far more variable than is the play of other species. In cultures where children can observe directly the sustenance activities of adults, children focus much of their play on those activities. For instance, young boys in hunter-gatherer cultures spend enormous amounts of time at play hunting—such as shooting at butterflies with bows and arrows—and develop great skill in the process (Konner, 1975; Morelli, personal communication).

23.

How did Groos explain play in evolutionary terms, and what evidence supports his theory?

A. & M. Shah / Animals Animals

Young predators at play
These lion cubs are playfully practicing maneuvers that will serve them well as they grow older.

24.

How do observations in two Mexican villages illustrate the role of play in the transmission of cultural skills and values from one generation to the next, and how might play promote new skills and knowledge?

Courtesy of Gilda Morelli

Play with a purpose

In their self-initiated play, children in all cultures exhibit their fascination with the tools and actions they see their elders use. This 11-month-old Efe boy is trying to cut a papaya with a huge, sharp knife.

25.

In Vygotsky's view, how does play help children acquire a conscious understanding of rules and social roles and help them learn to control their own behavior?

An example of how children's play reflects and perhaps helps transmit a culture's values and skills is found in a study by Douglas Fry (1992) of two Mexican villages. The two villages were observed to be alike in many ways, and the similarity was reflected in aspects of the children's play. In both communities boys made toy plows with sticks and used them to furrow the earth as their fathers worked at real plowing in the fields, and girls made pretend tortillas. In one respect, however, the two communities differed markedly. For generations in La Paz the people had prided themselves on their peacefulness and nonviolence, but the same was not true in San Andrés (the villages' names are pseudonyms). Often in San Andrés, but rarely in La Paz, children saw their parents fight physically, heard of fights or even murders among men stemming from sexual jealousy, and themselves were victims of beatings administered by their parents. In his systematic study of the everyday activities of 3- to 8-year-olds, Fry observed that the San Andrés children engaged in about twice as much serious fighting, and about three times as much play fighting, as the La Paz children. When fighting is common in a culture, fighting will apparently be understood intuitively by children as a skill to be practiced not just in anger but also in play, for fun.

Children's play can help create and advance culture as well as reflect it. When the computer revolution began in North America, children, who usually had no use for computers other than play, were in many families the first to become adept with the new technology. They taught their parents how to use computers. Some of the same children—as young adults, but still in the spirit of play—invented new and better computers and computer programs. Many years ago the Dutch cultural historian Johan Huizinga (1944/1970) wrote a book contending that much, if not most, of what we call "high culture"—including art, literature, philosophy, and legal systems—arose originally in the spirit of play in conditions where play was extended from childhood into adulthood.

Play as a Vehicle for Learning About Rules and Roles

In addition to practicing species-typical and culturally valued skills, children may, through play, acquire a more advanced understanding of the nature of rules and social roles and learn to control their own actions according to that understanding.

In his book *The Moral Judgment of the Child*, Piaget (1932/1965) argued that unsupervised play with peers is crucial to moral development. He observed that adult supervisors use their superior power to settle children's disputes, but when adults are not present, children argue out their disagreements and acquire a new understanding of rules based on reason rather than authority. They learn, for example, that rules of games like marbles are not immutable but are human contrivances designed to make the game more interesting and fair and can be changed if everyone agrees. By extension, the same is true of the social conventions and laws that govern life in democratic societies.

Like Piaget, Vygotsky connected play with learning about social rules. Vygotsky (1933/1978) contended that play, contrary to common belief, is not free and spontaneous but is always governed by rules that define the range of permissible actions for each participant. In real life, young children behave spontaneously—they cry when they are hurt, laugh when they are happy, and express their truly felt desires. But in play they must suppress their spontaneous urges and behave in accordance with the rules of the game or the role they have agreed on.

Consider, for example, children playing "house," in which one child is the mommy, another is the baby, and another is the dog. To play this game, each child must keep in mind a conscious conception of how a mommy, a baby, or a dog behaves and must govern his or her actions in accordance with that conception. Play, then, according to Vygotsky, has this paradoxical quality: Children freely enter into it, but in doing so they give up some of their freedom. In Vygotsky's view, play in humans evolved at least partly as a means of practicing self-discipline—the ability to govern one's own actions in accordance with a conscious understanding of rules and roles—which is essential for life in all human societies.

Consistent with Vygotsky's view, researchers have found that young children put great effort into planning and enforcing rules in their socio-dramatic play (Furth, 1996; Garvey, 1990). Children who break the rules—who act like themselves rather than the role they have agreed to play—are sharply reminded by the others of what they are supposed to be doing: "Dogs don't sit at the table; you have to get under the table." Also in line with Vygotsky's view, researchers have found positive correlations between the amount of sociodramatic play children engage in and subsequent ratings of their social competence (Connolly & Doyle, 1984; Howes & Matheson, 1992).

The Special Value of Age-Mixed Play

In age-graded school settings, such as recess, children play almost entirely with others who are about the same age as themselves. But in neighborhood settings in our culture (Ellis & others, 1981), and even more so in cultures that don't have age-graded schools (Whiting & Edwards, 1988), children often play in groups with age spans of several years. Indeed, as Konner (1975) has pointed out, the biological underpinnings of human play must have evolved under conditions in which age-mixed play predominated. Hunter-gatherer communities are small and births within them are widely spaced, so a given child would rarely have had more than one or two potential playmates within a year of his or her own age.

Psychologists have so far paid relatively little attention to age-mixed play, but what work has been done suggests that such play is often qualitatively different from play among age mates. One difference is that it is less competitive; there is less concern about who is best (Feldman & Gray, 1999; D. Greenberg, 1992). An 11-year-old has nothing to gain by proving himself or herself stronger, smarter, or more skilled than a 7-year-old, and the 7-year-old has no chance of proving the reverse. Konner (1972) noted that age-mixed rough-and-tumble play among the !Kung children whom he observed might better be called "gentle-and-tumble," because an implicit rule is that participants must control their movements so that they do not hurt a younger child. Children work at developing their skills with reduced concern about winning or losing. Similar observations have been made about age-mixed physical play in our culture (Feldman & Gray, 2001; M. Greenberg, 1992).

Age-mixed play may offer other advantages as well. In age-mixed settings all children, regardless of how temperamentally bold or timid they are, can be leaders with younger children and followers with older children (Feldman, 1997; Stoneman & others, 1984). Young children are exposed to new knowledge, ideas, and skills in their interactions with older children, and older children consolidate their knowledge, and elaborate upon it in their own minds, through explaining it to younger children (D. Greenberg, 1992; Pratt, 1986).

My own special interest in age-mixed play derives from observations at a particular ungraded alternative school—the Sudbury Valley School in Framingham, Massachusetts. At this school, which has been operating for over 30 years, students are admitted without regard to ability and range in age from 4 years through young adulthood. They are not assigned to grades or classes, have no academic requirements, and are not evaluated in any formal way. The staff-to-student ratio is lower than that in the surrounding public schools, and staff members refrain from intervening in students' activities unless invited. The students are free all day to do as they please, within the bounds of their democratically established rules for preserving peace, and most of what they do can be categorized as play and informal conversation. Much of their play is age-mixed and entails practice of physical,

Let's pretend

In sociodramatic play, children plan out situations and abide by the rules and roles they invent.

26.

What unique features of age-mixed play may make it particularly valuable to children's development?

27.

How do observations at a particular school suggest that age-mixed play can be a powerful vehicle of education?

Sharing an interest
These members of the Sudbury Valley School appear to be equally intent on completing their project correctly. Free age mixing is one of the key elements of the educational philosophy of this non-traditional school.

Courtesy of Peter Gray / The Sudbury Valley School

intellectual, and social skills that are valued by our culture (Feldman & Gray, 2001; Gray & Feldman, 1997). Follow-up studies of the graduates indicate that they have done very well in higher education and careers and appear to be highly responsible adults (Gray & Chanoff, 1986; Greenberg & Sadofsky, 1992). These observations suggest that the play instincts that evolved to provide a basis for education in hunter-gatherer cultures can also provide a basis for education in our own more complex culture if the setting allows unfettered age mixing and self-directed exploration of the culture's artifacts, skills, and ways of thinking.

Gender Differences in Social Development

Life is not the same for girls and boys. That is true not just in our culture but in every culture that has been studied (Maccoby, 1998; Whiting & Edwards, 1988). To some degree, the differences are biological in origin, mediated by hormones (discussed in Chapter 6). But, as the anthropologist Margaret Mead (1935) noted long ago, the differences also vary from culture to culture and over time within a given culture in ways that cannot be explained by biology alone.

The words *sex* and *gender* are in some contexts used as synonyms, but in typical psychological usage *sex* refers to the clear-cut biological basis for categorizing people as male or female, while *gender* refers to the entire set of differences attributed to males and females, which can vary across cultures (Deaux, 1985). You were born one sex or the other, but from the moment of birth—from the moment that someone announced, "It's a girl!" or "It's a boy!"—you also had a gender. Immediately, in the minds of all who heard the announcement, you were tied through a web of mental associations to all kinds of "girlish" or "boyish" traits, activities, and material belongings. Biological sex differences combined with cultural models and expectations produce the gender differences observed in any given culture.

Gender Differences in Interactions with Caregivers

28.

What gender differences have been observed in young infants? In our culture, what are some ways in which girls and boys are treated differently by adults, and how might such treatment promote different developmental consequences?

Even in early infancy, boys and girls, on average, behave somewhat differently from one another. Newborn boys are more irritable and less responsive to caregivers' voices and faces than are newborn girls (Hittelman & Dickes, 1979; Osofsky & O'Connell, 1977). By 6 months of age, boys squirm more and show more facial expressions of anger than do girls when confined in an infant seat, and girls show more facial expressions of interest and less fussing than do boys when interacting with their mothers (Weinberg & others, 1999). By 13 to 15 months of age, girls are more likely than are boys to comply with their mothers' requests (Kochanska & others, 1998), and that difference persists throughout childhood and adolescence (Maccoby, 1998).

Parents and other caregivers behave differently toward girls and boys, beginning at birth. They are, on average, more gentle with girls than with boys; they are more likely to talk to girls and to jostle boys (Maccoby, 1998). Such differences in treatment may in part reflect caregivers' sensitivity and responsiveness to actual differences in the behaviors and preferences of the infant girls and boys, but it also probably reflects adult expectations that are independent of the infants' behaviors and preferences. In one study, mothers were asked to hold a 6-month-old female infant, who in some cases was dressed as a girl and introduced as Beth, and in other cases was dressed as a boy and introduced as Adam (Culp & others, 1983). The mothers talked to Beth more than to Adam, and gave Adam more direct gazes unaccompanied by talk.

Other research suggests that, regardless of the child's age, adults offer help and comfort more often to girls than to boys and more often expect boys to solve problems on their own. In one experiment, college students were quicker to call for help for a crying infant if they thought it was a girl than if they thought it was a boy (Hron-Stewart, 1988). In another study, mothers of 2-year-old daughters helped the children in problem-solving tasks more than did mothers of 2-year-old sons (Hron-Stewart, 1988). Theorists have speculated that the relatively warmer treatment of girls and greater expectations of self-reliance for boys may lead girls to become more affectionate and sociable and boys to become more self-reliant than they otherwise would (Dweck & others, 1978; MacDonald, 1992).

Cross-cultural research indicates that the degree to which boys and girls are treated differently from each other varies in accordance with the degree of difference in the culture's adult male and female roles. In general, boys are expected to manifest more fortitude and aggression than girls, and that expectation is greater in polygynous cultures, where male-male competition for wives is often brutal, than in monogamous cultures, where men are relatively more peaceful (Low, 1989). In general, girls are expected to be more obedient and less assertive than boys, and that expectation is greater in societies where women lack political and economic power than it is in societies where women's power approaches men's (Low, 1989). In general, girls are expected more often than boys to care for younger siblings and perform domestic chores, and boys are given more time and freedom to play on their own (Huston & others, 1986; Whiting & Edwards, 1988), but that difference, too, varies across cultures in ways that correspond with adult roles. Gilda Morelli (1997) has discussed this issue as it pertains to two cultural groups—the Lese and the Efe—that exist side by side in Zaire. The Lese live in farming communities where women and men have sharply different roles, and men rarely take any part in child care or other domestic chores. The Efe, in contrast, live in hunter-gatherer groups where women and men have different roles away from camp (women gather and men hunt) but often work together at cooking and other chores within the camp. Predictably, the gender difference in task assignment to young children is much greater among the Lese than among the Efe.

Gender Differences in Interactions with Peers

Children are not passively molded by adults to behave according to their culture's conception of male and female; they actively mold themselves. By the age of 4 or 5, they have learned quite clearly their culture's stereotypes of male and female roles (Levy & Fivush, 1993; Williams & Best, 1990) and recognize that they themselves are one gender or the other and always will be, an understanding referred to as *gender identity* (Kohlberg, 1966). Once they have this understanding, children in all cultures seem to become concerned about projecting themselves as clearly male or female. They attend more closely to people of their own gender and model their own behavior accordingly, often in ways that exaggerate the male-female differences they see. When required to carry out a chore that they regard as gender-inappropriate, they often do so in a style that clearly distinguishes them from the other gender. For example, in a culture where fetching water is considered women's

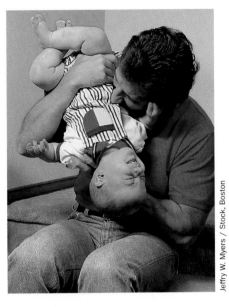

My tough little boy

Researchers have found that fathers generally play more vigorously with their infant sons than with their infant daughters.

29.

What relationships have been observed, across cultures, between the differential treatment of girls and boys and the adult roles available to men and to women?

30.

How do children mold themselves according to their understanding of gender differences?

Richard Hutchings / PhotoEdit

Sex-segregated play

Even in preschool, girls tend to play with girls and boys with boys. The little girl looking at the truck might want to join the two boys, but she will probably stay with the girls.

31.

Why, according to some research findings, do preschool girls often withdraw from preschool boys in play? Later in childhood, why might boys avoid playing with girls more than the reverse?

work, young boys who are asked to fetch water carry it in a manner different from that employed by women and girls (Whiting & Edwards, 1988). From a biological perspective, gender is not an arbitrary concept but is linked to sex, which is linked to reproduction. A tendency toward gender identity may well have evolved as an active assertion of one's sex as well as a means of acquiring culture-specific gender roles. By acting "girlish" and "boyish," girls and boys clearly announce that they are on their way to becoming sexually viable women and men.

In all cultures that have been studied to date, boys and girls play primarily with others of their own sex (Maccoby, 1998; Whiting & Edwards, 1988), and, at least in our culture, such segregation is more common in activities structured by children themselves than in activities structured by adults (Berk & Lewis, 1977; Maccoby, 1990). Even 3-year-olds have been observed to prefer same-sex playmates to opposite-sex playmates (Maccoby & Jacklin, 1987), but the peak of gender segregation, observed in many different settings and cultures, occurs in the age range of 8 to 11 (Gray & Feldman, 1997; Hartup, 1983; Whiting & Edwards, 1988).

Among very young children the tendency to avoid the other sex is stronger in girls than in boys (La Freniere & others, 1984), which may result at least in part from an early gender difference in mode of communication and exertion of power. Girls are more likely than boys to attempt to influence an activity through polite suggestions rather than direct commands, and boys are less likely than girls to respond to polite suggestions, with the result that girls find it difficult to influence boys (Maccoby, 1990; Serbin & others, 1984).

Later in childhood, however, at least in our culture, the tendency of boys to avoid girls becomes stronger than that of girls to avoid boys and is reinforced by social sanctions for violators (Finnan, 1982; Levy & others, 1995; Thorne, 1993). On elementary school playgrounds, Barrie Thorne (1986, 1993) found that boys who preferred to play with girls were much more likely to be taunted and shunned by both gender groups than were girls who preferred to play with boys. Adults, too, evaluate cross-gender behavior far more negatively in boys than in girls (Martin, 1990). Perhaps the difference reflects the culture's overall view that male roles are superior to female roles, which might also help explain why, over the past 40 years, many women in our culture have moved into roles that were once regarded as the exclusive domain of men, while relatively few men have moved into roles traditionally considered feminine.

Girls and boys tend to play differently as well as separately, and the differences are in some ways consistent from culture to culture (Geary, 1999; Whiting & Edwards, 1988). Some social scientists consider boys' and girls' peer groups to be so distinct as to constitute separate subcultures, each with its own values, directing its members along different developmental lines (Maccoby, 1998; Maltz & Borker, 1982). The *world of boys* has been characterized as consisting of relatively large, hierarchically organized groups in which individuals or coalitions attempt to prove their superiority or dominance through competitive games, teasing, and boasting. A prototypical boys' game is king of the hill, the goal of which is to stand on top and push everyone else down. The *world of girls* has been characterized as consisting of smaller, more intimate groups, in which cooperative forms of play predominate and competition, although not absent, is more subtle. A prototypical girls' game is jump rope, the goal of which is to keep the action going as long as possible through the coordinated activities of the rope twirlers and the jumper.

The "two-worlds" concept may exaggerate the typical differences in the social experiences of boys and girls. Most research supporting the concept has been conducted in age-segregated settings, such as school playgrounds and summer camps. At home and in neighborhoods children often play in age-mixed groups. As noted earlier, age-mixed play generally centers less on winning and losing than does same-age play, so age mixing reduces the difference in competitiveness between boys' and girls' play. Moreover, several studies indicate that girls and boys play together more often in age-mixed groups than in age-segregated groups (Ellis & others, 1981; Gray & Feldman, 1997; Whiting & Edwards, 1988).

Whether or not they play together, boys and girls are certainly interested in each other. On school playgrounds, for example, the separate boys' and girls' groups interact frequently, usually in teasing ways (Thorne, 1993). That interest begins to peak, and interactions between the sexes takes on a new dimension, as children enter adolescence.

32.

How can girls' and boys' peer groups be thought of as separate subcultures, and why might this idea be an exaggeration?

A lack of symmetry
We are much more accepting of the little girl who dresses and acts like a boy (left-hand photo) than we are of the litle boy who dresses and acts like a girl. Why?

SECTION SUMMARY

Socialization in childhood involves learning how to abide by social expectations and to please other people. Certain instinctive tendencies in infants and toddlers—including the tendencies to give, help, and empathize—contribute to this development. By the age of 3, children have internalized rules and moral guidelines from their caregivers and can to some degree control their own behavior accordingly. Induction, as a disciplinary technique, uses children's capacities for empathy and self-control. In contrast, power assertion interferes with children's ability to take responsibilty for their own behavior. Inductive styles of discipline and cooperative behavior in children correlate positively with each other, and research suggests that a causal relation between the two goes in both directions. Cooperative children elicit more induction, more affection, and less power assertion from caregivers than do uncooperative children; and an affectionate, inductive style of parenting promotes cooperative behavior.

In most cultures, children over 4 or 5 years old spend more time with other children than with adults, and much of that time is devoted to play. Like other young mammals, children play in ways that help develop stamina and species-typical physical skills. Children also incorporate the skills and values of the adult culture into their play. All play involves implicit or explicit rules, and through play children learn to abide by socially shared rules and expectations. Outside of school settings, most play is age-mixed. Age-mixed play is less competitive than same-age play. It offers younger children opportunities to learn from older children, and it enables older children to practice leadership and nurturance.

Boys and girls behave somewhat differently from each other even on the day they are born, and caregivers treat them differently. Girls are generally expected to be more obedient and to do more domestic work than are boys, and across cultures the degree of this difference correlates with the degree to which adult men and women differ in power and occupational roles. In all cultures, children tend to segregate themselves by gender in their play and to play in gender-specific ways. Girls' play is generally more cooperative and less rough and competitive than is boys' play.

ADOLESCENCE: BREAKING OUT OF THE COCOON

Adolescence is the transition period from childhood to adulthood. It begins with the first signs of puberty (the physical changes leading to reproductive capacity), and it ends when the person is viewed by himself or herself, and by others, as a full member of the adult community. Defined this way, adolescence in our culture begins earlier and ends later than it did in times past or still does in many other cultures.

33.

What are two reasons why adolescence is longer today in our culture than in times past or in some other cultures?

The physical changes of puberty include a growth spurt in body height, as well as the more specific changes in sexual organs and body shape toward the adult forms. In present-day North America the average age at which the growth spurt begins is 10½ in girls and 12½ in boys (Eveleth & Tanner, 1990). In contrast, 120 years ago in North America it began an average of 4 years later in both sexes, and even today it begins about 4 years later in many nonindustrialized cultures (Eveleth & Tanner, 1990). Likewise, *menarche*—a girl's first menstruation—typically occurs between ages 12 and 13 in North America today but occurred most often between ages 16 and 17 in the nineteenth century and still occurs at that age in such cultural groups as the !Kung hunter-gatherers (Konner, 1981; Zacharias & Wurtman, 1969). The early onset of puberty in industrialized cultures is believed to stem primarily from more food intake and less disease.

Acceptance by self and others into adulthood—the end of adolescence—typically comes slowly in our culture and has no clear-cut markers. In traditional societies, where adult roles are clearly defined and are learned through the child's direct involvement in the adult world, the transition to adulthood may coincide with one or another of the physical changes near the end of puberty and be officially marked by puberty rites or other celebrations. But our culture lacks such rites, and our laws dole out adult privileges and responsibilities inconsistently over a wide age span. In the United States minimum legal ages in most states are 16 for driving a car, 18 for voting, 21 for purchasing alcohol, and anywhere from 12 to 19 for marrying, depending on sex, place of residence, and whether parental permission has been granted. More important, the age at which people actually begin careers or families in our culture—often seen as marks of entry into adulthood—varies greatly. It is not uncommon to hear people in their late twenties, especially those in graduate school, refer to themselves as "kids," a tacit acknowledgment of their sense that they are still in some ways adolescents. If you prefer to define adolescence as the teenage years, as many people do, you can think of this section as about adolescence and youth, with *youth* defined as a variable period after age 19 that precedes one's settling into routines of career or family.

Establishing an Independent Identity

In Erikson's life-span theory (summarized in Table 12.1, page 453), adolescence is the stage of *identity crisis*, the goal of which is to give up one's childhood identity and establish a new identity—including a sense of purpose, a career orientation, and a set of values—appropriate for entry into adulthood (Erikson, 1968). Many developmental psychologists disagree with Erikson's specific definition of identity and with his idea that the search for identity necessarily involves a "crisis," but nearly all agree that adolescence is a period in which young people either consciously or unconsciously act in ways designed to move themselves from childhood toward adulthood.

Breaking Away from Parental Control

"I said, 'Have a nice day,' to my teenage daughter as she left the house, and she responded, 'Will you *please* stop telling me what to do!'" That joke, long popular among parents of adolescents, could be matched by the following, told by an adolescent: "Yesterday, I tried to really communicate with my mother. I told her how important it is that she trust me and not try to govern everything I do. She responded, 'Oh, sweetie, I'm so glad we have the kind of relationship in which you can be honest and tell me how you really feel. Now please if you are going out, wear your warmest coat and be back by 10:30.'"

Adolescence is often characterized as a time of rebellion against parents. But it rarely involves out-and-out rejection. Surveys taken at various times and places over the past several decades have shown that most adolescents admire their parents, accept their parents' religious and political convictions, and claim to be more or less at peace with them (Adelson, 1986; Offer & Schonert-Reichl, 1992). Rather, the typical rebellion is aimed specifically at the immediate controls that parents hold over the child's behavior. At the same time that adolescents are asking to be treated more like adults, parents may fear new dangers that can accompany this period of life—such as those associated with sex, alcohol, drugs, and automobiles—and try to tighten controls instead of loosening them. So adolescence is often marked by conflicts centering on parental authority (Smetana & Asquith, 1994). For both sons and daughters, increased conflict with parents is linked more closely to the physical changes of puberty than to chronological age (Steinberg, 1989). If puberty comes earlier or later than usual, so does the increase in conflict.

Establishing More Intimate Relationships with Peers

As young people gain a feeling of independence from parents, they look increasingly to their peers for clues as to how to behave and for emotional support. A number of studies, such as that described in Figure 12. 7 (page 478), suggest that conformity to peers increases during the same years that a sense of dependence on parents decreases. Other studies indicate that after the age of 12 or 13 both boys and girls spend much more time talking with peers, often in intimate and caring ways, than they did before that age (Gray & Feldman, 1997; Kelly & Hansen, 1987), although, as noted earlier, girls have a head start on this kind of communication.

When asked to describe the meaning of friendships, adolescents of both genders talk about the sharing of thoughts, feelings, and secrets, whereas younger children are more likely to talk about playing together and sharing material things (Berndt, 1992; Damon & Hart, 1992). In a study in which children and adolescents were asked to describe their network of personal friendships, fourth-graders indicated that their parents were their most frequent providers of emotional support, seventh-graders indicated that they received almost equal support from their parents and friends, and tenth-graders indicated that they received most of their emotional support from friends (Furman & Buhrmester, 1992).

In addition to providing emotional support, adolescent peer groups help break down the gender barriers that were erected in childhood. This is one of the main

34.

What is the typical nature of the so-called adolescent rebellion against parents?

35.

How do young people's relationships with peers change during adolescence, and how do peer groups promote the emergence of romantic relationships?

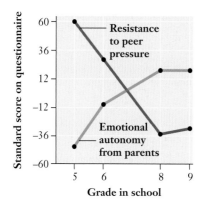

FIGURE **12.7** *Changes in perceived dependence on parents and peers during adolescence*
On the basis of responses to questionnaire items, the sense of *emotional autonomy from parents* (including feeling independent from parents and no longer idealizing them) increased, and *resistance to peer pressure* decreased, from fifth through eighth grade. The latter change was assessed with questions that asked the young person to choose between two hypothetical courses of action, one suggested by the youngster's best friends and the other representing what the youngster really thought he or she should do. (Adapted from Steinberg & Silverberg, 1986.)

36.

How have psychologists attempted to account for adolescents' heightened recklessness and violence in terms of (a) characteristics of the adolescents' mind, (b) society's limited adult roles for young people, (c) adolescents' concern for acceptance by their peers, and (d) the possible evolutionary function of such behavior?

conclusions of a classic study conducted by Dexter Dunphy (1963) in Sydney, Australia. By gaining the confidence of a large number of adolescents, Dunphy was able to chart the membership of many peer groups and study them by direct observation as well as by questionnaires. He found two varieties of such groups, which he labeled *cliques* and *crowds*. A clique was a close-knit group, consisting of from three to nine individuals, who saw themselves as best friends and who spent great amounts of time together throughout the week. A crowd was a larger group consisting of several cliques who got together for parties or other planned occasions, usually on weekends.

Younger adolescents' cliques were exclusively of one sex or the other, but their crowds usually consisted of a combination of girls' and boys' cliques. The clique leaders were usually the earliest to begin dating, and the crowds were often made up of cliques to which dating couples belonged. In the crowd, boys and girls could interact in a setting made more secure by the presence of their best same-sex friends. In later adolescence, as more individuals began to date regularly, single-sex cliques tended to break apart and new, more loosely associated groups, consisting of two or more pairs of dating couples, would take their place.

Recent studies in North America suggest that processes similar to those documented by Dunphy 40 years ago still operate (Brown & others, 1994; Steinberg & Morris, 2001). One study, which used questionnaires to track the experiences of a large sample of high school students from grade 9 through 11, revealed that over time the number of opposite-sex peers in an adolescent's social network tended to increase, and, at any given time, that number was positively correlated with the likelihood that the adolescent would become involved in a romantic relationship by the end of that year (Connolly & others, 2000).

Increased Rates of Recklessness and Delinquency

A century ago, in the first textbook of adolescent psychology, G. Stanley Hall (1904) proposed that adolescence is inherently a time of "storm and stress." Since then, many psychologists have taken issue with that characterization. In non-Western cultures, where there is greater continuity of life from childhood to adulthood and less emphasis on independance, adolescence is apparently less troublesome than it is in Western cultures (Rothbaum & others, 2000; Schlegel & Barry, 1991). Even in Western cultures, not all young people experience adolescence as a stressful and turbulent time. Still, on a statistical basis, at least in Western cultures, people are much more likely to experience emotional difficulties and to engage in disruptive or dangerous actions during adolescence than at any other time of life. Most dramatic are the increased rates of recklessness and delinquency. Rates of theft, assault, murder, reckless driving, unprotected sex, illicit drug use, and general disturbing of the peace are all much higher in adolescence and youth than at any other time of life (Arnett, 1995, 1999; Campos & others, 1995). The adolescent peak in recklessness and delinquency is particularly sharp in males, as exemplified in the graphs in Figure 12.8.

What causes the increased rates of recklessness and delinquency? Some psychologists have addressed this question by attempting to discern the underlying cognitive and motivational characteristics of the adolescent's mind that differentiate it from either the child's or the adult's. Adolescents have been described as having a *myth of invulnerability*—that is, a false sense that they are protected from the mishaps and diseases that can happen to other people (Elkind, 1978). They have also been described as *sensation seekers*, who enjoy the adrenaline rush associated with risky behavior, and as having heightened *aggressiveness*, which leads them to be easily provoked. Reasonably sound evidence has been compiled concerning all these ideas (Arnett, 1992, 1995), but such concepts leave one wondering why adolescents have such seemingly maladaptive characteristics, which can lead to grief to themselves and others.

FIGURE 12.8 *Evidence of heightened recklessness and aggressiveness in adolescence and youth*
The top graph is based on an analysis of traffic fatalities in the United States in 1970 by Wilson and Daly (1985, p. 69). The high rate of death for young drivers is probably due to inexperience as well as recklessness, but inexperience can't explain why the rate is so much higher for young men than for young women. The bottom graph, from Campbell (1995, p. 100), shows the rate of arrests for assault in 1989 in the United States, as reported by the U.S. Department of Justice.

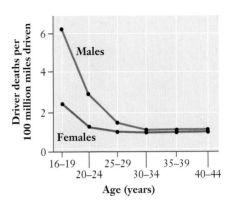

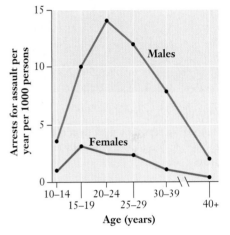

One line of explanation focuses on culture. Terrie Moffitt (1993), for example, suggests that the high rate of delinquency is a pathological side effect of the early onset of puberty and delayed acceptance into legitimate adult society that characterize modern cultures. She cites evidence that the adolescent peak in violence and crime is greater in modern cultures than in more traditional cultures, where puberty usually comes later and where young people are more fully integrated into adult activities. According to Moffitt, young people past puberty, who are biologically adults, are motivated to enter the adult world in whatever ways are available to them. Sex, alcohol, and crime are understood as adult activities. Crime, in particular, is taken seriously by adults and brings adolescents into the adult world of lawyers, courtrooms, and probation officers. Crime can also bring money and material goods that confer adultlike status.

Moffitt's theory makes considerable sense, but it does not account well for the risky activities of adolescents that are decidedly not adultlike. Adults do not "surf" on the tops of fast-moving trains or drive around wildly in stolen cars and deliberately crash them, as adolescents in various cities have been observed to do (Arnett, 1995). In a theory that is in some ways the opposite of Moffitt's, Judith Harris (1995, 1998) suggests that adolescents engage in risky and delinquent activities not to join the adult world but to set themselves apart from it. Just as they dress differently from adults, they also act differently. According to Harris, their concern is not with acceptance by adults but with acceptance by their own peers—the next generation of adults. Harris agrees with Moffitt that our culture's segregation of adolescents from adult society contributes to the problem, but she disagrees on the mechanism. To Moffitt it does so by reducing the chance that adolescents can find safe, legitimate ways to behave as adults; to Harris it does so by producing adolescent subcultures whose values are relatively unaffected by those of adults.

Neither Moffitt nor Harris addresses the question of why risky and delinquent activities are so much more readily pursued by young males than by young females or why they occur (albeit to a reduced degree) in cultures that do not segregate adolescents from adults. Even in hunter-gatherer communities, young males take risks that appear foolish to their elders and die at disproportionate rates from such mishaps as falling from trees that they have climbed too rapidly (Hewlett, 1988). To address such issues, Margo Wilson and Martin Daly (1985; Daly & Wilson, 1990) have discussed what they call "the young-male syndrome" from an evolutionary perspective, focusing on the potential value of such behavior for reproduction. As discussed in Chapter 3, among mammals in general, the number of potential offspring a male can produce is more variable than the number a female can produce and is more closely tied to status. In our species' history, males who took risks to achieve higher status among their peers may well have produced more offspring, on average, than those who didn't, so genes promoting that tendency may have been passed along. In Wilson and Daly's view, train surfing, wild driving, careless tree climbing, and seemingly senseless acts of violence are best understood as ways by which young men gain status by proving their fearlessness and valor.

In support of their thesis, Wilson and Daly point to evidence that a high proportion of violence among young human males is triggered by signs of disrespect or challenges to status. One young man insults another, and the other responds by punching, knifing, or shooting him. Such actions are more likely to occur if other young men are present than if they aren't. No intelligent person whose real goal was murder would choose to kill in front of witnesses, but young men who commit murder do so regularly in front of witnesses. Young men also drive more recklessly when another young man is in the car than when they drive alone, while young women's driving appears to be unaffected by the presence or absence of passengers (Jackson & Gray, 1976). Of course, not all young males are reckless or violent, but that does not contradict Wilson and Daly's thesis. Young men who see safer paths to high status—such as college, inherited wealth, or prestigious jobs—have less need to risk their lives for prestige and are less likely to do so.

Females also exhibit a peak in violence during adolescence and youth, although it is a much smaller peak than men's (see Figure 12.8). Anne Campbell (1995, 1999) has argued that when young women do fight physically, they, like young men, do so for reasons that can be understood from an evolutionary perspective. According to Campbell's evidence, young women fight most often in response to gossip or insults about their alleged sexual activities that could tarnish their standing with men or in instances when one woman appears to be trying to attract another's boyfriend.

An Expanded Moral Vision and a Moral Sense of Self

Adolescence seems to bring out both the worst and the best in people. Adolescents can be foolhardy and violent, but they can also be heroic and work valiantly toward making the world better. Recent American history, for example, reveals the extraordinary effects of adolescent idealists who worked and showed courage in such endeavors as marches for civil rights, protests and rallies aimed at protecting the environment, and volunteer work to help the needy.

Over the past 30 years or more, much of the psychological research on moral development has centered on a theory developed by Lawrence Kohlberg. Kohlberg was intrigued by Piaget's idea (discussed in Chapter 11) that logical reasoning develops over a series of stages in childhood and culminates, at adolescence, in the capacity for abstract, formal thought. Kohlberg suggested that the ability to reason about moral issues may also develop through stages, which derive at least partly from the person's more general logical ability. In his research, Kohlberg assessed moral reasoning by posing hypothetical moral dilemmas to people and asking them how they believe the protagonist should act and why. In one dilemma, for example, a man must decide whether or not to steal a certain drug under conditions in which that theft is the only way to save his wife's life. To evaluate the level of moral reasoning, Kohlberg was concerned not with whether people answered yes or no to such dilemmas but with the reasons they gave to justify their answers. Drawing partly on such research and partly on concepts gained from the writings of moral philosophers, Kohlberg proposed that moral reasoning develops through the stages outlined in Table 12.2 (based on Kohlberg, 1984; Rest, 1986).

As you study the table, notice the logic underlying Kohlberg's theory. Each successive stage takes into account a broader portion of the social world than does the previous one. The sequence begins with thought of oneself alone (Stage 1) and then progresses to encompass other individuals directly involved in the action (Stage 2), others who will hear about and evaluate the action (Stage 3), society at large (Stage 4), and, finally, universal principles that concern all of humankind (Stage 5). According to Kohlberg, the stages represent a true developmental progression in the sense that to reach any given stage, a person must first pass through the preceding ones. Thinking within one stage, and discovering the limitations of that way of thinking, provides the impetus for progression to the next. Kohlberg did not claim that everyone goes through the entire sequence; in fact, his research

Taking a chance
Risk taking reaches a peak in adolescence and young adulthood, especially among males.

37.

How did Kohlberg assess moral reasoning, how can his stages be described as the successive broadening of one's social perspective, and how does his theory explain adolescent idealism?

TABLE 12.2 *Kohlberg's stages of moral reasoning*

The quotations in each stage description exemplify how a person at that stage might justify a man's decision to steal an expensive drug that is needed to save his wife's life.

Stage 1: Obedience and punishment orientation

Reasoners in this stage focus on direct consequences to themselves. An action is bad if it will result in punishment, good if it will result in reward. "If he lets his wife die, he will get in trouble."

Stage 2: Self-interested exchanges

Reasoners here understand that different people have different self-interests, which sometimes come into conflict. To get what you want, you have to make a bargain, giving up something in return. "It won't bother him much to serve a little jail term if he still has his wife when he gets out."

Stage 3: Interpersonal accord and conformity

Reasoners here try to live up to the expectations of others who are important to them. An action is good if it will improve a person's relationships with significant others, bad if it will harm those relationships. "His family will think he's an inhuman husband if he doesn't save his wife."

Stage 4: Law-and-order morality

Reasoners here argue that to maintain social order, each person should resist personal pressures and feel duty-bound to follow the laws and conventions of the larger society. "It's a husband's duty to save his wife. When he married her he vowed to protect her."

Stage 5: Human-rights and social-welfare morality

Reasoners here balance their respect for laws with ethical principles that transcend specific laws. Laws that fail to promote the general welfare or that violate ethical principles can be changed, reinterpreted, or in some cases flouted. "The law isn't really set up for these circumstances. Saving a life is more important than following this law."

Note: The quotations are based on examples in Kohlberg (1984) and Rest (1986). A sixth stage, which emphasized universal ethical principles almost to the exclusion of other considerations, has been dropped in current versions, because of failure to find people who reason in accordance with it.

suggested that few go beyond Stage 4 and many stop at Stage 2 or Stage 3. Nor did he link his stages to specific ages, but he did contend that adolescence and young adulthood are the times when advancement into the higher stages is most likely to occur. Figure 12.9 illustrates the results of one long-term study, using Kohlberg's system, that supports his theory about the sequence of stages.

Kohlberg's theory is about moral reasoning, which is not the same thing as moral action. He recognized that a person might be a high-powered moral philosopher without being a moral person, or vice versa, yet he argued that the ability to think abstractly about moral issues does help account for the idealism and moral commitment of youth. In one of several studies supporting that contention, young people who scored at Stage 5 on Kohlberg's test were found to participate more often in public protests related to moral issues than those who scored at lower stages (Haan & others, 1968). Most of Kohlberg's studies were of males in the United States, and a good deal of current research and debate centers on whether Kohlberg's theory applies equally well to females and to people in other cultures.

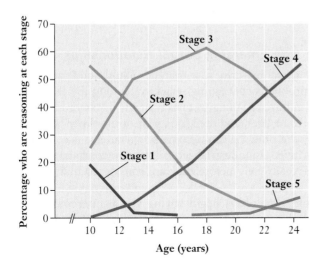

FIGURE 12.9
Results of a longitudinal study of moral reasoning
This graph, based on a longitudinal study of males from a relatively high socioeconomic background, shows the percentage of subjects at each age who were reasoning at each of Kohlberg's stages. Notice the sharp drop in the two most primitive stages of reasoning (Stages 1 and 2) through early adolescence, the rise and fall in Stage 3, and the consistent rise in Stage 4 reasoning over the adolescent and young-adult years. Very little Stage 5 reasoning was found, but it, too, increased with age. (Adapted from Colby & others, 1983.)

38.

What conclusions were drawn from a study of exceptionally morally committed young people residing in a particular impoverished community?

Strat Douthat / AP / Wide World Photos

Young heroes

In the 1960s many young Americans, black and white together, risked their lives in the effort to end segregation in the South. Among those murdered in that effort were the three young men remembered here.

Another way to study moral development is to identify individuals who have distinguished themselves through moral actions and then to try to understand how their experiences and thoughts may contribute to their moral commitment. Daniel Hart and his colleagues (1995) took this approach in a study of 15 exceptionally morally committed young people residing in low-income, inner-city neighborhoods in Camden, New Jersey. They had resisted the temptations of crime, drugs, and violence around them and were volunteering large amounts of time to improving their community and the lives of those within it. Extensive interviews revealed that these adolescents and youths were motivated not by a selfless sense of duty or abstract principles of right and wrong, as Kohlberg's theory might predict, but, rather, by their intense personal investment in doing the right thing. Being moral and setting a good example for others was a core aspect of their self-image, so their extensive volunteerism was an act of self-assertion, not of self-denial. It felt good to them to help, and it would hurt them not to.

What led these 15 to develop moral self-images? In some cases a particular life event apparently played a role. For example, one 17-year-old African-American became committed to civic action and personal morality after his older sister had been murdered. He developed the view that young people saw too many bad examples, and he became determined to be, himself, a good example. Reflective thought led him to define himself as one who sets a good example, and this in turn affected his behavior. It may have been even more critical for these 15 young people to have at least one parent who exemplified moral virtue and maintained a warm relationship with the adolescent. In describing themselves, nearly all the morally committed adolescents referred to aspects of a parent that they had internalized and made part of their own self-images. Other studies of morally committed people, of various ages and from a variety of backgrounds, have likewise revealed the value of good parental models (Colby & Damon, 1995; Rosenhan, 1970; Snyder & Omoto, 1992). Young people may reject the specific controls that their parents attempt to exert over them, yet they guide their own actions by the values and virtues they perceive in their parents.

Sexual Explorations

Adolescence is first and foremost the time of sexual blooming. Pubertal hormones make the body reproductively functional and act on the brain to heighten greatly the level of sexual desire (discussed in Chapter 6). Girls and boys who previously watched and teased one another from the safety of their same-sex groups become motivated to move closer together, to get to know each other, to touch in ways that aren't just teasing. The new thoughts and actions associated with all these changes can bring on fear, exhilaration, dread, pride, shame, and bewilderment—sometimes all at once.

Problems Associated with Emerging Sexual Relationships

The prolonged period of sexual maturity that precedes adulthood in modern cultures may create special problems concerning sexuality. Among the !Kung and in many other preindustrial cultures a young woman typically does not have her first menstrual cycle until age 16 or later, and then for a year or more her cycles are infertile (Konner, 1981). By the time she can become pregnant, she is considered an adult and most likely is married. In industrialized cultures, in contrast, most young people are fully mature sexually long before they are considered mature in other ways.

The majority of young Americans begin having sexual intercourse in their teenage years, and many begin early in those years (DeRidder, 1993). As a culture, we glorify sex and present highly sexual images of teenagers in advertisements and

39.

How do societal attitudes contribute to problems in adolescents' sexual relationships? How might the persistent double standard influence males' and females' responses on surveys of sexual activity?

Gay pride

For those whose sexual orientation is not the culture's ideal, the sexual awakening of adolescence can be especially difficult. Houston Area Teen Coalition of Homosexuals is one of a large number of social and support groups set up by and for members of gay and lesbian communities. These groups offer opportunities for education, empowerment, comfort, and recreation to homosexual men and women of all ages, races, and cultures.

movies; yet, at the same time, we typically disapprove of sex among the real teenagers of everyday life. Teenage sex is associated in the public mind with delinquency, and, indeed, the youngest teenagers to have intercourse are often those most involved in delinquent or antisocial activities (Capaldi & others, 1996). Earliest intercourse usually occurs surreptitiously, without benefit of adult advice and without a condom or other protection against pregnancy or sexually transmitted infections, with the result that roughly half of all teenage pregnancies occur within 6 months of the first sexual activity (DeRidder, 1993; McClellan, 1987). Nearly one-third of all sexually active young females in the United States become pregnant at least once during their teenage years, a rate that is much higher than that in any other developed country (DeRidder, 1993; Gordon & Gilgun, 1987). Such nations as Canada, England, France, the Netherlands, and Sweden have lower rates of teenage pregnancy despite comparable rates of teenage sex, apparently because teenage sex is discussed more openly there and sex education is more readily available than in the United States (DeRidder, 1993; Jones & others, 1985; Ketting & Visser, 1994).

Problems also arise from the persistent double standard regarding sexuality for girls and boys. Not just in our culture, but essentially everywhere, boys are more often encouraged in their sexual adventures, and more likely to feel proud of them, than are girls (Gordon & Gilgun, 1987; Michael & others, 1994). Boys more often than girls say that they are eager to have sex for the sheer pleasure of it, and girls more often than boys equate sex with love or say they would have intercourse only with someone they would marry. One index of the double standard is found in the results of sex surveys, in which young men routinely report having two or three times as many different opposite-sex partners as do young women, a mathematical discrepancy too large to be accounted for by prostitutes or hypersexual females who aren't sampled by the survey (Einon, 1994; T. Smith, 1992). For every male partner in a heterosexual act there must be a female partner, so either lots of young men are having sex with women from Mars or someone is exaggerating. Some researchers have concluded that both sexes exaggerate: Males overstate their promiscuity, and females overstate their chastity (Einon, 1994). Thus the questionnaire results may tell us more about attitudes than about actual behavior.

Although there can't be a true sex difference in actual amount of heterosexual intercourse, there is clearly a sex difference in who is pressuring whom to have sex. One sad consequence is the high frequency of date rape. In one survey, 6 percent of incoming college women said they had been raped during their high school or junior high years, and an additional 33 percent said they had experienced at least one serious form of sexual victimization short of full rape (Himelein & others, 1994). To some degree, such events may be attributable to social pressure experienced by young men to have sexual intercourse. They may also have heard from peers, and from society at large, that the woman's resistance is a natural part of the process, or even that women secretly want to be forced—a notion belied by studies showing that all forms of sexual coercion are extremely negative, and often traumatic, experiences for the victim (Gordon & Gilgun, 1987).

Sexual Restraint and Promiscuity as Products of Evolution and Life Conditions

40.

How is the sex difference in desire for uncommitted sex explained by the evolutionary theory of parental investment?

In culture after culture, young men are more eager than young women to have sexual intercourse in the absence of any long-term commitment (Buss, 1994b, 1995; Symons, 1979). Why? The standard evolutionary explanation is founded on the *theory of parental investment*, developed by Robert Trivers (1972) to account for sex differences in courtship and mating in all animal species. According to the theory (discussed more fully in Chapter 3), the sex that pays the greater cost in bearing and rearing young will—in any species—be the more discriminating sex in choosing when and with whom to copulate, and the sex that pays the lesser cost will be the more aggressive in seeking copulation with multiple partners. The theory can be applied to humans in a straightforward way. Sexual intercourse can cause pregnancy in women but not in men, so a woman's interest frequently lies in reserving intercourse until she can afford to be pregnant and has found a mate who will help her and their potential offspring over the long haul. In contrast, a man loses little and may gain much—in the economics of natural selection—through uncommitted sexual intercourse with many women. Some of those women may succeed in raising his children, sending copies of his genes into the next generation, at great cost to themselves and no cost to him.

For the reason just given, natural selection may well have produced an instinctive tendency for women to be more sexually restrained than men. The key word here, however, is *tendency*. Great variation on this score exists within each sex, both across cultures and within any given culture (Belsky & others, 1991; Small, 1993). As in any game of strategy, the most effective approach that either men or women can take in matters of courtship and sex depends very much on the strategy taken by the other sex. In communities where women successfully avoid and shun men who seek to behave promiscuously, promiscuity proves fruitless for men and the alternative strategy of fidelity works best. Conversely, in communities where men rarely stay to help raise their offspring, a woman who waits for "Mr. Right" may wait forever.

41.

How can sexual restraint and promiscuity be understood as adaptive strategies to different life conditions, for both sexes? What evidence suggests that the presence or absence of a father at home in childhood may tip the balance toward one strategy or the other?

Some researchers have theorized that evolution may have predisposed humans to be sensitive to cues in childhood that predict whether one or the other sexual strategy will be more successful. One such cue may be the presence or absence of a caring father at home. According to a theory proposed by Patricia Draper and Henry Harpending (1982), the presence of a caring father leads girls to grow up assuming that men are potentially trustworthy providers and boys to grow up assuming that they themselves will be such providers, and these beliefs, in turn, promote sexual restraint and the seeking of long-term commitments in both sexes. If a caring father is not present, according to the theory, girls grow up assuming that men are untrustworthy "cads" rather than "dads," which leads them to flaunt their sexuality to extract what they can from men in short-term relationships; and boys grow up assuming that long-term commitment to a mate and care of children are not their responsibility, which leads them to go from one sexual conquest to another.

In support of their theory, Draper and Harpending (1982, 1988) cite cross-cultural evidence that promiscuity prevails among both men and women in cultures where men devote little care to young and that sexual restraint prevails in cultures where men devote much care. They also present evidence that, even within a given culture and social class, adolescents raised by a mother alone are more promiscuous than those raised by a mother and father together. In one study (Hetherington, 1972), teenage girls who were members of the same community playground group

Culver Pictures

Stock, Boston

and were similar to one another in socioeconomic class were observed for their degree of flirtatiousness, both with boys on the playground and with an adult male interviewer. Girls who were raised by a mother alone—after divorce early in the girl's childhood—were, on average, much more flirtatious than girls who still had a father at home. More recently, researchers have found that girls who were raised by a mother alone showed more rapid pubertal development and reached sexual maturity at an earlier age than did otherwise comparable girls who were raised by both a mother and a father (Ellis & others, 1999). Since early puberty generally correlates with early onset of sexual activity, this finding is consistent with Draper and Harpending's theory.

That theory is still controversial. The evidence supporting it comes entirely from correlational studies, which, as you know, can support but never prove specific cause-effect relationships. Yet the theory does seem to account well for many research observations (Bereczkei & Csanaky, 1996), and it illustrates nicely the attempt on the part of many psychologists to understand the life course in terms of alternative strategies that are at least partially prepared by evolution but brought selectively to the fore by life experiences.

A matter of time and place

Victorians were probably somewhat less concerned with propriety, and contemporary Western couples are probably somewhat more ambivalent about sexual freedom, than these illustrations suggest. Nevertheless, permissible sexual behavior varies greatly from culture to culture. Across cultures, sexual promiscuity correlates positively with a high divorce rate and low rate of paternal support of children.

SECTION SUMMARY

Adolescence is a longer life phase in modern societies, with puberty coming earlier and acceptance as an adult coming later than in traditional societies. In modern Western cultures, adolescence is a period of breaking away from parental control, establishing more intimate relationships with peers, exploring romantic relationships, and establishing an adult identity. Recklessness and delinquency reach a peak in adolescence, especially among young men. Psychologists have attempted to explain this change in terms of the culture's lack of meaningful roles for adolescents, the relative segregation of adolescents from adult society, and an evolved drive among young males to achieve high status within their peer group.

Many adolescents commit much time and energy to moral pursuits. According to Kohlberg's theory of moral development, adolescence is the period during which many people begin to think in terms of moral principles that extend beyond their own immediate interests and close relationships. Moreover, some adolescents develop self-images that include a strong moral component, which they then work to live up to.

Sexual explorations in adolescence are often problematic, in part because of the culture's ambiguous messages concerning teenage sex and the differing sexual motives of young men and young women. Consistent with Trivers's theory of parental investment, young men are generally more strongly motivated for uncommitted sexual intercourse than are young women. However, great variation in that drive exists within each sex. Correlational evidence supports a theory proposing that the presence of a caring father at home leads to later sexual maturation and a more conservative sexual strategy among young women than occurs when there is no father at home.

ADULTHOOD: FINDING SATISFACTION IN LOVE AND WORK

Freud (1935/1960) defined emotional maturity as the capacity to love and work. Similarly, Erikson proposed that establishing intimate, caring relationships and finding fulfillment in work are the main tasks of early and middle adulthood (Stages 6 and 7 in Table 12.1). Some psychologists believe that adult development follows a predictable sequence of crises or problems to be resolved (Erikson, 1963; Levinson, 1986), while others contend that the course of adulthood in our modern culture is extraordinarily variable and unpredictable (Neugarten, 1979, 1984). But in essentially every psychological theory of adult development, caring and working are the two threads that weave the fabric of adulthood.

Love and Family

We are a romantic species. In every culture for which data are available, people describe themselves as falling in love (Fisher, 1992; Jankowiak & Fischer, 1991). We are also a marrying species. In every culture, adults of child-producing age enter into long-term unions sanctioned by law or social custom, in which the two members implicitly or explicitly promise to care for each other and the offspring they produce (Fisher, 1992; Rodseth & others, 1991), although cultures vary greatly in the degree to which people abide by those promises. Love and marriage do not necessarily go together, but they often do, and in most cultures their combination is considered ideal. In some cultures people fall in love and then get married; in others they get married—through an arrangement made by the couple's parents—and then (if fate works as hoped for) fall in love. Researchers have attempted to understand the underlying psychological elements of romantic love and to learn why some marriages are happy and others are not.

Romantic Love Viewed as Adult Attachment

Looking at romantic love from a developmental perspective, researchers have argued that it is similar in form, and perhaps in underlying mechanism, to the attachment that infants develop with their parents (Hazan & Shaver, 1994; Zeifman & Hazan, 1997). Close physical contact, caressing, and gazing into each other's eyes are crucial to the early formation of both types of relationships, and cooing and baby talk are common. A sense of fusion with the other reigns when all is well, and a feeling of exclusivity—that the other person could not be replaced by anyone else—prevails. The partners feel most secure and confident when they are together and may show physiological evidence of distress when separated (Feeney & Kirkpatrick, 1996). The emotional bond is not simply a by-product of shared pleasures. In long-married couples it may exist even when the two have few interests in common. Sometimes the bond reveals its full intensity only after separation or divorce or the death of one partner. Common experiences in such cases are intense anxiety, depression, and feelings of emotional loneliness or emptiness that are not relieved even by highly supportive friends and an active social life (Stroebe & others, 1996; Weiss, 1975).

Like infants' attachments with their caregivers, the attachments that adults form with romantic partners can be classed as *secure* (characterized by comfort), *anxious* (characterized by excessive worry about love or lack of it from the partner), or *avoidant* (characterized by little expression of intimacy or by ambivalence in commitment). Studies using questionnaires and interviews have revealed continuity between people's descriptions of their adult romantic attachments and their recollections of their childhood relationships with their parents (Feeney & Noller, 1990; Hazan & Shaver, 1987, 1994; Kotler, 1985). People who recall their relationships with parents as warm and secure typically describe their romantic relationships in similar terms, and those who recall anxieties and ambiguities in their relationships with parents tend to describe analogous anxieties and ambiguities in

42.

How is romantic love like infant attachment, and what evidence suggests continuity in attachment quality between infancy and adulthood?

Frank Siteman / Stock, Boston

T. J. Florian / Rainbow

Cultural connections

Research on successful marriage may misrepresent the lives of couples in traditional societies. Contrast the two couples shown here and think about what might constitute marital success for people living outside modern industrial societies.

their romances. Such continuity could stem from a number of possible causes, including a tendency for adult experiences to color one's memories of childhood. Hazan and Shaver (1994), however, interpret it as support for a theory developed by Bowlby (1982), who suggested that people form mental models of close relationships based on their early experiences with their primary caregivers and then carry those models into their adult relationships.

Ingredients of Marital Success

In the sanitized version of the fairy tale (but not in the Grimm brothers' original), love allows the frog prince and the child princess to transform each other into perfect human adults who marry and live happily ever after. Reality is not like that. Between half and two-thirds of new marriages in North America are predicted to end in divorce (Gottman, 1998), and even among couples who don't divorce, many are unhappy in marriage. Why do some marriages work while others fail? To answer that question, researchers have systematically compared happily and unhappily married couples.

Intimacy, commitment, and style of solving mutual problems are surely key ingredients. In interviews and on questionnaires, happily married partners consistently say that they *like* each other; they think of each other not just as husband and wife but also as best friends and confidants (Buehlman & others, 1992; Lauer & Lauer, 1985). They use the term *we* more than *I* as they describe their activities, and they tend to value their interdependence more than their independence. They also talk about their individual commitment to the marriage, their willingness to go more than halfway to carry the relationship through hard times. Happily married couples apparently argue as much as unhappily married couples, but they argue more constructively (Gottman, 1994; Gottman & Krokoff, 1989). They genuinely listen to each other, focus on solving the problem rather than "winning" or proving the other wrong, show respect rather than contempt for each other's views, refrain from bringing in past hurts or grievances that are irrelevant to the current issue, and intersperse their arguments with positive comments and humor to reduce the tension.

At least in our culture, women most often feel the brunt of responsibility for repair and maintenance of relationships (Gottman, 1994, 1998). Wives more often than husbands think about and confront their partners concerning relationship problems, whereas husbands tend more often to avoid or deny such problems. Wives also, more frequently than husbands, notice and respond to their partner's

43.

What are some characteristics of happily married couples? In what ways might marital happiness depend even more on the husband's capacity to adjust than on the wife's?

unspoken needs (Gottman, 1979, 1994). Perhaps that helps explain why, in unhappy marriages, the wife typically feels more unhappy, and manifests more physiological and psychological distress, than does the husband (Gottman, 1994; Levenson & others, 1993). Such observations bring to mind the differing styles of interaction and communication shown by boys and girls in their separate play groups. Success in marriage may often depend on the husband's willingness and ability to acquire some of the intimacy skills that he practiced less, as a child, than did his wife.

The obligations associated with parenting can strain a marriage. Several studies have shown that marital satisfaction—especially in women—tends to decline during the child-rearing years and to increase again after the children leave home (Cavanaugh, 1993; Doherty & Jacobson, 1982). With children there is less time for a couple to be intimate with each other, and children themselves can be a source of dispute. Yet marital harmony may be especially important during the child-rearing years. Discord between parents is a prime source of children's feelings of insecurity, and harmonious couples are warmer and more sensitive toward their children than are contentious couples (Gable & others, 1992). Researchers have found an especially strong correlation between men's sensitive involvement with their children and the satisfaction of both partners with their marriage (Gable & others, 1992; Levy-Shiff, 1994).

Employment

Most adults in the United States, both men and women, work outside the home even if they have young children. From the perspective of recent American history, this fact represents a social change. In 1960 only 19 percent of married women with children under 6 years old were employed outside the home, compared with 61 percent in 1996 (Bureau of Labor Statistics, 1997). From a broader and longer-term perspective, however, there is nothing new about women's going out to work. In our evolutionary history as hunter-gatherers, women apparently left camp daily to forage for food for their families—sometimes taking their young children and other times leaving them in others' care at camp (Konner, 1982; Morelli & Tronick, 1991). In most subsequent cultures, women as well as men have worked at jobs other than child care and domestic chores.

Work, of course, is first and foremost a means of making a living, but it is more than that. It occupies an enormous portion of adult life. Work can be boring and back-breaking or exciting and back-building. At its best, work is for adults what play is for children. It brings them into social contact with their peers outside the family, poses interesting problems to solve and challenges to meet, promotes development of physical and intellectual skills, and is fun. In surveys of workers, people most often say they enjoy their work if it is (a) complex rather than simple, (b) varied rather than routine, and (c) not closely supervised by someone else (Galinsky & others, 1993; Kohn, 1980; Kohn & Slomczynski, 1990). Sociologist Melvin Kohn refers to this much-desired constellation of job characteristics as *occupational self-direction*. A job high in occupational self-direction is one in which the worker makes many choices and decisions throughout the workday.

Effects of Occupational Self-Direction on Workers and Their Children

44.

What is occupational self-direction, and what effects does it have on workers and their children?

In a massive, long-term study involving questionnaires and psychological tests, conducted in both the United States and Poland, Kohn and his colleague Kazimierz Slomczynski (1990) found that workers in jobs high in occupational self-direction not only enjoyed their work more but also changed psychologically in certain ways, relative to other workers. Over their time in the job, they became more intellectually flexible, not just at work but in their approach to all of life. They began to value self-direction more than they previously did, in others as well as in themselves. They became less authoritarian and more democratic in their ap-

Donald Dietz / Stock, Boston

proach to child rearing; that is, they became less concerned with obedience for its own sake and more concerned with their children's ability to make decisions. Kohn and Slomczynski also tested the workers' children and found that parents whose jobs were high in self-direction tended to have children who were more self-directed and less conforming than children in otherwise-comparable families. Thus the job apparently affected the psychology not just of the workers but also of the workers' children, mediated by the change in parenting style.

All these effects occurred regardless of the salary level or general prestige level of the job. In general, blue-collar jobs were not as high in self-direction as white-collar jobs, but when they were as high, they had the same effects. Kohn and Slomczynski contend that the effects they observed on parenting may be adaptive for people whose social class determines the kinds of jobs available to them. In settings where people must make a living by obeying others, it may be sensible to raise children to obey and not question. In settings where people's living depends on their own decision making, however, it makes more sense to raise children to question authority and think independently.

Balancing Out-of-Home and At-Home Work

Women more often than men hold two jobs—one outside the home and the other inside. Although men today spend more time at housework and child care than they did 35 years ago (Gilbert, 1994), the average man is still much less involved in these tasks than the average woman. Even in families in which the husband and wife work equal hours outside the home, the wife still usually does most of the child rearing, grocery shopping, cooking, and housecleaning (Calasanti & Bailey, 1991; Deutsch, 2000). Career women, more than career men, feel torn between the obligations of career and family. In one study, women business executives and college professors rated themselves as worse parents than their husbands did, even though the women in fact spent more time at parenting than their husbands did (Biernat & Wortman, 1991).

Despite the traditional stereotype of who "belongs" where—or maybe because of it—a recent study found that wives enjoyed their out-of-home work more than their at-home work, whereas the opposite was true for husbands. Reed Larson and his colleagues (1994) asked 55 working-class and middle-class married parents of school-age children to wear pagers as they went about their daily activities. The pagers beeped at random times during the daytime and evening hours, and at each beep the person filled out a form to describe his or her activity and emotional state just prior to the beep. Over the whole set of reports, wives and husbands did not differ in their self-rated happiness, but wives rated themselves happier at work than at home and husbands rated themselves happier at home than at work. These results held even when the specific type of activity reported at work or at home was the

45.

What was found in a study of husbands' and wives' emotional states in work at home and out of home, and how was this result explained?

Jodi L. Buren Photo

The daughter track

Most women, whether employed outside the home or not, assume the social identity of caregiver. For Charlas Rhodes, 51, shown with her 71-year-old mother, Arena Whytus, this has meant leaving a job and moving to another city so that her mother would not have to live in a nursing home. Although she gets little sleep and has virtually no social life, Rhodes says she has no regrets and feels blessed by the opportunity to care for her mother.

same for the two. When men did laundry or vacuumed at home, they said they enjoyed it; when women did the same, they more often said they were bored or angry. Why this difference?

The men's greater enjoyment of housework might stem simply from their doing it less than their wives, but that explanation doesn't hold for the women's greater enjoyment of out-of-home work. Even the wives who worked out of home for as many hours as their husbands, at comparable jobs, enjoyed that work more than their husbands did. Larson and his colleagues suggest that both differences derived from the men's and women's differing perceptions of their choices and obligations. Men enjoyed housework because they didn't really consider it their responsibility; they did it by choice and as a gallant means of "helping out." Women did housework because they felt they had to; if they didn't do it, nobody else would, and visitors might assume that a dirty house was the woman's fault. Conversely, the men had a greater sense of obligation, and reduced sense of choice, concerning their out-of-home work. They felt it was their duty to support their family in this way. Although the wives did not experience more actual on-the-job choice in Kohn's sense of occupational self-direction than their husbands did, they apparently had a stronger global belief that their out-of-home work was optional. As Larson and his colleagues point out, the results after all do match a certain traditional stereotype: Men "slave" at work and come home to relax, and women "slave" at home and go out to relax. What's interesting is that the very same activity can be slaving for one and relaxing for the other, depending apparently on the feeling of obligation or choice.

Growing Old

According to current projections of life expectancy, and taking into account the greater longevity of college graduates compared with the rest of the population, the majority of you who are reading this book will live past your eightieth birthday. How will you change as you grow beyond middle adulthood into old age?

Some young people fear old age. There is no denying that aging entails loss. We lose gradually our youthful looks and some of our physical strength, agility, sensory acuity, and mental quickness. We lose some of our social roles (especially those related to employment) and some of our authority (as people take us less seriously). We lose loved ones who die before us, and, of course, with the passing of each year we lose a year from our own life expectancy. Yet, if you ask the elderly, old age is not as bad as it seems to the young. In one study, the ratings that younger adults gave for their expected life satisfaction in late adulthood were much lower than the actual life-satisfaction scores obtained from people who had reached old age (Borges & Dutton, 1976). Self-ratings of life satisfaction and self-esteem are, on average, as high in old age as they are at any other time in adulthood (Charles & others, 2001; Diener & Suh, 1998). As we age, our priorities and expectations change to match realities, and along with losses there are gains. We become in some ways wiser, mellower, and more able to enjoy the present moment.

A Shift in Motivation for Activities and Relationships

Much past research and writing on aging centered on the extent to which people choose to disengage themselves from activities and social involvements as they grow older. Some researchers supported a *disengagement theory* of aging, arguing that elderly people gradually and by choice withdraw from active involvement with the world around them and attend increasingly to their subjective inner worlds of memories, thoughts, dreams, and feelings (Cumming & Henry, 1961; Jung, 1969). Others held an *activity theory* of aging, contending that elderly people prefer to remain active and pointing to evidence that those who are most active and involved in the external world are also, by their own reports, the happiest (Botwinick, 1984). According to that theory, when disengagement occurs, it usually comes not from choice but from constraints such as illness, forced retirement, the death of friends, and societal prejudices that limit opportunities for and hospitality toward the elderly.

More recently, research has shifted from the question of whether or not elderly people prefer to be active to more subtle questions about the kinds of activities they choose and the motives underlying those choices. From such research, Laura Carstensen (1992; Carstensen & others, 1999) has developed what she calls the *socioemotional selectivity theory* of adult development and aging. According to Carstensen, as people grow older—or, more precisely, as they see that they have fewer years left—they become gradually more concerned with enjoying the present and less concerned with activities that function primarily to prepare for the future. Young people are motivated to explore new pathways and meet new people, despite the disruptions and fears associated with the unfamiliar. Such activities provide new skills, information, social contacts, and prestige that may prove useful in the future. But with fewer years left, the balance shifts. The older one is, the less sense it makes to sacrifice present routines, comforts, and pleasures for possible future gain. According to Carstensen, this idea helps us understand many of the specific changes observed in the elderly.

As people grow older, they devote less attention and energy to casual acquaintances and strangers and more to people with whom they already have close emotional ties. Long-married couples grow closer. Husband and wife become more concerned with enjoying each other and less concerned with trying to improve, impress, or dominate each other, and satisfaction with marriage becomes greater (Levenson & others, 1993). Ties with children, grandchildren, and long-time friends also grow stronger and more valued with age, and at the same time the person's broader social network becomes less valued and shrinks in size. Such changes have been observed not just among the elderly but also among younger people whose life expectancy is shortened by AIDS or another terminal illness (Carstensen & Fredrickson, 1998).

Research on employment satisfaction reveals that people who have worked for many years at a job usually enjoy the job more as they grow beyond middle adulthood (Rybash & others, 1995). This greater job satisfaction is demonstrated not only by self-reports but also by reduced absenteeism and improved job performance (Human Capital Initiative, 1993; Rhodes, 1983; Warr, 1992). Of course, there are many possible reasons why older workers tend to enjoy their jobs more than do younger workers. Among them are the improved skill and status achieved through previous years at work. However, the primary reason, according to the workers' own reports, appears to lie in their changed attitude toward the job, a change that is consistent with Carstensen's socioemotional selectivity theory. As workers grow older, they become, on average, less concerned with the rat race of advancement and impressing others and more concerned with the day-to-day work itself and the pleasant social relationships associated with it (Levinson, 1978; Rybash & others, 1995).

Approaching Death

The one certainty of life is that it ends in death. Surveys have shown that fear of death typically peaks in the person's fifties, which is when people often begin to see some of their peers dying from such causes as heart attack and cancer (Karp, 1988; Riley, 1970). Older people have less fear of death. They are more likely to accept it as inevitable; and death in old age, when a person has lived a full life, seems less unfair than it did earlier.

Various theories have been offered regarding the stages or mental tasks involved in preparing for death. On the basis of her experience with caring for dying patients, Elisabeth Kübler-Ross (1969) proposed that people go through five stages when they hear that they are incurably ill and will soon die: (1) *denial*—"The diagnosis can't be right," or "I'll lick it," (2) *anger*—"Why me?" (3) *bargaining*—"If I do such-and-such, can I live longer?" (4) *depression*—"All is lost," and (5) *acceptance*—"I am prepared to die." Another theory is that preparation for death consists of reviewing one's life and trying to make sense of it (Butler, 1975).

46.

How does Carstensen's theory of aging differ from the earlier disengagement and activity theories, and what observations are explained by her theory?

Macduff Everton / The Image Works

Socioemotional satisfaction
As people grow older, they tend to become more interested in enjoying the present and less future-oriented than they were when they were younger.

As useful as such theories may be in understanding individual cases, research shows that there is no universal approach to death. Each person faces it differently. One person may review his or her life; another may not. One person may go through one or several of Kübler-Ross's stages but not all of them, and others may go through them in different sequences (Kastenbaum, 1985). The people whom I have seen die all did it in pretty much the way they did other things in life. When my mother discovered that she would soon die—at the too-young age of 62—it was very important to her that her four sons be around her, not so we could comfort her as much as so she could tell us some of the things she had learned about life that we might want to know. She spent her time talking about what, from her present perspective, seemed important and what did not. She reviewed her life not to justify it but to tell us why some things she did worked out and others didn't. She had been a teacher all her life, and she died one.

SECTION SUMMARY

Theories of adult psychological development focus on love (or caring) and work. Romantic love in adulthood includes elements of attachment that are in some ways like infants' attachments with their caregivers, and variations in adult attachment quality are similar to those seen in infants. Beyond attachment, successful marriage requires commitment, a sincere respect for each other, and the use of constructive means to resolve disagreements. The husband's sensitivity and capacity for intimacy may be particularly predictive of a happy marriage.

The most satisfying jobs for most workers are those that offer the most occupational self-direction. Workers who move into jobs that are high on this dimension become more flexible and democratic in their thinking and attitudes, a development that, in turn, influences the way that they interact with their children. One study, with couples who both worked outside the home, found that the wives were happier at their out-of-home jobs than they were when doing housework and that the opposite was true of the husbands. This result may be related to the sense of obligation, and reduced sense of choice, that women feel toward housework and that men feel toward out-of-home employment.

Old age is accompanied by many losses, yet self-reported life satisfaction is generally as high or higher for the elderly as for any other age group. According to the socioemotional selectivity theory, as people approach the end of their lives, their priorities change. They become less concerned with preparing for the future and more concerned with enjoying the present, including their already established routines and relationships.

CONCLUDING THOUGHTS

This chapter has run the life course, from birth to death. As you review it, you might organize your thinking around the following two themes:

47.

What two themes that have run throughout the chapter are proposed as vehicles around which to organize a review?

1. Development as a product of evolution The universal characteristics of human beings at each life phase are evolved adaptations that promote survival and reproduction, either immediately within that phase or through their effects in helping the individual prepare for challenges ahead. In your review, think about how this idea might apply to (a) the nature of infants' attachments to caregivers; (b) the characteristics of toddlers that influence their sharing, helping, and complying with requests; (c) the nature of children's play, including differences between that of girls and that of boys; (d) the tendency of children to attend to gender stereotypes and mold their behavior accordingly; (e) the heightened risk taking and, sometimes, aggressiveness of adolescence and youth; (f) the differences between young men and young women in courtship style; (g) the attachment bonds that form between adults in love; and (h) the changes in priorities that arise in old age. As you think about each of these topics, you may well decide that the evolutionary accounts offered for some are more complete or compelling than those offered for others. You may think of alternative explanations, either founded in evolutionary theory or not.

2. Development as adaptation to the specifics of one's social environment
Evolution has endowed us not with rigid instincts but with tendencies, drives, and potential life strategies that are facilitated, inhibited, selected, or redirected in accordance with our experiences in our social environment. Researchers have found many reliable correlations between aspects of a person's social environment and the person's development. How might these correlations be understood as adaptive changes that help the person meet the specific social conditions of his or her life? Think about this question as it might apply to behavioral changes or differences associated with (a) caregiver responsiveness or unresponsiveness to infants' signs of distress; (b) cultural and individual differences in sleeping arrangements for infants and young children; (c) differing styles of parental discipline of children; (d) age-mixed compared with age-segregated play environments; (e) cultural differences in the degree to which children witness violence among adults; (f) cultural differences in the degree to which girls and boys are treated differently from each other; (g) social-class differences that alter the chance of adolescents' achieving status through nonrisky means; (h) good parental models for moral development in adolescence; (i) conditions that may alter sexual strategy toward either promiscuity or restraint; and (j) occupational self-direction in adulthood. As you review, you may find that some of the explanations just called for are lacking or incomplete, or you may decide that the correlational evidence does not warrant the cause-effect inference implied. In such cases, how might future research fill the gaps and assess causal relationships?

Further Reading

Wendy Craig (2000). *Childhood social development: The essential readings.* Malden, MA: Blackwell.

The 13 articles in this collection are representative of current theory and research about social development and are quite readable by the nonspecialist. Their topics include infant-mother attachment, parenting, friendships and peer relations, gender differences in development, moral reasoning, aggression, and development of antisocial behavior.

Peter J. La Freniere (2000). *Emotional development: A biosocial perspective.* Belmont, CA: Wadsworth.

This engaging, clearly written textbook shows how the interweaving of biological dispositions and social experiences accounts for the development of emotions, and for individual differences in that development, from infancy to adolescence.

Judith Rich Harris (1998). *The nurture assumption: Why children turn out the way they do.* New York: Free Press.

This highly controversial, highly engaging book challenges the long-standing assumption that the manner in which parents nurture their
children—within the normal range of variation—has much effect on how children turn out. Harris exposes the flaws in classic research studies that purport to show parental effects and suggests that peers are more influential than parents.

Eleanor Maccoby (1998). *The two sexes: Growing apart, coming together.* Cambridge, MA: Harvard University Press.

This book is about the ways in which a person's gender influences his or her life from infancy to adulthood. The first seven chapters are concerned with the biological, social, and cognitive factors that lead boys and girls to play separately and differently and to develop differently. The final three chapters are about the coming together of the two genders in adolescence and adulthood.

John M. Gottman (1994). *What predicts divorce? The relationship between marital processes and marital outcomes.* Hillsdale, NJ: Erlbaum.

A leading researcher summarizes the results of many years' research on the psychological variables that influence, or at least correlate with, marital happiness, strife, and divorce.

Looking Ahead

A theme of the chapter you have just read is that psychological development is in part a process of adapting to the specifics of one's social environment. We turn next to a two-chapter unit on social psychology, which focuses explicitly on the social environment. Social psychology deals with the processes through which people perceive, understand, and are influenced by one another.

Le Marché de Limbé (detail), Philome Obin

The Person in a World of People

We humans are social beings through and through. We are motivated to understand others; we are concerned about what others think of us; and our understanding of ourselves is strongly affected by our perception of what others think of us. This two-chapter unit is on social psychology— the attempt to understand human thought and behavior in relation to the social contexts in which they occur. The first chapter is about the mental processes involved in understanding others, ourselves, and the social world in general. The second is about some of the ways in which the presence or activities of other people, real or imagined, influence our behavior.

Chapter 13

Las Meninas, Diego Velasquez

Social Perception and Attitudes

We humans are intensely social animals. We are designed, by evolution, to depend on one another for even our most basic needs. We are not good, for example, at obtaining food alone; we need the help of others and the knowledge that is shared by members of a human community. Throughout our evolutionary history, to be thrown out of the tribe was tantamount to death. We are also thinking animals—thinking social animals. Most of what we think about is other people, ourselves, our relationships with other people, and the social conventions and norms that are essential aspects of life in any human society.

This is the first of a two-chapter sequence on *social psychology,* the subfield of psychology that deals most explicitly with how people are influenced by each other. This chapter focuses on *person perception,* the processes by which people perceive and understand each other and themselves, and on *attitudes,* the evaluative beliefs that people have about their social world and the entities within it. The next chapter focuses on the effects of those perceptions and beliefs on the person's emotions and actions.

Four themes run through this chapter. The first is that *biases* in social perceptions and attitudes can lead people to make judgments that are objectively untrue or unfair. The second theme is that social perceptions and attitudes serve life-promoting *functions* for the individual. The third is that *culture* plays a powerful role in shaping our social perceptions and attitudes; some social-psychological phenomena that occur reliably in North America and western Europe do not occur so reliably in other cultures, and vice versa. The fourth theme is that social perceptions and attitudes are influenced by both *automatic* and *controlled* mental processes (introduced in Chapter 8). To the degree that a mental process occurs unconsciously, quickly, and with little or no apparent effort, we say that the process is automatic. To the degree that the process occurs consciously and takes time and effort, we say that it is controlled. As you read, you might think about ways in which bias, adaptive function, culture, and automatic versus controlled processing contribute to your own social perceptions and attitudes.

PERCEIVING AND EVALUATING OTHER PEOPLE

One of social psychology's pioneers, Fritz Heider (1958), pointed out long ago that humans are natural psychologists—or *naïve psychologists,* to use his term. Heider contended that humans are naturally interested in assessing the personality characteristics and attitudes of other humans they encounter. From an evolutionary perspective, this drive to understand others has clear adaptive functions. Other individuals can help us or hurt us in our life endeavors. Understanding others helps us predict their behavior and decide how to interact with them. Consistent with Heider's general view, researchers have found that people untrained in psychology

---

Perceiving and Evaluating Other People

Forming Impressions About People from Their Behavior

Effects of Prior Information and Physical Appearance

Effects of Stereotypes

Person Perceptions as Self-Fulfilling Prophecies

Perceiving and Evaluating the Self

Seeing Ourselves Through the Eyes of Others

Comparing and Contrasting Ourselves to Others

Seeing Ourselves and Others as One: Social Identity

Attitudes: Beliefs Tinged with Emotion

Attitudes as Aspects of the Self

Attitudes as Social Norms

Attitudes as Rationalizations to Attain Cognitive Consistency

Attitudes as Guides to Action

Attitudes as Products of Information Processing

are often remarkably accurate and quick at assessing others' personalities by observing their behavior (Ambady & others, 1995; Funder, 1995).

Yet, as Heider himself pointed out, the accuracy of our judgments of others sometimes suffers from certain consistent mistakes, or *biases*. These biases occur most often when we are not using our full mental resources, or have only limited information with which to reason, or have unconscious motives for reaching particular conclusions. Such biases interest social psychologists for two reasons. First, they provide clues about the mental processes that contribute to accurate as well as inaccurate perceptions and judgments. In this regard, social psychologists' interest in biases is analogous to perceptual psychologists' interest in visual illusions, which (as discussed in Chapter 8) provide clues to understanding normal, accurate visual perception. Second, an understanding of bias can promote social justice. By identifying and teaching others to recognize psychological tendencies that contribute to prejudice and unfair treatment of people, social psychologists can help improve the social world.

Forming Impressions About People from Their Behavior

Actions are directly observable and thoughts are not. Therefore, our judgments about the personalities of people we encounter must be based primarily on what we observe of their actions. As "naïve psychologists" we intuitively, in our everyday experiences, form impressions of people's personalities on the basis of their actions. For example, if a new acquaintance smiles at you, you do not simply register the fact that she smiled; rather, you interpret the smile in terms of its meaning and use that interpretation to infer something about her personality. Depending on the context and any prior information you have about her, you might decide that the smile represents friendliness, or smugness, or guile. What you carry away from the encounter is not so much a memory that the person smiled as a memory that she was friendly, smug, or deceitful. That memory is added to your growing impression of her and may affect your future interactions with her.

Any such judgment about another person is, in essence, a claim about causation. It is an implicit claim that the person's behavior is caused in part by some more or less permanent characteristic of the person, such as friendliness or deceitfulness. In normal English usage, any claim about causation is called an *attribution*. In the study of person perception, an **attribution** is any claim about the cause of someone's behavior. As Heider (1958) pointed out, a major problem in judging someone's personality on the basis of his or her action is that of determining the degree to which the action truly represents something unique and lasting about the person or, instead, represents a normal human response to a particular situation or set of circumstances.

The Logic of Attributing Behavior to the Person or the Situation

If you see a man running and screaming and then see that a tiger is chasing him, you might logically attribute his fear to the situation rather than to any special aspect of his personality; almost anyone would be afraid of a loose and charging tiger. To build a useful picture of a person on the basis of the person's actions, you must decide which actions imply something unique about the person and which actions would be expected of anyone under similar circumstances. Heider noted that when behavior is clearly appropriate to the environmental situation, people commonly attribute the behavior to the situation rather than to the behaving person's personality.

In line with Heider's general ideas about attributions, Harold Kelley (1967, 1973) developed a logical model for judging whether a particular action should be attributed to some characteristic of the acting person or to something about the immediate environment. The essence of the model is that the perceiver considers three questions in making an attribution: (1) Does this person regularly behave this way in this situation? (2) Do many other people regularly behave this way in this

1.

What are two reasons for social psychologists' focus on biases in person perception?

2.

How does the process of attribution contribute to person perception?

3.

According to the logic outlined by Kelley, when should an attribution be made to the person and when should it be made to the situation?

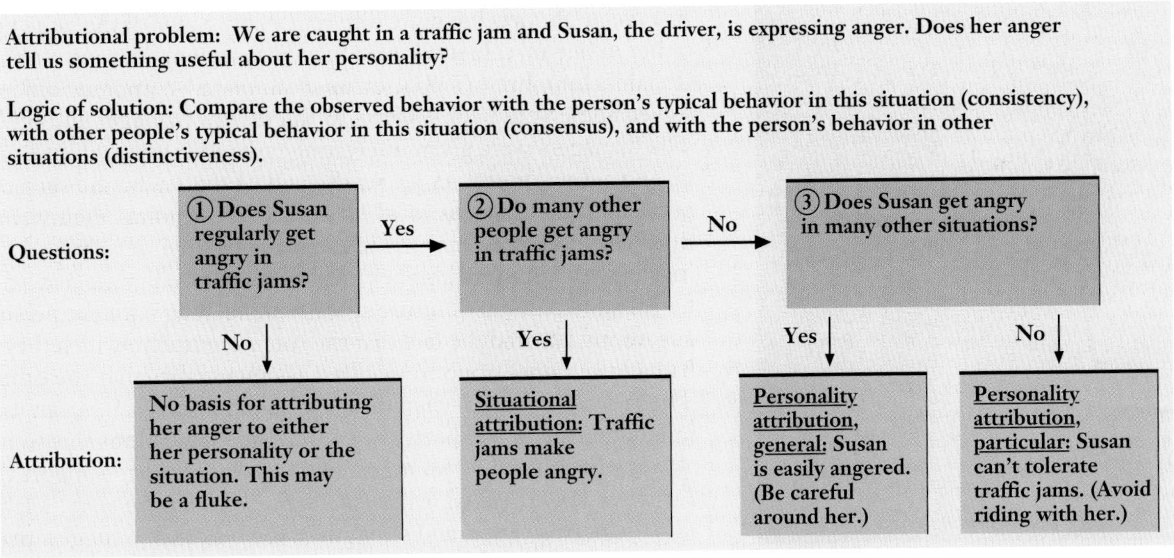

Attributional problem: We are caught in a traffic jam and Susan, the driver, is expressing anger. Does her anger tell us something useful about her personality?

Logic of solution: Compare the observed behavior with the person's typical behavior in this situation (consistency), with other people's typical behavior in this situation (consensus), and with the person's behavior in other situations (distinctiveness).

Questions:	① Does Susan regularly get angry in traffic jams?	→ Yes →	② Do many other people get angry in traffic jams?	→ No →	③ Does Susan get angry in many other situations?	
	↓ No		↓ Yes		↓ Yes	↓ No
Attribution:	No basis for attributing her anger to either her personality or the situation. This may be a fluke.		<u>Situational attribution:</u> Traffic jams make people angry.		<u>Personality attribution, general:</u> Susan is easily angered. (Be careful around her.)	<u>Personality attribution, particular:</u> Susan can't tolerate traffic jams. (Avoid riding with her.)

FIGURE 13.1
The logic behind an attribution
According to Kelley, our decision to attribute an observed behavior to internal causes (the person) or external causes (the situation) depends, ideally, on our answers to three questions. Although Kelley did not specify a sequence for asking the questions, this flowchart depicts the most efficient sequence and the attribution that would follow each combination of yes and no answers. In Kelley's original model the three questions shown here were described, respectively, as issues of consistency, consensus, and distinctiveness.

situation? (3) Does this person behave this way in many other situations? For a fully worked-out illustration of the model, linking the answers to these questions to the attribution that would logically follow, examine Figure 13.1.

There is nothing surprising in this model. It is simply a statement of the logic that you or I or anyone else—with sufficient motivation and information—would use in deciding whether or not an observed bit of behavior tells us something interesting about the person. It states explicitly the logic that leads us to conclude that a man's repeated fearful reaction to a gentle poodle tells us more about the man than does his fearful reaction to a loose and raging tiger.

Not surprisingly, a number of research studies have shown that when people are asked to explain the cause of a particular behavior and are given sufficient information to answer the three questions, they usually do make attributions that accord with the model just described (McArthur, 1972). But often people lack the information, the time, or the motivation to make a logical attribution. In that case they may take shortcuts in their reasoning, which may result in certain consistent errors, or biases.

The Person Bias in Attributions

In his original writings about attribution, Heider (1958) noted that people tend to give too much weight to personality and not enough to the environmental situation when they make attributions about others' actions. Concerning the example in Figure 13.1, they tend to ignore the traffic jam and attribute Susan's anger too heavily to her personality. Subsequently, other researchers confirmed the existence of this *person bias* in attribution. For instance, in one experiment male college students listened to a student who they were told was assigned to read a political statement written by someone else (Gilbert & Jones, 1986). Even when the assignment was made by the observers themselves, so they could be sure that the reader had not chosen it himself, observers tended to rate the reader as politically liberal when the statement he read was liberal and as politically conservative when the statement was conservative. Although there was no logical reason to assume that the statement had anything to do with the reader's own political beliefs, the students made that attribution.

Some of the most socially relevant examples of the person bias have to do with the effects of a person's social role on others' perceptions of the person. When we observe a police officer, nurse, teacher, or student carrying out his or her duties, we tend—in accord with the person bias—to attribute the action to the individual's personality and to ignore the constraints that the role places on how the person can

4.

What evidence supports the existence of a person bias in attributions, and why is the bias often called the "fundamental attribution error"?

A victim of bias?

Leonard Nimoy called his autobiography *I Am Not Spock*. He has apparently often encountered the fundamental attribution error.

5.

What conditions seem to promote a person bias or a situation bias, and how did an experiment demonstrate the effects of these conditions?

act. We might develop quite different impressions of the same person if we saw him or her in out-of-role situations. In an experiment demonstrating this effect of roles, Ronald Humphrey (1985) set up a simulated corporate office and randomly assigned some volunteer subjects to the role of manager and others to that of clerk. The managers were given interesting tasks and responsibilities, and the clerks were given routine, boring tasks. At the end of the study, the subjects rated various aspects of the personalities of all subjects, including themselves. Compared with those in the clerk role, those in the manager role were judged by others more positively; they were rated higher in leadership, intelligence, assertiveness, supportiveness, and likelihood of future success. In keeping with the person bias, the subjects apparently ignored the fact that the role assignment, which they knew was random, had allowed one group to manifest characteristics that the other group could not. The bias did not hold when the subjects rated themselves, but it did hold when they rated others who had been assigned to the same role as themselves.

By the mid-1970s so much evidence appeared to support the person bias that Lee Ross (1977) called it the *fundamental attribution error*, a label designed to signify the pervasiveness and strength of the bias and to suggest that it underlies many other social-psychological phenomena. That label is still in use despite growing evidence that the bias may not be quite as fundamental as Ross and others thought.

Conditions That Promote a Person Bias or a Situation Bias

The studies that supported the pervasiveness of the person bias may themselves have been biased. Volunteers for psychological studies tacitly agree to cooperate with the researcher. In experiments on attributions, they may believe that their task is to make some sort of attribution about the performer's personality or attitudes even with insufficient information (Leyens & others, 1996). In real life, the same people might not make judgments about a person's characteristics on the basis of such scanty information as the person's reciting of an assigned statement or playing of an assigned role.

When volunteers are invited to explain samples of behavior in whatever terms they choose, they most often give explanations that cannot be classed as either person attributions or situation attributions (Malle & others, 2000). In one such study (Lewis, 1995), many of the attributions were stated in terms of the goals of the action, such as "She is typing diligently at the computer in order to finish a term paper that is due tomorrow." A goal lies in both the person and the environment: The environment sets the challenge (the paper is due), and the person wants to meet the challenge. In real life people are not just interested in judging others' personalities; they are also interested in the challenges that are set by various situations and in the ways that people go about meeting those challenges.

Other research suggests that even in the laboratory the person bias depends very much on the conditions of the study. It occurs most frequently when (a) the subjects' task or goal is clearly to assess the personality of the target individual and (b) the subjects are provided with little opportunity or motivation to bring their controlled reasoning powers to bear on the problem, so they rely primarily on automatic mental processes. In one such experiment, female college students observed a silent videotape in which a young woman being interviewed was behaving very nervously (Krull, 1993). The subjects were told that the interview topic might or might not be highly anxiety-provoking (the possible topics ranged from world travel to sexual fantasies) but were not told the topic of the interview they saw. To manipulate the subjects' goal, some were told that their task would be to judge how anxious the woman was in her everyday life and others were told that their task would be to judge the degree to which the interview topic was anxiety-provoking. To manipulate the opportunity for controlled thought, some subjects in each of the two goal groups were kept cognitively busy with another task (rehearsing an eight-digit number) as they watched the video and others were permitted to devote their full attention to the video.

After watching the video, all subjects were asked to judge (a) the degree to which the interviewee was an anxious person in her everyday life and (b) the degree to which the topic of the interview was one that would provoke anxiety in most people. Only those subjects who were kept cognitively busy showed evidence of biased reasoning. The others attributed the woman's anxiety about equally to her personality and to the situation. Of the cognitively busy subjects, only those who had been asked in advance to evaluate the person manifested the typical person bias. They judged the woman to be a very anxious person and judged the interview topic to be only moderately anxiety-provoking. Most interesting, the cognitively busy subjects who had been asked to judge the interview topic manifested an opposite bias—a **situation bias** rather than a person bias. They rated the interview topic as highly anxiety-producing and the woman as only a moderately anxious person.

On the basis of this and other evidence, the researchers proposed a two-stage model of the process of making attributions (Krull & Erickson, 1995, elaborating on a model proposed earlier by Gilbert, 1989). The first stage is rapid and automatic and typically leads to a judgment that is biased in accordance with the reasoner's goal—a person bias if the goal is to judge the person and a situation bias if the goal is to judge the situation. The second stage is slower, is controlled, and doesn't occur if the person is mentally busy with another task or is not motivated to devote mental resources to the task. At this stage the person corrects the automatic attribution by taking into account the entity (situation or person) that is not the direct target of the attributional goal. The model is illustrated, with a new example, in Figure 13.2.

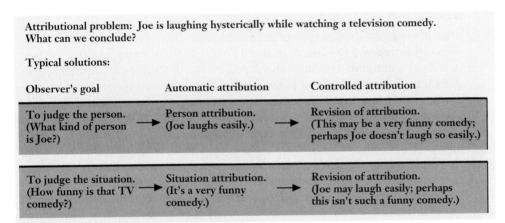

Attributional problem: Joe is laughing hysterically while watching a television comedy. What can we conclude?

Typical solutions:

Observer's goal	Automatic attribution	Controlled attribution
To judge the person. (What kind of person is Joe?)	Person attribution. (Joe laughs easily.)	Revision of attribution. (This may be a very funny comedy; perhaps Joe doesn't laugh so easily.)
To judge the situation. (How funny is that TV comedy?)	Situation attribution. (It's a very funny comedy.)	Revision of attribution. (Joe may laugh easily; perhaps this isn't such a funny comedy.)

FIGURE **13.2** *Attributions as products of the observer's goal and mode of mental processing* According to the model of attributions proposed by Krull and Erickson (1995), the person bias and situation bias depend on the observer's goal and the relative absence of controlled thought. Automatic mental processes lead one to attribute an action to the person when the implicit goal is to evaluate the person (Joe in this example) and to the situation when the implicit goal is to evaluate the situation (the television comedy in this example). Controlled processes, if brought to bear, can correct the bias in either case.

A Cross-Cultural Difference in Attributions

You have just read evidence that people tend to manifest a person bias when their task or goal is to evaluate the person. Other evidence suggests that, other things being equal, people in Western cultures are more inclined toward the person bias than are people in Eastern cultures. Western philosophies, religions, and political ideologies tend to emphasize the idea that people are in charge of their own destinies, so people growing up in Western cultures may learn to attribute behavior more to the person than to the situation (Jellison & Green, 1981). If so, then in Eastern cultures—such as those of India, China, and Japan, where philosophies and religions emphasize the role of fate or circumstances in controlling one's destiny—people might make relatively fewer person attributions and more situation attributions. To test this theory, Joan Miller (1984) asked middle-class children and adults in the United States and in a Hindu community in India to think of an action by someone they knew and then to explain why the person had acted in that way. As predicted, the Americans made more attributions to personality and fewer to the situation than did the Indians. This difference was greater for adults—who would

6.

What is some evidence that the person bias may be partly a product of Western culture?

FIGURE **13.3** *Cultural differences in making attributions*

When asked to explain a particular behavior produced by a particular person, the proportion of attributions to internal disposition (personality or attitude) was greater among people in the United States than it was among Hindus in India, and this difference was greater for adults than for children. (Data from Miller, 1984. The proportions were determined by dividing the number of internal attributions by the total number of internal plus external attributions for each group; the many attributions that were neither clearly internal nor clearly external were ignored.)

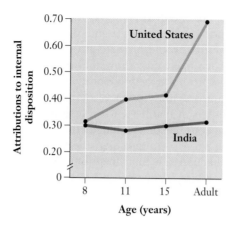

presumably have incorporated the cultural norms more strongly—than it was for children (see Figure 13.3).

Similar results have been found in comparisons of people raised in North America with those raised in China, Japan, or Korea (Morris & Peng, 1994; Norenzayan & Nisbett, 2000). As part of their study of Chinese attributional styles, Michael Morris and Kaiping Peng (1994) analyzed the content of every article published in the *New York Times* and every article published in the *World Journal*, a Chinese-language newspaper published in New York, concerning two specific mass murders that took place in 1991. The researchers found that the articles in the *Times* focused most heavily on personality characteristics of the murderers—their traits, attitudes, character flaws, mental disorders, and so on. In contrast, the articles in the Chinese newspaper focused most heavily on the life situations of the murderers—their living conditions, their social relationships, and the frustrations that might have provoked their actions.

The Actor-Observer Discrepancy in Attributions

Many studies suggest that the person bias is weaker, and the situation bias is stronger, when people make attributions about their own behavior than when they make attributions about someone else's. This difference is referred to as the ***actor-observer discrepancy*** (Nisbett & others, 1973). The person who performs an action (the *actor*) commonly attributes the action to the situation—"I am whistling because it is a beautiful day," or "I read those political statements because I was asked to read them." In contrast, another person (the *observer*) who sees the same action is likely to attribute it to the actor's internal characteristics—"She is whistling because she is a cheerful person," or "He read those statements because he is politically liberal."

7.

What are two hypotheses as to why people more frequently make person attributions about others than about themselves, and what is some evidence for each hypothesis?

What causes the actor-observer discrepancy? According to one hypothesis, people know from experience that their own behavior changes from one situation to another, but they do not have as much evidence that the same is true of others. For example, you may assume that your psychology professor's calm demeanor in the classroom is indicative of his or her behavior everywhere and thus attribute it to personality, but this may be only because you haven't seen your professor at home, in traffic court, or on the softball diamond. Consistent with this "knowledge-across-situations" hypothesis, people usually judge the behavior of their close friends as more flexible—more determined by the situation and less by unvarying personality traits—than the behavior of people whom they know less well (Prentice, 1990; Sande & others, 1988).

Another hypothesis holds that the actor-observer discrepancy stems from a basic characteristic of visual perception: Our eyes point outward, away from ourselves. When we watch someone *else* perform an action, our eyes focus on the actor, not the environment to which the actor is responding, so we tend to see the act as caused by the person rather than the situation. But when we perform an action, we see the surrounding environment, not ourselves, so we tend to attribute causal properties to the situation. Consistent with this "visual-orientation" hypothesis, one experimenter found that the actor-observer discrepancy was reversed when the actor and the observer watched videotaped replays of the action from reversed visual orientations (Storms, 1973). When people watched themselves on videotape, they attributed relatively more of their behavior to their own traits and less to the situation. When people watched a videotape of another person's performance from that person's perspective—so that they saw the environment as the person would see it—they attributed relatively more of the behavior to the situation and less to the person.

Effects of Prior Information and Physical Appearance

Thus far we have been considering how people judge the characteristics of another individual on the basis of their impressions, accurate or not, of what caused that individual's behavior. But judgments relating behavior to character go in both directions. People not only assess character from behavior; they also interpret behavior in terms of what they already know—or think they know—about the person's character.

Using a Schema to Interpret a Person's Actions

The organized set of information or beliefs that we have about any entity or event is referred to by cognitive psychologists as a *schema* (discussed in Chapter 9). Thus, to know a person, even slightly, accurately or inaccurately, is to have a mental schema for that person. Even before we meet a person, we may already have a schema of him or her based on what we have heard and supplemented by our imagination. That knowledge can influence our interpretation of the person's behavior and bias the attributions we make.

A classic experiment demonstrating this biasing effect of prior knowledge involved perception of a guest lecturer by students in a course at MIT (Kelley, 1950). Before the guest arrived, half the students received a written biographical sketch of the guest that included the statement, "People who know him consider him to be a very warm person, industrious, critical, practical, and determined." The other half received the same sketch except that the words "very warm" were replaced by "rather cold." After the guest had appeared and led a 20-minute discussion, the students were asked to fill out a form evaluating his performance. The main results were that the students who had received the sketch containing the words "very warm" took greater part in the discussion and rated the guest and his performance more positively than did the students who had received the sketch containing the words "rather cold." Thus, the two groups responded differently to the same lecturer and made different attributions about his performance depending on the initial schema set up for them.

First impressions are often hard to change because people tend to interpret new information so as to make it consistent with those impressions (Asch, 1946; Park, 1986). Our smile looks friendly to those who think we are kind, smug to those who think we are aloof, and deceitful to those who think we are untrustworthy. Because of others' interpretations, our smile tends to confirm rather than dispute their prior impression of us.

The Attractiveness Bias

Often the first impression we gain of others is based purely on their physical appearance, and, like any first impression, it can bias our subsequent judgments. Consistent with folktales in which the good people (the princesses and princes) are beautiful and the bad people (the witches and ogres) are ugly, experiments have shown that physically attractive people are commonly judged as more intelligent, competent, sociable, and moral than less attractive people (Dion, 1986; Eagly & others, 1991). In one experiment, fifth-grade teachers were given report cards and photographs of children whom they did not know and were asked to rate each child's intelligence and achievement. The teachers rated physically attractive children as brighter and more successful than unattractive children with identical report cards (Clifford & Walster, 1973). In a similar experiment, adults more frequently attributed a child's misbehavior to environmental circumstances if the child was physically attractive and to the child's personality if the child was not

---

8.

How can a preexisting schema bias interpretations of a person's behavior, and how was such an effect demonstrated in an experiment at MIT? Why do first impressions often resist change?

9.

How have researchers documented biasing effects of (a) physical attractiveness and (b) facial maturity on the attributions that people make about a person?

attractive (Dion, 1972). In yet another study, which analyzed actual court cases, judges regularly gave longer prison sentences to unattractive persons than to attractive persons convicted of comparable crimes (Stewart, 1985).

The Baby-Face Bias

Another pervasive bias, although less well known, concerns a person's facial maturity. Some people, regardless of their age, have facial features resembling those of a baby—a round rather than elongated head, a forehead protruding forward rather than sloping back, large eyes, and a small jawbone (see Figure 13.4). In a series of experiments conducted in both the United States and Korea, baby-faced adults were perceived as more naïve, honest, helpless, kind, and warm than mature-faced adults of the same age and sex, even though the perceivers could tell that the baby-faced persons were not really younger (McArthur & Berry, 1987; Zebrowitz & others, 1993). Leslie Zebrowitz and Susan McDonald (1991) found that the baby-face bias, like the attractiveness bias, can influence the outcome of actual small-claims court cases. Baby-faced defendants were much more frequently found innocent in cases involving intentional wrongdoing than were mature-faced defendants, but they were neither more nor less frequently found innocent in cases involving negligence (such as performing a contracted job incompetently). Apparently, judges find it hard to think of baby-faced persons as deliberately causing harm but do not find it hard to think of them as incompetent or forgetful.

Zebrowitz (1996) has also found evidence that differences in facial maturity between men and women may contribute to differences in how the two sexes are perceived. Women, on average, are more baby-faced than men, and women are also, on average, judged as kinder, more naïve, more emotional, and less socially dominant than men. In an experiment, Zebrowitz and her colleagues presented college students with schematic drawings of men's and women's faces in which facial maturity was varied by altering the size of the eyes and the length of the jaw (Friedman & Zebrowitz, 1992). When the typical differences between men's and women's faces were present, students judged the man as more dominant and less warm than the woman. But when the faces were equivalent on the maturity dimensions, the students judged the two as equal in dominance and warmth. Zebrowitz did not suggest that facial features are the sole determinant of the different perceptions people have of women and men under more natural conditions, but she did suggest that such features may contribute to the difference.

The ethologist Konrad Lorenz (1943, 1971) suggested long ago that infants' facial features act as *sign stimuli* (a concept discussed in Chapter 3) to elicit in us an

10.

How might a sex difference in facial features contribute to perceived psychological differences between women and men?

FIGURE **13.4**
Who would deceive you?
Adults whose faces are babyish (left) are commonly seen as more naïve, honest, helpless, kind, and warm than are mature-faced adults (right). The characteristics of a baby face include a round head, large forehead, large eyes, short nose, and small chin.

innate response of compassion and caring. He also noted that the same features lead us to perceive some animal species (such as bunnies and pandas) as particularly cute, innocent, and needing care, regardless of the animals' actual behaviors. Zebrowitz's work suggests that we generalize this response not just to babies and animals but also to adult humans whose faces resemble those of babies. For another example, see Figure 13.5.

From an evolutionary perspective, it is noteworthy that human adults of both sexes are much more baby-faced than the adults of our closest primate relatives. The typical adult human face is more like that of an infant chimpanzee than like that of an adult chimpanzee. This difference is generally attributed to the expanded cranial cavity that came with enlargement of the brain in humans. But I wonder if that is the whole explanation. In the course of human evolution individuals who had babyish faces may have been treated more benignly than those who had more mature faces, and perhaps this helped promote our species' evolution toward baby-facedness. This is speculation, but it is supported by evidence that baby-faced children and adolescents are less often physically abused than are their age mates who have more mature faces (McCabe, 1984). As further speculation, perhaps the protective effect was of greater value for girls and women than for boys and men—for reasons having to do with the general sex difference in strength and aggressiveness—leading to sex difference in baby-facedness observed today. (Can you imagine any ways to test this theory? Send me an e-mail if you can.)

FIGURE 13.5 *The evolution of innocence in Mickey Mouse*
Mickey Mouse began life, in the 1928 cartoon *Steamboat Willie*, as a mischievous, teasing character who delighted in cranking a goat's tail. In response to social pressure from citizens concerned about Mickey's moral effects on children, the Walt Disney Company made him increasingly innocent over the years. As part of this change, Disney artists made him look more innocent and cute by augmenting his juvenile features. According to measurements made by Stephen Jay Gould, over a 50-year period Mickey's eye size increased from 27 to 42 percent of his head length, his head length increased from 43 to 48 percent of his body length, and the apparent vault of his forehead increased markedly as a result of the gradual migration of his front ear toward the back of his head. (Based on S. J. Gould, 1980, pp. 96–97.)

Effects of Stereotypes

We all carry in our heads schemas not just for individual persons but also for whole groups of people. You may have schemas for men, women, Asians, African-Americans, Californians, Catholics, and college professors. Such schemas are called *stereotypes.* The first person to use the term *stereotype* in this way was the journalist Walter Lippmann (1922), who defined it as "the picture in the head" that a person may have of a particular group or category of people. Some stereotypes may accurately portray the distinguishing characteristics of a group, others may exaggerate those characteristics, and still others may be total fabrications. Later in this chapter and the next, you will encounter some ideas about how stereotypes are acquired and the psychological and social functions they may serve. For now, however, our concern is with the effects of stereotypes on perceptions of individuals. Whether or not a stereotype accurately portrays the average member of a particular group, it can bias our assessment of any individual member who differs (as everyone does) from the average.

The Problem of Identifying Stereotypes

At one time, psychologists in the United States had no difficulty identifying people's stereotypes of various ethnic groups. All they had to do was ask. Typically they asked respondents to check off, on a list of traits, those that best characterized the group in question. In one such study in the early 1930s, Princeton University students described black people as *superstitious* (84 percent checked this trait) and *lazy*

11.

What is the distinction among public, private, and implicit stereotypes, and how do psychologists identify implicit stereotypes?

Overcoming a stereotype

We tend to stereotype people who look different from us or from what we conceive as the norm. This woman, Barbara Tiemann, has a genetic condition called Turner's syndrome and is a past president of the Turner's Syndrome Society. Because women with this condition look different, many people mistakenly assume that they are intellectually slow. The society serves as a support group to help members deal with this kind of stereotyping.

12.

How have researchers shown that stereotypes can lead to prejudice and discrimination even in the absence of conscious prejudice? What different roles do automatic and controlled mental processes play in reactions to stereotyped individuals?

(75 percent), Jews as *shrewd* (79 percent) and *mercenary* (49 percent), and Germans as *scientifically minded* (84 percent) and *industrious* (65 percent) (Katz & Braly, 1933). A decade later, after World War II broke out, the prominent stereotypes of blacks and Jews were little changed, but that of Germans changed to include the traits *arrogant* and *cruel* (Seago, 1947).

Today it is not so easy for psychologists to assess stereotypes. People in our culture, particularly college students, are sensitized to the harmful effects of stereotypes and are reluctant to admit holding them, especially negative ones about socially oppressed groups. Some social psychologists today distinguish among three levels of stereotypes: public, private, and implicit (Dovidio & others, 1994). The *public* level is what we say to others about the group. The *private* level is what we consciously believe but generally do not say to others. The *implicit* level is the set of learned mental associations that can guide our judgments and actions without our awareness, whether or not the associations coincide with our conscious beliefs. Much recent research on stereotypes has centered on the implicit level.

As you may recall from Chapter 9, cognitive psychologists often use a method called *priming* to learn how knowledge is organized in people's minds. The premise behind this method is that any concept presented to a person activates (primes) in the person's mind the entire set of concepts that are closely associated with that concept. Priming the mind with one concept makes the related concepts more easily retrievable from long-term memory into working memory. For example, the word *apple*, presented as a prime, enables a typical person to respond more quickly to yes-or-no questions about such related concepts as *red*, *round*, *pie*, and *fruit*. A person whose task is to press one button for *yes* or a different button for *no* will respond a few milliseconds faster to the question "Is *red* a color?" after seeing the word *apple* as a prime than after seeing *banana* as a prime.

Social psychologists have adopted the priming method to identify people's implicit stereotypes. So that subjects do not consciously counteract the effects of the primes and suppress their stereotypes, the primes are either presented as irrelevant distractors or flashed so quickly that they are registered unconsciously but are not consciously perceived (a procedure discussed in Chapter 8). The priming stimuli in experiments dealing with stereotypes of black people and white people are in some cases words—such as *BLACK* or *WHITE*—and in other cases pictures of black or white faces.

Such studies reveal that implicit stereotypes are very much alive, even in persons who don't subscribe to the stereotypes in their explicit statements on questionnaires (Dovidio & others, 1996; Kawakami & Dovidio, 2001). Priming the concept of a black person typically leads white subjects to respond more quickly to questions about such concepts as *lazy*, *hostile*, *musical*, and *athletic*; and priming the concept of a white person leads them to respond more quickly to such concepts as *conventional*, *materialistic*, *ambitious*, and *intelligent*. Although positive and negative traits appear in both stereotypes, the experiments reveal that the implicit stereotypes white students have of blacks are significantly more negative than those they have of whites (Dovidio & others, 1986; Fazio & others, 1995). Conversely, in one study black Americans manifested significantly more negative stereotypes of whites than of blacks (Fazio & others, 1995).

Effects of Implicit Stereotypes on Actions and Judgments

Implicit stereotypes can promote prejudicial actions and attributions toward the stereotyped group, even in people who are not consciously prejudiced. In one study, John Dovidio and his colleagues (1997) found that white college students' nonverbal signs of discomfort (rate of eye blinks and failure to make eye contact) when interviewed by black interviewers correlated significantly and quite strongly with their implicit negative stereotypes of black people, which had been assessed using a priming method. In contrast, the same study revealed no correlation between the measures of discomfort and the students' explicit views of black people, which had been assessed with a questionnaire.

Linda Haas Photography

In an earlier study, Patricia Devine (1989) worked with white college students as subjects. Half were primed to activate their stereotypes of black men. Then all subjects heard a story about a man named Donald who engaged in actions that might or might not be attributed to hostility. The story did not mention Donald's race. Devine assumed that subjects in the stereotype-primed condition would have in their unconscious mind the image of a black man as they heard the story, and she predicted that they would interpret Donald's actions in terms of that stereotype. Consistent with Devine's prediction, those in the stereotype-primed condition rated Donald higher in hostility and unfriendliness than did those in the unprimed condition. This was as true of subjects who manifested the least prejudice on a questionnaire designed to assess explicit prejudice toward blacks as it was of those who manifested the most prejudice by that measure.

Other studies have shown that college students more often make biased attributions based on stereotypes when they are tired or mentally preoccupied than when they are refreshed and able to bring their full conscious attention to the attributional task (Bodenhausen & others, 1999; Gilbert & Hixon, 1991). Stereotypes apparently provide automatic shortcuts to judgment in situations where we lack the information, time, mental resources, or motivation to evaluate logically the facts of the individual case. Overcoming prejudice, therefore, is like resisting any well-learned habit. Devine and Margo Monteith (1993, 1999) have found that people who consciously dispute the culture's stereotypes feel discomfort or guilt when they find themselves reacting automatically in stereotype-consistent ways. They suggest that this discomfort can lead people to work deliberately at countering their automatic reactions and eventually overcoming them.

Person Perceptions as Self-Fulfilling Prophecies

Our beliefs and expectations—whether they are initially true or false—can to some degree create reality by influencing the behavior of ourselves and others. Such effects are sometimes called *self-fulfilling prophecies* (Merton, 1948). In George Bernard Shaw's play *Pygmalion* (upon which the musical *My Fair Lady* was based), the impoverished cockney flower girl Eliza Doolittle becomes a fine lady in large part because of her response to the expectations of others. Professor Higgins assumes that she is capable of learning to talk and act like a fine lady, and Colonel Pickering assumes that she is truly noble at heart. Their actions toward Eliza lead her to respond in ways that transform their assumptions into realities.

A number of experiments have affirmed the "Pygmalion effect." When person A is led to believe that person Z has a particular characteristic, A's behavior toward Z can lead Z to manifest that characteristic. In one such experiment, Robert Rosenthal and Lenore Jacobson (1968) led elementary school teachers to believe that certain students would show a spurt in intellectual growth during the next few months, as indicated by a special test that all students had taken. In reality, the students labeled "spurters" had been selected not on the basis of a test score but at random. Yet when all the students were tested 8 months later, the selected students showed significantly greater gains in IQ and academic performance than did their classmates. Subsequent research on this *Pygmalion in the classroom* effect indicates that it occurs through differences in the ways that teachers behave toward students whom they believe will excel compared with the other students. Teachers are warmer toward those students, give them more time to answer difficult questions, give them more challenging work, and notice and reinforce more often their self-initiated efforts (Cooper & Good, 1983; Rosenthal, 1994). In short, either consciously or unconsciously, they establish for those students a better learning environment, one in which the teachers' expectations of the students become self-fulfilling prophecies.

Other researchers have documented self-fulfilling effects of cultural stereotypes. J. Michael Palardy (1969) identified, with a survey, a group of first-grade teachers who believed that boys learn to read more slowly than do girls and another

13.

What is some evidence that beliefs about a person or a group can affect that person or group in such a way as to become a self-fulfilling prophecy?

group who believed that boys and girls learn to read at equal rates. Then, 5 months later, he examined the reading achievement scores of students who had subsequently entered the classrooms of the two groups of teachers. The results conformed with the teachers' expectations. The boys scored lower in reading than the girls in classrooms where the teacher believed in the sex difference but not in classrooms where the teacher did not believe in the sex difference. Other research suggests that parents' beliefs about biologically based sex differences in math, sports, and social relationships can influence the development of their sons and daughters in the expected directions (Jacobs & Eccles, 1992).

The perceptions and misperceptions of others can affect not just the behavior of the target person but also that person's *self-concept*, the topic to which we now turn.

SECTION SUMMARY

As intuitive psychologists, people form impressions of others' personalities by observing others' behaviors. In line with Kelley's model, distinctive behaviors (those that differ most from the way that a typical person would behave in similar circumstances) are most informative of personality. Nondistinctive behaviors are more reasonably attributed to the situation than to anything unique about the person. Often, however, people do attribute nondistinctive behaviors to personality. This person bias, or "fundamental attribution error," occurs in experiments in which the subjects' goal is to assess the personality of someone performing an action. When the goal is to assess the situation that provokes the action, the opposite bias—the situation bias—occurs. Both of these biases are especially strong when subjects are kept mentally occupied so that their judgments are based on automatic rather than controlled thought processes.

Other studies indicate that the person bias is more characteristic of people in Western cultures than in Eastern cultures. Moreover, the person bias is weaker, and the situation bias is stronger, when people make attributions about their own behavior than when they make attributions about someone else's. This so-called actor-observer discrepancy might derive from the more extensive knowledge that people have of themselves than of others, or it might derive from the fact that people's eyes are focused on the person when they watch another perform an action and on the situation when they themselves perform an action.

Preexisting beliefs about a person can influence the way in which that person's behavior is judged. Physical appearance is one source of such beliefs. For example, baby-faced people are viewed as more naïve, innocent, and incompetent than are mature-faced people, and their behavior is judged in that light. First impressions are also affected by cultural stereotypes concerning race, gender, age, and other ways of categorizing people. Experiments involving the technique of priming have revealed that even people who are not consciously prejudiced carry the culture's racial stereotypes in their heads and that those stereotypes can bias judgments about a person's actions.

Preexisting beliefs can sometimes result in self-fulfilling prophecies. In one experiment, teachers were falsely informed that certain of their students had performed exceptionally well on a test of academic potential. The teachers subsequently behaved differently toward those students than toward others, in ways that led those students to achieve more than they otherwise would have.

PERCEIVING AND EVALUATING THE SELF

Self-awareness is often described as one of the hallmarks of our species, though it is difficult to judge the degree to which members of other species may be aware of themselves as entities. At about 15 months of age, human infants stop treating their image in a mirror as if it were another child and begin to treat it as a reflection of themselves. If a researcher surreptitiously places a bright red spot of rouge on the child's nose before placing the child in front of the mirror, the 15-month-old responds by touching his or her *own* nose to feel or rub off the rouge; a younger child, by contrast, touches the mirror or tries to look behind it to find the red-nosed child (Lewis & Brooks-Gunn, 1979). The only other animals besides ourselves who have passed the rouge test of self-recognition are the other apes—chimpanzees, bonobos, orangutans, and at least one gorilla and one gibbon (Parker & others, 1994; Ujhelyi & others, 2000). Other animals, including all species of monkeys tested so far, continue to treat the mirror image as another animal—a creature to threaten and try to chase away—no matter what their age or how much experience they have had with mirrors.

Research with chimpanzees suggests that for them social interaction is crucial for self-recognition. Chimpanzees raised in isolation from others of their kind did not learn to make self-directed responses to their mirror images, whereas those raised with other chimps did (Gallup & others, 1971). Many psychologists and sociologists have argued that the self-concept, for humans as well as chimps, is fundamentally a *social* product. To become aware of yourself, you must first become aware of others of your species and then become aware, perhaps from how others treat you, that you are one of them. In humans, self-awareness includes awareness not just of the physical self, reflected in mirror images, but also of one's own personality and character, reflected psychologically in the reactions of other people.

It's me

By pointing to her own nose as she looks at herself in the mirror, this child demonstrates her understanding that the mirror image is indeed of her.

Seeing Ourselves Through the Eyes of Others

Many years ago the sociologist Charles Cooley (1902/1964) coined the term *looking-glass self* to describe what he considered to be a very large aspect of each person's self-concept. The "looking glass" to which he referred is not an actual mirror but other people who react to us. He suggested that we all naturally infer and imagine what others think of us from their reactions, and we use those inferences and images to build our own self-concepts. As Eliza Doolittle said to Colonel Pickering in *Pygmalion:* "You see, really and truly, . . . the difference between a lady and a flower girl is not how she behaves but how she's treated. I shall always be a flower girl to Professor Higgins, because he always treats me as a flower girl, and always will; but I know I can be a lady to you, because you always treat me as a lady, and always will."

From a functionalist perspective, it makes sense that our self-concepts should be founded largely on what others think of us. Our self-concepts allow us to predict how others will respond to us so that we can fit into society in ways consistent with others' expectations. A flower girl who thought she was a fine lady but could convince nobody else of it would be in for a hard time.

Effects of Others' Appraisals on Self-Understanding

The concept of the looking-glass self may help explain the effects that teachers' beliefs have on their pupils' behavior, discussed in the previous section. Children treated as if they have a particular quality may incorporate that quality into their self-concepts and therefore express it more fully in their actions. Studies in which children were asked to describe themselves have confirmed that their self-descriptions change in accordance with evaluations by their teachers and peers (Cole, 1991; Jussim, 1991). Moreover, in experiments where children were told explicitly that they were a certain kind of person, they responded by behaving in accordance with the attribute they were told they had.

In one such experiment, some children were told in the course of classroom activity that they *were* neat and tidy (*attribution condition*); others were told that they *should be* neat and tidy (*persuasion condition*); and still others were given no special treatment (*control condition*). The result was that those in the attribution condition showed significantly greater gains in neatness, as measured by the absence of littering, than did those in either of the other conditions (Miller & others, 1975). Similarly, children who were told that they were good at math showed greater improvements in math scores than did those who were told that they should try to

14.

What evidence in contemporary psychology supports, and delimits, Cooley's concept of the looking-glass self?

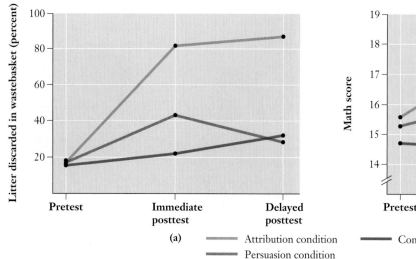

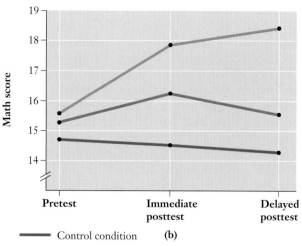

(a)

Attribution condition   Control condition   (b)

Persuasion condition

FIGURE **13.6**   *Effect of attribution compared with persuasion*

(a) Fifth-graders who were repeatedly told that they were neat and tidy (attribution condition) showed greater gain in use of the wastebasket than did those in the other conditions. (b) Second-graders who were repeatedly told that they were good at math (attribution condition) showed greater improvement in math scores than did those in the other conditions. In each case, the students were tested three times: once right before (pretest), once immediately after (immediate posttest), and once a few weeks after (delayed posttest) the experimental conditions were in effect. (Adapted from Miller & others, 1975.)

15.

What might lead us to develop multiple self-concepts, and why might they be useful?

become good at math (see Figure 13.6). In these experiments the change in behavior presumably occurred because of a direct effect of the appraisals on the children's self-concepts, which they then strove to live up to.

Of course, people's self-concepts are not always as moldable as the experiments just cited might suggest. The effects are strongest with young children and with characteristics for which people do not already have firm self-beliefs. Adolescents and adults often respond to such appraisals in ways that seem designed to correct what they perceive to be another person's misperception of them (Swann, 1987)—Pygmalion in reverse. In one experiment, adults who perceived themselves as dominant became all the more dominant in their behavior if their conversation partner initially thought they were submissive, and those who perceived themselves as submissive became all the more submissive if their partner initially thought they were dominant (Swann & Hill, 1982). As another example, Zebrowitz and her colleagues (1998) have found that baby-faced teenage boys and young men often behave in ways that seem to be designed to counteract the baby-face stereotype. For instance, in World War II and the Korean War, baby-faced soldiers undertook more dangerous missions and won more military awards, on average, than did mature-faced soldiers, apparently to counteract others' expectations that they lacked courage (Collins & Zebrowitz, 1995).

Social Roles and Multiple Selves

You have read of evidence that the raw material for self-understanding lies in one's social interactions with others. But any given person may have quite different kinds of interactions with different groups. As William James (1890/1950) put it long ago, "Many a youth who is demure enough before his parents and teachers, swears and swaggers like a pirate among his 'tough' young friends." From such observations, James argued that each person has not just one self-concept but many, each corresponding to his or her relationship with a different person or set of people. Psychologists who emphasize the relationship between self-concepts and *social roles* have expanded on this idea. Each of us plays a number of different roles in society, and we have a somewhat different concept of ourselves associated with each. I am a *father, son, neighbor,* and *college professor* to different people. When I think of myself in each role, different sets of traits and abilities come to mind. My understanding of myself in each role is mediated partly by the larger society's stereotype of what fathers, sons, neighbors, and college professors are like and partly by the specific expectations of the individuals to whom I am those things.

Research has shown that people's self-descriptions vary depending on which of their social roles has been mentally activated. Such work has led to weblike models of the self-concept, in which some self-perceived traits are attached to specific roles (the nodes in the web) while others are attached to several or all roles, tying the nodes together (Hoelter, 1985; Rosenberg, 1988). For example, a person might see herself or himself as *authoritative* in the role of employer, *submissive* in the role of daughter or son, *companionable* in the role of wife or husband, and *caring* in all these roles. For this person, the trait of being caring ties the roles together and is a source of consistency in the self-concept (see Figure 13.7). Self-report studies suggest that such consistent traits lead to a general sense of the self that cuts across roles, and people feel most comfortable in those roles where the role-specific self most closely matches the general self (Roberts & Donahue, 1994).

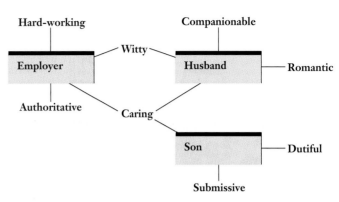

FIGURE 13.7 *The multiple nature of the self-concept*
The self-concept can be represented as a web with different nodes for one's different social roles. Some self-perceived traits may be tied to just one role (such as husband or employer), and others may be tied to several or all of one's roles.

You might expect that having multiple self-concepts, each associated with a different role, would be psychologically stressful, but research suggests that the opposite is more often true (Dance & Kuiper, 1987; Linville, 1985, 1987). The sense of having multiple roles and a wide variety of traits seems to protect a person from depression when one role is lost or diminished in importance—as might happen in a divorce, or when children grow up and leave home, or when a job is lost. Moreover, the sense of having many roles and traits to draw on apparently adds to a person's confidence in his or her ability to handle new situations (Sande & others, 1988).

Comparing and Contrasting Ourselves to Others

Although our self-concepts are to some degree sketched out for us by others' perceptions and the roles we occupy in society, we do not passively accept those sketches. Rather, we use the sketches as models, actively selecting from among them and modifying them to build our own self-concepts. As part of that process, we compare ourselves to others.

In perception everything is relative to some frame of reference, and in self-perception the frame of reference is other people. To see oneself as short, conscientious, or good at math is to see oneself as those things *compared with other people*. The process of comparing ourselves with others to identify our unique characteristics and evaluate our abilities is called *social comparison*. A direct consequence of social comparison is that the self-concept varies depending on the *reference group*, the group against whom the comparison is made. If the reference group against which I evaluated my height was made up of professional basketball players, I would see myself as short, but if it was made up of jockeys, I would see myself as tall.

In one series of studies that illustrates the role of the reference group, children's self-descriptions were found to focus on traits that most distinguished them from others in their group (McGuire & McGuire, 1988). Thus, children in racially homogeneous classrooms rarely mentioned their race, but those in racially mixed classrooms quite commonly did, especially if their race was in the minority. Children who were unusually tall or short compared with others in their group more frequently mentioned height, and children with opposite-gender siblings more frequently mentioned their gender than did other children (see Figure 13.8).

16.

What is some evidence that people construct a self-concept by comparing themselves with a reference group and that a change in reference group can alter self-esteem?

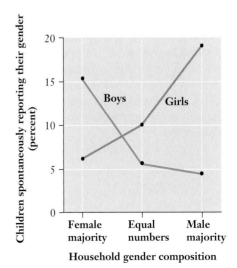

FIGURE 13.8 *Evidence that children define themselves in terms of differences from their reference group*
As shown here, children were more likely to mention their gender when describing themselves if their gender was in the minority in their household than they were if it was in the majority. (Adapted from McGuire & McGuire, 1988.)

"Of course you're going to be depressed if you keep comparing yourself with successful people."

Effect of the Reference Group on Self-Evaluation

The evaluative aspect of social comparison can be charged with emotion. We are pleased with ourselves when we feel that we measure up to the reference group and distressed when we don't. A change of reference group, therefore, can dramatically affect our self-esteem. Many first-year college students who earned high grades in high school feel crushed when their marks are only average or less compared with those of their new reference group of college classmates. Researchers have found that academically able students at nonselective schools typically have higher academic self-concepts than do equally able students at highly selective schools (Marsh, 1991; Marsh & others, 2000), a phenomenon aptly called the *big-fish-in-little-pond effect*. William James (1890/1950), reflecting on extreme instances of selective comparisons, wrote: "So we have the paradox of the man shamed to death because he is only the second pugilist or second oarsman in the world. That he is able to beat the whole population of the globe minus one is nothing; he has 'pitted' himself to beat that one and as long as he doesn't do that nothing else counts."

In a follow-up of James's century-old idea, Victoria Medvec and her colleagues (1995) analyzed the televised broadcasts of the 1992 Summer Olympics for the amounts of joy and agony expressed by the silver and bronze medalists after each event. The main finding was that the silver medalists (the second-place finishers) showed less joy and more agony than did the bronze medalists (the third-place finishers), whom they had defeated. This seemingly paradoxical finding makes sense if we assume that the groups were implicitly making different comparisons. The silver medalists had almost come in first, so the prominent comparison to them—after the contest if not before—was likely that of themselves to the gold medalists, and in that comparison they were losers. In contrast, the bronze medalists had barely made it into the group that received a medal at all, so the prominent comparison in their minds was likely that of themselves to the nonmedalists, and in that they were winners.

The Better-Than-Average Phenomenon

The radio humorist Garrison Keillor describes his mythical town of Lake Wobegon as a place where "all the children are above average." We smile at this statistical impossibility partly because we recognize the same bias in ourselves. Repeated surveys have found that most college students rate themselves as better students than the average college student, and in one survey 94 percent of college instructors rated themselves as better teachers than the average college instructor (Alicke & others, 1995; Cross, 1977). What causes such apparent self-delusion?

One possible cause, which hasn't been pursued by researchers as far as I know, is the complimentary nature of the feedback we typically receive from other people. Norms of politeness as well as other considerations of self-interest encourage people to praise each other and inhibit even constructive criticism: "If you can't say something nice, say nothing at all" is one of our mores. Since we build our self-concepts at least partly from others' appraisals of us, we are likely to construct positively biased self-concepts to the degree that the appraisals we hear are biased in that direction.

Another cause of the better-than-average phenomenon may lie in the differing criteria for success that different people have in any given endeavor. The majority of people may truly be "above average" if the criteria are allowed to vary from person to person in accordance with their unique views of the task. One student considers himself an above-average scholar because he plays such a constructive role in class discussions, another because he relates what he learns in class to practical problems in his life, another because he gets high scores on tests, and yet another

---

17.

How might the better-than-average phenomenon be explained by (a) biased feedback from others, (b) people's differing criteria of success, (c) the self-serving attributional bias, and (d) the inability of the incompetent to assess competence?

because he disdains "grubbing for grades" and spends time reading books that are not assigned. One instructor sees herself as better than average because she treats her students as individuals, another because she explains the subject matter clearly, another because she has high standards and is the toughest grader in her department, and yet another because she has never failed anyone. Consistent with this interpretation of the better-than-average phenomenon, researchers have found it to be stronger for endeavors in which the criteria of success are not well defined than for those (such as speed of running) in which the criteria are more uniform (Dunning & others, 1989). It is hard to know to what degree people define their criteria differently in order to view themselves in a better light or to what extent their differing goals and criteria stem from truly differing conceptions of the task. Although psychologists have tended to focus mostly on the former possibility, it seems likely that both factors are involved.

People may also maintain an elevated view of themselves by systematically biasing the attributions they make about their successes and failures. Earlier you read of the actor-observer effect in attributions, the tendency for people to attribute their own actions to the situation and others' actions to the person. That effect is best assessed with actions that are neutral on the dimension of success or failure. When success or failure enters the picture, another bias comes into play, the *self-serving attributional bias*—the tendency of people to attribute their successes to their own qualities and their failures to the situation. In one study, students who performed well on an examination attributed their high grades to their own ability and hard work, whereas those who performed poorly attributed their low grades to bad luck, the unfairness of the test, or other factors beyond their control (Bernstein & others, 1979). In another study, essentially the same result was found for college professors who were asked to explain why a paper they had submitted to a scholarly journal had been either accepted or rejected (Wiley & others, 1979). My favorite examples of the self-serving bias come from people's formal reports of automobile accidents, such as the following (quoted by Greenwald, 1980): "The telephone pole was approaching. I was attempting to swerve out of its way when it struck my front end." Clearly, a reckless telephone pole caused this accident; the skillful driver just couldn't get out of its way in time.

The people who most markedly overestimate their own abilities on a task are those who are objectively poorest at that task. Justin Kruger and David Dunning (1999) demonstrated this in experiments in which students evaluated their own abilities, compared to others, in humor, logical thinking, and grammar, and were also given objective tests of their abilities in those realms. In each case, those who were objectively the worst grossly overestimated their abilities, and those who were the best slightly underestimated their abilities (see Figure 13.9). A possible explanation, suggested by Kruger and Dunning, is that those who are most incompetent lack the knowledge necessary to realize that they are incompetent. They can't tell the difference between good performance and poor and therefore don't see that others perform better than they do. As Charles Darwin (1871/1965) put it long ago, "Ignorance more frequently begets confidence than the reverse."

Cultural Dependence of the Self-Serving Bias

The better-than-average and self-serving effects just described are so common in North America that some psychologists take their absence as a sign of psychological depression. Depressed people, according to some reports (Peterson & Seligman, 1984), evaluate themselves more accurately than do nondepressed people: If depressed individuals are average at some task, they see themselves as average; if they cause an accident, they blame themselves. As you will discover in

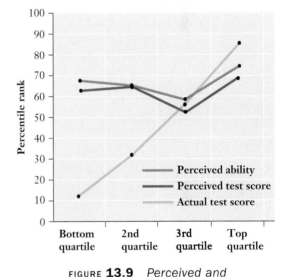

FIGURE **13.9** *Perceived and measured logical reasoning ability*
In an experiment, students took a test of logical reasoning and immediately afterward estimated, on a percentile scale, how well they thought they did on the test and how skilled they were in "general logical reasoning" compared to their classmates. As shown here, those with the lowest scores greatly overestimated their performance and skill. Similar findings occurred in other experiments having to do with sense of humor and grammatical ability. (Kruger & Dunning, 1999, p. 1125.)

18.

What evidence suggests that the self-enhancing biases observed in Western culture may not characterize people everywhere?

Chapter 15, some personality theorists believe that certain illusions are normal and healthy.

But what is true in the West is not necessarily true everywhere. Sometimes what Western psychologists report to be human nature is not *human* nature but *Western* nature. Hazel Markus and Shinobu Kitayama (1991) asked university students in the United States and Japan to estimate what percentage of their classmates had higher intellectual abilities than their own. The average response for the Americans was 30 percent, consistent with the better-than-average phenomenon, but the average for the Japanese was 50 percent, which of course is what the average would have to be for both groups if they were estimating accurately.

In another study, Michael Bond and Tak-Sing Cheung (1983) asked university students in the United States, Hong Kong, and Japan to describe themselves in an open-ended way by completing 20 statements, each of which began with the words *I am.* They then analyzed the statements for evaluative content and found that the ratio of positive to negative self-statements was nearly 2 to 1 for the American students, 1 to 1 for the Hong Kong students, and 1 to 2 for the Japanese students. In other words, the Japanese students showed a *self-effacing bias* that was as strong as the Americans' self-enhancing bias. In Japan—according to sociologists and psychologists—the ideal person is not someone who thinks highly of himself or herself but someone who is aware of his or her deficiencies and is working hard to overcome them (Heine & others, 1999).

Seeing Ourselves and Others as One: Social Identity

You have been reading of evidence that the self-concept is social in that others are involved in its construction: We see ourselves reflected in others' reactions to us, and we understand ourselves by comparing our properties with those of others. But the self-concept is social in another sense as well. Others are not just involved in its construction; they are also part of its contents. We describe and think of ourselves not just in terms of our individual characteristics—"I am *short,* . . . *adventurous,* . . . *somewhat shy*"—but also in terms of the groups to which we belong and with which we identify—"I am a *French Canadian,* . . . *Roman Catholic,* . . . *member of the University Marching Band.*" Self-descriptions that pertain to the person as a separate individual are referred to as **personal identity,** and those that pertain to the social categories or groups to which the person belongs are referred to as **social identity** (Tajfel, 1972).

19.

What value might lie in our flexible ability to think of ourselves in terms of both personal and social identities?

Adult self-concepts are relatively consistent from situation to situation, but they are not rigid (Oakes & others, 1994). We think of ourselves differently at different times, in ways that help us meet the ever-changing challenges of social life. Sometimes, for some purposes, we find it most useful to think of our unique properties and motives; other times, for other purposes, we find it most useful to think of ourselves as interchangeable components of a larger unit, the group. Our evolution as a social species entailed a continuous balance between the need to compete and assert ourselves as individuals and the need to cooperate with others, which may have selected for a capacity to hold both personal and social identities (Guisinger & Blatt, 1994). In evolutionary history the groups with which we cooperated included some that may have been lifelong, such as the family and tribe, and others that were more ephemeral, such as a hunting party organized to track down a particular antelope. Today the relatively permanent groups with which we identify may include our family, ethnic group, religious affiliation, and occupational colleagues. The temporary groups include the various teams and coalitions with which we affiliate for particular ends, for periods ranging from minutes to years. When we see some interest in common, we can be remarkably adept at forgetting our differences and thinking of ourselves and our group-mates as one (an idea pursued more fully in Chapter 14).

Relationships of Social Identity to Self-Esteem

Our feelings about ourselves depend not just on our personal achievements but also on the achievements of the groups with which we identify, even when we ourselves play little or no role in those achievements. Social psychologists have found, for example, that sports fans' feelings about themselves rise and fall as "their" team wins and loses (Hirt & others, 1992). Similarly, people feel good about themselves when their town, university, or place of employment achieves high rank or praise.

In some situations, the very same event—high achievement by other members of our group—can temporarily raise or lower our self-esteem, depending on whether our social identity or personal identity is most active. When our social identity predominates, our group-mates are part of us and we experience their success as ours. When our personal identity predominates, our group-mates are the reference group against which we measure our own accomplishments, so their success may diminish our view of ourselves. Social psychologists have demonstrated both of these effects by priming people to think in terms of either their social or their personal identities as they hear of high accomplishments by others in their group (Brewer & Weber, 1994). You read previously that students at highly selective schools think worse of themselves as scholars than do equally able students at less selective schools because of the difference in their relative standing in their reference group. A subsequent study indicated that this is true for those who think primarily in terms of their personal identities but not for those who think primarily in terms of their social identities (McFarland & Buehler, 1995). When the social identity is foremost, self-feelings are elevated, not diminished, by evidence of group-mates' excellent performances. Graceful winners of individual achievement awards know this intuitively, and to promote good feelings, they activate their group-mates' social identities by describing the award as belonging properly to the whole group.

Other studies reveal that the better-than-average phenomenon and the self-serving attributional bias apply at least as much to our judgments about our groups as to those about ourselves as individuals (Rubin & Hewstone, 1998). In fact, the concept of social identity first became prominent in social psychology when Henri Tajfel (1972, 1982) used it to explain people's strong bias in favor of their own groups over other groups in all sorts of judgments. He argued that we exaggerate the virtues of our own groups to build up the part of our self-esteem that derives from our social identities. Tajfel and others showed that the bias is so strong that we apply it even when we have no realistic basis at all for assuming that our group differs from another. In one laboratory experiment, people who knew they had been assigned to one of two groups by a purely random process—a coin toss—nevertheless rated their own group more positively than they did the other group (Locksley

20.

How does the distinction between social identity and personal identity help explain (a) the two opposing effects that our group-mates' excellent performance can have on our self-esteem and (b) extensions of the self-serving bias to attributions about our group-mates?

Jules Feiffer © 1992

& others, 1980). You don't need a degree in psychology to know that the fans of opposing baseball teams see the same plays differently, in ways that allow them all to leave the game believing that theirs was the better team, regardless of the score. Strike three is attributed by one group to the pitcher's sparkling fastball and by the other to the umpire's unacknowledged need for eyeglasses.

Cross-Cultural Differences in the Balance of Social Identity and Personal Identity

Although both personal and social identities exist among people everywhere, these two aspects of the self are differentially strengthened or weakened by different cultures. Harry Triandis (1995), one of the pioneers of cross-cultural research in psychology, distinguishes between *individualist cultures*, which strengthen personal identities, and *collectivist cultures*, which strengthen social identities. Individualist cultures predominate in western Europe, North America, and Australia, where philosophical and political traditions emphasize personal freedom, self-determination, and individual competition. Collectivist cultures predominate in Asia and in parts of Africa and Latin America, where philosophical and political traditions emphasize the inherent connectedness and interdependence of people within such groups as the family, workplace, village, and nation. Whereas people in individualist cultures tend to define their lives in terms of self-fulfillment, those in collectivist cultures tend to define theirs in terms of fulfilling their duties to, and promoting the welfare of, the groups of which they are members.

Each type of culture has its benefits and costs from the perspective of individual psychology. Individualist cultures may foster personal freedom and creativity at a cost of loneliness and insecurity, and collectivist cultures may foster a sense of belonging and security at a cost of reduced individual initiative and freedom. Collectivist cultures typically have less conflict within groups but more conflict between groups than is the case for individualist cultures (Triandis, 1995). In cultures where group identities are strong, the distinction between "we" and "they" is greater than in cultures where group identities are weak.

Consistent with Triandis's view are numerous studies indicating that people in Eastern cultures such as Japan, Korea, China, and India describe themselves differently than do people in Western cultures (Markus & Kitayama, 1991, 1994). The former describe themselves more often in terms of their social groups and roles and less often in terms of consistent personality traits that cut across their groups and roles. Asked to describe themselves, they are more likely to make such statements as "I am a student at University X" or "I am the eldest daughter in my family" and less likely to make such statements as "I am easygoing" or "I am ambitious." They are also more likely to attribute their achievements to their group rather than to themselves as individuals (Chen & others, 1998). When they do describe themselves with personality traits, they typically delimit the traits to particular social contexts—"I am easygoing with my friends," "I am ambitious at work" (Cousins, 1989). William James's idea that people have multiple self-concepts related to their multiple roles seems to be even more true of people in collectivist cultures than of those in individualist cultures.

21.

How does Triandis characterize individualist and collectivist cultures, and what differences have been found between the two in people's self-descriptions?

Noboru Hashimoto / Sygma

Walking a line between two cultures

Masako Owada was born in Japan, attended a public high school in Massachusetts, graduated from Harvard in 1985, distinguished herself as a brilliant executive in Japanese foreign trade, and then, in 1993, after much hesitation, accepted the marriage proposal of Japanese Crown Prince Naruhito. Her new role required that she give up much of her Western independence and refrain from expressing her own ideas directly and publicly.

SECTION SUMMARY

Our self-concepts are social constructs. We acquire them in part from other people's reactions to us and beliefs about us. For that reason we may have multiple self-concepts, each related to a different social role and a different group with which we interact. We also construct aspects of our self-concepts by comparing ourselves to others. We may see ourselves as good or bad at a given task depending on the abilities of the reference group with which we compare ourselves.

People in Western cultures tend to have inflated views of themselves, a phenomenon that may be explained in part by biased feedback from others, by people's varying definitions of success, by the self-serving attributional bias, and by the inability of the incompetent to judge their own incompetence. Some studies indicate that such self-inflation does not occur in Asian cultures, perhaps due to cultural traditions that promote a more communal, less individualistic outlook.

In every culture, people describe themselves partly in ways that emphasize their unique personal traits—their personal identity—and partly in ways that emphasize the groups to which they belong—their social identity. Depending on which identity is primed, a person's self-esteem may increase or decrease on hearing of the outstanding performance of other members of his or her group. Many studies have demonstrated that social identity is stronger, and personal identity weaker, in Eastern cultures (and in other collectivist cultures) than in Western cultures.

ATTITUDES: BELIEFS TINGED WITH EMOTION

Thus far in this chapter we have been discussing the ways in which people evaluate other people and themselves. In doing so, we have been implicitly discussing attitudes. An *attitude* is any belief or opinion that has an evaluative component—that something is good or bad, likable or unlikable, moral or immoral, attractive or repulsive. Attitudes tie individuals cognitively and emotionally to their entire social world. We all have attitudes about countless objects, people, events, and ideas, ranging from our feelings about a particular brand of toothpaste to those about democracy or religion. People in our society devote enormous effort to modifying other people's attitudes. Advertising, political campaigning, and the democratic process itself (in which people speak freely in support of their views) are, in essence, attempts to change other people's attitudes.

From a functional perspective, attitudes must exist because they serve certain purposes, or fulfill certain needs, for the people who hold them. Specifically, psychologists have proposed that attitudes serve four relatively separable functions (Herek, 1986; Katz, 1960; Maio & Olson, 2000). Attitudes serve (a) a *value-expressive function* to the degree that they are part of a person's self-concept and help give meaning to the person's life; (b) a *social-adjustive function* to the degree that they are shared by one's social group and help the person get along with that group; (c) a *defensive function* to the degree that they provide a sense of consistency and harmony and help calm the person's anxieties or boost the person's self-esteem; and (d) a *utilitarian function* to the degree that they actually guide the person's behavior toward or away from objects or events in a useful way that increases rewards and decreases punishments. A given attitude may serve any or all of these four functions. For example, your attitude about parenthood is value-expressive if it contains your cherished beliefs about your own present or future role as a parent; social-adjustive if it helps you get along in a social environment where others share a certain view of parenthood; defensive if it helps protect you from conscious or unconscious fears of becoming or not becoming a parent; and utilitarian if it plays a useful role in your decisions about marriage, conception, and child rearing. In what follows we will consider some ideas about attitudes that pertain to each of these functions, beginning with the value-expressive and ending with the utilitarian.

22.

What are four different functions that attitudes may serve?

Attitudes as Aspects of the Self

When people describe themselves, they often include—along with their personality traits and the groups they belong to—their most central attitudes, or values. ***Values*** are the general, relatively abstract attitudes that people claim as guiding principles behind their more specific attitudes and actions; they can be thought of as the *principled* component of the self-concept. Values pertain to one's sense of right and wrong and one's goals for self and society. They pertain to such concepts as freedom, equality, personal achievement, helping others, and respect for tradition.

23.

What evidence led Schwartz to conclude that values can be characterized by a universal structure pertaining to basic human social needs? What are the two dimensions of that structure, and what cross-cultural difference did Schwartz observe?

The Value Wheel: A Universal Structure?

In an extensive cross-cultural study of values, Israeli psychologist Shalom Schwartz (1992) surveyed thousands of primary and secondary school teachers in 20 countries around the globe. He chose teachers because they are literate (able to fill out questionnaires) and because he assumed that they, as conveyors of values to children and adolescents, would hold values representative of the culture at large. Each teacher filled out a form rating each of 56 values in terms of its importance "as a guiding principle" of his or her life. Schwartz then analyzed the responses to assess the degree to which each value correlated positively or negatively with each other value in the list. (Two values correlate positively if people who rate one high or low tend to rate the other in the same direction. Two values correlate negatively if people tend to rate them in opposite directions.) The final result of this analysis was the wheel-like structure of values portrayed in Figure 13.10. The wheel is segmented into 10 *value categories*, each representing a cluster of values that correlate strongly and positively with each other. The categories are arranged so that each one is flanked by the categories that correlate most positively with it and lies opposite those that correlate most negatively with it. The figure tells you, for example, that *self-direction* correlates most strongly in a positive direction with *universalism* and *stimulation* (which flank *self-direction* in the wheel) and most strongly in a negative direction with *security, conformity, tradition,* and *power* (which lie opposite *self-direction*). This general pattern of correlations occurred within each of the cultures Schwartz studied, suggesting that the pattern is universal.

To explain the universality of the value wheel, Schwartz (1992, 1996) suggested that the value types derive from basic human social needs and motives that relate logically to one another as similars or opposites, as depicted by the wheel. To judge the pattern for yourself, make your way around the wheel and consider how each value could promote a person's survival and how it either supports or opposes other values in the wheel. For example, a decision to act in accordance with self-direction

FIGURE 13.10 *The value wheel*
The universal pattern of values proposed by Schwartz is based on the degree to which values support or oppose one another. Each value category occupies a wheel segment adjacent to the categories that correlate most positively with it and opposite those that correlate most negatively with it. Conformity and tradition occupy the same segment because they each correlate about equally strongly with benevolence and security. The value categories are further grouped into four clusters that define two dimensions of the wheel: self-enhancement versus self-transcendence and openness to change versus conservation. Hedonism is marked off with dashed rather than solid lines because it straddles the openness-to-change and self-enhancement clusters. (Based on Figure 1.1 in Schwartz, 1996, p. 5.)

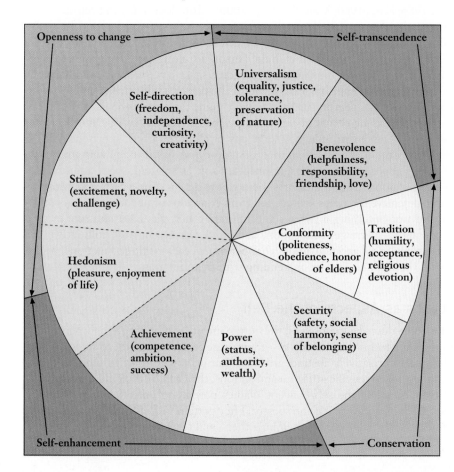

values is likely to be quite consistent with stimulation and universalism values but inconsistent with security and conformity values.

Schwartz concluded that value types cluster into four general categories (also shown in the figure) that form two polar dimensions. One dimension is *self-enhancement* (promotion of one's personal welfare) versus *self-transcendence* (promotion of the welfare of one's social groups and the larger world). The other dimension is *conservation* (holding on to familiar ways of doing things) versus *openness to change* (exploring new ways of doing things).

Although the overall pattern of correlations shown by the value wheel occurred in every culture, the importance assigned to specific value types varied from culture to culture. As you might predict, teachers in relatively collectivist cultures, such as Taiwan, gave the highest rankings to values that fall under security and conformity (conservation), whereas those in individualist cultures, such as New Zealand, placed relatively more weight on self-direction and stimulation (openness to change). But contrary to what you might predict, collectivist and individualist cultures did not differ reliably on the dimension of self-enhancement versus self-transcendence. This finding is consistent with other studies suggesting that people in collectivist cultures value helping others as a duty arising from tradition and social norms, whereas people in individualist cultures value helping others as a free, personal choice (Markus & Kitayama, 1994; Moghaddam & others, 1993).

Values as Predictors of Actions

You certainly can't predict everything people will do by knowing their stated values, but you can make some general predictions that are reliable on a statistical basis. In studies of Israeli citizens, Schwartz (1996) found that people's relative ratings of the value types shown in Figure 13.10 correlated significantly with measurable aspects of their behavior. People who rated the openness-to-change values highest most often supported liberal political candidates, and those who rated the conservation values highest most often supported conservative candidates. In a laboratory game pitting people's tendency to cooperate against their tendency to compete, people who rated the self-transcendence values highest chose most often to cooperate with others, and people who rated the self-enhancement values highest chose most often to compete.

In research that preceded Schwartz's, Milton Rokeach, one of the pioneers in the study of values, found similar correlations between people's relative ranking of particular values and their real-world behaviors. For example, he found that white college students who ranked *equality* especially high were more likely than other white college students to make eye contact when speaking with a black person, to join a political group supporting equal rights, and to participate in a rally for equal rights (Rokeach, 1980).

Attitudes as Social Norms

Values and other attitudes are properties not just of the individual person but also of the social groups to which the person belongs. It is not hard to think of many reasons why an interacting group of individuals would have attitudes in common. People living in the same conditions and communicating with one another are exposed to similar information, are subject to the same persuasive messages, may have come together partly because of preexisting similar attitudes, and may have modified their attitudes to gain greater acceptance in the group.

The best-known study of the effects of a social group on attitude change was initiated in 1934, in the midst of the Great Depression, by Theodore Newcomb (1943) at Bennington College in Vermont, which then was a small women's college. Bennington at that time had a politically liberal faculty but drew most of its students from wealthy, politically conservative families. Most first-year students shared their parents' conservative views, but with each year at the college they became more liberal. In the 1936 presidential election, for example, 62 percent of the

24.

What is some evidence that people's values can be used to predict their behavior?

25.

How did a long-term study at Bennington College and follow-up studies of Bennington graduates illustrate the role of social forces in attitude change?

first-year students, 43 percent of the sophomores, and only 15 percent of the juniors and seniors favored Alf Landon, the conservative Republican, over the liberal Democrat, Franklin Roosevelt. By the time the first-year students became juniors and seniors, they too had become politically liberal.

Certainly the economic crisis, the Depression, played a role in the attitude change that Newcomb observed, but more directly influential were the views expressed by the dominant members of the college. People who occupied the most prestigious positions—the faculty, older students, and leaders of various campus organizations—were politically liberal, and new students could gain social acceptance by shifting their expressed attitudes in that direction. In interviews, many students said that at first they expressed liberal attitudes at least partly to make friends and gain prestige, but over time the attitudes became part of their private as well as public ways of thinking. The relatively few students who remained conservative throughout their 4 years said that they felt socially isolated and not really part of the college community. In follow-ups, 25 years after the initial study and again 25 years after that, the Bennington graduates whom Newcomb had first studied were located and interviewed again (Alwin & others, 1991; Newcomb & others, 1967). The follow-up studies showed that most of the graduates retained their liberal views throughout their lives. Their self-reports suggested that they remained liberal at least partly because they continued to associate primarily with people whose views were like their own.

Other researchers have focused on regional differences and generational differences in attitudes (Cohen, 1996; Duncan & Agronick, 1995; Schuman & Scott, 1989). Such work suggests that lifelong attitudes tend to jell during young adulthood. Young adults who experience similar events and a shared social environment to help them interpret those events tend to acquire and maintain similar attitudes.

Attitudes as Rationalizations to Attain Cognitive Consistency

A century ago, Sigmund Freud began developing his controversial theory that human beings are fundamentally irrational. What pass for reasons, according to Freud, are most often rationalizations designed to calm our anxieties and boost our self-esteem. You will read more about Freud's view in Chapter 15. A more moderate view, to be pursued now, is that we are rational but the machinery that makes us so is by no means perfect. The same mental machinery that produces logic can produce pseudo-logic.

In the 1950s, Leon Festinger (1957) proposed what he called the *cognitive dissonance theory,* which ever since has been one of social psychology's most central ideas. According to the theory, we have, built into the workings of our mind, a mechanism that creates an uncomfortable feeling of *dissonance,* or lack of harmony, when we become aware of some inconsistency among the various attitudes, beliefs, and items of knowledge that constitute our mental store. Just as the discomfort of hunger motivates us to seek food, the discomfort of cognitive dissonance motivates us to seek ways to resolve contradictions or inconsistencies among our cognitions. Such a mechanism could well have evolved to serve adaptive functions related to logic. Inconsistencies imply that we are mistaken about something, and mistakes can lead to danger. Suppose you have a favorable attitude about sunbathing, but you learn that overexposure to the sun's ultraviolet rays is the leading cause of skin cancer. The discrepancy between your preexisting attitude and your new knowledge may create a state of cognitive dissonance every time you think about lying in the sun. To resolve the dissonance, you might change your attitude about sunbathing from positive to negative or you might bring in a third cognition: "Sunbathing is relatively safe, in moderation, if I use a sunscreen lotion."

As with all of our psychological machinery, our dissonance-reducing mechanism does not always function adaptively. Just as our hunger can lead us to eat things that aren't good for us, our dissonance-reduction drive can lead us to avoid or reduce dissonance in illogical and maladaptive ways. Those are the effects that particularly intrigued Festinger and many subsequent social psychologists.

Avoiding Dissonant Information

I once heard a person cut off a political discussion with the words, "I'm sorry, but I refuse to listen to something I disagree with." People don't usually come right out and say that, but have you noticed how often they seem to behave that way? Given a choice of books or articles to read, lectures to attend, or documentaries to watch, people generally choose those that they believe will support their existing views. That observation is consistent with the cognitive dissonance theory. One way to avoid dissonance is to avoid situations in which we might discover facts or ideas that run counter to our current views. If we avoid listening to or reading about the evidence that ultraviolet rays can cause skin cancer, we can blithely continue to enjoy sunbathing. People certainly don't always avoid dissonant information, but a considerable body of research indicates that they very often do (Frey, 1986; Jonas & others, 2001).

Paul Sweeney and Kathy Gruber (1984) conducted a study during the 1973 Senate Watergate hearings that documented this phenomenon. (The hearings uncovered illegal activities associated with then-president Richard Nixon's reelection campaign against George McGovern.) By interviewing the same voters before, during, and after the hearings, Sweeney and Gruber discovered that (a) Nixon supporters avoided news about the hearings (but not other political news) and were as strongly supportive of Nixon after the hearings as they were before; (b) McGovern supporters eagerly sought out information about the hearings and were as strongly opposed to Nixon afterward as they were before; and (c) previously undecided voters paid moderate attention to the hearings and were the only group whose attitude toward Nixon was significantly influenced (in a negative direction) by the hearings. So, consistent with the dissonance theory, all but the undecideds approached the hearings in a way that seemed designed to protect or strengthen, rather than challenge, their previous view.

Firming Up an Attitude to Be Consistent with an Action

We make most of our choices in life with less-than-absolute certainty. We vote for a candidate not knowing for sure if he or she is best, buy one car even though some of the evidence favors another, or choose to major in psychology even though some other fields have their attractions. After we have irrevocably made one choice or the other—after we have cast our ballot, made our down payment, or registered for our courses and the deadline for schedule changes is past—any lingering doubts would be discordant with our knowledge of what we have done; so, according to the cognitive dissonance theory, we should be motivated to set them aside.

26.

How does the cognitive dissonance theory explain people's attraction to some information and avoidance of other information?

27.

How does the cognitive dissonance theory explain why people are more confident about a choice just after they have made it than just before?

Dissonance abolished

This couple may have agonized long and hard before signing on the dotted line, but once they signed, they set their doubts aside and focused on the positive qualities of their new home. According to the cognitive dissonance theory, people are generally more confident about the correctness of their choices after those choices are made than before.

A number of studies have shown that people do tend to set their doubts aside after making a decision. Even in the absence of new information, people suddenly become more confident of their choice after acting on it than they were before. For example, in one study, bettors at a horse race were more confident that their horse would win if they were asked immediately after they had placed their bet than if they were asked immediately before (Knox & Inkster, 1968). In another study, voters who were leaving the polling place spoke more positively about their favored candidate than did those who were entering (Frenkel & Doob, 1976).

Changing an Attitude to Justify an Action

Sometimes people behave in ways that run counter to their attitude and then are faced with the dissonant cognitions, "I believe *this*, but I did *that*." They can't undo their deed, but they can relieve dissonance by modifying—maybe even reversing—their attitude. More than 200 years ago, the great inventor, statesman, and master of practical psychology Benjamin Franklin recognized this phenomenon and used it to his advantage. Franklin (1818/1949) describes in his autobiography how he changed the attitude of a political opponent who was trying to block his appointment to a high office:

> I did not like the opposition of this new member, who was a gentleman of fortune and education with talents that were likely to give him in time great influence. . . . I did not, however, aim at gaining his favour by paying any servile respect to him, but after some time took this other method. Having heard that he had in his library a certain very scarce and curious book, I wrote a note to him expressing my desire of perusing that book and requesting he do me the favour of lending it to me for a few days. He sent it immediately; and I returned it in about a week with another note expressing strongly my sense of the favour. When we next met in the House, he spoke to me (which he had never done before), and with great civility. And he ever afterwards manifested a readiness to serve me on all occasions, so that we became great friends, and our friendship continued to his death. This is another instance of the truth of an old maxim I had learned, which says, "He that has once done you a kindness will be more ready to do you another than he whom you yourself have obliged."

According to the cognitive dissonance theory, what might have happened in the former opponent's mind to change his attitude toward Franklin? He received Franklin's request to borrow the book, and for reasons of which he may not have been fully aware, such as the simple habit of courtesy, he did not turn it down. But once he sent the book to Franklin, he was thrown into a state of cognitive dissonance. One thought, *I do not like Ben Franklin*, was discordant with another, *I have just lent Franklin a very valuable book*. The second of these could not be denied, since that was objective fact, so dissonance could best be relieved by changing the first: *Ben Franklin isn't really a bad sort. At least I know he's honest. If he weren't honest, I certainly wouldn't have lent him that valuable book.* Such thinking reduced or erased the dissonance and set the stage for new, friendlier behaviors toward Franklin in the future.

Notice that, according to this analysis, the man changed his attitude toward Franklin because he saw the decision to lend the book as his own choice and he saw no good reason why he should have made that choice if he didn't like Franklin. If Franklin had paid him or threatened him to get him to lend the book, the lending of it would not have created dissonance with the belief that he disliked Franklin. He would say, "I lent the book to Franklin only because he paid me" or " . . . only because he threatened me." Since either of these would have been sufficient justification, no dissonance would have resulted and no attitude change would have been necessary.

The effect illustrated by Franklin's story is an instance of what is now called the ***insufficient-justification effect,*** defined as a change in attitude that occurs because, without the change, the person cannot justify his or her already completed action. Many dozens of experiments have demonstrated this effect and have helped identify the conditions required for its occurrence (Harmon-Jones & Mills, 1999).

28.

How does the cognitive dissonance theory explain why people who behave in a manner contrary to their attitude are likely to change their attitude?

Conditions That Optimize the Insufficient-Justification Effect

One requirement for the insufficient-justification effect to occur is that there be no obvious, high incentive for performing the counterattitudinal action. In an early demonstration of this, Leon Festinger and James Carlsmith (1959) gave college students a boring task (loading spools into trays and turning pegs in a pegboard) and then offered to "hire" them to tell another student that the task was exciting and enjoyable. Some students were offered $1 for their role in recruiting the other student, and others were offered $20 (a princely sum at a time when the minimum wage in the United States was $1 an hour). The result was that those in the $1 condition changed their attitude toward the task and later recalled it as truly enjoyable, whereas those in the $20 condition continued to recall it as boring. Presumably, students in the $1 condition could not justify their lie to the other student on the basis of the little they were promised, so they convinced themselves that they were not lying. Those in the $20 condition, in contrast, could justify their lie: "I said the task was enjoyable when it was actually boring, but who wouldn't tell such a small lie for $20?"

Another essential condition for the insufficient-justification effect is that subjects must perceive their action as stemming from their own free choice. Otherwise, they could justify the action—and relieve dissonance—simply by saying, "I was forced to do it." In one experiment demonstrating the requirement of free choice, students were asked to write essays expressing support for a bill in the state legislature that most students personally opposed (Linder & others, 1967). Students in the *free-choice condition* were told clearly that they didn't have to write the essays, but they were encouraged to do so and none refused. Students in the *no-choice condition* were simply told to write the essays, and all complied. After writing the essays, all students were asked to describe their personal attitude toward the bill. Only those in the free-choice condition showed a significant shift in the direction of favoring the bill; those in the no-choice condition remained as opposed to it as did those who had not written essays at all. Using essentially the same procedure, other researchers found that students in the free-choice condition not only changed their attitude more than did those in the no-choice condition but also manifested more psychological discomfort and physiological arousal as they wrote their essays, a finding consistent with the view that they were experiencing greater dissonance (Elkin & Leippe, 1986; Elliot & Devine, 1994).

29.

How have researchers identified three conditions that increase the likelihood that the insufficient-justification effect will occur?

Research also indicates that the insufficient-justification effect is strongest when the action to be justified would, from the viewpoint of the original attitude, be expected to cause harm to others or to oneself. In this case, the thought underlying the attitude change might be, "I would not deliberately do something harmful; therefore I must believe that what I did is helpful." In one experiment, for example, students who wrote essays counter to their initial attitude showed greater attitude change if they were led to believe that their essays could influence policy than if they were led to believe that their essays could not influence policy (Scher & Cooper, 1989). Other experiments, however, have shown that some degree of dissonance-induced discomfort and attitude change can occur even when subjects know that their counterattitudinal statements will be immediately discarded and nobody will know what they had written (Harmon-Jones, 2000).

Taking all this research into account, modern-day Ben Franklins who want to change someone's attitude by inducing the person to behave in a way that contradicts the old attitude are most likely to succeed if they (a) minimize any obvious incentive for the behavior, (b) maximize the appearance of free choice, and (c) choose a behavior that would seem harmful if viewed from the perspective of the old attitude.

Using Attitudes to "Justify" Injustice

Perhaps we develop unrealistic attitudes not only to explain our own otherwise-inexplicable actions but also to make sense of the chaos and injustice we observe in the world around us. Melvin Lerner (1980) summarized evidence that, at least in our culture, people tend to believe life is fair, a tendency he labeled the ***just-world bias***. In line with Freud's general way of thinking, Lerner suggested that we believe life is fair because to believe otherwise would induce more anxiety than we can tolerate. Unconsciously we may reason: "If life is *not* fair, then no matter how I behave, or how worthy I am, something terrible could happen to me. I can't bear that idea, so life must be fair." The just-world bias may motivate us to work hard and take precautions that indeed do promote our survival and well-being, and for that reason it may be adaptive. However, it may promote truly unfair negative attitudes toward people who suffer from mistreatment or misfortune.

To maintain the illusion that life is fair and predictable, we may distort our explanations of others' misfortunes to make it seem that people deserve what happens to them, a phenomenon called *blaming the victim* (Lerner & Goldberg, 1999; Ryan, 1971). If millions of Jews were killed in the Holocaust, they must have done something to bring it on or failed to do something to prevent it. If black Americans suffer from poverty and discrimination, it must somehow be their fault. If gay people suffer from discrimination, harassment, and AIDS, homosexuality must be evil. If my neighbor contracts Lyme disease, she was foolish to have gone walking in the woods. Numerous studies have shown that victims of rape, robbery, terrorism, accidents, illnesses, poverty, and social injustice often suffer doubly, once from the misfortune itself and again from the subtle or not-so-subtle blame they receive from others for "causing" or "allowing" the misfortune to happen (Lerner & Miller, 1978; Maes, 1998). In one laboratory experiment, college students evaluated another student's character less favorably if they believed she was going to receive a series of painful electric shocks as part of the experiment than they did if they believed she wasn't (Lerner & Simmons, 1966).

Attitudes as Guides to Action

As you have seen, attitudes can help us define ourselves, adjust to a social group, and rationalize our actions or beliefs. But common sense tells us that the most basic function of attitudes is to guide our behavior effectively. Presumably, we seek out those objects, people, events, and activities about which we have positive attitudes and avoid those about which we have negative attitudes.

Social psychologists first became interested in attitudes because they conceived of them as mental guides of behavior (Allport, 1935). But early research on the topic was most remarkable for its failure to find reliable relationships between attitudes and actions. In one classic study, for instance, students in a college course filled out a questionnaire aimed at assessing their attitudes toward cheating, and later in the semester they were asked to grade their own true-false tests (Corey, 1937). The tests had already been graded secretly by the instructor, so cheating could be detected. The result was that a great deal of cheating occurred and no correlation at all was found between the attitude measure and actual cheating. A strong correlation was found, however, between cheating and the student's true score on the test: The lower the true score, the more likely the student was to try to raise it by cheating.

Subsequent studies, however, have revealed many examples of reliable correlations between attitudes and behavior. Among these are Schwartz's study correlating people's expressed values with their subsequent choice to cooperate or compete and Rokeach's study correlating privileged people's ranking of equality as a value with their subsequent actions toward members of a discriminated-against group. Today essentially all social psychologists agree that attitudes do play a role in people's behavioral choices and the question is, "*When*, or under what conditions, do they play that role?"

Attitudes Must Be Retrieved from Memory to Affect Behavior

Attitudes, like any other cognitions, are stored in long-term memory and can influence a person's behavioral choice only if recalled into working memory at the time the choice is made. Behavior occurs in a continuous flow, and we rarely stop to think about each of our relevant attitudes before we act. In Corey's experiment on cheating, the students who cheated may have been immediately overwhelmed by their poor performance on the test, which reminded them strongly of their negative attitudes toward failing a course but did not remind them of their negative attitudes toward cheating. Perhaps with more time to think about it, or with more immediate inducement to think about it, fewer would have cheated and a correlation would have been found between their anticheating attitudes and their behavior.

This line of reasoning suggests that cues reminding a person of his or her attitudes at the time of action would increase the attitude-behavior correlation. Indeed, experiments have shown that if people are presented with a task that requires them to think about their attitude on an issue shortly before they must act on it, the correlation between the attitude and the behavior increases markedly (Aronson, 1992; Snyder & Swann, 1976). Other experiments have shown that the presence of a mirror can promote attitude-behavior consistency (Wicklund & Frey, 1980). Apparently their physical reflection reminds people of all aspects of themselves, including their central attitudes, or values. In one experiment, for example, trick-or-treaters were told to help themselves to a specific amount of candy, under conditions in which they believed nobody could see them. They took extra candy more often if no mirror was present than they did if a mirror was present behind the candy bowl (Beaman & others, 1979).

Russell Fazio (1986, 1990) has argued that the strongest attitude-behavior correlation occurs when the attitude is acquired through direct experience with its object, because then the object automatically reminds the person of the attitude. If you have a negative attitude toward bacon because on one or more occasions you ate it and got sick, then the sight and smell of bacon will automatically elicit your negative attitude and you won't eat it. However, if you have a negative attitude toward bacon only because you read that it is high in nitrates and nitrates are bad for you, your attitude will not be elicited automatically by the sight and smell of bacon. In that case you will need some other cue, extrinsic to the bacon, to remind you of the attitude, or you will need to rely on a habit of checking your set of food-related attitudes

30.

How did an early study demonstrate attitude-behavior inconsistency?

Save the Children

Translating attitudes into actions
Ads such as this encourage readers to put their money where their values are.

31.

How can the presence of a mirror increase attitude-behavior consistency? According to Fazio, what kinds of attitudes are most likely to be recalled at appropriate times to help control behavior?

whenever you eat. Only after repeated rehearsal would your intellectually derived attitude about bacon come automatically to mind when you saw or smelled it.

A Theory of Planned Behavior

When people make conscious decisions about how to behave, their attitudes are not the only thoughts they take into account. As a general framework for thinking about the decision-making process, Icek Ajzen (1985, 1991) proposed what he calls a **theory of planned behavior.** Planned behavior is defined as that which follows from one's conscious intention to behave in a particular way. According to the theory, in developing a behavioral intention, people take into account the following three types of cognitions: (a) their *attitude,* defined as their personal desire to behave that way or not; (b) the *subjective norm,* defined as their belief about what others who are important at the moment would think about the action; and (c) their *perceived control,* defined as their sense of their own ability or inability to carry out the action (see Figure 13.11). Suppose you have a strongly favorable attitude about becoming an astronaut but fail to act on it because others in your social world would think you strange for pursuing that line of work or because you doubt that you have the ability for it or could raise the funds needed for training. Your choice, in that case, is controlled by the subjective norm or by your perceived lack of control, despite your attitude.

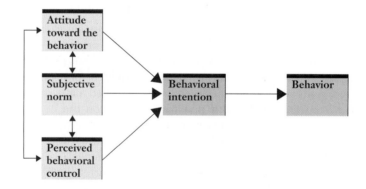

32.

According to the theory of planned behavior, what two kinds of thoughts might inhibit people from behaving according to their attitudes?

FIGURE **13.11**
A theory of planned behavior
According to Ajzen's theory, the decision to behave in a certain way is a product of three categories of cognitions. (Adapted from Ajzen, 1987.)

Research based on Ajzen's model has shown that, depending on innumerable factors, any of the three inputs to behavioral intention may account for most of the variability among people in their behavior. In a study of dieting and weight loss, for instance, perceived control (confidence in the ability to stay on a diet) was a better predictor of weight loss than was either attitude (desire to lose weight) or the subjective norm (belief about whether others thought one should lose weight or not) (Schifter & Ajzen, 1985). In a study of decisions about how much time to spend studying, some students were most influenced by the subjective norm (their view of what other students believe is an appropriate amount of study time) whereas others were most influenced by their own attitudes (Miller & Grush, 1986). Not surprisingly, a number of studies have shown that the subjective norm contributes more to behavioral intention among people who identify strongly with the reference group than among those who don't identify strongly (Terry & others, 1999, 2000).

Attitudes as Products of Information Processing

In the previous discussions you have already encountered some ideas about the origins of attitudes. To some degree we inherit attitudes from our sociocultural environment. To some degree we manufacture attitudes to create illusions of consistency. To the degree that we use attitudes for utilitarian functions—to guide our behavior toward or away from particular objects and events—it makes sense that we would also construct attitudes from actual information available to us about those objects and events. In some cases this construction process is automatic, engaging no or little conscious thought, and in other cases the process is deeply thoughtful.

Attitudes Through Classical Conditioning: No Thought

Classical conditioning, a basic learning process discussed in Chapter 4, can be thought of as an automatic attitude-forming system. A new stimulus (the conditioned stimulus) is paired with a stimulus that already elicits a particular reaction (the unconditioned stimulus), and, as a result, the new stimulus comes to elicit, on future presentations, a reaction similar to that elicited by the original stimulus. Using the language of the present chapter, we can say that Pavlov's dog entered the experiment with a preexisting positive attitude toward meat powder. When Pavlov preceded the meat powder on several occasions with the sound of a bell, the dog acquired a positive attitude toward that sound. The dog now salivated and wagged its tail when the bell rang, and if given a chance, it would have learned to ring the bell itself.

The neural mechanisms underlying classical conditioning evolved, presumably, because in evolutionary history such conditioning produced adaptive reactions more often than maladaptive ones. Conditioning leads us to approach objects and events that have been linked in our experience to pleasant, life-promoting occurrences, and it leads us to avoid objects and events that have been linked to unpleasant, life-threatening occurrences. In today's world, however, where many of the stimulus links we experience are the creations of advertisers and others who want to manipulate us, classical conditioning can have maladaptive consequences. All those ads in which cigarettes, beer, and expensive gas-guzzling cars are paired with beautiful people, happy scenes, and lovely music are designed to exploit our most thoughtless attitude-forming system, classical conditioning. The advertisers want us to salivate, wag our tails, and run out and buy their products. Apparently the technique works; if it didn't, they wouldn't continue spending money on such ads. Laboratory experiments have shown that it is easy to condition positive attitudes, in university students, toward a fictitious brand of mouthwash, or other product, by pairing the brand with pleasant, though irrelevant, scenes (Grossman & Till, 1998).

Direct evidence that classical conditioning can create attitudes in the absence of conscious thought comes from experiments in which the unconditioned stimulus is presented too rapidly for conscious detection. In one such experiment, subjects viewed slides of a woman engaged in various mundane activities, such as shopping. Each slide was preceded by a quickly flashed scene (9 milliseconds' duration) designed to induce either a positive or a negative emotional reaction. Among the positive scenes were kittens, a bridal couple, and a child with a Mickey Mouse doll. Among the negative scenes were a werewolf, a bucket of snakes, and a depiction of open-heart surgery. After all the

33.

How do advertisers use classical conditioning to influence our attitudes, and how did one experiment demonstrate that classical conditioning can influence attitudes without requiring conscious thought?

Her royal pleasure

John B. Watson, the founder of behaviorism (discussed in Chapters 1 and 4), became an advertising specialist after leaving academia. This ad, created by Watson, helped sell a skin cream by associating it with the wealth and beauty of the queen of Spain. According to the fine print, the queen uses Pond's vanishing and cold creams and "has expressed her royal pleasure in them."

slides had been viewed, the subjects who had been presented with the positive scenes evaluated the woman more favorably than did the other group, even though neither group, when questioned, could recall having seen any of the quickly flashed scenes (Krosnick & others, 1992).

Attitudes Through Heuristics: Superficial Thought

34.

What are some examples of decision rules (heuristics) that people use with minimal thought to evaluate messages?

Beyond simple classical conditioning is the more sophisticated but still relatively automatic process of using certain *decision rules*, or *heuristics*, to evaluate information and develop attitudes (Chen & Chaiken, 1999). Heuristics are shortcuts to a full, logical elaboration of the information in a message. Examples of such rules include the following: (a) If there are a lot of numbers and big words in the message, it must be well documented. (b) If the message is phrased in terms of values that I believe in, it is probably right. (c) Famous or successful people are more likely than unknown or unsuccessful people to be correct. (d) If most people believe this, it is probably true. We learn to use such rules, presumably, because they often allow us to make useful judgments with minimal expenditures of time and mental energy. The rules become mental habits, which we use implicitly, without conscious awareness that we are using them. Advertisers, of course, exploit these mental habits, just as they exploit the process of classical conditioning. They sprinkle their ads with irrelevant data and high-sounding words such as *integrity*, and they hire celebrities to endorse their products.

Attitudes Through Logical Analysis of the Message: Systematic Thought

Sometimes, of course, we think logically. Generally, we are most likely to do so for issues that really matter to us. In a theory of persuasion called the **elaboration likelihood model**, Richard Petty and John Cacioppo (1986) proposed that a major determinant of whether a message will be processed systematically (through logical analysis of the content) or superficially is the personal relevance of the message. According to Petty and Cacioppo, we tend to be *cognitive misers*; we reserve our elaborative reasoning powers for messages that seem most relevant to us, and we rely on mental shortcuts to evaluate messages that seem less relevant to us. Much research supports this proposition (Petty & Wegener, 1999).

35.

How did an experiment support the idea that people tend to reserve systematic thought for messages that are personally relevant to them and to use decision rules for other messages?

In one experiment on the role of personal relevance in persuasion, Richard Petty and his colleagues (1981) presented college students with messages in favor of requiring students to pass a set of comprehensive examinations in order to graduate. Different groups of students received different messages, which varied in (a) the *strength* of the arguments, (b) the alleged *source* of the arguments, and (c) the *personal relevance* of the message. The weak argument consisted of slightly relevant quotations, personal opinions, and anecdotal observations; the strong argument contained well-structured statistical evidence that the proposed policy would improve the reputation of the university and its graduates. In some cases the arguments were said to have been prepared by high school students and in other cases by the Carnegie Commission on Higher Education. Finally, the personal relevance was varied by stating in the high-relevance condition that the proposed policy would take effect the following year, so current students would be subject to it, and in the low-relevance condition that it would begin in 10 years. After hearing the message, students in each condition were asked to rate the extent to which they agreed or disagreed with the proposal.

Figure 13.12 shows the results. As you can see, in the high-relevance condition the quality of the arguments was most important. Students in that condition tended to be persuaded by strong arguments and not by weak ones, regardless of the alleged source. Thus, in that condition, students must have listened to and evaluated the arguments. In the low-relevance condition, the quality of the arguments had much less effect, and the source of the arguments had much more. Apparently, when the policy was not going to affect them, students did not attend carefully to the arguments but, instead, relied on the simple decision rule that experts (mem-

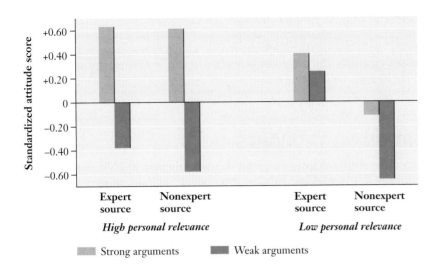

In this graph, movement above the horizontal axis indicates agreement with the persuasive message, and movement below the axis indicates disagreement. When the issue was of high personal relevance (left half of graph), the strength or weakness of the arguments had more impact than did the source of the arguments; but when the issue was of low personal relevance (right half of graph), the reverse was true. (Adapted from Petty & others, 1981.)

bers of the Carnegie Commission) are more likely to be right than are nonexperts (high school students).

There is no surprise in Petty and Cacioppo's theory or in the results supporting it. The idea that people think more logically about issues that directly affect them than about those that don't was a basic premise of philosophers who laid the foundations for democratic forms of government. And, to repeat what is by now a familiar refrain, our mental apparatus evolved to keep us alive and promote our welfare in our social communities; it is no wonder that we use our minds more fully for that than for other purposes.

SECTION SUMMARY

Attitudes can serve value-expressive, social-adjustive, defensive, and utilitarian functions. The value-expressive function is served especially by central attitudes, or values, that are part of one's self-concept. Schwartz found that values tend to cluster into 10 categories that can be arranged in a wheel in which similar values lie adjacent to one another and contradictory values lie opposite one another. This value structure appears to be universal, but the relative importance of each value category varies from culture to culture.

The social-adjustive function of attitudes was demonstrated in a classic study by Newcomb at Bennington College. New students changed their initially conservative attitudes to match the liberal attitudes of the older students and professors as a means of gaining social acceptance.

The defensive function of attitudes is illustrated by studies of cognitive dissonance. To avoid the discomfort that arises from awareness of inconsistency in their beliefs and actions, people will (a) avoid information that contradicts their present attitudes and (b) alter their attitudes to match their actions. People are especially likely to alter an attitude to match an action when they have no easy alternative means of explaining why they did what they did (the insufficient-justification effect). Another example of the defensive use of attitudes derives from the just-world bias: To convince themselves that the world is fair (and they are safe), people develop negative, blaming attitudes toward those who suffer.

Attitudes serve a utilitarian function to the degree that they guide behavior in useful ways. Some attitudes, such as those derived from classical conditioning, automatically come into play in response to the object of the attitude, but attitudes that are acquired intellectually must be recalled and thought about if they are to influence behavior. Anything that reminds a person of his or her attitudes—such as the presence of a mirror—tends to increase the consistency between attitudes and actions. According to the theory of planned behavior, the intention to behave in a particular way is influenced not just by one's own attitude but also by the subjective norm (one's sense of what others would think of one for behaving that way) and perceived control (one's confidence in one's own capacity to behave that way).

> Attitudes can be acquired through classical conditioning (no thought), simple heuristics (superficial thought), or logical analysis of the message (systematic thought). According to the elaboration likelihood model, we typically reserve our effortful logical capacities for issues that are personally important to us and acquire most of our other attitudes through conditioning and heuristics.

36.

How might a review of this chapter be organized around the four themes proposed at the chapter's outset?

CONCLUDING THOUGHTS

At the outset of this chapter you read that four themes would run through it—the themes of biases, functions, cultural differences, and automatic versus controlled processes in social perception and thought. To review the chapter, it would be useful, now, to reflect on each theme:

1. **Biases in social perception and thought**   A bias, as the term is used in this chapter, is any consistent manner of perception or interpretation that does not reflect the objective information or a purely logical analysis of it. You might think about each bias discussed in the chapter with the following questions in mind: What evidence was presented for the existence of the bias? In what contexts does the bias seem to occur or not occur? What, if any, functions might the bias serve for the person manifesting it? What harm might result from this bias, either to the person who manifests it or to the objects of the biased perception or thought? You will not find the answers to all these questions for every bias described in the chapter, but in most cases you will at least find hints. Apply such questions to the person bias, situation bias, actor-observer discrepancy, biasing effects of first impressions, attractiveness bias, baby-face bias, biasing effects of stereotypes, biasing effects of others' appraisals on self-concept, big-fish-in-little-pond effect, better-than-average effect, self-serving attributional bias, insufficient-justification effect, and just-world bias.

2. **Value of a functionalist perspective**   From the functionalist perspective, the first question asked about any consistent human tendency is how it might serve the needs of the individual who manifests that tendency. Some of the ideas in this chapter were presented quite explicitly from that perspective, and others were not. As you review each of the phenomena described in the chapter, think about whether and how it serves the individual. Concerning the biases in person perception, you might well conclude that some do serve useful functions for the perceiver and that others may be nonadaptive side effects of the ways that our minds work. Concerning self-perception, think about the potential survival-promoting values of the looking-glass self, the capacity for multiple self-concepts, the use of social comparison to understand oneself, the better-than-average effect, and the capacity to shift back and forth between thinking of oneself as a separate individual and as a cog in a larger unit (the group). Concerning attitudes, think again about the four basic functions that social psychologists identify—the self-defining (or value-expressive), social-adjustive, defensive (particularly reduction of cognitive dissonance), and utilitarian functions.

3. **Effects of culture on social perception and thought**   The human mind evolved to meet the social needs of our hunter-gatherer ancestors. But every individual person's mind is honed, through development, to meet the requirements of life within that person's culture. Social psychologists have only recently begun to examine social perception and attitudes systematically across cultures, and in this chapter you have sampled some of the first fruits of that research. You have seen evidence that the person bias in attributions, once thought to be so basic that it was called the "fundamental attribution error," may not occur in other cultures, or at least may not occur as reliably in them as in ours. You have also seen evidence that cultures may vary on a dimension of individualism versus collectivism that influ-

ences the balance between the personal and social self-concepts and the degree to which people value freedom and individual creativity compared with tradition and devotion to one's social responsibilities. We will gain a richer understanding of the range of human social nature through further systematic study and comparison of people from widely varying cultures.

4. Automatic versus controlled mental processes Automatic (unconscious) mental processes have to some degree been made the villain of this chapter, and controlled (conscious), deliberate processes the hero. You have read evidence that (a) the person and situation attributional biases stem from automatic processes and can be corrected with controlled processes; (b) implicit stereotypes can automatically lead people to react in discriminatory ways, but controlled processes can keep those reactions in check; (c) people often fail to abide by their values unless they use conscious processes to recall them when making a behavioral choice; and (d) advertisers and others can manipulate people by pulling the strings to their automatic processes unless people counteract them with controlled processes. As you think about all this, however, imagine what life would be like if we had to make conscious decisions about every step we took as we went from moment to moment in an hour or a day. Fortunately, our automatic processes can take care of most of those decisions and free our controlled processes to work on the decisions we deem most worthy of conscious thought. Wisdom lies in knowing when to trust and when not to trust the automatic processes of our minds.

Further Reading

Donald C. Pennington (2000). *Social cognition*. London: Routledge.

This brief introductory text focuses primarily on attribution, impression formation, and prejudice. In these areas it simply and clearly describes classic social-psychological theories and research.

Penelope J. Oakes, S. Alexander Haslam, & John C. Turner (1994). *Stereotyping and social reality*. Oxford: Blackwell.

This is a clear, thought-provoking review of social-psychological research and ideas on stereotyping. The authors' thesis is that stereotyping is an essential aspect of social reality in multigroup cultures. Defined as schemas for representing group differences, stereotypes can be positive as well as negative, are intimately related to social identity, provide useful guides for behavior in intergroup relationships, and can change to meet changing social realities.

Roy F. Baumeister (Ed.) (1999). *The self in social psychology.* Philadelphia: Psychology Press.

This is a collection of classic articles dealing with the social psychology of the self. Included are articles on self-knowledge, self-esteem, self-presentation

(a topic discussed in the next chapter), self-control, and cultural variation in the self-concept.

Alice H. Eagly & Shelly Chaiken (1993). *The psychology of attitudes.* Orlando, FL: Harcourt Brace Jovanovich.

The major psychological models of attitude structure, function, and origin—and the evidence for and against each model—are discussed fully and clearly in this scholarly textbook.

Fathali M. Moghaddam, Donald M. Taylor, & Stephen C. Wright (1993). *Social psychology in cross-cultural perspective.* New York: Freeman.

This brief and lively paperback can be read as a manifesto for the cross-cultural movement in social psychology. The authors develop a strong case that cross-cultural study not only allows researchers to test the applicability of traditional social-psychological ideas to other cultures but also prompts new questions, new ideas, and new ways of answering questions.

Looking Ahead

Because we are concerned about what others think of us, other people greatly influence our behavior. The next chapter is about that influence. It deals with such topics as self-conscious emotions, audience effects, conformity, group decision making, compliance, and cooperation.

La Pomarrosa, René Portocarrera

Social Influences on Behavior

Like chimpanzees, wolves, and most species of ants, humans live and function in groups and depend on one another for survival. During our long evolutionary history as hunter-gatherers each person's survival depended on acceptance by the group. A person cast out of the tribe to face life alone could not fend off predators, obtain all the needed food, or accumulate all the knowledge needed to survive for long or to raise children to maturity. No wonder our drive to be accepted by others is as strong as our drive to eat.

One requirement of any social species is the existence of *socially binding drives* that motivate individuals to come together and stay together. Group members must be attracted to one another, or averse to being alone, or drawn together by common survival interests. If nothing drew and kept individuals together, there would be no group. A second requirement is *behavioral coordination* across the members of the group. The group members must act in ways that coincide with, or complement, or at least do not interfere with the actions of the other members. If each individual acted in a manner completely unaffected by the others, they could not function as a group. A third and most basic requirement, which undergirds the other two, is *mutual beneficence*. Group members must, over the long haul, help one another more than they harm one another. Such help, after all, is the ultimate reason for the group's existence. Mutual beneficence requires that competition and aggression be at least somewhat muted within the group and that cooperation be enhanced.

This chapter is about aspects of human psychology that are most integrally tied to our tendency to live and function in groups. It is particularly concerned with the problems of behavioral coordination and mutual beneficence in human social life. The chapter is divided into four main sections, which deal, respectively, with (a) how emotions help people get along with each other, (b) how people are influenced by the presence and actions of other people, (c) the human tendency to comply with others' requests, and (d) conditions that promote cooperation or conflict among individuals and groups.

1.

What characteristics make a species social?

EMOTIONS AS FOUNDATIONS FOR SOCIAL BEHAVIOR

The preceding chapter described humans as *thinking* social beings. But we are also *feeling* social beings, and feeling may be more basic to our social nature than is thinking. We don't as a rule figure out, logically, that we need others for certain purposes. Rather, we feel drawn to others. We feel lonely without them, good when they approve of us, awful when they disapprove of us.

Getting along with others while still asserting one's individual wants and avoiding exploitation is a delicate balancing act. Natural selection has built into our brains a complex set of mechanisms that help us keep that balance, and through

2.

By what general means do emotions contribute to social life?

development and learning we tune these mechanisms to meet the particular group requirements of the culture in which we are raised. Many of these mechanisms, when active, produce effects that we experience as emotions.

Think about your experiences with various emotions. What brought on and how did you resolve your most recent intense episodes of anger, love, jealousy, grief, guilt, embarrassment, and joy? If you are like most people, your most intense emotions revolve around relationships with other people. In an analysis of hundreds of written accounts of people's own experiences of particular emotions, Phillip Shaver and his colleagues (1992) calculated the percentages of episodes, for each emotion, that had to do primarily with relationships with other people. The results were 100 percent for love, 91 percent for anger, 90 percent for sadness, 56 percent for joy, and 47 percent for fear.

Historically, psychologists have thought and written more about emotions' harmful effects than about their helpful effects. As most of us know all too well, strong emotions can disrupt our sleep, digestion, and ability to concentrate on anything other than the object of the emotion and can drive us to say or do things we later regret. Emotions can even become so chronically disruptive as to be diagnosed as disorders (discussed in Chapter 16). But our capacity for emotions would not have evolved if emotions did not, in our evolutionary history, serve adaptive purposes. Emotions are crucial elements of our tool kit for meeting the requirements of social life—social binding, behavioral coordination, and mutual beneficence. Emotions operate toward these ends through two means. First, the overt expressions of emotion—on one's face, in one's posture, or in one's tone of voice—serve as social signals that allow others in the group to discern the psychological state or desires of the emotional person and respond accordingly. Second, emotional feelings that pertain to relationships—such as feelings of shame, guilt, or loneliness—can motivate those who are feeling the emotions to behave in ways that help mend a damaged relationship or build a new one.

Emotional Expressions as Social Signals and Regulators of Behavior

3.

In general, how might a person's emotional expressions help promote his or her welfare within a group?

Like other social primates, our evolutionary ancestors communicated their moods and behavioral intentions nonverbally through bodily movements, facial expressions, and vocal grunts and cries. The emergence of language in our species did not replace the already existing system of nonverbal communication but, rather, added a new layer of communication on top of it. In his book *The Expression of the Emotions in Man and Animals*, Charles Darwin (1872/1965) made the case that specific facial expressions of emotion are universal in humans and serve similar communicative functions in all cultures (discussed in Chapter 3). Following Darwin's lead, researchers studying communication in humans and other species have documented many examples in which emotional expressions serve as signals that influence others in ways that benefit the signaler and perhaps also those that respond to the signal (for example, Eibl-Eibesfeldt, 1989). Expressions of sadness or helplessness elicit care or aid from others. Expressions of love signal a readiness for intimacy of one sort or another. Expressions of happiness help cement relationships in a positive way by signaling one's desire to share one's joy with the other. Angry expressions serve as a threat, leading another to back off or to repair the relationship in some way. For social interactions to meet the requirements of behavioral coordination and mutual beneficence, each individual must have clues about the intentions and desires of the others. For people—as well as for other primates—nonverbal expressions of emotion are often the most reliable clues available.

The Happy Smile as a Social Signal

If emotional expressions are social signals, then we might expect them to occur most often in social contexts, especially in the presence of those who are targets of the emotional feeling. People might *feel* particular emotions in private as much as they do when others are present, but they might express the emotion more in the latter case. The strongest evidence to date that this is so derives from studies of smiling. As discussed in Chapter 3, researchers have distinguished between two kinds of smiles: the *happy smile*, which involves wrinkles ("crow's feet") around the eyes, and the *greeting smile*, which is easier to fake, does not involve the eyes, and signals not happiness but, rather, one's friendly or nonaggressive intent. Further research, however, suggests that even the happy smile occurs most often in social settings and may function primarily as a social signal saying, in essence, "I am happy and I want to share that happiness with you," or "I am happy to be with you."

In one series of studies, people in a variety of natural settings were observed to smile frequently when socially engaged and hardly at all when not. Bowlers smiled when facing their colleagues in the pit but not when facing the pins, fans at a hockey game smiled when looking at their friends next to them but not when looking at the game, and pedestrians on the sidewalk smiled when looking at each other but not when looking anywhere else (Kraut & Johnston, 1979). In those observations, no distinction was made between different types of smiles, but the almost complete lack of smiles when not socially engaged— even after a strike in bowling, or after a goal by the home team in hockey, or during beautiful weather when walking along the sidewalk—suggests that even the happy smile was used primarily as a social signal.

In another study, television films of gold-medal winners in the 1992 Olympic Games were analyzed for the presence of happy smiles during and near the time that the awards were presented (Fernández-Dols & Ruiz-Belda, 1995). Presumably, these first-place winners were immensely happy throughout the period in which they were filmed, yet they rarely smiled except when they were socially engaged with the authorities who made the award or with their admiring public. During those periods of engagement, they manifested happy smiles 48 percent of the time and greeting smiles 28 percent of the time.

Emotional Contagion

Coordinated social action is more likely to occur if the individuals share a common mood than if they don't, and one function of emotional signals is to help a mood spread from one person to another (Hatfield & others, 1994). Sadness in one person tends to induce sadness in others nearby, and that is part of the mechanism of empathy by which others become motivated to help the one in distress (discussed in Chapter 12). Anger expressed in the presence of potential allies may lead to shared anger that helps in the recruitment of allies into a common cause. Likewise, fear in one person tends to induce fear in others nearby, placing them all in a state of heightened vigilance and thereby adding a measure of protection for the whole group.

One of the most contagious of all emotional signals is laughter, as evidenced by the regularity of mutual laughter in everyday interactions and the effectiveness of laugh tracks in inducing laughter in audiences (Provine, 1996). The easy spread of laughter apparently helps put a group into a shared mood of playfulness, which reduces the chance that one person will be offended by the remarks or actions of another. In addition to coordinating people's actions, shared moods seem to promote bonds of affection or attachment among those who share the moods, which contribute to the long-term stability of social relationships and groups.

Political leaders often achieve their status at least partly through their ability to manipulate others' emotions, and their own emotional expressions are part of that process. Former U.S. president Ronald Reagan was known to many political

4.

What evidence suggests that the smile of happiness is a social signal?

Vittoriano Rastelli / Corbis

A poker face is hard to keep
We tend automatically to signal our emotions when in the company of others. Only through conscious effort can we refrain from giving away our hand.

5.

What is the value, for group life, of the spread of sadness, anger, fear, and laughter from one person to another? How might emotional contagion figure into the rise of a group leader?

Emotional contagion
Many American citizens, regardless of their political views, found it hard not to feel good when they saw Ronald Reagan looking like this.

pundits as "the great communicator," and a psychological study conducted shortly after he became president adds credence to that label. University students—some of whom claimed to support Reagan and others of whom claimed to oppose him—watched film clips of Reagan expressing happiness, anger, or fear as he spoke to the American public about events that faced the nation (McHugo & others, 1985). In some cases the sound track was kept on, in others it was turned off, and in all cases the students' own emotional reactions were recorded by measuring their heart rate, their sweating, and the movements of particular facial muscles. Regardless of whether they claimed to be his supporters or opponents, and regardless of whether they could or could not hear what he was saying, the students' bodily changes indicated that they were responding to Reagan's performance with emotions similar to those he was displaying.

More recently, researchers have found that the spread of emotions can occur completely unconsciously. In one study, a face expressing happiness or anger was flashed on a screen too quickly for subjects to see it consciously, yet subjects responded with the same facial expression that had been flashed (Dimberg & others, 2000).

How Our Self-Conscious Emotions Make Us Socially Acceptable

In the marathon dance of social life, we must be aware of our own moves as well as those of others so that we don't step on anyone's toes. If we fail at this—if we hurt others or offend them—we risk rejection. As pointed out in Chapter 13, self-consciousness appears to be secondary to our consciousness of others, and its primary function appears to be to help us get along with others. When we stumble in the dance, we feel *guilt, shame,* or *embarrassment*; when we dance well, we feel *pride*. These four emotions are called the **self-conscious emotions**, because they are linked to thoughts about the self or one's own actions, although they are brought on by social experiences (Fisher & Tangney, 1995). The feelings of guilt, shame, and embarrassment are painful, and the pain may motivate us to make amends and try to avoid stumbling in the future. Conversely, the feeling of pride rewards us for dancing well.

The self-conscious emotions have been studied primarily by two means. One is to observe them in very young children, who are less adept than older children or adults at hiding them and whose emotions can be manipulated relatively easily in the laboratory. The other means is to ask adults to describe one or more of their previous experiences with a particular emotion: What brought it on? How did you feel? What effects did it have on your behavior and others'? How was the emotion resolved?

Guilt as a Motivator of Relationship Repair

When adults are asked to describe episodes in their lives that led them to experience guilt, they most often tell about incidents in which they hurt or disappointed someone they cared about (Baumeister & others, 1995; Tangney, 1995). Typical guilt stories involve neglecting, offending, or being disloyal to a relationship partner. In one study, Roy Baumeister and his colleagues (1995) asked university students to write out two episodes in which they caused someone else to become angry at them, one in which they responded with guilt and one in which they didn't.

6.

What differing functions are proposed for (a) guilt, (b) shame, and (c) embarrassment, and what evidence supports each proposed function?

Compared with the nonguilt stories, the guilt stories were far more likely to involve selfish behavior toward a victim who was respected by and had a mutually giving relationship with the transgressor and to end with an apology, with a behavioral change designed to make amends, or with both. Another study revealed that people who are most able to perceive events from another person's perspective are also most prone to experience guilt after an interpersonal conflict (Leith & Baumeister, 1998). When people perceive that they have hurt a valued partner, they respond with guilt, which motivates them to behave in ways that bring the relationship back into balance.

Shame as a Motivator of Social Withdrawal

While guilt focuses our attention on another person's feelings and our role in causing those feelings, shame focuses our attention on some real or imagined flaw in ourselves—a flaw in appearance, ability, or moral character (Lindsay-Hartz & others, 1995; Tangney, 1999). In one research study, 3-year-olds manifested more evidence of shame in response to failing an easy task than to failing a difficult one, already showing a link between shame and self-perceived lack of ability (Lewis, 1991). In another study, university students were asked to describe one episode in which they experienced shame and another in which they experienced guilt (Tangney, 1995). Compared with the guilt stories, the shame stories expressed more deeply felt pain and were more difficult for the students to tell. In the guilt episodes students saw themselves as relatively powerful—capable of either hurting or helping another person and motivated now to help. In the shame stories they saw themselves as blemished and powerless, motivated not to help but to disappear or hide. Stories of shame suggest that it often occurs in situations where it may truly be in the person's best interest to hide from negative judgment. Expressions of shame may also help communicate the person's feelings of self-derogation and powerlessness, which may induce compassion, perhaps even guilt, in those who would judge or punish the person.

Embarrassment as a Rectifier of Awkward Situations

When undergraduates were asked to write separate essays describing their experiences of embarrassment, shame, and guilt, the embarrassment essays far more often than the others focused on trivial or humorous incidents, not serious misconduct or deeply negative self-evaluations (Tangney & others, 1996). Embarrassment most often follows the inadvertent violation of a social norm or the receipt of unexpected or undesired attention from others. A guest walks into the bathroom and finds it occupied; an after-dinner speaker notices that he has gravy on his necktie; a young girl is asked by her grandmother to sing in front of strangers; a student is complimented too effusively by a professor in front of classmates. Unlike guilt, embarrassment most often involves acquaintances or strangers, whose reactions are not predictable, rather than close friends or family. Even toddlers as young as 15 months old have been observed to show signs of embarrassment when made the center of attention (Lewis, 1995). The human display of embarrassment is similar in form and function to the appeasement displays shown by other primates (Keltner & Anderson, 2000). As noted in Chapter 3, apes and monkeys grin and turn their heads away or down as a nonverbal way of saying, "No offense was meant; please don't attack me."

The function of embarrassment appears to lie primarily in its communicative value. The blush and the sheepish grin, which crests just after the head and eyes have turned aside, are clear and immediate signals that what just happened is the result of circumstance, or blunder, or someone else's doing and is not a deliberate attempt by the self to disrupt the others' activities or become the center of attention (Miller, 1995). The sheepish or silly grin of embarrassment seems to say, nonverbally, "How silly of me," or "What a foolish thing this is that happened."

Ondrea Barbe / Corbis

Embarrassment

Blushing, grinning sheepishly, looking down or to the side, and touching one's own face (as if symbolically hiding behind the hand) are common components of the human display of embarrassment.

Some people try to hide their embarrassment, but others—who know its power—may cultivate it and use it more or less deliberately for good effect. Several studies have shown that people are more attracted to those who manifest embarrassment in awkward situations than to those who don't (Keltner & Buswell, 1997). Embarrassment indicates concern for others' reactions and lack of haughtiness. In one experiment, subjects saw a video depicting a shopper bumping into a grocery display and then either expressing embarrassment or not as he began to pick up what he had knocked down (Semin & Manstead, 1982). The viewers who saw the embarrassment version rated the man as more likable than those who saw the calm, nonembarrassment version. In another experiment, a woman solicited volunteers for a research project from different sections of a sociology class under different conditions (Levin & Arluke, 1982). In one condition she read her request calmly, without embarrassment. In another condition she "accidentally" dropped her papers midway through, expressed embarrassment, and then continued her reading. She obtained significantly more volunteers in the second condition than in the first.

Pride, Self-Esteem, and Social Acceptability

7.

When is it safe to express pride? What functions may be served by (a) the expression of pride and (b) the feeling of pride?

In the dance of social life, we experience guilt at ignoring our partner too long, shame at our chronic lack of grace, and embarrassment when we accidentally bump a person we don't know very well. These reactions are useful; they help keep others from throwing us out despite our flaws. But sometimes we seem to do everything right, and then we experience *pride*. We throw our shoulders back, hold our head high, speak in richer tones, and strut a little as we dance, inviting others to admire us. As long as those others do indeed admire us, this drawing of attention to ourselves is useful; it adds to the cohort who may wish to make alliances with us for mutual benefit in the future.

Pride seems to be most directly opposite to shame. While shame focuses our attention on our own flaws and failures, pride focuses it on our own beauty and successes. While shame is felt and manifested as a desire to shrivel up and disappear, pride is felt and manifested as a desire to swell up and be seen by as many others as possible (Mascolo & Fischer, 1995). Just as 2-year-olds react with shame when they fail at a task or are criticized, they react with pride when they succeed or are praised (Stipek, 1995). The good feeling of pride is a self-reward for virtuous, diligent, or skillful behavior and an inducement to continue such behavior in the future. The expression of pride is perhaps best understood functionally as an advertisement of self-confidence that invites others to feel confident in us also.

8.

What is the sociometer theory of self-esteem, and what evidence supports the theory?

Closely related to pride is *self-esteem*, which can be defined as one's more-or-less sustained sense of liking oneself. According to a theory proposed by Mark Leary (1999; Leary & others, 1995), our self-esteem functions as a "sociometer," a gauge of the degree to which we are likely to be accepted or rejected by other people. In support of the sociometer theory, Leary and his colleagues (1995) described research in which they asked people to rate the degree to which particular real or hypothetical occurrences in their lives (such as rescuing a child, winning an award, or failing a course) would raise or lower their self-esteem, and also to rate the degree to which those same occurrences would raise or lower other people's opinions of them. They found that the two sets of ratings were essentially identical. Further support for the theory comes from studies in which people described experiences that had raised or lowered their self-esteem (Baumeister & others, 1998). Stories about gaining self-esteem most often entailed satisfying associations with other people, and stories about losing self-esteem most often involved experiences of being rejected or ostracized.

The ultimate, evolutionary purpose of our capacity for self-esteem, according to the sociometer theory, is to motivate us to act in ways that will promote our continued acceptance by others. What we call self-esteem, then, is actually our best guess about the degree to which others hold us in esteem. A decline in self-esteem may motivate us to either change our ways or seek a more compatible social group that approves of our way. Conversely, an increase in self-esteem may motivate us to continue on our present path, perhaps even more vigorously than before.

All in all, the self-conscious emotions provide much of the foundation for our experience of social pressure. They are evolved vehicles for prompting us to take others' feelings and expectations into account before we choose one action or another.

SECTION SUMMARY

Emotional expressions serve as social signals. They occur much more often when other people are present than when one is alone. Emotional expressions help people who are together understand each other's desires and needs, and this understanding improves their ability to cooperate. Emotional contagion, which can occur automatically and unconsciously, may help to coordinate the activities of a group by moving its members into the same mood.

The self-conscious emotions—guilt, shame, embarrassment, and pride—appear to serve functions related to social acceptance. Guilt is strongest after we hurt someone whom we care about, and it motivates us to make amends and thereby to preserve the relationship. Shame is strongest when we feel inadequate and powerless, and it motivates us to hide and refrain from drawing attention when others' judgments are likely to be negative. Embarrassment most often follows the inadvertent violation of a social norm; it wards off blame by signaling that the violation was not intentional. Pride, the opposite of shame, occurs in response to successes that are likely to be appreciated by others, and its expression appears designed to attract attention. A long-lasting sense of pride is called self-esteem. According to the sociometer theory, self-esteem relates quite directly to the likelihood of being approved of by other people whom we care about.

Kurt Lewin

A pioneer in social psychology, Lewin was known for his ability to identify problems in the social environment and study them within a theoretical framework.

SOCIAL PRESSURE: HOW OUR CONCERN FOR OTHERS' JUDGMENTS AFFECTS OUR ACTIONS

Social psychology is often defined (in the words of Gordon Allport, 1968) as "an attempt to understand and explain how the thought, feeling, and behavior of individuals are influenced by the actual, imagined, or implied presence of others." We experience these influences as *social pressure,* which can be defined as the entire set of psychological forces that are exerted on us by other people or by our beliefs about other people. We care deeply about what others think of us—especially if the others are nearby or are part of our social group—and that is a powerful source of pressure to do what we believe others want us to do.

The concept of social pressure has long figured into the broadest, most encompassing theories in social psychology. Kurt Lewin (1951), one of social psychology's pioneers, developed a theory, called *field theory,* that is based on an analogy between social pressure and physical force. According to this theory, each person exists in a continuously changing field of forces that push or pull the person in various directions. Some of these forces are understood by the person as coming from within—these are the person's own self-perceived desires, goals, and abilities. Other forces, which constitute social pressure, are perceived by the person as coming from the social environment. These forces consist primarily of the person's perception of or beliefs about other people's expectations or desires concerning his or her behavior. For an illustration and further elaboration of Lewin's field theory, see Figure 14.1, page 540.

Building on Lewin's use of analogies from physics, Bibb Latané (1981) developed a theory, known as *social impact theory,* aimed at predicting the amount of social pressure a person will feel at any given time. According to the theory, the factors that determine social pressure are the number, strength, and immediacy of the sources of that pressure. The *number of sources* is simply the number of people perceived by the target person as exerting pressure. The *strength of a source* is the

9.

How does the concept of social pressure figure into Lewin's field theory of behavior?

10.

According to Latané's social impact theory, what general factors increase and decrease the amount of social pressure a person experiences?

FIGURE **14.1**
Lewinian diagram of the life space
Lewin viewed the person as subject to a field of forces that push him or her toward or away from various goals. In this simplified diagram, goal 1 might be going to a party this evening, and goal 2 might be spending the evening studying; force 1 might be the person's own wish, and forces 2, 3, and 4 might be the person's perceptions of the desires of friends, family, and professors, respectively.

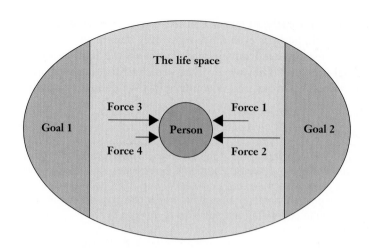

degree to which that person's opinions are valued by the target person. The *immediacy of a source* is the physical or psychological proximity of that person to the target person, measured either in physical distance or as prominence in memory. Social pressure grows or declines directly with an increase or decrease in the number, strength, and immediacy of its sources. The theory states further that the impact of any given pressure source on any given target decreases as the *number of targets* increases. For example, a child feels less impact if scolded along with others in a group than if scolded alone.

To illustrate the principles of social impact theory, Latané used the results of experiments on stage fright. Stage fright increases as the strength (in this case, status) and number of people in the audience increase (Figure 14.2a) and is greater if the audience is immediately present (can be seen by the performer) than if the audience is not immediately present (as in the case of a television audience). Further, stage fright decreases as the number of performers who share the stage increases (Figure 14.2b).

The propositions of social impact theory are useful because they summarize an enormously wide range of observations. Regardless of the kind of social impact—be it stage fright before an audience, shame from a scolding, persuasion from a salesperson, or an urge to conform when others are all behaving in a particular way—the amount of influence on the person increases as the strength, immediacy, and number of individuals perceived as exerting the influence increases, and it decreases as the number of perceived other targets increases.

FIGURE **14.2**
Experimental findings supporting Latané's model of social impact
These findings on the effects of audience status, audience size, and number of performers on stage fright come from two different studies. The results in (a) are from an experiment in which subjects imagined themselves reciting a poem in front of various audiences and then adjusted the brightness of a light to match their anticipated level of anxiety. Those in (b) are from a study in which college students who performed either alone or in groups of various sizes in an actual talent show estimated—using Stevens's method of magnitude estimation, described in Chapter 7—the degree of anxiety they had felt while on stage. (Graph [a] is adapted from Latané, 1981; graph [b] is adapted from Jackson & Latané, 1981.)

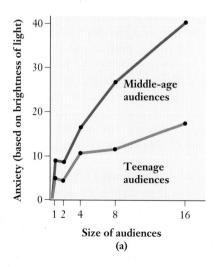

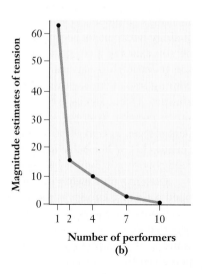

Social Facilitation and Interference: Effects of an Audience

Social pressure to perform a task well can, depending on conditions, either improve or worsen our performance. In some of the earliest experiments in social psychology, people performed tasks better when one or more observers were present than they did when alone. In one experiment, college students who had achieved skill at a task involving eye-hand coordination (moving a hand-held pointer to follow a moving target) subsequently performed it more accurately when observed by a group of graduate students than when tested alone (Travis, 1925). The enhancing effect of an audience on task performance was soon accepted as a general law of behavior and was given a name—*social facilitation.* Other early experiments, however, demonstrated an opposite effect—*social interference* (also called *social inhibition*), a decline in performance when observers are present. For example, students who were asked to develop arguments opposing the views of certain classical philosophers developed better arguments when they worked alone than when they worked in the presence of observers (Allport, 1920). The presence of observers also reduced performance in solving math problems (Moore, 1917), learning a finger maze (Husband, 1931), and memorizing lists of nonsense syllables (Pressin, 1933).

Why did social facilitation occur in some experiments and social interference occur in others? In reviewing the experiments, Robert Zajonc (1965) noticed that social facilitation usually occurred with relatively simple or well-learned tasks and social interference usually occurred with tasks that were more complex or involved learning something new. From this observation, Zajonc proposed the following generalization: *The presence of others facilitates performance of dominant (habitual, simple, or instinctive) actions and interferes with performance of nondominant (nonhabitual, complex, or unnatural) actions.*

Zajonc explained both effects by linking them to a more general phenomenon—the effect of high drive or arousal on performance. As discussed in Chapter 6, high arousal—no matter how it is produced—typically improves performance of simple or well-learned tasks and worsens performance of complex or poorly learned tasks. According to Zajonc, the primary effect of the presence of others is an increase in arousal, which facilitates dominant activities and interferes with nondominant activities (see Figure 14.3). Evidence for the theory comes from studies showing that (a) the presence of observers does typically increase arousal in a person performing a task (Cacioppo & others, 1990; Zajonc, 1980) and (b) either facilitation or interference can occur in the same task, depending on the performer's skill. As an example of the latter, in one experiment expert pool players performed better when they were watched conspicuously by a group of four observers than when they thought they were not being observed, and the opposite was true for novice pool players (Michaels & others, 1982).

Zajonc did not explain why arousal increases when another person is present, but subsequent research indicates, as you might expect, that the effect depends greatly on the performer's concern about being evaluated. Social facilitation and social interference both declined when the audience was blindfolded or did not pay attention to the performer (Cottrell & others, 1968) and increased when the audience was high in status or expertise and was present explicitly to evaluate (Geen, 1980, 1991). Other research suggests that social interference occurs not just through the negative effect that high arousal can have on performance but also through a shift in attention. The audience

11.

How does Zajonc's theory use the construct of arousal to explain the effects of an audience on performance? According to the theory, why are some performances improved and others worsened by an audience? What further evidence suggests that the arousal stems from evaluation anxiety?

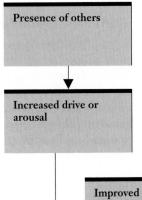

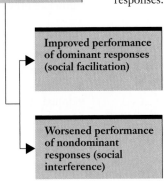

FIGURE **14.3** *Zajonc's theory of social facilitation and interference* This theory relates social facilitation and interference to a more general effect of high arousal or drive on dominant (habitual) and nondominant (nonhabitual) responses.

Challenge, not threat
When the performer is an expert, like Tiger Woods, the presence of an audience improves performance. Such an audience would worsen performance for a novice.

Duomo / Corbis

12.

How do the concepts of challenge and threat figure into a revised theory of social facilitation and interference?

makes the performer self-conscious, with the result that thoughts about the self and the image one is projecting detract from ability to perform the task (Baumeister & Showers, 1986). People who suffer from test anxiety know that a similar interfering effect can occur when taking a test (Sarason & Sarason, 1990). The mind becomes flooded with thoughts about failing and how others will react to the failure, and those thoughts interfere with the ability to concentrate on the problems posed by the test.

A recent modification of Zajonc's theory distinguishes between two types of audience-induced arousal—*challenge* and *threat* (Blasovich & others, 1999). The added pressure to perform well is experienced as a challenge when the person feels that he or she has the capacity to perform well, and it is otherwise experienced as a threat. James Blasovich and his colleagues (1999) found that the feelings of challenge and threat are accompanied by different patterns of physiological response. Heart rate increases in both cases, but blood pressure increases during threat and not during challenge (in the latter case, the blood vessels dilate to accommodate the increased blood flow). In experiments, Blasovich and his colleagues found that the challenge pattern of physiological response reliably accompanies social facilitation and the threat pattern reliably accompanies social interference.

Impression Management: Behavior as Performance

Social pressure influences not just our ability to perform specific tasks; it also—and more importantly—influences our choices of what to say and do in front of other people. Because we care what others think of us, we strive to influence their thoughts. To that end, we behave differently when witnesses are present than when we are alone, and differently in front of some witnesses than in front of others. Social psychologists use the term ***impression management*** to refer to the entire set of ways by which people consciously and unconsciously modify their behavior to influence others' impressions of them (Schlenker, 1980).

Humans as Actors and as Politicians

13.

How do the theatrical and political metaphors differ from each other in their portrayal of the purpose of impression management? According to the latter, why do we want to look "good"?

Poets and philosophers have always been aware of, and have frequently ridiculed, the human concern for appearances. As Shakespeare put it, "All the world's a stage, and all the men and women merely players." The sociologist Erving Goffman developed an entire approach to thinking about human behavior based on this metaphor. In a classic book entitled *The Presentation of Self in Everyday Life,* Goffman (1959) portrayed us as actors, playing at different times on different stages to different audiences, always trying to convince our current audience that we are who we are playing. The metaphor is useful, but if carried too far, it may suggest more duplicity, more conscious deception, than is warranted by what we know of impression management (Schlenker & Pontari, 2000). There need not be a division in our minds between the images we are trying to project and our sincere beliefs about ourselves. At any given moment we may simply be trying to exhibit our best selves, or those aspects of our selves that seem most appropriate and useful to meet the moment's needs.

An alternative metaphor, which may be more useful here, is that the human being is an *intuitive politician* (suggested by Tetlock, 1991). We perform in front of others not just to tell a good story or portray a character but to achieve real-life ends that may be selfish or noble or both at once. To do what we want to do in life, we need the approval and cooperation of other people—their votes, as it were—and to secure those votes, we perform and compromise in various ways. We are *intuitive* politicians in that we campaign for ourselves and our interests quite naturally, often without consciousness of our political ingenuity and strategies.

Depending on our needs, our capacities, and our audience, we may at any given time portray ourselves as pitiful, enraged, stern, or even irrational and unpredictable. These can be effective strategies for certain ends. For some people these strategies may even become regular ploys. But most of us, most of the time, try to make ourselves look *good* to other people. We want to come across as attractive, friendly, competent, rational, trustworthy, and moral because we know that others will be more inclined to collaborate with us if they see these qualities in us than if they don't. We also want to look *modest*, so people will think we are understating, not overstating, our virtues. And we want to look *sincere*, not like we are putting on a show or trying to ingratiate ourselves. We may or may not be conscious of our delicate balancing act between showing off and appearing modest, or between sincerity and ingratiation, but the act requires effort nevertheless. The degree to which we exert such effort and the manner in which we exert it depend on our audience, on our own personality characteristics, and on the norms of the culture to which we have adapted.

Impressing Acquaintances More Than Close Friends

In general, we are more concerned with impression management with new acquaintances than with familiar friends and companions (Leary & Kowalski, 1995; Tice & others, 1995). That concern makes sense in light of our understanding that first impressions can have long-lasting effects (discussed in Chapter 13). We have less need to manage impressions with close friends because they already know us well. A slip will not so seriously harm our reputation with friends as it will with strangers, and friends may see through our act no matter how clever the performance. In one research study, college students kept a diary of their self-perceived desire to impress others as they went through a week of daily life (Leary & others, 1994). They rated the degree to which they had wanted to appear likable, competent, ethical, and attractive to each person with whom they interacted for at least 10 minutes. As predicted, the students rated themselves as more concerned with all aspects of impression management with unfamiliar than with familiar same-sex companions. This relationship did not hold, however, for opposite-sex companions. When opposite-sex young singles interact, the effects of familiarity may be offset by the potential for romance, which may elevate the desire to impress.

Other research shows, not surprisingly, that dating partners are much more concerned with making a good impression on each other than are married partners. Dating partners rate themselves as most intimate and secure in their relationship when they have a highly favorable impression of each other, but married partners rate themselves as most intimate and secure when they have a "true" impression of each other—that is, when each sees the other as the other sees himself or herself (Swann & others, 1994). To feel comfortable in marriage, the two partners must feel that they can "be themselves" and not be rejected for it.

FIVE DISTINGUISHED PROFESSORS, EACH TRYING TO LOOK LIKE A MORE DISTINGUISHED PROFESSOR THAN THE OTHER FOUR

© Sidney Harris

14.

What evidence suggests that people are more concerned with impressing new acquaintances and dating partners than with impressing close friends and spouses? How do these differences make sense in terms of the functions of impression management?

Individual and Cultural Differences in Impression Management

Styles of impression management vary from person to person depending on personality (discussed in Chapter 15). For example, *shy* or *socially inhibited* people lack confidence in their ability to make a good impression and chronically fear making a bad impression, so they avoid meeting new people and tend to behave unobtrusively (Shepperd & Arkin, 1990).

Another personality dimension clearly associated with impression management is **self-monitoring,** which has to do with the degree to which people project a varied impression of themselves as they go from audience to audience. *High self-monitors* watch themselves vigilantly to assess how they must look to others present, and they modify their behavior to please their current audience. *Low self-monitors* are less vigilant in self-scrutiny and maintain greater consistency in behavior from one audience to another.

Some years ago, Mark Snyder (1974) developed a test of self-monitoring, made up of questions primarily about respondents' acting ability, conformity, and concern for others' immediate approval. Those who rank high on each of these factors are considered high self-monitors, and those who rank low are considered low self-monitors (see Table 14.1). In a series of studies using that test, researchers have identified certain consistent differences in the social lives and preferences of people who score high or low (Gangestad & Snyder, 2000). Highs typically have more friends than do lows, but their friendships are less intimate and more compartmentalized (Snyder & Smith, 1986). Highs tend to choose friends who appear attractive (and who thereby add, like a suit of clothes, to the impression that the high self-monitor makes on others) or who share some particular activity or interest with them; lows tend to choose friends who share their most consistent values and attitudes (Jamiesen & others, 1987). The high-self-monitoring style seems well adapted for a life lived on many different theatrical stages or political arenas. In contrast, the low-self-monitoring style seems well adapted for life on a single stage, with one rather consistent agenda and set of collaborators.

Styles of self-presentation also depend on cultural norms. For example, people in Asian cultures are more likely to express shame and less likely to express pride than are people in Western cultures, and this difference probably stems from cultural expectations (Okano, 1994). In cultures such as Japan it is considered most appropriate to hide one's pride and exhibit one's shame, while the opposite is true in the United States. The individualist orientation of Western cultures also encourages people to "be themselves" as they go from one situation to another, whereas the collectivist orientation of many other cultures (discussed in Chapter 13), in-

15.

What differences have been observed between people who score high and those who score low on the self-monitoring test? How might these be understood in terms of differing lifestyles?

16.

How might cultural expectations promote different impression-management styles in Western and Asian cultures?

TABLE **14.1** *Sample questions from the self-monitoring scale*

1. I can make impromptu speeches even on topics about which I have almost no information. (*T*)*
2. When I am uncertain how to act in a situation, I look to the behavior of others for cues. (*T*)
3. I rarely need the advice of my friends to choose movies, books, or music. (*F*)
4. Even if I am not enjoying myself, I often pretend to be having a good time. (*T*)
5. I would not change my opinions (or the way I do things) in order to please someone else or win their favor. (*F*)
6. I never have been good at games like charades or improvisational acting. (*F*)

*The *T* or *F* in parentheses is the response (True or False) that indicates high self-monitoring.

Source: From "Self-monitoring of expressive behavior" by M. Snyder, 1974, *Journal of Personality and Social Psychology, 30*, pp. 526–537.

cluding most Asian cultures, encourages people to change their behavior to meet the expectations of the group with which they are involved (Markus & Kitayama, 1991; Triandis, 1995).

Following Others' Examples to Be Right and to Be Liked

Other people influence our behavior not just through their roles as audience and judge but also through the examples they set. There are two general reasons why we tend to conform to others' examples.

One reason has to do with information and pragmatics. If other people cross bridge A and avoid bridge B, they may know something about the bridges that we don't know. To be safe, we had better stick with bridge A too. If other people say rhubarb leaves are poisonous, then to be safe, in the absence of better information, we shouldn't eat them, and we should probably tell our children they are poisonous. One of the great advantages of social life and culture lies in the sharing of information. We don't all have to learn everything from scratch, by trial and error. Rather, we can follow the examples of others and profit from trials and errors that may have occurred generations ago. Social influence that works through providing clues about the objective nature of an event or situation is referred to as *informational influence.*

The other general reason for conforming is to promote group cohesion and acceptance by the group. As was noted at the beginning of the chapter, social groups can exist only if some degree of behavioral coordination exists among the group members. Conformity is fundamental to coordination. Just as emotions tend to spread from person to person in a group, so do other aspects of cognition and behavior. We tend to adopt the ideas, myths, and habits of our group because doing so generates a sense of closeness with others, promotes our acceptance by them, and enables the group to function as a unit. We all cross bridge A because we are the bridge A people, and proud of it! If you cross bridge B, you may look like you don't want to be one of us or you may look strange to us. Better cross A. Social influence that works through the person's desire to be part of a group or to be approved of by others is called *normative influence.* Under some conditions, normative influences can lead people to say or do things that are objectively ridiculous, as demonstrated in a famous series of experiments conducted by Solomon Asch in the 1950s.

Asch's Experiments: Basic Procedure and Finding

Asch's original purpose was to demonstrate the limits of conformity (Asch, 1952). Previous experiments had shown that people will conform to others' judgments when the objective evidence is ambiguous (Sherif, 1936), and Asch expected to demonstrate that they will not conform when the evidence is clear-cut. But his results surprised him and changed the direction of his research.

Asch's (1956) procedure was as follows: A college-student volunteer was brought into the lab and seated with six to eight other students, and the group was told that their task was to judge the lengths of lines. On each trial they were shown one standard line and three comparison lines and were asked to judge which comparison line was identical in length to the standard (see Figure 14.4). As a perceptual task, this was almost absurdly easy; in previous tests, subjects performing the task alone almost never made mistakes. But, of course, this was not really a perceptual task; it was a test of conformity. Unbeknownst to the real subject, the others in the group were confederates of the experimenter and had been

17.

What are two classes of reasons why people tend to conform to examples set by others?

18.

How did Asch demonstrate that a tendency to conform can lead people to disclaim the evidence of their own eyes?

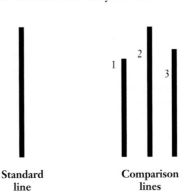

Standard
line

Comparison
lines

FIGURE **14.4** *Sample stimuli used by Asch to study conformity*
The task on each trial was to select the comparison line that was identical in length to the standard. On critical trials, the confederates unanimously made a specific wrong choice (either 1 or 3, in this example). (Adapted from Asch, 1956.)

FIGURE **14.5** *A perplexed subject in Asch's experiment*
It is not hard to tell who the real subject is in this photograph taken during a critical trial in one of Asch's experiments.

William Vandivert / *Scientific American*

instructed to give a specific wrong answer on certain prearranged "critical" trials. Choices were stated out loud by the group members, one at a time in the order of seating, and seating had been arranged so that the real subject was always the next to last to respond (see Figure 14.5). The question of interest was this: On the critical trials, would subjects be swayed by the confederates' wrong answers?

Of more than 100 subjects tested, 75 percent were swayed by the confederates on at least 1 of the 12 critical trials in the experiment. Some of the subjects conformed on every trial, others on only one or two. On average, subjects conformed on 37 percent of the critical trials. That is, on more than one-third of the trials on which the confederates gave a wrong answer, the subject also gave a wrong answer, usually the same wrong answer as the confederates had given. Asch's experiment has since been replicated dozens of times, in at least 17 different countries (Bond & Smith, 1996). The results reveal some decline in conformity in North America after the 1950s and some variation across cultures, but they still reveal a considerable amount of conformity whenever and wherever the experiment is conducted.

Was the Influence Informational or Normative?

Did Asch's subjects conform as a result of *informational* or *normative* influence? That is, did the subjects use the majority response as evidence regarding the objective lengths of the lines, or did they conform out of fear of looking different or nonnormative to the others present? When Asch (1956) questioned the subjects after the experiment, very few said that they had actually seen the lines as the confederates had seemed to see them, but many said that they had been led to doubt their own perceptual ability. They made such comments as "I thought that maybe because I wore glasses there was some defect"; "At first I thought I had the wrong instructions, then that something was wrong with my eyes and my head"; and "There's a greater probability of eight being right [than one]." Such statements suggest that to some degree the subjects did yield because of informational influence; they may have believed that the majority was right.

19.

What evidence led Asch to conclude that conformity in his experiments was caused more by normative than by informational influences?

But maybe these comments were rationalizations. Maybe the real reasons for conformity had more to do with a desire to be liked or accepted by the others (normative influence) than with a desire to be right. To test this possibility, Asch (1956) repeated the experiment under conditions in which the confederates responded out loud as before, but the subjects responded privately in writing. To accomplish this, Asch arranged to have the real subjects arrive "late" to the experiment and be told that although no more subjects were needed, they might participate in a different way by listening to the others and then writing down, rather than voicing aloud, the answer they believed to be correct. In this condition, the amount of conformity dropped to about one-third of that in the earlier experiments. Apparently, the primary influence on Asch's subjects was normative. Their conformity was motivated more by the desire to be liked or accepted by the group than by the desire to give an objectively correct answer. When subjects did not have to respond publicly, their answers in the critical trials rarely reflected conformity.

Experiments following Asch's indicate that conformity is most often motivated by normative influences when the perceptual task is easy (as in Asch's original experiment) and by informational influences when the task is difficult or ambiguous (Campbell & Fairey, 1989; Campbell & others, 1986). With an apparently easy task, people expect everyone to give the same response, so failure to side with the majority could be judged by others as a sign of abnormality or perverseness. With a difficult or ambiguous task, people expect responses to vary, so there is less stigma attached to being different; in that case the primary motive for conformity stems from the assumption that the others may be right.

The Liberating and Thought-Provoking Effects of a Nonconformist

When Asch (1956) changed his procedure so that a single confederate gave a different answer from the others, the amount of conformity on the line-judging task dropped dramatically—to about one-fourth of that in the unanimous condition. This effect occurred regardless of how many other confederates there were (from 2 to 14) and regardless of whether the dissenter gave the right answer or a different wrong answer from the others. Any response that differed from the majority encouraged the real subject to resist the majority's influence and to give the correct answer.

Since Asch's time, other experiments, using more difficult tasks or problems than Asch's, have shown that a single dissension from the majority can have beneficial effects not just through reducing normative pressure to conform but also through informational means, by shaking people out of their complacent view that the majority must be right (Nemeth, 1986). When people hear a dissenting opinion, they become motivated to examine the evidence more closely, which can lead to a better solution.

Conformity as a Basis for Failing to Help a Person in Need

Conformity can lead us not only to deny the evidence of our senses but also to fail to help a person whom we otherwise would help. A man lies ill on the sidewalk in full view of hundreds of passers-by who all fail to stop and ask if he needs help. A woman is brutally beaten in front of witnesses who fail to come to her aid or even to call the police. How can such incidents occur?

In many experiments, social psychologists have found that a given person is much more likely to help in an emergency if he or she is the only witness than if one or more other witnesses are also present (Latané & Nida, 1981). In one experiment, for example, college students filling out a questionnaire were interrupted by the sound of the researcher, behind a screen, falling and crying out, "Oh . . . my foot . . . I . . . can't move it; oh . . . my ankle . . . I can't get this thing off me" (Latané & Rodin, 1969). In some cases the student was alone, and in other cases two students sat together filling out questionnaires. The remarkable result was that 70 percent of those who were alone went to the aid of the researcher, but only 20 percent of those who were in pairs did so. Apparently an accident victim is better off with just one potential helper present than with two! Why? Part of the answer probably has to do with diffusion of responsibility. The more people present, the less any one person feels it is his or her responsibility to help (Schwartz & Gottlieb, 1980). But conformity also seems to contribute.

20.

What valuable effects can a single nonconformist have on others in the group?

Passing by
Researchers have found that the presence of other witnesses decreases the likelihood that any given witness will try to help a person who may be in need.

David McNew / Liaison / Newsmakers

21.

How can the failure of multiple bystanders to help a person in need be explained as an example of conformity stemming from both informational and normative influences?

Gerry Gropp / Sipa Press

Save the forest

Members of a group who initially share an opinion are likely to hold that opinion even more strongly after they have met and discussed it than they did before.

22.

How has group polarization been demonstrated, and what are some natural social circumstances in which it is likely to occur?

If you are the only witness to an incident, you decide whether it is an emergency or not, and whether you can help or not, using information from the victim. But if other witnesses are present, you look also at them. You wait just a bit to see what they are going to do, and chances are you find that they do nothing (because they are waiting to see what you are going to do). Their inaction is a source of information that may lead you to question your initial judgment: Maybe this is not an emergency, or if it is, maybe nothing can be done. Their inaction also establishes an implicit social norm. If you spring into action, you might look foolish to the others, who seem so complacent. Thus, each person's inaction can promote inaction in others through both informational and normative influences.

These interpretations are supported by experiments showing that the inhibiting effect of others' presence is reduced or abolished by circumstances that alter the informational and normative influences of the other bystanders. If the bystanders indicate, by voice or facial expressions, that they *do* interpret the situation as an emergency, then their presence has a much smaller or no inhibiting effect on the target person's likelihood of helping (Bickman, 1972). If the bystanders know each other well—and thus have less need to manage their impressions in front of each other, or know that each shares a norm of helping—they are more likely to help than if they don't know each other well (Rutkowski & others, 1983; Schwartz & Gottlieb, 1980).

Social Pressure in Group Discussions

When people get together to discuss an idea or make a decision, their explicit goal usually is to share information. But whether they want to or not, group members also influence one another through normative social pressure. Such pressure can occur whenever one person expresses an opinion or takes a position on an issue in front of another: Are you with me or against me? It feels good to be with, uncomfortable to be against. There is unstated pressure to agree.

Group Discussion Can Make Attitudes More Extreme

When a group is evenly split on an issue, the result is often a compromise (Burnstein & Vinokur, 1977). Each side partially convinces the other side, so the majority leave the room with a more moderate view on the issue than they had when they entered the room. However, if the group is not evenly split—if all or a large majority of the members argue on the same side of the issue—discussion typically pushes that majority toward a more extreme view in the same direction as their initial view. This phenomenon is called *group polarization.*

Group polarization has been demonstrated in many experiments, with a wide variety of problems or issues for discussion. In one experiment, mock juries evaluated traffic-violation cases that had been constructed to produce either high or low initial judgments of guilt. After group discussion the jurors rated the high-guilt cases as indicating even higher levels of guilt, and the low-guilt cases as indicating even lower levels of guilt, than they had before the discussion (Myers & Kaplan, 1976). In other experiments, researchers divided people into groups based on their initial view on a controversial issue and found that discussions held separately by each group widened the gap between the groups (see Figure 14.6). In one experiment, for example, discussion caused groups favoring a strengthening of the military to favor it even more strongly and groups favoring a paring down of the military to favor that more strongly (Minix, 1976; Semmel, 1976).

Group polarization can have socially important consequences. When students whose political views are barely to the right of center get together to form a Young Conservatives club, their views are likely to shift further toward the right; similarly, a Young Liberals club is likely to shift to the left. Prisoners who enter jail with little respect for the law and spend their time talking with other prisoners who share that view are likely to leave prison with even less respect for the law than they had be-

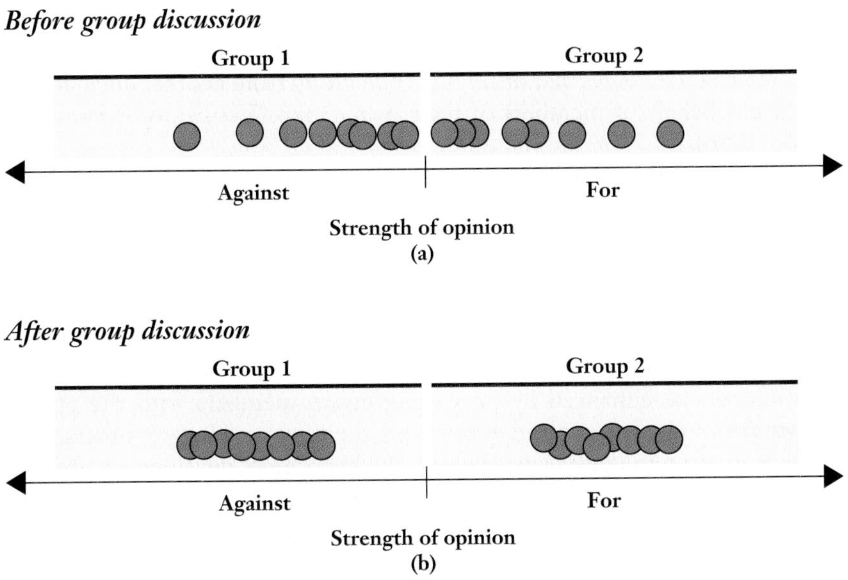

Before group discussion

Group 1   Group 2

Against   For

Strength of opinion
(a)

After group discussion

Group 1   Group 2

Against   For

Strength of opinion
(b)

FIGURE 14.6 *Schematic illustration of group polarization*
Each circle represents the opinion of one individual. When the individuals are divided into two groups on the basis of the direction of their initial position (a) and then discuss the issue with other members of their group, the majority move toward a more extreme position than they held before (b).

fore. Professors who believe that students are getting lazier each year are likely to become even more convinced of that after having lunch with other professors who also hold that view. Everyday observations suggest that such shifts are indeed quite common.

What Causes Group Polarization?

By now it should be no surprise to you that social psychologists have proposed two classes of explanations for group polarization—informational and normative. *Informational* explanations focus on the pooling of arguments that occurs during group discussion. People vigorously put forth arguments favoring the side toward which they lean and tend to withhold arguments that they might be able to think of favoring the other side. As a result, the group members hear a disproportionate number of arguments on the side of their initial leaning, which may persuade them to lean further in that direction (Kaplan, 1987; Vinokur & Burnstein, 1974). Moreover, simply hearing others repeat one's own arguments in the course of discussion can have a validating effect. People become more convinced of the soundness of their own logic and the truth of the "facts" they know when they hear the logic and facts repeated by another person (Brauer & others, 1995).

Normative explanations attribute group polarization to people's concerns about being approved of by other group members. One might expect normative influences to cause opinions within a group to become more similar to one another, but not more extreme. In fact, as illustrated in Figure 14.6, they do become more similar as well as, on average, more extreme. Several variations of normative hypotheses have been offered to explain why opinions within a like-minded group become more extreme.

One suggestion, which we can call the *one-upmanship hypothesis*, is that group members vie with one another to become the most vigorous supporter of the position that most people favor; this competition pushes the group as a whole toward an increasingly extreme position. This hypothesis is supported by evidence that people indeed do admire points of view that are more extreme but in the same direction as their own (Levinger & Schneider, 1969; Myers, 1982). Thus, by adopting increasingly extreme positions, group members may hope to enhance their standing in the group.

Another suggestion, which we can call the *group-stereotyping hypothesis*, is that people actually do shift their position toward what they believe to be the average view of the group but they misperceive that average. They think that the group as a whole has a more extreme position than it actually does, and they shift their own

23.

How might group polarization be explained in terms of (a) informational and (b) normative influences?

opinion toward that perceived extreme. This view is supported by evidence that people do, as part of the process of stereotyping (discussed in Chapter 13), exaggerate the characteristics that distinguish one group from another, including the attitudes and beliefs of members of their own group (Keltner & Robinson, 1996; Mackie, 1986).

Closely related to the group-stereotyping hypothesis is the *intergroup-conflict hypothesis*, which states that people shift toward a more extreme view not to become extreme members of their own group but to distinguish themselves clearly from the opposing group. The Young Liberals become more liberal to show clearly that they are not like those hard-hearted conservatives in the other club, and the Young Conservatives become more conservative to show that they are not like those soft-headed liberals. This hypothesis is supported by research showing that group polarization can be enhanced by presenting group members with the opinions of another group that is perceived as opposing their group (Hogg & others, 1990).

As is so often the case in psychology, the hypotheses developed by different researchers are not contradictory to one another and probably all have a grain or more of truth to them. Group polarization in any given instance might result from any or all of these informational and normative influences.

Conditions That Lead to Good or Bad Group Decisions

24.

How did Janis explain some White House policy blunders with his group-think theory? How can the tendency toward groupthink be countered?

Decisions made by groups are sometimes better and sometimes worse than decisions made by individuals working alone. To the degree that the group decision arises from the sharing of the best available evidence and logic, it is likely to be better. To the degree that it arises from collective ignorance, selective withholding of arguments on the less-favored side, false perceptions of others' views, and participants' attempts to outdo one another or to distinguish themselves from another group, the group decision may be worse than the decision most group members would make alone.

In a book entitled *Groupthink*, Irving Janis (1982) analyzed some of the most misguided policy decisions made in the U.S. White House. Among them were the decision to invade Cuba in 1961 (an episode commonly known as the Bay of Pigs fiasco), to escalate the Vietnam war during the late 1960s, and to cover up the Watergate burglary in the early 1970s. Janis contends that each of these decisions came about because a tightly knit clique of presidential advisers, whose principal concerns were upholding group unity and pleasing their leader (Presidents Kennedy, Johnson, and Nixon, respectively), failed to examine critically the choice that their leader seemed to favor and instead devoted their energy to defending that choice and suppressing criticisms of it. To refer to such processes, Janis coined the term **groupthink,** which he defined as "a mode of thinking that people engage in when they are deeply involved in a cohesive ingroup, when the members' striving for unanimity overrides their motivation to realistically appraise alternative courses of action." More recently, many other ill-advised decisions, including the decision to launch the U.S. space shuttle *Challenger* in below-freezing weather, have been attributed to groupthink ('t Hart, 1990; Moorhead & others, 1991). The tendency toward groupthink appears to be strongest when the group members feel threatened by opposing groups and begin to define their task as defending their view rather than seeking the best solution to the problem (Turner & Horvitz, 2001).

A number of experiments conducted both before and after Janis published his groupthink model have affirmed it. In one, actual bomber crews—each con-

The Challenger *explosion*

The flawed decision making that Irving Janis called *groupthink* has been implicated in the 1986 explosion of the U.S. space shuttle *Challenger*. In striving for unanimity in the decision to launch, managers ignored engineers' warnings about the dangers of launching after a night of subfreezing temperatures.

A. Tannenbaum / Sygma

sisting of a pilot, a navigator, and a gunner who were used to working together—were given problems to solve individually or as a group. As individuals the navigators were best at solving the problems, but working in a group the navigators were relatively ineffective because both they and the gunners deferred to the pilots, who held the highest status in the crew (Torrance, 1954). Other experiments have shown that the ability of groups to solve problems and make effective decisions is improved if (a) the leaders refrain from advocating a view themselves and instead encourage group members to present their own views and challenge one another (Leana, 1985; Neck & Moorhead, 1995) and (b) the groups focus on the problem to be solved rather than on developing group cohesion (Callaway & Esser, 1984; Mullen & others, 1994).

SECTION SUMMARY

Social pressure—which arises from one's beliefs about what other people expect or want one to do—is the central concept in Lewin's field theory and Latané's social impact theory. According to Latané, the amount of pressure experienced by a target of social pressure increases as the number, strength, and immediacy of the sources of that pressure increase, and it decreases as the number of targets of that pressure increases.

Social pressure to perform well, induced by the presence of an audience, typically improves performance on well-learned or habitual tasks (social facilitation) and worsens performance on poorly learned or novel tasks (social interference). We are not, however, passive victims of social pressure. Through conscious and unconscious means, we strive to manage the impressions that others form of us so as to promote ourselves and achieve our desired goals. Some people, referred to as high self-monitors, are more vigilant than others in assessing how they appear and in modifying their words and actions to impress their current audience.

People also influence one another by the examples they set. We conform to others' examples for informational reasons (to take advantage of others' knowledge) and for normative reasons (to be accepted by the group). In Asch's classic experiments, subjects who heard others all give a specific wrong answer in a simple task of length judgment often conformed by giving the same wrong answer. The conformity largely disappeared when the subjects were allowed to make their judgments privately, suggesting that it was caused by normative more than informational influences. Other research indicates that the tendency for bystanders to refrain from helping someone in need when other bystanders are present can be explained as conformity stemming from both informational and normative influences.

When like-minded people discuss a topic, their opinions typically shift toward a more extreme version of their initial view. Experiments have demonstrated that such group polarization of opinion can be explained by a combination of informational and normative influences. More generally, groups that are overly concerned with unanimity and cohesiveness, at the expense of frankness, often make poor decisions—a social phenomenon called groupthink.

INFLUENCE OF OTHERS' REQUESTS

One of the least subtle yet most potent forms of social influence is the direct request. If the request is small and made politely, we tend to comply automatically (Langer & others, 1978), and this tendency increases when our attention is otherwise occupied (Cialdini, 1993). But even if the request is onerous or offensive, people often find it hard to look a requester in the eye and say no. The tendency to comply usually serves us well. Most requests are reasonable, and we know that in the long run doing things for others pays off, as others in turn do things for us. But there are people who—out of selfishness, or because their jobs demand it, or because they are working for causes in which they sincerely believe—will exploit our tendency to comply. It is useful to know their techniques so that we give when we want to give and buy what we want to buy rather than succumb to pressure.

Sales Pressure: Some Principles of Compliance

Robert Cialdini (1987, 2001) is a social psychologist who has devoted more than lip service to the idea of combining real-world observations with laboratory studies. To learn about compliance from the real-world experts, he took training in how to sell encyclopedias, automobiles, and insurance; infiltrated advertising agencies and fund-raising organizations; and interviewed recruiters, public-relations specialists, and political lobbyists. He learned their techniques, extracted what seemed to be basic principles, and showed those principles in operation under the controlled conditions of experimental research. The following paragraphs describe a sample of compliance principles taken largely from Cialdini's work but also much studied by other social psychologists.

Cognitive Dissonance as a Force for Compliance

Chapter 13 contains an extensive discussion of the theory of cognitive dissonance. The basic idea of the theory is that people are made uncomfortable by contradictions among their beliefs, or between their beliefs and their actions, and thus are motivated to change their beliefs or actions to maintain consistency. According to Cialdini's analysis, a number of standard sales tricks make use of cognitive dissonance to elicit compliance.

One such trick, called the *four-walls technique,* is a questioning strategy that induces the potential customer to make statements that are consistent with the idea that owning the product would be a good thing. The customer's own statements set up cognitive walls, which more or less box the customer into agreeing to the deal when it is finally proposed. This is the technique of telemarketers and door-to-door salespeople, who begin as if conducting a survey, with questions such as these (from Cialdini, 1987): (a) "Do you feel that a good education is important for your children?" (b) "Do you think that children who do their homework will get a better education?" (c) "Do you believe that a good set of reference books can help children do their homework?" (d) "Well, then, it sounds like you'll want to hear about the fine set of encyclopedias I have to offer at an excellent price. May I tell you about it?" After expressing a favorable attitude toward education and reference books in response to the first three questions, most people find it hard to say no to the fourth.

Another common sales trick, the *foot-in-the-door technique,* relies on getting the potential customer to grant an initial small request, which prepares the customer psychologically to grant a subsequent larger request. To my chagrin, I was outwitted—once—by a clever gang of driveway sealers who used this technique on me. One day while I was raking leaves in front of my house, these men pulled up in their truck and asked if they could have a drink of water. I, of course, said yes; how could I say no to a request like that? Then they got out of the truck and one said,

25.

How can the four-walls and the foot-in-the-door sales techniques be explained in terms of cognitive dissonance?

A foot in the door

If the homeowner here agrees to the first request, to sign a petition, she may then find it hard to turn down a second, larger request, to donate time or money to the cause.

Bondan Hrynewych / Stock, Boston

"Oh, if you have some lemonade or soda, that would even be better; we'd really appreciate that." Well, all right, I did have some lemonade. As I brought it to them, one of the men pointed to the cracks in my driveway and commented that they had just enough sealing material and time to do my driveway that afternoon, and they could give me a special deal. Normally, I would never have agreed to a bargain like that on the spot; but I found myself unable to say no. I ended up paying far more than I should have, and they did a very poor job. I had been taken in by what I now see clearly to be a novel twist on the foot-in-the-door sales technique.

The basis of the foot-in-the-door technique is that people are more likely to agree to a large request if they have already agreed to a small one. The driveway sealers got me twice on that: Their request for water primed me to agree to their request for lemonade, and their request for lemonade primed me to agree to their deal about sealing my driveway. Cialdini (1987) has argued that the foot-in-the-door technique works largely through the principle of cognitive dissonance. Having agreed, apparently of my own free will, to give the men lemonade, I must have justified that action to myself by thinking, *These are a pretty good bunch of guys*, and that thought was dissonant with any temptation I might have had a few moments later, when they proposed the driveway deal, to think, *These people may be cheating me.* So I pushed the latter thought out of my mind before it fully registered.

In cases like my encounter with the driveway sealers, the foot-in-the-door technique may work because compliance to the first request induces a sense of trust, commitment, or compassion toward the person making that request. In other cases it may work by inducing a sense of commitment toward a particular product or cause (Burger, 1999). The technique has proved to be especially effective in soliciting donations for political causes or charities. People who first agree to make a small donation, such as by signing a petition or giving a few minutes of their time, are subsequently more willing than they otherwise would be to make a much larger donation (Bell & others, 1994; Cialdini, 2001; Freedman & Fraser, 1966). Apparently the small donation leads the person to develop a firmer sense of support for the cause—"I contributed to it, so I must believe in it"—which in turn promotes willingness to make a larger donation.

The Reciprocity Norm as a Force for Compliance

Anthropologists and sociologists have found that people all over the world abide by a *reciprocity norm* (Gouldner, 1960). That is, people everywhere feel obliged to return favors. This norm is so ingrained that people may even feel driven to reciprocate favors that they didn't want in the first place. Cialdini (1993) suggests that this is why the technique known as *pregiving*—such as pinning a flower on the lapel of an unwary stranger before asking for a donation or giving a free bottle of furniture polish to a potential vacuum-cleaner customer—is effective. Having received the gift, the victim finds it hard to turn away without giving something in return.

Notice that pregiving works through a means that is opposite to that proposed for the foot-in-the-door technique. The foot-in-the-door target is first led to make a small donation, which induces a sense of commitment and thereafter a larger donation. The reciprocity target, in contrast, is first presented with a gift, which leads to a felt need to give something back. If the two procedures were combined, they should tend to cancel each other out. The contribution would be seen as payment for the gift, reducing any further need to reciprocate, and the gift would be seen as justification for the contribution, reducing cognitive dissonance and thereby reducing the psychological drive to become more committed to the cause.

26.

How can the effectiveness of pregiving be explained in terms of the reciprocity norm? What evidence supports the theory that pregiving operates through a means opposite to that of the foot-in-the-door technique?

The reciprocity norm
The free sample may lead this man to purchase the product in part by inducing in him a need to reciprocate in some way.

Bill Aron / Photo Edit

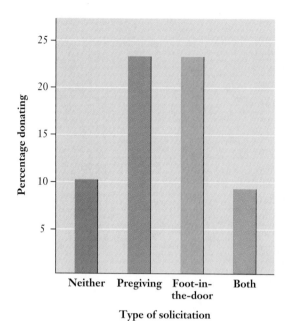

FIGURE 14.7 *Evidence that the pregiving and foot-in-the-door techniques work in ways that oppose each other*
In this field experiment, involving actual door-to-door solicitation to support an AIDS foundation, the pregiving and foot-in-the-door techniques were effective when each was used alone, but the two together were ineffective. The results support the theory that the two techniques work through psychological mechanisms that, when combined, cancel each other out. (Data from Bell & others, 1994.)

An experiment involving actual door-to-door solicitation of funds for a local AIDS foundation showed that in fact the two techniques do cancel each other out (Bell & others, 1994). Each person who was solicited first heard the same standard spiel about the foundation's good work. Some were then immediately asked for a donation (*control condition*). Others were given an attractive brochure containing "life-saving information about AIDS" (*pregiving condition*), or were asked to sign a petition supporting AIDS education (*foot-in-the-door condition*), or both (*combined condition*), before they were asked for a donation. As shown in Figure 14.7, pregiving and foot-in-the-door techniques markedly increased the frequency of giving when either was used alone but had no effect beyond that of the control condition when the two were used in combination. This finding not only provides practical information for fund-raisers but also supports the proposed theories about the mechanisms of the two effects. If the two techniques operated simply by increasing the amount of interaction between the solicitor and the person being solicited, then the combined condition should have been most effective.

Psychological Reactance as a Force Opposing Compliance

27.

How can an understanding of psychological reactance help one gain another's compliance?

Balancing our tendency to comply is our tendency to assert our independence and freedom. When pressure to behave in a certain way is too blatant, it can have the opposite of its intended effect—a phenomenon called ***psychological reactance*** (Brehm & Brehm, 1981). An intuitive understanding of the reactance principle leads most people to soften the way they make requests so as to prevent refusal to comply by preserving the appearance of choice. When a teacher says to the class, "Would you all please take out your pencils and answer the following questions," the class knows that this isn't a question, or even a request, but a command—yet the gentle phrasing helps prevent reactance by maintaining the superficial appearance of choice.

Clever salespeople may exploit the reactance principle not just by softening their sales pitch but by acting as if they are trying to prevent you from making a particular purchase. They may act as if they would rather not sell you that particular item, implying, perhaps, that very few of them are left, thus threatening your freedom to own one. In one experiment conducted long ago, children who were given a choice of candies overwhelmingly picked the one that was placed farthest away and under a wire screen (Wright, 1937). Apparently, the ruse that the experimenter was trying to hide that piece made it more attractive. With adults the attempt to hide the forbidden item must be less obvious, but the idea is the same. When a group of college students were led to believe that their cafeteria would be closing down for a while because of a fire, they rated its food more favorably than they had before the announcement (West, 1975).

Conditions That Promote Obedience: Milgram's Experiments

Obedience refers to those cases of compliance in which the person making the request is perceived as an authority figure or leader and the request is perceived as an order or command. Obedience can be a good thing. Obedience to parents and teachers is part of nearly everyone's social training. Running an army, an orchestra, a hospital, or any enterprise involving large numbers of people would be almost impossible if people did not routinely carry out the instructions given to them by their leaders or bosses. But obedience has its dark side. Most tragic are the cases in which people obey a leader who is evil, unreasonable, or sadly mistaken. Under what conditions, short of physical threat, will people obey an order to hurt a person whom they do not want to hurt? That is the central question behind a series of experiments performed by Stanley Milgram at Yale University in the early 1960s, which are now perhaps the best known of all experiments in social psychology.

Milgram's Basic Procedure and Finding

Let us suppose that you are a volunteer who has answered Milgram's ad to participate in a psychological experiment. You enter the laboratory and meet the experimenter and another person, who is introduced to you as a volunteer subject like yourself. The experimenter, a stern and expressionless man, explains that this is a study of the effects of punishment on learning and that one of you will serve as teacher and the other as learner. You draw slips of paper to see who will play which role and find that your slip says "teacher." The other subject, a pleasant middle-aged man, will be the learner. You watch while his arms are strapped into a chair and electrodes are taped to his wrist (see Figure 14.8). The experimenter explains that the straps will prevent excessive movement while the learner is shocked and that the electrode paste on the skin has been applied "to avoid blisters and burns." While he is being strapped in, the learner expresses some apprehension, saying that he is concerned because he has a heart condition.

After observing this part of the procedure, you—the teacher—are taken to an adjoining room, from which you can communicate with the learner through an intercom. Your job is to read off the questions on a test of verbal memory and to give the learner an electric shock whenever he gives a wrong answer. The shock generator in front of you has 30 switches, labeled with voltage designations from 15 to 450 volts. Additional labels next to the switches describe the shocks as ranging from "Slight shock" to "Danger, severe shock," followed by two switches labeled "XXX."

As the experiment progresses, the learner makes frequent mistakes, and at each mistake you give him a stronger shock than you gave before. The learner receives the early shocks silently, but when you get to 75 volts, he responds with an audible "unghh," and at stronger shocks his protests become more extreme. At 150 volts he cries out, "Experimenter, get me out of here! I won't be in the experiment any more! I refuse to go on!" At 180 volts he hollers, "I can't stand the pain!" By 270 volts his response to each shock is an agonized scream, and at 300 volts he shouts in desperation that he will no longer provide answers in the memory test. The experimenter instructs you to continue anyway and to treat each nonresponse as a wrong answer. At 315 and 330 volts the learner screams violently, and then, most frightening of all, from 345 volts on, the learner makes no sound at all. He does not respond to your questions, and he does not react to the shock.

At various points you look to the experimenter and ask if he should check on the learner or if the experiment should be terminated. You might even plead with the experimenter to let you quit giving shocks. At each of these junctures, the experimenter responds firmly with well-rehearsed prompts. First, he says, "Please continue." If you still protest, he responds, "The experiment requires that you continue." This is followed, if necessary, by "It is absolutely essential that you continue" and "You have no other choice; you must go on." These prompts are always used in sequence. If you still refuse to go on after the last prompt, the experiment is discontinued. In reality—as you, sitting comfortably and reading this book, have probably figured out—the learner receives no shocks. He is a confederate of the experimenter, trained to play his role. But you, as a subject in the experiment, do not know that. You believe that the learner is suffering, and at some point you begin to think that his life may be in danger. What do you do? If you are like the majority of people, you will go on with the experiment to the very end and eventually give the

28.

How did Milgram demonstrate that a remarkably high percentage of people would follow a series of orders to hurt another person?

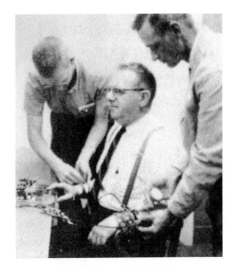

FIGURE **14.8** *The "learner" in Milgram's obedience experiments* While being strapped into a chair and fitted with electrodes, this pleasant man— the "learner"—mentioned that he had a heart condition.

learner the strongest shock on the board—450 volts, "XXX." In a typical rendition of this experiment, 65 percent (26 out of 40) of the subjects continued to the very end of the series. They did not find this easy to do. Many pleaded with the experimenter to let them stop, and almost all of them showed signs of great tension, such as sweating and nervous tics, yet they went on.

Why didn't they quit? There was no reason to fear retribution for halting the experiment. The experimenter, although stern, did not look physically aggressive. He did not make any threats. The $5 pay for participating was so small as to be irrelevant; and all subjects had been told that the $5 was theirs just for showing up. So why didn't they quit?

Explaining the Finding

Upon first hearing about the results of Milgram's experiment, people are tempted to suggest that the volunteers must have been in some way abnormal to give painful, perhaps deadly, shocks to a middle-aged man with a heart condition. But that explanation doesn't hold up. The experiment was replicated dozens of times, using many different groups of subjects, with essentially the same results each time. Milgram (1974) himself found the same results for women as for men and the same results for college students, professionals, and workers of a wide range of ages and backgrounds. Others repeated the experiment outside the United States, and the consistency from group to group was far more striking than the differences (A. G. Miller, 1986). No category of person has been found immune from the tendency to obey at a high rate in the Milgram experiment. Another temptation is to interpret the results as evidence that people in general are sadistic. But nobody who has seen Milgram's film of subjects actually giving the shocks would conclude that. The subjects showed no pleasure in what they were doing, and they were obviously upset by their belief that the learner was in pain. How, then, can the results be explained? Milgram (1974) and other social psychologists (A. G. Miller, 1986) have identified some facilitating factors, including:

29.

Why does Milgram's finding call for an explanation in terms of the social situation rather than in terms of unique personality characteristics of the subjects?

* ***Preexisting beliefs about authority and the value of science***   The volunteer comes to the laboratory as a product of a social world that effectively, and usually for beneficent reasons, trains people to obey legitimate authorities and to play by the rules. An experimenter, especially one at such a reputable institution as Yale University, must surely be a legitimate authority in the context of the laboratory. In addition, the volunteer arrives with a degree of faith in the value of scientific research, which Milgram referred to as an *overarching ideology*, analogous to the overarching political or religious ideologies that motivate people to make much greater voluntary sacrifices when, for example, they join an army. Thus, the person enters the laboratory highly prepared to do what the experimenter asks. Consistent with the idea that prior beliefs about the legitimacy of the experiment contributed to this obedience, Milgram found that when he moved the experiment from Yale to a downtown office building, under the auspices of a fictitious organization, Research Associates of Bridgeport, the percentage who were fully obedient dropped somewhat—from 65 to 48 percent.

30.

How might the high rate of obedience in Milgram's experiments be explained in terms of the subjects' preexisting beliefs, the experimenter's demeanor, the proximity of the experimenter, the lack of a model for rebellion, and the incremental nature of the task?

* ***The experimenter's self-assurance and acceptance of responsibility***   Obedience is predicated on the assumption that the person giving orders is in control and responsible and that your role is essentially that of a cog in a wheel. The preexisting beliefs mentioned above helped prepare subjects to accept the cog's role, but the experimenter's unruffled self-confidence during what seemed to be a time of crisis no doubt helped subjects to continue accepting that role as the experiment progressed. To reassure themselves, they often asked the experimenter questions like "Who is responsible if that man is hurt?" and the experimenter routinely answered that he was responsible for anything that might happen. The importance of attributing responsibility to the experimenter was shown directly in an experiment conducted by another researcher (Tilker,

1970), patterned after Milgram's. Obedience dropped sharply when subjects were told beforehand that they, the subjects, were responsible for the learner's well-being.

+ *The immediacy of the experimenter and the distance of the learner*   If you think of Milgram's subjects in relation to social impact theory, you can picture them as caught between two conflicting social forces. On one side was the experimenter demanding that the experiment be continued, and on the other was the learner asking that it be stopped. Not only did the experimenter have the greater initial authority (higher strength), but he was also physically closer and perceptually more prominent (higher immediacy). He was standing in the same room with the subject while the learner was in another room, out of sight. To test the importance of immediacy, Milgram (1974) varied the placement of the experimenter or the learner. In one variation, the experimenter left the room when the experiment began and communicated with the subject by telephone, using the same verbal prompts as in the original study; in this case, only 23 percent obeyed to the end, compared with 65 percent in the original condition. In another variation, the experimenter remained in the room with the subject, but the learner was also brought into that room; in this case, 40 percent obeyed to the end. In still another variation, the subject was required to hold the learner's arm on the shock plate while the shock was administered (see Figure 14.9), with the result that 30 percent obeyed to the end. Thus, any change that moved the experimenter farther away from the subject, or the learner closer to the subject, tended to tip the balance away from obedience.

+ *The absence of an alternative model of how to behave*   Milgram's subjects were in a novel situation. Unlike the subjects in Asch's experiments, those in most variations of Milgram's experiment saw no other subjects who were in the same situation as they, so there were no examples of how to respond to the experimenter's orders. In two variations, however, a model was provided in the form of another ostensible subject, actually a confederate of the experimenter, who shared with the real subject the task of giving shocks (Milgram, 1974). When the confederate refused to continue at a specific point and the experimenter asked the real subject to take over the whole job, only 10 percent of the real subjects obeyed to the end. When the confederate continued to the end, 93 percent of the real subjects did too. In an unfamiliar and stressful situation, having a model to follow has a potent effect. (For a summary of the results of the variations in Milgram's experiments, see Figure 14.10.)

FIGURE **14.9**   *Giving a shock while in close proximity to the learner*
In one of Milgram's experiments, subjects were required to hold the learner's arm on the shock plate each time a shock was given. Fewer obeyed in this condition than when the learner received shocks in another room.

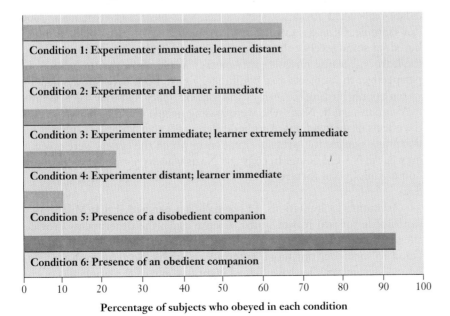

Condition 1: Experimenter immediate; learner distant

Condition 2: Experimenter and learner immediate

Condition 3: Experimenter immediate; learner extremely immediate

Condition 4: Experimenter distant; learner immediate

Condition 5: Presence of a disobedient companion

Condition 6: Presence of an obedient companion

0   10   20   30   40   50   60   70   80   90   100

Percentage of subjects who obeyed in each condition

FIGURE **14.10**   *Results of Milgram's obedience experiments*
Of the first four conditions, in which the subject was alone, the greatest degree of compliance occurred when the experimenter and the subject were in the same room and the learner was invisible in another room. Obedience dropped with decreased immediacy of the experimenter and increased immediacy of the learner. The most extreme results occurred in the two conditions in which the subject was accompanied by a confederate of the researcher masquerading as another subject. In at least 90 percent of these cases, the real subject followed the example—either disobedience or obedience—set by the confederate.

◆ *The sequential nature of the task*   At the very beginning of the experiment, Milgram's subjects had no compelling reason to quit. After all, the first few shocks were very weak, and subjects had no way of knowing how many errors the learner would make or how strong the shocks would become before the experiment ended. Although Milgram did not use the term, we might think of his method as a very effective version of the foot-in-the-door technique. Having complied with earlier, smaller requests (giving weaker shocks), subjects found it hard to refuse new, larger requests (giving stronger shocks). The technique was especially effective in this case because each shock was only a little stronger than the previous one. At no point were subjects asked to do something radically different from what they had already done. To refuse to give the next shock would be to admit that it was probably also wrong to have given the previous shocks—a thought that would be dissonant with subjects' knowledge that they indeed had given those shocks.

Critiques of Milgram's Experiments

31.

How has Milgram's research been criticized on grounds of ethics and real-world validity, and how has the research been defended?

Because of their dramatic results, Milgram's experiments immediately attracted much attention and criticism from psychologists and other scholars. Some critics focused on ethics (for example, Baumrind, 1964). They were disturbed by such statements as this one made in Milgram's (1963) initial report: "I observed a mature and initially poised businessman enter the laboratory smiling and confident. Within 20 minutes he was reduced to a twitching, stuttering wreck, who was rapidly approaching a point of nervous collapse." Was the study of sufficient scientific merit to warrant inflicting such stress on subjects, leading some to believe that they might have killed a man?

Milgram took great care to protect his subjects from psychological harm. Before leaving the lab, they were fully informed of the real nature and purpose of the experiment; they were informed that most people in this situation obey the orders to the end; they were reminded of how reluctant they had been to give shocks; and they were reintroduced to the learner, who offered further reassurance that he was fine and felt well disposed toward them. In a survey made a year after their participation, 84 percent of Milgram's subjects said they were glad to have participated, and fewer than 2 percent said they were sorry (Milgram, 1964). Psychiatric interviews of 40 of the former subjects revealed no evidence of harm (Errera, 1972). Still, such research would not be approved today by the ethics review boards at most research institutions.

Other critics denied Milgram's view that laboratory experiments can help elucidate real-world atrocities, such as the Nazi Holocaust (Saltzman, 2000). Some (for example, Orne & Holland, 1968) argued that Milgram's subjects must have believed, at some level of their consciousness, that they could not really be hurting the learner, because no sane experimenter would allow that to happen. From that perspective, the subjects' real conflict may have been between the belief that they weren't really hurting the learner and the possibility that they were. Unlike subjects in Milgram's study, Nazis who were gassing people could have had no doubt about the effects of their actions. Another difference is that Milgram's subjects had no opportunity, outside the stressful situation in which the orders were given, to reflect on what they were doing. In contrast, Nazis who were murdering people would go home at night and then return to the gas chambers and kill more people the next day.

Accepting its limitations, I personally am persuaded that Milgram's work was worthwhile for two reasons. First, science aside, the experiments provide a moral allegory for our time that prompts us to think about obedience and resist the temptation to surrender our moral authority to others. Second, from a scientific position, Milgram's studies have helped identify some of the principles of compliance and obedience. Preexisting beliefs about the legitimacy of the endeavor, the authority's confident manner, the immediacy of the authority, the lack of alternative models, and the incremental nature of tasks may contribute to real atrocities in much the same way that they contributed to obedience in Milgram's studies, even when the motives and specific conditions are very different.

SECTION SUMMARY

Social pressure derives not just from the presence, expectations, and examples of others but also from their overt requests. Techniques used by expert sales personnel and fund-raisers to gain compliance have been dissected in social-psychological laboratories. The four-walls and foot-in-the-door techniques both appear to operate by inducing cognitive dissonance that can be relieved by complying with the request. The technique of pregiving appears to work by inducing an urge to reciprocate. Sales pressure that threatens one's sense of freedom may induce a rebellious state of psychological reactance. Salespeople occasionally exploit that tendency by acting as if they would rather not sell a particular item.

Requests from authority figures may be construed as orders, and in that case compliance is called obedience. In a famous series of experiments, Milgram found that subjects would obey the orders of an experimenter to give what appeared to be painful, possibly dangerous electric shocks to an innocent victim. The tendency to obey was increased by (a) the subjects' acceptance of the experimenter as a legitimate authority figure, (b) the immediate presence of the experimenter, (c) the lack of the immediate presence of the victim, (d) the lack of an alternative model of how to behave, and (e) (probably) the sequential nature of the task (starting with weak shocks and working gradually upward).

TO COOPERATE OR NOT: THE DILEMMA OF SOCIAL LIFE

32.

What are the defining characteristics of a social dilemma, and why are such dilemmas critical to human survival?

From an evolutionary perspective, the fundamental purpose of sociability is cooperation. Individual ants, wolves, chimpanzees, and humans live and work with others of their kind because they can fulfill certain life-sustaining needs better through cooperation than they could alone. At the same time that they are teammates working for common ends, however, the members of a group are also individuals with self-interests that can run counter to those of the group as a whole. The tension between acting for the good of the group (*cooperation*) and acting for one's own selfish good at the expense of the others (*defection*) is epitomized in social dilemmas. A **social dilemma** exists whenever a particular course of action or inaction will benefit the individual but harm the others in the group and cause more harm than good to everyone if everyone takes that course.

The significance of social dilemmas for the survival of our species was dramatically illustrated by the ecologist Garrett Hardin (1968) with an allegory that he called the *tragedy of the commons*. Hardin compared our whole planet with the common grazing land that used to lie at the center of New England towns. When the number of cattle grazing the pasture began to reach its carrying capacity, each farmer was faced with a dilemma: "Should I add another cow to my herd? One more cow will only slightly hurt the pasture and my neighbors, and it will significantly increase my profits. But if everyone adds a cow, the pasture will fail and all the cattle will die." The dilemma becomes a tragedy if all the farmers reason: "It is not my increase in cattle, but everyone else's, that will determine the fate of the commons. I will lose if everyone increases his herd, but I will lose even more if everyone except me increases his herd." So they all add a cow, the pasture gives out, the cattle die, and the townspeople all suffer the loss.

We are all constantly involved in social dilemmas, some so grand in scale as to encompass all members of our species as a single group and others much smaller in scale. Here's a grand one: Sound logic tells me that the pollution I personally add to the earth's atmosphere by driving a gasoline-burning automobile does not seriously

A modern tragedy of the commons

The oceans are common fishing grounds where thousands of people make their living. When too many fish are caught, the supply diminishes and valued species may even become extinct. Each fisherman can reason, logically, that his catch contributes very little to the problem. The diminished supply of fish is caused by the thousands of other fishermen.

Darren McCollester / Newsmakers

damage the air. It is the pollution of the millions of cars driven by people other than me that does most of the damage. So I keep driving, everyone else does too, and the pollution keeps getting worse.

Here's a social dilemma of smaller scale, more typical of the kind that most of us actually experience as a dilemma: If you are part of a team of students working on a project to which everyone is supposed to contribute and for which everyone will receive the same grade, you might benefit by slacking off and letting others do the work. That way you could spend your time on other courses, where your grade depends only on your own effort. But if everyone in your group reasoned that way, the group project would not get done and you, along with the others in your group, would fail.

Another example, intermediate in scale, is that of public television, which depends on voluntary contributions from its viewers. Any individual viewer might reason that his or her contribution or lack of it won't make or break the station and might decide, therefore, to leave the contributing to others. If everyone reasoned that way, the station would disappear.

Every project that depends on group effort or voluntary contributions poses a social dilemma. In each case, *social working*, or *contributing*, is the individual's cooperative solution, and *social loafing*, or *free riding*, is the noncooperative solution. We are all involved in social dilemmas every day. What are the factors that lead us to cooperate or not in any given instance? Let's first look more closely at the logic of social dilemmas, as exemplified in laboratory games, and then at some human psychological adaptations for resolving real-life social dilemmas.

The Logic of Social Dilemmas Exemplified in Games

To study the logic of social dilemmas, stripped of some of their real-world complexity, social scientists have invented a variety of social-dilemma games (Kollock, 1998). Going further—stripping away also the emotions, values, and norms that human subjects carry with them—some social scientists use computer programs rather than humans as the players. Such studies help researchers understand the underlying logic of the dilemmas and develop hypotheses about real-life conditions that would tip the balance, logically, toward or away from cooperation.

The One-Trial Prisoner's Dilemma Game

33.

What are the features of prisoner's dilemma games, and how do they put each player into a social dilemma?

The most common social-dilemma games used by researchers are two-person games called **prisoner's dilemma games**. They are called that because of their historical origin in a hypothetical dilemma in which each of two prisoners must choose between remaining silent and confessing. If both remain silent, both will get a short prison sentence based on other charges. If both confess, they will both get a moderately long sentence. If only one confesses, that one will be granted immunity and get no sentence but the partner will get a very long sentence. They can neither communicate nor learn the other's choice until both have chosen.

In prisoner's dilemma games played in the psychology laboratory, the consequence for one choice or the other is not a reduced or increased prison sentence but a monetary reward. Figure 14.11 shows a typical payoff matrix for a two-person game. On each trial, each player can choose either to cooperate for the common good or to defect from the common good. Neither learns of the other's choice until both have responded, and the payoff to each player depends on the combination of their two responses. As in all prisoner's dilemma games, the payoff matrix has the following characteristics: (a) The *highest individual payoff* goes to the player who defects while the other cooperates ($5 in the example); (b) the *lowest individual payoff* goes to the player who cooperates while the other defects ($0 in the example); (c) the *highest total payoff* to the two players combined occurs if both cooperate ($3 + $3 = $6 in the example); and (d) the *lowest total payoff* occurs if they both defect ($1 + $1 = $2 in the example).

The game is a social dilemma because the highest individual payoff to either player comes from defecting, but the highest total payoff to the two combined comes from cooperating. If the other player defects, you will get more for defecting ($1) than for cooperating ($0); if the other cooperates, you will still get more for defecting ($5) than for cooperating ($3); but if you both defect, you will each get less ($1) than you would if you had both cooperated ($3).

In the *one-trial* version of the game, each player plays only once with a given other player. When the players are anonymous to each other, are not allowed to discuss their choices, and see their task as winning as much for themselves as they can, they usually defect. A person or a computer program that always defects on one-trial prisoner's dilemma games will necessarily win more money than any person or program that sometimes or always cooperates. Logic tells both players to defect, so they both do and get $1 each. What a pity they are so logical. If they were illogical, they might have both cooperated and received $3 each!

The Iterative Prisoner's Dilemma Game: The Power of Reciprocity

If two players play the same prisoner's dilemma game repeatedly (iteratively) with each other for a series of trials rather than just once, the logic changes. Cooperation becomes a reasonable choice even when the only goal is to maximize one's own profits. Each player might now reason: "If I cooperate on this trial, maybe that will convince the other player to cooperate on the next. We'll both do a lot better over time if we cooperate and get $3 each per trial than if we defect and get $1 each per trial." In other words, logic and selfishness, which lead players to defect in the one-trial game, can lead them to cooperate in the iterative game.

In order to identify the best strategy in an iterative prisoner's dilemma game (the strategy that maximizes one's own earnings), Robert Axelrod (1984) held two round-robin tournaments played by computer programs. The programs were submitted by various experts on game strategy, including social scientists, mathematicians, and teenage computer hacks. Each program was made to play a series of trials with each other program, using the payoff system shown in Figure 14.11. The objective was to see which program would accumulate the most total points in the tournament. Some of the programs were very complicated, able to remember all the previous plays of the other player and take them into account in deciding on the next play. But in the end, the simplest program won both tournaments.

The winning program, sent in by psychologist Anatol Rapoport, was called Tit-for-Tat (or TFT). It consisted of just two rules: (1) The first time you meet a new program, cooperate with it. (2) After that, do on each trial what the other program did on its most recent previous trial with you.

Notice that TFT is incapable of "beating" any other program in head-to-head competition. It never cooperates less often than the other program does, and therefore it can never win more points in play with another program than that program

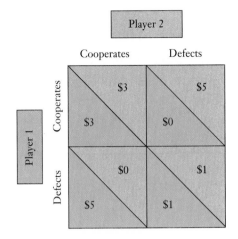

FIGURE 14.11 *Sample payoff matrix for a prisoner's dilemma game* On each trial, each player must decide whether to cooperate or defect, without knowing in advance what the other player will do. The payoff to each player depends on the combination of the two players' decisions. In this example, the possible payoffs to player 1 are shown in the blue portions of the matrix, and the possible payoffs to player 2 are shown in the green portions.

34.

Why are players more likely to cooperate in an iterative (repeated) prisoner's dilemma game than in a one-trial game?

35.

Why was the TFT program so successful in Axelrod's prisoner's dilemma tournaments?

wins in play with it. The TFT program won the tournament not by beating other programs in individual encounters but by getting them to cooperate with it. Other programs earned at least as many points as TFT in their games with TFT, but they did not do so well in their games with each other, and that is why TFT earned the most points in the end.

Why is TFT so effective in eliciting cooperation? According to Axelrod's analysis, there are four reasons: (1) TFT is *nice*. By cooperating from the start, it encourages the other player to cooperate. (2) TFT is *not exploitable*. By reciprocating every failure to cooperate with its own failure to cooperate on the next turn, it discourages the other player from defecting. (3) TFT is *forgiving*. It resumes cooperating with any program as soon as that program begins to cooperate with it. (4) TFT is *transparent*. It is so simple that other programs quickly figure out its strategy and learn that they are best off cooperating with it. Studies since Axelrod's have shown that TFT is highly effective in eliciting cooperation not just from other computer programs but also from human subjects in the laboratory (Komorita & Parks, 1999; Sheldon, 1999). People, like computer programs, figure out rather quickly that their best strategy when playing with TFT is to cooperate.

Decline in Cooperation as Number of Players Increases

Prisoner's dilemma games involve just two players, but other social-dilemma games—including those called *public-goods games*—can involve any number. In a typical public-goods game, each player is given a sum of money and then, under conditions of anonymity, must choose whether to keep the money or contribute it to a common pool (the public good). Then, if and only if at least a certain percentage (say, 75 percent) have contributed, all players, including those who haven't contributed, receive a reward that is substantially greater than the amount each person was asked to contribute. In such games, each individual player's choice to contribute or not is more significant (has a bigger effect on the percentage contributing) if the total number of players is small than if it is large, so the temptation to refrain from contributing becomes greater as the number of players increases. With few players, each one might logically reason: "I'd better contribute or we won't reach the needed percentage to win the reward." But with many players, each might logically reason: "My contribution will have little effect on the total pool of contributions, so my best strategy is to keep my money and hope enough others will contribute to produce the reward."

The result is that many more rewards are won in such games when group size is small than when it is large, whether the game is played by real people or by computer programs (Glance & Huberman, 1994; Komorita & Parks, 1995). The same

36.

Logically, why might we expect small groups to cooperate more than large ones, and what evidence indicates that indeed they do?

A social dilemma in dining out

When diners agree before a meal to split the bill equally, a temptation may be created in each one to "cheat" by ordering a more expensive meal than he or she normally would. Since the added expense created by any one person's expensive meal is shared by the whole group, the temptation to order an expensive meal increases as the number of diners increases. But if everyone orders an expensive meal, then everyone pays dearly in the end.

Michael Grecco / Stock, Boston

thing happens in experiments in which groups of people are asked to exert effort for a common goal. People work harder in small groups than in large ones (Karau & Williams, 1995, 2001). You are more likely to contribute to a course project for a common grade if you are one member on a team of 3 than if you are one on a team of 30.

Human Adaptations for Dealing with Social Dilemmas

In real life, and sometimes even in laboratory games, people cooperate more in social dilemmas than would be expected if their choices were based just on immediate self-interest. Many people work hard on group projects even in large groups. Many people contribute to public television. Some people (though not nearly enough) even choose to ride a bicycle or use public transportation, rather than drive a car, to reduce pollution and help save the planet. What are the forces that lead us to cooperate in such "illogical" ways?

Evolution, cultural history, and our own individual experiences have combined to produce in us decision-making mechanisms that are not limited to an immediate cost-benefit analysis. Consciously or unconsciously, thoughtfully or automatically, we take into account factors that have to do with not just our short-term interests but also our long-term interests, which often reside in maintaining good relationships with other people. Many of the aspects of our social nature that you have already read about in this and the previous chapter can be thought of as adaptations for cooperating in social dilemmas. Some examples follow.

Accountability and Reputation as Forces for Cooperation

In the iterative prisoner's dilemma game, people and computer programs using the TFT strategy do well by cooperating because cooperation induces future cooperation toward themselves from other players. By cooperating, players greatly increase their long-term earnings at the expense of slightly reduced short-term earnings on any given play. The strategy works only because the other players can identify who did or did not cooperate, can remember that information from one trial to the next, and are inclined to respond to each player in accordance with that player's previous action toward them. In human terms, we would say that TFT is successful because each player is *accountable* for his or her actions. Through that accountability, TFT establishes a *reputation* as one who helps others and reciprocates help given by others but who won't be exploited by those who fail to reciprocate.

When the players of laboratory social-dilemma games are free to choose the partners for their play, they favor those who have already developed a reputation for cooperation (Sheldon & others, 2000; Wedekind & Milinski, 2000). The TFT strategy does especially well in this situation because it attracts partners who seek to cooperate and repels potential partners who seek to compete (Van Lange & Visser, 1999).

In laboratory games, the factors of accountability, reputation, and reciprocity are neatly confined to the specific actions allowed by the game. But in real life they are not confined; they spill out everywhere. If I help a person today, I don't know how many people will eventually hear of it, or exactly what they will think of me for it, or how it will affect their future behavior toward me. Ten years from now that person's second cousin, who somehow heard of my help, may be in a position to help me in return and be more inclined to do so because of what he had heard. Such stories of long-range, unanticipated reciprocity are easy to find in everyone's autobiography. Because there is no way to predict how or when reciprocity may occur, it hardly even pays to think about reciprocity when we have an opportunity to help another without too much sacrifice to ourselves. It may be more efficient in such cases to help automatically, and that indeed describes fairly well what most people do in the absence of factors that inhibit helping (Cialdini, 2001).

Lorne Resnick / Stone

Should I drive or cycle to work?
For some people it is easy to resolve this dilemma in the cooperative direction. Bicycle commuting not only helps preserve the earth's atmosphere but is also good regular exercise.

37.

Why is TFT especially successful in situations where players can choose their partners? How do real-life social dilemmas differ from laboratory games with respect to the factors of accountability, reputation, and reciprocity?

38.

How do human emotions figure into social-dilemma payoffs in such a way as to encourage mutual cooperation and discourage defection?

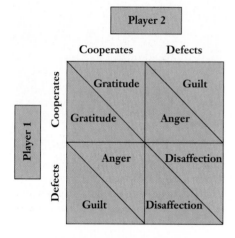

FIGURE **14.12** *Matrix of emotional payoffs in a social dilemma*
Shown here is a sample of the emotions that each person in a real-life social dilemma might experience after cooperating or defecting and learning what the other person did.

39.

What is some evidence that social identity can lead to helping others even in the absence of reciprocity?

How Emotions Promote Cooperation

The discussion of emotions at the beginning of the chapter is relevant to the problem of resolving social dilemmas. Our capacity for empathy certainly promotes helping. To the degree that we feel another's suffering or joy, we are motivated to relieve the former and produce the latter. Moreover, as Randolph Nesse (1990) has pointed out, the immediate benefits and costs of cooperating or defecting in real-life social dilemmas are not simply material gains and losses but also emotional gains and losses. Our evolutionary history and cultural training, combined, have endowed us with emotions that tend to reward us for cooperating and punish us for cheating (see Figure 14.12):

◆ *When we cooperate with someone who likewise cooperates,* we experience the pleasant feelings of gratitude, friendship, love, and pride. These reinforce our bond with the other person and promote future cooperation.

◆ *When we fail to cooperate with someone who likewise fails to cooperate,* we may experience disaffection or in some cases even hatred, either of which motivates us to avoid interacting with that person in the future.

◆ *When we cooperate with someone who fails to cooperate,* we experience anger. Anger motivates us to seek retribution, and its expression warns the other person that the defection has been detected and will not be tolerated.

◆ *When we fail to cooperate with someone who cooperates,* we experience guilt. Guilt motivates us to make amends, and its expression is a signal to the other that we feel bad about our defection and will cooperate in the future. Both guilt and anger are forces for change in an unbalanced relationship. Depending on which feeling is stronger, they may move the relationship toward mutual cooperation or mutual defection in the future.

In sum, emotions promote cooperation and reduce interactions that involve defection by (a) motivating mutual cooperators to interact more frequently with each other in the future, (b) motivating mutual defectors to avoid each other in the future, and (c) motivating those in an unbalanced relationship to change their relationship one way or the other, so they either both cooperate and interact more frequently or both defect and move apart.

Social Identity as a Force for Cooperation

As discussed in Chapter 13, people everywhere have two different ways of thinking about themselves, which serve different functions. One is *personal identity*, which entails thought of oneself as an independent person with self-interests distinct from those of other people. The other is *social identity*, which entails thought of oneself as a more or less interchangeable member of a larger entity, the group, whose interests are shared by all members. Evolutionarily, the two modes of self-thought may have arisen from our need to survive both as individuals and as groups (Guisinger & Blatt, 1994). If I save myself but destroy the group on which I depend, I will in the long run destroy myself. We don't logically think the issue through each time but, rather, tend automatically to cooperate more when we think of the others as members of our group than when we don't.

Many experiments have shown that people in all types of social-dilemma games cooperate much more when they think of the other players as group-mates than when they think of them as separate individuals or as members of other groups (Dawes & Messick, 2000). In one study, for example, players differing in age cooperated much more if they were introduced to each other as citizens of the same town than if they were introduced as representatives of different age groups (Kramer & Brewer, 1984). In another study, allowing previously unacquainted players to meet and talk with one another for a while before the game greatly increased their subsequent cooperation, even though the game was structured so that nobody could tell who was cooperating and who wasn't (Dawes, 1991). Apparently the increased cooperation came from an increased caring about the other players, which came from having met with them as a group. In yet another study, simply referring to a set of unacquainted players as a "group," rather than as a set of individuals, increased their cooperation (Wit & Wilke, 1992).

Group Against Group: The Tragic Side of Social Identity

Identification with a group increases people's willingness to help members of their own group but *decreases* their willingness to help members of another group. Groups playing social-dilemma games with other groups are far more likely to defect than are individuals playing with other individuals, even when the payoffs to individuals for cooperating or not are identical in the two conditions (Insko & others, 1987, 1994; Schopler & others, 1991). In real life, as in the laboratory, interactions between groups are typically more hostile than interactions between individuals (Hoyle & others, 1989). All too often the hostility becomes extreme.

Rattlers versus Eagles
What at first were friendly competitions, such as the tug-of-war shown here, degenerated into serious hostility and aggression between the two groups of boys in Sherif's field study at Robbers Cave.

Conflict Among Boys at Robbers Cave

In order to learn about intergroup conflict and possible ways to resolve it under natural conditions, Muzafer Sherif and his colleagues (1961, 1966) conducted a now-famous study with 11- and 12-year-old boys at a 3-week camping program in Oklahoma's Robbers Cave Park (an area once used as a hideout by Jesse James). To establish two groups, the researchers divided the boys into two separate cabins and assigned separate tasks to each group, such as setting up camping equipment and improving the swimming area. Within a few days, with little adult intervention, each cabin of boys acquired the characteristics of a distinct social group. Each group had its own leaders, its own rules and norms of behavior, and its own name—the Eagles and the Rattlers.

When the groups were well established, the researchers proposed a series of competitions—an idea that the boys eagerly accepted. They would compete for valued prizes in such games as baseball, touch football, and tug-of-war. As Sherif had predicted from previous research, the competitions promoted three changes in the relationships among the boys within and between groups:

1. *Within-group solidarity* As the boys worked on plans to defeat the other group, they set aside their internal squabbles and differences, and their loyalty to their own group became even stronger than it was before.

2. *Negative stereotyping of the other group* Even though the boys had all come from the same background (white, Protestant, and middle class) and had been assigned to the groups on a purely random basis, they began to see members of the other group as very different from themselves and as very similar to one another in negative ways. For example, the Eagles began to see the Rattlers as dirty and rough, and in order to distinguish themselves from that group they adopted a "goodness" norm and a "holier-than-thou" attitude.

3. *Hostile between-group interactions* Initial good sportsmanship collapsed. The boys began to call their rivals names, accuse them of cheating, and cheat in retaliation. After being defeated in one game, the Eagles burned one of the Rattlers' banners, which led to an escalating series of raids and other hostilities. What at first was a peaceful camping experience turned gradually into something verging on intertribal warfare.

40.

What changes occurred within and between two groups of boys as a result of intergroup competitions at a summer camp?

Resolving the Conflict by Creating Common Goals

In the final phase of their study, Sherif and his colleagues tried to reduce hostility between the two groups, a more difficult task than provoking it. In two previous studies similar to the one at Robbers Cave, Sherif had tried a number of procedures to reduce hostility, all of which had failed. Peace meetings between leaders failed because those who agreed to meet lost status within their own group for conceding to the enemy. Individual competitions (similar to the Olympic Games) failed because the boys turned them into group competitions by tallying the total victories for each group (just as we find with the international Olympics). Sermons on brotherly love and forgiveness failed because, while claiming to agree with the messages, the boys simply did not apply them to their own actions.

At Robbers Cave, the researchers tried two new strategies. The first involved joint participation in pleasant activities. Hoping that mutual enjoyment of noncompetitive activities would lead the boys to forget their hostility, the researchers brought the two groups together for such activities as meals, movies, and shooting firecrackers. This didn't work either. It merely provided opportunities for further hostilities. Meals were transformed into what the boys called "garbage wars."

The second new strategy, however, was successful. This involved the establishment of **superordinate goals**, defined as goals that were desired by both groups and could be achieved best through cooperation between the groups. The researchers created one such goal by staging a breakdown in the camp's water supply. In response to this crisis, boys in both groups volunteered to explore the mile-long water line to find the break, and together they worked out a strategy to divide their efforts in doing so. Two other staged events similarly elicited cooperation. By the end of this series of cooperative adventures, hostilities had nearly ceased, and the two groups were arranging friendly encounters on their own initiative, including a campfire meeting at which they took turns presenting skits and singing songs. On their way home, one group treated the other to milkshakes with money left from its prizes.

Research since Sherif's suggests that the intergroup harmony brought on by superordinate goals involves the fading of group boundaries (Bodenhausen, 1991; Gaertner & others, 1990). The groups merge into one, and each person's social identity expands to encompass those who were formerly excluded. The boys at Robbers Cave might say, "I am an Eagle [or a Rattler], but I am also a member of the larger camp group of Eagles plus Rattlers—the group that together found the leak in the camp's water supply."

Intergroup Strife in the Real World

The history of humankind can be read as a sad, continuing tale of intergroup strife that often becomes intergroup atrocity. The capacity that allows us to think of our group as "us" allows us to think of another group as "them." At times, when conditions are ripe, "them" becomes "the enemy," or even "the evil ones" or "the worthless ones." History has proved repeatedly that members of one group can define those of another as subhuman or worse, and then the feelings of compassion and empathy that normally occur among humans are shut off (for example, Goldhagen, 1996). It becomes possible then for one group to enslave, torture, or systematically eliminate another.

Every instance of intergroup atrocity has its own shameful history and must be understood in terms of that history. It must be understood in terms of the specific economic interests, norms, prejudices, myths, religious beliefs, and propaganda of the time. This is the job of historians. The task of psychologists is to discover what aspects of human nature are played upon by the historical forces that promote intergroup atrocity. Certainly our capacity for social identity—our capacity to define ourselves not just as individuals but as members of one group and not another—is part of it. Closely related to this is our tendency to subscribe to the normative beliefs and myths of our group, which unite the group and are components of group

41.

How did Sherif and his colleagues succeed in promoting peace between the two groups of boys?

42.

What does history tell us about intergroup atrocities, and how might psychological research complement historical research in understanding them?

identity. At times of strife, or in response to the self-interests of the group or its leaders, the normative beliefs can include myths about the evil or degraded nature of another group. Also tied to this is a tendency (discussed earlier) for social identity to become stronger when one group sees its self-interest as being at odds with that of another.

If there is hope for the long-term survival and well-being of our species, it surely lies in an understanding of the common needs of people everywhere and the establishment of superordinate goals. Perhaps, just perhaps, nations and groups within nations will learn to cooperate to stop the pollution of our common atmosphere and oceans, and the international drug trade, and diseases such as AIDS that spread worldwide, and the famines that strike periodically, and . . . Perhaps such goals will bring us together and lead us to think of all humankind as members of one tribe spinning together on a small and fragile planet.

SECTION SUMMARY

Many of the choices we make every day can be characterized as social dilemmas, which pit our own self-interest against that of the larger group. A social dilemma exists whenever a particular course of action or inaction will (a) benefit the individual who takes that course, (b) harm the others in the group, and (c) cause more harm than good to everyone in the group if everyone takes that course. In the laboratory, social dilemmas are often formulated as games, such as prisoner's dilemma games. In one-trial prisoner's dilemma games, self-interest favors defection regardless of what one expects the other player to do. In iterative (repeated-trial) games, in contrast, self-interest favors cooperation if, by cooperating, one can induce others to cooperate. The Tit-for-Tat strategy is especially effective because it rewards others for cooperating and punishes them for defecting.

Accountability and concern for reputation promote cooperation. People are more likely to help others who have a reputation for cooperation than those who have a reputation for defection. Moreover, certain emotions seem designed to promote cooperation in social dilemmas. Gratitude rewards us for mutual cooperation; guilt motivates us to make amends when we have failed to reciprocate others' help; anger motivates us to avoid people who consistently fail to cooperate with us.

Social identity has a dual effect on cooperation. It promotes cooperation among people who see themselves as part of the same social group, but it reduces cooperation and promotes hostility among people who see themselves as part of different groups. In Sherif's famous Robbers Cave experiment, the hostility that was generated between two groups of boys at a summer camp was reduced only by the procedure of establishing superordinate goals, which, in effect, merged the two groups into a single larger group with interests in common. The recognition of common interests is perhaps the most powerful force for reducing intergroup conflict.

Fun for all

At work and at play, positive goal interdependence has been found to be extremely effective in breaking down barriers between groups.

CONCLUDING THOUGHTS

This chapter opened by noting three general requirements for social life in any animal species: (1) mechanisms of attraction, which draw and hold individuals together; (2) mechanisms of behavioral coordination, which enable a group to function in some ways as a unit rather than as a collection of individuals; and (3) mechanisms of mutual beneficence, which help ensure that individuals gain more than they lose by being group members. Had this chapter been about the social ecology of a species of ants, you would have read of rather rigid instincts, or fixed action patterns—triggered by stimuli emanating from other individual ants and the environment—that fulfill the three requirements of group functioning. In humans the requirements are met not by rigid instincts but by biologically prepared drives, tendencies, and capacities, which can play themselves out in a wide variety of ways and are activated not by stimuli as such but by the meanings that people learn to attach to them. This chapter was about some of those drives, tendencies, and

43.

What, again (see question 1), are the three general requirements of social life, and how can each of the particular ideas discussed in the chapter be related to one or more of these requirements?

capacities as they are understood by social psychologists. One useful way to review it is to map the specific ideas discussed in the chapter back onto the three requirements of social life.

1.   Mechanisms that draw and hold people together   Beyond the attachment mechanisms that bind family members, lovers, and close friends together (discussed in Chapter 12) are mechanisms that can connect any set of people into a functional group. Compassion, empathy, the self-conscious emotions by which people avoid offending each other, and emotional contagion all help unite people who are in proximity with one another. The fluid capacity for social identity enables a person to think of any given set of others as a group to which he or she belongs, and social identity is manifested as attraction and favoritism toward those who are perceived as members of one's group. Individuals have a vital interest in acceptance and approval by others, which leads them to behave in ways that help bind groups together. Such concerns provide the foundation for what is experienced as social pressure, which manifests itself in impression management, evaluation anxiety, and instances of conformity, group polarization, groupthink, and compliance with others' requests. According to the sociometer theory, self-esteem is a barometer of the degree to which we believe others accept and approve of us, so it, too, is an aspect of our social binding system.

2.   Mechanisms of behavioral coordination within groups   Essentially every concept in this chapter pertains directly or indirectly to behavioral coordination in groups of people. Emotional contagion and all varieties of conformity, compliance, and obedience are ways by which individuals in a group coordinate their moods and actions, enabling them to function as a unit. Shared beliefs, or norms, likewise add to the uniformity and predictability of behavior within a group, so that individuals can get along without interfering intolerably with one another. All the processes that lead people to care about one another's judgments also lead them to behave in ways that support rather than contravene the common goals of the group. Thus, impression management, accountability, and social pressure in general are part of our species' behavioral coordinating system.

3.   Mechanisms that promote mutual beneficence   The ultimate function of group life in any social species is to promote the survival and reproduction of the individual members. In human evolution, those benefits included protection from predators, protection from other groups of humans, and cooperation in such endeavors as finding food, building shelters, rearing children, and sharing information relevant to all life functions. Individuals are unlikely to remain loyal to a group if they are consistently exploited, so group life requires mechanisms that guard against that. Perhaps the most central of these is the capacity for personal identity (discussed in Chapter 13), by which people keep their own needs distinct from those of the group. Anger, brought on by the perception of being exploited, and guilt, brought on by that of exploiting another, are emotional mechanisms for maintaining mutually beneficent relationships. The reciprocity norm exists in every human culture and is surely based on aspects of our biological nature. Beyond the calculations of give-and-take within pairs of individuals is the tallying of each person's beneficence to the group as a whole. People who give to the group—in natural social dilemmas—are deemed more valuable and are more likely in the long run to receive the group's support than are those who don't. Thus, accountability promotes beneficence. Beyond the domain usually studied by psychologists (and beyond the scope of this book) is the whole set of specific cultural norms and institutions that build upon and add to our biologically prepared capacities for mutually beneficial behaviors—including religions, moral philosophies, and codified systems of law and punishment.

Further Reading

Mark Leary & Robin Kowalski (1995). *Social anxiety*. New York: Guilford.

In this clear account, social anxiety is defined as a normal aspect of human psychology linked to people's adaptive concern for social acceptance. The book begins with chapters on impression management and the conditions that provoke social anxiety. Subsequent chapters deal with individual differences in social anxiety and means of treating extreme cases of it.

Robert Cialdini (2001). *Influence: Science and practice* (4th ed.). Boston: Allyn & Bacon.

This fun-to-read paperback, full of anecdotes as well as references to research, has chapters on reciprocity, cognitive consistency, conformity, friendliness, and authority as means of influencing people and gaining compliance. After reading it, you will never be quite as susceptible to sales pressure as you were before.

Stanley Milgram (1974). *Obedience to authority: An experimental view*. New York: Harper & Row.

This is a fascinating, firsthand account of one of the most famous series of experiments in social psychology. Milgram describes his reasons for initiating the research, his findings in many variations of the basic experiment, and his interpretations of and reactions to the findings.

Robert Axelrod (1984). *The evolution of cooperation*. New York: Basic Books.

The first half of this brief, nontechnical book tells the story of Axelrod's computer tournaments of a prisoner's dilemma game and presents his analysis of the success of the Tit-for-Tat strategy. The second half presents examples of the reciprocity principle in evolution and modern-day life. One chapter tells how a "live-and-let-live" reciprocity norm emerged between opposing lines in trench warfare in World War I and operated against officers' commands to shoot.

Elliot Aronson (2000). *Nobody left to hate: Teaching compassion after Columbine*. New York: Worth.

On April 20, 1999, two students at Columbine High School in Littleton, Colorado, killed 12 other students and a teacher before turning their guns on themselves. In this brief book, written in the aftermath of that tragedy, a leading social psychologist brings classic social-psychological theories and findings to bear on the problem of how schools might be restructured to promote greater empathy and cooperation and to reduce the exclusion and humiliation that many students experience.

Looking Ahead

As you have seen in this chapter and the previous one, social psychologists attempt to explain behavior in terms of the social environment within which it occurs. Their goal usually is to identify general principles that characterize most people's responses to particular social situations; they are relatively unconcerned with individual differences among people. In the next chapter, on theories of personality, we turn to the opposite approach—the attempt to explain behavior in terms of inner characteristics that differ from one person to the next.

L'Epouvante de L'Oiseau Porte-Malheur, Joan Miro

Personality and Disorders

We do not all approach life in the same way. We differ in our emotions, motives, and styles of thinking and behaving, and these differences give each of us a unique personality. Although most of these differences are healthy and add spice to our lives, some create problems for the differing individual and are classed as mental disorders. This final unit has three chapters. The first is about ways of describing and explaining normal personality differences. The second is about identifying mental disorders and understanding their origins. And the third is about methods that psychologists and psychiatrists have developed to help people overcome or live with their mental problems or disorders.

Chapter 15

Woman with Beret, Pablo Picasso

Personality

Personality refers to a person's general style of interacting with the world, especially with other people—whether one is withdrawn or outgoing, excitable or placid, conscientious or careless, kind or stern. A basic assumption of the personality concept is that people do differ from one another in their styles of behavior, in ways that are at least relatively consistent across time and place. Most chapters of this book have emphasized the ways in which we are similar to one another. In this chapter, we turn explicitly to differences among us.

Most people are fascinated by human differences. Such fascination is natural and useful. In everyday life we take for granted those aspects of a person that can be attributed to human nature and focus, instead, on the aspects that distinguish one person from another. Attention to differences helps us decide whom we want for partners and friends and enables us to get along with each other. *Personality psychologists* make a scientific study of such differences. Using questionnaires and other formal tools, they conduct research to measure personality differences and explain their origins. They try to relate personality to the varying roles and habitats that people occupy in the social world, and they try to describe objectively the mental processes that underlie the differences. In this chapter we will examine these endeavors.

The chapter is divided into three main parts. The first is concerned with the basic concept of personality traits and with questions about their validity, stability, and biological bases. The second is concerned with the adaptive functions of personality: How might individual differences prepare people for life within different niches of the social environment? The third section is about the unconscious and conscious mental processes that may underlie and help explain the behavioral differences among individuals.

PERSONALITY AS BEHAVIORAL DISPOSITIONS, OR TRAITS

What are the first three adjectives that come to mind when you describe your own personality? Do those adjectives apply to you in all settings, or only in some? How clearly do they distinguish you from other people you know? Do you have any idea why you have those characteristics?

The most central concept in personality psychology is the *trait*, which can be defined as a relatively stable predisposition to behave in a certain way. Traits are considered to be part of the person, not part of the environment. People carry their traits with them from one environment to another, although the actual manifestation of a trait in the form of behavior usually requires some perceived cue or trigger in the environment. For example, the trait of aggressiveness might be defined as an inner predisposition to argue or fight. That predisposition is presumed to stay with

1.

What is a trait, and how do traits differ from states?

573

the person in all environments, but actual arguing or fighting is unlikely to occur unless the person perceives provocations in the environment. Aggressiveness or kindness or any other personality trait is, in that sense, analogous to the physical trait of "meltability" in margarine. Margarine melts only when subjected to heat (a characteristic of the environment); but some brands need less heat than do others to melt, and that difference lies in the margarine, not in the environment.

It is useful to distinguish *traits* from *states*. States of motivation and emotion (discussed in Chapter 6) are, like traits, defined as inner entities that can be inferred from observed behavior. But while traits are enduring, states are temporary. In fact, a trait might be defined as an enduring attribute that describes one's likelihood of entering temporarily into a particular state. The personality trait of aggressiveness describes the likelihood that a person will enter a hostile state, much as the physical trait of meltability describes the likelihood that a brand of margarine will enter a liquid state.

Traits are not characteristics that people have or lack in all-or-none fashion but, rather, are dimensions along which people differ by degree. If we measured aggressiveness or any other trait in a large number of people, our results would approximate a normal distribution (illustrated in Figure 3.10), in which the majority of people are near the middle of the range and few are at the extremes. Traits describe how people differ from others on particular dimensions, but they are not themselves explanations of those differences. To say that a person is high in aggressiveness simply means that the person tends to argue or fight a lot, in situations that would not provoke such behavior in most people. The trait is inferred from the behavior. It would be meaningless, then, for me to say that Harry argues and fights a lot *because* he is highly aggressive. That would be just the same as saying, "Harry argues and fights a lot because he argues and fights a lot."

2.

Why is a trait considered to be a description rather than an explanation of behavior?

Trait Theories: Efficient Systems for Describing Personalities

In everyday life we use an enormous number of personality descriptors. Gordon Allport (1937), one of the pioneers of personality psychology, identified 18,000 such terms in a standard English dictionary. Most of them have varying meanings, many of which overlap with the meanings of other terms. Consider, for example, the various connotations and overlapping meanings of *affable, agreeable, amiable, amicable, companionable, congenial, convivial, cordial, friendly, genial, gracious, hospitable, kind, sociable, warmhearted,* and *welcoming*. Naturally enough, personality psychologists have long been interested in devising a more efficient vocabulary for describing personality. The goal of **trait theories** is to specify a manageable set of distinct personality dimensions that can be used to summarize the fundamental psychological differences among individuals.

The Idea That Traits Are Hierarchically Organized

3.

How are surface traits inferred from behavior, and how are central traits inferred from surface traits?

A basic assumption underlying all trait theories is that behaviors and traits are linked to one another in a hierarchical fashion, as exemplified in Figure 15.1. At the bottom of the hierarchy are specific behaviors, which might be observed directly by the researcher or (more often) assessed from participants' self-descriptions on questionnaires. At the next level up are **surface traits**, each of which is linked directly to a set of related behaviors. For instance, a person who argues a lot in many different situations might be said to have the surface trait of high argumentativeness. At the highest level, linking related surface traits, are **central traits**, considered to be the fundamental dimensions of personality. In Figure 15.1, *argumentativeness, pugnaciousness,* and *competitiveness* are three surface traits that are linked by the central trait *aggressiveness*. The assumption behind this hierarchy is that the tendencies to argue, to engage in physical fights (pugnaciousness), and to compete in other ways all correlate positively with one another, so the three surface traits can be understood as aspects of a single central trait. Of course, that assumption might be wrong. If re-

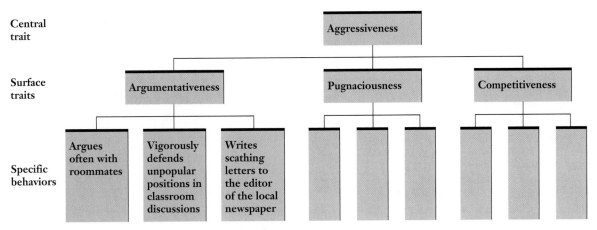

Central trait

Surface traits

Specific behaviors

Aggressiveness

Argumentativeness

Pugnaciousness

Competitiveness

Argues often with roommates

Vigorously defends unpopular positions in classroom discussions

Writes scathing letters to the editor of the local newspaper

FIGURE **15.1** *Hierarchical relationship among behaviors, surface traits, and a central trait*
In trait theories, surface traits are inferred from people's behaviors, and central traits are inferred by identifying surface traits that correlate with one another. (Adapted from Eysenck, 1982.)

search showed that people who argue a lot are not above average in their tendency to fight physically or to compete in other ways, but are above average in their tendency to read a lot and think deeply about issues, then *argumentativeness* would have to be ascribed to a different central trait—perhaps one labeled *thoughtfulness* or *intellectuality*.

A trait theory is basically a statement that specifies (a) the set of central traits that is deemed most useful for describing the psychological differences among individuals, (b) the surface traits that are linked to each central trait, and (c) an objective means for measuring the surface traits and central traits, usually involving a questionnaire on which the person describes his or her own behaviors in a fashion that permits objective scoring. To generate such a theory, researchers build the hierarchy from the bottom up. First, they collect a large amount of data about the specific behaviors of a large number of people. Then they use statistical means to determine which classes of behaviors correlate most strongly with one another, indicating surface traits, and which surface traits correlate most strongly with one another, indicating central traits. Finally, after generating a hierarchical set of proposed traits and giving them names, they develop a questionnaire that can be used reliably to measure the degree to which any given person manifests each of the traits specified by the theory.

The primary goal of any trait theory is to account for the greatest amount of meaningful variation among individuals while minimizing the number of separate central-trait dimensions used. In the ideal theory, the central traits are nonredundant; that is, they are independent dimensions that do not correlate with one another.

Two Early Trait Theories: Cattell's and Eysenck's

The first well-known trait theory was developed by Raymond Cattell (1950). Cattell's undergraduate degree was in chemistry, and his goal in psychology was to develop a sort of chemistry of personality. Just as an infinite number of different molecules can be formed from a finite number of atoms, Cattell argued that an infinite number of different personalities can be formed from a finite number of traits. To pursue this idea, he needed to identify these elements of personality (central traits) and develop a way to measure them.

Cattell began his research by condensing the 18,000 or so English adjectives describing personality down to about 170 that he took to be logically different from one another. These were his initial set of surface traits. He had large numbers of people rate themselves on each of the surface traits and then used factor analysis (described in Chapter 10) to determine which surface traits correlated most with one another. By finding clusters of surface traits that correlated strongly with one another within the cluster but not across clusters, Cattell identified a preliminary

4.

How did Cattell and Eysenck develop their trait theories, and how do the two theories differ from each other?

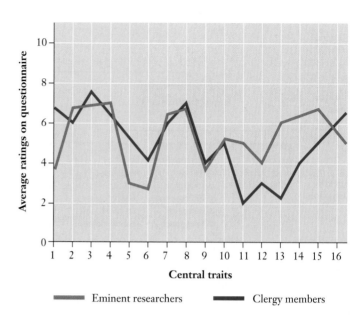

FIGURE **15.2** *Personality profiles of scientists and clergy members*
Shown here are the average ratings on each of the central traits, or factors, in Cattell's 16 PF Questionnaire for a group of well-known scientists and a group of clergy members. The 16 traits indicated along the horizontal axis are those listed in Table 15.1. For each dimension, a high score indicates tendency toward the left-hand term in Table 15.1, and a low score indicates tendency toward the right-hand term. By comparing the two curves, you can find differences between the average personalities of the two groups. For example, the researchers are, on average, lower in sociability (factor 1) and higher in radicalism (factor 13) than are the clergy members. (Adapted from Cattell, 1965.)

TABLE **15.1** *Cattell's 16 source traits, or personality factors*

1. Sociable–unsociable
2. Intelligent–unintelligent
3. Emotionally stable–unstable
4. Dominant–submissive
5. Cheerful–brooding
6. Conscientious–undependable
7. Bold–timid
8. Sensitive–insensitive
9. Suspicious–trusting
10. Imaginative–practical
11. Shrewd–naïve
12. Guilt proclivity–guilt rejection
13. Radicalism–conservatism
14. Self-sufficiency–group adherence
15. Self-disciplined–uncontrolled will
16. Tense–relaxed

Note: In this table, descriptive terms have been substituted for the technical terms that Cattell coined for each trait.

Source: Adapted from *Personality and mood by questionnaire* (pp. 53–54) by R. B. Cattell, 1973, San Francisco: Jossey-Bass.

5.

Why is the Big Five theory generally preferred over Cattell's or Eysenck's trait theory today?

set of central traits and gave each a name. Then he developed various questionnaires aimed at assessing these traits and used the questionnaire results to modify the set of central traits. The upshot of his research, which spanned many years, was the identification of 16 central traits, listed in Table 15.1, and a questionnaire called the *16 PF Questionnaire* to measure them (Cattell, 1950, 1973). (*PF* stands for *personality factors*, which was Cattell's term for central traits.) The questionnaire consists of nearly 200 statements about specific aspects of behavior, such as "I like to go to parties." For each statement the respondent must select one of three possible answers—*yes, occasionally,* or *no.* The 16 PF Questionnaire is still used today, both as a clinical tool for assessing personality characteristics of clients in psychotherapy and as a research tool in studies of personality. For an example of the questionnaire's use in research, see Figure 15.2.

Another pioneering trait theorist, Hans Eysenck (1952), collected data quite similar to Cattell's but employed factor analysis somewhat differently, in a way that resulted in a smaller number of central traits. In fact, Eysenck's early studies suggested that just two traits accounted for much of the consistent variation among individuals. One trait, which he labeled *introversion–extroversion,* is related to a person's tendency to avoid or seek excitement in the external environment. Extroverts are sociable and adventurous; introverts are relatively unsociable and introspective and prefer quieter activities. The second trait, which he labeled *neuroticism–stability,* pertains to one's tendency to become emotionally upset. The surface traits associated with neuroticism include moodiness, anxiety, suggestibility, and low willpower; and the opposites are associated with stability. Subsequently, Eysenck identified a third personality dimension, which he labeled *psychoticism–nonpsychoticism,* which is associated with aggression and lack of concern for others, at one end, and with peaceableness and empathy at the other end. To measure people's positions along each of these dimensions, Eysenck developed a questionnaire called the *Eysenck Personality Inventory,* which, like Cattell's 16 PF Questionnaire, is still used for both clinical and research purposes.

The Big Five Theory

Many trait researchers today find Cattell's 16-factor theory overly complex, with redundant factors, and Eysenck's three-dimensional theory oversimplified, with too few traits to capture enough of the meaningful differences among personalities. Using newer versions of the methods pioneered by Cattell and Eysenck, researchers have subsequently conducted many factor-analytic studies—in various countries, in several languages, with children as well as adults—and have found re-

TABLE 15.2 *The Big Five personality factors*

- *Neuroticism–stability (N):* worrying–calm; vulnerable–hardy; self-pitying–self-satisfied; impatient–patient.
- *Extroversion–introversion (E):* Sociable–reserved; fun-loving–sober; talkative–quiet; spontaneous–self-controlled.
- *Openness to experience–nonopenness (O):* Imaginative–unimaginative; independent–conforming; curious–incurious; broad interests–narrow interests.
- *Agreeableness–antagonism (A):* Courteous–rude; selfless–selfish; trusting–suspicious; cooperative–uncooperative.
- *Conscientiousness–undirectedness (C):* Careful–careless; reliable–undependable; persevering–lax; ambitious–aimless.

Note: After each central trait are listed some of the surface traits whose intercorrelation provided the basis for inferring the central trait. The traits are measured with the NEO Personality Inventory, which consists of a set of self-statements—such as *I often crave excitement*—to which the person responds on a 5-point scale ranging from "Strongly agree" to "Strongly disagree."

Source: Adapted from Costa & McCrae, 1992, p. 3, and McCrae & Costa, 1985, p. 85.

markably consistent results (Benet-Martínez & John, 1998; Digman, 1989; Goldberg, 1990, 1993; McCrae & Costa, 1997). The result is the *Big Five theory* of personality, which posits that the most efficient set of central traits for describing personalities consists of the five listed in Table 15.2. Paul Costa and Robert McCrae have developed a widely used questionnaire—called the *NEO Personality Inventory* (where *N*, *E*, and *O* stand for three of the traits)—to measure the five central traits and the surface traits associated with each. Table 15.2 identifies some of the surface traits associated with each central trait and presents (in a footnote) a sample item from the NEO Personality Inventory.

As you study the table, notice that the first two personality dimensions are the same as the two most strongly emphasized by Eysenck (*neuroticism* and *extroversion*). The other three are *openness to experience*, *agreeableness*, and *conscientiousness*. The contention of many trait researchers today is that if you want to choose a convenient number of trait terms that will most efficiently summarize the measurable personality differences among people, these are the terms you should choose. Nearly all the thousands of adjectives commonly used to describe personalities correlate at least to some degree, in factor-analytic studies, with one or another of these five traits.

Questions About the Predictive Value of Traits

You now have some understanding of how personality psychologists identify and measure traits, and you know that traits describe but do not explain psychological differences. So what do we learn from trait measures? Do they tell us what the person will be like tomorrow or 30 years from now? Do they allow us to predict, with any degree of accuracy, how individuals will meet real-life challenges? Are personality traits consistent across situations, as trait theorists assume, or would it be better to think of traits as specific to particular situations?

The Stability of Personality Measures over Time

If you ever have the opportunity to attend the twenty-fifth reunion of your high school class, don't miss it; it is bound to be a remarkable experience. Before you stands a person who claims to be your old friend Marty, whom you haven't seen for 25 years. The last time you saw Marty, he was a skinny kid with lots of hair, wearing floppy sneakers and a sweatshirt. What you notice first are the differences: This Marty is not skinny, he has very little hair, and he isn't wearing sneakers. But within 10 minutes you have the almost eerie knowledge that you are talking with the same person with whom you used to play basketball behind the school. The voice is the same, the sparkle in the eyes, the quiet sense of humor, the way of walking. And when it is Marty's turn to stand up and speak to the group, he, who always was the most nervous about speaking before the class, is still most reluctant to do so. There's no doubt about it—this Marty, who now has two kids older than he was when you last saw him, is the same Marty you always knew.

But that is all impression. Is he really the same? Perhaps Marty is in some sense *your* construction, and it is your construction that has not changed over the years. Or maybe it's just the situation. This, after all, is a high school reunion held in your old school gymnasium, and maybe you've all been transported back in your minds and are coming across much more like your old selves than you normally would. Maybe you're all trying to be the same kids you were 25 years ago, if only so that your former classmates will recognize you. Clearly, if we really want to answer the question of how consistent personality is over long periods, we've got to be more scientific.

By now, many studies have been conducted in which people fill out personality questionnaires, or are rated on personality characteristics by family members or friends, at widely separated times in their lives. The results indicate a rather high stability of personality throughout adulthood. The correlation coefficients on repeated measures of the Big Five traits typically range from 0.50 to 0.70, even with time spans between the first and second tests of 30 or 40 years (Costa & McCrae, 1994). Such stability apparently cannot be dismissed as resulting from a consistent bias in how individuals fill out personality questionnaires, as similar consistency is found even when the people rating the participants' personalities are not the same in the second test as in the first (Mussen & others, 1980).

Such studies also indicate that personality is considerably more stable after about age 30 than before that (Costa & McCrae, 1994; Roberts & Del Vecchio, 2000). Some of the changes that occur with age are relatively consistent across individuals and constitute what is commonly summarized as increased maturity. For instance, on measures of the Big Five, in many different cultures, people have been found to become, on average, somewhat less neurotic, less extroverted, less open to experience, more conscientious, and more agreeable between their late teenage years and age 30 (Costa & others, 2000; McCrae & others, 2000). In addition, irregular changes of all sorts, which vary from person to person, also occur more before age 30 than later on. People are more likely to change in either direction on any given personality trait before age 30 than after (McCrae & Costa, 1994).

Why might personality change less after one's twenties than before? One possibility is that, with maturity, personality becomes less responsive to the molding effects of environmental conditions than it was before; it becomes "set like plaster" (Costa & McCrae, 1994). Another possibility, not incompatible with the first, is that conditions of life (which do the molding) generally vary less after age 30 than before. Some research indicates that personality indeed can change, at least to some degree, at any age in response to such life changes as those brought on by a change in career, or marital status, or chronic illness (Caspi & Roberts, 1999; Helson & Stewart, 1994).

The Relation of Personality Measures to People's Actual Behavior

In theory, personality measures could be highly *reliable* (consistent from one test to the next) but not at all *valid* (see Chapter 2, page 43). A test is valid to the degree that its scores are true measures of the intended characteristics, from which accurate predictions can be drawn. Do scores on personality tests predict anything about people's actual behavior? The general answer is a qualified yes.

Countless studies have shown that personality-test scores allow one to make better-than-chance predictions about the choices individuals will make in life and how they will respond to real-life situations and challenges. People who score as *extroverts* on personality questionnaires, compared with those who score as introverts,

6.

What is the evidence that as one grows older, personality (a) becomes more stable and (b) changes in certain consistent ways?

7.

What are two ways to explain the increased stability of traits after age 30?

8.

What evidence indicates that personality tests are to some degree valid? What are some examples of successful predictions based on such tests?

have been found to (a) be less disturbed by sudden loud sounds or other intense stimuli (Eysenck, 1990; Geen, 1984; Matthews & Gilliland, 1999; Stelmack, 1990); (b) choose to live with and work with more people (Diener & others, 1992); (c) prefer a wider range of sexual activities (Eysenck, 1976); and (d) look people directly in the eye and talk more at group meetings (Mobbs, 1968; Patterson & Holmes, 1966). People who score high on *conscientiousness* have been found to be more sexually faithful to their spouses (Buss, 1996), to receive higher ratings for job performance (Goodstein & Lanyon, 1999), and to smoke less, drink less, and live longer (Friedman & others, 1995) than do those who score low on that trait. People who score high on *openness to experience* have been found to change careers more often in middle adulthood (McCrae & Costa, 1985) and to perform better in job training programs (Goodstein & Lanyon, 1999) than do those who score low on that trait.

Reliable relationships have even been found between some types of personality ratings in early childhood and behaviors observed several or many years later. In one long-term study conducted in New Zealand, a personality rating of low self-control at age 3 was found to correlate significantly with likelihood of being fired from a job and likelihood of being convicted of a crime by age 21 (Caspi, 2000). In another study, more young adults who in middle childhood scored high on measures of behavioral inhibition (fear of new people and situations) were still living with their parents than were those who scored as less inhibited (Gest, 1997). Still other studies have revealed significant correlations between measures of behavioral inhibition in infancy and avoidance of new people and experiences later in childhood and adolescence (Kagan, 1994).

Of course, personality differences do not reveal themselves equally well in all settings. When you watch people in familiar roles and settings, conforming to learned, socially agreed-upon behavioral norms—at their jobs, or in the classroom, or at formal functions such as weddings and funerals—the common influence of the situation may override individual personality styles. Avshalom Caspi and Terrie Moffitt (1991, 1993) have suggested, with some evidence, that personality differences are most clearly revealed when people are in novel, ambiguous, stressful situations and in life transitions, where there are no or few cues as to what actions are appropriate. According to Caspi and Moffitt (1993), in the absence of cues as to how to behave, "the reticent become withdrawn, the irritable become aggressive, and the capable take charge."

Situation-Specific Dispositions: If-Then Relationships

A person's scores on a handful of global personality traits, such as the Big Five, provide at best a very rough first approximation of the person. As one personality theorist put it, trait theories deal with "the psychology of the stranger" (McAdams, 1994). They may be useful in describing someone we barely know, but they don't come close to the precise descriptions we can give of our closest friends and ourselves.

To move beyond the psychology of the stranger, we must acknowledge that people differ not just in global traits but also in their tendencies to manifest particular traits in particular situations (Mischel, 1984; Van Heck & others, 1994). One person might be shy at parties but outspoken at formal meetings, while another might be the opposite. Similarly, a person might be agreeable with work colleagues but argumentative with family and neighbors, or conscientious about his health but not about keeping his promises to others. Walter Mischel (1968, 1984) has long contended that describing personality in terms of traits that are specific to particular situations is far more useful in predicting behavior than are global-trait statements about the person's overall degree of extroversion, agreeableness, or conscientiousness.

A stressful situation

First day on campus for first-year students is the kind of event that brings out personality differences.

9.

Why might personality differences be most apparent in novel situations or life transitions?

Elizabeth Crews

Are traits consistent across situations?

Do people usually show the same traits in different contexts of their lives, as this woman seems to? After 30 years of controversy, researchers still disagree. Some emphasize sameness across situations; others focus on differences due to situation.

Elizabeth Crews

10.

What evidence supports Mischel's concept of situation-specific dispositions?

In his initial argument for describing people in terms of situation-specific traits, Mischel (1968) referred to a classic study of morality conducted by Hugh Hartshorne and Mark May (1928). Thousands of schoolchildren were provided with opportunities to be dishonest in a wide variety of situations, under conditions in which they did not know that their dishonesty could be detected. The differing situations offered opportunities or temptations for various forms of dishonesty—such as lying to parents, falsifying school records, cheating on tests at school, and stealing money at club meetings. Hartshorne and May found that correlations within any given type of situation were quite high but correlations across different situations were low. Children who cheated on a test, for example, were quite likely to cheat on another test but were only a little more likely than average to steal money.

Subsequently, Mischel and his colleagues documented the situation specificity of personality traits in research studies of their own. In one study, Mischel and Phillip Peake (1982) assessed repeatedly, by direct observation, 19 different forms of behavior presumed to be related to the trait of conscientiousness in a group of students at Carleton College in Minnesota. Included were measures of regularity of class attendance, promptness in completing assignments, bed neatness, and neatness of class notes. They found high consistency within any one of these measures but relatively low consistency across measures. For instance, students who kept neat notes for one class were very likely to keep neat notes for another class but only slightly more likely than average to keep their beds neat. In yet another study, Mischel and his colleagues found that children with social adjustment problems at a summer camp were not well described by such global traits as "aggressive" or "withdrawn" but were quite well described and differentiated from one another by terms that referred to the social situations that prompted them to act aggressively or to withdraw (Mischel & Shoda, 1995; Shoda & others, 1994). For sample findings from that study, see Figure 15.3.

When Mischel began writing about situation-specific personality characteristics, he and his colleagues saw their argument as one of fundamental opposition to global-trait theories. As advocates of the *social-learning*, or *social-cognitive*, approach to personality (discussed later in this chapter), they maintained that personality characteristics are learned habits of thinking and behaving, which are acquired and manifested in particular social situations. Today most personality theorists under-

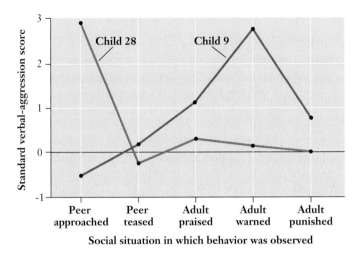

FIGURE **15.3** *Situation-specific profiles of verbal aggression for two children*
Shoda, Mischel, and Wright (1994) recorded various categories of behaviors among children at a summer camp in various social situations. Shown here are results concerning verbal aggressiveness for two children. Zero on the *y* axis represents the average aggressiveness for all the children observed. If these two children were described simply in terms of their overall level of verbal aggressiveness, they would appear to be similar to each other—both somewhat more verbally aggressive than the average child. The two children appear very different, however, when the situations are included in the description. Child 28 was highly aggressive to peers who approached him in a friendly manner but not particularly aggressive in other situations, and child 9 was highly aggressive to adults but not to peers. (Adapted from Shoda & others, 1994, Figure 1, p. 678.)

stand that both the global-trait and situation-specific approaches to personality are valid and serve different purposes. Traits (including the Big Five) can be found that yield a statistically significant degree of cross-situational generality. This fact is most important to trait theorists, whose goal is to develop convenient ways to describe overall differences among people—the types of differences that may not predict a specific action in a specific situation but generally predict behavior averaged over a large set of situations. Traits also show a considerable degree of situational specificity, and this fact is most important to social-cognitive theorists, such as Mischel, whose goal is to predict how individuals will behave in particular situations.

Biological Foundations of Traits

Where do traits come from? To some degree, at least, global traits such as the Big Five appear to derive from inherited physiological qualities of the nervous system.

A Physiological Theory of Extroversion–Introversion

The personality dimension that to date has been most fully studied from a physiological perspective is extroversion–introversion. Many years ago, Hans Eysenck (1967; Eysenck & Eysenck, 1985) proposed that individual differences in this trait stem from differences in the arousability of higher parts of the brain. In particular, he proposed that the brains of extroverts are less easily aroused than are those of introverts. He proposed further that all people seek an optimal level of brain arousal but extroverts require more stimulation to achieve that level than do introverts. Extroverts seek stimulating environments to increase their arousal level toward the optimum, while introverts avoid stimulating environments to prevent their arousal level from exceeding the optimum. Another way of stating this is to say that introverts, with their easily aroused nervous systems, are well designed for functioning in calm environments, while extroverts, with their less easily aroused nervous systems, are well designed for functioning in highly stimulating environments.

Consistent with Eysenck's theory, researchers have found that introverts typically outperform extroverts on tasks that require focused concentration in relatively unstimulating environments, such as vigilance tasks, and extroverts typically perform better on tasks that require attention to many stimuli at once in a relatively arousing environment (Lieberman & Rosenthal, 2001; Matthews & Gilliland, 1999). Other experiments suggest that introverts react more strongly than do extroverts to intense stimuli of all sorts. Introverts, compared to extroverts, have been found to (a) show greater disruption in performance on a learning task when loud noise is present (Geen, 1984); (b) exhibit a greater physiological arousal response to sudden noise (Doucet & Stelmack, 2000; Stelmack, 1990); (c) salivate more profusely when lemon juice is squirted into their mouths

11.

How did Eysenck explain the difference between introverts and extroverts in terms of a basic property of the nervous system, and how has research supported his explanation?

(Eysenck & Eysenck, 1967); and (d) be less tolerant of painful electric shocks (Bartol & Costello, 1976).

Another study, using PET neuroimaging, showed that the frontal lobes of the cerebral cortex of introverts were more active than those of extroverts in the absence of external stimulation (Johnson & others, 1999). And, in yet another study, a high dose of caffeine worsened performance on a learning task for introverts, presumably by producing too much arousal, but improved performance for extroverts, presumably by bringing their arousal level up toward the optimum (Corr & others, 1995).

Some other studies, however, have produced results that are inconsistent with Eysenck's theory, and new variations of the theory have been presented to explain the discrepant results (Depue & Collins, 1999; Matthews & Gilliland, 1999). Perhaps the most accurate conclusions at this point are that a difference in arousability accounts for some but not all of the behavioral differences between introverts and extroverts and that most but not all introverts have more easily aroused nervous systems than do most extroverts.

The Heritability of Traits

12.

How have twin and adoption studies (described in Chapter 10) been used to assess the heritability of personality? What are the results of such studies?

How heritable are personality traits? As discussed in Chapter 10, *heritabilty* refers to the degree to which individual differences derive from differences in genes rather than from differences in environmental experiences. Numerous research studies—using the behavior-genetics methods described in Chapter 10—have shown that the traits identified by trait theories are at least moderately heritable. The most common approach in these studies has been to administer standard personality questionnaires to pairs of identical twins and fraternal twins (who are no more similar genetically than are ordinary siblings). The usual finding is that identical twins are much more similar than are fraternal twins on every personality dimension measured, similar enough to lead to an average heritability estimate of roughly 0.40 to 0.50 for most traits, including all the Big Five (Loehlin, 1992; McGue & Bouchard, 1998). As explained in Chapter 10, a heritability of 0.50 means that about 50 percent of the variability among individuals is due to genetic differences and the remainder is due to a combination of environmental differences and measurement error.

Such findings have been criticized on the grounds that parents and others may treat identical twins more similarly than fraternal twins, and similar treatment may lead to similar personality. To get around that possibility, researchers at the University of Minnesota, led by David Lykken, gave personality tests to twins who had been separated in infancy and raised in different homes, as well as to twins raised in the same home (Bouchard, 1991, 1994; Tellegen & others, 1988). Their results were consistent with the previous studies: The identical twins were more similar to each other than were the fraternal twins on essentially every measure, whether they had been raised in the same home or in different homes, again leading to heritability scores averaging close to 0.50. Subsequent studies, by other researchers in several different countries, have produced similar results (Plomin & Caspi, 1999).

Even traits that seem as if they should be heavily affected by learning have been found to be highly heritable. For example, the heritability of *traditionalism*—a measure of conservative values and respect for discipline and authority—was estimated to be about 0.60 (Tellegen & others, 1988). Other researchers have even found high heritability of quite specific beliefs or attitudes. For example, one study revealed a heritability coefficient of about 0.50 for support of or opposition to the death penalty (Tesser, 1993). Such results suggest that genetic predispositions

Sipress / The Funny Times

"I was a good boy, grandpa was a good boy, his father was a good boy. In fact, since the dawn of history, there have only been good boys in this family. That's why you have to be a good boy."

influence which attitudes a person is most likely to attend to and pick up from the smorgasbord of attitudes available in the social environment.

Relative Lack of Shared Effect of the Family Environment

In the past it was common for psychologists to attribute almost all personality characteristics to the examples and training that people gain from their mothers and (to a lesser degree) their fathers (Harris, 1998). A common assumption was that people raised in the same family have similar personalities not just because of their shared genes but also because of their shared family environment. Perhaps the most surprising finding in the Minnesota study, confirmed since by other studies, is that this assumption is not true. Being raised in the same family had an almost negligible effect on measures of personality (McGue & Bouchard, 1998; Turkheimer & Waldron, 2000). Twin pairs who had been raised in different families were, on average, as similar to—and as different from—each other as were twin pairs who had been raised in the same family.

The contradiction between this finding and long-standing beliefs about the influence of parents is dramatically illustrated by some of the explanations that twins gave for their own behavioral traits (Neubauer & Neubauer, 1996). When one young man was asked to explain his almost pathological need to keep his environment neat and clean, he responded, "My mother. When I was growing up she always kept the house perfectly ordered. . . . I learned from her. What else could I do?" When his identical twin brother, who had grown up in a different home in a different country but was also compulsively neat and clean, was asked the same question, he said, "The reason is quite simple. I'm reacting to my mother, who was a complete slob!" In this case the similarity of the twins in their compulsive tendency was almost certainly the result of their shared genetic makeup, yet each one blamed this tendency on his adoptive mother.

The results of such studies of twins do not mean that the environment is unimportant in personality differentiation, or even that the family environment is unimportant. It does mean, however, that those aspects of the environment that contribute to personality differentiation must be nearly as different, on average, for individuals who grow up in the same family as for those who grow up in different families. Two children raised in the same family may experience that environment very differently from each other. Sandra Scarr and her colleagues (1981) earlier came to a similar conclusion through a different route. They compared nontwin, adopted children with both their biological and their adoptive siblings and found that biological siblings were far more similar than were adoptive siblings. In fact, for most personality measures, they found that the children were no more similar to their adoptive siblings than any two randomly compared children were to each other. Later in the chapter we will examine some possible causes of the large individual differences in personality found among children raised in the same family.

Single Genes and the Physiology of Traits

Thus far the study of personality heritability has been largely distinct from the study of the physiological bases for personality. The next step, just now beginning at a number of laboratories, is to link the behavior-genetics and physiological approaches. If genes affect personality, they presumably do so primarily by influencing the physiological characteristics of the nervous system in one way or another.

One of the many routes by which genes might affect personality is through their influences on neurotransmission in the brain. In recent years, several laboratories have reported small but significant correlations between specific personality characteristics and genes that alter neurotransmission. One group of researchers (Lesch & others, 1996) found a significant relationship between neuroticism and a gene allele that increases the action of the neurotransmitter serotonin; and another group (Benjamin & others, 1996, 1998) found a significant relationship between the trait of novelty seeking—which includes elements of impulsiveness, excitability, and extravagance—and an allele that decreases the action of the neurotransmitter

13.

What evidence suggests that being raised in the same home does not promote similarity of personality?

Identical twins

Research indicates that identical twins raised in different homes are nearly as similar to each other in personality as those raised in the same home.

14.

How might variation in single genes influence personality?

DILBERT by Scott Adams

dopamine. Attempts to replicate these findings, however, have thus far produced inconsistent and largely negative results (Herbst & others, 2000; Samochowiec & others, 2001). It seems inevitable that, with time, researchers will find direct relationships between the effects of individual genes and personality variations, but the first chapter of this story is not yet clear.

SECTION SUMMARY

Personality psychology is the study of psychological differences among people. Trait theories are attempts to specify the dimensions, or traits, that most efficiently describe those differences. To identify traits, researchers collect data about the behavioral tendencies of large numbers of people—mostly with questionnaires—and then look for patterns of correlations among those tendencies. Behavioral tendencies that correlate with one another are considered to be part of the same surface trait, and surface traits that correlate with one another are considered to be part of the same central trait. Using this approach, Cattell developed a trait theory that specified 16 central traits, and Eysenck developed one that specified just two (and later three) central traits. The trait theory that is most accepted today is the Big Five theory, which specifies the five central traits listed in Table 15.2. Personality researchers measure traits with questionnaires that ask individuals to report on their own behavioral tendencies that are relevant to each trait.

Using such measures, researchers have found that personality traits are quite stable, especially after age 30. People who take personality tests at various times in their lives tend to score similarly each time they are tested. On average, however, as people age they tend (on measures of the Big Five) to show gradual reductions in neuroticism, extroversion, and openness and gradual increases in conscientiousness and agreeableness. Personality measures are valid in that they correlate moderately well with indices of everyday behavior, such as sociability and work performance. A limitation, however, is that the measures do not specify the contexts in which people's assessed traits are most likely to manifest themselves. Two people may score similarly on extroversion, for example, but one may be most extroverted in formal social situations and the other most extroverted in informal social situations. Mischel and other advocates of the social-cognitive approach to personality prefer to describe people in terms of situation-specific traits rather than global traits.

Biologically oriented psychologists have attempted to explain traits in terms of heritable qualities of the nervous system. Eysenck suggested that introverts seek placid environments because their nervous systems are easily aroused and extroverts seek stimulating environments because their nervous systems are not easily aroused. Studies of twins—including those raised in separate adoptive homes—indicate that roughly half the variability in personality traits stems from genetic variability. The same studies indicate that the same home environment does not generally affect siblings' personalities in the same way. For instance, twins raised in the same home are, on average, not more similar to each other in personality than are twins raised in different homes. In recent years researchers have attempted to identify specific genes that contribute to personality through known effects on the brain, but so far the results have been inconsistent.

PERSONALITY AS ADAPTATION TO LIFE CONDITIONS

Why are people different from one another in personality? As you may recall from Chapter 3, psychologists and biologists distinguish between two different types of answers to *why* questions. One type, referred to as *proximate explanation*, focuses on causal mechanisms that operate in the lifetime of the individual to produce the phenomenon in question. Proximate explanations of personality differences focus on ways by which differing genes and experiences work to make us different. The other type of answer, referred to as *ultimate explanation*, focuses on function, or evolutionary survival value, rather than mechanisms. How might personality differences help individuals survive longer and produce more offspring than they would if all individuals were identical in personality? Why were genetic, developmental, and learning mechanisms that ensure diversity favored by natural selection over mechanisms that would have made us more uniform? These are the questions we turn to now.

15.

How does an ultimate explanation of personality variability differ from a proximate one?

Advantages of Being Different from One Another

It is conceivable that variability in personality has no adaptive advantage. Perhaps the kinds of differences that personality theorists study simply represent a degree of randomness that could not be weeded out by natural selection. Perhaps; but I doubt it.

As noted in Chapter 3, sexual reproduction itself seems to be an adaptation that ensures the diversity of offspring. Mixing half of one parent's genes in a random manner with half of the other parent's genes leads to an essentially infinite number of possible new gene combinations in the offspring. From a purely biomechanical point of view, cloning is a far simpler and less costly form of reproduction than is sexual reproduction, so it is hard to imagine why sexual reproduction would have evolved and persisted if there were no advantage in diversity. It seems equally unlikely that learning mechanisms and other developmental mechanisms that lead us to become different in response to different environmental conditions would have evolved if they produced no survival advantage. Research on dozens of species of other animals, ranging from ants to octopuses to chimpanzees, has revealed, in every species tested, individual differences in behavioral styles that can be described in terms very similar to those that are used to describe human personality differences (Gosling, 2001). Personality appears to be a basic, biological aspect of animal existence.

Diversifying One's Investment in Offspring

One way to think about the value of genetic diversity and personality differences is through an analogy between producing offspring and investing money (Miller, 1997). Investors who put all their money in one company risk going broke if that company suddenly collapses. Smart investors diversify: They invest in a variety of stocks, bonds, and other financial instruments, which are likely to respond differently to economic forces, so that when one goes down, another goes up or at least doesn't go down as rapidly as the first. Diversified investment greatly reduces the potential for dramatic loss while maintaining the potential for substantial gains over the long run.

From the perspective of evolution by natural selection, producing offspring is an investment, the goal of which is to send multiple copies of one's genes into future generations. Since conditions of survival and reproduction vary in unpredictable ways over time, the chance that an individual's genes will die out can be reduced if the offspring differ from one another in some of their operating characteristics. Therefore, over the course of evolution, mechanisms that ensure diversity of offspring—even the random diversity that results from genetic mixing in sexual reproduction—would be favored by natural selection.

16.

How does an analogy to financial investment explain the value of producing offspring who differ from one another in personality?

Occupying Alternative Niches

17.

How might the availability of different niches help explain the evolution of trait differences within a species, and how is this illustrated in two experiments with pumpkinseed sunfish?

Conditions of life vary not only over time but also across available habitats, ways of making a living, and social roles at any given time. Borrowing a term from biology, we can refer to particular habitats, occupations, and roles as *niches*. Genetic diversity and developmental flexibility may allow individuals to occupy different niches, thereby reducing competition among individuals for the limited number of positions that any given niche can support. Numerous examples of such adaptive diversity have been documented in nonhuman animals. As illustration, consider two examples of diversity among pumpkinseed sunfish.

In many lakes, pumpkinseeds can be found in two distinct habitats. One habitat is shoreline areas containing much vegetation such as water lilies, and the other is the deeper, open-water region. The two habitats impose quite different life conditions on the fish. The food is different and the means of avoiding predation are different. The shoreline fish are quite sedentary, as their best strategy is to remain quiet and hidden among the plants (see Figure 15.4). In contrast, the open-water fish must swim rapidly to escape predators. The open-water and shoreline fish differ in form as well as behavior. In contrast to the disklike shape of the shoreline pumpkinseeds, the open-water pumpkinseeds are more tapered at each end, which enables them to swim faster.

To assess the source of this variation, Beren Robinson and David Wilson (in Wilson, 1994, 1998) captured both varieties of sunfish from a specific lake, bred them in separate experimental ponds, and raised the offspring in cages placed either in vegetation near the shore or in open water. The results demonstrated both genetic and environmental influences. As evidence of a genetic effect, within each rearing environment the offspring of pumpkinseeds caught in the open water were more tapered than were the offspring of those caught near the shoreline. As evidence of an environmental effect, the offspring of each parental group were more tapered if raised in open water than if raised near the shore.

FIGURE 15.4 *Pumpkinseed sunfish*
Pumpkinseeds differ in shape and in boldness, in ways that help them to occupy and exploit different niches.

In other work, Wilson and his colleagues (1993; Wilson, 1998) showed that pumpkinseeds differ along a bold–cautious dimension similar to the extroversion–introversion dimension in people. Fish were identified as bold or cautious on the basis of their tendency to approach (and get caught in) or to avoid wire traps placed in their shoreline habitat in a small experimental pond. Pumpkinseeds caught by the trap were considered bold and those that avoided the traps (and were later caught by seining) were considered cautious. Subsequent study of the two groups of fish in laboratory tanks demonstrated the consistency and generality of the trait difference. Compared with the cautious fish, the bold fish (a) adapted more readily to the tank, as shown by a quicker return to normal feeding, (b) more frequently swam off on their own rather than staying close to the other fish, and (c) were more likely to approach rather than avoid a human observer. In addition, analysis of the stomach contents of freshly caught bold and cautious fish revealed a striking difference in their diets. The bold fish had eaten far more copepods (tiny crustaceans), which are most plentiful in the shoreline areas where vegetation is least dense and the risk of predation by fish and birds is greatest.

One can well imagine the advantages and disadvantages of being either cautious or bold, among pumpkinseeds or any other vertebrate species. Caution reduces the risk of sudden death through predation or accident, but it also confines one's life to a relatively narrow niche. Boldness may be especially valuable when the narrow niche occupied by cautious individuals is nearly filled, so the risks entailed in exploring new objects, areas, and life strategies are offset by the potential for finding new, needed resources. Parents who produce offspring that differ from each other in their degree of caution or boldness are hedging their bets, much like investors who invest in a combination of conservative and high-risk bonds and stocks. Not surprisingly, variation along the cautious–bold dimension has been observed in many species of animals (Gosling, 2001).

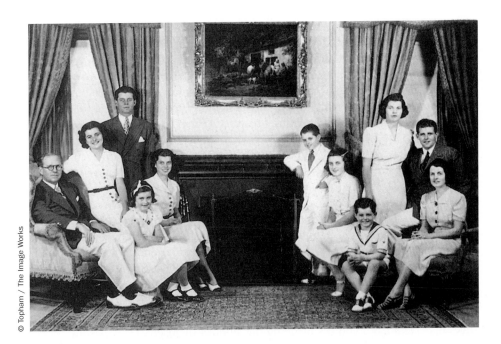

© Topham / The Image Works

A family famous for boldness

The members of the Kennedy clan are well known for their willingness to take risks in their political and personal lives. This photograph, taken in 1938, shows Joseph Kennedy (far left) with his wife Rose (far right) and their children (left to right): Patricia, John (who became the thirty-fifth president of the United States), Jean, Eunice, Robert, Kathleen, Edward, Rosemary, and Joseph. The subsequent histories of these people and of their own children offer repeated examples of triumphs and tragedies resulting from risky actions.

Personality Traits as Alternative Problem-Solving Strategies

From an evolutionary perspective, personality traits in humans can be thought of as alternative general strategies for solving problems related to survival and reproduction (Buss, 1991, 1996). Consistent with this view, David Buss (1996) has found significant correlations between many measures of the Big Five trait dimensions and mating strategies. For instance, variation along the conscientiousness–undirectedness dimension correlates with one's tendency to be sexually faithful or unfaithful to one's mate, and variation along the antagonism–agreeableness dimension correlates with one's tendency to become aggressive, or not, toward sexual rivals. As an exercise, you might return to Table 15.2 (page 577) and think of ways in which each of the Big Five traits may influence one's approach to a wide range of problems that can enhance or reduce one's ability to survive and reproduce, depending on conditions that are not always predictable. From an evolutionary perspective, what might be the advantages and disadvantages of lying toward either end of each trait dimension? Your speculations will no doubt generate many hypotheses, and you might think further about how such hypotheses could be tested through research.

The finding that individual differences on trait dimensions are partly heritable and partly the product of differential environmental experience is consistent with the evolutionary perspective. In an environment that varies unpredictably, the chances that at least some offspring will survive are enhanced if they are genetically inclined toward different life strategies, as some pumpkinseed sunfish are genetically inclined toward shore and others toward open water. Genetic inclinations need to be flexible, however, so that individuals can move along a personality dimension in a direction compatible with their life situation. Pumpkinseeds that are genetically inclined to be cautious and people who are genetically inclined toward introversion can become more bold and extroverted if their condition of life promotes or requires such adaptation. (If I had to make my living selling books rather than writing them, even I might become a tiny bit extroverted.)

18.

How might both heritable and nonheritable variation on the Big Five dimensions be explained in terms of alternative life strategies?

Adapting to the Family Environment

The first social environment to which most new human beings must adapt is that of the family into which they are born. The first view of other people, the first attempts at communication, the first emotional attachments, the first strivings for acceptance and approval, and the first competitions with others for resources occur most often within the context of the family. Children come into the world with nervous systems predisposed for behaving in certain ways, but those ways of behaving are first exercised and built upon within the family. Not surprisingly, personality psychologists from Sigmund Freud on have emphasized the role of the early family environment in the development of each individual's unique personality.

Some psychologists contend that the family may not play as big a role in personality development as was previously believed (Harris, 1998; Rowe, 1994). That contention stems primarily from the research indicating that people who were raised in the same home typically score, on average, just about as differently from each other on personality tests as do equally related people who were raised in different homes. To the degree that siblings are similar to each other in global personality traits, that similarity seems to come mainly from their shared genes, not from their shared home environment.

19.

What are some ways by which the personality-forming experiences of children raised in the same family may differ?

One response to such findings has been to suggest that siblings raised in the same home, by the same parents, might nevertheless experience quite different environments (Dunn & Plomin, 1990; Vernon & others, 1997). Some differences may stem from chance events: One child has an accident that leads to extensive care from the parents which is not given to the other, or one child is assigned to a warm and caring teacher at school and another is assigned to a harsh one. Other differences may stem from choices made by the siblings themselves. Preexisting differences in personality may lead them to choose very different sets of friends and activities, which may lead them to diverge even further in personality. Preexisting personality differences can also lead them to interpret the same objective events quite differently, with different consequences for further personality development: A parent's consistent demand that chores be done might be understood by one child as a caring act designed to instill good work habits and by another as harsh discipline. Judy Dunn and Robert Plomin (1990) have summarized evidence that siblings indeed do have different experiences for all these kinds of reasons.

Sibling Contrast: Carving Out a Unique Niche Within the Family

"And then, as soon as I had carved out my niche, they went and had another kid."

Differences between siblings growing up in the same family may become exaggerated because siblings tend to define themselves as different from one another and to accentuate their differences through their behavioral choices (Sulloway, 1996). When people are asked to describe their brother or sister, they commonly start off by saying, in effect, "Oh, he (or she) is entirely different from me," and then proceed to point out how (Dunn & Plomin, 1990). Parents likewise tend to focus more on differences than on similarities when they describe two or more of their children (Schachter, 1982). This within-family emphasis on the differences between siblings is referred to as *sibling contrast*. Possibly related to sibling contrast is a strong tendency for siblings with two parents to identify more strongly with different parents; this is referred to as *split-parent identification*. If the first child identifies more strongly with the mother, the second typically identifies more strongly with the father, and vice versa. Sibling contrast and split-parent identification have been documented as highly reliable phenomena in questionnaires filled out by parents as well as in those filled out by the siblings themselves (Schachter, 1982).

20.

How might sibling contrast and split-parent identification be useful in reducing sibling rivalry and diversifying parental investment? What evidence supports the reduced sibling rivalry hypothesis?

Why do family members accentuate the differences rather than the similarities between siblings? A possible answer, proposed by Frances Schachter (1982), is that sibling contrast and split-parent identification are devices by which parents and children consciously or unconsciously strive to reduce sibling rivalry, which can be highly disruptive to family functioning. If siblings are seen by themselves and their parents as having very different abilities, needs, and dispositions, then the siblings are less likely to compete with each other and more likely to be valued and rewarded separately for their unique characteristics. If Joan is understood to be re-

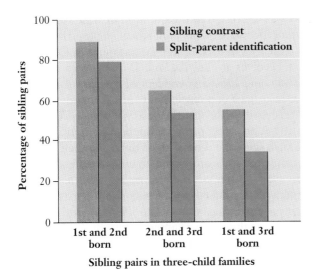

FIGURE **15.5** *Sibling contrast and split-parent identification in three-child families*

Mothers were asked to compare pairs of their children by stating whether the two were similar or different on each of various personality dimensions and by stating which parent each child identified with more strongly. *Sibling contrast* (maroon bars), here, refers to the percentage of times that the mothers said "different" rather than "alike" in response to questions about personality, and *split-parent identification* (blue bars) refers to the percentage of times two siblings were said by the mother to identify with different parents (one with the mother and one with the father) rather than with the same parent. (Data from Schachter, 1982, pp. 128 and 141.)

served and scholarly and her sister Mary is understood to be outgoing and athletic, then Joan and Mary can be appreciated by their parents and by each other for their separate traits rather than viewed as competitors on the same dimension—a competition that one or the other would have to lose. From an evolutionary perspective, such differentiation may promote the survival of the two siblings and other members of their family not only by reducing rivalry but also by diversifying the parental investment (Lalumière & others, 1996; Sulloway, 1996). To the degree that Joan and Mary move into different life niches, they will compete less with each other for limited resources both within the family and in the larger environment outside the family, and they may develop separate skills through which they can help each other and the family as a whole.

In support of the view that sibling contrast and split-parent identification serve to reduce sibling rivalry, Schachter (1982) found that both phenomena are much stronger for adjacent pairs of siblings than for pairs who are separated in birth order (Figure 15.5) and stronger for same-sex pairs of siblings than for opposite-sex pairs. It seems reasonable that siblings who are the same sex and adjacent to each other in birth order would be most subject to implicit comparisons and possible rivalries and would therefore have the greatest need to reduce rivalry through contrast and split-parent identification. The observation that sibling contrast and split-parent identification are strongest for the first two children in a family is likewise consistent with the rivalry-reduction hypothesis. The first two children are likely to experience the greatest degree of sibling rivalry because for a period of time they are the only two children being compared. When third and subsequent children come along, multiple comparisons can be made, so the intensity of comparisons between any two, and the potential for rivalry between them, may be somewhat muted.

Influence of Birth Order on Personality

With the exception of twins, children within a family all differ from one another in one important way—birth order. Birth order certainly affects children's lives within the family. Earlier-born children, simply by virtue of being older, are—at least for some period of time—bigger, stronger, more knowledgeable, and more competent than their later-born siblings. Because of this, earlier-born children are likely to dominate later-borns and may often be called upon to help care for them. Firstborns in particular occupy a special position. They are *first*: first in competitions, first in receiving new privileges and responsibilities, first to grow up. Do these differences in childhood experiences have lasting consequences for personality? One person who thinks they do is Frank Sulloway, a historian of science who became interested in this topic as a result of his interest in scientific revolutions.

21.

What differences between the niches of firstborn and later-born children might be expected to produce personality differences? What consistent birth-order differences in personality did Sulloway find in his analyses of historical data?

A brilliant, rebellious lastborn
Voltaire, the eighteenth-century satirist and leading critic of the Catholic Church—whose literary work sometimes led to periods of imprisonment or exile—was, according to Sulloway, reacting against his sanctimonious, pious eldest brother, his father's favorite son.

22.

How do correlations between birth order and personality measures support Sulloway's theory?

Sulloway was interested in the question of why, at any given point in history, some people support and others oppose the revolutionary new scientific theories of their time—theories such as Copernicus's idea that the earth revolves around the sun, Darwin's idea of evolution by natural selection, and Einstein's concept of special relativity. With the help of other historians of science, he identified hundreds of scientists and other intellectuals who, over the past 500 years of Western history, were on record as either supporting or opposing a particular revolutionary or innovative scientific idea of their time. He then classified these people according to birth order and found, overall, that later-borns were far more likely to support such ideas than were firstborns. For example, the odds that a later-born person relative to a firstborn supported the new scientific idea were 5.4 to 1 for Copernicus's theory and 4.6 to 1 for Darwin's theory. In a subsequent study, Sulloway also found that later-borns were disproportionately likely to support liberal political causes and firstborns were disproportionately likely to support conservative political causes.

Largely on the basis of these historical studies, Sulloway (1996) developed the theory that children's experiences within the family have long-lasting effects, such that firstborns tend to be conservative and traditional throughout their lives and later-borns tend to be more open to new ideas and more likely to rebel against established ways. Because firstborns are, for a while, the only child in their family, they identify strongly with their parents, and in doing so they develop strong respect for authority and for conventional ways of doing things. Later-born children enter a family that already has at least one older child. They cannot compete with the firstborn child at the activities that are most sanctioned by their parents, so they are motivated to explore new activities and new ways of thinking. The status quo does not favor them, so they look for ways to shake things up. They also tend to identify with the underdog; they know what it is like to be dominated by their more powerful older siblings. Such forces, according to Sulloway, lead later-borns to be much more supportive than firstborns of new ideas and liberal political causes.

Over the past several decades, psychologists have conducted dozens of research studies on the relationship between birth order and scores on standard personality tests. When only the best, most well-controlled studies are included, the results tell a fairly consistent story. Relatively small but reliable effects are found that are, in their direction, consistent with Sulloway's theory (Paulhus & others, 1999; Sulloway, 1996). Consistent with the drive of later-borns to find new ways of doing things and with firstborns' interest in preserving the status quo, later-borns typically score higher than firstborns on the personality trait of *openness to experience*. Later-borns also tend to score higher than firstborns on *agreeableness*. According to Sulloway, this may be because in interactions with older siblings later-borns cannot win by intimidation, so they learn to get along with others and form coalitions to preserve their interests. Firstborns, however, tend to be more responsible, achievement-oriented, and organized than later-borns, and they score higher than later-borns on the personality trait of *conscientiousness*. Sulloway suggests that these effects may derive from firstborns' early caretaking roles in the family, their early identification with parents, and their more predictable life course.

At this point it is uncertain why the effects of birth order on personality measures are relatively small compared to the very large effects that Sulloway documented in his historical study. Another limitation of Sulloway's theory is that essentially all the work related to it has been confined to middle- and upper-class people in Western cultures. It remains to be seen whether birth-order effects occur similarly, differently, or not at all in other cultures, especially in cultures that emphasize interdependence and conformity within the family rather than independence and individuality.

Adapting to One's Gender

Human beings, like other sexually reproducing animals, come in two varieties—female and male. If you have read the previous chapters of this book, you have already read a good deal about sex differences. For instance, in Chapter 3 you read of the different problems that females and males must solve in mating and of their possible different strategies for solving them. In Chapter 12 you read of differences in how the two sexes are treated, how they are expected to behave, and how they typically do behave at each life stage in our culture and in other cultures. As is pointed out in Chapter 12, psychologists generally use the word *sex* to refer to the clear-cut biological differences between males and females and the word *gender* to refer to the differences that may be heavily influenced by cultural forces and expectations.

One way to think about gender is in terms of niches to which we must adapt. The female and male niches are defined partly by biological sex: Females play one role in sexual reproduction, males another. The gender niches are further defined and elaborated upon socially in ways that vary at least somewhat from culture to culture. Females and males are understood by the culture to have different attributes and to be best suited for different social roles. We choose neither our sex nor our gender. Pure chance normally decides sex—X, you're a female; Y, you're a male. Then, throughout life, most of us live with that assignment. The X or the Y affects the hormones that act on our cells and the social environment that acts on our selves. What consequences might all this have for personality?

Some Gender Differences in Personality

Standard personality tests do reveal relatively consistent differences, small to moderate in size, between men and women in average scores on many personality traits. In a review of such studies, Alan Feingold (1994) classified the results in terms of the Big Five trait dimensions. Most of the studies had been conducted in the United States, but Feingold also analyzed the results of several done in Canada, China, Finland, Germany, Poland, and Russia. The largest and most consistent gender difference by far was on the *agreeableness–antagonism* dimension. In essentially every study relevant to this dimension, in every country, women scored as more agreeable, less antagonistic, than men. The average difference across all studies was nearly one standard deviation, which (as explained in the Statistical Appendix, page A-5) means that about 84 percent of women scored higher on agreeableness than the average man. This result is in line with the findings of many studies, conducted in a wide range of cultures, indicating that women are consistently more concerned than men with developing and maintaining positive social relationships (Kashima & others, 1995; Taylor & others, 2000).

Feingold's review turned up evidence for smaller differences on other Big Five dimensions. Women scored slightly but significantly higher than men on indices of *neuroticism*, primarily because women reported higher levels of anxiety. Women also scored slightly but significantly higher on *conscientiousness*. *Openness* showed no consistent gender difference at all, and *extroversion* showed mixed results, depending on the nature of the measure. Measures focusing on sociability or gregariousness showed higher extroversion scores for women than for men, and measures focusing on assertiveness or dominance in social interactions showed the opposite. Feingold found no evidence of change with time in any of these gender differences over a 40-year period of studies conducted in the United States, from 1952 through 1992, and no consistent evidence of a difference between the U.S. findings and those for the other countries.

Another trait that has shown pronounced sex differences is *sensation seeking*, a disposition to take risks for the thrill involved. On personality tests of sensation seeking, men score higher than women in every culture that has been studied (Zuckerman, 1994). With age, from middle adolescence to late adulthood, sensation

23.

What differences have researchers found between women and men on personality traits?

24.

What evidence suggests that gender alters the relationship between personality and life satisfaction?

seeking declines for both genders, and the difference between the two diminishes somewhat beginning at about age 30 (Zuckerman & others, 1978). Many other studies have likewise shown that boys and men engage in more risky actions of a wide variety of types—ranging from daredevil physical activities to speaking out at public meetings—than do girls and women (Byrnes & others, 1999).

Gender not only influences the kind of personality one develops but may also affect the relationship of personality to life satisfaction (Rothbart & Bates, 1998). For example, researchers have found that shyness or behavioral inhibition correlates positively with feelings of emotional distress and unhappiness in young men but not in young women (Gest, 1997). That difference is not present in early childhood but seems to emerge in adolescence and reach a peak in young adulthood. A possible explanation lies in cultural expectations that make life more difficult for shy or inhibited young men than for similarly shy or inhibited young women. In our culture and all others that have been studied, men are expected to initiate romantic and sexual relationships and to be more assertive or dominant in social interactions of all types, and shyness or lack of assertion is considered more attractive in women than in men. In other respects, too, personality dispositions that run counter to stereotypes can have emotional costs. For instance, women who have a relatively competitive orientation toward others, rather than an orientation emphasizing similarity and agreeableness, typically score lower on measures of self-esteem than do other women, while the opposite is true for men (Josephs & others, 1992).

Evolutionary and Cultural Foundations of Gender Differences

25.

How might gender differences in personality be understood in terms of the differing biological and cultural niches of males and females?

As noted earlier, personality measures are merely descriptions, not explanations, of psychological differences among people. What accounts for the just-described average differences between women and men on personality measures? In addressing that question, some psychologists focus on evolutionary history and others focus on the present-day pressures and expectations of the cultures in which we develop.

Evolutionary theorists can point to the long history of evolution in which males and females were subject, generation after generation, to different reproductive challenges. Females' greater role in child care, and perhaps a need for cooperative relationships with other adults in relation to child care, may have led to selection for personality qualities promoting nurturance, cooperation, and caution; and males' greater need to compete in order to reproduce may have led to selection for competitiveness, aggressiveness, and risk taking (as described in Chapter 3).

Recently, Shelley Taylor and her colleagues (2000) have amassed considerable evidence that male and female mammals in general, including humans, tend to respond differently to stressful situations. Whereas males tend to respond to stress by becoming more aggressive, females tend to respond by becoming more nurturant and more motivated to strengthen social connections. According to Taylor, females are more likely than males to attempt to placate their rivals rather than intimidate them and are more likely than males to look to friends for comfort and support. This difference, of course, is not all-or-none, but a matter of degree, and there is considerable overlap between the sexes. Oxytocin, a hormone whose levels are higher in females than in males, tends to promote affiliation; testosterone, which is higher in males, tends to promote aggression.

Cultural theorists, in contrast, point to the different experiences, expectations, role models, and opportunities provided by the culture for girls and boys—all the differences discussed in Chapter 12. From the cultural perspective, the relevant niches to think about are not those existing in past generations of humans and prehumans but are those in existence right now (Bussey & Bandura, 1999). The immediate causes of gender differences in personality are not hormones but social forces that encourage girls to develop the nurturant, agreeable, and conscientious aspects of their nature and boys to develop their competitive, aggressive, and risk-taking aspects.

Cultural theorists such as Alice Eagly and Wendy Wood (1999) contend that the effect of biology on present-day gender differences in personality is indirect and historical. Biological sex differences may have contributed to the original development of cultural practices and expectations that differ for women and men, and those practices and expectations may, in turn, have promoted gender divergence in personality development in each succeeding generation. For instance, the greater physical strength of men may have led men to assume positions of power in early cultures, and women's roles in childbirth and nursing may have led women to assume nurturing positions. As life changed over generations—such that power became less tied to physical strength and women's lives were less consumed by childbirth and infant care—the concepts that men are dominant and women are nurturant may have lived on as self-fulfilling cultural beliefs, passed on by training and example to each new generation.

Oooh, call on me
Educational researchers have found that boys more readily put their hands up to be called on than do girls, whether or not they know the answer. Beginning at an early age, boys are quicker than girls to take risks and to show off.

At present there is no convincing way to determine the degree to which the observed gender differences in personality stem from hormonal effects on neural development, resulting from evolutionary history, or from learning within gender-specific niches provided by the culture. Cross-cultural differences in the personality distinctions between men and women provide some evidence for effects of culture. But the directions of the personality distinctions, if not the extents, are quite similar across cultures. That cross-cultural similarity may reflect both the direct effects of hormones and the effects of cultural roles and expectations that don't differ greatly from one culture to another.

The evolutionary and cultural theories do make different predictions about the future. Some Western cultures have taken large strides toward breaking down gender stereotypes and opening up social roles more equivalently to both sexes. If gender differences in personality diminish considerably as a result of such changes, that will support the cultural theory. At present, the evidence is mixed as to whether or not men and women are becoming more similar in personality as their social roles are becoming more equitable. Some analyses have shown no change in male-female personality differences over recent decades (Feingold, 1994; Lueptow & others, 1995), but one analysis has suggested that the gender difference in risk taking is growing smaller (Byrnes & others, 1999). It will be interesting to see what the evidence suggests a generation or two from now.

SECTION SUMMARY

From an evolutionary perspective, the production of offspring who differ from one another in their predilections and dispositions may be an adaptation that increases the chance that at least some will survive in a diverse, ever-changing, competitive environment. Thus, some pumpkinseed sunfish are adapted for life near the shore and others for life in deeper water. Among the shoreline fish, some are bolder than others. The differences reduce competition among the pumpkinseeds and allow more of them to survive within the pond than would be possible if they were all identical. Similarly, differences among people in traits such as the Big Five may have come about because such diversity allows people to occupy different niches in the human social world.

Personality differences among siblings derive partly from genetic differences and partly from experiences that lead siblings to occupy different niches. The phenomena of sibling contrast and split-parent identification may accentuate differences among siblings and thereby reduce sibling rivalry. Birth order may also promote differences among siblings. Research suggests that firstborn children tend to accept the norms of the world into which they are born and later-born children tend to rebel against them. The difference may stem from the fact that firstborns have a head start in occupying the niches favored by parents, and therefore later-borns may do better by seeking or creating alternative niches.

Personality also correlates in some ways with gender; girls and women tend to be more agreeable, more conscientious, more anxious, and less risk-prone than boys and men. Evolutionary theorists attempt to explain these differences in terms of natural selection based on females' greater role in child care and males' greater need to compete in order to reproduce. Cultural theorists attempt to explain the differences in terms of the differing roles, expectations, and training that cultures provide for males and females.

PERSONALITY AS MENTAL PROCESSES

Trait theories, such as the Big Five theory, are useful as very general schemes for describing human psychological differences and thinking about their possible functions. Such theories are not, however, of much use for developing in-depth understandings of individual persons. The differences among us in our ways of thinking and acting are far richer, subtler, and more interesting than can possibly be captured by a handful of central traits.

We turn now to quite a different mode of thinking about personality—one that examines the processes and contents of the mind to find the source of personality and its behavioral expressions. Freud pioneered this approach. He developed an elaborate model of the mind that was aimed at explaining people's varying ways of coping with the psychological stresses of daily life. Many other theorists—mostly clinicians—subsequently modified Freud's model or developed alternative models. The theories that emerged are commonly classed into three general types: *psychodynamic*, *social cognitive*, and *humanistic*. In this final section of the chapter we will examine some of the basic premises of, and research generated by, these types of personality theories. Each class of theories is also associated with a set of explanations for psychological disorders and a set of psychotherapy techniques, which are discussed in Chapters 16 and 17.

The Psychodynamic Perspective: Unconscious Motives and Defenses

Before you began studying psychology, your image of a typical psychologist might have been a caricature of Sigmund Freud, stroking his beard and murmuring in a Viennese accent, "Hmm, I wonder what he really meant by that." Freud more or less founded psychotherapy, and from his experiences with patients he developed the first extensive theory of personality. As a young physician in the late nineteenth century, Freud found reason to believe that many of his patients' complaints were rooted not in organic disease but in mental conflicts of which the patients themselves were unaware. On the basis of this insight, he developed an approach to psychotherapy and a theory of personality, both of which he called ***psychoanalysis***. Freud's theory was the first of what today are called ***psychodynamic theories***—personality theories that emphasize the interplay of mental forces (the word *dynamic* refers to energy or force).

Two guiding premises of psychodynamic theories are that (a) people are often unconscious of their motives and (b) processes called *defense mechanisms* work within the mind to keep unacceptable or anxiety-producing motives and thoughts out of consciousness. According to psychodynamic theories, personality differences lie in variations in people's unconscious motives, in how those motives are manifested, and in the ways that people defend themselves from anxiety.

Unconscious Motivation

Freud proposed that the main causes of behavior lie deeply buried in the unconscious mind, that is, in the part of the mind that affects the individual's conscious thought and action but is not itself open to conscious inspection. The reasons peo-

Keystone / The Image Works

Sigmund Freud

The founder of psychoanalysis viewed himself as a detective whose task was to use cues in people's behavior to uncover the secrets of their unconscious minds.

26.

What characteristics of the mind underlie personality differences, according to psychodynamic theories?

ple give to explain their behavior often are not the true causes. To illustrate this idea, Freud (1912/1932) drew an analogy between everyday behavior and the phenomenon of posthypnotic suggestion.

In a demonstration of posthypnotic suggestion, a person is hypnotized and given an instruction such as "When you awake, you will not remember what happened during hypnosis. However, when the clock chimes, you will walk to the back of the room, pick up the umbrella lying there, and open it." When awakened, the subject appears to behave in a perfectly normal, self-directed way until the clock chimes. At this signal the subject consciously senses an irresistible impulse to perform the commanded action, and consciously performs it, but has no conscious memory of the origin of the impulse (the hypnotist's command). If asked why he or she is opening the umbrella, the subject may come up with a plausible though clearly false reason, such as "I thought I should test it because it may rain later." According to Freud, the real reasons behind our everyday actions are likewise hidden in our unconscious minds, and our conscious reasons are cover-ups, plausible but false rationalizations that we believe to be true.

Freud believed that to understand his patients' actions, problems, and personality, he had to learn about the content of their unconscious minds. But how could he do that when the unconscious, by definition, consists only of information that the patient cannot talk about? He claimed that he could do it by *analyzing* certain aspects of their speech and other observable behavior to draw inferences about their unconscious motives. This is where the term *psychoanalysis* comes from. His technique was to sift the patient's behavior for clues to the unconscious. In detectivelike fashion he collected clues and tried to piece them together into a coherent story about the unconscious causes of the person's conscious thoughts and actions.

Because the conscious mind always attempts to act in ways that are consistent with conventional logic, Freud reasoned that the elements of thought and behavior that are *least* logical would provide the best clues to the unconscious. They would represent elements of the unconscious mind that leaked out relatively unmodified by consciousness. Freud therefore paid particular attention to his patients' slips of the tongue and other mistakes as clues to the unconscious. He also asked them to describe their dreams and to report in uncensored fashion whatever thoughts came to mind in response to particular words or phrases. These methods are described more fully, with examples, in Chapter 17.

Sex and Aggression as Motivating Forces in Freud's Theory

Unlike most modern psychologists, Freud considered drives to be analogous to physical forms of energy that build up over time and must somehow be released. To live peaceably in society (especially in the Victorian society that Freud grew up in), one must often control one's direct expressions of the sexual and aggressive drives, so these are the drives that are most likely to build up and exert themselves in indirect ways. Freud concluded from his observations that much of human behavior consists of disguised manifestations of sex and aggression and that personality differences lie in the different ways that people disguise and channel these drives. Over time, Freud (1933/1964) came to define these drives increasingly broadly. He considered the sex drive to be the main pleasure-seeking and life-seeking drive and the aggressive drive to be the force that lies behind all sorts of destructive actions, including actions that harm oneself.

Social Drives as Motivating Forces in Other Psychodynamic Theories

Freud viewed people as basically asocial, forced into society more by necessity than by desire and interacting principally in terms of sex, aggression, and displaced forms of these drives. In contrast, most psychodynamic theorists since Freud's time have viewed people as inherently social beings whose motives for interacting with others extend well beyond sex and aggression.

27.

How is the concept of unconscious motivation illustrated by posthypnotic suggestion?

28.

How did Freud draw inferences about the content of his clients' unconscious minds?

29.

Why, according to Freud, are sex and aggression especially significant drives in personality formation?

30.

What drives or human needs provide a basis for personality differences in (a) Horney's theory, (b) object relations theories, (c) Adler's theory, and (d) Erikson's theory?

Karen Horney

One of the first psychoanalysts to offer a rebuttal to Freud's ideas about women, Horney argued that psychoanalysis must consider facts about women's social circumstances as well as their anatomy.

One such theorist was Karen Horney (1855–1952), who focused on *security* as an inborn human need that can be filled only by other people. The most fundamental emotion in her theory is *basic anxiety*, defined as "the feeling a child has of being isolated and helpless in a potentially hostile world" (Horney, 1945). Parents influence a child's lifelong personality through the ways in which they succeed or fail in relieving the child's basic anxiety and helping the child feel secure. A child who finds security in relating to parents will continue to find security in other relationships throughout life. A child who fails to find security in relating to parents will grow up feeling insecure and distrustful of others (Horney, 1937). This distrust may manifest itself in any of three unhappy personality styles: avoiding others, consistently giving in to others, or dominating others.

Thematically related to Horney's theory are more recent *object relations theories* of personality (Ingram & Lerner, 1992; Kernberg, 1976), which derive partly from John Bowlby's ideas concerning the emotional attachments that infants make with their caregivers (discussed in Chapter 12). Object relations theories focus on the potentially conflicting human drives to be in close emotional relationships with other people (the objects of attachment) and yet be autonomous and independent. According to object relations theories, the way people respond to others throughout life depends on the nature of their early attachments. For instance, inconsistent approval from attachment objects early in childhood—veering from fawning admiration to rejection—may result in an excessive need for others' approval later in life. This need restricts the person's capacity to behave independently and also limits the person's relationships with others. Seeing others primarily as sources of approval, the person fails to empathize with or respond to others' needs, a condition referred to as a *narcissistic personality* (Kohut, 1971).

Alfred Adler (1870–1937), a contemporary of both Freud and Horney, developed a psychodynamic theory that centers on people's drive to feel competent. Adler (1930) contended that everyone begins life with a feeling of inferiority, which stems from the helpless and dependent nature of early childhood, and that the manner in which people learn to cope with or to overcome this feeling provides the basis for their lifelong personality. While Horney emphasized emotional attachments as means of overcoming early anxieties, Adler emphasized the role of personal achievements. People who become overwhelmed by a sense of inferiority will develop either an *inferiority complex*, and go through life acting inadequate and dependent, or a *superiority complex*, and go through life trying to prove they are better than others as a means of masking their inferiority. Psychologically healthy people have neither of these complexes but, rather, have a mature sense of their own abilities and worth (experienced as self-esteem) and can direct those abilities toward socially useful achievements.

Perhaps the most all-encompassing psychodynamic theory is Erik Erikson's theory of psychosocial development, which posits that different motives, each accompanied by its own set of needs from the social environment, become paramount at different stages of development (described in Table 12.1 on page 453). Infants need security, children need independence and opportunities to become competent at various skills, adolescents need to develop an adult identity, young adults need intimacy, and older adults need to care for others. At each stage the manner in which these needs are met influences the personality that enters the next stage.

In all psychodynamic theories, including Freud's, the first few years of life are especially critical in forming the personality. One's earliest attempts to satisfy drives result in positive or negative responses from others that, taken together, have lifelong effects on how those drives are subsequently manifested.

The Mind's Defenses Against Anxiety

A central idea in psychodynamic theories is that mental processes of self-deception, referred to as **defense mechanisms**, operate to reduce one's consciousness of wishes, memories, and other thoughts that would threaten one's self-esteem or in other ways provoke a strong sense of insecurity, or anxiety. The theory of defense mechanisms was most thoroughly developed by Anna Freud (1936/1946), Sigmund's daughter, who was also a prominent psychoanalyst. Some examples of defense mechanisms are repression, displacement, reaction formation, projection, and rationalization.

Repression is the process by which anxiety-producing thoughts are pushed out or kept out of the conscious mind. The most dramatic examples of repression reported in the clinical literature occur with young children. An example from my own experience concerns a young friend who, at age 5, witnessed a person with a knife attack his father. A day later, when his father tried to talk to him about the incident, the boy appeared to have no memory of it at all; he didn't know what his father was talking about. Given the circumstances, it seems unlikely that the boy was pretending not to remember. The thought that his father (who was his only caregiving parent) might be killed was apparently so threatening that he had repressed the entire incident.

Repression provides the basis for most of the other defense mechanisms. Freud visualized repression as a damming up of a pool of mental energy. Just as water will leak through any crack in a dam, repressed wishes and memories will leak through the barriers separating the unconscious mind from the conscious mind. When such thoughts leak through, however, the mind can still defend itself by distorting the ideas in ways that make them less threatening. The other defense mechanisms are means to such distortion.

Displacement occurs when an unconscious wish or drive that would be unacceptable to the conscious mind is redirected toward a more acceptable alternative. For example, a child long past infancy may still have a desire to suck at the mother's breast—a desire that is now threatening and repressed, because it violates the child's conscious assessment of what is proper and possible. The desire might be displaced toward sucking on a lollipop, an action that is symbolically equivalent to the original desire but more acceptable and realistic. In some cases, displacement may direct one's energies toward activities that are particularly valued by society, such as artistic, scientific, or humanitarian endeavors. In these cases displacement is referred to as *sublimation*. A highly aggressive person might perform valuable service in a competitive profession, such as being a trial lawyer, as sublimation of the drive to beat others. As another example, Freud (1910/1947) suggested that Leonardo da Vinci's fascination with painting Madonnas was a sublimation of his desire for his mother, which had been frustrated by his separation from her.

Reaction formation is the turning of a frightening wish into its safer opposite. For example, a young woman who unconsciously hates her mother and wishes her dead may consciously experience these feelings as intense love for her mother and strong concern for her safety. Psychodynamic theorists have long speculated that *homophobia*—the irrational fear and hatred of homosexuals—may often stem from reaction formation. People who have a tendency toward homosexuality but fear it may protect themselves from recognizing it by vigorously separating themselves from homosexuals (West, 1977). In a study supporting that explanation, men who scored as highly homophobic on a questionnaire were subsequently found, through direct physical measurement, to show more penile erection while watching a male homosexual video than did other men, even though they denied experiencing any sexual arousal while watching the video (Adams & others, 1996).

Projection occurs when a person consciously experiences an unconscious drive or wish as though it were someone else's. A person with intense, unconscious anger may project that anger onto her friend—she may feel that it is her friend, not she, who is angry. In an early study of projection conducted at college fraternity houses, Robert Sears (1936) found that men who were rated by their fraternity brothers as extreme on a particular characteristic, such as stinginess, but who denied that trait in themselves tended to rate others as particularly high on that same characteristic.

Rationalization is the use of conscious reasoning to explain away anxiety-provoking thoughts or feelings. A man who cannot face his own sadistic tendencies

31.

How, specifically, do repression, displacement, reaction formation, projection, and rationalization each serve to defend against anxiety?

Defense!!!

The rerouting of aggression into sports—an example of Freud's construct *sublimation*—offers rewards to players and fans alike. Although Freud based his notion of defenses on observations of disordered behavior, he recognized their adaptive functions in everyday life.

may rationalize the beatings he gives his children by convincing himself that children need to be beaten and that he is only carrying out his fatherly duty. Psychodynamic theories encourage us to be wary of conscious logic, since it often serves to mask true feelings and motives.

The concept of psychological defenses is one of the most well-accepted of Freud's ideas today. Controlled research studies have shown that at least some of the classic defense mechanisms do exist (Baumeister & others, 1998). In addition, many modern ideas about social cognition are based implicitly on the concept of psychological defenses (Westen, 1998). Examples discussed in Chapter 13 include the self-serving biases, which lead people to think they are more competent and ethical than they actually are, and the just-world bias, which leads people to think that life is more fair than it actually is.

From an evolutionary perspective, we might think of defense mechanisms as serving for anxiety a function analogous to that which endorphins serve for pain (Goleman, 1985; Nesse & Lloyd, 1992). As discussed in Chapter 6, endorphins are chemicals produced by the body that reduce the sense of pain from physical wounds and are released especially at those times when it is best to ignore wounds. As is true of pain, anxiety generally promotes survival but in some conditions is more harmful than helpful. To the degree that defenses help us worry less about things that aren't worth worrying about or that we can't do much about anyway, they are adaptive. However, to the degree that they distort our understanding of realistic matters that we could do something about, they are not adaptive. I am perhaps well off defending myself from thoughts of becoming wrinkled as I grow old, as there is little I can or am likely to do about that anyway. However, for survival's sake I am probably best off not defending myself from realistic thoughts that certain enjoyable activities and tasty foods are dangerous or harmful and therefore I should avoid them.

Evidence That Some Defensive Styles Are Healthier Than Others

In the late 1930s, an ambitious longitudinal study was begun of male sophomores at Harvard University. Each year until 1955, and less often after that, the men filled out an extensive questionnaire concerning such issues as their work, ambitions, social relationships, emotions, and health. Nearly 30 years after the study began, when the men were in their late forties, a research team led by George Vaillant (1995) interviewed in depth 95 of these men, randomly selected. By systematically analyzing the content and the style of their responses in the interview and on the previous questionnaires, the researchers rated the extent to which each man used specific defense mechanisms.

Vaillant divided the various defense mechanisms into categories according to his judgment of the degree to which they would promote either ineffective or effective behavior. *Immature defenses* were those presumed to distort reality the most and to lead to the most ineffective behavior. Projection was included in this category. *Intermediate defenses* (referred to by Vaillant as "neurotic defenses"), including repression and reaction formation, were presumed to involve less distortion of reality and to lead to somewhat more effective coping. *Mature defenses* were presumed to involve the least distortion of reality and to lead to the most adaptive behaviors. One of the most common of the mature defenses was *suppression*, which involves the conscious avoidance of negative thinking. Suppression differs from repression in that the negative information remains available to the conscious mind and can be thought about constructively when the person chooses to do so. Another defense in the mature category was humor, which, according to Freud and other psychodynamic theorists, reduces fear by making fun of feared ideas (for a comparable view, see the discussion of the evolution of laughter in Chapter 3).

Consistent with Vaillant's expectations, the men who used the most mature defenses were the most successful on all measures of ability to love and work (Freud's criteria for mature adulthood). They were also, by their own reports, the happiest.

32.

Under what conditions are defenses likely to be adaptive or maladaptive?

33.

What relationships did Vaillant find between defensive styles and measures of life satisfaction?

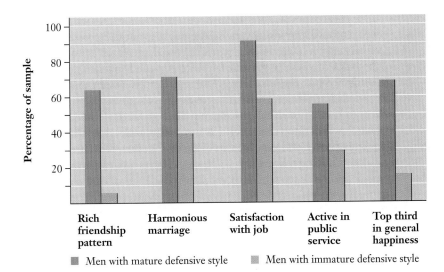

FIGURE **15.6** *Love, work, and happiness in men with mature and immature defensive styles* Harvard alumni who were classed as using primarily mature defenses were more frequently rated as having rich friendships, a good marriage, satisfaction with their work, active involvement in public service, and a high degree of happiness than were those who were classed as using primarily immature defenses. (Data from Vaillant, 1977.)

Some comparisons between the men who used mainly mature defenses and those who used mainly immature defenses are shown in Figure 15.6. Subsequently, Vaillant found similar results in two other longitudinal studies: one of men from a working-class background and the other of women who had been identified in childhood as unusually bright (Vaillant & Vaillant, 1992). Such correlations do not prove that mature defenses help cause successful coping, but they do show that mature defenses and such success tend to go together. Vaillant (1995) also found, not surprisingly, that as the Harvard men matured—from age 19 into their forties—the average maturity of their defenses increased. Immature defenses such as projection declined, and mature defenses such as suppression and humor increased.

The Social-Cognitive Perspective: Learned Beliefs and Habits

Social-cognitive theories of personality, sometimes called *social-learning* or *social-cognitive-learning theories*, draw both from clinical psychologists' experiences with their clients and from academic psychologists' research on learning, cognition, and social influence. In place of the instinctive, unconscious motives posited by psychodynamic theories as the prime shapers of personality, social-cognitive theories emphasize the roles of beliefs and habits of thought that are acquired through one's unique experiences in the social environment. These learned beliefs and habits may be conscious, but they may also become so ingrained and automatic as to exert their influence without the person's conscious awareness. Thus, to social-cognitive theorists, the term *unconscious* generally refers to automatic mental processes (in the same sense as discussed in earlier chapters in this book), not to thoughts that are actively barred from consciousness by defense mechanisms. Much of the personality research within the social-cognitive tradition has focused on learned beliefs and habits of thinking that increase or decrease people's ability to take control of their lives and accomplish the tasks they would like to accomplish (Bandura, 2001).

Beliefs About the Locus of Control over Desired Effects

If there is a principal founder of the social-cognitive perspective on personality, it is Julian Rotter, who wrote the first book explicitly describing a social-cognitive approach to personality (Rotter, 1954/1980). While still in high school, Rotter became fascinated by the writings of Alfred Adler and especially by Adler's idea that people's beliefs about their own abilities influence their efforts and achievements (Rotter, 1982). In his own early research, Rotter found that people behaved differently at various tasks or games in the laboratory, depending on whether they believed that success depended on skill or luck (Rotter & others, 1961). To the degree

34.

How do social-cognitive theories differ, in general, from psychodynamic theories?

35.

What, in Rotter's research, predicted people's improvement or failure to improve in laboratory tasks? How did this lead to Rotter's concept of locus of control?

The Card Players, Paul Cézanne

Skill or luck?

People approach an activity—such as a game of cards—very differently depending on whether they believe its potential rewards are controlled by skill or luck. This insight lay behind Rotter's concept of locus of control.

that they believed that success depended on skill (which it did), they worked hard and improved. To the degree that they believed that success depended on luck, they did not work hard and did not improve. Partly on the basis of these observations, Rotter argued that people's behavior depends not just on the objective relationship between their responses and rewards but also on their subjective beliefs about that relationship.

In many life situations it is not clear to what degree we have control over rewards. For example, it is not completely clear that studying hard will lead to a good grade on an exam or that diet and exercise will prevent us from having a heart attack. Rotter (1966) suggested that in such situations people tend to behave according to a generalized disposition (a personality trait), acquired from past experience, to believe that rewards either are or are not usually controllable by their own efforts. He referred to this disposition as **locus of control** and developed a questionnaire designed to measure it. Table 15.3 shows sample test items from Rotter's locus-of-control questionnaire. People whose answers reflect a belief that individuals control their own rewards (and, by extension, their own fate) are said to have an *internal* locus of control. People whose answers reflect a belief that rewards (and fate) are controlled by factors outside the self are said to have an *external* locus of control.

TABLE **15.3** *Sample test items from Rotter's locus-of-control scale*

The task on each item is to decide which alternative (*a* or *b*) seems more true. The actual test consists of 23 items similar to those shown here.

Item: a. In the long run, people get the respect they deserve in this world.
       b. Unfortunately, an individual's work often passes unrecognized, no matter how hard he or she tries.
Item: a. I have often found that what is going to happen will happen.
       b. Trusting to fate has never turned out as well for me as making a decision to take a definite course of action.
Item: a. In the case of the well-prepared student, there is rarely if ever such a thing as an unfair test.
       b. Many times exam questions tend to be so unrelated to course work that studying is really useless.

Note: For the items shown here, *internal* locus of control is indicated by choosing *a* for the first and third items and *b* for the second item.

Source: "Generalized expectancies for internal versus external locus of control of reinforcement" by J. B. Rotter, 1966, *Psychological Monographs: General and Applied, 80* (Whole no. 609), p. 11.

36.

What sorts of behaviors correlate with an internal locus of control?

Since its development, hundreds of studies have shown consistent, though usually not very high, correlations between scores on Rotter's locus-of-control scale and actual behavior in various situations. People who score toward the internal end of the scale are, on average, more likely than those who score toward the external end to try to control their own fate. They are more likely to take preventive health care measures (Reich & others, 1997); to seek information on how to protect themselves during a tornado warning (Sims & Baumann, 1972); to resist group pressures to conform in laboratory tests of conformity (Crowne & Liverant, 1963); and to prefer games of skill over games of chance (Schneider, 1972).

Other research has indicated that people who score toward the internal end of the scale are, on average, less anxious and more content with life than those who score toward the external end (Phares, 1978, 1984). Of course, as with all correlational research, we cannot be sure what is cause and what is effect. Does a sense of control promote hard work, success, and happiness; or do hard work, success, and happiness promote a sense of control? Most social-cognitive theorists would contend that both causal hypotheses are correct to some degree.

Beliefs About One's Own Ability to Perform Specific Tasks

Another pioneer of the social-cognitive perspective on personality is Albert Bandura, who, like Rotter, earned a degree in clinical psychology and then went on to a career of laboratory research. Some of Bandura's early research on social learning is described in Chapter 4. Much of Bandura's more recent research centers on people's beliefs about their own ability to perform specific tasks, which he refers to as *self-efficacy*. People who expect that they can perform a certain task are said to have high self-efficacy about the task, and people who expect the opposite are said to have low self-efficacy about it.

Self-efficacy may sound similar to locus of control, but Bandura (1997) considers the two to be distinct. Self-efficacy refers to the person's sense of his or her own ability, while locus of control refers to the person's sense of whether or not that ability will produce rewards. Although self-efficacy and an internal locus of control usually go together, they do not always. If you believe, for example, that you are skilled at math but that the skill is worthless (perhaps because it is unrecognized by your math professor or others in society), then you have high self-efficacy but an external locus of control in that area. Conversely, if you believe that skill at math would bring rewards but that you don't have the skill, then you have low self-efficacy and an internal locus of control in that area. Self-efficacy may be quite specific to a very narrow range of tasks or quite general over a broad range of tasks (Cervone, 1997; Welch & West, 1995). For instance, a person might have high or low self-efficacy for intellectual tasks in general or for athletic tasks in general.

Bandura and his colleagues have repeatedly demonstrated that improved self-efficacy for a task predicts improvement in actual performance of the task. In one study, for example, various treatments were used to help people overcome their fear of snakes. The subjects who claimed after treatment that they now expected to be able to pick up and handle a large snake were indeed most likely to succeed at the task, regardless of which treatment they had received (Bandura & others, 1977). Correlations between changes in self-efficacy and changes in performance have likewise been found for such diverse tasks as arithmetic problems (Schunk & Hanson, 1985) and physical exertion on an exercise machine (Bandura & Cervone, 1983).

Bandura's concept of self-efficacy implies that educational and child-rearing methods highlighting the person's abilities or successes will lead to greater success than methods highlighting inabilities or failures. This implication is based on the assumption that self-efficacy helps *cause* improved performance and is not simply a by-product of it. Perhaps the most compelling evidence for this assumption comes from experiments in which subjects were asked to solve problems that were actually unsolvable. Those subjects who were misled into believing that they could solve the problems, and who therefore developed high self-efficacy concerning them, persisted longer at trying to solve the problems than did those who had not been deceived in this way (Bandura, 1982; Schunk, 1984). Such studies provide a plausible chain through which self-efficacy may affect success on solvable problems:

High self-efficacy → increased effort or persistence → success

The Power of Positive Thinking

Much has been written, by psychologists and nonpsychologists alike, about the benefits of a positive, optimistic outlook on life (Cousins, 1977; Peale, 1956; Seligman, 1990). You have just read of research indicating that people who believe in their own abilities and believe that their abilities will be rewarded are on average more successful than people who don't have those beliefs.

A number of psychologists have developed questionnaires designed to assess people's general tendency to think positively or negatively. C. Rick Snyder (1994) and his colleagues developed a questionnaire to assess hope, which they construe as a belief in one's ability to solve solvable problems (generalized self-efficacy) combined with a belief that most problems in life are solvable. Martin Seligman (1990)

37.

How does self-efficacy differ from locus of control?

38.

What evidence supports the theory that high self-efficacy (a) predicts high performance and (b) may help cause high performance?

39.

What evidence supports the value of optimism, and through what mechanism might optimism produce its beneficial effects?

and his colleagues developed a questionnaire to assess the degree to which people explain negative events in their lives in a pessimistic or optimistic manner (discussed in relation to theories of depression in Chapter 16). Michael Scheier and Charles Carver (1993) developed a questionnaire to assess dispositional optimism, the tendency to believe in a rosy future. On the questionnaire, people indicate the degree to which they agree or disagree with such statements as "In uncertain times, I usually expect the best."

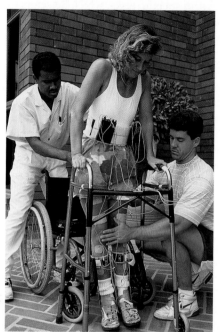

A. Ramey / Stock, Boston

Optimism

The belief that one can overcome adversity may become a self-fulfilling prophesy if that belief leads to effective actions. This woman, the victim of a drunk driver, works hard at strengthening her legs so she can walk again.

Correlational studies using all these questionnaires have shown that, in general, people with an optimistic style of thought tend to cope more effectively with life's stressors than do people who have a pessimistic style (Peterson, 2000; Schneider, 2001; Snyder, 1994). In one such study, Scheier and his colleagues (1989) used their questionnaire to assess dispositional optimism in middle-aged men who were about to undergo coronary artery bypass surgery. They found that those who scored high on optimism before the surgery made quicker recoveries than did those who scored low, even when the medical conditions that led to surgery were equivalent. The optimists were quicker to sit up on their own, to walk, to resume vigorous exercise, and to get back to work full-time than were the pessimists. The most likely explanation for this and other positive correlations with optimism is that optimistic thinking leads people to devote attention and energy to solving their problems or recovering from their disabilities, which in turn leads to positive results. Pessimists are relatively more likely to say, "It won't work out anyway, so why try?" A more controversial idea is that optimistic thinking and psychological equanimity in general may facilitate physical health and recovery through direct effects on body chemistry (discussed in Chapter 16).

Adaptive and Maladaptive Optimism and Pessimism

Before concluding that optimism is always best, before rushing out to trade the clear lenses on our glasses for rose-tinted ones, we should consider a potential hazard of optimism. Health psychologists have long pointed out the danger of unrealistic, self-delusional forms of optimism. Many people, especially adolescents and young adults, optimistically believe that they are invulnerable to such catastrophes as AIDS, lung cancer, drug addiction, or maiming through an automobile accident and fail to take precautions to avoid such dangers (Schwarzer, 1994; Weinstein, 1980, 1982). Optimism of this sort, which in the psychodynamic tradition is called *defensive optimism*, may reduce anxiety by diverting thoughts away from fearful possibilities but may also lead to serious harm. The optimistic belief that you can control your fate through active self-care usually leads to constructive behaviors, but the optimistic belief that fate will protect you without your participation can lead to dangerously imprudent behaviors.

Just as optimism can be adaptive or maladaptive, depending on whether or not it translates into constructive action, so can pessimism. In research on the cognitive underpinnings of success in college, Julie Norem and her colleagues found students who use apparently opposite mental strategies to perform well academically (Norem & Illingworth, 1993). Some students use an adaptive form of optimism. They believe they will do well; and that belief, coupled with their thoughts about

40.

What seems to differentiate adaptive from maladaptive optimism and adaptive from maladaptive pessimism?

TALES OF THE OVERLY OPTIMISTIC...

I THINK I CAN
I THINK I CAN
I THINK I CAN
I THINK I CAN
I THINK I CAN...

WILEY 1-2

the positive consequences of doing well, motivates them to work hard and actually do well. Other students, however, use an adaptive form of pessimism. They believe they will not do well, despite having done well in the past; and that belief, along with thoughts about the negative consequences of failure, motivates them to work hard to avoid failure. As a result, and apparently to their surprise, they not only pass but achieve high grades. Still, the optimists are probably better off in the long run than the pessimists. One study of adjustment to college life revealed that the pessimists' constant anxiety about failure led them to focus too narrowly on grades and lose the intrinsic pleasure of academic work (Cantor & Harlow, 1994).

The Humanistic Perspective: The Self and Life's Meanings

Social-cognitive theories of personality, with their emphasis on styles of thinking, are sometimes criticized for not considering the person as a whole, unique, integrated entity. The concepts in such theories derive largely from laboratory research, in which one group is compared with another on some task or measure and no attempt is made to understand any one individual in depth. In contrast, *humanistic theories* of personality attempt to focus attention on the whole, unique person, especially on the person's conscious understanding of his or her self and the world. They are called *humanistic* because they center on an aspect of human nature that seems to distinguish us clearly from other animals—our tendency to create belief systems, meaningful stories about ourselves and our world, and to govern our lives in accordance with those stories.

While social-cognitive theorists view beliefs primarily as internal causes of the person's actions in the physical world, humanistic theorists are interested in beliefs for their own sake, as part of the person's experiences. *Phenomenology* is the study of conscious perceptions and understandings, and humanistic theorists use the term *phenomenological reality* to refer to each person's conscious understanding of his or her world. Humanistic theorists commonly claim that one's phenomenological reality is one's real world; it provides the basis for the person's contentment or lack of contentment and for the meaning that he or she finds in life. In the words of one of the leaders of humanistic psychology, Carl Rogers (1980): "The only reality you can possibly know is the world as you perceive and experience it. . . . And the only certainty is that those perceived realities are different. There are as many 'real worlds' as there are people."

41.

How, in general, do humanistic theories differ from social-cognitive theories? How does the concept of phenomenological reality figure into humanistic theories?

Carl Rogers

Rogers's humanistic theory centers on the self-concept and the ways in which it can be distorted by socially imposed conditions of worth.

42.

What human drive is posited by Rogers's self theory?

43.

How are research findings concerning people's use of medical advice consistent with Rogers's theory?

Self-actualization

Humanistic theorists draw an analogy between the self-actualization process in humans and the inner growth potential of all living things. This beech tree has long been using its environment to promote its own growth, and these children have for a much shorter time been doing the same.

44.

What is Maslow's theory about the relationship among various human needs, and how might the theory be reconciled with an evolutionary perspective?

Being One's Self; Making One's Own Decisions

According to most humanistic theories, a central aspect of one's phenomenological reality is the *self-concept*, the person's understanding of who he or she is. Carl Rogers referred to his own version of humanistic theory as *self theory*. He claimed that at first he avoided the construct of self because it seemed unscientific but was forced to consider it through listening to his clients in therapy sessions. Person after person would say, in effect, "I feel I am not being my real self"; "I wouldn't want anyone to know the real me"; "I wonder who I am." From such statements, Rogers (1959) gradually came to believe that a concept of self is a crucial part of a person's phenomenological reality and that a common goal of people is to "discover their real selves" and "become their real selves." According to Rogers, people often are diverted from becoming themselves by the demands and judgments placed upon them by other people, particularly by authority figures such as parents and teachers. To be oneself, according to Rogers, is to live life according to one's own wishes rather than someone else's.

As would be predicted by Rogers's theory, researchers have found that people who feel as if a decision is fully their own, made freely by themselves, are more likely to follow through and act on it effectively than are people who feel that someone else made the decision for them. People who think and talk about their intention to lose weight, stop smoking, or take prescribed medicines on schedule as "following the doctor's orders" are less likely to succeed at such goals than are people who think and talk about the decision as their own (Ryan & Deci, 2000; Williams & others, 1995, 1996). These findings have induced some medical professionals to avoid giving orders and to provide information and suggestions in such a way as to make it clear that any decision on how to act is up to the patient. Experiments indicate that such tactics do increase the likelihood that people will follow a healthful medical regimen (Williams & Deci, 1996).

Self-Actualization and Maslow's Hierarchy of Human Needs

Humanistic theorists use the term **self-actualization** to refer to the process of becoming one's full self, that is, realizing one's dreams and capabilities. The specific route to self-actualization will vary from person to person and from time to time within a person's lifetime, but for each individual the route must be self-chosen.

Rogers (1963, 1977) often compared self-actualization in humans to physical growth in plants. A tree growing on a cliff by the sea must battle against the wind and saltwater and does not grow as well as it would in a more favorable setting, yet its inner potential continues to operate and it grows as well as it can under the circumstances. Nobody can tell the tree how to grow; its growth potential lies within itself. Humanistic theorists hold that full growth, full actualization, requires a fertile environment. But the direction of actualization and the ways of using the environment must come from within the organism. In the course of evolution, organisms have acquired the capacity to use the environment in ways that maximize growth. In humans, the capacity to make free, conscious choices that promote positive psychological growth is the actualizing tendency. To grow best, individuals must be permitted to make those choices and must trust themselves to do so.

Another humanistic psychologist, Abraham Maslow (1970), suggested that to self-actualize, one must satisfy five sets of needs that can be arranged in a hierarchy (see Figure 15.7). From bottom to top, they are (1) physiological needs (the minimal essentials for life, such as food and water); (2) safety needs (protection from dangers in the environment); (3) attachment needs (belongingness and love); (4) esteem

FIGURE **15.7** *Maslow's hierarchy of human needs*
According to Maslow, needs at the lower portion of the hierarchy must be at least relatively satisfied before people can satisfy needs higher up. The most psychologically healthy people are those whose deficiency needs are sufficiently satisfied to free their energies for self-actualization.

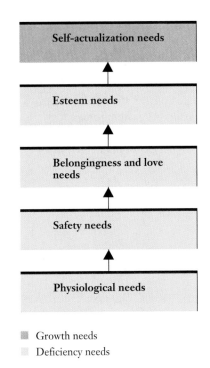

Growth needs
Deficiency needs

needs (competence, respect from others and the self); and (5) self-actualization needs. In Maslow's view, the self-actualization needs encompass the needs for self-expression, creativity, and "a sense of connectedness with the broader universe." Maslow argued that a person can focus on higher needs only if lower ones, which are more immediately linked to survival, are sufficiently satisfied so that they do not claim the person's full attention and energy.

Maslow's needs hierarchy makes some sense from an evolutionary perspective. The physiological and safety needs are most basic in that they are most immediately linked to survival. If one is starving or dehydrated, or if a tiger is charging, then survival depends immediately upon devoting one's full resources to solving that problem. The social needs for belongingness, love, and esteem are also linked to survival, though not in quite as direct and immediate a fashion. We need to maintain good social relationships with others to ensure their future cooperation in meeting our physiological and safety needs and in helping us reproduce. The self-actualization needs are best construed, from an evolutionary perspective, as *self-educative needs*. Playing, exploring, and creating can lead to the acquisition of skills and knowledge that help one later in such endeavors as obtaining food, fending off predators, attracting mates, and securing the goodwill and protection of the community. From this perspective, self-actualization is not ultimately higher than the other needs but is part of the long-term human system for satisfying those needs.

The Life Story or Personal Myth as a Basis for Personality

People strive to make sense of their lives as a whole, and they may establish goals and make choices in accordance with that larger conception. One way to learn about individual people, which is gaining increasing acceptance by psychologists, is to ask them to tell their life stories. On the basis of his analysis of many such stories, Dan McAdams (1993, 1994) contends that the formats of the stories generally share certain characteristics, though the contents vary greatly. Each story contains themes and subthemes, morals, subordinate characters who influence the main character (the self), conflicts that get resolved, and a relatively consistent narrative tone (such as serious or lighthearted). The stories are not simply chronological chains of events but, rather, are integrated wholes in which events are related to one another with themes pertaining to larger life purposes or a sense of personal destiny. The integrating themes are creations of the storyteller.

McAdams refers to the self-told story as a **personal myth** because it seems to provide for the individual what religious myths provide for whole cultures. It gives a sense of direction and meaning to life. People understand and explain individual events in their lives in terms of how they fit into their larger life stories, and they make new decisions that are consistent with their stories. In their research, McAdams and his colleagues have found positive correlations between the coherence of people's life stories and measures of their mental health (Baerger & McAdams, 1999).

The personal myth changes with time and experience, usually gradually but sometimes dramatically and quickly. As circumstances change, the story may change to accommodate the new situation (Baumeister, 1994; McAdams, 1994). For instance, a couple's first meeting may be understood and described in romantic terms as part of their life destiny when the couple is happily married, but years

45.

How is the life-story conception of personality consistent with the humanistic theorists' focus on phenomenology and a holistic approach to the person?

46.

How does the life-story approach to personality differ from the trait approach in its conclusions about the modifiability of personality in adulthood?

later, when the couple is divorced, the same meeting might be described as an interfering accident, a digression from the meaningful life course (Vaughan, 1986). From a phenomenological perspective, neither understanding is right or wrong; each is a way of making sense of one's current and ongoing life.

In a study of personal transformation, William Miller and Janet C'deBaca (1994) advertised for volunteers "who have been transformed in a relatively short period of time—who have had a deep shift in core values, feelings, attitudes, or actions." They had no trouble finding people who claimed to have had such an experience at some time in their lives, and they interviewed extensively 55 such people. Each story of change was different, but some common themes emerged. In general, these people saw themselves as acquiring over a short period of time, often less than 24 hours, a dramatic and lasting new insight, a new way of understanding themselves and their purpose in life. Usually they described themselves as emotionally distressed before the new insight and relieved and happy after it. Usually they described the change as liberating and involving a shift in values. Most often the shift was from worldly values—such as wealth, achievement, adventure, fitting in, and attractiveness—to social and spiritual values—such as honesty, generosity, personal peace, and obedience to God's will. Such changes occurred for different people at very different ages and in response to a wide variety of life events.

If personality is defined phenomenologically as one's self-told story, then personality can apparently change dramatically at any time in adulthood. Traits such as the Big Five, measured by standard personality tests, may not change much as people grow older and move from one life experience to another. But through their personal myths people can apparently acquire new ways of understanding and employing those traits at any time in life—new meanings, new self-definitions, and new life goals.

The Cultural Relativity of Personality Theories

47.

In what ways are psychodynamic, humanistic, and social-cognitive theories all limited by their focus on a nonrepresentative sample of humanity?

Personality theories are commonly presented by their proponents as if they apply to human beings in general, but the observations on which the theories are based usually do not justify such generality. The theories are products of the minds of psychologists and psychiatrists raised and trained in Western Europe and North America. They are designed largely to explain the behavior and verbal statements of the small subgroups of people within those cultures who seek out psychotherapy or serve as subjects in psychology laboratories at universities. Such people represent a relatively small minority of the human beings on earth, and theories derived from that minority may not apply to everyone.

Consider, for example, the group of patients who inspired Freud's psychoanalytic theory of personality. For the most part they were wealthy citizens of Vienna who had the leisure and inclination to reflect on their childhoods, on subtleties of their sex lives and social interactions, and on other such topics that might have been of less concern to people struggling to put food on the table. Those patients were also, almost by definition, people who suffered from some form of anxiety, which led them to seek Freud out for psychotherapy. Freud's theory, with its focus on anxiety and manifestations of the sex drive, might be understood as a sort of generalized personal myth, helpful to his clients and others like them in making sense of their concerns but hardly a universal theory of human nature.

Similarly, almost all humanistic and social-cognitive theorists have been highly educated North Americans and Europeans, brought up in philosophical traditions focusing on individuality and self-determination. As Hope Landrine (1992) has pointed out, middle-class Westerners, especially North Americans—the kind of people who would have gone to Carl Rogers for therapy—tend to think of the *self* as a kind of god. The self is implicitly understood as a spirit that resides within the person, that makes decisions, that speaks to the person, that should be listened to and followed, that should be exalted and praised.

As described in Chapter 13, people in non-Western cultures are less likely than Westerners to think of themselves as separate entities from their families, communities, and other social settings (Cross & Markus, 1999). Their gods, to be praised and listened to, are more likely to reside outside themselves than inside and to be shared by other members of the community. The godlike autonomous self may be a meaningful part of the personal myth of people raised in middle- to upper-class Western cultures but not so meaningful for those raised in other cultures. Cross-cultural research conducted to date suggests that such self-related cognitive constructs as internal locus of control, self-efficacy, and personal optimism do not have the same meanings to people raised in non-Western traditions as to those raised in Western traditions (Heine & Lehman, 1995; Smith & others, 1995). In one study, for example, an optimistic belief in one's own abilities correlated positively with problem solving for Caucasian Americans but not for Asian-Americans (Chang, 1996). In fact, among the Asian-Americans, those who expressed pessimism about their own abilities performed somewhat better than those who expressed optimism.

Trait theories of the person achieve a degree of universality by focusing on very general dispositions, which characterize people everywhere. Theories that add more specific mental content to the description of the person—including the psychodynamic, social-cognitive, and humanistic theories described in this chapter—are likely to apply to some groups more than to others.

Cultural relativity
of personality training

In the American art class (left-hand photo), a major goal is to allow children to express their individuality. In the Chinese art class (right-hand photo), a major goal is to impart traditional Chinese artistic methods so that the children's paintings will resemble the model. Such differences in expectations and training lead children in China and the United States to develop different personality styles.

SECTION SUMMARY

Whereas trait theories attempt to describe the differences among individuals in terms of a relatively small number of central traits, other theories—classed as psychodynamic, social cognitive, and humanistic—attempt to explain individual differences in terms of people's mental processes and beliefs.

Freud's psychodynamic theory, called psychoanalysis, posits that the main causes of human behavior lie in the unconscious mind, especially in the unconscious aspects of the sexual and aggressive drives. Freud believed that individuals' unconscious minds can be understood by analyzing clues that occur in slips of the tongue, dreams, and uncensored thoughts. All psychodynamic theories focus on the unconscious mind, but the theories after Freud's place relatively less emphasis on sex and aggression and more on other drives. Horney's theory and object relations theories focus on the drive for secure interpersonal relationships; Adler's theory focuses on the drive to feel competent; and Erikson's theory posits a set of social motives, each of which becomes more active at a particular life stage. A central concept of all psychodynamic theories is that of defense mechanisms—psychological processes designed to reduce anxiety by minimizing one's consciousness of upsetting ideas. Vaillant classified defense mechanisms according to the degree to which they distort reality and found, in a long-term study, that men who used the most mature defenses (that is, who distorted reality the least) were, on average, happiest and most successful.

Social-cognitive theories attempt to account for individual differences in terms of learned beliefs or habits of thought that predispose people to react in particular ways. Internal locus of control refers to the tendency to believe that one's fate depends on one's own actions. Self-efficacy refers to one's sense of competence in performing certain tasks or sets of tasks. Optimism refers to one's tendency to believe that things will work out for the best, and pessimism refers to one's tendency to expect the worst. Research has shown that all these beliefs promote effective functioning to the degree that they lead people to work hard at tasks and to take appropriate precautions.

Humanistic theories focus on people's phenomenological reality—that is, on their conscious understandings of themselves and their world—and on the value of acting in accordance with one's own wishes and motives. Rogers found evidence that people feel best and function best when they feel that they are "being themselves," or behaving in accordance with their own wishes. Maslow posited a needs hierarchy, with self-actualizing needs—having to do with being fully oneself—at the top. McAdams and others have studied personality by having people tell their own life stories. From the humanistic perspective, such stories, or personal myths, are important aspects of the person, whether or not they are objectively true.

Psychodynamic, social-cognitive, and humanistic theories have been developed primarily by Western psychologists working with psychiatric patients or university students. The theories emphasize Western values of individuality and autonomy that may not apply so well to the rest of the world.

CONCLUDING THOUGHTS

In this chapter you read of ideas about how personality can be described, why personalities differ across individuals, and how personality differences might be understood in terms of mental processes. Two general ideas might help you organize your thinking as you review the particular ideas of the chapter:

48.

What two general themes are proposed for organizing a review of the specific ideas of the chapter?

1. The varying purposes of personality theories   Different personality theories have been developed to serve different purposes. Trait theorists try to distill the essential personality dimensions common to all people, while clinical theorists try to discover the mental processes and beliefs that help or hinder people in coping with life's demands.

Trait theories, such as the Big Five theory, are attempts to describe human diversity in personality objectively and efficiently, by identifying a set of global traits and a means of measuring them. The trait measures, usually made with questionnaires, are used in studies comparing one group of people with another, such as firstborns with later-borns, men with women, or people in one career with those in another. They are also used clinically (as explained in Chapter 17) as a first approximation to describing the personality of individuals. Trait theories do not explain personality but just describe its elements.

Psychodynamic, humanistic, and social-cognitive theories, in contrast, were designed to explain the particular behaviors, emotions, and thoughts of individual people, especially of people undergoing psychotherapy. Psychodynamic theories explain personality in terms of unconscious motives and defenses against anxiety. Humanistic theories explain personality in terms of people's subjective understanding of themselves and their world and their strivings for self-actualization. Social-cognitive theories also attempt to explain the behavior of individuals in terms of their beliefs but take a less holistic approach than do either humanistic or psychodynamic theories. Social-cognitive theorists are more often academic research psychologists than clinicians, and their interest tends to center more on a specific mental construct (such as locus of control) than on individuals as whole entities.

2.   A functionalist perspective on individual differences   Because of the close tie between personality research and clinical research, personality theories have often been concerned with distinctions between healthy (or adaptive) and unhealthy (or maladaptive) personality styles. This concern is reflected in such distinctions as that between mature and immature defenses or between adaptive and maladaptive forms of optimism. Another way to think about personality differences is as adaptations for or to different niches or different strategies for solving life's problems, in which case two quite different styles might be equally healthy or adaptive. In this chapter you saw examples of this functionalist view reflected especially in research and theories concerning the effects of birth order and gender on personality. As you review each of the dimensions of personality differences discussed in the chapter—including differences in defensive style, locus of control, and optimistic versus pessimistic thinking, as well as the Big Five traits—think about ways in which variation in either direction could be either adaptive or maladaptive, depending on one's life circumstances.

Further Reading

William Wright (1998). *Born that way: Genes, behavior, personality.* New York: Knopf.

This book is about the revolution in psychology's understanding of personality that was brought about by the Minnesota twin study and other behavioral-genetic research beginning in the late 1970s. It is not so much about science as about the researchers themselves and the antigene political climate they had to contend with in order to conduct and publish their studies. It is lively, inspiring, and fun to read.

Frank Sulloway (1996). *Born to rebel: Birth order, family dynamics, and creative lives.* New York: Pantheon.

Sulloway elaborates here on his theory of the influence of birth order on personality and presents the historical and psychological evidence from which he developed it. The narrative is enriched by illustrations from the lives of many well-known rebels and reformers whose dispositions originated, according to Sulloway, in their interactions with their older siblings.

Sigmund Freud (1901; reprinted 1960). *The psychopathology of everyday life* (J. Strachey, Ed.; A. Tyson, Trans.). New York: Norton.

This is one of Freud's most popular and fun-to-read books. It is full of anecdotes having to do with forgetting, slips of the tongue, and bungled actions. In each anecdote, Freud argues that an apparent mistake was really an expression of an unconscious wish.

Martin E. P. Seligman (1990). *Learned optimism.* New York: Knopf.

In this book for nonspecialists, Seligman, a leading social-cognitive researcher, distinguishes between pessimistic and optimistic explanatory styles, discusses the origins and life consequences of these styles, and suggests applications for child rearing and self-improvement.

Dan P. McAdams (1993). *The stories we live by: Personal myths and the making of the self.* New York: Morrow.

On the basis of his extensive interviewing of people about their life stories and his study of autobiographies, McAdams describes how personal myths develop, how they change with experience, and how they guide and create experience. One particularly interesting segment deals with the evolution of Karen Horney's personal story, beginning when she was a young girl, and the role that story played in her career as a pioneering psychoanalyst.

Looking Ahead

The personality theories you have read about in this chapter were all developed at least partly as a way of understanding people's psychological problems. The remaining two chapters focus directly on such problems. Chapter 16 deals with issues of defining, categorizing, and explaining mental disorders. Chapter 17 deals with the treatment of mental disorders, and there you will see how various theories of personality specify different approaches to psychotherapy.

Chapter 16

Melancholy, Edvard Munch

Mental Disorders

A theme running through this book is that psychological processes are usually adaptive; that is, they usually promote survival and well-being. Drives and emotions, including those experienced as discomforting or painful, typically motivate survival-enhancing actions; perceptions provide useful information to guide such actions; and thoughts produce effective plans for actions. But sometimes these processes break down and become maladaptive: Drives become too strong, too weak, or misdirected; emotions become overwhelming; perceptions become inaccurate; thoughts become confused; and behavior becomes ineffective. All of us experience such disturbances occasionally to some degree and accept them as a normal part of life. But sometimes such disturbances are so strong, prolonged, or recurrent that they seriously interfere with a person's ability to live a satisfying life. Then the person is said to have a mental disorder.

BASIC CONCEPTS

Mental disorder is a fuzzy concept, impossible to define in a precise way. This should come as no surprise. Most concepts, if you think about them, are fuzzy. Try to define precisely, for example, such an everyday concept as a chair. Some things are clearly chairs, and others, like the rock you sometimes sit on in the park, are only "sort of" chairs. Every attempt to define *mental disorder* raises controversy.

The most frequently used definition today is that which appears in the current (fourth, text-revised) edition of the *Diagnostic and Statistical Manual of Mental Disorders*, referred to as *DSM-IV*, the American Psychiatric Association's official guide for diagnosing mental disorders. This definition treats mental disorders as analogous to medical diseases and borrows from medicine the terms *symptom* and *syndrome*. A *symptom* is any characteristic of a person's actions, thoughts, or feelings that could be a potential indicator of a mental disorder; and a *syndrome* is a constellation of interrelated symptoms manifested by a given individual. According to *DSM-IV* (American Psychiatric Association, 2000), a syndrome may be taken as evidence of a mental disorder if, and only if, it satisfies the following criteria:

+ *Clinically significant detriment* The syndrome must involve *distress* (painful feelings) or *impairment of functioning* (interference with ability to work, play, or get along with people) or both, and it must be *clinically significant*, meaning that the distress or impairment must be serious enough to warrant professional treatment.

+ *Internal source* The source of distress or impairment must be located within the person, that is, in the person's biology, mental structure (ways of perceiving, thinking, or feeling), or learned habits, and not just in the person's immediate environment. The disturbance in biology or way of thinking or acting

1.

How is the concept of mental disorder defined by the American Psychiatric Association, and what ambiguities lie in that definition?

Cleo Freelance / Jeroboam, Inc.

Mental distress or mental disorder?

Feelings of sadness, pessimism, and low self-esteem are evident here, but is the source of the distress the situation or something inside the person? This question is central to defining the concept mental disorder.

may have been caused by past environmental circumstances and may be aggravated by present circumstances, but the distress cannot be simply an expectable reaction to present circumstances, such as despondency brought on by poverty or a period of grief brought on by the death of a loved one.

+ ***Involuntary manifestation***   The syndrome cannot be understood as a deliberate, voluntary decision to act in a manner contrary to the norms of society. Thus, a person who voluntarily undergoes starvation to protest a government policy is not considered to have a mental disorder.

Although these criteria are useful guidelines for thinking about and identifying mental disorders, they are by nature ambiguous and in some cases seem to be contradicted by the descriptions of particular disorders in *DSM-IV* (Widiger, 1997a, 1997b; Widiger & Sankis, 2000). Just how "distressing" or "impairing" must a syndrome be to be considered "clinically significant"? Since all behavior involves an interaction between the person and the environment, how can we tell whether the impairment is really within the person, rather than just in the environment? For example, in the case of someone living in poverty or experiencing discrimination, how can we tell if the person's actions are normal responses to those conditions or represent something more? When people claim they are deliberately choosing to behave in a way that violates social norms and could behave normally if they wanted to, how do we know when to believe them? Who has the right to decide whether a person is or is not mentally disordered: the person, the person's family, a psychiatrist or psychologist, a court of law, a health insurance administrator who must approve or not approve payment for therapy? These are tough questions that can never be answered strictly scientifically. The answers always represent human judgments, and they are always tinged by the social values and pragmatic concerns of those doing the judging.

Categorization and Diagnosis of Mental Disorders

We humans are inveterate categorizers. Rarely do we see an unfamiliar object or event as completely new and unique; instead, we see it as a member of some familiar category—a chair, a fruit, a party. Our world is more predictable and describable when we can relate each new object and event to a familiar category, even if the categories are fuzzy and the boundaries arbitrary. This same response applies in the realm of mental disorders. Beginning long before the era of modern psychology and psychiatry, people everywhere have had systems for categorizing and labeling their psychological miseries. In keeping with the common Western practice of likening mental disorders to physical diseases, the process of assigning a label to a person's mental disorder is referred to as *diagnosis*.

Classification and diagnosis are essential to the scientific study of mental disorders. Without a system to identify people whose disorders are similar to each other, the accumulation of knowledge about causes, effective treatments, and eventual outcomes would be impossible. But such a system is useful only to the degree that it is reliable and valid.

The Quest for Reliability: Development of DSM-IV

The *reliability* of a diagnostic system refers to the extent to which different diagnosticians, all trained in the use of the system, reach the same conclusion when they independently diagnose the same individuals. If you have ever gone to two different doctors with a physical complaint and been given two different, nonsynonymous labels for your disease, you know that, even in the realm of physical disorders, diagnosis is by no means completely reliable.

From the late-nineteenth to the mid-twentieth century, various methods of categorizing and labeling mental disorders emerged in Europe and North America. One commonly used system divided mental disorders into two main categories:

2.

What does reliability mean with reference to a diagnostic system, and how did the developers of recent versions of the DSM strive to increase reliability?

neuroses, in which anxiety is the underlying problem but the person is still in touch with reality, and *psychoses*, in which marked distortions in perception or thought render the person seriously out of touch with reality. Within these broad categories, certain terms for more specific disorders also became common, such as *phobia* as a type of neurosis and *schizophrenia* as a type of psychosis. But in general there was no agreed-upon way of defining these or other classes of disorders, and thus no agreed-upon diagnostic system.

To promote more effective communication in the rapidly growing mental health field, the American Psychiatric Association published, in 1952, the first edition of the *Diagnostic and Statistical Manual of Mental Disorders (DSM)*, which was intended to be a standardized system for labeling and diagnosing mental disorders. The first revision of the manual, *DSM-II*, appeared in 1968. Both editions were quite slim; diagnostic categories were defined briefly, in general terms, and much was left to the judgment of individual diagnosticians. Many of the categories were based on tenuous assumptions about the inner causes of the disorders, taken largely from Freud's psychoanalytic theory. For example, some disorders within the general category "neuroses" were defined in terms of unconscious anxiety and defenses against it, even though anxiety was not an observable symptom. The result was that studies aimed at assessing diagnostic reliability with those versions of the DSM revealed very little of it. For some categories, in fact, reliability was barely greater than would be expected if the labels had been assigned randomly (Matarazzo, 1983; Spitzer & Fleiss, 1974). Clearly, the manual needed major revision.

Hundreds of psychiatrists, clinical psychologists, and other mental health professionals worked in teams to create *DSM-III*, a much thicker volume published in 1980. Their goal was to define mental disorders as objectively as possible so as to remove as much guesswork as possible from the task of diagnosis and thereby increase diagnostic reliability. To do this, they dropped *DSM-II* categories that were based on unobservable symptoms or inferred causes (including the overriding categories "neuroses" and "psychoses") and formulated new categories in terms of symptoms that an unbiased clinician or researcher could observe in the subject or learn from the subject by asking appropriate questions. To test alternative ways of diagnosing each disorder, they conducted field studies in which subjects who might have a particular disorder were diagnosed independently by a number of clinicians or researchers using each of several alternative diagnostic systems. In general, the systems that produced the greatest reliability—that is, the greatest agreement among the diagnosticians as to who had or did not have a particular disorder—were retained. As a result, the diagnostic reliability of *DSM-III* was quite high—comparable in many cases to the levels achieved in diagnosing physical disorders (Matarazzo, 1983; Segal & Coolidge, 2001). The manual was updated somewhat and reissued as *DSM-III-R* in 1987. The fourth edition, *DSM-IV*, also a relatively minor revision but based on extensive research, appeared in 1994 and was slightly modified in 2000. (The modified version is referred to as the text-revised edition of *DSM-IV*.)

As an example of diagnostic criteria specified in *DSM-IV*, consider those for *anorexia nervosa*, an eating disorder that can result in self-starvation. The person must (a) refuse to maintain body weight at or above a minimally normal weight for age and height; (b) express an intense fear of gaining weight or becoming fat; (c) manifest a disturbance in the experience of her or his own body weight or shape, show an undue influence of body weight or shape on self-evaluation, or deny the seriousness of the current low body weight; and (d) if a postpubertal female, have missed at least three successive menstrual periods (a condition brought on by a lack of body fat). If any of these criteria are not met, a diagnosis of anorexia nervosa would not be made. Notice that all these criteria are based on observable characteristics or self-descriptions by the person being diagnosed; none rely on inferences about underlying causes or unconscious symptoms that could easily result in disagreement among diagnosticians who have different perspectives.

3.

How can the validity of the DSM be improved through research and further revisions?

The Question of Validity

The *validity* of a diagnostic system is an index of the extent to which the categories it identifies are clinically meaningful (see Chapter 2 for a more general discussion of both validity and reliability). Do two people with the same diagnosis truly suffer in similar ways? Does their suffering stem from similar causes? Does the label help predict the future course of the disorder and help in deciding on a beneficial treatment? To the degree that questions like these can be answered in the affirmative, a diagnostic system is valid.

Some psychologists and psychiatrists argue that the creators of *DSM-III* and *DSM-IV* sacrificed validity for the sake of reliability (Wakefield, 1992). They contend that the effort to attain agreement among different diagnosticians led to an emphasis on superficial symptoms at the expense of more basic underlying symptoms or causes, which must be inferred through subjective clinical judgments. Others, however—especially those who are engaged in systematic research on mental disorders—counter that reliability is a prerequisite for validity (Wilson, 1993). In order to conduct the research needed to determine whether or not a diagnosis is

---

TABLE **16.1**   *Summary of DSM-IV categories of mental disorders*

Anxiety disorders* Disorders in which fear or anxiety is a prominent symptom. Examples: *generalized anxiety disorder, phobias, obsessive-compulsive disorder, panic disorder,* and *posttraumatic stress disorder.*

Mood disorders* Disorders marked by depression or mania. Examples: *major depression, dysthymia, bipolar disorder,* and *cyclothymia.*

Somatoform disorders* Disorders involving physical (somatic) symptoms arising from unconscious psychological processes. Examples: *conversion disorder* and *somatization disorder.*

Substance-related disorders* Disorders brought on by drugs such as alcohol, amphetamines, cocaine, or opiates. Examples: intoxicating effects, withdrawal effects, dependence (the intense craving for the drug), and effects of brain damage caused by prolonged use of the drug.

Dissociative disorders* Disorders in which a part of one's experience is separated off (dissociated) from one's conscious memory or identity. Examples: *psychogenic amnesia, fugue states,* and *dissociative identity disorder.*

Schizophrenia and other psychotic disorders* *Schizophrenia* is marked by delusions, hallucinations, disorganized thought and speech, and flattened or inappropriate affect. Another psychotic disorder is *delusional disorder,* which involves persistent delusions (usually of persecution) *not* accompanied by other disruptions of thought or mood that would lead to a diagnosis of schizophrenia.

Sexual and gender identity disorders *Sexual disorders* are those of sexual functioning, and include *paraphilias* (in which bizarre imagery or acts are necessary for sexual excitement, such as *fetishism, exhibitionism,* and *sexual sadism*) and *psychosexual dysfunctions* (inability to become sexually aroused or to complete intercourse in a satisfying way). *Gender identity disorders* involve a strong and persistent desire to be, or appear to be, a member of the other gender.

Eating disorders Disorders marked by extreme undereating, overeating, or purging or by excessive concern about gaining weight. Examples: *anorexia nervosa* and *bulimia nervosa.*

Sleep disorders Disorders include *insomnia* (too little sleep), *hypersomnia* (too much sleep), *sleep-wake disorder* (inability to establish a sleep-wake cycle corresponding with the 24-hour day), and disorders involving sleepwalking, fear of sleep, or fear of nightmares.

Impulse control disorders not elsewhere specified Disorders characterized by impulsive behaviors that are harmful to the self or others. Examples: *intermittent explosive disorder* (outbursts of aggression resulting in assault or property destruction), *kleptomania* (impulsive stealing), *pyromania* (impulsive setting of fires), and *pathological gambling.*

Disorders usually first diagnosed in infancy, childhood, or adolescence A diverse group of disorders that always or almost always first appear before adulthood. Examples: various forms of mental retardation, learning disorders, and language development disorders.

Delirium, dementia, amnestic, and other cognitive disorders A diverse group of disorders of perception, memory, and thought that stem from known damage to the brain. Examples: disorders due to strokes, physical trauma to the brain, and degenerative brain diseases such as *Alzheimer's disease.*

Adjustment disorder Maladaptive, excessive emotional reaction to an identified stressful event that occurred within the previous 6 months.

Personality disorders† Disorders involving inflexible, maladaptive personality traits. Examples: *antisocial personality disorder* (a history of antisocial acts and violation of others' rights, with no sense of guilt), *histrionic personality disorder* (excessively emotional, overly dramatic attention seeking), and *narcissistic personality disorder* (unwarranted sense of self-importance and demand for constant attention or admiration).

*The first six categories in the list correspond with major sections of this chapter.

†Because personality disorders involve a person's long-standing style of thinking and acting rather than a change in the person, they are categorized on a separate dimension, or axis (Axis II), from the other categories (which comprise Axis I).

Source: Diagnostic and statistical manual of mental disorders (4th, text-revised ed.). American Psychiatric Association, 2000.

valid, by the criteria listed above, one must first form a tentative, reliable diagnostic system. To determine whether people suffering from anorexia nervosa, for example, have similar histories, experience similar outcomes, and benefit from similar treatment, one must first have a consistent way of deciding who falls into the population to be studied. The results of such studies can lead to new means of diagnosis, or new subcategories that describe variations within the original category, leading to increased validity.

Robert Spitzer, who led the task force that created *DSM-III* and *DSM-III-R*, and who served as special adviser in the creation of *DSM-IV*, routinely refers to the diagnoses in the *DSM* as "hypotheses to be tested" (Wilson, 1993). The results of research based on each version of the manual led to the changes incorporated into the next version, and current and future research will eventuate in further changes. Psychiatry has moved past its early tendency toward dogma and become increasingly amenable to science—an enterprise in which the presumption of ignorance, not knowledge, is the driving force. In the subsequent sections of this chapter, you will read about the results of research studies concerning causes and outcomes of various disorders that were diagnosed by *DSM-III-R* or *DSM-IV* criteria; the results partly confirm and partly challenge the validity of those diagnostic systems.

The main categories of *DSM-IV*, most of which were also included in *DSM-III* and *DSM-III-R*, are listed in Table 16.1.

Prevalence of Mental Disorders

Since the development of *DSM-III*, two large-scale studies have assessed the prevalence of various mental disorders in the general population in the United States. In each study, the data were collected by trained interviewers and were analyzed using either *DSM-III* (first study, Robins & Regier, 1991) or *DSM-III-R* (second study, Kessler & others, 1994) criteria. The results for the most common disorders, mostly from the second study, are depicted in Figure 16.1. The graph shows the percentages of men and women who had manifested each disorder at some point in their lives by the time they were interviewed. You may wish to look back at this figure as you read, later in the chapter, about the various disorders and about possible explanations of the sex differences in prevalence that are shown in the figure.

FIGURE **16.1** *Lifetime prevalence of various mental disorders*
Most of these data come from diagnostic interviews of a cross section of the population in the United States, ages 15 to 54 years, conducted between late 1990 and early 1992, analyzed according to *DSM-III-R* criteria (Kessler & others, 1994). The data for obsessive-compulsive disorder, bipolar disorder, and schizophrenia come from an earlier survey study that used *DSM-III* criteria (Robins & Regier, 1991), as those disorders were not fully assessed in the more recent study. Notice the large sex difference in the prevalence of many of the disorders.

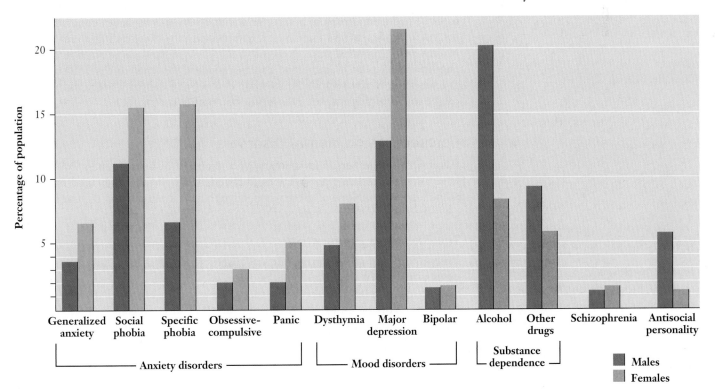

4.

What are some negative consequences of labeling a person as mentally disordered, and what is recommended as a partial solution?

A Danger in Labeling

Diagnosing and labeling may be essential for the scientific study of mental disorders, but labels can be harmful. Research studies (discussed in Chapter 17) have shown that a label implying mental disorder can blind clinicians and others to qualities of the person that are not captured by the label, can reduce the esteem accorded to the person by others, and can reduce the labeled person's self-esteem.

To reduce, at least somewhat, the likelihood of such effects, the American Psychiatric Association (2000) recommends that clinicians apply diagnostic labels only to people's disorders, not to people themselves. For example, a client or patient might be referred to as *a person who has schizophrenia* or *who suffers from alcoholism* but should not be referred to as *a schizophrenic* or *an alcoholic*. The distinction might at first seem subtle, but if you think about it, you may agree that it is not so subtle in psychological impact. If we say "John has schizophrenia," we tend to be reminded that John is first and foremost a person, with qualities like those of other people, and that his having schizophrenia is just one of many things we could say about him. In contrast, the statement "John is a schizophrenic" tends to imply that everything about him is summed up by that label. As I talk about specific disorders in the remainder of this chapter and the next, I will attempt to follow this advice even though it produces some awkward wording at times. I also urge you to add, in your mind, yet another step of linguistic complexity. When I refer to "a person who has schizophrenia," you should read this statement as "a person *who has been diagnosed by someone as having* schizophrenia," keeping in mind that diagnostic systems are never completely reliable.

Medical Students' Disease

The ability of labels to cause psychological harm demonstrates the power of suggestion, which also underlies *medical students' disease*. This disease, which could also be called *introductory psychology students' disease*, is characterized by a strong tendency to relate personally to, and find in oneself, the symptoms of any disease or disorder described in a textbook. Medical students' disease was described by the nineteenth-century humorist Jerome K. Jerome (1889/1982) in an essay about his own discomfort upon reading a textbook of medical diagnoses. After explaining his discovery that he must have typhoid fever, St. Vitus's dance, and a multitude of diseases he had never heard of before, he wrote, "The only malady I concluded I had *not* got was housemaid's knee. . . . I had walked into that reading-room a happy, healthy man. I crawled out a decrepit wreck." As you read about specific disorders later in this chapter, brace yourself against medical students' disease. Everyone has at least some of the symptoms, to some degree, of essentially every disorder that can be found in this chapter, *DSM-IV*, or any other compendium.

Perspectives on Mental Disorders

Clinicians, researchers, and scholars with a variety of backgrounds and interests have adopted different perspectives, different ways of describing and explaining mental disorders. None of these perspectives have a monopoly on the truth; rather, each accounts for different aspects of a very complex phenomenon.

The Biological Perspective

5.

How do the biological, psychodynamic, cognitive, behavioral, and sociocultural perspectives differ from each other in their accounts of the origins of mental disorders? What kinds of terms does each perspective use to describe disorders?

From the *biological perspective*, mental disorders are fundamentally physical diseases—diseases of the brain. This perspective motivates the attempt to find measurable abnormalities in the brain that correlate with observed disorders and to develop treatments in the form of drugs or other direct means to alter the brain. The brain disease may result from genes or from such environmental assaults as poisons (including alcohol or other drugs consumed by the mother while pregnant), birth difficulties (such as oxygen deprivation during birth), and viruses or bacteria that attack the brain.

Consistent with the idea that genes play a role in mental disorders, numerous studies—some of which are summarized later in the chapter—have shown that the genetic kin of people with a given mental disorder have a higher-than-average probability of developing either the same disorder or another disorder, regardless of whether or not they had been raised in the same home (Faraone & others, 1999). Some genes appear to predispose people to particular mental disorders, and other genes appear to predispose people to mental disorder in general or to a set of such disorders (Eley, 1997).

The Psychodynamic, Cognitive, and Behavioral Perspectives

Mental disorders, by definition, involve disturbances in people's emotions, thoughts, and behavior. Such disturbances may not just be evidence of a mental disorder; they may also be causes of the disorder. They may prevent the person from behaving in ways that would help bring rewards or relieve misery.

Psychodynamic theories, such as that developed by Sigmund Freud (introduced in Chapter 15), propose that mental disorders arise from mental conflicts and drives that the person has been unable to resolve or coordinate with the realities of life and that therefore generate anxiety. To defend against the anxiety, the person may repress or mask the conflicts and drives, and that process may result in the maladaptive ways of thinking and behaving that lead to a diagnosis of mental disorder. The psychodynamic therapist's task (discussed in Chapter 17) is to help the person become aware of and talk about the conflicts and drives that underlie the disordered thinking and action, so that he or she can begin to resolve the conflicts consciously and direct the drives toward more useful ends. Many psychodynamic theories hold that the conflicts and anxieties that have such crippling effects originate from traumatic (highly stressful) experiences in early childhood.

While psychodynamic theories are concerned with the role of hidden conflicts and drives, *cognitive* and *behavioral theories* are more concerned, respectively, with the person's conscious thoughts and actions. From the cognitive and behavioral perspectives (which are often combined), mental disorders are learned, maladaptive habits of thinking and acting that have been acquired through the person's interaction with the environment. For example, such maladaptive thoughts as "Nobody likes me" or "Anything I do will fail" may have been learned from demanding parents or through other social interactions, and such maladaptive habits as excessive drinking or avoidance of anxiety-provoking social encounters may have been learned through operant conditioning, based on the short-term pleasure or relief produced by such drinking or avoidance. Various procedures for replacing such undesired habits with desired habits have been developed, and these are described in Chapter 17.

The Sociocultural Perspective

Mental disorders are products not only of the person and the person's immediate environment but also of the larger culture within which the person develops. The kinds of psychological distress that people experience, the ways in which they express that distress, and the ways in which other people respond to a distressed person vary greatly from culture to culture and over time in any given culture. The *sociocultural perspective* brings insights from social psychology, sociology, and anthropology to the attempt to understand these variations.

The most striking evidence of cross-cultural variation in mental disorders can be found in *culture-bound syndromes*—expressions of mental distress that are almost completely limited to specific cultural groups. A syndrome called *koro*, for example, marked by an incapacitating fear that the penis will withdraw into the abdomen and cause death, occurs in occasional epidemics among men in Southeast Asia but is almost nonexistent anywhere else (Tseng & others, 1992). Examples closer to home are *anorexia nervosa*, marked by an extraordinary preoccupation with thinness and a refusal to eat, sometimes to the point of death by starvation;

The four temperaments
The ancient Greek physician Hippocrates promulgated the belief that disturbed emotions and behavior are caused by an imbalance in the body's fluids. A melancholy (gloomy) temperament was attributed to an excess of black bile, a choleric (angry) temperament to an excess of yellow bile, a sanguine (cheerful) temperament to an excess of blood, and a phlegmatic (apathetic) temperament to an excess of phlegm.

6.

How do the examples of anorexia and bulimia illustrate the value of the sociocultural perspective?

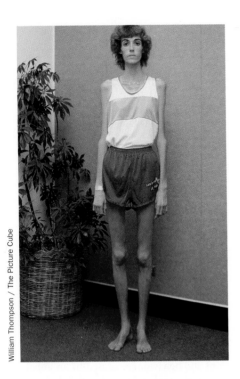

William Thompson / The Picture Cube

A syndrome of our times

Over the last 40 years anorexia nervosa became increasingly prevalent in Western cultures, but it is still rare in non-Western cultures.

and *bulimia nervosa*, marked by periods of extreme binge eating followed by self-induced vomiting, misuse of laxatives or other drugs, or other means to undo the effects of the binge.

From the sociocultural perspective, it is no coincidence that these eating disorders began to appear with some frequency in the 1970s in North America and western Europe, primarily among adolescent girls and young women of the middle and upper social classes, and that their prevalence increased rapidly through the 1970s and 1980s (Gordon, 1990). During that period, for social and historical reasons that are beyond the scope of this book, Western culture became increasingly obsessed with dieting and the ideal of female thinness. At present, more than 50 percent of women in Western industrialized cultures report some symptoms of an eating disorder and approximately 2 percent meet the *DSM-IV* criteria for anorexia nervosa or bulimia nervosa (Porzelius & others, 2001). As other parts of the world have become more Westernized in habits and values, eating disorders have begun to spread (Castillo, 1997).

As you will see later in this chapter, the sociocultural perspective is concerned not just with culture-bound syndromes but also with how the culture labels and reacts to manifestations of mental distress and with how those labels and reactions affect the afflicted person.

A Framework for Thinking About Multiple Causation

The perspectives just described emphasize different ways of thinking about the causes of mental disorders, but theorists of all perspectives recognize that any given disorder is likely to have multiple causes. A disorder typically arises from a preexisting susceptibility coupled with a triggering set of circumstances, and the consequences of the disorder may help perpetuate it. Accordingly, a general framework for thinking about causes recognizes three main categories.

Predisposing causes are those that were in place well before the onset of the disorder and make the person susceptible to the disorder. Genetically inherited characteristics are most often mentioned in this category. But learned beliefs and habitual patterns of reacting to or thinking about stressful situations may also be included here, as may the sociocultural conditions under which one acquires such beliefs and habits. A young woman reared in upper-class, Western society is more likely to have acquired beliefs and values that predispose her to anorexia nervosa than is a young woman from a rural community in China.

Precipitating causes are the immediate events in a person's life that bring on the disorder. Any loss, such as the death of a loved one or the loss of a job; any real or perceived threat to one's well-being, such as physical disease; any new responsibilities, such as might occur as a result of marriage or job promotion; or any large change at all in the day-to-day course of life can, in the sufficiently predisposed person, bring on the mood or behavioral change that leads to diagnosis of a mental disorder. Precipitating causes are often talked about under the rubric of *stress*, a term that sometimes refers to the life event itself and sometimes to the worry, anxiety, hopelessness, or other negative experiences that accompany the life event (Lazarus, 1993). When the predisposition is very high, a seemingly trivial event can be sufficiently stressful to bring on a mental disorder. When the predisposition is very low, even an extraordinarily high degree of loss, threat, or change may fail to bring on a mental disorder. Figure 16.2 depicts this inverse relationship.

Maintaining causes are those consequences of a disorder that help keep it going once it begins. In some cases, a person may gain rewards, such as extra atten-

---

7.

How can the causes of mental disorders be categorized into three types?

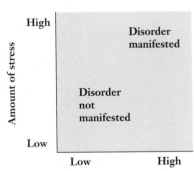

FIGURE **16.2** *Inverse relationship between predisposition and stress in initiating a mental disorder*
The amount of stress needed to bring on a mental disorder decreases as the predisposition to the disorder increases.

tion, which help maintain the maladaptive behavior. More often, the negative consequences of the disorder help maintain it. For example, a sufferer of depression may withdraw from friends, and lack of friends may perpetuate the depression. Poor diet, irregular sleep patterns, and lack of exercise brought on by the disorder may also, through physiological means, help prolong the disorder. Expectations associated with a particular disorder may also play a maintaining role. In a culture that regards a particular disorder as incurable, a person diagnosed with that disorder may simply give up trying to change for the better.

What Accounts for Apparent Sex Differences in Prevalence?

Little difference occurs between men and women in the prevalence of mental disorder when all disorders are combined, but as you saw in Figure 16.1, large sex differences are found for specific disorders. In particular, women are much more likely than men to be diagnosed with anxiety and mood disorders, and men are much more likely than women to be diagnosed with alcohol and other drug-use disorders and with antisocial personality disorder. In theory, such differences might arise directly from biological differences between men and women, or they might arise from the different roles and expectations that society ascribes to men and women. Within the sociocultural category of causes, specific explanations have centered on self-report biases, observer biases, and sex differences in life experiences.

Differences in Reporting or Suppressing Psychological Distress

The diagnosis of anxiety and mood disorders necessarily depends to a great extent on self-report. Men, who are supposed to be the "stronger" sex, may be less inclined than women to admit mental distress in interviews or questionnaires. Supporting this view, experiments have shown that when men and women are subjected to the same stressful situation, such as a school examination, men report less anxiety than do women even though they show physiological signs of distress that are as great as, or greater than, those shown by women (Polefrone & Manuck, 1987). Men might also use alcohol and illegal drugs to suppress their mental distress or might express it in the form of anger rather than fear or sadness. Anger is the one negative emotion that in our society is more acceptable in men than in women (Hyde, 1986), and it is the only common negative emotion that does not correspond directly to a major category in the *DSM*. A person who expresses severe distress in terms of fear or sadness may receive a diagnosis of an anxiety or mood disorder, but a person who expresses it in terms of anger usually will not.

Bias in Diagnosis

Diagnosticians may, to some degree, find a disorder more often in one sex than in the other because they *expect* to find it there. To test this possibility, Maureen Ford and Thomas Widiger (1989) mailed a fictitious case history to several hundred clinical psychologists throughout the United States and asked them to make diagnoses using *DSM-III* criteria. For some the case history was constructed to resemble the criteria for *antisocial personality*, a disorder found more often in men than in women. For others it was constructed to resemble the criteria for *histrionic personality*, a disorder found more often in women. (For a brief description of these personality disorders, look at the last entry in Table 16.1 on page 614.) Each of these case histories was written in duplicate forms, one

8.

From the sociocultural perspective, what are three possible ways to account for sex differences in the prevalence of specific mental disorders?

Hysterical or angry?

Even today the word "hysterical" may come to mind more quickly when we view an angry woman than when we view an angry man. That same bias may contribute to the more frequent diagnosis of histrionic personality in women than in men.

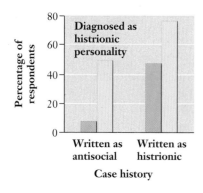

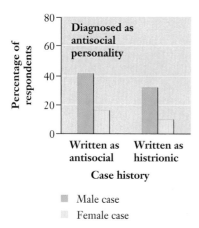

■ Male case
□ Female case

FIGURE **16.3** *Evidence of a gender bias in diagnosis*
In this study, case histories were more likely to be diagnosed as antisocial personality if they described a fictitious male patient and as histrionic personality if they described a fictitious female patient, regardless of which disorder the case history was designed to resemble. (Data from Ford & Widiger, 1989.)

describing a male patient and the other describing a female patient. As you can see in Figure 16.3, the diagnoses were strongly affected by the patient's sex. Given the exact same case histories, the male was far more likely than the female to receive a diagnosis of antisocial personality, and the female was far more likely than the male to receive a diagnosis of histrionic personality.

Might a similar bias have operated in the survey of the prevalence of disorders, shown in Figure 16.1 on page 615? That question is hard to answer. On the one hand, the interviewers were trained to ask questions and record data using a standard format, and diagnoses were then made from those data by a computer program, which presumably had no gender bias programmed into it. On the other hand, there is no way to rule out the possibility that interviewers unconsciously interpreted and recorded responses differently depending on the gender of the person they were interviewing.

Differences in Stressfulness of Men's and Women's Experiences

A third approach has been to assume that to some degree sex differences in mental disorders are real and to search for possible causes in the different social experiences of men and women. Women in our culture are more likely than men to live in poverty, to experience discrimination, to have been sexually or physically abused in childhood, and to be physically abused by their spouses—all of which can contribute to depression, anxiety, and various other disorders (Koss, 1990; Strickland, 1992). Moreover, some psychologists have argued that the traditional role of wife and mother in our society is more conducive to anxiety and depression than is the role of husband and father (Barnett & Baruch, 1987). The wife and mother spends more time in isolation from other adults and performs jobs that are accorded little prestige by society at large. She is often made to feel responsible for events over which she has little real control, such as her children's illnesses, accidents, or poor school performance. The combination of high demands, low real control, and low prestige is the ideal mix for creating both anxiety and depression. Consistent with this view, in a study in which a large sample of married couples in the United States kept diaries for 6 weeks, the women reported many more distressing experiences than did the men (Almeida & Kessler, 1998).

SECTION SUMMARY

Disturbances in emotions and thoughts that cause prolonged, serious distress or impairment of functioning are referred to as mental disorders. The American Psychiatric Association has developed an extensive manual, DSM-IV, for classifying and diagnosing categories of mental disorders. Because the criteria specified by DSM-IV are relatively objective, the diagnostic system is relatively reliable.

Mental disorders are described and studied from a variety of perspectives. The biological perspective focuses on the roles of genes and observable abnormalities in the brain. The psychodynamic perspective focuses on the roles of unconscious mental conflicts and drives that interfere with the person's ability to function adaptively. The cognitive and behavioral perspectives focus on learned habits of thought and action that interfere with adaptive functioning in the person's current environment. The sociocultural perspective focuses on the influences that a culture's beliefs and practices can have on the mental disorders that people develop within that culture. A useful framework for thinking about the multiple causation of any given instance of mental disorder distinguishes among predisposing causes, precipitating causes, and maintaining causes.

Women are much more likely than men to be diagnosed with anxiety and mood disorders; men are much more likely than women to be diagnosed with alcohol or drug-use disorders and antisocial personality disorder. Attempts to explain these gender differences from the sociocultural perspective have focused on sex differences in the willingness to report psychological distress, on possible bias in diagnosis, and on differences in daily experiences of men and women.

ANXIETY DISORDERS

The rabbit crouches, frozen in the grass, minimizing its chance of being detected. Its sensory systems are at maximum alertness, all tuned to the approaching dog. With muscles tense, the rabbit is poised to leap away at the first sign that it has been detected; its heart races, and its adrenal glands secrete hormones that help prepare the body for extended flight if necessary. Here we see fear operating adaptively, as it was designed to operate by evolution.

We humans differ from the rabbit on two counts: Our biological evolution added a massive, thinking cerebral cortex atop the more primitive structures that organize fear; and our cultural evolution led us to develop a habitat far different from that of our ancestors. Our pattern of fear is not unlike the rabbit's, but it can be triggered by an enormously greater variety of both real and imagined stimuli, and in many cases the fear is not adaptive. Fear is not adaptive when it causes a job candidate to freeze in an interview, or overwhelms a student's mind during an examination, or constricts the life of a person who can vividly imagine the worst possible consequence of every action.

Anxiety disorders are those in which fear or anxiety is the most prominent symptom. Although *fear* and *anxiety* can be used as synonyms, fear is more often used when the feared stimulus or event is specific and present, and anxiety is more often used when the stimulus or event is vague, not identifiable, or in the future. Cognitively, anxious people worry excessively, especially about their own lack of ability to cope with unpredictable future dangers (Barlow, 1991). The treatment of these and other disorders is discussed in Chapter 17; but it is worth noting here that anxiety disorders are, as a group, the easiest disorders to treat and have the best long-term prognosis (chance of recovery).

Among the classes of anxiety disorders recognized by *DSM-IV* are generalized anxiety disorder, phobias, obsessive-compulsive disorder, panic disorder, and post-traumatic stress disorder.

Generalized Anxiety Disorder

Generalized anxiety is called *generalized* because it is not focused on any one specific threat; instead, it attaches itself to various threats, real and imagined. Sufferers of *generalized anxiety disorder* worry more or less continuously, about multiple issues, and associated with their worry they experience muscle tension, irritability, difficulty in sleeping, and sometimes gastrointestinal upset due to overactivity of the autonomic nervous system. They worry about the same kinds of issues that most of us worry about—family members, money, work, illness—but to a far greater extent and with much less provocation (Barlow, 1988).

By *DSM-III-R* or *DSM-IV* criteria, roughly 5 percent of people in North America suffer from generalized anxiety disorder at some time in their lives (American Psychiatric Association, 2000; Kessler & others, 1994). This percentage underestimates the actual number who suffer from generalized anxiety, because the *DSM* diagnostic criteria are quite stringent: The generalized anxiety must seriously impair daily functioning for at least 6 months and occur independently of other diagnosable mental disorders.

Research suggests that generalized anxiety disorder is moderately heritable and that the genes promoting it may be the same as those promoting major depression (Smoller & others, 2000). In large-scale twin studies, the identical twins of people suffering from either generalized anxiety disorder or major depression had equally elevated prevalences of both disorders (Kendler & others, 1992, 1995). Other studies have shown that people who suffer from one of these disorders frequently suffer at some point in their lives from the other (Mineka & others, 1998).

On the environmental side, frequent, unpredictable traumatic experiences in childhood can apparently predispose a person to generalized anxiety disorder (Torgersen, 1986), and the disorder typically first appears in adulthood following a

9.

How can the onset of generalized anxiety disorder be explained in terms of predisposing and precipitating causes?

major life change, such as getting a new job or having a baby, or a disturbing event such as an accident or illness (Blazer & others, 1987). Researchers approaching the disorder from a cognitive perspective suggest that *hypervigilance*—a persistent tendency to scan the environment for signs of impending danger and to disregard cues indicative of safety—may provide the link between early trauma and generalized anxiety disorder (Beck & Emery, 1985; Eysenck, 1992). Consistent with this view, people who develop generalized anxiety disorder are apparently hypervigilant before the onset of the disorder and continue to be so when the disorder is in remission (Eysenck, 1992).

Taking all these findings into account, the typical etiology (description of causes) of generalized anxiety disorder might be summarized as follows:

Genetic predisposition and/or early traumatic experiences →
hypervigilance → generalized anxiety disorder following a life change or
other disturbing event

Surveys taken at various times, using comparable measures, indicate that the average level of generalized anxiety in Western cultures has increased sharply over the past 50 years (Twenge, 2000). From a sociocultural perspective, that increase may be attributable to the reduced stability of the typical person's life. In a world of rapid technological change, we can't be sure that the job skills needed today will still be useful tomorrow. In a world of frequent divorce and high mobility, we can't be sure that the people we are attached to now will be with us in the future. In a world of rapidly changing values and expectations, we have difficulty judging right from wrong or safe from unsafe. Such threats may be felt only dimly and lead not to conscious articulation of specific fears but to generalized anxiety. And, unlike the predator that scares the rabbit one minute and is gone the next, these threats are with us always.

Phobias

In contrast to generalized anxiety, a **phobia** is an intense, irrational fear that is very clearly related to a particular category of object or event. In **specific phobias** (formerly called *simple phobias*) the fear is of something specific, such as a particular type of animal (such as snakes), substance (such as blood), or situation (such as heights or being closed in). In **social phobias**, the fear is of being scrutinized or evaluated by other people; included here are fears of public speaking, of eating in public places, and of meeting new people. Usually a phobia sufferer is aware that the fear is irrational but still cannot control it. The person knows full well that the neighbor's kitten won't claw anyone to death, that people don't ordinarily drown in ankle-deep water, or that the crowd of 10-year-olds at the corner won't attack. People with phobias suffer doubly—from the fear itself and from knowing how irrational they are to have such a fear.

Probably everyone has some irrational fears, and, as in all other anxiety disorders, the difference between the normal condition and the disorder is an arbitrary one of degree, not kind. Specific phobias are usually of things that many people fear to some extent, such as snakes, spiders, blood, darkness, or heights; and social phobias may simply be extreme forms of shyness (Marks, 1987). Specific phobias are much more often diagnosed in females than in males, whereas social phobias are diagnosed about equally often in the two sexes (American Psychiatric Association, 2000; Barlow, 1988), and these facts are consistent with the idea that phobias lie on a continuum with normal fears. Men and boys are much less likely than women and girls to report fears of such things as spiders and darkness but are about equally likely to report shyness. The sex difference in specific phobias could stem from the fact that boys in our society are more strongly encouraged than are girls to overcome or to hide their childhood fears (Fodor, 1982).

As with most other mental disorders, little is known about how phobias usually arise. Behaviorists, from John B. Watson (1924) on, have argued that phobias are

10.

What evidence links phobias to normal fears, and how might phobias be explained in terms of learning, evolution, and culture?

acquired by classical conditioning, through experiences in which the now-feared stimulus had been paired with some unconditionally fearful stimulus. A problem with this interpretation is that people with phobias are, on average, no more likely than people without phobias to recall having had any specific experiences with the feared object or event that could have provided the basis for such learning (Craske, 1999; McNally & Steketee, 1985). It also does not explain such findings as this: In a survey in Burlington, Vermont, where there are no dangerous snakes, the single most common specific phobia was of snakes (Agras & others, 1969). If phobias are acquired by conditioning, why aren't phobias of such things as automobiles or (in Burlington) icy sidewalks more common?

Another theory, first proposed by Martin Seligman (1971), is that people are genetically prepared to be wary of—and to learn easily to fear—objects and events that would have posed realistic dangers during most of our evolutionary history (discussed in Chapter 4). This idea is helpful in understanding why phobias of snakes, darkness, and heights are more common than those of automobiles and electric outlets. Research has shown that people can acquire strong fears of such evolutionarily significant objects and events through means other than direct conditioning (Mineka & Zinbarg, 1996). Simply observing others respond fearfully to them, or reading or hearing fearful stories about them, can initiate or contribute to a phobia. The fact that some people acquire phobias and others don't in the face of similar experiences probably stems from a variety of predisposing factors, including genetic temperament and prior experiences (Craske, 1999).

Consistent with the sociocultural perspective, phobias can take different forms in different cultures. For example, a social phobia common in Japan but almost nonexistent in the West is *taijin kyofusho*, an incapacitating fear of offending or harming others through one's own awkward social behavior or imagined physical defect (Kirmayer, 1991). The focus of cognition for a sufferer of this phobia is on the harm to others, not on embarrassment to the self, as in social phobias in the West. *Taijin kyofusho* is described by Japanese psychiatrists as a pathological exaggeration of the modesty and sensitive regard for others that, at lower levels, are considered proper in Japan.

Obsessive-Compulsive Disorder

An *obsession* is a disturbing thought that intrudes repeatedly on a person's consciousness even though the person recognizes it as irrational. A *compulsion* is a repetitive action that is usually performed in response to an obsession. Most people experience moderate forms of these, especially in childhood. I remember a period in sixth grade when, while reading in school, the thought would repeatedly enter my mind that reading could make my eyes fall out. The only way I could banish this thought and go on reading was to close my eyelids down hard—a compulsive act that I fancied might push my eyes solidly back into their sockets. Of course, I knew that both the thought and the action were irrational, yet the thought kept intruding, and the only way I could abolish it for a while was to perform the action. Like most normal obsessions and compulsions, this one did not really disrupt my life, and it simply faded with time.

People who are diagnosed with **obsessive-compulsive disorder** are those for whom such thoughts and actions are severe, prolonged, and disruptive of normal life. To meet *DSM-IV* criteria for this disorder, the obsessions and compulsions must consume more than an hour per day of the person's time and seriously interfere with work or social relationships (American Psychiatric Association, 2000). An obsessive-compulsive disorder is similar to a phobia in that it involves a specific irrational fear, and it is different primarily in that the fear is of something that exists only as a thought and can be reduced only by performing some ritual. People with obsessive-compulsive disorder, like those with phobias, suffer also from their

Charles Nes / Stone

A dreadful view

Phobia comes from a Greek word meaning "flight" or "fear." If you experience such feelings when viewing this scene, you have some sense of what a person with a height phobia feels when looking out a second-story window.

11.

How is an obsessive-compulsive disorder similar to and different from a phobia?

12.

What evidence links obsessive-compulsive disorder with excessive neural activity in a portion of the basal ganglia of the brain?

knowledge of the irrationality of their actions and go to great lengths to hide them from other people.

The obsessions experienced by people diagnosed with this disorder are similar to, but stronger than, the kinds of obsessions experienced by people in the general population (Rachman & DeSilva, 1978). The most common obsessions concern disease, disfigurement, or death, and the most common compulsions involve checking or cleaning. People with checking compulsions may spend hours each day repeatedly checking doors to be sure they are locked, the gas stove to be sure it is turned off, automobile wheels to be sure they are on tight, and so on. People with cleaning compulsions may wash their hands every few minutes, scrub everything they eat, and sterilize their dishes and clothes in response to their obsessions about disease-producing germs and dirt. Some compulsions, however, bear no apparent logical relationship to the obsession that triggers them. For example, a woman obsessed by the thought that her husband would die in an automobile accident could in fantasy protect him by dressing and undressing in a specific pattern 20 times every day (Marks, 1987).

Brain imaging studies reveal that people diagnosed with obsessive-compulsive disorder exhibit heightened neural activity in the *caudate nucleus* of the brain, a portion of the basal ganglia (discussed in Chapter 5) known to be involved in the initiation of learned, habitual motor activities (Rapaport, 1991). Drugs that increase the activity of the neurotransmitter serotonin in the brain reduce the neural activity in the caudate nucleus and also reduce the obsessions and compulsions in people diagnosed with the disorder (Kronig & others, 1999). Such work does not necessarily indicate that obsessive-compulsive disorder derives originally from an overactive caudate nucleus. The heightened neural activity could well be part of the mechanism for producing obsessions and compulsions without being the initial cause. Obsessive-compulsive disorder is often treated successfully by behavioral and cognitive therapy procedures (discussed in Chapter 17), and people who recover from the disorder through such nondrug treatments show the same decline in activity in the caudate nucleus as do people who recover through drugs (Baxter & others, 1992; Schwartz & others, 1996).

Panic Disorder

Panic is a feeling of helpless terror, such as one might experience if cornered by a predator. For people who suffer from **panic disorder**, this sense of terror comes at unpredictable times, unprovoked by any specific threat in the environment. Because the panic is unrelated to any specific situation or idea, the panic victim, unlike the victim of a phobia or an obsessive-compulsion, cannot avoid it by avoiding certain situations or relieve it by engaging in certain rituals. Panic attacks usually last several minutes and are usually accompanied by high physiological arousal (including rapid heart rate and shortness of breath) and a fear of losing control and behaving in some frantic, desperate way (Craske, 1999). Between attacks the victim may experience almost constant anxiety about having another attack. The victim especially fears having an attack in a public place, where embarrassment or humiliation might follow a loss of control in front of others. As a result, the majority of panic-attack victims develop *agoraphobia*, an intense fear of public places, sometime after their first panic attack (Craske, 1999).

Twin studies indicate that panic disorder is at least moderately heritable (Smoller & others, 2000). On the environmental side, the panic victim commonly experiences the first attack shortly after some stressful event or life change (Breier & others, 1986). In the laboratory or clinic, panic attacks can be brought on in people with the disorder by lactic acid injection, high doses of caffeine, carbon dioxide inhalation, and other procedures that increase heart and breathing rates (Hecker & Thorpe, 1992). This has led to the view that a maintaining cause, if not a predisposing cause, of the disorder is a learned tendency to interpret physiological

13.

What learned thought pattern might be a maintaining cause of panic disorder?

arousal as catastrophic (Clark, 1988). One treatment, used by cognitive therapists, is to help the person learn to interpret each attack as a temporary physiological condition rather than a sign of mental derangement or impending doom.

Posttraumatic Stress Disorder

Unlike the other anxiety disorders, ***posttraumatic stress disorder*** is directly and explicitly tied to a traumatic incident or set of incidents that the affected person has experienced. It is most common in torture victims, concentration camp survivors, people who have been violently assaulted, people who have survived a dreadful accident, and soldiers who have experienced the horrors of battle. The disorder may begin immediately after the traumatic experience or later, sometimes many months later. It typically involves painful and uncontrollable reliving of the traumatic events, both in nightmares and in daytime thoughts. Other common symptoms are sleeplessness, high arousal, irritability, guilt (perhaps for surviving when others didn't), emotional numbing, and depression (Biedel & Turner, 1997; Foa & Riggs, 1995). In an effort to relieve such symptoms, posttraumatic stress victims may turn to alcohol or street drugs, which often compound the problem.

People who are exposed repeatedly, or over a long period of time, to distressing conditions are apparently more likely to develop posttraumatic stress symptoms than are those exposed to a single short-term highly traumatic incident. One study revealed that the incidence of posttraumatic stress disorder among Vietnam War veterans correlated more strongly with long-term exposure to the daily stressors and dangers of the war—such as heat, insects, loss of sleep, sight of dead bodies, and risk of capture by the enemy—than with exposure to a single short-term atrocity (King & others, 1995). Likewise, children exposed to repeated abuse in their homes are particularly prone to manifest posttraumatic stress symptoms (Roesler & McKenzie, 1994).

Not everyone exposed to extraordinary stress develops posttraumatic stress symptoms. Social support apparently helps protect people from the aftereffects of trauma, and this may help explain why posttraumatic symptoms are more prevalent among veterans of unpopular wars, such as the Vietnam War, than among veterans of more popular wars, such as World War II (Card, 1987). Genes also play a role in determining who develops posttraumatic symptoms and who does not (Paris, 2000). For instance, a study of twin pairs who fought in Vietnam revealed that identical twins were more similar to each other in the incidence and type of such symptoms than were fraternal twins (True & others, 1993).

14.

How does posttraumatic stress disorder differ from other anxiety disorders?

15.

What sorts of conditions may be particularly conducive to posttraumatic stress disorder?

SECTION SUMMARY

Anxiety disorders entail feelings of fear or worry that are disproportionate to the realistic dangers of the person's current environment. DSM-IV identifies five main categories of such disorders. Generalized anxiety disorder involves more-or-less continuous worry about daily life experiences; it seems to involve a state of hypervigilance that may have been brought on by traumatic events suffered in childhood or by a generally unpredictable environment. Phobias—including specific phobias and social phobias—are intense, irrational fears of particular types of objects or events. The feared objects or events are typically those that would have posed some realistic threat to our evolutionary ancestors. People who suffer from obsessive-compulsive disorder regularly experience an obsessive, fearful thought that can be temporarily relieved by engaging in some compulsive action such as hand washing. The disorder seems to be associated with an abnormality in the basal ganglia of the brain. Panic disorder involves the repeated experience of a sense of terror that comes at unpredictable times, unprovoked by specific environmental threats. People with this disorder often suffer chronically from an intense fear of their next attack and for this reason are often afraid to leave their homes. Posttraumatic stress disorder involves the painful, uncontrollable reliving of one or more traumatic experiences, along with such additional symptoms as sleeplessness, high arousal, irritability, and guilt. Genetic predisposition plays a role in all five categories of anxiety disorders, and the same genes that predispose a person for generalized anxiety also predispose a person for depression.

MOOD DISORDERS

Mood refers to a prolonged emotional state that colors many, if not all, aspects of a person's thought and behavior. It is useful (though oversimplified) to think of a single dimension of mood, running from depression at one end to elation at the other. Because we all have tasted both, we have an idea of what they are like. Both are normal experiences, but at times either of them can become so intense or prolonged as to promote harmful, even life-threatening, actions. Severe depression can keep a person from working, lead to withdrawal from friends, or even provoke suicide. Severe elation, called *mania*, can lead to outrageous behaviors that turn other people away or to dangerous acts that stem from a false sense of security and bravado. *DSM-IV* identifies two main categories of **mood disorders**: **depressive disorders**, characterized by prolonged or extreme depression, and **bipolar disorders**, characterized by alternating episodes of depression and mania.

Depression

16.

How does depression differ from generalized anxiety?

Much has been written about the differences and similarities between depression and generalized anxiety. As was noted earlier, the two disorders often coexist in the same people and seem to be predisposed by the same genes. Both also involve a shared cluster of negative feelings (Mineka & others, 1998; Zinbarg & others, 1992). Two major distinctions between them are that (a) anxiety is more likely than depression to be accompanied by physiological arousal and hypervigilance and (b) depression is more likely than anxiety to entail an absence of pleasure and a sense of hopelessness (Clark & Watson, 1991). Behaviorally, anxiety is associated with active engagement in life and depression is associated with disengagement (Barlow, 1991). Cognitively, the anxious individual worries about what might happen in the future, while the depressed individual feels that all is already lost (see Table 16.2). The sense of worthlessness and hopelessness typical of depressed thinking is captured in the following quotation from Norman Endler (1982), a highly respected psychologist describing his own bout with depression:

> I honestly felt subhuman, lower than the lowest vermin. . . . I could not understand why anyone would want to associate with me, let alone love me. . . . I was positive that I was a fraud and a phony. . . . I couldn't understand how I had written the books and journal articles that I had and how they had been accepted for publication. I must have conned a lot of people.

Other symptoms of depression—beyond the main ones of sadness, self-blame, sense of worthlessness, and absence of pleasure—may include increased or decreased sleep, increased or decreased appetite, and either agitated or retarded motor symptoms. Agitated symptoms include repetitive, aimless movements such as hand wringing or pacing, and retarded symptoms include slowed speech and slowed body movements. To warrant a *DSM-IV* diagnosis of a depressive disorder, the symptoms must be either very severe or very prolonged and not attributable directly to a specific life experience.

Two main classes of depressive disorders are distinguished. **Major depression** is characterized by very severe symptoms that last essentially without remission for at least 2 weeks. **Dysthymia** is characterized by less severe symptoms that last for at least 2 years. Quite often, bouts of major depression are superimposed over a more chronic state of dysthymia, in which case the person is said to have *double depression*. As shown in Figure 16.1, both major depression and dysthymia are quite prevalent, and both are diagnosed more often in women than in men.

TABLE 16.2 *Comparison of anxious thoughts with depressive thoughts*

Anxious thoughts
What if I get sick and become an invalid?
Something will happen to someone I care about.
Something might happen that will ruin my appearance.
I am going to have a heart attack.

Depressed thoughts
I'm worthless.
I'm a social failure.
I have become physically unattractive.
Life isn't worth living.

Source: Adapted from Beck & others, 1987.

Biological Bases for Depression

In the 1950s researchers discovered that many sufferers from depression could be treated successfully with drugs that act in the brain to increase the action of a group of neurotransmitters known as *monoamines*. In other research, drugs that reduce sharply the level of brain monoamines were found to induce feelings of depression in some previously undepressed people (but not in all such people). Such findings led to the *monoamine theory of depression*, which holds that depression results from too little activity at brain synapses where monoamines are the neurotransmitters (Schildkraut, 1965).

The three major monoamine transmitters in the brain are *dopamine*, *norepinephrine*, and *serotonin*, all of which are known from nonhuman animal research to be involved in neural mechanisms underlying motivation and arousal. Research on the neurochemistry of depression has focused especially on the roles of norepinephrine and serotonin, since drugs that selectively augment the activity of just one or the other of these transmitters are effective in treating depression (Feeney & Nutt, 1999). A frequently prescribed drug for depression today is fluoxetine, sold by the trade name *Prozac*. This drug (discussed further in Chapter 17) acts specifically at synapses where serotonin is the transmitter. It blocks the reuptake of serotonin back into the presynaptic terminal and thereby prolongs the action of serotonin on the postsynaptic neuron. (See Chapter 5 for a general discussion of how drugs can alter synaptic transmission.)

Despite many years of research motivated by the monoamine theory, the theory is now very much in doubt (Hirschfeld, 2000). One problem with the theory is that it does not explain the delayed effectiveness of drug treatments. Antidepressant drugs begin to enhance the activity of norepinephrine or serotonin (or both) immediately after they are taken, yet they do not begin to relieve depression until 2 weeks or more of continuous treatment have elapsed. During that period the nervous system makes many adjustments to the influence of the drug, including adjustments that counteract the drug's initial effects on the activity of neurotransmitters. There is reason to think that antidepressant drugs no longer increase the activity of monoamines by the time the depression begins to be relieved. It is also not clear why drugs that act just on norepinephrine or just on serotonin should each be effective in treating depression in the same individuals, given that these transmitters are known to act on anatomically and functionally different parts of the brain. Presently, researchers are trying to learn about the long-term biochemical adjustments that the brain makes in response to antidepressant drugs as a route to understanding how the drugs alleviate depression (Sandler, 2001; Shelton, 2000).

As is the case for nearly every other mental disorder, there is good evidence that heredity plays a role in predisposition for depression. The more closely related two people are, the more similar they are, on average, in their history of depression or lack of it and in the specific types of depressive symptoms they exhibit (Kendler & others, 1996). One study involving over 1000 pairs of female twins provided evidence that heredity affects depression by influencing the way the person responds to highly stressful life events (Kendler, 1998; Kendler & others, 1995). Among women who had not recently experienced such an event, the incidence of depression was low regardless of degree of genetic risk for the disorder; but among those who had recently experienced such an event, the incidence of depression rose much more sharply for those who were at high genetic risk than for those who were not. For the results and more about the methods of this study, see Figure 16.4 on page 628.

17.

What is some evidence for and against the monoamine theory of depression?

Depression

As expressed in this woodcut by Edvard Munch, the world looks bleak to a depressed person.

18.

How did a study of twins provide evidence that genetic predisposition for depression may alter one's response to stressful experiences?

FIGURE **16.4** *Depression as influenced by genetic predisposition and stressful experiences*
In this study of female twins, the genetic liability for major depression was ranked (in the order shown in the figure's key) in accordance with whether or not the co-twin had a history of major depression and whether or not the co-twin was genetically identical. A severely stressful event was defined as assault, serious marital problems, divorce or breakup of a marriage or other romantic relationship, or death of a close relative. As shown here, the women who had experienced a severely stressful event were far more likely to experience the onset of major depression within a month after that event than were those who had not experienced a severely stressful event. This effect of stress was greater for those who were more genetically liable than for those who were less genetically liable. (Adapted from Kendler & others, 1995, p. 837.)

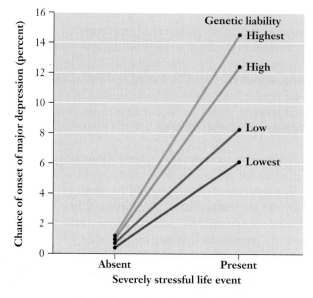

Identical co-twins of people with a history of major depression

Nonidentical co-twins of people with a history of major depression

Nonidentical co-twins of people with no history of major depression

Identical co-twins of people with no history of major depression

19.

Why should we be somewhat skeptical about interpreting correlations between stressful life events and depression in cause-effect terms? What sorts of studies seem to provide the best evidence that stressful events can help cause depression?

Situational Bases for Depression

Many research studies, like that depicted in Figure 16.4, reveal positive correlations between the onset of depression and stressful life events reported as occurring within a few months prior to the depression. Such studies are usually taken as evidence that stressful events help bring on depression, but we should not automatically accept that interpretation. In most cases the measure of stressful events comes from reports made by depressed and nondepressed people who are asked to recall or check off events that happened to them over a specified period of time (Kessler, 1997). Depression itself can lead people to recall more negative events or to interpret events more negatively than they otherwise would (Cohen & others, 1988). For example, depression might lead a person to remember a cold as a "serious illness" and to place a check next to that item on an inventory of stressful experiences. Moreover, people who are predisposed for depression may also be predisposed to behave in ways that bring on stressful life events (Hammen, 1991; Kendler, 1998). A stressful event such as being in a traffic accident, or being fired from a job, or being abandoned by a lover or spouse may not just "happen" but may be partly caused by one's own actions. Thus, at least in theory, an observed relationship between reported stressful events and depression could be due to biased reporting or to some general behavioral difference between those who are prone to depression and those who are not.

Perhaps the best evidence that stressful events can bring on depression comes from studies that follow people, over time, after they have experienced some stressful event that was presumably out of their control, such as the death of a spouse (Umberson & others, 1992) or job loss due to general layoff rather than lack of ability (Dew & others, 1987). Such studies provide rather compelling evidence that stressful events indeed can bring on depression (Kessler, 1997).

The Dawn of Psychiatry...

YOU SEEM TO BE DEPRESSED

The kinds of experiences that appear to be most often associated with depression are *losses* that permanently change the nature of one's life—such as loss of a spouse or other close daily companion, loss of a job that one has held for a long time, loss in status, loss in income, or permanent loss in health. Such events interrupt one's life routines and render ineffective well-established ways of satisfying one's needs and desires. Studies of monkeys and apes indicate that they also manifest depressed mood and behavior when they lose a parent or mate or are forced out of a high position in the colony's dominance hierarchy (Goodall, 1986; Nesse & Williams, 1994; Suomi, 1991). Theorizing from an evolutionary perspective, Randolph Nesse (2000; Nesse & Williams, 1994) has suggested that depression may be an exaggerated form of a response to loss that in less extreme form is adaptive. A depressed mood slows us down, makes us think realistically rather than optimistically, makes us turn away from goals that we can no longer hope to achieve, and signals to others that this is a time in life when we need some help. A depressed mood also can lead to a kind of soul-searching, the end result of which may be the establishment of new, more realistic goals and a new approach to life.

Cognitive Bases for Depression

Although stressful life events can increase one's chance of becoming depressed, only a minority of people who experience such events actually become sufficiently depressed to warrant a clinical diagnosis. This observation—that different individuals respond very differently to the same objective experiences—is the starting point for cognitive theories of depression. Such theories hold that depression stems not so much from the objective events themselves as from the way those events are interpreted.

One of the first to emphasize the role of cognition in depression was Aaron Beck (1967), a psychiatrist who observed that his depressed clients held consistently pessimistic views of themselves, their world, and the future and that they seemed to maintain these views by distorting their perceptions of their experiences in negative ways. They would mentally exaggerate bad experiences and minimize or overlook good ones. Beck developed a mode of therapy (discussed in Chapter 17) that centers on training depressed people to assess their experiences more optimistically.

Following Beck, Martin Seligman and Lyn Abramson developed a more specific cognitive theory of depression, which has undergone a number of revisions and is now called the *hopelessness theory* (Abramson & others, 1989). According to this theory, depression results from a pattern of thinking about negative experiences that reduces or eliminates any hope that life will get better. More specifically, the theory holds that people who are most prone to depression consistently attribute negative experiences to causes that are *stable* (unlikely to change) and *global* (applicable to a wide sphere of endeavors), and that people who are least prone to depression attribute negative experiences to causes that are *unstable* (likely to change) and/or *specific* (applicable to a narrow sphere of activities and experiences).

20.

How might moderate depression be interpreted as an adaptive response to loss?

21.

According to the hopelessness theory, what patterns of thinking predispose a person for depression? What is some evidence for and against the theory?

For instance, a failing grade on a test might trigger one student to think, "I am incompetent," and another student to think, "I didn't study hard enough for that test." The first attribution is stable and global (incompetence is the kind of trait that stays with a person and affects all realms of life), and the second is unstable and specific (study habits can change and the lack of study applied only to this one test). According to the hopelessness theory, the first student is more likely to become depressed after receiving the failing grade than is the second.

Seligman and his colleagues have developed an *attributional-style questionnaire* to assess people's routine ways of explaining their negative and positive experiences, and they and others have used it in research aimed at testing the hopelessness theory. Depressed people do clearly make attributions in a manner consistent with the theory (Seligman & others, 1988), but that observation by itself does not show that the attributional style is a cause of depression; it could simply be a symptom of depression.

Other research suggests strongly that the negative style of thinking does play a causal role in the onset of depression. In one study, first-year, nondepressed college students—who had no prior history of clinical depression—filled out the attributional-style questionnaire and then were assessed for depression at various times over a 2½-year follow-up period (Alloy & others, 1999). Of those whose attributional style placed them in the "high risk for depression" category, 17 percent developed a major depressive disorder during the follow-up period. In contrast, only 1 percent of those in the low-risk category developed such a disorder. In other studies, people who learned, through cognitive therapy, to change their way of thinking to the more positive style were significantly less likely than otherwise comparable control subjects to become depressed during a follow-up period of many months (DeRubeis & Hollon, 1995; Gillham & others, 1995).

Depression Breeds Depression

Most of us, when we are in a depressed mood, are able to relieve it through our own thoughts and actions. After a certain period of gloom, we grab our bootstraps and pull ourselves up, using such means as positive thinking, problem solving, talking with friends, or engaging in activities that we especially enjoy. But severely depressed people—those who qualify for a diagnosis of major depression—typically don't do those things. Their patterns of thought and action continue to work against their recovery, rather than for it. Figure 16.5 depicts what might be called the vicious triangle of severe depression, in which a person's mood, thought, and action interact in such a way as to keep him or her in a depressed state. Depressed mood promotes negative thinking and withdrawal from enjoyable activities; negative thinking promotes depressed mood and withdrawal from enjoyable activities; and withdrawal from enjoyable activities promotes depressed mood and negative thinking. Each corner of the triangle supports the others.

Each corner of the triangle also corresponds to a different therapeutic approach to breaking the triangle of depression (described more fully in Chapter 17). Drug therapy attempts to elevate mood through direct action on the brain, and this in turn should increase positive thinking and actions. Behavioral therapy attempts to get the person to act in ways that bring more pleasure and a greater sense of control, and this in turn should improve mood and promote positive thoughts. Cognitive therapy attempts to change the person's way of thinking in a positive direction, and this in turn should improve behavior and mood.

Bipolar Disorders

Major depression and dysthymia are sometimes called *unipolar disorders*, because they are characterized by mood changes in only one direction—downward from normal. Bipolar disorders (also called *manic-depression*) are characterized by mood swings in both directions: downward in *depressive episodes* and upward in *manic episodes*. Such episodes may last anywhere from a few days to several months, and

22.

How can depression be depicted as a vicious triangle, and how do different approaches to treating depression correspond with the triangle's corners?

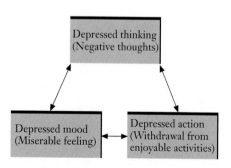

FIGURE **16.5** *The vicious triangle of severe depression*
Mood, thought, and behavior feed on one another to maintain the depressed state.

23.

How are manic states experienced, and what is some evidence linking mild manic (hypomanic) episodes to heightened creativity?

periods of normal mood may occur in between. *DSM-IV* identifies two main varieties of bipolar disorders, which differ in degree. **Bipolar disorder** (in the singular) is the more severe variety, and **cyclothymia** is the less severe variety, in which the mood changes are not as great. The high phase in cyclothymia is less disabling than that in bipolar disorder and is technically referred to as *hypomania* rather than *mania*. The manic and hypomanic episodes in bipolar disorders typically involve inordinate feelings of power, confidence, and energy, as illustrated by the following quotation from a woman describing her own disorder (Fieve, 1975):

> When I start going into a high, I no longer feel like an ordinary housewife. Instead, I feel organized and accomplished, and I begin to feel I am my most creative self. I can write poetry easily. I can compose melodies without effort. I can paint. . . . I have countless ideas about how the environmental problem could inspire a crusade for the health and betterment of everyone. . . . I don't seem to need much sleep. . . . I feel sexy and men stare at me. Maybe I'll have an affair, or perhaps several. I feel capable of speaking and doing good in politics.

The feeling of enhanced ability and creativity during hypomanic and mild manic episodes is probably not entirely an illusion. A number of studies have found a disproportionately high incidence of cyclothymia among eminently creative artists and writers and have shown that those individuals produced their best work during manic episodes (Andreasen, 1987; Jamison, 1995). In another study, people with cyclothymia, selected only on the basis of their clinical diagnosis, were found to be more creative in their regular work and home life than were a control group with no diagnosed mental disorder (Richards & others, 1988). In the same study, however, people with the more serious bipolar disorder were not more creative than those in the control group. Apparently, the disorganization of thought and action that accompanied their more extreme bouts of mania offset any creative advantage that they may have enjoyed.

The positive experiences accompanying some hypomanic states should not blind us to the extraordinarily disruptive effects that bipolar disorders have on the affected individuals and their families. Mania may be accompanied by bizarre thoughts and dangerous behaviors, such as jumping off a building in the false belief that one can fly; and even hypomania may be accompanied by spending sprees, absence from work, or sexual escapades that the affected person later regrets. Moreover, not all people with bipolar disorders experience the hypomanic or manic state as euphoric. Some experience it as a time of extraordinary irritability, suspiciousness, or destructive rage (Carroll, 1991). The depressed phase of bipolar disorder entails mood and behavioral changes that are similar to those experienced by sufferers of unipolar depression.

Research with twins and adoptees to assess heritability has shown that the predisposition to bipolar disorder is strongly influenced by genes (Kelsoe, 1997). Stressful life events may help bring on manic and depressive episodes in people who are predisposed (Ambelus, 1987; Hlastala & others, 2000), but the evidence for such effects is not as strong as it is for unipolar depression. Bipolar disorder, unlike unipolar depression, can usually be controlled with the drug lithium, but how lithium works is as yet unknown (Manji & Lenox, 2000).

Corbis-Bettman

Ups and downs of a composer
Like many highly creative people, composer Robert Schumann suffered from a mood disorder. He attempted suicide twice during bouts of severe depression and eventually died, in 1856, from self-starvation in an asylum. His depression waxed and waned over long cycles, and during two prolonged periods, in 1840 and 1849, he was hypomanic (exhibited moderate mania). Those were his most productive years by far. He composed 24 musical works in 1840 and 27 in 1849. (Jamison, 1995.)

SECTION SUMMARY

Mood disorders include depressive and bipolar disorders. Major depression is characterized by intense sadness, feelings of worthlessness, and absence of pleasure that last for at least 2 weeks. Dysthymia is characterized by less severe symptoms that last for at least 2 years.

Antidepressant drugs typically raise the level of monoamine neurotransmitters (particularly norepinephrine and serotonin) in the brain. This fact led, early on, to the theory—now doubted—that depression is caused by an undersupply of one or more of the monoamine neurotransmitters. Genes that predispose a person for depression appear to work largely by increasing one's sensitivity to stressful life events. Major depression is especially likely to be triggered by serious losses, such as the death of a spouse or a permanent decline in health. From an evolutionary perspective, depression may be an exaggerated response that in less extreme form helps one reassess one's goals following a major setback.

Cognitively, people who are most prone to depression are those who attribute their failures and losses to causes that are stable (unlikely to change) and global (widespread). Changing one's way of interpreting such events has been shown to reduce the occurrence of depression. Major depression, unlike normal low mood, traps a person in a vicious cycle in which negative thoughts, depressed action (withdrawal from enjoyable activities), and depressed mood all reinforce one another.

Bipolar disorders—including the less extreme cyclothymia—involve alternating episodes of depression and mania (or the milder hypomania). During manic episodes people typically experience inordinately high levels of energy and unrealistic, often dangerous, feelings of power and confidence. Some creative people have done their best work during periods of hypomania. Bipolar disorder is quite strongly heritable, but the initiation of episodes of depression and mania in predisposed individuals may be triggered by stressful life experiences.

PSYCHOLOGICAL INFLUENCES ON PHYSICAL SYMPTOMS AND DISEASES

The brain is responsible not just for thoughts and emotion but also for sensation, movement, and the regulation of many biological systems within the body. It is not surprising, therefore, that experiences that affect our thoughts and emotions can also affect our bodily functions and our manner of experiencing those functions.

Somatoform Disorders

Somatoform literally means "bodily form," and **somatoform disorders** are those in which the person experiences bodily ailments in the absence of any physical disease that could cause them. The most dramatic category of somatoform disorder, of the several categories described in *DSM-IV*, is **conversion disorder**, in which the person temporarily loses some bodily function, perhaps (in the most dramatic cases) becoming blind, deaf, or partially paralyzed in ways or under conditions that cannot be explained in terms of physical damage to the affected organs or their neural connections (for example, see Figure 16.6).

Conversion disorders are rare in North America and western Europe today, but they were relatively common in these places 100 years ago and earlier. Such disorders were prominent in Sigmund Freud's practice in the late-nineteenth and early-twentieth centuries, and they played a major role in his development of psychoanalytic theory. As a neurologist, Freud saw many patients with physical complaints and disabilities that appeared to have no medical explanation. He concluded that such symptoms were products of the patients' unconscious minds that served to protect them from anxiety-producing activities and experiences (discussed further in Chapter 17).

Today, the most dramatic examples of conversion disorder are generally found in people raised in non-Western cultures who have been exposed to highly traumatic events. An example of this is the high rate of psychologically based blindness discovered among Cambodian women who managed to emigrate to the United States after the Khmer Rouge reign of terror in Cambodia in the 1970s (Rozée & Van Boemel, 1989). All these women mani-

24.

How did Freud interpret conversion disorders? Why are somatoform disorders in general and conversion disorders in particular much affected by culture?

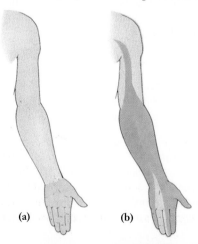

FIGURE **16.6**   *A conversion disorder*
Glove anesthesia—the experience of no sensation in the hand but continued sensation in all other parts of the arm, as shown in (a)—cannot result from nerve damage, because no nerves innervate the hand without innervating part of the arm. The actual areas of sensory loss that would occur if specific nerves were damaged are shown in (b). Thus, whenever glove anesthesia occurs, it is most likely a conversion disorder.

(a)   (b)

fested posttraumatic stress syndrome brought on by the tortures they suffered and witnessed. Many of them had seen their own children being slowly tortured and murdered. One woman described the onset of her blindness in these words: "My family was killed in 1975 and I cried for 4 years. When I stopped crying I was blind." Another described becoming blind "from the smoke" as she was looking at the cooking pot in a forced-labor camp where she was held—a pot that, she knew, often contained human flesh, rats, and worms, which the women were forced to cook for themselves and other inmates to eat.

A less dramatic category of somatoform disorder described in *DSM-IV* is ***somatization disorder***, which is characterized by a long history of dramatic complaints about many different medical conditions, most of which are vague and unverifiable, such as dizziness, heart palpitations, and nausea. No reliable information exists on the prevalence of somatization disorder, because there is usually no way to determine whether such complaints derive from undetectable physical diseases or from purely psychological origins. On the basis of cross-cultural and historical research, Arthur Kleinman (1988) has argued that somatization and depression may be two ways of feeling and expressing the same underlying problem. According to Kleinman, a sense of hopelessness is usually experienced as depression in Western cultures today but in the past was more often experienced as physical aches and pains, as it still is in China and many other parts of the world.

More generally, cross-cultural and historical research suggests that the prevalence and precise nature of all categories of somatoform disorders are very much affected by cultural beliefs (Castillo, 1997; Shorter, 1992). Few people in North America or Europe today believe that a person can be stricken suddenly blind, deaf, or paralyzed without a medical cause, so those forms of somatoform disorders are much rarer in the West now than they were in the nineteenth century and earlier. Moreover, as disorders purely of mood or emotion become more legitimized by a culture, the incidence of somatoform disorders of all types tends to go down and that of anxiety and mood disorders tends to go up. The more Westernized a culture, apparently, the more its people express their misery in psychological rather than physical terms (Kleinman & Cohen, 1977).

Bart Bartholemew / NYT Pictures

Traumatic blindness

This woman is one of many Cambodian women whose acute vision problems have been tied to seeing atrocities committed by, and being tortured by, the Khmer Rouge. Because of cultural differences and problems with diagnosis, Western psychologists have just begun to develop ways of treating the disorder.

Psychological Factors Affecting Medical Condition

You have just read of disorders in which bodily pain or disability is experienced in the absence of any medical explanation. We turn now to a different category of psychological effects on the body—cases in which one's behavior or emotions precipitate or influence the course of a disease that clearly does have a physical, medical basis. The harm-producing behavior or emotions do not technically constitute a mental disorder, yet a category—called *psychological factors affecting medical condition*—is reserved for them in a section of *DSM-IV* devoted to clinically significant conditions other than mental disorders.

Typical of the evidence that psychological state can affect physical health are studies showing that recent widowers and widows are much more vulnerable to essentially all types of physical diseases during the months following the death of their spouses than are otherwise-comparable men and women who have not lost a spouse (Kaprio & others, 1987). In one study (Prigerson & others, 1997), 150 men and women whose spouses were terminally ill were identified and then were assessed for psychological state and physical health from the time just before they were widowed until 25 months afterward. On the basis of interviews conducted 6 months after their widowhood, a subgroup were identified who manifested what

25.

What evidence did a study of widows and widowers provide for an effect of psychological state on medical condition? What are possible mechanisms for such effects?

the researchers called *traumatic grief*—a syndrome similar to posttraumatic stress syndrome combined with extraordinary yearning for the deceased spouse, bitterness, and survival guilt. Although the members of this subgroup were not physically less healthy than the other subjects before the spouse's death or at the 6-month interview, by 25 months of widowhood they had developed significantly more incidences of flu, heart disease, and cancer than had the less traumatized group.

It is not hard to imagine possible mechanisms through which traumatic grief or other disruptive psychological states can affect a person's health. The most obvious possibility is that the affected person may fail to take good physical care of himself or herself. Bereavement is often associated with poor diet, poor sleep patterns, increased smoking, increased alcohol consumption, and failure to take prescribed medicines (Cohen & Herbert, 1996). There is also evidence that psychological states can affect health more directly through the brain's effects on internal organs and the immune system.

Personality, Negative Emotions, and Cardiovascular Disease

In the 1950s, two California cardiologists, Meyer Friedman and Ray Rosenman, observed that many of their heart-attack patients (most of whom were men) were similar to one another in personality. They seemed to be competitive, aggressive, easily irritated, impatient workaholics, constantly concerned with deadlines and getting ahead. Friedman and Rosenman coined the terms *Type A* to refer to this constellation of behaviors and *Type B* to refer to the opposite constellation of more easygoing behaviors that they believed would be associated with low risk for heart attack. After conducting several preliminary studies that yielded results consistent with their hypothesis, Friedman and Rosenman received a government grant to conduct a large-scale study.

As subjects for their study, they recruited 3100 businessmen, none of whom had heart disease. On the basis of an interview procedure that took into account not just the subjects' literal answers to questions but also their manner of answering (such as irritation in their voices), Friedman and Rosenman's team of researchers classified the subjects as best they could into Type A and Type B groups. Then they followed the subjects medically, for a period of 9 years, and found that the Type A subjects developed cardiovascular diseases at double the frequency of the Type B subjects. This difference was highly significant statistically and could not be accounted for by a difference between the two subject groups in any other known risk factor such as smoking, diet, weight, or cholesterol level. Friedman and Rosenman (1974) wrote a book on their findings, which became a best-seller, and by the late-1970s *Type A* was a familiar term. In some corners, "I'm Type A" became a kind of boast, meaning "I'm so hard-working and competitive that I'm likely to have a heart attack."

Subsequent attempts to corroborate Friedman and Rosenman's finding produced mixed results. Some found a relation between Type A behavior and heart disease, some found none, and some found that certain other characteristics predicted heart attack more reliably than did the Type A constellation. A systematic review of such studies concluded that (a) Type A is moderately but reliably predictive of heart disease in men and probably also in women (though relatively few studies have included women); (b) the hurried lifestyle and job-involvement aspects of Type A are not predictive of heart disease, but the irritability and hostility are; (c) depression and anxiety, which are not part of the definition of Type A, are also predictive of heart disease; and (d) these effects are not mediated by other known risk factors, such as smoking or high cholesterol (Booth-Kewley & H. Friedman, 1987).

In sum, the evidence today is that prolonged or frequent negative emotions in general can increase one's risk for heart disease but that a hard-working, constantly rushed person who enjoys what he or she is doing is not at special risk (H. Friedman & others, 1994; Suinn, 2001). Nobody knows just how negative emotions promote heart disease, but most researchers assume that the effect is mediated through the autonomic nervous system and endocrine system, both of which

26.

How did two heart specialists find evidence for their hypothesis that a set of behaviors designated Type A promotes heart disease? How have subsequent studies altered our understanding of the psychological factors that promote heart disease?

© Randy Glasbergen, 1997

GLASBERGEN

"I'm learning how to relax, doctor—but I want to relax *better* and *faster*! I want to be on the cutting edge of relaxation!"

have direct influences on the circulatory system and are altered during emotional states (discussed in Chapter 6). Among other things, negative emotions increase blood pressure (Ewart & Kolodner, 1994), and consistently high blood pressure can contribute to heart disease.

Emotional Distress and Suppression of the Body's Defenses Against Diseases

An increasing number of well-controlled studies suggest that emotional distress shuts down some of the body's defenses against viruses and other pathogens and in that way makes us more vulnerable to infectious diseases such as colds and flu (Cohen, 1996; Kiecolt-Glaser & Glaser, 2001).

In one study, 394 healthy men and women agreed, for the sake of science, to have a fluid containing known respiratory viruses dribbled into their nostrils and then to remain quarantined for 6 days while researchers assessed their medical condition (Cohen & others, 1991). At the outset of the study, each volunteer filled out a set of questionnaires aimed at assessing the degree of psychological distress he or she had experienced recently. The result was that the more distress people reported at the outset of the study, the more likely they were to develop a cold within the 6-day period (see Figure 16.7). The colds were real, not imagined; they were assessed by direct viral counts as well as by external symptoms. Moreover, the relation between distress and the incidence of colds could not be accounted for by any other risk factors the researchers measured, including smoking, alcohol consumption, diet, and quality of sleep.

Because of the correlational nature of this study, we cannot be certain that increased emotional distress was a cause of the increased susceptibility to colds. Perhaps people who are prone to emotional distress are also constitutionally susceptible to colds. Other research, however, has shown more directly that emotional distress can suppress the body's immune response (Cohen & others, 2001; Maier & others, 1994). In one study, people given frustrating cognitive tasks (including difficult mental arithmetic) manifested a temporary decline in production of T-cells, a class of white blood cells known to be involved in fighting disease organisms (Manuck & others, 1991). This effect occurred only in subjects who showed other physiological signs of distress in response to the tasks. In other studies, laboratory animals subjected to various long-term stressful conditions showed long-term declines in immune responses to infectious agents (Ader & Cohen, 1993; Cohen & others, 1992).

If you think about this from an evolutionary perspective, you might wonder why we, and other mammals, are constructed in such a manner that our disease-fighting capacity is reduced in times of emotional distress. A plausible answer, proposed by Steven Maier and his colleagues (1994), begins with a reminder that the body's stress response is fundamentally a fight-or-flight response. Its purpose is to shift as many as possible of the body's resources toward muscular energy to enable

27.

What is some evidence that one's emotional state can alter the chance of catching a cold and that this may be mediated by effects on the immune system?

28.

From an evolutionary perspective, why might psychological distress inhibit immune function?

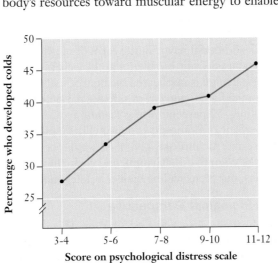

FIGURE **16.7** *Relation between psychological distress and subsequent development of a cold* The psychological distress score was based on a combination of recent stressful life events and negative emotions reported by volunteer subjects on questionnaires. As the degree of psychological distress increased, so did the percentage of subjects who developed a cold within 6 days of deliberate exposure to respiratory viruses. (From Cohen & others, 1991.)

fight or flight, and to do so, it partly shuts down many physiological functions that are not essential for dealing with the immediate emergency. The physiological mechanisms for resisting disease use a great deal of bodily energy, so it makes sense that these would be suppressed or partly suppressed when dealing with something like a charging tiger. The sympathetic nervous system and adrenal hormones mediate much of the body's response to stress, and, as part of that response, they suppress energy-consuming aspects of the body's defense against disease, including production of white blood cells. Unfortunately, that ancient stress response continues to be triggered off in us when we experience anger, fear, or dread in response to situations or events that can't be dealt with by fight or flight and that plague us for longer periods of time than a charging tiger would.

SECTION SUMMARY

Our thoughts and emotions can affect our bodily functions. Somatoform disorders—including conversion disorder and somatization disorder—are manifested as bodily ailments in the absence of any physical disease that could cause them. Such disorders are relatively common in cultures that do not distinguish between medical and psychological problems as sharply as do modern Western cultures. Psychological factors can also affect the onset and maintenance of actual medical conditions, and these influences are apparently as common in the West as elsewhere. Traumatic grief predisposes people for a variety of life-threatening diseases; chronic anger, anxiety, and depression increase the risk of cardiovascular diseases; and emotional distress interferes with the immune response, increasing people's chances of developing colds and other infectious diseases.

PSYCHOACTIVE-SUBSTANCE-USE DISORDERS

A *psychoactive substance* is a drug that acts on the brain and affects a person's emotions, perceptions, or thoughts. A ***psychoactive-substance-use disorder*** involves the abuse of or dependence on such a drug. ***Drug abuse*** implies persistent use of the drug in a way that is harmful to the self or society. ***Drug dependence*** (which in *DSM-IV* is a synonym for *addiction*) implies that the person feels compelled—for physiological or psychological reasons or both—to take the drug on a regular basis and feels severe distress without it. A person who repeatedly drives while drunk, or who drinks despite awareness that alcohol is exacerbating a stomach ulcer, or who periodically misses work because of a drinking spree is said to abuse alcohol. A person who feels that he or she cannot get through the day without drinking is said to be dependent on alcohol. In *DSM-IV* separate abuse and dependence disorders are listed for alcohol, cocaine, opiates (such as heroin), and a variety of other drugs.

It would be hard to overestimate the problems that drugs cause for individuals and society. Drugs that cannot be obtained legally—especially cocaine and heroin—wreak additional havoc in the form of murders, robberies, and wasted lives. But the most abused drug by far, today as well as in the past, is alcohol. In the United States, alcohol is implicated in about 55 percent of automobile fatalities, 50 percent of homicides, 30 percent of suicides, 65 percent of drownings, 50 percent of deaths by falling, 52 percent of fires leading to death, 60 percent of child-abuse cases, and 85 percent of domestic violence (FitzGerald, 1988; National Institute of Alcohol Abuse and Alcoholism, 1987). As we discuss substance-use disorders from the biological, cognitive-behavioral, and sociocultural perspectives in the following paragraphs, our focus will be on alcohol dependence and abuse.

The Biological Perspective

Psychoactive drugs alter mood, thought, or behavior by altering the biology of the brain. Such alterations can be classified into three types of drug effects—intoxicating effects, withdrawal effects, and permanent effects.

Intoxicating effects are the short-term effects for which the drug is usually taken, which may last for minutes or hours after a single dose. (For a summary of such effects and their physiological mechanisms for many drugs, see Table 5.1 in Chapter 5.) The intoxicating effects of alcohol include relief from anxiety, slowed thinking, poor judgment, slurred speech, and uncoordinated movements. Beyond reducing anxiety, alcohol can have varying, sometimes contrary effects on emotion: It can promote happiness or sadness, goodwill or pugnaciousness. Such extremes in emotion may be due to the dulling effect of alcohol on logic and long-range thinking. Lacking the modulating effects of long-term thinking, the person reacts more strongly than usual to emotion-arousing cues in the immediate environment, a condition called *alcohol myopia* (Steele & Josephs, 1990). If cues in the environment promote happiness, the intoxicated person will feel elated; if they promote sadness, the person will sob.

Withdrawal effects occur after the drug is removed from the system. Usually such effects occur only when withdrawal follows a long period of continuous or frequent drug use. These effects apparently result from adaptation to the drug such that the brain functions in some ways more normally with the drug than without it. (For a more complete discussion, see Chapter 5.) In a person who is physiologically addicted to alcohol, withdrawal effects begin to occur within 8 to 20 hours after alcohol has been cleared from the body. These symptoms—referred to as *delirium tremens* (or *DTs*)—reflect an extraordinarily overactive brain. They include hallucinations; feelings of panic; muscle tremors ("the shakes"); sweating, high heart rate, and other signs of autonomic arousal; and sometimes brain seizures. Delirium tremens is not only frightening but truly dangerous. When not treated medically, it results in death in between 15 and 50 percent of instances (Light, 1986).

Permanent effects are irreversible forms of brain damage that can result from frequent drug use or that can occur in a developing fetus if the mother uses the drug during pregnancy. One permanent effect of long-term, heavy alcohol use is *alcohol amnesic disorder* (also called *Korsakoff's syndrome*), which entails severe memory impairment and difficulties with motor coordination associated with damage to various areas of the brain, including parts of the limbic system. Another permanent effect of alcohol is *fetal alcohol syndrome*, a condition of mental retardation and physical abnormalities in a child that stems from the mother's consumption of large amounts of alcohol during pregnancy.

Twin and adoption studies indicate that genes contribute considerably to one's susceptibility to alcohol dependence (McGue, 1999). Such studies also suggest that more than one type of alcohol dependence exists and that different types have different degrees of heritability (Cloninger, 1990; Pickens & others, 1991). In at least some cases, the genetic predisposition seems to work by heightening alcohol's pleasurable effects and/or reducing its unpleasant effects through such means as enhancing the effect that alcohol has on the production of endorphins (Gianoulakis & others, 1996).

The Behavioral and Cognitive Perspectives

Consuming alcohol or taking any drug is a learned, voluntary action. Behaviorists have long described addictive behavior in terms of operant conditioning. From this view, the short-term pleasure or relief caused by the drug is a powerful reinforcer for continued drug use. Classical conditioning may also come into play. As described in Chapter 4, cues associated with an environment in which a drug is frequently taken can become conditioned stimuli for physiological responses that tend to counteract the drug effect (Siegel & others, 1988). The responses feel like withdrawal symptoms and thus induce the craving. This phenomenon has been used to

29.

What are three classes of effects that psychoactive drugs can have on the brain, and how is each exemplified by consequences of alcohol?

Alcoholics Anonymous

In A.A. groups, people must meet as equals to share their experiences and strengths and to help one another recover from alcohol misuse. The core of the recovery program is a series of twelve steps, the most basic of which is admitting that one suffers from alcoholism.

30.

How do behavioral theorists describe addiction in terms of conditioning, and how do cognitive theorists describe it in terms of learned expectancies?

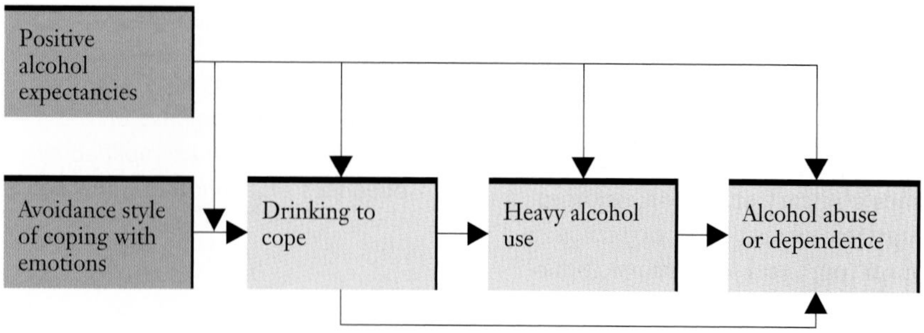

FIGURE **16.8**
A cognitive model of alcoholism
In this model, positive alcohol expectancies plus a tendency to avoid confronting one's own strong emotions are predisposing causes of alcohol abuse or dependence. (Adapted from Cooper & others, 1988.)

explain why a person who has been drug-free and has felt no craving for it during a long stay in a treatment center may suddenly experience an intense craving upon returning to the environment in which he or she had habitually taken the drug.

From a cognitive perspective, the act of taking a drug requires a decision to take it, and that decision is based in part on a person's beliefs or expectancies concerning the drug and its effects. In a longitudinal study, researchers found that they could predict which nondrinking teenagers would become alcohol abusers on the basis of their beliefs about alcohol (Roehling & others, 1987). Those who believed that alcohol has valued effects—such as making a person more sociable, powerful, or sexually vital—were more likely to be alcohol abusers 1 or 2 years later than were those who did not have such beliefs. Other studies have suggested that a critical step in the development of alcoholism occurs when a person begins to use alcohol not just socially but as a way of coping with negative emotions (Cooper & others, 1988; Laurent & others, 1997). Once the person thinks of alcohol as a general way of quieting negative emotions, its use increases and the person is well on the path to alcohol abuse or dependence. On the basis of such research, M. Lynne Cooper and her colleagues (1988, 1995) proposed a cognitive model of alcoholism in which the predisposing causes are (a) positive expectancies about the effects of alcohol and (b) a learned fear of negative emotions or a tendency to avoid such emotions (see Figure 16.8).

31.

What is some evidence that cultural traditions affect the prevalence of alcoholism?

The Sociocultural Perspective

If the likelihood of abusing alcohol or other drugs is related to a person's beliefs about the substance, where do these beliefs come from? They come from family, friends, and the entire social environment to which the person is exposed. Research has shown that most young people who abuse alcohol or other drugs were first encouraged to do so by their peers and that the ability to resist such peer pressure is directly related to the strength and cohesiveness of family ties (Oetting & Beauvais, 1988; Zucker & Gomberg, 1986). Other studies have revealed large cultural and subcultural differences in alcohol abuse and dependence that correspond to cultural traditions. In the United States, the lowest rates of alcoholism are found among ethnic Jews, Chinese, Japanese, Italians, and Greeks, all of whom have traditions of strong negative sanctions against heavy drinking or drunkenness (Peele, 1988; Vaillant, 1983). Among such groups alcohol may be used for religious purposes or as a beverage to accompany a meal, but drinking to get drunk is not accepted. Cultural beliefs probably also contribute to the large difference between men and women in prevalence of diagnosed alcoholism (shown in Figure 16.1); in practically every culture, drunkenness is viewed as less acceptable in women than in men.

SECTION SUMMARY

Issues of drug abuse and dependence are illustrated here with examples concerning alcohol. Biologically, alcohol alters mood, thought, and behavior through its intoxicating effects (including alcohol myopia), withdrawal effects, and permanent effects (including Korsakoff's syndrome and fetal alcohol syndrome). Susceptibility to alcohol dependence is strongly affected by genes. From a behavioral perspective, alcoholism is partly explained as operant conditioning reinforced by the pleasure or relief that alcohol offers and the classical conditioning of counteractive responses that induce alcohol craving. From a cognitive perspective, alcoholism is partly explained in terms of learned alcohol expectancies and an avoidant style of coping with negative emotions. From a sociocultural perspective, differences in alcohol use and abuse are understood in terms of varying cultural traditions and mores.

DISSOCIATIVE DISORDERS

Dissociation is the process by which a period of a person's life, ranging from a few minutes to years, becomes separated from the rest of his or her conscious mind in such a way that it cannot be recalled or can be recalled only under special conditions. Dissociation can be produced in many people through hypnosis. Hypnosis is a state in which a person voluntarily relinquishes control of his or her own mental activities to another person (the hypnotist) and, as a result, experiences the perceptions, emotions, and memories that are suggested by the hypnotist (Kihlstrom, 1985). The state can be induced by a variety of techniques, most of which include instructions to relax and to fix attention on a specific sight or sound over a period of time. In general, people who easily become engrossed in imaginative activity are more easily hypnotized than other people (Kihlstrom, 1985). When a hypnotized person is given the suggestion that, upon awakening, he or she will remember nothing of what happened until a certain signal occurs, the hypnotized person typically reports remembering nothing until a certain signal is given (Hilgard, 1977). Dissociative disorders can reasonably be thought of as conditions in which a person undergoes such hypnosislike experiences in the course of his or her everyday life (Bliss, 1986).

Varieties of *dissociative disorders* are distinguished in *DSM-IV* according to their complexity. In the simplest type, *dissociative amnesia*, memory loss is the only prominent symptom. The amnesia may be selective for a specific traumatic experience, or it may be more global and include loss of memory for all facts about the self, including one's own name and place of residence. A second level of complexity occurs in those rare cases diagnosed as *dissociative fugue*. Here the person not only loses memory of his or her previous identity but wanders away from home and develops a new identity that is quite separate from the earlier one (the term *fugue* stems from the Latin word *fugere*, "to flee"). When the fugue ends, perhaps days or months later, the person regains his or her original identity, with all its associated memories, and at the same time loses memory of everything that happened during the fugue. The most complex and intriguing variety of dissociative disorder is *dissociative identity disorder*, formerly called *multiple-personality disorder*, which is the focus of the rest of this section.

Identifying Dissociative Identity Disorder

Let us assume that you are a clinical psychologist or psychiatrist interviewing a new client. Before you sits a demure, exhausted-looking young woman who speaks in earnest tones about her complete devotion to her husband and child and about the headaches that she has been experiencing lately. Then, at a difficult moment in the conversation, she closes her eyes, and when she opens them, you see before you a new person. She sits and speaks differently, and the expression on her face is that of a different person. No longer demure and exhausted, she is vivacious and talkative. She looks you in the eye, speaks with confidence, and calls you "Doc." This woman has no headaches, and she claims to have no children or husband either. "I can't be bothered with that. Life is too short," she says, and gives you a wink. This woman calls herself by a different name from the other one. She knows the other, though, and speaks of her with a combination of contempt and pity as a person who has never learned how to live. She knows the husband and child, too, and doesn't like them at all. In later sessions, as you get to know both of these women better, you find that although the second woman knows about the first, the first woman knows nothing of the second. The first talks about "losing time" (discovering that time has passed without her knowing what happened); about finding herself in strange places such as hotel rooms; and about finding dresses that had mysteriously appeared in her closet—garish ones that she would never buy herself.

32.

How is dissociation exemplified by hypnosis?

Michael Newman / Photo Edit

A state of heightened suggestibility

Because hypnosis is a state of heightened suggestibility, memories that come to mind in this state are often constructions that accord with the hypnotist's suggestions or expectations. To induce a hypnotic state in this woman, the therapist asks her to fix her visual attention entirely on a spot on the ceiling and her auditory attention entirely on his voice. Some researchers contend that cases of dissociative identity disorder are often products of hypnotic suggestion.

Gerald Martineau / The Washington Post

The integrated "Eve"

After many years of psychotherapy, Chris Sizemore—the real "Eve"—overcame her dissociative identity disorder. Here she is shown with a painting she made to symbolize the three personalities that were apparent when she first entered therapy.

33.

What evidence links dissociative identity disorder with childhood abuse coupled, perhaps, with an inborn ability to dissociate?

The account just described is based on the book *The Three Faces of Eve*, written by two psychiatrists, Corbett Thigpen and Hervey Cleckley (1957), about a woman they had treated for dissociative identity disorder. The first personality is referred to as Eve White, the second as Eve Black. Later, a third, more mature and stable personality emerges, referred to as Jane. Still later, after the book was completed, new personalities continued to emerge—22 in all—over a period of nearly 20 years (McKellar, 1979). Eventually, after many years of therapy, the woman overcame the disorder and since 1974 has been one person—the integrated person whom she considers to be her real self (Sizemore, 1989).

Dissociative identity disorder is defined in *DSM-IV* as a disorder in which two or more distinct personalities or self-identities are manifested by the same person at different times. The switch from one identity to another apparently occurs automatically, usually in response to some environmental provocation. At the time of Thigpen and Cleckley's book, this disorder was believed to be extraordinarily rare. In fact, prior to 1970 only about 100 cases could be found in the psychiatric literature (Boor, 1982), but by 1999 that number had increased to about 30,000 in North America alone (Ross, 1999). In most reported cases, the personality change is not as obvious as that described for Eve. At present, much debate exists concerning the nature and causes of the disorder. The two most common but opposing views on the subject will be described here.

The Childhood-Trauma Theory of Dissociative Identity Disorder

Most people diagnosed with dissociative identity disorder are women who report having been severely abused or in other ways traumatized repeatedly in childhood (Ross, 1999). In one report, for example, Phillip Coons and his colleagues (1988) described 50 cases of dissociative identity disorder that had been diagnosed at their Indiana clinic. Of these, 46 were women and 48 reported that they had been physically or sexually abused repeatedly and severely in childhood, most often by their parents. Of the two patients who had not been abused as children, one was a man whose mother had been diagnosed with schizophrenia and the other was a woman whose disorder originated in her early twenties at a time when she was repeatedly beaten by her husband. Except for this woman, all the patients presented memories suggesting that they had begun a pattern of dissociation sometime before the age of 10. Large-scale studies in the Netherlands and Canada have likewise found that the vast majority of people diagnosed with dissociative identity disorder are women and that the vast majority (of either sex) claimed to have been repeatedly tortured or sexually abused beginning in early childhood (Boon & Draijer, 1993; Ross & others, 1989).

Such findings have led to and supported the theory that dissociative identity disorder typically begins in early childhood as a way of coping with repeated abuse (Bliss, 1986; Ross, 1999). The child learns that she can feel less pain and cope with the abuse better if she imagines that it is happening to someone other than herself—someone who is better equipped to deal with the pain. With practice, these periods of imagination take on the character of hypnoticlike trances, which are dissociated from the child's other, more normal experiences. Over time, the trance states become more elaborate and take on the form of distinct personalities that have their own sets of thoughts, feelings, or memories. For example, a child being tortured might construct a masochistic personality who "enjoys" the torture or a tough personality who "can take it." Having learned to produce new personalities to deal with such extreme conditions, the individual may use the same personalities or may develop new ones to deal with the more normal problems of life.

Not everyone who is abused repeatedly in childhood develops multiple personalities. Another prerequisite may be an inborn capacity for vivid fantasy and ability to dissociate. Consistent with this view, dissociative identity patients often report a rich fantasy life and are extremely easy to hypnotize compared with people who suffer from other mental disorders or have no disorder (Bliss, 1986).

The Culturally Conditioned Iatrogenic Theory of Dissociative Identity Disorder

The dramatic increase in the number of reported cases of dissociative identity disorder began shortly after the appearance of a popular book (Schreiber, 1973) and television movie (Petrie, 1976) about a woman (known as Sybil) who was diagnosed with the disorder. Even today, only a relatively small number of psychiatrists and clinical psychologists claim to have seen any cases of the disorder, but a few—who are strong believers in the childhood-trauma model—have reported seeing dozens or even hundreds of such cases. In the great majority of cases, the personality changes reported by therapists who identify the disorder are quite subtle, nothing like the dramatic changes described in books about Eve and Sybil. Most patients themselves—and their family members—are unaware of the patient's multiple identities until they are "discovered" in the course of therapy. In many cases that discovery is made in response to much prodding and suggestions by the therapist, often with the aid of hypnosis. Many of the memories reported by patients with dissociative identity disorder seem quite implausible. (According to one estimate, 25 percent of such patients recall instances of torture by satanic cults [Mulhern, 1991], even though federal law enforcement officials have been unable to verify the existence of such cults [Bottoms & others, 1996; Lilienfeld & others, 1999].) Very little effort has been made to find evidence—aside from the memories that are recalled in the course of therapy—that patients actually began dissociating before they started therapy or that they experienced the severe abuse that they describe.

These facts have led some researchers and clinicians to argue that many if not most cases of dissociative identity disorder are at least partly iatrogenic in nature (Lilienfield & others, 1999; Spanos, 1994). *Iatrogenic* means doctor-induced or induced by the course of treatment. The iatrogenesis is not deliberate but emerges from the therapist's genuine desire to help the suffering person. It also depends on a cultural milieu that predisposes the patient and therapist to believe in the childhood-trauma theory of dissociative identity disorder.

Suppose that a woman suffering from diffuse psychological problems enters therapy. Her behavior during a few sessions suggests to the therapist the possibility of dissociative identity disorder, and at some point the therapist presents this possibility to her. The patient, who is highly suggestible and has faith in the therapist and therapy, thinks hard about her past to find memories that seem to fit with the diagnosis. Instances in which she behaved or felt differently from her usual ways of behaving or feeling may come to mind, and in reconstructing these instances, she may recall the alteration as greater than it actually was. She might also, in the spirit of helping her therapy, construct memories of child abuse that did not happen in the extreme form that she remembers. (The malleable nature of memories, especially memories of childhood, is discussed in Chapter 10.) As part of the therapy, the therapist may at some point—with or without the aid of hypnosis—"invite" one of the patient's alternative selves to emerge and talk with the therapist. Over the course of therapy the patient develops increasingly vivid memories of past abuse and dissociations and becomes ever better at producing alternative personalities in the therapist's office. With time and practice, the patient may begin dissociating outside the therapist's office as well as during therapy sessions.

Both theories may be correct to some degree. The question of whether most cases of dissociative identity disorder begin in childhood as a way of coping with abuse or begin in adulthood in response to therapists' suggestions and encouragement has yet to be answered. That answer can come only from research aimed at finding corroborating evidence, in the daily lives and histories of the patients, that is independent of memories that patients recall or construct in the course of therapy.

34.

What reasoning suggests that dissociative identity disorder may be produced by psychotherapy?

SECTION SUMMARY

Dissociation, which can be produced by hypnosis, is a process in which a period of a person's life is separated from the rest of his or her conscious experience in such a way that it cannot later be recalled or can be recalled only under special conditions. People who suffer from dissociative disorders experience such dissociations in their everyday lives in a manner that interferes with their ability to function effectively. The most well-known such disorder is dissociative identity disorder, in which the person manifests two or more distinct self-identities at different times. According to the childhood-trauma theory, the dissociation begins in early childhood as a means of coping with severe physical or sexual abuse. According to the culturally conditioned iatrogenic theory, the disorder begins in the therapist's office when a therapist who believes in the childhood-trauma theory and a suggestible patient work together to construct memories and behaviors in the patient that are consistent with the therapist's belief.

SCHIZOPHRENIA

John sits alone in his dismal room, surrounded by plastic bags of garbage that he has hoarded during late-night excursions onto the street. He is unkempt and scrawny. He has no appetite and hasn't eaten a proper meal in weeks. He lost his job months ago. He is afraid to go out during the day because he sees in every passing face a spy who is trying to learn, by reading his mind, the secret that will destroy him. He hears voices telling him that he must stay away from the spies, and he hears his own thoughts as if they were broadcast aloud for all to hear. He sits still, trying to keep calm, trying to reduce the volume of his thoughts. John's disorder is diagnosed as schizophrenia.

Characteristics and Variations of the Disorder

Schizophrenia is a serious and relatively prevalent disorder. It is found in roughly 1 percent of people at some time in their lives (Kessler & others, 1994). It accounts for a higher percentage of the inpatient population of mental hospitals than any other diagnostic category. The disorder seems to be equally prevalent in males and females, but, for unknown reasons, it typically is more severe and strikes earlier in males than in females (Salyers & Mueser, 2001). The most frequent age range for first symptoms is 18 to 25 for men and 26 to 45 for women (Straube & Oades, 1992). Sometimes people make a full recovery from schizophrenia, sometimes they make a partial recovery, and sometimes the disorder takes a deteriorating course throughout the person's life.

The label *schizophrenia* was first used by the Swiss psychiatrist Eugen Bleuler (1911/1950), whose writings are still a valuable source of information and insight about the disorder. The term comes from the Greek words *schizo*, which means "split," and *phrenum*, which means "mind," so it literally means "split mind." Bleuler believed, as do many theorists today, that schizophrenia entails a split among such mental processes as attention, perception, emotion, motivation, and thought, such that these processes operate in relative isolation from one another, leading to bizarre and disorganized thoughts and actions. Bleuler's term has caused many nonpsychologists to confuse schizophrenia with dissociative identity disorder. The mind of a person with schizophrenia is *not* split among more than one personality; dissociation is not a symptom of schizophrenia.

Symptoms

No two sufferers of schizophrenia have quite the same symptoms. But to receive the *DSM-IV* diagnosis of **schizophrenia**, the person must manifest a serious, long-lasting decline in ability to work, care for himself or herself, and connect socially

Art by a person diagnosed with schizophrenia

This piece by Adolf Wölfi typifies the unusual personal symbolism and eerie rhythmical forms that characterize the artwork of many patients with schizophrenia.

35.

What are the main classes of symptoms of schizophrenia?

with others, and the person must manifest at least two out of the following five categories of symptoms: delusions, hallucinations, disorganized speech, grossly disorganized or catatonic behavior, and negative symptoms.

Delusions are false beliefs held in the face of compelling evidence to the contrary. Common types of delusions in schizophrenia are *delusions of persecution*, which are beliefs that others are plotting against one; *delusions of grandeur*, which are beliefs in one's own extraordinary importance, for example, that one is the queen of England; and *delusions of being controlled*, such as believing one's thoughts or movements are being controlled by radio waves or by invisible wires in puppetlike fashion. Often several delusions occur together in a single delusional scenario.

Hallucinations are false sensory perceptions—hearing or seeing things that aren't there. The most common hallucinations are auditory, usually the hearing of voices. Hallucinations and delusions typically work together to support one another. For example, a man who has a delusion of persecution may repeatedly hear the voice of his persecutor insulting or threatening him. When asked to describe the source of the voices, people with schizophrenia typically say that they come from inside their own heads, and some even say that the voices are produced (against their will) by their own vocal apparatus (Smith, 1992). Consistent with these reports, people with schizophrenia can usually stop the voices by such procedures as humming to themselves, counting, or holding their mouths wide open in a way that immobilizes the vocal apparatus (Bick & Kinsbourne, 1987). These same procedures also prevent people who don't have schizophrenia from vividly imagining the sound of a spoken word (Reisberg & others, 1989) and hearing hallucinated voices under hypnotic suggestion (Bick & Kinsbourne, 1987). Apparently, auditory hallucinations in schizophrenia occur through the same mechanism that produces vividly imagined speech sounds in everyone; the difference is that during a schizophrenic hallucination the person experiences the sound as truly audible and as a phenomenon separate from his or her own thoughts.

Disorganized speech refers to characteristics of the person's speech that are assumed to reflect an underlying disorganization in thought. In some instances, the person jumps wildly from one idea to another in a manner not guided by logic but by such factors as simple word associations—a pattern referred to as *overinclusion*. A classic example is this greeting to Bleuler (1911/1950) from one of his patients: "I wish you a happy, joyful, healthy, blessed and fruitful year, and many good wine-years to come as well as a healthy and good apple-year, and sauerkraut and cabbage and squash and seed year." Notice that, once the patient's mind hooked onto fruit (in "fruitful year"), it entered into a chain of associations involving fruit and vegetables that had little to do with the original intent of the statement. Another variety of formal thought disturbance is known as *paralogic*, in which reasoning is superficially based on rules of logic but in fact is flawed in ways that are obvious to others. Paralogic may help support a delusion, as in the case of a woman who supported her claim to be the Virgin Mary this way: "The Virgin Mary is a virgin. I am a virgin. Therefore, I am the Virgin Mary" (Arieti, 1966).

Grossly disorganized behavior refers to behaviors that are strikingly inappropriate for the situation (such as wearing many overcoats on a hot day or behaving in a silly manner at a solemn social occasion) or ineffective in obtaining the apparent goal (such as failure in preparing a simple meal or in dressing oneself). *Catatonic behavior* refers to periods of marked unresponsiveness to the environment, which may involve active resistance (such as becoming stiff when someone tries to help the person dress), or excited motor activity related to the environment, or a complete lack of movement or apparent awareness of the environment, in the form of a *catatonic stupor* (see Figure 16.9).

Negative symptoms involve an absence of, or reduction in, expected behaviors, thoughts, feelings, and drives. They include a general slowing down of bodily movements, poverty of speech (slow, labored, unspontaneous speech), flattened affect (reduction in or absence of emotional expression), loss of basic drives such

FIGURE **16.9**
A person in a catatonic stupor
People with schizophrenia withdraw from their environment in various ways. One of the most extreme forms of withdrawal is the catatonic stupor, in which the person may remain motionless for hours on end in an uncomfortable position.

Grunnitus / Monkmeyer

as hunger, and loss of the pleasure that normally comes from fulfilling drives. The majority of people with schizophrenia manifest negative symptoms to some degree, and for many these are the most prominent symptoms. I once asked a dear friend, who was suffering from schizophrenia and was starving himself, why he didn't eat. His answer, in labored but thoughtful speech, was essentially this: "I have no appetite. I feel no pleasure from eating or anything else. I keep thinking that if I go long enough without eating, food will taste good again and life might be worth living."

Variations of the Disorder

36.

How have researchers attempted to classify subtypes of schizophrenia according to symptoms?

Two different people diagnosed with schizophrenia can differ greatly from each other, with little overlap in the kinds of symptoms they show. Studies using factor analysis to determine which symptoms correlate most strongly with each other suggest three different clusters of symptoms: *positive symptoms* (primarily delusions and hallucinations), *disorganized symptoms* (disorganized speech and behavior), and *negative symptoms* (as defined above) (Toomey & others, 1997). Positive symptoms tend to come and go; patients often experience remission from them for many months between episodes. These symptoms are also most responsive to antipsychotic drugs. The disorganized and negative symptoms, in contrast, are more constant and less responsive to drugs (Salyers & Mueser, 2001).

Various subcategories of schizophrenia have been proposed, based on the prevalence of specific symptoms or symptom clusters. The subcategories described in *DSM-IV* include *paranoid type*, characterized mainly by delusions of persecution and grandeur and often by hallucinations; *catatonic type*, characterized mainly by nonreaction to the environment; and *disorganized type*, characterized by disorganized speech, disorganized behavior, and either inappropriate or flattened affect. However, no system of subcategories has proved very satisfactory. The symptoms appear in a huge number of different combinations and may change over time in a given person, thereby defying attempts at classification.

Biological Bases

Because of its high prevalence and debilitating effects, schizophrenia has been more fully studied than any other mental disorder to determine its possible biological underpinnings. All such studies are complicated by the fact that the disorder comes in so many different forms, which may have different biological bases.

Role of Heredity

Schizophrenia was one of the first mental disorders to be studied extensively by behavior geneticists, and the evidence now is overwhelming that genes play a role in predisposing some people for the disorder (Gottesman, 1991).

37.

How did a classic study in Denmark provide evidence for the heritability of schizophrenia? In general, how do the varying rates of concordance for schizophrenia among different classes of relatives support the contention that heredity affects susceptibility for the disorder?

One now-classic study, conducted in Denmark, began with the identification of a group of adults who had been adopted in infancy and who later (in adolescence or adulthood) were hospitalized for schizophrenia (Kety & others, 1976). For comparison, the researchers also selected a group of adoptees who did not have schizophrenia or any other diagnosed mental disorder but were similar to those in the schizophrenia group in other ways, such as age and socioeconomic class. Then they tracked down the biological and adoptive parents, siblings, and half-siblings of both groups and asked them to participate in an extensive psychiatric interview. The purpose of the interview (unknown to the interviewee) was to look for signs of schizophrenia. To prevent bias, the interviews were conducted and evaluated by a team of psychiatrists who were blind (uninformed) as to whether the interviewee was a biological or adoptive relative or was related to an individual who did or did not have schizophrenia. The main results are shown in Figure 16.10. Only the biological relatives of the adoptees with schizophrenia manifested significantly more evidence of schizophrenia than any other group, and they were about four times as likely as the others to show such symptoms.

Many other studies have shown that liability for schizophrenia is very much affected by one's degree of genetic relatedness to a person with that disorder. In such studies, persons in the original group identified as having the disorder are referred to as the *index cases*. The relatives of the index cases can then be studied to see what percentage of them have the disorder. This percentage is referred to as the ***concordance*** for the disorder, for the class of relatives studied. A separate concordance measure can be calculated for identical and fraternal twins (or any other class of relatives studied) and used to estimate heritability. The average concordances found in many such studies, for various classes of relatives, are shown in Table 16.3.

All in all, the results show that genetic differences among individuals play a substantial role in predisposition for schizophrenia but are by no means the sole determinants. Of particular interest is the fact that the average concordance for schizophrenia between identical twins—shown in the table to be 48 percent—is much less than the 100 percent that would be predicted if genetic variation alone were involved. To some degree reduced concordance could come from misdiagnosis, because any errors in diagnosing either the index cases or their twins would reduce the measured concordance below its true value. But some pairs of discordant identical twins have been studied over many years, and no doubt exists in those cases that one manifests the disorder and the other does not (Wahl, 1976). Recent research suggests that many different genes probably play a role in the predisposition for schizophrenia, and some progress has been made in identifying the chromosomal locations of some of them (Brzustowicz & others, 2000; Wright & others, 1996). There is also evidence that genetic relatives who are concordant for schizophrenia tend to manifest similar symptoms (Kendler & others, 1997). To date, however, nobody knows just how any given gene predisposes a person for schizophrenia or contributes to specific symptoms.

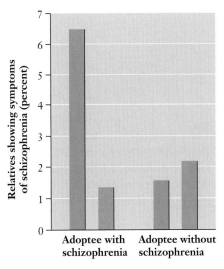

FIGURE **16.10** *Results of an adoption study of the heritability of schizophrenia*
Kety, Rosenthal, and their colleagues looked for signs of schizophrenia in the biological and adoptive relatives of adoptees who either had or had not become schizophrenic. The results here are the percentage of relatives who showed either schizophrenia or a milder disorder now called schizotypical personality disorder. (Data from Kety & others, 1976.)

TABLE **16.3** *Concordance rates for schizophrenia*

Relationship to a person who has schizophrenia	Average percentage found to have schizophrenia (concordance)
Relatives in same generation	
Identical twin	48%
Fraternal twin	17
Nontwin brother or sister	9
Half-sibling	6
First cousin	2
Relatives in later generations	
Child of two parents with schizophrenia	46
Child of one parent with schizophrenia	13
Grandchild of one person with schizophrenia	5
Niece or nephew of one person with schizophrenia	4

Sources: I. I. Gottesman, 1991. *Schizophrenia genesis: The origins of madness*, p. 96. New York: Freeman.

Other Congenital Influences

Prenatal or birth traumas may also play a causal role in schizophrenia. People with schizophrenia are unusually likely to have had a difficult birth, involving oxygen deprivation or other trauma to the brain (DeLisi & others, 1988; Weinberger, 1995). Birth records of identical twins, only one of whom developed schizophrenia, reveal that in most cases the afflicted twin was born second and had a lower birth weight (indicative of a less favorable uterine position) than the co-twin (Wahl, 1976). Prenatal lack of nutrition can also predispose a child for schizophrenia. People born in the western Netherlands between October 15 and December 31, 1945, shortly after the end of a severe famine brought on by a Nazi blockade, have manifested twice the rate of schizophrenia observed in other people born in the Netherlands (Susser & others, 1996).

38.

What evidence suggests that birth traumas, prenatal lack of nutrition, and prenatal viral infections can enhance one's susceptibility to schizophrenia?

Prenatal viral infections may also play a role (Torrey, 1988). Several studies have shown that people born in late winter or early spring have about a 20 percent greater risk for schizophrenia than do those born in late summer or early fall (Mortensen & others, 1999). A plausible explanation for this is that the brain is especially vulnerable to damage from viral infections during the last 3 months before birth and such infections are more common in winter than in summer.

Brain Chemistry

By the early 1970s a great deal of evidence had accrued for the *dopamine theory of schizophrenia*, the theory that schizophrenia arises from overactivity at brain synapses where dopamine is the neurotransmitter. The most compelling support for the theory came from the discovery that the clinical effectiveness of various drugs in reducing the positive symptoms of schizophrenia was directly proportional to the drugs' effectiveness in blocking dopamine release at synaptic terminals (Seeman & Lee, 1975). Other support came from the finding that drugs such as cocaine and amphetamine, which increase the action of dopamine in the brain, can greatly exacerbate the symptoms of schizophrenia in people with the disorder (Davis, 1974) and at higher doses can even induce such symptoms in people who do not have the disorder (Griffith & others, 1972).

Today few, if any, researchers accept the original, simple form of the dopamine theory. One major flaw in the theory is that it does not explain the disorganized and negative symptoms of schizophrenia, which are not well treated by the classical antipsychotic drugs and are not typically exacerbated by drugs that increase that action of dopamine. Modern theories suggest that unusual patterns of dopamine activity, perhaps including overactivity in some areas of the brain and underactivity in others, may provide a physiological basis for schizophrenia (Goldsmith & others, 1997; Okubo & others, 1997). Decreased dopamine activity in the prefrontal cortex—an area known to be important for working memory, attention, and planning (discussed in Chapters 5 and 9)— may provide a basis for the disorganized and negative symptoms of schizophrenia (Kurumaji & Yoshira, 2000). Newer antipsychotic drugs, such as clozapine, have smaller effects than the traditional drugs on dopamine but are at least as effective as the traditional drugs in treating positive symptoms of schizophrenia and, unlike the traditional drugs, also reduce somewhat the negative and disorganized symptoms of the disorder. These drugs may exert their actions through a long-term stabilizing effect on dopamine-using synapses, coupled, perhaps, with effects on other transmitter systems (Hertel & others, 1999; O'Connor, 1998; Roth & Meltzer, 1995).

Brain Structure

Many dozens of studies using brain imaging techniques have shown reliable, but often subtle, structural differences between the brains of people with schizophrenia and the brains of people without schizophrenia. The most common finding is enlargement of the cerebral ventricles (fluid-filled spaces in the brain) accompanied by a reduced amount of neural tissue surrounding the ventricles (Weinberger, 1995). Decreased neural mass has been found particularly in the temporal and frontal lobes of the cerebral cortex and in the thalamus (Andreasen & others, 1994; Marsh & others, 1997). Such abnormalities are found especially often in patients whose disorder is characterized by severe negative symptoms (Brown & Pluck, 2000). Abnormalities have also been found in the varieties and arrangements of neurons within portions of the cerebral cortex (Akbarian & others, 1996; Weinberger, 1995). Evidence to date suggests that the brain abnormalities do not suddenly appear when the clinical symptoms first appear (generally in young adulthood) but, rather, are present well before that time, perhaps as early as or earlier than birth (Weinberger, 1995).

39.

What early evidence supported the dopamine theory of schizophrenia? What evidence lends doubt to the simple form of the dopamine theory?

Disorder in the brain

In these PET scans, the blue areas are cerebral ventricles and the green represents relatively low levels of neural activity. The brains are oriented so that the front is at the top. Notice that the brain of the person with schizophrenia (on the left) has less activity in the frontal lobes (more green) and larger cerebral ventricles than the brain of the person without schizophrenia.

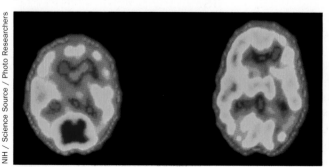

NIH / Science Source / Photo Researchers

Behavioral Precursors of Schizophrenia

If the neural basis for schizophrenia is present well before the first diagnosable episode of the disorder, one might expect to find some behavioral differences between people who are vulnerable to schizophrenia and those who are not. Despite extensive research, no behavioral precursors of schizophrenia have been identified that are so reliable that they can be used to predict, with high probability, that a given individual will develop the disorder. However, certain *average* differences have been found between the behavior of young people who later develop the disorder and that of those who don't.

The most fully studied differences have to do with attention. People who have been diagnosed with schizophrenia show certain deficits in attention even after they recover from all overt symptoms of schizophrenia (Green, 1993). For example, they perform poorly at tasks in which they must press a button whenever a particular stimulus pattern appears on a screen (Nuechterlein & others, 1992). In other research, an unusually high percentage of children who were genetically at risk for schizophrenia (because one of their parents had the disorder) were found to show attention deficits similar to those seen in adults with schizophrenia (Cornblatt & Erlenmeyer-Kimling, 1985; Green, 1993). More recently, a long-term study of at-risk children has produced strong evidence of a correlation between deficits in attention, verbal memory, and gross motor skills in childhood and schizophrenia in adulthood (Erlenmeyer-Kimling & others, 2000). Such findings are consistent with the idea that defects in brain frontal-lobe structures that are involved in organizing perceptions, thoughts, and actions contribute to one's vulnerability to schizophrenia.

In studies of home movies taken by the parents of children who later developed schizophrenia, Elaine Walker and her colleagues (1993, 1994) found certain statistically reliable differences between the children who later developed schizophrenia and their same-sex siblings who did not. The former showed a higher frequency of subtly unusual movements and postures before the age of 2, which tended to disappear after that, and relatively more facial expressions indicative of negative emotions throughout their childhood.

40.

What average behavioral differences have been observed between children who later develop schizophrenia and children who do not?

Influences of Family and Culture

Given a certain degree of biological predisposition for schizophrenia, the actual manifestation and the life course of the disorder may depend on one's daily experiences. There is evidence that the course of the disorder is affected by stressful life events (Fowles, 1992; Pallanti & others, 1997), by the family one is brought up in, and by the larger culture in which one resides. Our focus here is on the effects of family and culture.

Effects of the Family

What characteristics of a child's home life might increase or decrease the chance of the child's eventually developing schizophrenia? In an attempt to answer that question, researchers in Finland have for many years been studying the home environment and psychological development of two groups of adopted children. One group is genetically at relatively high risk for schizophrenia because their biological mothers were diagnosed with the disorder, and the other group is at relatively low risk because neither of their biological parents was diagnosed with the disorder. It is still too early to know who in each group will eventually develop schizophrenia, but the results so far are intriguing. Among the high-risk children, those whose adoptive parents communicated in a relatively disorganized, hard-to-follow, or highly emotional manner manifested more schizophreniclike thought patterns, in a test of such thinking, than did those whose adoptive parents communicated in a calmer, more organized fashion (Wahlberg & others, 1997). This relationship was not found among the low-risk children; among them, the degree of such thought was unrelated to the measure of communicative style in their adoptive parents. The

41.

What evidence suggests, tentatively, that the family environment may promote schizophrenic-like symptoms in those who are genetically predisposed for the disorder but not in those who are not genetically predisposed?

Family visit at a group home

Rose Hill, in Michigan, is a high quality group home and rehabilitation center for people with schizophrenia and other serious mental disorders. Today is family day, and John (at left) is being visited by his mother (next to him) and father (far right). In western cultures, where home care of a person with a serious mental disorder can be highly disruptive, family members may often be able to maintain warmer relationships with the preson if he or she resides in a safe, caring, therapeutic environment outside the family's home than they could if he or she lived at home with the family.

Dwight Cendroski

42.

How has expressed emotion by family members been linked to relapse of schizophrenia?

43.

What cross-cultural difference has been observed in rate of recovery from schizophrenia, and what are some possible explanations for that difference?

results suggest that a degree of disordered communication at home that does not harm most children may have damaging effects on a child who is genetically predisposed for schizophrenia.

Other research has centered on a concept referred to as *expressed emotion*, defined as criticisms and negative attitudes or feelings expressed about and toward a person with schizophrenia by family members with whom that person lives. Many studies indicate that, other things being equal, the greater the expressed emotion, the greater the likelihood that the diagnosed person's symptoms will worsen and the person will require hospitalization (Hooley & Hiller, 2001).

Cause-effect inferences based on all such correlational studies must be interpreted cautiously. It is possible that the behavior of people who eventually develop schizophrenia, or who manifest repeated relapses of the disorder, affects the family members, producing disordered communication or expressed emotion in them, rather than the other way around. However, consistent with the theory that expressed emotion promotes relapse, a number of experiments have shown that support and training for family members, aimed at creating a more stable and accepting home environment and reducing expressed emotion, significantly reduces the rate of relapse (Hooley & Hiller, 2001).

Cross-Cultural Differences in Rate of Recovery

Perhaps the most striking evidence for environmental influences on the course of schizophrenia comes from comparisons made across cultures. In the late 1970s, the World Health Organization initiated an ambitious cross-cultural study of schizophrenia involving locations in 10 countries (Jablensky & others, 1992). Three of the countries—Colombia, Nigeria, and India—were identified as relatively nonindustrialized, developing countries. The others were identified as developed countries—England, Ireland, Denmark, the United States, Japan, Czechoslovakia (before it was divided), and Russia (then part of the Soviet Union). Using agreed-upon criteria and cross-cultural reliability checks, the researchers diagnosed new cases of schizophrenia in each location, classed them according to symptom types and apparent severity, and reassessed each case through interviews conducted 1 year and 2 years later. In all, 1379 patients were included in the study.

The results showed considerable cross-cultural consistency. The relative prevalence of the various symptoms, the average age of onset of the disorder, and the sex difference in age of onset (later for women than for men) were similar from location to location despite wide variations in the ways that people lived. However, the study also revealed a remarkable cross-cultural difference, which had been more than hinted at by earlier, less systematic studies: The patients in developing countries were much more likely to recover during the 2-year follow-up period than were those in developed countries. This was true for every category of schizophrenia that was identified and for nearly every index of recovery that was used.

When all categories were combined, 63 percent of patients in the developing countries, compared with only 37 percent in the developed countries, showed a full recovery by the end of the 2-year period (Jablensky & others, 1992).

Why should people in less industrialized countries fare better after developing schizophrenia than people in more industrialized countries? The cross-cultural study revealed some reliable differences in treatment between the two classes of countries. Patients in the less industrialized countries were more likely than those in the industrialized countries to receive non-Western folk or religious treatments, less likely to be hospitalized, and less likely to receive antipsychotic drugs over prolonged periods (Jablensky & others, 1992). Some controversial studies in Europe and the United States have suggested that prolonged use of antipsychotic drugs, while dampening immediate symptoms, may impede full recovery (Warner, 1985).

Most researchers interested in cross-cultural differences in schizophrenia outcome, however, have focused not on these differences but on differences in the prevailing attitude toward the disorder and those who have it. Cross-cultural research shows that family members in nonindustrialized countries are more accepting and less critical of individuals diagnosed with schizophrenia than are those in industrialized countries. They show less expressed emotion, as defined earlier, which might account for the better recovery rate (Jenkins & Karno, 1992). Many plausible reasons for this attitude difference have been suggested (Jenkins & Karno, 1992; Lin & Kleinman, 1988; Weisman, 1997). People in less industrialized countries are less likely to call the disorder "schizophrenia" or to think of it as permanent and are more likely to refer to it with terms such as "a case of nerves," which sound more benign and tie it to experiences that everyone has had. They place relatively less value on personal independence and more on interdependence and family ties, which may lead them to feel less resentful and more nurturing toward a family member who needs extra care. They are more likely to live in large, extended families, which means that more people share in providing the extra care. Finally, in a less industrialized country a person with schizophrenia is more able to play an economically useful role. The same person who could not hold a job at a factory or in an office can perform useful chores on the family farm or at the family trade. Being less stigmatized, less cut off from the normal course of human activity, may increase the chance of a full recovery.

Family business

In nonindustrialized countries people often live and work together in large extended families. In such a setting, a person with a serious mental disorder—who would not be able to hold a job away from home—can nevertheless contribute to the family's economy. Partly for that reason, the person may not be regarded as a burden to family members to the degree that the same person would in a developed country.

Susan Meiselas / Magnum Photos, Inc.

SECTION SUMMARY

Schizophrenia is a debilitating disorder of cognition. Its symptoms fall into three broad clusters: (1) positive symptoms (including delusions and hallucinations); (2) disorganized symptoms (disorganized speech, thought, and behavior); and (3) negative symptoms (slow bodily movements, labored speech, lack of emotional expression, and loss of basic drives). People with the disorder can vary greatly in the relative prominence of any of these symptom categories.

Twin and adoption studies show that genes contribute considerably to a person's vulnerability to schizophrenia. Other congenital influences on vulnerability include birth trauma, prenatal undernutrition, and, apparently, prenatal viral infections. The positive symptoms of the disorder can be relieved with drugs that block the release or effects of dopamine, suggesting that these symptoms may be due to overactivity of brain neurons that use dopamine as their neurotransmitter. Newer antipsychotic drugs reduce the negative and disorganized symptoms to some degree, as well as the positive symptoms, by means that are not well understood. Neuroimaging studies indicate that many people with schizophrenia have larger cerebral ventricles and somewhat smaller masses of neural tissue in the frontal and temporal cortical lobes than people without the disorder, and researchers have found that adults who develop schizophrenia often showed some deficits in attention, memory, and behavioral organization in childhood, well before they developed the disorder.

A long-term study of adopted children has suggested that those who are genetically at high risk for schizophrenia are more likely to develop the disorder—or some of the symptoms of it—if they grow up in a family characterized by a disorganized style of communication than if they grow up in a more harmonious family. Other research has shown that people who are in remission from schizophrenia show higher rates of relapse if their family members manifest a critical, hostile emotional attitude toward the patients than if they are more accepting. Cross-cultural research suggests that rates of full recovery from schizophrenia are higher in developing countries than in developed countries, a result that may derive from cultural differences in family structure, employment possibilities, attitudes toward mental disorders, and beliefs about the value of helping family members.

CONCLUDING THOUGHTS

Here are three final ideas that may help you organize your thoughts as you reflect on what you have read in this chapter:

1. The multiple causes of mental disorders By this time in your study of psychology, you are no doubt used to the idea that human feelings, thoughts, and actions emerge from the interaction of many causes. This idea also applies to the feelings, thoughts, and actions that lead to the diagnosis of a mental disorder. The differences among us that are considered disorders—no less than the differences that are considered normal—are caused by differences in our genes and in our past and present environments. Any claim to have found *the* cause of generalized anxiety, depression, schizophrenia, or another major class of disorder is of doubtful validity.

One way to review this chapter would be to think about each disorder in relation to the three classes of causes—predisposing, precipitating, and maintaining—that were introduced near the beginning of the chapter. How might genes operate through the person's physiology to predispose him or her to the disorder? How might learned ways of thinking or acting predispose a person to the disorder? How might specific stressful events in life interact with the predisposition to precipitate the disorder? How might the disordered behavior itself, or people's reactions to it, help maintain the disorder once it begins? For each disorder, think about the relationship between the research or ideas described and the possible answers to these questions. Note too that similar stressful events can result in different kinds of symptoms—and different diagnosed disorders—for different individuals or at different times for any given individual.

2. The continuum between normality and abnormality Although a diagnosis of a mental disorder is categorical (all or none), the symptoms on which diagnoses are made are not; they vary in degree throughout the population. Thus, any decision as to whether a particular person does or does not have a mental disorder is based on arbitrary criteria as to how severe or prolonged each symptom must be in order to call the syndrome a disorder.

As you review each disorder described in the chapter, think about its symptoms in relation to the moods, emotions, thoughts, and behaviors that all of us manifest to some degree. Doing so helps remove some of the mystique from the concept of mental disorder and helps us identify with people whose troubles are like ours, only stronger. Thinking of disorders in terms of extremes of normal processes has also helped scientists understand them better. For example, in this chapter you read about evidence (a) relating the symptoms of phobias and obsessive-compulsive disorders to normal fears, thoughts, and actions; (b) relating the symptoms of depression and bipolar disorders to normal despondency and elation; and (c) relating the hallucinations experienced in schizophrenia to a normal capacity for vivid mental imagery.

3. An evolutionary view of mental disorder The evolutionary theme running through this book maintains that behavior is generally functional; it promotes survival and reproduction. But mental disorder is dysfunctional; it reduces one's ability to work and interact with others effectively in survival-promoting ways. Why, then, do mental disorders exist?

One possible partial answer is that mental disorders are a cost the species pays for the general value that lies in diversity. The previous chapter, on personality, dealt with individual difference within the range generally considered healthy, not disordered, and the case was made that natural selection may have favored diversity because those who are different from average can exploit niches and make unique contributions that provide rewards in return. Such diversity stems from diversity in genes and from behavioral mechanisms that are capable of being modified through experience. Variation in capacity for anxiety, or compulsiveness, or sadness within a certain range may be beneficial; but the coin tosses that distribute genes and experiences will sometimes produce those characteristics at pathological levels.

Further Reading

Dale Peterson (Ed.) (1982). *A mad people's history of madness.* Pittsburgh: University of Pittsburgh Press.

In this fascinating collection of excerpts from autobiographies written over the past 500 years, people who either were, or were regarded as, seriously mentally disordered describe their suffering, the reactions of others, and their own efforts toward recovery. Some of the excerpts are from well-known books that have helped shape reforms in the understanding and treatment of people with mental disorders.

Stephen Schwartzberg (2000). *Casebook of psychological disorders: The human face of emotional distress.* Boston: Allyn & Bacon.

This book introduces readers to mental disorders by describing case histories, including one each of posttraumatic stress disorder, panic disorder, bipolar disorder, conversion disorder, dissociative identity disorder, and schizophrenia. Each case is discussd respectfully and compassionately and includes a description of the person's psychological difficulties and history and the therapist's diagnosis and treatment plan.

Kay Jamison (1995). *An unquiet mind.* New York: Knopf.

In this autobiography, Kay Jamison—a leading researcher of mood disorders—describes her own experiences as a sufferer of bipolar disorder. The book includes an especially vivid description of her first full-blown manic episode, which happened in her first year as an assistant professor, and a moving discussion of how she came to terms with the disorder and has managed to live with it.

Stephen Faraone, Ming Tsuang, & Debby Tsuang (1999). *Genetics of mental disorders: A guide for students, clinicians, and researchers.* New York: Guilford.

This book discusses clearly and insightfully the rationale and methods of twin and adoption studies of mental disorder heritability and of modern methods to identify specific genes involved in such disorders. Also included are chapters on mathematical models of inheritance, how genetic analysis can refine the categories of mental disorders, and clinical uses of genetic information.

Scott Lilienfeld (1998). *Looking into abnormal psychology: Contemporary readings.* Pacific Grove, CA: Brooks/Cole.

This is a collection of 40 articles that deal with controversial issues concerning mental disorders. The articles are taken mostly from popular sources such as Scientific American *and* Discover, *and many of them are written by well-known psychologists. Among the articles are one by Nesse on the evolutionary basis for mood and anxiety disorders and one by Strickland on women and depression.*

Looking Ahead

I hope you didn't catch medical students' disease from this chapter, but in case you did, don't worry: The next chapter is on treatment. Of course, real mental disorders are serious problems, and effective means for treating them are among the most valuable contributions that psychology has made and is continuing to make to human welfare.

Chapter 17

Evening, Pierre Bonnard

Treatment

Throughout this book you have read of psychology as a *science*. Perhaps you have discovered that psychology is a vast, complex, and fascinating science in which every finding generates far more questions than it answers. If your experience reading this book has been anything like my experience writing it, your attitude right now might be one of respect for what research psychologists have accomplished, coupled with awe concerning the amount they have yet to learn about the human mind and behavior.

But psychology is not just a science; it is also a *practice*. Practitioners in psychology attempt to apply psychological ideas and findings in ways designed to make life more satisfying for individuals or society as a whole. This last chapter is about *clinical psychology*, the field of practice and research that is directed toward helping people who suffer from psychological problems and disorders. The chapter consists of five main sections, which deal, respectively, with (a) the social problem of providing care for the seriously disturbed; (b) methods of clinical assessment (how clinicians try to determine what is wrong); (c) biological approaches to treatment (especially drugs); (d) some major forms of psychotherapy (psychodynamic, humanistic, cognitive, and behavioral); and (e) research concerned with the effectiveness of psychotherapy and the factors that lead to its success or failure.

CARE AS A SOCIAL ISSUE

The existence of mental suffering, like that of physical suffering, raises social and moral questions. Who, if anyone, is responsible for caring for those who cannot care for themselves? Should society assume the task of helping relieve suffering in individuals, or should society merely assume the task of protecting those who don't suffer from those who do?

What to Do with the Severely Disturbed?

Through most of history, Western cultures felt little obligation toward people with mental disorders. During the Middle Ages, and even into the seventeenth century, people with serious mental disorders—the kind called "madness" or "lunacy" (and today most commonly diagnosed as schizophrenia)—were often considered to be in league with the devil, and "treatment" commonly consisted of torture, hanging, burning at the stake, or being sent to sea in "ships of fools" to drown or be saved, depending upon divine Providence. By the eighteenth century, such "religious" views had waned somewhat and a more secular attitude began to prevail, which attributed mental disorders not to supernatural powers but to the basic degeneracy and unworthiness of the disordered people themselves. The principal treatment for those who couldn't care for themselves was to put them out of the way of decent

1.

How has Western society's response to people with serious mental disorders changed since the Middle Ages? What were the goals of the moral-treatment and deinstitutionalization movements?

653

Life in a nineteenth-century mental hospital

One source of pressure for mental hospital reform in early-nineteenth-century England were portraits, such as this, drawn by George Cruikshank. The man shown here had been bound to the wall by foot-long chains for 12 years at the time of the portrait.

society in places that were called "hospitals" but in reality were dark, damp, miserable dungeons, where inmates were frequently kept chained to the walls, alive but in a state that was perhaps worse than death.

Attempts at Reform: In and Out of Asylums

Not until the beginning of the nineteenth century did humanitarian reform begin to occur in a significant way. The best-known leader of reform in Europe was Philippe Pinel (1745–1826), who, as director of a large mental hospital in Paris, unchained the inmates, transferred them to sunny and airy rooms, and gave them access to the hospital grounds for exercise. Under these conditions some inmates who had been deemed permanently and hopelessly deranged recovered sufficiently to be released from the hospital. In the United States, the leading reformer was Dorothea Dix (1802–1887), a Boston schoolteacher who visited dozens of jails and almshouses where people with mental disorders were housed and publicized the appalling conditions she found. As this *moral-treatment movement* grew, it spurred the building of large, state-supported asylums for the mentally disordered. The idea behind such institutions was high-minded: to provide kindly care and protection for those unable to care for themselves. Unfortunately, public sympathy was rarely sustained at this high level, at least not in the tangible form of financial support. Almost invariably the asylums became overcrowded and understaffed, and reverted to conditions not unlike those that had appalled Pinel and Dix. As recently as the 1940s, the following report could be written about a state mental institution in Philadelphia (Deutsch, 1948):

> The male "incontinent ward" was like a scene out of Dante's Inferno. Three hundred nude men stood, squatted and sprawled in this bare room. . . . Winter or summer, these creatures never were given any clothing at all. . . . Many patients [in another ward] had to eat their meals with their hands. . . . Four hundred patients were herded into a barn-like day room intended for only 80. There were only a few benches; most of the men had to stand all day or sit on the splintery floor. . . . The hogs in a nearby pigpen were far better fed, in far greater comfort than these human beings.

By the mid-1950s, disenchantment with large state institutions led to a new kind of reform movement in the United States—a movement to *deinstitutionalize* people with mental disorders, to get them back into the community. This new movement was inspired partly by the development of effective antipsychotic drugs and partly by a general mood of optimism in the nation, a feeling that everyone could "make it" if given the chance. President John F. Kennedy gave the movement a boost in 1961, by encouraging Congress to pass legislation to establish community-based mental health centers (Bassuk & Gerson, 1978). By the early 1970s, hundreds of such centers were in operation, offering transitional homes and outpatient care to patients capable of living in the community.

Unfortunately, the dream of the community mental health movement, like the earlier dream of asylums, has remained mostly unrealized. The number of chronic patients in state mental institutions has been greatly reduced, but it is debatable whether the quality of life for former patients has been improved. They have generally not been integrated into the community but are living on its fringes. They are often found in run-down rooming houses, understaffed nursing homes, and, as in the days of Dorothea Dix, in jails (Abram & Teplin, 1991; Lamb, 2000; Smith & others, 1993). Many are homeless; according to one estimate, 25 percent of homeless people in the United States suffer from schizophrenia (Lehman, 1998).

Dorothea Dix

This Boston schoolteacher's crusade resulted in new asylums for the mentally ill and improved conditions in existing institutions.

Hospital "Treatment" from a Patient's-Eye View: Rosenhan's Study

In the midst of the movement toward deinstitutionalization, David Rosenhan (1973), a psychologist at Stanford University, published a study that helped sensitize the general public to continuing problems in mental hospitals. In the study, Rosenhan and seven other sane individuals feigned mental illness to gain admission at a total of 12 different psychiatric hospitals. After making an appointment, each appeared at a hospital admitting office and complained of a single symptom—hearing voices that said, "Empty, hollow, thud." They answered all other questions about their problems and history honestly. Once in the hospital, they behaved as normally as possible, and when asked about the voices, they said that they no longer heard them. None of these pseudopatients was ever detected as an impostor by hospital staff, though real patients often saw through the ruse and said things like, "You're not really mentally ill; you must be a reporter studying the hospital." Perhaps the main reason that they remained undetected is that the staff had very little contact with them; the pseudopatients' total time with psychiatrists and psychologists averaged less than 7 minutes per day, including group meetings. Even in hospitals that were adequately funded and staffed, staff members who could have spent more time interacting with patients chose instead to stay inside the glass "cage" that separated them from patients.

Even more striking than the minuscule amount of interaction with staff was the dehumanizing nature of the interactions that did occur. When pseudopatients (or real patients) approached them to ask questions, staff members commonly averted their eyes and walked away or gave a reply that was irrelevant to the question. In other ways as well, staff members communicated an attitude that patients were not to be taken seriously as thinking individuals. They talked about patients in front of them as if the patients were not there. A nurse unbuttoned her uniform and adjusted her brassiere in front of a ward of male patients, not to be seductive but because she felt no need to show normal social decorum in front of patients. Some attendants beat or verbally abused patients in front of other patients but stopped immediately when other staff members approached. As Rosenhan put it, "Staff are credible witnesses, patients are not." The pseudopatients' normal behaviors were frequently interpreted in terms of mental illness. For example, no staff member ever asked the pseudopatients why they were so often writing in notebooks (which they did to record their experiences), yet a subsequent inspection of the hospital records showed that their "writing behavior" was regularly described as part of their pathological symptomatology. All in all, staff members seemed unable to look through the label *mentally ill*, or through the bizarre symptoms that patients sometimes show, to see that patients are not always crazy and are usually capable of normal human interactions.

Bright Spots

Within the past three decades, a number of highly successful programs for helping seriously disordered individuals have been developed, both in and out of mental hospitals, which illustrate what can be done when the will is present and political obstacles are overcome.

In one now-classic study within the state mental hospital system in Illinois, Gordon Paul and Robert Lentz (1977) selected 84 very dysfunctional patients who had been hospitalized for an average of 17 years, each with a diagnosis of schizophrenia, and assigned them randomly to different treatments. One group continued to receive *standard hospital treatment*, emphasizing custodial care and drug therapy. A second group was assigned to *milieu therapy*, which involved close interaction between staff and patients, increased respect for patients (who were referred to as residents), heightened expectations concerning the responsibilities of both staff and patients, a degree of democratic decision making in the ward, and reduction or elimination of antipsychotic drugs wherever possible. A third group was

2.

How did Rosenhan study the experiences of patients in mental hospitals, and what did he find?

3.

How did Paul and Lentz show that people who had been long-term mental patients could profit from a therapeutic environment that was quite different from the standard hospital treatment?

Reaching out

In some communities social workers seek out people who are in need, get to know them as individuals, and help them gain access to useful services and means of support.

assigned to *social-learning therapy*, which involved most of the elements of milieu therapy plus a highly directed effort to teach patients the social skills they would need to live outside the hospital. Patients in this group were engaged in organized, skill-learning activities during 85 percent of their waking hours. In contrast, those in the standard ward spent only 5 percent of their waking hours in classes, therapy sessions, or other organized activities.

The staff-to-patient ratio and the proportion of professional to nonprofessional staff were the same in all three wards. The study continued for 5 years, by which time 97 percent of the patients in the social-learning ward, 71 percent in the milieu ward, and 46 percent in the standard ward had been able to leave the hospital and live in the community for at least 18 months. By other measures as well—including improved behavior in the ward and reduced total cost per patient—the social-learning ward was far more successful than the standard ward.

More recently, some communities have developed intensive intervention programs for seriously disturbed people outside mental hospitals. Such programs actively reach out to the mentally disabled, offering them training in daily living and advocating for them as they attempt to secure housing, employment, and other necessities. Rather than wait for the disabled to come to them, they go to the disabled. Well-designed research studies have shown that such programs can be highly effective in reducing the need for hospitalization and in increasing the proportion of patients who eventually recover from their disorders (Drake & others, 2001; Test & others, 1991). They are expensive, but no more so than custodial care in a mental hospital (Lehman & others, 1999; Levine & others, 1993). Other studies have shown that support, training, and crisis intervention provided to families caring for a person with schizophrenia sharply reduce the need for hospitalization (Lehman, 1998). Despite such evidence, the majority of people with schizophrenia and their families in the United States do not receive such services (Drake & others, 2001; Lehman & others, 1998).

Structure of the Mental Health System

Public concern about mental health generally centers on the most severely disordered individuals. But most people who seek mental health services have much milder problems. The kinds of services they seek depend on such factors as the severity of their disorders, what they can afford, and the services available in their community.

Places of Treatment

Public and private *mental hospitals* still exist. They provide custodial care for patients who cannot care for themselves or be cared for by family members at home. In addition, they provide brief hospitalization (typically 2 to 4 weeks) to stabilize individuals during acute psychotic attacks. The number of people in mental hospitals in the United States dropped from about 560,000 in 1955 to about 62,000 in 1997 (Lamb, 2000).

Today the majority of psychiatric inpatients are in *general hospitals* rather than mental hospitals, sometimes in special psychiatric wards but more often not (Kiesler, 1993). A general hospital is often preferred by patients whose stay will be short. Among other things, less stigma is associated with hospitalization there, and its location near the patient's home makes visiting easier for family members and friends. *Nursing homes* now care for many older chronic mental patients who in former times would have been in mental hospitals (Grob, 2000). Nursing homes usually do not employ specialized personnel for treating such people, and living conditions vary widely from one home to another.

4.

Where and from whom can mental health services be obtained?

Gary Wagner / Stock, Boston

Halfway houses, usually located in residential areas of cities, are places where people who have been discharged from a hospital reside during their transition back to the community. The halfway house (or *group home*, as it is often called) provides a place to sleep, eat, and socialize; staff may also provide help in finding employment and a permanent place to live. Residents are expected to leave the house during the day to work, look for work, or go to school. Such houses are usually run by nonprofessionals who consult regularly with government-employed psychiatrists, psychologists, and social workers.

The majority of people who seek psychological help do not need inpatient care. When they can afford it, or when their health insurance covers it, they most often seek treatment in the *private offices* of psychiatrists, clinical psychologists, or psychiatric social workers. Others may seek help in publicly supported settings. *Community mental health centers* offer free or low-cost services, including psychotherapy, support groups, and telephone crisis hotlines. In addition, such centers often sponsor classes, initiate legislation, and engage in other activities aimed at preventing psychological problems in the community. A national survey in the United States found that 72 percent of patients of mental health professionals were seen in private offices, 16 percent were seen in community mental health centers, and 12 percent were seen in such settings as medical school clinics and public hospitals (Howard & others, 1996).

Providers of Treatment

Psychotherapy and other mental health services are provided by an array of professionals with various kinds of training:

- *Psychiatrists* have a medical degree, obtained through standard medical school training, followed by special training and residency in psychiatry. They can work in any of the settings described above but most often choose hospitals and private practice. They are the only mental health specialists who can regularly prescribe drugs.

- *Clinical psychologists* usually have a doctoral degree in psychology, with training in research and clinical practice. Many are employed by universities as teachers and researchers in addition to having their own clinical practices. As clinicians they may work in any of the settings described above.

- *Counseling psychologists* usually have a doctoral degree from a counseling program. Their training is similar to that of clinical psychologists but generally entails less emphasis on research and more on practice. They may work in any of the settings described above. In general, counseling psychologists are more likely than are psychiatrists or clinical psychologists to work with people who have problems of living that do not warrant a diagnosis of mental disorder.

- *Counselors* usually have a master's degree from a counseling program. They may work in any of the above settings but are more likely to work in a school or other institution, with people who are dealing with school- or job-related problems. They receive less training in research and psychological assessment procedures than do doctoral-level clinical or counseling psychologists.

- *Psychiatric social workers* usually have a master's degree in social work, followed by advanced training and experience working with people who have psychological problems. They may be employed in any of the settings described above, but they are most often employed by public social work agencies and commonly visit people in their homes to offer support and guidance.

- *Psychiatric nurses* usually have a bachelor's or master's degree in nursing, followed by advanced training in the care of mental patients. They usually work in hospitals and may conduct psychotherapy sessions as well as provide more typical nursing services.

Help for psychological problems is also provided by many people other than mental health professionals. Such help is often found in religious organizations and in self-help organizations, such as Alcoholics Anonymous, where people with specific kinds of problems help each other.

Recipients of Treatment

As was discussed in Chapter 16, the American Psychiatric Association (2000) has defined mental disorders as psychological problems that are sufficiently distressing or disruptive to warrant professional help. Such disorders are described in the association's official diagnostic manual, *DSM-IV* (*Diagnostic and Statistical Manual of Mental Disorders*, fourth edition). A large-scale national survey conducted in the 1980s, however, revealed that most people in the United States who have mental disorders by *DSM* criteria do not seek or receive formal treatment (Howard & others, 1996).

The study revealed that somewhat fewer than half of adults with a mental disorder had ever in their lives obtained any formal treatment for a mental problem or disorder and only about half of those (less than a quarter of the total) had ever obtained such treatment from a mental health professional. The percentage of individuals with a diagnosable disorder who had seen a mental health professional varied with sex, education, race, and income level. The figure was 25 percent for women compared with 20 percent for men; 43 percent for college graduates compared with 11 percent for persons with less than a high school education; 27 percent for whites compared with 17 percent for nonwhites; and 37 percent for individuals earning over $35,000 compared with 20 percent for those earning under $10,000. Figure 17.1 shows the relationship found between income level and (a) incidence of mental disorder, (b) likelihood of seeing a mental health professional among those who had a *DSM*-diagnosable mental disorder, and (c) likelihood of seeing a mental health professional among those who did not have a *DSM*-diagnosable mental disorder. The higher the income, the less the incidence of mental disorder; and the higher the income, the greater the likelihood of seeing a mental health professional, regardless of whether or not the person had a diagnosable mental disorder.

According to the same study, roughly 2 million of the 7 million people in the United States who visited a mental health professional within a 6-month period had never in their lives qualified for a *DSM* diagnosis of mental disorder. Those people most often were seeking help with some life problem, such as a marital difficulty. The majority of the rest suffered from anxiety disorders, major depression, substance (drug or alcohol) abuse or dependence, or some combination of these (Howard & others, 1996).

5.

According to a survey conducted in the United States, how does the obtaining of mental health care vary with sex, education, race, and income?

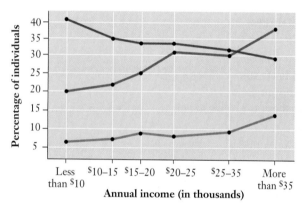

At least one diagnosable
mental disorder

At least one visit to a mental health
specialist, given a mental disorder

At least one visit to a mental health
specialist, given no mental disorder

FIGURE **17.1**
Relation of income level to mental disorder and treatment
People in higher income brackets are less likely to have a *DSM*-diagnosable mental disorder but more likely to visit a mental health specialist, whether or not they have a disorder, than are people in lower income brackets. The data shown here come from a national mental health survey conducted in the United States in the early 1980s (Howard & others, 1996).

SECTION SUMMARY

Through most of Western history, public concern with the seriously mentally disordered was limited largely to keeping such people away from the rest of society. In the eighteenth and nineteenth centuries, public asylums and mental hospitals were built with the stated intention of providing care and treatment, but the reality for most patients was neglect and abuse. The deinstitutionalization movement, begun in the 1950s, reduced the number of inmates in such institutions but increased the numbers of seriously mentally disordered people among the homeless and in nursing homes and jails. Controlled studies have shown that seriously mentally disordered people can function outside of institutions if they and their families receive reliable help and support with problems of daily living, but such services are not available to the majority who could use them.

Today, places of treatment for mental disorders include mental hospitals, general hospitals, nursing homes, halfway houses, private offices of mental health profession-

als, and community mental health centers. Providers of treatment include psychia-trists, clinical psychologists, counseling psychologists, counselors, psychiatric social workers, and psychiatric nurses. Most people who have a DSM-IV-diagnosable mental disorder do not seek treatment from any mental health professional. The more edu-cated and wealthier a person is, the more likely he or she is to seek and obtain such treatment.

CLINICAL ASSESSMENT

Assessment is the process by which a mental health professional gathers and inter-prets information about a client for the purposes of developing a plan of treatment. Diagnosis—defined in Chapter 16 as the classifying and labeling of a disorder ac-cording to some standard set of guidelines, such as those in *DSM-IV*—is only one goal of assessment. In fact, some clinicians deliberately avoid such labeling except when it is required for bureaucratic purposes, such as filing for insurance reim-bursement. The more important goal is to understand the person as a unique indi-vidual with a unique set of life circumstances, ways of thinking, and ways of behaving. Assessment ideally occurs not only before treatment but throughout it, to monitor changes and determine when treatment should be modified or discon-tinued. Assessment is far from an exact science; it often has a sizable subjective component. Yet many studies have shown that the tests and measures used for psy-chological assessment do produce valid, clinically useful information (Meyer & others, 2001).

Clinicians who have different theoretical orientations have different views as to what kinds of information are most useful in assessment. To a psychodynamically oriented clinician, what the client *doesn't* say (and thus may be repressing) may be as revealing as what he or she *does* say. To a humanistic clinician, the client's conscious perceptions and beliefs (his or her phenomenological world) are most useful, whether they are objectively accurate or not. To a cognitively oriented clinician, the client's habitual patterns of thinking are crucial. And to a behaviorally oriented clinician, objective facts about the client's actual behaviors and the settings in which they occur are most important. Some of the assessment aids available to clinicians are described below.

Assessment Interviews and Objective Questionnaires

George Kelly (1958), a clinical psychologist whose ideas helped found the human-istic and cognitive traditions, once offered the following simple advice about clini-cal assessment: "If you want to know what is going on in a person's mind, ask him; he may tell you."

The *assessment interview* is by far the most common assessment procedure. It is basically a dialogue through which the clinician tries to learn about the client. The dialogue may be unstructured, leaving to the client the task of deciding what is important or unimportant; or it may be a highly structured set of questions asked by the clinician and answered by the client. The interview typically touches on the client's immediate symptoms, home and work environment, personal history, fam-ily history, and other information that seems relevant to the client's problem. The client's nonverbal behaviors, such as long pauses, body tension, or emotional ex-pressions may also be taken into account in interpreting his or her verbal responses.

To supplement interviews, *objective questionnaires* have been developed to help clients report their feelings, thoughts, and behaviors. Some of these are simply lists of adjectives or brief, descriptive statements; the client is asked to check off those that apply to himself or herself. Others use a multiple-choice format in which the client chooses from among several possible statements the one that most

6.

What are the advantages of interviews and objective questionnaires for assessing a client's condition?

TABLE 17.1
Sample items from the Beck Depression Inventory

The client's task on each item is to pick out the one statement that best describes how he or she has been feeling for the past week.

Item (pessimism)

I am not particularly discouraged about the future.
I feel discouraged about the future.
I feel I have nothing to look forward to.
I feel that the future is hopeless and that things cannot improve.

Item (sense of failure)

I do not feel like a failure.
I feel I have failed more than the average person.
As I look back on my life, all I can see is a lot of failures.
I feel I am a complete failure as a person.

Source: BDI by Aaron T. Beck, 1978, New York: Harcourt Brace Jovanovich.

7.

How was the MMPI developed, and why was it revised? What is the purpose of its clinical, content, and validity scales?

applies to himself or herself. Some cover a broad range of possible symptoms or characteristics. Others, such as the *Beck Depression Inventory* illustrated in Table 17.1, focus on a narrow range of symptoms associated with a particular class of disorder. Objective questionnaires offer a degree of standardization that is useful for clinical research or for any comparison of one client with others. In addition, they are in some ways less subject to bias than are face-to-face interviews, in which the clinician's way of asking the questions may influence the client's answers. However, they require a client who is literate, reflective, and motivated to answer honestly.

A Psychometric Personality Test: The MMPI

Psychometric personality tests are objective questionnaires that have been developed through psychometric methods (discussed in Chapter 15) to assess a wide range of personality characteristics. Chapter 15 described the use of such tests in research on normal personality differences. By far the most commonly used psychometric personality test for clinical assessment is the *Minnesota Multiphasic Personality Inventory*, abbreviated **MMPI**.

The original purpose of the MMPI—developed at the University of Minnesota in the late 1930s—was to provide an objective means of diagnosing mental disorders, uncontaminated by the biases of any particular clinician (Hathaway & McKinley, 1943). As the test was being developed, all potential questions were pretested on groups of people who had already been diagnosed as having a specific mental disorder and on a large control group with no diagnosed disorder (the so-called Minnesota normals). Questions that were commonly answered differently by a group diagnosed with a disorder than by the controls were kept, and the others were thrown out. The goal was to identify questions that would distinguish different diagnosed groups from each other and from the control group.

Despite its frequent use, or perhaps because of it, the original version of the MMPI was often criticized. Some argued, for example, that the test was culturally biased, producing false signs of disorder in people whose backgrounds were different from those of the mostly white, middle-class Minnesotans with whom the test was developed (Gynther, 1972). Consider the statement "People say insulting and vulgar things about me." A response of *true* was scored as a sign of paranoia even in a member of a discriminated-against minority (Pervin, 1980). In the late 1980s the test was revised on the basis of results obtained from a large, representative sample of U.S. citizens, with the aim of updating the content, reducing the cultural bias, and increasing the test's validity (Butcher, 1990, 1999).

The revised test, MMPI-2, contains 567 statements about the self, to which the person must reply *true* or *false*. Most statements contribute to a score on one or more of 10 *clinical scales* and 15 *content scales*. In some cases the relationship between a statement and the clinical scale to which it contributes is obvious. Thus, the response *true* to the statement "The future seems hopeless to me" adds a point to the clinical scale measuring depression. In other cases, the relationship is not obvious. For example, answering *false* to "At times I feel like swearing" also contributes to the clinical scale measuring depression. This is because in the research on which the scale was built, depressed people responded *false* to that item significantly more often than did nondepressed people. The content scales are similar to the clinical scales but contain only statements that are obviously related to the characteristic being measured. Thus, the content scales assess most directly what people choose to say about their psychological condition.

In addition, the test has several *validity scales* designed to assess honesty and care in completing the test. The *L* scale was designed to assess lying (or lack of frankness) motivated by the attempt to make a good impression. For example, the response *true* to the statement "I never get angry" adds a point to the L scale, on the assumption that everyone gets angry at times. The F scale was designed to assess the tendency to "fake bad," that is, to exaggerate problems or to claim nonexistent symptoms. The response *true* to "Everything smells the same" adds a point to the F scale, as actual inability to discriminate among different odors is practically nonexistent. High scores on the L, F, and other validity scales can also reflect random responses, which might stem from carelessness or from insufficient reading or reasoning ability. Whatever their cause, high scores on the validity scales imply that the answers to other questions cannot be trusted and the results should be either thrown out or interpreted with caution.

Projective Tests

The interviews and objective questionnaires just described rely on the person's conscious mind to supply accurate information about the self. But, according to psychodynamic theories (introduced in Chapter 15), defense mechanisms may hide the person's most clinically significant motives and emotions from his or her conscious mind, rendering them unreportable in interviews or objective tests. For this reason, many clinicians use *projective tests*, which are designed to provide clues about the unconscious mind. Projective tests are an outgrowth of the technique of *free association*, originally developed by Freud as a means of learning about his patients' unconscious minds. In free association generally, clients are asked to free their minds from the constraints of conventional logic and to say at once whatever comes to mind in response to particular words or other stimuli. In most projective tests the person views ambiguous pictures and is asked to say quickly, without logical explanation, what each picture brings to mind.

Taking a projective test is a bit like responding to a work of art. If you look at a painting or a piece of sculpture, you may see something quite different in it from what another person sees. Your interpretation says something about yourself. In psychodynamic terms, you are *projecting* some aspect of yourself onto the work of art. Unconscious thoughts that would never get past your defense mechanisms and into conscious expression if you were talking about yourself may be freely expressed in the guise of artistic interpretation.

The projective tests most commonly used are the **Rorschach Test** and the **Thematic Apperception Test (TAT)**. In the Rorschach test, the visual stimuli are symmetrical inkblots, and the task is to say what each inkblot looks like. In the TAT,

8.

Why and how do clinicians use projective tests?

The Rorschach and TAT tests

In the Rorschach test, people say what they see in the inkblots. In the TAT, they tell a brief story for each picture. The rationale of both tests is that people project their unconscious wishes and memories into their perceptions or stories.

the stimuli are pictures of ambiguous scenes that include one or more persons, and the task is to tell a story about what might be happening in the picture. Clinicians have developed standard procedures for scoring projective tests, with guidelines for coding the content of the client's responses (Exner, 1993; Rose & others, 2001). For example, standard scoring for the Rorschach test includes methods for rating the degree of morbidity (tendency to see death and decay) and aggressiveness (tendency to see conflict) in each response. The validity of such systems is still very much debated (Garb & others, 1998; Wood & others, 1996).

The MMPI-2 and Rorschach are today the two most commonly used clinical assessment tests (Butcher & Rouse, 1996). Some clinicians use both of them, arguing that each has a separate set of strengths, which can be used to help offset the weaknesses of the other (Ganellen, 1996). All objective and projective tests, however, depend on comparing the individual's responses to a standard, modal way of responding collected from a comparison group of people without disorders. Any unique background or cultural difference between the person being tested and the comparison group would tend to make the test invalid. Increasingly, separate tests or separate scoring systems are being used for people from cultures different from the groups on which the original tests and scoring systems were based (Castillo, 1997; Mezzich & others, 1996).

Behavioral Monitoring

9.

How does behavioral monitoring contribute to both assessment and treatment?

The term **behavioral monitoring** refers to any system for counting or recording actual instances of desired or undesired behaviors. In Paul and Lentz's experiment comparing treatments for hospitalized patients, noted earlier, staff members charted each patient's progress by keeping daily counts of the person's positive and negative actions (defined according to his or her symptoms). In a less formal way, ward nurses or other observers in any mental hospital keep a daily log of patients' activities to assess improvement or deterioration.

Behavior therapists who work with noninstitutionalized clients emphasize *self-monitoring*, in which clients keep written records of their own actions that they are trying to increase or decrease. Thus, a person trying to eliminate a hand-washing compulsion might keep a record of each instance of hand washing, or a person with an eating disorder might keep a record of each food eaten and the amount consumed.

The very process of keeping records heightens awareness of the behavior, which in itself can alleviate the problem. In addition, the records and graphs can provide a strong incentive for change—everyone likes to see evidence of improvement.

Assessment of Brain Damage and Neuropsychological Functioning

If there is a reason to think that brain damage might underlie a patient's psychological difficulties, the location of damage might be assessed through such means as an EEG or a brain imaging technique (CAT scan, MRI scan, or PET scan).

The *EEG (electroencephalogram)*, as discussed in Chapter 6, is a measure of the pattern of electrical activity of the brain, taken through electrodes attached to the scalp. It can be analyzed for abnormal patterns that indicate possible brain damage. The scanning techniques are newer, much more costly methods. In making a *CAT scan (CAT* stands for *computerized axial tomography*), multiple x-rays of the brain are taken from various angles and analyzed by a computer to produce pictures of individual sections of the brain, which can be inspected to find anatomical abnormalities. With an *MRI (magnetic resonance imaging) scan*, pictures of brain sections are constructed on the basis of electromagnetic radiation given off by specific molecules in the brain when the brain is subjected to a strong magnetic field (discussed in Chapter 5). With a *PET (positron emission tomography) scan*, images are produced that reflect the pattern of blood flow and rate of oxygen use across sections of the brain (discussed in Chapter 5).

A person with suspected or confirmed brain damage might also be given *neuropsychological tests* aimed at identifying specific functional deficits that often accompany brain damage. The most frequently used set of such tests, the *Halstead–Reitan battery*, includes tests of motor control (such as moving the index finger rapidly up and down), perception (such as identifying objects by touch), and cognition (answering items from a standard IQ test) (Reitan & Wolfson, 1985). The person may then be given special training to compensate for deficits and might also be treated with drugs or even surgery if such treatment is warranted to prevent further damage (as in the case of a potentially lethal tumor).

10.

What is the purpose of neuropsychological tests such as the Halstead–Reitan battery?

SECTION SUMMARY

Assessment procedures and tools are used by mental health professionals to learn about clients' symptoms, problems, and strengths. The most common procedure is the assessment interview. Objective questionnaires, such as the Beck Depression Inventory, may be used to supplement an interview. Psychometric personality tests are objective questionnaires that assess a wide range of personality characteristics. Examples are the MMPI and MMPI-2, which were developed by comparing the responses to a large set of true-false questions made by people with known disorders with the responses of people without such disorders. Both tests contain validity scales as well as clinical and content scales. Projective tests—such as the Rorschach test and the Thematic Apperception Test—require the client to free-associate in response to ambiguous stimuli. The purpose of such tests is to learn about aspects of the client that he or she may not be conscious of. Behavioral monitoring refers to any system for recording instances of specific desired or undesired behaviors. Assessment for brain damage may involve electroencephalography, brain scanning (with the CAT, MRI, or PET methods), and neuropsychological testing.

BIOLOGICAL TREATMENTS

Once a person has undergone clinical assessment and a mental disorder has been diagnosed, the disorder might be treated by biological means (most often drugs), psychological means (psychotherapy of one form or another), or both. Biological treatments attempt to relieve the disorder by directly altering bodily processes. In the distant past, such treatments included drilling holes in the skull to let out bad spirits and bloodletting to drain diseased humors. Today, in decreasing order of extent of use, the three main types of biological treatments are drugs, electroconvulsive shock therapy, and psychosurgery.

Drugs

A new era in the treatment of mental disorders began in the early 1950s when two French psychiatrists, Jean Delay and Pierre Deniker (1952), reported that they had reduced or abolished the psychotic symptoms of schizophrenia with a drug called *chlorpromazine*. Today, a plethora of drugs is available for treating essentially all major varieties of mental disorders.

Drugs for mental disorders have been far from unmixed blessings, however. They are not magic bullets that zero in on and correct a disordered part of the mental machinery while leaving the rest of the machinery untouched. Like drugs used in general medicine, drugs used to treat mental disorders nearly always produce undesirable side effects. Some of the drugs are also addictive, and the attempt to withdraw from them sometimes produces symptoms worse than those for which the drug was prescribed. As you read of the three categories of drugs described below, notice their drawbacks as well as their benefits.

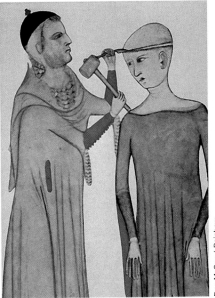

Dan McCoy / Rainbow

Madness as possession

This twelfth-century painting probably depicts trephination (piercing the skull to permit evil spirits to escape). With the revival of the medical model in the late Middle Ages, people gave up the use of trephination and other brutal treatments that were based on the belief that abnormal behavior indicates possession.

11.

What is known about the mechanisms, effectiveness, and limitations of drugs used to treat schizophrenia, generalized anxiety, and depression?

Antipsychotic Drugs

Antipsychotic drugs are used to treat schizophrenia and other disorders in which psychotic symptoms predominate. Chlorpromazine (sold as Thorazine), belonging to a chemical class called *phenothiazines*, was the first such drug, but now many others exist as well. As described in Chapter 16, most antipsychotic drugs seem to produce their effects by decreasing the activity of the neurotransmitter dopamine at certain synapses in the brain. Many well-designed experiments have shown that such drugs really do reduce or abolish the hallucinations, delusions, and bizarre actions that characterize the active phase of schizophrenia and that they prevent or forestall the recurrence of such symptoms when they are taken continually (Ashton, 1987). For the results and methods of one early study showing the effectiveness of chorpromazine, see Figure 17.2. Nevertheless, serious problems remain with antipsychotic drugs.

One problem is that although the drugs relieve the positive symptoms of schizophrenia (hallucinations, delusions, and bizarre behavior) in many patients, they often fail to relieve the negative symptoms (flattened affect, poverty of speech and thought, and lack of motivation) and in some cases make them worse (Carpenter & others, 1985; Fowles, 1992). Thus, although the drugs help make it possible for someone with schizophrenia to live outside the hospital, they usually do not restore the zest or pleasure that should come from doing so. Life becomes more normal but not necessarily happier.

Moreover—and this is why many people with schizophrenia refuse to take them—the drugs can produce very unpleasant and potentially harmful side effects. Through direct action on the autonomic nervous system, they can produce dizziness, nausea, dry mouth, blurred vision, constipation, sexual impotence in men, and disrupted menstrual cycles in women (McKim, 2000). Through effects on motor-control areas in the brain, they can produce symptoms akin to Parkinson's disease (shaking and difficulty in controlling voluntary movements) (Klein & others, 1980). In addition, about 40 percent of patients who take antipsychotic drugs for long periods of time eventually develop a serious and often irreversible motor disturbance called *tardive dyskinesia*, manifested as involuntary jerking of the tongue, face, and sometimes other muscles (Karon, 1989). A far more controversial problem is that antipsychotic drugs may, in some people, reduce the chance of eventual full recovery—an idea supported by a considerable amount of correlational research and at least one experimental study (Warner, 1985). Prolonged use of the drugs causes the brain to undergo a permanent biochemical adjustment that effectively increases its sensitivity to dopamine (Rupniak, Kilpatrick, & others, 1984; Rupniak, Mann, & others, 1984). This change probably provides the basis for tardive dyskinesia (Lickey & Gordon, 1991), and some suggest that it might also provide a basis for the exacerbation of schizophrenia itself (Breggin, 1997).

Some of the more recently developed antipsychotic drugs operate through different chemical mechanisms than do the traditional antipsychotic drugs and do not produce the same side effects. The most fully studied of these drugs is *clozapine*, which, compared with traditional antipsychotic drugs, has a smaller blocking effect on dopamine and a greater blocking effect on various other transmitters, including serotonin (McKim, 2000). Unlike traditional antipsychotic drugs, clozapine reduces the negative symptoms of schizophrenia as well as the positive symptoms, and it does not cause tardive dyskinesia or other motor problems (Kane, 1992; Trimble, 1996). Unfortunately, however, clozapine produces a potentially lethal

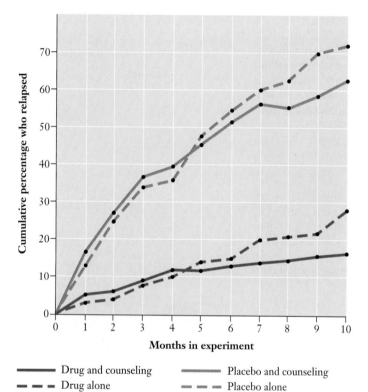

Drug and counseling   Placebo and counseling
- - - Drug alone   - - - Placebo alone

FIGURE 17.2 *Effects of antipsychotic drug treatment and counseling on rate of relapse among people with schizophrenia*
In this experiment, 374 patients with schizophrenia were randomly assigned to treatment with either an antipsychotic drug (chlorpromazine) or a placebo, following a 2-month period during which all had received the drug. Within each of these two groups, half received regular counseling, which focused on their social and vocational roles, and half received no regular counseling. As shown here, the rate of relapse (defined as sufficient worsening of symptoms to require rehospitalization) was much less for those receiving the antipsychotic drug than for those receiving the placebo. Counseling produced a smaller, but still significant, beneficial effect, beginning after the sixth month. (Adapted from Hogarty & Goldberg, 1973.)

blood disorder in some people, so continuous, very expensive monitoring of blood changes is required. For that reason, clozapine is usually used today only for patients who respond especially poorly to traditional drugs or are at high risk for tardive dyskinesia.

Antianxiety Drugs

Among the most frequently prescribed psychoactive drugs are those used to treat anxiety; they are commonly referred to as *tranquilizers*. At one time, barbiturates such as phenobarbital were often prescribed as tranquilizers, and many people became seriously addicted to them. During the 1960s, barbiturates were replaced by a new, safer group of antianxiety drugs belonging to a chemical class called *benzodiazepines*, including *chlordiazepoxide* (sold as Librium) and *diazepam* (sold as Valium). According to some estimates, by 1975 more than 10 percent of adults in the United States and western Europe were taking these drugs on a regular basis (Lickey & Gordon, 1991; Lipman, 1989). Since then their use has declined somewhat (Pincus & others, 1998), partly because of growing recognition that they are not as safe as they were once thought to be.

Benzodiazepines are most effective against generalized anxiety and are usually not effective against phobias, obsessive-compulsive disorder, and panic disorder (Lipman, 1989). Biochemically, the drugs appear to produce their tranquilizing effects by augmenting the action of the neurotransmitter GABA (gamma-aminobutyric acid) in the brain (McKim, 2000). GABA is an inhibitory transmitter, so its increased action decreases the excitability of neurons on which it acts. Side effects of benzodiazepines at high doses include drowsiness and a decline in motor coordination. More important, the drugs potentiate the action of alcohol, so that an amount of alcohol that would otherwise be safe can produce a coma or death in people taking a benzodiazepine. (If you're taking such a drug, don't drink!) In addition, benzodiazepines are now known to be at least moderately addictive, and very unpleasant withdrawal symptoms—sleeplessness, shakiness, anxiety, headaches, and nausea—occur in those who stop taking them after having taken high doses for a long time (Bond & Lader, 1996). These symptoms subside within about 2 weeks, but they drive many people back to the pills before the end of that period.

Antidepressant Drugs

In line with the monoamine theory of depression (discussed in Chapter 16), most antidepressant drugs are believed to reduce depression by increasing the availability of monoamine neurotransmitters—especially serotonin and norepinephrine—in synapses in the brain. One class of such drugs forms a chemical group referred to as *tricyclics*, of which *imipramine* (sold as Tofranil) and *amitriptyline* (sold as Elavil) are examples. Tricyclics block the reuptake of serotonin and norepinephrine (and, to a lesser extent, dopamine) molecules into the presynaptic neuron after their release into the synapse, thereby prolonging the action of the transmitter molecules on the postsynaptic neuron (Stahl, 2000). The side effects of tricyclics—which can include fatigue, dry mouth, and blurred vision—are not as severe as those of antipsychotic drugs, but are still a problem for many people.

A more recently developed class of antidepressants is the *selective serotonin reuptake inhibitors (SSRIs)*, which block the reuptake of serotonin but not that of other monoamine transmitters (see Figure 17.3 on page 666; Stahl, 2000). One often-prescribed SSRI is *fluoxetine* (sold as Prozac). The side effects of these drugs are considerably milder than those of the tricyclics, and partly for that reason physicians often prescribe SSRIs for people who complain of problems that do not warrant a diagnosis of mental disorder, such as normal feelings of sadness or even shyness. The drugs seem to alter personality in the direction of elevated mood and confidence, and much has been written both for

"...so I said," Hold on Doc, later for the family therapy, let's just put the whole kit n'kaboodle on anti-depressants!"

SIPRESS

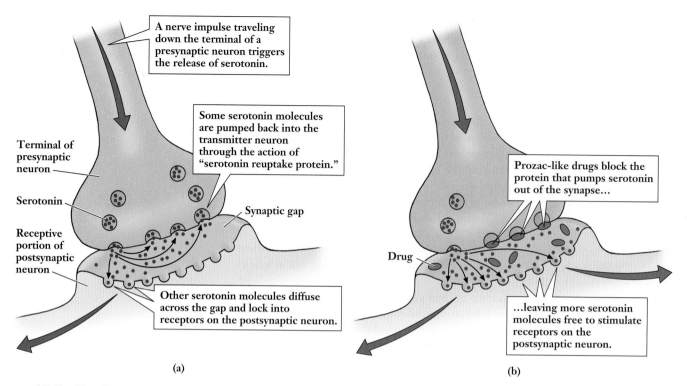

A nerve impulse traveling down the terminal of a presynaptic neuron triggers the release of serotonin.

Some serotonin molecules are pumped back into the transmitter neuron through the action of "serotonin reuptake protein."

Terminal of presynaptic neuron

Serotonin

Receptive portion of postsynaptic neuron

Synaptic gap

Other serotonin molecules diffuse across the gap and lock into receptors on the postsynaptic neuron.

Prozac-like drugs block the protein that pumps serotonin out of the synapse...

Drug

...leaving more serotonin molecules free to stimulate receptors on the postsynaptic neuron.

(a)   (b)

FIGURE **17.3** *How Prozac and other SSRI antidepressant drugs work*
When serotonin is released into a synapse, its action is normally cut short by reuptake into the presynaptic neuron. Selective serotonin reuptake inhibitors block this reuptake and thereby increase the action of serotonin on the postsynaptic neuron.

and against their use for such purposes (Concar, 1994; Kramer, 1994). Today—primarily because of the popularity of the SSRIs—antidepressants are the most frequently prescribed of all psychoactive drugs in the United States (Pincus & others, 1998). Some research, however, suggests that the SSRIs may not be as effective as the tricyclics in treating severe depression (Moeller & Volz, 2000).

Placebo Effects

To be approved for clinical use, a drug must be shown to be more effective than a placebo in treating the condition for which it is intended. A *placebo* (as discussed in Chapter 2) is an inactive substance that is indistinguishable in appearance from the drug. To test a drug's efficacy in treating a mental disorder, a large number of people diagnosed with the disorder must agree to take part in an experiment, and then each person is assigned randomly to either the drug or the placebo condition. The experiment is double-blind (as discussed in Chapter 2)—that is, neither the subjects nor the researchers who evaluate them are told who is receiving the drug or the placebo. When such experiments are conducted to test drugs for anxiety disorders or depression, the typical result is that both groups improve considerably over time, but the drug group improves somewhat more than does the placebo group (Enserink, 1999; Joffe & others, 1996; Kirsch, 2000). For example, in one set of experiments on treatments for depression, 46 percent of subjects receiving a placebo and 65 percent of those receiving an antidepressant drug showed a certain, clinically significant degree of improvement over the months of treatment (Walach & Maidhof, 1999). The difference between the two groups, though small, was statistically significant.

Why do anxious and depressed people who receive a placebo improve as much as they do? Anxiety and depression are characterized by feelings of helplessness and hopelessness. In fact, for some people those feelings *are* the disorder. Simply participating in a treatment experiment—meeting regularly with someone who seems to care and taking what *might* be a useful drug—may restore feelings of control and hope and produce expectations of improvement. These feelings and expectations may promote life changes that lead to partial or full recovery from the disorder. All such effects, which derive from the sense that one's disorder is being treated, are referred to as *placebo effects*.

12.

How might the strong placebo effects found in treatment of anxiety and depression be explained? Why has it been difficult to prove that the effects of antidepressants are not simply placebo effects?

In addition to placebo effects, some improvement typically occurs over time even with no treatment at all. Depression and anxiety are disorders that tend to come and go. Improvement that would occur without any treatment, not even placebo treatment, is referred to as *spontaneous remission*. According to one analysis, roughly 25 percent of the improvement shown by groups of people receiving antidepressant drugs may be attributable to spontaneous remission, 50 percent may be attributable to the placebo effect, and the remaining 25 percent may be attributable to the specific effects that antidepressant drugs have on the brain (Kirsch & Sapirstein, 1999).

A serious limitation of placebo-controlled studies of psychoactive drugs is that patients are often able to figure out—according to the presence or absence of side effects—whether they are receiving the active drug or the placebo (Enserink, 1999). A few researchers (e.g., Kirsch & Sapirstein, 1999) have gone so far as to suggest that antidepressant drugs may work better than placebos only because they are more effective than typical placebos in inducing placebo effects! People experience the side effects and feel all the more certain that they are receiving an active drug, a belief that gives them hope for recovery. The best way to determine whether a drug effect is more than a placebo effect would be to conduct experiments with so-called active placebos—that is, with substances that mimic the side effects of the drug without producing the specific effect in the brain that is presumed to be the basis for the drug's effectiveness. The few such studies that have been conducted have generally shown that active placebos are as effective as standard antidepressant drugs in relieving depression, but the experiments have been criticized on the grounds that the substances used as active placebos might indeed have antidepressant effects through their action on the brain (Hamburg, 2000; Kirsch, 2000).

Other Biologically Based Treatments

The increased use of drugs, coupled with the increased understanding and acceptance of psychotherapy, has led to the abandonment of most nondrug biological therapies for mental disorders. The two such treatments still occasionally used are electroconvulsive shock therapy and, in very rare cases, psychosurgery.

Electroconvulsive Shock Therapy

Electroconvulsive shock therapy, or *ECT*, is used primarily in cases of severe depression that do not respond to psychotherapy or antidepressant drugs. To the general public this treatment often seems barbaric, a remnant of the days when victims of mental disorders were tortured to exorcise the demons, and indeed it once was a brutal treatment. The brain seizure induced by the shock would cause muscular contractions so violent that they sometimes broke bones. Today, however, ECT is administered in a way that is painless and quite safe (Fink, 2000). Before receiving the shock, the patient is given drugs that block nerve and muscle activity so that no pain will be felt and no damaging muscle contractions will occur. Then an electric current is passed through the patient's skull, which touches off a seizure in the brain that lasts a minute or so. Usually such treatments are given in a series, one every 2 or 3 days for about 2 weeks.

Overall, about 70 percent of people who are suffering from major depression and have not been helped by psychotherapy and drug treatments experience remission with ECT (Weiner & Coffey, 1988). In some cases, the remission is permanent; in others, depression recurs after several months or more, and then another series of treatments may be given. Nobody knows how ECT produces its antidepressant effect. In nonhuman animals, such shocks cause immediate release of monoamines and certain other neurotransmitters, followed by longer-lasting changes in transmitter production and in the sensitivity of postsynaptic receptors (Nutt & Glue, 1993). Most theories of the effects of ECT focus on one or another of those long-term changes (Kapur & Mann, 1993; Sackeim, 1988).

13.

Under what conditions and how is ECT used to treat depression? Why is it often administered just to the right hemisphere?

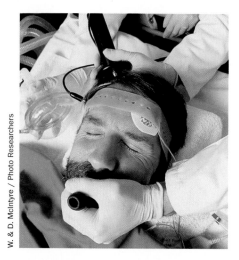

Electroconvulsive therapy
ECT is the treatment of choice for very severe depression that does not respond to drug therapy. This man has been anesthetized (so he is unconscious), given a muscle relaxant (so he will not show muscle spasms when the shock is given), and provided with a tube so that his breathing will not be impeded. The shock will be applied to the right side of his brain through the two black leads shown in the photo. Unilateral right-hemisphere ECT disrupts memory much less than does ECT applied across the whole brain.

14.

Why are prefrontal lobotomies no longer performed, and why are less drastic forms of psychosurgery occasionally performed?

Clinicians and researchers have long been concerned about the possibility that ECT can produce permanent brain damage. This concern is fueled by evidence of brain damage in laboratory animals subjected to intense electroconvulsive shocks. To date there is no evidence that such damage occurs with the shock levels used in clinical treatment, but temporary disruptions in cognition, especially in memory, are known to occur. When ECT is applied in the traditional manner—*bilaterally*, with the current running across both of the brain's hemispheres—the patient typically loses memory for events that occurred a day or two before the treatment. With a series of treatments, some memories for earlier events may also be lost, but these usually return within a month after the last treatment (Calev & others, 1993).

Many clinicians today prefer to apply ECT *unilaterally* to the right hemisphere only, because that produces little apparent memory loss. Controversy exists as to whether the unilateral procedure is as effective against depression as the bilateral procedure; it seems to be so when relatively high shock levels are used but not when low levels are used (Sackeim & others, 1993). Even at the relatively higher shock levels, the right-hemisphere treatment causes very little loss of conscious, verbal memories, although it may cause some loss of pictorial memories, as measured by the recognition of geometric designs seen before the shocks (Sachs & Gelenberg, 1988). Unilateral left-hemisphere treatment—which is rarely used—reduces verbal memories almost as much as bilateral treatment does and, according to some (but not all) studies, is less effective in relieving depression (Abrams, 1993; Sackeim, 1989). Such findings are consistent with other evidence (discussed in Chapter 5) that the left hemisphere is more involved in verbal processes and the right in visuospatial processes and emotion.

Psychosurgery

A treatment of last resort today is *psychosurgery*, the surgical cutting or production of lesions in portions of the brain to relieve a mental disorder. From the late 1930s into the early 1950s, tens of thousands of men and women were subjected to an operation called *prefrontal lobotomy*, in which the front portions of the brain's frontal lobes were surgically separated from the rest of the brain. Individuals with severe cases of schizophrenia, bipolar disorder, depression, obsessive-compulsive disorder, and pathological violence were subjected to the operation. Prefrontal lobotomy was so highly regarded that in 1949 the Portuguese neurologist who developed the technique, Egas Moniz, was awarded the Nobel Prize. By the mid-1950s, however, prefrontal lobotomies had gone out of style, partly because newly developed drug treatments offered an alternative and partly because of mounting evidence that, although lobotomy relieved people of their incapacitating emotions, it left them incapacitated in new ways (Valenstein, 1986). The anterior portions of the prefrontal lobes are a critical part of the brain's circuitry for integrating plans with action (see Chapter 5), and lobotomized patients showed lifelong deficits in the ability to make plans and behave according to them.

Refined versions of psychosurgery began to be used in the 1960s and continue to be used in rare cases today. The new procedures involve destruction of very small areas of the brain by applying radio-frequency current through fine wire electrodes implanted temporarily into the brain. In the most common such operation, called a *cingulotomy*, the cingulum (a small structure in the limbic system known to be involved in emotionality) is partly destroyed. Follow-up studies indicate that these electrode operations have (a) only rarely left the patient worse off after treatment than he or she was before, (b) often reduced or abolished the symptoms of major depression and obsessive-compulsive disorder, and (c) generally *not* been successful in treating the main symptoms of schizophrenia (Baer & others, 1995; Trimble, 1996; Valenstein, 1980). Because of their irreversible nature, such operations are generally considered appropriate only when the disorder has persisted for at least 10 years, all the more conventional treatments (including drugs) have failed, and the patient is desperate to the point of being suicidal (Trimble, 1996).

SECTION SUMMARY

Biological treatments for mental disorders include drug treatments, electroconvulsive shock therapy, and (in very rare cases) psychosurgery.

Traditional antipsychotic drugs, such as chlorpromazine, greatly reduce the positive symptoms of schizophrenia, apparently by decreasing the action of dopamine in the brain, but they do not reduce the negative symptoms. They also produce unpleasant and damaging side effects, including—after long-term use—tardive dyskinesia, an irreversible motor disturbance. The newer antipsychotic drug clozapine is effective against the negative as well as positive symptoms of schizophrenia and does not cause tardive dyskinesia, but it can cause a lethal blood disorder.

The most common antianxiety drugs are the benzodiazepines, which are believed to work by augmenting the action of the inhibitory neurotransmitter GABA. Side effects of these drugs include drowsiness and a decline in motor coordination. The drugs also interact with alcohol in a manner that is sometimes lethal. The traditional antidepressant drugs, including the tricyclics, augment the action of serotonin and norepinephrine in the brain by blocking their reuptake into presynaptic neurons. Their side effects include fatigue, dry mouth, and blurred vision. A group of newer antidepressants, the SSRIs, selectively block the reuptake of serotonin and produce relatively few and mild side effects.

Researchers have found it difficult to prove that antianxiety and antidepressant drugs have their therapeutic effects through their specific actions on brain transmitters because of the large placebo effects that occur in double-blind experiments. Depressed or anxious people taking inactive placebos improve almost as much as do those taking the drugs, and some researchers suggest that the incremental efficacy of the drugs may derive from their being more effective than chemically inactive placebos in producing placebo effects: People who experience a drug's side effects become convinced that they are being treated with a real drug, and that conviction may lead them to feel better.

Electroconvulsive shock therapy, used to treat otherwise intractable cases of severe depression, is much safer today than in the past. By administering the shock just to the right hemisphere, clinicians can reduce the loss of memories that otherwise results from such treatments. Prefrontal lobotomies, which were once rather common, are no longer performed, but in rare cases a much more refined psychosurgical procedure—in which a very small area of the limbic system is destroyed—is used to treat severe depression or obsessive-compulsive disorder that has not responded to any other treatment.

VARIETIES OF PSYCHOTHERAPY

From a physiological perspective, mental disorders are dysfunctions in the brain, potentially correctable with drugs or other means of altering the brain's activity. From a *psychological* perspective, mental disorders are dysfunctional ways of feeling, thinking, and behaving. **Psychotherapy** refers to any formal, theory-based, systematic treatment for mental problems or disorders that uses psychological rather than physiological means and is conducted by a trained therapist. Psychotherapy normally involves dialogue between the person in need and the therapist, and its aim is usually to restructure some aspect of the person's way of feeling, thinking, or behaving. If you have ever helped a child overcome a fear, encouraged a friend to give up a bad habit, or cheered up a despondent roommate, you have engaged in a process akin to psychotherapy, though less formal.

By one count, more than 400 nominally different forms of psychotherapy have appeared over the years (Karasu, 1986). Here we will limit ourselves to the approaches most often taught in clinical psychology and psychiatric programs and most often practiced by those trained in such programs. We will examine psychodynamic, humanistic, cognitive, behavioral, group, and family approaches to therapy. Today many, if not most, psychotherapists are *eclectic* in orientation, using

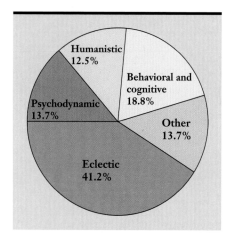

FIGURE **17.4**   *The theoretical orientations of a sample of psychotherapists*
Shown here are the results of a large survey that asked a representative sample of American psychotherapists to identify their theoretical orientation (data from Smith, 1982). There is reason to think that the percentage who consider themselves to be eclectic is even higher now than when this survey was taken (Hollanders, 2000).

techniques that they consider most appropriate from more than one of the classic varieties (see Figure 17.4). But we will focus here on the pure forms of each type and examine especially the work of the pioneers who first developed them.

Psychoanalysis and Other Psychodynamic Therapies

The term ***psychoanalysis*** was coined by Sigmund Freud, about a hundred years ago, to refer both to his theory of personality (discussed in Chapter 15) and to his approach to psychotherapy. ***Psychodynamic therapy*** refers more broadly to any therapy approach, including Freud's, that is based on the premise that psychological problems are manifestations of unconscious mental conflicts and that conscious awareness of those conflicts and insight into their origins are keys to recovery. Here we will look primarily at Freud's own version of psychoanalysis.

Unconscious Wishes and Repressed Memories as Bases for Mental Disorder

As described in Chapter 15, Freud contended that many of our most emotionally charged memories and wishes are unconscious. To protect ourselves from the anxiety they would create if we thought consciously about them, we actively keep them out of consciousness through repression and other defense mechanisms. In particular, we repress wishes and early childhood memories having to do with sex and aggression, as expressions of these drives are especially likely to run counter to social standards, provoke anger or rejection in others, and in that way threaten our existence.

On the basis of his experiences with patients, Freud postulated that emotional disorders (which he called *neuroses*) arise from an interaction between two categories of experiences. The first and most basic category consists of *predisposing experiences*, which typically occur in the first 5 to 6 years of life and relate to infantile sexual wishes and conflicts. The second category consists of *precipitating experiences*, which occur later and most immediately bring on the emotional breakdown. Precipitating experiences activate repressed memories and wishes that are connected with one or more predisposing experiences, stirring up the repressed material so that it threatens to enter consciousness. To defend against those memories and wishes, the mind responds in ways that lead to a diagnosis of mental disorder.

Routes to the Unconscious: Free Associations, Dreams, and Mistakes

Freud believed that to understand his patients' actions and problems, he had to learn about the content of their unconscious minds. But how could he do that if, by definition, the unconscious consists only of information that the patient cannot talk about? He could do it by analyzing certain aspects of the patient's speech and other observable behavior. This is where the term *psychoanalysis* comes from. His technique was to treat the patient's behavior as clues to the unconscious. Like a detective, he collected clues and tried to piece them together into a coherent story about the unconscious causes of the person's conscious thought and behavior.

What sorts of clues would be most useful? Since the conscious mind always attempts to act in ways that are consistent with conventional logic, Freud reasoned that the elements of thought and behavior that are least logical would provide the

15.

In Freud's theory, how do childhood experiences contribute to mental disorder?

best clues to the unconscious. They would represent elements of the unconscious mind that leaked out relatively unmodified by consciousness.

To encourage a flow of such clues, Freud developed the technique of *free association*. He instructed patients to sit back (or lie down on a couch), relax, free their minds, refrain from trying to be logical or "correct," and report every image and idea that entered their awareness in response to stimulus words that he (Freud) would provide or simply in response to their own previous words or thoughts. As an exercise, you might try this yourself: Relax, free your mind from what you have just been reading or thinking about, and write down the words or ideas that come immediately to your mind in response to each of the following: *liquid, horse, soft, potato*. Now, when you examine your set of responses to these words, do you find they make any sense that wasn't apparent when you produced them? Do you feel they give you any clues to your unconscious mind?

Freud also used the technique of asking patients to describe their dreams to him. According to Freud, dreams are the purest exercises of free association. During sleep, conventional logic is largely absent, and the forces that normally hold down unconscious ideas are weakened. Still, even in dreams the unconscious is partially disguised. Freud distinguished the underlying, unconscious meaning of the dream (the *latent content*) from the dream as it is consciously experienced and remembered by the dreamer (the *manifest content*). The analyst's task in interpreting a dream is the same as that in interpreting any other form of free association: to see through the disguises and uncover the latent content from the manifest content. The disguises in dreams come in many forms. Some are unique to a particular person, but some are universal (which, according to Freud, makes the analyst's job much easier). These universal disguises have become known as *Freudian symbols*, some of which were described by Freud (1900/1953) as follows (also see Figure 17.5 on page 672):

> The Emperor and Empress (or King and Queen) as a rule really represent the dreamer's parents; and a Prince or Princess represents the dreamer himself or herself. . . . All elongated objects, such as sticks, tree-trunks, and umbrellas (the opening of these last being comparable to an erection) may stand for the male organ—as well as all long, sharp weapons, such as knives, daggers, and pikes. . . . Boxes, cases, chests, cupboards, and ovens represent the uterus, and also hollow objects, ships, and vessels of all kinds. Rooms in dreams are usually women; if the various ways in and out of them are represented, this interpretation is scarcely open to doubt. In this connection interest in whether the room is open or locked is easily intelligible. There is no need to name explicitly the key that unlocks the room.

Still another route to the unconscious for Freud was to analyze mistakes, especially slips of the tongue, that occur in everyday behavior. In Freud's view, mistakes are never simply random accidents but are expressions of unconscious wishes. In one of his most popular books, *The Psychopathology of Everyday Life*, Freud (1901/1995) backed up this claim with numerous examples of such errors, along with his interpretations. For example, he reported an incident in which a young woman, complaining about the disadvantages of being a woman, stated, "A woman must be pretty if she is to please the men. A man is much better off. As long as he has his *five straight limbs* he needs no more." According to Freud, this slip involved a fusion of two separate clichés, *four straight limbs* and *five senses*, which would not have occurred had it not expressed an idea that was on the woman's mind (either unconscious or conscious) that she consciously would have preferred to conceal. In another context the same statement could have been a deliberate, slightly off-color joke; but Freud claims that in this case it was an honest slip of the tongue, as evidenced by the woman's embarrassment upon realizing what she had said.

16.

How did Freud use people's free associations, dreams, and "mistakes" as routes to learning about their unconscious minds?

The original therapeutic couch

This photograph of Freud's consulting room shows the couch on which patients reclined while he sat, out of their line of sight, listening to their free associations. Contemporary psychoanalysts have generally abandoned the couch in favor of a more egalitarian face-to-face encounter.

Edmund Engelman

FIGURE 17.5   *Freudian symbols in a work of art painted four centuries before Freud*
This is a detail from *The Garden of Earthly Delights*, painted in the late fifteenth century by the Dutch artist Hieronymus Bosch. It is believed to represent Bosch's conception of decadence or hell. Notice the dreamlike (nightmarish) quality and the numerous Freudian symbols.

17.

According to Freud's theory, how do resistance and transference contribute to the therapeutic process?

18.

According to Freud's theory, how do insights into the patient's unconscious conflicts bring about a cure?

Roles of Resistance and Transference in Psychoanalysis

Freud found that patients often resist the therapist's attempt to bring their unconscious memories or wishes into consciousness. The **resistance** may manifest itself in such forms as refusing to talk about certain topics, "forgetting" to come to therapy sessions, or arguing incessantly in a way that diverts the therapeutic process. Freud assumed that resistance stems from the more general defensive processes by which people protect themselves from becoming conscious of anxiety-provoking thoughts. Resistance provides clues that therapy is going in the right direction, toward critical unconscious material; but it can also slow down the course of therapy or even bring it to a halt. To avoid too much resistance, the therapist must present interpretations gradually, when the patient is ready to accept them.

Freud also observed that patients often express strong emotional feelings—sometimes love, sometimes anger—toward the therapist. Freud believed that the true object of such feelings is usually not the therapist but some other significant person in the patient's life whom the therapist symbolizes. Thus, **transference** is the phenomenon by which the patient's unconscious feelings about a significant person in his or her life are experienced consciously as feelings about the therapist. Freud considered transference to be especially useful in psychoanalysis because it provides an opportunity for the patient to become aware of his or her strong emotions. With help from the analyst, the patient can gradually become aware of the origin of those feelings and their true target.

Relationship Between Insight and Cure

Psychoanalysis is essentially a process in which the analyst makes inferences about the patient's unconscious conflicts and relays that information to the patient. How does such knowledge help? In Freud's theory, it helps by making conscious the dis-

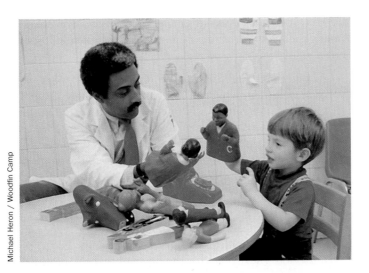

Play therapy

In this extension of psychodynamic therapy, children use dolls and other toys to express their feelings. The therapist uses the child's actions as clues for understanding the child's feelings and motives. If the therapist joins in the play, as in this example, he must be careful to play only in a way that is responsive to and does not direct the child's actions.

turbing wishes and memories that are the source of the neurotic symptoms. Once conscious, they can be expressed and experienced directly, or, if they are unrealistic, the conscious mind can modify them into healthier pursuits. At the same time, the patient is freed of the defenses that had kept that material repressed and has more psychic energy for other activities. But for all this to happen, the patient must truly accept the insights, viscerally as well as intellectually. The analyst cannot just tell the patient about his or her unconscious conflicts but must lead the patient gradually in such a way that he or she actually experiences the emotions and arrives at the insights himself or herself.

Case Example: Freud's Analysis of the Rat Man

All the just-described ideas about psychoanalysis can be made more vivid with a case example. One of Freud's most famous and illustrative cases is that of a 29-year-old man referred to in the case history as the Rat Man.

This patient came to Freud complaining of various fears, obsessions, and compulsions that had begun 6 years earlier and had prevented him from completing his university studies and going on to a career. One of the most revealing symptoms was an obsessive fantasy of a horrible torture applied to both his father and the woman whom the Rat Man was courting, in which a pot of hungry rats strapped against the victims' buttocks would chew their way out through the only available opening. Freud used this fantasy along with many other clues to interpret the Rat Man's problems. Here I will sketch the outlines of Freud's interpretation and some of the evidence on which he based it. You can decide for yourself from the sketch or, better yet, from Freud's original case history (Freud, 1909/1963) whether or not the interpretation seems plausible.

According to Freud (1909/1963), the *precipitating cause* of the Rat Man's disorder was his conflict over whether or not to marry the woman he had been courting since the age of 20. Unable to decide consciously, he had allowed his unconscious mind to resolve the conflict by making him too ill (producing his neurotic symptoms) to complete his studies and start a career (which were prerequisites for marriage). The *predisposing cause* was an unconscious conflict, originating in early childhood, between love and hatred for his father. These two causes were linked. The Rat Man's conflict about marrying the woman was a reenactment of his love-hate feelings toward his father. To marry her would be an act of hatred against his father, and to spurn her would be an act of love toward him.

The connection between these two conflicts had been cemented by the death of the Rat Man's father shortly after the Rat Man had begun to court the woman in question. He unconsciously and irrationally believed that he had caused his father's death by continuing the relationship with the woman against his father's wishes. Yet he also imagined unconsciously and irrationally that his father was still alive and

19.

How does the case of the Rat Man exemplify Freud's concepts of precipitating and predisposing causes, and how did free association, dream analysis, and transference contribute to Freud's analysis of the Rat Man?

that he could murder his father once more by following through with the marriage. Among the many converging lines of evidence that led Freud to these conclusions were the following:

+ At one point Freud asked the Rat Man to free-associate to the concept *rats* (*Ratten* in German), and the man immediately came up with *rates* (*Raten* in German), meaning "installments" or "money." The Rat Man had previously mentioned that the woman had little money and that his father wanted him to marry a certain wealthy cousin. These facts suggested to Freud that the rat fantasy was related to the father's opposition to the woman.

+ At another point the Rat Man described his mother's account of an event that took place when he was about 4 years old. His father had begun to beat him for having bitten his nurse. He responded with such a torrent of angry words that his father, shaken, stopped the beating and never beat him again. In Freud's analysis, this incident had great significance. Freud assumed that biting the nurse was a sexual act for the boy and that the beating contributed to the Rat Man's lifelong fear of his father's reactions to his sexual wishes. At the same time, his apparent power over his father—his anger had made the father stop the beating—helped stamp into the Rat Man the unconscious fear that he could kill his father through anger. From that time until his psychoanalysis, the Rat Man never consciously experienced anger toward his father. In addition, Freud saw direct symbolic links between this early childhood incident and the rat-torture obsession: rats, biting into and destroying his woman friend and his father, symbolized another small, biting beast—the boy who had once bitten first his beloved nurse and then, with angry words, his father.

+ Transference also entered into the analysis. The Rat Man reported a fantasy in which Freud wanted him to marry his (Freud's) daughter and a dream in which Freud's daughter had two spots of dung on her face instead of eyes. Freud interpreted the dung as symbolic of money, and he interpreted the fantasy and dream as a symbolic reconstruction of the man's conflict, with Freud replacing the Rat Man's father in urging him to marry a wealthy relative. At another point—which Freud regarded as the major breakthrough—the Rat Man became irrationally angry at Freud, jumping up from the couch and shouting abusive words at him. Reflecting on this incident later, the Rat Man recalled that his sudden anger was accompanied by a fear that Freud would beat him and that he had jumped up to defend himself. By this time in the analysis, it took little convincing for the Rat Man to share Freud's view that this was a reenactment of the incident in which his father had beaten him and he had responded so angrily.

This transference experience helped the Rat Man overcome his resistance to the idea that he felt fear and anger toward his father. The Rat Man's conscious acceptance of those feelings led, according to Freud, to recovery from his neurotic symptoms. In a sad footnote to the case, Freud (1923/1963) added that after a short period as a healthy man, the Rat Man was killed as an officer in World War I.

Post-Freudian Psychodynamic Psychotherapies

20.

How do modern variations of psychodynamic psychotherapy differ from Freud's psychoanalysis?

Few psychotherapists today practice psychoanalysis as Freud did, but many make use of his basic ideas. Many varieties of psychodynamic psychotherapy have been developed. All share certain aspects of Freud's approach, including the bringing of troublesome feelings into consciousness, the attribution of present troubles to mental conflicts stemming from past experiences, and the use of the therapist-client relationship as a model for understanding the client's relationships outside therapy (Jones & Pulos, 1993). The most common modification today, motivated largely by economic considerations, is to reduce the number of sessions required for analysis by using methods that get more quickly at unconscious material. So-called short-term psychodynamic psychotherapies attempt to accomplish in 10 to 40 sessions the task that usually takes hundreds of sessions in classic psychoanalysis. The couch is dispensed with, and the client and analyst sit face to face. The analyst more actively calls the client's attention to relevant material and ideas, and sometimes uses techniques such as role playing to facilitate transference and speed the therapeutic process.

Other variations differ from Freud's psychoanalysis in their theoretical underpinnings as well as their methods. Some psychodynamic therapists pay less attention than did Freud to early childhood and repressed memories and pay more attention to the client's adult experiences, relationships, and defenses against anxiety. These therapies aim to discover and expose ways by which defenses interfere with the client's current life. By breaking down the defenses, even without uncovering their origins, the therapist helps the client develop a healthier range of responses. Still other variations, called *non-Freudian psychodynamic therapies*, are based on alternative psychodynamic personality theories—such as Adler's, Jung's, or Horney's (discussed in Chapter 15)—that emphasize mental conflicts different from those deemed important by Freud. In Adlerian therapy, for example, the client's feeling of inferiority and the conflicts engendered by that feeling are considered to be most significant.

Hippocrates, March 2000

"Of course I'm feeling uncomfortable. I'm not allowed on the couch."

Humanistic Therapy

As described in Chapter 15, the humanistic view of the person emphasizes the inner potential for positive growth—the so-called actualizing potential. For this potential to exert its effects, people must be conscious of their inner feelings and desires and not deny or distort them. Humanistic therapy is similar to psychodynamic therapy in that both attempt to help clients become more aware of their feelings and wishes. From the humanistic view, however, these are likely to be positive and life-promoting rather than socially unacceptable and irrational. The main goal of humanistic therapy is to help clients become aware of their own feelings and wishes, so that they can gain control of their own lives rather than operate in accordance with their perceptions of what others expect. By far the most common humanistic therapy is that developed by Carl Rogers.

Rogers's Client-Centered Therapy

Rogers called his therapeutic approach *client-centered therapy*, because it focuses on the thoughts, abilities, and insights of the client rather than those of the therapist. The client, not the therapist, figures out what is wrong, makes plans for improvement, and decides when improvement has occurred. The therapist in this case is not an analyst, not a detective trying to infer things about the client that the client doesn't know, but instead is a compassionate yet professional person who acts as a sounding board for the client's ideas and emotions. How those ideas and emotions sound and feel to the client, not to the therapist, is most important.

From Rogers's perspective, psychological problems originate when people learn from their parents or other authorities to deny their own feelings and to distrust their own ability to make decisions. As a result of such learning, they look to others as guides to how to feel and act, but at the same time they rebel inside or feel resentful about living according to others' preferences. The client-centered therapist tries to provide a context within which clients can become aware of and accept their own feelings and learn to trust their own decision-making abilities. To do so, the therapist must display empathy, unconditional positive regard, and genuineness (Rogers, 1951).

Empathy refers to the therapist's attempt to comprehend what the client is saying or feeling at any given moment from the client's point of view rather than as an outside observer. As part of the attempt to achieve and manifest such empathy, the

21.

What is the primary goal of humanistic psychotherapy?

22.

In Rogers's humanistic therapy, what is the role of the client and what is the role of the therapist?

23.

Why are empathy, unconditional positive regard, and genuineness essential aspects of Rogers's approach to psychotherapy?

Michael Rougier / *LIFE Magazine*, © Time Warner, Inc

Carl Rogers

The inventor of client-centered therapy was a charismatic individual who personally embodied the empathy and genuineness that are the essence of his method of therapy.

therapist frequently reflects back the ideas and feelings that the client expresses. A typical exchange might go like this:

Client: *My mother is a mean, horrible witch!*

Therapist: *I guess you're feeling a lot of anger toward your mother right now.*

To an outsider, the therapist's response here might seem silly, a statement of the obvious. But to the client and therapist fully immersed in the process, the response serves several purposes. First, it shows the client that the therapist is listening and trying to understand. Second, it distills and reflects back to the client the feeling that seems to lie behind the client's words—a feeling of which the client may or may not have been fully aware at the moment. Third, it offers the client a chance to correct the therapist's understanding. By clarifying things to the therapist, the client clarifies them to himself or herself.

Unconditional positive regard implies a belief on the therapist's part that the client is worthy and capable even when the client may not feel or act that way. By expressing positive feelings about the client regardless of what the client says or does, the therapist creates a safe, nonjudgmental environment for the client to explore and express all of his or her thoughts and feelings. Through experiencing the therapist's positive regard, clients begin to feel more positive about themselves, and this is essential if they are going to take charge of their lives. Unconditional positive regard does not imply agreement with everything the client says or approval of everything the client does, but it does imply faith in the client's underlying capacity to make appropriate decisions. Consider the following hypothetical exchange:

Client: *Last semester in college I cheated on every test.*

Therapist: *I guess what you're saying is that last semester you did something against your values.*

Notice that the therapist has said something positive about the client in relation to the misdeed without condoning the misdeed. The shift in focus from the negative act to the client's positive values affirms the client's inner worth and potential ability to make constructive decisions.

Genuineness reflects the belief that it is impossible to fake empathy and positive regard, that the therapist must really feel them. If the therapist's words and feelings don't match, the words will not be believable to the client. The capacity for genuine empathy and positive regard toward all clients might seem to be a rare quality, but Rogers suggests that it can be cultivated by deliberately trying to see things as the client sees them.

Case Example: Rogers's Treatment of a Silent and Bitter Young Man

Rogers's greatest challenge as a therapist came when, as part of a research study, he conducted client-centered therapy with severely withdrawn inpatients in a state mental hospital (Rogers, 1967). One of these individuals was Jim, a 28-year-old man who had been hospitalized for 2½ years with a diagnosis of schizophrenia. Prior to the two sessions excerpted below, Rogers had met with Jim once a week for months, and most of that time had been spent in silence. According to Rogers, these two sessions marked a turning point, because for the first time Jim began to express how he felt.

24.

How did Rogers use empathy, unconditional positive regard, and genuineness to help a man who had been diagnosed with schizophrenia?

[At about 40 minutes into the session, marked mostly by silence.]

Jim: *I just ain't no good to nobody, never was and never will be.*

Rogers: *Feeling that now, hm? . . . Those really are lousy feelings. Just feel that you're no good at all, hm?*

Jim: *Yeah.* [Muttering in a low, discouraged voice.] *That's what this guy I went to town with just the other day told me.*

Rogers: *This guy that you went to town with really told you that you were no good? Is that what you're saying? Did I get that right?*

Jim: *M-hm.*

Rogers: *I guess the meaning of that, if I get it right, is that here's somebody that meant something to you and what does he think of you? Why, he's told you that he thinks you're no good at all. And that just really knocks the props out from under you.* [Jim weeps quietly.] *It just brings the tears.*

[Silence of 20 seconds.]

Jim: [Defiantly.] *I don't care though.*

Rogers: *You tell yourself you don't care at all, but somehow I guess some part of you cares because some part of you weeps over it.*

[This is followed by more silence, more weeping, and more reflection by Rogers on how it must hurt to feel that someone thinks you're no good. The next session also begins with lots of silence, punctuated by bitter statements in which Jim says that he wants to die. We pick up the conversation as Rogers breaks a long silence by asking whether Jim's wish to die is related to the comment discussed in the previous session.]

Rogers: *Can't help but wonder whether it's still true that some things this friend said to you—are those still part of the thing that makes you feel so awful?*

Jim: *In general, yes.*

Rogers: *M-hm.*

[Silence of 47 seconds, interrupted by another comment from Rogers. Then:]

Jim: *I ain't no good to nobody, or I ain't no good for nothin', so what's the use of living?*

Rogers: *M-hm. I guess a part of that is—here I'm kind of guessing and you can set me straight, I guess a part of that is that you felt, "I tried to be good for something as far as he was concerned. I really tried. And now—If I'm no good to him, if he feels I'm no good, then that proves I'm just no good to anybody." Is that, uh—anywhere near it?*

Jim: *Oh, well, other people have told me that, too.*

Rogers: *Yeah, m-hm. I see. So you feel if, if you go by what others—what several others have said, then, you are no good. No good to anybody.*

[This is followed by more silence, interrupted by a few comments along the same track. Then:]

Jim: [Muttering in discouraged tone.] *That's why I want to go, 'cause I don't care what happens.*

Rogers: *M-hm, m-hm . . . You don't care what happens. And I guess I'd just like to say—I care about you. And, I care what happens.*

[Silence of 30 seconds, and then Jim bursts into tears.]

Rogers: [Tenderly.] *Somehow that just—makes the feelings pour out.* [Silence of 35 seconds.] *And you just weep and weep. And feel so badly.*

Commenting on the transaction above, Rogers (1967) wrote:

> Jim Brown, who sees himself as stubborn, bitter, mistreated, worthless, useless, hopeless, unloved, unlovable, experiences my caring. In that moment his defensive shell cracks wide open, and can never be quite the same. When someone cares for him, and when he feels and experiences this caring, he becomes a softer person whose years of stored up hurt come pouring out in anguished sobs. He is not the shell of hardness and bitterness, the stranger to tenderness. He is a person hurt beyond words, and aching for the love and caring which alone can make him human. This is evident in his sobs. It is evident too in his returning to my office [shortly after the session], partly for a cigarette, partly to say spontaneously that he will return.

After this session, according to Rogers, Jim gradually became more open, spontaneous, and optimistic at their meetings. After several months, he was able to leave the hospital and support himself with a job. Eight years later, on his own initiative, Jim called Rogers to tell him that he was still employed, had friends, was content with life, and that his feelings toward Rogers were still important, even though they had not been in touch during all that time (Meador & Rogers, 1973).

Cognitive Therapy

25.

How does cognitive therapy differ from psychodynamic therapy and from humanistic therapy?

Cognitive therapy begins with the assumption that people disturb themselves through their habitual ways of thinking. Maladaptive beliefs and thoughts make reality seem worse than it is and in that way produce anxiety or depression. The goal of cognitive therapy is to identify maladaptive ways of thinking and replace them with adaptive ways that provide a base for more effective coping with the real world. Unlike psychoanalysis, cognitive therapy generally centers on conscious thoughts, though such thoughts may be so ingrained and automatic as to occur with little conscious effort.

Cognitive therapy is similar to humanistic therapy in its focus on conscious mental experiences, but in other respects it is different. Whereas humanistic therapy is client-centered, cognitive therapy is problem-centered. That is, whereas humanistic therapists try to help their clients understand themselves better as whole persons, cognitive therapists focus more directly on their clients' specific problems. Compared with either humanistic or psychodynamic therapists, cognitive therapists adopt more of a let's-get-down-to-business attitude. Most cognitive therapists are quite directive and relate to their clients somewhat like a teacher to a student. The cognitive therapist's task is to help clients identify and correct their faulty reasoning. Most cognitive therapists even assign homework to be completed between one session and the next. The two best-known pioneers of cognitive therapy are Albert Ellis and Aaron Beck.

Ellis's Rational-Emotive Therapy

26.

How does Ellis explain people's emotions in terms of their beliefs?

After trying the psychodynamic and the humanistic approaches to therapy and becoming disenchanted with both, Albert Ellis began in 1955 to develop his own approach, which he labeled *rational-emotive therapy (RET)* (Ellis, 1986, 1993). The basic premise of RET is that negative emotions arise from people's irrational interpretations of their experiences, not from the objective experiences themselves. Ellis gives humorous names to certain styles of irrational thinking. Thus, *musturbation* is the irrational belief that one *must* have some particular thing or *must* act in some particular way in order to be happy or worthwhile. If a client says, "I must get all A's this semester in college," Ellis might respond, "You're musturbating again." *Awfulizing*, in Ellis's vocabulary, is the mental exaggeration of setbacks or inconveniences. A client who feels bad for a whole week because of a dent in her new car might be told, "Stop awfulizing." Ellis is notoriously direct in his approach to correcting what he sees as clients' irrational views, quite the opposite of Rogers.

The following dialogue between Ellis (1962) and a client not only illustrates Ellis's style but also makes explicit his theory of the relationship between thoughts and emotions. The client has just complained that he was unhappy because some men with whom he played golf didn't like him.

Ellis: *You think you were unhappy because these men didn't like you?*

Client: *I certainly was!*

Ellis: *But you weren't unhappy for the reason you think you were.*

Client: *I wasn't? But I was!*

Ellis: *No, I insist: You only think you were unhappy for that reason.*

Client: *Well, why was I unhappy then?*

Ellis: *It's very simple—as simple as A, B, C, I might say. A in this case is the fact that these men didn't like you. Let's assume that you observed their attitude correctly and were not merely imagining they didn't like you.*

Client: *I assure you that they didn't. I could see that very clearly.*

Ellis: *Very well, let's assume they didn't like you and call that A. Now, C is your unhappiness—which we'll definitely have to assume is a fact, since you felt it.*

Client: *Damn right I did!*

Ellis: *All right, then: A is the fact that the men didn't like you, and C is your unhappiness. You see A and C and you assume that A, their not liking you, caused your unhappiness. But it didn't.*

Client: *It didn't? What did, then?*

Ellis: *B did.*

Client: *What's B?*

Ellis: *B is what you said to yourself while you were playing golf with those men.*

Client: *What I said to myself? But I didn't say anything.*

Ellis: *You did. You couldn't possibly be unhappy if you didn't. The only thing that could possibly make you unhappy that occurs from without is a brick falling on your head, or some such equivalent. But no brick fell. Obviously, therefore, you must have told yourself something to make you unhappy.*

In this dialogue, Ellis invokes his famous *ABC theory of emotions: A* is the *activating event* in the environment, *B* is the *belief* that is triggered in the client's mind when the event occurs, and *C* is the emotional *consequence* of that belief (see Figure 17.6). Therapy proceeds by changing B, the belief. In this particular example, the man suffers because he believes irrationally that he must be liked by everyone (an example of musturbation), so if someone doesn't like him, he is unhappy. The first step will be to convince the man that it is irrational to expect everyone to like him and that there is little or no harm in not being liked by everyone. The next step, after the man admits to the belief's irrationality, will be to help him get rid of the belief, so that it doesn't recur in his thinking. That takes hard work. Long-held beliefs do not simply disappear once they are recognized as irrational. They have become habits that occur automatically unless they are actively resisted. Ellis gives his clients homework designed to train them to catch and correct themselves each time the habitual thought pattern appears.

Albert Ellis

Founder of rational-emotive therapy
Albert Ellis is a colorful individual who, in his practice, took a highly assertive role with clients. He would refer to their maladaptive, irrational thoughts with such terms as "musterbation" and "awfulizing."

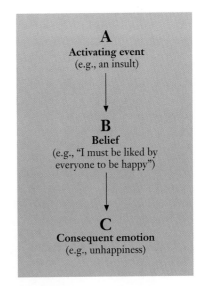

A
Activating event
(e.g., an insult)

↓

B
Belief
(e.g., "I must be liked by everyone to be happy")

↓

C
Consequent emotion
(e.g., unhappiness)

FIGURE **17.6**
The ABC's of Ellis's theory
Ellis and other cognitive therapists contend that our emotional feelings stem not directly from events that happen to us but rather from our interpretation of those events. By changing our beliefs—the cognitions we use for interpreting what happens—we can alter our emotional reactions.

Beck's Cognitive Therapy

Aaron Beck began to develop a cognitive approach to the treatment of depression in 1960, after observing that his depressed clients routinely distorted their experiences in ways that helped them maintain negative views of themselves, their world, and their future (Beck, 1976, 1991). He observed that they would minimize positive experiences, maximize negative experiences, and misattribute negative experiences to their own deficiencies when they were not really at fault. In later work, Beck and his associates also identified patterns of thinking that promote anxiety (such as exaggerating the likelihood that accidents or diseases will occur), and they expanded their cognitive therapy to include clients with anxiety disorders (Beck & Emery, 1985).

In therapy sessions, Beck's approach is gentler than is Ellis's. Instead of telling his clients directly about their irrational thoughts, he leads them, with a Socratic style of questioning, to discover and correct the thoughts themselves. He prefers this approach because it is less threatening than the direct approach and because it helps show clients that they can correct their own thoughts and need not always depend on the therapist. Beck's approach is illustrated by the following case summary.

Case Example: Beck's Treatment of a Depressed Young Woman

The client in this case (from Beck & Young, 1985) was Irene, a 29-year-old married woman with two young children, who was diagnosed with major depression. She had not been employed outside her home since marriage, and her husband, who had been in and out of drug-treatment centers, was also unemployed. She was socially isolated and felt that people looked down on her because of her poor control over her children and her husband's drug record. She was treated for three sessions by Beck and then was treated for a longer period by another cognitive therapist.

During the first session, Beck helped her to identify a number of her automatic (habitual) negative thoughts, including *Things won't get better. Nobody cares for me. I am stupid.* By the end of the session, she accepted Beck's suggestion to try to invalidate the first of those thoughts by doing certain things for herself, before the next session, that might make life more fun. She agreed to take the children on an outing, visit her mother, go shopping, read a book, and find out about joining a tennis group—all things that she claimed she would like to do. Having completed that homework, she came to the second session feeling more hopeful. However, she began to feel depressed again when, during the session, she misunderstood a question that Beck asked her, which, she said, made her "look dumb." Beck responded with a questioning strategy that helped her to distinguish between the *fact* of what happened (not understanding a question) and her *belief* about it (looking dumb) and then to correct that belief:

> **Beck:**   *OK, what is a rational answer [to why you didn't answer the question]? A realistic answer?*
>
> **Irene:**   *I didn't hear the question right, that is why I didn't answer it right.*
>
> **Beck:**   *OK, so that is the fact situation. And so, is the fact situation that you look dumb or you just didn't hear the question right?*
>
> **Irene:**   *I didn't hear the question right.*
>
> **Beck:**   *Or is it possible that I didn't say the question in such a way that it was clear?*
>
> **Irene:**   *Possible.*
>
> **Beck:**   *Very possible. I'm not perfect so it's very possible that I didn't express the question properly.*
>
> **Irene:**   *But instead of saying you made a mistake, I would still say I made a mistake.*
>
> **Beck:**   *We'll have to watch the video to see. Whichever. Does it mean if I didn't express the question, if I made the mistake, does it make me dumb?*

27.

How does Beck's treatment of a depressed woman illustrate his approach to identifying and correcting maladaptive, automatic patterns of thought?

Will McIntyre / Photo Researchers

A pioneer of cognitive therapy

Aaron Beck's approach to therapy is gentler than Ellis's, but not less teacher-like. Beck typically leads clients, through a Socratic style of questioning, to discover the irrationality of their thoughts.

Irene: *No.*

Beck: *And if you made the mistake, does it make you dumb?*

Irene: *No, not really.*

Beck: *But you felt dumb?*

Irene: *But I did, yeah.*

Beck: *Do you still feel dumb?*

Irene: *No. Right now I feel glad. I'm feeling a little better that at least somebody is pointing all these things out to me because I have never seen this before. I never knew that I thought that I was that dumb.*

As homework between the second and third sessions, Beck gave Irene the assignment of catching, writing down, and correcting her own dysfunctional thoughts, using the form shown in Figure 17.7. Subsequent sessions were aimed at eradicating each of her depressive thoughts, one by one, and reinforcing the steps she was taking to improve her life. Progress was rapid. Irene felt increasingly better about herself, as measured by the Beck Depression Inventory (illustrated in Table 17.1, page 660). During the next several months, she (a) joined a tennis league, (b) got a job as a waitress, (c) took a college course in sociology and did well in it, and (d) left her husband after trying and failing to get him to develop a better attitude toward her or to join her in couple therapy. By this time, according to Beck, she was cured of her depression, had created for herself a healthy environment, and no longer needed therapy.

FIGURE 17.7 *Homework sheet for cognitive therapy*
The purpose of this homework is to enable clients to become aware of and correct the automatic thoughts that contribute to their emotional difficulties. (Adapted from Beck & Young, 1985.)

	SITUATION	EMOTION(S)	AUTOMATIC THOUGHT(S)	RATIONAL RESPONSE	OUTCOME
DATE	Describe: 1. Actual event leading to unpleasant emotion, or 2. Stream of thoughts, daydream, or recollection, leading to unpleasant emotion.	1. Specify sad/ anxious/ angry, etc. 2. Rate degree of emotion, 1–100.	1. Write automatic thought(s) that preceded emotion(s). 2. Rate belief in automatic thought(s), 0–100%.	1. Write rational response to automatic thought(s). 2. Rate belief in rational response, 0–100%.	1. Rerate belief in automatic thought(s), 0–100%. 2. Specify and rate subsequent emotions, 0–100.
7/15	Store clerk didn't smile at me when I paid for purchase.	Sad – 60 Anxious – 40	Nobody likes me – 70% I look awful – 80%	Maybe the clerk was having a bad day or maybe she never smiles at customers – 70%	1. 20% 30% 2. Pleasure – 25

Explanation: When you experience an unpleasant emotion, note the situation that seemed to stimulate the emotion. (If the emotion occurred while you were thinking, daydreaming, etc., please note this.) Then note the automatic thought associated with the emotion. Record the degree to which you believe this thought: 0% = not at all, 100% = completely. In rating degree of emotion: 1 = a trace, 100 = the most intense possible.

Behavior Therapy

Behavior therapy is the psychotherapy approach rooted originally in the laboratory research of such pioneers as Ivan Pavlov, John B. Watson, and B. F. Skinner, who formulated principles of classical and operant conditioning in terms of relationships between stimuli and responses (see Chapter 4).

In principle, and in line with their philosophical forebears, behavior therapists might prefer to ignore mental phenomena such as thoughts and emotions and concentrate only on direct relationships between observable aspects of the environment (stimuli) and observable behaviors (responses); but in practice they cannot. After all, clients in behavior therapy, like those in any other form of psychotherapy, complain about such mental phenomena as fears, anxiety, obsessive thoughts, and depressed feelings. To deal with these problems, within the theoretical framework of behaviorism, behavior therapists have traditionally spoken of mental events as covert responses (hidden responses) that follow the same laws of conditioning as overt responses.

Contemporary behavior therapists, however, increasingly use language similar to that of cognitive therapists in describing mental events. In fact, behavior and cognitive therapies have to a considerable degree merged to form what is often called ***cognitive-behavior therapy***. This merging parallels a similar progression in academic research laboratories, where studies of learning have shifted from a stimulus–response emphasis to one that focuses on mental processes as mediators between stimuli and responses (see Chapters 4 and 9). Using the terminology of modern cognitive psychology, Chris Brewin (1996) has suggested that cognitive therapists are generally concerned with *explicit* cognitions, the memories and beliefs that people can state verbally and think about consciously, while behavior therapists are concerned with *implicit* cognitions, the mental associations and habit memories that govern behavior automatically but are not available for conscious inspection. In other respects, behavior and cognitive therapies have always shared certain characteristics. Both commonly claim to be problem-centered more than client-centered; their focus is on helping the person overcome specific problems, not on treating the "whole person." Both usually characterize these problems as learned ways of thinking or acting and take the approach that what has been learned can be unlearned. Both monitor the patient's behavior closely over time and advocate the changing of techniques if improvement does not occur rather quickly. In the following sections we will look at several of the most common behavior therapy techniques, beginning with those most closely related to principles of classical and operant conditioning.

Exposure Treatments to Eliminate Unwanted Fears

Behavior therapy has proved especially successful in treating specific phobias, in which the person fears something well defined, such as high places or a specific type of animal (Emmelkamp, 1994). From a behavioral perspective, fear is a reflexive response, which through classical conditioning can come to be triggered by various nondangerous as well as dangerous stimuli. An unconditioned stimulus for fear is one that elicits the response even if the individual has had no previous experience with the stimulus; a conditioned stimulus for fear is one that elicits the response only because the stimulus was previously paired with some fearful event in the person's experience (see Chapter 4). Opinions may differ as to whether a particular fear, such as a fear of snakes, is unconditioned or conditioned (unlearned or learned), but in practice this does not matter because the treatment is the same in either case.

A characteristic of the fear reflex, whether conditioned or unconditioned, is that it declines and gradually disappears if the eliciting stimulus is presented many times or over a prolonged period in a context where no harm comes to the person. In the case of an unconditioned fear reflex—such as the startle response to a sudden noise—the decline is called *habituation*. In the case of a conditioned fear reflex, the

28.

How and why has behavior therapy become increasingly similar to cognitive therapy, and in what respects have the two always been similar?

Spencer Grant / Stock, Boston

Hanging in the balance
By exposing their clients in safe ways to situations that frighten them, behavior therapists help clients overcome fears and phobias.

29.

What is the theoretical rationale for exposure treatments to eliminate fears?

decline that occurs when the conditioned stimulus is presented repeatedly without the unconditioned stimulus is called *extinction* (discussed in Chapter 4). For example, if a person fears all dogs because of once having been bitten, then prolonged exposure to various dogs (the conditioned stimuli) in the absence of being bitten (the unconditioned stimulus) will result in loss of the fear.

Any treatment for an unwanted fear or phobia that involves exposure to the feared stimulus to habituate or extinguish the fear response is referred to as an ***exposure treatment*** (Foa & Kozak, 1986). Varieties of exposure treatments can be ranked along a continuum in accordance with the gradualness versus suddenness of the exposure and the amount of fear the person is expected to experience during the exposure (Marks, 1972).

At the gradual end of the continuum is ***systematic desensitization***, originated by Joseph Wolpe (1958). In this technique, clients are first trained in muscle relaxation until they can relax easily. Then they are asked to employ the relaxation technique to remain relaxed while imagining a scene that would normally elicit a small degree of anxiety. When they can imagine that scene without becoming tense, they gradually move on through increasingly frightening scenes, again imagining each while relaxing. For example, a woman afraid of heights might be asked to relax while imagining first that she is looking out a second-floor window, then a third-floor window, and so on, until she can relax while imagining that she is looking down from the top of a skyscraper. An assumption here is that the ability to relax while imagining the previously feared situation will generalize, so that the person will be able to relax in the actual situation. Research involving long-term follow-up has shown that systematic desensitization and variations of it can be highly effective in treating simple phobias and can often be accomplished in a single session (Öst, 1989; Zinbarg & others, 1992).

At the other end of the continuum is ***flooding***, a procedure in which the person is "flooded" with the stimulus and the accompanying fear until it declines and disappears (Marks, 1972). For example, a person who is afraid of dogs might be induced to sit in the same room with several dogs until the fear is gone. In some cases, flooding is accomplished through imagination rather than actual exposure to the feared stimulus. The therapist teaches the client techniques for vivid imagining, and then the client imagines the feared object or event until it is no longer feared. Imaginal flooding has proved useful in treating posttraumatic stress disorder (Saigh

30.

How do the exposure treatments of systematic desensitization, flooding, and exposure homework differ from one another?

Fear of flying

Airline pilot Tom Bunn (left) and a friend encourage a man who has chosen flooding as a means of overcoming his fear of flying. Through an organization called SOAR, Bunn offers his services to individuals with airplane phobias.

Rick Friedman / Black Star

FIGURE **17.8**   *Comparison of three treatments for phobias*
Ninety-nine patients suffering from phobias were randomly assigned to one of three treatment groups. Those in the *relaxation* group (actually a pseudo-treatment group) were asked to practice relaxation exercises every day and to avoid exposing themselves to the situations that they feared. Those in the *self-exposure* group were given homework that involved exposing themselves to the feared situation every day for a specified period of time. Those in the *clinician + self-exposure* group were treated just like those in the self-exposure group but in addition had six 90-minute sessions of exposure to the feared situation with the clinician present. During the 8-week treatment period, all patients met six times with a therapist to learn the techniques and report on their use of the techniques. The measure of fear shown here was a rating—by another therapist, who was blind as to the patients' treatment condition—of the degree to which each patient continued to avoid the feared situations. Other measures, including the subjects' own measures of the fear they experienced when exposed to the initially feared situation, showed similar patterns of improvement. (Adapted from Al-Kubaisy & others, 1992.)

& others, 1996). In one clinical study, for example, Vietnam War veterans who suffered from memories of traumatic war experiences were asked to hold those memories vividly in mind, not shut them off, for 40-minute periods during 19 sessions (Keane & Kaloupek, 1982). With time, they became able to think and talk about the memories without experiencing the paralyzing anxiety they had experienced at the beginning.

In between systematic desensitization and flooding are exposure methods in which the client, either alone (as homework) or with a therapist present, exposes himself or herself to the feared situation for controlled amounts of time. For the methods and results of one clinical study involving exposure treatment for phobias, see Figure 17.8 (Al-Kubaisy & others, 1992). Exposure homework has also proved useful in treating obsessive-compulsive disorder (Foster & Eisler, 2001). In one case, for example, a woman whose fear of soil, dust, and grease led her to spend most of her day washing her hands and cleaning her house (dusting and polishing everything an average of seven times a day) was given systematic homework in which she was at first asked to leave just one item uncleaned for an hour and a half and then was asked to leave increasingly larger portions of the house uncleaned for increasingly longer periods of time (Marks & others, 1988). Gradually the anxiety and cleaning compulsion subsided.

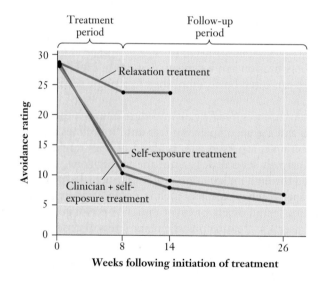

31.

How can maladaptive habits be interpreted in terms of operant conditioning and eliminated by use of aversive stimuli?

Aversion Treatment to Eliminate Bad Habits

From the behavioral perspective, much of what we do can be understood as *habit*. A habit is a learned action that has become so ingrained that the person performs it unconsciously and may even feel compelled to perform it. Most habits are good; they permit us to do automatically things that are beneficial. Stepping on the automobile brake in response to a red traffic light is a habit that saves many lives every day. But some habits—such as habitual drinking, overeating, gambling, or compulsive hand washing (in obsessive-compulsive disorder)—are harmful. No matter how such behaviors originated, they persist at least partly because they are followed immediately by pleasure or relief from discomfort. The person addicted to alcohol feels pleasure or relief from withdrawal symptoms after a drink, the compulsive gambler experiences a thrill when placing a bet, and the obsessive-compulsive hand washer experiences relief from the fear of germs after washing his or her hands. Thus, such behaviors can be understood at least partly in terms of operant conditioning, the process by which responses that are followed either by positive reinforcement (something pleasant) or by negative reinforcement (removal of something unpleasant) are likely to occur again in the future (see Chapter 4).

Aversion treatment

In an attempt to eliminate this man's tobacco addiction, the therapist is trying to make him sick. Do you think the client will learn that smoking a cigarette produces nausea, or only that smoking two cigarettes does?

A behavioral analysis suggests that the basic obstacle to getting rid of bad habits is that operant responses are controlled more by their immediate effects than by their long-term effects. A person might know that drinking alcohol in quantity eventually destroys the liver and brain, that gambling is in the end a losing proposition, and that repeated hand washing wastes time and may eat away the skin; yet such behaviors persist because knowledge of the long-term harm they bring is less effective in controlling them than is the short-term pleasure or relief they bring. To eliminate such harmful habits, the person must somehow change the reinforcement contingencies, and this is where aversion treatment comes in.

Put simply, *aversion treatment* is the application of an aversive (painful or unpleasant) stimulus immediately after the person has made the unwanted habitual response or immediately after the person has experienced cues that would normally elicit the response. Thus, a compulsive gambler might be given shocks to the fingers while reaching out onto a simulated gambling table to place a bet, or an alcohol addict might be given a drug that induces nausea after taking a drink (Clarke, 1988). Such treatment can be understood in terms of either operant or classical conditioning (see Chapter 5). In operant-conditioning terms, the aversive stimulus is punishment for behaving in the objectionable way or for initiating such behavior. In classical-conditioning terms, the aversive stimulus is an unconditioned stimulus for an avoidance reaction, which becomes conditioned to a cue, such as the sight of the gambling table or the smell of alcohol, that previously elicited attraction.

Aversion treatment has always been controversial, partly because of ethical questions associated with deliberately hurting a person (even when the person agrees to the procedure) and partly because of its mixed results. Learned aversions often do not generalize beyond the specific conditions in which the learning occurs. This limitation may stem from the fact that conditioning depends on cues indicating that the aversive stimulus will follow. Clients may experience the learned aversion only as long as they know that they are connected to the shock generator or that they have taken the illness-inducing drug.

A well-documented illustration of this point involves the use of the drug *Antabuse* to treat alcohol addiction. Antabuse reacts with alcohol in a person's body to induce severe flushing, dizziness, nausea, and headaches shortly after alcohol is consumed. In the early days of Antabuse treatment, behavior therapists believed that people who drank alcohol after taking the drug would develop a conditioned aversion to alcohol, which they would retain even without further Antabuse treatment. Unfortunately, however, experience has shown that most people suffering from long-term alcoholism avoid alcohol when on Antabuse but go back to it quickly after they stop taking the drug (Forrest, 1985). Today, Antabuse is recognized as an effective first-stage treatment for alcoholism, a means of helping the client keep sober while other treatments are begun. The drug is not recommended for long-term treatment because it induces some feelings of illness even when the person is sober (Littrell, 1991).

THE FAR SIDE By GARY LARSON

Professor Gallagher and his controversial technique of simultaneously confronting the fear of heights, snakes, and the dark.

32.

How does the treatment of alcohol addiction with Antabuse illustrate a general limitation of aversion treatment?

33.

What are the therapeutic uses of token economies, contingency contracts, assertiveness training, and modeling?

Some Other Behavioral Techniques

In addition to the exposure and aversion treatments described above, behavior therapists have developed an arsenal of other techniques to help people cultivate constructive behaviors and eradicate destructive ones. Among them are the following:

+ *Token economies* A token economy is essentially a monetary-exchange system adapted for use in a mental hospital or other institution where patients are confined. Its purpose is to provide a direct incentive for patients to do things that are deemed good for them or others. Thus, patients may receive tokens for such activities as making their beds, helping out in the kitchen, or helping other patients in specified ways, and they can cash in the tokens for desired privileges, such as movies or treats at the hospital commissary. This technique helps combat the lethargy, boredom, and dependence that are so common in mental hospitals (Ayllon & Azrin, 1968), and it was a component of the successful social-learning program for people with schizophrenia in the study by Paul and Lentz (1977), described on pages 655–656.

+ *Contingency contracts* A contingency contract is a formal, usually written agreement between two or more people in which certain specified services or rewards provided by one party are made contingent upon the actions of the other. For example, a contingency contract between a therapist and a client might specify that the therapist will meet with the client each week only if the client completes the agreed-upon homework. As another example, a family therapist might help an embattled husband and wife work out a contract in which one party agrees to behave in certain ways toward the other (say, continue to live in the same house) only if the other behaves in certain ways (say, takes specific steps toward getting a job or overcoming a drug addiction). To be effective, a contingency contract must clearly spell out the behaviors expected and the consequences for meeting or not meeting those expectations.

+ *Assertiveness and social skills training Assertiveness* can be defined as the ability to express one's own desires and feelings and to maintain one's rights in interactions with others, while at the same time respecting the others' rights. A high percentage of people in therapy are there partly because they lack the assertiveness or social skills necessary for effective and comfortable social interaction. Because of this lack, they may either avoid other people or, when with others, fail to assert their own feelings, wishes, and opinions. In either case, they feel lonely, because they have not made real emotional contact with others. Assertiveness and social skills training includes all direct methods by which a therapist attempts to teach a client to be more assertive, effective, and comfortable in social interactions. At first the therapist may demonstrate social skills or methods of assertion or may give the client phrases to memorize and practice—such as "Well, that's not a bad idea, but today I would really rather _____." Later, role-playing sessions might be introduced, in which the person plays out, with the therapist or with other clients in a group, various scenes requiring assertion (such as asking for a raise, refusing a sexual advance, or explaining to parents that one's mail is private) or social skills (such as asking for or accepting a date).

+ *Modeling* As a therapy technique, *modeling* is the process of teaching a person to do something by having that person watch someone else do it (discussed more generally in Chapter 4). As part of assertiveness training, a therapist might model (demonstrate) ways to be assertive. In the realm of fear reduction, Albert Bandura and his colleagues (1982) have shown in many experiments that people can overcome snake or spider phobias by watching others handle the feared creature during several sessions and then being asked to approach or handle it themselves.

Alvis Uptis / The Image Bank

Assertiveness training

In this technique, widely used in business organizations, individuals learn the skills necessary for effective social interaction.

Therapies Involving More Than One Client

Psychotherapy is not always a two-person interaction, involving a single client and a therapist. In group, couple, and family therapies the therapist works with more than one person at a time.

Group Therapies

In group therapy a therapist meets regularly with a number of clients, who usually don't know one another outside the therapy sessions. Group therapy is often preferred over individual therapy not only because it is less costly in therapists' time but also because of therapeutic benefits in the interactions among group members (Dies, 1992).

All the just-described varieties of individual therapy have been modified for use with groups. In *group psychodynamic therapy* the interactions among group members provide clues to each person's unconscious motives and defenses and provide opportunities for insight as to how those motives and defenses affect each person's ability to relate to others (Wolf & Kutash, 1990). *Humanistic client-centered groups* offer clients the opportunity to express themselves honestly to one another in a safe environment, where the therapist's reflections help clarify what each person is saying (Rogers, 1970). The assumption is that the group interaction can help clients identify and learn to express their own wishes and goals and thereby begin the process of self-actualization. *Group cognitive* and *behavioral therapies* offer opportunities for people to practice new ways of thinking and behaving with one another (Lazarus, 1968). The therapist can see firsthand how maladaptive thoughts and habits affect group members' interactions and can ask the members to try out new ways of thinking and behaving with one another. Group members might also be asked to role-play various parts with one another to practice social skills and assertiveness.

Regardless of theoretical orientation, group therapy also offers clients the opportunity to encourage, praise, and in other ways support one another's progress. Groups are often created for people who suffer from the same disorder or who have shared a similar traumatic experience (such as the death of a spouse or a child). In such groups people can learn immediately that their problem and their way of reacting to it are not entirely unique, a discovery that can itself be helpful by making each person feel less isolated. By sharing their successes as well as failures in coping with their disorder or loss, group members may provide one another with useful insights and ideas. This principle is most clearly manifested in *self-help support groups*—such as Alcoholics Anonymous, Gamblers Anonymous, Weight Watchers, and groups for people suffering from specific diseases, such as AIDS or breast cancer—which are often run not by professional therapists but by people who themselves have suffered from the same problem as the other group members. Recent surveys suggest that 3 to 4 percent of the adult population in North America takes part in some type of self-help support group in the course of a year, making this the most prevalent of all varieties of psychological treatment (Davison & others, 2000).

34.
How might the special value of the group be used in psychodynamic, humanistic, and cognitive-behavioral group therapies?

Couple and Family Therapies

The basic premise behind couple and family therapies is that the disorder or problem lies not in a single individual but in the interactions of two or more individuals whose lives are intertwined. In *couple therapy* a married or cohabiting couple see the therapist together, and in *family therapy* a whole family may be seen together. By observing the interactions of the couple or family members, the therapist can gain insights about their habitual ways of relating to one another. The couple or family might also be videotaped while engaged in some interaction, such as planning a vacation together, so that the participants can then observe themselves from one another's perspectives. One family member might be domineering, another might be submissive but resentful, and still another might be a useful scapegoat for others'

35.
What are some assumptions and practices of couple and family therapies?

Couple therapy

A basic premise of marriage or couple therapy is that disorder lies in the interaction between the two partners. A common difficulty in such therapy, possibly represented here, is that of maintaining the equal engagement of both partners and avoiding a situation in which one partner feels excluded and picked on by an alliance between the other partner and the therapist.

problems. For example, parents who are socially anxious might cite the fears of one of their children as a reason for not inviting visitors to the house. To calm their own anxiety, the parents might reinforce their child's fears.

Most family therapies are based on a *family systems perspective*, which views each person's behavioral style and problems as in part an accommodation to the needs of the family as a whole (Glick & others, 2000). Through offering insights concerning how each family member is affecting the others, and through practice in changing their ways of relating to one another, the therapy aims to alter the family system in directions that are beneficial to each of its members. In addition, some family therapists take an *intergenerational approach*, which focuses on ways by which family members' behaviors may be affected by events in previous generations. For example, a domineering father might be attempting to mimic the behavior of his own much-admired and feared father or grandfather. As an aid in identifying such effects, family members working with the therapist might construct a chart, called a *genogram*, which depicts the family members' relatives for a generation or more back and something about the current family members' perceptions or beliefs about each of them (McGoldrick & Gerson, 1985).

SECTION SUMMARY

The major classic varieties of psychotherapy are psychodynamic, humanistic, cognitive, and behavior therapies.

Psychodynamic therapies, including Freudian psychoanalysis, typically use the techniques of free association, dream analysis, analysis of the client's slips of the tongue and other mistakes, and analysis of the client's resistance and transference of feelings to gain insight into the client's unconscious mental conflicts. An assumption of psychoanalysis is that such conflicts arise from childhood experiences pertaining to sex and aggression. Insight concerning the nature and origins of such conflicts allows the client to resolve them and to abandon irrational, maladaptive ways of thinking and acting. Post-Freudian psychodynamic therapies share many of the premises of psychoanalysis but usually place less emphasis on childhood sexuality and use methods designed to reduce the number of sessions required to achieve insight.

The most common form of humanistic therapy is client-centered therapy, developed by Carl Rogers. The main goal of this approach is to help clients learn to value themselves and to trust their own decision-making abilities. The therapist's task is not to provide insights and advice but to help clients arrive at their own insights and discover their own feelings, desires, and strengths. This is done by listening compassionately and trying to understand the clients as they talk about themselves and their experiences.

The primary assumption of cognitive therapy is that people disturb themselves though their beliefs and habitual ways of thinking. The goal of cognitive therapy is to replace maladaptive beliefs and thoughts with adaptive ones, which lead to more effective actions and reduce anxiety and depression. Cognitive therapists typically give their clients homework aimed at changing their ways of thinking. Some cognitive therapists, such as Albert Ellis, are quick to point out to clients their irrational beliefs and thoughts; others, such as Aaron Beck, lead their clients through Socratic questioning to discover these for themselves.

Behavior therapy uses basic principles of learning—particularly principles of classical conditioning, operant conditioning, and modeling—to help people change their habitual, maladaptive ways of responding to aspects of their environment. Among the most successful behavior therapy techniques are exposure treatments, in which irrational fears are eliminated (habituated or extinguished) by exposing the client to the feared object or situation under safe conditions. Other behavioral techniques include aversion treatments to eliminate bad habits and token economies, contingency contracts, and assertiveness and social skills training aimed at reinforcing and teaching adaptive ways of behaving.

*In group therapies a therapist meets with a number of clients at once, who inter-
act with one another as well as with the therapist. Each of the major classic varieties
of psychotherapy can be conducted with groups as well as individually. The most prevalent therapy groups, however, are self-help support groups, in which people who share
some disorder, disease, problem, or similar traumatic experience meet regularly to discuss their experiences and to offer one another advice and emotional support. Couple
and family therapies treat the couple or family as a unit and attempt to understand the
roles that each person's feelings and actions play within that unit.*

EVALUATING PSYCHOTHERAPIES

You have just read about several major varieties of psychotherapy. Do they work?
That might seem like a strange question at this point. After all, didn't Freud cure
the Rat Man, didn't Rogers help the silent young man, didn't Beck and his associates cure the depressed young woman, and haven't behavior therapists cured many
people of their fears and bad habits? But case studies—even thousands of them—
showing that people are better off at the end of therapy than at the beginning cannot tell us for sure that therapy works. Maybe those people would have improved
anyway, without therapy. An adage about the common cold goes like this: "Treat a
cold with the latest remedy and you'll get rid of it in 7 days; leave it untreated and
it'll hang on for a week." Maybe psychological problems or disorders are often like
colds in this respect. Everyone has peaks and valleys in life, and people are most
likely to start therapy while in one of
the valleys (see Figure 17.9). Thus, even
if therapy has no effect, most people
will feel better at some point after entering it than they did when they began
(a point that was made earlier in this
chapter in the discussion of drug treatments). The natural tendency for both
therapist and client is to attribute the
improvement to the therapy.

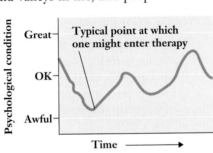

    The only way to know if psychotherapy really works is to perform controlled
experiments, in which groups of people undergoing therapy are compared with
otherwise-similar control groups who are not undergoing therapy.

A Classic Example of a Therapy Outcome Experiment

One of the earliest well-controlled experiments on therapy outcome was conducted
at a psychiatric outpatient clinic in Philadelphia (Sloane & others, 1975). The subjects were 94 men and women, ages 18 to 45, who sought psychotherapy at the
clinic. Most of these individuals suffered from anxiety disorders. Each was assigned
by a random procedure to one of three groups. One group received once-a-week
sessions of *behavior therapy* for 4 months (including such procedures as systematic
desensitization and assertiveness training) from one of three highly experienced behavior therapists. The second group received the same amount of *psychoanalytical
psychotherapy* (including such procedures as probing into childhood memories,
dream analysis, and interpretation of resistance) from one of three highly experienced psychoanalytically oriented therapists. The members of the third group, the
no-therapy group, were placed on a waiting list and given no treatment during the
4-month period but were called periodically to let them know that they would
eventually be accepted for therapy.

    To measure treatment effectiveness, all subjects, including those in the no-
therapy group, were assessed both before and after the 4-month period by psychiatrists who were uninformed of the groups to which the subjects had been assigned.

36.

*Why must we rely on experiments
rather than case studies to assess the
effectiveness of psychotherapy?*

FIGURE 17.9
The peaks and valleys of life
If a person enters psychotherapy while in a
valley, he or she is likely to feel better after
a time even if the therapy is ineffective.

37.

*How did an experiment in Philadelphia
demonstrate the effectiveness of
behavior therapy and psychoanalytic
psychotherapy?*

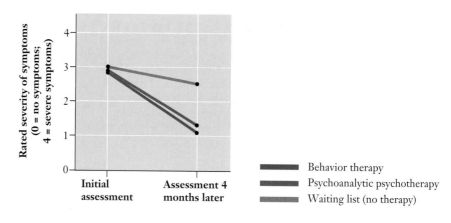

FIGURE **17.10**   *Results of the Philadelphia experiment*
Psychiatrists rated the severity of each subject's symptoms before and after a 4-month treatment period. As shown here, those in the two therapy groups improved more than did those who were placed on the waiting list. (Adapted from Sloane & others, 1975.)

As illustrated in Figure 17.10, all three groups improved during the 4-month period, but the treatment groups improved significantly more than did the control group. Moreover, the two treatment groups did not differ significantly from each other in degree of improvement.

General Conclusions from Many Therapy Outcome Experiments

Over the past three decades or so, hundreds of therapy outcome experiments have been conducted, each of which compared one or more groups of people receiving psychotherapy with a control group that did not receive therapy. Large collections of such studies have been analyzed by statistical means, and the analyses have supported the following conclusions:

38.

What are four general conclusions from therapy outcome experiments?

1. *Psychotherapy helps.* On average, people in treatment improve more than do those not in treatment. When hundreds of separate experiments are combined, the results indicate that about 75 to 80 percent of people in psychotherapy showed greater improvement than did the average person in a nontherapy control group (Lipsey & Wilson, 1993; Shadish & others, 2000; Smith & others, 1980).

2. *No single type of therapy stands out as clearly better overall than any other type.* When all studies are combined, each of the varieties of psychotherapy discussed in the previous section—psychodynamic, humanistic, cognitive, behavior, group, and family—appears to be about as effective as each of the other varieties (Lipsey & Wilson, 1993; Wampold & others, 1997).

3. *Some types of therapy appear to work better than other types for specific kinds of disorders or problems.* The results of one early analysis supporting this conclusion are illustrated in Table 17.2. As you can see in the table, fear and anxiety seem to be treated more effectively by behavior therapy and cognitive therapy than by psychodynamic therapies, whereas the reverse seems true for achievement problems and addictions; and humanistic therapy seems best for raising self-esteem. Other analyses of multiple experiments suggest that cognitive therapies are more effective than psychodynamic psychotherapies in treating depression (Dobson, 1989; Svartberg & Stiles, 1991). The results of such comparisons must be interpreted cautiously, because the experiments that are combined differ in many more ways than just the type of therapy employed. Nevertheless, such analyses do offer interesting hypotheses to test in future large-scale single experiments.

4. *The therapist matters.* Experiments in which different psychotherapists treat different groups of patients indicate that some therapists produce consistently better results than do others, even when they are ostensibly using the same therapy procedures. This difference among therapists apparently does not lie so much in their degrees of training and experience as in their personalities

TABLE **17.2** *Average effectiveness of various therapy types in treating various problems*

Type of therapy	Type of Problem				
	Fear or anxiety	Self-esteem	Addiction	Social behavior	Work or school achievement
Psychodynamic	0.78	0.66	1.05	0.94	1.24
Humanistic	0.61	0.99	*	0.45	0.54
Cognitive	1.67	0.65	0.53	*	0.28
Cognitive-behavioral	1.78	0.73	*	1.23	0.60
Behavioral	1.12	0.23	0.75	0.42	0.45

Note: This table is based on an analysis that combined the results of several hundred therapy outcome experiments. The measure of effectiveness, the *standard effect size*, was calculated for each experiment by subtracting the outcome measure for the control group from that for the therapy group and dividing the difference by the standard deviation of the scores. Shown here are the average standard effect sizes for various types of therapy for various types of problems. Any score above zero indicates that the average person in the treatment groups improved more than did the average person in the control groups, and a score of 1.0 indicates that 84.13 percent of the people in the treatment groups improved more than did the average person in the control groups. (For further explanation of standardized scores, see the Statistical Appendix at the back of the book.)

Note: Asterisks indicate too few studies to warrant inclusion.

Source: Adapted from *The benefits of psychotherapy* (p. 97) by M. L. Smith, G. V. Glass, & T. I. Miller, 1980, Baltimore, MD: John Hopkins University Press.

and motivation to help. Therapists who are warm, understanding, and strongly motivated to help consistently produce more improvement in their clients than do those who are not (Lambert & Okiishi, 1997; Luborsky & others, 1997; Mohr, 1995; Najavits & Strupp, 1994).

The Role of Nonspecific Factors in Therapy Outcome

The observation that the effectiveness of therapy may depend on the personal qualities of the therapist suggests that certain *nonspecific factors*, which are unrelated to the specific principles on which the therapy is based, may be critical to therapy outcome. Many such factors have been proposed (Ford & Urban, 1998), but they fall into two general categories: support and hope.

Support includes acceptance, empathy, encouragement, and guidance. By devoting time to the client, listening warmly and respectfully, and not being shocked at the client's statements or actions, any good psychotherapist communicates the attitude that the client is a worthwhile human being, and this support may directly enhance the client's self-esteem and indirectly lead to other improvements as well. Moreover, almost any caring therapist, regardless of theoretical orientation, will start sessions by asking the client how things have gone since the last meeting; the anticipation of such reporting may encourage clients to work on self-improvement so that they can give a better report. In addition, most therapists make at least some commonsense suggestions that have little to do with their theories, of the sort that anyone's wise friend or relative might make, but carrying more weight because they come from a recognized authority.

Many studies have demonstrated the value of such support. In a long-term study at the Menninger Clinic, Robert Wallerstein (1989) found that contemporary psychoanalysts, in fact, provided more support and less insight to their clients than would be expected from psychoanalytic theory, and that support even without insight seemed to produce stable therapeutic gains. In another study, college professors with no training in psychology or methods of therapy, but with reputations for good rapport with students, proved able to help depressed college students in twice-a-week therapy sessions as effectively as highly trained and experienced clinical psychologists (Strupp & Hadley, 1979). Such results have led one well-known psychodynamic therapist, Hans Strupp (1989), to conclude that "the first and foremost task for the therapist is to create an accepting and empathic context, which in itself has great therapeutic value because for many people it is a novel and deeply gratifying experience to be accepted and listened to respectfully."

39.

What is some evidence that the most important ingredients of psychotherapy may be the offering of support and hope?

Hope, the second category of nonspecific factors, may come partly from the sense of support but may also come from faith in the therapy process. Most psychotherapists believe in what they do. They speak with authority and confidence about their methods, and they offer scientific-sounding theories or even data to back up their confidence. Thus, clients also come to believe that the therapy will work. Many studies have shown that people who believe they will get better have an improved chance of getting better, even if the specific reason for the belief is false. As discussed earlier, this is the basis for the placebo effect in studies of drugs. The term *placebo effect* is now often used to refer to any improvement that comes from a person's belief in the treatment rather than from other therapeutic factors. The placebo effect is an element that all sought-after healing procedures have in common, whether provided by psychotherapists, medical doctors, faith healers, or folk healers.

How much of the improvement observed in psychotherapy is due to the client's belief in the process (hope)? That is hard to answer. In tests of drug treatments, the psychological effects of hope and the direct chemical effects of the drug can, at least in theory, be separated by using a placebo pill, but in psychotherapy—where the whole treatment is psychological—no clear distinction can be made between hope as a nonspecific side effect of psychotherapy and hope as a specific goal of psychotherapy (Kirsch & Lynn, 1999). Some experiments on therapy outcome include a *placebo group* who receive pseudopsychotherapy that is designed to provide the element of hope without providing the specific elements deemed important to the therapy being tested. For example, in one study systematic desensitization was compared with a made-up placebo treatment called *systematic ventilation*, in which people talked about their fears in systematic ways (Kirsch & others, 1983). In general, in such experiments the placebo group does better than nontreated controls but not as well as those receiving the more standard form of psychotherapy being tested (Barker & others, 1988; Lipsey & Wilson, 1993). But it is hard to interpret such results (Nathan & others, 2000). On the one hand, hope may not be raised as fully in placebo groups as in therapy groups; on the other, placebo treatments may include elements that could produce therapeutic effects through means other than hope. For example, talking about fears in systematic ventilation could have therapeutic value.

My own most general conclusion from the psychotherapy studies is reminiscent of ideas about human nature that you have encountered elsewhere in this book: We are social animals who need positive regard and encouragement from other people in order to function well. When these are insufficient in our everyday interactions with others, a supportive and hope-inspiring psychotherapist can help.

SECTION SUMMARY

Many experiments have shown that people undergoing psychotherapy improve more than do those assigned to a nontherapy control group. Taken as a whole, such studies reveal that the standard varieties of psychotherapy are all about equally effective, though some may be more effective than others for particular disorders. Certain nonspecific factors, which fall into the categories of support and hope and which cut across all the varieties of psychotherapy, may be at least as influential in promoting improvement as are the specific practices that vary from one type of therapy to another.

CONCLUDING THOUGHTS

The best way to review this chapter is to think about the principles underlying each approach to treatment, about the potential problems of each, and about the evidence concerning the effectiveness of each. As a start in that review, the following ideas may be useful:

1. Self-knowledge and self-acceptance as goals of psychodynamic and humanistic therapies   The psychodynamic and humanistic approaches to treatment focus less on the person's specific symptoms or problems and more on the person as a whole than do the other approaches. A psychoanalyst or other psychodynamic therapist who is asked to describe the purpose of therapy might well respond with the Socratic dictum: Know thyself. The goal of such therapies is to enable clients to learn about aspects of themselves that were previously unconscious, so that they can think and behave in ways that are more rational and integrated than they did before.

Most humanistic therapists would agree with the Socratic dictum, but they would add, and place greater emphasis on, a second dictum: Accept thyself. Humanistic therapists argue that people often learn to dislike or deny important aspects of themselves, because of real or imagined criticism from other people. The task for the humanistic therapist is to help clients regain their self-esteem, so that they can regain control of their lives.

2. Biological, behavior, and cognitive therapies as derivatives of basic approaches to psychological research   Biological, behavior, and cognitive therapies focus more closely on clients' specific symptoms than do psychodynamic and humanistic therapies. These three approaches differ from one another, however, in that they emphasize different levels of causation of behavior. In that respect, they mirror the approaches taken by research psychologists who focus on (a) physiological mechanisms, (b) the role of environmental stimuli and learned habits, and (c) the role of cognitive mediators of behavior.

Biological treatments are founded on the knowledge that everything psychological is a product of the nervous system. Drugs, electroconvulsive therapy, and psychosurgery all involve attempts to help a person overcome psychological problems or disorders by altering the nervous system in some way. Behavioral treatments are founded on the knowledge that people acquire, through conditioning, habitual and sometimes maladaptive ways of responding to stimuli in the world around them. The goal of behavior therapy is to eliminate the maladaptive responses and replace them with useful responses. Cognitive treatments are founded on the knowledge that people interpret and think about stimuli in their environment and that those interpretations and thoughts affect the way they feel and behave. The goal of cognitive therapy is to replace maladaptive ways of thinking with useful ways of thinking.

3. Psychotherapy and science   Two questions can be asked about the relationship between psychotherapy and science: (a) Is psychotherapy a science? (b) Has science shown that psychotherapy works? These are fundamentally different questions.

The first question concerns the degree to which the techniques used in psychotherapy are based on scientific principles and can be described objectively. Most psychotherapists would respond that their practice is a blend of science and art—that it is based on theories that stem from scientific research but that it also involves a great deal of intuition, not unlike the sort of intuition that is critical to any prolonged interaction between two human beings. Each client is a distinct individual with distinct problems and needs, who does not necessarily fit snugly with the statistically derived principles that have emerged from scientific research. One way to compare the various psychotherapy approaches is on the degree to which they emphasize empathy and intuition compared with the rigorous application of laboratory-derived principles. Rogers's humanistic therapy lies at one end of this spectrum and behavior therapy lies at the other.

The second question concerns the use of scientific methods to evaluate psychotherapy. The history of psychotherapy has often been marked by feuds among advocates of one approach or another, each arguing that theirs is the only valid way. As increasingly well-controlled outcome studies have been conducted, the feuds have died down considerably. Evidence has mounted that all the well-established psychotherapies work about equally well, on a statistical basis, though some may be more effective than others in treating certain kinds of problems. Such findings have led to increased recognition of the nonspecific therapeutic factors shared by the various approaches and have also inspired a movement toward eclecticism, in which therapists draw from each tradition those methods that seem most appropriate to the client's specific needs.

Further Reading

Michael H. Stone (1997). *Healing the mind: A history of psychiatry from antiquity to the present.* New York: Norton.

This is a clear, chronological account of ideas and discoveries relevant to treatments for mental disorders from ancient times up to 1996. These developments are described in the context of larger intellectual trends or schools of thought, both within and outside mainstream psychology.

Stephen A. Mitchell & Margaret J. Black (1995). *Freud and beyond: A history of modern psychoanalytic thought.* New York: Basic Books.

This is a lucid account of psychoanalytic theories of the person and techniques for psychotherapy from Freud on. The authors dispel the myth that psychoanalytic thought has been static since Freud.

Frank Dumont & Raymond J. Corsine (Eds.) (2000). *Six therapists and one client* (2nd ed.). New York: Springer.

In this book six different well-known therapists—one of whom is Albert Ellis—describe how they would treat the same client, a socially withdrawn man who suffers from a variety of fears and other psychological problems.

Each account of treatment is followed by a critique by another expert therapist. Reading this book will give you a good idea of the various ways that psychotherapists think about their work.

Robyn M. Dawes (1994). *House of cards: Psychology and psychotherapy built on myth.* New York: Free Press.

Contrary to what you might infer from the title, this is not a general case against clinical psychology, but it is a case against those aspects of it that are built on intuition and fad rather than evidence. If you wish to think about clinical psychology from a scientific perspective, this is a good place to begin.

Stephen M. Stahl (2000). *Essential psychopharmacology* (2nd ed.). Cambridge, England: Cambridge University Press.

This is a straightforward, up-to-date introduction to the neurochemistry and drug treatment of mental disorders. It begins with basic neurotransmitter mechanisms and continues through chapters on mood disorders, anxiety disorders, and psychotic disorders. It is chock full of colorful drawings that illustrate basic principles and that in themselves can provide a quick understanding.

Looking Ahead

I hope you have enjoyed this book and found it to be a useful survey of the vast field of psychology. Perhaps the book has helped you decide on areas of psychology that you would like to study further, through either additional courses or your own reading. If you look over the offerings of the psychology department at your college or university, you will probably find that the courses map quite readily onto the various parts of this book. I hope you do pursue the areas that interest you most.

Statistical Appendix

Statistical procedures are tools for dealing with data. Some people find them fascinating for their own sake, just as some become intrigued by the beauty of a saw or a hammer. But most of us, most of the time, care about statistics only to the extent that they help us answer questions. Statistics become interesting when we want to know our batting average, or the chance that our favorite candidate will be elected, or how much money we'll have left after taxes. In psychology, statistics are interesting when they are used to analyze data in ways that help answer important psychological questions.

Some of the basics of statistics are described in Chapter 2. The main purpose of the first three sections of this appendix is to supplement that discussion and make it more concrete by providing some examples of statistical calculations. The fourth section (Supplement on Psychophysical Scaling) supplements the discussion of Fechner's and Stevens's work in the section on psychophysics in Chapter 7.

ORGANIZING AND SUMMARIZING A SET OF SCORES

This section describes some basic elements of descriptive statistics: the construction of frequency distributions, the measurement of central tendency, and the measurement of variability.

Ranking the Scores and Depicting a Frequency Distribution

Suppose you gave a group of people a psychological test of introversion-extroversion, structured such that a low score indicates introversion (a tendency to withdraw from the social environment) and a high score indicates extroversion (a tendency to be socially outgoing). Suppose further that the possible range of scores is from 0 to 99, that you gave the test to 20 people, and that you obtained the scores shown in the left-hand column of Table A.1. As presented in that column, the scores are hard to describe in a meaningful way; they are just a list of numbers. As a first step toward making some sense of them, you might rearrange the scores in *rank order*, from lowest to highest, as shown in the right-hand column of the table. Notice how the ranking facilitates your ability to describe the set of numbers. You can now see that the scores range from a low of 17 to a high of 91 and that the two middle scores are 49 and 50.

A second useful step in summarizing the data is to divide the entire range of possible scores into equal intervals and determine how many scores fall in each interval.

TABLE A.1 *Twenty scores unranked and ranked*

Scores in the order they were collected	The same scores ranked
58	17
45	23
23	31
71	36
49	37
36	41
61	43
41	45
37	45
75	49
91	50
54	54
43	57
17	58
63	61
73	63
31	71
50	73
45	75
57	91

TABLE **A.2** *Frequency distribution formed from scores in Table A.1*

Interval	Frequency
0– 9	0
10–19	1
20–29	1
30–39	3
40–49	5
50–59	4
60–69	2
70–79	3
80–89	0
90–99	1

FIGURE **A.1** *A frequency distribution depicted by a bar graph*

This graph depicts the frequency distribution shown in Table A.2. Each bar represents a different interval of possible scores, and the height of each bar represents the number of scores that occurred in that interval.

Table A.2 presents the results of this process, using intervals of 10. A table of this sort, showing the number of scores that occurred in each interval of possible scores, is called a ***frequency distribution***. Frequency distributions can also be represented graphically, as shown in Figure A.1. Here, each bar along the horizontal axis represents a different interval, and the height of the bar represents the frequency (number of scores) that occurred in that interval.

As you examine Figure A.1, notice that the scores are not evenly distributed across the various intervals. Rather, most of them fall in the middle intervals (centering around 50), and they taper off toward the extremes. This pattern would have been hard to see in the original, unorganized set of numbers.

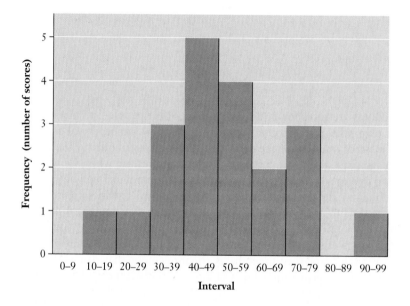

Shapes of Frequency Distributions

The frequency distribution in Figure A.1 roughly approximates a shape that is referred to as a ***normal distribution*** or *normal curve*. A perfect normal distribution (which can be expressed by a mathematical equation) is illustrated in Figure A.2a. Notice that the maximum frequency lies in the center of the range of scores and that the frequency tapers off—first gradually, then more rapidly, and then gradually again—symmetrically on the two sides, forming a bell-shaped curve. Many measures in nature are distributed in accordance with a normal distribution. Height (for people of a given age and sex) is one example. A variety of different factors (different genes and nutritional factors) go into determining a person's height. In most cases, these different factors—some promoting tallness and some shortness—average themselves out, so that most people are roughly average in height (accounting for the peak frequency in the middle of the distribution). A small proportion of people, however, will have just the right combination of factors to be much taller or much shorter than average (accounting for the tails at the high and low ends of the distribution). In general, when a measure is determined by several independent factors, the frequency distribution for that measure at least approximates the normal curve. The results of most psychological tests also form a normal distribution if the test is given to a sufficiently large group of people.

But not all measures are distributed in accordance with the normal curve. Consider, for example, the set of scores that would be obtained on a test of English vocabulary if some of the people tested were native speakers of English and others were not. You would expect in this case to find two separate groupings of scores.

The native speakers would score high and the others would score low, with relatively few scores in between. A distribution of this sort, illustrated in Figure A.2b, is referred to as a *bimodal distribution*. The **mode** is the most frequently occurring score or range of scores in a frequency distribution; thus, a bimodal distribution is one that has two separate areas of peak frequencies. The normal curve is a *unimodal distribution*, because it has only one peak in frequency.

Some distributions are unimodal, like the normal distribution, but are not symmetrical. Consider, for example, the shape of a frequency distribution of annual incomes for any randomly selected group of people. Most of the incomes might center around, let's say, $20,000. Some would be higher and some lower, but the spread of higher incomes would be much greater than that of lower incomes. No income can be less than $0, but no limit exists to the high ones. Thus, the frequency distribution might look like that shown in Figure A.2c. A distribution of this sort, in which the spread of scores above the mode is greater than that below, is referred to as a *positively skewed distribution*. The long tail of the distribution extends in the direction of high scores.

As an opposite example, consider the distribution of scores on a relatively easy examination. If the highest possible score is 100 points and most people score around 85, the highest score can only be 15 points above the mode, but the lowest score can be as much as 85 points below it. A typical distribution obtained from such a test is shown in Figure A.2d. A distribution of this sort, in which the long tail extends toward low scores, is called a *negatively skewed distribution*.

Measures of Central Tendency

Perhaps the most useful way to summarize a set of scores is to identify a number that represents the center of the distribution. Two different centers can be determined—the median and the mean (both described in Chapter 2). The **median** is the middle score in a set of ranked scores. Thus, in a ranked set of nine scores, the fifth score in the ranking (counting in either direction) is the median. If the data set consists of an even number of scores, determining the median is slightly more complicated because two middle scores exist rather than one. In this case, the median is simply the midpoint between the two middle scores. If you look back at the list of twenty ranked scores in Table A.1, you will see that the two middle scores are 49 and 50; the median in this case is 49.5. The **mean** (also called the *arithmetic average*) is found simply by adding up all of the scores and dividing by the total number of scores. Thus, to calculate the mean of the twenty introversion-extroversion scores in Table A.1, simply add them (the sum is 1020) and divide by 20, obtaining 51.0 as the mean.

Notice that the mean and median of the set of introversion-extroversion scores are quite close to one another. In a perfect normal distribution, these two measures of central tendency are identical. For a skewed distribution, on the other hand, they can be quite different. Consider, for example, the set of incomes shown in Table A.3 on page A-4. The median is $19,500, and all but one of the other incomes are rather close to the median. But the set contains one income of $900,000, which is wildly different from the others. The size of this income does not affect the median. Whether the highest income were $19,501 (just above the median) or a trillion dollars, it still counts as just one income in the ranking that determines the median. But this income has a dramatic effect on the mean. As shown in the table, the mean of these incomes is $116,911. Because the mean is most affected by extreme scores, it will always be higher than the median in a positively skewed distribution and lower than the median in a negatively skewed distribution. In a positively skewed distribution the most extreme scores are high scores (which raise the mean above the median), and in a negatively skewed distribution they are low scores (which lower the mean below the median).

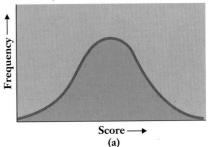

Normal, unimodal distribution

(a)

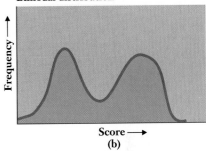

Bimodal distribution

(b)

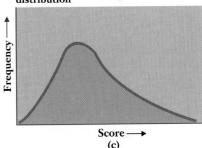

Positively skewed, unimodal distribution

(c)

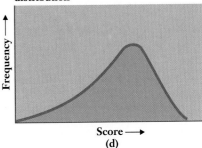

Negatively skewed, unimodal distribution

(d)

FIGURE **A.2** *Four differently shaped frequency distributions*
You can imagine that each of these curves was formed from a set of bars similar to those in Figure A.1, but the bars would be narrower and more numerous (the intervals would be smaller) and the data sets would be much larger.

TABLE A.3 *Sample incomes, illustrating how the mean can differ greatly from the median*

Rank	Income
1	$15,000
2	16,400
3	16,500
4	17,700
5	(19,500)
6	21,200
7	22,300
8	23,600
9	900,000
	Total: $1,052,200

Mean = $1,052,200 ÷ 9 = $116,911

Median = $19,500

Which is more useful, the mean or the median? The answer depends on one's purpose, but in general the mean is preferred when scores are at least roughly normally distributed, and the median is preferred when scores are highly skewed. In Table A.3 the median is certainly a better representation of the set of incomes than is the mean, because it is typical of almost all of the incomes listed. In contrast, the mean is typical of none of the incomes; it is much lower than the highest income and much higher than all the rest. This, of course, is an extreme example, but it illustrates the sort of biasing effect that skewed data can have on a mean. Still, for certain purposes, the mean might be the preferred measure even if the data are highly skewed. For example, if you wanted to determine the revenue that could be gained by a 5 percent local income tax, the mean income (or the total income) would be more useful than the median.

Measures of Variability

The mean or median tells us about the central value of a set of numbers, but not about how widely they are spread out around the center. Look at the two frequency distributions depicted in Figure A.3. They are both normal and have the same mean, but they differ greatly in their degree of spread or variability. In one case the scores are clustered near the mean (low variability), and in the other they are spread farther apart (high variability). How might we measure the variability of scores in a distribution?

One possibility would be to use the *range*—that is, simply the difference between the highest and lowest scores in the distribution—as a measure of variability. For the scores listed in Table A.1, the range is 91 − 17 = 74 points. A problem with the range, however, is that it depends on just two scores, the highest and lowest. A better measure of variability would take into account the extent to which all of the scores in the distribution differ from each other.

One measure of variability that takes all of the scores into account is the **variance**. The variance is calculated by the following four steps: (1) Determine the mean of the set of scores. (2) Determine the difference between each score and the mean; this difference is called the *deviation*. (3) Square each deviation (multiply it by itself). (4) Calculate the mean of the squared deviations (by adding them up and dividing by the total number of scores). The result—the mean of the squared deviations—is the variance. This method is illustrated for two different sets of scores in Table A.4. Notice that the two sets each have the same mean (50), but most of the scores in the first set are much closer to the mean than are those in the second set. The result is that the variance of the first set (25.5) is much smaller than that of the second set (729).

FIGURE A.3 *Two normal distributions*

These normal distributions, superimposed on one another, have identical means but different degrees of variability.

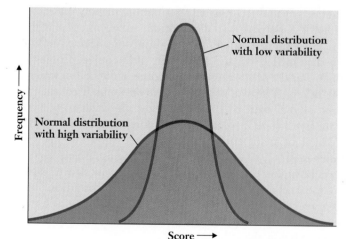

TABLE A.4 *Calculation of the variance and standard deviation for two sets of scores that have identical means*

First set of scores			*Second set of scores*		
Score	Deviation (Score – 50)	Squared deviation	Score	Deviation (Score – 50)	Squared deviation
42	–8	64	9	–41	1681
44	–6	36	19	–31	961
47	–3	9	31	–19	361
49	–1	1	47	–3	9
52	+2	4	56	+6	36
54	+4	16	70	+20	400
55	+5	25	78	+28	784
57	+7	49	90	+40	1600
Total = 400		Total = 204	Total = 400		Total = 5832
Mean = 400/8 = 50		Mean = 204/8 = 25.5	Mean = 400/8 = 50		Mean = 5832/8 = 729

Variance = Mean squared deviation = 25.5   Variance = Mean squared deviation = 729

Standard deviation = $\sqrt{\text{Variance}} = \sqrt{25.5} = 5.0$ Standard deviation = $\sqrt{\text{Variance}} = \sqrt{729} = 27.0$

Because the variance is based on the squares of the deviations, the units of variance are not the same as those of the original measure. If the original measure is points on a test, then the variance is in units of squared points on the test (whatever on earth that might mean). To bring the units to their original form, all we need to do is take the square root of the variance. The square root of the variance is the **standard deviation**, which is the measure of variability that is most commonly used. Thus, for the first set of scores in Table A.4, the standard deviation = $\sqrt{25.5}$ = 5.0; for the second set, the standard deviation = $\sqrt{729}$ = 27.0.

CONVERTING SCORES FOR PURPOSES OF COMPARISON

Are you taller than you are heavy? That sounds like a silly question, and it is. Height and weight are two entirely different measures, and comparing them is like the proverbial comparison of apples and oranges. But suppose I worded the question this way: Relative to other people of your gender and age group, do you rank higher in height or in weight? Now that is an answerable question. Similarly, consider this question: Are you better at mathematical or at verbal tasks? This, too, is meaningful only if your mathematical and verbal skills are judged relative to those of other people. Compared to other people, do you rank higher in mathematical or in verbal skills? To compare different kinds of scores with each other, we must convert each score into a form that directly expresses its relationship to the whole distribution of scores from which it came.

Percentile Rank

The most straightforward way to see how one person compares to others on a given measure is to determine the person's **percentile rank** for that measure. The percentile rank of a given score is simply the percentage of scores that are equal to that score or lower, out of the whole set of scores obtained on a given measure. For example, in the distribution of scores in Table A.1, the score of 37 is at the 25th percentile, because five of the twenty scores are at 37 or lower (⁵⁄₂₀ = ¼ = 25%). As another example in the same distribution, the score of 73 is at the 90th percentile because eighteen of the twenty scores are lower ($^{18}/_{20} = ^9/_{10} = 90\%$). If you had available the heights and weights of a large number of people of your age and gender, you could answer the question about your height compared to your weight by determining your percentile rank on each. If you were at the 39th percentile in height and the 25th percentile in weight, then, relative to others in your group, you would be taller than you were heavy. Similarly, if you were at the 94th percentile on a test of math skills and the 72nd percentile on a test of verbal skills, then, relative to the group who took both tests, your math skills would be better than your verbal skills.

Standardized Scores

Another way to convert scores for purposes of comparison is to *standardize* them. A **standardized score** is one that is expressed in terms of the number of standard deviations that the original score is from the mean of original scores. The simplest form of a standardized score is called a **z score**. To convert any score to a z score, you first determine its deviation from the mean (subtract the mean from it), and then divide the deviation by the standard deviation of the distribution. Thus,

$$z = \frac{\text{score} - \text{mean}}{\text{standard deviation}}$$

For example, suppose you wanted to calculate the z score that would correspond to the test score of 54 in the first set of scores in Table A.4. The mean of the distribution is 50, so the deviation is $54 - 50 = +4$. The standard deviation is 5.0. Thus, $z = ^4/_5 = +0.80$. Similarly, the z score for a score of 42 in that distribution would be $^{(42\,-\,50)}/_5 = -^8/_5 = -1.60$. Remember, the z score is simply the number of standard deviations that the original score is away from the mean. A positive z score indicates that the original score is above the mean, and a negative z score indicates that it is below the mean. A z score of +0.80 is 0.80 standard deviation above the mean, and a z score of -1.60 is 1.60 standard deviations below the mean.

Other forms of standardized scores are based directly on z scores. For example, College Board (SAT) scores were originally (in 1941) determined by calculating each person's z score, then multiplying the z score by 100 and adding the result to 500 (DuBois, 1972). That is,

$$\text{SAT score} = 500 + 100(z)$$

Thus, a person who was directly at the mean on the test ($z = 0$) would have an SAT score of 500; a person who was 1 standard deviation above the mean ($z = +1$) would have an SAT score of 600; a person who was 2 standard deviations above the mean would have 700; and a person who was 3 standard deviations above the mean would have 800. (Very few people would score beyond 3 standard deviations from the mean, so 800 was set as the highest possible score.) Going the other way, a person who was 1 standard deviation below the mean ($z = -1$) would have an SAT score of 400, and so on. (Today, a much broader range of people take the SAT tests than in 1941, when only a relatively elite group applied to colleges, and the scoring system has not been restandardized to maintain 500 as the average score. The result is that average SAT scores are now considerably less than 500.)

Wechsler IQ scores (discussed in Chapter 10) are also based on z scores. They were standardized—separately for each age group—by calculating each person's z score on the test, multiplying that by 15, and adding the product to 100. Thus,

$$\text{IQ} = 100 + 15(z)$$

This process guarantees that a person who scores at the exact mean achieved by people in the standardization group will have an IQ score of 100, that one who scores 1 standard deviation above that mean will have a score of 115, that one who scores 2 standard deviations above that mean will have a score of 130, and so on.

Relationship of Standardized Scores to Percentile Ranks

If a distribution of scores precisely matches a normal distribution, one can determine percentile rank from the standardized score, or vice versa. As you recall, in a normal distribution the highest frequency of scores occurs in intervals close to the mean, and the frequency declines with each successive interval away from the mean in either direction. As illustrated in Figure A.4, a precise relationship exists between any given z score and the percentage of scores that fall between that score and the mean.

As you can see in the figure, slightly more than 34.1% of all scores in a normal distribution will be between a z score of +1 and the mean. Since another 50% will fall below the mean, a total of slightly more than 84.1% of the scores in a normal distribution will be below a z score of +1. By using similar logic and examining the figure, you should be able to see why z scores of −3, −2, −1, 0, +1, +2, and +3, respectively, correspond to percentile ranks of about 0.1, 2.3, 15.9, 50, 84.1, 97.7, and 99.9, respectively. Detailed tables have been made that permit the conversion of any possible z score in a perfect normal distribution to a percentile rank.

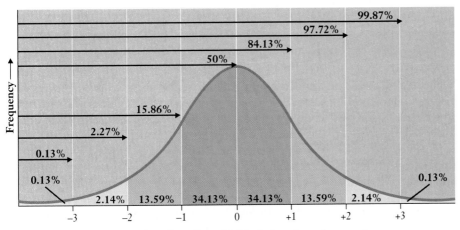

z score (number of standard deviations from the mean)

FIGURE A.4 *Relationship between z score and percentile rank for a normal distribution*
Because the percentage of scores that fall between any given z score and the mean is a fixed value for data that fit a normal distribution, it is possible to calculate what percentage of individuals would score less than or equal to any given z score. In this diagram, the percentages above each arrow indicate the percentile rank for z scores of -3, -2, -1, 0, +1, +2, and +3. Each percentage is the sum of the percentages within the portions of the curve that lie under the arrow.

CALCULATING A CORRELATION COEFFICIENT

The basic meaning of the term *correlation* and how to interpret a correlation coefficient are described in Chapter 2. As explained there, the correlation coefficient is a mathematical means of describing the strength and direction of the relationship between two variables that have been measured mathematically. The sign (+ or −) of the correlation coefficient indicates the direction (positive or negative) of the relationship; and the absolute value of the correlation coefficient (from 0 to 1.00, irrespective of sign) indicates the strength of the correlation. To review the difference between a positive and negative correlation, and between a weak and strong correlation, look back at Figure 2.2 and the accompanying text. Here, as a supplement to the discussion in Chapter 2, is the mathematical means for calculating the most common type of correlation coefficient, called the *product-moment correlation coefficient*.

To continue the example described in Chapter 2, suppose you collected both the IQ score and GPA (grade-point average) for each of ten different high school students and obtained the results shown in the "IQ score" and "GPA" columns of

TABLE **A.5** *Calculation of a correlation coefficient (r)*

Students (ranked by IQ)	IQ score	GPA	z_{IQ}	z_{GPA}	Cross-products $(z_{IQ}) \times (z_{GPA})$
1	82	2.0	−1.77	−0.66	1.17
2	91	1.2	−1.01	−1.71	1.73
3	93	2.3	−0.84	−0.26	0.22
4	97	2.2	−0.51	−0.39	0.20
5	104	3.0	+0.08	+0.66	0.05
6	105	1.8	+0.17	−0.92	−0.16
7	108	3.5	+0.42	+1.32	0.55
8	109	2.6	+0.51	+0.13	0.07
9	118	2.5	+1.26	0.00	0.00
10	123	3.9	+1.68	+1.84	3.09
	Sum = 1030	Sum = 25.0			Sum = 6.92
	Mean = 103	**Mean = 2.5**			**Mean = 0.69 = r**
	SD = 11.88	**SD = 0.76**			

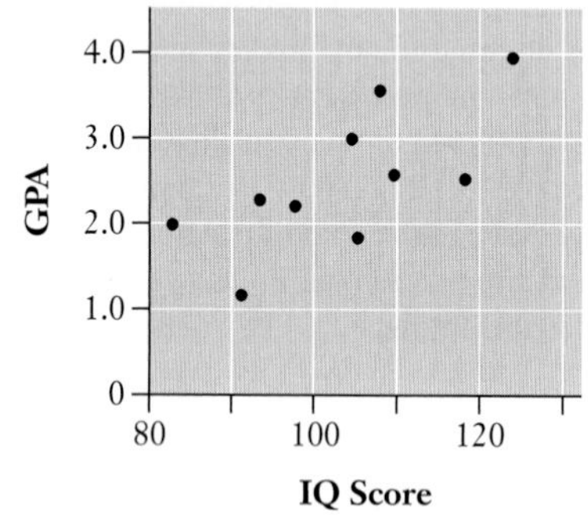

FIGURE **A.5** *Scatter plots relating GPA to IQ*

Each point represents the IQ and the GPA for one of the ten students whose scores are shown in Table A.5. (For further explanation, refer to Figure 2.2 in Chapter 2.)

Table A.5. As a first step in determining the direction and strength of correlation between the two sets of scores, you might graph each pair of points in a *scatter plot*, as shown in Figure A.5 (compare this figure to Figure 2.2). The scatter plot makes it clear that, in general, the students with higher IQs tended to have higher GPAs, so you know that the correlation coefficient will be positive. However, the relationship between IQ and GPA is by no means perfect (the plot does not form a straight line), so you know that the correlation coefficient will be less than 1.00.

The first step in calculating a correlation coefficient is to convert each score to a z score, using the method described in the section on standardizing scores. Each z score, remember, is the number of standard deviations that the original score is away from the mean of the original scores. The standard deviation for the ten IQ scores in Table A.5 is 11.88, so the z scores for IQ (shown in the column marked z_{IQ}) were calculated by subtracting the mean IQ score (103) from each IQ and dividing by 11.88. The standard deviation for the ten GPA scores in Table A.5 is 0.76, so the z scores for GPA (shown in the column marked z_{GPA}) were calculated by subtracting the mean GPA (2.5) from each GPA and dividing by 0.76.

To complete the calculation of the correlation coefficient, you multiply each pair of z scores together, obtaining what are called the *z-score cross-products*, and then determine the mean of those cross-products. The product-moment correlation coefficient, *r*, is, by definition, the mean of the z-score cross-products. In Table A.5, the z-score cross-products are shown in the right-hand column, and the mean of them is shown at the bottom of that column. As you can see, the correlation coefficient in this case is +0.69—a rather strong positive correlation.

SUPPLEMENT ON PSYCHOPHYSICAL SCALING

This section should *not* be read as a supplement to Chapter 2. It concerns two issues discussed in the section on psychophysical scaling in Chapter 7.

Derivation of Fechner's Law from Weber's Law

In Chapter 7, I described Ernst Weber's law, according to which the just-noticeable difference (jnd) between a comparison stimulus and a standard stimulus is directly proportional to the physical magnitude of the standard stimulus (M). As a formula, this is

$$jnd = kM$$

I then noted that Gustav Fechner used Weber's law to derive a law of psychophysical scaling, according to which the magnitude of a sensory experience (S) is directly proportional to the logarithm of the physical magnitude of the stimulus (M). As a formula, this is

$$S = c \log M$$

Here I will use the numbers shown in Table A.6 to demonstrate the logic of Fechner's derivation of his law from Weber's. The logic begins with the assumption that every jnd is subjectively equal to every other jnd. Thus, the sensory scale in the left-hand column of the table is a jnd scale, and each step in that scale produces an equal change in the magnitude of sensory experience (S). The example is for loudness of a 2000-Hz sound, for which the Weber fraction (k) is $\frac{1}{10}$ and the minimal intensity that can be heard is 1 sound-pressure unit. With these assumptions, Weber's law predicts that the intensity that will be 1 jnd above the minimum will be 1.10 units (1 + $\frac{1}{10}$th of 1 = 1.10). Similarly, the intensity that will be 2 jnd's above threshold will be 1.21 units (1.10 + $\frac{1}{10}$th of 1.10 = 1.21).

Continuing in this way, it is possible to derive the physical intensity of the stimulus that would be any given number of jnd's above threshold. The results, for 5 jnd's, are shown in the middle column of the table. Notice that each successive jnd step involves a greater increase in the physical intensity than did the step before. For example, going from 0 to 1 jnd above threshold requires an addition of 0.10 physical unit, whereas going from 4 to 5 jnd's requires an addition of 0.15 physical unit (1.61 − 1.46 = 0.15). Thus, the relationship between the first and second columns is not linear. The third column of the table shows the logarithms (to base 10) of the numbers in the middle column. (If you have a calculator, you can check them yourself. The logarithm of 1 is 0, that of 1.1 is 0.041, and so on.) Notice that now, after the logarithmic transformation, the numbers do form a linear relationship with the numbers in the first column. Each jnd step corresponds with an increase of approximately 0.041 log unit. Thus, in line with Fechner's law, each constant step in sensory magnitude corresponds with a constant step in the logarithm of the physical intensity of the stimulus.

TABLE A.6 *Demonstration that a jnd sensory scale is linearly related to the logarithm of the physical stimulus (log M)*

S in jnd units	M in sound-pressure units if $k = \frac{1}{10}$	Log M
0	1.00	0
1	1.10	0.041
2	1.21	0.082
3	1.33	0.123
4	1.46	0.164
5	1.61	0.205

Illustration Showing That Stevens's Power Law Preserves Sensory Ratios

At the end of Chapter 7, I described Stevens's power law, which states that the magnitude of a sensory experience (S) is directly proportional to the physical magnitude of the stimulus (M) raised by a constant power (p). As a formula, this is

$$S = cM^p$$

I then pointed out (as had Stevens) that our sensory systems may have evolved to operate according to a power law because such a law preserves constant sensory ratios as the overall physical intensity of stimulation waxes or wanes. For example, as a sound becomes closer (and therefore more intense), we hear its various pitches as maintaining the same ratios of intensity to each other as before, and thus we hear it as the same sound. As another example, as light fades in the evening, the relative brightness of one object compared to another in the visual scene remains constant. To make this more concrete, I mentioned in Chapter 7 that, according to Stevens's power law, every eightfold change in light intensity causes a twofold change in apparent brightness, no matter where on the intensity continuum we start from. Following are calculations proving that point.

For brightness estimations, $p = \frac{1}{3}$ (as shown in Table 7.4). Let S_1 be the sensory magnitude for a stimulus whose physical magnitude is M, and let S_2 be the sensory magnitude for a stimulus that is physically eight times as intense as S_1 (that is, whose physical magnitude is $8M$). In accordance with the power law,

$$S_1 = cM^{\frac{1}{3}} \text{ and } S_2 = c(8M)^{\frac{1}{3}}$$

The ratio of S_2/S_1 can now be calculated as follows:

$$\frac{S_2}{S_1} = \frac{c(8M)^{\frac{1}{3}}}{cM^{\frac{1}{3}}} = \frac{(8M)^{\frac{1}{3}}}{M^{\frac{1}{3}}} = (8M/M)^{\frac{1}{3}} = 8^{\frac{1}{3}} = 2$$

Thus, regardless of the value of the original stimulus magnitude (M), an eightfold increase in that magnitude will produce a doubling of the sensory magnitude, or an eightfold decrease will produce a halving of the sensory magnitude. So, if the physical intensity of each part of a visual scene decreases to one-eighth what it was before, the sensory intensity experienced from each part of the scene will be cut in half and each part of the scene will maintain the same ratio of sensory intensity to each other part as it had before.

Glossary

A

absolute threshold In psychophysics, the faintest (lowest-intensity) stimulus of a given sensation (such as sound or light) that an individual can detect. For contrast, see *difference threshold*. (p. 264)

accommodation In Piaget's theory of cognitive development, the change that occurs in an existing mental scheme or set of schemes as a result of the assimilation of the experience of a new event or object. See also *assimilation*. (p. 418)

action potentials Neural impulses; the all-or-nothing electrical bursts that begin at one end of the axon of a neuron and move along the axon to the other end. (p. 165)

actor-observer discrepancy The observation that a person who performs an action (the actor) is likely to attribute the action to the environmental situation, whereas the person who observes the same action (the observer) is likely to attribute it to the actor's inner characteristics (personality). See also *attribution*. (p. 502)

additive color mixing The mixing of colored lights (lights containing limited ranges of wavelengths) by superimposing them to reflect off the same surface. It is called *additive* because each light adds to the total set of wavelengths that are reflected to the eye. For contrast, see *subtractive color mixing*. (p. 283)

algorithm A rule specifying a set of steps that, if followed correctly, is guaranteed to solve a particular class of problem. For contrast, see *heuristic*. (p. 398)

alleles Different genes that can occupy the same locus on a pair of chromosomes and thus can potentially pair with one another. (p. 58)

altruism In sociobiology, a type of helping behavior in which an individual increases the survival chance or reproductive capacity of another individual while *decreasing* its own survival chance or reproductive capacity. For contrast, see *cooperation*. (p. 88)

amplitude The amount of physical energy or force exerted by a physical stimulus at any given moment. For sound, this physical measure is related to the psychological experience of loudness. (p. 254)

amygdala A brain structure that is part of the limbic system and is particularly important for evaluating the emotional and motivational significance of stimuli and generating emotional responses. (pp. 152, 226)

analogy In ethology and comparative psychology, any similarity among species that is not due to common ancestry but has evolved independently because of some similarity in their habitats or lifestyles. For contrast, see *homology*. (p. 76)

anxiety disorders The class of mental disorders in which fear or anxiety is the most prominent symptom. It includes *generalized anxiety disorder, obsessive-compulsive disorder, panic disorder, phobias,* and *post-traumatic stress disorder.* (p. 621)

aphasia Any loss in language ability due to brain damage. See also *Broca's aphasia, Wernicke's aphasia.* (p. 162)

arousal response A pattern of measurable physiological changes (including tense muscles, increased heart rate, and secretion of certain hormones) that helps prepare the body for the possible expenditure of a large amount of energy. (p. 202)

assertiveness training In behavior therapy, a direct method of training people to express their own desires and feelings and to maintain their own rights in interactions with others, while at the same time respecting the others' rights. (p. 686)

assessment In clinical practice, the process by which a mental health professional gathers and compiles information about a client for the purpose of describing the person's problems or disorder and developing a plan of treatment. (p. 659)

assessment interview A dialogue through which a mental health professional learns about a client. (p. 659)

assimilation In Piaget's theory of cognitive development, the process by which experiences are incorporated into the mind or, more specifically, into mental schemes. See also *accommodation*. (p. 418)

association areas Areas of the cerebral cortex that receive input from the primary or secondary sensory areas for more than one sensory modality (such as vision and hearing) and are involved in associating this input with stored memories, in the processes of perception, thought, and decision making. (p. 154)

association by contiguity See *law of association by contiguity*.

association by similarity See *law of association by similarity*.

attachment The long-lasting emotional bonds that infants develop toward their principal caregivers. More broadly, the long-lasting emotional bonds that any individual develops toward any other individual or object. (p. 456)

attention In perception, the process or set of processes by which the mind chooses from among the various stimuli that strike the senses at any given moment, allowing only some of those stimuli to enter into higher stages of information processing. (p. 331) In the modal model of the mind, the process that controls the flow of information from the sensory store into working memory. More broadly, any focusing of mental activity along a specific track, whether that track consists purely of inner memories and knowledge or is based on external stimuli. (p. 328)

attitude Any belief or opinion that has an evaluative component—a belief that something is good or bad, likable or unlikable, attractive or repulsive. (p. 497)

attribution In social cognition, any inference about the cause of a person's behavioral action or set of actions. More generally, any inference about the cause of any observed action or event. (p. 498)

auditory masking The phenomenon by which one sound (usually a lower-frequency sound) tends to prevent the hearing of another sound (usually a higher-frequency sound). (p. 259)

autism A congenital (present-at-birth) disorder, typically marked by severe deficits in social interaction, severe deficits in language acquisition, a tendency to perform repetitive actions, and a restricted focus of attention and interest. (pp. 44, 432)

autonomic motor system The set of motor neurons that act upon visceral muscles and glands. (p. 147)

aversion treatment In behavior therapy, a method for eliminating an undesired habit by applying some painful or unpleasant stimulus immediately after the unwanted response occurs or immediately after the person has experienced stimuli that would normally elicit the response. (p. 685)

axon A thin, tubelike extension from a neuron that is specialized to carry neural impulses (action potentials) to other cells. (p. 144)

axon terminal A swelling at the end of an axon that is designed to release a chemical substance (neurotransmitter) onto another neuron, muscle cell, or gland cell. (p. 144)

B

basal ganglia The large masses of gray matter in the brain that lie on each side of the thalamus; they are especially important for the initiation and coordination of deliberate movements. (p. 152)

basilar membrane A flexible membrane in the cochlea of the inner ear; the wavelike movement of this structure in response to sound stimulates the receptor cells for hearing. See also *hair cells*. (p. 256)

behavior The observable actions of an individual person or animal. (p. 3)

behavior therapy The psychotherapy approach based on the philosophy of behaviorism and rooted in basic behavioral research on learning. In this approach, psychological problems are considered to stem from learned habits, and learning techniques are used to treat them. (p. 682)

behavioral monitoring Any assessment procedure that involves counting or recording actual instances of desired or undesired behaviors. (p. 662)

behaviorism A school of psychological thought that holds that the proper subject of study is observable behavior, not the mind, and that behavior should be understood in terms of its relationship to observable events in the environment rather than in terms of hypothetical events within the individual. (pp. 14, 98)

bias A technical term referring to nonrandom (directed) effects on research results, caused by some factor or factors extraneous to the research hypothesis. For contrast, see *error*. (p. 42)

biased sample A subset of the population under study that is not representative of the population as a whole. (p. 43)

binocular disparity The cue for depth perception that stems from the separate (disparate) views that the two eyes have of any given visual object or scene. The farther away the object is, the more similar are the two views of it. (p. 308)

biofeedback training A variety of operant conditioning in which a signal, such as a tone or light, is made to come on whenever a certain desirable physiological change occurs, and the person is instructed to try to keep the signal on for increasing periods of time. It is used as a treatment for such problems as headaches and high blood pressure. (p. 110)

bipolar cells The class of neurons in the retina that receive input from the receptor cells (rods and cones) and form synapses on ganglion cells (which form the optic nerve). (p. 280)

bipolar disorder A mood disorder characterized by episodes of extreme depression alternating with episodes of extreme mania. (p. 626)

blind In scientific research, the condition in which those who collect the data are deliberately kept uninformed about aspects of the study's design (such as which subjects have had which treatment) that could lead them either unconsciously or consciously to bias the results. See also *bias, observer-expectancy effect*. (p. 46)

blind spot The place in the retina of the eye where the axons of visual sensory neurons come together to form the optic nerve. Because the blind spot lacks receptor cells, light that strikes it is not seen. (p. 278)

blood-brain barrier The tight capillary walls and the surrounding glial cells that prevent many chemical substances from entering the brain from the blood. (p. 181)

bottom-up processes In theories of perception, mental processes that bring the individual stimulus features recorded by the senses together to form a perception of the larger object or scene. For contrast, see *top-down processes*. (p. 297)

brainstem The primitive, stalklike portion of the brain that can be thought of as an extension of the spinal cord into the head; it consists of the medulla, pons, and midbrain. (p. 150)

Broca's aphasia A specific syndrome of loss in language ability that occurs due to damage in a particular part of the brain called *Broca's area*; it is characterized by telegraphic speech in which the meaning is usually clear but the small words and word endings that serve grammatical purposes are missing; also called *nonfluent aphasia*. For contrast, see *Wernicke's aphasia*. (p. 162)

C

catatonic behavior A symptom of schizophrenia in which the person is unresponsive to the environment. It may take the form of active resistance, excited motor activity, or a complete lack of movement or awareness of the environment. (p. 643)

cell body The widest part of a neuron, which contains the cell nucleus and the other basic machinery common to all cells. (p. 144)

cell membrane The thin, porous outer covering of a neuron or other cell that separates the cell's intracellular fluid from extracellular fluid. (p. 166)

central drive system According to the central-state theory of drives, a set of neurons in the brain that, when active, most directly promotes a specific motivational state, or drive. (p. 190)

central executive In Baddeley's theory, a component of the mind responsible for coordinating all the activities of working memory and for bringing new information into working memory. (p. 336)

central nervous system The brain and spinal cord. (p. 144)

central-state theory of drives The theory that the most direct physiological bases for motivational states, or drives, lie in neural activity in the brain. According to most versions of this theory, different drives correspond to activity in different, localizable sets of neurons. See also *central drive system*. (p. 190)

central traits In trait theories of personality, the relatively small set of basic traits (personality characteristics) that are inferred from statistical intercorrelations among various surface traits. See also *surface traits*. (p. 574)

cerebellum The relatively large, conspicuous, convoluted portion of the brain attached to the rear side of the brainstem; it is especially important for the coordination of rapid movements. (p. 151)

cerebral cortex The outermost, evolutionarily newest, and (in humans) by far the largest portion of the brain; it is divisible into two hemispheres (right and left), and each hemisphere is divisible into four lobes—the occipital, temporal, parietal, and frontal. (p. 153)

chromosomes The structures within the cell nucleus that contain the genetic material (DNA). (p. 56)

chunking A strategy for improving the ability to remember a set of items by grouping them mentally to form fewer items. (p. 343)

circadian rhythm Any cyclic physiological or behavioral change in a person or other living thing that has a period of about 1 day even in the absence of external cues signaling the time of day. (p. 213)

classical conditioning A training procedure or learning experience in which a neutral stimulus (the conditioned stimulus) comes to elicit a reflexive response through its being paired with another stimulus (usually an unconditioned stimulus) that already elicits that reflexive response; originally studied by Pavlov. See also *conditioned response, conditioned stimulus, unconditioned response, unconditioned stimulus*. (p. 100)

client-centered therapy The humanistic approach to psychotherapy developed by Rogers, in which the therapist refrains from offering advice or leading the course of therapy, but rather listens to the client with empathy and respect and reflects the client's thoughts and feelings back to him or her. (p. 675)

clinical psychology The field of practice and research that is directed toward helping people who suffer from psychological problems and disorders. (p. 643)

closure principle See *Gestalt principles of grouping*.

cochlea A coiled structure in the inner ear in which the receptor cells for hearing are located. (p. 256)

cochlear implant A type of hearing aid used to treat sensorineural deafness; it transforms sounds into electrical impulses and directly stimulates the tips of auditory neurons within the cochlea. (p. 257)

coding In sensation, the process by which information about the quality and quantity of a stimulus is preserved in the pattern of action potentials sent through sensory neurons to the central nervous system. (p. 236)

cognitive-behavior therapy The psychotherapy approach that stems from a union of cognitive and behavioral theory; it usually characterizes psychological problems as learned habits of thought and action, and its approach to treatment is to help people change those habits. See also *behavior therapy, cognitive therapy*. (p. 682)

cognitive dissonance theory Festinger's theory that people seek to relieve the discomfort associated with the awareness of inconsistency between two or more of one's own cognitions (beliefs or bits of knowledge). (p. 520)

cognitive map The mental representation of the spatial layout of a familiar environment, inferred from the individual's ability to move in that environment as if guided by a map. (p. 126)

cognitive psychology The study of people's ability to acquire, organize, remember, and use knowledge to guide behavior; it involves the construction of hypothetical mental processes to explain observable behavior. (pp. 20, 118)

cognitive therapy An approach to psychotherapy that begins with the assumption that people disturb themselves through their own thoughts and that they can overcome their problems through changing the way they think about their experiences. (p. 678)

common movement principle See *Gestalt principles of grouping*.

concept A rule or other form of mental information for categorizing stimuli into groups. (p. 119)

concordance In behavioral genetics research, an index of heritability that is found by identifying a set of individuals who have a particular trait or disorder and then determining the percentage of some specific class of their relatives (such as identical twins) who have the same trait or disorder. (p. 645)

concrete-operational scheme In Piaget's theory, the type of mental stimulus that allows a child to think logically about reversible actions (operations) but only when applied to objects with which the child has had direct (concrete) experience. See also *operation*. (p. 420)

conditioned reflex In classical conditioning, a reflex that occurs only because of previous conditions in the individual's experience; a learned reflex. For contrast, see *unconditioned reflex*. (p. 100)

conditioned response In classical conditioning, a reflexive response that is elicited by a stimulus (the conditioned stimulus) because of the previous pairing of that stimulus with another stimulus (the unconditioned stimulus) that already elicits a reflexive response. For contrast, see *unconditioned response*. (p. 100)

conditioned stimulus In classical conditioning, a stimulus that comes to elicit a reflexive response (the conditioned response) because of its previous pairing with another stimulus (the unconditioned stimulus) that already elicits a reflexive response. For contrast, see *unconditioned stimulus*. (p. 100)

conduction deafness Deafness that occurs when the ossicles of the middle ear become rigid and cannot carry sounds inward from the tympanic membrane to the cochlea. (p. 257)

cones The class of receptor cells for vision that are located in and near the fovea of the retina, operate in moderate to bright light, and are most important for the perception of color and fine detail. For contrast, see *rods*. (p. 277)

cone vision The high-acuity color vision that occurs in moderate to bright light and is mediated by cones in the retina; also called *photopic* or *bright-light vision*. See *cones*. For contrast, see *rod vision*. (p. 278)

consciousness In perception, the experiencing of percepts or other mental events in such a manner that one can report on them to others. (p. 325)

content morphemes Words, including nouns, verbs, adjectives, and adverbs, that are most essential to the meaning of a sentence. For contrast, see *grammatical morphemes*. (p. 435)

context-dependent memory The improved ability to retrieve information from memory that occurs when an individual is in the same environment as that in which the memory was originally encoded. (p. 351) *contingency contract* In behavior therapy, a formal, usually written agreement in which certain specified services or rewards provided by one party are made contingent upon the actions of the other party. (p. 686)

control processes In the modal model of the mind, the mental processes that operate on information in the memory stores and move information from one store to another. See *attention, encoding, retrieval.* (p. 326)

conversion disorder A category of somatoform disorder in which the person, for psychological reasons, loses some bodily function. (p. 632)

cooperation In sociobiology, a type of helping behavior in which interaction among two or more individuals increases the survival chance or reproductive capacity of each individual involved in the interaction. For contrast, see *altruism.* (p. 88)

cornea The curved, transparent tissue at the front of the eyeball that helps to focus light rays as they first enter the eye. (p. 276)

corpus callosum A massive bundle of axons connecting the right and left hemispheres of the higher parts of the brain, including the cerebral cortex. (p. 159)

correlation coefficient A numerical measure of the strength and direction of the relationship between two variables. (pp. 39, A-7)

correlational study Any scientific study in which the researcher observes or measures (without directly manipulating) two or more variables to find relationships between them. Such studies can identify lawful relationships but cannot determine whether change in one variable is the cause of change in another. (p. 35)

cranial nerve A nerve that extends directly from the brain. See *nerves.* For contrast, see *spinal nerve.* (p. 147)

creole language A new language, with grammatical rules, that develops from a pidgin language in colonies established by people who had different native languages. See *pidgin language.* (p. 442)

critical period A relatively restricted time period in an individual's development during which a particular form of learning can best occur. See *imprinting.* (p. 135)

crystallized intelligence In Cattell's theory, the variety of intelligence that derives directly from previous experience. It includes one's accumulated knowledge and verbal skills. For contrast, see *fluid intelligence.* (p. 373)

cultural psychology The study of the relationship between the culture in which a person develops and the person's thoughts, feelings, and behavior. Cultural psychologists may focus on just one culture or may compare people living in different cultures. (p. 19)

cyclothymia A mood disorder similar to bipolar disorder but involving less extreme depression and mania. See *bipolar disorder.* (p. 631)

D

dark adaptation The increased visual sensitivity that occurs when the eyes are exposed for a period of time to dimmer light than was present before the adaptation period. For contrast, see *light adaptation.* (p. 279)

deductive reasoning Logical reasoning from the general to the specific; the reasoner begins by accepting the truth of one or more general premises or axioms and uses them to assert whether a specific conclusion is true, false, or indeterminate. For contrast, see *inductive reasoning.* (p. 393)

defense mechanisms In psychoanalytic theory, self-deceptive means by which the mind defends itself against anxiety. See *displacement, projection, rationalization, reaction formation, repression, sublimation.* (p. 596)

delusion A false belief that is maintained despite compelling evidence to the contrary. (p. 643)

dendrites The thin, tubelike extensions of a neuron that typically branch repeatedly near the neuron's cell body and are specialized for receiving signals from other neurons. (p. 144)

dependent variable In an experiment, the variable that is believed to be dependent upon (affected by) another variable (the independent variable). In psychological experiments, it is usually some measure of behavior. (p. 34)

depressive disorders The class of mood disorders characterized by prolonged or frequent bouts of depression. See *dysthymia, major depression.* (p. 626)

deprivation experiment An experiment in which animals are raised in ways that deprive them of some of their usual experiences in order to determine what experiences are essential (or not) for a particular species-typical behavior to develop. (p. 75)

descriptive statistics Mathematical methods for summarizing sets of data. (p. 38)

descriptive study Any study in which the researcher describes the behavior of an individual or set of individuals without systematically investigating relationships between specific variables. (p. 36)

deterministic fallacy The mistaken belief that genes control, or determine, behavior in a manner that is independent of environmental influences. (p. 90)

developmental psychology The branch of psychology that charts changes in people's abilities and styles of behaving as they get older and tries to understand the factors that produce or influence those changes. (p. 409)

difference threshold In psychophysics, the minimal difference that must exist between two otherwise similar stimuli for an individual to detect them as different; also called the *just-noticeable difference (jnd).* (p. 266)

differential lighting of surfaces A pictorial cue for perceiving depth in which the amount of light reflecting on different surfaces indicates the position of objects relative to the light source. (p. 312)

direct-perception theory The theory that perceptual mechanisms register directly the critical stimulus relationships that are present in the external environment, such that perception is not dependent upon mental inference. For contrast, see *unconscious-inference theory of perception.* (p. 317)

discrimination training The procedure, in both classical and operant conditioning, by which generalization between two stimuli is diminished or abolished by reinforcing the response to one stimulus and extinguishing the response to the other. See *extinction, generalization, reinforcement.* (p. 103)

discriminative stimulus In operant conditioning, a stimulus that serves as a signal that a particular response will produce a particular reinforcer. (p. 113)

disorganized speech A symptom of schizophrenia in which the person's speech contains loose associations and logical inconsistencies that are believed to reflect an underlying disorganization in thought. (p. 643)

displacement The defense mechanism by which a drive is diverted from one goal to another that is more realistic or acceptable. Also called *sublimation* in cases where the goal toward which the drive is diverted is highly valued by society. (p. 597)

dissociation A process by which some portion of a person's experiences are cut off mentally from the rest of his or her experiences, such that they cannot be recalled or can be recalled only under special conditions. (p. 639)

dissociative disorders The class of mental disorders that are characterized by dissociation. They include *dissociative identity disorder, dissociative amnesia,* and *dissociative fugue.* (p. 639)

dissociative identity disorder A mental disorder in which two or more distinct personalities or self-identities are manifested in the same person at different times. Formerly called *multiple-personality disorder.* (p. 639)

dominance In animal colonies, a condition established by one animal over another by prevailing in an aggressive encounter between the two. (p. 87)

dominance hierarchy A system of social organization in which the individuals in a group are ranked from lowest to highest, with each being dominant to those lower in rank and submissive to those higher. (p. 87)

dominant gene A gene that will produce its observable effects in either the homozygous or the heterozygous condition. (p. 59)

double-blind experiment An experiment in which both the observer and the subjects are blind with respect to the subjects' treatment conditions. See also *blind.* (p. 46)

drive See *motivational state.*

drug abuse The persistent taking of a drug in a way that is harmful to the self or that causes one to behave in a way that is harmful or threatening to others. (p. 636)

drug dependence The condition, which may or may not stem from physiological withdrawal symptoms, in which a person feels compelled to take a particular drug on a regular basis; also called *drug addiction.* (p. 636)

drug tolerance The phenomenon by which a drug produces successively smaller physiological and behavioral effects, at any given dose, if it is taken repeatedly. (p. 182)

dualism The philosophical theory that two distinct systems—the material body and the immaterial soul—are involved in the control of behavior. For contrast, see *materialism.* (p. 4)

dysthymia A mental disorder characterized by feelings of depression that are less severe than those in major depression but which last for at least a 2-year period. See also *major depression.* (p. 626)

E

echoic memory Sensory memory for the sense of hearing. (p. 330)

ecological perspective In research on learning, the view that different learning mechanisms have developed through natural selection to serve different survival needs and that these mechanisms are best understood in relation to daily life in the natural environment. More generally, the view that behavioral or mental capacities are best understood by considering how they serve the individual's needs in the environment. (p. 130)

elaboration The process of thinking about an item of information in such a way as to tie the item mentally to other information in memory, which helps to encode the item into long-term memory; also called *elaborative rehearsal.* (p. 341)

elaboration likelihood model A theory of persuasion postulating that people are more likely to think logically about a message (that is, elaborate upon the message) if it is personally relevant than if it is not. (p. 528)

electroencephalogram (EEG) A record of the electrical activity of the brain that can be obtained by amplifying the weak electrical signals picked up by recording electrodes pasted to the person's scalp. It is usually described in terms of wave patterns. (p. 208)

emotion A subjective feeling, the intensity of which is typically related to the degree of physiological arousal that accompanies it. (p. 221)

empiricism The idea that all human knowledge and thought ultimately come from sensory experience; the philosophical approach to understanding the mind that is based on that idea. For contrast, see *nativism.* (p. 6)

encoding In the modal model of the mind, the mental process by which long-term memories are formed. See also *long-term memory.* (p. 328)

encoding rehearsal Any active mental process by which a person strives to encode information into long-term memory. For contrast, see *maintenance rehearsal.* (p. 341)

encoding-specificity principle The principle that the stimuli that were most prominent in a person's experience at the time of encoding a specific item of information into long-term memory are powerful cues for subsequent retrieval of that item from long-term memory. (p. 350)

endocrine glands Glands that are specialized to secrete hormones into the circulatory system. (p. 177)

endorphins Chemicals produced in the body that act like morphine in inhibiting pain. (p.251)

environmentality The proportion of the variability in a particular characteristic, in a particular group of individuals, that is due to environmental rather than genetic differences among the individuals. For contrast, see *heritability.* (p. 378)

episodic memory Explicit memory of past events (episodes) in one's own life. For contrast, see *semantic memory, implicit memory.* (p. 356)

error A technical term referring to random variability in research results. For contrast, see *bias.* (p. 42)

ethology The study of animal behavior in the natural environment, which uses evolutionary adaptation as its primary explanatory principle. (pp. 15, 71)

excitatory synapse A synapse at which the neurotransmitter increases the likelihood that an action potential will occur, or increases the rate at which they are already occurring, in the neuron on which it acts. For contrast, see *inhibitory synapse.* (p. 169)

experiment A research design for testing hypotheses about cause-effect relationships, in which the researcher manipulates one variable (the independent variable) in order to assess its effect on another variable (the dependent variable). (p. 34)

explicitation In Karmiloff-Smith's theory, the mental process by which previously implicit memories are transformed into explicit memories. (p. 425)

explicit memory The class of memory that can be consciously recalled and used to answer explicit questions about what one knows or remembers. See *episodic memory, semantic memory*. For contrast, see *implicit memory*. (p. 355)

exposure treatment Any method of treating fears—including flooding and systematic desensitization—that involves exposing the client to the feared object or situation (either in reality or imagination) so that the process of extinction or habituation of the fear response can occur. (p. 683)

extinction In classical conditioning, the gradual disappearance of a conditioned reflex that results when a conditioned stimulus occurs repeatedly without the unconditioned stimulus. (p. 102) In operant conditioning, the decline in response rate that results when an operant response is no longer followed by a reinforcer. (p. 111) See *classical conditioning, operant conditioning*.

eyebrow flash A momentary raising of the eyebrows, lasting about one-sixth of a second, which is a nonverbal sign of greeting in cultures throughout the world. (p. 73)

F

fact An objective statement, usually based on direct observation, that reasonable observers agree is true. In psychology, facts are usually particular behaviors, or reliable patterns of behaviors, of persons or animals. (p. 31)

factor analysis A statistical procedure for analyzing the correlations among various measurements (such as test scores) taken from a given set of individuals; it identifies hypothetical, underlying variables called *factors* that could account for the observed pattern of correlations and assesses the degree to which each factor is adequately measured by each of the measurements that was used in the analysis. (p. 372)

Fechner's law The idea that the magnitude of the sensory experience of a stimulus is directly proportional to the logarithm of the physical magnitude of the stimulus. For contrast, see *power law*. (p. 267)

field study Any scientific research study in which data are collected in a setting other than the laboratory. (p. 36)

field theory Lewin's broad social psychological theory that each person exists in a field of psychological forces—made up of the person's own desires, goals, and abilities and the person's perceptions of others' expectations or judgments—that act simultaneously to push or pull the person in various directions. (p. 539)

figure In perception, the portion of a visual scene that draws the perceiver's attention and is interpreted as an object rather than as the background. For contrast, see *ground*. (p. 302)

fixed action pattern Ethologists' term for a behavior that occurs in essentially identical fashion among most members of a species (though it may be limited to one sex or the other), is elicited by a specific environmental stimulus, and is typically more complex than a reflex. (p. 71)

flooding A behavior therapy technique for treating phobias in which the person is presented with the feared object or situation until the fear response is extinguished or habituated. (p. 683)

fluid intelligence In Cattell's theory, the variety of intelligence that enables one to perceive relationships independent of previous specific practice or instruction concerning those relationships. For contrast, see *crystallized intelligence*. (p. 373)

fMRI See *functional magnetic resonance imaging*.

foot-in-the-door technique A technique for gaining compliance in which one first asks for some relatively small contribution or favor before asking for a larger one. Complying with the first request predisposes the person to comply with the second. (p. 552)

formal-operational scheme In Piaget's theory, the type of mental stimulus that allows a person to reason about abstract concepts and hypothetical ideas. See also *operation, schemes*. (p. 420)

four-walls technique A sales trick in which the salesperson asks a set of leading questions that cause the potential customer to say things that would contradict (and cause cognitive dissonance with) a subsequent refusal to purchase the product that the salesperson is trying to sell. (p. 552)

fovea The pinhead-size area of the retina of the eye in which the cones are concentrated and that is specialized for high visual acuity. (p. 277)

fraternal twins Two individuals who developed simultaneously in the same womb, but who originated from separate zygotes (fertilized eggs) and are therefore no more genetically similar to one another than are nontwin siblings; also called *dizygotic twins*. For contrast, see *identical twins*. (p. 58)

free association In psychoanalysis, the procedure in which a patient relaxes, frees his or her mind from the constraints of conscious logic, and reports every image and idea that enters his or her awareness. (p. 661)

free nerve endings The sensitive tips of sensory neurons, located in the skin and other peripheral tissues, that are *not* surrounded by specialized end organs and are involved in the sense of pain. (p. 248)

frequency For any form of energy that changes in a cyclic or wavelike way, the number of cycles or waves that occur during a standard unit of time. For sound, this physical measure is related to the psychological experience of pitch. (p. 254)

frequency distribution A table or graph depicting the number of individual scores, in a set of scores, that fall within each of a set of equal intervals. (p. A-2)

frontal lobe The frontmost lobe of the cerebral cortex, bounded in the rear by the parietal and temporal lobes; it contains the motor area and parts of the association areas involved in planning and making judgments. (pp. 154, 226)

functionalism A school of psychological thought, founded by William James and others, that focuses on understanding the functions, or adaptive purposes, of mental processes. For contrast, see *structuralism*. (pp. 11, 69)

functional magnetic resonance imagining (fMRI) A method for visually displaying brain activity that is based on the fact that protons in certain molecules can be made to resonate and give off radio waves indicating relative amounts of neural activity in each portion of the brain. (p. 163)

G

ganglion cells The sensory neurons for vision; their cell bodies are located in the retina, and their axons run by way of the optic nerve into the brain. (p. 280)

gate-control theory Melzack and Wall's theory that pain will be experienced only if the input from peripheral pain neurons passes through a "gate" located at the point that the pain-carrying neurons enter the spinal cord or lower brainstem. (p. 250)

gender identity A person's subjective sense of being male or female. (p. 473)

general intelligence In Spearman's theory of intelligence (and in other theories based on Spearman's), the underlying mental ability that affects performance on a wide variety of mental tests and accounts for the statistical correlation among scores on such tests; also called *g*. (p. 372)

generalization In classical conditioning, the phenomenon by which a stimulus that resembles a conditioned stimulus will elicit the conditioned response even though it has never been paired with the unconditioned stimulus. (p. 103) In operant conditioning, the phenomenon by which a stimulus that resembles a discriminative stimulus will increase the rate at which the animal produces the operant response, even though the response has never been reinforced in the presence of that stimulus. (p. 118)

generalized anxiety disorder A mental disorder characterized by prolonged, severe anxiety that is not consistently associated in the person's mind with any particular object or event in the environment or any specific life experience. (p. 621)

genotype The set of genes inherited by the individual. See also *phenotype*. (p. 55)

Gestalt principles of grouping The rules, proposed by Gestalt psychologists, concerning the manner by which the perceptual system groups sensory elements together to produce organized perceptions of whole objects and scenes. They include the principles of (a) *proximity* (nearby elements are grouped together), (b) *similarity* (elements that resemble one another are grouped together), (c) *closure* (gaps in what would otherwise be a continuous border are ignored), (d) *good continuation* (when lines intersect, those segments that would form a continuous line with minimal change in direction are grouped together), (e) *common movement* (elements moving in the same direction and velocity are grouped together), and (f) *good form* (elements are grouped in such a way as to form percepts that are simple and symmetrical). (p. 301)

Gestalt psychology A school of psychological thought, founded in Germany, which emphasizes the idea that the mind must be understood in terms of organized wholes, not elementary parts. For contrast, see *structuralism*. (pp. 12, 300)

gland Any bodily structure designed to secrete a chemical substance. See also *endocrine glands*. (p. 147)

good continuation principle See *Gestalt principles of grouping*.

good form principle See *Gestalt principles of grouping*.

grammar The entire set of rules that specify the permissible ways that smaller units can be arranged to form morphemes, words, phrases, and sentences in a language. (p. 436)

grammatical morphemes The class of words, suffixes, and prefixes that serve primarily to fill out the grammatical structure of a sentence rather than to carry its main meaning. For contrast, see *content morphemes*. (p. 435)

grossly disorganized behavior A symptom of schizophrenia in which the person's behaviors are strikingly inappropriate for the situation. (p. 643)

ground In perception, the portion of a visual scene that is interpreted as the background rather than as the object of attention. For contrast, see *figure*. (p. 302)

group polarization The tendency for a group of people who already share a particular opinion to hold that opinion more strongly—or in a more extreme form—after discussing the issue among themselves. (p. 548)

groupthink A model of thinking in which members of a group are more concerned with group cohesiveness and unanimity than with realistic appraisal of the actions being considered. (p. 550)

H

habituation The decline in the magnitude or likelihood of a reflexive response that occurs when the stimulus is repeated several or many times in succession. (p. 99)

hair cells The receptor cells for hearing, which are arranged in rows along the basilar membrane of the cochlea in the inner ear. (p. 256)

hallucination A false sensory perception; the experience of seeing, hearing, or otherwise perceiving something and believing it to be present when in fact it is not present. (p. 643)

helping In sociobiology, any behavior that increases the survival chance or reproductive capacity of another individual. See also *altruism*, *cooperation*. (p. 87)

heritability The proportion of the variability in a particular characteristic, in a particular group of individuals, that is due to genetic rather than environmental differences among the individuals. For contrast, see *environmentality*. (p. 378)

heritability coefficient A measure of heritability, which can vary from 0 (no heritability) to 1 (complete heritability); specifically, variance due to genes divided by total variance. See *heritability*. (p. 378)

heterozygous The condition in which a pair of genes occupying the same locus on a pair of chromosomes are different from one another. For contrast, see *homozygous*. (p. 58)

heuristic A shortcut in problem solving; a rule for reducing the number of mental operations (or information-processing steps) taken to solve a problem. For contrast, see *algorithm*. (p. 398)

higher-order stimuli In direct-perception theory, those stimulus relationships that the perceptual system detects directly with no mental calculations necessary. (p. 317)

hippocampus A structure in the limbic system of the brain that is essential for encoding explicit memories for long-term storage. (p. 152)

homeostasis The constancy in the body's internal environment that must be maintained through the expenditure of energy. (p. 189)

homology In ethology and comparative psychology, any similarity among species that exists because of the species' common ancestry. For contrast, see *analogy*. (p. 76)

homozygous The condition in which a pair of genes occupying the same locus on a pair of chromosomes are identical to one another. For contrast, see *heterozygous*. (p. 58)

hormone Any chemical substance that is secreted naturally by the body into the blood and can influence physiological processes at specific target tissues (such as the brain) and thereby influence behavior. (p. 177)

humanistic psychology An approach to understanding the human personality that emphasizes (a) the person's subjective mental experiences, (b) a holistic view of the person, and (c) the person's inner drive toward higher psychological growth. (pp. 18, 603)

humanistic theories Personality theories that attempt to focus attention on the whole, unique person, especially on the person's conscious understanding of his or her self and the world. (p. 603) *hypothalamus* A small brain structure lying just below the thalamus, connected directly to the pituitary gland and to the limbic system, that is especially important for the regulation of motivation, emotion, and the internal physiological conditions of the body. (p. 153)

hypothesis A specific prediction about what will be observed in a research study, usually derived from a more general conception or theory. See also *theory*. (p. 31)

I

iconic memory Sensory memory for the sense of vision. (p. 329)

identical twins Two individuals who are genetically identical to one another because they originated from a single zygote (fertilized egg); also called *monozygotic twins*. For contrast, see *fraternal twins*. (p. 58)

implicit memory Memory that influences one's behavior or thought but does not itself enter consciousness. See *priming*, *procedural memory*. For contrast, see *explicit memory*. (p. 356)

impression management The entire set of ways by which people either consciously or unconsciously attempt to influence other people's impressions (perceptions and judgments) of them. (p. 542)

imprinting Ethologists' term for a relatively sudden and irreversible form of learning that can occur only during some critical period of the individual's development. See *critical period*. (p. 135)

incentive Any object or end that exists in the external environment and toward which behavior is directed. Also called a *reinforcer*, *reward*, or *goal*. (p. 188)

independent variable In an experiment, the condition that the researcher varies in order to assess its effect upon some other variable (the dependent variable). In psychology, it is usually some condition of the environment or of the organism's physiology that is hypothesized to affect the individual's behavior. (p. 33)

induction In Hoffman's typology of discipline styles, a form of verbal reasoning in which a parent (or other caregiver) induces the child to think about his or her actions and the consequences they have for other people. (p. 466)

inductive reasoning Logical reasoning from the specific to the general; the reasoner begins with a set of specific observations or facts and uses them to infer a more general rule to account for those observations or facts; also called *hypothesis construction*. For contrast, see *deductive reasoning*. (p. 391)

inferential statistics Mathematical methods for helping researchers determine how confident they can be in drawing general conclusions (inferences) from specific sets of data. (p. 38)

informational influence The class of social influence that derives from the use of others' behavior or opinions as information in forming one's own judgment about the objective nature of an event or situation. For contrast, see *normative influence*. (p. 545)

inhibitory synapse A synapse at which the neurotransmitter decreases the likelihood that an action potential will occur, or decreases the rate at which they are already occurring, in the neuron upon which it acts. For contrast, see *excitatory synapse*. (p. 169)

inner ear The portion of the ear lying farthest inward in the head; it contains the cochlea (for hearing) and the vestibular apparatus (for the sense of balance). (p. 256)

insufficient-justification effect A change in attitude that serves to justify an action that seems unjustified in the light of the previously held attitude. (p. 522)

interneuron A neuron that exists entirely within the brain or spinal cord and carries messages from one set of neurons to another. (p. 144)

interview A self-report method of data collection in which the individual being studied (or assessed) answers questions in an oral dialogue; often used for clinical assessment. (p. 37)

intoxicating effects of a drug The relatively short-term effects on mood and behavior that stem from the immediate physiological effects of a drug and that subside as the amount of the drug in the body diminishes. (p. 637)

introspection The process of looking inward to examine one's own conscious experience; the method used by Titchener and other structuralists. (p. 10)

iris The colored (usually brown or blue), doughnut-shaped, muscular structure in the eye, located behind the cornea and in front of the lens, that controls the size of the pupil and in that way controls the amount of light that can enter the eye's interior. (p. 276)

J

just-noticeable difference (jnd) See *difference threshold*.

just-world bias The tendency to believe that life is fair, which can lead people to assume that individuals who suffer misfortune deserve their misfortune. (p. 524)

K

kin selection theory of altruism The sociobiological theory that apparent acts of altruism have come about through natural selection because such actions are disproportionately directed toward close genetic relatives and thus promote the survival of others who have the same genes. See also *altruism*. (p. 88)

L

laboratory study Any research study in which the subjects are brought to a specially designated area (laboratory) that has been set up to facilitate the researcher's ability to control the environment or collect data. (p. 36)

language-acquisition device (LAD) Chomsky's term for the special, innate characteristics of the human mind that allow children to learn their native language; it includes innate knowledge of basic aspects of grammar that are common to all languages and an innate predisposition to attend to and remember the critical, unique aspects of the language. (p. 442)

language-acquisition support system (LASS) The term used by social-learning theorists to refer to the simplification of language and the use of gestures that occur when parents or other language users speak to young children, which helps children learn language; developed as a complement to Chomsky's concept of the LAD (language-acquisition device). (p. 444)

latent learning Learning that is not demonstrated in the subject's behavior at the time that the learning occurs but can be inferred from its effect on the subject's behavior at some later time. (p. 127)

law of association by contiguity Aristotle's principle that if two environmental events (stimuli) occur at the same time or one right after the other (contiguously), those events will be linked together in the mind. (pp. 101, 349)

law of association by similarity Aristotle's principle that objects, events, or ideas that are similar to one another become linked (associated) in the person's mind (structure of memory), such that the thought of one tends to elicit the thought of the other. (p. 349)

law of complementarity The observation that certain pairs of limited-wavelength lights that produce different colors (such as red and green) alone will produce the perception of white (no color) when mixed. See also *additive color mixing*. (p. 283)

law of effect Thorndike's principle that responses that produce a satisfying effect in a particular situation become more likely to recur in that situation, and responses that produce a discomforting effect become less likely to recur in that situation. (p. 107)

learning The process or set of processes through which sensory experience at one time can affect an individual's behavior at a future time. (p. 97)

leptin A hormone produced by fat cells that acts in the brain to inhibit hunger and regulate body weight. (p. 196)

lesion Any localized area of damage in biological tissue, such as in the brain. (p. 191)

light adaptation The decreased visual sensitivity that occurs when the eyes are exposed for a period of time to brighter light than was present before the adaptation period. For contrast, see *dark adaptation*. (p. 279)

lightness constancy The tendency to perceive a surface as having the same degree of lightness or darkness regardless of the amount of light that illuminates it; also called *whiteness constancy*. (p. 316)

limbic system An interconnected set of brain structures (including the amygdala and hippocampus) that form a circuit wrapped around the thalamus and basal ganglia, underneath the cerebral cortex. These structures are especially important for the regulation of emotion and motivation and are involved in the formation of long-term memories. (p. 152)

linear perspective A pictorial cue for perceiving depth in which the convergence of parallel lines indicates the distance of objects. Parallel lines appear to converge as they become more distant. (p. 312)

linguistic relativity Whorf's theory that people who have different native languages perceive the world differently and think differently from each other because of their different languages. (p. 400)

localization of function The concept that different, localizable parts of the brain serve different, specifiable functions in the control of mental experience and behavior. (p. 7)

locus In genetics, a position on a chromosome that contains the DNA of a single gene. (p. 58)

locus of control According to Rotter, a person's perception of the typical source of control over rewards. *Internal locus of control* refers to the perception that people control their own rewards through their own behavior, and *external locus of control* refers to the perception that rewards are controlled by external circumstances or fate. (p. 600)

long-term memory In the modal model of the mind, information that is retained in the mind for long periods (often throughout life). For contrasts, see *sensory memory, working memory*. (p. 328)

long-term potentiation (LTP) A process by which repeated activation of synapses results in strengthening of those synapses. (p. 172)

loudness The quality of the psychological experience (sensation) of a sound that is most directly related to the amplitude of the physical sound stimulus. (p. 254)

LTP See *long-term potentiation*.

M

maintaining causes of a mental disorder Those consequences of a mental disorder—such as the way other people treat the person who has it—that help keep the disorder going once it begins. See also *precipitating* and *predisposing causes of a mental disorder*. (p. 618)

maintenance rehearsal Any active mental process by which a person strives to hold information in short-term memory for a period of time. For contrast, see *encoding rehearsal*. (p. 341)

major depression A mental disorder characterized by severe depression that lasts essentially without remission for at least 2 weeks. (p. 626)

materialism Hobbes's theory that nothing exists but matter and energy. For contrast, see *dualism*. (p. 6)

mean The arithmetic average of a set of scores, determined by adding the scores and dividing the sum by the number of scores. (pp. 39, A-3)

median The center score in a set of scores that have been rank-ordered. (pp. 39, A-3)

medulla The lowest portion of the brainstem, bounded at one end by the spinal cord and at the other by the pons. It is responsible, with the pons, for organizing reflexes more complex than spinal reflexes. (p. 150)

meiosis The form of cell division involved in producing egg or sperm cells, which results in cells that are genetically dissimilar and that each have half the number of chromosomes of the original cell. (p. 56)

melatonin A hormone secreted by the pineal gland that contributes to the daily rhythm of sleep and arousal. (p. 219)

memory 1. The mind's ability to retain information over time. 2. Information retained in the mind over time. (p. 326)

memory stores In cognitive psychology, hypothetical constructs that are conceived of as places where information is held in the mind. (p. 326)

mental disorder A disturbance in a person's emotions, drives, thought processes, or behavior that (a) involves serious and relatively prolonged distress and/or impairment in ability to function, (b) is not simply a normal response to some event or set of events in the person's environment, and (c) is not explainable as an effect of poverty, prejudice, or other social forces that prevent the person from behaving adaptively, nor as a deliberate decision to act in a way that is contrary to the norms of society. (p. 611)

mental set A habit of perception or thought, stemming from previous experience, that can either help or hinder a person in solving a new problem. (p. 395)

method of magnitude estimation Stevens's psychophysical method in which people are asked to estimate the magnitude of a subjective experience (such as the perceived loudness of a sound), usually by assigning a number to it. (p. 268)

midbrain The upper portion of the brainstem, bounded at its lower end by the pons and at its upper end by the thalamus, that contains neural centers that organize basic movement patterns. (p. 150)

middle ear The air-filled cavity separated from the outer ear by the eardrum; its main structures are three ossicles (tiny bones) that vibrate in response to sound waves and stimulate the inner ear. (p. 256)

mind 1. The entire set of an individual's sensations, perceptions, memories, thoughts, dreams, motives, emotional feelings, and other subjective experiences. (p. 3) 2. In cognitive psychology, the set of hypothesized information-processing steps that analyze stimulus information and organize behavioral responses. (pp. 17–18)

mitosis The form of cell division involved in normal body growth, which produces cells that are genetically identical to each other. (p. 56)

MMPI The *Minnesota Multiphasic Personality Inventory*. A psychometric personality test that is commonly used for clinical assessment. See *assessment, psychometric personality test*. (p. 660)

modal model of the mind A depiction of the mind as a set of memory storage compartments and control processes for manipulating and moving information. It has long served as the standard framework for thinking about the human mind. (p. 326)

mode The most frequently occurring score in a set of scores; in a frequency distribution, the interval that contains the highest frequency of scores. (p. A-3)

modeling The process of teaching a person what to do, or how to do it, by having the person watch another person (the model) engage in that behavior. (p. 686)

monogamy A mating system in which one female and one male bond only with each other. For contrast, see *polyandry, polygyny, polygynandry*. (p. 81)

monozygotic twins See *identical twins*.

mood disorders A class of mental disorders characterized by prolonged or extreme disruptions in mood. It includes the *depressive disorders* and *bipolar disorders*. (p. 626)

moon illusion The illusion by which the moon appears larger when seen near the horizon and smaller when seen near the zenith, even though it is objectively the same size and distance from the viewer in either location. (p. 315)

morphemes The smallest meaningful units of a verbal language; words, prefixes, or suffixes that have discrete meanings. (p. 435)

motion parallax The cue for depth perception that stems from the changed view one has of a scene or object when one's head moves sideways to the scene or object; the farther away an object is, the smaller is the change in view. (p. 311)

motivation The entire constellation of factors, some inside the organism and some outside, that cause an individual to behave in a particular way at a particular time. See also *incentive, motivational state*. (p. 187)

motivational state An internal, reversible condition in an individual that orients the individual toward one or another type of goal (such as food or water). This condition is not observed directly but is inferred from the individual's behavior; also called a *drive*. (p. 187)

motor neuron A neuron that carries messages from the brain or spinal cord, through a nerve, to a muscle or gland. (p. 144)

Müller-Lyer illusion A visual size illusion in which a horizontal line looks longer if attached at each end to an outward-extending, V-shaped object, and looks shorter if attached at each end to an inward-extending, V-shaped object. (p. 314)

mutations Errors that occasionally and unpredictably occur during DNA replication, producing a "replica" that is different from the original. Mutations are believed to be the original source of all genetic variability. (p. 67)

myelin sheath A casing of fatty cells wrapped tightly around the axon of some neurons. (p. 144)

N

nativism The idea that certain elementary ideas are innate to the human mind and do not need to be gained through experience; the philosophical approach to understanding the mind that is based on that idea. For contrast, see *empiricism*. (p. 6)

natural selection The selective breeding that results from the obstacles to reproduction that are imposed by the natural environment; it is the driving force of evolution. See *selective breeding*. (p. 66)

naturalistic fallacy The mistaken belief that whatever is natural (and particularly whatever is a product of natural selection) is right, good, or moral. (p. 89)

naturalistic observation Any data-collection procedure in which the researcher records subjects' ongoing behavior in a natural setting, without interfering with that behavior. (p. 37)

nature-nurture debate The long-standing controversy as to whether the differences among people are principally due to their genetic differences (nature) or differences in their past and present environment (nurture). (p. 377)

negative contrast effect In operant conditioning, the decline in response rate, when the size of a reinforcer (or reward) is reduced, to a rate below that which occurs for subjects that had been receiving the smaller reinforcer all along. For contrast, see *positive contrast effect*. (p. 124)

negative punishment In operant conditioning, the type of punishment in which the *removal* of a stimulus (such as taking food or money) when a response occurs decreases the likelihood that the response will recur. For contrast, see *positive punishment*. (p. 115)

negative reinforcement In operant conditioning, the condition in which a response results in *removal* of a negative reinforcer. See *negative reinforcer*. (p. 115)

negative reinforcer In operant conditioning, a stimulus (such as electric shock or loud noise) that is *removed* after a response and whose removal increases the likelihood that the response will recur. (p. 115)

negative symptoms The class of symptoms of schizophrenia that are characterized by the absence of, or reduction in, expected behaviors, thoughts, feelings, and drives. (p. 643)

nerve A large bundle containing the axons of many neurons. Located in the peripheral nervous system, nerves connect the central nervous system with muscles, glands, and sensory organs. (p. 146)

neural convergence In a sensory system, the funneling of the activity of many receptor cells upon fewer sensory neurons; high convergence increases sensitivity at the expense of acuity. More generally, any case in which a single neuron receives synaptic input from more than one other neuron. (p. 281)

neurohormone A chemical substance that is similar to a neurotransmitter in that it is secreted from the axon terminals of neurons but is classed as a hormone because it is secreted into blood vessels rather than onto other neurons. (p. 178)

neurons Single cells in the nervous system that are specialized for carrying information rapidly from one place to another and/or integrating information from various sources; also called *nerve cells*. (p. 144)

neurotransmitter A chemical substance released from the axon terminal of a neuron, at a synapse, that influences the activity of another neuron, a muscle cell, or a glandular cell; also called a *transmitter*. (p. 144) *nonregulatory drive* Any motivational state (such as the sex drive) that serves some function *other than* that of preserving some constancy of the body's internal environment. For contrast, see *regulatory drive*. (p. 190)

normal distribution A bell-shaped frequency distribution in which the mean, median, and mode are identical and the frequency of scores tapers off symmetrically on both sides, as defined by a specific mathematical equation. See *frequency distribution*. (pp. 64, A-2)

normative influence The class of social influence that derives from people's concern about what others will think of them if they behave in a certain way or express a certain belief. For contrast, see *informational influence*. (p. 545)

nucleus In neuroanatomy, a cluster of cell bodies of neurons within the central nervous system (not to be confused with the cell nucleus within each cell). (p. 150)

O

object permanence Piaget's term for the understanding that an object still exists even when it is out of view. (p. 414)

objective questionnaire In clinical assessment or in personality research, a questionnaire on which a client or research subject checks off adjectives or statements that describe his or her own behaviors, thoughts, or feelings. (p. 659)

observational learning Learning by watching others. See also *modeling*. (p. 128)

observational method Any data-collection procedure in which the researcher directly observes the behavior of interest rather than relying on subjects' self-descriptions. (p. 37)

observer-expectancy effect Any bias in research results that derives from the researcher's desire or expectation that a subject or set of subjects will behave in a certain way. See *bias, subject-expectancy effect*. (p. 44)

obsessive-compulsive disorder A mental disorder characterized by a repeated, disturbing, irrational thought (the *obsession*) that can only be terminated (temporarily) by performing some action (the *compulsion*). (p. 623)

occipital lobe The rearmost lobe of the cerebral cortex, bounded in front by the temporal and parietal lobes; it contains the visual area of the brain. (p. 154)

occlusion A pictorial cue for perceiving depth in which the closer object occludes (cuts off) part of the view of the more distant object. (p. 311)

operant conditioning A training or learning process by which the consequence of a behavioral response affects the likelihood that the individual will produce that response again; also called *instrumental conditioning*. (pp. 106, 109)

operant response Any behavioral response that produces some reliable effect on the environment that influences the likelihood that the individual will produce that response again; also called *instrumental response*. (pp. 106, 109)

operation Piaget's term for a reversible action that can be performed either in reality or mentally upon some object or set of objects. For example, rolling a clay ball into a clay sausage is an operation, because the sausage can be rolled back again to form the ball. (p. 418)

opponent-process theory of color vision A theory designed by Hering to explain the law of complementarity, it holds that units (neurons) that mediate the perception of color are excited by one range of wavelengths and inhibited by another (complementary) range of wavelengths. According to the theory, such units cancel out the perception of color when two complementary wavelength ranges are superimposed. See also *law of complementarity*. (p. 287)

optic nerve The cranial nerve that contains the sensory neurons for vision, which run from the eye's retina into the brain. (p. 278)

outer ear The pinna (the visible, external portion of the ear) and the auditory canal (the air-filled opening that extends inward from the pinna to the middle ear). (p. 255)

overjustification effect The phenomenon in which a person who initially performs a task for no reward (except the enjoyment of the task) becomes less likely to perform that task for no reward after a period during which he or she has been rewarded for performing it. (p. 125)

P

panic disorder A mental disorder characterized by the repeated occurrence of panic attacks at unpredictable times and with no clear relationship to environmental events. Each attack involves an intense feeling of terror, which usually lasts several minutes and is accompanied by signs of high physiological arousal. (p. 624)

parallel processing In perception, the early (unconscious) steps in the analysis of sensory information that act simultaneously on all (or at least many) of the stimulus elements that are available at any given moment. For contrast, see *serial processing*. (p. 298)

parasympathetic division of the autonomic motor system The set of motor neurons that act upon visceral muscles and glands and mediate many of the body's regenerative, growth-promoting, and energy-conserving functions. For contrast, see *sympathetic division of the autonomic motor system*. (p. 148)

parental investment The time, energy, and risk to survival involved in producing, feeding, and otherwise caring for each offspring. (p. 82)

parietal lobe The lobe of the cerebral cortex that lies in front of the occipital lobe, above the temporal lobe, and behind the frontal lobe; it contains the somatosensory area of the brain. (p. 154)

partial reinforcement In operant conditioning, any condition in which the response sometimes produces a reinforcer and sometimes does not. See *reinforcer*. (p. 111)

percentile rank For any single score in a set of scores, the percentage of scores in the set that are equal to or lower than that score. (pp. A-5 to A-6)

perception The recognition, organization, and meaningful interpretation of sensory stimuli. For contrast, see *sensation*. (pp. 233, 275)

peripheral nervous system The entire set of cranial and spinal nerves that connect the central nervous system (brain and spinal cord) to the body's sensory organs, muscles, and glands. (p. 144)

permanent effects of a drug Irreversible forms of bodily damage, including brain damage, that result from drug use. (p. 637)

person bias The tendency to attribute a person's behavior too much to the person's inner characteristics (personality) and not enough to the environmental situation. Sometimes called the fundamental attribution error. For contrast, see *situation bias*. (p. 499)

person perception In social psychology, the processes by which people perceive and understand each other and themselves. (p. 497) *personal identity* The portion of the self-concept that pertains to the self as a distinct, separate individual. For contrast, see *social identity*. (p. 514)

personal myth The ever-changing self-told story of an individual that gives a sense of direction and meaning to one's life. (p. 605)

personality The relatively consistent patterns of thought, feeling, and behavior that characterize each person as a unique individual. (p. 573)

PET See *positron emission tomography*.

phenomenological reality Humanistic theorists' term for each person's conscious understanding of his or her world. (p. 603)

phenomenology The study of subjective mental experiences; a theme of humanistic theories of personality. (p. 603)

phenotype The observable properties of an individual's body and behavior. See also *genotype*. (p. 55)

pheromone A chemical that is released by an animal and that acts on other members of the species to promote some specific behavioral or physiological response. (p. 241)

phobia Any mental disorder characterized by a strong, irrational fear of some particular category of object or event. (p. 622)

phonemes The various vowel and consonant sounds that provide the basis for a spoken language. (p. 262)

phonological loop In Baddeley's theory, a component of working memory responsible for holding verbal information. (p. 336)

photoreceptors Specialized light-detecting cells connected to the nervous system in many multicellular animals. (p. 276) In humans and other vertabrates, the photoreceptors are rods and cones.

physiological psychology The study of the physiological mechanisms, in the brain and elsewhere, that mediate behavior and psychological experiences. (p. 17)

pictorial cues for depth perception The depth cues that operate not only when viewing real scenes but also when viewing pictures. They include *occlusion, relative image size for familiar objects, linear perspective, texture gradient, differential lighting of surfaces,* and (for outdoor scenes) *position relative to the horizon.* (pp. 311–312)

pidgin language A primitive system of communication that emerges when people with different native languages colonize the same region; it uses words from the various native languages and has either no or minimal grammatical structure. See also *creole language*. (p. 442)

pineal gland An endocrine gland, located above the brainstem, that secretes the hormone melatonin. (p. 218)

pitch The quality of the psychological experience (sensation) of a sound that is most related to the frequency of the physical sound stimulus. (p. 254)

PKU Abbreviation for *phenylketonuria*, a genetic disorder caused by a recessive gene and characterized by the body's inability to break down phenylalanine (an amino acid found in most protein-containing foods). (p. 62)

placebo In drug studies, an inactive substance given to subjects assigned to the nondrug group. More generally, any treatment that alters a person's behavior or feelings through the power of suggestion. (p. 46)

polyandry A mating system in which one female bonds with more than one male. For contrast, see *monogamy, polygyny, polygynandry*. (p. 81)

polygenic characteristic Any trait or characteristic for which the observed variation is affected by many genes. (p. 64)

polygynandry A mating system in which members of a group consisting of more than one male and more than one female mate with one another. For contrast, see *monogamy, polygyny, polyandry*. (p. 81)

polygyny A mating system in which one male bonds with more than one female. For contrast, see *monogamy, polyandry, polygynandry*. (p. 81)

pons The portion of the brainstem that is bounded at its lower end by the medulla and its upper end by the midbrain and is responsible, with the medulla, for organizing reflexes more complex than spinal reflexes. (p. 150)

Ponzo illusion A visual size illusion in which two converging lines cause objects between the two lines to look larger near the converging ends of the lines and smaller near the diverging ends. (p. 314)

position relative to the horizon A pictorial cue for perceiving depth in which objects nearer the horizon seem farther away than objects displaced from the horizon. (p. 312)

positive contrast effect In operant conditioning, the increase in response rate, when the size of the reinforcer (or reward) is increased, to a rate that increases above that which occurs for subjects that had been receiving the larger reinforcer all along. For contrast, see *negative contrast effect*. (p. 124)

positive punishment In operant conditioning, the type of punishment in which the *presentation* of a stimulus (such as an electric shock or scolding) when a response occurs decreases the likelihood that the response will recur. For contrast, see *negative punishment*. (p. 115)

positive reinforcement In operant conditioning, the condition in which a response results in a positive reinforcer. (p. 115)

positive reinforcer In operant conditioning, a stimulus (such as food or money) that is presented after a response and that increases the likelihood that the response will recur. (p. 115)

positron emission tomography (PET) A method for visually displaying brain activity that is based upon the uptake of a radioactive form of oxygen into active areas of the brain. (p. 163)

posttraumatic stress disorder A mental disorder that is directly and explicitly tied to a particular traumatic incident or set of incidents (such as torture) that the affected person has experienced. (p. 625)

power law In psychophysics, Stevens's idea that the intensity of a sensation is directly proportional to the intensity of the physical stimulus raised by a constant power. For contrast, see *Fechner's law*. (p. 269)

preattentive processing The analysis, at an unconscious level, in which the mind determines which stimuli are worth passing into working memory. (p. 331)

precipitating causes of a mental disorder The events that most immediately bring on a mental disorder in a person who is sufficiently predisposed for the disorder. See also *maintaining* and *predisposing causes of a mental disorder*. (p. 618)

predisposing causes of a mental disorder Those conditions that are in place well before the onset of a mental disorder and that make the person susceptible to the disorder. They may include genetic predisposition, early childhood experiences, and the sociocultural environment in which one develops. See also *maintaining* and *precipitating causes of a mental disorder*. (p. 618)

preoperational scheme In Piaget's theory, mental structures that permit the child to symbolize objects and events that are absent, but do not permit the child to think about the operations that can be performed on objects. See also *operation, schemes*. (p. 419)

primary motor area An area in the rear part of the frontal lobe of the cerebral cortex that is directly involved in the control of movements, especially finely coordinated movements of small muscles, as in the fingers and vocal apparatus. (p. 154)

primary reinforcer In operant conditioning, a stimulus, such as food or water, that is innately reinforcing. See *reinforcer*. For contrast, see *secondary reinforcer*. (p. 114)

primary sensory areas Specialized areas of the cerebral cortex that receive input from sensory nerves and tracts by way of the relay nuclei in the thalamus. They include the visual area (in the occipital lobe), auditory area (in the temporal lobe), and somatosensory area (in the parietal lobe). (p. 154)

primary visual cortex The area in the rearmost part of the occipital lobe that receives input from the optic nerves (by way of the thalamus) and sends output to other visual-processing areas of the brain. (p. 293)

priming The implicit memory process by which a stimulus (the priming stimulus) activates (makes more retrievable) one or more memories that already exist in a person's mind. See *implicit memory*. (p. 334)

prisoner's dilemma games A class of laboratory games in which the tendency to compete can be pitted against the tendency to cooperate. In such games, the highest combined payoff to the two players occurs if both choose the cooperative response, but the highest individual payoff goes to a player who chooses the competitive response on a play in which the other chooses the cooperative response. (p. 560)

proactive interference The loss of memory for one set of information that results from the prior learning of another (usually similar) set of information. For contrast, see *retroactive interference*. (p. 347)

procedural memory The class of implicit memory that enables a person to perform specific learned skills or habitual responses. See *implicit memory*. (p. 357)

projection The defense mechanism by which a person consciously experiences his or her own unconscious emotion or wish as though it belongs to someone else or to some part of the environment. (p. 597)

projective tests Psychological tests involving free association, in which the person being tested is presented with an ambiguous stimulus and is asked to tell a story or to say quickly, without logical explanation, what the stimulus looks like. See also *free association, projection*. (p. 661)

prosopagnosia A deficit in the ability to recognize faces; generally results from damage to a particular part of the lower temporal cortex. (p. 295)

proximate explanations Explanations of behavior that state the immediate environmental conditions or the mechanisms within the individual that cause the behavior to occur. For contrast, see *ultimate explanations*. (p. 69)

proximity principle See *Gestalt principles of grouping*.

psychoactive-substance-use disorder The class of mental disorders characterized by drug abuse or dependence. (p. 636)

psychoanalysis 1. The theory of the mind developed by Freud, which emphasizes the roles of unconscious mental processes, early childhood experiences, and the drives of sex and aggression in personality formation; also called *psychoanalytic theory*. (pp. 18, 594) 2. Freud's therapy technique in which such methods as free association, dream analysis, and analysis of transference are used to learn about the person's unconscious mind; the goal is to make the unconscious conscious. (p. 670)

psychodynamic theories of personality Any theory that describes personality and its development in terms of inner mental forces that are often in conflict with one another and are shaped by experiences in early childhood. (p. 594)

psychodynamic therapy Any approach to psychotherapy that is based on the premise that psychological problems are manifestations of inner mental conflicts and that conscious awareness of those conflicts is a key to recovery. See also *psychoanalysis*. (p. 670)

psychological reactance A social psychological phenomenon in which too much pressure to respond a certain way pushes the person to behave in the opposite way. (p. 554)

psychology The science of behavior and the mind. (p. 3)

psychometric personality test An objective questionnaire that has been developed through systematic, statistically based methods (usually involving factor analysis) to assess a wide range of personality characteristics. See *MMPI*. (p. 660)

psychophysics The scientific study of the relationship between physical characteristics of stimuli and the psychological (sensory) experiences that the stimuli produce. (p. 263)

psychotherapy Any formal, theory-based, systematic treatment for mental problems or disorders that uses psychological means (such as dialogue or training) rather than physiological means (such as drugs) and is conducted by a trained therapist. (p. 669)

punishment In operant conditioning, the process through which the consequence of a response *decreases* the likelihood that the response will recur. For contrast, see *reinforcement*. (p. 115)

pupil The hole in the center of the iris of the eye through which light passes. See *iris*. (p. 276)

Q

qualitative variation Variation in the precise kind of energy present. (p. 236)

quantitative variation Variation in the amount or intensity of energy present. (p. 236)

questionnaire A self-report method of data collection or clinical assessment method in which the individual being studied (or assessed) checks off items on a printed list, answers multiple-choice questions, or writes out answers to essay questions aimed at producing a self-description. (p. 37)

R

rational-emotive therapy (RET) A type of cognitive therapy developed by Albert Ellis, based on the idea that people's irrational interpretations of their experiences, not the experiences themselves, cause their negative emotions. (p. 678)

rationalization The defense mechanism by which a person uses conscious reasoning to justify or explain away his or her harmful or irrational behaviors or thoughts. (p. 597)

reaction formation The defense mechanism by which the mind turns a frightening wish into its safer opposite. (p. 597)

receptive field For any neuron in the visual system, the portion of the retina that, when stimulated by light, results in a change in electrical activity in the neuron. More generally, a property of a neuron in any sensory system; it is the area of sensory tissue (or set of receptor cells) that, when stimulated by an appropriate stimulus, produces an electrical change in the neuron in question. (p. 280)

receptor potential The electrical change that occurs in a receptor cell (such as a rod or cone in the eye, or a hair cell in the inner ear) in response to the energy of a physical stimulus (such as light or sound). (p. 236)

receptors Specialized biological structures—which in some cases are separate cells and in other cases are the sensitive tips of sensory neurons—that respond to physical stimuli by producing electrical changes that can initiate neural impulses. (p. 235)

recessive gene A gene that will produce its observable effects only in the homozygous condition, that is, only when paired with a gene that is identical to it. (p. 59)

reciprocity norm The widespread sense of obligation that people have to return favors. (p. 553)

reciprocity theory of altruism The sociobiological theory that apparent acts of altruism have come about through natural selection because they are actually forms of long-term cooperation rather than true altruism. See also *altruism, cooperation.* (p. 88)

reference group A group of people with whom an individual compares himself or herself for the purpose of self-evaluation. See also *social comparison.* (p. 511)

reflex A simple, relatively automatic, stimulus-response sequence mediated by the nervous system. (p. 98)

reflexology An approach to understanding human behavior, developed by physiologists in the nineteenth century, that was based on the premise that all behavior occurs through reflexes. (p. 6)

regulatory drive Any motivational state (such as hunger or thirst) that helps maintain some constancy of the body's internal environment that is necessary for survival. For contrast, see *nonregulatory drive.* (p. 190)

reinforcement In operant conditioning, the presentation of a positive reinforcer or removal of a negative reinforcer when a response occurs, which increases the likelihood that the subject will repeat the response. See *negative reinforcer, positive reinforcer.* For contrast, see *punishment.* (p. 115)

reinforcer In operant conditioning, any stimulus change that occurs after a response and tends to *increase* the likelihood that the response will be repeated. See *negative reinforcer, positive reinforcer.* (p. 109)

relative image size for familiar objects A pictorial cue for perceiving depth in which one infers the distance of familiar objects on the basis of their known actual sizes and the size of their retinal images. (p. 311)

reliability The capacity of a measurement system to produce similar results each time it is used with a particular subject or set of subjects under a particular set of conditions. (p. 43)

REM (rapid-eye-movement) sleep The recurring stage of sleep during which the EEG resembles that of an alert person, rapid eye movements occur, the large muscles of the body are most relaxed, and true dreams are most likely to occur. It is sometimes called *emergent stage 1.* For contrast, see *slow-wave sleep.* (p. 210)

repression The defense mechanism by which the mind prevents anxiety-provoking ideas from becoming conscious. (p. 597)

resistance Attempts by a patient to avoid bringing unconscious memories or wishes into consciousness. (p. 672)

resting potential The constant electrical charge that exists across the membrane of an inactive neuron. (p. 166)

retina A thin membrane of cells that lines the rear interior of the eyeball; it contains the receptor cells for vision (rods and cones). (p. 276)

retrieval In the modal model of the mind, the mental process by which long-term memories are brought into working memory, where they become part of the flow of thought. See also *long-term memory, working memory.* (p. 328)

retrieval cue A word, phrase, or other stimulus that helps one retrieve a specific item of information from long-term memory. (p. 349)

retroactive interference The loss of memory for one set of information that results from the subsequent learning of another (usually similar) set of information. For contrast, see *proactive interference.* (p. 347)

reversible figure A visual stimulus (usually a picture) in which any given part is seen sometimes as the *figure* and other times as the *ground.* (p. 302)

rhodopsin The photochemical in rods that undergoes structural changes in response to light and thereby initiates the transduction process for rod vision. (p. 278)

rods The class of receptor cells for vision that are located in the peripheral portions of the retina (away from the fovea) and are most important for seeing in very dim light. For contrast, see *cones.* (p. 272)

rod vision The low-acuity, high-sensitivity, noncolor vision that occurs in dim light and is mediated by rods in the retina of the eye. For contrast, see *cone vision.* (p. 278)

Rorschach test A widely use projective test in which symmetrical inkblots are presented and the person is asked what the inkblots look like. (p. 661)

S

schema The mental representation of a concept; the information stored in long-term memory that allows a person to identify a group of different events or items as members of the same category. (p. 352)

schemes Piaget's term for the mental entities that provide the basis for thought and that change in a stagelike way through development. They contain information about the actions that one can perform on objects, either in reality or symbolically in the mind. (p. 418)

schizophrenia A serious class of mental disorder that is characterized by disrupted perceptual and thought processes, often including hallucinations and delusions. (p. 642)

science An approach to answering questions that is based on the systematic collection and logical analysis of objectively observable data. (p. 3)

script A variety of schema that represents in memory the temporal organization of a category of event (such as the sequence of occurrences at a typical birthday party). (p. 352)

secondary reinforcer In operant conditioning, a stimulus that has acquired reinforcing capacity through previous training, usually through serving as a discriminative stimulus for some other reinforced response. See *reinforcer.* For contrast, see *primary reinforcer.* (p. 114)

selective breeding The mating of those members of a strain of animals or plants that manifest a particular characteristic, which may or may not be done deliberately, to affect the genetic makeup of future generations of that strain; can be used to assess *heritability.* (p. 64)

self-actualization In humanistic psychology, the fulfillment of drives that go beyond one's survival needs and pertain to psychological growth, creativity, and self-expression. (p. 604)

self-conscious emotions The feelings of guilt, shame, embarrassment, and pride, which are linked to thoughts about the self or one's own actions. (p. 536)

self-efficacy A person's subjective sense of his or her own ability to perform a particular task or set of tasks. (p. 601)

self-monitoring A personality characteristic defined as sensitivity to other people's immediate reactions to oneself, combined with a desire and ability to control those reactions. (p. 544)

self-report method A data-collection method in which the people being studied are asked to rate or describe their own behaviors or mental states. See also *interview, questionnaire.* (p. 37)

self-serving attributional bias The tendency of people to attribute their successes to their own qualities and their failures to the situation. (p. 513)

semantic memory One's storehouse of explicit general knowledge, that is, of knowledge that can be expressed in words and is not mentally tied to specific experiences in one's own life. Semantic memory includes, but is not limited to, one's knowledge of word meanings. For contrasts, see *episodic memory, implicit memory.* (p. 357)

sensation The psychological experience associated with a sound, light, or other simple stimulus and the initial information-processing steps by which sense organs and neural pathways take in stimulus information from the environment. For contrast, see *perception.* (p. 233)

sensorimotor scheme In Piaget's theory, the type of mental structure that enables an infant to act on objects that are immediately present but does not permit thought about objects that are absent. See also *schemes.* (p. 419)

sensorineural deafness Deafness due to damage to the cochlea, the hair cells, or the auditory neurons. (p. 257)

sensory adaptation The temporary decrease in sensitivity to sensory stimulation that occurs when a sensory system is stimulated for a period of time, and the temporary increase in sensitivity that occurs when a sensory system is not stimulated for a period of time. See also *dark adaptation, light adaptation.* (p. 237)

sensory areas of the cerebral cortex See *primary sensory areas.*

sensory memory In the modal model of the mind, the memory trace that preserves the original information in a sensory stimulus for a brief period (less than 1 second for sights and up to 3 seconds for sounds) following the termination of the stimulus; it is experienced as if one is still sensing the original stimulus. For contrasts, see *long-term memory, working memory.* (p. 327)

sensory neuron A neuron that carries messages from a sensory organ, through a nerve, into the brain or spinal cord. (pp. 144, 235)

serial processing The steps in the processing of sensory information that operate sequentially, an item at a time, on the available sensory information. For contrast, see *parallel processing.* (p. 298)

shape constancy The tendency to perceive an object as having the same shape even though the retinal image changes shape when the object is viewed from different positions. (p. 316)

shaping An operant-conditioning procedure in which successively closer approximations to the desired response are reinforced until the response finally occurs. See *reinforcement.* (p. 111)

short-term memory See *working memory.* (p. 327)

sign stimulus Ethologists' term for any stimulus (well-defined environmental event) that elicits a fixed action pattern. See *fixed action pattern.* (p. 72)

similarity principle See *Gestalt principles of grouping.*

situation bias The tendency to attribute a person's behavior too much to the environmental situation and not enough to the person's inner characteristics. For contrast, see *person bias.* (p. 501)

size constancy The perceptual ability to see an object as the same size despite change in image size as it moves farther away or closer. (p. 313)

skeletal motor system The set of peripheral motor neurons that act upon skeletal muscles. (p. 147)

skeletal muscles The muscles attached to bones, which produce externally observable movements of the body when contracted. For contrast, see *visceral muscles.* (p. 147)

slow-wave sleep Stages 2, 3, and 4 of sleep, characterized by the prominent occurrence of slow (delta) waves in the EEG. For contrast, see *REM (rapid-eye-movement) sleep.* (p. 211)

social-cognitive theories of personality Theories of personality that emphasize the roles of beliefs and habits of thought that are acquired through one's unique experiences in the social environment. Also called *social-learning* or *social-cognitive-learning theories.* (p. 599)

social comparison Any process in which an individual evaluates his or her own abilities, characteristics, ideas, or achievements by comparing them with those of other people. See also *reference group.* (p. 511)

social development The person's developing capacity for social relationships and the effects of those relationships on further development. (p. 451)

social dilemma A situation in which a particular action will (a) benefit the individual who takes it, (b) harm the individuals who don't, and (c) cause more harm than benefit to everyone if everyone takes it. See *prisoner's dilemma games.* (p. 559)

social ecology The entire network of interactions and interdependencies among people, institutions, and cultural constructs to which the developing person must adapt psychologically. (p. 454)

social facilitation The tendency to perform a task better in front of others than when alone. For contrast, see *social interference.* (p. 541)

social identity The portion of the self-concept that pertains to the social categories or groups of which the person is a part. For contrast, see *personal identity.* (p. 514)

social impact theory Latané's social psychological theory concerning the amount of social impact that the actual or imagined presence of others will have on a person. (p. 539)

social interference The tendency to perform a task worse in front of others than when alone. For contrast, see *social facilitation.* (p. 541)

socialization The process whereby infants and children learn, from caregivers and other people, their culture's values, morals, and manners. (p. 463)

social phobia Any phobia in which the basic fear is of being scrutinized or evaluated by other people. For contrast, see *specific phobia.* (p. 622)

social pressure The entire set of psychological forces that are exerted on an individual by other people or by the individual's beliefs about other people. (p. 539)

social psychology The branch of psychology that attempts to understand how the behavior and subjective experiences of individuals are influenced by the actual or imagined presence of other people. (pp. 20, 497)

social referencing The process by which infants use the nonverbal emotional expressions of a caregiver as cues to guide their behavior. (p. 412)

social skills training In behavior therapy, a direct method for training people to interact more effectively with other people. See also *assertiveness training*. (p. 686)

sociobiology The study of social systems in animals from an evolutionary perspective. (p. 81)

somatization disorder A category of somatoform disorder that is characterized by vague, unverifiable complaints about many different medical conditions. (p. 633)

somatoform disorders The class of mental disorders in which the person experiences bodily ailments in the absence of any physical disease that could cause them. It includes *conversion disorder* and *somatization disorder*. (p. 632)

somatosensation The set of senses that derive from the whole body—such as from the skin, muscles, and tendons—as opposed to those senses that come from the special sensory organs of the head. (p. 147)

span of short-term memory The number of pronounceable items of information (such as single, randomly chosen digits) that a person can retain in short-term (working) memory at any given time through rote rehearsal. (p. 337)

spatial frequency The number of repetitions, per unit distance, of the repeating elements of the image of a pattern on the retina of the eye. (p. 292)

species-typical behavior Any behavior pattern that is so characteristic of a given species of animal that it can be used to help identify that species. (p. 71)

specific phobia Any phobia in which the feared object is a well-defined category of object (such as snakes) or environmental situations (such as heights) other than other people. See also *phobia*. For contrast, see *social phobia*. (p. 622)

spinal nerve A nerve that extends directly from the spinal cord. See *nerve*. For contrast, see *cranial nerve*. (p. 147)

spontaneous recovery In both classical and operant conditioning, the return—due to passage of time with no further testing or training—of a conditioned response that had previously undergone extinction. (p. 103)

standard deviation A measure of the variability in a set of scores, determined by taking the square root of the variance. (pp. 39, A-5)

standardized score A score that is expressed in terms of the number of standard deviations the original score is from the mean of the original scores. (p. A-6)

statistical significance A statistical statement of how small the likelihood is that an obtained result occurred by chance. By convention, research findings are said to be *statistically significant* if the probability is less than 5 percent that the data could have come out as they did if the research hypothesis were wrong. (p. 41)

stereotypes Mental concepts that people have for particular groups of people (such as races or ethnic groups) that exaggerate the differences between groups, minimize the differences among individual members of the same group, and may provide a basis for prejudice and discrimination. (p. 505)

strange-situation test A test of an infant's attachment to a particular familiar person, in which the infant's behavior is observed in an unfamiliar room while the familiar person and a stranger move in and out of the room in a preplanned way. (p. 458)

stress-induced analgesia The reduced sensitivity to pain that occurs when one is subjected to highly arousing (stressful) conditions. (p. 252)

Stroop interference effect Named after J. Ridley Stroop, the effect by which a printed color word (such as the word *red*) interferes with a person's ability to name the color of ink in which the word is printed if the ink color is not the same as the color named by the word. (p. 335)

structuralism A school of psychological thought, founded principally by Titchener, whose goal was to identify the basic elements of the mind and to determine how those elements combine with one another to produce more complex thoughts. For contrast, see *functionalism*. (p. 10)

subject-expectancy effect Any bias in research results that derives from subjects' expectations or beliefs about how they should feel or behave in response to the variables imposed in the study. See also *bias, observer-expectancy effect*. (p. 46)

sublimation See *displacement*.

subtractive color mixing The mixing of pigments whereby each pigment absorbs a different set of wavelengths of light that would otherwise be reflected to the eye. For contrast, see *additive color mixing*. (p. 282)

superordinate goals The goals shared by two or more groups, which tend to foster cooperation among the groups. (p. 566)

surface traits Traits (personality characteristics) that are most directly inferred from a person's external behavior. See also *central traits*. (p. 574)

sympathetic division of the autonomic motor system The set of motor neurons that act upon visceral muscles and glands and mediate many of the body's responses to stressful stimulation, preparing the body for possible "fight or flight." For contrast, see *parasympathetic division of the autonomic motor system*. (p. 147)

symptom In clinical psychology or psychiatry, any characteristic of a person's actions, thoughts, or feelings that could be a potential indicator of a mental disorder. (p. 611)

synapse The functional connection through which neural activity in the axon of one neuron influences the action of another neuron, a muscle cell, or a glandular cell. (p. 144)

syndrome In clinical psychology or psychiatry, the entire pattern of symptoms manifested in an individual's behavior and self-statements, which, collectively, may constitute evidence of a mental disorder. (p. 611)

syntax The set of grammatical rules for a given language that specifies how words can be arranged to produce phrases and sentences. (p. 436)

systematic desensitization A behavior therapy technique for eliminating phobias or fears in which the client is first trained to relax and then to imagine various versions of the feared object or scene, progressing from weak to stronger forms of it, while remaining relaxed. (p. 683)

T

temporal lobe The lobe of the cerebral cortex that lies in front of the occipital lobe and below the parietal and frontal lobes and that contains the auditory area of the brain. (p. 154) *temporal-lobe amnesia* The loss in memory abilities that occurs as a result of damage to structures in the limbic system that lie under the temporal lobe of the cerebral cortex. (p. 359)

test In psychology, a data collection method in which stimuli or problems are deliberately presented by the researcher for the subject to respond to. (p. 37)

texture gradient A pictorial cue for perceiving depth in which the gradual change in size and density of textured elements (such as pebbles or blades of grass) indicates depth. (p. 312)

thalamus The brain structure that sits directly atop the brainstem; it functions as a sensory relay station, connecting incoming sensory tracts to special sensory areas of the cerebral cortex. (p. 151)

Thematic Apperception Test (TAT) A widely used projective test in which pictures involving one or more people are presented, and the person being tested is asked to tell a story about what might be happening in each picture. (p. 661)

theory A belief or set of interrelated beliefs that one has about some aspect of the universe, which is used to explain observed facts and to predict new ones. See also *hypothesis*. (p. 31)

theory of planned behavior The theory that a person's behavioral intention, and hence behavior, is influenced by (a) the person's own attitude toward the behavior, (b) the person's belief about other's attitudes toward the behavior, and (c) the person's sense of his or her own ability to carry out the behavior. (p. 526)

three-primaries law The observation that one can choose three limited-wavelength lights (called *primaries*) and, by mixing them in differing proportions, match any color that the human eye can see. See also *additive color mixing*. (p. 283)

token In operant conditioning, a secondary reinforcer (such as money) that can be saved and turned in later for another reinforcer. See *secondary reinforcer*. (p. 114)

token economy An exchange system, adapted for use in a mental hospital or other institution, in which tokens are awarded for behaving in specific ways deemed desirable and the tokens can in turn be exchanged for goods or privileges. (p. 686)

tolerance See *drug tolerance*.

top-down processes In theories of perception, mental processes that bring preexisting knowledge or expectations about an object or scene to bear upon the perception of that object or scene. For contrast, see *bottom-up processes*. (p. 297)

tract A bundle of neural axons coursing together within the central nervous system; analogous to a *nerve* in the peripheral nervous system. (p. 149)

trait A hypothetical, relatively stable, inner characteristic that influences the way a person responds to various environmental situations. (p. 573)

trait theories of personality Theories of personality that are based on the idea that people can be described and differentiated in terms of hypothetical underlying personality dimensions, called *traits*, which can be measured by questionnaires or other quantitative means. (p. 574)

transduction The process by which a receptor cell (such as a rod or cone in the eye, or a hair cell in the inner ear) produces an electrical change in response to the energy of a physical stimulus (such as light or sound). (p. 236)

transference The phenomenon by which a patient's unconscious feelings about a significant person in his or her life are experienced consciously as feelings about the therapist. (p. 672)

trichromatic theory of color vision Theory proposed independently by Young and Helmholtz to explain the three-primaries law of color vision; it holds that the human ability to perceive color is mediated by three different types of receptors, each of which is most sensitive to a different range of wavelengths. See also *three-primaries law*. (p. 285)

U

ultimate explanations Functional explanations of behavior that state the role that the behavior plays or once played in survival and reproduction, that is, explanations of why the potential for the behavior was favored by natural selection. For contrast, see *proximate explanations*. (p. 69)

unconditioned reflex A reflex that does not depend upon previous conditions in the individual's experience; an unlearned reflex. For contrast, see *conditioned reflex*. (p. 100)

unconditioned response A reflexive response that does not depend upon previous conditioning or learning. For contrast, see *conditioned response*. (p. 100)

unconditioned stimulus A stimulus that elicits a reflexive response without any previous training or conditioning. For contrast, see *conditioned stimulus*. (p. 100)

unconscious-inference theory of perception The theory that perception is the end result of unconscious reasoning processes in which the mind uses sensory information as cues to infer the characteristics of objects or scenes that are being perceived. For contrast, see *direct-perception theory*. (p. 308)

V

validity The degree to which a measurement system actually measures the characteristic that it is supposed to measure. (p. 43)

values The general, relatively abstract attitudes that people claim as guiding principles behind their more specific attitudes and actions; the *principled* component of the self-concept. (p. 517)

variance A measure of the variability of a set of scores, determined by obtaining the difference (deviation) between each score and the mean, squaring each deviation, and calculating the mean of the squared deviations. (p. A-4)

vestigial characteristics Inherited characteristics of anatomy or behavior that are no longer useful to the species but were presumably useful at an earlier time in evolution. (p. 80)

visceral muscles Internal muscles, such as those of the heart, arteries, and gastrointestinal tract. For contrast, see *skeletal muscles*. (p. 147)

visual agnosia A condition caused by damage to specific portions of the occipital and temporal lobes of the cortex, in which people cannot make sense of what they see. (p. 294)

visual constancies Those characteristics of objects or scenes that remain constant in our visual perception of them despite changes in the retinal image. They include *size constancy*, *shape constancy*, and *lightness constancy*. (p. 316)

visual form agnosia A variety of agnosia in which people can identify some elements of what they see but cannot perceive an object's shape. (p. 294)

visual object agnosia A variety of agnosia in which people can identify and draw the shapes of objects but cannot identify the objects. (p. 294)

visual texture A repeating visual pattern that characterizes the surface of a visual object or scene. (p. 292) *visuospatial sketch pad* In Baddeley's theory, a component of working memory responsible for holding visual and spatial information. (p. 336)

W

Weber's law The idea that, within a given sensory modality (such as vision), the difference threshold (amount that the stimulus must be changed in magnitude to be perceived as different) is a constant proportion of the magnitude of the original stimulus. (p. 267)

Wernicke's aphasia A specific syndrome of loss of language ability that occurs due to damage in a particular part of the brain called *Wernicke's area*. Speech in a person with this disorder typically retains its grammatical structure but loses its meaning due to the speaker's failure to provide meaningful content words (nouns, verbs, adjectives, and adverbs); also called *fluent aphasia*. For contrast, see *Broca's aphasia*. (p. 162)

"what" pathway The lower portions of the occipital and temporal lobes of the cortex. Damage here on both sides of the brain interferes with the ability to identify objects. (p. 294)

"where" pathway The upper portions of the occipital and parietal lobes of the cortex. Damage here on both sides of the brain interferes with the ability to locate objects and guide one's own actions. (p. 295)

withdrawal effects The physiological, mental, and behavioral disturbances that can occur when a long-term user of a drug stops taking the drug. (p. 637)

working memory In the modal model, the memory store that is considered to be the main workplace of the mind. Among other things, it is the seat of conscious thought and reasoning. For contrast, see *sensory memory*, *long-term memory*. (p. 327)

Y

Yerkes-Dodson law The idea that the optimal degree of arousal for performing a task depends on the nature of the task. High arousal is best for easy tasks and low arousal is best for difficult tasks. (p. 220)

Z

z score The simplest form of a standardized score; it is the score minus the mean divided by the standard deviation. (p. A-6)

zone of proximal development Vygotsky's term for the difference between what a child can do alone and what the child can do in collaboration with a more competent other. (p. 428)

zygote The single cell that is formed when an egg and sperm cell unite; the first, single-cell form of a newly developing individual. (p. 58)

References

Abram, K. M., & Teplin, L. A. (1991). Co-occurring disorders among mentally ill jail detainees. *American Psychologist, 46*, 1036–1045.

Abrams, R. (1993). ECT technique: Electrode placement, stimulus type, and treatment frequency. In C. E. Coffey (Ed.), *The clinical science of electroconvulsive therapy.* Washington, DC: American Psychiatric Press.

Abramson, L. Y., Matelsky, G. I., & Alloy, L. B. (1989). Hopelessness depression: A theory-based subtype of depression. *Psychological Review, 96*, 358–372.

Adams, D. B., Gold, A. R., & Burt, A. D. (1978). Rise in female-initiated sexual activity at ovulation and its suppression by oral contraceptives. *The New England Journal of Medicine, 299*, 1145–1150.

Adams, H. E., Wright, L. W., & Lohr, B. A. (1996). Is Homophobia associated with homosexual arousal? *Journal of Abnormal Psychology, 105*, 440–445.

Adamson, R.E. (1952). Functional fixedness as related to problem solving. *Journal of Experimental Psychology, 44*, 288–291.

Adelson, J. (1986). *Inventing adolescence: The political psychology of everyday schooling.* New Brunswick, NJ: Transaction Books.

Ader, R., & Cohen, N. (1993). Psychoneuroimmunology: Conditioning and stress. *Annual Review of Psychology, 44*, 53–85.

Adkins-Regan, E. (1981). Early organizational effects of hormones: An evolutionary perspective. In N. T. Adler (Ed.), *Neuroendocrinology of reproduction.* New York: Plenum Press.

Adler, A. (1930). Individual psychology. In C. Murchison (Ed.), *Psychologies of 1930.* Worcester, MA: Clark University Press.

Adler, E., Hoon, M. A., Mueller, K. L., Chandrashekar, J., Ryba, N. J. P., & Zuker, C. S. (2000). A novel family of mammalian taste receptors. *Cell, 100*, 693–702.

Agras, S., Sylvester, D., & Oliveau, D. (1969). The epidemiology of common fears and phobias. *Comprehensive Psychiatry, 10*, 151–156.

Ahluvalia, T., & Schaefer, C. E. (1994). Implications of transitional object use: A review of empirical findings. *Psychology, a Journal of Human Behavior, 31* (2), 45–57.

Ainsworth, M. D. S. (1979). Attachment as related to mother-infant interaction. *Advances in the Study of Behaviour, 9*, 2–52.

Ainsworth, M. D. S. (1989). Attachments beyond infancy. *American Psychologist, 44*, 709–716.

Ainsworth, M. D. S., Blehar, M. C., Waters, E., & Wall, S. (1978). *Patterns of attachment: A psychological study of the strange situation.* Hillsdale, NJ: Erlbaum.

Ajzen, I. (1985). From intentions to actions: A theory of planned behavior. In J. Kuhl & J. Beckmann (Eds.), *Action control: From cognition to behavior.* Heidelberg: Springer.

Ajzen, I. (1987). Attitudes, traits, and actions: Dispositional prediction of behavior in personality and social psychology. In L. Berkowitz (Ed.), *Advances in experimental social psychology* (Vol. 20). Orlando, FL: Academic Press.

Ajzen, I. (1991). The theory of planned behavior. *Organizational Behavior and Human Decision Processes, 50*, 179–211.

Akbarian, S., Kim, J. J., Potkin, S. G., Hetrick, W. P., Bunney, W. E., & Jones, E. G. (1996). Maldistribution of interstitial neurons in prefrontal white matter of the brains of schizophrenic patients. *Archives of General Psychiatry, 53*, 425–436.

Akerstedt, T., & Fröberg, J. E. (1977). Psychophysiological circadian rhythms in women during 72 hours of sleep deprivation. *Waking and Sleeping, 1*, 387–394.

Alicke, M. D., Klotz, M. L., Breitenbecher, D. L., Yurak, T. J., & Vredenburg, D. S. (1995). Personal contact, individuation, and the better-than-average effect. *Journal of Personality and Social Psychology, 68*, 804–825.

Al-Kubaisy, T., Marks, I. M., Logsdail, S., Marks, M. P., Lovell, K., Sungur, M., & Araya, R. (1992). Role of exposure homework in phobia reduction: A controlled study. *Behavior Therapy, 23*, 599–621.

Allison, T., & Cicchetti, D. V. (1976). Sleep in mammals: Ecological and constitutional correlates. *Science, 194*, 732–734.

Allman, J., & Brothers, L. (1994). Faces, fear and the amygdala. *Nature, 372*, 613–614.

Alloy, L. B., Abramson, L. Y., & Francis, E. L. (1999). Do negative cognitive styles confer vulnerability to depression? *Current Directions in Psychological Science, 8*, 128–132.

Allport, F. H. (1920). The influence of the group upon association and thought. *Journal of Experimental Psychology, 3*, 159–182.

Allport, G. W. (1935). Attitudes. In C. Murchison (Ed.), *Handbook of social psychology.* Worcester, MA: Clark University Press.

Allport, G. W. (1937). *Personality: A psychological interpretation.* New York: Holt.

Allport, G. W. (1968). The historical background of modern social psychology. In G. Lindzey & E. Aronson (Eds.), *The handbook of social psychology* (2nd ed., Vol. 1). Reading, MA: Addison-Wesley.

Almeida, D. M., & Kessler, R. C. (1998). Everyday stressors and gender differences in daily distress. *Journal of Personality and Social Psychology, 75*, 670–680.

Alwin, D. F., Cohen, R. L., & Newcomb, T. M. (1991). *Political attitudes over the life span: The Bennington women after fifty years.* Madison: University of Wisconsin Press.

Ambady, N., Hallahan, M., & Rosenthal, R. (1995). On judging and being judged accurately in zero-acquaintance situations. *Journal of Personality and Social Psychology, 69,* 518–529.

Ambelas, A. (1987). Life events and mania: A special relationship? *British Journal of Psychiatry, 150,* 235–240.

American Psychiatric Association. (1994). *Diagnostic and statistical manual of mental disorders* (4th ed.). Washington, DC: Author.

American Psychiatric Association. (2000). *Diagnostic and statistical manual of mental disorders* (4th ed., text-revised). Washington, DC: Author.

American Psychological Association. (1992). Ethical principles of psychologists and code of conduct. *American Psychologist, 47,* 1597–1611.

Anderson, C. A., Lindsay, J. J., & Bushman, B. J. (1999). Research in the psychological laboratory: Truth or triviality? *Current Directions in Psychological Science, 8,* 3–9.

Anderson, J. R. (2000). *Learning and memory* (2nd ed.) New York: Wiley.

Anderson, R. H., Fleming, D. E., Rhees, R. W., & Kinghorn, E. (1986). Relationships between sexual activity, plasma testosterone, and the volume of the sexually dimorphic nucleus of the preoptic area in prenatally stressed and non-stressed rats. *Brain Research, 370,* 1–10.

Andrasik, F. (2000). Biofeedback. In D. I. Mostofsky & D. H. Barlow (Eds.), *The management of stress and anxiety in medical disorders.* Needham Heights, MA: Allyn & Bacon.

Andreasen, N. C. (1987). Creativity and mental illness: Prevalence rates in writers and their first-degree relatives. *American Journal of Psychiatry, 144,* 1288–1292.

Andreasen, N. C., Arndt, S., Swayze, V., Cizadlo, T., Flaum, M., O'Leary, D., Ehrhardt, J. C., & Yuh, W. T. C. (1994). Thalamic abnormalities in schizophrenia visualized through magnetic resonance image averaging. *Science, 266,* 294–298.

Anglin, J. M. (1977). *Word, object, and conceptual development.* New York: Norton.

Antrobus, J. (2000). Theories of dreaming. In M. H. Kryger, T. Roth, & W. C. Dement (Eds.), *Principles and practice of sleep medicine* (3rd ed.). Philadelphia: W. B. Saunders.

Archambault, A., O'Donnell, C., & Schyns, P. G. (1999). Blind to object changes: When learning the same object at different levels of categorization modifies perception. *Psychological Science, 10,* 249–255.

Arditi, A. (1986). Binocular vision. In K. R. Boff, L. Kaufman, & J. P. Thomas (Eds.), *Handbook of perception and human performance.* New York: Wiley.

Arieti, S. (1966). Schizophrenic cognition. In P. Hook & J. Zubin (Eds.), *Psychopathology of schizophrenia.* New York: Grune & Stratton.

Arnett, J. (1992). Reckless behavior in adolescence: A developmental perspective. *Developmental Review, 12,* 339–373.

Arnett, J. (1995). The young and the reckless: Adolescent reckless behavior. *Current Directions in Psychological Science, 4,* 67–71.

Arnett, J. J. (1999). Adolescent storm and stress, reconsidered. *American Psychologist, 54,* 317–326.

Aronson, E. (1992). The return of the repressed: Dissonance theory makes a comeback. *Psychological Inquiry, 3,* 303–311.

Asch, S. E. (1946). Forming impressions of personality. *Journal of Abnormal and Social Psychology, 41,* 258–290.

Asch, S. E. (1952). *Social psychology.* Englewood Cliffs, NJ: Prentice–Hall.

Asch, S. E. (1956). Studies of independence and conformity: I. A minority of one against a unanimous majority. *Psychological Monographs: General and Applied, 70*(9, Whole No. 416).

Aschoff, J. (1969). Desynchronization and resynchronization of human circadian rhythms. *Aerospace Medicine, 40,* 844–849.

Ash, M. G. (1985). Gestalt psychology: Origins in Germany and reception in the United States. In C. E. Buxton (Ed.), *Points of view in the modern history of psychology.* New York: Academic Press.

Ashby, F. G., Isen, A. M., & Turken, U. (1999). A neuropsychological theory of positive affect and its influence on cognition. *Psychological Review, 106,* 529–550.

Atkin, O. (1980). *Models of architectural knowledge.* London: Pion.

Atkinson, R. C. (1975). Mnemotechnics in second-language learning. *American Psychologist, 30,* 821–828.

Atkinson, R. C., & Shiffrin, R. M. (1968). Human memory: A proposed system and its control processes. In K. W. Spence & J. T. Spence (Eds.), *The psychology of learning and motivation: Advances in research and theory* (Vol. 2). New York: Academic Press.

Atkinson, R. C., & Shiffrin, R. M. (1971, August). The control of short-term memory. *Scientific American,* pp. 82–90.

Awh, E., Jonides, J., Smith, E. E., Schumacher, E. H., Koeppe, R. A., & Katz, S. (1996). Dissociation of storage and retrieval in verbal working memory: Evidence from positron emission tomography. *Psychological Science, 7,* 25–31.

Axel, R. (1995, October). The molecular logic of smell. *Scientific American, 273,* 154–159.

Axelrod, R. (1984). *The evolution of cooperation.* New York: Basic Books.

Ayllon, T., & Azrin, N. H. (1968). *The token economy: A motivational system for therapy and rehabilitation.* New York: Appleton-Century-Crofts.

Baddeley, A. (1986). *Working Memory.* Oxford: Clarendon.

Baddeley, A. (2000). Short-term and working memory. In E. Tulving & F. I. M. Craik (Eds.), *The Oxford handbook of memory.* New York: Oxford University Press.

Baddeley, A., Gathercole, S., & Papagno, C. (1998). The phonological loop as a language learning device. *Psychological Review, 105,* 158–173.

Baddeley, A., Thomson, N., & Buchanan, M. (1975). Word length and the structure of short-term memory. *Journal of Verbal Learning and Verbal Behavior, 14,* 575–589.

Baer, L., Rauch, S. L., Ballantine, T., Martuza, R., Cosgrove, R., Cassem, E., Giriunas, I., Manzo, P. A., Dimino, C., & Jenike, M. A. (1995). Cingulotomy for intractable obsessive-compulsive disorder. *Archives of General Psychiatry, 52,* 384–392.

Baerger, D. R., & McAdams, D. P. (1999). Life story coherence and its relation to psychological well-being. *Narrative Inquiry, 9,* 69–96.

Bahrick, H. P., Bahrick, P. O., & Wittlinger, R. P. (1975). Fifty years of memory for names and faces. *Journal of Experimental Psychology: General, 104,* 54–75.

Bailey, C. H., & Chen, M. (1989). Time course of structural changes at identified sensory neuron synapses during long-term sensitization in aplysia. *Journal of Neuroscience, 9,* 1774–1781.

Bailey, J. M., & Pillard, R. C. (1991). A genetic study of male sexual orientation. *Archives of General Psychiatry, 48,* 1089–1096.

Bailey, J. M., Pillard, R. C., Neale, M. C., & Agyei, Y. (1993). Heritable factors influence sexual orientation in women. *Archives of General Psychology, 50,* 217–223.

Baillargeon, R. (1987). Object permanence in 3½- and 4½-month-old infants. *Developmental Psychology, 23,* 655–664.

Baillargeon, R. (1993). The object concept revisited: New directions in the investigation of infants' physical knowledge. In C. E. Granrud (Ed.), *Visual perception and cognition in infancy.* Hillsdale, NJ: Erlbaum.

Baillargeon, R. (1994). How do infants learn about the physical world? *Current Directions in Psychological Science, 3,* 133–140.

Baillargeon, R. (1998). Infants' understanding of the physical world. In M. Sabourin, F. Craik, & M. Robert (Eds.), *Advances in psychological science* (Vol. 2). Hove, UK: Psychology Press.

Bakeman, R., Adamson, L. B., Konner, M., & Barr, R. (1990). !Kung infancy: The social context of object exploration. *Child Development, 61,* 794–809.

Bakin, J. S., South, D. A., & Weinberger, N. M. (1996). Induction of receptive field plasticity in the auditory cortex of the guinea pig during instrumental avoidance conditioning. *Behavioral Neuroscience, 110,* 905–913.

Baldwin, D. A. (2000). Interpersonal understanding fuels knowledge acquisition. *Current Directions in Psychological Science, 9,* 40–45.

Baldwin, D. A., Markman, E. M., & Melartin, R. L. (1993). Infants' ability to draw inferences about nonobvious object properties: Evidence from exploratory play. *Child Development, 64,* 711–728.

Ball, G. F., & Hulse, S. H. (1998). Birdsong. *American Psychologist, 53,* 37–58.

Bancroft, J. (1978). The relationship between hormones and sexual behavior in humans. In J. B. Hutchinson (Ed.), *Biological determinants of sexual behavior.* New York: Wiley.

Bandura, A. (1969). *Principles of behavior modification.* New York: Holt, Rinehart & Winston.

Bandura, A. (1982). Self-efficacy mechanisms in human agency. *American Psychologist, 37,* 122–147.

Bandura, A. (1997). *Self-efficacy: The exercise of control.* New York: Freeman.

Bandura, A. (2001). Social cognitive theory: An agentic perspective. *Annual Review of Psychology, 52,* 1–26.

Bandura, A., Adams, N. E., & Beyer, J. (1977). Cognitive processes mediating behavioral change. *Journal of Personality and Social Psychology, 35,* 125–139.

Bandura, A., & Cervone, D. (1983). Self-evaluative and self-efficacy mechanisms governing the motivational effects of goal systems. *Journal of Personality and Social Psychology, 45,* 1017–1028.

Bandura, A., Cioffi, D., Taylor, C. B., & Brouillard, M. E. (1988). Perceived self-efficacy in coping with cognitive stressors and opioid activation. *Journal of Personality and Social Psychology, 55,* 479–488.

Bandura, A., O'Leary, A., Taylor, C. B., Gauthier, J., & Gossard, D. (1987). Perceived self-efficacy and pain control: Opioid and nonopiod mechanisms. *Journal of Personality and Social Psychology, 53,* 563–571.

Bandura, A., Reese, L., & Adams, N. E. (1982). Microanalysis of action and fear arousal as a function of differential levels of perceived self-efficacy. *Journal of Personality and Social Psychology, 43,* 5–21.

Barker, S. L., Funk, S. C., & Houston, B. K. (1988). Psychological treatment versus nonspecific factors: A meta-analysis of conditions that engender comparable expectations for improvement. *Clinical Psychology Review, 8,* 579–594.

Barkow, J. H., Cosmides, L., & Tooby, J. (1992). *The adapted mind: Evolutionary psychology and the generation of culture.* New York: Oxford University Press.

Barlow, D. H. (1988). *Anxiety and its disorders: The nature and treatment of anxiety and panic.* New York: Guilford Press.

Barlow, D. H. (1991). Disorders of emotion. *Psychological Inquiry, 2,* 58–71.

Barnett, R. C., & Baruch, G. K. (1987). Social roles, gender, and psychological distress. In R. C. Barnett, L. B. Biener, & G. K. Baruch (Eds.), *Gender and stress.* New York: Free Press.

Baron-Cohen, S. (1995). *Mindblindness: An essay on autism and theory of mind.* Cambridge, MA: Bradford Books/MIT Press.

Baron-Cohen, S., Leslie, A. M., & Frith, U. (1985). Does the autistic child have a "theory of mind"? *Cognition, 21,* 37–46.

Barry, H., III, & Paxson, L. (1971). Infancy and early childhood: Cross-cultural codes, 2. *Ethnology, 10,* 466–508.

Barsh, G. S., Farooqi, S., & O'Rahilly, S. (2000). Genetics of body-weight regulation. *Nature, 404,* 644–651.

Bartlett, F. C. (1932). *Remembering: A study in experimental and social psychology.* Cambridge, England: Cambridge University Press.

Bartol, C. R., & Costello, N. (1976). Extraversion as a function of temporal duration of electric shock: An exploratory study. *Perceptual and Motor Skills, 42,* 1174.

Bartoshuk, L. M., & Beauchamp, G. K. (1994). Chemical senses. *Annual Reviews of Psychology, 45,* 419–449.

Bartsch, K., & Wellman, H. M. (1995). *Children talk about the mind.* New York: Oxford University Press.

Basbaum, A. I., & Fields, H. L. (1984). Endogenous pain control systems: Brainstem spinal pathways and endorphin circuitry. *Annual Review of Neuroscience, 7,* 309–338.

Basbaum, A. I., & Jessell, T. M. (2000). The perception of pain. In E. R. Kandel, J. H. Schwartz, & T. M. Jessell (Eds.), *Principles of neuroscience* (4th ed.). New York: McGraw-Hill.

Bassuk, E. L., & Gerson, S. (1978, February). Deinstitutionalization and mental health services. *Scientific American,* pp. 46–53.

Bateson, P. (2000). What must be known in order to understand imprinting? In C. Heyes & L. Huber (Eds.), *The evolution of cognition.* Cambridge, MA: MIT Press.

Baumeister, R. E. (1994). The crystallization of discontent in the process of major life change. In T. F. Heatherton & J. L. Weinberger (Eds.), *Can personality change?* Washington, DC: American Psychological Association.

Baumeister, R. F., Dale, K., & Sommer, K. L. (1998). Freudian defense mechanisms and empirical findings in modern social psychology: Reaction formation, projection, displacement, undoing, isolation, sublimation, and denial. *Journal of Personality, 66,* 1081–1124.

Baumeister, R. F., Dori, G. A., & Hastings, S. (1998). Belongingness and temporal bracketing in personal accounts of changes in self-esteem. *Journal of Research in Personality, 32,* 222–235.

Baumeister, R. F., & Showers, C. J. (1986). A review of paradoxical performance effects: Choking under pressure in sports and mental tests. *European Journal of Social Psychology, 16,* 361–383.

Baumeister, R. F., Stillwell, A. M., & Heatherton, T. F. (1995). Personal narratives about guilt: Role of action control and interpersonal relationships. *Basic and Applied Social Psychology, 17,* 173–198.

Baumgart, F., Gaschler-Markefski, B., Woldorff, M. G., Heinze, H., & Scheich, H. (1999). A movement-sensitive area in auditory cortex. *Nature, 400,* 724–726.

Baumrind, D. (1964). Some thoughts on ethics of research: After reading Milgram's "Behavioral study of obedience." *American Psychologist, 19,* 421–423.

Baumrind, D. (1967). Child care practices anteceding three patterns of preschool behavior. *Genetic Psychology Monographs, 75,* 43–88.

Baumrind, D. (1971). Current patterns of parental authority. *Developmental Psychology Monograph, 4,* 1–103.

Baumrind, D. (1986). *Familial antecendents of social competence in middle childhood.* Unpublished monograph, University of California, Institute of Human Development, Berkeley.

Baxter, L. R., Schwartz, J. M., Bergman, K. S., Szuba, M. P., Guze, B. H., Mazziotta, J. C., Alazrake, A., Selin, C. E., Ferng, H., Munford, P., & Phelps, M. E. (1992). Caudate glucose metabolic rate changes with both drug and behavior therapy for obsessive-compulsive disorder. *Archives of General Psychiatry, 49,* 681–689.

Beaman, A. L., Klentz, B., Diener, E., & Svanum, S. (1979). Self-awareness and transgression in children: Two field studies. *Journal of Personality and Social Psychology, 37,* 1835–1846.

Beck, A. T. (1967). *Depression: Clinical, experimental, and theoretical aspects.* New York: Harper & Row.

Beck, A. T. (1976). *Cognitive therapy and the emotional disorders.* New York: International Universities Press.

Beck, A. T. (1991). Cognitive therapy: A 30-year retrospective. *American Psychologist, 46,* 368–375.

Beck, A. T., & Emery, G. (1985). *Anxiety disorders and phobias: A cognitive perspective.* New York: Basic Books.

Beck, A. T., & Young, J. E. (1985). Depression. In D. H. Barlow (Ed.), *Clinical handbook of psychological disorders: A step-by-step treatment manual.* New York: Guilford Press.

Beck, M., & Galef, B. G. (1989). Social influences on the selection of a protein-sufficient diet by Norway rats (*Rattus norvegicus*). *Journal of Comparative Psychology, 103,* 132–139.

Becklen, R., & Cervone, D. (1983). Selective looking and the noticing of unexpected events. *Memory & Cognition, 11,* 601–608.

Bell, A. P., Weinberg, M. S., & Hammersmith, S. K. (1981). *Sexual preference: Its development in men and women.* Bloomington: Indiana University Press.

Bell, R. A., Cholerton, M., Fraczek, K. E., Rohlfs, G. S., & Smith, B. A. (1994). Encouraging donations to charity: A field study of competing and complementary factors in tactic sequencing. *Western Journal of Communication, 58,* 98–115.

Belsky, J., Steinberg, L., & Draper, P. (1991). Childhood experience, interpersonal development, and reproductive strategy: An evolutionary theory of socialization. *Child Development 62,* 647–670.

Benet-Martínez, V., & John, O. P. (1998). *Los Cinco Grandes* across cultures and ethnic groups: Multitrait multimethod analysis of the Big Five in Spanish and English. *Journal of Personality and Social Psychology, 75,* 729–750.

Benjamin, J., Ebstein, R. P., & Lesch, K. (1998). Genes for personality traits: Implications for psychology. *International Journal of Neuropsychopharmacology, 1,* 153–168.

Benjamin, J., Li, L., Patterson, C., Greenberg, B. D., Murphy, D. L., & Hamer, D. H. (1996). Population and familial association between the D4 dopamine receptor gene and measures of novelty seeking. *Nature Genetics, 12,* 81–84.

Bereczkei, T., & Csanaky, A. (1996). Evolutionary pathway of child development: Lifestyles of adolescents and adults from father-absent families. *Human Nature, 7,* 257–280.

Berk, L. E. (1994, November). Why children talk to themselves. *Scientific American,* pp. 78–83.

Berk, L. E., & Lewis, N. G. (1977). Sex role and social behavior in four school environments. *The Elementary School Journal, 77,* 205–217.

Berkeley, G. (1710; reprinted 1820). *A treatise concerning the principles of human knowledge.* In *The works of George Berkeley* (3 vols.). London: Richard Priestley.

Berko, J. (1958). The child's learning of English morphology. *Word, 14,* 150–177.

Berndt, T. J. (1992). Friendship and friends' influence in adolescence. *Current Directions in Psychological Science, 1,* 156–159.

Bernstein, I. L. (1991). Flavor aversion. In R. C. Doty, L. M. Bartoshuk, & J. B. Snow (Eds.), *Smell and taste in health and disease.* New York: Raven.

Bernstein, W. M., Stephan, W. G., & Davis, M. H. (1979). Explaining attributions for achievement: A path analytic approach. *Journal of Personality and Social Psychology, 37,* 1810–1821.

Berry, J. W. (1971). Ecological and cultural factors in spatial perceptual development. *Canadian Journal of Behavioural Science, 3,* 324–336.

Bertenthal, B. I., Campos, J. J., & Barrett, K. C. (1984). Self-produced locomotion: An organizer of emotional, cognitive, and social development in infancy. In R. N. Emde & R. J. Harmon (Eds.), *Continuities and discontinuities in development.* New York: Plenum Press.

Bick, P. A., & Kinsbourne, M. (1987). Auditory hallucinations and subvocal speech in schizophrenic patients. *American Journal of Psychiatry, 144,* 222–225.

Bickerton, D. (1984). The language bioprogram hypothesis. *Behavioral and Brain Sciences, 7,* 173–221.

Bickman, L. (1972). Social influence and diffusion of responsibility in an emergency. *Journal of Experimental Social Psychology, 8,* 438–445.

Biedel, D. C., & Turner, S. M. (1997). Anxiety disorders. In S. M. Turner & M. Hersen (Eds.), *Adult psychopathology and diagnosis* (3rd ed.). New York: Wiley.

Biederman, I. (1987). Recognition-by-components: A theory of human image understanding. *Psychological Review, 94,* 115–147.

Biederman, I. (1988). Aspects and extensions of a theory of human image understanding. In Z. W. Pylyshyn (Ed.), *Computational processes in human vision: An interdisciplinary perspective.* Norwood, NJ: Ablex.

Biederman, I. (1989). Higher-level vision. In N. Osherson, H. Lasnik, S. Kosslyn, J. Hollerbach, E. Smith, & N. Bloch (Eds.), *An invitation to cognitive science,* Cambridge, MA: MIT Press.

Biederman, I., & Shiffrar, M. M. (1987). Sexing day-old chicks: A case study and expert systems analysis of a difficult perceptual-learning task. *Journal of Experimental Psychology: Learning, Memory, and Cognition, 13,* 640–645.

Biernat, M., & Wortman, C. B. (1991). Sharing of home responsibilities between professionally employed women and their husbands. *Journal of Personality and Social Psychology, 60,* 844–860.

Biklen, D. (1990). Communication unbound: Autism and praxis. *Harvard Educational Review, 60,* 291–314.

Binet, A., & Henri, V. (1896). La psychologie individuelle. *Année Psychologie, 11,* 163–169.

Binet, A., & Simon, T. (1916; reprinted 1973). *The development of intelligence in children.* New York: Arno Press.

Birkhead, T. R., & Moller, A. P. (1992). *Sperm competition in birds: Evolutionary causes and consequences.* London: Academic Press.

Bitterman, M. E. (1975). The comparative analysis of learning. *Science, 188,* 699–709.

Bitterman, M. E. (2000). Cognitive evolution: A psychological perspective. In C. Heyes & L. Huber (Eds.), *The evolution of cognition.* Cambridge, MA: MIT Press.

Bivens, J. A., & Berk, L. E. (1990). A longitudinal study of the development of elementary school children's private speech. *Merrill-Palmer Quarterly, 36,* 443–463.

Bjorklund, D. F., & Pellegrini, A. D. (2000). Child development and evolutionary psychology. *Child Development, 71,* 1687–1708.

Blasovich, J., Mendes, W. B., Hunter, S. B., & Salomon, K. (1999). Social "facilitation" as challenge and threat. *Journal of Personality and Social Psychology, 77,* 68–77.

Blazer, D., Hughes, D., & George, L. D. (1987). Stressful life events and the onset of a generalized anxiety syndrome. *American Journal of Psychiatry, 144,* 1178–1183.

Bleuler, E. P. (1911; reprinted 1950). *Dementia praecox, or the group of schizophrenias* (J. Zinkin, Trans.). New York: International Universities Press.

Bligh, S., & Kupperman, P. (1993). Facilitated communication evaluation procedure accepted in a court case. *Journal of Autism and Developmental Disorders, 23,* 553–557.

Bliss, E. L. (1986). *Multiple personality, allied disorders, and hypnosis.* Oxford: Oxford University Press.

Bliss, T. V. P., & Lømo, T. (1973). Long-lasting potentiation of synaptic transmission in the dentate area of the anaesthetized rabbit following stimulation of the perforant path. *Journal of Physiology (London), 232,* 331–356.

Bloom, L. M., & Lahey, M. (1978). *Language development and language disorders.* New York: Wiley.

Blumenthal, A. L. (1985). Wilhelm Wundt: Psychology as the propaedeutic science. In C. E. Buxton (Ed.), *Points of view in the modern history of psychology.* New York: Academic Press.

Blurton-Jones, N. G. (1967). An ethological study of some aspects of social behavior of children in nursery school. In D. Morris (Ed.), *Primate ethology.* Chicago: Aldine.

Blurton-Jones, N. G., & Konner, M. J. (1973). Sex differences in the behavior of Bushman and London two- to five-year-olds. In J. Crook & R. Michael (Eds.), *Comparative ecology and behavior of primates.* New York: Academic Press.

Bodenhausen, G. V. (1991). Identity and cooperative social behavior: Pseudospeciation or human integration? *World Futures, 31,* 95–106.

Bodenhausen, G. V., Macrae, C. N., & Sherman, J. W. (1999). On the dialectics of discrimination: Dual processes in social stereotyping. In S. Chaiken & Y. Trope (Eds.), *Dual-process theories in social psychology.* New York: Guilford.

Boivin, D. B., Duffy, J. F., Kronauer, R. E., & Czeisler, C. A. (1996). Dose-response relationships for resetting of human circadian clock by light. *Nature, 379,* 540–542.

Bolyard, K. J., & Rowland, W. J. (1996). Context-dependent response to red coloration in stickleback. *Animal Behaviour, 52,* 923–927.

Bond, A. J., & Lader, M. H. (1996). *Understanding drug treatment in mental health care.* New York: Wiley.

Bond, M. H., & Cheung, T. (1983). College students' spontaneous self-concept: The effect of culture among respondents in Hong Kong, Japan, and the United States. *Journal of Cross-Cultural Psychology, 14,* 153–171.

Bond, R., & Smith, P. B. (1996). Culture and conformity: A meta-analysis of studies using Asch's (1952b, 1956) line judgment task. *Psychological Bulletin, 119,* 111–137.

Boor, M. (1982). The multiple personality epidemic. *Journal of Nervous and Mental Disease, 170,* 302–304.

Booth-Kewley, S., & Friedman, H. S. (1987). Psychological predictors of heart disease: A quantitative review. *Psychological Bulletin, 101,* 343–362.

Borbély, A. (1986). *The secrets of sleep.* New York: Basic Books.

Borges, M. A., & Dutton, L. J. (1976). Attitudes toward aging. *The Gerontologist, 16,* 220–224.

Bottoms, B. L., Shaver, P. R., & Goodman, G. S. (1996). An analysis of ritualistic and religion-related child abuse allegations. *Law and Human Behavior, 20,* 1–34.

Botwinick, J. (1984). *Aging and behavior: A comprehensive integration of research findings* (3rd ed.). New York: Springer-Verlag.

Bouchard, T. J. (1991). A twice-told tale: Twins reared apart. In W. M. Gove & D. Cicchetti (Eds.), *Thinking clearly about psychology: Vol. 2. Personality and psychopathology.* Minneapolis: University of Minnesota Press.

Bouchard, T. J. (1994). Genes, environment, and personality. *Science, 264,* 1700–1701.

Bouton, M. E. (1994). Context, ambiguity, and classical conditioning. *Current Directions in Psychological Science, 3,* 49–53.

Bowlby, J. (1958). The nature of the child's tie to his mother. *International Journal of Psychoanalysis, 39*, 35–373.

Bowlby, J. (1973). *Attachment and loss: Vol. 2 Separation: Anxiety and anger.* New York: Basic Books.

Bowlby, J. (1982). *Attachment and loss* (2nd ed.). New York: Basic Books.

Bowmaker, J. K., & Dartnall, H. J. A. (1980). Visual pigments of rods and cones in a human retina. *Journal of Physiology (London), 298*, 501–511.

Bradshaw, G. L., & Anderson, J. R. (1982). Elaborative encoding as an explanation of levels of processing. *Journal of Verbal Learning and Verbal Behavior, 21*, 165–174.

Bradshaw, M. F., Leach, R., Hibbard, P. B., van der Willigen, R., & Rushton, S. K. (1999). In M. A. Grealy & J. A. Thomson (Eds.), *Studies in perception and action V.* Mahwah, NJ: Erlbaum.

Brand, P., & Yancey, P. (1993). *Pain: The gift nobody wants.* New York: HarperCollins.

Bransford, J. D., Stein, B. S., Vye, N. J., Franks, J. J., Auble, P. M., Mezynski, K. J., & Perfetto, G. A. (1982). Different approaches in learning: An overview. *Journal of Experimental Psychology: General, 111*, 390–398.

Brauer, M., Judd, C. M., & Gliner, M. D. (1995). The effects of repeated expressions on attitude polarization during group discussions. *Journal of Personality and Social Psychology, 68*, 1014–1029.

Bray, G. A., & Gallagher, T. F., Jr. (1975). Manifestation of hypothalamic obesity in man: A comprehensive investigation of eight patients and a review of the literature. *Medicine (Baltimore), 54*, 301–330.

Bray, G. A., & Popkin, B. M. (1998). Dietary fat intake does affect obesity! *American Journal of Clinical Nutrition, 68*, 1157–1173.

Breggin, P. (1997). *Brain-disabling treatments in psychiatry: Drugs, electroshock, and the role of the FDA.* New York: Springer.

Breggin, P. R. (1991). *Toxic psychiatry.* New York: St. Martin's Press.

Brehm, S. S., & Brehm, J. W. (1981). *Psychological reactance: A theory of freedom and control.* New York: Academic Press.

Breier, A., Charney, D. S., & Heninger, G. R. (1986). Agoraphobia with panic attacks. *Archives of General Psychiatry, 43*, 1029–1036.

Bretherton, I., Golby, B., & Cho, E. (1997). Attachment and the transmission of values. In J. E. Grusec & L. Kuczynski (Eds.), *Parenting and children's internalization of values: A handbook of contemporary theory.* New York: Wiley.

Brewer, M. B., & Weber, J. G. (1994). Self-evaluation effects of interpersonal versus intergroup social comparison. *Journal of Personality and Social Psychology, 66*, 268–275.

Brewin, C. R. (1996). Theoretical foundations of cognitive-behavior therapy for anxiety and depression. *Annual Review of Psychology, 47*, 33–57.

Broadbent, D. E. (1958). *Perception and communication.* London: Pergamon.

Broccia, M., & Campos, J. J. (1989). Maternal emotional signals, social referencing, and infants' reactions to strangers. In N. Eisenberg (Ed.), *Empathy and related emotional responses* (New Directions for Child Development, No. 44). San Francisco: Jossey-Bass.

Brody, N. (1992). *Intelligence* (2nd ed.). San Diego, CA: Academic Press.

Bronfenbrenner, U. (1979). *The ecology of human development.* Cambridge, MA: Harvard University Press.

Bronfenbrenner, U. (1986). Ecology of the family as a context for human development: Research perspectives. *Developmental Psychology, 22*, 723–742.

Brown, B. B., Mory, M., & Kinney, D. (1994). Casting crowds in a relational perspective: Caricature, channel, and context. In R. Montemayor, G. Atam, & T. Gullotta (Eds.), *Advances in adolescent development: Vol. 5. Personal relationships during adolescence.* Newbury Park, CA: Sage.

Brown, C. H. (1994). Sound localization. In R. R. Fay & A. N. Popper (Eds.), *Comparative hearing: Mammals.* New York: Springer-Verlag.

Brown, J. R., Ye, H., Bronson, R. T., Dikkes, P., & Greenberg, M. E. (1996). A defect in nurturing in mice lacking the immediate early gene fosB. *Cell, 86*, 297–309.

Brown, R. (1973). *A first language.* Cambridge, MA: Harvard University Press.

Brown, R., & Hanlon, C. (1970). Derivational complexity and order of acquisition in child speech. In J. R. Hayes (Ed.), *Cognition and the development of language.* New York: Wiley.

Brown, R. G., & Pluck, G. (2000). Negative symptoms: The "pathology" of motivation and goal-directed behaviour. *Trends in Neuroscience, 23*, 412–417.

Brownell, K., Greenwood, M. R. C., Stellar, E., & Shrager, E. E. (1986). The effects of repeated cycles of weight loss and regain in rats. *Physiology and Behavior, 38*, 459–464.

Bruce, D. (1991). Integrations of Lashley. In G. A. Kimble, M. Wertheimer, & C. White (Eds.), *Portraits of pioneers in psychology.* Hillsdale, NJ: Erlbaum.

Bruce, V., & Young, A. (1998). *In the eye of the beholder: The science of face perception.* Oxford: Oxford University Press.

Bruner, J. S. (1983) *Child's talk: Learning to use language.* New York: Norton.

Brzustowicz, L. M., Hodgkinson, K. A., Chow, E. W. C., Honer, W. G., & Bassett, A. S. (2000). Location of a major susceptibility locus for familial schizophrenia on chromosome 1q21–q22. *Science, 288*, 678–682.

Buck, L. B. (2000a). The molecular architecture of odor and pheromone sensing in mammals. *Cell, 100*, 611–618.

Buck, L. B. (2000b). Smell and taste: The chemical senses. In E. R. Kandel, J. H. Schwartz, & T. M. Jessell (Eds.), *Principles of neuroscience* (4th ed.). New York: McGraw-Hill.

Buehlman, K. T., Gottman, J. M., & Katz, L. F. (1992). How a couple views their past predicts their future: Predicting divorce from an oral history interview. *Journal of Family Psychology, 5*, 295–318.

Bureau of Labor Statistics. (1997). Labor force statistics from the current population survey. Internet: http://stats.bls.gov/news.

Burger, J. M. (1999). The foot-in-the-door compliance procedure: A multiple-process analysis and review. *Personality and Social Psychology Review, 3*, 303–325.

Burgess, C. A., Kirsch, I., Shane, H., Niederauer, K. L., Graham, S. M., & Bacon, A. (1998). Facilitated communication as an ideomotor response. *Psychological Science, 9,* 71–74.

Burnstein, E., & Vinokur, A. (1977). Persuasive argumentation and social comparison as determinants of attitude polarization. *Journal of Social Psychology, 13,* 315–332.

Bushnell, I. W., R., Sai, F., & Mullin, J. T. (1989). Neonatal recognition of the mother's face. *British Journal of Developmental Psychology, 7,* 3–15.

Buss, D. M. (1991). Evolutionary personality psychology. *Annual Review of Psychology, 42,* 459–491.

Buss, D. M. (1994a). The strategies of human mating. *American Scientist, 82,* 238–250.

Buss, D. M. (1994b). *The evolution of desire: Strategies of human mating.* New York: Basic Books.

Buss, D. M. (1995). Psychological sex differences: Origins through sexual selection. *American Psychologist, 50,* 164–168.

Buss, D. M. (1996). Social adaptation and five major factors of personality. In J. S. Wiggins (Ed.), *The five-factor model of personality: Theoretical perspectives.* New York: Guilford Press.

Buss, D. M. (1998). The psychology of human mate selection: Exploring the complexity of the strategic repertoire. In C. Crawford & D. L. Krebs (Eds.), *Handbook of evolutionary psychology: Ideas, issues, and applications.* Mahwah, NJ: Erlbaum.

Bussey, K., & Bandura, A. (1999). Social cognitive theory of gender development and differentiation. *Psychological Review, 106,* 676–713.

Butcher, J. N. (1990). *The MMPI-2 in psychological treatment.* New York: Oxford University Press.

Butcher, J. N. (1999). *A beginner's guide to the MMPI-2.* Washington, DC: American Psychological Association.

Butcher, J. N., & Rouse, S. V. (1996). Personality: Individual differences and clinical assessment. *Annual Review of Psychology, 47,* 87–111.

Butler, R. N. (1975). *Why survive?* New York: Harper & Row.

Butterfield, E. C., & Siperstein, G. N. (1974). Influence of contingent auditory stimulation upon non-nutritional suckle. *Proceedings of the third symposium on oral sensation and perception: The mouth of the infant.* Springfield, IL: Charles C. Thomas.

Byne, W. (1994, May). The biological evidence challenged. *Scientific American,* pp. 50–55.

Byrne, R. W., & Russon, A. E. (1998). Learning by imitation: A hierarchical approach. *Behavioral and Brain Sciences, 21,* 667–721.

Byrnes, J. P., Miller, D. C., & Schafer, W. D. (1999). Gender differences in risk taking: A meta-analysis. *Psychological Bulletin, 125,* 367–383.

Cabib, S., Orsini, C., Le Moal, M., & Piazza, P. V. (2000). Abolition and reversal of strain differences in behavioral responses to drugs of abuse after a brief experience. *Science, 289,* 463–465.

Cacioppo, J. T., Berntson, G. G., & Klein, D. J. (1992). What is an emotion? The role of somatovisceral afference, with special emphasis on somatovisceral "illusions." *Review of Personality and Social Psychology,* Vol. 13.

Cacioppo, J. T., Rourke, P. A., Marshall-Goodell, B. S., Tassinary, L. G., & Baron, R. S. (1990). Rudimentary physiological effects of mere observation. *Psychophysiology, 27,* 177–186.

Caggiula, A. R., & Hoebel, B. G. (1966). "Copulation-reward site" in the posterior hypothalamus. *Science, 153,* 1284–1285.

Calasanti, T. M., & Bailey, C. A. (1991). Gender inequality and the division of household labor in the United States and Sweden: A socialist-feminist approach. *Social Problems, 38,* 34–53.

Calev, A., Pass, H. L., Shapira, B., Fink, M., Tubi, N., & Lerer, B. (1993). ECT and memory. In C. E. Coffey (Ed.), *The clinical science of electroconvulsive therapy.* Washington, DC: American Psychiatric Press.

Callaway, M. R., & Esser, J. K. (1984). Groupthink: Effects of cohesiveness and problem-solving procedures on group decision making. *Social Behavior and Personality, 12,* 157–164.

Campbell, A. (1995). A few good men: Evolutionary psychology and female adolescent aggression. *Ethology and Sociobiology, 16,* 99–123.

Campbell, A. (1999). Staying alive: Evolution, culture, and women's intrasexual aggression. *Behavioral and Brain Sciences, 22,* 203–252.

Campbell, J. D., & Fairey, P. J. (1989). Informational and normative routes to conformity: The effect of faction size as a function of norm extremity and attention to the stimulus. *Journal of Personality and Social Psychology, 57,* 457–468.

Campbell, J. D., Tesser, A., & Fairey, P. J. (1986). Conformity and attention to the stimulus: Some temporal and contextual dynamics. *Journal of Personality and Social Psychology, 51,* 315–324.

Campbell, K. (1970). *Body and mind.* Notre Dame, IN: University of Notre Dame Press.

Campfield, L. A., & Smith, F. J. (1990). Systemic factors in the control of food intake: Evidence for patterns as signals. In E. M. Stricker (Ed.), *Handbook of behavioral neurobiology: Vol. 10. Neurobiology of food and fluid intake.* New York: Plenum Press.

Campos, J. J., Anderson, D. I., Barbu-Roth, M. A., Hubbard, E. M., Hertenstein, M. J., & Witherington, D. (2000). Travel broadens the mind. *Infancy, 1,* 149–219.

Campos, J. J., Bertenthal, B. I., & Kermoian, R. (1992). Early experience and emotional development: The emergence of wariness of heights. *Psychological Science, 3,* 61–64.

Cannon, W. B. (1927). The James-Lange theory of emotions: A critical examination and an alternative theory. *American Journal of Psychology, 39,* 106–124.

Cannon, W. B. (1932; reprinted 1963). *The wisdom of the body.* New York: Norton.

Cantor, N., & Harlow, R. E. (1994). Personality, strategic behavior, and daily-life problem solving. *Current Directions in Psychological Science, 3,* 169–172.

Capaldi, D. M., Crosby, L., & Stoolmiller, M. (1996). Predicting the timing of first sexual intercourse for at-risk adolescent males. *Child Development, 67,* 344–359.

Card, J. J. (1987). Epidemiology of PTSD in a national cohort of Vietnam veterans. *Journal of Clinical Psychology, 43,* 6–27.

Carpenter, P. A., Just, M. A., & Shell, P. (1990). What one intelligence test measures: A theoretical account of the processing in the Raven Progressive Matrices Test. *Psychological Review, 97,* 404–431.

Carpenter, W. T., Jr., Heinrichs, D. W., & Alphs, L. D. (1985). Treatment of negative symptoms. *Schizophrenia Bulletin, 11,* 440–452.

Carr, S., Dabbs, J., & Carr, T. (1975). Mother-infant attachment: The importance of the mother's visual field. *Child Development, 46,* 331–338.

Carroll, B. J. (1991). Psychopathology and neurobiology of manic-depressive disorders. In B. J. Carroll & J. E. Barrett (Eds.), *Psychopathology and the brain.* New York: Raven Press.

Carroll, J. L., Shmidt, J. L., & Sorensen, R. (1992). Careers in psychology: Or what can I do with a bachelor's degree? *Psychological Reports, 71,* 1151–1154.

Carroll, M. A., Schneider, H. G., & Wesley, G. R. (1985). *Ethics in the practice of psychology.* Englewood Cliffs, NJ: Prentice-Hall.

Carstensen, L. L. (1995). Evidence for a life-span theory of socioemotional selectivity. *Current Directions in Psychological Science, 4,* 151–156.

Carstensen, L. L., & Fredrickson, B. L. (1998). Influence of HIV status and age on cognitive representations of others. *Health Psychology, 17,* 494–503.

Carstensen, L. L., Isaacowitz, D. M., & Charles, S. T. (1999). Taking time seriously: A theory of socioemotional selectivity. *American Psychologist, 54,* 165–181.

Case, R. (1992). Neo-Piagetian theories of intellectual development. In H. Beilin & P. B. Pufall (Eds.), *Piaget's theory: Prospects and possibilities.* Hillsdale, NJ: Erlbaum.

Case, R., Kurland, M., & Goldberg, J. (1982). Operational efficiency and the growth of short-term memory span. *Journal of Experimental Child Psychology, 33,* 386–404.

Cashdan, E. (1994). A sensitive period for learning about food. *Human Nature, 5,* 279–291.

Caspi, A. (2000). The child is father of the man: Personality continuities from childhood to adulthood. *Journal of Personality and Social Psychology, 78,* 158–172.

Caspi, A., & Moffitt, T. E. (1991). Individual differences are accentuated during periods of social change: The sample case of girls at puberty. *Journal of Personality and Social Psychology, 61,* 157–168.

Caspi, A., & Moffitt, T. E. (1993). When do individual differences matter? A paradoxical theory of personality coherence. *Psychological Inquiry, 4,* 247–271.

Caspi, A., & Roberts, B. W. (1999). Personality continuity and change across the life course. In L. A. Pervin & O. John (Eds.), *Handbook of personality: Theory and research* (2nd ed.). New York: Guilford.

Castillo, R. J. (1997). *Culture and mental illness: A client-centered approach.* Pacific Grove, CA: Brooks/Cole.

Cattell, R. B. (1943). The measurement of adult intelligence. *Psychological Bulletin, 40,* 153–193.

Cattell, R. B. (1950). *Personality: A systematic, theoretical, and factual study.* New York: McGraw-Hill.

Cattell, R. B. (1965). *The scientific analysis of personality.* Baltimore: Penguin.

Cattell, R. B. (1971). *Abilities: Their structure, growth, and action.* Boston: Houghton Mifflin. (Revised edition: Amsterdam: North-Holland, 1987)

Cattell, R. B. (1973). *Personality and mood by questionnaire.* San Francisco: Jossey-Bass.

Cavanaugh, J. C. (1993). *Adult development and aging* (2nd ed.). Belmont, CA: Wadsworth.

Ceci, S. J. (1993). Contextual trends in intellectual development. *Developmental Review, 13,* 403–435.

Ceci, S. J. (1996). *On intelligence: A bioecological treatise on intellectual development.* Cambridge, MA: Harvard University Press.

Ceraso, J. (1967, October). The interference theory of forgetting. *Scientific American,* pp. 117–124.

Cervone, D. (1997). Social-cognitive mechanisms and personality coherence: Self-knowledge, situational beliefs, and cross-situational coherence in perceived self-efficacy. *Psychological Science, 8,* 43–50.

Chagnon, N. A. (1979). Mate competition, favoring close kin, and village fissioning among the Yanomamö Indians. In N. A. Chagnon & W. Irons (Eds.), *Evolutionary biology and human social behavior: An anthropological perspective.* North Scituate, MA: Duxbury Press.

Chang, E. C. (1996). Cultural differences in optimism, pessimism, and coping: Predictors of subsequent adjustment in Asian American and Caucasian American college students. *Journal of Counseling Psychology, 43,* 113–123.

Charles, S. T., Reynolds, C. A., & Gatz, M. (2001). Age-related differences and change in positive and negative affect over 23 years. *Journal of Personality and Social Psychology, 80,* 136–151.

Chase, W. G., & Simon, H. A. (1973). Perception in chess. *Cognitive Psychology, 4,* 55–81.

Chater, N. (1996). Reconciling simplicity and likelihood principles in perceptual organization. *Psychological Review, 103,* 566–581.

Chaudhari, N., Landin, A. M., & Roper, S. D. (2000). A metabotropic glutamate receptor variant functions as a taste receptor. *Nature Neuroscience, 3,* 113–119.

Chen, S., & Chaiken, S. (1999). The heuristic-systematic model in its broader context. In A. Chaiken & Y. Trope (Eds.), *Dual-process theories in social psychology.* New York: Guilford.

Chen, Y., Brockner, J., & Katz, T. (1998). Toward an explanation of cultural differences in in-group favoritism: The role of individual versus collective primacy. *Journal of Personality and Social Psychology, 75,* 1490–1502.

Cherry, E. C. (1953). Some experiments on the recognition of speech, with one and with two ears. *Journal of the Acoustical Society of America, 25,* 975–979.

Cherry, E. C., & Taylor, W. K. (1954). Some further experiments on the recognition of speech with one and two ears. *Journal of the Acoustical Society of America, 26,* 554–559.

Chesler, P. (1969). Maternal influence in learning by observation in kittens. *Science, 166,* 901–903.

Chi, M. T. H., Bassok, M., Lewis, M. W., Reimann, P., & Glaser, R. (1989). Self-explanations: How students study and use examples in learning to solve problems. *Cognitive Science, 13,* 145–182.

Chi, M. T. H., de Leeuw, N., Chiu, M., & LaVancher, C. (1994). Eliciting self-explanations improves understanding. *Cognitive Science, 18,* 439–477.

Chi, M. T. H., & Glaser, R. (1985). Problem-solving ability. In R. J. Sternberg (Ed.), *Human abilities: An information-processing approach.* New York: Freeman.

Chomsky, N. (1957). *Syntactic structures.* The Hague: Mouton.

Chomsky, N. (1965). *Aspects of a theory of syntax.* Cambridge, MA: MIT Press.

Chomsky, N. (1968). *Language and mind.* New York: Harcourt Brace Jovanovich.

Cialdini, R. B. (1987). Compliance principles of compliance professionals: Psychologists of necessity. In M. Zanna, J. M. Olson, & C. P. Herman (Eds.), *Social influence: The Ontario symposium* (Vol. 5). Hillsdale, NJ: Erlbaum.

Cialdini, R. B. (1993). *Influence: Science and practice* (3rd ed.). New York: HarperCollins.

Cialdini, R. B. (2001). *Influence: Science and practice* (4th ed.). Boston: Allyn & Bacon.

Clark, D. M. (1988). A cognitive model of panic attacks. In S. Rachman & J. D. Maser (Eds.), *Panic: Psychological perspectives.* Hillsdale, NJ: Erlbaum.

Clark, E. (1973). What's in a word? On the child's acquisition of semantics in his first language. In T. Moore (Ed.), *Cognitive development and the acquisition of language.* New York: Academic Press.

Clark, E. (1987). The principle of contrast: A constraint on language acquisition. In B. MacWhinney (Ed.), *Mechanisms of language acquisition.* Hillsdale, NJ: Erlbaum.

Clark, E. V. (1995). Language acquisition: The lexicon and syntax. In J. L. Miller & P. D. Eimas (Eds.), *Speech, language, and communication.* San Diego, CA: Academic Press.

Clark, L. A., & Watson, D. (1991). Tripartite model of anxiety and depression: Psychometric evidence and taxonomic implications. *Journal of Abnormal Psychology, 100,* 316–336.

Clarke, J. C. (1988). *Alcoholism and problem drinking: Theories and treatment.* New York: Pergamon Press.

Clement, C. A., & Falmagne, R. J. (1986). Logical reasoning, world knowledge, and mental imagery: Interconnections in cognitive processes. *Memory & Cognition, 14,* 299–307.

Clifford, M. M., & Walster, E. (1973). The effects of physical attractiveness on teacher expectation. *Sociology of Education, 46,* 248–258.

Cloninger, C. R. (1990). Genetic epidemiology of alcoholism: Observations critical to the design and analysis of linkage studies. In C. R. Cloninger & H. Begleiter (Eds.), *Genetics and biology of alcoholism.* Plainview, NY: Cold Spring Harbor Laboratory Press.

Clutton-Brock, T. H., & Vincent, A. C. J. (1991). Sexual selection and the potential reproductive rates of males and females. *Nature, 351,* 58–60.

Cohen, D. (1996). Law, social policy, and violence: The impact of regional cultures. *Journal of Personality and Social Psychology, 70,* 961–978.

Cohen, L. H., Towbes, L. C., & Flocco, R. (1988). Effects of induced mood on self-reported life events and perceived and received social support. *Journal of Personality and Social Psychology, 55,* 669–674.

Cohen, R. A., & Albers, H. E. (1991). Disruption of human circadian and cognitive regulation following a discrete hypothalamic lesion: A case study. *Neurology, 41,* 726–729.

Cohen, S. (1996). Psychological stress, immunity, and upper respiratory infections. *Current Directions in Psychological Science, 5,* 86–90.

Cohen, S., & Herbert, T. B. (1996). Health psychology: Psychological factors and physical disease from the perspective of human psychoneuroendocrinology. *Annual Review of Psychology, 47,* 113–142.

Cohen, S., Kaplan, J. R., Cunnick, J. E., Manuck, S. B., & Rabin, B. S. (1992). Chronic social stress, affiliation, and cellular immune response in nonhuman primates. *Psychological Science, 3,* 301–304.

Cohen, S., Miller, G. E., & Rabin, B. S. (2001). Psychological stress and antibody response to immunization: A critical review of the human literature. *Psychosomatic Medicine, 63,* 7–18.

Cohen, S., Tyrrell, D. A. J., & Smith, A. P. (1991). Psychological stress and susceptibility to the common cold. *New England Journal of Medicine, 325,* 606–612.

Colby, A., & Damon, W. (1995). The development of extraordinary moral commitment. In M. Killen & D. Hart (Eds.), *Morality in everyday life: Developmental perspectives.* Cambridge, England: Cambridge University Press.

Colby, A., Kohlberg, L., Gibbs, J., & Lieberman, M. (1983). A longitudinal study of moral judgment. *Monographs of the Society for Research in Child Development, 48*(Whole Nos. 1 & 2).

Cole, D. A. (1991). Change in self-perceived competence as a function of peer and teacher evaluation. *Developmental Psychology, 27,* 682–688.

Cole, M., Gay, J., Glick, J., & Sharp, D. W. (1971). *The cultural context of learning and thinking.* New York: Basic Books.

Cole, M., & Means, B. (1981). *Comparative studies of how people think.* Cambridge, MA: Harvard University Press.

Collins, A., & Loftus, E. (1975). A spreading-activation theory of semantic processing. *Psychological Review, 82,* 407–428.

Collins, M. A., & Zebrowitz, L. A. (1995). The contributions of appearance to occupations outcomes in civilian and military settings. *Journal of Applied Social Psychology, 25,* 129–163.

Collins, W. A., Maccoby, E. E., Steinberg, L., Hetherington, E. M., & Bornstein, M. H. (2000). Contemporary research on parenting: The case for nature and nurture. *American Psychologist, 55,* 218–232.

Commons, M. L., Grossberg, S., & Staddon, J. E. R. (Eds.). (1991). *Neural network models of conditioning and action.* Hillside, NJ: Erlbaum.

Compas, B. E., Hinden, B. R., & Gerhardt, C. A. (1995). Adolescent development: Pathways and processes of risk and resilience. *Annual Review of Psychology, 46,* 265–293.

Concar, D. (1994, March). Design your own personality. *New Scientist,* pp. 22–26.

Connolly, J., Furman, W., & Konarski, R. (2000). The role of peers in the emergence of heterosexual romantic relationships in adolescence. *Child Development, 71,* 1395–1408.

Connolly, J. A., & Doyle, A. (1984). Relation of social fantasy play to social competence in preschoolers. *Developmental Psychology, 20,* 797–806.

Conway, M. A., Gardiner, J. M., Perfect, T. J., Anderson, S. J., & Cohen, G. M. (1997). Changes in memory awareness during learning: The acquisition of knowledge by psychology undergraduates. *Journal of Experimental Psychology: General, 126,* 393–413.

Cooley, C. H. (1902; reprinted 1964). *Human nature and the social order*. New York: Schocken Books.

Coons, P. M., Bowman, E. S., & Milstein, V. (1988). Multiple personality disorder: A clinical investigation of 50 cases. *Journal of Nervous and Mental Disease, 176*, 519–527.

Cooper, H. M., & Good, T. L. (1983). *Pygmalion grows up: Studies in the expectation communication process*. New York: Longman.

Cooper, M. L., Frone, M. R., Russel, M., & Mudar, P. (1995). Drinking to regulate positive and negative emotions: A motivational model of alcohol use. *Journal of Personality and Social Psychology, 69*, 990–1005.

Cooper, M. L., Russell, M., & George, W. H. (1988). Coping, expectancies, and alcohol abuse: A test of social learning foundations. *Journal of Abnormal Psychology, 97*, 218–230.

Corballis, M. C. (1999). Phylogeny from apes to humans. In M. C. Corballis & S. E. G. Lea (Eds.), *The descent of mind: Psychological perspectives on hominid evolution*. Oxford: Oxford University Press.

Corbetta, M., Miezin, F., Dobmeyer, S., Shulman, G., & Petersen, S. (1991). Selective and divided attention during visual discrimination of shape, colour and speed: Functional anatomy by positron emission tomography. *Journal of Neuroscience, 11*, 2383–2402.

Coren, S., & Ward, L. M. (1989). *Sensation and perception* (3rd ed.). New York: Harcourt Brace Jovanovich.

Corey, S. M. (1937). Professed attitudes and actual behavior. *Journal of Educational Psychology, 28* 271–280.

Corr, P. J., Pickering, A. D., & Gray, J. A. (1995). Sociability/impulsivity and caffeine-induced arousal: Critical flicker/fusion frequency and procedural learning. *Personality and Individual Differences, 18*, 713–730.

Costa, P. T., & McCrae, R. R. (1994). Set like plaster? Evidence for the stability of adult personality. In T. F. Heatherton & J. L. Weinberger (Eds.), *Can personality change?* Washington, DC: American Psychological Association.

Costa, P. T., McCrae, R. R., Martin, T. A., Oryol, V. E., Senin, I. G., Rukavishnikov, A. A., Shimonaka, Y., Nakazato, K., Gondo, Y., Takayama, M., Allik, J., Kallasmaa, T., & Realo, A. (2000). Personality development from adolescence through adulthood: Further cross-cultural comparisons of age differences. In V. J. Molfese & D. Molfese (Eds.), *Temperament and personality development across the life span*. Hillsdale, NJ: Erlbaum.

Cottrell, N. B., Wack, D. L., Sekerak, G. J., & Rittle, R. H. (1968). Social facilitation of dominant responses by the presence of an audience and the mere presence of others. *Journal of Personality and Social Psychology, 9*, 245–250.

Coughlin, L. D., & Patel, V. L. (1987). Processing of critical information by physicians and medical students. *Journal of Medical Education, 62*, 818–828.

Cousins, N. (1977, May 23). Anatomy of an illness (as perceived by the patient). *Saturday Review*, Nos. 4–6, pp. 48–51.

Cousins, S. D. (1989). Culture and self-perception in Japan and the United States. *Journal of Personality and Social Psychology, 56*, 124–131.

Cowan, N., Nugent, L. D., Elliott, E. M., & Saults, J. S. (2000). Persistence of memory for ignored lists of digits: Areas of developmental constancy and change. *Journal of Experimental Child Psychology, 76*, 151–172.

Cox, M. J., Owen, M. T., Henderson, V. K., & Margand, N. A. (1992). Prediction of infant-father and infant-mother attachment. *Developmental Psychology, 28*, 474–483.

Crabbe, J. C., Phillips, T. J., Buck, K. J. Cunningham, C. L., & Belknap, J. K. (1999). Identifying genes for alcohol and drug sensitivity: Recent progress and future directions. *Trends in Neuroscience, 22*, 173–179.

Crabbe, J. C., Wahlsten D., & Dudek, B. C. (1999b). Genetics of mouse behavior: Interactions with the laboratory environment. *Science, 284*, 1670–1672.

Craig, J. C., & Rollman, G. B. (1999). Somesthesis. *Annual Reviews of Psychology, 50*, 305–331.

Craik, F. I., & Tulving, E. (1975). Depth of processing and the retention of words in episodic memory. *Journal of Experimental Psychology: General, 104*, 268–294.

Craik, F. I., & Watkins, M. J. (1973). The role of rehearsal in short-term memory. *Journal of Verbal Learning and Verbal Behavior, 12*, 599–607.

Craske, M. G. (1999). *Anxiety disorders: Psychological approaches to theory and treatment*. Boulder, CO: Westview.

Crawford, C. J. (1994). Parenting in the Basque country: Implications of infant and childhood sleeping location for personality development. *Ethos, 22*, 42–82.

Cross, P. (1977). Not *can* but *will* college teachers be improved? *New Directions for Higher Education, 17*, 1–15.

Cross, S. E., & Markus, H. R. (1999). The cultural construction of personality. In L. A. Pervin & O. John (Eds.), *Handbook of personality: Theory and research* (2nd ed.). New York: Guilford.

Crowne, D. P., & Liverant, S. (1963). Conformity under varying conditions of personal commitment. *Journal of Abnormal and Social Psychology, 66*, 547–555.

Culebras, A., & Moore, J. T. (1989). Magnetic resonance findings in REM sleep behavior disorder. *Neurology, 39*, 1519–1523.

Culp, R. E., Cook, A. S., & Housley, P. C. (1983). A comparison of observed and reported adult-infant interactions: Effects of perceived sex. *Sex Roles, 9*, 475–479.

Cumming, E., & Henry, W. (1961). *Growing old: The process of disengagement*. New York: Basic Books.

Curtiss, S. (1977). *Genie: A psycholinguistic study of a modern-day "wild child."* New York: Academic Press.

Curtiss, S. (1989). The independence and task-specificity of language. In M. H. Bornstein & J. S. Bruner (Eds.), *Interaction in human development*. Hillsdale, NJ: Erlbaum.

Cutting, J. E., Proffitt, D. R., & Kozlowski, L. T. (1978). A biomechanical invariant for gait perception. *Journal of Experimental Psychology: Human Perception and Performance, 4*, 357–372.

Czeisler, C. A., Johnson, M. P., Duffy, J. E. Brown, E. N., Ronda, J. M., & Kronauer, R. E. (1990). Exposure to bright light and darkness to treat physiologic maladaptation to night work. *New England Journal of Medicine, 322*, 1253–1259.

Czeisler, C. A., Kronauer, R. E., Allen, J. S., Duffy, J. F., Jewett, M. E., Brown, E. N., & Ronda, J. M. (1989). Bright light induction of strong (type O) resetting of the human circadian pacemaker. *Science, 244*, 1328–1333.

Daly, M., & Wilson, M. (1988). *Homicide.* New York: de Gruyter.

Daly, M., & Wilson, M. (1990). Killing the competition. *Human Nature, 1,* 81–107.

Damon, W., & Hart, D. (1992). Self-understanding and its role in social and moral development. In M. H. Bornstein & M. E. Lamb (Eds.), *Developmental psychology: An advanced textbook* (3rd ed.). Hillsdale, NJ: Erlbaum.

Damsma, G., Pfaus, J. G., Wenkstern, D., Phillips, A. G., & Fibiger, H. C. (1992). Sexual behavior increases dopamine transmission in the nucleus accumbens and striatum of male rats: Comparison with novelty and locomotion. *Behavioral Neurosciences, 106,* 181–191.

Dance, K. A., & Kuiper, N. A. (1987). Self-schemata, social roles, and a self-worth contingency model of depression. *Motivation and Emotion, 11,* 251–268.

Darwin, C. (1859; reprinted 1963). *The origin of species.* New York: Washington Square Press.

Darwin, C. (1871). *The descent of man.* London: John Murray.

Darwin, C. (1872; reprinted 1965). *The expression of the emotions in man and animals.* Chicago: University of Chicago Press.

Darwin, C. T., Turvey, M. T., & Crowder, R. G. (1972). An auditory analogue of the Sperling partial report procedure: Evidence for brief auditory storage. *Cognitive Psychology, 3,* 255–267.

Dasen, P. R., & Heron, A. (1981). Cross-cultural tests of Piaget's theory. In H. C. Triandis & A. Heron (Eds.), *Handbook of cross-cultural psychology: Vol. 4. Developmental psychology.* Boston: Allyn & Bacon.

Daum, I., Channon, S., & Canavar, A. (1989). Classical conditioning in patients with severe memory problems. *Journal of Neurology and Neurosurgery Psychiatry, 52,* 47–51.

Davidoff, J., Davies, I., & Roberson, D. (1999). Colour categories in a stone-age tribe. *Nature, 398,* 203–204.

Davidson, J. M. (1980). Hormones and sexual behavior in the male. In D. T. Krieger & J. C. Hughes (Eds.), *Neuroendocrinology.* Sunderland, MA: Sinauer.

Davidson, J. M., Camargo, C. A., & Smith, E. R. (1979). Effects of androgen on sexual behavior in hypogonadal men. *Journal of Clinical Endocrinology and Metabolism, 48,* 955–958.

Davidson, J. M., & Myers, L. S. (1988). Endocrine factors in sexual psychophysiology. In R. C. Rosen & J. G. Beck (Eds.), *Patterns of sexual arousal: Psychophysiological processes and clinical applications.* New York: Guilford Press.

Davidson, R. J., Ekman, P., Saron, C. D., Senulis, J. A., & Friesn, W. V. (1990). Approach-withdrawal and cerebral asymmetry: Emotional expression and brain physiology I. *Journal of Personality and Social Psychology, 58,* 330–341.

Davies, N. B. (1991). Mating systems. In J. R. Krebs & N. B. Davies (Eds.), *Behavioural ecology III.* Oxford: Blackwell Scientific Publications.

Davis, C. M. (1928). Self selection of diet in newly weaned infants: An experimental study. *American Journal of Diseases of Children, 36,* 651–679.

Davis, J. M. (1974). A two-factor theory of schizophrenia. *Journal of Psychiatric Research, 11,* 25–30.

Davis, M. (1992). The role of the amygdala in fear and anxiety. *Annual Review of Neuroscience, 15,* 353–375.

Davison, K. P., Pennebaker, J. W., & Dickerson, S. S. (2000). Who talks? The social psychology of illness support groups. *American Psychologist, 55,* 205–217.

Dawes, R. M. (1991). Social dilemmas, economic self-interest, and evolutionary theory. In D. R. Brown & J. E. K. Smith (Eds.), *Frontiers of mathematical psychology.* New York: Springer-Verlag.

Dawes, R. M., & Messick, D. M. (2000). Social dilemmas. *International Journal of Psychology, 35,* 11–116.

Deary, I. J. (2000). Simple information processing and intelligence. In R. J. Sternberg (Ed.), *Handbook of intelligence.* Cambridge, England: Cambridge University Press.

Deaux, K. (1985). Sex and gender. *Annual Review of Psychology, 36,* 49–81.

de Boysson-Bardies, B. (1999). *How language comes to children.* Cambridge, MA: MIT Press.

DeCasper, A. J., & Fifer, W. P. (1980). Of human bonding: Newborns prefer their mothers' voices. *Science, 208,* 1174–1176.

Deci, E. L., Koestner, R., & Ryan, R. M. (1999). A meta-analytic review of experiments examining the effects of extrinsic rewards on intrinsic motivation. *Psychological Bulletin, 125,* 627–668.

Deci, E. L., & Ryan, R. M. (1991). A motivational approach to self: Integration in personality. In R. Dienstbier (Ed.), *Nebraska Symposium on Motivation: Perspectives on Motivation* (Vol. 38, pp. 237–288). Lincoln: University of Nebraska Press.

DeGalan, J., & Lampert, S. (2000). *Great jobs for psychology majors* (3rd ed.). Lincolnwood, IL: NTC Contemporary Publishing.

de Groot, A. D. (1965). *Thought and choice in chess.* The Hague: Mouton.

DeJonge, F. H., Louwerse, A. L., Ooms, M. P., Evers, P., Endert, E., & Van de Poll, N. E. (1989). Lesions of the SDN-POA inhibit sexual behavior of male Wistar rats. *Brain Research Bulletin, 23,* 483–492.

Delay, J., & Deniker, P. (1952). Trente-huit cas de psychoses traitées par la cure prolongée et continué de 4560 RP. *Comptes Rendus Congrès des Médecins Aliénistes et Neurologistes de France et des Pays de Langue Française, 50,* 497–502.

DeLisi, L. E., Dauphinais, I. D., & Gershon, E. S. (1988). Perinatal complications and reduced size of brain limbic structures in familial schizophrenia. *Schizophrenia Bulletin, 14,* 185–191.

Dement, W. C. (1972). *Some must watch while some must sleep.* San Francisco: Freeman.

Dement, W. C. (1979). The relevance of sleep pathologies to the function of sleep. In R. Drucker-Colin, M. Shkurovich, & M. B. Sterman (Eds.), *The functions of sleep.* New York: Academic Press.

Dennett, D. C. (1994). Language and intelligence. In J. Khalfa (Ed.), *What is intelligence?* Cambridge, England: Cambridge University Press.

Depue, R. A., & Collins, P. F. (1999). Neurobiology of the structure of personality: Dopamine, facilitation of incentive motivation, and extraversion. *Behavioral and Brain Science, 22,* 491–569.

DeRidder, L. M. (1993). Teenage pregnancy: Etiology and educational interventions. *Educational Psychology Review, 5,* 87–107.

DeRubeis, R. J., & Hollon, S. D. (1995). Explanatory style in the treatment of depression. In G. M. Buchanan & M. E. P. Seligman (Eds.), *Explanatory style.* Hillsdale, NJ: Erlbaum.

Descartes, R. (1637; reprinted 1972). *Treatise of man* (T. S. Hall, Trans.). Cambridge, MA: Harvard University Press.

Descartes, R. (1649; reprinted 1985). *The passions of the soul.* In J. Cottingham, R. Stoothoff, & D. Murdoch (Eds. and Trans.), *The philosophical writings of Descartes* (Vol. 1, pp. 324–404). Cambridge, England: Cambridge University Press.

Deutsch, A. (1948). *The shame of the states.* New York: Harcourt, Brace.

Deutsch, F. M. (2001). Equally shared parenting. *Current Directions in Psychological Science, 10,* 25–28.

Deutsch, J. A. (1990). Food intake: Gastric factors. In E. M. Stricker (Ed.), *Handbook of behavioral neurobiology: Vol. 10. Neurobiology of food and fluid intake.* New York: Plenum Press.

De Valois, R. L., & De Valois, K. K. (1988). *Spatial vision.* Oxford: Oxford University Press.

De Valois, R. L., Abramov, I., & Jacobs, G. H. (1966). Analysis of response patterns of LGN cells. *Journal of the Optical Society of America, 56,* 96–97.

de Villiers, J. G., & de Villiers, P. A. (1979). *Language acquisition.* Cambridge, MA: Harvard University Press.

Devine, P. G. (1989). Stereotypes and prejudice: Their automatic and controlled components. *Journal of Personality and Social Psychology, 56,* 5–18.

Devine, P. G., & Monteith, M. J. (1993). The role of discrepancy-associated affect in prejudice reduction. In D. M. Mackie & D. L. Hamilton (Eds.), *Affect, cognition, and stereotyping: Interactive processes in group perception.* San Diego, CA: Academic Press.

Devine, P., & Monteith, M. J. (1999). Automaticity and control in stereotyping. In S. Chaiken & Y. Trope (Eds.), *Dual-process theories in social psychology.* New York: Guilford.

de Waal, F. (1997). *Bonobo: The forgotten ape.* Berkeley: University of California Press.

Dew, M. A., Bromet, E. H., & Schulberg, H. C. (1987). A comparative analysis of two community stressors' long-term mental health effects. *American Journal of Community Psychology, 15,* 167–184.

DeWitt, L. A., & Samuel, A. G. (1990). The role of knowledge-based expectations in music perception: Evidence from musical restoration. *Journal of Experimental Psychology: General, 119,* 123–144.

Dewsbury, D. A. (1988). The comparative psychology of monogamy. In D. W. Leger (Ed.), *Comparative perspectives in modern psychology. Nebraska Symposium on Motivation, 1987.* Lincoln: University of Nebraska Press.

Dias, M. G., & Harris, P. L. (1988). The effect of make-believe play on deductive reasoning. *British Journal of Developmental Psychology, 6,* 207–221.

Dickinson, A. (1989). Expectancy theory in animal conditioning. In S. B. Klein & R. R. Mowrer (Eds.), *Contemporary learning theories: Pavlovian conditioning and the status of learning theory.* Hillsdale, NJ: Erlbaum.

Dickinson, A., & Balleine, B. (1995). Motivational control of instrumental action. *Current Directions in Psychological Science, 4,* 162–167.

Dickinson, A., & Balleine, B. W. (2000). Causal cognition and goal-directed action. In C. Heyes & L. Huber (Eds.), *The evolution of cognition.* Cambridge, MA: MIT Press.

Dickinson, A., & Dawson, G. R. (1987). The role of the instrumental contingency in motivational control of performance. *Quarterly Journal of Experimental Psychology, 39B,* 77–93.

Diener, E., Sandvik, E., Pavot, W., & Fujita, F. (1992). Extraversion and subjective well-being in a U.S. national probability sample. *Journal of Research in Personality, 26,* 205–215.

Diener, E., & Suh, M. E. (1998). Subjective well-being and age: An international analysis. In K. W. Schaie & M. P. Lawton (Eds.), *Annual review of gerontology and geriatrics: Vol. 17. Focus on emotion and adult development.* New York: Springer.

Dies, R. (1992). The future of group therapy. *Psychotherapy, 29,* 58–64.

Digman, J. M. (1989). Five robust trait dimensions: Development, stability, and utility. *Journal of Personality, 57,* 195–214.

Dillon, K. M. (1993). Facilitated communication, autism, and Ouija. *Skeptical Inquirer, 17,* 281–287.

DiMascio, A., Weissman, M. M., Prusoff, B. A., Neu, C., Zwilling, M., & Klerman, G. L. (1979). Differential symptom reduction by drugs and psychotherapy in acute depression. *Archives of General Psychiatry, 36,* 1450–1456.

Dimberg, U., Thunberg, M., & Elmehed, K. (2000). Unconscious facial reactions to emotional facial expressions. *Psychological Science, 11,* 86–89.

Dion, K. K. (1972). Physical attractiveness and evaluation of children's transgressions. *Journal of Personality and Social Psychology, 24,* 207–213.

Dion, K. K. (1986). Stereotyping based on physical attractiveness: Issues and conceptual perspectives. In C. P. Herman, M. P. Zanna, & E. T. Higgins (Eds.), *Physical appearance, stigma, and social behavior: The Ontario symposium* (Vol. 3). Hillsdale, NJ: Erlbaum.

Dobson, K. (1989). A meta-analysis of the efficacy of cognitive therapy for depression. *Journal of Consulting and Clinical Psychology, 57,* 414–429.

Doherty, W., & Jacobson, N. (1982). Marriage and the family. In B. B. Wolman (Ed.), *Handbook of developmental psychology.* Englewood Cliffs, NJ: Prentice-Hall.

Donenberg, G. R. (1998). Guilt and abnormal aspects of parent-child interactions. In J. Bybee (Ed.), *Guilt and children.* San Diego: Academic Press.

Doob, L. W. (1990). Forward. In M. H. Segall, P. R. Dasen, J. W. Berry, & Y. H. Poortinga, *Human behavior in global perspective: An introduction to cross-cultural psychology.* New York: Pergamon Press.

Doty, R. L., Shaman, P., Applebaum, S. L., Giberson, R., Siksorski, L., & Rosenberg, L. (1984). Smell identification ability: Changes with age. *Science, 226,* 1441–1443.

Doucet, C., & Stelmack, R. M. (2000). An event-related potential analysis of extraversion and individual differences in cognitive processing speed and response execution. *Journal of Personality and Social Psychology, 78,* 956–964.

Dovidio, J. F., Brigham, J. C., Johnson, B. T., & Gaertner, S. L. (1996). Stereotyping, prejudice, and discrimination. In C. N. Macrae, C. Stangor, & M. Hewstone (Eds.), *Stereotypes and stereotyping.* New York: Guilford Press.

Dovidio, J. F., Evans, N., & Tyler, R. B. (1986). Racial stereotypes: The contents of their cognitive representations. *Journal of Experimental Social Psychology, 22,* 22–37.

Dovidio, J. F., Johnson, C., Gaertner, S. L., Validzic, A., Howard, A., & Eisinger, N. (1994, April). *Racial bias and the role of implicit and explicit attitudes.* Paper presented at the annual meeting of the Eastern Psychological Association, Providence, RI.

Dovidio, J., Kawakami, K., Johnson, C., Johnson, B., & Howard, A. (1997). On the nature of prejudice: Automatic and controlled processes. *Journal of Experimental Social Psychology, 33,* 510–540.

Drake, R. E., Goldman, H. H., Leff, H. S., Lehman, A. F., Dixon, L., Mueser, K. T., & Torrey, W. C. (2001). Implementing evidence-based practices in routine mental health service settings. *Psychiatric Services, 52,* 179–182.

Draper, P., & Harpending, H. (1982). Father absence and reproductive strategy: An evolutionary perspective. *Journal of Anthropological Research, 38,* 255–273.

Draper, P., & Harpending, H. (1988). A sociobiological perspective on the development of human reproductive strategies. In K. B. MacDonald (Ed.), *Sociobiological perspectives on human development.* New York: Springer-Verlag.

Dronkers, N. F., Pinker, S., & Damasio, A. (2000). Language and the aphasias. In E. R. Kandel, J. H. Schwartz, & T. M. Jessell (Eds.), *Principles of Neural Science* (4th ed.). New York: McGraw-Hill.

Duffy, V. B., & Bartoshuk, L. M. (1996). Sensory factors in feeding. In E. D. Capaldi (Ed.), *Why we eat what we eat: The psychology of eating.* Washington, DC: APA.

Duggan, J. P., & Booth, D. A. (1986). Obesity, overeating, and rapid gastic emptying in rats with ventromedial hypothalamic lesions. *Science, 231,* 609–611.

Dulac, C. (2000). The physiology of taste, vintage 2000. *Cell, 100,* 607–610.

Duncan, J., Seitz, R. J., Kolodny, J., Bor, D., Herzog, H., Ahmed, A., Newell, F. N., & Emslie, H. (2000). A neural basis for general intelligence. *Science, 289,* 457–460.

Duncan, L. E., & Agronick G. S. (1995). The intersection of life stage and social events: Personality and life outcomes. *Journal of Personality and Social Psychology, 69,* 558–568.

Duncker, K. (1945). On problem-solving. *Psychological Monographs, 58*(Whole No. 270).

Dunn, J., & Plomin, R. (1990). *Separate lives: Why siblings are so different.* New York: Basic Books.

Dunning, D., Meyerowitz, J. A., & Holzberg, A.D. (1989). Ambiguity and self-evaluation: The role of idiosyncratic trait definitions in self-serving assessments of ability. *Journal of Personality and Social Psychology, 57,* 1082–1090.

Dunphy, D. C. (1963). The social structure of urban adolescent peer groups. *Sociometry, 26,* 230–246.

Dweck, C. S., Davidson, W., Nelson, S., & Enna, B. (1978). Sex differences in learned helplessness: II. The contingencies of evaluative feedback in the classroom. III. An experimental analysis. *Developmental Psychology, 14,* 268–276.

Dworkin, B. R. (1993). *Learning and physiological regulation.* Chicago: University of Chicago Press.

Eacott, M. J. (1999). Memory for events in early childhood. *Current Directions in Psychological Science, 8,* 46–49.

Eagle, M., Wolitzky, D. L., & Klein, G. S. (1966). Imagery: Effect of a concealed figure in a stimulus. *Science, 151,* 837–839.

Eagly, A. H., Ashmore, R. D., Makhijani, M. G., & Longo, L. C. (1991). What is beautiful is good, but . . .: A meta-analytic review of research on the physical attractiveness stereotype. *Psychological Bulletin, 110,* 109–128.

Eagly, A. H., & Wood, W. (1999). The origins of sex differences in human behavior: Evolved dispositions versus social roles. *American Psychologist, 54,* 408–423.

Eaton, W. O., & Ritchot, K. F. M. (1995). Physical maturation and information-processing speed in middle childhood. *Developmental Psychology, 31,* 967–972.

Ebbinghaus, H. (1885; reprinted 1913). *Memory: A contribution to experimental psychology* (H. A. Ruger & C. E. Bussenius, Trans.). New York: Teachers College Press.

Edeline, J., Pham, P., & Weinberger, N. M. (1993). Rapid development of learning-induced receptive field plasticity in the auditory cortex. *Behavioral Neuroscience, 107,* 539–551.

Edelman, G. M. (1987). *Neural Darwinism.* New York: Basic Books.

Eibl-Eibesfeldt, I. (1961, December). The fighting behavior of animals. *Scientific American,* pp. 112–121.

Eibl-Eibesfeldt, I. (1975). *Ethology: The biology of behavior* (2nd ed.). New York: Holt, Rinehart & Winston.

Eibl-Eibesfeldt, I. (1989). *Human ethology.* New York: de Gruyter.

Eichenbaum, H. (1997b). How does the brain organize memories? *Science, 277,* 330–331.

Eimas, P. D. (1975). Speech perception in early infancy. In L. B. Cohen & P. Salapafek (Eds.), *Infant perception.* New York: Academic Press.

Einon, D. (1994). Are men more promiscuous than women? *Ethology and Sociobiology, 15,* 131–143.

Eisenberg, N. (2000). Emotion, regulation, and moral development. *Annual Review of Psychology, 51,* 665–697.

Ekman, P. (1973). Cross-cultural studies of facial expression. In P. Ekman (Ed.), *Darwin and facial expression.* New York: Academic Press.

Ekman, P. (1992). Facial expressions of emotion: New findings, new questions. *Psychological Science, 3,* 34–38.

Ekman, P., & Friesen, W. V. (1975). *Unmasking the face.* Englewood Cliffs, NJ: Prentice-Hall.

Ekman, P., & Friesen, W. V. (1982). Measuring facial movements with the facial action coding system. In P. Ekman (Ed.), *Emotion in the human face.* Cambridge, England: Cambridge University Press.

Ekman, P., Friesen, W. V., O'Sullivan, M., & many others (1987). Universals and cultural differences in the judgments of facial expressions of emotion. *Journal of Personality and Social Psychology, 53,* 712–717.

Ekman, P., Levenson, R. W., & Friesen, W. V. (1983). Autonomic nervous system activity distinguishes among emotions. *Science, 221,* 1208–1210.

Eley, T. C. (1997). General genes: A new theme in developmental psychopathology. *Current Directions in Psychological Science, 6,* 90–95.

Elkin, R., & Leippe, M. (1986). Physiological arousal, dissonance, and attitude change: Evidence for a dissonance-arousal link and a "don't remind me" effect. *Journal of Personality and Social Psychology, 51,* 55–65.

Elkind, D. (1978). Understanding the young adolescent. *Adolescence, 13,* 127–134.

Elliot, A. J., & Devine, P. G. (1994). On the motivational nature of cognitive dissonance: Dissonance as psychological discomfort. *Journal of Personality and Social Psychology, 67,* 382–394.

Ellis, A. (1962). *Reason and emotion in psychotherapy.* New York: Lyle Stuart.

Ellis, A. (1986). Rational-emotive therapy. In I. L. Kutash & A. Wolf (Eds.), *Psychotherapist's casebook.* San Francisco: Jossey-Bass.

Ellis, A. (1993). Fundamentals of rational-emotive therapy for the 1990s. In W. Dryden & L. K. Hill (Eds.), *Innovations in rational-emotive therapy.* Newbury Park, CA: Sage.

Ellis, B. J., McFadyen-Ketchum, S., Dodge, K. A., Pettit, G. S., & Bates, J. E. (1999). Quality of early family relationships and individual differences in the timing of pubertal maturation in girls: A longitudinal test of an evolutionary model. *Journal of Personality and Social Psychology, 77,* 387–401.

Ellis, L., & Ames, M. A. (1987). Neurohormonal functioning and sexual orientation: A theory of homosexuality-heterosexuality. *Psychological Bulletin, 101,* 233–258.

Ellis, L., Ames, M. A., Peckham, W., & Burke, D. (1988). Sexual orientation of human offspring may be altered by severe maternal stress during pregnancy. *Journal of Sex Research, 25,* 152–157.

Ellis, S., Rogoff, B., & Cromer, C. (1981). Age segregation in children's social interactions. *Developmental Psychology, 17,* 399–406.

Emde, R. N., Biringen, Z., Clyman, R. B., & Oppenheim D. (1991). The moral self of infancy: Affective core and procedural knowledge. *Developmental Review, 11,* 251–270.

Emde, R. N., & Buchsbaum, H. K. (1990). "Didn't you hear my mommy?" Autonomy with connectedness in moral self emergence. In D. Cicchetti, & M. Beeghly (Eds.), *The self in transition: Infancy to childhood.* Chicago: University of Chicago Press.

Emmelkamp, P. (1994). Behavior therapy with adults. In A. Bergin & S. Garfield (Eds.), *Handbook of psychotherapy and behavior change* (4th ed.). New York: Wiley.

Endler, J. A. (1986). *Natural selection in the wild.* Princeton, NJ: Princeton University Press.

Endler, N. S. (1982). *Holiday of darkness: A psychologist's personal journey out of his depression.* New York: Wiley.

Engel, S. A. (1999). Using neuroimaging to measure mental representations: Finding color-opponent neurons in visual cortex. *Current Directions in Psychological Science, 8,* 23–27.

Enserink, M. (1999). Can the placebo be the cure? *Science, 284,* 238–240.

Epstein, R. (1991). Skinner, creativity, and the problem of spontaneous behavior. *Psychological Science, 2,* 362–370.

Erckmann, W. J. (1983). The evolution of polyandry in shorebirds: An evolutionary hypothesis. In S. K. Wasser (Ed.), *Social behavior of female vertebrates.* New York: Academic Press.

Ericsson, K. A. (1998) The scientific study of expert levels of performance: General implications for optimal learning and creativity. *High Ability Studies, 9,* 75–100.

Ericsson, K. A., & Chase, W. G. (1982). Exceptional memory. *American Scientist, 70,* 607–615.

Ericsson, K. A., & Delaney, P. F. (1999). Long-term working memory as an alternative to capacity models of working memory in everyday skilled performance. In A. Miyake & P. Shah (Eds.), *Models of working memory: Mechanisms of active maintenance and executive control.* Cambridge, England: Cambridge University Press.

Ericsson, K. A., & Faivre, I. A. (1988). What's exceptional about exceptional abilities? In L. K. Obler & D. Fein (Eds.), *The exceptional brain: Neuropsychology of talent and special abilities.* New York: Guilford Press.

Ericsson, K. A., & Kintsch, W. (1995). Long-term working memory. *Psychological Review, 102,* 211–245.

Ericsson, K. A., Krampe, R. T., & Tesch-Römer, C. (1993). The role of deliberate practice in the acquisition of expert performance. *Psychological Review, 100,* 363–406.

Ericsson, K. A., & Lehmann, A. C. (1996). Expert and exceptional performance: Evidence of maximal adaptation to task constraints. *Annual Review of Psychology, 47,* 273–305.

Erienmeyer-Kimling, L., Rock, D., Roberts, S. A., Janal, M., Kestenbaum, C., Cornblatt, B., Adamo, U. H., & Gottesman, I. I. (2000). Attention, memory, and motor skills as childhood predictors of schizophrenia-related psychoses: The New York high-risk project. *American Journal of Psychiatry, 157,* 1416–1422.

Eriksen, C. W., & Collins, J. F. (1967). Some temporal characteristics of visual pattern perception. *Journal of Experimental Psychology, 74,* 476–484.

Erikson, E. H. (1963). *Childhood and society* (2nd ed.). New York: Norton.

Erikson, E. H. (1968). *Identity: Youth and crisis.* New York: Norton.

Errera, P. (1972). Statement based on interviews with forty "worst cases" in the Milgram obedience experiments. In J. Katz (Ed.), *Experimentation with human beings: The authority of the investigator, subject, professions, and state in the human experimentation process.* New York: Russell Sage Foundation.

Essock-Vitale, S. M., & McGuire, M. T. (1980). Predictions derived from the theories of kin selection and reciprocation assessed by anthropological data. *Ethology and Sociobiology, 1,* 233–243.

Etscorn, F., & Stephens R. (1973). Establishment of conditioned taste aversions with a 24-hour CS-US interval. *Physiological Psychology, 1,* 251–253.

Eveleth, P. B., & Tanner, J. M. (1990). *Worldwide variation in human growth* (2nd ed.). Cambridge, England: Cambridge University Press.

Everson, C. A. (1993). Sustained sleep deprivation impairs host defense. *American Journal of Physiology, 265,* R1148–R1154.

Everson, C. A., Bergmann, B. M., & Rechtschaffen, A. (1989). Sleep deprivation in the rat: III. Total sleep deprivation. *Sleep, 12,* 13–21.

Ewart, C. K., & Kolodner, K. B. (1994). Negative affect, gender, and expressive style predict elevated ambulatory blood pressure in adolescents. *Journal of Personality and Social Psychology, 66,* 596–605.

Exner, J. E. (1993). *The Rorschach: A comprehensive system: Vol. I. Basic foundations* (3rd ed.). New York: Wiley.

Eysenck, H. J. (1952). *The scientific study of personality.* London: Routledge & Kegan Paul.

Eysenck, H. J. (1967). *The biological basis of personality*. Springfield, IL: Charles C. Thomas.

Eysenck, H. J. (1976). *Sex and personality*. London: Open Books.

Eysenck, H. J. (1982). Development of a theory. In H. J. Eysenck (Ed.), *Personality, genetics, and behavior: Selected papers*. New York: Praeger.

Eysenck, H. J. (1990). Biological dimensions of personality. In L. A. Pervin (Ed.), *Handbook of personality: Theory and research*. New York: Guilford Press.

Eysenck, H. J., & Eysenck, M. W. (1985). *Personality and individual differences: A natural science approach*. New York: Plenum Press.

Eysenck, M. W. (1992). *Anxiety: The cognitive perspective*. Hillsdale, NJ: Erlbaum.

Eysenck, S. B. G., & Eysenck, H. J. (1967). Salivary response to lemon juice as a measure of introversion. *Perceptual and Motor Skill, 24*, 1047–1051.

Fagen, R. M., & George, T. K. (1977). Play behavior and exercise in young ponies (*Equus caballus*). *Behavioral Ecology and Sociobiology, 2*, 267–269.

Fancher, R. E. (1985). *The intelligence men: Makers of the IQ controversy*. New York: Norton.

Farah, M. J. (1989). The neuropsychology of mental imagery. In J. W. Brown (Ed.), *Neuropsychology of visual perception*. Hillsdale, NJ: Erlbaum.

Farah, M. J. (1989). *Visual Agnosia*. Cambridge, MA: MIT Press.

Farah, M. J., Wilson, K. D., Drain, M., & Tanaka, J. N. (1998). What is "special" about face perception? *Psychological Review, 105*, 482–498.

Faraone, S. V., Tsuang, M. T., & Tsuang, D. W. (1999). *Genetics of mental disorders: A guide for students, clinicians, and researchers*. New York: Guilford.

Farooqi, I. S., Jebb, S. A., Langmack, G., Lawrence, E., Cheetham, C. H., Prentice, A. M., Hughes, I. A., McCamish, M. A., & O'Rahilly, S. (1999). Effects of recombinant leptin therapy in a child with congenital leptin deficiency. *New England Journal of Medicine, 341*, 879–884.

Faust, I. M. (1984). Role of the fat cell in energy balance physiology. In A. J. Stunkard & E. Stellar (Eds.), *Eating and its disorders*. New York: Raven Press.

Fazio, R. H. (1986). How do attitudes guide behavior? In R. M. Sorrentino & E. T. Higgins (Eds.), *Handbook of motivation and cognition: Foundations of social behavior*. New York: Guilford Press.

Fazio, R. H. (1990). Multiple processes by which attitudes guide behavior: The mode model as an integrative framework. *Advances in Experimental Social Psychology, 23*, 75–109.

Fazio, R. H., Jackson, J. R., Dunton, B. C., & Williams, C. J. (1995). Variability in automatic activation as an unobtrusive measure of racial attitudes: A bona fide pipeline? *Journal of Personality and Social Psychology, 69*, 1013–1027.

Fechner, G. T. (1860; translated edition 1966). *Elements of psychophysics*. (H. E. Alder, Trans.). New York: Holt, Rinehart & Winston.

Feder, H. H. (1984). Hormones and sexual behavior. *Annual Reviews of Psychology, 35*, 165–200.

Feeney, A., & Nutt, D. J. (1999). The neuropharmacology of serotonin and noradrenaline in depression. *International Journal of Psychiatry in Clinical Practice, 3, Supplement 2*, S3–S8.

Feeney, B. C., & Kirkpatrick, L. A. (1996). Effects of adult attachment and presence of romantic partners on physiological responses to stress. *Journal of Personality and Social Psychology, 70*, 255–270.

Feeney, J. A., & Noller, P. (1990). Attachment style as a predictor of adult romantic relationships. *Journal of Personality and Social Psychology, 58*, 281–291.

Feingold, A. (1994). Gender differences in personality: A meta-analysis. *Psychological Bulletin, 116*, 429–456.

Feldman, J. (1997). *The educational opportunities that lie in self-directed age mixing among children and adolescents*. Unpublished doctoral dissertation, Department of Psychology, Boston College, Chestnut Hill, MA.

Feldman, J., & Gray, P. (1999). Some educational benefits of freely chosen age mixing among children and adolescents. *Phi Delta Kappan, 80*, 507–512.

Feldman, J., & Gray, P. (2001). Qualities of age-mixed interactions among adolescents and children at an ungraded democratic school. Manuscript submitted for publication.

Feng, A. S., & Ratnam, R. (2000). Neural basis of hearing in real-world situations. *Annual Reviews of Psychology, 2000*, 699–725.

Fernandez, G., Weyerts, H., Schrader-Bolsche, M., Tendolkar, I., Smid, H. G., Tempelmann, C., Hinrichs, H., Sheich, H., Elger, C. E., Mangun, G. R., & Heinze, H. J. (1998). Successful verbal encoding into episodic memory engages the posterior hippocampus: A parametrically analyzed functional magnetic resonance imaging study. *Journal of Neuroscience, 18*, 1841–1847.

Fernández-Dols, J., & Ruiz-Belda, M. (1995). Are smiles a sign of happiness? Gold medal winners at the Olympic Games. *Journal of Personality and Social Psychology, 69*, 1113–1119.

Ferster, D., Chung, S., & Wheat, H. (1996). Orientation selectivity of thalamic input to simple cells of cat visual cortex. *Nature, 380*, 249–252.

Festinger, L. (1957). *A theory of cognitive dissonance*. Stanford, CA: Stanford University Press.

Festinger, L., & Carlsmith, J. M. (1959). Cognitive consequences of forced compliance. *Journal of Abnormal and Social Psychology, 58*, 203–210.

Field, T. (1990). *Infancy*. Cambridge, MA: Harvard University Press.

Field, T. (1996). Attachment and separation in young children. *Annual Review of Psychology, 47*, 541–561.

Field, T., Woodson, R., Greenberg, R., & Cohen, D. (1982). Discrimination and imitation of facial expressions by neonates. *Science, 218*, 179–181.

Fieve, R. R. (1975). *Mood swing*. New York: W. Morrow.

Fink, M. (2000). Electroshock revisited. *American Scientist, 88*, 162–167.

Finnan, C. R. (1982). The ethnography of children's spontaneous play. In G. Spindler (Ed.), *Doing the ethnography of schooling: Educational anthropology in action*. New York: Holt, Rinehart & Winston.

Fiorani, M., Rosa, M. G. P., Guttass, R., & Rocha-Miranda, C. E. (1992). Dynamic surrounds of receptive fields in primate striate cortex: A physiological basis for perceptual completion. *Proceedings of the National Academy of Sciences (USA) 89*, 8547–8551.

Fischler, M. A., & Firschein, O. (1987). *Intelligence: The eye, the brain, and the computer*. Reading, MA: Addison-Wesley.

Fisher, H. E. (1992). *Anatomy of love: The natural history of monogamy, adultery, and divorce*. New York: Norton.

Fisher, K. W., & Tangney, J. P. (1995). Self-conscious emotions and the affect revolution: Framework and overview. In J. P. Tangney & K. W. Fischer (Eds.), *Self-conscious emotions: The psychology of shame, guilt, embarrassment, and pride*. New York: Guilford Press.

FitzGerald, K. W. (1988). *Alcoholism: The genetic inheritance*. Garden City, NY: Doubleday.

Flaherty, C. F. (1996). *Incentive relativity*. New York: Cambridge University Press.

Flavell, J. H. (1999). Cognitive development: Children's knowledge about the mind. *Annual Review of Psychology, 50*, 21–45.

Flynn, J. R. (1987). Massive IQ gains in 14 nations: What IQ tests really measure. *Psychological Bulletin, 101*, 171–191.

Flynn, J. R. (1999). Searching for justice: The discovery of IQ gains over time. *American Psychologist, 54*, 5–20.

Foa, E. B., & Kozak, M. J. (1986). Emotional processing of fear: Exposure to corrective information. *Psychological Bulletin, 99*, 20–35.

Foa, E. B., & Riggs, D. S. (1995). Posttraumatic stress disorder following assault: Theoretical considerations and empirical findings. *Psychological Science, 4*, 61–65.

Fodor, I. G. (1982). Gender and phobia. In I. Al-Issa (Ed.), *Gender and psychopathology*. New York: Academic Press.

Fontaine, R. P. (1994). Play as physical flexibility training in five Ceboid primates. *Journal of Comparative Psychology, 108*, 203–212.

Forbes, J. F., & Weiss, D. S. (1992). The cosleeping habits of military children. *Military Medicine, 157*, 196–200.

Ford, D. H., & Urban, H. B. (1998). *Contemporary models of psychotherapy: A comparative analysis* (2nd ed.). New York: Wiley.

Ford, M. R., & Widiger, T. A. (1989). Sex bias in the diagnosis of histrionic and antisocial personality disorders. *Journal of Consulting and Clinical Psychology, 57*, 301–305.

Forgatch, M. S., & DeGarmo, D. S. (1999). Parenting through change: An effective prevention program for single mothers. *Journal of Consulting and Clinical Psychology, 67*, 711–724.

Forrest, G. G. (1985). Antabuse treatment. In T. E. Bratter & G. G. Forrest (Eds.), *Alcoholism and substance abuse: Strategies for clinical intervention*. New York: Free Press.

Foss, J. D., & Hakes, D. T. (1978). *Psycholinguistics: An introduction to the psychology of language*. Englewood Cliffs, NJ: Prentice-Hall.

Foster, P. S., & Eisler, R. M. (2001). An integrative approach to the treatment of obsessive-compulsive disorder. *Comprehensive Psychiatry, 42*, 24–31.

Foulkes, D. (1985). *Dreaming: A cognitive-psychological analysis*. Hillsdale, NJ: Erlbaum.

Fowles, D. C. (1992). Schizophrenia: Diathesis-stress revisited. *Annual Review of Psychology, 43*, 303–336.

Fox, N. A., & Davidson, R. J. (1988). Patterns of brain electrical activity during facial signs of emotion in 10-month-old infants. *Developmental Psychology, 24*, 230–236.

Frandsen, A. N., & Holder, J. R. (1969). Spatial visualization in solving complex verbal problems. *Journal of Psychology, 73*, 229–233.

Frankel, K. A., & Bates, J. E. (1990). Mother-toddler problem solving: Antecedents of attachment, home behavior, and temperament. *Child Development, 61*, 810–819.

Franklin, B. (1818; reprinted 1949). *The autobiography of Benjamin Franklin*. Berkeley: University of California Press.

Freedman, J. L, & Fraser, S. C. (1966). Compliance without pressure: The foot-in-the-door technique. *Journal of Personality and Social Psychology, 4*, 195–202.

Freedman, M. S., Lucas, R. J., Soni, B., von Schantz, M., Muñoz, M., David-Gray, Z., & Foster, R. (1999). Regulation of mammalian circadian behavior by non-rod, non-cone, ocular photoreceptors. *Science, 284*, 502–504.

Freidman, M., & Rosenman, R. H. (1974). *Type A behavior and your heart*. New York: Knopf.

Frenkel, O. J., & Doob, A. N. (1976). Post-decision dissonance at the polling booth. *Canadian Journal of Behavioural Science, 8*, 347–350.

Freud, A. (1936; reprinted 1946). *The ego and the mechanisms of defense* (C. Baines, Trans.). New York: International Universities Press.

Freud, S. (1901; reprinted 1990). *The psychopathology of everyday life* (A. Tyson, Trans.). In J. Strachey (Ed.), *The standard edition of the complete psychological works of Sigmund Freud*. New York: Norton.

Freud, S. (1909; reprinted 1963). Notes upon a case of obsessional neurosis. In P. Rieff (Ed.), *Three case histories*. New York: Collier Books.

Freud, S. (1910; reprinted 1947). *Leonardo da Vinci: A study in psychosexuality*. New York: Random House.

Freud, S. (1912; reprinted 1932). A note on the unconscious in psychoanalysis. In J. Rickman (Ed. 1), *A general selection from the works of Sigmund Freud*. London: Hogarth Press.

Freud, S. (1923; reprinted 1963). [Note appended to the 1963 reprint of "Notes upon a case of obsession neurosis."] In P. Rieff (Ed.), *Three case histories*. New York: Collier Books.

Freud, S. (1933; reprinted 1964). *New introductory lectures on psychoanalysis*. In J. Strachey (Ed. & Trans.), *The standard edition of the complete works of Sigmund Freud* (Vol. 20). London: Hogarth Press.

Freud, S. (1935; reprinted 1960). *A general introduction to psychoanalysis*. New York: Washington Square Press.

Frey, D. (1986). Recent research on selective exposure to information. *Advances in Experimental Social Psychology, 19*, 41–80.

Friedman, H., & Zebrowitz, L. A. (1992). The contribution of typical sex differences in facial maturity to sex role stereotypes. *Personality and Social Psychology Bulletin, 18*, 430–438.

Friedman, H. S., Tucker, J. S., Schwartz, J. E., Martin, L. R., Tomlinson-Keasey, C., Wingard, D. L., & Criqui, M. H. (1995). Childhood conscientiousness and longevity: Health behaviors and cause of death. *Journal of Personality and Social Psychology, 68*, 696–703.

Friedman, J. M. (1997). The alphabet of weight control. *Nature, 385*, 119–120.

Friedman, S. (1972). Habituation and recovery of visual response in the alert human newborn. *Journal of Experimental Child Psychology, 13*, 339–349.

Friedman-Hill, S. R., Robertson, L. C., & Treisman, A. (1995). Parietal contributions to visual feature binding: Evidence from a patient with bilateral lesions. *Science, 269*, 853–855.

Fritsch, J. (1999, June 8). A closer look at those who stay slim. *New York Times*, p. C8.

Fritz, J., Bisenberger, A., & Kotrschal, K. (2000). Stimulus enhancement in greylag geese: Socially mediated learning of an operant task. *Animal Behaviour, 59,* 1119–1125.

Fry, D. P. (1992). "Respect for the rights of others is peace": Learning aggression versus nonaggression among the Zapotec. *American Anthropologist, 94,* 621–639.

Fuller, J. L., & Thompson, W. R. (1978). *Foundations of behavior genetics.* New York: Wiley.

Fulton, S., Woodside, B., & Shizgal, P. (2000). Modulation of brain reward by leptin. *Science, 287,* 125–128.

Funder, D. C. (1995). On the accuracy of personality judgment: A realistic approach. *Psychological Review, 102,* 652–670.

Furman, W., & Buhrmester, D. (1992). Age and sex differences in perceptions of networks of personal relationships. *Child Development, 63,* 103–115.

Furrow, D., Nelson, K., & Benedict, H. (1979). Mothers' speech to children and syntactic development: Some simple relationships. *Journal of Child Language, 6,* 423–442.

Furth, H. G. (1996). *Desire for society: Children's knowledge as social imagination.* New York: Plenum.

Fuson, K. C., & Kwon, Y. (1992). Learning addition and subtraction: Effects of number words and other cultural tools. In J. Bideaud, C. Meljac, & J. Fischer (Eds.), *Pathways to number: Children's developing numerical abilities.* Hillsdale, NJ: Erlbaum.

Futuyma, D. J. (1997). *Evolutionary biology* (3rd ed.). Sunderland, MA: Sinauer.

Gable, S., Belsky, J., & Crnic, K. (1992). Marriage, parenting, and child development: Progress and prospects. *Journal of Family Psychology, 5,* 276–294.

Gabrieli, J. D. E. (1998). Cognitive neuroscience of human memory. *Annual Review of Psychology, 49,* 87–115.

Gabrieli, J. D. E., Corkin, S., Mickel, S. F., & Growdon, J. H. (1993). Intact acquisition and long-term retention of mirror-tracing skill in Alzheimer's disease and in global amnesia. *Behavioral Neuroscience, 107,* 899–910.

Gadian, D. G., Aicardi, J., Watkins, K. E., Porter, D. A., Mishkin, M., & Vargha-Khadem, F. (2000). Developmental amnesia associated with early hypoxic-ischaemic injury. *Brain, 123,* 499–507.

Gaertner, S. L., Mann, J. A., Dovidio, J. F., Murrell, A. J., & Pomare, M. (1990). How does cooperation reduce intergroup bias? *Journal of Personality and Social Psychology, 59,* 692–704.

Gaffan, E. A., Hansel, M. C., & Smith, L. E. (1983). Does reward depletion influence spatial memory performance? *Learning and Memory, 14,* 58–74.

Galanter, E. (1962). Contemporary psychophysics. In R. Brown, E. Galanter, E. Hess, & G. Mandler (Eds.), *New directions in psychology.* New York: Holt, Rinehart & Winston.

Galef, B. G. (1991). A contrarian view of the wisdom of the body as it relates to dietary self-selection. *Psychological Review, 98,* 218–223.

Galef, B. G., & Whiskin, E. E. (1997). Effects of social and asocial learning on longevity of food-preference traditions. *Animal Behaviour, 53,* 1313–1322.

Galef, B. G., Jr. (1985). Social learning in wild Norway rats. In T. D. Johnston & A. T. Pietrewicz (Eds.), *Issues in the ecological study of learning.* Hillsdale, NJ: Erlbaum.

Galef, B. G., Jr., & Clark, M. M. (1971). Social factors in the poison avoidance and feeding behavior of wild and domesticated rat pups. *Journal of Comparative and Physiological Psychology, 75,* 341-357.

Galinsky, E., Bond, J. T., & Friedman, D. E. (1993). *The changing workforce: Highlights of the national study.* New York: Families and Work Institute.

Gallistel, C. R. (1990). *The organization of learning.* Cambridge, MA: MIT Press.

Gallup, G. G., McClure, M. K., Hill, S. D., & Bundy, R. A. (1971). Capacity for self–recognition in differentially reared chimpanzees. *Psychological Record, 21,* 69–74.

Galton, F. (1869; reprinted 1962). *Hereditary genius: An inquiry into its laws and consequences.* Cleveland, OH: World Publishing.

Galton, F. (1876). The history of twins as a criterion of the relative powers of nature and nurture. *Royal Anthropological Institute of Great Britain and Ireland Journal, 6,* 391–406.

Galton, F. (1885). On the anthropometric laboratory at the late international health exhibition. *Journal of the Anthropological Institute, 14,* 205–219.

Ganellen, I. B. (Ed.). (1996). *Integrating the Rorschach and the MMPI-2 in personality assessment.* Mahwah, NJ: Erlbaum.

Gangestad, S. W., & Snyder, M. (2000). Self-monitoring: Appraisal and reappraisal. *Psychological Bulletin, 126,* 530–555.

Garb, H. N., Florio, C. M., & Grove, W. M. (1998). The validity of the Rorschach and the Minnesota Multiphasic Personality Inventory: Results from meta-analyses. *Psychological Science, 9,* 402–404.

Garcia, J., Brett, L. P., & Rusiniak, K. W. (1989). Limits of Darwinian conditioning. In S. B. Klein & R. R. Mowrer (Eds.), *Contemporary learning theories: Instrumental conditioning theory and the impact of biological constraints on learning.* Hillsdale, NJ: Erlbaum.

Garcia, J., McGowan, B. K., Ervin, F. R., & Koelling, R. A. (1968). Cues—their relative effectiveness as a function of the reinforcer. *Science, 160,* 794–795.

Garcia, J., McGowan, B. K., & Green, K. F. (1972). Biological constraints on conditioning. In A. H. Black & W. G. Prokasy (Eds.), *Classical conditioning II: Current research and theory.* New York: Appleton-Century-Crofts.

Gardner, R. A., & Gardner, B. T. (1978). Comparative psychology and language acquisition. In K. Slazinger & F. L. Denmark (Eds.), Psychology: The state of the art. *Annals of the New York Academy of Sciences, 309,* 37–76.

Gardner, R. A., & Gardner, B. T. (1989). A cross-fostering laboratory. In R. A. Gardner, B. T. Gardner, & T. E. Van Cantfort (Eds.), *Teaching sign language to chimpanzees.* Albany: State University of New York Press.

Garland, D. J., & Barry, J. R. (1991). Cognitive advantage in sports: The nature of perceptual structures. *American Journal of Psychology, 104,* 211–228.

Garvey, C. (1990). *Play: enlarged edition.* Cambridge, MA: Harvard University Press.

Gazzaniga, M. S. (1998, July). The split brain revisited. *Scientific American*, pp. 50–55.

Geary, D. C. (1999). Evolution and developmental sex differences. *Current Directions in Psychological Science, 8*, 115–120.

Geary, D. C. (2000). Evolution and proximate expression of human paternal investment. *Psychological Bulletin, 126*, 55–77.

Geen, R. G. (1980). The effects of being observed on performance. In P. B. Paulus (Ed.), *Psychology of group influence.* Hillsdale, NJ: Erlbaum.

Geen, R. G. (1984). Preferred stimulation levels in introverts and extraverts: Effects on arousal and performance. *Journal of Personality and Social Psychology, 45*, 1303–1312.

Geen R. G. (1991). Social motivation. *Annual Review of Psychology, 42*, 377–399.

Gelman, D., Foote, D., & Talbot, M. (1992, February 24.). Born or bred? *Newsweek.*

Gescheider, G. A. (1976). *Psychophysics: Methods and theory.* Hillsdale, NJ: Erlbaum.

Gest, S. D. (1997). Behavioral inhibition: Stability and associations with adaptation from childhood to early adulthood. *Journal of Personality and Social Psychology, 72*, 467–475.

Ghez, C., & Krakauer, J. (2000). The Organization of Movement. In E. R. Kandel, J. H. Schwartz, & T. M. Jessell (Eds.), *Principles of Neural Science* (4th ed.). New York: McGraw-Hill.

Ghez, C., & Thach, W. T. (2000). The cerebellum. In E. R. Kandel, J.H. Schwartz, & T. M. Jessell (Eds.), *Principles of Neural Science* (4th ed.). New York: McGraw-Hill.

Gianoulakis, C., Krishnan, B., & Thavundayil, J. (1996). Enhanced sensitivity of pituitary β-endorphin to ethanol in subjects at high risk for alcoholism. *Archives of General Psychiatry, 53*, 250–257.

Gibbs, W. W. (1996, August). Gaining on fat. *Scientific American*, pp. 88–94.

Gibson, E. J. (1969). *Principles of perceptual learning and its development.* Englewood Cliffs, NJ: Prentice-Hall.

Gibson, E. J. (1971). Perceptual learning and the theory of word perception. *Cognitive Psychology, 2*, 351–358.

Gibson, E. J., & Walk, R. D. (1960, April). The visual cliff. *Scientific American*, pp. 64–71.

Gibson, J. J. (1966). *The senses considered as perceptual systems.* Boston: Houghton Mifflin.

Gibson, J. J. (1979). *The ecological approach to visual perception.* Boston: Houghton Mifflin.

Gilbert, C. D., & Wiesel, T. N. (1992). Receptive field dynamics in adult primary visual cortex. *Nature, 356*, 150–152.

Gilbert, D. T. (1989). Thinking lightly about others: Automatic components of the social inference process. In J. S. Uleman & J. A. Bargh (Eds.), *Unintended thought.* New York: Guilford Press.

Gilbert, D. T., & Hixon, J. G. (1991). The trouble of thinking: Activation and application of stereotypic beliefs. *Journal of Personality and Social Psychology, 60*, 509–517.

Gilbert, D. T., & Jones, E. E. (1986). Perceiver-induced constraint: Interpretations of self-generated reality. *Journal of Personality and Social Psychology, 50*, 269–280.

Gilbert, L. A. (1994). Current perspective on dual-career families. *Current Directions in Psychological Science, 3*, 101–105.

Gilchrist, A., Kossyfidis, C., Bonato, F., Agostini, T., Cataliotti, J., Li, X., Spehar, B., Annan, V., & Economou, E. (1999). An anchoring theory of lightness perception. *Psychological Review, 106*, 795–834.

Gillham, J. E., Revish, K. J., Jaycox, L. H., & Seligman, M. E. P. (1995). Prevention of depressive symptoms in schoolchildren: Two-year follow-up. *Psychological Science, 6*, 343–351.

Gladue, B. A. (1994). The biopsychology of sexual orientation. *Current Directions in Psychological Science, 3*, 150–154.

Glance, N. S., & Huberman, B. A. (1994, March). The dynamics of social dilemmas. *Scientific American*, pp. 76–81.

Gleitman, L. R., & Gillette, J. (1995). The role of syntax in verb learning. In P. Fletcher & B. MacWhinney (Eds.), *The handbook of child language.* Cambridge, MA: Basil Blackwell.

Glendinning, J. I. (1994). Is the bitter rejection response always adaptive? *Physiology and Behavior, 56*, 1217–1227.

Glick, I. D., Berman, E. M., Clarkin, J. F., & Rait, D. S. (2000). *Marital and family therapy* (4th ed.). Washington, DC: American Psychiatric Press.

Glickman, S. E., Frank, L. G., Licht, P., Yalcinkaya, T., Siiteri, P. K., & Davidson, J. (1992). Sexual differentiation of the female spotted hyena: One of nature's experiments. *Annals of the New York Academy of Sciences, 662*, 135–159.

Glisky, E. L., Schacter, D. L., & Tulving, E. (1986). Computer learning by memory-impaired patients: Acquisition and retention of complex knowledge. *Neuropsychologia, 24*, 313–328.

Goffman, E. (1959). *The presentation of self in everyday life.* Garden City, NY: Doubleday.

Goldberg, L. R. (1990). An alternative "description of personality": The big-five factor structure. *Journal of Personality and Social Psychology, 59*, 1216–1229.

Goldberg, L. R. (1993). The structure of phenotypic personality traits. *American Psychologist, 48*, 26–34.

Goldenthal, P., Johnston, R. E., & Kraut, R. E. (1981). Smiling, appeasement, and the silent bared-teeth display. *Ethology and Sociobiology, 2*, 127–133.

Goldhagen, D. J. (1996). *Hitler's willing executioners: Ordinary Germans and the Holocaust.* New York: Knopf.

Goldsmith, H. H., Bradshaw, D. L., & Riesser-Danner, L. A. (1986). Temperament as a potential developmental influence on attachment. In J. V. Lerner & R. M. Lerner (Eds.), *Temperament and social interaction in infants and children.* San Francisco: Jossey-Bass.

Goldsmith, S. K., Shapiro, R. M., & Joyce, J. N. (1997). Disrupted pattern of D2 dopamine receptors in the temporal lobe in schizophrenia. *Archives of General Psychiatry, 54*, 649–658.

Goleman, D. (1985). *Vital lies, simple truths.* New York: Simon & Schuster.

Golinkoff, R. M., Mervis, C. B., & Hirsh-Pasek, K. (1994). Early object labels: The case for a developmental lexical principles framework. *Journal of Child Language, 21*, 125–155.

Golinkoff, R. M., Shuff-Bailey, M., Olguin, R., & Ruan, W. (1995). Young children extend novel words at the basic level: Evidence for the principle of categorical scope. *Developmental Psychology, 31,* 494–507.

Gomes, H., Sussman, E., Ritter, W., Kurtzberg, D., Cowan, N., & Vaughan, H. G. (1999). Electrophysiological evidence for developmental changes in the duration of sensory memory. *Developmental Psychology, 35,* 294–302.

Gonzalez, M. F., & Deutsch, J. A. (1981). Vagotomy abolishes cues of satiety produced by gastric distension. *Science, 212,* 1283–1284.

Goodale, M. A., & Murphy, K. (1997). Action and perception in the visual periphery. In P. Their & H. O. Karnath (Eds.), *Parietal lobe contributions to orientation in 3D space.* Heidelberg: Springer-Verlag.

Goodall, J. (1986). *The chimpanzees of Gombe.* Cambridge, MA: Harvard University Press.

Goodall, J. (1988). *In the shadow of man* (Rev. ed.). Boston: Houghton Mifflin.

Goodman, J. C., McDonough, L., & Brown, N. B. (1998). The role of semantic context and memory in the acquisition of novel nouns. *Child Development, 69,* 1330–1344.

Goodstein, L. D., & Lanyon, R. I. (1999). Applications of personality assessment to the workplace: A review. *Journal of Business and Psychology, 13,* 291–322.

Goossens, F. A., & van Ijzendoorn, M. H. (1990). Quality of infants' attachments to professional caregivers: Relation to infant-parent attachment and day-care characteristics. *Child Development, 61,* 550–567.

Gopnik, A. (1993). How we know our minds: The illusion of first-person knowledge of intentionality. *Behavioral and Brain Sciences, 16,* 1–14.

Gopnik, A., & Astington, J. W. (1988). Children's understanding of representational change and its relation to the understanding of false belief and the appearance-reality distinction. *Child Development, 59,* 26–37.

Gopnik, M. (1999). Familial language impairment: More English evidence. *Folia Phoniatrica et Logopaedica, 51,* 5–19.

Gopnik, M., & Crago, M. B. (1991). Familial aggregation of a developmental language disorder. *Cognition, 39,* 1–50.

Gordon, R. A. (1990). *Anorexia and bulimia: Anatomy of a social epidemic.* Cambridge, MA: Basil Blackwell.

Gordon, S., & Gilgun, J. F. (1987). *Adolescent sexuality.* In V. B. Van Hasselt & M. Hersen (Eds.), *Handbook of adolescent psychology.* New York: Pergamon Press.

Gorski, R. A. (1996). Gonadal hormones and the organization of brain structure and function. In D. Magnusson (Ed.), *The lifespan development of individuals: Behavioral, neurobiological, and psychosocial perspectives.* Cambridge, England: Cambridge University Press.

Gorski, R. A., Harlan, R. E., Jacobson, C. D., Shryne, J. E., & Southham, A. M. (1980). Evidence for the existence of a sexually dimorphic nucleus in the preoptic area of the rat. *Journal of Comparative Neurology, 193,* 529–539.

Gosling, S. D. (2001). From mice to men: What can we learn about personality from animal research? *Psychological Bulletin, 127,* 45–86.

Gottesman, I. I. (1991). *Schizophrenia genesis: The origins of madness.* New York: Freeman.

Gottman, J. M. (1979). *Marital interaction: Experimental investigations.* New York: Academic Press.

Gottman, J. M. (1994). *What predicts divorce? The relationship between marital processes and marital outcomes.* Hillsdale, NJ: Erlbaum.

Gottman, J. M. (1998). Psychology and the study of marital processes. *Annual Review of Psychology, 49,* 169–197.

Gottman, J. M., & Krokoff, L. J. (1989). Marital interaction and satisfaction: A longitudinal view. *Journal of Consulting and Clinical Psychology, 57,* 47–52.

Goudie, A. J. (1990). Conditioned opponent processes in the development of tolerance to psychoactive drugs. *Progress in Neuro-Psychopharmacology and Biological Psychiatry, 14,* 675–688.

Gould, E., Reeves, A. J., Graziano, M. S. A., & Gross, C. G. (1999). Neurogenesis in the neocortex of adult primates. *Science, 286,* 548–552.

Gould, J. L. (1982). *Ethology: The mechanisms and evolution of behavior.* New York: Norton.

Gould, S. J. (1980). A biological homage to Mickey Mouse. In *The panda's thumb: More reflections in natural history.* New York: Norton.

Gould, S. J. (1983). Hyena myths and realities. In S. J. Gould (Ed.), *Hen's teeth and horse's toes: Further reflections in natural history.* New York: Norton.

Gould, S. J., & Eldredge, N. (1993). Punctuate equilibrium comes of age. *Nature, 366,* 223–227.

Gould-Beierle, K. L. & Kamil, A. C. (1999). The effect of proximity on landmark use in Clark's nutcrackers. *Animal Behaviour, 58,* 477–488.

Gouldner, A. W. (1960). The norm of reciprocity: A preliminary statement. *American Sociological Review, 25,* 161–178.

Graham, C. H., Sperling, H. G., Hsia, Y., & Coulson, A. H. (1961). The determination of some visual functions of a unilaterally color-blind subject: Methods and results. *The Journal of Psychology, 51,* 3–32.

Grant, P. R. (1991, October). Natural selection and Darwin's finches. *Scientific American, 265,* 82–87.

Gray, P., & Chanoff, D. (1986). Democratic schooling: What happens to young people who have charge of their own education? *American Journal of Education, 94,* 182–213.

Gray, P., & Feldman, J. (1997). Patterns of age mixing and gender mixing among children and adolescents at an ungraded democratic school. *Merrill-Palmer Quarterly, 43,* 67–86.

Green, D. M. (1964). Psychoacoustics and detection theory. In J. A. Swets (Ed.), *Signal detection and recognition by human observers.* New York: Wiley.

Green, M. F. (1993). Cognitive remediation in schizophrenia: Is it time yet? *American Journal of Psychiatry, 150,* 178–187.

Greenberg, D. (1992). Sudbury Valley's secret weapon: Allowing people of different ages to mix freely at school. In *The Sudbury Valley School experience* (3rd ed.). Framingham, MA: Sudbury Valley School Press.

Greenberg, D., & Sadofsky, M. (1992). *Legacy of trust: Life after the Sudbury Valley School experience.* Framingham, MA: Sudbury Valley School Press.

Greenberg, J. H. (1978). Generalizations about numeral systems. In J. H. Greenberg (Ed.), *Universals of human language: Vol. 3. Word structure*. Stanford, CA: Stanford University Press.

Greenberg, M. (1992). On the nature of sports at S.V.S. and the limitations of language in describing S.V.S. to the world. In *The Sudbury Valley School Experience* (3rd ed.). Framingham, MA: Sudbury Valley School Press.

Greenfield, P. M. (1998). The cultural evolution of IQ. In U. Neisser (Ed.), *The rising curve: Long-term gains in IQ and related measures*. Washington, DC: APA.

Greenfield, P. M., & Smith, J. H. (1976). *The structure of communication in early language development*. New York: Academic Press.

Greenwald, A. G. (1980). The totalitarian ego: Fabrication and revision of personal history. *American Psychologist, 35*, 603–618.

Greenwald, A. G. (1992). New look 3: Unconscious cognition reclaimed. *American Psychologist, 47*, 766–779.

Greenwald, A. G., Draine, S. C., & Abrams, R. L. (1996). Three cognitive markers of unconscious semantic activation. *Science, 273*, 1699–1702.

Gregory, R. L. (1968, November). Visual illusions. *Scientific American*, pp. 66–76.

Gregory, R. L. (1996). *Eye and brain: The psychology of seeing* (5th ed.). Princeton, NJ: Princeton University Press.

Greulich. W. W. (1957). A comparison of the physical growth and development of American-born and native Japanese children. *American Journal of Physical Anthropology, 15*, 489–515.

Griffin, D. R. (1986). *Listening in the dark: The acoustic orientation of bats and men*. Ithaca, NY: Cornell University Press.

Griffith, J. D., Cavanaugh, J., Held, N. N., & Oates, J. A. (1972). Dextroamphetamine: Evaluation of psychotomimetic properties in man. *Archives of General Psychiatry, 26*, 97–100.

Grilo, C. M., & Pogue-Geile, M. F. (1991). The nature of environmental influences on weight and obesity: A behavior genetic analysis. *Psychological Bulletin, 110*, 520–537.

Grob, G. N. (2000). Mental health policy in late twentieth-century America. In R. W. Menninger & J. C. Nemiah (Eds.), *American psychiatry after World War II*. Washington, DC: American Psychiatric Press.

Grodzinsky, Y. (2000). The neurology of syntax: Language use without Broca's area. *Behavioral and Brain Sciences, 23*, 1–71.

Groos, K. (1898). *The play of animals*. New York: Appleton.

Groos, K. (1901). *The play of man*, New York: Appleton.

Gross, C. G. (1998). *Brain, vision, memory: Tales in the history of neuroscience*. Cambridge, MA: MIT Press.

Grossman, R. P., & Till, B. D. (1998). The persistence of classically conditioned brand attitudes. *Journal of Advertising, 27*, 23–31.

Grossman, S. P. (1979). The biology of motivation. *Annual Review of Psychology, 30*, 209–242.

Grüsser, O. J., & Grüsser-Cornehls, U. (1986). Physiology of vision. In R. F. Schmidt (Ed.), *Fundamentals of sensory physiology* (3rd ed.). New York: Springer-Verlag.

Guisinger, S., & Blatt, S. J. (1994). Individuality and relatedness: Evolution of a fundamental dialectic. *American Psychologist, 49*, 104–111.

Guthrie, E. R. (1952). *The psychology of learning*. New York: Harper & Row.

Guyote, M. J., & Sternberg, R. J. (1981). A transitive-chain theory of syllogistic reasoning. *Cognitive Psychology, 13*, 461–525.

Gynther, M. D. (1972). White norms and black MMPIs: A prescription for discrimination? *Psychological Bulletin, 78*, 386–402.

Haan, N., Smith, M. B., & Block, J. (1968). The moral reasoning of young adults: Political-social behaviour, family background and personality correlated. *Journal of Personality and Social Psychology, 10*, 183–201.

Haimov, I., & Lavie, P. (1996). Melatonin—a soporific hormone. *Current Directions in Psychological Science, 5*, 106–111.

Haller, W., Nitschke, J. B., & Miller, G. A. (1998). Lateralization in emotion and emotional disorders. *Current Directions in Psychological Science, 7*, 26–32.

Halpern, A. R. (1986). Memory for tune titles after organized or unorganized presentation. *American Journal of Psychology, 99*, 57–70.

Halpern, A. R., & Zatorre, R. J. (1999). When that tune runs through your head: A PET investigation of auditory imagery for familiar melodies. *Cerebral Cortex, 9*, 697–704.

Hamburg, S. R. (2000). Antidepressants are not placebos. *American Psychologist, 55*, 761–762.

Hamill, J. F. (1990). *Ethno-logic: The anthropology of human reasoning*. Urbana and Chicago: University of Illinois Press.

Hamilton, W. D. (1964). The genetical theory of social behaviour, I, II. *Journal of Theoretical Biology, 12*, 12–45.

Hamilton, W. D., Axelrod, R., & Tanese, R. (1990). Sexual reproduction as an adaptation to resist parasites: A review. *Proceedings of the National Academy of Sciences of the U.S.A., 87*, 3566–3573.

Hammen, C. (1991). The generation of stress in the course of unipolar depression. *Journal of Abnormal Psychology, 100*, 555–561.

Hara, T. J. (1994). Olfaction and gustation in fish: An overview. *Acta Physiologica Scandinavica, 152*, 207–217.

Hardin, G. (1968). The tragedy of the commons. *Science, 162*, 1243–1248.

Harlow, H. F. (1959, June). Love in infant monkeys. *Scientific American*, pp. 68–74.

Harmon-Jones, E. (2000). Cognitive dissonance and experienced negative affect: Evidence that dissonance increases experienced negative affect even in the absence of aversive consequences. *Personality and Social Psychology Bulletin, 26*, 1490–1501.

Harmon-Jones, E., & Mills, J. (Eds.) (1999). *Cognitive dissonance: Progress on a pivotal theory in social psychology*. Washington, DC: American Psychological Association.

Harper, L. V., & Sanders, K. M. (1975). The effect of adults' eating on young children's acceptance of unfamiliar foods. *Journal of Experimental Child Psychology, 20*, 206–214.

Harris, J. R. (1995). Where is the child's environment? A group socialization theory of development. *Psychological Review, 102*, 458–489.

Harris, J. R. (1998). *The nurture assumption: Why children turn out the way they do*. New York: Simon & Schuster.

Harrison, L. (1975). Cro-magnon woman—in eclipse. *Science Teacher, 42*, 8–10.

Hart, D., Yates, M., Fegley, S., & Wilson, G. (1995). Moral commitment in inner-city adolescents. In M. Killen & D. Hart (Eds.), *Morality in everyday life: Developmental perspectives.* Cambridge, England: Cambridge University Press.

Hartshorne, H., & May, M. (1928). *Studies in deceit.* New York: Macmillan.

Hartup, W. W. (1983). Peer relations. In E. M. Hetherington (Ed.), P. H. Mussen (Series Ed.), *Handbook of child psychology, Vol. 4: Socialization, personality, and social development.* New York: Wiley.

Hasler, A. D., & Larsen, J. A. (1955, August). The homing salmon. *Scientific American,* pp. 72–76.

Hatfield, E., Cacioppo, J. T., & Rapson, R. L. (1994). *Emotional contagion.* Cambridge, England: Cambridge University Press.

Hathaway, S. R., & McKinley, J. C. (1943). *MMPI manual.* New York: Psychological Corporation.

Hawkins, H. L., & Presson J. C. (1986). Auditory information processing. In K. R. Boff, L. Kaufman, & J. P. Thomas (Eds.), *Handbook of perception and human performance: Vol. II. Cognitive processes and performance.* New York: Wiley.

Hay, D. (1985). *Essentials of behaviour genetics.* Melbourne: Blackwell.

Hay, D. F., & Murray, P. (1982). Giving and requesting: Social facilitation of infants' offers to adults. *Infant Behavior and Development, 5,* 301–310.

Hazan, C., & Shaver, P. R. (1987). Romantic love conceptualized as an attachment process. *Journal of Personality and Social Psychology, 52,* 511–524.

Hazan, C., & Shaver, P. R. (1994). Attachment as an organizational framework for research on close relationships. *Psychological Inquiry, 5,* 1–22.

Heath, R. G. (1972). Pleasure and brain activity in man. *Journal of Nervous and Mental Disease, 154,* 3–18.

Hebb, D. (1958). *A textbook of psychology.* Philadelphia: Saunders.

Hécaen, H., & Albert, M. L. (1978). *Human neuropsychology.* New York: Wiley.

Hecht, S., & Mandelbaum, M. (1938). Rod-cone dark adaptation and vitamin A. *Science, 88,* 219–221.

Hecker, J. E., & Thorpe, G. L. (1992). *Agoraphobia and panic: A guide to psychological treatment.* Boston: Allyn & Bacon.

Heckler, S. (1994). Facilitated communication: A response by child protection. *Child Abuse and Neglect, 18,* 495–503.

Hefferline, R. F., Keenan, B., & Harford, R. A. (1959). Escape and avoidance conditioning of human subjects without their observation of the response. *Science, 130,* 1338–1339.

Heider, F. (1958). *The psychology of interpersonal relations.* New York: Wiley.

Heiman, M. (1987). Learning to learn: A behavioral approach to improving thinking. In D. N. Perkins, J. Lockhead, & J. Bishop (Eds.), *Thinking: The Second International Conference.* Hillsdale, NJ: Erlbaum.

Heine, S. J., & Lehman, D. R. (1995). Cultural variation in unrealistic optimism: Does the West feel more invulnerable than the East. *Journal of Personal and Social Psychology, 68,* 595–607.

Heine, S. J., Lehman, D. R., Markus, H. R., & Kitayama, S. (1999). Is there a universal need for positive self-regard? *Psychological Review, 106,* 766–794.

Helmholtz, H. von (1852). On the theory of compound colors. *Philosophical Magazine, 4,* 519–534.

Helmholtz, H. von (1962). *Helmholtz's treatise on physiological optics.* (J. P. C. Southall, Ed. and Trans.). New York: Dover. (Originally published in the *Handbuch der physiologischen optik,* 1867.)

Helson, R., & Stewart, A. (1994). Personality change in adulthood. In T. F. Heatherton & J. L. Weinberger (Eds.), *Can personality change?* Washington, DC: American Psychological Association.

Henderson, J. M., & Hollingworth, A. (1999). High-level scene perception. *Annual Review of Psychology, 50,* 243–271.

Hendricks, B., Marvel, M. K., & Barrington, B. L. (1990). The dimensions of psychological research. *Teaching of Psychology, 17,* 76–82.

Henry, J. L. (1986). Role of circulating opioids in the modulation of pain. In D. D. Kelly (Ed.), *Stress-induced analgesia* (Vol. 467 of the *Annals of the New York Academy of Sciences*). New York: New York Academy of Sciences.

Herbst, J. H., Zonderman, A. B., McCrae, R. R., & Costa, P. T. (2000). Do the dimensions of the temperament and character inventory map a simple genetic architecture? Evidence from molecular genetics and factor analysis. *American Journal of Psychiatry, 157,* 1285–1290.

Herdt, G., & Boxer, A. (1993). *Children of horizons.* New York: Beacon Press.

Herek, G. M. (1986). The instrumentality of attitudes: Toward a neofunctional theory. *Journal of Social Issues, 42,* 99–114.

Hering, E. (1878; translated edition 1964). *Outlines of a theory of the light sense.* (L. M. Hurvich and D. Jameson, Trans.) Cambridge, MA: Harvard University Press.

Herness, M. S., & Gilbertson, T. A. (1999). Cellular mechanisms of taste transduction. *Annual Reviews of Physiology, 61,* 837–900.

Herrnstein, R. J. (1990). Levels of stimulus control: A functional approach. *Cognition, 37,* 133–166.

Herrnstein, R. J., & Murray, C. (1994). *The bell curve: Intelligence and class structure in American life.* New York: Free Press.

Hershenson, M. (1989). The most puzzling illusion. In M. Hershenson (Ed.), *The moon illusion.* Hillsdale, NJ: Erlbaum.

Hertel, P., Fagerquist, M. V., & Svensson, T.H. (1999). Enhanced cortical dopamine output and antipsychotic-like effects of raclopride by alpha-2 and adrenoceptor blockade. *Science, 286,* 105–107.

Hetherington, E. M. (1972). Effects of father absence on personality development in adolescent daughters. *Developmental Psychology, 7,* 313–326.

Hewlett, B. S. (1988). Sexual selection and paternal investment among Aka pygmies. In L. Betzig, M. B. Mulder, & P. Turke (Eds.), *Human reproductive behavior: A Darwinian perspective.* Cambridge, England: Cambridge University Press.

Hewlett, B. S., Lamb, M. E., Shannon, D., Leyendecker, B., & Schölmerich, A. (1998). Culture and early infancy among central African foragers and farmers. *Developmental Psychology, 34,* 653–661.

Higgins, E. T., & Chaires, W. M. (1980). Accessibility of interrelational constructs: Implications for stimulus encoding and creativity. *Journal of Experimental Social Psychology, 16,* 348–361.

Hilgard, E. R. (1977). *Divided consciousness: Multiple controls in human action and thought.* New York: Wiley.

Hill, J. O., & Peters, J. C. (1998). Environmental contributions to the obesity epidemic. *Science, 280,* 1371–1374.

Hill, P. M., & McCune-Nicolich, L. (1981). Pretend play and patterns of cognition in Down's Syndrome children. *Child Development, 52,* 217–250.

Hilts, P. J. (1995). *Memory's ghost.* New York: Simon & Schuster.

Himelein, M. J., Vogel, R. E., & Wachowiak, D. G. (1994). Nonconsensual sexual experience in precollege women: Prevalence and risk factors. *Journal of Counseling and Development, 72,* 411–415.

Hinson, R. E., Poulos, C. X., Thomas, W., & Cappell, H. (1986). Pavlovian conditioning and addictive behavior: Relapse to oral self-administration of morphine. *Behavioral Neuroscience, 100,* 368–375.

Hirata, S., & Morimura, N. (2000). Naive chimpanzees' (*Pan troglodytes*) observation of experienced conspecifics in a tool-using task. *Journal of Comparative Psychology, 114,* 291–296.

Hirschfeld, R. M. A. (2000). History and evolution of the monoamine hypothesis of depression. *Journal of Clinical Psychiatry, 61,* 4–6.

Hirsh-Pasek, K., & Golinkoff, R. M. (1991). Language comprehension: A new look at some old themes. In N. A. Karsnegor, D. M. Rumbaugh, R. L. Schiefelbusch, & M. Studdert-Kennedy (Eds.), *Biological and behavioral determinants of language development.* Hillsdale, NJ: Erlbaum.

Hirst, W., Spelke, E. S., Reaves, C. C., Caharack, G., & Neisser, U. (1980). Dividing attention without alternation or automaticity. *Journal of Experimental Psychology: General, 109,* 98–117.

Hirt, E. R., Zillman, D., Erickson, G. A., & Kennedy, C. (1992). The costs and benefits of allegiance: Changes in fans' self-described competence after team victory versus team defeat. *Journal of Personality and Social Psychology, 63,* 724–738.

Hittelman, J. H., & Dickes, R. (1979). Sex differences in neonatal eye contact time. *Merrill-Palmer Quarterly, 25,* 171–184.

Hlastala, S. A., Frank, E., Kowalski, K., Sherrill, J. T., Tu, X. M., Anderson, B., & Kupfer, D.J. (2000). Stressful life events, bipolar disorder, and the "kindling model." *Journal of Abnormal Psychology, 109,* 777–786.

Hobbes, T. (1651; reprinted 1962). Leviathan. In W. Molesworth (Ed.), *The English works of Thomas Hobbes* (Vol. 3, pp. 1–714). London: Scientia Aalen.

Hobson, J. A. (1987). (1) Sleep, (2) Sleep, functional theories of, (3) Dreaming. All in G. Adelman (Ed.), *Encyclopedia of neuroscience.* Boston: Birkhäuser.

Hobson, J. A. (1988). *The dreaming brain.* New York: Basic Books.

Hobson, J. A. (1995). *Sleep.* New York: Scientific American Library.

Hochberg, J. (1971). Perception II: Space and movement. In J. W. Kling & L. A. Riggs (Eds.), *Woodworth & Schlosberg's experimental psychology* (3rd ed.). New York: Holt, Rinehart & Winston.

Hoebel, B. G., Monaco, A. P., Hernandez, L., Aulisi, E. F., Stanley, B. G., & Lenard, L. G. (1983). Self-injection of amphetamine directly into the brain. *Psychopharmacology, 81,* 158–163.

Hoelter, J. W. (1985). The structure of self-conception: Conceptualization and measurement. *Journal of Personality and Social Psychology, 49,* 1392–1407.

Hoelzel, A. R., Le Boeuf, B. J., Reiter, J., & Campagna, C. (1999). Alpha-male paternity in elephant seals. *Behavioral Ecology and Sociobiology, 46,* 298–306.

Hoffman, C., Lau, I., & Johnson, D. R. (1986). The linguistic relativity of person cognition: An English-Chinese comparison. *Journal of Personality and Social Psychology, 51,* 1097–1105.

Hoffman, D. D. (1998). *Visual intelligence: How we create what we see.* New York: Norton.

Hoffman, M. L. (1975). Developmental synthesis of affect and cognition and its interplay for altruistic motivation. *Developmental Psychology, 11,* 607–622.

Hoffman, M. L. (1982). Development of prosocial motivation: Empathy and guilt. In N. Eisenberg (Ed.), *The development of prosocial behavior.* New York: Academic Press.

Hoffman, M. L. (1983). Affective and cognitive processes in moral internalization. In E. T. Higgins, D. N. Ruble, & W. W. Hartup (Eds.), *Social cognition and social development.* Cambridge, England: Cambridge University Press.

Hoffman, M. L. (1998). Varieties of empathy-based guilt. In J. Bybee (Ed.), *Guilt and children.* San Diego: Academic Press.

Hofsten, C. von, & Siddiqui, A. (1993). Using the mother's actions as a reference for object exploration in 6- and 12-month-old infants. *British Journal of Developmental Psychology, 11,* 61–74.

Hogarty, G. E., & Goldberg, S. C. (1973). Drug and sociotherapy in the aftercare of schizophrenic patients: One-year relapse rates. *Archives of General Psychiatry, 28,* 54–64.

Hogg, M. A., Turner, J. C., & Davidson, B. (1990). Polarized norms and social frames of reference: A test of the self-categorization theory of group polarization. *Basic and Applied Social Psychology, 11,* 77–100.

Hohmann, G., & Fruth, B. (2000). Use and function of genital contacts among female bonobos. *Animal Behaviour, 60,* 107–120.

Hollanders, H. (2000). Eclecticism/integration: Some key issues and research. In S. Plamer & R. Woolfe (Eds.), *Integrative and eclectic counselling and psychotherapy.* London: Sage.

Hollis, K. L. (1997). Contemporary research on Pavlovian conditioning. *American Psychologist, 52,* 956–965.

Honig, K. M., & Townes, B. D. (1976). Infants' attachment to inanimate objects: A cross-cultural study. *American Academy of Child Psychiatry Journal, 15,* 49–61.

Hood, B. M., Willen, J. D., & Driver, J. (1998). Adult's eyes trigger shifts of visual attention in human infants. *Psychological Science, 9,* 131–134.

Hood, D. C. (1998). Lower-level visual processing and models of light adaptation. *Annual Review of Psychology, 49,* 503–535.

Hooley, J. M., & Hiller, J. B. (2001). Family relationships and major mental disorder: Risk factors and preventive strategies. In B. R. Sarason & S. Duck (Eds.). *Personal relationships: Implications for clinical and community psychology.* Chichester, England: Wiley.

Horn, J. L. (1985). Remodeling old models of intelligence. In B. B. Wolman (Ed.), *Handbook of intelligence: Theories, measurements, and applications.* New York: Wiley.

Horne, J. A. (1979). Restitution and human sleep: A critical review. *Physiological Psychology, 7,* 115–125.

Horne, J. A. (1988). *Why we sleep: The functions of sleep in humans and other mammals.* Oxford: Oxford University Press.

Horney, K. (1937). *The neurotic personality of our time.* New York: Norton.

Horney, K. (1945). *Our inner conflicts.* New York: Norton.

Hornik, R., Risenhoover, N., & Gunnar, M. (1987). The effects of maternal positive, neutral, and negative affective communications on infant responses to new toys. *Child Development, 58,* 937–944.

Hosobuchi, Y., Rossier, J., Bloom, F. E., & Guillemin, R. (1979). Stimulation of human periaqueductal gray for pain relief increases immunoreactive beta-endorphin in ventricular fluid. *Science, 203,* 279–281.

Hothersall, D. (1995). *History of psychology* (3rd ed.). New York: McGraw-Hill.

Howard, K. I., Cornille, T. A., Lyons, J. S., Vessey, J. T., Lueger, R. J., & Saunders, S. M. (1996). Patterns of mental health service utilization. *Archives of General Psychiatry, 53,* 696–703.

Howes, C., & Hamilton, C. E. (1992a). Children's relationships with caregivers: Mothers and child care teachers. *Child Development, 63,* 859–866.

Howes, C., & Hamilton, C. E. (1992b). Children's relationships with child care teachers: Stability and concordance with parental attachments. *Child Development, 63,* 867–878.

Howes, C., & Matheson, C. C. (1992). Sequences in the development of competent play with peers: Social and pretend play. *Developmental Psychology, 28,* 961–974.

Howes, C., & Segal, J. (1993). Children's relationships with alternative caregivers: The special case of maltreated children removed from their homes. *Journal of Applied Developmental Psychology, 14,* 71–81.

Hoyle, R. H., Pinkley, R. L., & Insko, C. A. (1989). Perceptions of social behavior: Evidence for differing expectations for interpersonal and intergroup interactions. *Personality and Social Psychology Bulletin, 15,* 365–376.

Hrdy, S. B. (1981). *The woman that never evolved.* Cambridge, MA: Harvard University Press.

Hrdy, S. B. (1997). Raising Darwin's consciousness: Female sexuality and the prehominid origins of patriarchy. *Human Nature, 8,* 1–49.

Hron-Stewart, K. M. (1988, April). *Gender differences in mothers' strategies for helping toddlers solve problems.* Paper presented at the biennial International Conference on Infancy Studies, Washington, DC.

Hubel, D. H. (1996). A big step along the visual pathway. *Nature, 380,* 197–198.

Hubel, D. H., & Wiesel, T. N. (1962). Receptive fields, binocular interaction, and functional architecture of the cat's visual cortex. *Journal of Physiology (London), 160,* 106–154.

Hubel, D. H., & Wiesel, T. N. (1979, September). Brain mechanisms of vision. *Scientific American,* pp. 150–162.

Hudspeth, A. J. (2000a). Hearing. In E. R. Kandel, J. H. Schwartz, & T. M. Jessell (Eds.), *Principles of neuroscience* (4th ed). New York: McGraw-Hill.

Hudspeth, A. J. (2000b). Sensory transduction in the ear. In E. R. Kandel, J. H. Schwartz, & T. M. Jessell (Eds.), *Principles of neuroscience* (4th ed). New York: McGraw-Hill.

Huff, D. (1954). *How to lie with statistics.* New York: Norton.

Hughes, H. C. (1999). *Sensory exotica: A world beyond human experience.* Cambridge, MA: MIT Press.

Huizinga, J. (1944; reprinted 1970). *Homo ludens: A study of the play-element in culture.* London: Paladin.

Human Capital Initiative. (1993). *Vitality for life: Psychological research for productive aging.* Washington, DC: American Psychological Society.

Humphrey, R. (1985). How work roles influence perception: Structural-cognitive processes and organizational behavior. *American Sociological Review, 50,* 242–252.

Hunt, E. (1995). The role of intelligence in modern society. *American Scientist, 83,* 356–368.

Hunt, M. (1993). *The story of psychology.* New York: Doubleday.

Hurvich, L. M., & Jameson, D. (1957). An opponent-process theory of color vision. *Psychological Review, 64,* 384–404.

Husband, R. W. (1931). Analysis of methods in human maze learning. *Journal of Genetic Psychology, 39,* 258–278.

Huston, A. C., Carpenter, C. J., & Atwater, J. B. (1986). Gender, adult structuring of activities, and social behavior in middle childhood. *Child Development, 57,* 1200–1209.

Hyde, J. S. (1986). Gender differences in aggression. In J. S. Hyde & M. C. Linn (Eds.), *The psychology of gender.* Baltimore: Johns Hopkins University Press.

Hyman, I. E., & Pentland, J. (1996). The role of mental imagery in the creation of false childhood memories. *Journal of Memory and Language, 35,* 101–117.

Ingram, D. H., & Lerner, J. A. (1992). Horney's theory: An object relations theory. *American Journal of Psychoanalysis, 52,* 37–44.

Inhelder, B., & Piaget, J. (1958). *The growth of logical thinking from childhood to adolescence.* New York: Basic Books.

Inoue-Nakamura, N., & Matsuzawa, T. (1997). Development of stone tool use by wild chimpanzees (*Pan troglodytes*). *Journal of Comparative Psychology, 111,* 159–173.

Insko, C. A., Pinkley, R. L., Hoyle, R. H., Dalton, B., Hong, G., Slim, R. M., Landry, P., Holton, B., Ruffin, P. F., & Thibaut, J. (1987). Individual versus group discontinuity: The role of intergroup contact. *Journal of Experimental Social Psychology, 23,* 250–267.

Insko, C. A., Schopler, J., Graetz, K. A., Drigotas, S. M., Currey, D. P., Smith, S. L., Brazil, D., & Bornstein, G. (1994). Interindividual-intergroup discontinuity in the prisoner's dilemma game. *Journal of Conflict Resolution, 38,* 87–116.

Irwin, D. E. (1992). Memory for position and identity across eye movements. *Journal of Experimental Psychology: Learning, Memory, and Cognition, 18,* 307–317.

Isen, A. M., Daubman, K. A., & Nowicki, G. P. (1987). Positive effect facilitates creative problem solving. *Journal of Personality and Social Psychology, 52,* 1122–1131.

Izard, C. E., Fantauzzo, C. A., Castle, J. M., Haynes, O. M., Rayias, M. F., & Putnam, P. H. (1995). The ontogeny and significance of infants' facial expressions in the first 9 months of life. *Developmental Psychology, 31,* 997–1013.

Jablensky, A., Sartorius, N., Ernberg, G., Anker, M., Korten, A., Cooper, J. E., Day, R., & Bertelsen, A. (1992). Schizophrenia: Manifestations, incidence and course in different cultures. A World Health Organization ten-country study. *Psychological Medicine, Monograph Supplements* (Whole Vol. 20).

Jackendoff, R. (1994). *Patterns in the mind: Language and human nature.* New York: BasicBooks/HarperCollins.

Jackson, J. M., & Lantané, B. (1981). All alone in front of all those people: Stage fright as a function of number and type of co-performers and audience. *Journal of Personality and Social Psychology, 40,* 73–85.

Jackson, T. T., & Gray, M. (1976). Field study of risk-taking behavior of automobile drivers. *Perceptual and Motor Skills 43,* 471–474.

Jacobs, J. E., & Eccles, J. S. (1992). The impact of mothers' gender-role stereotypic beliefs on mothers' and children's ability perceptions. *Journal of Personality and Social Psychology, 63,* 932–944.

Jacobson, J. W., Mulick, J. A., & Schwartz, A. A. (1995). A history of facilitated communication: Science, pseudoscience, and antiscience. *American Psychologist, 50,* 750–765.

James, W. (1884, January). Some omissions of introspective psychology. *Mind, 9,* 1–26.

James, W. (1890; reprinted 1950). *The principles of psychology.* New York: Dover.

Jamiesen, D. W., Lydon, J. E., & Zanna, M. P. (1987). Attitude and activity preference similarity: Differential bases of interpersonal attraction for low and high self-monitors. *Journal of Personality and Social Psychology, 53,* 1052–1060.

Jamison, K. R. (1995, February). Manic-depressive illness and creativity. *Scientific American,* pp. 62–67.

Janal, M. N., Colt, E. W. D., Clark, W. C., & Glusman, M. (1984). Pain sensitivity, mood and plasma endocrine levels in man following long-distance running: Effects of naloxone. *Pain, 19,* 13–25.

Janis, I. (1982). *Groupthink: Psychological studies of policy decisions and fiascoes* (2nd ed.). Boston: Houghton Mifflin.

Jankowiak, W. R., & Fischer, E. F. (1991). A cross-cultural perspective on romantic love. *Ethnology, 31,* 149–155.

Janowsky, J. S., Shimamura, A. P., & Squire, L. R. (1989). Source memory impairment in patients with frontal lesions. *Neuropsychologia, 27,* 1043–1056.

Janssen, P., Vogels, R., & Orban, G. A. (2000). Selectivity for 3D shape that reveals distinct areas within macaque inferior temporal cortex. *Science, 288,* 2054–2056.

Jellison, J. M., & Green, J. (1981). A self-presentation approach to the fundamental attribution error: The norm of internality. *Journal of Personality and Social Psychology, 40,* 643–649.

Jencks, C. (1979). *Who gets ahead? The determinants of economic success in America.* New York: Basic Books.

Jenkins, H. M., Barrera, F. J., Ireland, C., & Woodside, B. (1978). Signal-centered action patterns of dogs in appetitive classical conditioning. *Learning and Motivation, 9,* 272–296.

Jenkins, J. H., & Karno, M. (1992). The meaning of expressed emotion: Theoretical issues raised by cross-cultural research. *American Journal of Psychiatry, 149,* 9–21.

Jensen, A. R. (1980). *Bias in mental testing.* New York: Free Press.

Jerome, J. K. (1889; reprinted 1982). *Three men in a boat (to say nothing of the dog).* London: Pavilion Books.

Joffe, R., Sokolov, S., & Streiner, D. (1996). Antidepressant treatment of depression: A meta-analysis. *Canadian Journal of Psychiatry, 41,* 613–616.

Johansson, G. (1994). Spatio-temporal differentiation and integration in visual motion perception. In G. Jansson, S. S. Bergström, & W. Epstein (Eds.), *Perceiving objects and events.* Hillsdale, NJ: Erlbaum. (Article originally published in 1976.)

Johnson, D. L., Wiebe, J. S., Gold, S. M., Andreasen, N. C., Hichwa, R. D., Watkins, G. L., & Ponto, L. L. B. (1999). Cerebral blood flow and personality: A positron emission tomography study. *American Journal of Psychiatry, 156,* 252–257.

Johnson, G. R. (1987). In the name of the fatherland: An analysis of kin term usage in patriotic speech and literature. *International Political Science Review, 8,* 165–174.

Johnson, M. H., & Horn, G. (1988). Development of filial preferences in dark-reared chicks. *Animal Behaviour, 36,* 675–783.

Johnson, M. K., Hashtroudi, S., & Lindsay, D. S. (1993). Source monitoring. *Psychological Bulletin, 114,* 3–28.

Johnson-Laird, P. N. (1985). Deductive reasoning ability. In R. J. Sternberg (Ed.), *Human abilities: An information-processing approach.* New York: Freeman.

Johnson-Laird, P. N., Byrne, R. M. J., & Schaeken, W. (1994). Why models rather than rules give a better account of propositional reasoning: A reply to Bonatti and to O'Brien, Braine, and Yang. *Psychological Review, 101,* 734–739.

Johnson-Laird, P. N., Legrenzi, P., Girotto, V., & Legrenzi, M. S. (2000). Illusions in reasoning about consistency. *Science, 288,* 531–532.

Johnston, T. D., & Pietrewicz, A. T. (Eds.). (1985). *Issues in the ecological study of learning.* Hillsdale, NJ: Erlbaum.

Jonas, E., Schulz-Hardt, S., Frey, D., & Thelen, N. (2001). Confirmation bias in sequential information search after primary decisions: An expansion of dissonance theoretical research on selective exposure to information. *Journal of Personality and Social Psychology, 80,* 557–571.

Jones, B. E. (2000). Basic mechanisms of sleep-wake states. In M. H. Kryger, T. Roth, & W. C. Dement (Eds.), *Principles and practice of sleep medicine* (3rd ed.). Philadelphia: W. B. Saunders.

Jones, E. E., & Pulos, S. M. (1993). Comparing the process in psychodynamic and cognitive-behavioral therapies. *Journal of Consulting and Clinical Psychology, 61,* 306–316.

Jones, E. F., Forrest, J. D., Goldman, N., Henshaw, S. K., Lincoln, R., Rosoff, J. I., Westoff, C. F., & Wulf, D. (1985). Teenage pregnancy in developed countries: Determinants and policy implications. *Family Planning Perspectives, 17,* 53–63.

Josephs, R. A., Markus, H. R., & Tafarodi, R. W. (1992). Gender and self-esteem. *Journal of Personality and Social Psychology, 63,* 391–402.

Jouvet, M. (1972). The role of monoamines and acetylcholine-containing neurons in the regulation of the sleep-waking cycle. *Ergebnisse der Physiologie, 64,* 166–307.

Julesz, B. (1995). *Dialogues on perception.* Cambridge, MA: MIT Press.

Jung, C. G. (1969). *The structure and dynamics of the psyche.* Princeton, NJ: Princeton University Press.

Jussim, L. (1991). Social perception and social reality: A reflection-construction model. *Psychological Review, 98* 54–73.

Kagan, J. (1976). Emergent themes in human development. *American Scientist, 64,* 186–196.

Kagan, J. (1994). *Galen's prophesy: Temperament in human nature.* New York: Basic Books.

Kagan, J., Snidman, N., & Arcus, D. M. (1992). Initial reactions to unfamiliarity. *Current Directions in Psychological Science, 1,* 171–174.

Kahneman, D., & Treisman, A. (1984). Changing views of attention and automaticity. In R. Parasuraman & D. R. Davies (Eds.), *Varieties of attention.* New York: Academic Press.

Kail, R. (1991). Development of processing speed in childhood and adolescence. *Advances in Child Development and Behavior, 13,* 151–183.

Kail, R. (1993). The role of a global mechanism in developmental change in speed of processing. In M. L. Howe & R. Pasnak (Eds.), *Emerging themes in cognitive development: Vol. 1. Foundations.* New York: Springer-Verlag.

Kail, R., & Bisanz, J. (1992). The information-processing perspective on cognitive development. In R. J. Sternberg & C. A. Berg (Eds.), *Intellectual development.* New York: Cambridge University Press.

Kaitz, M., Good, A., Rokem, A. M., & Eidelman, A. I. (1987). Mothers' recognition of their newborns by olfactory cues. *Developmental Psychobiology, 20,* 587–591.

Kamil, A. C., & Balda, R. P. (1990). Spatial memory in seed-catching corvids. *Psychology of Learning and Motivation, 26,* 1–25.

Kandel, E. R. (2000a). Cellular mechanisms of learning and the biological basis of individuality. In E. R. Kandel, J.H. Schwartz, & T. M. Jessell (Eds.), *Principles of Neural Science* (4th ed.). New York: McGraw-Hill.

Kandel, E. R. (2000b). Nerve cells and behavior. In E. R. Kandel, J.H. Schwartz, & T. M. Jessell (Eds.), *Principles of Neural Science* (4th ed.). New York: McGraw-Hill.

Kane, J. M. (1992). Atypical neuroleptics for the treatment of schizophrenia. In J. Lindenmayer & S. R. Kay (Eds.), *New biological vistas on schizophrenia.* New York: Brunner/Mazel.

Kanizsa, G. (1976, April). Subjective contours. *Scientific American,* pp. 48–52.

Kano, T. (1992). *The last ape: Pygmy chimpanzee behavior and ecology.* Standford, CA: Stanford University Press.

Kant, I. (1781; reprinted 1965). Critique of pure reason (J. Watson, Trans.). In B. Rand (Ed.), *Modern classical philosophers.* Boston: Houghton Mifflin.

Kaplan, M. F. (1987). The influencing process in group decision making. In C. Hendrick (Ed.), *Review of personality and social psychology: Vol. 8. Group processes.* Newbury Park, CA: Sage.

Kaprio, J., Koskenvuo, M., & Rita, H. (1987). Mortality after bereavement: A prospective study of 95,647 widowed persons. *American Journal of Public Health, 77,* 283–287.

Kapur, S., & Mann, J. J. (1993). Antidepressant action and the neurobiologic effects of ECT: Human studies. In C. E. Coffey (Ed.), *The clinical science of electroconvulsive therapy.* Washington, DC: American Psychiatric Press.

Karádi, Z., Oomura, Y., Nishino, H., Scott, T. R., Lénárd, L., & Aou, S. (1990). Complex attributes of lateral hypothalamic neurons in the regulation of feeding of alert rhesus monkeys. *Brain Research Bulletin, 25,* 933–939.

Karasu, T. B. (1986). The specificity versus nonspecificity dilemma: Toward identifying therapeutic change agents. *American Journal of Psychiatry, 143,* 687–695.

Karau, S. J., & Williams, K. D. (1995). Social loafing: Research findings, implications, and future directions. *Current Directions in Psychological Science, 4,* 134–140.

Karau, S. J., & Williams, K. D. (2001). Understanding individual motivation in groups: The collective effort model. In M. E. Turner (Ed.), *Groups at work: Theory and research.* Mahwah, NJ: Erlbaum.

Karmiloff-Smith, A. (1984). Children's problem solving. In M. E. Lamb, A. L., Brown, & B. Rogoff (Eds.), *Advances in developmental psychology* (Vol. 3). Hillsdale, NJ: Erlbaum.

Karmiloff-Smith, A. (1992). *Beyond modularity: A developmental perspective on cognitive science.* Cambridge, MA: MIT Press.

Karmiloff-Smith, A. (1994). Précis of beyond modularity: A developmental perspective on cognitive science. *Behavioral and Brain Sciences, 17,* 693–745.

Karni, A., Tanne, D., Rubenstein, B. S., Askenasy, J. J. M., & Sagi, D. (1994). Dependence on REM sleep of overnight improvement of a perceptual skill. *Science, 265,* 679–682.

Karon, B. P. (1989). Psychotherapy versus medication for schizophrenia: Empirical comparisons. In S. Fisher & R. P. Greenberg (Eds.), *The limits of biological treatments for psychological distress: Comparisons with psychotherapy and placebo.* Hillsdale, NJ: Erlbaum.

Karp, D. (1988). A decade of reminders: Changing age consciousness between fifty and sixty years old. *The Gerontologist, 28,* 727–738.

Kashima, Y., Yamaguchi, S., Kim, U., Choi, S., Gelfand, M. J., & Yuki, M. (1995). Culture, gender, and self: A perspective from individualism-collectivism research. *Journal of Personality and Social Psychology, 69,* 925–937.

Kastenbaum, R. (1985). Dying and death. In J. E. Birren & K. W. Schaie (Eds.), *Handbook of the psychology of aging* (2nd ed.). New York: Van Nostrand-Reinhold.

Katz, D. (1960). The functional approach to the study of attitudes. *Public Opinion Quarterly, 24,* 163–204.

Katz, D., & Braly, K. (1933). Racial stereotypes of one hundred college students. *Journal of Abnormal and Social Psychology, 28,* 280–290.

Kaufman, A. S. (1990). *Assessing adolescent and adult intelligence.* Boston: Allyn & Bacon.

Kaufman, L., & Kaufman, J. H. (2000). Explaining the moon illusion. *Proceedings of the National Academy of Sciences (USA), 97,* 500–505.

Kaufman, L., & Rock, I. (1962, July). The moon illusion. *Scientific American,* pp. 120–130.

Kaufman, L., & Rock, I. (1989). The moon illusion thirty years later. In M. Hershenson (Ed.), *The moon illusion.* Hillsdale, NJ: Erlbaum.

Kavaliers, M., Choleris, E., Colwell, D. D., & Ossenkopp, K. (1999). Learning to cope with biting flies: Rapid NMDA-mediated acquisition of conditioned analgesia. *Behavioral Neuroscience, 113,* 126–135.

Kawakami, K., & Dovidio, J. (2001). The reliability of implicit stereotyping. *Personality and Social Psychology Bulletin, 27,* 212–225.

Kay, P., & Kempton, W. (1984). What is the Sapir-Whorf hypothesis? *American Anthropologist, 86,* 65–79.

Keane, T. M., & Kaloupek, D. G. (1982). Imaginal flooding in the treatment of posttraumatic stress disorder. *Journal of Consulting and Clinical psychology, 50,* 138–140.

Keefe, F. J., & France, C. R. (1999). Pain: Biopsychosocial mechanisms and management. *Current Directions in Psychological Science, 8,* 137–141.

Keesey, R. E., & Corbett, S. W. (1984). Metabolic defense of the body weight set-point. In A. J. Stunkard & E. Stellar (Eds.), *Eating and its disorders.* New York: Raven Press.

Kegl, J. (1994). The Nicaraguan Sign Language Project: An overview. *Signpost, 7,* 24–31.

Kelley, H. H. (1950). The warm-cold variable in first impressions of persons. *Journal of Personality, 18,* 431–439.

Kelley, H. H. (1967). Attribution theory in social psychology. In D. Levine (Ed.), *Nebraska Symposium on Motivation, 1967.* Lincoln: University of Nebraska Press.

Kelley, H. H. (1973). The process of causal attribution. *American Psychologist, 28,* 107–128.

Kelly, G. A. (1958). The theory and technique of assessment. *Annual Review of Psychology, 9,* 323–352.

Kelly, J. A., & Hansen, D. J. (1987). Social interactions and adjustment. In V. B. Van Hasselt & M. Hersen (Eds.), *Handbook of adolescent psychology.* New York: Pergamon.

Kelsoe, J. R. (1997). The genetics of bipolar disorder. *Psychiatric Annals, 27,* 285–292.

Keltner, D., & Anderson, C. (2000). Saving face for Darwin: The functions and uses of embarrassment. *Current Directions in Psychological Science, 9,* 187–192.

Keltner, D., & Buswell, B. N. (1997). Embarrassment: Its distinct form and appeasement functions. *Psychological Bulletin, 122,* 250–270.

Keltner, D., & Robinson, R. J. (1996). Extremism, power, and the imagined basis of social conflict. *Current Directions in Psychological Science, 5,* 101–105.

Kempermann, G., & Gage, F. H. (1999, May). New nerve cells for the adult brain. *Scientific American,* pp. 48–53.

Kendler, H. H. (1987). *Historical foundations of modern psychology.* Philadelphia: Temple University Press.

Kendler, K. S. (1998). Major depression and the enviroment: A psychiatric genetic perspective. *Pharmacopsychiatry, 31,* 5–9.

Kendler, K. S., Karkowski-Shuman, L., O'Neill, A., Straub, R. E., MacLean, C. J., & Walsh, D. (1997). Resemblance of psychotic symptoms and syndromes in affected sibling pairs from the Irish study of high-density schizophrenia families: Evidence for possible etiologic heterogeneity. *American Journal of Psychiatry, 154,* 191–198.

Kendler, K. S., Kessler, R. C., Walters, E. E., MacLean, C., Neale, M. C., Heath, A., C., & Eaves, L. J. (1995). Stressful life events, genetic liability, and the onset of an episode of major depression in women. *American Journal of Psychiatry, 152,* 833–842.

Kendler, K. S., Lindon, J. E., Walters, E. E., Neale, M. C., Heath, A. C., & Kessler, R. C. (1996). The identification and validation of distinct depressive syndromes in a population-based sample of female twins. *Archives of General Psychiatry, 53,* 391–399.

Kendler, K. S., Neal, M. C., Kessler, R. C., Heath, A. C., & Eaves, L. J. (1992). Major depression and generalized anxiety disorder: Same genes, (partly) different environments? *Archives of General Psychiatry, 49,* 716–722.

Kendler, K. S., Walters, E. E., Neale, M.C., Kessler, R. C., Heath, A. C., & Eaves, L. J. (1995). The structure of the genetic and environmental risk factors for six major psychiatric disorders in women: phobia, generalized anxiety disorders, panic disorder, bulimia, major depression, and alcoholism. *Archives of General Psychiatry, 52,* 374–383.

Kendler, T. S. (1972). An ontogeny of mediational deficiency. *Child Development, 43,* 1–17.

Kendrick, K. M., Lévy, F., & Keverne, E. B. (1992). Changes in sensory processing of olfactory signals induced by birth in sheep. *Science, 256,* 833–836.

Keppel, G., Postman, L., & Zavortink, B. (1968). Studies of learning to learn? VIII. The influence of massive amounts of training upon the learning and retention of paired-associate lists. *Journal of Verbal Learning and Verbal Behavior, 7,* 790–796.

Kermoian, R., & Campos, J. J. (1988). Locomotor experience: A facilitator of spatial cognitive development. *Child Development, 59,* 908–917.

Kernberg, O. (1976). *Object relations theory and clinical psychoanalysis.* New York: Jason Aronson.

Kessler, R. C. (1997). The effects of stressful life events on depression. *Annual Review of Psychology, 48,* 191–214.

Kessler, R. C., McGonagle, K. A., Zhao, S., Nelson, C. B., Hughes, M., Eshleman, S., Wittchen, H., & Kendler, K. S. (1994). Lifetime and 12-month prevalence of *DSM-III-R* psychiatric disorders in the United States. *Archives of General Psychiatry, 51,* 8–19.

Ketterson, E. D., & Nolan, V. (1994). Male parental behavior in birds. *Annual Review of Ecology and Systematics, 25,* 601–628.

Ketting, E., & Visser, A. P. (1994). Contraception in the Netherlands: The low abortion rate explained. *Patient Education and Counseling, 23,* 161–171.

Kety, S. S., Rosenthal, D., Wender, P. H., Schulsigner, F., & Jacobson, B. (1976). Mental illness in the biological and adoptive families of adopted individuals who have become schizophrenic. *Behavior Genetics, 6,* 219–225.

Khorsroshahi, F. (1989). Penguins don't care, but women do: A social identity analysis of a Whorfian problem. *Language in Society, 18,* 505–525.

Kiecolt-Glaser, J. K., & Glaser, R. (2001). Stress and immunity: Age enhances the risks. *Current Directions in Psychological Science, 10,* 18–21.

Kiesler, C. A. (1993). Mental health policy and mental hospitalization. *Current Directions in Psychological Science, 2,* 93–95.

Kihlstrom, J. F. (1985). Hynosis. *Annual Reviews of Psychology, 36,* 385–418.

Kimberg, D. Y., D'Esposito, M., & Farah, M. J. (1997). Cognitive functions in the prefrontal cortex—working memory and executive control. *Current Directions in Psychological Science, 6,* 185–192.

King, A. C., Oman, R. J., Brassington, G. S., Bliwise, D. L., & Haskell, W. L. (1997). Moderate-intensity exercise and self-rated quality of sleep in older adults. *JAMA, Journal of the American Medical Association, 277* (1), 32–37.

King, B. M., Smith, R. L., & Frohman, L. A. (1984). Hyperinsulinemia in rats with ventromedial hypothalamic lesions: Role of hyperphagia. *Behavioral Neuroscience, 98,* 152–155.

King, D. W., King, L. A., Gudanowski, D. M., & Vreven, D. L. (1995). Alternative representations of war zone stressors: Relationships to posttraumatic stress disorder in male and female Vietnam veterans. *Journal of Abnormal Psychology, 104*, 184–196.

Kinsey, A. C., Pomeroy, W. B., Martin, C. E., & Gebhard, P. H. (1953). *Sexual behavior in the human female.* Philadelphia: Saunders.

Kinsey, A., C., Pomeroy, W. B., & Martin, C. E. (1948). *Sexual behavior in the human male.* Philadelphia: Saunders.

Kirmayer, L. J. (1991). The place of culture in psychiatric nosology: *Taijin kyofusho* and DSM-III-R. *Journal of Nervous and Mental Disease, 179*, 19–28.

Kirsch, I. (2000). Are drug and placebo effects in depression additive? *Biological Psychiatry, 47*, 733–735.

Kirsch, I., & Lynn, S. J. (1999). Automaticity in clinical psychology. *American Psychologist, 54*, 504–515.

Kirsch, I., & Saperstein, G. (1998). Listening to prozac but hearing placebo: A meta-analysis of antidepressant medication. *Prevention and Treatment, 1*, Article 0002a.

Kirsch, I., & Sapirstein, G. (1999). Listening to Prozac but hearing placebo: A meta-analysis of antidepressant medications. In I. Kirsch (Ed.), *How expectancies shape experience.* Washington, DC: American Psychological Association.

Kirsch, I., Tennen, H., Wickless, C., Saccone, A. J., & Cody, S. (1983). The role of expectancy in fear reduction. *Behavior Therapy, 14*, 520–533.

Kissin, B. 1986). *Conscious and unconscious programs in the brain.* New York: Plenum Press.

Kleiman, D. G. (1977). Monogamy in mammals. *Quarterly Review of Biology, 52*, 39–69.

Klein, D. F., Gittelman, R., Quitkin, F., & Rifkin, A. (1980). *Diagnosis and drug treatment of psychiatric disorders: Adults and children* (2nd ed.). Baltimore: Williams & Wilkins.

Kleinman, A. (1988). *Rethinking psychiatry: From cultural category to personal experience.* New York: Free Press.

Kleinman, A., & Cohen, A. (1977, March). Psychiatry's global challenge. *Scientific American,* pp. 86–89.

Klinke, R. (1986). Physiology of hearing. In R. F. Schmidt (Ed.), *Fundamentals of sensory physiology.* New York: Springer-Verlag.

Kluger, M. J. (1991). Fever: Role of pyrogens and cryogens. *Physiological Reviews, 71*, 93–127.

Klüver H., & Bucy, P. C. (1937). "Psychic blindness" and other symptoms following temporal lobectomy in rhesus monkeys. *American Journal of Physiology, 119*, 352–353.

Knowlton, B. J., Ramus, S. J., & Squire, L. R. (1992). Intact artificial grammar learning in amnesia: Dissociation of classification learning and explicit memory for specific instances. *Psychological Science, 3*, 172–179.

Knowlton, B. J., & Squire, L. R. (1993). The learning of categories: Parallel brain systems for item memory and category knowledge. *Science, 262*, 1747–1749.

Knox, R. E., & Inkster, J. A. (1968). Postdecision dissonance at post time. *Journal of Personality and Social Psychology, 8*, 319–323.

Kochanska, G. (1995). Children's temperament, mother's discipline, and security of attachment: Multiple pathways to emerging internalization. *Child Development, 66*, 597–615.

Kochanska, G., Tjebkes, T. L., & Forman, D. R. (1998). Children's emerging regulation of conduct: Restraint, compliance, and internalization from infancy to the second year. *Child Development, 69*, 1378–1389.

Koffka, K. (1935). *Principles of Gestalt psychology.* New York: Harcourt Brace Jovanovich.

Kohlberg, L. (1966). A cognitive-developmental analysis of children's sex-role concepts and attitudes. In E. E. Maccoby (Ed.), *The development of sex differences.* Stanford, CA: Stanford University Press.

Kohlberg, L. (1984). *The psychology of moral development.* San Francisco: Harper & Row.

Kohlberg, L., Yaeger, J., & Hjertholm, E. (1968). Private speech: Four studies and a review of theories. *Child Development, 39*, 691–736.

Köhler, W. (1917; reprinted 1973). *Intelligenzprüfungen an Anthropoiden* (3rd ed.). Berlin: Springer.

Kohn, M. L. (1980). Job complexity and adult personality. In N. J. Smelser & E. H. Erikson (Eds.), *Theories of work and love in adulthood.* Cambridge, MA: Harvard University Press.

Kohn, M. L., & Slomczynski, K. M. (1990). *Social structure and self-direction: A comparative analysis of the United States and Poland.* Cambridge, MA: Basil Blackwell.

Kohut, H. (1971). *The analysis of the self: A systematic approach to the treatment of narcissistic personality disorders.* Madison, CT: International Universities Press.

Kollock, P. (1998). Social dilemmas: The anatomy of cooperation. *Annual Review of Sociology, 24*, 183–214.

Komorita, S. S., & Parks, C. D. (1995). Interpersonal relations: Mixed-motive interaction. *Annual Review of Psychology, 46*, 183–207.

Komorita, S. S., & Parks, C. D. (1999). Reciprocity and cooperation in social dilemmas: Review and future directions. In D. B. Budescu, I. Erev, & R. Zwick (Eds.), *Games and human behavior: Essays in honor of Amnon Rapaport.* Mahwah, NJ: Erlbaum.

Konner, M. (1972). Aspects of the developmental ethology of a foraging people. In N. G. Blurton-Jones (Ed.), *Ethological studies of child behavior.* Cambridge, England: Cambridge University Press.

Konner, M. (1975). Relations among infants and juveniles in comparative perspective. In M. Lewis & L. A. Rosenblum (Eds.), *The origins of behavior: Vol. 4. Friendship and peer relations.* New York: Wiley.

Konner, M. (1981). Evolution of human behavior development. In R. H. Munroe, R. L. Munroe, & B. B. Whiting (Eds.), *Handbook of cross-cultural psychology.* New York: Garland.

Konner, M. J. (1976). Maternal care, infant behavior and development among the !Kung. In R. B. Lee & I. DeVore (Eds.), *Kalahari hunter-gatherers: Studies of the !Kung San and their neighbors.* Cambridge, MA: Harvard University Press.

Konner, M. J. (1982). *The tangled wing: Biological constraints on the human spirit.* New York: Harper & Row.

Koodsma, D. E., & Byers, B. E. (1991). The functions of bird song. *American Zoologist, 31*, 318–328.

Koss, M. P. (1990). The women's mental health research agenda: Violence against women. *American Psychologist, 45*, 374–380.

Kosslyn, S. M. (1973). Scanning visual images: Some structural implications. *Perception and Psychophysics, 14*, 90–94.

Kosslyn, S. M. (1980). *Image and mind*. Cambridge, MA: Harvard University Press.

Kosslyn, S. M., & Koenig, O. (1992). *Wet mind: The new cognitive neuroscience*. New York: Free Press.

Kotler, T. (1985). Security and autonomy within marriage. *Human Relations, 38,* 299–321.

Kraemer, G. W. (1992). A psychobiological theory of attachment. *Behavioral and Brain Sciences, 15,* 493–541.

Krakauer, J., & Ghez, C. (2000). Voluntary movement. In E. R. Kandel, J.H. Schwartz, & T. M. Jessell (Eds.), *Principles of Neural Science* (4th ed.). New York: McGraw-Hill.

Kramer, P. D. (1994). *Listening to Prozac*. London: Fourth Estate.

Kramer, R. M., & Brewer, M. B. (1984). Effect of group identity on resource use in a simulated common dilemma. *Journal of Personality and Social Psychology, 46,* 1044–1057.

Kraut, R. E., & Johnston, R. E. (1979). Social and emotional messages of smiling: An ethological approach. *Journal of Personality and Social Psychology, 37,* 1539–1553.

Kronig, M. H., Apter, J., Asnis, G., Brystritsky, A., et al., (1999). Placebo-controlled multicenter study of sertraline treatment for obsessive-compulsive disorder. *Journal of Clinical Psychopharmacology, 19,* 172–176.

Krosnick, J. A., Betz, A. L., Jussim, L. J., & Lynn, A. R. (1992). Subliminal conditioning of attitudes. *Personality and Social Psychology Bulletin, 18,* 152–162.

Kruger, J., & Dunning, D. (1999). Unskilled and unaware of it: How difficulties in recognizing one's own incompetence lead to inflated self-assessments. *Journal of Personality and Social Psychology, 77,* 1121–1134.

Krull, D. S. (1993). Does the grist change the mill? The effect of perceiver's inferential goal on the process of social inference. *Personality and Social Psychology Bulletin, 19,* 340–348.

Krull, D. S., & Erickson, D. J. (1995). Inferential hopscotch: How people draw social inferences from behavior. *Current Directions in Psychological Science, 4,* 35–38.

Kryter, K. D. (1985). *The effects of noise on man* (2nd ed.). Orlando, FL: Academic Press.

Kübler-Ross, E. (1969). *On death and dying*. New York: Macmillan.

Kuczaj, S. A. (1977). The acquisition of regular and irregular past tense forms. *Journal of Verbal Learning and Verbal Behavior, 16,* 589–600.

Kuffler, S. W. (1953). Discharge patterns and functional organization of mammalian retina. *Journal of Neurophysiology, 16,* 37–68.

Kuhl, P. K. (1987). Perception of speech and sound in early infancy. In P. Salapatek & L. Cohen (Eds.), *Handbook of infant perception: Vol. 2. From perception to cognition*. Orlando, FL: Academic Press.

Kuhl, P. K., Andruski, J. E., Christovich, I. A., Kozhevnikova, E. V., Ryskina, V. L., Stolyarova, E. I., Sundberg, U., & Lacerda, F. (1997). Cross-language analysis of phonetic units in language addressed to infants. *Science, 277,* 684–686.

Kurihara, K., & Kashiwayanagi, M. (1998). Introductory remarks on umami taste. *Annals of the New York Academy of Sciences, 855,* 393–397.

Kurland, J. A. (1979). Paternity, mother's brother, and human sociality. In N. A. Chagnon & W. Irons (Eds.), *Evolutionary biology and human social behavior: An anthropological perspective*. North Scituate, MA: Duxbury Press.

Kurumaji, A., & Yoshiro, O. (2000). D1 dopamine receptors, schizophrenia, and antipsychotic medications. In M. S. Lidow (Ed.), *Neurotransmitter receptors in actions of antipsychotic medications: Pharmacology and toxicology*. BocaRaton, FL: CRC Press.

Kyllonen, P. C., & Christal, R. E. (1990). Reasoning ability is (little more than) working-memory capacity?! *Intelligence, 14,* 389–433.

LaBerge, D. (1995). *Attentional processing: The brain's art of mindfulness*. Cambridge, MA: Harvard University Press.

Lack, D. (1968). *Ecological adaptations for breeding in birds*. London: Methuen.

La Freniere, P., Strayer, F. F., & Gauthier, R. (1984). The emergence of same-sex affiliative preferences among preschool peers: A developmental/ethological perspective. *Child Development, 55,* 1958–1965.

Laird, J. D. (1974). Self-attribution of emotion: The effects of expressive behavior on the quality of emotional experience. *Journal of Personality and Social Psychology, 29,* 475–486.

Lalumière, M. L., Quinsey, V. L., & Craig, W. M. (1996). Why children from the same family are so different from one another: A Darwinian note. *Human Nature, 7,* 281–290.

Lamb, H. R. (2000). Deinstitutionalization and public policy. In R. W. Menninger & J. C. Nemiah (Eds.), *American psychiatry after World War II*. Washington, DC: American Psychiatric Press.

Lambert, M. J., & Okiishi, J. C. (1997). The effects of the individual psychotherapist and implications for future research. *Clinical Psychology: Science and Practice, 4,* 66–75.

Lancaster, J. B. (1971). Play-mothering: The relations between juvenile females and young infants among free-ranging vervet monkeys (*Cercopithecus aethiops*). *Folia Primatologica, 15,* 161–182.

Land, M. F., & Furnald, R. D. (1992). The evolution of eyes. *Annual Review of Neuroscience, 15,* 1–29.

Landrine, H. (1992). Clinical implications of cultural differences: The referential verses the indexical self. *Clinicial Psychology Review, 12,* 401–415.

Landrum, E., Davis, S., & Landrum, T. (2000). *The psychology major: Career options and strategies for success*. Upper Saddle River, NJ: Prentice-Hall.

Langer, E. J., Blank, A., & Chanowitz, B. (1978). The mindlessness of ostensibly thoughtful action. *Journal of Personality and Social Psychology, 36,* 635–642.

Larson, R. W., Richards, M. H., & Perry-Jenkins M. (1994). Divergent worlds: The daily and emotional experience of mothers and fathers in the domestic and public spheres. *Journal of Personality and Social Psychology, 67,* 1034–1046.

Lashley, K. S. (1930). Basic neural mechanisms in behavior. *Psychological Review, 37,* 1–24.

Lashley, K. S. (1951). The problem of serial order in behavior. In L. A. Jeffress (Ed.), *Cerebral mechanisms in behavior*. New York: Wiley.

Latané, B. (1981). The psychology of social impact. *American Psychologist, 36*, 343–356.

Latané, B. & Nida, S. (1981). Ten years of research on group size and helping. *Psychological Bulletin, 89*, 308–324.

Latané, B., & Rodin, J. (1969). A lady in distress: Inhibiting effects of friends and strangers on bystander intervention. *Journal of Experimental Social Psychology, 5*, 189–202.

Lauer, J., & Lauer, R. (1985, June). Marriages made to last. *Psychology Today*, pp. 22–26.

Laurent, J., Catanzaro, S. J., & Callan, M.K. (1997). Stress, alcohol-related expectancies and coping preferences: A replication with adolescents of the Cooper et al. (1992) model. *Journal of Studies on Alcohol, 58*, 644–651.

Lave, J. (1988). Cognition in practice: Mind, mathematics, and culture in everyday life. Cambridge, England: Cambridge University Press.

Lazarus, A. A. (1968). Behavior therapy in groups. In G. M. Gazda (Ed.), *Basic approaches to group psychotherapy and counseling*. Springfield, IL: Charles C. Thomas.

Lazarus, R. S. (1993). From psychological stress to the emotions: A history of changing outlooks. *Annual Review of Psychology, 44*, 1–21.

Leana, C. R. (1985). A partial test of Janis' groupthink model. Effects of group cohesiveness and leader behavior on defective decision making. *Journal of Management, 11*, 5–17.

Leary, M. R. (1999). Making sense of self-esteem. *Current Directions in Psychological Science, 8*, 32–35.

Leary, M. R., & Kowalski, R. M. (1995). *Social anxiety*. New York: Guilford Press.

Leary, M. R., Nezlek, J. B., Downs, D., Radford-Davenport, J., Martin, J., & McMullen, A. (1994). Self-presentation in everyday interactions: Effects of target familiarity and gender composition. *Journal of Personality and Social Psychology, 67*, 664–673.

Leary, M. R., Tambor, E. S., Terdal, S. K., & Downs, D. L. (1995). Self-esteem as an interpersonal monitor: The sociometer hypothesis. *Journal of Personality and Social Psychology, 68*, 518–530.

LeDoux, J. E. (1992). Emotion and the amygdala. In J. P. Aggleton (Ed.), *The amygdala: Neurobiological aspects of emotion, memory, and mental dysfunction*. New York: Wiley-Liss.

LeDoux, J. E. (1996). *The emotional brain: The mysterious underpinnings of emotional life*. New York: Simon & Schuster.

LeDoux, J. E., Romanski, L., & Xagoraris, A. (1989). Indelibility of subcortical emotional memories. *Journal of Cognitive Neuroscience, 1*, 238–243.

Lehman, A. F. (1998). Public health policy, community services, and outcomes for patients with schizophrenia. *The psychiatric clinics of North America, 21*, 221–231.

Lehman, A. F., Dixon, L., Hoch, J. S., DeForge, B., Kernan, E., & Frank, R. (1999). Cost-effectiveness of assertive community treatment for homeless persons with severe mental illness. *British Journal of Psychiatry, 174*, 346–352.

Lehman, A. F., Steinwachs, D. M., & survey co-investigators of the PORT project (1998). Patterns of usual care for schizophrenia: Initial results from the schizophrenia patient outcomes research team (PORT) client survey. *Schizophrenia Bulletin, 24*, 11–20.

Leibel, R. L., Rosenbaum, M., & Hirsch, J. (1995). Changes in energy expenditure resulting from altered body weight. *New England Journal of Medicine, 332*, 621–628.

Leith, K. P., & Baumeister, R. F. (1998). Empathy, shame, guilt, and narratives of interpersonal conflicts: Guilt-prone people are better at perspective taking. *Journal of Personality, 66*, 1–37.

Lenneberg, E. H. (1969). *Biological foundations of language*. New York: Wiley.

Lennie, P. (1998). Single units and visual cortical organization. *Perception, 27*, 889–935.

Lepper, M. R., & Greene, D. (1978). Overjustification research and beyond: Toward a means-end analysis of intrinsic and extrinsic motivation. In M. R. Lepper & D. Greene (Eds.), *The hidden costs of reward: New perspectives on the psychology of human motivation*. New York: Wiley.

Lerner, M. J. (1980). *The belief in a just world: A fundamental delusion*. New York: Plenum Press.

Lerner, M. J., & Goldberg, J. H. (1999). When do decent people blame victims? The differing effects of the explicit/rational and implicit/experiential cognitive systems. In S. Chaiken & Y. Trope (Eds.), *Dual-process theories in social psychology*. New York: Guilford.

Lerner, M. J., & Miller, D. T. (1978). Just world research and the attribution process: Looking back and looking ahead. *Psychological Bulletin, 85*, 1030–1051.

Lerner, M. J., & Simmons, C. H. (1966). The observer's reaction to the "innocent victim": Compassion or rejection? *Journal of Personality and Social Psychology, 4*, 203–210.

Lerner, M. R., Gyorgyi, T. K., Reagan, J., Roby-Shemkovitz, A., Rybczynski, R., & Vogt, R. (1990). Peripheral events in moth olfaction. *Chemical Senses, 15*, 191–198.

Lesch, K.-P., Bengel, D., Heils, A., Sabol, S. Z., Greenberg, B. D., Petri, S., Benjamin, J., Clemens, R. M., Hamer, D. H., & Murphy, D. L. (1996). Association of anxiety-related traits with a polymorphism in the serotonin transporter gene regulation region. *Science, 274*, 1527–1531.

Leslie, A. M. (1987). Pretense and representation: The origins of "theory of mind." *Psychological Review, 94*, 412–426.

Leslie, A. M. (1991). The theory of mind impairment in autism: Evidence for a modular mechanism of development? In A. Whiten (Ed.), *Natural theories of mind: Evolution, development and simulation of everyday mindreading*. Cambridge, MA: Basil Blackwell.

Leslie, A. M. (1994). Pretending and believing: Issues in the theory of ToMM. *Cognition, 50*, 211–238.

Leslie, A. M., & Thaiss, L. (1992). Domain specificity in conceptual development: Neuropsychological evidence from autism. *Cognition, 43*, 225–251.

LeVay, S. (1991). A difference in hypothalamic structure between heterosexual and homosexual men. *Science, 253*, 1034–1037.

LeVay, S., & Hamer, D. H. (1994, May). Evidence for a biological influence in male homosexuality. *Scientific American*, pp. 44–49.

Levenson, R. W. (1992). Autonomic nervous system differences among emotions. *Psychological Science, 3*, 23–27.

Levenson, R. W., Carstensen, L. L., & Gottman, J. M. (1993). Long-term marriage: Age, gender, and satisfaction. *Psychology and Aging, 8*, 301–313.

Levenson, R. W., Ekman, P., & Friesen, W. V. (1990). Voluntary facial action generates emotion-specific nervous system activity. *Psychophysiology, 27,* 363–384.

Levin, J., & Arluke, A. (1982). Embarrassment and helping behavior. *Psychological Reports, 51,* 999–1002.

Levine, J. D., Gordon, N. C., & Fields, H. L., (1979). The role of endorphins in placebo analgesia. *Advances in Pain Research and Therapy, 3,* 547–550.

Levine, K., Shane, H. C., & Wharton, R. H. (1994). What if . . . : A plea to professionals to consider the risk-benefit ratio of facilitated communication. *Mental Retardation, 31,* 300–307.

Levine, M., Toro, P. A., & Perkins, D. V. (1993). Social and community interventions. *Annual Review of Psychology, 44,* 525–558.

Levinger, G., & Schneider, D. J. (1969). Test of the "risk is a value" hypothesis. *Journal of Personality and Social Psychology, 11,* 165–169.

Levinson, D. J. (1978). *The seasons of a man's life.* New York: Ballantine.

Levinson, D. J. (1986). The conception of adult development. *American Psychologist, 41,* 3–13.

Levinson, S. C. (1996). Relativity in spatial conception and description. In J. Gumperz & S. C. Levinson (Eds.), *Rethinking linguistic relativity.* Cambridge, England: Cambridge University Press.

Levitt, M. J. (1991). Attachment and close relationships: A life-span perspective. In J.L. Gewirtz & W.M. Kurtines (Eds.), *Intersections with attachment.* Hillsdale, NJ: Erlbaum.

Levy, G. D., & Fivush, R. (1993). Scripts and gender: A new approach for examining gender-role development. *Developmental Review, 13,* 126–146.

Levy, G. D., Taylor, M. G., & Gelman, S. A. (1995). Traditional and evaluative aspects of flexibility in gender roles, social conventions, moral rules, and physical laws. *Child Development, 66,* 515–531.

Levy-Shiff, R., (1994). Individual and contextual correlates of marital change across the transition to parenthood. *Developmental Psychology, 30,* 591–601.

Lewicka, M. (1998). Confirmation bias: Cognitive error or adaptive strategy of action control? In M. Kofta, G. Weary, & G. Sedek (Eds.), *Personal control in action: Cognitive and motivational mechanisms.* New York: Plenum.

Lewin, K. (1951). *Field theory in social science: Selected theoretical papers by Kurt Lewin* (D. Cartwright, Ed.). New York: Harper & Row.

Lewis, J. W., Cannon, J. T., & Liebeskind, J. C. (1980). Opioid and nonopioid mechanisms of stress analgesia. *Science, 208,* 623–625.

Lewis, M. (1991). Self-conscious emotions and the development of self. *Journal of the American Psychoanalytic Association (Supplement), 39,* 45–73.

Lewis, M. (1995). Embarrassment: The emotion of self-exposure and evaluation. In J. P. Tangney & K. W. Fischer (Eds.), *Self-conscious emotions: The psychology of shame, guilt, embarrassment, and pride.* New York: Guilford Press.

Lewis, M., Alessandri, S. M., & Sullivan, M. W. (1990). Violation of expectancy, loss of control, and anger expressions in young infants. *Developmental Psychology, 26,* 745–751.

Lewis, M., & Brooks-Gunn, J. (1979). *Social cognition and the acquisition of self.* New York: Plenum Press.

Lewis, P. T. (1995). A naturalistic test of two fundamental propositions: Correspondence bias and the actor-observer hypothesis. *Journal of Personality, 63,* 88–111.

Lewontin, R., & Gould, S. J. (1978). The spandrels San Marco and the Pangolossian paradigm: A critique of the adaptationalist programme. *Proceedings of the Royal Society of London, 205,* 581–598.

Leyens, J-P., Yzerbyt, V., & Corneille, O. (1996). The role of applicability in the emergence of the overattribution bias. *Journal of Personality and Social Psychology, 70,* 219–229.

Liable, D. J., & Thompson, R. A. (2000). Mother-child discourse, attachment security, shared positive affect, and early conscience development. *Child Development, 71,* 1424–1440.

Lichtman, A. H., & Fanselow, M. S. (1990). Cats produce analgesia in rats on the tail-flick test: Naltrexone sensitivity is determined by the nociceptive test stimulus. *Brain Research, 553,* 91–94.

Lickey, M. E., & Gordon, B. (1991). *Medicine and mental illness: The use of drugs in psychiatry.* New York: Freeman.

Lieberman, D. A. (2000). *Learning: Behavior and cognition* (3rd. ed.). Belmont, CA: Wadsworth.

Lieberman, M. D., & Rosenthal, R. (2001). Why introverts can't always tell who likes them: Multitasking and nonverbal decoding. *Journal of Personality and Social Psychology, 80,* 294–310.

Light, W. J. H. (1986). *Neurobiology of alcohol abuse.* Springfield, IL: Charles C. Thomas.

Lilenfeld, S. O., Lynn, S. J., Kirsh, I., Chaves, J. F., Sarbin, T. R., Ganaway, G. K., & Powell, R. A. (1999). Dissociative identity disorder and the sociocognitive model: Recalling the lessons of the past. *Psychological Bulletin, 125,* 507–523.

Lillard, A. S., & Flavell, J. H. (1990). Young children's preference for mental state versus behavioral descriptions of human action. *Child Development, 61,* 731–741.

Lillard, A. S., & Flavell, J. H. (1992). Young children's understanding of different mental states. *Developmental Psychology, 28,* 626–634.

Lin, K., & Kleinman, A. M. (1988). Psychopathology and clinical course of schizophrenia: A cross-cultural perspective. *Schizophrenia Bulletin, 14,* 555–567.

Linder, D. E., Cooper, J., & Jones, E. E. (1967). Decision freedom as a determinant of the role of incentive magnitude in attitude change. *Journal of Personality and Social Psychology, 6,* 245–254.

Lindsay, P. H., & Norman, D. A. (1977). *Human information processing* (2nd ed.). New York: Academic Press.

Lindsay-Hartz, J., de Rivera, J., & Mascolo, M. F. (1995). Differentiating guilt and shame and their effects on motivation. In J. P. Tangney & K. W. Fischer (Eds.), *Self-conscious emotions: The psychology of shame, guilt, embarrassment, and pride.* New York: Guilford Press.

Linville, P. W. (1985). Self-complexity and affective extremity: Don't put all of your eggs in one cognitive basket. *Social Cognition, 3,* 94–120.

Linville, P. W. (1987). Self-complexity as a cognitive buffer against stress-related illness and depression. *Journal of Personality and Social Psychology, 52,* 663–676.

Lipman, R. S. (1989). Pharmacotherapy of the anxiety disorders. In S. Fischer & R. P. Greenberg (Eds.), *The limits of biological treatments for psychological distress: Comparisons with psychotherapy and placebo.* Hillsdale, NJ: Erlbaum.

Lippmann, W. (1922; reprinted 1960). *Public opinion*. New York: Macmillan.

Lipsey, M. W., & Wilson, D. B. (1993). The efficacy of psychological, educational, and behavioral treatment. *American Psychologist, 48,* 1181–1209.

Littrell, J. (1991). *Understanding and treating alcoholism: Vol. 2. Biological, psychological and social aspects of alcohol consumption and abuse.* Hillsdale, NJ: Erlbaum.

Lively, S. E., Logan, J. S., & Pisoni, D. B. (1993). Training Japanese listeners to identify English /r/ and /l/. II. The role of phonetic environment and talker variability in learning new perceptual categories. *Journal of the Acoustical Society of America, 94,* 1242–1255.

Livingston, D. (1857). *Missionary travels and researches in South Africa.* London: John Murray.

Locke, J. (1690; reprinted 1975). *An essay concerning human understanding* (P. Nidditch, Ed.). Oxford: Clarendon.

Locke, J. L. (1983). *Phonological acquisition and change.* New York: Academic Press.

Lockman, J. J., & McHale, J. P. (1989). Object manipulation in infancy: Developmental and contextual determinants. In J. L. Lockman & N. Hazen (Eds.) *Action in social context: Perspectives on early development.* New York: Plenum Press.

Locksley, A., Ortiz, V., & Hepburn, C. (1980). Social categorization and discriminatory behavior: Extinguishing the minimal intergroup discrimination effect. *Journal of Personality and Social Psychology, 39,* 773–783.

Loehlin, J. C. (1992). *Genes and environment in personality development.* Newbury Park, CA: Sage.

Loehlin, J. C., Vandenberg, S., & Osborne, R. (1973). Blood group genes and Negro-White ability differences. *Behavior Genetics, 3,* 263–270.

Loehlin, J. C., Willerman, L., & Horn, J. M. (1988). Human behavior genetics. *Annual Review of Psychology, 39,* 101–133.

Loftus, E. F. (1992). When a lie becomes memory's truth: Memory distortion after exposure to misinformation. *Current Directions in Psychological Science, 1,* 121–123.

Loftus, E. F. (1997). Memory for a past that never was. *Current Directions in Psychological Science, 6,* 60–65.

Loftus, E. F. & Palmer, J. C. (1974). Reconstruction of automobile destruction: An example of the interaction between language and memory. *Journal of Verbal Learning and Verbal Behavior, 13,* 585–589.

Loftus, E. F., & Pickrell, J. E. (1995). The formation of false memories. *Psychiatric Annals, 25,* 720–725.

Lorenz, K. Z. (1943). Die angeborenen Formen möglicher Erfahrung. *Zeitschrift für Tierpsychologie, 5,* 235–409.

Lorenz, K. Z. (1966). *On aggression.* New York: Harcourt, Brace & World.

Lorenz, K. Z. (1971). *Studies in animal and human behavior* (Vol. 2). Cambridge, MA: Harvard University Press.

Lorenz, K. Z. (1974). Analogy as a source of knowledge. *Science, 185,* 229–234.

Low, B. S. (1989). Cross-cultural patterns in the training of children: An evolutionary perspective. *Journal of Comparative Psychology, 103,* 311–319.

Low, B. S. (2000). *Why sex matters: A Darwinian look at human behavior.* Princeton, NJ: Princeton University Press.

Lozoff, B., Wolf, A. W., & Davis, N. S. (1984). Cosleeping in urban families with young children in the United States. *Pediatrics, 74,* 171–182.

Luborsky, L., McLellan, A. T., Diguer, L., Woody, G., & Seligman, D. A. (1997). The psychotherapist matters: Comparison of outcomes across twenty-two therapists and seven patient samples. *Clinical Psychology: Science and Practice, 4,* 53–65.

Lueptow, L. B., Garovich, L., & Lueptow, M. B. (1995). The persistence of gender stereotypes in the face of changing sex roles: Evidence contrary to the sociocultural model. *Ethology and Sociobiology, 16,* 509–530.

Luo, C. R. (1999). Semantic competition as the basis of Stroop Interference: Evidence from color-word matching tasks. *Psychological Science, 10,* 35–40.

Luria, A. R. (1971). Towards the problem of the historical nature of psychological processes. *International Journal of Psychology, 6,* 259–272.

Lynn, B. L., & Perl, E. R. (1996). Afferent mechanisms of pain. In L. Kruger (Ed.), *Pain and touch.* San Diego, CA: Academic Press.

Maccoby, E. E. (1990). Gender and relationships: A developmental account. *American Psychologist, 45,* 513–520.

Maccoby, E. E. (1998). *The two sexes: Growing up apart, coming together.* Cambridge, MA: Harvard University Press.

Maccoby, E. E. & Jacklin, C. N. (1987). Gender segregation in childhood. In H. W. Reese (Ed.), *Advances in child development and behavior* (Vol. 20). Orlando, FL: Academic Press.

MacDonald, K. (1992). Warmth as a developmental construct: An evolutionary analysis. *Child Development, 63,* 753–773.

Macfarlane, A. (1975). Olfaction in the development of social preferences in the human neonate. In *Ciba Foundation Symposium No. 33: Parent-infant interaction.* New York: Elsevier.

Macfarlane, A. J. (1975). Olfaction in the development of social preferences in the human neonate. *Ciba Foundation Symposium, 33,* 103–117.

MacKay, D. G. (1973). Aspects of the theory of comprehension, memory and attention. *Quarterly Journal of Experimental Psychology, 25,* 22–40.

MacKay, D. G. (1980). Psychology, prescriptive grammar, and the pronoun problem. *American Psychologist, 35,* 444–449.

Mackie, D. M. (1986). Social identification effects in group polarization. *Journal of Personality and Social Psychology, 50,* 720–728.

Mackintosh, N. J., & Dickinson, A. (1979). Instrumental (Type II) conditioning. In A. Dickinson & R. A. Boakes (Eds.), *Mechanisms of learning and motivation.* Hillsdale, NJ: Erlbaum.

MacWhinney, B. (1998). Models of the emergence of language. *Annual Review of Psychology, 49,* 1999–2227.

Maes, J. (1998). Eight stages in the development of research on the construct of belief in a just world. In L. Montada & M. J. Lerner (Eds.), *Responses to victimization and belief in a just world.* New York: Plenum.

Maier, S. F., Watkins, L. R., & Fleshner, M. (1994) Psychoneuroimmunology: The interface between behavior, brain, and immunity. *American Psychologist, 49,* 1004–1017.

Maio, G. R., & Olson, J. M. (Eds.) (2000). *Why we evaluate: Functions of attitudes.* Mahwah, NJ: Erlbaum.

Malcolm, J. R. (1985). Paternal care in Canids. *American Zoologist, 25,* 853–859.

Maldonado, R., Saiardi, A., Valverde, O., Samad, T. A., Roques, B. P., & Borrelli, E. (1997). Absence of opiate rewarding effects in mice lacking dopamine D2 receptors. *Nature, 388,* 586–589.

Malle, B. F., Knobe, J., O'Laughlin, M. J., Pearce, G. E., & Nelson, S. E. (2000). Conceptual structure and social functions of behavioral explanations: Beyond person-situation attributions. *Journal of Personality and Social Psychology, 79,* 309–326.

Maltz, D. N., & Borker, R. A. (1982). A cultural approach to male-female miscommunication. In J. J. Gumperz (Ed.), *Language and social identify.* Cambridge, England: Cambridge University Press.

Mani, S. K., Allen, J. M. C., Clark, J. H., Blaustein, J. D., & O'Malley, B. W. (1994). Convergent pathways for steroid hormone- and neurotransmitting-induced rat sexual behavior. *Science, 265,* 1246–1249.

Manji, H. K., & Lenox, R. H. (2000). The nature of bipolar disorder. *Journal of Clinical Psychology, 61 (Supplement 13),* 42–57.

Mäntylä, T. (1986). Optimizing cue effectiveness: Recall of 500 and 600 incidentally learned words. *Journal of Experimental Psychology: Learning, Memory, and Cognition, 12,* 66–71.

Manuck, S. B., Cohen, S., Rabin, B. S., Muldoon, M. F., & Bachen, E. A. (1991). Individual differences in cellular immune response to stress. *Psychological Science, 2,* 111–115.

Maquet, P., Laureys, S., Peigneux, P., Fuchs, S., Petiau, C., Phillips, C., Aerts, J., Del Fiore, G., Degueldre, C., Meulemans, T., Luxen, A., Franck, G., Van Der Linden, M., Smith, C., & Cleeremans, A. (2000). Experience-dependent changes in cerebral activation during REM sleep. *Nature Neuroscience, 3,* 831–836.

Marcus, G. F., Pinker, S., Ullman, M., Hollander, M., Rosen, T. J., & Xu, F. (1992). Overregularization in language acquisition. *Monographs of the Society for Research in Child Development, 57.*

Maren, S. (1999). Long-term potentiation in the amygdala: A mechanism for emotional learning and memory. *Trends in Neuroscience, 22,* 561–567.

Marks, I. M. (1972). Flooding (implosion) and allied treatments. In S. Agras (Ed.), *Behavior modification: Principles and clinical applications.* Boston: Little, Brown.

Marks, I. M. (1987). *Fears, phobias, and rituals: Panic, anxiety, and their disorders.* New York: Oxford University Press.

Marks, I. M., Lelliott, P., Basoglu, M., Noshirvani, H., Monteiro, W., Cohen, D., & Kasvikis, Y. (1988). Clomipramine, self-exposure and therapist-aided exposure for obsessive-compulsive rituals. *British Journal of Psychiatry, 152,* 522–534.

Markus, H. R. & Kitayama, S. (1991). Culture and the self: Implications for cognition, emotion and motivation. *Psychological Review, 98,* 224–253.

Markus, H. R., & Kitayama, S. (1994). A collective fear of the collective: Implications for selves and theories of selves. *Personality and Social Psychology Bulletin, 20,* 568–579.

Marler, P. (1970). A comparative approach to vocal learning. Song development in white-crowned sparrows. *Journal of Comparative and Physiological Psychology, 7,* 1–25.

Marlowe, W. B., Mancall, E. L., & Thomas, J. J. (1975). Complete Klüver-Bucy syndrome in man. *Cortex, 11,* 53–59.

Marr, D. B., & Sternberg, R. J. (1987). The role of mental speed in intelligence. A triarchic perspective. In P. A. Vernon (Ed.), *Speed of information-processing and intelligence.* Norwood, NJ: Ablex.

Marschark, M., & Hunt, R. R. (1989). A reexamination of the role of imagery in learning and memory. *Journal of Experimental Psychology: Learning, Memory, and Cognition, 15,* 710–720.

Marsh, H. W. (1991). The failure of high-ability high schools to deliver academic benefits: The importance of academic self-concept and educational aspirations. *American Educational Research Journal, 28,* 445–480.

Marsh, H. W., Kong, C., & Hau, K. (2000). Longitudinal multilevel models of the big-fish–little-pond effect on academic self-concept: Counterbalancing contrast and reflected-glory effects in Hong Kong schools. *Journal of Personality and Social Psychology, 78,* 337–349.

Marsh, L., Harris, D., Lim, K. O., Beal, M., Hoff, A. L., Minn, K., Csernansky, J. G., DeMent, S., Faustman, W. O., Sullivan, E. V., & Pfefferbaum, A. (1997). Structural magnetic resonance imaging abnormalities in men with severe chronic schizophrenia and an early age at clinical onset. *Archives of General Psychiatry, 54,* 1104–1112.

Martin, C. L. (1990). Attitudes and expectations about children with nontraditional and traditional gender roles. *Sex Roles, 22,* 151–165.

Martin, G., & Pear, J. (1996). *Behavior modification: What it is and how to do it* (5th ed.). Upper Saddle River, NJ: Prentice-Hall.

Mascolo, M. F., & Fischer, K. W. (1995). Developmental transformations in appraisals for pride, shame, and guilt. In J. P. Tangney & K. W. Fischer (Eds.), *Self-conscious emotions: The psychology of shame, guilt, embarrassment, and pride.* New York: Guilford Press.

Masland, R. H. (1996). Unscrambling color vision. *Science, 271,* 616–617.

Maslow, A. H. (1970). *Motivation and personality* (2nd ed.). New York: Harper & Row.

Massaro, D., & Cowan, N. (1993). Information processing models: Microscopes of the mind. *Annual Review of Psychology, 44,* 383–425.

Masters, W. H., Johnson, V. E., & Kolodny, R. C. (1992). *Human sexuality* (4th ed.). New York: HarperCollins.

Matarazzo, J. D. (1983). The reliability of psychiatric and psychological diagnosis. *Clinical Psychology Review, 3,* 103–145.

Matlin, M. W., & Foley, H. J. (1997) *Sensation and perception* (4th ed.). Boston: Allyn & Bacon.

Matthews, G., & Gilliland, K. (1999). The personality theories of H. J. Eysenck and J. A. Gray: A comparative review. *Personality and Individual Differences, 26,* 583–626.

Maurer, D., & Maurer, C. (1988). *The world of the newborn.* New York: Basic Books.

McAdams, D. (1993). *The stories we live by: Personal myths and the making of the self.* New York: Morrow.

McAdams, D. (1994). Can personality change? Levels of stability and growth in personality across the life span. In T. F. Heatherton & J. L. Weinberger (Eds.), *Can personality change?* Washington, DC: American Psychological Association.

McArthur, L. Z. (1972). The how and what of why: Some determinants and consequences of causal attribution. *Journal of Personality and Social Psychology, 22,* 171–193.

McArthur, L. Z., & Berry, D. S. (1987). Cross-cultural agreement in perceptions of babyfaced adults. *Journal of Cross-Cultural Psychology, 18,* 165–192.

McCabe, V. (1984). Abstract perceptual information for age level: A risk factor for maltreatment? *Child Development, 55,* 267–276.

McClellan, M. C. (Ed.) (1987). *Summary and implications in teenage pregnancy.* Bloomington, IN: Phi Delta Kappa.

McClelland, D. C. (1993). Intelligence is not the best predictor of job performance. *Current Directions in Psychological Science, 2,* 5–6.

McClintock, M. K. (1971). Menstrual synchrony and suppression. *Nature, 299,* 244–245.

McClintock, M. K. (2000). Human pheromones: Primers, releasers, signalers, or modulators. In K. Wallen & J. E. Schneider (Eds), *Reproduction in context.* Cambridge, MA: MIT Press.

McClintock, M. K., & Herdt, G. (1996). Rethinking puberty: The development of sexual attraction. *Current Directions in Psychological Science, 6,* 178–183.

McCloskey, M., & Palmer, E. (1996). Visual representation of object location: Insights from localized impairments. *Current Directions in Psychological Science, 5,* 25–28.

McCrae, R. R., & Costa, P. T. (1985). Openness to experience. In R. Hogan & W. H. Jones (Eds.), *Perspectives in personality* (Vol. 1). Greenwich, CT: JAI Press.

McCrae, R. R., & Costa, P. T. (1994). The stability of personality: Observations and evaluations. *Current Directions in Psychological Science, 3,* 173–175.

McCrae, R. R., & Costa, P. T. (1997). Personality trait structure as a human universal. *American Psychologist, 52,* 509–516.

McCrae, R. R., Costa, P. T., Ostendorf, F., Angleitner, A., Hrebíčková, M., Avia, M. D., Sanz, J., Sánchez-Bernardos, M. L., Kusdil, M. E., Woodfield, R., Saunders, P. R., & Smith, P. B. (2000). Nature over nurture: Temperament, personality, and life span development. *Journal of Personality and Social Psychology, 78,* 173–186.

McFarland, C., & Buehler, R. (1995). Collective self-esteem as a moderator of the frog-pond effect in reactions to performance feedback. *Journal of Personality and Social Psychology, 68,* 1055–1070.

McGarrigle, J., & Donaldson, M. (1975). Conservation accidents. *Cognition, 3,* 341–350.

McGoldrick, M., & Gerson, R. (1985). *Genograms and family assessment.* New York: Norton.

McGue, M. (1999). The behavioral genetics of alcoholism. *Current Directions in Psychological Science, 8,* 109–115.

McGue, M., & Bouchard, T. J. (1998). Genetic and environmental influences on human behavioral differences. *Annual Review of Neuroscience, 21,* 1–24.

McGue, M., Bouchard, T. J., Iacono, W. G., & Lykken, D. T. (1993). Behavioral genetics of cognitive ability: A life-span perspective. In R. Plomin & G. E. McClearn (Eds.), *Nature, nurture, and psychology.* Washington, DC: American Psychological Association.

McGuire, W. J., & McGuire, C. V. (1988). Content and process in the experience of self. In L. Berkowitz (Ed.), *Advances in experimental social psychology* (Vol. 21). Orlando, FL: Academic Press.

McHugo, G. J., Lanzetta, J. T., Sullivan, D. G., Masters, R. D., & Englis, B. G. (1985). Emotional reactions to a political leader's expressive displays. *Journal of Personality and Social Psychology, 49,* 1513–1529.

McKellar, P. (1979). *Mindsplit: The psychology of multiple personality and the dissociated self.* London: Dent & Sons.

McKim, W. A. (2000). *Drugs and behavior: An introduction to behavioral pharmacology* (4th ed.). Upper Saddle River, NJ: Prentice Hall.

McNally, R. J., & Steketee, G. S. (1985). Etiology and maintenance of severe animal phobias. *Behavioral Research and Therapy, 23,* 431–435.

McNeil, J. E., & Warrington, E. K. (1993). Prosopagnosia: A face-specific disorder. *Quarterly Journal of Experimental Psychology, 46A,* 1–10.

McShane, D., & Berry, J. W. (1988). Native North Americans: Indian and Inuit abilities. In S. H. Irvine & J. W. Berry (Eds.), *Human abilities in cultural context.* Cambridge, England: Cambridge University Press.

Mead, M. (1935). *Sex and temperament in three primitive societies.* New York: Wm. Morrow.

Meador, B. D., & Rogers, C. R. (1973). Client-centered therapy. In R. Corsini (Ed.), *Current psychotherapies.* Itasca, IL: Peacock.

Meaney, M. J., Stewart, J., & Beatty, W. W. (1985). Sex difference in social play: The socialization of sex roles. *Advances in the Study of Behavior, 15,* 1–58.

Meddis, R. (1977). *The sleep instinct.* London: Routledge & Kegan Paul.

Medvec, V. H., Madey, S., & Gilovich, T. (1995). When less is more: Counterfactual thinking and satisfaction among Olympic medalists. *Journal of Personality and Social Psychology, 69,* 603–610.

Meisel, R. L., & Sachs, B. D. (1994). The physiology of male sexual behavior. In E. Knobil & J. Neill (Eds.), *The physiology of reproduction.* New York: Raven Press.

Melchior, C. L. (1990). Conditioned tolerance provides protection against ethanol lethality. *Pharmacology Biochemistry and Behavior, 37,* 205–206.

Meltzoff, A. N. (1995). Understanding the intentions of others: Re-enactment of intended acts by 18-month-old children. *Developmental Psychology, 31,* 838–850.

Melzack, R. (1992, April). Phantom limbs. *Scientific American,* pp. 120–126.

Melzack, R., & Wall, P. D. (1965). Pain mechanisms: A new theory. *Science, 150,* 971–979.

Melzack, R., & Wall, P. D. (1996). *The challenge of pain: Updated second edition.* New York: Penguin.

Merbs, S. L., & Nathans, J. (1992). Absorption spectra of human cone pigments. *Nature, 356,* 433–435.

Mercer, D. (1986). *Biofeedback and related therapies in clinical practice.* Rockville, MD: Aspen Systems.

Merton, R. (1948). The self-fulfilling prophesy. *Antioch Review, 8,* 193–210.

Mervis, C. M., & Bertrand, J. (1994). Acquisition of the novel name-nameless category (N3C) principle. *Child Development, 65,* 1646–1662.

Metzger, R. L., Boschee, P. F., Haugen, T., & Schnobrich, B. L., (1979). The classroom as a learning context: Changing rooms affects performance. *Journal of Educational Psychology, 71,* 440–442.

Meyer, G. J., Finn, S. E., Kay, G. G., Moreland, K. L., Dies R. R., Eisman, E. J., Kubiszyn, T. W., & Reed, G. M. (2001). Psychological testing and psychological assessment: A review of evidence and issues. *American Psychologist, 56,* 128–165.

Meyer-Bahlburg, H. F. L., Ehrhardt, A. A., Rosen, L. R., & Gruen, R. S. (1995). Prenatal estrogens and the development of homosexual orientation. *Developmental Psychology, 31*, 12–21.

Meyering, T. C. (1989). *Historical roots of cognitive science: The rise of a cognitive theory of perception from antiquity to the nineteenth century.* Boston: Kluwer Academic Publishers.

Mezzich, J. E., Kleinman, A., Fabrega, H., & Parron, D. L. (1996). *Culture and psychiatric diagnosis: A DSM-IV perspective.* Washington, DC: American Psychiatric Press.

Michael, R. T., Gagnon, J. H., Laumann, E. O., & Kolata, G. (1994). *Sex in America: A definitive survey.* Boston: Little, Brown.

Michaels, C. F., & Carello, C. (1981). *Direct perception.* Englewood Cliffs, NJ: Prentice-Hall.

Michaels, J. W., Blommel, J. M., Brocato, R. M., Linkous, R. A., & Rowe, J. S. (1982). Social facilitation and inhibition in a natural setting. *Replications in Social Psychology, 2*, 21–24.

Miles, L. (1983). Apes and language: The search for communicative competence. In J. de Luce & H. T. Wilder (Eds.), *Language in primates.* New York: Springer-Verlag.

Milgram, S. (1963). Behavioral study of obedience. *Journal of Abnormal and social Psychology, 67*, 371–378.

Milgram, S. (1964). Issues in the study of obedience: A reply to Baumrind. *American Psychologist, 19*, 848–852.

Milgram, S. (1974). *Obedience to authority: An experimental view.* New York: Harper & Row.

Miller, A. G. (1986). *The obedience experiments: A case study of controversy in social science.* New York: Praeger.

Miller, E. M. (1997). Could nonshared environmental variance have evolved to assure diversification through randomness? *Evolution and Human Behavior, 18*, 195–221.

Miller, G. E. (1956). The magic number seven plus or minus two: Some limits on our capacity for processing information. *Psychological Review, 63*, 81–97.

Miller, J. G. (1984). Culture and the development of everyday social explanations. *Journal of Personality and Social Psychology, 46*, 961–978.

Miller, J.G. (1999). Cultural psychology: Implications for basic psychological theory. *Psychological Science, 10*, 85–91.

Miller, K. F., Smith, C. M., Zhu, J., & Zhang, H. (1995). Preschool origins of cross-national differences in mathematical competence: The role of number-naming systems. *Psychological Science, 6*, 56–60.

Miller, L. E., & Grush, J. E. (1986). Individual differences in attitudinal versus normative determination of behavior. *Journal of Experimental Social Psychology, 22*, 190–202.

Miller, L. K. (1999). The savant syndrome: Intellectual impairment and exceptional skill. *Psychological Bulletin, 125*, 31–46.

Miller, L. T., & Vernon, P. A. (1992). The general factor in short-term memory, intelligence, and reaction time. *Intelligence, 16*, 5–29.

Miller, N. E. (1986). The morality and humaneness of animal research on stress and pain. *Annals of the New York Academy of Sciences, 467*, 402–404.

Miller, R. (1995). Embarrassment and social behavior. In J. P. Tangney & K. W. Fischer (Eds.), *Self-conscious emotions: The psychology of shame, guilt, embarrassment, and pride.* New York: Guilford Press.

Miller, R. L., Brickman, P., & Bolen, D. (1975). Attribution versus persuasion as a means for modifying behavior. *Journal of Personality and Social Psychology, 31*, 430–441.

Miller, W. R., & C'deBaca, J. (1994). Quantum change: Toward a psychology of transformation. In T. F. Heatherton & J. L. Weinberger (Eds.), *Can personality change?* Washington, DC: American Psychological Association.

Milner, A. D., & Goodale, M. A. (1995). *The visual brain in action.* Oxford: Oxford University Press.

Milner, B. (1965). Memory disturbance after bilateral hippocampal lesions. In P. Milner & S. Glickman (Eds.), *Cognitive processes and the brain.* Princeton, NJ: Van Nostrand.

Milner, B. (1970). Memory and the medial temporal regions of the brain. In K. H. Pribram & D. E. Broadbent (Eds.), *Biology of memory.* New York: Academic Press.

Milner, B. (1984). *Temporal lobes and memory disorders.* Paper presented at the American Psychological Association Convention, Toronto, Canada.

Milner, P. M. (1991). Brain-stimulation reward: A review. *Canadian Journal of Psychology, 45*, 1–36.

Mineka, S., Davidson, M., Cook, M., & Keir, R. (1984). Observational conditional of snake fear in rhesus monkeys. *Journal of Abnormal Psychology, 93*, 355–372.

Mineka, S., Watson, D., & Clark, L. A. (1998). Comorbidity of anxiety and unipolar mood disoders. *Annual Review of Psychology, 49*, 377–412.

Mineka, S., & Zinbarg, R. (1996). Conditioning and ethological models of anxiety disorders: Stress-in-dynamic-context anxiety models. In D.A. Hope (Ed.), *Perspectives on anxiety, panic, and fear. Nebraska Symposium on Motivation* (Vol. 43). Lincoln: Nebraska University Press.

Minix, D. A. (1976). *The rule of the small group in foreign policy decision making: A potential pathology in crisis decisions?* Paper presented to the Southern Political Science Association. (For description, see D. G. Myers, 1982.)

Mischel, W. (1968). *Personality and assessment.* New York: Wiley.

Mischel, W. (1984). Convergences and challenges in the search for consistency. *American Psychologist, 39*, 351–364.

Mischel, W., & Peake, P. K. (1982). Beyond déjà vu in the search for cross-situational consistency. *Psychological Review, 89*, 730–755.

Mischel, W., & Shoda, Y. (1995). A cognitive-affective system theory of personality: Reconceptualizing situations, dispositions, dynamics, and invariance in personality structure. *Psychological Review, 102*, 246–268.

Mitchell, K. J., & Johnson, M. K. (2000). Source monitoring: Attributing mental experiences. In E. Tulving & F. I. M. Craik (Eds.), *The Oxford handbook of memory.* New York: Oxford University Press.

Miura, I. T., Okamoto, Y., Kim, C. C., Chang, C., Steere, M., & Fayol, M. (1994). Comparisons of children's cognitive representation of number: China, France, Japan, Korea, Sweden, and the United States. *International Journal of Behavioral Development, 17*, 401–411.

Miyake, M., & Shah, P. (Eds.) (1999). *Models of working memory: Mechanisms of active maintenance and executive control.* Cambridge, England: Cambridge University Press.

Mobbs, N. A. (1968). Eye contact in relation to social interaction/extraversion. *British Journal of Social and Clinical Psychology, 7*, 305–306.

Moeller, H., & Volz, H. (2000). Achievements and future possibilities in the drug treatment of depression. In K. J. Palmer (Ed.), *Drug treatment issues in depression.* Kwai Chung, Hong Kong: Adis International Publications.

Moffitt, T. E. (1993). Adolescence-limited and life-course-persistent antisocial behavior: A developmental taxonomy. *Psychological Review, 100,* 674–701.

Mogenson, G. J., & Yim, C. C. (1991). Neuromodulatory functions for the mesolimbic dopamine system: Electrophysiological and behavioral studies. In P. Willner & J. Scheel-Krüger (Eds.), *The mesolimbic dopamine system: From motivation to action.* New York: Wiley.

Moghaddam, F. M., Taylor, D. M., & Wright, S. C. (1993). *Social psychology in cross-cultural perspective.* New York: Freeman.

Mohr, D. C. (1995). Negative outcome in psychotherapy: A critical review. *Clinical Psychology: Science and Practice, 2,* 1–27.

Money, J., & Ehrhardt, A. (1972). *Man and woman, boy and girl.* Baltimore: Johns Hopkins University Press.

Montgomery, G., & Kirsch, I. (1996). Mechanisms of placebo pain reduction: An empirical investigation. *Psychological Science, 7,* 174–176.

Moore, B. C. J. (1997). *An introduction to the psychology of hearing.* San Diego, CA: Academic Press.

Moore, C., & Corkum, V. (1994). Social understanding at the end of the first year of life. *Developmental Review, 14,* 349–372.

Moore, G. E. (1903). *Principia ethica.* Cambridge, England: Cambridge University Press.

Moore, H. T. (1917). Laboratory tests of anger, fear, and sex interests. *American Journal of Psychology, 28,* 390–395.

Moorhead, G., Ference, R., & Neck, C. P. (1991). Group decision fiascoes continue: Space shuttle *Challenger* and a revised groupthink framework. *Human Relations, 44,* 539–550.

Moray, N. (1959). Attention in dichotic listening: Effective cues and the influence of instructions. *Quarterly Journal of Experimental Psychology, 11,* 56–60.

Morelli, G. A. (1997). Growing up female in a farmer community and forager community. In M. E. Morbeck, A. Galloway, & A. L. Zihlman (Eds.), *The evolving female: A life history perspective.* Princeton, NJ: Princeton University Press.

Morelli, G. A., Rogoff, B., Oppenheim, D., & Goldsmith, D. (1992). Cultural variation in infants' sleeping arrangements: Questions of independence. *Developmental Psychology, 28* 604–613.

Morelli, G. A., & Tronick, E.Z. (1991). Parenting and child development in the Efe foragers and the Lese farmers of Zaïre. In M. H. Bornstein (Ed.), *Cultural approaches to parenting.* Hillsdale, NJ: Erlbaum.

Morgan, C. T. (1943). *Physiological psychology.* New York: McGraw-Hill.

Morris, M. W., & Peng, K. (1994). Culture and cause: American and Chinese attributions for social and physical events. *Journal of Personality and Social Psychology, 67,* 949–971.

Mortensen, P. B., Pedersen, C. B., Wesergaard, T., Wohlfahrt, J., Ewald, H., Mors, O., Andersen, P. K., & Melbye, M. (1999). Effects of family history and place and season of birth on the risk of schitzophrenia. *New England Journal of Medicine, 340,* 603–608.

Mosko, S., McKenna, J., Dickel, M., & Hunt, L. (1993). Parent-infant cosleeping: The appropriate context for the study of infant sleep and implications for sudden infant death syndrome (SIDS) research. *Journal of Behavioral Medicine, 16,* 589–610.

Mowrer, O. H. (1960). *Learning theory and behavior.* New York: Wiley.

Mozell, M. M., Smith, B., Smith, P., Sullivan, L., & Sender, P. (1969). Nasal chemoreception in flavor identification. *Archives of Otolaryngology, 90,* 367–373.

Muir, D., & Field, J. (1979). Newborn infants orient to sounds. *Child Development, 50,* 431–436.

Mulder, R. A. (1994, November). Faithful philanderers. *Natural History, 103,* 57–62.

Mulhern, S. (1991). Satanism and psychotherapy: A rumor in search of an inquisition. In J. T. Richardson, J. Best, & D. G. Bromley (Eds.). *The satanism scare.* New York: Aldine.

Mullen, B., Anthony, T., Salas, E., & Driskell, J. E. (1994). Group cohesiveness and quality of decision making: An integration of tests of the groupthink hypothesis. *Small Group Research, 25,* 189–204.

Mundy, P., Sigman, M., & Kasari, C. (1990). A longitudinal study of joint attention and language development in autistic children. *Journal of Autism and Developmental Disorders, 20,* 115–128.

Muntz, W. R. A. (1964, May). Vision in frogs. *Scientific American,* pp. 110–119.

Murdock, G. P. (1981). *Atlas of world cultures.* Pittsburgh, PA: University of Pittsburgh Press.

Mussen, P., Eichorn, D. H., Honzik, M. P., Bieher, S. L., & Meredith, W. (1980). Continuity and change in women's characteristics over four decades. *International Journal of Behavioral Development, 3,* 333–347.

Myers, D. G. (1982). Polarizing effects of social interaction. In H. Brandstatter, J. H. Davis & G. Stocker-Kreichgauer (Eds.), *Group decision making.* New York: Academic Press.

Myers, D. G., & Kaplan, M. F. (1976). Group-induced polarization in simulated juries. *Personality and Social Psychology Bulletin, 2,* 63–66.

Nader, K., Bechara, A., & van der Kooy, D. (1997). Neurobiological constraints on behavioral models of motivation. *Annual Review of Psychology, 48,* 85–114.

Naigles, L. (1990). Children use syntax to learn verb meanings. *Journal of Child Language, 17,* 357–374.

Najavits, L. M., & Strupp, H. (1994). Differences in the effectiveness of psychodynamic therapists: A process-outcome study. *Psychotherapy, 31,* 114–123.

Nakagawa, M., Lamb, M. E., & Miyaki, K. (1992). Antecedents and correlates of the strange situation behavior of Japanese infants. *Journal of Cross-Cultural Psychology, 23,* 300–310.

Nathan, P. E., Stuart, S. P., & Dolan, S. L. (2000). Research on psychotherapy efficacy and effectiveness: Between Scylla and Charybdis? *Psychological Bulletin, 126,* 964–981.

National Institute of Alcohol Abuse and Alcoholism. (1987). *Alcohol and health.* Rockville, MD; Author.

Navitt, G. A., Dittman, A. H., Wuinn, T. P., & Moody, W. J. (1994). Evidence for peripheral olfactory memory in imprinting in salmon. *Proceedings of the National Academy of Sciences, USA, 91,* 4288–4292.

Neck, C. P., & Moorhead, G. (1995). Groupthink remodeled: The importance of leadership, time pressure, and methodical decision-making procedures. *Human Relations, 48,* 537–557.

Neisser, U. (1998). Introduction: Rising test scores and what they mean. In U. Neisser (Ed.), *The rising curve: Long-term gains in IQ and related measures.* Washington, DC: APA.

Neitz, J., Neitz, M., & Kainz, P. M. (1996). Visual pigment gene structure and the severity of color vision defects. *Science, 274,* 801–804.

Nemeth, C. J. (1986). Differential contributions of majority and minority influence. *Psychological Review, 93,* 23–32.

Nesse, R. M. (1990). Evolutionary explanations of emotions. *Human Nature, 1,* 261–289.

Nesse, R. M. (2000). Is depression an adaptation? *Archives of General Psychiatry, 57,* 14–20.

Nesse, R. M., & Lloyd, A. T. (1992). The evolution of psychodynamic mechanisms. In J. H. Barkow, L. Cosmides, & J. Tooby (Eds.), *The adapted mind: Evolutionary psychology and the generation of culture.* Oxford: Oxford University Press.

Nesse, R. M., & Williams, G. C. (1994). *Why we get sick: The new science of Darwinian medicine.* New York: Random House.

Neubauer, P. B., & Neubauer, A. (1996). *Nature's thumbprint: The new genetics of personality* (2nd ed.). New York: Columbia University Press.

Neugarten, B. L. (1979). Time, age, and the life cycle. *American Journal of Psychiatry, 136,* 887–894.

Neugarten, B. L. (1984). Interpretive social science and research on aging. In A. Rossi (Ed.), *Gender and the life course.* Chicago: Aldine.

Newcomb, T. M. (1943). *Personality and social change: Attitude formation in a student community.* New York: Dryden.

Newcomb, T. M., Koenig, K., Flacks, R., & Warwick, D. (1967). *Persistence and change: Bennington College and its students after 25 years.* New York: Wiley.

Newman, J., & Layton, B. D. (1984). Overjustification: A self-perception perspective. *Personality and Social Psychology Bulletin, 10,* 419–425.

Newsom, C., Favell, J. E., & Rincover, A. (1983). Side effects of punishment. In S. Axelrod & J. Apsche (Eds.), *The effects of punishment on human behavior.* New York: Academic Press.

Nisbett, R. E., Caputo, C., Legant, P., & Marecek, J. (1973). Behavior as seen by the actor and as seen by the observer. *Journal of Personality and Social Psychology, 27,* 154–164.

Nishida, T. (Ed.). (1990). *The chimpanzees of the Mahale Mountains: Sexual and life history strategies.* Tokyo: University of Tokyo Press.

Norem, J. K., & Illingworth, K. S. S. (1993). Strategy-dependent effects of reflecting on self and tasks: Some implications of optimism and defensive pessimism. *Journal of Personality and Social Psychology, 65,* 822–835.

Norenzayan, A., & Nisbett, R. E. (2000). Culture and cognition. *Current Directions in Psychological Science, 9,* 132–135.

Novin, D., Robinson, B. A., Culbreth, L. A., & Tordoff, M. G. (1983). Is there a role for the liver in the control of food intake? *American Journal of Clinical Nutrition, 9,* 233–246.

Nowak, M. A., & Sigmund, K. (1992). Tit for tat in heterogeneous populations. *Nature, 355,* 250–253.

Nowlis, G. H., & Frank, M. (1977). Qualities in hamster taste: Behavioral and neural evidence. In J. LeMagnen & P. MacLeod (Eds.), *Olfaction and taste* (Vol. 6). Washington, DC: Information Retrieval.

Nuechterlein, K. H., Dawson, M. E., Gitlin, M., Ventura, J., Goldstein, M. J., Snyder, K. S., Yee, C.M., & Mintz, J. (1992). Developmental processes in schizophrenic disorders: Longitudinal studies of vulnerability and stress. *Schizophrenia Bulletin, 18,* 387–425.

Numan, M., & Numan, M. J. (1995). Importance of pup-related sensory inputs and maternal performance for the expression of fos-like immunoreactivity in the preoptic area and ventral bed nucleus of the stria terminalis of postpartum rats. *Behavioral Neuroscience, 109,* 135–149.

Nutt, D. J., & Glue, P. (1993). The neurobiology of ECT: Animal studies. In C. E. Coffee (Ed.), *The clinical science of electroconvulsive therapy.* Washington, DC: American Psychiatric Press.

Nyberg, L., & Cabeza, R. (2000). Brain imaging of memory. In E. Tulving & F. I. M. Craik (Eds.), *The Oxford handbook of memory.* New York: Oxford University Press.

Oakes, L. M., & Tellinghuisen, D. J. (1994). Examining in infancy: Does it reflect active processing? *Developmental Psychology, 30,* 748–756.

Oakes, P. J., Halsam, S. A., & Turner, J. C. (1994). *Stereotyping and social reality.* Oxford: Blackwell.

Ochs, E., & Schieffelin, B. (1995). The impact of language socialization on grammatical development. In P. Fletcher & B. MacWhinney (Eds.), *The handbook of child language.* Cambridge, MA: Basil Blackwell.

O'Connor, F. L. (1998). The role of seratonin and dopamine in schizophrenia. *Journal of the American Psychiatric Nurses Association, 8,* 175–183.

O'Connor, T. G., Deater-Deckard, K., Fulker, D., Rutter, M., & Plomin, R. (1998). Genotype-environment correlations in late childhood and early adolescence: Antisocial behavioral problems and coercive parenting. *Developmental Psychology, 34,* 970–981.

Oetting, E. R., & Beauvais, F. (1988). Common elements in youth drug abuse: Peer clusters and other psychosocial factors. In S. Peele (Ed.), *Visions of addiction: Major contemporary perspectives on addiction and alcoholism.* Lexington, MA: Lexington Books.

Offer, D., & Schonert-Reichl, K. A. (1992). Debunking the myths of adolescence: Findings from recent research. *Journal of the American Academy of Child and Adolescent Psychiatry, 31,* 1003–1013.

Ogbu, J. U. (1986). The consequences of the American caste system. In U. Neisser (Ed.), *The school achievement of minority children: New perspectives.* Hillsdale, NJ: Erlbaum.

Ogbu, J. U. (1994). From cultural difference to differences in cultural frame of reference. In P. M. Greenfield & R. R. Cocking (Eds.), *Cross-cultural roots of minority child development,* Hillsdale, NJ: Erlbaum.

Öhman, A. (1986). Face the beast and fear the face: Animal and social fears as prototypes for evolutionary analysis of emotion. *Psychophysiology, 23,* 123–145.

Okano, K. (1994). Shame and social phobia: A transcultural viewpoint. *Bulletin of the Menninger Clinic, 58,* 323–338.

Okano, Y., Eisensmith, R. C., & many others (1991). Molecular basis of phenotypic heterogeneity in phenylketonuria. *New England Journal of Medicine, 324,* 1232–1238.

Okubo, Y., Suhara, T., Suzuki, K., Kobayashi, K., Inoue, O., Terasaki, O., Someya, Y., Sassa, T., Sudo, Y., Matsushima, E., Iyo, M., Tateno, Y., & Toru, M. (1997). Decreased prefrontal dopamine D1 receptors in schizophrenia revealed by PET. *Nature, 385*, 634–638.

Olds, J. (1956, October). Pleasure centers in the brain. *Scientific American*, pp. 105–116.

Olds, J., & Milner, P. (1954). Positive reinforcement produced by electrical stimulation of the septal area and other regions of the rat brain. *Journal of Comparative and Physiological Psychology, 47*, 419–427.

Olds, M. E., & Fobes, J. L. (1981). The central basis of motivation: Intracranial self-stimulation studies. *Annual Review of Psychology, 32*, 523–574.

Olson, D. J., Kamil, A. C., Balda, R. P., & Nims, P. J. (1995). Performance of four seed-caching corvid species in operant tests of nonspatial and spatial memory. *Journal of Comparative Psychology, 109*, 173–181.

Oring, L. W. (1995, August). The early bird gives the sperm: Spotted sandpipers on a Minnesota lake reveal the secrets of their breeding success. *Natural History, 104*, 58–61.

Orne, M. T., & Holland, C.G. (1968). On the ecological validity of laboratory deception. *International Journal of Psychiatry, 6*, 282–293.

Osofsky, J. D., & O'Connell, E. J. (1977). Patterning of newborn behavior in an urban population. *Child Development, 48*, 532–536.

Öst, L. G. (1989). One-session treatment for specific phobias. *Behavioral Research and Therapy, 27*, 1–7.

Overmann, S. R. (1976). Dietary self-selection by animals. *Psychological Bulletin, 83*, 218–235.

Page, D., Mosher, R., Simpson, E. M., Fisher, E. M. C., Mardon, G., Pollack, J., McGillivray, B., Chapelle, A., & Brown, L. (1987). The sex-determinating region of the human Y chromosome encodes a finger protein. *Cell, 51*, 1091–1104.

Paivio, A. (1971). *Imagery and verbal processes*. New York: Holt, Rinehart & Winston. (Reprinted 1979, Hillsdale, NJ: Erlbaum.)

Paivio, A. (1986). *Mental representations: A dual coding approach*. New York: Oxford University Press.

Paivio, A., Smythe, P. C., & Yuille, J. C. (1968). Imagery *versus* meaningfulness of nouns in paired-associate learning. *Canadian Journal of Psychology, 22*, 427–441.

Palardy, J. M. (1969). What teachers believe—what children achieve. *Elementary School Journal, 69*, 370–374.

Pallanti, S., Quercioli, L., & Pazzagli, A. (1997). Relapse in young paranoid schizophrenic patients: A prospective study of stressful life events, P300 measures, and coping. *American Journal of Psychiatry, 154*, 792–798.

Papagno, C., & Vallar, G. (1995). Verbal short-term memory and vocabulary learning in polyglots. *Quarterly Journal of Experimental Psychology, 38A*, 98–107.

Papousek, H. (1969). Individual variability in learned responses in human infants. In R. J. Robinson (Ed.), *Brain and early behavior*. New York: Academic Press.

Paris, J. (2000). Predispositions, personality traits, and posttraumatic stress disorder. *Harvard Review of Psychiatry, 8*, 175–183.

Parish, A. R. (1996). Female relationships in bonobos (*Pan Paniscus*): Evidence for bonding, cooperation, and female dominance in a male-philopatric species. *Human Nature, 7*, 61–96.

Park, B. (1986). A method for studying the development of impressions of real people. *Journal of Personality and Social Psychology, 51*, 907–917.

Park, C. (1967). *The siege: The first eight years of an autistic child*. Boston: Little, Brown.

Parker, S. T., Mitchell, R. W., & Boccia, M. L. (Eds.). (1994). *Self-awareness in animals and humans: Developmental perspectives*. Cambridge, England: Cambridge University Press.

Parks, T. E., & Rock, I. (1990). Illusory contours from pictorially three-dimensional inducing elements. *Perception, 19*, 119–121.

Parmelee, A. H., Wenner, W. H., Akiyama, Y., Schultz, M., & Stern, E. (1967). Sleep states in premature infants. *Developmental Medicine and Child Neurology, 9*, 70–77.

Pascual-Leone, J. (1970). A mathematical model for the transition rule in Piaget's developmental stages. *Acta Psychological, 32*, 301–345.

Pashler, H. E. (1998). *The psychology of attention*. Cambridge, MA: MIT Press.

Pattatucci, A. M. L., & Hamer, D. H. (1995). Development and familiarity of sexual orientation in females. *Behavior Genetics, 25*, 407–420.

Patterson, F., & Linden, E. (1981). *The education of Koko*. New York: Holt, Rinehart & Winston.

Patterson, M., & Holmes, D. S. (1966). Social interaction, correlates of MPI extraversion-introversion scale. *American Psychologist, 21*, 724–725.

Paul, G. L., & Lentz, R. J. (1977). *Psychosocial treatment of chronic mental patients: Milieu versus social-learning programs*. Cambridge, MA: Harvard University Press.

Paulesu, E., Frith, C. D., & Frackowiak, R. S. J. (1993). The neural correlates of the verbal components of working memory. *Nature, 362*, 342–345.

Paulhus, D. L., Trapnell, P. D., & Chen, D. (1999). Birth order effects on personality and achievement within families. *Psychological Science, 10*, 482–488.

Pavlov, I. P. (1927; reprinted 1960). *Conditioned reflexes* (G. V. Anrep, Ed. & Trans.). New York: Dover.

Peale, N. V. (1956). *The power of positive thinking*. Englewood Cliffs, NJ: Prentice-Hall.

Pearson, K. & Gordon, J. (2000). Locomotion. In E. R. Kandel, J.H. Schwartz, & T. M. Jessell (Eds.), *Principles of Neural Science* (4th ed.). New York: McGraw-Hill.

Pecoraro, N. C., Timberlake, W. D., & Tinsley, M. (1999). Incentive downshifts evoke search repertoires in rats. *Journal of Experimental Psychology: Animal Behavior Processes, 25*, 153–167.

Pederson, D. R., Gleason, K. E., Moran, G., & Bento, S. (1998). Maternal attachment representations, maternal sensitivity, and the infant-mother relationship. *Developmental Psychology, 34*, 925–933.

Peele, S. (1988). A moral vision of addiction: How people's values determine whether they become and remain addicts. In S. Peele (Ed.), *Visions of addiction: Major contemporary perspectives on addiction and alcoholism*. Lexington, MA: Lexington Books.

Penfield, W., & Faulk, M. E. (1955). The insula. Further observation on its function. *Brain, 78*, 445–470.

Penfield, W., & Perot, P. (1963). The brain's record of auditory and visual experience. *Brain, 86,* 595–696.

Perner, J. (1991). *Understanding the representational mind.* Cambridge, MA: Bradford Books/MIT Press.

Pervin, L. A. (1980). *Personality: Theory, assessment, and research* (3rd ed.). New York: Wiley.

Pessoa, L., Thompson, E., & Noë, A. (1998). Finding out about filling-in: A guide to perceptual completion for visual science and the philosophy of perception. *Behavioral and Brain Sciences, 21,* 723–802.

Peterson, C. (2000). The future of optimism. *American Psychologist, 55,* 44–55.

Peterson, C., & Seligman, E. P. (1984). Causal explanations as a risk factor for depression: Theory and evidence. *Psychological Review, 91,* 347–374.

Petrie, D. (Director). (1976). *Sybil* [film]. New York: NBC/Lorimar.

Pettito, L. A., & Marentette, P. F. (1991). Babbling in the manual mode: Evidence for the ontogeny of language. *Science, 251,* 1493–1496.

Petty, R. E., & Cacioppo, J. T. (1986). The elaboration likelihood model of persuasion. In L. Berkowitz (Ed.), *Advances in experimental social psychology* (Vol. 19). New York: Academic Press.

Petty, R. E., Cacioppo, J. T., & Goldman, R. (1981). Personal involvement as a determinant of argument-based persuasion. *Journal of Personality and Social Psychology, 41,* 847–855.

Petty, R. E., & Wegener, D. T. (1999). The elaboration likelihood model: Current status and controversies. In S. Chaiken & Y. Trope (Eds.), *Dual-process theories in social psychology.* New York: Guilford.

Pfaff, D., & Modianos, D. (1985). Neural mechanisms of female reproductive behavior. In N. Adler, D. Pfaff, & R. W. Goy (Eds.), *Handbook of behavioral neurobiology: Vol. 7. Reproduction.* New York: Plenum Press.

Pfennig, D. W., & Sherman, P. W. (1995, June). Kin recognition. *Scientific American,* pp. 98–103.

Pfungst, O. (1911; reprinted 1965). *Clever Hans: The horse of Mr. von Osten* (C. L. Rahn, Trans.). New York: Holt, Rinehart & Winston.

Phares, E. J. (1978). Locus of control. In H. London & J. E. Exner (Eds.), *Dimensions of personality.* New York: Wiley.

Phares, E. J. (1984). *Introduction to personality.* Columbus, OH: Merrill.

Phillips, A. G., Pfaus, J. G., & Blaha, C. D. (1991). Dopamine and motivated behavior: Insights provided by *in vivo* analyses. In P. Willner & J. Scheel-Krüger (Eds.), *The mesolimbic dopamine system: From motivation to action.* New York: Wiley.

Phillips, D. P. (1989). The neural coding of simple and complex sounds in the auditory cortex. In J. S. Lund (Ed.), *Sensory processing in the mammalian brain: Neural substrates and experimental strategies.* Oxford: Oxford University Press.

Piaget, J. (1923). *The language and thought of the child* (M. Worden, Trans.). New York: Harcourt, Brace & World.

Piaget, J. (1927). *The child's conception of physical causality* (M. Worden, Trans.). New York: Harcourt, Brace & World.

Piaget, J. (1932; reprinted 1965). *The moral judgment of the child.* New York: Free Press.

Piaget, J. (1936; reprinted 1963). *The origins of intelligence in the child.* New York: Norton.

Piaget, J. (1952). *The origins of intelligence in children.* New York: International University Press.

Piaget, J. (1962). *Play, dreams and imitation in childhood.* New York: Norton.

Piaget, J. (1970). *Genetic epistemology* (E. Duckworth, Trans.). New York: Norton.

Pickens, R. W., Svikis, D. S., McGue, M., Lykken, D. T., Heston, L. L., & Clayton, P. J. (1991). Heterogeneity in the inheritance of alcoholism. *Archives of General Psychology, 48,* 19–28.

Pierrel, R., & Sherman, J. G. (1963, February). Train your rat the Barnabus way. *Brown Alumni Monthly,* pp. 8–14.

Pincus, H. A., Tanielian, T. L., Marcus, S. C., Olfson, M., Zarin, D. A., Thompson, J., & Zito, J. M. (1998). Prescribing trends in psychotropic medications. *Journal of the American Medical Association, 279,* 526–531.

Pinker, S. (1994). *The language instinct.* New York: Morrow.

Pinker, S. (1997). *How the mind works.* New York: Norton.

Pinker, S., & Bloom, P. (1992). Natural language and natural selection. In J. H. Barkow, L. Cosmides, & J. Tooby (Eds.), *The adapted mind-Evolutionary psychology and the generation of culture.* New York: Oxford University Press.

Pitman, R. K., van der Kolk, B. A., Orr, S. P., & Greenberg, M. S. (1990). Naloxone-reversible analgesic response to combat-related stimuli in posttraumatic stress disorder. *Archives of General Psychiatry, 47,* 541–544.

Pleim, E. T., & Barfield, R. J. (1988). Progesterone versus estrogen facilitation of female sexual behavior by intracranial administration to female rats. *Hormones and Behavior, 22,* 150–159.

Plomin, R., & Caspi, A. (1999). Behavioral genetics and personality. In L. A. Pervin & O. John (Eds.), *Handbook of personality: Theory and research* (2nd ed.). New York: Guilford.

Plomin, R., & Daniels, D. (1987). Why are children in the same family so different from one another: *Behavioral and Brain Sciences, 10,* 1–60.

Plomin, R., DeFries, J. C., & McClearan, G. E. (1990). *Behavioral genetics: A primer* (2nd ed.). New York: Freeman.

Polefrone, J., & Manuck, S. (1987). Gender differences in cardiovascular and neuroendocrine response to stressors. In R. C. Barnett, L. Biener, & G. K. Baruch (Eds.), *Gender and stress.* New York: Free Press.

Porter, R. H. (1991). Human reproduction and the mother-infant relationship: The role of odors. In T. V. Getchell, R. L. Doty, L. M., Bartoshuk, & J. B. Snow (Eds.), *Smell and taste in health and disease.* New York: Raven Press.

Porzelius, L. K., Dinsmore, B. D., & Staffelbach, D. (2001). In M. Hersen & V. B. Van Hasselt (Eds.), *Advanced abnormal psychology* (2nd ed.). New York: Klewer Academic/Plenum.

Potts, W. K., Manning, C. J., & Wakeland, E. K. (1991). Mating patterns in seminatural populations of mice influenced by MHC genotype. *Nature, 352,* 619–621.

Power, T. G. (2000). *Play and exploration in children and animals.* Mahwah, NJ: Erlbaum.

Prabu, D. (1998). News concreteness and visual-verbal association: Do news pictures narrow the recall gap between concrete and abstract news? *Human Communication Research, 25,* 180–201.

Pratt, D. (1986). On the merits of multiage classrooms. *Research in rural Education, 3,* 111–115.

Premack, D. (1990). The infant's theory of self-propelled objects. *Cognition, 36,* 1–16.

Prentice, D. (1990). Familiarity and differences in self- and other-representations. *Journal of Personality and Social Psychology, 59,* 369–383.

Pressin, J. (1933). The comparative effects of social and mechanical stimulation on memorizing. *American Journal of Psychology, 45,* 263–270.

Preti, G., Cutler, W. B., Garcia, C. R., Huggins, G. R., & Lawley, H. J. (1986). Human axillary secretions influence women's menstrual cycles: The role of donor extract of females. *Hormones and Behavior, 20,* 474–482.

Preuschoft, S., & van Hooff, J. (1997). The social function of "smile" and "laughter": Variations across primate species and societies. In U. Segerstrale & P. Molnar (Eds.), *Nonverbal communication: Where nature meets culture.* Mahwah, NJ: Erlbaum.

Price, D. D. (2000). Psychological and neural mechanisms of the affective dimension of pain. *Science, 288,* 1769–1772.

Prigerson, H. G., Bierhals, A. J., Stanislav, V. K., Reynolds, C. F., Shear, M. K., Day, N., Beery, L. C., Newsom, J. T., & Jacobs, S. (1997). Traumatic grief is a risk factor for mental and physical morbidity. *American Journal of Psychiatry, 154,* 616–623.

Prior, K. (1985). *Don't shoot the dog: The new art of teaching and training.* New York: Bantam.

Pritchard, T. C. (1991). The primate gustatory system. In T. V. Getchell, R. L. Doty, L. M. Bartoshuk, & J. B. Snow (Eds.), *Smell and taste in health and disease.* New York: Raven Press.

Profet, M. (1992). Pregnancy sickness as adaptation: A deterrent to maternal ingestion of teratogens. In J. H. Barkow, L. Cosmides, & J. Tooby (Eds.), *The adapted mind: Evolutionary psychology and the generation of culture.* Oxford: Oxford University Press.

Provine, R. R. (1996). Laughter. *American Scientist, 84,* 38–45.

Rachels, J. (1990). *Created from animals: The moral implications of Darwinism.* Oxford: Oxford University Press.

Rachman, S. J., & DeSilva, P. (1978). Abnormal and normal obsessions. *Behavioral Research and Therapy, 16,* 223–248.

Ramachandran, V. S. (1992, May). Blind spots. *Scientific American,* pp. 84–91.

Ramsay, D. S., & Woods, S. C. (1997). Biological consequences of drug administration: Implications for acute and chronic tolerance. *Psychological Review, 104.* 170–193.

Rapaport, J. L. (1991). Basal ganglia dysfunction as a proposed cause of obsessive-compulsive disorder. In B. J. Carroll & J. E. Barrett (Eds.), *Psychopathology and the brain.* New York: Raven Press.

Raugh, M. R., & Atkinson, R. C. (1975). A mnemonic method for learning a second-language vocabulary. *Journal of Educational Psychology, 67,* 1–16.

Rauschecker, J. P. (1999). Making brain circuits listen. *Science, 285,* 1686–1687.

Rauschecker, J. P., Tian, B., & Hauser, M. (1995). Processing of complex sounds in the macaque nonprimary auditory cortex. *Science, 268,* 111–114.

Razran, G. A. (1939). A quantitative study of meaning by a conditioned salivary technique (semantic conditioning). *Science, 90,* 89–91.

Reber, A. S. (1989). Implicit learning and tacit knowledge. *Journal of Experimental Psychology: General, 118,* 219–235.

Recanzone, G. H., Merzenich, M. M., Jenkins, W. M., Grajski, K. A. & Dinse, H. R. (1992). Topographic reorganization of the hand representation in cortical area 3b of owl monkeys trained in a frequency-discrimination task. *Journal of Neurophysiology, 67,* 1031–1056.

Redican, W. K. (1982). An evolutionary perspective on human facial displays. In P. Ekman (Ed.), *Emotion in the human face.* Cambridge, England: Cambridge University Press.

Ree, M. J., & Earles, J. A. (1992). Intelligence is the best predictor of job performance. *Current Directions in Psychological Science, 1,* 86–89.

Rees, J. A., & Harvey, P. H. (1991). The evolution of mating systems. In V. Reynolds & J. Kellett (Eds.), *Mating and marriage.* Oxford: Oxford University Press.

Reich, J. W., Erdal, K. J., & Zautra, A. (1997). Beliefs about control and health behaviors. In D. S. Gochman (Ed.), *Handbook of health behavior research: I. Personal and social determinants.* New York: Plenum.

Reisberg, D., Smith, J. D., Baxter, D. A., & Sonenshine, M. (1989). "Enacted" auditory images are ambiguous; "pure" auditory images are not. *Quarterly Journal of Experimental Psychology: Human Experimental Psychology, 41,* 619–641.

Reiser, M. F. (1991). *Memory in mind and brain: What dream imagery reveals.* New York: Basic Books.

Reitan, R. M., & Wolfson, D. (1985). *The Halstead-Reitan neuropsychological test battery: Theory and clinical interpretation.* Tucson, AZ: Neuropsychology Press.

Rende, R. D., Plomin, R., & Vandenberg, S. G. (1990). Who discovered the twin method? *Behavior Genetics, 20,* 277–285.

Rescorla, R. A. (1988). Pavlovian conditioning: It's not what you think it is. *American Psychologist, 43,* 151–160.

Rescorla, R. A., & Wagner, A. R. (1972). A theory of Pavlovian conditioning. Variations in effectiveness of reinforcement and non-reinforcement. In A. Black & W. F. Prokasky, Jr. (Eds.), *Classical conditioning II.* New York: Appleton-Century-Crofts.

Rest, J. R. (1986). *Moral development: Advances in research and theory.* New York: Praeger.

Reuter-Lorenz, P. A., & Miller, A. C. (1998). The cognitive neuroscience of human laterality: Lessons from the bisected brain. *Current Directions in Psychological Science, 7,* 15–20.

Reynolds, D. V. (1969). Surgery in the rat during electrical analgesia induced by focal brain stimulation. *Science, 164,* 444–445.

Rheingold, H. L. (1982). Little children's participation in the work of adults, a nascent prosocial behavior. *Child Development, 53,* 114–125.

Rheingold, H. L., Hay, D. F., & West, M. J. (1976). Sharing in the second year of life. *Child Development, 47,* 1148–1158.

Rhodes, S. R. (1983). Age-related differences in work attitudes and behavior: A review and conceptual analysis. *Psychological Bulletin, 93,* 328–367.

Richards, R., Kinney, D. K., Lunde, I., Benet, M., & Merzel, A. P. C. (1988). Creativity in manic-depressives, cyclothymes, their normal relatives and control subjects. *Journal of Abnormal Psychology, 97,* 281–288.

Richter, C. P. (1942–1943). Total self regulatory functions in animals and human beings. *Harvey Lecture Series, 38,* 63–103.

Richter, C. P., & Eckert, J. F. (1938). Mineral metabolism of adrenalectomized rats studied by the appetite method. *Endocrinology, 22,* 214–224.

Ridley, M. (1994). *The red queen: Sex and the evolution of human nature.* New York: Macmillan.

Riggs, L. A. (1965). Visual acuity. In C. H. Graham (Ed.), *Vision and visual perception.* New York: Wiley.

Riley, J. W., Jr. (1970). What people think about death. In O. B. Brim, Jr., H. E. Freeman, S. Levine, & N. A. Scotch (Eds.), *The dying patient.* New York: Russell Sage Foundation.

Rime, B., Philippot, P., & Cisamolo, D. (1990). Social schemata of peripheral changes in emotion. *Journal of Personality and Social Psychology, 59,* 38–49.

Rissman, E. F. (1995). An alternative animal model for the study of female sexual behavior. *Current Directions in Psychological Science, 4,* 6–10.

Robbins, R. W., Gosling, S.D., & Craik, K. H. (1999). An empirical analysis of trends in psychology. *American Psychologist, 54,* 117–128.

Roberts, B. W., & DelVecchio, W. F. (2000). The rank-order consistency of personality traits from childhood to old age: A quantitative review of longitudinal studies. *Psychological Bulletin, 126,* 3–25.

Roberts, B. W. & Donahue, E. M. (1994). One personality, multiple selves: Integrating personality and social roles. *Journal of Personality, 62,* 200–218.

Robertson, S. I. (1999). *Types of thinking.* London: Routledge.

Robins, L. N., & Regier, D. A. (Eds.) (1991). *Psychiatric disorders in America.* New York: Free Press.

Robinson, R. G., Kubos, K. L., Starr, L. B., Rao, K., & Price, T. R. (1984). Mood disorders in stroke patients: Importance of location of lesion. *Brain, 107,* 81–93.

Rochat, P. (1989). Object manipulation and exploration in 2- to 5-month-old infants. *Developmental Psychology, 25,* 871–884.

Rock, I. (1995). *Perception.* New York: Scientific American Books.

Rock, I., & Gutman, D. (1981). The effect of inattention on form perception. *Journal of Experimental Psychology: Human Perception and Performance, 7,* 275–285.

Rodier, P. M. (2000, February). The early origins of autism. *Scientific American,* 56–63.

Rodin, J., Schank, D., & Striegel-Moore, R. (1989). Psychological features of obesity. *Medical Clinics of North America, 73,* 47–66.

Rodseth, L., Wrangham, R. W., Harrigan, A. M., & Smuts, B. B. (1991). The human community as a primate society. *Current Anthropology, 32,* 221–252.

Roehling, P. V., Smith, G. T., Goldman, M. S., & Christiansen, B. A. (1987). *Alcohol expectancies predict adolescent drinking: A three year longitudinal study.* Paper presented at the 95th annual convention of the American Psychological Association, New York.

Roesler, T. A., & McKenzie, N. (1994). Effects of childhood trauma on psychological functioning in adults sexually abused as children. *Journal of Nervous and Mental Disease, 182,* 145–150.

Rogers, C. R. (1951). *Client-centered therapy: Its current practice, implications, and theory.* Boston: Houghton Mifflin.

Rogers, C. R. (1959). A theory of therapy, personality, and interpersonal relationships, as developed in the client-centered frame-work. In S. Koch (Ed.), *Psychology: A study of a science* (Vol. 3). New York: McGraw-Hill.

Rogers, C. R. (1963). The actualizing tendency in relation to "motives" and to consciousness. In M. R. Jones (Ed.), *Nebraska Symposium on Motivation.* Lincoln: University of Nebraska.

Rogers, C. R. (1970). *Carl Rogers on encounter groups.* New York: Harper & Row.

Rogers, C. R. (1977). *Carl Rogers on personal power.* New York: Delacorte Press.

Rogers, C. R. (1980). *A way of being.* Boston: Houghton Mifflin.

Rogers, C. R. (Ed.). (1967). *The therapeutic relationship and its impact: A study of psychotherapy with schizophrenics.* Madison: University of Wisconsin Press.

Rogers, T. B., Kuiper, N. A., & Kirker, W. S. (1977). Self-reference and the encoding of personal information. *Journal of Personality and Social Psychology, 35,* 677–688.

Rogoff, B. (1990). *Apprenticeship in thinking: Cognitive development in social context.* New York: Oxford University Press.

Rogoff, B. (1993). Children's guided participation and participatory appropriation in sociocultural activity. In R. H. Wozniak & K. W. Fisher (Eds.), *Development in context: Acting and thinking in specific environments.* Hillsdale, NJ: Erlbaum.

Rokeach, M. (1980). Some unresolved issues in theories of beliefs, attitudes, and values. In M. M. Page (Ed.), *1979 Nebraska Symposium on Motivation.* Lincoln: University of Nebraska Press.

Rolls, E. T. (1982). Feeding and reward. In B. G. Hoebel & D. Novin (Eds.), *The neural basis of feeding and reward.* Brunswick, ME: Haer Institute.

Rolls, E. T., Critchley, H. D., Browning, A., & Hernadi, I. (1998). The neurophysiology of taste and olfaction in primates, and umami flavor. *Annals of the New York Academy of Sciences, 855,* 426–437.

Rolls, E. T., Murzi, E., Yaxley, S., Thorpe, S. J., & Simpson, S. J. (1986). Sensory-specific satiety: Food-specific reduction in responsiveness of ventral forebrain neurons after feeding in the monkey. *Brain Research, 368,* 79–86.

Rose, S. (1973). *The conscious brain.* New York: Knopf.

Rose, T., Kaser-Boyd, N., & Maloney, M. P. (2001). *Essentials of Rorschach assessment.* New York: Wiley.

Rosenberg, S. (1988). Self and others: Studies in social personality and autobiography. In L. Berkowitz (Ed.), *Advances in experimental social psychology* (Vol. 21). Orlando, FL: Academic Press.

Rosenhan, D. (1970). The natural socialization of altruistic autonomy. In J. Macaulay & L. Berkowitz (Eds.), *Altruism and helping behavior.* New York: Academic Press.

Rosenhan, D. L. (1973). On being sane in insane places. *Science, 179,* 250–258.

Rosenthal, R. (1976). *Experimenter effects in behavioral research* (Enlarged ed.). New York: Irvington.

Rosenthal, R. (1994). Interpersonal expectancy effects: A 30-year perspective. *Current Directions in Psychological Science, 3,* 176–179.

Rosenthal, R., & Jacobson, L. (1968). *Pygmalion in the classroom.* New York: Holt, Rinehart & Winston.

Ross, C. A. (1999). Dissociative disorders. In Millon, T., Blaney, P. H., & Davis, R.D. (Eds.), *Oxford textbook of psychopathology.* New York: Oxford University Press.

Ross, C. A., Norton, O. R., & Wozney, K. (1989). Multiple personality disorder: An analysis of 236 cases. *Canadian Journal of Psychiatry, 34,* 413–418.

Ross, L. (1977). The intuitive psychologist and his shortcomings: Distortions in the attribution process. In L. Berkowitz (Ed.), *Advances in experimental social psychology.* New York: Academic Press.

Roth, B. L., & Meltzer, H. Y. (1995). In F. E. Bloom & D. J. Kupfer (Eds.), *Psychopharmacology: The fourth generation of progress.* New York: Raven Press.

Rothbart, M. K., & Bates, J. (1998). Temperament. In N. Eisenberg (Ed.), *Handbook of child psychology* (5th ed.), Vol. 3. *Social, emotional, and personality development.* New York: Wiley.

Rothbaum, F., Weisz, J., Pott, M., Miyake, K., & Morelli, G. (2000). Attachment and culture: Security in the United States and Japan. *American Psychologist, 55,* 1093–1104.

Rotter, J. B. (1954; reprinted 1973, 1980). *Social learning and clinical psychology.* New York: Johnson Reprint Co.

Rotter, J. B. (1966). Generalized expectancies for internal versus external locus of control of reinforcement. *Psychological Monographs: General and Applied, 80* (Whole No. 609).

Rotter, J. B. (1982). Brief autobiography of the author. In J. B. Rotter (Ed.), *The development and application of social learning theory: Selected papers.* New York: Praeger.

Rotter, J. B., Liverant, S., & Crowne, D. P. (1961). The growth and extinction of expectancies in change of controlled and skilled tasks. *Journal of Psychology, 52,* 161–177.

Rowe, D. C. (1994). *The limits of family influence: Genes, experience, and behavior.* New York: Guilford Press.

Rozée, P. D., & Van Boemel, G. V. (1989). The psychological effects of war trauma and abuse on older Cambodian refugee women. *Women & Therapy, 8,* 23–50.

Rozin, P., & Kalat, J. (1971). Specific hungers and poison avoidance as adaptive specializations of learning. *Psychological Review, 78,* 459–486.

Rozin, P., & Schull, J. (1988). The adaptive-evolutionary point of view in experimental psychology. In R. L. Atkinson, R. J. Hernstein, G. Lindzey, & R. D. Luce (Eds.), *Steven's Handbook of Experimental Psychology* (2nd ed.). New York: Wiley.

Rubin, M., & Hewstone, M. (1998). Social identity theory's self-esteem hypothesis: A review and some suggestions for clarification. *Review of Personality and Social Psychology, 2,* 40–62.

Rubin, N., Nakayama, K., & Shapley, R. (1996). Enhanced perception of illusory contours in the lower versus upper visual hemifields, *Science, 271,* 651–653.

Ruff, H. A. (1986). Components of attention during infants' manipulative exploration. *Child Development, 75,* 105–114.

Ruff, H. A. (1989). The infant's use of visual and haptic information in the perception and recognition of objects. *Canadian Journal of Psychology, 43,* 302–319.

Runeson, S., & Frykholm, G. (1986). Kinematic specification of gender and gender expression. In V. McCabe & G. J. Balzano (Eds.), *Event cognition: An ecological perspective.* Hillsdale, NJ: Erlbaum.

Rupniak, N. M. J., Kilpatrick, G., Hall, M. D., Jenner, P., & Marsden, C. D. (1984). Differential alterations in striatal dopamine receptor sensitivity induced by repeated administration of clinically equivalent doses of haloperidol, sulpiride or clozapine in rats. *Psychopharmacology, 84,* 512–519.

Rupniak, N. M. J., Mann, S., Hall, M. D., Fleminger, S., Kilpatrick, G., Jenner, P., & Marsden, C. D. (1984). Differential effects of continuous administration of haloperidol or sulpiride on striatal dopamine function in the rat. *Psychopharmacology, 84,* 503–511.

Russell, M. J., Switz, G. M., & Thompson, K. (1980). Olfactory influences on the human menstrual cycle. *Pharmacology, Biochemistry, and Behavior, 13,* 737–738.

Rutkowski, G. K., Gruder, C. L., & Romer, D. (1983). Group cohesiveness, social norms, and bystander intervention. *Journal of Personality and Social Psychology, 44,* 545–552.

Ryan, R. M., & Deci, E. L. (2000). Self-determination theory and the facilitation of intrinsic motivation, social development, and well-being. *American Psychologist, 55,* 68–78.

Rybash, J. M., Roodin, P. A., & Hoyer, W. J. (1995). *Adult development and aging* (3rd ed.). Dubuque, IA: Brown & Benchmark.

Rymer, R. (1993). *Genie: An abused child's flight from silence.* New York: HarperCollins.

Sackeim, H. A. (1988). Mechanisms of action of electroconvulsive therapy. In A. J. Frances & R. E. Hales (Eds.), *Review of psychiatry* (Vol. 7). Washington, DC: American Psychiatric Press.

Sackeim, H. A. (1989). The efficacy of electroconvulsive therapy in the treatment of major depressive disorder. In S. Fisher & R. P. Greenberg (Eds.), *The limits of biological treatments for psychological distress.* Hillsdale, NJ: Erlbaum.

Sackeim, H. A., Prudic, J., Devanand, D. P., Kiersky, J. E., Fitzsimons, L., Moody, B. J., McElhiney, M. C., Coleman, E. A., & Settembrino, J. M. (1993). Effects of stimulus intensity and electrode placement on the efficacy and cognitive effects of electroconvulsive therapy. *New England Journal of Medicine, 328,* 839–846.

Sacks, O. (1970). *The man who mistook his wife for a hat, and other clinical tales.* New York: Harper & Row.

Sacks, O. (1995). *An anthropologist on Mars: Seven paradoxical tales.* New York: Knopf.

Saigh, P. A., Yule, W., & Inamdar, S. C. (1996). Imaginal flooding of traumatized children and adolescents. *Journal of School Psychology, 34,* 163–183.

Salthouse, T. A. (1994). The nature of the influence of speed on adult age differences in cognition. *Developmental Psychology, 30,* 240–259.

Saltzman, A. L. (2000). The role of the obedience experiments in holocaust studies: The case for renewed visibility. In T. Blass (Ed.), *Obedience to authority: Current perspectives on the Milgram paradigm.* Mahwah, NJ: Erlbaum.

Salyers, M. P., & Mueser, K. T. (2001). Schizophrenia. In M. Hersen & V. B. Van Hasselt (Eds.), *Advanced abnormal psychology* (2nd ed.) New York: Klewer Academic/Plenum.

Samochowiec, J., Rybakowski, F., Czerski, P., Zakrzewska, M., Stepien, G., Pelka-Wysiecka, J., Horodnicki, J., Rybakowski, J. K., & Hauser, J. (2001). Polymorphisms in the dopamine, serotonin, and norepinephrine transporter genes and their relationship to temperamental dimensions measured by the temperament and character inventory of healthy volunteers. *Neuropsychobiology, 43,* 248–253.

Samuel, A. G. (1991). A further examination of attentional effects in the phonemic restoration illusion. *Quarterly Journal of Experimental Psychology, 43A,* 679–699.

Sande, G. N., Goethals, G. R., & Radloff, C. E. (1988). Perceiving one's own traits and others': The multifaceted self. *Journal of Personality and Social Psychology, 54,* 13–20.

Sandler, M. (2001). Neurotrophins: Possible role in affective disorders. *Human Psychopharmacology: Clinical Experimental, 16,* 61–64.

Sanford, E. C. (1917/1982). Professor Sanford's morning prayer. In U. Neisser (Ed.), *Memory observed: remembering in natural contexts.* New York: Freeman. (Originally written as a letter in 1917; published in Neisser's book in 1982.)

Sapir, E. (1941; reprinted 1964). *Culture, language, and personality.* Berkeley: University of California Press.

Sarason, I. G., & Sarason, B. R. (1990). Test anxiety. In H. Leitenberg (Ed.), *Handbook of social and evaluation anxiety.* New York: Plenum Press.

Savage-Rumbaugh, E. S., & Fields, W. M. (2000). Linguistic, cultural, and cognitive capacities of bonobos. (*Pan paniscus*). *Culture and Psychology, 6,* 131–153.

Savage-Rumbaugh, E. S., McDonald, K., Sevcik, R. A., Hopkins, B., & Rupert, E. (1986). Spontaneous symbol acquisition and communicative use by pygmy chimpanzees. *Journal of Experimental Psychology: General, 115,* 211–235.

Savage-Rumbaugh, S., Murphy, J., Sevcik, R. A., Brakke, K. E., Williams, S., & Rumbaugh, D. M. (1993). Language comprehension in ape and child. *Monographs of the Society for Research on Child Development,* (3 & 4).

Saxe, G. B. (1988). The mathematics of child street vendors. *Child Development, 59,* 1415–1425.

Scarborough, E., & Furumoto, L. (1987). *Untold lives: The first generation of American women psychologists.* New York: Columbia University Press.

Scarr, S., & Carter-Saltzman, L. (1983). Genetics and intelligence. In J. L. Fuller & E. C. Simmel (Eds.), *Behavior genetics: Principles and applications.* Hillsdale, NJ: Erlbaum.

Scarr, S., & McCartney, K. (1983). How people make their own environments: A theory of genotype–environment effects. *Child Development, 54,* 424–435.

Scarr, S., Weber, P. L., Weinberg, R. A., & Wittig, M. A. (1981). Personality resemblance among adolescents and their parents in biologically related and adoptive families. *Journal of Personality and Social Psychology, 40,* 885–898.

Schab, F. R. (1990). Odors and remembrance of things past. *Journal of Experimental Psychology: Learning, Memory, and Cognition, 16,* 648–655.

Schachter, F. F. (1982). Sibling deidentification and split-parent identification: A family tetrad. In M. E. Lamb & B. Sutton-Smith (Eds.), *Sibling relationships: Their nature and significance across the lifespan.* Hillsdale, NJ: Erlbaum.

Schachter, S. (1971). *Emotion, obesity, and crime.* New York: Academic Press.

Schafe, G. E., Sollars, S. I., & Bernstein, I. L. (1995). The CS-US interval and taste aversion learning: A brief look. *Behavioral Neuroscience, 109,* 799–802.

Schank, R. C., & Abelson, R. P. (1977). *Scripts, plans, goals and understanding.* Hillsdale, NJ: Erlbaum.

Scharf, B. (1964). Partial masking. *Acustica, 14,* 16–23.

Scheier, M. F., & Carver, C. S. (1993). On the power of positive thinking: The benefits of being optimistic. *Current Directions in Psychological Science, 2,* 26–30.

Scheier, M. F., Matthews, K. A., Owens, J. F., Magovern, G. J., Lefebvre, R., Abbott, R. C., & Carver, C. S. (1989). Dispositional optimism and recovery from coronary artery bypass surgery: The beneficial effects of optimism on physical and psychological well-being. *Journal of Personality and Social Psychology, 57,* 1024–1040.

Schieffelin, B., & Ochs, E. (1983). A cultural perspective on the transition from prelinguistic to linguistic communication. In R. Golinkoff (Ed.), *The transition from prelinguistic to linguistic communication.* Hillsdale, NJ: Erlbaum.

Schifter, D. E., & Ajzen, I. (1985). Intention, perceived control, and weight loss: An application of the theory of planned behavior. *Journal of Personality and Social Psychology, 49,* 849–851.

Schildkraut, J. J. (1965). The catecholamine hypothesis of affective disorders: A review of supporting evidence. *American Journal of Psychiatry, 122,* 509–522.

Schiller, P. H. (1994). Area V4 of the primate visual cortex. *Current Directions in Psychological Science, 3,* 89–92.

Schlenker, B. R. (1980). *Impression management: The self-concept, social identity,* and *interpersonal relations.* Monterey, CA: Brooks/Cole.

Schlenker, B. R., & Pontari, B. A. (2000). The strategic control of information: Impression management and self-presentation in daily life. In A. Tesser, R. B. Felson, & J. M. Suls (Eds.), *Psychological perspectives on self and identity.* Washington, DC: American Psychological Association.

Schmidt, F. L., & Hunter, J. E. (1992). Development of a causal model of processes determining job performance. *Current Directions in Psychological Science, 1,* 89–92.

Schmidt, F. L., Ones, D. S., & Hunter, J. E. (1992). Personnel selection. *Annual Review of Psychology, 43,* 627–670.

Schnapf, J. L., & Baylor, D. A. (1987, April). How photoreceptor cells respond to light. *Scientific American,* pp. 40–47.

Schneider, B. H., Atkinson, L., & Tardif, C. (2001). Child-parent attachment and children's peer relations: A quantitative review. *Developmental Psychology, 37,* 86–100.

Schneider, J. M. (1972). Relationship between locus of control and activity preferences: Effects of masculinity, activity, and skill. *Journal of Consulting and Clinical Psychology, 38,* 225–230.

Schneider, J. W., & Hacker, S. L. (1973). Sex role imagery and use of the generic "man" in introductory texts: A case of the sociology of sociology. *The American Sociologists, 8,* 12–18.

Schneider, S. L. (2001). In search of realistic optimism: Meaning, knowledge, and warm fuzziness. *American Psychologist, 56*, 250–263.

Schopler, J., Insko, C. A., Graetz, K. A., Drigotas, S. M., & Smith, V. A. (1991). The generality of the individual-group discontinuity effect: Variations in positivity-negativity of outcomes, players' relative power, and the magnitude of outcomes. *Personality and Social Psychology Bulletin, 17*, 612–624.

Schreiber, F. R. (1973). *Sybil*. New York: Warner.

Schretlen, D., Pearlson, G. D., Anthony, J. C., Aylward, E. H., Augustine, A. M., Davis, A., & Barta, P. (2000). Elucidating the contributions of processing speed, executive ability, and frontal lobe volume to normal age-related differences in fluid intelligence. *Journal of the International Neuropsychological Society, 6*, 52–61.

Schröder, I. (1993). Concealed ovulation and clandestine copulation: A female contribution to human evolution. *Ethology and Sociobiology, 14*, 381–389.

Schuman, H., & Scott, J. (1989). Generations and collective memories. *American Sociological Review, 54*, 359–381.

Schunk, D. H. (1984). Self-efficacy perspective on achievement behavior. *Educational Psychologist, 19*, 48–58.

Schunk, D. H., & Hanson, A. R. (1985). Peer models: Influence on children's self-efficacy and achievement. *Journal of Educational Psychology, 77*, 313–322.

Schwartz, J. M., Stoessel, P. W., Baxter, L. R., Martin, K. M., & Phelps, M. E. (1996). Systematic changes in cerebral glucose metabolic rate after successful behavior modification treatment of obsessive-compulsive disorder. *Archives of General Psychiatry, 53*, 109–113.

Schwartz, S. H. (1992). Universals in the content and structure of values: Theoretical advances and empirical tests in 20 countries. *Advances in Experimental Social Psychology, 25*, 1–65.

Schwartz, S. H. (1996). Value priorities and behavior: Applying a theory of integrated value systems. In C. Seligman, J. M. Olson, & M. Zanna (Eds.), *The psychology of values: The Ontario Symposium* (Vol. 8). Mahwah, NJ: Erlbaum.

Schwartz, S. H., & Gottlieb, A. (1980). Bystander anonymity and reactions to emergencies. *Journal of Personality and Social Psychology, 39*, 418–430.

Schwartz-Giblin, S., McEwen, B. S., & Pfaff, D. W. (1989). Mechanisms of female reproductive behavior. In F. R. Brush & S. Levine (Eds.), *Psychoendocrinology*. San Diego, CA: Academic Press.

Schwartzman, H. (1978). *Transformations: The anthropology of children's play*. New York: Plenum Press.

Schwarzer, R. (1994). Optimism, vulnerability, and self-beliefs as health-related cognitions: A systematic overview. *Psychology and Health, 9*, 161–180.

Scott, J. P. (1963). The process of primary socialization in canine and human infants. *Monograph of the Society for Research in Child Development, 28*, 1–47.

Scott, J. P., & Fuller, J. L. (1965). *Genetics and the social behavior of the dog*. Chicago: University of Chicago Press.

Scott, S. K., Young, A. W., Calder, A. J., Hellawell, D. J., Aggleton, J. P., & Johnson, M. (1997). Impaired auditory recognition of fear and anger following bilateral amygdala lesions. *Nature, 385*, 254–257.

Scribner, S. (1977). Modes of thinking and ways of speaking: Culture and logic reconsidered. In P. N. Johnson-Laird & P. C. Wason (Eds.), *Thinking: Readings in cognitive science*. Cambridge, England: Cambridge University Press.

Scribner, S. (1986). Thinking in action: Some characteristics of practical thought. In R. J. Sternberg & R. K. Wagner (Eds.), *Practical intelligence: Nature and origins of competence in the everyday world*. Cambridge, England: Cambridge University Press.

Seago, D. W. (1947). Stereotypes: Before Pearl Harbor and after. *Journal of Social Psychology, 23*, 55–64.

Searle, L. V. (1949). The organization of hereditary maze-brightness and maze-dullness. *Genetic Psychology Monographs, 39*, 279–325.

Sears, R. R. (1936). Experimental studies of projection: I. Attributions of traits, *Journal of Social Psychology, 7*, 151–163.

Sechenov, I. M. (1863; reprinted 1935). Reflexes of the brain. In A. A. Subkow (Ed. & Trans.), *I. M. Sechenov: Selected works*. Moscow: State Publishing House for Biological and Medical Literature.

Seeman, P., & Lee, T. (1975). Antipsychotic drugs: Direct correlation between clinical potency and presynaptic action on dopamine neurons, *Science, 188*, 1271–1219.

Segal, D. L., & Coolidge, F. L. (2001). Diagnosis and classification. In M. Hersen & V. B. Van Hasselt (Eds.), *Advanced abnormal psychology* (2nd ed.). New York: Klewer Academic/Plenum.

Segall, M. H., Dason, P. R., Berry, J. W., & Poortinga, Y. H. (1990). *Human behavior in global perspective: An introduction to cross-cultural psychology*. New York: Pergamon Press.

Seifer, R., Schiller, M., Sameroff, A. J., Resnick, S., & Riordan, K. (1996). Attachment, maternal sensitivity, and infant temperament during the first year of life. *Developmental Psychology, 32*, 12–25.

Selfe, L. (1977). *Nadia: A case of extraordinary drawing ability in an autistic child*. London: Academic Press.

Seligman, M. E. P. (1971). Phobias and preparedness. *Behavior Therapy, 2*, 307–320.

Seligman, M. E. P. (1990). *Learned optimism*. New York: Knopf.

Seligman, M. E. P., Castellon, C., Cacciola, J., Schulman, P., Luborsky, L., Ollove, M., & Downing, R. (1988). Explanatory style change during cognitive therapy for unipolar depression. *Journal of Abnormal Psychology, 97*, 13–18.

Semin, G. R., & Manstead, A. S. R. (1982). The social implications of embarrassment displays and restitution behavior. *European Journal of Social Psychology, 12*, 367–377.

Semmel, A. K. (1976). *Group dynamics and foreign policy process: The choice-shift phenomenon*. Paper presented to the Southern Political Science Association. (For description, see D. G. Myers, 1982.)

Senghas, A. (1994, November). The development of Nicaraguan Sign Language via the language acquisition process. *Proceedings for the Boston University Conference on Language Development, 1994*.

Serbin, L., Sprafkin, C., Elman, M., & Doyle, A. B. (1984). The early development of sex differentiated patterns and social influence. *Canadian Journal of Social Science, 14*, 350–363.

Sereno, M. I., Dale, A. M., Reppas, J. B., Kwong, K. K., Belliveau, J. W., Brady, T. J., Rosen, B. R., & Tootell, R. B. H. (1995). Borders of multiple visual areas in humans revealed by functional magnetic imaging. *Science, 268*, 889–892.

Sevcik, R. A., & Savage-Rumbaugh, E. S. (1994). Language comprehension and use by great apes. *Language and Communication, 14,* 37–58.

Shadish, W. R., Matt, G. E., Navarro, A. M., & Phillips, G. (2000). The effects of psychological therapies under clinically representative conditions: A meta-analysis. *Psychological Bulletin, 126,* 512–529.

Shapiro, C. M., Bortz, R., Mitchell, D., Bartell, P., & Jooste, P. (1981). Slow-wave sleep: A recovery period after exercise. *Science, 214,* 1253–1254.

Shearman, L. P., Sathyanarayanan, S., Weaver, D. R., Maywood, E. S., Chaves, I., Zheng, B., Kume, K., Lee, C. C., van der Horst, G., Hastings, M. H., & Reppert, S. M. (2000). Interacting molecular loops in the mammalian circadian clock. *Science, 288,* 1013–1019.

Sheldon, K. M. (1999). Learning the lessons of tit-for-tat: Even competitors can get the message. *Journal of Personality and Social Psychology, 77,* 1245–1253.

Sheldon, K. M., Sheldon, M. S., & Osbaldiston, R. (2000). Prosocial values and group assortation within an *N*-person Prisoner's Dilemma Game. *Human Nature, 11,* 387–404.

Shelton, R. C. (2000). Cellular mechanisms in the vulnerability to depression and response to antidepressants. *The Psychiatric Clinics of North America, 23,* 713–729.

Shepperd, J. A., & Arkin, R. M. (1990). Shyness and self-presentation. In W. R. Crozier (Ed.), *Shyness and embarrassment: Perspectives from social psychology.* Cambridge, England: Cambridge University Press.

Sherif, M. (1936). *The psychology of social norms.* New York: Harper.

Sherif, M. (1966). *In common predicament: Social psychology of intergroup conflict and cooperation.* Boston: Houghton Mifflin.

Sherif, M., Harvey, O. J., White, B. J., Hood, W. E., & Sherif, C. S. (1961). *Intergroup conflict and cooperation: The Robbers Cave experiment.* Norman: University of Oklahoma Book Exchange.

Sherman, P. W. (1977). Nepotism and the evolution of alarm calls. *Science, 197,* 1246–1253.

Sherwin, B. B., & Gelfand, M. M. (1987). Androgen enhances sexual motivation in females: A prospective cross-study of sex hormone administration in the surgical menopause. *Psychosomatic Medicine, 47,* 339–351.

Sherwin, B. B., Gelfand, M. M., & Brender, W. (1985). The role of androgen in the maintenance of sexual functioning in oophorectomised women. *Psychosomatic Medicine, 49,* 397–409.

Shettleworth, S. J. (1972). Constraints on learning. In D. S. Lehrman, R. A. Hinde, & E. Shaw (Eds.), *Advances in the study of behavior* (Vol. 4). New York: Academic Press.

Shiffrin, R. M., & Schneider, W. (1977). Controlled and automatic information processing: II. Perceptual learning, automatic attending, and a general theory. *Psychological Review, 84,* 127–190.

Shoda, Y., Mischel, W., & Wright, J. C. (1994). Intraindividual stability in organization and patterning of behavior: Incorporating psychological situations into the idiographic analysis of personality. *Journal of Personality and Social Psychology, 67,* 674–687.

Shorter, E. (1992). *From paralysis to fatigue: A history of psychosomatic illness in the modern era.* New York: Free Press.

Siegel, S. (1999). Drug anticipation and drug addiction. The 1998 H. David Archibald Lecture. *Addiction, 94,* 1113–1124.

Siegel, S., Krank, M. D., & Hinson, R. E. (1988). Anticipation of pharmacological and nonpharmacological events. Classical conditioning and addictive behavior. In S. Peele (Ed.), *Visions of addiction: Major contemporary perspectives on addiction and alcoholism.* Lexington, MA: Lexington Books.

Siegler, R. S. (1983). How knowledge influences learning. *American Scientist, 71,* 631–638.

Siegler, R. S. (2000). The rebirth of children's learning. *Child Development, 71,* 26–35.

Siegler, R. S., & Crowley, K. (1994). Constraints on learning in nonprivileged domains. *Cognitive Psychology, 27,* 194–226.

Siegler, R. S., & Jenkins, E. (1989). *How children discover new strategies.* Hillsdale, NJ: Erlbaum.

Sigman, M., & Whaley, S. E. (1998). The role of nutrition in the development of intelligence. In U. Neisser (Ed.), *The rising curve: Long-term gains in IQ and related measures.* Washington, DC: APA.

Silver, R., LeSauter, J., Tresco, P. A., & Lehman, M. N. (1996). A diffusible coupling signal from the transplanted suprachiasmatic nucleus controlling circadian locomotor rhythms. *Nature, 382,* 810–813.

Simon, H. A. (1992). What is an explanation of behavior? *Psychological Science, 3,* 150–161.

Sims, J. H., & Baumann, D. D. (1972). The tornado threat: Coping styles of the north and south. *Science, 176,* 1386–1392.

Siqueland, R. R., & Lipsitt, L. P. (1966). Conditioned headturning in human newborns. *Journal of Experimental Child Psychology, 3,* 356–376.

Sizemore, C. C. (1989). *A mind of my own.* New York: Wm. Morrow.

Skinner, B. F. (1938). *The behavior of organisms.* New York: Appleton-Century-Crofts.

Skinner, B. F. (1953). *Science and human behavior.* New York: Macmillan.

Skinner, B. F. (1966). The phylogeny and ontogeny of behavior. *Science, 153,* 1205–1213.

Skinner, B. F. (1971). *Beyond freedom and dignity.* New York: Knopf.

Skinner, B. F. (1974). *About behaviorism.* New York: Knopf.

Skov, R. B., & Sherman, S. J. (1986). Information-gathering processes: Diagnosticity, hypothesis confirmation strategies and perceived hypothesis confirmation. *Journal of Experimental Social Psychology, 22,* 93–121.

Slagsvold, T., Svein, D., & Lampe, H. M. (1999). Does female aggression prevent polygyny? An experiment with pied flycatchers (*Ficedula hypoleuca*). *Behavioral Ecology and Sociobiology, 45,* 403–410.

Sloane, R. B., Staples, F. R., Cristo, A. H., Yorkston, N. J., & Whipple, K. (1975). *Psychotherapy versus behavior therapy.* Cambridge, MA: Harvard University Press.

Small, M. F. (1993). *Female choices: Sexual behavior of female primates.* Ithaca, NY: Cornell University Press.

Smetana, J. G., & Asquith, P. (1994). Adolescents' and parents' conceptions of parental authority and personal autonomy. *Child Development, 65,* 1147–1162.

Smith, C. (1995). Sleep states and memory processes. *Behavior and Brain Research, 69,* 137–145.

Smith, D. (1982). Trends in counseling and psychotherapy. *American Psychologist, 37,* 802–809.

Smith, E. E. (2000). Neural bases of human working memory. *Current Directions in Psychological Science, 2,* 45–49.

Smith, E. E., & Jonides, J. (1999). Storage and executive processes in the frontal lobes. *Science, 283,* 1657–1661.

Smith, G. B., Schwebel, A. I., Dunn, R. L., & McIver, S. D. (1993). The role of psychologists in the treatment, management, and prevention of chronic mental illness. *American Psychologist, 48,* 966–971.

Smith, J. D. (1992). The auditory hallucinations of schizophrenia. D. Reisberg (Ed.), *Auditory imagery.* Hillsdale, NJ: Erlbaum.

Smith, L. B., Thelen, E., Titzer, R., & McLin, D. (1999). Knowing in the context of acting: The task dynamics of the A-not-B error. *Psychological Review, 106,* 235–260.

Smith, M. L., Glass, G. V., & Miller, T. I. (1980). *The benefits of psychotherapy.* Baltimore: Johns Hopkins University Press.

Smith, P. B., Trompenaars, F., & Dugan, S. (1995). The Rotter Locus of Control Scale in 43 countries: A test of cultural relativity. *International Journal of Psychology, 30,* 377–400.

Smith, T. W. (1992). Discrepancies between men and women in reporting number of sexual partners: A summary from four countries. *Social Biology, 39,* 203–211.

Smoller, J. W., Finn, C., & White, C. (2000). The genetics of anxiety disorders: An overview. *Psychiatraic Annals, 30,* 745–753.

Smuts, B. (1992). Male aggression against women. An evolutionary perspective. *Human Nature, 3,* 1–44.

Snow, C. E. (1984). Parent-child interaction and the development of communicative ability. In R. L. Schiefelbusch & J. Pickar (Eds.), *The acquisition of communicative competence.* Baltimore: University Park Press.

Snyder, C. R. (1994). *The psychology of hope: You can get there from here.* New York: Free Press.

Snyder, F., & Scott, J. (1972). The psychophysiology of sleep. In N. S. Greenfield & R. A. Sternbach (Eds.), *Handbook of psychophysiology.* New York: Holt, Rinehart & Winston.

Snyder, M. (1974). Self-monitoring of expressive behavior. *Journal of Personality and Social Psychology, 30,* 526–537.

Snyder, M. (1981). Seek and ye shall find: Testing hypotheses about other people. In E. T. Higgins, C. P. Herman, & M. P. Zanna (Eds.), *Social cognition: The Ontario symposium on personality and social psychology* (pp. 277–303). Hillsdale, NJ: Erlbaum.

Snyder, M., & Omoto, A. M. (1992). Volunteerism and society's response to the HIV epidemic. *Current Directions in Psychological Science, 1,* 113–116.

Snyder, M., & Smith, D. (1986). Personality and friendship: The friendship worlds of self-monitoring. In V. Derlega & B. A. Winstead (Eds.), *Friendship and social interaction.* New York: Springer-Verlag.

Snyder, M., & Swann, W. B. (1976). When actions reflect attitudes: The politics of impression management. *Journal of Personality and Social Psychology, 34,* 1032–1042.

Snyderman, M., & Rothman, S. (1987). Survey of expert opinion on intelligence and aptitude testing. *American Psychologist, 42,* 137–144.

Sodian, B., Taylor, C., Harris, P. L., & Perner, J. (1991). Early deception and the child's theory of mind: False trials and genuine markers. *Child Development, 62,* 468–483.

Sommer, S. (2000). Sex-specific predation on a monogamous rat, *Hypogeomys antimena* (Muridae: Nesomyinae). *Animal Behaviour, 59,* 1087–1094.

Sorce, J. F., Emde, R. N., Campos, J., & Klinnert, M.D. (1985). Maternal emotional signaling: Its effect on the visual cliff behavior of 1-year-olds. *Developmental Psychology, 21,* 195–200.

Spanagel, R., & Weiss, R. (1999). The dopamine hypothesis of reward: Past and current status. *Trends in Neuroscience, 22,* 521–527.

Spanos, N. P. (1994). Multiple identity enactments and multiple personality disorder: A sociocognitive perspective. *Psychological Bulletin, 116,* 143–165.

Spearman, C. (1904). The proof and measurement of association between two things. *American Journal of Psychology, 15,* 72–101.

Spearman, C. (1927). *The abilities of man.* New York: Macmillan.

Spelke, E. S., Breinlinger, K., Macomber, J., & Jacobson, K. (1992). Origins of knowledge. *Psychological Review, 99,* 605–632.

Spelke, E. S., Hirst, W. C., & Neisser, U. (1976). Skills of divided attention. *Cognition, 4,* 215–230.

Spelke, E. S., Katz, G., Purcell, S., Ehrlich, S., & Breinlinger, K. (1994). Early knowledge of object motion: Continuity and inertia. *Cognition, 51,* 131–176.

Spencer, H. (1879). *The data of ethics.* New York: Crowell.

Sperling, G. (1960). The information available in brief visual presentations. *Psychological Monographs, 74* (Whole No. 498).

Spitz, H. H. (1997). *Nonconscious movements: From mystical messages to facilitated communication.* Mahwah, NJ: Erlbaum.

Spitzer, R. L., & Fleiss, J. L. (1974). A reanalysis of the reliability of psychiatric diagnosis. *British Journal of Psychiatry, 125,* 341–347.

Spock, B., & Rothenberg, M. B. (1985). *Dr. Spock's baby and child care* (Rev. & updated ed.). New York: Pocket Books.

Squire, L. R. (1992). Memory and the hippocampus: A synthesis from findings with rats, monkeys, and humans. *Psychological Review, 99,* 195–231.

Squire, L. R., Knowlton, B., & Musen, G. (1993). The structure and organization of memory. *Annual Review of Psychology, 44,* 453–495.

Stahl, S. M. (2000). *Essential psychopharmacology.* Cambridge, England: Cambridge University Press.

Stanley, B. G., & Gillard, E. R. (1994). Hypothalamic neuropeptide Y and the regulation of eating behavior and body weight. *Current Directions in Psychological Science, 3,* 9–15.

Steele, C. M., & Josephs, R. A. (1990). Alcohol myopia: Its prized and dangerous effects. *American Psychologist, 45,* 921–933.

Steinberg, L. (1989). Pubertal maturation and parent-adolescent distance: An evolutionary perspective. In G. R. Adams, R. Montemayor, & T. P. Gullota (Eds.), *Biology of adolescent behavior and development.* Newbury Park, CA: Sage.

Steinberg, L., & Morris, A. S. (2001). Adolescent development. *Annual Review of Psychology, 52,* 83–110.

Steinberg, L., & Silverberg, S. B. (1986). The vicissitudes of autonomy in early adolescence. *Child Development, 57,* 841–851.

Stellar, E. (1954). The physiology of emotion. *Psychological Review, 61*, 5–22.

Stellar, J. R., & Stellar, E. (1985). *The neurobiology of motivation and reward*. New York: Springer-Verlag.

Stelmack, R. M. (1990). Biological bases of extraversion: Psychophysiological evidence. *Journal of Personality, 58*, 293–311.

Steriade, M. (1996). Awakening the brain. *Nature, 383*, 24–25.

Steriade, M., McCormick, D. A., & Sejnowski, T. J. (1993). Thalamocortical oscillations in the sleeping and aroused brain. *Science, 262*, 679–685.

Stern, K., & McClintock, M. K. (1998). Regulation of ovulation by human pheromones. *Nature, 392*, 177–179.

Sternberg, R. J. (1985). *Beyond IQ: A triarchic theory of human intelligence*. Cambridge, England: Cambridge University Press.

Sternberg, R. J. (1986b). Intelligence is mental self-government. In R. J. Sternberg & D. K. Detterman (Eds.), *What is intelligence? Contemporary viewpoints on its nature and definition*. Norwood, NJ: Ablex.

Stevens, S. S. (1962). The surprising simplicity of sensory metrics. *American Psychologist, 17*, 29–39.

Stevens, S. S. (1975). *Psychophysics: Introduction to its perceptual, neural, and social prospects*. New York: Wiley.

Stewart, J. E., II (1985). Appearance and punishment: The attraction-leniency effect in the courtroom. *Journal of Social Psychology, 125*, 373–378.

Stipek, D. (1995). The development of pride and shame in toddlers. In J. P. Tangney & K. W. Fischer (Eds.), *Self-conscious emotions: The psychology of shame, guilt, embarrassment, and pride*. New York: Guilford Press.

Stoddart, D. M. (1990). *The scented ape*. Cambridge, England: Cambridge University Press.

Stoneman, Z., Brody, G. H., & MacKinnon, C. (1984). Naturalistic observations of children's activities and roles while playing with their siblings and friends. *Child Development, 55*, 617–627.

Stoolmiller, M. (1999). Implications of the restricted range of family environments for estimates of heritability and nonshared environment in behavior-genetic adoption studies. *Psychological Bulletin, 125*, 392–409.

Storms, M. D. (1973). Videotape and the attribution process: Reversing actors' and observers' points of view. *Journal of Personality and Social Psychology, 27*, 165–175.

Straube, E. R. & Oades, R. D. (1992). *Schizophrenia: empirical research and findings*. San Diego, CA: Academic Press.

Streri, A. (1993). *Seeing, reaching, touching: The relations between vision and touch in infancy* (T. Pownall & S. Kingerlee, Trans.). Cambridge, MA: MIT Press.

Stricker, E. M. (1973). Thirst, sodium appetite, and complementary physiological contributions to the regulation of intravascular fluid volume. In A. N. Epstein, H. R. Kissileff, & E. Stellar (Eds.), *The neuropsychology of thirst: New findings and advances in concepts*. Washington, DC: Winston.

Stricker, E. M. (1982). The central control of food intake: A role for insulin. In B. G. Hoebel & D. Novin (Eds.), *The neural basis of feeding and reward*. Brunswick, ME: Haer Institute.

Strickland, B. R. (1992). Women and depression. *Current Directions, 1*, 132–135.

Stroebe, W., Stroebe, M., Abakoumkin, G., & Schut, H. (1996). The role of loneliness and social support in adjustment to loss: A test of attachment versus stress theory. *Journal of Personality and Social Psychology, 70*, 1241–1249.

Stroop, J. R. (1935). Studies of interference in serial verbal reactions. *Journal of Experimental Psychology, 18*, 643–662.

Strupp, H. H. (1989). Psychotherapy: Can the practitioner learn from the researcher? *American Psychologist, 44*, 717–724.

Strupp, H. H., & Hadley, S. W. (1979). Specific vs. nonspecific factors in psychotherapy: A controlled study of outcome. *Archives of General Psychiatry, 36*, 1125–1136.

Stunkard, A., Sorensen, T., Hanis, C., Teasdale, T., Chakraborty, R., Schull, W., & Schulsinger, F. (1986). An adoption study of human obesity. *New England Journal of Medicine, 314*, 193–198.

Suinn, R. M. (2001). The terrible twos—anger and anxiety: Hazardous to your health. *American Psychologist, 56*, 27–36.

Sulloway, F. J. (1996). *Born to rebel: Birth order, family dynamics, and creative lives*. Pantheon Books: New York.

Suomi, S. J. (1991). Adolescent depression and depressive symptoms: Insights from longitudinal studies with rhesus monkeys. *Journal of Youth and Adolescence, 20*, 273–287.

Susser, E., Neugebauer, R., Hoek, H. W., Brown, A. S., Lin, S., Labovitz, D., & Gorman, J. M. (1996). Schizophrenia after prenatal famine. *Archives of General Psychiatry, 53*, 25–31.

Sutherland, S., (1991). Only four possible solutions. *Nature, 353*, 389–390.

Sutton, S. K., & Davidson, R. J. (1997). Prefrontal brain asymmetry: A biological substrate of the behavioral approach and inhibition systems. *Psychological Science, 8*, 204–210.

Svartberg, M., & Stiles, T. C. (1991). Comparative effects of short-term psychodynamic psychotherapy: A meta-analysis. *Journal of Consulting and Clinical Psychology, 59*, 704–714.

Svirsky, M. A., Robbins, A. M., Kirk, K. I., Pisoni, D. B., & Miyamoto, R. T. (2000). Language development in profoundly deaf children with cochlear implants. *Psychological Science, 11*, 153–158.

Swann, W. B. (1987). Identity negotiation: Where two roads meet. *Journal of Social Psychology, 53*, 1038–1051.

Swann, W. B., De La Ronde, C., & Hixon, J. G. (1994). Authenticity and positivity strivings in marriage and courtship. *Journal of Personality and Social Psychology, 66*, 857–869.

Swann, W. B., & Hill, C. A. (1982). When our identities are mistaken: Reaffirming self-conceptions through social interaction. *Journal of Personality and Social Psychology, 43*, 59–66.

Swanson, H. L. (1999). What develops in working memory? A life span perspective. *Developmental Psychology, 35*, 986–1000.

Sweeney, P. D., & Gruber, K. L. (1984). Selective exposure: Voter information preferences and the Watergate affair. *Journal of Personality and Social Psychology, 46*, 1208–1221.

Symons, D. (1979). *The evolution of human sexuality*. Oxford: Oxford University Press.

Tajfel, H. (1972). Social categorization. In S. Moscovici (Ed.), *Introduction à la psychologie sociale* [Introduction to social psychology] (Vol. 1), Paris: Larousse.

Tajfel, H. (1982). Social psychology of intergroup relations. *Annual Review of Psychology, 33,* 1–39.

Takahashi, J. S., & Zatz, M. (1982). Regulation of circadian rhythmicity. *Science, 217,* 1104–1111.

Tanabe, T., Iino, M., & Takagi, S. F. (1975). Discrimination of odors in olfactory bulb, pyriform-amygdaloid areas and orbitofrontal cortex of the monkey. *Journal of Neurophysiology, 38,* 1284–1296.

Tang, Y., Shimizu, E., Dube, G. R., Rampon, C., Kerchner, G. A., Zhou, M., Liu, G., & Tsien, G. Z. (1999). Genetic enhancement of learning and memory in mice. *Nature, 401,* 63–69.

Tangney, J. P (1995). Shame and guilt in interpersonal relationships. In J. P. Tangney & K. W. Fischer (Eds.), *Self-conscious emotions: The psychology of shame, guilt, embarrassment, and pride.* New York: Guilford. Press.

Tangney, J. P. (1999). The self-conscious emotions: Shame, guilt, embarrassment and pride. In T. Dalgleish & M. Power (Eds.), *Handbook of cognition and emotion.* New York: Wiley.

Tangney, J. P., Miller, R. S., Flicker, L., & Barlow, D. H. (1996). Are shame, guilt, and embarrassment distinct emotions? *Journal of Personality and Social Psychology, 70,* 1256–1269.

Taylor, S. E., Klein, L. C., Lewis, B. P., Gruenewald, T. L., Gurung, R. A. R., & Updegraff, J. A. (2000). Biobehavioral responses to stress in females: Tend-and-befriend, not fight-or-flight. *Psychological Review, 107,* 411–429.

Tellegen, A., Lykken, D. T., Bouchard, T. J., Wilcox, K. J., Segal, N. L., & Rich, S. (1988). Personality similarity in twins reared apart and together. *Journal of Personality and Social Psychology, 54,* 1031–1039.

Terman, G. W., Shavit, Y., Lewis, J. W., Cannon, J. T., & Liebeskind, J. C. (1984). Intrinsic mechanisms of pain inhibition: Activation by stress. *Science, 226,* 1270–1277.

Terry, D. J., Hogg, M. A., & White, K. M. (1999). The theory of planned behavior: Self-identity, social identity, and group norms. *British Journal of Social Psychology, 38,* 225–244.

Terry, D. J., Hogg, M. A., & White, K. M. (2000). Attitude-behavior relations: Social identity and group membership. In D. J. Terry & M. A. Hogg (Eds.), *Attitudes, behavior, and social context: The role of norms and group membership.* Mahwah, NJ: Erlbaum.

Tesser, A. (1993). The importance of heritability in psychological research: The case of attitudes. *Psychological Reviews, 100,* 129–142.

Test, M. A. Knoedler, W. H., Allness, D. J., Burke, S. S., Brown, R. L., & Wallisch, L. S. (1991). Long-term community care through an assertive continuous treatment team. In C. A. Tamminga & S. C. Shulz (Eds.), *Advances in neuropsychiatry and psychopharmacology: Vol. 1. Schizophrenia research.* New York: Raven Press.

Tetlock, P. E. (1991). An alternative metaphor in the study of judgment and choice: People as politicians. *Theory and Psychology, 1,* 451–475.

't Hart, P. (1990). *Groupthink in government: A study of small groups and policy failure.* Amsterdam: Swets & Zeitlinger.

Thigpen, C. H., & Cleckley, H. M. (1957). *The three faces of Eve.* New York: Popular Library.

Thomson, J. R., & Chapman, R. S. (1977). Who is "Daddy" revisited: The status of two-year-olds' over-extended words in use and comprehension. *Journal of Child Language, 4,* 359–375.

Thorndike, E. L. (1898). Animal intelligence: An experimental study of associative processes in animals. *Psychological Review Monograph Supplements, 2,* 4–160.

Thorndike, E. L. (1913). *Educational psychology.* New York: Teachers College Press.

Tice, D. M., Butler, J. L., Muraven, M. B., & Stillwell, A. M. (1995). When modesty prevails: Differential favorability of self-presentation to friends and strangers. *Journal of Personality and Social Psychology, 69,* 1120–1138.

Tilker, H. A. (1970). Socially responsible behavior as a function of observer responsibility and victim feedback. *Journal of Personality and Social Psychology, 14,* 95–100.

Tinbergen, N. (1951). *The study of instinct.* New York: Oxford University Press.

Tinbergen, N. (1952, December). The curious behavior of the stickleback. *Scientific American,* pp. 22–26.

Tizard, B., & Hodges, J. (1978). The effect of early institutional rearing on the development of eight-year-old children. *Journal of Child Psychology and Psychiatry, 19,* 99–118.

Tobias, J., & Seddon, N. (2000) Territoriality as a paternity guard in the European robin, *Erithacus rubecula. Animal Behaviour, 60,* 165–173.

Tolman, E. C. (1948). Cognitive maps in rats and men. *The Psychological Review, 55,* 189–208.

Tolman, E. C., & Honzik, C. H. (1930a). "Insight" in rats. *University of California Publications in Psychology, 4,* 215–232.

Tomasello, M., Call, J., & Hare, B. (1998). Five primate species follow the joint visual gaze of conspecifics. *Animal Behaviour, 55,* 1063–1069.

Tomasello, M., Kruger, A. C., & Ratner, H. H. (1993). Cultural learning. *Behavioral and Brain Sciences, 16,* 495–552.

Toni, N., Buchs, P., Nikonenko, I., Bron, C. R., & Muller, D. (1999). LTP promotes formation of multiple spine synapses between a single axon terminal and a dendrite. *Nature, 402,* 421–425.

Toomey, R., Kremen, W. S., Simpson, J. C., Samson, J. A., Seidman, L. J., Lyons, M. J., Faraone, S. V., & Tsuang, M. T. (1997). Revisiting the factor structure for positive and negative symptoms: Evidence from a large heterogeneous group of psychiatric patients. *American Journal of Psychiatry, 154,* 371–377.

Torgersen, S. (1986). Childhood and family characteristics in panic and generalized anxiety disorder. *American Journal of Psychiatry, 143,* 630–639.

Torrance, E. P. (1954). Some consequences of power differences on decision-making in permanent and temporary three-man groups. *Research Studies, State College of Washington, 22,* 130–140.

Torrey, E. F. (1988). Stalking the schizovirus. *Schizophrenia Bulletin, 14,* 223–229.

Travis, L. E. (1925). The effect of a small audience upon eye-hand coordination. *Journal of Abnormal and Social Psychology, 20,* 142–146.

Treisman, A. (1986, November). Features and objects in visual processing. *Scientific American,* pp. 114B–125B.

Treisman, A. (1998). Feature binding, attention and object perception. *Philosophical Transactions of the Royal Society of London, Series B, 353,* 1295–1306.

Treisman, A., & Gormican, S. (1988). Feature analysis in early vision: Evidence from search asymmetries. *Psychological Review, 95,* 15–48.

Triandis, H. C. (1995). *Individualism and collectivism.* Boulder, CO: Westview.

Trimble, M. R. (1996). *Biological psychiatry* (2nd ed.). New York: Wiley.

Trivers, R. L. (1971). The evolution of reciprocal altruism. *Quarterly Review of Biology, 46,* 35–57.

Trivers, R. L. (1972) Parental investment and sexual selection. In B. Campbell (Ed.), *Sexual selection and the descent of man.* Chicago: Aldine.

Tronick, E. Z., Morelli, G. A., & Ivey, P. K. (1992). The Efe forager infant and toddler's pattern of social relationships: Multiple and simultaneous. *Developmental Psychology, 28,* 568–577.

Troutt-Ervin, E. D. (1990). Application of keyword mnemonics to learning terminology in the college classroom. *Journal of Experimental Education, 59,* 31–41.

True, W. R., Rice, J., Eisen, S. A., Heath, A. C., Goldberg, J., Lyons, M. J., & Nowak, J. (1993). A twin study of genetic and environmental contributions to liability for posttraumatic stress symptoms. *Archives of General Psychiatry, 50,* 257–264.

Trut, L. N. (1999). Early canid domestication: The farm-fox experiment. *American Scientist, 87,* 160–169.

Tryon, R. C. (1942). Individual differences. In F. A. Moss (Ed.), *Comparative psychology* (Rev. ed.). New York: Prentice-Hall.

Tseng, W., Mo, K., Li, L., Chen, G., Ou, L., & Zheng, H. (1992). Koro epidemics in Guangdong, China. *Journal of Nervous and Mental Disorders, 180,* 117–123.

Tsien, J. Z. (2000, April). Building a brainier mouse. *Scientific American,* pp. 62–68.

Tsien, J. Z., Huerta, P. T., & Tonegawa, S. (1996). The essential role of hippocampal CA1 NMDA receptor-dependent synaptic plasticity in spatial memory. *Cell, 87,* 1327–1338.

Tulving, E. (1974). Recall and recognition of semantically encoded words. *Journal of Experimental Psychology, 102,* 778–787.

Tulving, E. (1985). How many memory systems are there? *American Psychologist, 40,* 385–398.

Tulving, E. (2000). Concepts of memory. In E. Tulving & F. I. M. Craik (Eds.), *The Oxford handbook of memory.* New York: Oxford University Press.

Tulving, E., & Schacter, D. L. (1990). Primary and human memory systems. *Science, 247,* 301–306.

Turkheimer, E., & Waldron, M. (2000). Nonshared environment: A theoretical, methodological, and quantitative review. *Psychological Bulletin, 126,* 78–108.

Turner, H. S., & Watson, T. S. (1999). Consultant's guide for the use of time-out in the preschool and elementary classroom. *Psychology in the Schools, 36,* 135–148.

Turner, M. E., & Horvitz, T. (2001). The dilemma of threat: Group effectiveness and ineffectiveness under adversity. In M. E. Turner (Ed.), *Groups at work: Theory and research.* Mahwah, NJ: Erlbaum.

Tversky, A., & Kahneman, D. (1973). Availability: A heuristic for judging frequency and probability. *Cognitive Psychology, 5,* 207–232.

Tversky, A., & Kahneman, D. (1974). Judgment under uncertainty: Heuristics and biases. *Science, 185,* 1124–1131.

Twenge, J. M. (2000). The age of anxiety? Birth cohort change in anxiety and neuroticism, 1952–1993. *Journal of Personality and Social Psychology, 79,* 1007–1021.

Tyler, C. W., & Clarke, M. B. (1990). The autostereogram. *Proceedings of the International Society for Optical Engineering, 1256,* 182–197.

Ujhelyi, M., Merker, B., Buk, P., & Geissmann, T. (2000). Observations on the behavior of Gibbons (*Hylobates leucogenys, H. gabriellae,* and *H. lar*) in the presence of mirrors. *Journal of Comparative Psychology, 114,* 253–262.

Umberson, D., Wortman, C. B., & Kessler, R. C. (1992). Widowhood and depression: Explaining long-term gender differences in vulnerability. *Journal of Health and Social Behavior, 33,* 10–24.

Ungerleider, L. G., & Haxby, J. V. (1994). "What" and "where" in the human brain. *Current Opinion in Neurobiology, 4,* 157–165.

Ungerleider, L. G., & Mishkin, M. (1982). Two cortical visual systems. In D. J. Ingle, M. A. Goodale, & R. J. W. Mansfield (Eds.), *Analysis of visual behavior.* Cambridge, MA: MIT Press.

Uttal, W. R. (1973). *The psychobiology of sensory coding.* New York: Harper & Row.

Vaidya, C. J., Gabrieli, J. D. E., Keane, M. M., & Monti, L. A. (1995). Perceptual and conceptual memory processes in global amnesia. *Neuropsychology, 9,* 580–591.

Vaillant, G. E. (1977). *Adaptation to life.* Boston: Little, Brown.

Vaillant, G. E. (1983). *The natural history of alcoholism.* Cambridge, MA: Harvard University Press.

Vaillant, G. (1995). *Adaptation to life* (2nd ed.). Cambridge, MA: Harvard University Press.

Vaillant, G. E., & Vaillant, C. O. (1992). Empirical evidence that defensive styles are independent of environmental influence. In G. E. Vaillant (Ed.), *Ego mechanisms of defense: A guide for clinicians and researchers.* Washington, DC: American Psychiatric Press.

Valenstein, E. S. (1973). *Brain control: A critical examination of brain stimulation and psychosurgery.* New York: Wiley.

Valenstein, E. S. (1986). *Great and desperate cures: The rise and decline of psychosurgery and other radical treatments for mental illness.* New York: Basic Books.

Valenstein, E. S. (Ed.) (1980). *The psychosurgery debate: Scientific, legal, and ethical perspectives.* San Francisco: Freeman.

Vance, E. B., & Wagner, N. N. (1976). Written descriptions of orgasm: A study of sex differences. *Archives of Sexual Behavior, 5,* 87–98.

van den Boom, D. C. (1991). The influence of infant irritability on the development of the mother-infant relationship in the first six months of life. In J. K. Nugent, M. M. Lester, & T. B. Brazelton (Eds.), *The cultural context of infancy* (Vol. 2). Norwood, NJ: Ablex.

van den Boom, D. C. (1994). The influence of temperament and mothering on attachment and exploration: An experimental manipulation of sensitive responsiveness among lower-class mothers with irritable infants. *Child Development, 65,* 1457–1477.

Van Essen, D. C., Anderson, C. H., & Felleman, D. J. (1992). Information processing in the primitive visual system: An integrated systems perspective. *Science, 255,* 419–423.

Van Heck, G. L., Perugini, M., Caprara, G., & Fröger, J. (1994). The big five as tendencies in situations. *Personality and Individual Differences, 16,* 715–731.

van Hooff, J. A. (1972). A comparative approach to the phylogeny of laughter and smiling. In R. A. Hinde (Ed.), *Nonverbal communication.* Cambridge, England: Cambridge University Press.

van Hooff, J. A. (1976). The comparison of facial expression in man and higher primates. In M. von Cranach (Ed.), *Methods of inference from animal to human behaviour.* Chicago: Aldine.

Van Itallie, T. B., & Kissileff, H. R. (1990). Human obesity: A problem in body energy economics. In E. M. Stricker (Ed.), *Handbook of behavioral neurobiology: Vol. 10. Neurobiology of food and fluid intake.* New York: Plenum Press.

Van Lange, P. A. M., & Visser, K. (1999). Locomotion in social dilemmas: How people adapt to cooperative, tit-for-tat, and noncooperative partners. *Journal of Personality and Social Psychology, 77,* 762–773.

Vargha-Khadem, F., Gadian, D. G., Watkins, K. E., Connelly, A., Van Paesschen, W., & Mishkin, M. (1997). Differential effects of early hippocampal pathology on episodic and semantic memory. *Science, 277,* 376–380.

Vaughan, D. (1986). *Uncoupling.* New York: Oxford University Press.

Vernon, P. A., Jang, K. L., Harris, J. A., & McCarthy, J. M. (1997). Environmental predictors of personality differences: A twin and sibling study. *Journal of Personality and Social Psychology, 72,* 177–183.

Vernon, P. A., & Kantor, L. (1986). Reaction time correlations with intelligence test scores obtained under either timed or untimed conditions. *Intelligence, 9,* 357–374.

Vernon, P. A., Wickett, J. C., Bazana, P. G., & Stelmack, R. M. (2000). The neuropsychology and psychophysiology of human intelligence. In R. J. Sternberg (Ed.), *Handbook of intelligence.* Cambridge, England: Cambridge University Press.

Vernon, P. E. (1961). *The structure of human abilities* (2nd ed.). London: Methuen.

Vinokur, A., & Burnstein, E. (1974). Effects of partially shared persuasive arguments on group-induced shifts: A group problem-solving approach. *Journal of Personality and Social Psychology, 29,* 305–315.

Volkova, V. D. (1953). On certain characteristics of the formation of conditioned reflexes to speech stimuli in children. *Fiziologicheskii Zhurnal USSR, 39,* 540–548.

Voss, J. F., & Post, T. A. (1988). On the solving of ill-structured problems. In M. T. H. Chi, R. Glaser, & M. J. Farr (Eds.), *The nature of expertise.* Hillsdale, NJ: Erlbaum.

Vygotsky, L. S. (1933; reprinted 1978). Play and its role in the mental development of the child. In M. Cole, V. John-Steiner, S. Scribner, & E. Sourberman (Eds.), *Mind and society.* Cambridge, MA: Harvard University Press.

Vygotsky, L. S. (1934; reprinted 1962). *Thought and language* (E. Haufmann & G. Vaker, Eds. & Trans.). Cambridge, MA: MIT Press.

Vygotsky, L. S. (1935; reprinted 1978). Interaction between learning and development. In M. Cole, V. John-Steiner, S. Scribner, & E. Souberman (Eds.), *Mind in society: The development of higher psychological processes.* Cambridge, MA: Harvard University Press.

Wade, N. J., & Swanston, M. (1991). *Visual perception: An introduction.* London: Routledge.

Wahl, O. F. (1976). Monozygotic twins discordant for schizophrenia: A review. *Psychological Bulletin, 83,* 91–106.

Wahlberg, K., Wynne, L. C., Oja, H., Keskitalo, P., Pykäläinen, L., Lahti, I., Moring, J., Naarala, M., Sorri, A., Seitamaa, M., Läksy, K., Kolassa, J., & Tienari, P. (1997). Gene-environment interaction in vulnerability to schizophrenia: Findings from the Finnish adoptive family study of schizophrenia. *American Journal of Psychiatry, 154,* 355–362.

Wahlsten, D. (1999). Single-gene influences on brain and behavior. *Annual Review of Psychology, 50,* 599–624.

Wakefield, J. C. (1992). Disorder as harmful dysfunction: A conceptual critique of *DSM-III-R*'s definition of mental disorder. *Psychological Review, 99,* 232–247.

Walach, H., & Maidhof, C. (1999). Is the placebo effect dependent on time? A meta-analysis. In I. Kirsch (Ed.), *How expectancies shape experience.* Washington, DC: American Psychological Associaiton.

Walden, T. A. (1991). Infant social referencing. In J. Garber & K. A. Dodge (Eds.), *The development of emotion regulation and dysregulation.* Cambridge, England: Cambridge University Press.

Walker, E. F., Grimes, K. E., Davis, D. M., & Smith, A. J. (1993). Childhood precursors of schizophrenia: Facial expressions of emotion. *American Journal of Psychiatry, 150,* 1654–1660.

Walker, E. F., Savoie, T., & Davis, D. (1994). Neuromotor precursors of schizophrenia. *Schizophrenia Bulletin, 20,* 441–451.

Wallace, P. (1977). Individual discrimination of humans by odor. *Physiology and Behavior, 19,* 577–579.

Wallach, H. (1948). Brightness constancy and the nature of achromatic colors. *Journal of Experimental Psychology, 38,* 310–324.

Wallen, K. (1990). Desire and ability: Hormones and the regulation of female sexual behavior. *Neuroscience and Biobehavioral Reviews, 14,* 233–241.

Wallerstein, R. S. (1989). The psychotherapy research project of the Menninger Foundation: An overview. *Journal of Consulting and Clinical Psychology, 57,* 195–205.

Wampold, B. E., Mondin, G. W., Moody, M., Stich, F., Bensen, K., & Ahn, H. N. (1997). A meta-analysis of outcome studies comparing bona fide psychotherapies: Empirically, "all must have prizes." *Psychotherapy Bulletin, 122,* 203–215.

Ward, I. L. (1992). Sexual behavior: The product of perinatal hormonal and prepubertal social factors. In A. A. Gerall, H. Moltz, & I. L. Ward (Eds.), *Handbook of behavioral neurobiology: Vol. 11. Sexual differentiation,* New York: Plenum Press.

Ward, I. L., Bennett, A. L., Ward, O. B., Hendricks, S. E., & French, J. A. (1999). Androgen threshold to activate copulation differs in male rats prenatally exposed to alcohol, stress, or both factors. *Hormones and Behavior, 36,* 129–140.

Warner, R. (1985). *Recovery from schizophrenia*. London: Routledge & Kegan Paul.

Warr, P. (1992). Age and occupational well-being. *Psychology and Aging, 7*, 37–45.

Warren, R. M. (1970). Perceptual restoration of missing speech sounds. *Science, 167*, 392–393.

Warren, R. M. (1984). Perceptual restoration of obliterated sounds. *Psychological Bulletin, 96*, 371–383.

Wason, P. C. (1960). On the failure to eliminate hypotheses in a conceptual task. *Quarterly Journal of Experimental Psychology, 12*, 129–140.

Wasserman, E. A. (1995). The conceptual abilities of pigeons. *American Scientist, 83*, 246–255.

Waters, E., Hamilton, C. E., & Weinfield, N. S. (2000). The stability of attachment security from infancy to adolescence and early adulthood: General introduction. *Child Development, 71*, 678–683.

Watkins, L. R., & Maier, S. F. (2000). The pain of being sick: Implications of immune-to-brain communication for understanding pain. *Annual Reviews of Psychology, 51*, 29–57.

Watson, J. B. (1913). Psychology as the behaviorist views it. *Psychological Review, 20*, 158–177.

Watson, J. B. (1924). *Behaviorism*. Chicago: University of Chicago Press.

Watson, J. B. (1936). John Broadus Watson. In C. Murchison (Ed.), *A history of psychology in autobiography* (Vol. 3). New York: Russell & Russell.

Watson, J. S. (1972). Smiling, cooing, and "the game." *Merrill-Palmer Quarterly, 18*, 323–339.

Watt, R. J. (1988). *Visual processing: Computational psychophysical, and cognitive research*. Hillsdale, NJ: Erlbaum.

Waugh, N. C., & Norman, D. A. (1965). Primary memory. *Psychological Review, 72*, 89–104.

Waxman, S. R., & Markow, D. B. (1995). Words as invitations to form categories: Evidence from 12- to 13-month-old infants. *Cognitive Psychology, 29*, 257–302.

Webb, W. B. (1982). Some theories about sleep and their clinical implications. *Psychiatric Annals, 11*, 415–422.

Weber, E. H. (1834). *De pulen, resorptione, auditu et tactu: Annotationes anatomicae et physiologicae*. Leipzig: Koehler.

Wedekind, C., & Füri, S. (1997). Body odour preferences in men and women: Do they aim for specific MHC combinations or simply heterozygosity? *Proceedings of the Royal Society of London, Series B, 264*, 1471–1479.

Wedekind, C., & Milinski, M. (2000). Cooperating through image scoring in humans. *Science, 288*, 850–852.

Wedekind, C., Seebeck, T., Bettens, F., & Paepke, A. J. (1995). MHC-dependent mate preference in humans. *Proceedings of the Royal Society of London, Series B, 260*, 245–249.

Weinberg, M. K., Tronick, E. Z., Cohn, J. F., & Olson, K. L. (1999). Gender differences in emotional expressivity and self-regulation during early infancy. *Developmental Psychology, 35*, 175–188.

Weinberger, D. R. (1995). Schizophrenia: From neuropathology to neurodevelopment. *Nature, 346*, 552–557.

Weiner, J. (1994). *The beak of the finch: A story of evolution in our time*. New York: Knopf.

Weiner, R. D., & Coffey, C. E. (1988). Indications for use of electroconvulsive therapy. In A. J. Frances & R. E. Hales (Eds.), *Review of Psychiatry* (Vol. 7). Washington, DC: American Psychiatric Press.

Weinstein, N. D. (1980). Unrealistic optimism about future events. *Journal of Personality and Social Psychology, 39*, 806–820.

Weinstein, N. D. (1982). Unrealistic optimism about susceptibility to health problems. *Journal of Behavioral Medicine, 5*, 441–460.

Weiskrantz, L. (1956). Behavioral changes associated with ablation of the amygdaloid complex in monkeys. *Journal of Comparative Physiology and Psychology, 49*, 381–391.

Weisman, A. (1997). Understanding cross-cultural prognostic variability in schizophrenia. *Cultural Diversity and Mental Health, 3*, 3–35.

Weiss, R. S. (1975). *Marital separation*. New York: Basic Books.

Welch, D. C., & West, R. L. (1995). Self-efficacy and mastery: Its application to issues of environmental control, cognition, and aging. *Developmental Review, 15*, 150–171.

Welsh, M. C., Bennington, B. F., Ozonoff, S., Rouse, B., & McCabe, E. R. B. (1990). *Child Development, 61*, 1697–1713.

Werker, J. F., & Desjardins, R. N. (1995). Listening to speech in the 1st year of life: Experiential influences on phoneme perception. *Current Directions in Psychological Science, 4*, 76–81.

Werker, J. F., & Tees, R. C. (1992). The organization and reorganization of human speech perception. *Annual Review of Neuroscience, 15*, 377–402.

Werker, J. F., & Tees, R. C. (1999). Influences on infant speech processing: Toward a new synthesis. *Annual Review of Psychology, 50*, 509–535.

Werker, J. J., Gilbert, J. H. V., Humphrey, K., & Tees, R. C. (1981). Developmental aspects of cross-language speech perception. *Child Development, 52*, 349–355.

Wertheimer, M. (1912; reprinted 1965). Experimentelle Studien über das Sehen von Bewegung (M. D. Boring, Trans.). In R. J. Herrnstein & E. G. Boring (Eds.), *A source book in the history of psychology*. Cambridge, MA: Harvard University Press.

Wertheimer, M. (1923; reprinted 1938). Principles of perceptual organization. In W. D. Ellis (Ed. & Trans.), *A source-book of Gestalt psychology*. New York: Harcourt Brace.

West D. J. (1977). *Homosexuality re-examined*. Minneapolis: University of Minnesota Press.

West S. G. (1975). Increasing the attractiveness of college cafeteria food: A reactance theory perspective. *Journal of Applied Psychology, 60*, 656–658.

Westen, D. (1998). The scientific legacy of Sigmund Freud: Toward a psychodynamically informed psychological science. *Psychological Bulletin, 124*, 333–371.

Whalen, P. J. (1998). Fear, vigilance, and ambiguity: Initial neuroimaging studies of the human amygdala. *Current Directions in Psychological Science, 7*, 177–188.

Wheeler, M. A. (2000). Episodic memory and autonoetic awareness. In E. Tulving & F. I. M. Craik (Eds.), *The Oxford handbook of memory*. New York: Oxford University Press.

Wheeler, M. A., Stuss, D. T., & Tulving, E. (1997). Toward a theory of episodic memory: The frontal lobes and autonoetic consciousness. *Psychological Bulletin, 121*, 331–354.

Whiten, A. (1998). Imitation of the sequential structure of actions by chimpanzees (*Pan troglodytes*). *Journal of Comparative Psychology, 112,* 270–281.

Whiten, A., Goodall, J., McGrew, W. C., Nishida, T., Reynolds, V., Sugiyama, Y., Tutin, C. E. G., Wrangham, R. W., & Boesch, C. (1999). Culture in chimpanzees. *Nature, 399,* 682–685.

Whiting, B. B., & Edwards, C. P. (1988). *Children of different worlds: The formation of social behavior.* Cambridge, MA: Harvard University Press.

Whiting, J. W. M. (1971). *Causes and consequences of the amount of body contact between mother and infant.* Paper read at the annual meetings of the American Anthropological Association, New York.

Whorf, B. (1956). *Language, thought, and reality.* New York: Wiley.

Wickens, D. D. (1972). Characteristics of word encoding. In A. W. Melton & E. Martin (Eds.), *Coding processes in human memory.* Washington, DC: Winston & Sons.

Wicklund, R. A., & Frey, D. (1980). Self-awareness theory: When the self makes a difference. In D. M. Wegner & R. R. Vallacher (Eds.), *The self in social psychology.* New York: Oxford University Press.

Widiger, T. A. (1997a). The construct of mental disorder. *Clinical Psychology: Science and Practice, 4,* 262–266.

Widiger, T. A. (1997b). Mental disorders as discrete clinical conditions: Dimensional versus categorical classification. In S. M. Turner & M. Hersen (Eds.), *Adult psychopathology and diagnosis* (3rd ed.). New York: Wiley.

Widiger, T. A., & Sankis, L. M. (2000). Adult psychopathology: Issues and controversies. *Annual Review of Psychology, 51,* 377–404.

Wiessner, P. (1982). Risk, reciprocity and social influences on !Kung San economics. In E. Leacock & R. Lee (Eds.), *Politics and history in band societies.* Cambridge, England: Cambridge University Press.

Wigdor, A. K., & Green, B. F. (1991). *Performance assessment in the workplace.* Washington, DC: National Academy Press.

Wiley, M. G., Crittenden, K. S., & Birg, L. D. (1979). Why a rejection? Causal attributions of a career achievement event. *Social Psychology Quarterly, 42,* 214–222.

Wilkins, L., & Richter, C. P. (1940). A great craving for salt by a child with cortico-adrenal insufficiency. *JAMA, Journal of the American Medical Association, 114,* 866–868.

Wilkinson, G. S. (1988). Reciprocal altruism in bats and other mammals. *Ethology and Sociobiology, 9,* 85–100.

Willatts, P. (1999). Development of means-end behavior in young infants: Pulling a support to retrieve a distant object. *Developmental Psychology, 35,* 651–667.

Williams, G. C., & Deci, E. L. (1996). Internalization of biopsychosocial values by medical students: A test of self-determination theory. *Journal of Personality and Social Psychology, 70,* 767–779.

Williams, G. C., Grow, V. M., Freedman, Z. R., Ryan, R. M., & Deci, E. L. (1996). Motivational predictors of weight loss and weight-loss maintenance. *Journal of Personality and Social Psychology, 70,* 115–126.

Williams, G. C., Rodin, G. C., Ryan, R. M., Grolnick, W. S., & Deci, E. L. (1995). Compliance or autonomous regulation: New insights about adherence to medical regimens. *Journal of General Internal Medicine, Supplement, 10*(4), 116.

Williams, J. E., & Best, D. L. (1990). *Measuring sex stereotypes: a multination study, revised edition.* Newbury Park, CA: Sage.

Wilson, D. S. (1994). Adaptive genetic variation and human evolutionary psychology. *Ethology and Sociobiology, 15,* 219–235.

Wilson, D. S. (1998). Adaptive individual differences within single populations. *Philosophical Transactions of the Royal Society of London, 353,* 199–205.

Wilson, D. S., Coleman, K., Clark, A. B., & Biederman, L. (1993). Shy-bold continuum in pumpkinseed sunfish (*Lepomis gibbosus*): An ecological study of a psychological trait. *Journal of Comparative Psychology, 70,* 250–260.

Wilson, M. (1993). *DSM-III* and the transformation of American psychiatry: A history. *American Journal of Psychiatry, 150,* 399–410.

Wilson, M., & Daly, M. (1985). Competitiveness, risk taking, and violence: The young male syndrome. *Ethology and Sociobiology, 6,* 59–73.

Wimer, R. E., & Wimer, C. C. (1985). Animal behavior genetics: A search for the biological foundations of behavior. *Annual Review of Psychology, 36,* 171–218.

Wimmer, H., & Perner, J. (1983). Beliefs about beliefs: Representation and constraining function of wrong beliefs in young children's understanding of deception. *Cognition, 13,* 103–128.

Wing, L., Gould, J., Yeates, S. R., & Brierley, L. (1977). Symbolic play in severely mentally retarded and in autistic children. *Journal of Child Psychology and Psychiatry, 18,* 167–178.

Winklegren, I. (1992). How the brain "sees" borders where there are none. *Science, 256,* 1520–1521.

Winn, P. (1995). The lateral hypothalamus and motivated behavior: An old syndrome reassessed and a new perspective gained. *Current Directions in Psychological Science, 4,* 182–187.

Wise, R. A. (1996). Addictive drugs and brain stimulation reward. *Annual Review of Neuroscience, 19,* 319–340.

Wise, R. A., & Rompre, P. (1989). Brain dopamine and reward. *Annual Review of Psychology, 40,* 191–225.

Wise, R. A., Spindler, J., & Legault, L. (1978). Major attenuation of food reward with performance-sparing doses of pimozide in the rat. *Canadian Journal of Psychology, 32,* 77–85.

Wishart, J. G., & Bower, T. G. R. (1984). Spatial relations and the object concept: A normative study. In L. P. Lipsitt & C. Rovee-Collier (Eds.), *Advances in infancy research* (Vol. 3). Norwood, NJ: Ablex.

Wit, A. P., & Wilke, H. A. M. (1992). The effect of social categorization on cooperation in three types of social dilemmas. *Journal of Economic Psychology, 13,* 135–151.

Witty, P. A., & Jenkins, M. D. (1935). Intra-race testing and Negro intelligence. *Journal of Psychology, 1,* 179–192.

Wolf, A., & Kutash, I. L. (1990). Psychoanalysis in groups. In I. L. Kutash & A. Wolf (Eds.), *The group psychotherapist's handbook: Contemporary theory and technique.* New York: Columbia University Press.

Wolf, A. W., & Lozoff, B. (1989). Object attachment, thumbsucking, and passage to sleep. *Journal of the American Academy of Child and Adolescent Psychiatry, 28,* 287–292.

Wolfe, J. B. (1936). Effectiveness of token-rewards for chimpanzees. *Comparative Psychology Monographs, 12* (Whole No. 60).

Wolpe, J. (1958). *Psychotherapy by reciprocal inhibition.* Stanford, CA: Stanford University Press.

Wood, D. M., & Emmett-Oglesby, M. W. (1989). Mediation in the nucleus accumbens of the discriminative stimulus produced by cocaine. *Pharmacology, Biochemistry, and Behavior, 33,* 453–457.

Wood, J. M., Nezworski, T., & Stejskal, W. J. (1996). The comprehensive system for the Rorschach: A critical examination. *Psychological Science, 7,* 3–17.

Woods, S. C., Schwartz, M. W., Baskin, D. G., & Seeley, R. J. (2000). Food intake and the regulation of body weight. *Annual Review of Psychology, 51,* 255–277.

Woods, S. C., Seeley, R. J., Porte, D., & Schwartz, M. W. (1998). Signals that regulate food intake and energy homeostasis. *Science, 280,* 1378–1387.

Woolf, C. J., & Salter, M. W. (2000). Neuronal plasticity: Increasing the gain in pain. *Science, 288,* 1765–1768.

Woolley, J. D. (1995). Young children's understanding of fictional versus epistemic mental representations: Imagination and belief. *Child Development, 66,* 1011–1021.

Wrangham, R. W. (1993). The evolution of sexuality in chimpanzees and bonobos. *Human Nature, 4,* 47–79.

Wright, H. F. (1937). *The influence of barriers upon strength of motivation.* Durham, NC: Duke University Press.

Wright, P., Donaldson, P. T., Underhill, J. A., Choudhuri, K., Doherty, D. G., & Murray, R. M. (1996). Genetic association of the HLA DRB1 gene locus on chromosome 6p21.3 with schizophrenia. *American Journal of Psychiatry, 153,* 1530–1533.

Wulff, S. B. (1985). The symbolic and object play of children with autism: A review. *Journal of Autism and Developmental Disorders, 15,* 139–148.

Wyrwicka, W. (1996). *Imitation in human and animal behavior.* New Brunswick, NJ: Transaction Books.

Yalcinkaya, T. M., Siiteri, P. K., Vigne, J., Licht, P., Pavgi, S., Frank, L. G., & Glickman, S. E. (1993). A mechanism for virilization of female spotted hyenas in utero. *Science, 260,* 1929–1931.

Yamazaki, K., Beauchamp, G. K., Fung-Win, S., Bard, J., & Boyse, E. A. (1994). Discrimination of odor types determined by the major histocompatibility complex among outbred mice. *Proceedings of the National Academy of Sciences, USA, 91,* 3735–3738.

Yamazaki, K., Beauchamp, G. K., Kupniewski, D., Bard, J., Thomas, L., & Boyse, E. A. (1988). Familial imprinting determines H-2 selective mating preferences. *Science, 240,* 1331–1332.

Yerkes, R. M., & Dodson, J. D. (1908). The relation of strength of stimulus to rapidity of habit-formation. *Journal of Comparative and Neurological Psychology, 18,* 459–482.

Yirmiya, N., Solomonica-Levi, D., & Shulman, C. (1996). The ability to manipulate behavior and to understand manipulation of beliefs: A comparison of individuals with autism, mental retardation, and normal development. *Developmental Psychology, 32,* 62–69.

Yoshihara, T., Honma, S., & Honma, K. (1996). Effects of restricted daily feeding on neuropeptide Y release in the rat paraventricular nucleus. *American Journal of Physiology, 270,* E596–560.

Young, S. K., Fox, N. A., & Zahn-Waxler, C. (1999). The relations between temperament and empathy in 2-year-olds. *Developmental Psychology, 35,* 1189–1197.

Zacharias, I., & Wurtman, R. J. (1969). Age at menarche: Genetic and environmental influences. *New England Journal of Medicine, 280,* 868–875.

Zahn-Waxler, C., & Radke-Yarrow, M. (1990). The origins of empathic concern. *Motivation and Emotion, 14,* 107–130.

Zahn-Waxler, C., Radke-Yarrow, M., Wagner, E., & Chapman, M. (1992). Development of concern for others. *Developmental Psychology, 28,* 126–136.

Zajonc, R. B. (1965). Social facilitation. *Science, 149,* 269–274.

Zajonc, R. B. (1980). Compresence. In P. B. Paulus (Ed.), *Psychology of group influence.* Hillsdale, NJ: Erlbaum.

Zajonc, R. B., Murphy, S. T., & Inglehart, M. (1989). Feeling and facial efference: Implications of the vascular theory of emotion. *Psychological Review, 96,* 395–416.

Zaragoza, M. S. & Mitchell, K. J. (1996). Repeated exposure to suggestion and the creation of false memories. *Psychological Science, 7,* 294–300.

Zebrowitz, L. A. (1996). Physical appearance as a basis of stereotyping. In C.N. Macrae, C. Stangor, & M. Hewstone (Eds.), *Stereotypes and stereotyping.* New York: Guilford Press.

Zebrowitz, L. A., Andreoletti, C., Collins, M. A., Lee, S. Y., & Blumenthal, J. (1998). Bright, bad, babyfaced boys: Appearance stereotypes do not always yield self-fulfilling prophecy effects. *Journal of Personality and Social Psychology, 75,* 1300–1320.

Zebrowitz, L. A., & McDonald, S. M. (1991). The impact of litigants' baby-facedness and attractiveness on adjudications in small claims courts. *Law and Human Behavior, 15,* 603–623.

Zebrowitz, L. A., Montepare, J. M., & Lee, H. K. (1993). They don't all look alike: Differentiating same vs. other race individuals. *Journal of Personality and Social Psychology, 65,* 85–101.

Zeifman, D., & Hazen, C. (1997). Attachment: The bond in pair-bonds. In J. A. Simpson & D. T. Kenrick (Eds.), *Evolutionary social psychology.* Mahwah, NJ: Erlbaum.

Zentall, T. R. (2000). Symbolic representation by pigeons. *Current Directions in Psychological Science, 9,* 118–123.

Zhao, H., & Santos-Sacchi, J. (1999). Auditory collusion and a coupled couple of outer hair cells. *Nature, 399,* 359–362.

Zinbarg, R. E., Barlow, D. H., Brown, T. A., & Hertz, R. M. (1992). Cognitive-behavioral approaches to the nature and treatment of anxiety disorders. *Annual Review of Psychology, 43,* 235–267.

Zucker, R. A., & Gomberg, E. S. L. (1986). Etiology of alcoholism reconsidered: The case for a biopsychosocial process. *American Psychologist, 41,* 783–793.

Zuckerman, M. (1994). *Behavioral expressions and biosocial bases of sensations seeking.* New York: Cambridge University Press.

Zuckerman, M., Eysenck, S., & Eysenck, M. (1978). Sensation seeking in England and America: Cross-cultural, age, and sex comparison. *Journal of Consulting and Clinical Psychology, 70,* 371–377.

Zwislocki, J. J. (1981). Sound analysis in the ear: A history of discoveries. *American Scientist, 69,* 184–192.

Illustration Credits

Front Matter

p. vi (author photo) Scott Finer, Finer Photography. (The part opener images depicted in the table of contents are credited with the part openers below.)

Part Openers

1 Giorgio De Chirico, *Anxiety of Waiting*, Scala / Art Resource NY **p. viii, facing p. 1**
2 Marc Chagall. *Pont Marie*. © 1998 Artists Rights Society (ARS), New York/ADAGP, Paris. Photo © Christie's Images. **pp. viii, 50**
3 Jean Dubuffet, *Visage macule de rouge*. 1954. © Art Resource NY **pp. ix, 140**
4 Robert Delaunay, *Ménage de Cochon (Ménage Electrique)*. Musée d'Art Moderne / Centre Pompidou, Paris / Art Resource NY **pp. x, 230**
5 Jacob Lawrence, *The Library* (detail). 1960. National Museum of American Art, Washington, DC. Photo Art Resource. **pp. x, 322**
6 Zinadia Serebriakova. *The House of Cards* (detail). Russian State Museum, St. Petersburg. © 1998 Artists Rights Society (ARS), New York / ADAGP, Paris. Photo © Scala / Art Resource, NY. **pp. xi, 406**
7 Philome Obin, *Le Marché de Limbe*. Christie's Images. **pp. xii, 494**
8 Joan Miro, *L'Epouvante de L'Oiseau Porte-Malheur*. 1965. © Art Resource NY **pp. xii, 570**

Chapter 1

Opener (p. 2) Juan Gris, *The Book*. 1913. © Giraudon / Art Resource NY; **Fig. 1.2** Descartes, R. (1972). *Treatise of Man*. Cambridge, MA: Harvard University Press; **p. 23 (top)**. Adapted from Rose, S. (1973). *The conscious brain*. New York: Alfred A. Knopf, Inc. Copyright by Stephen Rose. Reprinted by permission of Alfred A. Knopf, Inc.

Chapter 2

Opener (p. 28) Wassily Kandinsky. *4 × 5 = 20*. Photo © Christie's Images; **p. 30 (top)** Pfungst, O. (1965). *Clever horse: The horse of Mr. Von Osten*. New York: Holt, Rinehart & Winston; **Fig. 2.2** Di Mascio, A., et al. (1979). Differential symptom reduction by drugs and psychotherapy in acute depression. *Archives of General Psychiatry, 36*, 1453. Copyright © 1979, American Medical Association; **p. 45** Enrico Ferorelli.

Chapter 3

Opener (p. 52) Franz Marc, *The Monkey*. 1911. Frieze, oil on canvas. SuperStock; **Fig. 3.2** Pueschel, S. M., & Goldstein, A. (1983). Genetic counseling. In J. L. Maton & J. A. Mulick (Eds.), *Handbook of Mental Retardation*. London: Pergamon Press PLC. Reprinted with permission; **Fig. 3.6 (left and right)** Scott, J. P. & Fuller, J. L. (1965). *Genetic and social behavior of the dog*. Chicago: University of Chicago Press; **Fig. 3.8** Hay, D. (1985). *Essentials of genetics*. Boston: Blackwell Scientific Publications; **p. 64 (bottom)** L. N. Trut (1999). *American Scientist*; **Fig. 3.13** Tinbergen, N. (1951). *The study of instinct*. Oxford: Oxford University Press. Copyright © by N. Tinbergen; **Fig. 3.14** Ekman, P. & Friesen, W. (1975). *Unmasking the face*. Englewood Cliffs, NJ: Prentice Hall; **Fig. 3.15** Eibl-Eibesfeldt, I. (1989). *Human ethology*. Hawthorne, NY: Walter de Gruyter, Inc.; **Fig. 3.16** Eibl-Eibesfeldt, I. (1975). *Human ethology*. Hawthorne, NY: Holt, Rinehart & Winston; **Fig. 3.17** Eibl-Eibesfeldt, I. (1961, December). The fighting behavior of animals. *Scientific American, 205*, 7. Copyright 1961 by Scientific American, Inc. All rights reserved; **Fig. 3.19** Lorenz, K. (1974). Analogy as a source of knowledge. *Science, 185*, 229–234. Copyright © 1974 The Nobel Foundation; **Fig. 3.22** Eibl-Eibesfeldt, I. (1975). *Human ethology*. Hawthorne, NY: Holt, Rinehart & Wintson; **p. 83** *Natural History*, August 1995, p. 57. Photo by Tom Vezo; **p. 84** *Natural History*, November 1994, p. 60. Photo by C. Allan Morgan.

Chapter 4

Opener (p. 96) François-Edouard Picot, *Le duc de Bordeaux chez la duchesse d'Angoulême à Villeneuve l'Etang*. 1826. © Giraudon / Art Resource NY; **Fig. 4.4** Pavlov, I. P. (1927/1960) *Conditioned reflexes*. New York: Dover; **Figs. 4.5 and 4.6** Thorndike, E. L. (1898). Animal intelligence: An experimental study of the associate processes in animals. *The Psychological Review Monograph Supplements, 2*, 4–160; **Fig. 4.15** Dickinson, A., & Dawson, G. R. (1987). The role of the instrumental contingency in motivational control of performance. *Quarterly Journal of Experimental Psychology, 39B*, 77–93. Reproduced with permission. Copyright © 1987 by the Experimental Psychology Society and Lawrence Erlbaum Associates Ltd, Hove, UK; **Fig. 4.16** Tolman, E. C., & Honzik, C. H. (1930). "Insight" in rats. *University of California Publications in Psychology, 4*, 215–232; **Fig. 4.17** Tolman, E. C., & Honzik, C. H. (1930). Introduction and removal of reward and maze performance in rats. *University of California Publications in Psychology, 4*, 267; **p. 128** Tetsuro Matsuzawa, Primate Institute, Kyoto University. From Matsuzawa, T. (1994). Field experiments on use of stone tools in the wild. In R. Wraugham, F. de Waal, and P. Heltne (Eds.), *Chimpanzee cultures* (pp. 351–370). Cambridge, MA: Harvard University Press; **p. 132** James Balog.

Chapter 5

Opener (p. 142) Andy Warhol, *Yarn*. 1983. © The Andy Warhol Foundation for the Visual Arts / Art Resource NY; **Figs. 5.7 and 5.8** Illustrations by David Macaulay from *The amazing brain* by Robert Ornstein and Richard Thompson. Illustrations copyright © 1984 by David A. Macaulay. Reprinted by permission of Houghton Mifflin Co. All rights reserved; **Fig 5.10** From *The conscious brain* by Steven Rose. Copyright © 1973 by Steven Rose. Reprinted by permission of Alfred A. Knopf, Inc.; **Fig. 5.11** Reprinted with the permission of Macmillan College Publishing Company from *The cerebral cortex of man* by Wilder Penfield and Theodore Rasmussen. Copyright © 1950 Macmillan College Publishing Company, copyright renewed © 1978 Theodore Rasmussen; **Fig. 5.12** Ghez, C. (1985). Voluntary movement. In E. R. Kandel & J. H. Schwartz (Eds.), *Principles of Neural Science* (3rd ed.). Norwalk, CT: Appleton & Lange; **Fig. 5.16** Gazzaniga, M. S. (1967, August). The split brain in man. *Scientific American*, 24–27. Copyright © 1967 by Scientific American, Inc. All rights reserved; **Fig. 5.19** Washington University; **Fig. 5.20** Adapted from John Koester. (1991). Membrane potential. In *Principles of neural science* (3rd ed., p. 85). New York: Elsevier.

Chapter 6

Opener (p. 188) Joaquin Sorolla y Bastida, *Boy with Grapes*, Museo Sorolla / Art Resource NY; **Fig. 6.2** Courtesy Bart Hoebel, Department of Psychology, Princeton University; **Fig. 6.8** Barnett, S. A. (1975). *The study of rat behavior* (rev. ed.). Chicago: University of Chicago Press; **Fig. 6.9** McClintock, M. K., & Herdt, G. (1996). Rethinking puberty: The development of sexual attraction. *Current Directions in Psychological Science, 2*, 181. Copyright © 1996 American Psychological Society. Reproduced by permission; **Fig. 6.11** Rosenzweig, Leihman, & Breedlov. *Biological Psychology*, 1996; **Fig. 6.12** Olds, J. (1956, October). Pleasure centers in the brain. *Scientific American*, 112; **Figs. 6.14 and 6.15** Snyder, F., & Scott, J. (1972). The psychophysiology of sleep. In N. S. Greenfield & R. A. Sternbach (Eds.), *Handbook of psychophysiology*. New York: Holt, Rinehart & Winston. Copyright © 1972 by Holt, Rinehart & Winston, Inc., reproduced by permission of the publisher; **Fig. 6.16** Shapiro, C. M., et al. (1981). Slow-wave sleep: A recovery period after exercise. *Science, 214*, 1252–1254. Copyright © 1981 by the AAAS; **Fig. 6.17** Aschoff, J. (1973). Desynchronization and resynchronization of human circadian rhythms. *Aerospace Medicine, 40*, 844–849; **Fig. 6.19** Askerstedt, T., & Fröberg, J. E. (1977). Psychophysiological circadian rhythms in women during 72 hours of sleep deprivation. *Waking and Sleeping, 1*, 387–394; **Fig. 6.20** Snyder, F., & Scott, J. (1972). The psychophysiology of sleep. In N. S. Greenfield & R. A. Sternbach (Eds.), *Handbook of psychophysiology*. New York: Holt, Rinehart & Winston. Copyright © 1972 by Holt, Rinehart & Winston, Inc., reproduced by permission of the publisher; **Fig. 6.27** Ekman, P., et al. (1983). Autonomic nervous system activity distinguishes among emotions. *Science, 221*, 1208–1210. Copyright © 1983 by the AAAS.

Chapter 7

Opener (p. 232) Hieronymus Bosch, *The Concert in the Egg*, Giraudon / Art Resource NY; **Fig. 7.1** Uttal, W. R. (1973). *The psychobiology of sensory coding*. New York: Harper & Row; **Fig. 7.3** Nowlis, G. H., & Frank, M. (1977). Qualities in hamster taste: Behavioral and neural evidence. In J. LeMagnen & P. MacLeod (Eds.), *Olfaction and taste* (Vol. 6). Washington, DC: Information Retrieval. By copyright permission of the Rockfeller University Press; **Fig. 7.11** Klinke, R. (1986). Physiology of hearing. In R. F. Schmidt (Ed.), *Fundamentals of sensory physiology*. New York: Springer-Verlag; **Fig. Fig. 7.15** Scharf, B. (1964). Partial masking. *Acustica*, 14, 16-23; **7.16** Robert S. Preston. Courtesy of J. E. Hawkins, Kresge Hearing Research Institute, University of Michigan Medical School; **Fig. 7.21** Stevens, S. S. (1962). The surprising simplicity of sensory metrics. *American Psychologist*, 17, 29–39. Copyright © 1962 by the American Psychological Association. Reprinted by permission.

Chapter 8

Opener (p. 274) Egyptian house facade with magic eye, painted wood. © Borromeo / Art Resource NY; **Fig. 8.3** Lindsay, P. H., & Norman, D. A. (1977). *Human information processing* (2nd ed.). New York: Harcourt Brace Jovanovich; **Fig. 8.5** Grusser, O. J., & Grusser-Cornehls, U. (1986). Physiology of vision. In R. F. Schmidt (Ed.), *Fundamentals of sensory physiology*. New York: Springer-Verlag; **Fig. 8.12** Bowmaker, J. K., & Dartnall, H. J. A. (1980). Visual pigments of rods and cones in a human retina. *Journal of Physiology*, 298, 501–511; **Fig. 8.15** Matlin, M. W. (1988). *Sensation and perception* (2nd ed.). Boston: Allyn & Bacon. Copyright © 1988 by Allyn and Bacon. Adapted by permission; **Fig. 8.16** De Valois, K. (1988). *Spatial vision*. New York: Oxford University Press; **Fig. 8.28** Rubin, E. E. (1915/1958). *Synoplevede figurer*. Copenhagen: Gyldendalske. Abridged trans. by M. Wertheimer in C. C. Bearslee & M. Wertheimer (Eds.), *Reading in perception*. Princeton, NJ: Van Nostrand; **Fig. 8.29** From Kanizsa, G. (1976). Subjective contours. *Scientific American*, 234, 48. Copyright © 1976 by Scientific American, Inc. All rights reserved; **Figs. 8.31 and 8.32** Biederman, I. (1985). Recognition-by-components: A theory of human image understanding. In *Computer vision, graphics, and image processing* (Vol. 32), pp. 29–73; **Fig. 8.33** From *Exploration in cognition* by Donald A. Norman and David E. Rumelhart. Copyright © 1975 by W. H. Freeman and Company. Reprinted with permission; **Fig. 8.34** Michaels, C. F., & Carello, C. (1981). *Direct perception*. Englewood Cliffs, NJ: Prentice Hall. Copyright © 1981. Reprinted by permission of Prentice Hall, Inc.; **Fig. 8.36** Rock, I. (1995). *Perception*. New York: Scientific American Books. Reproduced by permission. **p. 312 (top)** Alan Reingold; **Fig. 8.37** SPIE Vol. 1256 *Stereoscopic Displays and Applications* (1990); **Fig. 8.47** From *Exploration in cognition* by Donald A. Norman and David E. Rumelhart. Copyright © 1975 by W. H. Freeman and Company. Reprinted with permission.

Chapter 9

Opener (p. 324) René Magritte, *The Happy Donor (L'heureux donateur)*. 1966. Herscovici / © Art Resource NY; **Fig. 9.2** Erickson, C. W., and Collins, J. F. (1967). Some temporal characteristics of visual pattern perception. *Journal of Experimental Psychology*, 74 (4), 476–484. Copyright © 1967 by the American Psychological Association. Reprinted by permission; **Fig. 9.4** Rock, I., & Gutman, D. (1981). The effect of inattention on form perception. *Journal of Experimental Psychology: Human Perception and Performance*, 1, 275–285. Copyright © American Psychological Association. Reprinted by permission; **Fig. 9.5** Becklen, R., & Cervonne, D. (1983). Selective looking and the noticing of unexpected events. *Memory and Cognition*, 11, 601–608. Reprinted by permission of Psychonomic Society, Inc.; **Fig. 9.6** Eagle, M., et al. (1966). Imagery: Effect of a concealed figure in a stimulus. *Science*, 151, 838. Copyright © 1966 by the AAAS; **Fig. 9.8** Kosslyn, S. M. (1980). *Image and mind*. Cambridge, MA: Harvard University Press; **Fig. 9.10** Craik, F. I. M., & Tulving, E. (1975). Depth of processing and the retention of words in long-term memory. *Journal of Experimental Psychology: General*, 104, 274; **Fig. 9.12** Atkinson, R. C. (1975). Mnemotechnics in second language learning. *American Psychologist*, 30, 822. Copyright © 1975 by the American Psychological Association. Adapted by permission; **Fig. 9.13a** Ebbinghaus, H. (1885/1913). *Memory: A contribution to experimental psychology* (H. A. Ruger & C. E. Bussenius, Trans.). New York: Teachers College Press; **Fig. 9.13b** Bahrick, H. P., et al. (1975). Fifty years of memory for names and faces. *Journal of Experimental Psychology*, 104, 54–75. Copyright © 1975 by the American Psychological Association. Adapted by permission; **Fig. 9.14** Keppel, G., et al. (1968). Studies of learning to learn: VIII. The influence of massive amounts of training upon learning and retention of paired-associate lists. *Journal of Verbal Learning and Verbal Behavior*, 7, 790–796; **Fig. 9.15** Collins, A., & Loftus, E. (1975). A spreading-activation theory of semantic processing. *Psychological Review*, 82, 407–428. Copyright © 1975 by the American Psychological Association. Reprinted by permission.

Chapter 10

Opener (p. 366) Paul Klee. *The Gifted Boy*. Photo © SuperStock; **p. 369 (top)** From *L'Année Psychologique*, Paris, 1905. General Research Division, The New York Public Library, Astor, Lenox and Tilden Foundations; **(bottom)** R. L. Thorndike, E. P.

Hagen, & J. M. Sattler, Riverside Publishing Co., Chicago; **Fig. 10.3** Carpenter, P. A., Just, M. A., & Shell, P. (1990). What one intelligence test measures: A theoretical account of the processing in the Raven Progressive Matrices Test. *Psychological Review*, 97, 409. Reproduced by permission; **Fig. 10.7** McGue, M., Bouchard, T. J., Iacono, W. G., & Lyken, D. T. (1993). Behavioral genetics of cognitive ability: A life-span perspective. In R. Plomin & G. E. McClearn (Eds.), *Nature, nurture, and psychology*. Washington, DC: American Psychological Association. Reproduced by permission; **Fig. 10.10** Selfe, L. (1979). *Nadia*. New York: Academic Press. Reprinted by permission; **p. 403 (top)** Scarry, R. (1963). *Best word book ever*, © 1963 by Western Publishing Company, Inc.; **(bottom)** Scarry, R. (1980). *Best word book ever*, © 1980 by Western Publishing Company, Inc.

Chapter 11

Opener (p. 408) Kitagawa Utamaro, *Yamauba and Kintoki*. Eighteenth-century engraving. Giraudon / Art Resource NY; **Fig. 11.1** Baillargeon, R. (1987). Object permanence in 3½- and 4½-month-old infants. *Developmental Psychology*, 23, 655–664. Copyright © 1987 by the American Psychological Association. Adapted by permission; **Fig. 11.2 (p. 407)** Wishart, J. G., & Bower, T. G. R. (1984). Spatial relations and the object concept: A normative study. In L. P. Lipsitt & C. Rovee-Collier (Eds.), *Advances in infancy research*, Vol. 3. Norwood, NJ: Ablex. Reprinted with permission from Ablex Publishing Corporation; **Fig. 11.6** Siegler, R. S. (1983). How knowledge influences learning. *American Scientist*, 71, 631–638. Reprinted by permission of American Scientist, journal of Sigma Pi and The Scientific Research Society. **Fig. 11.11** Berko, J. (1958). The child's learning of English morphology. *Word*, 14, 155–177.

Chapter 12

Opener (p. 450) Diego Rivera. *Fin del Corrido* (mural, detail, from Court of Fiestas). Secretaria de Educación Pública de Mexico D. F. © Estate of Diego Rivera/Licensed by VAGA, New York, NY. Used by permission of Instituto Nacional de Bellas Artes, Mexico. Photo © Schalkwijk / Art Resource, NY; **Fig. 12.3** Harlow, H. (1959). Affectional responses in the infant monkey. *Science*, 130, 421–432. Copyright © 1959 by the AAAS; **Fig. 12.7** Steinberg, L., & Silverberg, S. B. (1986). The vicissitudes of autonomy in early adolescence. *Child Development*, 57, 841–851. Copyright © 1986 by The Society for Research in Child Development, Inc.; **Fig. 12.8 (top)** Wilson, M., & Daly, M. (1985). Competitiveness, risk taking, and violence: The young male syndrome. *Ethology and Sociobiology*, 6, 69. Reproduced by permission; **(bottom)** Campbell, A. (1995). A few good men: Evolutionary psychology and female adolescent aggression. *Ethology and Sociobiology*, 16, 100. Reproduced by permission; **Fig. 12.9** Colby, A., et al. (1983). A longitudinal study of moral judgment. *Monographs for The Society for Research in Child Development*, 148, 1–2. Copyright © 1983 by the Society for Research in Child Development, Inc.

Chapter 13

Opener (p. 496) Diego Velázquez, *Las Meninas*. 1665. Museo del Prado / Art Resource NY; **Fig. 13.6** Miller, R. L., et al. (1975). Attribution versus persuasions as a means for modifying behavior. *Journal of Personality and Social Psychology*, 31, 430–441. Copyright © 1975 by the American Psychological Association. Adapted by permission; **Fig. 13.8** McGuire, W. J., & McGuire, C. V. (1988). Content and process in the experience of self. In L. Berkowitz (Ed.), *Advances in experimental social psychology* (Vol. 21). New York: Academic Press; **Fig. 13.10** Schwartz, S. H. (1996). Value priorities and behavior: Applying a theory of integrated value systems. In C. Seligman, J. M. Olson, & M. Zanna (Eds.), *The psychology of values: The Ontario Symposium* (Vol. 8). Mahwah, NJ: Erlbaum. Reproduced by permission; **Fig. 13.11** Azjen, I. (1987). Attitudes, traits, and actions: Dispositional prediction of behavior in personality and psychology. In L. Berkowitz (Ed.), *Advances in experimental social psychology* (Vol. 20). New York: Academic Press; **Fig. 13.12** Petty, R. E., et al. (1981). Personal involvement as a determinant of argument-based persuasion. *Journal of Personality and Social Psychology*, 41, 847–855. Copyright © 1981 by the American Psychological Association. Reprinted by permission.

Chapter 14

Opener (p. 532) René Portocarrero, *La Pomarrosa* / Christie's Images; **Figs. 14.8, 14.9** From the film *Obedience* distributed by New York University Film Library; **p. 565** From *Social psychology* by Muzafer Sherif and Carolyn W. Sherif, Fig. 11.18a (p. 258): Copyright © 1969 by Muzafer Sherif and Carolyn Sherif, by permission of HarperCollins, Inc.

Chapter 15

Opener (p. 572) Pablo Picasso, *Femme au Beret (Woman with Beret)*. © 1998 Estate of Pablo Picasso / Artists Rights Society (ARS), New York. Christie's Images / SuperStock; **Fig. 15.1** Eysenck, J. J. (1982). Development of a theory. In J. J. Eysenck (Ed.), *Personality, genetics, and behavior: Selected papers*. New York: Praeger. Copyright © 1982 by Praeger Publishers, an imprint of Greenwood Publishing Group, Inc., Westport, CT. Reprinted with permission; **Fig. 15.2** Cattell, R. B. (1965). *The scientific* *analysis of personality.* Baltimore: Penguin; **Fig. 15.3** Shoda, Y., Mischel, W., & Wright, J. C. (1994). Intraindividual stability in organization and patterning of behavior: Incorporating psychological situations in the idiographic analysis of personality. *Journal of Personality and Social Psychology, 67,* 678 (Figure 1). Reproduced by permission; **p. 600** Paul Cézanne, *The Card Players,* 1892. Paris, Musée d'Orsay. Photo Erich Lessing / Art Resource.

Chapter 16

Opener (p. 610) Edvard Munch, *Melancholy.* Color woodcut. Museo Munch / Art Resource NY; **Table 16.2** Beck, A. T., Brown, G., Eidelson, J. I., Steer, R. A., & Riskind, J. H. (1987). Differentiating anxiety and depression: A test of the cognitive content-specificity hypothesis. *Journal of Abnormal Psychology, 96,* 181. Copyright © 1987 by the American Psychological Association. Reprinted by permission; **p. 627** Edvard Munch (1863–1944), *Despair,* SuperStock; **Fig. 16.4** Kendler, K. S., Kessler, R. C., Walters, E. E., MacLean, C., Neale, M. C., Health, A. C., & Eaves, L. J. (1995). Stressful life events, genetic liability, and the onset of an episode of major depression in women. *American Journal of Psychiatry, 53,* 837. Reproduced by permission; **Fig. 16.7** Cohen, S., Tyrell, D. A. J., & Smith, A. P. (1991). Psychological stress and susceptibility to the common cold. *The New England Journal of Medicine, 325,* 606–612. Reprinted with permission from *The New England Journal of Medicine;* **Fig. 16.8** Cooper, M. L., et al. (1988). Coping, expectancies and alcohol abuse: A test of social learning foundations. *Journal of Abnormal Psychology, 97,* 218–230. Copyright © 1988 by the American Psychological Association. Used by permission; **p. 642** Adolf Wolfi, Untitled (1915). The Prinzhorn Institute, University of Heidelberg.

Chapter 17

Opener (p. 652) Pierre Bonnard, *Evening (La Siesta* or *In a Southern Garden).* 1914. Giraudon / Art Resource NY; **Table 17.1** Beck, A. T. (1978). *BDI.* New York: Harcourt Brace Jovanovich. From the Beck Depression Inventory. Copyright © 1987 by Aaron T. Beck, M.D. Reproduced by permission of the publisher, The Psychological Corporation. All rights reserved; **Fig. 17.2** Hogarty, G. E., & Goldberg, S. C. (1973). Drug and sociotherapy in the aftercare of schizophrenic patients: One year relapse rates. *Archives of General Psychiatry, 28,* 54–64; **Fig. 17.3** Concar, D. (1994, March). Design your own personality. *New Scientist,* 24. Reproduced by permission; **Fig. 17.5** Hieronymous Bosch (1450–1516), *The Garden of Earthly Delights* (detail of Hell). Prado / Art Resource; **Fig. 17.7** Beck, A. T., & Young, J. E. (1985). Depression. In D. H. Barlow (Ed.), *Clinical handbook of psychological disorders: A step-by-step treatment manual.* New York: Guilford; **Fig. 17.8** Al-Kubaisy, T., Marks, I. M., Logsdail, S., Marks, M. P., Lovell, K., Sungur, M., & Araya, R. (1992). Role of exposure homework in phobia reduction: A controlled study. *Behavior Therapy, 23,* 614 (Figure 2). Adapted with permission; **17.10** Redrawn with permission of the publishers from *Psychotherapy versus behavior therapy,* edited by R. Bruce Sloane, Fred R. Staples, Allan H. Cristol, Neil J. Yorkston and Katherine Whipple. Cambridge, Mass.: Harvard University Press, copyright © 1975 by the Commonwealth Fund.

Name Index

Subject Index